AF855839

Texas Real Estate Forms Manual
2023 Edition

Volume 1

TEXAS REAL ESTATE FORMS MANUAL

2023 Edition

Volume 1

A project of the
Real Estate Forms Committee
of the
State Bar of Texas

Austin 2023

The use of the masculine gender in parts of this manual is purely for literary convenience and should, of course, be understood to include the feminine gender as well.

ISBN (print): 978-1-956363-34-0
ISBN (digital download): 978-1-956363-35-7
ISBN (online): 978-1-956363-36-4

The authors and the State Bar of Texas gratefully acknowledge permission of the copyright holder and publisher to reprint the following materials: ACORD 25 "Certificate of Liability Insurance," ACORD 28 "Evidence of Commercial Property Insurance," and ACORD 45 "Additional Interest Schedule."

Printed in the United States of America

2023 Edition

TEXAS REAL ESTATE FORMS MANUAL

2023 Edition

REAL ESTATE FORMS COMMITTEE

2022–2023

Contents
Volume 1

Preface

The State Bar of Texas is proud to publish the 2023 edition of the *Texas Real Estate Forms Manual*. The manual is written, reviewed, and approved by Texas attorneys who hail from every part of Texas and from every sort of real estate–related practice, enabling them to bring a broad range of experience and expertise to the manual. Committee members have given countless hours over the years toward maintaining the manual as the most up-to-date, comprehensive, and practical publication of its kind.

While there are remarkable individual contributions to various chapters, it is the policy of the committee not to single out any individual contributors because to do so would be to ignore the value of the collaborative process. Working alone and in pairs, in subcommittees, and in full meetings, the committee has identified and responded to changes in the law and enhanced the value of the material provided to the members of the State Bar of Texas.

The history of the manual is significant because it explains the depth of its contents. The original manual began in 1949 as a project of the San Antonio Bar Association to assemble a uniform set of legal real estate forms for sale to Texas lawyers. The State Bar assumed responsibility for the project in 1970 and has published several editions and dozens of supplements over the last half century.

The manual is now published as two softbound volumes and is available in online and downloadable versions that offer enhanced word-processing forms and a custom toolbar for greater ease in customizing the forms. The online and downloadable versions contain links to primary research, assisting practitioners in knowing the law and understanding how and why to approach a transaction in a certain way.

The 2023 edition of the manual stems from the passion for the law and its practice held by each member of the Real Estate Forms Committee. It would be difficult to exaggerate the contributions of this year's committee members or their boundless energy, care, diligence, and amazing (sometimes painful) attention to detail. The members maintained goodwill and a sense of humor throughout the countless hours during which the 2023 edition of the manual was developed. It has been a privilege to work with each of them.

Ed McCarthy, *Chair* • Christina Jenkins, *Vice-Chair* • Sara E. Dysart, *Chair Emeritus*

Preface

The State Bar of Texas is proud to publish the 2023 edition of the *Texas Real Estate Forms Manual*. This manual is written, reviewed, and approved by Texas attorneys who hail from every part of Texas and from every sort of real estate–related practice, enabling them to bring a broad range of expertise and experience to the manual. Committee members have spent countless hours over the years forming and maintaining the manual as the most up-to-date, comprehensive, and practical publication of its kind.

While there are remarkable individual contributions to various chapters, it is the policy of the committee not to single out any individual contributors because to do so would be to ignore the nature of the collaborative process. Working alone and in informal subcommittees, and in full meetings, the committee has identified and responded to changes in the law and evaluations of the material provided to the members of the State Bar of Texas.

The history of the manual is significant because it explains the depth of its contents. The original manual began in 1969 as a project of the San Antonio Bar Association to develop a uniform set of legal real estate forms for sale to Texas lawyers. The State Bar assumed responsibility for the project in 1976 and has published several editions and dozens of supplements over the past half century.

The manual is now published as two softbound volumes and is available online, with downloadable versions that offer enhanced word-processing functions and a custom toolbar for creating and customizing the forms. The online and downloadable versions contain links to primary resources, assisting practitioners in knowing the law and understanding how and why to approach a transaction in a certain way.

The 2023 edition of the manual stems from the passion for the law and its practice held by each member of the Real Estate Forms Committee. It would be difficult to exaggerate the contributions of this year's committee members or their boundless energy, care, diligence, and amazing (sometimes painful) attention to detail. The members maintained goodwill and a sense of humor through the countless hours during which the 2023 edition of the manual was developed. It has been a privilege to work with each of them.

Ed McCarthy, *Chair* • Christine Jenkins, *Vice-Chair* • Sara E. Dysart, *Chair Emeritus*

List of Chapters

Summary of Contents

A detailed chapter table of contents immediately precedes each chapter.

9 **Security Agreements**

Practice notes and related forms for the use of personal property as security in a real property transaction

10 **Ancillary Loan Documents**

Practice notes and forms for use ancillary to an original loan and for documenting subsequent transactions such as transfers or releases of liens

11 **Home Equity Loan Documents**

Practice notes and forms for documenting the use of homestead property to secure a home equity loan or reverse mortgage

12 **Federal Consumer Disclosure Documents**

Practice notes relating to federal lending regulations and examples of the model forms

13 **Residential Contracts for Deed**

Brief summary of law relating to contracts for deed

14 **Foreclosure Documents**

Practice notes and forms for use in foreclosing a real estate lien created by a deed of trust

[chapter 15 reserved]

16 **Water Rights Conveyancing Documents**

Practice notes and forms for use in conveying groundwater rights for on-site and off-site production, conveying surface water rights, and documenting the creation of liens on water rights

17 **Risk Allocation: Indemnity, Waiver, and Insurance**

Practice notes concerning the allocation of risk in real estate transactions, addressing the use of indemnities and waivers and the transfer of risk to third parties through the purchase of insurance

18 **Residential Construction Contract Documents**

Practice notes and forms for use in the construction of a new residence

19 **Commercial Construction Contract Documents**

Practice notes and form for use in new commercial construction

Introduction

The *Texas Real Estate Forms Manual* is organized according to steps involved in typical real estate transactions, insofar as possible. Each chapter contains a detailed table of contents; each except chapter 26 contains practice notes concerning the topic of the chapter. With the exception of chapters 2 and 27, the forms take up the greater part of each chapter.

§ 1 Practice Notes

The practice notes are short synopses of the law, designed to serve as a primer to the basic matters involved in a particular chapter. These notes are, at most, black-letter law and do not try to resolve questions in controversial areas. They bring together the Texas Property Code sections and other basic Texas and U.S. law relating to the topic treated in the chapter. For the attorney experienced with real estate law, these notes should serve as a reminder of some of the basics; for the attorney not so experienced with the law, they should provide an orientation to the major matters with which the attorney needs to be concerned when completing a particular transaction.

Although the notes are not intended as a treatise on the subject, they contain much important information that must be understood before the forms may be used responsibly.

§ 2 Forms

The forms (except those promulgated by governmental agencies) were prepared by members of the Real Estate Forms Committee of the State Bar of Texas, and great care has gone into their preparation. The forms represent the best thinking of the practicing attorneys on the committee. Perfection, however, is hard to achieve, and each attorney using these materials must depend on his or her own expertise and knowledge of the law.

The alternative situations that occur most often are covered in the forms. There is, however, no substitute in a particular transaction for the legal mind, and there is no end to the variations of legal problems. Thus, care should be taken to ensure that any form used fits the situation and treats the problems of that transaction.

1. Optional content

Within major sections of the text of forms, optional paragraphs or items are usually identified by boxed instructions. Additional optional clauses are collected under separate form numbers in each chapter where appropriate. Because the manual can cover only relatively common situations confronted in real estate transactions, language needed to address an atypical issue in a particular situation may not appear in the form. The user must take care to ensure both that language appearing in the form that is not appropriate for the particular transaction is eliminated and that any language needed for the particular transaction that does not appear in the form is added.

2. Typeface conventions

Two typefaces are used in the forms. Material in Times Roman (like most of this page) is appropriate for inclusion in a finished form. In contrast, Arial type is used for boxed instructions. When Arial type is used within the form itself (rather than in an instruction box), it appears in **boldface** for emphasis.

3. Bracketed material

Several types of bracketed material appear in the forms.

Choice of terms. In a bracketed statement such as "[Landlord/Tenant]," the user must choose between the terms or phrases within the brackets. The choices are separated by forward slash marks. Alternative letters or phrases may also be indicated by the use of brackets. A frequent example that appears in the forms is "[county/counties]," indicating a choice between the singular and plural forms of the word.

Optional words. In a phrase such as "Description of the Land [and Personal Property]," the user must determine whether to include the words "and Personal Property."

Substitution of terms. In a bracketed statement such as "[**name of buyer**]," the user is to substitute the name of the buyer rather than typing the bracketed material verbatim.

Instructions for use. Material such as "[**include if applicable:** . . .]" and "[**describe property**]" provides instructions for completing the finished form and should not be typed verbatim in the document.

Subtitles. The titles of some forms are followed by a bracketed subtitle that is not to be typed as part of the form title. In the title "Closing Instructions [from Borrower]," for example, the bracketed words simply distinguish the form from another similarly titled form in the same chapter for ease of reference.

4. Blank lines

Signature lines appear as blank lines. Spaces for dates and times that would be filled in *after* the document is prepared also appear as blank lines. If an actual date or time should be inserted in the form when it is prepared, "[**date**]" or "[**time**]" appears instead. Additional signature lines may be necessary in a given form and should be added by the user.

5. Language in boxes

Language in boxes is not to be typed in the finished document but constitutes instructions, usually either telling the user whether to use the form language following the box, describing what information should be included at that point in the finished document or attached to it, or providing cautionary reminders about use of the form language.

6. Form numbers

Forms are numbered in sequence within each chapter. All forms begin with the number of the chapter, which is followed by a hyphen and the number of the form within the chapter. Some forms consist only of clauses to be inserted in other forms. In these instances the clauses are numbered in sequence using the form number, followed by the number of the clause—for example, clause 5-6-2 in form 5-6. This system is used to permit future expansion of any chapter without requiring the rearrangement of the entire book.

7. Digital versions

The *Texas Real Estate Forms Manual* is available in two digital versions: online and downloadable. The online version, available by subscription, is accessible on a variety of platforms including PC, mobile phones, and tablets. The downloadable version contains the entire text of the manual as a single Adobe Acrobat PDF file.

Features of both versions include downloadable State Bar of Texas–copyrighted forms from the manual as editable Word files, as well as printable or downloadable PDF files of forms available from various agencies. In both versions, applicable Texas and federal case and statute citations in the practice notes and forms instructions are linked to case reports and main code sections cited via Fastcase online. Both versions are searchable and hyperlinked to allow for easy, rapid navigation to topics of interest.

Caveat: Note that the Word files of forms included in the digital versions contain instructional language as hidden text. Be aware that this language will be included in your completed forms unless you specifically delete it.

For more information about the online version, visit **www.texasbarpractice.com/texas-bar-books-online**. For more information about the digital download including usage notes, see the material at the end of this introduction titled "How to Download This Manual."

§ 3 Corrections and Updates

In drafting the manual, the members of the committee devoted a great deal of effort to making it error-free, but it undoubtedly contains some errors. We would appreciate your pointing out to us any errors you find in the manual, as well as any revisions you believe are advisable. Please mail any corrections or suggestions to the following address:

Director, Texas Bar Books
State Bar of Texas
P.O. Box 12487
Austin, Texas 78711-2487
books@texasbar.com

Periodic updating of the manual is planned to reflect changes in the law. It is also expected that, over time, additional topics will be covered and the scope of coverage of existing topics will be expanded. We welcome your suggestions about new topics that you would find helpful. Please send your suggestions to the address shown above.

How to Download This Manual

To install this manual's digital download—

1. go to **https://manage.texasbarpractice.com**;
2. if prompted to log in, do so; and
3. in the "Downloadables" column, click the download button for this manual's title.

For details, see the section below titled "Downloading and Installing."

Texas Real Estate Forms Manual Digital Download 2023

The downloadable version of the *Texas Real Estate Forms Manual* contains the entire text of the printed manual. If you have questions or problems with this product not covered in the documentation available via the URLs below, please contact Texas Bar Books at 800-204-2222, ext. 1499 for technical support or ext. 1411 for orders and accounts, or at **books@texasbar.com**.

Additional and Entity Licenses

The current owner of this manual may purchase additional and entity licenses for the digital download. Each additional license is for one additional lawyer and that lawyer's support team only. Additional and entity licenses are subject to the terms of the original license concerning permitted users of the printed manual and digital download. Please visit **www.texasbarpractice.com/knowledgebase/article/how-to-get-access-for-other-lawyers** for details.

Usage Tips and Other Information

For information on digital download licensing, installation, and usage, visit the Texas Bar Practice Knowledge Base at **www.texasbarpractice.com/knowledgebase**.

Downloading and Installing

Use of the digital download is subject to the terms of the license and limited warranty included in this documentation and on the digital download web pages. By accessing the digital download, you waive all refund privileges for this publication.

To install this manual's complete digital download, follow the instructions below.*

1. Go to **https://manage.texasbarpractice.com**:

   If the site prompts you to log you in, do so using the email address associated with this purchase.

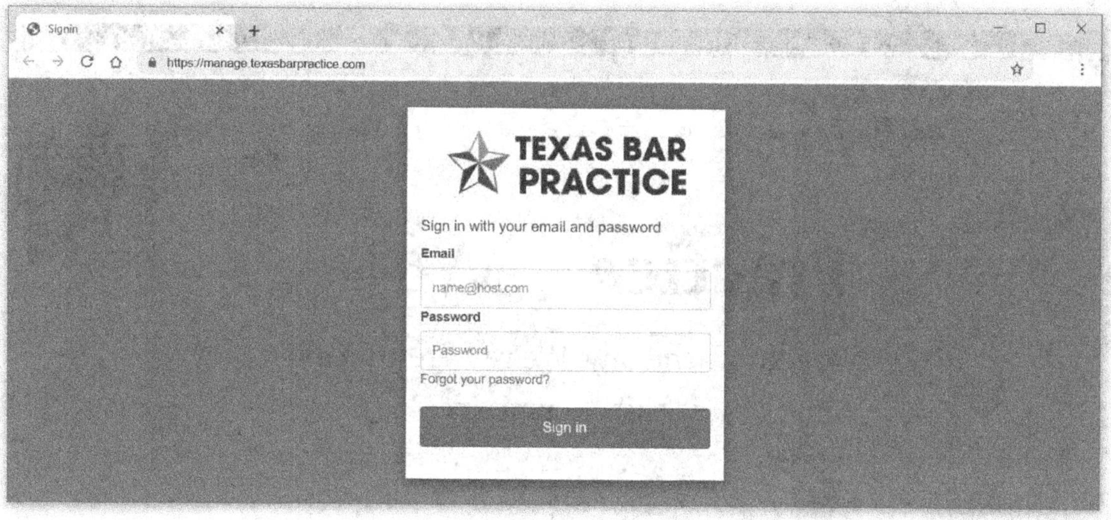

Once logged in, you should see the user icon in the upper right-hand corner of the page.

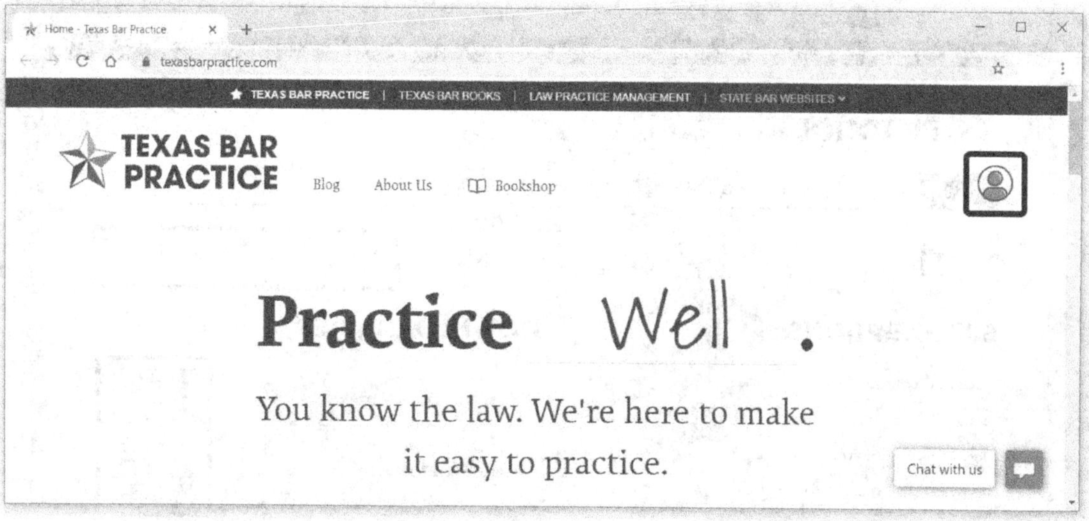

2. Go to your account:

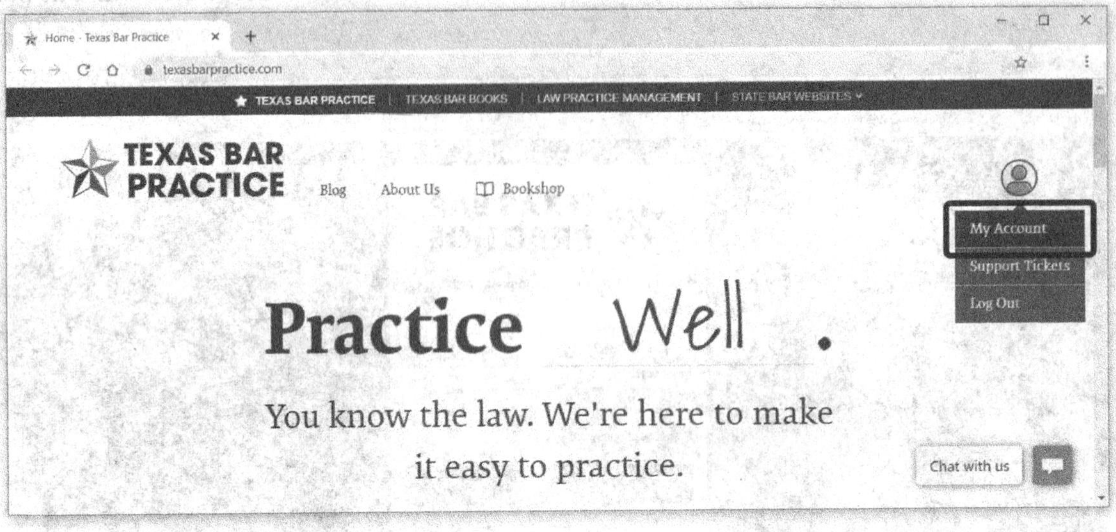

3. Select the library of the individual or organization associated with this download, and click the download button next to the manual's title.

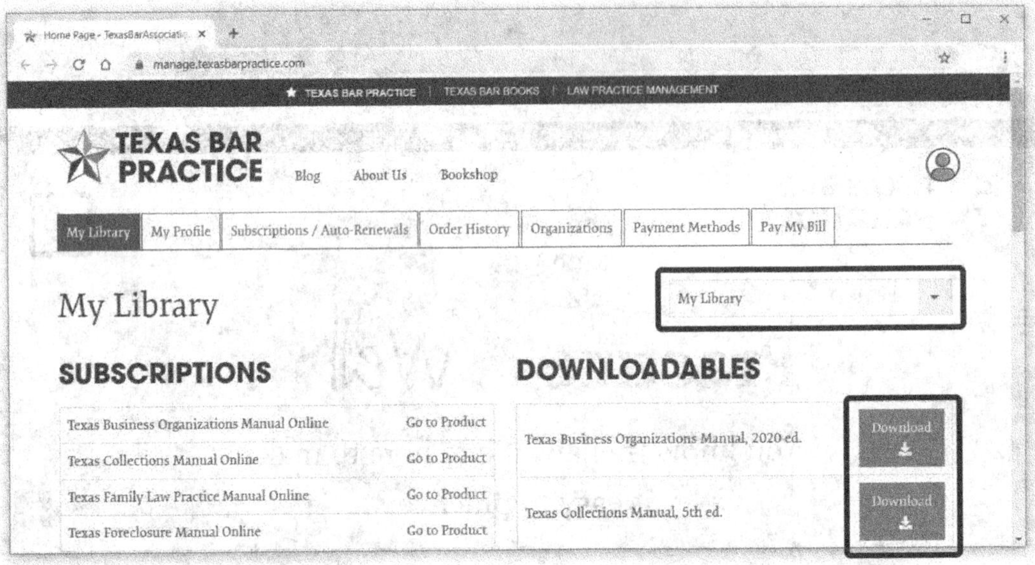

***Notes:**

- If you have never logged in to our site, the purchaser of this manual should follow the instructions at **www.texasbarpractice.com/knowledgebase/article/already-a-customer**.
- If you purchased the manual as an organization, see **www.texasbarpractice.com/knowledgebase/article/texas-bar-practice-account-types**.

If you need any assistance, you may chat with us online or email us at **books@texasbar.com**.

Preparing Word Forms for E-Filing (Windows)

Notes for Other Software

- *Word for Macintosh:* See the section titled "Remove Metadata" in the document named "Macintosh--How to Use the Word Forms" included with the digital download.
- *WordPerfect:* To remove metadata from forms saved as WordPerfect files (version X3 or later), launch the "Save Without Metadata" tool (File > Save Without Metadata, or Alt + F + M).

Using Word version 2007 or later, to remove personal information, hidden text, and other metadata before filing or sharing a document electronically, launch the "Inspect Document" tool.

1. Go to File > Info > Check for Issues > Inspect Document (Alt + F + I + I + I).

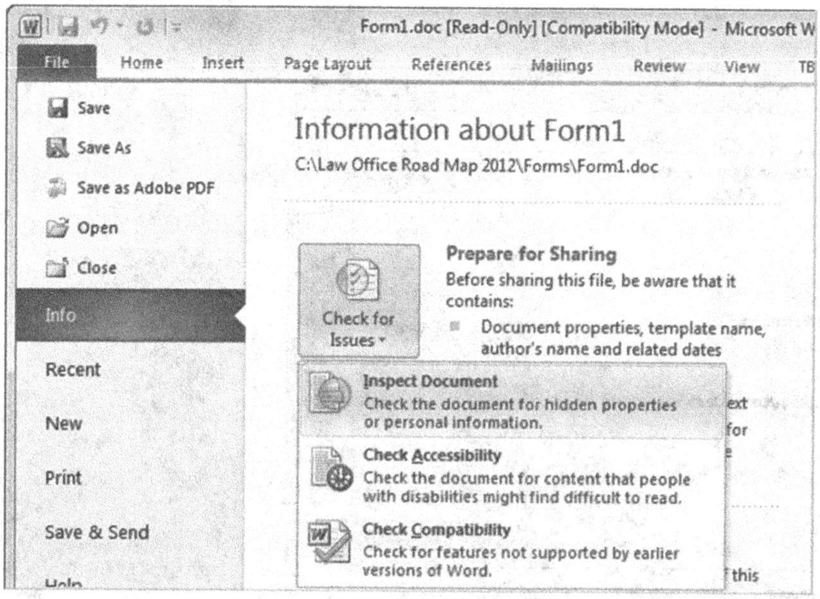

2. In the "Document Inspector" window that opens, select the categories desired by checking the appropriate boxes (be certain to check the "Hidden Text" box to ensure that any remaining red, hidden instructional text in the document will be also be detected) and click the "Inspect" button.

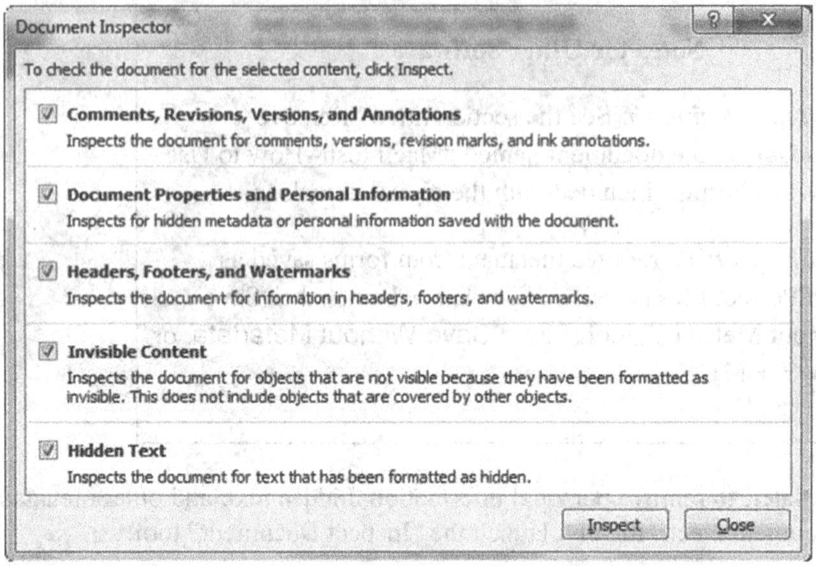

3. In the second "Document Inspector" window that opens, review and remove any metadata found as desired.

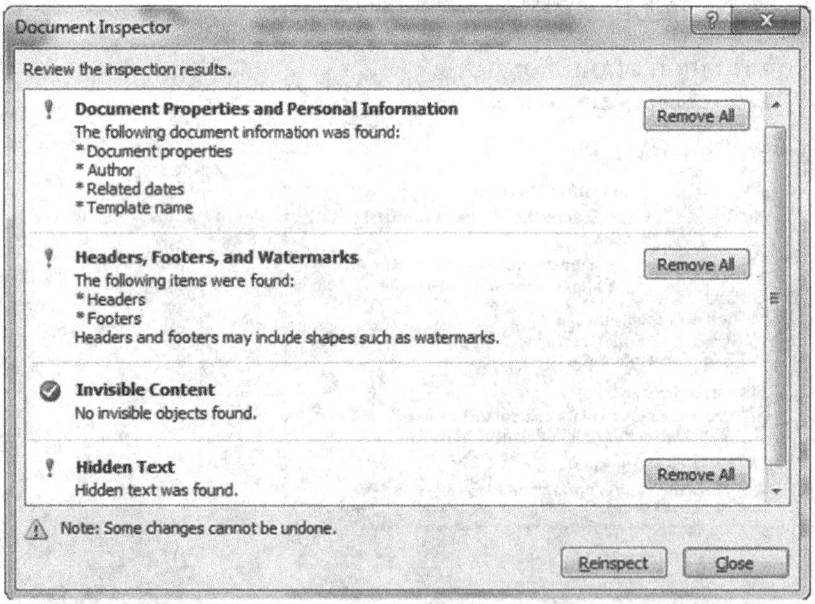

CAVEAT: Although the above steps should remove basic metadata and the form instructions from the Word forms, electronic files contain all manner of metadata. It's wise to familiarize yourself with the types of data stored by any software you use in the types of files you plan to share and reasonable measures available to remove that data before sharing.

License and Limited Warranty

Grant of license: The material in the digital product and in the documentation is copyrighted by the State Bar of Texas ("State Bar"). The State Bar grants you a nonexclusive license to use this material as long as you abide by the terms of this agreement.

Ownership: The State Bar retains title and ownership of the material in the digital files and in the documentation and all subsequent copies of the material regardless of the form or media in which or on which the original and other copies may exist. This license is not a sale of the material or any copy. The terms of this agreement apply to derivative works.

Permitted users: The material in these files is licensed to you for use by one lawyer and that lawyer's support team only. At any given time, the material in these files may be installed only on the computers used by that lawyer and that lawyer's support team. That lawyer may be the individual purchaser or the lawyer designated by the firm that purchased this product. You may not permit other lawyers to use this material unless you purchase additional licenses. **Lawyers, law firms, and law firm librarians are specifically prohibited from distributing these materials to more than one lawyer. A separate license must be purchased for each lawyer who uses these materials.** For information about special bulk discount pricing for law firms, please call 1-800-204-2222, ext. 1402, or 512-427-1402. Libraries not affiliated with firms may permit reading of this material by patrons of the library through installation on one or more computers owned by the library and on the library's network but may not lend or sell the files themselves. The library may not allow patrons to print or copy any of this material in such a way as would infringe the State Bar's copyright.

Copies: You may make a copy of the files for backup purposes. Otherwise, you may copy the material in the files only as necessary to allow use by the users permitted under the license you purchased. Copyright notices should be included on copies. You may copy the documentation, including any copyright notices, as needed for reference by authorized users, but not otherwise.

Transfer: You may not transfer any copy of the material in the files or in the documentation to any other person or entity unless the transferee first accepts this agreement in writing and you transfer all copies, wherever located or installed, of the material and documentation, including the original provided with this agreement. You may not rent, loan, lease, sublicense, or otherwise make the material available for use by any person other than the permitted users except as provided in this paragraph.

Limited warranty and limited liability: THE STATE BAR MAKES NO WARRANTIES, EXPRESS OR IMPLIED, CONCERNING THE MATERIAL IN THESE FILES, THE DOCUMENTATION, OR THIS AGREEMENT. THE STATE BAR EXPRESSLY DISCLAIMS ALL IMPLIED WARRANTIES, INCLUDING THE IMPLIED WARRANTIES OF MERCHANTABILITY AND OF FITNESS FOR A PARTICULAR PURPOSE. THE MATERIAL IN THE FILES AND IN THE DOCUMENTATION IS PROVIDED "AS IS."

THE STATE BAR SHALL NOT BE LIABLE FOR THE LEGAL SUFFICIENCY OR LEGAL ACCURACY OF ANY OF THE MATERIAL CONTAINED IN THESE FILES. NEITHER THE STATE BAR NOR ANY OF THE CONTRIBUTORS TO THE MATERIAL MAKES EITHER EXPRESS OR IMPLIED WARRANTIES WITH REGARD TO THE USE OR FREEDOM FROM ERROR OF THE MATERIAL. EACH USER IS SOLELY RESPONSIBLE FOR THE LEGAL EFFECT OF ANY USE OR MODIFICATION OF THE MATERIAL.

IN NO EVENT SHALL THE STATE BAR BE LIABLE FOR LOSS OF PROFITS OR FOR INDIRECT, SPECIAL, CONSEQUENTIAL, OR PUNITIVE DAMAGES, EVEN IF THE STATE BAR HAS BEEN ADVISED OF THE POSSIBILITY OF THOSE DAMAGES. THE STATE BAR'S AGGREGATE LIABILITY ARISING FROM OR RELATING TO THIS AGREEMENT OR THE MATERIAL IN THE FILES OR IN THE DOCUMENTATION IS LIMITED TO THE PURCHASE PRICE YOU PAID FOR THE LICENSED COPYRIGHTED PRODUCT. THIS AGREEMENT DEFINES YOUR SOLE REMEDY.

General provisions: This agreement contains the entire agreement between you and the State Bar concerning the license to use the material in the files. The waiver of any breach of any provision of this agreement does not waive any other breach of that or any other provision. If any provision is for any reason found to be unenforceable, all other provisions nonetheless remain enforceable.

Chapter 1

Ethics and Professional Conduct

Chapter 1

Ethics and Professional Conduct

§ 1.1 Introduction

The Texas Disciplinary Rules of Professional Conduct set the standard of conduct for Texas attorneys and are found in the Texas Government Code in title 2, subtitle G, appendix A, following section 84.004 of the Government Code. The rules are also available online at **www.texasbar.com/AM/Template.cfm?Section=Ethics_Resources**.

This chapter of the manual follows the attorney-client relationship from the initial client interview to the termination of the relationship, with examples of what a real estate attorney might do to document compliance with the rules. This chapter is very general and is not intended to be a substitute for a complete study of the rules.

The documents at the end of this chapter are examples only and provide general guidance, not "forms" for all transactions.

§ 1.1:1 The Texas Lawyer's Creed

On November 7, 1989, the Supreme Court of Texas and the Texas Court of Criminal Appeals adopted "The Texas Lawyer's Creed—A Mandate for Professionalism." An attorney adhering to the Creed agrees to advise a client of the contents of the Creed when undertaking a representation (article II, paragraph 1).

Recommended paragraphs for the disclosure about the Creed are found in the model engagement letters at forms 1-8, 1-9, and 1-10 in this chapter.

§ 1.1:2 Notice of Grievance Process

Section 81.079 of the Texas Government Code requires attorneys to notify clients of the grievance process. Notice must be provided by making available in the attorney's office grievance brochures prepared by the State Bar, by prominently posting a sign in the attorney's office describing the process, by including the information in a written contract for services, or by providing the information in a bill for services. Tex. Gov't Code § 81.079(b).

Example paragraphs for the disclosure about the Creed are found in the model engagement letters at forms 1-8, 1-9, and 1-10 in this chapter.

§ 1.2 Sources of Interpretation of Rules

Judicial decisions in Texas regarding ethical violations are referenced in the annotations to the Texas Disciplinary Rules of Professional Conduct.

The Professional Ethics Committee for the State Bar of Texas issues opinions on the rules and the Texas Code of Professional Responsibility (the predecessor to the rules). These opinions are published in the *Texas Bar Journal*.

An attorney may obtain informal explanations of the rules from the State Bar. A consultation with the disciplinary counsel's office may be not only informative but also probative of good faith should a question later arise. The telephone number of the attorney ethics line is 800-532-3947.

The Texas Center for Legal Ethics also maintains an online library, index, and text of all published opinions of the Committee on Professional Ethics; Texas cases dealing with ethics and professionalism; and a bibliography. The Center's website is at **www.legalethicstexas.com/Home**, and its phone number is 800-204-2222, ext. 1477. Tex. Disciplinary Rules Prof'l Conduct R. 1.05(c)(9) permits a lawyer to reveal confidential information to secure legal advice about the lawyer's compliance with the Texas Disciplinary Rules of Professional Conduct.

§ 1.3 Disciplinary Action

Article VIII of the Texas Disciplinary Rules of Professional Conduct (Maintaining the Integrity of the Profession) generally governs an attorney's conduct. Rule 8.04 sets out a comprehensive restatement of all forms of conduct that will subject an attorney to disciplinary action. Tex. Disciplinary Rules Prof'l Conduct R. 8.04, *reprinted in* Tex. Gov't Code Ann., tit. 2, subtit. G, app. A (Tex. State Bar R. art. X, § 9). It includes conduct controlled by the State Bar Act and the State Bar Rules. The rules govern attorneys who are admitted to practice in Texas or specially admitted for a particular proceeding. A licensed Texas attorney's conduct in another state may also be the subject of a Texas grievance procedure. Tex. Disciplinary Rules Prof'l Conduct R. 8.05.

The rules do not prescribe either disciplinary procedures or penalties for a violation. Tex. Disciplinary Rules Prof'l Conduct preamble ¶ 14. Possible sanctions are found instead in the Texas Rules of Disciplinary Procedure. These rules are reproduced in the Texas Government Code in title 2, subtitle G, appendix A-1, following section 84.004 of the Government Code. The rules are also available online at **www.texasbar.com/AM/Template.cfm?Section=Ethics_Resources**.

§ 1.4 Consulting Potential Client

§ 1.4:1 Attorney-Client Relationship

The relationship of attorney and client is one of agent and principal. *Duval County Ranch Co. v. Alamo Lumber Co.*, 663 S.W.2d 627, 633 (Tex. App.—Amarillo 1983, writ ref'd n.r.e.). It is created by consent and governed by the general rules covering agency. *Bar Ass'n of Dallas v. Hexter Title & Abstract Co.*, 175 S.W.2d 108, 115 (Tex. App.—Fort Worth 1943), *aff'd*, 179 S.W.2d 946 (Tex. 1944). The fiduciary obligations and responsibilities imposed on the attorney are predicated on the existence of the attorney-client relationship. *See Shropshire v. Freeman*, 510 S.W.2d 405 (Tex. App.—Austin 1974, writ ref'd n.r.e.).

The attorney-client relationship can be implied from the conduct of the parties. *Duval County Ranch Co.*, 663 S.W.2d at 633. A written contract or payment of a retainer is not necessary. For example, gratuitous services can establish an attorney-client relationship. *Prigmore v. Hardware Mutual Insurance Co. of Minnesota*, 225 S.W.2d 897, 899 (Tex. App.—Amarillo 1949, no writ). But the fact that an attorney had business dealings with someone does not establish an attorney-client relationship. *McGary v. Campbell*, 245 S.W. 106, 116 (Tex. App.—Beaumont 1922, writ dism'd w.o.j.).

The existence of an attorney-client relationship is a question of fact. *Jinks v. Moppin*, 80 S.W. 390, 393 (Tex. App. 1904, no writ).

§ 1.4:2 Areas of Concern When Consulting Potential Client

Consultation alone does not create an attorney-client relationship. Nevertheless, some duties attach during a consultation. *See* Tex. Disciplinary Rules Prof'l Conduct preamble ¶ 12.

During a consultation, an attorney must maintain the requirements of confidentiality and must be wary to avoid current and future conflicts. A consultation and certainly an investigation may impose additional duties such as advising the potential client of the statute of limitations. *See Villarreal v. Cooper*, 673 S.W.2d 631 (Tex. App.—San Antonio 1984, no writ). At least one state has held attorneys liable for negligently investigating the claim, even though the attorney refused to take the case. *See Togstad v. Vesely, Otto, Miller & Keefe*, 291 N.W.2d 686 (Minn. 1980). Further confusion may result if an attorney has a continuing or gratuitous relationship with a client. *See Bresette v. Knapp*, 159 A.2d 329 (Vt. 1960).

An attorney should consider declining bad or unwanted business as well as the unwanted client. An attorney is not ethically required to represent all who seek the attorney's advice. *See* Tex. Disciplinary Rules Prof'l Conduct R. 6.01 & cmts.

§ 1.4:3 Refusing Representation

A potential client may believe that an attorney-client relationship is created by the initial interview. If the attorney decides not to represent a person, this should be made clear. The attorney should consider sending a letter to confirm that the proposed representation will not be undertaken. Form 1-1 in this chapter is an example of a nonrepresentation letter. Tex. Disciplinary Rules Prof'l Conduct R. 1.15(d) requires the potential client's documents to be returned. They may be withheld only if other law, such as a lien, permits the withholding of documents and if the client will not be prejudiced by the retention. *See* Tex. Comm. on Prof'l Ethics, Op. 395 (1979). If the documents are particularly valuable, the attorney should consider having their receipt acknowledged.

§ 1.4:4 Advising Potential Client

If the attorney declines the representation, there is a question about whether the attorney should advise the nonclient of any rights or statutes of limitation. Some attorneys, as a matter of policy, will advise the nonclient of such matters if the attorney is aware of them. Other attorneys believe that advice implies some representation of the nonclient and therefore, as a matter of policy, do not offer any advice in the nonrepresentation letter.

§ 1.5 Establishing Attorney-Client Relationship

§ 1.5:1 Disclosure of Conflicts

An attorney must disclose all potential conflicts before accepting employment and those that arise during the course of employment. Nonlitigation conflicts are addressed specifically in rule 1.06, comments 13–16. Unfortunately, these comments merely provide examples and conclude that the question is "often one of proximity and degree." Tex. Disciplinary Rules Prof'l Conduct R. 1.06 cmt. 13. Relevant factors include the duration of the relationship and intimacy that an attorney has with a client, the duties performed, the likelihood a conflict will arise, and the likelihood of resulting prejudice.

The disclosure requirement includes all personal conflicts, conflicts with current clients, and conflicts with past clients. For examples of disclosures and waivers of specific types of conflicts of interest, see forms 1-2 through 1-7 in this chapter.

Rule 1.12(a) states that an attorney employed by an organization represents the entity. Because investors often ask real estate attorneys to form a limited liability company, partnership, corporation, or other entity, it is a good practice to clarify that the client is the entity and not the individual investors. Keep in mind that investors or prospective clients may have impliedly formed a general partnership (without a formal or written partnership agreement) before your engagement if they have already created an association to carry on a business for profit. See forms 1-5 and 1-6 for examples of letters pertaining to the formation of a partnership and a corporation.

In addition, rule 1.12(e) requires the attorney to inform shareholders and officers that the attorney will not represent them if their interests are adverse to the interests of the entity. *See* Tex. Disciplinary Rules Prof'l Conduct R. 1.12(e) & cmt. 4.

§ 1.5:2 Consent Required for Representation of Multiple Clients

A typical real estate transaction may involve sellers, purchasers, guarantors, lenders, title insurance companies, trustees, real estate brokers and agents, mortgage brokers, tenants, and lien claimants, as well as the attorneys. In addition, if any of the parties are limited liability companies, corporations, or partnerships, the individual officers, directors, shareholders, partners, members, managers, or venturers involved may have interests that diverge from those of the business entity. An attorney who provides legal counsel for more than one of the parties faces a potential conflict of interest that should be carefully examined before the attorney undertakes representation. Note that the initial client engagement may evolve during the transaction. For example, a buyer may assign a purchase and sale agreement to a newly formed entity for a closing that may or may not be directly affiliated with the initial client or its principals and want the attorney to carry on the representation. Also, sometimes situations arise where a lender may ask the opinion of the borrower's attorney on the authority of entities with whom the borrower's attorney is not directly engaged.

In examining the potential attorney-client relationship, the attorney should carefully consider the unique facts of the transaction and the purpose of the engagement. Representation may be analyzed under two theories: the traditional multiple-representation analysis (*see* Tex. Disciplinary Rules Prof'l Conduct R. 1.06) and the intermediaries analysis (*see* Tex. Disciplinary Rules Prof'l Conduct R. 1.07).

In many transactions, the multiple clients have adverse positions to each other but, because of economic constraints, want only one attorney to represent them in the transaction. Rule 1.06(a) prohibits an attorney from representing opposing parties in the same litigation. Rule 1.06(b) also prohibits an attorney from representing a client if the representation is substantially related and materially and directly adverse to the interest of another client of the attorney or if the attorney would be limited by other responsibilities. Notwithstanding the prohibition of rule 1.06(b), subsection (c) allows the attorney to represent multiple clients if the attorney believes each client's representation will not be materially affected and each client consents to the multiple representation after full disclosure.

Rule 1.07 may also affect the consent required for representation of multiple clients. Rule 1.07 can be read to require that an attorney obtain "each client's written consent" whenever "two or more parties with potentially conflicting interests" are represented by one attorney. One of the primary drafters of the rules has suggested that the literal language of rule 1.07 was in error and should be limited to situations in which an attorney mediates between clients, as illustrated by the comments to rule 1.07. *See* Robert P. Schuwerk & John F. Sutton, Jr., *A Guide to the Texas Disciplinary Rules of Professional Conduct*, 27A Hous. L. Rev., Oct. 1990, at 122.

If the attorney concludes that multiple representation is appropriate, obtaining written consent of the clients is advised. Form 1-3 in this chapter is a model letter for such a situation. See also forms 1-5, 1-6, and 1-7 for letters dealing with multiple representation. Separate engagement letters for each client may be appropriate in addition to the multiple-representation consent letter.

An additional problem that may arise is the division of the legal bill between multiple clients. Any representation of multiple clients will require a tailor-made consent agreement that clarifies the billing arrangement. See form 1-7 for an example of a consent agreement.

Further, if multiple parties are to receive cash or some other consideration, the attorney may have a duty to make sure all parties represented concur in the way the consideration is to be divided. *See* Tex. Disciplinary Rules Prof'l Conduct R. 1.08(f); *Quintero v. Jim Walter Homes, Inc.*, 709 S.W.2d 225, 229 (Tex. App.—Corpus Christi–Edinburg 1985, writ ref'd n.r.e.) (involves litigation but easily analogized to business settlements).

§ 1.5:3 Legal Fees

An attorney may not enter into an agreement for, charge, or collect an illegal or unconscionable fee. Tex. Disciplinary Rules Prof'l Conduct R. 1.04(a). A fee is unconscionable if a competent attorney could not form a reasonable belief that the fee is reasonable. Tex. Disciplinary Rules Prof'l Conduct R. 1.04(a). In borderline cases the comments specify two indications of unconscionability: the attorney's overreaching with a client, especially one susceptible to such a practice, and the attorney's failing to give the client at the outset of the representation a clear explanation of how the fee will be calculated. Tex. Disciplinary Rules Prof'l Conduct R. 1.04 cmt. 8. Rule 1.04(b) lists a number of factors that may be considered in determining the reasonableness of a fee.

An attorney may not divide a fee with another attorney who is not a member or employee of the same firm unless (1) the client consents in writing to the terms of the arrangement ahead of time, (2) the division is in proportion to the services rendered by each attorney or is with an attorney who assumes joint responsibility for the representation, *and* (3) the aggregate fee is not unconscionable. Tex. Disciplinary Rules Prof'l Conduct R. 1.04(f).

Unless the agreement is confirmed by an arrangement conforming to paragraph (f)(2) of rule 1.04, the attorney may not collect fees or expenses in connection with the agreement except for (1) the reasonable value of legal services provided and (2) the reasonable and necessary expenses actually incurred. Tex. Disciplinary Rules Prof'l Conduct R. 1.04(g).

An attorney may share fees with an "of counsel" attorney (Tex. Comm. on Prof'l Ethics, Op. 450 (1988)) or with a former partner or associate (Tex. Disciplinary Rules Prof'l Conduct R. 1.04(h)).

Fees paid in advance of the performance of work, as well as any of the client's other property that comes into the attorney's possession, must be held in trust by the attorney. Tex. Disciplinary Rules Prof'l Conduct R. 1.14. Attorneys must keep complete records of client account funds for at least five years after the conclusion of the representation. Tex. Disciplinary Rules Prof'l Conduct R. 1.14(a). If a client's funds either are of an amount or are held for a long enough time that the interest generated is likely to exceed the costs of setting up and maintaining an account, an individual account must be set up for the client. For a client's funds that are of a small amount or are likely to be held only for a short time, attorneys are required to maintain an interest-bearing account in which to pool the funds. Under the Interest on Lawyers' Trust Accounts (IOLTA) program, interest from these pooled accounts is paid to the Texas Equal

Access to Justice Foundation, which awards grants to organizations in Texas that serve the poor in legal matters. Attorneys must submit an annual IOLTA compliance statement to the foundation. State Bar Rules art. XI (1989) (found in the Texas Government Code in title 2, subtitle G, appendix A, following section 84.004 of the Government Code). See also the Rules Governing the Operation of the Texas Equal Access to Justice Program (reproduced in *Texas Rules of Court—State* (West 2021)).

Although generally each party to a transaction pays its own attorney's fees, there are certain circumstances in which a prevailing party may contractually recover fees from the opposing party or may be entitled to recover reasonable attorney's fees under Tex. Civ. Prac. & Rem. Code § 38.001. When such a fee-shifting circumstance is legally authorized, the party seeking a fee award must prove both the reasonableness and necessity of the requested attorney's fees. *Rohrmoos Venture v. UTSW DVA Healthcare, LLP*, 578 S.W.3d 469, 484 (Tex. 2019).

§ 1.5:4 Engagement Agreements Detailing Fee Arrangements

Rule 1.04(c) states:

> When the lawyer has not regularly represented the client, the basis or rate of the fee shall be communicated to the client, *preferably in writing*, before or within a reasonable time after commencing the representation.

Tex. Disciplinary Rules Prof'l Conduct R. 1.04(c) (emphasis added). Forms 1-8, 1-9, and 1-10 in this chapter are examples of engagement letters for real estate transactions. Form 1-16 may be used as a basis whenever the terms of the engagement change (whether fee, scope of engagement, conflicts, or other matters).

§ 1.5:5 Charging for Time and Expenses

As implied in rule 1.04(c), the attorney's fee basis is established by an agreement between the attorney and the client. The attorney should, however, carefully outline the fee basis to avoid a client's misunderstanding later. For example, the attorney might advise the client that there will be a fee to recover time previously spent to develop a limited partnership or other entity form, unbilled or unpaid time for research incurred on another matter, or initial consultation costs or that attorneys at the same firm may be substituted at different rates.

§ 1.5:6 Record Retention and Destruction

Neither the rules nor Texas case law specify if, or how long, an attorney must retain client records. To resolve the ambiguity, some attorneys adopt a record retention and destruction policy. If the existence of a policy is disclosed to the client in either the engagement letter or the closing letter, the client has the opportunity to obtain the records and the attorney has some authority to dispose of the documents. See forms 1-8, 1-9, 1-10, 1-14, and 1-15 in this chapter for an optional paragraph concerning retention and destruction of records. As attorneys move to digital offices, this paragraph could be modified to reflect that the attorney would not be required to maintain paper files or records or how they handle highly sensitive client information.

An attorney that routinely handles matters with highly sensitive information (e.g., Social Security numbers, driver's license numbers, passport numbers, or bank account numbers) may consider consulting an IT professional to understand vulnerabilities in their system, backup safety measures that may be best practices, and additional steps necessary to safeguard client information in order to comply with federal and state laws that govern data privacy or that impose notification requirements upon the unauthorized access or breach of the attorney's system.

§ 1.6 Representation of Client

§ 1.6:1 Duty to Keep Client Informed

Rule 1.03(a) requires an attorney to keep the client reasonably informed. In addition, the attorney has the duty to inform the client of relevant considerations and explain their legal significance to permit the client to make informed decisions. Tex. Disciplinary Rules Prof'l Conduct R. 1.03(b).

One way to meet these obligations is to routinely provide the client with copies of all pertinent correspondence, documents, and file memoranda; advise the client in writing of risks involved with the transaction, including the obvious; and document the business decisions made by the client.

§ 1.6:2 Confidentiality

An attorney may not knowingly reveal confidential information of a client or use such confidential information to the attorney's advantage or for the advantage of a third person. Tex. Disciplinary Rules Prof'l Conduct R. 1.05(b). The ethical duty to preserve a client's confidence is much broader than the attorney-client evidentiary privilege. This duty applies even if there is not yet an established attorney-client relationship—for instance, when a client comes in for an initial interview. *See* Tex. Disciplinary Rules Prof'l Conduct preamble ¶ 12. The obligation of confidentiality also continues after the termination of employment. Tex. Disciplinary Rules Prof'l Conduct R. 1.09(a)(2).

Rule 1.16, adopted effective July 1, 2021, authorizes an attorney to disclose a client's confidential information if the lawyer reasonably believes it is necessary to protect the client's interests. Tex. Disciplinary Rules Prof'l Conduct R. 1.16. This is limited to instances in which the attorney reasonably believes that the client has diminished capacity; that the client is at risk of substantial physical, financial, or other harm unless action is taken; and that the client cannot adequately act in the client's own interest.

§ 1.6:3 Business Interests with Clients

Rule 1.08(a) provides that an attorney may not enter into a business transaction with a client unless (1) the transaction and the terms on which the attorney acquires the interest in the transaction are fair and reasonable to the client and are fully disclosed in a manner that can be reasonably understood by the client, (2) the client is given reasonable opportunity to seek the advice of independent counsel in the transaction, and (3) the client *consents in writing*. Tex. Disciplinary Rules Prof'l Conduct R. 1.08(a). Comment 2 to rule 1.08 indicates that the rule does not apply to standard commercial transactions between the attorney and the client for products or services the client generally markets to others, because the attorney has no advantage in dealing with the client.

In cases in which the attorney and client are both personally involved in a business transaction, malpractice insurance claims might be denied because the policies may exclude coverage under such circumstances. The attorney's malpractice carrier can confirm if it provides such coverage or offers any special endorsements on a case-by-case basis (e.g., where an attorney is a part owner of a bank client and prepares loan documents on behalf of the bank).

See form 1-11 in this chapter for an example of a consent agreement for doing business with a client.

§ 1.6:4 Duty to Clarify Nonrepresentation

An attorney dealing on behalf of a client with a person not represented by an attorney may not state or imply that the attorney has no interest in the outcome of the matter. If the attorney believes an unrepresented person misunderstands the attorney's role, the attorney must correct this misunderstanding. Tex. Disciplinary Rules Prof'l Conduct R. 4.03. For example, an attorney might make a written nonrepresentation disclosure to a borrower when representing a lender. See form 1-12 in this chapter for an example of a nonrepresentation disclosure letter.

§ 1.6:5 Communication with Someone Represented by Counsel

An attorney may not communicate about the subject of the representation with someone the lawyer knows to be represented by counsel. Tex. Disciplinary Rules Prof'l Conduct R. 4.02. Likewise, the rules prohibit an attorney from encouraging a client to make such a communication. *See* Tex. Disciplinary Rules Prof'l Conduct R. 4.02 cmt. 2.

There are legally required exceptions to this rule, such as the sending of a foreclosure notice. *See* Tex. Prop. Code § 51.002.

§ 1.7 Issues Raised by Use of Technology

The Texas Disciplinary Rules of Professional Conduct do not specifically address issues raised by the use of technology in the practice of law. The ABA Model Rules of Professional Conduct provide some guidance on such issues, especially when there is no counterpart in the Texas rules.

§ 1.7:1 Confidentiality of Information

Rule 1.6(c) of the ABA Model Rules of Professional Conduct states: "A lawyer shall make reasonable efforts to prevent the inadvertent or unauthorized disclosure of, or unauthorized access to, information relating to the representation of a client." Comment 18 to this rule states, in part, that—

> [t]he unauthorized access to, or the inadvertent or unauthorized disclosure of, information relating to the representation of a client does not constitute a violation of paragraph (c) if the lawyer has made reasonable efforts to prevent the access or disclosure. Factors to be considered in determining the reasonableness of the lawyer's efforts include, but are not limited to, the sensitivity of the information, the likelihood of disclosure if additional safeguards are not employed, the cost of employing additional safeguards, the difficulty of implementing the safeguards, and the extent to which the safeguards adversely affect the lawyer's ability to represent clients (e.g., by making a device or important piece of software excessively difficult to use).

§ 1.7:2 Responsibilities Regarding Nonlawyer Assistant

Rule 5.03 of the Texas Disciplinary Rules of Professional Conduct is similar to rule 5.3 of the ABA Model Rules of Professional Conduct. Comment 3 to ABA rule 5.3 recognizes that the use of nonlawyers outside the firm may include—

> sending client documents to a third party for printing or scanning, and using an Internet-based service to

> store client information. When using such services outside the firm, a lawyer must make reasonable efforts to ensure that the services are provided in a manner that is compatible with the lawyer's professional obligations.

Tex. Comm. on Prof'l Ethics, Op. 572 (2006), addresses the use of an independent contractor for copying services. *See* 69 Tex. B.J. 793–94 (2006).

§ 1.7:3 Respect for Rights of Third Parties

Rule 4.4(b) of the ABA Model Rules of Professional Conduct states: "A lawyer who receives a document or electronically stored information relating to the representation of the lawyer's client and knows or reasonably should know that the document or electronically stored information was inadvertently sent shall promptly notify the sender." Comments 2 and 3 to this rule state the following:

> [2] Paragraph (b) recognizes that lawyers sometimes receive a document or electronically stored information that was mistakenly sent or produced by opposing parties or their lawyers. A document or electronically stored information is inadvertently sent when it is accidentally transmitted, such as when an email or letter is misaddressed or a document or electronically stored information is accidentally included with information that was intentionally transmitted. If a lawyer knows or reasonably should know that such a document or electronically stored information was sent inadvertently, then this Rule requires the lawyer to promptly notify the sender in order to permit that person to take protective measures. Whether the lawyer is required to take additional steps, such as returning the document or electronically stored information, is a matter of law beyond the scope of these Rules, as is the question of whether the privileged status of a document or electronically stored information has been waived. Similarly, this Rule does not address the legal duties of a lawyer who receives a document or electronically stored information that the lawyer knows or reasonably should know may have been inappropriately obtained by the sending person. For purposes of this Rule, "document or electronically stored information" includes, in addition to paper documents, email and other forms of electronically stored information, including embedded data (commonly referred to as "metadata"), that is subject to being read or put into readable form. Metadata in electronic documents creates an obligation under this Rule only if the receiving lawyer knows or reasonably should know that the metadata was inadvertently sent to the receiving lawyer.
>
> [3] Some lawyers may choose to return a document or delete electronically stored information unread, for example, when the lawyer learns before receiving it that it was inadvertently sent. Where a lawyer is not required by applicable law to do so, the decision to voluntarily return such a document or delete electronically stored information is a matter of professional judgment ordinarily reserved to the lawyer. See Rules 1.2 ["Scope of Representation and Allocation of Authority Between Client and Lawyer"] and 1.4 ["Communications"].

Texas Disciplinary Rules of Professional Conduct rules 1.02 ("Scope and Objectives of Representation") and 1.03 ("Communication") are the comparable Texas rules referenced in comment 3 above.

§ 1.8 Terminating Attorney-Client Relationship

§ 1.8:1 Termination by Parties

A client may always terminate the attorney-client relationship. An attorney must return any unearned portion of the fee and all pertinent papers and property. Tex. Disciplinary Rules Prof'l Conduct R. 1.15(d) cmt. 4; Tex. Comm. on Prof'l Ethics, Op. 395 (1979). However, rule 1.15(d) specifically provides that an attorney may retain papers relating to the client to the extent permitted by other law, but only if such retention will not prejudice the client in the subject matter of the representation. *See* Tex. Comm. on Prof'l Ethics Op. 411 (1984).

An attorney also may terminate the relationship; however, the attorney has a duty to minimize any adverse effects to the client. Tex. Disciplinary Rules Prof'l Conduct R. 1.15(b), (d). It is a good practice for an attorney to send a disengagement letter to record the date of the termination of the attorney-client relationship. See form 1-13 in this chapter for an example of a disengagement letter.

Tex. Disciplinary Rules Prof'l Conduct R. 1.15(a) sets out the circumstances under which the attorney must terminate the relationship with the client. An attorney must withdraw if continued representation will result in a violation of one of the Texas Disciplinary Rules of Professional Conduct or another law or if the attorney's physical, mental, or psychological condition materially impairs the attorney's fitness to represent the client. The attorney must also withdraw when discharged. When terminating the attorney-client relationship before completing the work for which the client contracted, the attorney should review rule 1.15 to be sure that good cause for withdrawal exists.

Withdrawal is permissible under the circumstances listed in rule 1.15(b). The rule provides that an attorney may withdraw if the client fails substantially to fulfill an obligation to the attorney, including the obligation to pay the attorney's fee as agreed, *and* a reasonable warning has been given that the attorney will withdraw unless the obligation is fulfilled. Tex. Disciplinary Rules Prof'l Conduct R. 1.15(b)(5). See form 1-13 for an example of a letter terminating the attorney-client relationship because of nonpayment of fees. At least one court in dicta has stated that by accepting employment an attorney implicitly represents that the attorney will see the task through to conclusion. *See Staples v. McKnight*, 763 S.W.2d 914 (Tex. App.—Dallas 1988, writ denied). By conditioning the commencement of work and continued performance on the payment of a fee, the attorney may avoid problems later.

§ 1.8:2 Termination Due to Other Considerations

The attorney-client relationship does not continue automatically once the purpose of the employment is completed. However, it is often difficult to determine when a matter is completed. Again, it is a good practice to send a disengagement letter to record the date of the completion of employment. See form 1-14 in this chapter for an example of a completion letter.

§ 1.9 Local Counsel Representation

In financing transactions involving multiple jurisdictions, due to either the location of the borrower or the location of collateral, the borrower is commonly required to provide opinions of local counsel. While all of the preceding rules apply in these situations, local counsel may have additional concerns, including the fact that they may be engaged by lead counsel, have little or no contact with the client, and have little or no knowledge of the overall transaction. Form 1-15, based on form 1-10, includes an additional provision in paragraph 1 that may be useful in a local counsel representation.

§ 1.10 Technological Competence

The Texas Supreme Court has amended the comment to rule 1.01, which addresses competent and diligent legal representation, to address technological competency. The revised comment indicates each lawyer "should strive to become and remain proficient and competent in the practice of law, *including the benefits and risks associated with relevant technology*." Tex. Disciplinary Rules Prof'l Conduct R. 1.01 & cmt. 8 (emphasis added). The comment is similar to a change made in the American Bar Association's model rule in 2012. See **www.americanbar.org/groups/professional_responsibility/publications/model_rules_of_professional_conduct/rule_1_1_competence/comment_on_rule_1_1/**.

§ 1.11 Duty to Report Ethical Violation; Peer Assistance Program Alternative

The Texas Lawyer's Creed states that a lawyer must "abide by the Texas Disciplinary Rules of Professional Conduct," and "[p]rofessionalism requires more than merely avoiding the violation of laws and rules." The Texas Lawyer's Creed—A Mandate for Professionalism, *reprinted in Texas Rules of Court—State* (West 2021).

Rule 8.03 of the Texas Disciplinary Rules of Professional Conduct requires attorneys to make a report when a substantial question arises about another lawyer's "honesty, trustworthiness or fitness":

> **8.03 Reporting Professional Misconduct**
>
> (a) Except as permitted in paragraphs (c) or (d), a lawyer having knowledge that another lawyer has committed a violation of applicable rules of professional conduct that raises a substantial question as to that lawyer's honesty, trustworthiness or fitness as a lawyer in other respects, shall inform the appropriate disciplinary authority.
>
> (b) Except as permitted in paragraphs (c) or (d), a lawyer having knowledge that a judge has committed a violation of applicable rules of judicial conduct that raises a substantial question as to the judge's fitness for office shall inform the appropriate authority.
>
> (c) A lawyer having knowledge or suspecting that another lawyer or judge whose conduct the lawyer is required to report pursuant to paragraphs (a) or (b) of this Rule is impaired by *chemical dependency on alcohol or drugs or by mental illness may report that person to an approved peer assistance program rather than to an appropriate disciplinary authority.* If a lawyer elects that option, the lawyer's report to the approved peer assistance program shall disclose any disciplinary violations that the reporting lawyer would otherwise have to dis-

close to the authorities referred to in paragraphs (a) and (b).

(d) This rule does not require disclosure of knowledge or information otherwise protected as confidential information:

(1) by Rule 1.05 or

(2) by any statutory or regulatory provisions applicable to the counseling activities of the approved peer assistance program.

(e) A lawyer who has been convicted or placed on probation, with or without an adjudication of guilt, by any court for barratry, any felony, or for a misdemeanor involving theft, embezzlement, or fraudulent or reckless misappropriation of money or other property—including a conviction or sentence of probation for attempt, conspiracy, or solicitation—must notify the chief disciplinary counsel within 30 days of the date of the order or judgment. The notice must include a copy of the order or judgment.

(f) A lawyer who has been disciplined by the attorney-regulatory agency of another jurisdiction, or by a federal court or federal agency, must notify the chief disciplinary counsel within 30 days of the date of the order or judgment. The notice must include a copy of the order or judgment. For purposes of this paragraph, "discipline" by a federal court or federal agency means a public reprimand, suspension, or disbarment; the term does not include a letter of "warning" or "admonishment" or a similar advisory by a federal court or federal agency.

Tex. Disciplinary Rules Prof'l Conduct R. 8.03 (emphasis added). The rule and the alternative method of reporting under rule 8.03(c) reflect the values of the Texas Lawyer's Creed; rule 8.03(c) allows attorneys to help each other without involving the disciplinary process.

§ 1.12 Texas Lawyers' Assistance Program

The only approved peer assistance program to which lawyers may make reports under rule 8.03(c) is the Texas Lawyers' Assistance Program (TLAP). *See* Tex. Health & Safety Code § 467.001(1)(A); Board of Directors Meeting Minutes, Jan. 20–21, 1989, State Bar of Texas. TLAP is available to lawyers, judges, and law students twenty-four hours a day, seven days a week, at 1-800-343-TLAP (8527). Information about attorney wellness and other related information is also available on TLAP's website, **www.tlaphelps.org**. If a lawyer is required to report under rule 8.03(a), that is, if he has knowledge "or suspects" another lawyer is "impaired by chemical dependency on alcohol or drugs or by mental illness," the report may instead be made to TLAP and discharges the reporting lawyer's duty to report. *See* Tex. Health & Safety Code § 467.005(b); Tex. Disciplinary Rules Prof'l Conduct R. 8.03(c). "Mental illness" encompasses Alzheimer's disease, dementia, and other cognitive disorders. American Psychiatric Association, *Diagnostic & Statistical Manual of Mental Disorders* 591 (5th ed. 2013).

Calling TLAP about a fellow lawyer in need is a way to help an attorney with a problem without getting that attorney into disciplinary trouble. The confidentiality of TLAP participants' information is ensured under Tex. Health & Safety Code § 467.007 and by TLAP policy. All communications by any person with the program (including staff, committee members, and volunteers) and all records received or maintained by the program are strictly protected from disclosure. TLAP does not report lawyers to disciplinary authorities. While the majority of calls to TLAP are self-referrals, referrals may also come from partners, associates, office staff, judges, court personnel, clients, family members, and friends. TLAP is respectful and discreet in its efforts to help impaired lawyers who are referred, and TLAP never discloses the identity of a caller trying to get help for another attorney. Furthermore, the Health and Safety Code provides that any person who "in good faith reports information or takes action in connection with a peer assistance program is immune from civil liability for reporting the information or taking the action." Tex. Health & Safety Code § 467.008.

Approximately half of all assistance provided by TLAP is given to attorneys suffering from anxiety, depression, or burnout. Additionally, TLAP helps lawyers, law students, and judges suffering problems such as prescription and other drug use, eating disorders, gambling addictions, cognitive impairment, codependency, and many other serious issues.

Once a lawyer, law student, or judge is connected to TLAP, the resources that can be provided directly to that person include—

1. direct peer support from TLAP staff attorneys;
2. self-help information;
3. connection to a trained peer support attorney who has overcome the particular problem at hand and who has signed a confidentiality agreement;
4. information about attorney-only support groups such as Lawyers Concerned for Lawyers (weekly meetings for alcohol, drug, depression, and other issues) and monthly wellness groups (professional speakers on various wellness topics in a lecture format), which take place in major cities across the state;
5. referrals to lawyer-friendly and experienced therapists, medical professionals, and treatment centers; and
6. assistance with financial resources needed to get help, such as the Sheeran-Crowley Memorial Trust, which is available to help attorneys in financial need with the costs of mental-health or substance abuse care.

§ 1.13 Additional Resources

Anglin, Michael W., and Claude E. Ducloux. "Conflicts of Interest—Who's Your Client?" In *Essentials for Business Law: Practical Considerations, 2019*. Austin: State Bar of Texas, 2019.

Axelrad, Mary S. "Ethics & Pitfalls." In *Advanced Real Estate Strategies Course, 2017*. Austin: State Bar of Texas, 2017.

Dillard, D. Diane. "Conflicts of Interest: Entity Creation and Other Sticky Situations." In *Real Estate Law 101, 2019*. Austin: State Bar of Texas, 2019.

———. "Engagement Agreements: The Top 20 Country Countdown with Tips for Ethical Compliance." In *Real Estate Law 101, 2015*. Austin: State Bar of Texas, 2015.

———. "Engagement Letters (What Could Go Wrong?)." In *Advanced Real Estate Strategies Course, 2007*. Austin: State Bar of Texas, 2007.

———. "Ethical Traps for the Unwary: The Top 20 Country Countdown With Tips for Ethical Compliance." In *Real Estate Law 101, 2021*. Austin: State Bar of Texas, 2021.

———. "Shoes for the Shoemaker's Children: Practical Forms and Suggestions for Ethical Compliance and Malpractice Prevention." In *Real Estate Law 101, 2012*. Austin: State Bar of Texas, 2012.

Falk, Sheryl, Robert Green, and Ryan Pavel. "Information Security for Real Estate Attorneys: Ethical Responsibilities and Best Practices." In *Advanced Real Estate Drafting Course, 2018*. Austin: State Bar of Texas, 2018.

Hanna, Jett. "Materials on Ethical and Malpractice Concerns in Real Estate Drafting." In *Advanced Real Estate Drafting Course, 2008*. Austin: State Bar of Texas, 2008.

Herring, Charles F., Jr. *Texas Legal Malpractice & Lawyer Discipline*. 17th ed. Texas Lawyer, 2018.

Howard, C. Elaine. "Ethical Issues in Negotiations." In *Advanced Real Estate Law Course, 2018*. Austin: State Bar of Texas, 2018.

Jacobus, Charles J. "Ethics: Positional Conflicts for Real Estate Lawyers." In *Advanced Real Estate Law Course, 2009*. Austin: State Bar of Texas, 2009.

Jacobus, Charles J., and Douglas W. Becker. "The Ethical Complications of Fee Attorney Relationships." In *Advanced Real Estate Law Course, 2007*. Austin: State Bar of Texas, 2007.

Johnson, Sam. "Ethical Issues in Representing Multiple Clients and Other Related Attorney Ethical Issues." In *Business Disputes, 2020*. Austin: State Bar of Texas, 2020.

Jolley, Rhonda G. "How We Communicate with Clients in the Digital Age: Remember the Fax Machine." In *Advanced Real Estate Law Course, 2019*. Austin: State Bar of Texas, 2019.

Knap, Pam, John Meredith, and Gregory W. Sampson. "New Rules and Ethics Opinions Affecting Your Practice." In *Law Practice Management Course, 2020*. Austin: State Bar of Texas, 2020.

Kulik, Thomas A. "Cloudy with a Chance of Rain: Ethical Legal Practice in an Increasingly Digital World." In *Advanced Estate Planning Strategies, 2018*. Austin: State Bar of Texas, 2018.

Maloney, Marilyn C. "The ABA ACREL ACMA Local Counsel Opinion Report." In *Advanced Real Estate Law Course, 2016*. Austin: State Bar of Texas, 2016.

———. "Top 10 Drafting Tips for Local Counsel Opinions and Related Engagement Letters in Real Estate Financings." In *Advanced Real Estate Drafting Course, 2018*. Austin: State Bar of Texas, 2018.

———. "You Won That RFP, Now What? Ethics & Pitfalls." In *Advanced Real Estate Strategies Course, 2017*. Austin: State Bar of Texas, 2017.

McCarthy, Edmond R., Jr. "Dual Representation and Ex Parte Communications: Ethical Issues in Water Law and Related Regulatory Scenarios." In *Advanced Real Estate Law Course, 2014*. Austin: State Bar of Texas, 2014.

Nunley, J. Ken, and Kelly P. Rogers. "Malpractice—Tips from the Trenches." In *Advanced Real Estate Law Course, 2005*. Austin: State Bar of Texas, 2005.

Panzer, Jason M. "Ethical Considerations in Drafting Contracts." In *14th Annual John Huffaker Agricultural Law Course, 2021*. Austin: State Bar of Texas, 2021.

Ritter, Chris. "Ten Tips for Lawyer Wellness in the Age of Quarantine." In *Advanced Real*

Estate Drafting Course, 2021. Austin: State Bar of Texas, 2021.

Wallenstein, James H. "ABA/ACREL Real Estate Opinion Letter Guidelines." In *Advanced Real Estate Drafting Course, 2004*. Austin: State Bar of Texas, 2004.

———. "Provisions Often Negotiated in Mortgage Loan Opinion Letters." In *Advanced Real Estate Law Course, 2008*. Austin: State Bar of Texas, 2008.

Weinberg, Gregg S. and Sara Wolfe. "Making Sure Your Engagement, Closing Letters and Other Correspondence Are Drafted in a Manner to Explain to Your Client What You Are Not Doing for Them." In *Advanced Real Estate Drafting Course, 2019*. Austin: State Bar of Texas, 2019.

Weller, Philip D. "Drafting Advance Waivers of Conflicts of Interest." In *Advanced Real Estate Law Course, 2009*. Austin: State Bar of Texas, 2009.

Westerheim, Suzanne Raggio. "Ethical Considerations in Drafting Fee Arrangements." In *Advanced Real Estate Drafting Course, 2015*. Austin: State Bar of Texas, 2015.

White, Mark D. "Dances with Wolves and Legal Ethics." In *Real Estate Law 101, 2019*. Austin: State Bar of Texas, 2019.

———. "Drafting Ethical Engagement Agreements." In *Business Disputes, 2018*. Austin: State Bar of Texas, 2018.

Form 1-1

This letter is furnished only as a basic example and should not be used as a standard form. The attorney must be careful to tailor the details of the letter to the facts of the particular case.

Letter Declining Representation

[Date]

[Name and address of potential client]

Re: **[state nature of representation]**

[Salutation]

First, let me thank you for contacting this firm about representing you in **[state nature of representation]**.

After reviewing the documents I have concluded that we are not the appropriate firm to handle this matter. Please understand that in declining this representation I am not expressing any opinion about your legal remedies in this situation, nor am I suggesting that a solution is or is not available.

See section 1.4:4 in this chapter concerning advising a potential client.

Include the following if applicable.

I strongly recommend that you contact another attorney who is familiar with real estate transactions.

Continue with the following.

Again, I appreciate the confidence you have expressed in our firm, and I hope that you are able to resolve this matter in a satisfactory manner. [**Include if applicable:** I am returning [**describe documents**] with this letter.]

Include the following if applicable.

Please sign and return the enclosed copy of this letter to confirm that you have received the enclosures.

Continue with the following.

Sincerely yours,

____

[**Name of attorney**]

Enc.

Include lines for potential client to sign and date if copy of letter is to be returned.

Form 1-2

This letter is furnished only as a basic example and should not be used as a standard form. The attorney must be careful to tailor the details of the letter to the facts of the particular case. See section 1.5:1 in this chapter concerning disclosing conflicts.

Letter Disclosing and Requesting Waiver of Potential Conflict with Current Client

[**Date**]

[**Name and address of prospective client**]

Re: [**describe transaction**]

[**Salutation**]

I would like to express my appreciation for the opportunity to represent [**name of corporation**] in connection with [**describe transaction**]. However, before I can serve as your counsel, it is important that you have a clear understanding of a potential ethical conflict that could exist in this matter. If you have any questions about any matter in this letter, please give me a call.

[**Describe potential conflict, e.g.,** Our firm has decided not to represent any clients with an adverse position to First Local Bank or a related party because we represent First Local Bank. We do not believe a borrower from First Local Bank is in an adverse position, and I assure you that we will represent your interests to the very best of our abilities. But if you should decide to sue the bank, our firm would not be able to represent you. Of course, we would not represent the bank in any matter adverse to you.]

Please give careful thought to the matter discussed in this letter and respond in the space below.

Sincerely yours,

____

[Name of attorney]

☐ I consent to the representation subject to the foregoing limitation.

☐ I do not consent to the representation.

____

[Name of prospective client]
Date:

Form 1-3

This letter is furnished only as a basic example and should not be used as a standard form. The attorney must be careful to tailor the details of the letter to the facts of the particular case. See section 1.5:2 in this chapter concerning representing multiple clients.

Letter Disclosing and Requesting Waiver of Potential Conflict for Multiple Representation of Title Company and Third Party

[**Date**]

[**Name and address of prospective client**]

Re: [**describe transaction**]

[**Salutation**]

I am pleased that you are considering employing our firm in connection with the above-referenced transaction. Although it is not common for a lawyer to represent more than one party in a transaction, dual representation is permitted by professional ethics guidelines as long as two conditions are met.

First, the lawyer must conclude, after a good-faith self-evaluation, that the lawyer can adequately represent the interests of each client. The multiple representation should not adversely affect the attorney's independent professional judgment on behalf of any client. Second, all clients must consent to the multiple representation after full disclosure is given by the lawyer.

The first condition has been satisfied because I believe that this firm can adequately represent each of you (although I hope you understand that we must reserve the right to with-draw from this dual representation if later events cause me in good faith to reach a different conclusion). This letter is intended to fulfill the second requirement mentioned above, that of disclosure and consent. Accordingly, I will review some of the possible effects that dual representation may have on you.

Conflicts of interest. If I determine that, because of differences between the parties, I can no longer represent each of you impartially, I will inform you of the conflict, and I must then withdraw from representation. If this occurs, I will no longer be able to represent any party to the transaction. Should I determine that this law firm must withdraw from the representation, I will, if you wish, assist the parties in obtaining new counsel. You would, of course, be responsible for payment of all accrued legal fees and any outstanding expenses. Likewise, I would return any unused portion of any advances that had been made. The need to obtain substitute counsel may involve additional legal fees and expenses.

Scope of employment. I am being hired solely to advise you on and document this real estate transaction. I am not responsible for and will not advise you on other transactions, nor will I give either of you any kind of tax advice with respect to this transaction. [**Include additional disclaimers appropriate to the facts.**]

Judgment calls. In all real estate closings, a seller or buyer must decide which title matters materially affect title to the property. These decisions are often routine; however, on occasion they require my exercising professional judgment in representing your sometimes competing interests. [**Describe examples of possible judgment calls appropriate to the facts.**]

Describe any specific conflicts possible in this transaction.

There are of course other potential problems that might develop. Although I assure you that I will try to act as fairly as possible in judgment-call matters, it is certainly possible that one of you may not concur with my judgment.

Confidential information. During the course of any representation a lawyer generally becomes aware of confidential information regarding the client. The confidential information may be a potential cloud on the title that one party does not want revealed to the other party. Another possible confidential matter may be the financial capacity of a party, which bears on the likelihood of that party's performance of its obligations.

Although I assure you that I will try to act discreetly within the bounds of fair dealing, it is certainly possible that either or both of you would prefer to eliminate any possibility of having your confidential information known by an attorney who is also representing the other party. Furthermore, neither of you will be protected by the attorney-client privilege concerning any information disclosed to me or another lawyer in this firm during our representation. The general rule is that, as between commonly represented clients, the privilege does not attach. Thus, confidential information that would be protected by the attorney-client privilege if we represented only one of you can be disclosed to the other party.

Of course, I would have declined the dual representation before now if I had not already concluded that I can adequately represent both of you in this transaction; however, I also understand that you may feel differently. Therefore, I would appreciate your giving careful thought to the matters discussed in this letter. If you consent to the multiple representation, please sign in the space below and return this letter to me. You should keep a copy of this letter for your records. I will be happy to answer any questions you might have.

Sincerely yours,

____

[Name of attorney]

I understand this disclosure and I consent to the proposed multiple representation.

____

[Name of prospective client]

Date:

Send letter to each prospective client for signature.

Form 1-4

This letter is furnished only as a basic example and should not be used as a standard form. The attorney must be careful to tailor the details of the letter to the facts of the particular case. See section 1.5:1 in this chapter concerning disclosing conflicts.

Letter Disclosing and Requesting Waiver of Potential Conflict with Former Client

[**Date**]

[**Name and address of former client**]

Re: [**describe transaction**]

[**Salutation**]

As you are aware, this firm previously represented you in connection with [**describe transaction**]. This firm has recently been asked to represent [**name of prospective client**] in a claim against you.

Rule 1.09 of the Texas Disciplinary Rules of Professional Conduct prohibits us from representing [**name of prospective client**] without your written consent. Before asking for your consent, we advise you that the claim against you [**describe adverse claim and the specific prohibition of rule 1.09(a)(1)–(3)**].

As this is a very serious matter and you may be compromising certain rights that you have under the Texas Disciplinary Rules of Professional Conduct, I suggest that you seek independent counsel in this matter before consenting to our representation of [**name of prospective client**]. Please give careful thought to the matters discussed in this letter and respond in the space below.

Sincerely yours,

____

[Name of attorney]

☐ I consent to the representation [**include if applicable:** subject to the following limitation: [**describe any limitation on representation to be imposed**]].

☐ I do not consent to the representation.

____

[Name of former client]
Date:

Form 1-5

This letter is furnished only as a basic example and should not be used as a standard form. The attorney must be careful to tailor the details of the letter to the facts of the particular case. See section 1.5:2 in this chapter concerning representing multiple clients.

Letter Disclosing Potential Risks and Requesting Consent of Individual [Partners/Members] to Representation of [Partnership/ Limited Liability Company]

[**Date**]

[**Names and addresses of all partner[s] or member[s]**]

Re: Proposed representation of [**name of partnership or limited liability company**] (the partnership/the company)

[**Salutation**]

In connection with your request that this law firm represent your [partnership/company], I want to make the following disclosures regarding potential ethical conflicts of interest involving our proposed representation.

Our representation of clients is governed by the Texas Disciplinary Rules of Professional Conduct. A lawyer has the duty to exercise independent professional judgment on behalf of each client. If a lawyer is requested to represent multiple clients in the same matter, two requirements must be met: The lawyer must be able to fulfill this duty for each client on an impartial basis, and the lawyer must obtain the consent of each client after explaining the possible risks involved in the multiple representation.

Concerning the representation of an entity, such as a corporation, limited liability company, partnership, joint venture, trust, or association, rule 1.12 of the Texas Disciplinary Rules of Professional Conduct provides, in part, as follows:

> A lawyer employed or retained by an organization represents the entity. While the lawyer in the ordinary course of working relationships may report to, and accept direction from, an entity's duly authorized constituents . . . the lawyer shall proceed as reasonably necessary in the best interest of the organization. . . .

Thus, as legal counsel to the entity, we will respond to the instructions of the purported representative authorized to act on behalf of the entity. For example, the managing partner or general partner of the partnership or the manager or managing member of the limited liability company that has the apparent authority and power to deal with this law firm. Further, this law firm has no responsibility to verify or investigate the representative's authority and will not bear any responsibility for discovering whether the representative is not in fact authorized or has committed acts of fraud, defalcation, forgery, or other criminal or civil liability actions.

If matters arise that cause any one [partner/member] to have a claim against another [partner/member], this law firm could not represent either [partner/member]. If matters arise that cause any [partner/member] to have a claim against the [partnership/company] or that cause the [partnership/company] to have a claim against an individual [partner/member], this law firm retains the right to require the [partnership/company] to engage other legal counsel to represent it in that claim.

Before consenting to our representation of the [partnership/company], please be aware of the following:

1. This law firm has represented one or more of the [partners/members] in matters unrelated to the [partnership/company]. These [partners/members], for whom unrelated legal counsel has been furnished, include **[name[s] of partner[s] or members[s]]**. Each of these [partners/members] is requested to execute a form consenting to this law firm's serving as counsel to the [partnership/company], because of potential conflicts of interest. At this time, we do not believe that our prior representation of individual [partners/members] will impair

our independent professional judgment on behalf of the [partnership/company]. However, if we determine that, because of differences between the [partnership/company] and the [partners/members], we can no longer represent the [partnership/company] impartially or if a conflict arises during our representation of the [partnership/company], we will inform you of such conflict, and we must then withdraw from representation. If this occurs, we will no longer be able to represent any party to the conflict. Should we determine that this law firm must withdraw from the representation, we will, if you wish, assist the [partnership/company] in obtaining new counsel. The [partnership/company] would, of course, be responsible for payment of all accrued legal fees and any outstanding expenses. Likewise, we would return any unused portion of any advances that had been made. The need to obtain substitute counsel may involve additional legal fees and expenses.

2. Representation of any entity automatically involves potential conflicts, because entities are nothing more than the joining of individuals or other entities with differing needs for what is initially perceived to be a common objective. Each individual should understand that when there is such diversity of interests, the lawyer for the organization cannot provide legal representation for constituent individuals and that discussions between the lawyer for the organization and an individual may not be privileged insofar as that individual is concerned.

3. Before agreeing to the contents of this letter, you are advised to obtain separate legal counsel for these matters. If you consent to this law firm's representation of the [partnership/company] as contemplated by this letter, please sign in the spaces below and return one copy of this letter to me.

Sincerely yours,

____

[Name of attorney]

We consent to your representation of the [partnership/company] under the terms and conditions outlined above.

____
[Name of partner or member]
Date:

Repeat signature blocks as necessary.

Form 1-6

This letter is furnished only as a basic example and should not be used as a standard form. The attorney must be careful to tailor the details of the letter to the facts of the particular case. See section 1.5:2 in this chapter concerning representing multiple clients.

Letter Disclosing Potential Risks and Requesting Consent to Representation of Corporate Entity

[**Date**]

[**Names and addresses of all shareholders**]

Re: Consent to multiple representation in organizing corporation and acting as its general counsel

[**Salutation**]

You have requested that this law firm represent all of you as initial investors in organizing [**name of corporation**] (the corporation). You have also requested that this firm serve as general counsel to the corporation following the incorporation.

Our representation of clients is governed by the Texas Disciplinary Rules of Professional Conduct. A lawyer has the duty to exercise independent professional judgment on behalf of each client. If a lawyer is requested to represent multiple clients in the same matter, two requirements must be met: The lawyer must be able to fulfill this duty for each client on an impartial basis, and the lawyer must obtain the consent of each client after explaining the possible risks involved in the multiple representation. Further, if at any time during the representation it is determined that because of differences between the joint clients a lawyer can no longer represent each of them impartially, then the lawyer must withdraw from representing all the clients.

At our initial conference, I advised each of you of your right to obtain separate legal counsel to represent you in all matters relating to the organization of the corporation. I am still recommending that course of action to you. Each of you indicated that you understood this but nevertheless wanted this firm to represent all of you. Based on the information you have provided, we have concluded that we can represent each of you impartially. In determining whether you should consent to this joint representation, however, you should carefully consider the following matters.

The first matter involves the attorney-client privilege. Although the law is not settled, we believe that any information disclosed by you to us during this representation will not be protected by the privilege in a subsequent legal proceeding asserted by or against one of you involving another of you. Moreover, we believe we cannot effectively represent each of you if information disclosed to us by one of you must be preserved in confidence. If we are to represent you, it will only be with the express understanding that each of you has waived the attorney-client privilege to the extent, but only to the extent, that the privilege might otherwise require us to withhold from your fellow shareholders information disclosed by one of you.

Second, at this time there does not appear to be any difference of opinion among you about the major issues involved in organizing the corporation. However, it may turn out that on further consultation you may have varying opinions about the corporation's capitalization or other organizational matters. There are many issues about which investors may disagree that we must explore with you. Should we determine that there are material differences on one or more of these issues that you cannot resolve amicably or that we conclude cannot be resolved on terms compatible with the best interests of each party involved, then we must at that time withdraw from the representation. If this occurs, we will, if you wish, assist each of you in obtaining new counsel. You would, of course, be responsible for payment of all accrued legal fees and any outstanding expenses. Likewise, we would return any unused portion of any advances that had been made. The need to obtain substitute counsel may involve additional legal fees and expenses.

Third, as you know, I have represented **[name]** in other legal matters. I do not believe that this prior representation will affect in any material manner my ability to represent each of you impartially. Nonetheless, you must understand that this prior representation may unconsciously bias me in favor of **[name]** in the event of any disagreement among you. Should I at any time determine that such a bias exists, then I must withdraw from the representation.

The fourth matter is that of ultimately allocating our fees and disbursements. Unless we receive joint instructions to the contrary, we will send our entire bill for fees and disbursements for organizing the corporation to **[name]**. You should enter into a written agreement for reimbursement of **[name]**.

When you have reached an agreement on the subject of fee payment, we will discuss with you whether we can ethically draft the agreement concerning fee payment. If not, we will recommend independent counsel for you. However, we cannot provide advice to any of you for any claim you may have or desire to assert against another for indemnity or reimbursement of fees and disbursements billed by us for this representation.

If you are willing to consent to our joint representation based on the disclosures and conditions listed above, please sign in the spaces below and return one copy of this letter to us.

Sincerely yours,

____
[Name of attorney]

We consent to your joint representation of us under the terms and conditions outlined above.

____
[**Name of shareholder**]
Date:

Repeat signature blocks as necessary.

Form 1-7

This letter is furnished only as a basic example and should not be used as a standard form. The attorney must be careful to tailor the details of the letter to the facts of the particular case. See section 1.5:2 in this chapter concerning representing multiple clients.

Letter Requesting Consent to Intermediary and Outlining Fee Agreement

[**Date**]

[**Names and addresses**]

Re: [**describe transaction**]

[**Salutation**]

You have inquired about hiring me to [**describe transaction**]. As you will recall, we have thoroughly discussed the risks and advantages involved in dual representation. Nevertheless, I believe that we should set out a few matters in more detail. Also, the Texas Disciplinary Rules of Professional Conduct require me to get your consent to this arrangement in writing.

As we discussed, since I will be acting as an intermediary, I will not be an advocate for either side. This role is different from the traditional one of an attorney in American society; I must remain impartial. The risks we discussed were [**list risks**].

Another matter we discussed involved the attorney-client privilege. Although the law is not settled, we believe that any information disclosed by you to us during this representation will not be protected by the privilege in a subsequent legal proceeding asserted by or against one of you involving the other. Moreover, I believe I cannot effectively represent both of you if information disclosed to me by one of you must be preserved in confidence. If I am to represent you, it will only be with the express understanding that each of you has waived the attorney-client privilege to the extent, but only to the extent, that the privilege might otherwise require me to withhold from one of you information disclosed by the other.

Because I am and will continue to be neutral, you, as clients, will assume greater responsibility for this transaction than you might ordinarily if you were each represented by counsel. For example, I am being hired solely to document the agreement between you. I am not responsible for and will not advise either of you of the risks or benefits of the transaction, nor am I giving either of you any kind of tax advice with respect to this transaction. I am not giving any other legal advice or opinions such as [**include additional disclaimers appropriate to the facts**]. Each of you must be sure that the transaction is one in which you want to participate and that it is structured the way you want it.

If I determine that intermediation is no longer appropriate I will so inform you, and I must then withdraw from representation. If this occurs, I will no longer be able to represent any party to the conflict. Should I determine that this law firm must withdraw from the representation, I will, if you wish, assist each of you in obtaining new counsel. You would, of course, be responsible for payment of all accrued legal fees and any outstanding expenses. Likewise, I would return any unused portion of any advances that had been made. The need to obtain substitute counsel may involve additional legal fees and expenses.

As we have discussed, our fees are charged on an hourly basis plus expenses. My fees are $[**amount**] per hour. The billing rate for my associate, [**name**], is $[**amount**] per hour. It is my understanding, and by your signature below you are confirming, that our fees are to be divided equally between you and paid at the closing. I, of course, do not guarantee or promise that any certain result will be obtained. I make no express warranties concerning this transaction, and I disclaim any implied warranties concerning it.

If you are willing to engage me for this joint representation under the terms outlined above, please return a signed copy of this letter for our files.

Sincerely yours,

____

[Name of attorney]

We consent to your joint representation of us under the terms and conditions outlined above.

____

[Name of client]

Date:

____

[Name of client]

Date:

Form 1-8

This letter is furnished only as a basic example and should not be used as a standard form. The attorney must be careful to tailor the details of the letter to the facts of the particular case. See sections 1.5:4 and 1.5:5 in this chapter concerning the basic engagement agreement.

Letter Detailing Basic Engagement Agreement and Fee Agreement

[**Date**]

[**Name and address of client**]

Re: [**describe transaction**]

[**Salutation**]

Please read this letter carefully. It describes the terms and conditions under which we will represent you concerning the above-referenced matter. Our policy requires that each client sign a copy of this letter agreeing to the terms and conditions described below before we can engage in representation. The terms and conditions of our engagement are as follows:

1. Our fees for legal services are based primarily on the hourly rates for each lawyer and legal assistant at the time the services are rendered. Our current rates are $[**amount**] per hour for [**name**], $[**amount**] per hour for [**name**], and $[**amount**] per hour for legal assistants. We review these hourly rates periodically and may adjust them. If such changes are necessary, you will be notified in writing [**number**] days before the change.

> Complete disclosure about the attorney's billing practices can avoid client misunderstandings later. For example, explain about travel time, multiple attorney conferences, research, billing for "forms" in the firm's form library, administrative overtime, etc. See sections 1.5:4 and 1.5:5 for additional information.

2. It is our policy to bill clients periodically for fees and out-of-pocket expenses. Each lawyer and legal assistant records the time required to perform services, and these time

records are the basis for the bills. These bills will generally describe services performed and the expenses incurred. For large expenses, we may request the supplier to bill you directly.

3. Because of the detailed nature of our statements, our clients do not usually have any questions about them. However, if any question should arise, please call us promptly so we can discuss the matter. Our hourly rates do not include any interest for slow payment. Because of this and the fact that we do not include a service charge for late payments, we must insist that our clients pay their bills promptly.

4. If during our representation we anticipate a significant increase in the level of our activity on your behalf—for example, trial preparation or trial—we may bill you more frequently. We will expect that such statements also will be paid promptly.

5. We require a deposit before we commence work for you. We have asked that you remit to and maintain with us during our representation a deposit of at least $[**amount**]. Unless deposits are large enough or will be held long enough to earn interest in excess of the cost of an individual account, we will place these funds in a State Bar of Texas Interest on Lawyers' Trust Account, the interest on which benefits the Texas Equal Access to Justice Foundation. The deposit will be applied to our final statement for fees and expenses or, at our discretion, to any past-due amounts. On the termination of our services, we will promptly refund the deposit, less any fees and expenses unpaid as of the date of our final bill.

6. Our agreement to provide legal representation in the above-referenced matter is conditioned not only on your execution of this engagement letter but also on payment of the requested deposit.

7. We retain the right to request a supplemental deposit, over and above the original deposit, in the event of an increase in our anticipated fees and expenses during our representation.

8. By your execution of this engagement letter, you agree that we are relieved from the responsibility of performing any further work should you fail to pay any statement for fees and expenses (including bills for expenses received from third parties) or for supplemental deposits within fifteen days of their receipt. In that event, you agree that we may move to withdraw as your counsel and that you will promptly execute any withdrawal motions to accomplish this.

9. By signing this engagement agreement, you are agreeing that this firm may retain papers relating to this matter to secure payment of any amount you owe us, to the extent permitted by law, but only if such retention will not prejudice your interests in the subject matter of the representation.

10. During our discussion about handling this matter, we may have provided you with certain estimates of the fees and expenses that will be required at certain stages of our representation. Such estimates are just that, and the fees and expenses required are ultimately a function of many conditions over which we have little or no control, particularly the extent to which other parties require our involvement on your behalf. The reason we submit our clients' bills shortly after the services are rendered is so they will have a means of monitoring and controlling their expenses. If you believe the expenses are mounting too rapidly, please contact us immediately so we can assist you in evaluating how they might be curtailed. If we do not hear from you, we assume that you approve of the overall level of activity in this matter.

11. In representing you, we recognize that we may be disqualified from representing any client in any matter related to our representation of you. We also recognize that we may be disqualified from representing any client in any matter in which confidential information concerning you and made available to us during our representation of you becomes material or relevant to another matter or in which use or knowledge of such information could be adverse to your interest.

Include the following if applicable.

You agree that, except as stated above, the firm will be entitled to represent the interests of any other client against you in business negotiations or other legal matters.

Continue with the following.

12. The Supreme Court of Texas has adopted and promulgated the Texas Lawyer's Creed. Although compliance with the Creed is voluntary, we have decided to adhere to its provisions. Please review the attached Texas Lawyer's Creed, and if you have any questions, we will be glad to discuss them with you.

13. You may discharge us from this representation at any time. We will be free to withdraw at any time and without cause, subject to reasonable notice under the circumstances and to approval by any court in which your matter may be pending. We will be entitled to receive compensation from you for all services rendered and all disbursements made, under the provisions of this agreement, up to the time of withdrawal. Circumstances may arise that will require us to withdraw from representation under the Texas Disciplinary Rules of Professional Conduct or other applicable professional standards. In such circumstances, as well as in the instances referred to above, we will cooperate in the transfer of the matter to other counsel of your choice.

14. As is true with all legal services, we cannot and do not guarantee the results of our representation. We make no express warranties concerning this transaction, and disclaim any implied warranties concerning it.

15. Attorneys, like other professionals who advise on personal financial matters, are required by a federal law (the Gramm-Leach-Bliley Act) to inform their clients of their policies regarding privacy of client information. Because attorneys have been and continue to be bound by professional standards of confidentiality that are even more stringent than those required by this new law, we have always protected our clients' right to privacy. In the course

of representing our clients, we receive all manner of significant personal financial information from them. As a client of the firm, you are advised that all information we receive from you will be held in confidence and not released to outside persons, except as agreed to by you or as required under applicable law. We retain records relating to professional services we provide to assist our clients with their professional needs and, in some cases, to comply with professional guidelines. To guard your nonpublic personal information, we maintain physical, electronic, and procedural safeguards that comply with our professional standards.

Our firm makes reasonable efforts to ensure the security of all electronic data including confidential records related to our clients and the electronic communications (such as email, texts, telephone calls, voice-over-internet calls, video calls, cellular telephone, Twitter, and social networking sites) relating to our clients, whether those communications are between our firm and our clients or our internal communications relating to client matters. We believe that employing such electronic records and communications, including the use of cloud storage of data and communications, improves the efficiency of our work and our communications with our clients. You understand that we cannot guarantee that any such electronic records or communications are not intercepted or accessed by unauthorized or unintended parties. Unless you specify otherwise in writing, our firm will continue to employ such electronic communications and record storage in performing our duties, and you understand and agree that we are not responsible for the unintended disclosure of any confidential information obtained by others through the interception or unauthorized access of such electronic records or communications.

Include the following if applicable.

At the end of our representation, please let us know if you need any documents from our files. We will retain documents for five years and then destroy them in accordance with our record-retention policy then in effect.

Continue with the following.

We discuss the terms and conditions of our engagement so candidly because you are entitled to know and we believe a candid discussion now should avoid any misunderstandings later. Please sign a copy of this letter in the space below, expressing your agreement to the terms and conditions set forth above. After we receive your signed copy of this letter and the required deposit, we will commence our representation in the matter.

Sincerely yours,

____

[Name of attorney]

Enc.

ACCEPTED AND AGREED TO ON ______________________.

____

[Name of client]

Include the following notice if notice is not otherwise provided as required by Tex. Gov't Code § 81.079. See section 1.1:2.

Notice to Clients

Texas law requires that all attorneys provide their clients with the following notice about the existence of the attorney grievance process: "The State Bar of Texas investigates and prosecutes professional misconduct committed by Texas attorneys. Although not every complaint against or dispute with a lawyer involves professional misconduct, the State Bar's Office of Chief Disciplinary Counsel will provide you with information about how to file a complaint. Please call 1-800-932-1900 toll-free for more information."

Continue with the following.

The Texas Lawyer's Creed

I am a lawyer. I am entrusted by the People of Texas to preserve and improve our legal system. I am licensed by the Supreme Court of Texas. I must therefore abide by the Texas Disciplinary Rules of Professional Conduct, but I know that professionalism requires more than merely avoiding the violation of laws and rules. I am committed to this creed for no other reason than it is right.

Our Legal System

A lawyer owes to the administration of justice personal dignity, integrity, and independence. A lawyer should always adhere to the highest principles of professionalism.

1. I am passionately proud of my profession. Therefore, "My word is my bond."

2. I am responsible to assure that all persons have access to competent representation regardless of wealth or position in life.

3. I commit myself to an adequate and effective pro bono program.

4. I am obligated to educate my clients, the public, and other lawyers regarding the spirit and letter of this Creed.

5. I will always be conscious of my duty to the judicial system.

Lawyer to Client

A lawyer owes to a client allegiance, learning, skill, and industry. A lawyer shall employ all appropriate means to protect and advance the client's legitimate rights, claims, and objectives. A lawyer shall not be deterred by any real or imagined fear of judicial disfavor or public unpopularity, nor be influenced by mere self-interest.

1. I will advise my client of the contents of this Creed when undertaking representation.

2. I will endeavor to achieve my client's lawful objectives in legal transactions and in litigation as quickly and economically as possible.

3. I will be loyal and committed to my client's lawful objectives, but I will not permit that loyalty and commitment to interfere with my duty to provide objective and independent advice.

4. I will advise my client that civility and courtesy are expected and are not a sign of weakness.

5. I will advise my client of proper and expected behavior.

6. I will treat adverse parties and witnesses with fairness and due consideration. A client has no right to demand that I abuse anyone or indulge in any offensive conduct.

7. I will advise my client that we will not pursue conduct which is intended primarily to harass or drain the financial resources of the opposing party.

8. I will advise my client that we will not pursue tactics which are intended primarily for delay.

9. I will advise my client that we will not pursue any course of action which is without merit.

10. I will advise my client that I reserve the right to determine whether to grant accommodations to opposing counsel in all matters that do not adversely affect my client's lawful objectives. A client has no right to instruct me to refuse reasonable requests made by other counsel.

11. I will advise my client regarding the availability of mediation, arbitration, and other alternative methods of resolving and settling disputes.

Lawyer to Lawyer

A lawyer owes to opposing counsel, in the conduct of legal transactions and the pursuit of litigation, courtesy, candor, cooperation, and scrupulous observance of all agreements and mutual understandings. Ill feelings between clients shall not influence a lawyer's conduct, attitude, or demeanor toward opposing counsel. A lawyer shall not engage in unprofessional conduct in retaliation against other unprofessional conduct.

1. I will be courteous, civil, and prompt in oral and written communications.

2. I will not quarrel over matters of form or style, but I will concentrate on matters of substance.

3. I will identify for other counsel or parties all changes I have made in documents submitted for review.

4. I will attempt to prepare documents which correctly reflect the agreement of the parties. I will not include provisions which have not been agreed upon or omit provisions which are necessary to reflect the agreement of the parties.

5. I will notify opposing counsel, and, if appropriate, the Court or other persons, as soon as practicable, when hearings, depositions, meetings, conferences or closings are canceled.

6. I will agree to reasonable requests for extensions of time and for waiver of procedural formalities, provided legitimate objectives of my client will not be adversely affected.

7. I will not serve motions or pleadings in any manner that unfairly limits another party's opportunity to respond.

8. I will attempt to resolve by agreement my objections to matters contained in pleadings and discovery requests and responses.

9. I can disagree without being disagreeable. I recognize that effective representation does not require antagonistic or obnoxious behavior. I will neither encourage nor knowingly permit my client or anyone under my control to do anything which would be unethical or improper if done by me.

10. I will not, without good cause, attribute bad motives or unethical conduct to opposing counsel nor bring the profession into disrepute by unfounded accusations of impropriety. I will avoid disparaging personal remarks or acrimony towards opposing counsel, parties and witnesses. I will not be influenced by any ill feeling between clients. I will abstain from any allusion to personal peculiarities or idiosyncrasies of opposing counsel.

11. I will not take advantage, by causing any default or dismissal to be rendered, when I know the identity of an opposing counsel, without first inquiring about that counsel's intention to proceed.

12. I will promptly submit orders to the Court. I will deliver copies to opposing counsel before or contemporaneously with submission to the Court. I will promptly approve the form of orders which accurately reflect the substance of the rulings of the Court.

13. I will not attempt to gain an unfair advantage by sending the Court or its staff correspondence or copies of correspondence.

14. I will not arbitrarily schedule a deposition, court appearance, or hearing until a good faith effort has been made to schedule it by agreement.

15. I will readily stipulate to undisputed facts in order to avoid needless costs or inconvenience for any party.

16. I will refrain from excessive and abusive discovery.

17. I will comply with all reasonable discovery requests. I will not resist discovery requests which are not objectionable. I will not make objections nor give instructions to a witness for the purpose of delaying or obstructing the discovery process. I will encourage witnesses to respond to all deposition questions which are reasonably understandable. I will neither encourage nor permit my witness to quibble about words where their meaning is reasonably clear.

18. I will not seek Court intervention to obtain discovery which is clearly improper and not discoverable.

19. I will not seek sanctions or disqualification unless it is necessary for protection of my client's lawful objectives or is fully justified by the circumstances.

Lawyer and Judge

Lawyers and judges owe each other respect, diligence, candor, punctuality, and protection against unjust and improper criticism and attack. Lawyers and judges are equally responsible to protect the dignity and independence of the Court and the profession.

1. I will always recognize that the position of judge is the symbol of both the judicial system and administration of justice. I will refrain from conduct that degrades this symbol.

2. I will conduct myself in Court in a professional manner and demonstrate my respect for the Court and the law.

3. I will treat counsel, opposing parties, the Court, and members of the Court staff with courtesy and civility.

4. I will be punctual.

5. I will not engage in any conduct which offends the dignity and decorum of proceedings.

6. I will not knowingly misrepresent, mischaracterize, misquote or miscite facts or authorities to gain an advantage.

7. I will respect the rulings of the Court.

8. I will give the issues in controversy deliberate, impartial and studied analysis and consideration.

9. I will be considerate of the time constraints and pressures imposed upon the Court, Court staff and counsel in efforts to administer justice and resolve disputes.

Form 1-9

This letter is furnished only as a basic example and should not be used as a standard form. The attorney must be careful to tailor the details of the letter to the facts of the particular case. See sections 1.5:4 and 1.5:5 in this chapter concerning the basic engagement agreement.

Letter Detailing Ongoing Engagement Agreement and Fee Agreement

[**Date**]

[**Name and address of client**]

Re: [**describe attorney engagement**]

[**Salutation**]

Please read this letter carefully. It describes the terms and conditions under which we will represent you on an ongoing basis. Our policy requires that each client sign a copy of this letter agreeing to the terms and conditions described below before we can engage in representation. The terms and conditions of our engagement are as follows:

1. Our fees for legal services are based primarily on the hourly rates for each lawyer and legal assistant at the time the services are rendered. Our current rates are $[**amount**] per hour for [**name**], $[**amount**] per hour for [**name**], and $[**amount**] per hour for legal assistants. We review these hourly rates periodically and may adjust them. If such changes are necessary, you will be notified in writing [**number**] days before the change.

> Complete disclosure about the attorney's billing practices can avoid client misunderstandings later. For example, explain about travel time, multiple attorney conferences, research, billing for "forms" in the firm's form library, administrative overtime, etc. See sections 1.5:4 and 1.5:5 for additional information.

2. It is our policy to bill clients periodically for fees and out-of-pocket expenses. Each lawyer and legal assistant records the time required to perform services, and these time

records are the basis for the bills. These bills will generally describe services performed and the expenses incurred. For large expenses, we may request the supplier to bill you directly.

3. Because of the detailed nature of our statements, our clients do not usually have any questions about them. However, if any question should arise, please call us promptly so we can discuss the matter. Our hourly rates do not include any interest for slow payment. Because of this and the fact that we do not include a service charge for late payments, we must insist that our clients pay their bills promptly.

4. If during our representation we anticipate a significant increase in the level of our activity on your behalf—for example, trial preparation or trial—we may bill you more frequently. We will expect that such statements also will be paid promptly.

5. We require a deposit before we commence work for you. We have asked that you remit to and maintain with us during our representation a deposit of at least $[**amount**]. Unless deposits are large enough or will be held long enough to earn interest in excess of the cost of an individual account, we will place these funds in a State Bar of Texas Interest on Lawyers' Trust Account, the interest on which benefits the Texas Equal Access to Justice Foundation. The deposit will be applied to our final statement for fees and expenses or, at our discretion, to any past-due amounts. On the termination of our services, we will promptly refund the deposit, less any fees and expenses unpaid as of the date of our final bill.

6. Our agreement to provide legal representation is conditioned not only on your execution of this engagement letter but also on payment of the requested deposit.

7. We retain the right to request a supplemental deposit, over and above the original deposit, during our representation.

8. By your execution of this engagement letter, you agree that we are relieved from the responsibility of performing any further work should you fail to pay any statement for fees

and expenses (including bills for expenses received from third parties) or for supplemental deposits within fifteen days of their receipt. In that event, you agree that we may move to withdraw as your counsel and that you will promptly execute any withdrawal motions to accomplish this.

9. By signing this engagement agreement, you are agreeing that this firm may retain papers relating to this matter to secure payment of any amount you owe us, to the extent permitted by law, but only if such retention will not prejudice your interests in the subject matter of the representation.

10. During our discussion about representing you, we may have provided you with certain estimates of the fees and expenses that will be required at certain stages of our representation. Such estimates are just that, and the fees and expenses required are ultimately a function of many conditions over which we have little or no control, particularly the extent to which other parties require our involvement on your behalf. The reason we submit our clients' bills shortly after the services are rendered is so they will have a means of monitoring and controlling their expenses. If you believe the expenses are mounting too rapidly, please contact us immediately so we can assist you in evaluating how they might be curtailed. If we do not hear from you, we assume that you approve of the overall level of activity in this matter.

11. In representing you, we recognize that we may be disqualified from representing any client in any matter related to our representation of you. We also recognize that we may be disqualified from representing any client in any matter in which confidential information concerning you and made available to us during our representation of you becomes material or relevant to another matter or in which use or knowledge of such information could be adverse to your interest.

Include the following if applicable.

You agree that, except as stated above, after our representation of you has terminated, the firm will be entitled to represent the interests of any other client against you in business negotiations or other legal matters.

Continue with the following.

12. The Supreme Court of Texas has adopted and promulgated the Texas Lawyer's Creed. Although compliance with the Creed is voluntary, we have decided to adhere to its provisions. Please review the attached Texas Lawyer's Creed, and if you have any questions, we will be glad to discuss them with you.

13. You may discharge us from this representation at any time. We will be free to withdraw at any time and without cause, subject to reasonable notice under the circumstances and to approval by any court in which we are your attorney of record. We will be entitled to receive compensation from you for all services rendered and all disbursements made, under the provisions of this agreement, up to the time of withdrawal. Circumstances may arise that will require us to withdraw from representation under the Texas Disciplinary Rules of Professional Conduct or other applicable professional standards. In such circumstances, as well as in the instances referred to above, we will cooperate in the transfer of the matter to other counsel of your choice.

14. As is true with all legal services, we cannot and do not guarantee the results of our representation. We make no express warranties concerning any matter in which we represent you, and disclaim any implied warranties.

15. Attorneys, like other professionals who advise on personal financial matters, are required by a federal law (the Gramm-Leach-Bliley Act) to inform their clients of their policies regarding privacy of client information. Because attorneys have been and continue to be bound by professional standards of confidentiality that are even more stringent than those required by this new law, we have always protected our clients' right to privacy. In the course

of representing our clients, we receive all manner of significant personal financial information from them. As a client of the firm, you are advised that all information we receive from you will be held in confidence and not released to outside persons, except as agreed to by you or as required under applicable law. We retain records relating to professional services we provide to assist our clients with their professional needs and, in some cases, to comply with professional guidelines. To guard your nonpublic personal information, we maintain physical, electronic, and procedural safeguards that comply with our professional standards.

Our firm makes reasonable efforts to ensure the security of all electronic data including confidential records related to our clients and the electronic communications (such as email, texts, telephone calls, voice-over-internet calls, video calls, cellular telephone, Twitter, and social networking sites) relating to our clients, whether those communications are between our firm and our clients or our internal communications relating to client matters. We believe that employing such electronic records and communications, including the use of cloud storage of data and communications, improves the efficiency of our work and our communications with our clients. You understand that we cannot guarantee that any such electronic records or communications are not intercepted or accessed by unauthorized or unintended parties. Unless you specify otherwise in writing, our firm will continue to employ such electronic communications and record storage in performing our duties, and you understand and agree that we are not responsible for the unintended disclosure of any confidential information obtained by others through the interception or unauthorized access of such electronic records or communications.

Include the following if applicable.

At the end of our representation, please let us know if you need any documents from our files. We will retain documents for five years and then destroy them in accordance with our record-retention policy then in effect.

Continue with the following.

We discuss the terms and conditions of our engagement so candidly because you are entitled to know and we believe a candid discussion now should avoid any misunderstandings later. Please sign a copy of this letter in the space below, expressing your agreement to the terms and conditions set forth above. After we receive your signed copy of this letter and the required deposit, we will commence our representation of you.

Sincerely yours,

____

[Name of attorney]

Enc.

ACCEPTED AND AGREED TO ON______________________.

____

[Name of client]

Include the following notice if notice is not otherwise provided as required by Tex. Gov't Code § 81.079. See section 1.1:2.

Notice to Clients

Texas law requires that all attorneys provide their clients with the following notice about the existence of the attorney grievance process: "The State Bar of Texas investigates and prosecutes professional misconduct committed by Texas attorneys. Although not every complaint against or dispute with a lawyer involves professional misconduct, the State Bar's Office of Chief Disciplinary Counsel will provide you with information about how to file a complaint. Please call 1-800-932-1900 toll-free for more information."

Continue with the following.

The Texas Lawyer's Creed

I am a lawyer. I am entrusted by the People of Texas to preserve and improve our legal system. I am licensed by the Supreme Court of Texas. I must therefore abide by the Texas Disciplinary Rules of Professional Conduct, but I know that professionalism requires more than merely avoiding the violation of laws and rules. I am committed to this creed for no other reason than it is right.

Our Legal System

A lawyer owes to the administration of justice personal dignity, integrity, and independence. A lawyer should always adhere to the highest principles of professionalism.

1. I am passionately proud of my profession. Therefore, "My word is my bond."

2. I am responsible to assure that all persons have access to competent representation regardless of wealth or position in life.

3. I commit myself to an adequate and effective pro bono program.

4. I am obligated to educate my clients, the public, and other lawyers regarding the spirit and letter of this Creed.

5. I will always be conscious of my duty to the judicial system.

Lawyer to Client

A lawyer owes to a client allegiance, learning, skill, and industry. A lawyer shall employ all appropriate means to protect and advance the client's legitimate rights, claims, and objectives. A lawyer shall not be deterred by any real or imagined fear of judicial disfavor or public unpopularity, nor be influenced by mere self-interest.

1. I will advise my client of the contents of this Creed when undertaking representation.

2. I will endeavor to achieve my client's lawful objectives in legal transactions and in litigation as quickly and economically as possible.

3. I will be loyal and committed to my client's lawful objectives, but I will not permit that loyalty and commitment to interfere with my duty to provide objective and independent advice.

4. I will advise my client that civility and courtesy are expected and are not a sign of weakness.

5. I will advise my client of proper and expected behavior.

6. I will treat adverse parties and witnesses with fairness and due consideration. A client has no right to demand that I abuse anyone or indulge in any offensive conduct.

7. I will advise my client that we will not pursue conduct which is intended primarily to harass or drain the financial resources of the opposing party.

8. I will advise my client that we will not pursue tactics which are intended primarily for delay.

9. I will advise my client that we will not pursue any course of action which is without merit.

10. I will advise my client that I reserve the right to determine whether to grant accommodations to opposing counsel in all matters that do not adversely affect my client's lawful objectives. A client has no right to instruct me to refuse reasonable requests made by other counsel.

11. I will advise my client regarding the availability of mediation, arbitration, and other alternative methods of resolving and settling disputes.

Lawyer to Lawyer

A lawyer owes to opposing counsel, in the conduct of legal transactions and the pursuit of litigation, courtesy, candor, cooperation, and scrupulous observance of all agreements and mutual understandings. Ill feelings between clients shall not influence a lawyer's conduct, attitude, or demeanor toward opposing counsel. A lawyer shall not engage in unprofessional conduct in retaliation against other unprofessional conduct.

1. I will be courteous, civil, and prompt in oral and written communications.

2. I will not quarrel over matters of form or style, but I will concentrate on matters of substance.

3. I will identify for other counsel or parties all changes I have made in documents submitted for review.

4. I will attempt to prepare documents which correctly reflect the agreement of the parties. I will not include provisions which have not been agreed upon or omit provisions which are necessary to reflect the agreement of the parties.

5. I will notify opposing counsel, and, if appropriate, the Court or other persons, as soon as practicable, when hearings, depositions, meetings, conferences or closings are canceled.

6. I will agree to reasonable requests for extensions of time and for waiver of procedural formalities, provided legitimate objectives of my client will not be adversely affected.

7. I will not serve motions or pleadings in any manner that unfairly limits another party's opportunity to respond.

8. I will attempt to resolve by agreement my objections to matters contained in pleadings and discovery requests and responses.

9. I can disagree without being disagreeable. I recognize that effective representation does not require antagonistic or obnoxious behavior. I will neither encourage nor knowingly permit my client or anyone under my control to do anything which would be unethical or improper if done by me.

10. I will not, without good cause, attribute bad motives or unethical conduct to opposing counsel nor bring the profession into disrepute by unfounded accusations of impropriety. I will avoid disparaging personal remarks or acrimony towards opposing counsel, parties and witnesses. I will not be influenced by any ill feeling between clients. I will abstain from any allusion to personal peculiarities or idiosyncrasies of opposing counsel.

11. I will not take advantage, by causing any default or dismissal to be rendered, when I know the identity of an opposing counsel, without first inquiring about that counsel's intention to proceed.

12. I will promptly submit orders to the Court. I will deliver copies to opposing counsel before or contemporaneously with submission to the Court. I will promptly approve the form of orders which accurately reflect the substance of the rulings of the Court.

13. I will not attempt to gain an unfair advantage by sending the Court or its staff correspondence or copies of correspondence.

14. I will not arbitrarily schedule a deposition, court appearance, or hearing until a good faith effort has been made to schedule it by agreement.

15. I will readily stipulate to undisputed facts in order to avoid needless costs or inconvenience for any party.

16. I will refrain from excessive and abusive discovery.

17. I will comply with all reasonable discovery requests. I will not resist discovery requests which are not objectionable. I will not make objections nor give instructions to a witness for the purpose of delaying or obstructing the discovery process. I will encourage witnesses to respond to all deposition questions which are reasonably understandable. I will neither encourage nor permit my witness to quibble about words where their meaning is reasonably clear.

18. I will not seek Court intervention to obtain discovery which is clearly improper and not discoverable.

19. I will not seek sanctions or disqualification unless it is necessary for protection of my client's lawful objectives or is fully justified by the circumstances.

Lawyer and Judge

Lawyers and judges owe each other respect, diligence, candor, punctuality, and protection against unjust and improper criticism and attack. Lawyers and judges are equally responsible to protect the dignity and independence of the Court and the profession.

1. I will always recognize that the position of judge is the symbol of both the judicial system and administration of justice. I will refrain from conduct that degrades this symbol.

2. I will conduct myself in Court in a professional manner and demonstrate my respect for the Court and the law.

3. I will treat counsel, opposing parties, the Court, and members of the Court staff with courtesy and civility.

4. I will be punctual.

5. I will not engage in any conduct which offends the dignity and decorum of proceedings.

6. I will not knowingly misrepresent, mischaracterize, misquote or miscite facts or authorities to gain an advantage.

7. I will respect the rulings of the Court.

8. I will give the issues in controversy deliberate, impartial and studied analysis and consideration.

9. I will be considerate of the time constraints and pressures imposed upon the Court, Court staff and counsel in efforts to administer justice and resolve disputes.

Form 1-10

This letter is furnished only as a basic example and should not be used as a standard form. The attorney must be careful to tailor the details of the letter to the facts of the particular case. See sections 1.5:4 and 1.5:5 in this chapter concerning the basic engagement agreement.

Letter Detailing Basic Engagement Agreement and Fee Agreement for Simple Matters

[**Date**]

[**Name and address of client**]

Re: [**describe transaction**]

[**Salutation**]

Thank you for asking me to represent you in the above-referenced matter. I consider it a privilege to do so. Please excuse the overly formal and detailed nature of this letter—it is intended to ensure that you know and understand the terms and conditions under which this firm will represent you.

1. Our fees for legal services are based primarily on the hourly rates for each lawyer and legal assistant at the time the services are rendered. Our current rates are $[**amount**] per hour for [**name**], $[**amount**] per hour for associates or contract lawyers, and $[**amount**] per hour for legal assistants.

> Complete disclosure about the attorney's billing practices can avoid client misunderstandings later. For example, explain about travel time, multiple attorney conferences, research, billing for "forms" in the firm's form library, administrative overtime, etc. See sections 1.5:4 and 1.5:5 for additional information.

2. It is our policy to bill clients periodically for fees and out-of-pocket expenses. These bills will generally describe services performed and the expenses incurred. If we are

confronted with unanticipated expenses, we may request the supplier to bill you directly for any third-party expenses.

3. Our statements are reasonably detailed, and consequently our clients do not usually have any questions about them. However, if you should ever have any question or comment, please do not hesitate to call us so that we can discuss the matter. Our hourly rates do not include any interest for slow payment. Because of this and the fact that we do not include a service charge for late payments, we must insist that our clients pay their bills promptly.

4. We require a [nonrefundable] retainer [when accepting work from new clients/before beginning work on a new matter]. Accordingly, we ask that you remit to [us/and maintain with us during our representation] a retainer of $[**amount**]. [**Include as applicable:** We will place these funds in our trust account./The retainer will be applied to our final statement for fees and expenses or, at our discretion, to any past-due amounts./On the termination of our services, we will promptly refund the retainer, less any fees and expenses unpaid as of the date of our final bill.]

5. You agree that we are relieved from the responsibility of performing any further work should you fail to pay any statement for fees and expenses (including bills for expenses received from third parties) or for supplemental retainers within fifteen days of their receipt. In that event, you agree that we may move to withdraw as your counsel and that you will promptly execute any withdrawal motions to accomplish this.

6. You agree that this firm may retain papers relating to this matter to secure payment of any amount you owe us, to the extent permitted by law, but only if such retention will not prejudice your interests in the subject matter of the representation.

7. During our discussions about handling this matter, we may have provided you with certain estimates of the fees and expenses that will be required at certain stages of our representation. Such estimates are just that, and the fees and expenses required are ultimately

a function of many conditions over which we have little or no control, particularly the difficulties we encounter during negotiations with other parties. The reason we submit our clients' bills shortly after the services are rendered is so they will have a means of monitoring and controlling their expenses. If you believe the expenses are mounting too rapidly, please contact us immediately so we can assist you in evaluating how they might be curtailed. If we do not hear from you, we assume that you approve of the overall level of activity in this matter.

Include the following if applicable.

8. The Supreme Court of Texas has adopted and promulgated the Texas Lawyer's Creed. Although compliance with the Creed is voluntary, we have decided to adhere to its provisions. Please review the attached Texas Lawyer's Creed, and if you have any questions, we will be glad to discuss them with you.

Continue with the following.

9. You may discharge us from this representation at any time. We will be free to withdraw at any time, with or without cause, subject to reasonable notice under the circumstances and to approval by any court that may become involved in your matter. We will be entitled to receive compensation from you for all services rendered and all disbursements made, under the provisions of this agreement, up to the time of withdrawal. Circumstances may arise that will require us to withdraw from representation under the Texas Disciplinary Rules of Professional Conduct or other applicable professional standards. In such circumstances, as well as in the instances referred to above, we will cooperate in the transfer of the matter to other counsel of your choice.

10. As is true with all legal services, we cannot and do not guarantee the results of our representation. We make no express warranties concerning this transaction, and disclaim any implied warranties concerning it.

11. Attorneys, like other professionals who advise on personal financial matters, are required by a federal law (the Gramm-Leach-Bliley Act) to inform their clients of their policies regarding privacy of client information. Because attorneys have been and continue to be bound by professional standards of confidentiality that are even more stringent than those required by this new law, we have always protected our clients' right to privacy. In the course of representing our clients, we receive all manner of significant personal financial information from them. As a client of the firm, you are advised that all information we receive from you will be held in confidence and not released to outside persons, except as agreed to by you or as required under applicable law. We retain records relating to professional services we provide to assist our clients with their professional needs and, in some cases, to comply with professional guidelines. To guard your nonpublic personal information, we maintain physical, electronic, and procedural safeguards that comply with our professional standards.

Our firm makes reasonable efforts to ensure the security of all electronic data including confidential records related to our clients and the electronic communications (such as email, texts, telephone calls, voice-over-internet calls, video calls, cellular telephone, Twitter, and social networking sites) relating to our clients, whether those communications are between our firm and our clients or our internal communications relating to client matters. We believe that employing such electronic records and communications, including the use of cloud storage of data and communications, improves the efficiency of our work and our communications with our clients. You understand that we cannot guarantee that any such electronic records or communications are not intercepted or accessed by unauthorized or unintended parties. Unless you specify otherwise in writing, our firm will continue to employ such electronic communications and record storage in performing our duties, and you understand and agree that we are not responsible for the unintended disclosure of any confidential information obtained by others through the interception or unauthorized access of such electronic records or communications.

Include the following if applicable.

At the end of our representation, please let us know if you need any documents from our files. We will retain documents for [five years/a limited time] and then destroy them in accordance with our record-retention policy then in effect.

Continue with the following.

We believe this candid discussion should prevent any misunderstandings later. Please sign a copy of this letter in the space below, expressing your agreement to the terms and conditions set forth above.

Sincerely yours,

____

[Name of attorney]

Enc.

ACCEPTED AND AGREED TO ON ____________________.

____

[Name of client]

Include the following notice if notice is not otherwise provided as required by Tex. Gov't Code § 81.079. See section 1.1:2.

Notice to Clients

Texas law requires that all attorneys provide their clients with the following notice about the existence of the attorney grievance process: "The State Bar of Texas investigates and prosecutes professional misconduct committed by Texas attorneys. Although not every complaint against or dispute with a lawyer involves professional misconduct, the State Bar's

Office of Chief Disciplinary Counsel will provide you with information about how to file a complaint. Please call 1-800-932-1900 toll-free for more information."

Include the following if applicable.

The Texas Lawyer's Creed

I am a lawyer. I am entrusted by the People of Texas to preserve and improve our legal system. I am licensed by the Supreme Court of Texas. I must therefore abide by the Texas Disciplinary Rules of Professional Conduct, but I know that professionalism requires more than merely avoiding the violation of laws and rules. I am committed to this creed for no other reason than it is right.

Our Legal System

A lawyer owes to the administration of justice personal dignity, integrity, and independence. A lawyer should always adhere to the highest principles of professionalism.

1. I am passionately proud of my profession. Therefore, "My word is my bond."

2. I am responsible to assure that all persons have access to competent representation regardless of wealth or position in life.

3. I commit myself to an adequate and effective pro bono program.

4. I am obligated to educate my clients, the public, and other lawyers regarding the spirit and letter of this Creed.

5. I will always be conscious of my duty to the judicial system.

Lawyer to Client

A lawyer owes to a client allegiance, learning, skill, and industry. A lawyer shall employ all appropriate means to protect and advance the client's legitimate rights, claims, and objectives. A lawyer shall not be deterred by any real or imagined fear of judicial disfavor or public unpopularity, nor be influenced by mere self-interest.

1. I will advise my client of the contents of this Creed when undertaking representation.

2. I will endeavor to achieve my client's lawful objectives in legal transactions and in litigation as quickly and economically as possible.

3. I will be loyal and committed to my client's lawful objectives, but I will not permit that loyalty and commitment to interfere with my duty to provide objective and independent advice.

4. I will advise my client that civility and courtesy are expected and are not a sign of weakness.

5. I will advise my client of proper and expected behavior.

6. I will treat adverse parties and witnesses with fairness and due consideration. A client has no right to demand that I abuse anyone or indulge in any offensive conduct.

7. I will advise my client that we will not pursue conduct which is intended primarily to harass or drain the financial resources of the opposing party.

8. I will advise my client that we will not pursue tactics which are intended primarily for delay.

9. I will advise my client that we will not pursue any course of action which is without merit.

10. I will advise my client that I reserve the right to determine whether to grant accommodations to opposing counsel in all matters that do not adversely affect my client's lawful objectives. A client has no right to instruct me to refuse reasonable requests made by other counsel.

11. I will advise my client regarding the availability of mediation, arbitration, and other alternative methods of resolving and settling disputes.

Lawyer to Lawyer

A lawyer owes to opposing counsel, in the conduct of legal transactions and the pursuit of litigation, courtesy, candor, cooperation, and scrupulous observance of all agreements and mutual understandings. Ill feelings between clients shall not influence a lawyer's conduct, attitude, or demeanor toward opposing counsel. A lawyer shall not engage in unprofessional conduct in retaliation against other unprofessional conduct.

1. I will be courteous, civil, and prompt in oral and written communications.

2. I will not quarrel over matters of form or style, but I will concentrate on matters of substance.

3. I will identify for other counsel or parties all changes I have made in documents submitted for review.

4. I will attempt to prepare documents which correctly reflect the agreement of the parties. I will not include provisions which have not been agreed upon or omit provisions which are necessary to reflect the agreement of the parties.

5. I will notify opposing counsel, and, if appropriate, the Court or other persons, as soon as practicable, when hearings, depositions, meetings, conferences or closings are canceled.

6. I will agree to reasonable requests for extensions of time and for waiver of procedural formalities, provided legitimate objectives of my client will not be adversely affected.

7. I will not serve motions or pleadings in any manner that unfairly limits another party's opportunity to respond.

8. I will attempt to resolve by agreement my objections to matters contained in pleadings and discovery requests and responses.

9. I can disagree without being disagreeable. I recognize that effective representation does not require antagonistic or obnoxious behavior. I will neither encourage nor knowingly permit my client or anyone under my control to do anything which would be unethical or improper if done by me.

10. I will not, without good cause, attribute bad motives or unethical conduct to opposing counsel nor bring the profession into disrepute by unfounded accusations of impropriety. I will avoid disparaging personal remarks or acrimony towards opposing counsel, parties and witnesses. I will not be influenced by any ill feeling between clients. I will abstain from any allusion to personal peculiarities or idiosyncrasies of opposing counsel.

11. I will not take advantage, by causing any default or dismissal to be rendered, when I know the identity of an opposing counsel, without first inquiring about that counsel's intention to proceed.

12. I will promptly submit orders to the Court. I will deliver copies to opposing counsel before or contemporaneously with submission to the Court. I will promptly approve the form of orders which accurately reflect the substance of the rulings of the Court.

13. I will not attempt to gain an unfair advantage by sending the Court or its staff correspondence or copies of correspondence.

14. I will not arbitrarily schedule a deposition, court appearance, or hearing until a good faith effort has been made to schedule it by agreement.

15. I will readily stipulate to undisputed facts in order to avoid needless costs or inconvenience for any party.

16. I will refrain from excessive and abusive discovery.

17. I will comply with all reasonable discovery requests. I will not resist discovery requests which are not objectionable. I will not make objections nor give instructions to a witness for the purpose of delaying or obstructing the discovery process. I will encourage witnesses to respond to all deposition questions which are reasonably understandable. I will neither encourage nor permit my witness to quibble about words where their meaning is reasonably clear.

18. I will not seek Court intervention to obtain discovery which is clearly improper and not discoverable.

19. I will not seek sanctions or disqualification unless it is necessary for protection of my client's lawful objectives or is fully justified by the circumstances.

Lawyer and Judge

Lawyers and judges owe each other respect, diligence, candor, punctuality, and protection against unjust and improper criticism and attack. Lawyers and judges are equally responsible to protect the dignity and independence of the Court and the profession.

1. I will always recognize that the position of judge is the symbol of both the judicial system and administration of justice. I will refrain from conduct that degrades this symbol.

2. I will conduct myself in Court in a professional manner and demonstrate my respect for the Court and the law.

3. I will treat counsel, opposing parties, the Court, and members of the Court staff with courtesy and civility.

4. I will be punctual.

5. I will not engage in any conduct which offends the dignity and decorum of proceedings.

6. I will not knowingly misrepresent, mischaracterize, misquote or miscite facts or authorities to gain an advantage.

7. I will respect the rulings of the Court.

8. I will give the issues in controversy deliberate, impartial and studied analysis and consideration.

9. I will be considerate of the time constraints and pressures imposed upon the Court, Court staff and counsel in efforts to administer justice and resolve disputes.

Form 1-11

This letter is furnished only as a basic example and should not be used as a standard form. The attorney must be careful to tailor the details of the letter to the facts of the particular case. See section 1.6:3 in this chapter concerning entering business transactions with clients.

Letter Requesting Client's Consent to Business Relationship with Attorney

[**Date**]

[**Name and address of client**]

Re: [**describe transaction**]

[**Salutation**]

You have inquired about my interest in investing in the above-referenced venture in addition to my performing the legal work for you on this project. I have given this matter considerable thought and will continue to do so. I will let you know my decision by [**date**].

Nevertheless, I think it is important that you consider the advisability of having me, your lawyer, as a business partner. Under rule 1.08(a) of the Texas Disciplinary Rules of Professional Conduct, a lawyer cannot enter into a business venture with a client unless (1) the transaction and terms on which the lawyer acquires an interest are fair and reasonable to the client, (2) these terms are fully disclosed to the client, (3) the client is given a reasonable opportunity to seek independent counsel, and (4) the client agrees in writing to the relationship. This rule protects the client from possible conflicts of interest that may occur if counsel is involved in the venture.

In this case the terms and conditions of the venture are well known to you because you were the one who suggested them. However, for purposes of clarity I will repeat them here. The terms are [**list terms**].

Although not required by our State Bar's rules of ethics, I must insist that you seek independent counsel before our entry into this venture.

Once you consult with an attorney, please put his or her name in the space I have provided and then sign and return the copy of this letter to signify your consent for me to have an interest in the venture.

Sincerely yours,

____

[Name of attorney]

I have consulted with ______________________________ and have availed myself of that attorney's advice. I knowingly agree to your participation in the venture described on the terms outlined in this letter, which I believe are fair and reasonable. I am also requesting you to act as legal counsel in this transaction, with the terms of the engagement to be outlined in a separate letter agreement.

ACCEPTED:

____

[Name of client]
Date:

Form 1-12

This letter is furnished only as a basic example and should not be used as a standard form. The attorney must be careful to tailor the details of the letter to the facts of the particular case. See section 1.6:4 in this chapter concerning clarifying nonrepresentation.

Nonrepresentation Letter When Representing Lender or Title Company

[**Date**]

[**Names and addresses of buyer and seller**]

Re: [**describe transaction**]

[**Salutation**]

I have represented [**name of lender or title company**] in the preparation of legal documents for use in closing the above-referenced transaction.

While I have acted solely on behalf of [**name of lender or title company**], [**name**], the buyer, and [**name**], the seller, acknowledge that the legal fees incurred in preparing the legal documents will be paid by the buyer or the seller even though I have not in any manner undertaken to assist or render legal advice to the buyer or the seller, except in the preparation of the legal documents. The buyer and the seller further acknowledge and understand that they may retain independent legal counsel to represent their individual interests in the referenced transaction.

The buyer and the seller specifically recognize that I do not have the responsibility to provide any truth-in-lending disclosures, any other truth-in-lending documents, or any other documents required by any regulations that apply to this transaction. The lender is responsible for providing those documents, and no charge may be made for providing them.

Please sign below to acknowledge that you have been advised of my representation of the [lender/title company] and that you understand that I am not your attorney.

Sincerely yours,

____

[**Name of attorney**]

Buyer:

____

[**Name of buyer**]
Date:

Seller:

____

[**Name of seller**]
Date:

Form 1-13

This letter is furnished only as a basic example and should not be used as a standard form. The attorney must be careful to tailor the details of the letter to the facts of the particular case. See section 1.8:1 in this chapter concerning terminating the attorney-client relationship.

Letter Terminating Attorney-Client Relationship

[**Date**]

[**Name and address of client**]

Re: [**describe transaction**]

[**Salutation**]

During the past [**time period**], it has been our pleasure to serve you as counsel in [**describe transaction**]. During that representation, you have paid substantial legal fees and related expenses. Unfortunately, contrary to our engagement agreement, you have not paid our statements in a timely manner for the past few months.

At this time, the outstanding and overdue fees and expenses total approximately $[**amount**]. Our firm desires to continue our relationship but does not have the ability to finance your legal representation. Moreover, you expressly agreed that payment of the hourly fees and expenses in this matter would be kept current.

We now provide you the opportunity to retain other counsel without jeopardizing your position. However, if we wait several more months, it is possible that circumstances will change and this opportunity will be lost. Consequently, as of [**date**], we will cease to represent you.

Your new counsel may wish to discuss this file with us. That would be to your advantage both substantively and economically. We are willing to do so as long as satisfactory arrangements are made to compensate us for the additional time and expense incurred. Also, it will be necessary to agree on a plan to pay the outstanding fees and expenses.

During our representation we have generated work that we are willing to share with your new counsel to the extent our legal obligations require us to do so in the absence of full payment of our fees and expenses.

If you wish us to continue representing you, satisfactory arrangements must be made to take care of the overdue fees and expenses, as well as the future fees and expenses.

I look forward to hearing from you and remain hopeful our representation can continue.

Sincerely yours,

____

[Name of attorney]

Form 1-14

This letter is furnished only as a basic example and should not be used as a standard form. The attorney must be careful to tailor the details of the letter to the facts of the particular case. Client files must be maintained and preserved for a period of five years after termination of representation. Tex. Disciplinary Rules Prof'l Conduct R. 1.14.

Letter for Completion of Attorney-Client Relationship

[**Date**]

[**Name and address of client**]

Re: [**describe transaction**]

[**Salutation**]

It has been our pleasure to serve you as counsel in [**describe transaction**]. According to our records, we have completed this matter, and we are closing this file.

You should already have a complete set of the relevant closing documents in your possession. If not, please let us know and we will be glad to send them to you.

> Describe any actions that the client may need to follow up on, such as UCC1 renewals, note extensions at maturity, etc.

> Include the following if applicable.

Please let us know if you need any other documents from our files. We will retain documents for five years and then destroy them in accordance with our record-retention policy then in effect.

> Continue with the following.

I look forward to the opportunity to represent you on other matters in the future.

Sincerely yours,

____

[**Name of attorney**]

Form 1-15

This letter is furnished only as a basic example and should not be used as a standard form. The attorney must be careful to tailor the details of the letter to the facts of the particular case. See sections 1.5:4 and 1.5:5 in this chapter concerning the basic engagement agreement.

Letter Detailing Basic Engagement Agreement and Fee Agreement for Local Counsel in Financing Transaction

[**Date**]

[**Name and address of client**]

Re: Local counsel representation

[**Salutation**]

Thank you for asking me to represent you in the above-referenced matter. I consider it a privilege to do so. Please excuse the overly formal and detailed nature of this letter—it is intended to ensure that you know and understand the terms and conditions under which this firm will represent you.

1. We have been engaged by you solely to provide local Texas law advice, as requested by your lead counsel, [**name of lead counsel**] ("Lead Counsel"). We have not been involved in the negotiations regarding any loan, guaranty, or security documents. You have asked that we provide opinions on your behalf to [**name of lender**] ("Lender"), and you consent to our doing so. It is possible that, in the course of the review of forms of documents to be executed, we will be required to provide drafting comments to conform to Texas law. You consent to our doing so. You understand that such comments may be helpful to the Lender rather than to you. Our primary contact on your behalf will be the Lead Counsel. You authorize the Lead Counsel to direct us on your behalf concerning our representation and to

approve all actions to be taken on your behalf. Similarly, you authorize us to transmit our advice and any documentation to the Lead Counsel for its approval.

2. Our fees for legal services are based primarily on the hourly rates for each lawyer and legal assistant at the time the services are rendered. Our current rates are $[**amount**] per hour for [**name**], $[**amount**] per hour for associates or contract lawyers, and $[**amount**] per hour for legal assistants.

> Complete disclosure about the attorney's billing practices can avoid client misunderstandings later. For example, explain about travel time, multiple attorney conferences, research, billing for "forms" in the firm's form library, administrative overtime, etc. See sections 1.5:4 and 1.5:5 for additional information.

3. It is our policy to bill clients periodically for fees and out-of-pocket expenses. These bills will generally describe services performed and the expenses incurred. If we are confronted with unanticipated expenses, we may request the supplier to bill you directly for any third-party expenses.

4. Our statements are reasonably detailed, and consequently our clients do not usually have any questions about them. However, if you should ever have any question or comment, please do not hesitate to call us so that we can discuss the matter. Our hourly rates do not include any interest for slow payment. Because of this and the fact that we do not include a service charge for late payments, we must insist that our clients pay their bills promptly.

5. We require a [nonrefundable] retainer [when accepting work from new clients/ before beginning work on a new matter]. Accordingly, we ask that you remit to [us/and maintain with us during our representation] a retainer of $[**amount**]. [**Include as applicable:** We will place these funds in our trust account./The retainer will be applied to our final statement for fees and expenses or, at our discretion, to any past-due amounts./On the termination of our services, we will promptly refund the retainer, less any fees and expenses unpaid as of the date of our final bill.]

6. You agree that we are relieved from the responsibility of performing any further work should you fail to pay any statement for fees and expenses (including bills for expenses received from third parties) or for supplemental retainers within fifteen days of their receipt. In that event, you agree that we may move to withdraw as your counsel and that you will promptly execute any withdrawal motions to accomplish this.

7. You agree that this firm may retain papers relating to this matter to secure payment of any amount you owe us, to the extent permitted by law, but only if such retention will not prejudice your interests in the subject matter of the representation.

8. During our discussions about handling this matter, we may have provided you with certain estimates of the fees and expenses that will be required at certain stages of our representation. Such estimates are just that, and the fees and expenses required are ultimately a function of many conditions over which we have little or no control, particularly the difficulties we encounter during negotiations with other parties. The reason we submit our clients' bills shortly after the services are rendered is so they will have a means of monitoring and controlling their expenses. If you believe the expenses are mounting too rapidly, please contact us immediately so we can assist you in evaluating how they might be curtailed. If we do not hear from you, we assume that you approve of the overall level of activity in this matter.

Include the following if applicable.

9. The Supreme Court of Texas has adopted and promulgated the Texas Lawyer's Creed. Although compliance with the Creed is voluntary, we have decided to adhere to its provisions. Please review the attached Texas Lawyer's Creed, and if you have any questions, we will be glad to discuss them with you.

Continue with the following.

10. You may discharge us from this representation at any time. We will be free to withdraw at any time, with or without cause, subject to reasonable notice under the circum-

stances and to approval by any court that may become involved in your matter. We will be entitled to receive compensation from you for all services rendered and all disbursements made, under the provisions of this agreement, up to the time of withdrawal. Circumstances may arise that will require us to withdraw from representation under the Texas Disciplinary Rules of Professional Conduct or other applicable professional standards. In such circumstances, as well as in the instances referred to above, we will cooperate in the transfer of the matter to other counsel of your choice.

11. As is true with all legal services, we cannot and do not guarantee the results of our representation. We make no express warranties concerning this transaction, and disclaim any implied warranties concerning it.

12. Attorneys, like other professionals who advise on personal financial matters, are required by a federal law (the Gramm-Leach-Bliley Act) to inform their clients of their policies regarding privacy of client information. Because attorneys have been and continue to be bound by professional standards of confidentiality that are even more stringent than those required by this new law, we have always protected our clients' right to privacy. In the course of representing our clients, we receive all manner of significant personal financial information from them. As a client of the firm, you are advised that all information we receive from you will be held in confidence and not released to outside persons, except as agreed to by you or as required under applicable law. We retain records relating to professional services we provide to assist our clients with their professional needs and, in some cases, to comply with professional guidelines. To guard your nonpublic personal information, we maintain physical, electronic, and procedural safeguards that comply with our professional standards.

Our firm makes reasonable efforts to ensure the security of all electronic data including confidential records related to our clients and the electronic communications (such as email, texts, telephone calls, voice-over-internet calls, video calls, cellular telephone, Twitter, and social networking sites) relating to our clients, whether those communications are between our firm and our clients or our internal communications relating to client matters. We believe that employing such electronic records and communications, including the use of cloud storage of data and communications, improves the efficiency of our work and our communications with our clients. You understand that we cannot guarantee that any such electronic records or communications are not intercepted or accessed by unauthorized or unintended parties. Unless you specify otherwise in writing, our firm will continue to employ such electronic communications and record storage in performing our duties, and you understand and agree that we are not responsible for the unintended disclosure of any confidential information obtained by others through the interception or unauthorized access of such electronic records or communications.

Include the following if applicable.

At the end of our representation, please let us know if you need any documents from our files. We will retain documents for [five years/a limited time] and then destroy them in accordance with our record-retention policy then in effect.

Continue with the following.

We believe this candid discussion should prevent any misunderstandings later. Please sign a copy of this letter in the space below, expressing your agreement to the terms and conditions set forth above.

Sincerely yours,

____

[Name of attorney]

Enc.

ACCEPTED AND AGREED TO ON ____________________.

____

[Name of client]

Include the following notice if notice is not otherwise provided as required by Tex. Gov't Code § 81.079. See section 1.1:2.

Notice to Clients

Texas law requires that all attorneys provide their clients with the following notice about the existence of the attorney grievance process: "The State Bar of Texas investigates and prosecutes professional misconduct committed by Texas attorneys. Although not every complaint against or dispute with a lawyer involves professional misconduct, the State Bar's Office of Chief Disciplinary Counsel will provide you with information about how to file a complaint. Please call 1-800-932-1900 toll-free for more information."

Include the following if applicable.

The Texas Lawyer's Creed

I am a lawyer. I am entrusted by the People of Texas to preserve and improve our legal system. I am licensed by the Supreme Court of Texas. I must therefore abide by the Texas Disciplinary Rules of Professional Conduct, but I know that professionalism requires more than merely avoiding the violation of laws and rules. I am committed to this creed for no other reason than it is right.

Our Legal System

A lawyer owes to the administration of justice personal dignity, integrity, and independence. A lawyer should always adhere to the highest principles of professionalism.

1. I am passionately proud of my profession. Therefore, "My word is my bond."

2. I am responsible to assure that all persons have access to competent representation regardless of wealth or position in life.

3. I commit myself to an adequate and effective pro bono program.

4. I am obligated to educate my clients, the public, and other lawyers regarding the spirit and letter of this Creed.

5. I will always be conscious of my duty to the judicial system.

Lawyer to Client

A lawyer owes to a client allegiance, learning, skill, and industry. A lawyer shall employ all appropriate means to protect and advance the client's legitimate rights, claims, and objectives. A lawyer shall not be deterred by any real or imagined fear of judicial disfavor or public unpopularity, nor be influenced by mere self-interest.

1. I will advise my client of the contents of this Creed when undertaking representation.

2. I will endeavor to achieve my client's lawful objectives in legal transactions and in litigation as quickly and economically as possible.

3. I will be loyal and committed to my client's lawful objectives, but I will not permit that loyalty and commitment to interfere with my duty to provide objective and independent advice.

4. I will advise my client that civility and courtesy are expected and are not a sign of weakness.

5. I will advise my client of proper and expected behavior.

6. I will treat adverse parties and witnesses with fairness and due consideration. A client has no right to demand that I abuse anyone or indulge in any offensive conduct.

7. I will advise my client that we will not pursue conduct which is intended primarily to harass or drain the financial resources of the opposing party.

8. I will advise my client that we will not pursue tactics which are intended primarily for delay.

9. I will advise my client that we will not pursue any course of action which is without merit.

10. I will advise my client that I reserve the right to determine whether to grant accommodations to opposing counsel in all matters that do not adversely affect my client's lawful objectives. A client has no right to instruct me to refuse reasonable requests made by other counsel.

11. I will advise my client regarding the availability of mediation, arbitration, and other alternative methods of resolving and settling disputes.

Lawyer to Lawyer

A lawyer owes to opposing counsel, in the conduct of legal transactions and the pursuit of litigation, courtesy, candor, cooperation, and scrupulous observance of all agreements and mutual understandings. Ill feelings between clients shall not influence a lawyer's conduct, attitude, or demeanor toward opposing counsel. A lawyer shall not engage in unprofessional conduct in retaliation against other unprofessional conduct.

1. I will be courteous, civil, and prompt in oral and written communications.

2. I will not quarrel over matters of form or style, but I will concentrate on matters of substance.

3. I will identify for other counsel or parties all changes I have made in documents submitted for review.

4. I will attempt to prepare documents which correctly reflect the agreement of the parties. I will not include provisions which have not been agreed upon or omit provisions which are necessary to reflect the agreement of the parties.

5. I will notify opposing counsel, and, if appropriate, the Court or other persons, as soon as practicable, when hearings, depositions, meetings, conferences or closings are canceled.

6. I will agree to reasonable requests for extensions of time and for waiver of procedural formalities, provided legitimate objectives of my client will not be adversely affected.

7. I will not serve motions or pleadings in any manner that unfairly limits another party's opportunity to respond.

8. I will attempt to resolve by agreement my objections to matters contained in pleadings and discovery requests and responses.

9. I can disagree without being disagreeable. I recognize that effective representation does not require antagonistic or obnoxious behavior. I will neither encourage nor knowingly permit my client or anyone under my control to do anything which would be unethical or improper if done by me.

10. I will not, without good cause, attribute bad motives or unethical conduct to opposing counsel nor bring the profession into disrepute by unfounded accusations of impropriety. I will avoid disparaging personal remarks or acrimony towards opposing counsel, parties and witnesses. I will not be influenced by any ill feeling between clients. I will abstain from any allusion to personal peculiarities or idiosyncrasies of opposing counsel.

11. I will not take advantage, by causing any default or dismissal to be rendered, when I know the identity of an opposing counsel, without first inquiring about that counsel's intention to proceed.

12. I will promptly submit orders to the Court. I will deliver copies to opposing counsel before or contemporaneously with submission to the Court. I will promptly approve the form of orders which accurately reflect the substance of the rulings of the Court.

13. I will not attempt to gain an unfair advantage by sending the Court or its staff correspondence or copies of correspondence.

14. I will not arbitrarily schedule a deposition, court appearance, or hearing until a good faith effort has been made to schedule it by agreement.

15. I will readily stipulate to undisputed facts in order to avoid needless costs or inconvenience for any party.

16. I will refrain from excessive and abusive discovery.

17. I will comply with all reasonable discovery requests. I will not resist discovery requests which are not objectionable. I will not make objections nor give instructions to a witness for the purpose of delaying or obstructing the discovery process. I will encourage witnesses to respond to all deposition questions which are reasonably understandable. I will neither encourage nor permit my witness to quibble about words where their meaning is reasonably clear.

18. I will not seek Court intervention to obtain discovery which is clearly improper and not discoverable.

19. I will not seek sanctions or disqualification unless it is necessary for protection of my client's lawful objectives or is fully justified by the circumstances.

Lawyer and Judge

Lawyers and judges owe each other respect, diligence, candor, punctuality, and protection against unjust and improper criticism and attack. Lawyers and judges are equally responsible to protect the dignity and independence of the Court and the profession.

1. I will always recognize that the position of judge is the symbol of both the judicial system and administration of justice. I will refrain from conduct that degrades this symbol.

2. I will conduct myself in Court in a professional manner and demonstrate my respect for the Court and the law.

3. I will treat counsel, opposing parties, the Court, and members of the Court staff with courtesy and civility.

4. I will be punctual.

5. I will not engage in any conduct which offends the dignity and decorum of proceedings.

6. I will not knowingly misrepresent, mischaracterize, misquote or miscite facts or authorities to gain an advantage.

7. I will respect the rulings of the Court.

8. I will give the issues in controversy deliberate, impartial and studied analysis and consideration.

9. I will be considerate of the time constraints and pressures imposed upon the Court, Court staff and counsel in efforts to administer justice and resolve disputes.

Form 1-16

This letter is furnished only as a basic example and should not be used as a standard form. The attorney must be careful to tailor the details of the letter to the facts of the particular case.

Letter Amending Engagement Agreement

[**Date**]

[**Name and address of client**]

Re: Amendment of engagement agreement dated [**date**]

[**Salutation**]

The purpose of this letter is to amend the engagement agreement dated [**date**] to [include a new adverse party/[add/restrict] the scope of services/[**other amendment**]]. Please read this letter carefully. It describes the terms and conditions under which we will represent you. Our policy requires that each client sign a copy of this letter agreeing to the terms and conditions described below before we can engage in representation.

[**Detail the reason for amending the agreement, including the new adverse party, revised scope of representation, or other new amendment.**]

Our fees for legal services are based primarily on the hourly rate for each lawyer and legal assistant at the time services are rendered. My current rate per hour is $[**amount**]. The current rate per hour for my associates ranges from $[**amount**] to $[**amount**]. We review these hourly rates periodically and may adjust them. The changes will apply automatically and be reflected on your next statement.

Please sign a copy of this letter in the space below, expressing your agreement to the terms and conditions set forth above. After we receive your signed copy of this letter, we will commence our representation in the matter.

Sincerely,

____

[Name of attorney]

ACCEPTED AND AGREED TO ON______________________________

____

[Name of client]

Chapter 2
Laws Affecting Real Estate

Chapter 2

Laws Affecting Real Estate

The following statutes and regulations affecting real estate are organized alphabetically by topic, with cross-references to other relevant sections where appropriate.

§ 2.1 Abandonment

The landlord's rights and obligations regarding personal property after a tenant abandons commercial leased premises are addressed in Tex. Prop. Code § 93.002(e). A landlord has a duty to mitigate damages if a tenant abandons leased premises. Tex. Prop. Code § 91.006. The general subject of unclaimed personal property and escheat is addressed in Tex. Prop. Code chs. 72–76.

§ 2.2 Abstracts of Judgment

A person in whose favor a judgment is rendered, or certain others on their behalf, may apply for an abstract of judgment. The Texas Property Code sets out the procedure for obtaining an abstract of judgment from the judge or justice of the peace who rendered the judgment or from the clerk of the court. The required contents of an abstract of judgment are located in Tex. Prop. Code § 52.003. Abstracts of judgment are recorded in the county's real property records. Tex. Prop. Code §§ 52.002–.003. See also sections 2.143 and 2.216 below.

Tex. Prop. Code § 52.0012 provides that a homestead affidavit and a certificate of mailing (both in the form prescribed by the statute) may be filed by a judgment debtor as a release of a judgment lien on homestead property, provided the judgment creditor does not file a contradicting affidavit within thirty days of the filing of the certificate of mailing.

For special restrictions on the filing of abstracts of judgment by inmates or their representatives, refer to Tex. Civ. Prac. & Rem. Code §§ 12.001–.007.

§ 2.3 Acceleration of Note

Tex. Civ. Prac. & Rem. Code § 16.038 provides that if the maturity date of a note is accelerated and subsequently rescinded or waived in accordance with the requirements of section 16.038 before the limitations period expires, then the acceleration is deemed rescinded and waived, and the note is governed by Tex. Civ. Prac. & Rem. Code § 16.035 as if no acceleration had occurred. A notice served under section 16.038 does not affect a lienholder's right to accelerate the maturity date of the debt in the future or waive past defaults. Section 16.038 does not create an exclusive method for waiver and rescission of acceleration or affect the accrual of a cause of action and the running of the related limitations period under Tex. Civ. Prac. & Rem. Code § 16.035(e) on any subsequent maturity date, accelerated or otherwise, of the note.

§ 2.4 Acknowledgments

Texas law provides one form of ordinary certificate of acknowledgment and six short-form certificates of acknowledgment. Tex. Civ. Prac. & Rem. Code §§ 121.007–.008. A notary may sign on behalf of a disabled person in certain circumstances. Tex. Gov't Code § 406.0165. There are specific requirements for proof of instruments. Tex. Civ. Prac. & Rem. Code §§ 121.005, 121.009–.011. Instruments may be recorded in Texas real property records if they contain an acknowledgment, a jurat, or a proof. Tex. Prop.

Code § 12.001. On the law of acknowledgments generally, see Tex. Civ. Prac. & Rem. Code §§ 121.001–.016. Instruments may be acknowledged using online notarization. An acknowledgment may be made by appearing in person before the notary or appearing by an interactive two-way audiovisual communication that meets the online notarization requirements. *See* Tex. Civ. Prac. & Rem. Code §§ 121.006, 121.016; Tex. Gov't Code ch. 406, subch. C; 1 Tex. Admin. Code ch. 87. See section 3.13 in this manual. Forms of acknowledgments are included in chapter 3. See also section 2.184 below.

§ 2.5 Ad Valorem Taxes

Both real and personal property are subject to ad valorem taxes in Texas. Tex. Tax Code § 11.01. Provisions for special assessments or exemptions that may apply to real property include those for a residence homestead (Tex. Tax Code §§ 11.13–.135, 23.013); charitable organizations improving property for low-income housing (Tex. Tax Code §§ 11.18(p), 11.181–.1826); agricultural use (Tex. Const. art. VIII, §§ 1–d, 1–d–1; Tex. Tax Code §§ 23.41–.60); timber production (Tex. Const. art. VIII, § 1–d–1; Tex. Tax Code §§ 23.59, 23.71–.79); restricted timber use land (Tex. Tax Code §§ 23.9801–.9807); open-space scenic, recreational, or park use (Tex. Const. art. VIII, § 1–d–1; Tex. Tax Code §§ 23.59, 23.81–.87); mandatory school-tax home exemption (Tex. Const. art. VIII); partially disabled and disabled veterans or their surviving spouses, surviving spouses of members of the armed services killed in action, and surviving spouses of first responders killed or fatally injured in the line of duty (Tex. Const. art. VIII, § 1–b; Tex. Tax Code §§ 11.133(b), 11.134); and solar or wind-powered energy devices (Tex. Tax Code § 11.27). There is also a provision dealing with the separate taxation of tax parcels in condominium projects (Tex. Prop. Code § 82.005). The word *grant* or *convey* in a deed implies a covenant that the estate is free of encumbrances at the time of execution of the conveyance. Tex. Prop. Code § 5.023. "Encumbrance" includes a tax, an assessment, and a lien on real property. Tex. Prop. Code § 5.024.

Owners taxed at a reduced rate under the agricultural-use amendment (Tex. Const. art. VIII, § 1–d), the open-space amendment (Tex. Const. art. VIII, § 1–d–1), or the special appraisal provisions of subchapters B–H of chapter 23 of the Tax Code should be alert to the potential tax liability that accrues if the land use changes or title is transferred and must disclose the reduced rate to a potential buyer using the statutorily prescribed form. Tex. Prop. Code § 5.010. The county appraisal district office is required to maintain a list of properties potentially subject to this type of rollback of taxes. *See* Tex. Tax Code §§ 23.51–.79. Lenders should be aware of the prohibitions against certain waivers and indemnities relating to the agricultural or open-space use exemption, described in more detail at section 2.160 below. In certain circumstances, taxing authorities may have the ability to waive penalties and interest on property erroneously omitted from taxation or granted improper tax exemptions. *See* Tex. Tax Code § 33.011.

Ad valorem tax liens take priority over most prior recorded liens. Tex. Tax Code §§ 32.01–.07. Certain redemption and possessory rights also apply to properties sold at tax foreclosures. *See generally* Tex. Tax Code ch. 34; see also section 2.213 below. A tax lien may also be transferred to a third party on payment of taxes authorized by the owner in accordance with Tex. Tax Code § 32.06. In some cases, property tax lenders will need to be licensed, are prohibited from lending to those eligible for the tax exemption for people over age sixty-five, will need to be cognizant of the regulations concerning advertising, and may be limited in selling a property tax loan in the secondary market. *See* Tex. Fin. Code ch. 351.

In counties having a population in excess of 250,000 and counties of less than 250,000 whose county commissioners opt to participate, an officer conducting a tax foreclosure sale of real property may not execute or deliver a deed to a purchaser who owes ad valorem taxes, whether on real or personal property. Tex. Tax Code § 34.015.

A tenant may contest a landlord's ad valorem tax assessment under certain circumstances. Tex. Tax Code §§ 41.413, 42.015. The property owner may have an obligation to send notices of appraised value to a tenant. Tex. Tax Code § 41.413(d).

When a governmental entity acquires the right to possession of taxable property by a court order issued in condemnation proceedings, takes possession of taxable property under a possession and use agreement, or acquires title to taxable property, taxes for the year of conveyance are prorated to the date of the order granting possession, the effective date of the possession and use agreement, or the date of conveyance. If taxes for the year have not yet been determined, the assessor for each taxing unit may base the proration on taxes for the prior year. The collector must accept the tax payment, and the transferor is relieved of further payment for that year. Tex. Tax Code § 26.11.

§ 2.6 Adverse Possession

Texas has adverse possession periods of three, five, ten, and twenty-five years, depending on different factors. *See* Tex. Civ. Prac. & Rem. Code §§ 16.021–.034. There is a special provision for "cotenant heirs" that provides for a ten-year adverse possession period followed by a five-year "waiting" period after filing certain affidavits. Tex. Civ. Prac. & Rem. Code § 16.0265.

§ 2.7 Affidavits of Heirship

If an ownership interest in real property is in the estate of a decedent who dies intestate, inheritance of the property may be established by an affidavit recorded in the real property records of the county in which the property is located that details the family history and heirship of the decedent and identifies the heirs-at-law under sections 201.001–.003 of the Texas Estates Code. Tex. Est. Code ch. 205. The Estates Code includes a form of affidavit of heirship. Tex. Est. Code § 203.002. See also section 2.296 below. A form of affidavit is furnished at form 26-1 in this manual. The practitioner may want to verify with a title insurance company that the affidavit will be sufficient evidence of inheritance for issuance of a title policy in the event of a future sale of the property interest.

§ 2.8 Affordable Housing Investments

The Internal Revenue Code provides for credits against federal income tax for owners of qualified low-income rental housing projects. *See* 26 U.S.C. § 42. In Texas that program is administered by the Texas Department of Housing and Community Affairs under Tex. Gov't Code ch. 2306 and the rules found in 10 Tex. Admin. Code ch. 49. Under the National Affordable Housing Act of 1990, 42 U.S.C. §§ 12701–12898a, certain HUD funds are available for nonprofit and community development organizations to build or preserve low-income housing. Those projects must also satisfy the HUD program requirements found in 24 C.F.R. pts. 91, 92. Affordable housing constructed with federal or state funds must meet specified handicapped-accessible standards. Tex. Gov't Code § 2306.514. Tex. Gov't Code § 2306.6711(g) provides for the allocation of housing tax credits in Fort Worth, Houston, Dallas, and San Antonio. A community land trust may be created to acquire and hold land for the benefit of developing and preserving long-term affordable housing in a municipality or county. Tex. Loc. Gov't Code ch. 373B.

§ 2.9 Agricultural Development Districts

The creation of agricultural development districts is authorized by chapter 60 of the Agriculture Code. Tex. Agric. Code ch. 60. Districts have the power of eminent domain and may issue bonds (Tex. Agric. Code § 60.058) and levy taxes (Tex. Agric. Code ch. 60, subcs. E, F). See also section 2.69 below.

§ 2.10 Agricultural Liens

Persons securing loans with agricultural products should be aware that the perfection and priority of agricultural liens may be subject to rules outside of chapter 9 of the Texas Uniform Commercial Code. For example, an agricultural lien granted under subchapter E of Texas Property Code chapter 70 has priority over certain prior liens if certain conditions are met. *See* Tex. Prop. Code § 70.4045. Similarly, the statutory trust created upon acceptance of commodities to which the Perishable Agricultural Commodities Act (PACA) applies may also have priority over certain previously filed UCC liens. *See* 7 U.S.C. § 499a–499s. The seller of commodities to which PACA applies may be in a position superior to all other creditors.

§ 2.11 Agricultural Use Exemption

See sections 2.5 above and 2.160 below.

§ 2.12 Aircraft Liens

Lien instruments covering aircraft should consider the aircraft registration requirements of the Federal Aviation Act of 1958 as amended (FAA), 49 U.S.C. §§ 44101–44113, and regulations found in 14 C.F.R. pt. 49. There are also provisions relating to aircraft storage, maintenance, and repair liens in Tex. Prop. Code §§ 70.301–.306.

§ 2.13 Alcoholic Beverages

There are a number of significant limitations on the transfer of and eligibility for alcoholic beverage permits under Texas law. *See* Tex. Alco. Bev. Code ch. 11. Businesses that sell alcohol are heavily regulated, and statutory control may extend to the physical structure of the business. *See, e.g.*, Tex. Alco. Bev. Code § 22.14. The Alcoholic Beverage Code also imposes location requirements applicable to the sale and consumption of alcoholic beverages. *See* Tex. Alco. Bev. Code §§ 101.75(a), 109.33.

§ 2.14 Alternative Dispute Resolution (ADR)

The Texas Alternate Methods of Dispute Resolution Act establishes alternative dispute resolution procedures, including mediation. Tex. Civ. Prac. & Rem. Code ch. 154. See section 2.19 below.

§ 2.15 Americans with Disabilities Act and Related Statutes

Title III of the Americans with Disabilities Act of 1990 (ADA), 42 U.S.C. §§ 12181–12189, creates minimum standards for accessibility in commercial and some types of residential buildings, including requirements relating to new construction; parking alterations; removing barriers from existing structures; installing telephone devices and other assistive listening devices for the deaf; providing auxiliary aids for conferences, seminars, and written materials offered to the public; and ensuring equivalent services and opportunities to disabled persons. Regulations under title III of the ADA pertaining to public accommodations, commercial facilities, and private entities are promulgated under 28 C.F.R. pt. 36. Architectural guidelines can be found in 36 C.F.R. pt. 1191.

Texas also has a state architectural-barriers statute that applies to certain commercial and residential facilities. Tex. Gov't Code ch. 469. Regulations promulgated under the statute are found at 16 Tex. Admin. Code ch. 68. The Human Resources Code permits guide trainers reasonable access to public facilities to train assistance animals and prohibits the denial of access to public facilities, commercial properties, or housing for disabled persons, including those who use assistance animals. Tex. Hum. Res. Code § 121.003. Affordable housing constructed with federal or state funds must meet specified handicapped-accessible standards. Tex. Gov't Code § 2306.514.

For current information on contractors and municipalities that are authorized to perform inspection functions, contact the Texas Department of Licensing and Regulation.

A set of procedures has been adopted for persons pursuing claims of failure to comply with ADA and similar standards, including required notice, opportunity to cure, evidentiary hearings, and abatement of actions. Tex. Hum. Res. Code § 121.0041.

See also section 2.97 below for additional statutes relating to disability access for residential properties.

§ 2.16 Annexation

Annexation and disannexation of real property by municipalities are governed generally by Tex. Loc. Gov't Code chs. 42, 43. Chapter 43 was revised in 2019 to eliminate unilateral annexations. *See* Acts 2019, 86th Leg., R.S., ch. 155 (H.B. 347), eff. May 24, 2019. A municipality may offer to a landowner to enter into an agreement in which the landowner consents to annexation. Tex. Loc. Gov't Code § 43.004. A municipality may contract with an owner of land that is located in the municipality's extraterritorial jurisdiction to guarantee the land's immunity from annexation for a period not to exceed forty-five years, including renewals or extensions. Tex. Loc. Gov't Code § 212.172(b), (d). If a municipality enters into an agreement with a landowner regarding annexation, the municipality must provide the landowner a written disclosure that includes required provisions. Any agreement regarding annexation that fails to provide such disclosure is void. Tex. Loc. Gov't Code § 212.172(b–1), (b–2).

§ 2.17 Antiquities

Chapter 191 of the Texas Natural Resources Code (the Antiquities Code) governs the location, protection, and preservation of "all sites, objects, buildings, pre-twentieth century shipwrecks, and locations of historical, archeological, educational, or scientific interest . . . in, on, or under any of the land in the State of Texas." Tex. Nat. Res. Code § 191.002. The Antiquities Code provides landowners with certain rights. *See* Tex. Nat. Res. Code §§ 191.094, 191.133. There are civil and criminal penalties for violation of provisions of the statute. *See* Tex. Nat. Res. Code §§ 191.171–.174.

§ 2.18 Appraisers

Appraisers are governed by Tex. Occ. Code ch. 1103, the Texas Appraiser Licensing and Certification Act. The Broker's and Appraiser's Lien on Commercial Real Estate Act provides for a lien and procedures to foreclose the lien for commissions and fees due and payable on the sale or lease of commercial real estate (as defined in the Act). *See* Tex. Prop. Code ch. 62. An appraiser or other person who intentionally or knowingly makes a materially false or misleading written statement in providing an appraisal of real property for compensation commits a criminal offense punishable under Tex. Penal Code § 32.32(b–1).

Except for an action for fraud or breach of contract, a person must bring suit for damages or other relief arising from an appraisal or appraisal review conducted by a real estate appraiser or appraisal firm not later than the earlier of (a) two years after the day the person knew or should have known the facts on which the action is based or (b) five years after the day the appraisal or appraisal review was completed. Tex. Civ. Prac. & Rem. Code § 16.013.

Appraisal management companies are defined and regulated by Tex. Occ. Code ch. 1104.

Creditors approved as sellers and servicers to government-sponsored enterprises Federal National Mortgage Association (Fannie Mae) and Federal Home Loan Mortgage Corporation (Freddie Mac) must represent and warrant that appraisals for all covered loans for which application is made on or after October 15, 2010, comply with certain appraiser independence requirements as defined in their respective seller and servicing guides. *See* Fannie Mae, Announcement SEL-2010-14 (Oct. 15, 2010), and Freddie Mac, Bulletin 2010-23 (Oct. 15, 2010).

Title XIV of the Dodd-Frank Wall Street Reform and Consumer Protection Act (Pub. L. No. 111-203, 124 Stat. 1376) contains extensive appraisal reform measures. Appraisal requirements are set out in Regulation Z (Truth in Lending) and 12 C.F.R. § 1026.42 for consumer credit transactions secured by a consumer's principal residence. The regulations are intended to ensure that real estate appraisals used to support creditors' underwriting decisions are based on the appraisers' independent professional judgment, free of any influence or pressure exerted by parties to the transactions.

§ 2.19 Arbitration

Arbitration is a dispute resolution process whereby one or more arbitrators make a decision, called an award, which is binding only if the parties so agree. In Texas, arbitrations can be governed by common law, the Texas Arbitration Act (TAA), and the Federal Arbitration Act (FAA). *See L.H. Lacy v. City of Lubbock*, 559 S.W.2d 348, 351 (Tex. 1977); Tex. Civ. Prac. & Rem. Code chs. 171, 172; 9 U.S.C. §§ 1–16. Some Texas statutes prohibit arbitration under certain circumstances. For example, in a contract for the construction or repair of improvements to real property in Texas, a provision requiring arbitration of disputes in another state is voidable. Tex. Bus. & Com. Code ch. 272. Also, in a contract for the sale or lease of goods worth $50,000 or less, a provision requiring arbitration in another state is voidable unless the provision is in bold-faced, capitalized, underlined, or otherwise conspicuous type. Tex. Bus. & Com. Code ch. 273. When an arbitration agreement is not governed by or enforceable under the TAA, it may be governed by relevant Texas common-law arbitration rules. *L.H. Lacy*, 559 S.W.2d at 352. The FAA applies when the dispute concerns a contract evidencing a transaction involving interstate commerce. *Jack B. Anglin Co. v. Tipps*, 842 S.W.2d 266, 269–70 (Tex. 1992). The FAA and TAA are not mutually exclusive and can both apply to an arbitration provision. *In re D. Wilson Construction Co.*, 196 S.W.3d 774, 779–80 (Tex. 2006). If the FAA applies, however, restrictions under Texas statutes, like the ones described above, can be preempted if the TAA would not allow enforcement of an arbitration agreement that the FAA would enforce. *In re D. Wilson Construction Co.*, 196 S.W.3d at 780.

§ 2.20 Architects

The Board of Architectural Examiners governs the activities of professional architects. Tex. Occ. Code ch. 1051.

An architect's lien against real estate is addressed in Tex. Prop. Code § 53.021(3). An architect's standard of care is addressed in Tex. Civ. Prac. & Rem. Code § 130.0021.

§ 2.21 Asbestos

See section 2.85 below.

§ 2.22 Assignment of Rent

Assignment of rents to a lienholder is governed by Tex. Prop. Code ch. 64, commonly referred to as the Texas Assignment of Rents Act, or TARA. An enforceable security instrument creates an assignment of rents arising from the real property described in the instrument. Tex. Prop. Code § 64.051. An assignment of rents creates a security interest in accrued and unaccrued rents, regardless of whether the assignment is referred to as an absolute assignment. Tex. Prop. Code § 64.051(b). The Act provides methods of enforcement, by notice to the assignor (Tex. Prop. Code § 64.054) or by notice to tenants (Tex. Prop. Code § 64.055). A form of notice is provided. Tex. Prop. Code § 64.056.

§ 2.23 Assumed Names

The circumstances under which assumed names should be filed are addressed in the Assumed Business or Professional Name Act, Tex. Bus. & Com. Code ch. 71. The circumstances under which an entity is considered to have fraudulently filed an assumed name and the penalties for doing so are addressed in Tex. Bus. & Com. Code § 71.203. See also section 2.113 below.

A financing statement that identifies a debtor by an assumed name or trade name may not be effective to perfect a security interest against the debtor unless the name used in the financing statement is so similar to the debtor's name that a search of the records of the filing office under the debtor's name, using the filing office's standard search logic, would disclose the financing statement that used a different assumed name or trade name. Tex. Bus. & Com. Code § 9.506(c). The Texas Business and Commerce Code provides rules for the name to be used in a financing statement for different types of debtors—for example, a debtor that is a decedent's estate, a trust or a trustee, an individual, or an organization. Tex. Bus. & Com. Code § 9.503.

§ 2.24 Astronomical Observatories

See section 2.188 below.

§ 2.25 Automatic Teller Machines (ATMs)

Public safety requirements for the design of and layout surrounding an unmanned teller machine are found at Tex. Fin. Code ch. 59, subch. D.

§ 2.26 Bankruptcy

In addition to the federal Bankruptcy Code, title 11 of the United States Code, property subject to bankruptcy protection will also be affected by the homestead and personal property exemptions of the Texas Constitution and Property Code. Tex. Const. art. XVI, § 50; Tex. Prop. Code chs. 41, 42. Assignment for the benefit of creditors is addressed in Tex. Bus. & Com. Code §§ 23.01–.33. Texas has also adopted the Uniform Fraudulent Transfer Act, Tex. Bus. & Com. Code ch. 24. The circumstances under which a judgment lien is canceled after a bankruptcy discharge are addressed in Tex. Prop. Code §§ 52.041–.043.

§ 2.27 Beaches

See section 2.43 below.

§ 2.28 Beauty Shop Leases

Lessors of premises used for beauty salons and parlors should be aware of the Texas Department of Licensing and Regulation regulations found in 16 Tex. Admin. Code § 83.114.

§ 2.29 Billboards

See section 2.189 below.

§ 2.30 Blind Trusts and Undisclosed Beneficiaries

A conveyance by a person designated as trustee is valid, even if the identity of the beneficiary has not been disclosed; the beneficiary may not set aside the conveyance of the property. Tex. Prop. Code § 101.001. A governmental entity may not purchase real property held in trust or sell real property to a trustee until the trustee submits a copy of the trust agreement and identifies the true owner of the property to the governmental entity. Tex. Gov't Code ch. 2252, subch. D.

§ 2.31 Brokers

Real estate brokers and salespersons are regulated by the Texas Real Estate Commission under the provisions of the Real Estate License Act, Tex. Occ. Code ch. 1101. The Broker's and Appraiser's Lien on Commercial Real Estate Act provides for a lien and procedures to foreclose the lien for commissions and fees due and payable on the sale or lease of commercial real estate (as defined in the Act). *See* Tex. Prop. Code ch. 62. See also section 2.69 below.

§ 2.32 Brownfields Statute

See section 2.287 below.

§ 2.33 Building Codes

The Plumbing License Law adopts the Uniform Plumbing Code and the International Plumbing Code. *See* Tex. Occ. Code ch. 1301. The International Residential Code applies to all construction, alteration, remodeling, enlargement, and repair of residential structures inside municipalities except the installation and maintenance of electrical components. *See* Tex. Loc. Gov't Code §§ 214.212–.213. The National Electrical Code regulates all residential electrical installation and maintenance. *See* Tex. Loc. Gov't Code § 214.214. See also section 2.297 below.

The National Electrical Code as it existed on May 1, 2001, was adopted by the Texas legislature as the municipal electrical construction code in Texas and applies to (1) all residential electrical construction applications and (2) commercial buildings in a municipality for which construction began after January 1, 2006. A municipality may establish procedures to adopt local amendments and to administer and enforce the code. Tex. Loc. Gov't Code § 214.214.

The International Building Code as it existed on May 1, 2012, has been adopted by the Texas legislature as the municipal commercial building code in Texas for commercial buildings in a municipality for which construction began after January 1, 2022. A municipality may establish procedures to adopt local amendments and to administer and enforce the code. Tex. Loc. Gov't Code § 214.216.

The International Residential Code as it existed on May 1, 2012, has been adopted by the Texas legislature as the municipal residential building code in Texas. A municipality may establish procedures to adopt local amendments and to administer and enforce the code. Tex. Loc. Gov't Code § 214.212.

§ 2.34 Business Organizations Code

Corporations, partnerships, limited partnerships, limited liability companies, registered limited liability partnerships, nonprofit corporations, and cooperative associations organized or qualified to do business in Texas on or after January 1, 2006, must comply with the Texas Business Organizations Code. Entities organized or qualified to do business before January 1, 2006, had the option to be governed by the Code on or after January 1, 2006. Effective January 1, 2010, all entities organized or qualified to do business in Texas must comply with the Code. *See generally* Tex. Bus. Orgs. Code ch. 402.

§ 2.35 Camping Resorts

The Texas Membership Camping Resort Act is found at Tex. Prop. Code ch. 222. See also section 2.147 below.

§ 2.36 Cash Proceeds

Those who receive in connection with their trade or business more than $10,000 in cash in a transaction or in several related transactions must report to the Internal Revenue Service the amount of currency received; the payor's name, address, and tax identification number; the date and nature of the transaction; and other information as the United States Secretary of the Treasury may prescribe. 26 U.S.C. § 6050I(a), (b); 26 C.F.R. § 1.6050I–1.

§ 2.37 Cemeteries

The location and operation of cemeteries are regulated by Tex. Health & Safety Code §§ 711.001–.062. The platting of cemetery lands, mausoleums, crematories, and columbariums is governed by Tex. Health & Safety Code § 711.034.

§ 2.38 Certificates of Convenience and Necessity

See sections 2.233, 2.254, and 2.292 below.

§ 2.39 Certification of Trust

A person other than a beneficiary is not required to inquire into the extent of the trustee's powers or the propriety of the exercise of those powers if the person deals with the trustee in good faith and obtains a certification of trust. Tex. Prop. Code § 114.081(b). Tex. Prop. Code § 114.086 describes the contents of such a certification and describes the instances in which a party may rely on the representations about the power of the trustee to take actions on behalf of the trust described in the certification. See section 10.15 in this manual.

§ 2.40 Certified Mail

See section 2.214 below.

§ 2.41 Child Support Liens

A lien for all child support due and owing, including any accrued interest, attaches by operation of law to all nonhomestead property of an obligor. Tex. Fam. Code § 157.312. A child support lien against real property is perfected by filing or delivering an abstract of judgment or a child support lien notice as provided by Tex. Fam. Code § 157.314. Tex. Fam. Code § 157.316. The lien is subject to the general requirements addressed in Tex. Fam. Code §§ 157.311–.331. Foreclosure is governed by Tex. Fam. Code § 157.323. Tex. Fam. Code § 157.318 sets out the provisions regarding duration and effect of child support liens. Tex. Fam. Code § 157.3171 provides a process that parallels and adopts portions of Tex. Prop. Code § 52.0012 to release an abstracted child support lien from homestead property.

§ 2.42 Choice of Law

Choice-of-law provisions in contracts of $1 million or more are enforceable under certain conditions. Tex. Bus. & Com. Code ch. 271. Tex. Bus. & Com. Code ch. 272 restricts the enforceability of choice-of-law provisions in contracts for the construction or repair of improvements to real property. For other types of contracts of $50,000 or less, a conspicuous legend informing the parties of the choice-of-law provision must be in the contract (if another state's laws are chosen). Tex. Bus. & Com. Code ch. 273. Choice-of-law provisions for contracts made solely over the Internet are governed by Tex. Bus. & Com. Code ch. 274.

§ 2.43 Coastal Properties

Two types of notices relating to coastal properties are required for real property transactions in the vicinity of coastal waters. First, persons entering into an executory contract to convey an interest in property located seaward of the Gulf Intracoastal Waterway must make the disclosure required by Tex. Nat. Res. Code § 61.025, either in the contract itself or in a notice delivered not less than ten days before the closing of the sale. With some exceptions, the notice must be provided to the purchaser or transferee in all conveyancing transactions, including nonjudicial foreclosure sales. *See* Tex. Att'y Gen. Op. No. JM-834 (1987). Second, if real property adjoins and abuts the tidally influenced waters of the state, the notice prescribed in Tex. Nat. Res. Code § 33.135 must be given in all written executory contracts. The statutory disclosure form prescribed by section 5.008(b) of the Texas Property Code also includes language regarding such coastal properties.

Chapter 61 of the Natural Resources Code (Texas Open Beaches Act) declares the public policy of the state is that the public has free and unrestricted right of ingress and egress to and from state-owned beaches bordering on the seaward shore of the Gulf of Mexico and the larger area extending from the line of mean low tide to the line of vegetation bordering on the Gulf of Mexico, to which the public has acquired a right of use or easement to or over by prescription or dedication or has established and retained a right by virtue of continuous right in the public under Texas common law. Chapter 61 contains provisions under which the commissioner of the General Land Office can (1) impose administrative penalties on persons constructing, maintaining, controlling, owning, or possessing improvements on public beaches; (2) order those improvements removed at the expense of the person constructing, maintaining, controlling, owning, or possessing them; (3) notify the State Board of Insurance that the improvements are not insurable; and (4) make determinations concerning the line of vegetation, including the ability to suspend a determination on the line of vegetation for up to three years. There are several provisions regarding public access to beaches, coastal erosion duties, erosion responses, and posting of private access in Tex. Nat. Res. Code chs. 33, 61.

See also section 2.297 below.

The Texas Constitution was amended in 2009 to further protect the right of the public to access and use public beaches. Tex. Const. art. I, § 33, defines "public beach" and grants to the public a permanent easement and the unrestricted right to use, and a right of ingress to and egress from, a public beach. Section 33 further authorizes the legislature to enact laws to protect the public's right to access and use a public beach and to protect the public beach easement from interference and encroachments, but it does not create a private right of enforcement. However, Texas law does not recognize the concept of a "rolling" public easement onto privately owned beachfront property, which would have the effect of allowing the public use easement to migrate onto previously unencumbered private property.

> Easements for public use of private dry beach property change size and shape along with the gradual and imperceptible erosion or accretion in the coastal landscape. But, avulsive events such as storms and hurricanes that drastically alter pre-existing littoral boundaries do not have the effect of allowing a public use easement to migrate onto previously unencumbered property.

Severance v. Patterson, 370 S.W.3d 705, 724–25 (Tex. 2012).

§ 2.44 Colonias

Colonias are housing developments in low-income regions, typically near the border between Texas and Mexico. The Texas Local Government Code contains subdivision platting requirements in counties located (1) within fifty miles of the international border regardless of the population of any city within the county or (2) within one hundred miles of the international border if a city located within the county has a population of more than 250,000. Tex. Loc. Gov't Code §§ 232.021–.043. See also Tex. Loc. Gov't Code §§ 232.071–.080 for alternate subdivision platting requirements applicable to certain other economically distressed areas. The Property Code contains restrictions on executory contracts (contracts for deed), a form of real estate transaction widely used in colonias. *See* Tex. Prop. Code §§ 5.061–.080. Colonia self-help centers are authorized in certain counties under Tex. Gov't Code §§ 2306.581–.590. See also section 2.57 below.

§ 2.45 Community Homes; Group Homes

The Community Homes for Disabled Persons Location Act, Tex. Hum. Res. Code §§ 123.001–.010, restricts in some circumstances the enforceability of restrictive covenants and zoning excluding such homes and provides for registration, licensing, and other regulation of such facilities.

§ 2.46 Community Property with Right of Survivorship

Spouses may create a right of survivorship in community property by executing a written agreement. Tex. Est. Code §§ 111.001–.002. The Estates Code also addresses the rights of personal representatives, purchasers, and creditors in this type of property.

§ 2.47 Condemnation and Eminent Domain

Condemnation is the right to take private property for public use; property may not be taken, damaged, or destroyed for or applied to public use without just and adequate compensation and due process. *See* U.S. Const. amends. V, XIV, § 1; Tex. Const. art. I, §§ 17, 19. Condemnation actions are governed by chapter 21 of the Texas Property Code. Before a governmental entity with eminent domain authority begins negotiating with a property owner to acquire real property, the entity must provide a landowner's bill of rights statement provided by Tex. Gov't Code § 402.031. The landowner's bill of rights provides that the property owner has a right to (1) notice of the proposed acquisition of the owner's property; (2) a bona fide good-faith effort to negotiate by the entity proposing to acquire the property; (3) an assessment of damages to the owner that will result from the taking of the property; (4) a hearing under chapter 21 of the Texas Property Code, including a hearing on the assessment of damages; (5) an appeal of a judgment in a condemnation proceeding, including an appeal of an assessment of damages; and (6) file a written complaint with the Texas Real Estate Commission regarding alleged misconduct by a registered easement or right-of-way agent acting on behalf of the entity exercising eminent domain authority. The attorney general will prepare a written statement that includes a bill of rights for a property owner whose real property may be acquired by a governmental or private entity through the use of the entity's eminent domain authority under chapter 21 of the Texas Property Code. A copy of the Texas Landowner's Bill of Rights can be found at **www.texasattorneygeneral.gov/sites/default/files/files/divisions/general-oag/landowners-bill-of-rights-2022.pdf**.

Some of the statutes authorizing condemnation are Tex. Transp. Code § 22.011 (airports and airspace), §§ 224.001–.008, 280.001, 314.011–.013 (highways and streets); Tex. Loc. Gov't Code §§ 251.001–.002 (public works or public use), §§ 331.001, 331.003 (parks and playgrounds), §§ 552.011, 552.013 (waterworks), § 571.004 (seawalls, levees, floodways, and the like); Tex. Nat. Res. Code § 111.019 (pipelines); Tex. Health & Safety Code § 711.033 (cemetery organizations); Tex. Educ. Code § 11.155 (school districts); Tex. Util. Code § 181.004 (utilities); Tex. Water Code § 49.222 (drainage districts); Tex. Gov't Code § 411.004 (providing eminent domain authority to counties for drainage); and Tex. Water Code ch. 54 (municipal utility districts ("MUDs")).

See also sections 2.148 and 2.200 below.

The comptroller is required to create an eminent domain database including the name, address, and representative of each entity authorized by the state to exercise the power of eminent domain. Tex. Gov't Code ch. 2206, subch. D. The database must identify the scope of eminent domain granted to the entity, the entity's website address, and whether the entity exercised its eminent domain authority in the past year. Entities with the power of eminent domain are required to submit an annual report to the comptroller to update the database, including whether or not the entity exercised its eminent domain authority in the past year. Failure to file a report may result in a civil penalty.

§ 2.48 Condominiums

A condominium is a form of real property ownership in which portions of the real property are designated for separate ownership and the remainder is designated for common ownership solely by the separate owners. A condominium exists only if one or more of the common elements are directly owned in undivided interests by the unit owners. If an entity separate from the unit owners (e.g., an incorporated property owners' association) owns all the common elements, the real property is not a condominium, even if the separate entity is owned by all the unit owners. Tex. Prop. Code § 82.003(a)(8).

The Texas Uniform Condominium Act (TUCA), Tex. Prop. Code ch. 82, governs the creation, operation, alteration, termination, and management of TUCA condominium projects created on or after January 1, 1994, but certain provisions of TUCA apply to those created before that date. Condominium projects created before January 1, 1994, are governed by portions of Tex. Prop. Code ch. 81 (the prior Condominium Act) and portions of TUCA, unless the owners of the project amend their declaration and submit it exclusively to the provisions of TUCA. *See* Tex. Prop. Code § 82.002. Tax certificates, receipts, or other statements evidencing payment of taxes or that taxes have not yet been calculated must be attached to a plat, replat, or amended plat or replat of a condominium before recording in accordance with Tex. Prop. Code § 82.051(g). The separate taxation of individual units of a condominium is addressed in Tex. Prop. Code § 82.005 and Tex. Tax Code § 25.09. Certain disclosures are required in a contract for sale of a condominium. Tex. Prop. Code §§ 82.156–.157. See chapter 24 in this manual.

§ 2.49 Confessions of Judgment

Confession-of-judgment provisions in contracts executed before a lawsuit is brought are not enforceable. Tex. Civ. Prac. & Rem. Code § 30.001.

§ 2.50 Confidentiality Notice

See section 2.69 below.

§ 2.51 Conspicuous Text

Several statutes require that certain notices and contractual provisions be set apart from and made more conspicuous than the surrounding text, either by using bold-faced type or some other method. A partial list of these provisions includes—

1. choice-of-law provisions designating another state and agreements to litigate or arbitrate in another state in contracts concerning goods valued at $50,000 or less (Tex. Bus. & Com. Code ch. 273);
2. Deceptive Trade Practices Act waivers (Tex. Bus. & Com. Code § 17.42);
3. the statutory statute-of-frauds notice for loans greater than $50,000 (Tex. Bus. & Com. Code § 26.02);
4. notices of cancellation for certain types of credit services agreements (Tex. Fin. Code § 393.202);
5. disclosures required in rental-purchase agreements (Tex. Bus. & Com. Code § 92.051(d));
6. certain language in homestead improvement contracts (Tex. Prop. Code § 41.007);
7. certain language in homestead lien affidavits (Tex. Prop. Code § 53.254);
8. certain notices relating to contracts for deed (Tex. Prop. Code §§ 5.062, 5.066, 5.074);
9. certain agreements between landlords and residential tenants concerning repairs (Tex. Prop. Code § 92.006);
10. certain notices in residential leases concerning the landlord's obligations to install safety devices (Tex. Prop. Code § 92.164);
11. certain notices in residential leases concerning the disabling of smoke alarms by tenants (Tex. Prop. Code § 92.2611);
12. various provisions in retail installment contracts (Tex. Fin. Code §§ 345.052, 345.081, 345.304);
13. home solicitation transaction cancellation notices (Tex. Bus. & Com. Code §§ 601.052–.053);
14. the business opportunity contract disclosure statement (Tex. Bus. & Com. Code § 51.151) (note that "business opportunity" does not include real estate syndications and certain other transactions (Tex. Bus. & Com. Code § 51.003(b)));
15. liability for rollback taxes (Tex. Prop. Code § 5.010(a));
16. the confidentiality notice required by the Property Code (Tex. Prop. Code § 11.008); and
17. material changes to prior or existing property and casualty insurance policies (Tex. Ins. Code § 551.1055(c)).

§ 2.52 Construction Accounts

Construction accounts are governed by Tex. Prop. Code ch. 162.

§ 2.53 Construction Contracts

Payment to contractors, subcontractors, and materialmen must be made within certain prescribed time periods. Tex. Prop. Code § 28.002. Waivers of this provision are generally void. Tex. Prop. Code § 28.006. Certain restrictions on indemnity agreements entered into with contractors are contained in Tex. Civ. Prac. & Rem. Code ch. 130. Restrictions on choice-of-law provisions and agreements to litigate or arbitrate in another state in some types of construction contracts are contained in Tex. Bus. & Com. Code ch. 272. Disclosures concerning home insulation are required of sellers of new homes by 16 C.F.R. § 460.16. Contractors are required to give owners a disclosure statement for residential construction contracts. Tex. Prop. Code § 53.255. See also sections 2.56, 2.132, and 2.166 below. Except in certain instances, contractors are not liable for design defects in (and may not warranty the accuracy or suitability of) plans, specifications, or other design documents provided to the contractor by a person other than the contractor's agents. Tex. Bus. & Com. Code §§ 59.001–.052. A person may recover attorney's fees as compensatory damages for breach of a construction contract. Tex. Civ. Prac. & Rem. Code § 38.0015.

§ 2.54 Construction Liability Claims on Public Projects

Construction defects in public buildings and public works are addressed in Tex. Gov't Code ch. 2272. *See* Acts 2019, 86th Leg., R.S., ch. 1287, § 1 (H.B. 1999), eff. June 14, 2019 (adding Tex. Gov't Code ch. 2272).

§ 2.55 Construction Payment Bond Claims

A surety company that has issued a construction payment bond is subject to requirements governing the claims process. *See* Tex. Ins. Code §§ 3503.051–.057.

§ 2.56 Consumer Laws

Many of the laws designed to protect consumers apply to real estate transactions, including—

1. the Deceptive Trade Practices–Consumer Protection Act (DTPA), Tex. Bus. & Com. Code §§ 17.41–.63 (including special provisions in section 17.42 limiting waivers of DTPA rights);

2. the Magnuson-Moss Warranty Act, 15 U.S.C. §§ 2301–2312 (applies to consumer products used for personal, family, or household purposes, including property intended to be attached to or installed in real property);

3. the Home Solicitation Transactions Act, Tex. Bus. & Com. Code ch. 601 (gives consumers the right to cancel a transaction involving real property);

4. the Real Estate License Act, Tex. Occ. Code ch. 1102 (requires the licensing of persons who inspect real property);

5. the Residential Service Company Act, Tex. Occ. Code ch. 1303 (regulates persons who sell residential service or maintenance contracts);

6. the Manufactured Housing Standards Act, Tex. Occ. Code ch. 1201 (requires the licensing of persons who install manufactured housing), Tex. Occ. Code ch. 1202 (regulates "industrialized housing" or modular homes);

7. the Truth in Lending Act, 15 U.S.C. §§ 1601–1667f, and its accompanying Regulation Z, 12 C.F.R. pt. 226 (requires certain consumer disclosures by creditors of the costs and terms of consumer credit and provides certain remedies for consumers, including the right of rescission of certain credit transactions secured by a lien on the consumer's principal dwelling); see also section 2.267 below; and

8. the Real Estate Settlement Procedures Act, 12 U.S.C. §§ 2601–2617, and its accompanying Regulation X, 24 C.F.R. pt. 3500 (requires certain consumer disclosures for mortgage loan transactions secured by a lien on one-to-four family residential real property that otherwise meet the definition of a "federally related mortgage loan" set out in 24 C.F.R. § 3500.2 and also prohibits unlawful kickbacks, referral fees, and unearned fees in connection

with federally related mortgage loans). See also section 2.209 below.

§ 2.57 Contracts for Deed

The requirements for creating an enforceable residential contract for deed, the notice requirements to enforce a default, and numerous requirements imposed on sellers under such a contract are found in subchapter D of chapter 5 of the Texas Property Code. Tex. Prop. Code §§ 5.061–.086. See section 2.62 below regarding DTPA actions for failure to deliver required disclosures.

The Real Estate Forms Committee has removed the instructions and explanations for residential contracts for deed. These transactions are heavily regulated, and in the majority of circumstances the risks and consequences of failure of compliance outweigh the usefulness of the transaction in light of the fact that the same result can be accomplished by a note, deed, and deed of trust.

§ 2.58 Copyrights

The U.S. copyright laws extend to visual arts and architectural works and prohibit modification or destruction of visual arts in certain circumstances. *See* 17 U.S.C. §§ 102, 106A. Owners of buildings may alter or destroy a building embodying an architectural work. 17 U.S.C. § 120(b).

§ 2.59 Corporations

Corporations may buy, sell, and otherwise deal with real property. Tex. Bus. Orgs. Code § 2.101. They are prohibited, however, from engaging in specified combinations of businesses: owning land and raising cattle and operating stockyards and packing meat; and operating both a petroleum-producing business and an oil pipeline business in the state. Tex. Bus. Orgs. Code § 2.007. A corporation cannot be organized to operate a bank, trust company, savings association, insurance company, cemetery company (except as authorized by the Health and Safety Code), or abstract or title company. Tex. Bus. Orgs. Code § 2.003.

Unless otherwise provided in the governing documents, the governing entity may authorize by resolution a disposition of property without the approval of the members or owners of the entity. Tex. Bus. Orgs. Code § 10.252. If a corporation conveys land under authority of its governing documents, the deed must be signed by an officer or attorney-in-fact. Tex. Bus. Orgs. Code § 10.253. A corporation may convey or mortgage its property for any lawful purpose, except if prohibited by law or by the corporation's charter or bylaws. No corporate seal is required for a valid deed. Tex. Bus. Orgs. Code § 10.251.

Condominium owners' associations for condominium regimes formed after December 31, 1993—and those formed before January 1, 1994, that opt to be governed exclusively by Texas Property Code chapter 82 under section 82.002(a)(1)—must be formed as for-profit or nonprofit corporations. Tex. Prop. Code § 82.101.

See also sections 2.34 above and 2.109, 2.156, 2.181, and 2.193 below.

§ 2.60 Covenants Not to Compete

Covenants not to compete are governed by the provisions of Tex. Bus. & Com. Code § 15.50.

§ 2.61 Criminal Record Checks of Employees

Criminal record checks of employees of residential dwelling projects are permitted under the provisions of Tex. Health & Safety Code ch. 765.

§ 2.62 Deceptive Trade Practices–Consumer Protection Act (DTPA)

The Texas Deceptive Trade Practices–Consumer Protection Act (Tex. Bus. & Com. Code §§ 17.41–.63) applies to certain types of real estate transactions. Waivers of the Act's protection are permitted only if in compliance with Tex. Bus. & Com. Code § 17.42. See also section 2.218 below. A violation of the provisions of the Texas Property Code pertaining to home improvement contracts may be brought as a DTPA action (Tex. Prop. Code § 41.007), as may a seller's failure to deliver a property disclosure statement before execution of some contracts for deed to convey residential property (Tex. Prop. Code § 5.069(d)). See also Tex. Prop. Code § 221.071 for a DTPA action under the Texas Timeshare Act (Tex. Prop. Code ch. 221).

§ 2.63 Deeds

The legal requirements for deeds are addressed in Tex. Prop. Code §§ 5.021–.023. See also chapter 5 in this manual.

Deeds transferring an interest in real property to or from an individual are required to include the confidentiality notice set out in Tex. Prop. Code § 11.008. See section 3.17 in this manual.

Instruments that correct a conveyance of real property should comply with Tex. Prop. Code §§ 5.027–.030. Whether the change to the instrument is material or nonmaterial will dictate the process needed to make the correction. See section 5.8 in this manual.

The Texas Real Property Transfer on Death Act authorizes an individual to execute and record a transfer on death deed to make a revocable transfer of the transferor's interest in real property to one or more designated beneficiaries, including alternate beneficiaries, effective at the transferor's death. *See* Tex. Est. Code ch. 114. In the 86th legislative session, the statutory forms for the transfer on death deed and the revocation of transfer on death deed were removed from chapter 114 of the Texas Estates Code. Acts 2019, 86th Leg., R.S., ch. 337, § 3.2 (S.B. 874), eff. Sept. 1, 2019. Tex. Gov't Code § 22.020 directs the Texas Supreme Court to promulgate forms for creating and revoking a transfer on death deed. The forms have yet to be promulgated. The Estates Code continues to authorize use of transfer on death deeds and revocation of transfer on death deeds but no longer prescribes statutory language. See section 5.11 in this manual.

§ 2.64 Deeds of Trust

Foreclosure of liens is addressed in Tex. Prop. Code ch. 51 and Tex. Bus. & Com. Code § 22.001. See also the separate discussion at section 2.107 below.

Deeds of trust transferring an interest in real property to or from an individual are required to include the confidentiality notice set out in Tex. Prop. Code § 11.008. See section 3.17 in this manual.

§ 2.65 Deficiency Litigation after Foreclosure

A suit for a deficiency following a foreclosure sale conducted under Tex. Prop. Code § 51.002 must be brought within two years and is governed by Tex. Prop. Code §§ 51.003–.005. See also section 2.107 below.

§ 2.66 Disaster Recovery Relief

The Texas Division of Emergency Management coordinates the state emergency management plan. Tex. Gov't Code ch. 418 lays out the responsibilities of the division.

§ 2.67 Disclaimer of Interest in Decedent's Estate

A person desiring to disclaim an interest in a decedent's estate must comply with Tex. Est. Code ch. 122.

§ 2.68 Disclosure of Interested Parties When Contracting with Governmental Entities

A governmental entity or state agency may not enter into a contract with a business entity if the contract requires a vote by the governing body of the governmental entity or state agency, the contract has a value of at least $1 million, or the contract is for services that would require a person to register as a lobbyist, unless the business entity submits a disclosure of interested parties to the governmental entity or state agency at the time the business entity submits the signed contract to the governmental entity or state agency. Tex. Gov't Code § 2252.908. The disclosure of interested parties must be submitted on an electronic form prescribed by the Texas Ethics Commission. *See* 1 Tex. Admin. Code ch. 46. The required Form 1295 and filing instructions can be found on the Texas Ethics Commission website at **www.ethics.state.tx.us/resources/FAQs/FAQ_Form1295.php**. See also section 2.226 below.

§ 2.69 Disclosures and Notices

Numerous statutory disclosure and notice requirements affect real estate transactions.

1. A seller of residential real property comprising not more than one dwelling unit must give the purchaser of the property a signed, written notice, substantially in statutory form, concerning the condition of the property, including known defects or malfunctions of building structural components and building materials; working condition of various systems, appliances, smoke detectors, and other enumerated items; and the existence of various undesirable conditions such as termite damage, lead-based paint, radon gas, and a single blockable main drain in a swimming pool or hot tub. The notice must be delivered on or before the effective date of any executory sales contract binding the purchaser and, if the seller fails to provide the notice by the effective date, the purchaser may rescind the contract for any reason within seven days after receiving the notice. Tex. Prop. Code § 5.008. The notice was revised effective September 1, 2019, to provide additional disclosures on previous flooding, previous water penetration, and flood risk. *See* Tex. Prop. Code § 5.008(b). See form 4-23 in this manual.

2. Real estate brokers have a number of disclosure obligations, including the nature of their principal-agent relationship, as well as any applicable intermediary status, to prospective buyers, sellers, landlords, and tenants; knowledge of latent defects; the advisability of obtaining a title policy; as well as nondisclosure requirements. Tex. Occ. Code §§ 1101.555–.559, 1101.651–.652; 22 Tex. Admin. Code chs. 535, 537.

3. A seller is obligated to make certain disclosures if the property is located in a water or utility district. Tex. Water Code §§ 49.452, 54.016(h)(4)(A). See form 4-19.

4. Sellers in certain municipalities must disclose the presence of restrictive covenants affecting the property. Tex. Loc. Gov't Code §§ 212.151–.157 (Enforcement of Land Use Restric-

tions Contained in Plats and Other Instruments). See form 4-12.

5. The presence of underground storage tanks must be disclosed to purchasers in accordance with 30 Tex. Admin. Code § 334.9. See form 4-11.

6. There are disclosure requirements in the Texas Timeshare Act, Tex. Prop. Code §§ 221.031–.036.

7. The Texas Membership Camping Resort Act has disclosure requirements. *See* Tex. Prop. Code § 222.006.

8. There are disclosures required by the Interstate Land Sales Full Disclosure Act, 15 U.S.C. §§ 1701–1720, and 24 C.F.R. pts. 1710–1720.

9. Disclosures concerning home insulation are required by 16 C.F.R. § 460.16. See form 4-7.

10. Disclosures concerning asbestos are required by 29 C.F.R. §§ 1910.1001 and 1926.1101. See the appropriate forms in chapters 25 and 26. See also form 4-9.

11. A seller of vacant land must include in the contract a certain bold-faced notice about potential rollback taxes. A number of exemptions apply, including an exemption if a separate paragraph in the contract addresses rollback tax liability. Tex. Prop. Code § 5.010. See form 4-15.

12. A seller of unimproved residential property must provide the buyer with a written disclosure of certain subsurface conditions, such as pipelines, in certain circumstances. This notice is not required if the seller is obligated under the contract to furnish a title insurance commitment and if the buyer is entitled to terminate if objections to the commitment are not cured before closing. Tex. Prop. Code § 5.013.

13. A seller of a single-family residence must give notice to a prospective buyer if the residence is subject to membership in a property owners' association, restrictive covenants have been recorded, and an assessment lien may be foreclosed for failure to pay assessments. Tex. Prop. Code § 5.012. See form 23-9.

14. A seller must disclose that the land may be included in the extraterritorial jurisdiction of a municipality and thereby subject to annexation. Tex. Prop. Code § 5.011. See form 4-16.

15. Contractors are required to give the owner a disclosure statement before the owner executes a residential construction contract. Tex. Prop. Code § 53.255. See form 18-1.

16. Residential mortgage loan originators have certain disclosure obligations to residential mortgage loan applicants, including the nature of the relationship between the residential mortgage loan originator and the applicant, the duties the residential mortgage loan originator has to the applicant, and how the residential mortgage loan originator will be compensated, as well as the terms under which an interest rate lock-in fee will be refundable. Tex. Fin. Code §§ 156.004, 156.304. The Savings and Mortgage Lending Commissioner by rule has promulgated a standard form entitled "Residential Mortgage Loan Originator Discloser." 7 Tex. Admin. Code § 80.9.

17. A seller of unimproved real property located outside a municipality's jurisdiction must provide a statutory notice to a purchaser that the extension of water or sewer services may require

additional expense and delay to obtain. Tex. Water Code § 13.257. See form 4-17.

18. Sellers of real property within an agricultural development district must give the purchaser written notice to that effect. Tex. Agric. Code § 60.063. The district must file a copy of the form for notice required by section 60.063 with the county clerk in each county in which all or part of the district is located. Tex. Agric. Code § 60.0631. The statute charges each agricultural district with the responsibility to prepare its own form.

19. Disclosures concerning home loans and high-cost home loans (loans with an interest rate of 12 percent or greater per year), including disclosures regarding individual or group credit life or disability insurance, are required by chapter 343 of the Finance Code. Tex. Fin. Code ch. 343. See also section 10.14 in this manual.

20. Texas Property Code section 11.008 provides that an instrument transferring an interest in real property to or from an individual must include a statutorily described notice that appears on the top of the first page of the instrument in twelve-point boldfaced type or twelve-point uppercase letters and reads substantially as follows:

    Notice of confidentiality rights: If you are a natural person, you may remove or strike any or all of the following information from any instrument that transfers an interest in real property before it is filed for record in the public records: your Social Security number or your driver's license number.

    Tex. Prop. Code § 11.008(c). "Instrument" is defined, for purposes of this statute, as "a deed, deed of trust, or any other record recorded by a county clerk related to real property, including a mineral lease, a mechanic's lien, and the release of a mechanic's lien."

    The validity of an instrument as between the parties to the instrument and the notice provided by the instrument is not affected by a party's failure to include the notice required under this section. Tex. Prop. Code § 11.008(d).

    The county clerk may not under any circumstance reject an instrument presented for recording solely because the instrument fails to comply with this section. Other than the duty to redact an individual's social security number as required by Tex. Gov't Code § 552.146, the county clerk has no duty to ensure that an instrument presented for recording does not contain an individual's social security number. Tex. Prop. Code § 11.008(e).

21. A person who proposes to sell or otherwise convey property located in a public improvement district established pursuant to chapters 372 (municipality) or 382 (county) of the Local Government Code must first give written notice to the purchaser. The purchaser must acknowledge receipt of the notice before the effective date of the contract. *See* Tex. Prop. Code § 5.014. If the notice is not timely provided, the purchaser may terminate the contract. Tex. Prop. Code § 5.0141. If the notice is provided before closing and the purchaser elects to close, the purchaser waives

its rights to terminate or seek damages. At closing, the seller and purchaser must execute a separate copy of the notice in recordable form to be recorded in the deed records in the county where the property is located. Tex. Prop. Code §§ 5.0142, 5.0143.

The form of notice may also be found in a service plan filed with the applicable municipality or county. Tex. Prop. Code § 5.0144. Whether a property is located in a public improvement district may be determined by review of the city or county website, the county appraisal district or county tax assessor's website if the county tax assessor-collector collects the taxes, or the state comptroller's website. Texas Property Code section 5.0145 sets out the remedies which may be available if notice is not given when required.

22. If all or part of a subdivision for which a plat is required under chapter 232 of the Local Government Code is located within a future transportation corridor identified in an agreement between the Texas Department of Transportation and a county under section 201.619 of the Transportation Code, each purchase contract or lease between the subdivider and a purchaser or lessee of land in the subdivision must contain a conspicuous statement that the land is located within the area of the alignment of a transportation project as shown in the final environmental decision document that is applicable to the future transportation corridor. Tex. Loc. Gov't Code § 232.0033. See form 4-20.

23. With a number of exceptions, a seller of property that will be conveyed subject to a lien must make required disclosures to the prospective purchaser at least seven days before the earlier of the effective date of the conveyance or the execution of the contract for the conveyance. The failure to give the notice does not invalidate a conveyance, but the purchaser may pursue other remedies available unless the person required to give notice reasonably believes and takes any necessary action to ensure that each lien for which notice was not provided will be released on or before the thirtieth day after the date on which title to the property is transferred. Among the excepted transactions for which the disclosure is not required are those in which the purchaser obtains a title policy and those in which the purchaser has purchased interests in real property four or more times during the preceding twelve months. Tex. Prop. Code § 5.016.

24. A person registered under the Residential Mortgage Loan Servicer Registration Act (Tex. Fin. Code ch. 158) and acting as a servicer of loans secured by a lien on residential real estate located in Texas must provide a statutory notice informing the borrower of each such residential mortgage loan that complaints about servicing of the loan should be sent to the Department of Savings and Mortgage Lending. Tex. Fin. Code § 158.101.

25. A person who sells property for which a certificate of mold remediation has been issued pursuant to section 1958.154 of the Texas Occupations Code must deliver to the purchaser copies of each certificate of mold remediation issued for the property with the preceding five years. Tex. Occ. Code § 1958.154.

26. A seller of commercial or residential property adjoining an impoundment of

water, including a reservoir or lake constructed and maintained under chapter 11 of the Texas Water Code that has storage capacity of at least 5,000 acre-feet at the impoundment's normal operating level, must give to the purchaser notice of fluctuations for various reasons, including an entity lawfully exercising its right to the water stored in the impoundment or drought or flood conditions. Tex. Prop. Code § 5.019. See form 4-21.

27. Certain for-profit entities may record an affidavit identifying one or more individuals authorized to transfer an estate or interest in real property on behalf of the entity. Tex. Prop. Code § 12.019(c). Further limitations and requirements are contained in Tex. Prop. Code § 12.019.

28. A landlord must provide a tenant a written notice whether the landlord is or is not aware that the dwelling rented to the tenant is located in a hundred-year flood plain. In addition, if a landlord knows that flooding has damaged any portion of the dwelling during the preceding five-year period, the landlord must provide an additional notice. The forms of notices are prescribed by statute. Tex. Prop. Code § 92.0135.

Other situations may require disclosures. See sections 2.5, 2.16, 2.42, 2.43, 2.48, 2.51, and 2.57 above and 2.104, 2.110, 2.116, 2.128, 2.129, 2.140, 2.144, 2.150, 2.177, 2.228, 2.267, and 2.280 below.

§ 2.70 Discrimination

A restriction in a deed or other instrument affecting real property that prohibits the use, sale, lease, or transfer on account of race, color, religion, or national origin is void and unenforceable. Tex. Prop. Code § 5.026. Municipalities may also adopt fair housing ordinances, which may have enforcement procedures and remedies that vary from state and federal law. Tex. Loc. Gov't Code § 214.903. The Texas Workforce Commission civil rights division has the authority to hear certain types of discrimination complaints. Tex. Lab. Code ch. 301. See also sections 2.15 above and 2.86 and 2.97 below.

Cities and counties may not prohibit housing discrimination against a person "because the person's lawful source of income to pay rent includes funding from a federal housing assistance program," but ordinances or regulations protecting veterans from discrimination may not be invalidated by cities or counties. Tex. Loc. Gov't Code § 250.007.

A person who owns real property or an interest in real property which includes in its chain of title a recorded conveyance instrument containing a discriminatory provision, or a person with permission from the owner, may request removal of the discriminatory provision by filing with the county clerk a motion verified by affidavit containing certain required information. A court having jurisdiction must rule on the motion, which may be ex parte and based on only the review of the questioned provision. The court's ruling and findings of fact must be filed with the county clerk. Tex. Prop. Code § 5.0261.

§ 2.71 Divorce

See section 2.98 below.

§ 2.72 Dodd-Frank Wall Street Reform and Consumer Protection Act

The Dodd-Frank Wall Street Reform and Consumer Protection Act, codified as amended in scattered sections of U.S.C. (Pub. L. No. 111-203, 124 Stat. 1376), is sweeping financial reform legislation intended in pertinent part to "protect consumers from abusive financial services practices" thought by Congress to have significantly contributed to the 2007–2009 national financial crisis. The Act, comprising some sixteen titles, was signed into law on July 21, 2010. It was extensively amended on May 28, 2018.

Titles IX (dealing with securitization of mortgage loans), X (establishing the Bureau of Consumer Financial Protection), and XIV (containing extensive amendments to the Truth in Lending Act, the Real Estate Settlement Procedures Act, and the Equal Credit Opportunity Act reforming residential mortgage origination, underwriting, appraisal, and servicing practices) are particularly pertinent to residential real estate finance transactions. See the discussion in chapter 12 in this manual.

§ 2.73 Dry Cleaners

Chapter 374 of the Health and Safety Code regulates performance standards for both existing and new dry cleaning facilities. Tex. Health & Safety Code ch. 374.

§ 2.74 Due-on-Sale Clauses

Due-on-sale provisions are addressed in the Garn-St. Germain Depository Institutions Act of 1982, 12 U.S.C. § 1701j–3, and the regulations promulgated thereunder at 12 C.F.R. § 34.5, including preemption of certain conflicting state laws.

§ 2.75 Durable Powers of Attorney

Durable powers of attorney are governed by Tex. Est. Code chs. 751–752. Unless a time limitation is specifically stated in the instrument creating it, the passage of time does not cause a durable power of attorney to lapse. Tex. Est. Code § 751.132(b). The durable power of attorney between spouses terminates on divorce or annulment except in certain situations. Tex. Est. Code § 751.132(a)(3). A court's appointment of a permanent guardian for the principal's estate terminates the durable power of attorney on the guardian's qualification. A court may suspend the powers of an agent under a durable power of attorney during the term of a temporary guardianship. Tex. Est. Code § 751.133.

A durable power of attorney must be in writing, be signed by a principal who is an adult, be acknowledged, and contain the following phrase or words of similar import: "This power of attorney is not affected by subsequent disability or incapacity of the principal." Tex. Est. Code § 751.0021(a). The attorney-in-fact or agent has a fiduciary duty to the principal to timely inform the principal of all actions taken, account for his actions, maintain appropriate records, and provide an accounting on demand by the principal. Tex. Est. Code § 751.101.

Tex. Est. Code § 751.051 sets forth a statutory form of durable power of attorney. When using the statutory form, the principal will need to initial each specific power to be granted or initial the line to grant all powers. A durable power of attorney that confers authority with respect to real property empowers the agent to perform those acts described in Tex. Est. Code § 752.102. Durable powers of attorney used in real estate transactions must be recorded in the county or counties in which the real property is located not later than thirty days after the instrument signed by the agent is recorded. *See* Tex. Est. Code § 751.151. Several other important requirements for such powers of attorney are addressed in the statute. A form of durable power of attorney for use in real estate transactions incorporating the statutory requirements is included in chapter 26 in this manual.

§ 2.76 Easements, Pipeline

Unless expressly provided otherwise, pipeline easements created by grant or power of eminent domain for the benefit of a single common carrier pipeline for which the power of eminent domain is available are presumed to create an easement in favor of the common carrier pipeline that extends a width of fifty feet as to each pipeline laid under the easement before January 1, 1994. Tex. Nat. Res. Code § 111.0194. The presumption is rebuttable. Persons who acquire pipeline easements and rights-of-way for others must be registered, licensed, or exempt from licensing by the Real Estate License Act. A notice promulgated by the Texas Real Estate Commission must be delivered to the grantor of the easement before the easement is granted. Tex. Occ. Code § 1101.653.

§ 2.77 Economically Distressed Counties

See section 2.44 above.

§ 2.78 Economic Development

The Texas Economic Development Act provides certain ad valorem tax benefits to encourage economic development. Tex. Tax Code ch. 313.

§ 2.79 Elderly Housing

See section 2.97 below.

§ 2.80 Electronic Commerce

Texas has adopted the Uniform Electronic Transactions Act, which is intended to facilitate electronic commerce. Tex. Bus. & Com. Code ch. 322. The Uniform Electronic Transactions Act does not apply to transactions that are otherwise covered by the laws governing the execution of wills and testamentary trusts or by the Uniform Commercial Code. Tex. Bus. & Com. Code § 322.003(b). Electronic funds transfers are governed by chapter 4A of the Uniform Commercial Code. Tex. Bus. & Com. Code ch. 4A.

§ 2.81 Electronic Filing of Documents

Statutes authorizing and otherwise relating to the electronic filing of documents in the public records include Tex. Loc. Gov't Code § 191.009 and ch. 195. Chapter 9 of the Texas Business and Commerce Code, while no longer explicitly authorizing electronic filing, is clearly written to accommodate it. For example, in most places the revision refers to "authenticating" rather than "signing" a record. The revised Code also provides that "communication of a record to a filing office . . . constitutes filing." Tex. Bus. & Com. Code § 9.516(a). Filing by means other than in writing is contemplated by Tex. Bus. & Com. Code § 9.525(a)(3); *see also* Tex. Bus. & Com. Code § 9.526(b).

Texas has also adopted the Uniform Real Property Electronic Recording Act. Tex. Prop. Code §§ 15.001–.008. Under the Act, a "document" includes information stored in an electronic or other medium that is retrievable in perceivable form. Tex. Prop. Code § 15.002(1). A document received by a county clerk in electronic form is eligible to be recorded in the real property records. If another law requires as a condition of recording that a document be on paper or other tangible medium, the requirement is satisfied by an electronic document that complies with the Act. Tex. Prop. Code § 15.004. An electronic signature is an electronic sound, symbol, or process attached to or logically associated with a document executed or adopted by a person with the intent to sign the document. Tex. Prop. Code § 15.002(4). An acknowledgment may be similarly satisfied by an electronic signature. Tex. Prop. Code § 15.004. Licensed attorneys, lending institutions, title insurance companies, and state agencies may record electronically. County clerks are authorized (but not required) to implement the Act. Tex. Prop. Code § 15.005. The Act also amends provisions of the Local Government Code pertaining to electronic recording and directs the Texas State Library and Archives

Commission to adopt rules to promote uniformity within the state and among other states that adopt similar laws. Tex. Prop. Code § 15.006.

The Electronic Government Task Force has launched an Internet portal to provide access to electronic government services in Texas. It is found at **www.texas.gov**; it provides forms and applications from various agencies and access to filing and payment of sales tax. Authority for oversight by the TexasOnline Authority is provided in Tex. Gov't Code ch. 2054.

§ 2.82 Eminent Domain

See section 2.47 above.

§ 2.83 Endangered Species Act

The Endangered Species Act can be found at 16 U.S.C. §§ 1531–1544. The provisions of the statute may limit the development of real property in areas that include the habitats of endangered species.

§ 2.84 Engineer's Liens against Real Estate

An engineer's lien against real estate is addressed in Tex. Prop. Code § 53.021(3).

§ 2.85 Environmental Laws

Numerous federal and state environmental statutes affect real estate transactions. Among the most important federal laws are—

1. the Comprehensive Environmental Response, Compensation, and Liability Act of 1980, as amended by the Superfund Amendments and Reauthorization Act of 1986, 42 U.S.C. §§ 9601–9675, relating primarily to liability for cleanup of inactive hazardous waste sites (see also sections 2.125 and 2.147 below);

2. the Resource Conservation and Recovery Act, as amended by the Hazardous and Solid Waste Amendments of 1984 and the Land Disposal Program Flexibility Act of 1996, 42 U.S.C. §§ 6901–6992k, relating primarily to active waste treatment, storage, or disposal facilities, including underground storage tanks (see also section 2.270 below);

3. the Federal Water Pollution Control Act, also known as the Clean Water Act, 33 U.S.C. §§ 1251–1387, governing, among other things, the regulation of wetlands, stormwater, and point-source water pollution (see also sections 2.243 and 2.295 below);

4. the federal Clean Air Act, 42 U.S.C. §§ 7401–7671q, requiring permits for many types of operations, regulating certain asbestos materials and emissions, and prohibiting certain types of chemicals, such as chlorofluorocarbons (CFCs), that deplete the ozone layer. The regulations dealing with CFCs are in 40 C.F.R. pt. 82. Related regulations include the asbestos-based National Emission Standards for Hazardous Air Pollutants at 40 C.F.R. pt. 61;

5. the Endangered Species Act, 16 U.S.C. §§ 1531–1544;

6. the Asbestos Hazard Emergency Response Act of 1986, 15 U.S.C. §§ 2641–2656, and regulations, 40 C.F.R. pt. 763;

7. asbestos regulations under the Occupational Safety and Health Act, 29 C.F.R. § 1910.1001 (general industry standard), and 29 C.F.R. § 1926.1101 (construction standard);

8. the Residential Lead-Based Paint Hazard Reduction Act of 1992, also

known as Title X of the Housing and Community Development Act (42 U.S.C. §§ 4851–4856) (see section 2.150 below);

9. the Safe Drinking Water Act, 42 U.S.C. §§ 300f to 300j–26; and

10. the Toxic Substances Control Act, 15 U.S.C. §§ 2601–2695d, regulating polychlorinated biphenyls and other substances.

Important state environmental statutes and regulations include—

1. the Solid Waste Disposal Act, Tex. Health & Safety Code ch. 361 (concerns the disposal of hazardous and certain nonhazardous wastes), including the statute regulating developments over abandoned landfills, Tex. Health & Safety Code §§ 361.531–.539 (see the separate discussion of this statute at section 2.144 below), and the voluntary cleanup program (also known as a Brownfields statute), Tex. Health & Safety Code §§ 361.601–.613 (see section 2.287 below);

2. the Texas Clean Air Act, Tex. Health & Safety Code ch. 382, requiring air permits for many types of industrial and construction operations and regulating air emissions and various other hazardous substances and activities;

3. the Texas Hazardous Substances Spill Prevention and Control Act, Tex. Water Code §§ 26.261–.267;

4. the Texas Underground and Aboveground Storage Act, as amended, Tex. Water Code §§ 26.341–.367 (see also section 2.270 below);

5. the Coastal Public Lands Management Act of 1973, as amended, Tex. Nat. Res. Code ch. 33, and regulations at 31 Tex. Admin. Code chs. 501–506 (see also section 2.43 above);

6. the Texas Environmental, Health, and Safety Audit Privilege Act, Tex. Health & Safety Code ch. 1101;

7. the Texas Asbestos Health Protection Act, Tex. Occ. Code ch. 1954;

8. the Texas Railroad Commission's Operator Cleanup Program and regulations at 16 Tex. Admin. Code § 3.91; and

9. Tex. Agric. Code ch. 63, providing enhanced safety oversight and inspections of ammonium nitrate storage facilities by permitting entry by local or state fire authorities and providing enhanced storage requirements.

In addition, there are numerous environmental provisions that bear on the ownership, operation, and development of real estate properties in the Texas Health and Safety Code, the Texas Natural Resources Code, the Texas Parks and Wildlife Code, and the Texas Water Code.

§ 2.86 Equal Credit Opportunity

The Equal Credit Opportunity Act, implemented by Regulation B, 12 C.F.R. § 202.16, provides a cause of action against a creditor who discriminates against an applicant for credit (1) on the basis of the applicant's race, color, religion, national origin, sex, marital status, or age (provided the applicant has the capacity to enter into a binding contract), (2) because all or part of the applicant's income derives from any public assistance program, or (3) because the applicant has in good faith exercised any right under the Consumer Credit Protection Act. *See* 15 U.S.C. §§ 1691–1691f. Regulation B also establishes rules for a creditor's collection, evaluation, and use of information in connection with a credit application and requires a creditor to notify applicants of action taken on their applications concerning the creditor's approval of, counteroffer to, or denial of credit generally within thirty days after receiving a completed application. Proper use of sample notification forms set out in Appendix C of Regulation B constitutes full compliance with various requirements of the Act. Effective July 21, 2011, model forms C1 through C5 were revised to include a notice that a credit score was used to make an adverse credit decision and to include certain information about credit scores to comply with amended content requirements of the Fair Credit Reporting Act. Notifications must be in writing and contain a statement of specific reasons for any adverse action taken on the credit application and a statutory notice set forth in section 701(a) of the Act. Creditors furthermore must provide consumers with a copy of any property appraisal report used to evaluate an application for credit that is to be secured by a lien on a dwelling. *See* 12 C.F.R. § 202.14.

§ 2.87 Equal Housing Opportunity

See sections 2.8 above and 2.97 below.

§ 2.88 Escheat

Escheat of real and personal property to the state is governed by Tex. Prop. Code ch. 71. See also section 2.1 above.

§ 2.89 Estate Tax Liens

An unpaid federal estate tax becomes a lien on the gross estate of the decedent. 26 U.S.C. § 6324(a)(1).

§ 2.90 Eviction

Eviction actions (also known as forcible-entry-and-detainer actions) are governed by Tex. Prop. Code ch. 24 and Tex. R. Civ. P. 500–507, 510.1–.13. Tex. Prop. Code ch. 24 permits an owner of a multifamily residential property to be represented by a nonlawyer in the appeal of an eviction suit for nonpayment of rent. Tex. Prop. Code § 24.011.

§ 2.91 Excavators

See section 2.271 below.

§ 2.92 Exempt Property and Liens

See section 2.26 above.

§ 2.93 Extraterritorial Jurisdiction

The extraterritorial jurisdiction of municipalities is governed by Tex. Loc. Gov't Code ch. 42. See also section 2.69 above.

§ 2.94 Failed Depository Institutions

If a bank, savings and loan association, or other depository institution is placed in receivership or conservatorship, one may record at any time an affidavit or memorandum of a sale, transfer, purchase, or acquisition agreement between the receiver or conservator and another depository institution. If the transfer involves an interest in land or in a mortgage vested according to the real property records in the failed depository institution, a recorded affidavit or memorandum is constructive notice of the transfer. Tex. Prop. Code § 12.018.

§ 2.95 Fair Credit Reporting Act

The federal Fair Credit Reporting Act has been amended to require any financial institution that (1) extends credit to an individual and (2) regularly and in the ordinary course of business reports negative information to a credit bureau to give a clear and conspicuous written notice to its individual customers about reporting negative information.

The term *financial institution* is broadly defined to include "any institution the business of which is engaging in financial activities as described in section 1843(k)" of the Bank Holding Company Act of 1956, whether affiliated with a bank or not. 15 U.S.C. § 6809(3)(a). Thus the term *financial institution* includes not only institutions regulated by federal banking agencies but also other entities, such as merchant creditors and debt collectors, that extend credit to individuals and report negative information. *See* 16 C.F.R. § 313.3(k).

A financial institution must give the required notice to an individual customer before, or no later than thirty days after, reporting the negative information to a credit bureau. After giving the notice, the institution may report additional negative information to a credit bureau for the same transaction, extension of credit, account, or customer without giving additional notice. If a financial institution gives a customer a notice before reporting negative information, the institution is not required to actually report negative information about the customer to a credit bureau. A financial institution generally may give the notice about reporting negative information on or with any notice of default, billing statement, or other material provided to an individual customer as long as the notice is clear and conspicuous. The notice may not be included in the initial disclosures required to be given by section 127(a) of the federal Truth in Lending Act (15 U.S.C. § 1637(a)).

A financial institution complies with the notice requirement if the institution uses a model notice promulgated by the Board of Governors of the Federal Reserve System. The format of a model notice may be rearranged. For model notices, see clauses 14-7-2 and 14-7-3 in this manual.

Creditors also are required to give a "risk-based pricing" notice when, based on the consumer's credit report, the creditor provides credit to the consumer on materially less favorable terms than terms available to a substantial proportion of consumers through that creditor. Creditors who conduct periodic reviews of existing accounts and increase the annual percentage rate of interest charged consumers based on findings of a deteriorated consumer credit report must also provide the consumer with an account review risk-based pricing notice. Effective July 21, 2011, the notices must contain the credit score of the consumer and certain information about credit scores if a credit score of the consumer is used in setting the material terms of the credit. Model forms in 12 C.F.R. pt. 222 app. H may be used for compliance with risk-based pricing and credit score disclosure requirements. Consumers who receive a risk-based pricing notice must be informed that they are entitled to a free consumer credit report to confirm the report's accuracy or to dispute the accuracy or completeness of any information in the report. As an alternative to providing a risk-based pricing notice, creditors instead may provide all credit applicants with a free credit score and certain required information about credit scores.

§ 2.96 Fair Debt Collection Practices

The federal Fair Debt Collection Practices Act (15 U.S.C. §§ 1692–1692p) and the Texas Debt Collection Practices Act (Tex. Fin. Code §§ 392.001–.404) regulate efforts to collect debts from consumers. Each act requires collection notices to contain information about the debt and how to dispute it. Attorneys are subject to most provisions of each act. However, an attorney collecting a debt on behalf of a client is not considered a "third-party debt collector" under the Texas Debt Collection Practices Act unless the attorney employs nonattorneys who regularly solicit debts for collection or make frequent contact with debtors to collect or adjust debts. Tex. Fin. Code § 392.001(7). Each act also prohibits types of communications that might be considered harassment. Creditors and debt collectors usually have the right to collect on a debt from the assets of a decedent's estate but, effective August 29, 2011, are prohibited from contacting relatives of a deceased debtor, other than a spouse or legal representative of the estate, who may lack either the authority to pay the debt from the decedent's estate or the legal obligation to pay the debt. *See* 76 Fed. Reg. 44,915 (July 27, 2011). Trustees and substitute trustees are not considered debt collectors. Tex. Prop. Code § 51.0075(b).

§ 2.97 Fair Housing

The federal Fair Housing Act (42 U.S.C. §§ 3601–3631) and the Texas Fair Housing Act (Tex. Prop. Code §§ 301.001–.171) forbid (1) discrimination in the sale, rental, or financing of housing on the basis of race, color, religion, national origin, sex, handicap, or familial status; (2) the refusal to permit modifications of existing premises at the expense of the handicapped person or reasonable accommodations in rules, policies, practices, or services, if necessary to afford handicapped persons equal opportunity for, or full enjoyment of, the use of the premises; and (3) the failure to make special accommodations for handicapped persons in certain multifamily dwellings designed and constructed for first occupancy after March 13, 1991. Regulations setting out the particular handicapped access requirements for new multifamily housing structures can be found at 24 C.F.R. § 100.205. Municipalities may also adopt fair housing ordinances, which may have enforcement procedures and remedies that vary from state and federal law. Tex. Loc. Gov't Code § 214.903.

The Texas Fair Housing Act and the federal Fair Housing Act both prohibit housing that is limited specifically to the elderly and that excludes families and young children, unless certain minimum design and eligibility requirements are met. The state requirements can be found in 40 Tex. Admin. Code §§ 819.121–.135. The federal requirements can be found at 24 C.F.R. §§ 100.300–.308 and 42 U.S.C. § 3607(b)(2).

§ 2.98 Family Law

The Texas Family Code has several provisions that relate to real property transfers, including enforcement of a division of property (Tex. Fam. Code §§ 9.006–.014); right to future property (Tex. Fam. Code § 9.011); division of property following a decree of divorce (Tex. Fam. Code §§ 9.201–.205); the Uniform Premarital Agreement Act (Tex. Fam. Code §§ 4.001–.010); partition or exchange of community property (Tex. Fam. Code §§ 4.101–.106); rules of marital property liability (Tex. Fam. Code §§ 3.201–.203); homestead rights (Tex. Fam. Code §§ 5.001–.108); child support liens (Tex. Fam. Code §§ 157.311–.331); and prohibition by a temporary restraining order of the transfer, assignment, mortgage, encumbrance, or alienation of any real property of the parties to a dissolution of marriage without the prior authorization of the court (Tex. Fam. Code § 6.501(a)). The Texas Constitution also addresses the issue of separate and community property between spouses. Tex. Const. art. XVI, § 15. Tex. Fam. Code § 7.006(b) provides that a written agreement incident to divorce or annulment may be set out in the final decree or incorporated by reference, each of which will have equal effect and validity.

§ 2.99 Federal Lien Registration Act

Texas has adopted the Uniform Federal Lien Registration Act, Tex. Prop. Code §§ 14.001–.007, which governs the procedures for filing notices of federal liens, including tax liens, against real property. See also section 2.100 below.

§ 2.100 Federal Tax Liens

If notice of a junior federal tax lien has been filed at least thirty days before a scheduled foreclosure sale, written notice of the sale under a deed of trust, forfeiture under a contract for deed, or receipt of a deed in lieu of foreclosure must be given, by registered or certified mail or by personal service, to the Internal Revenue Service at least twenty-five days before the transfer. Without this notice, the transfer will be made subject to the federal tax lien. If proper notice is given, the United States is limited to a right to redeem the property within 120 days after the date of sale. *See* 26 U.S.C. § 7425(d)(1); 26 C.F.R. §§ 301.7425–1 to –4. See the form of notice to the IRS of nonjudicial sale in chapter 14 in this manual.

§ 2.101 Fences and Gates

The Texas Agriculture Code sets out certain requirements for cleared and cultivated lands, including the maintenance of fences of adequate substance and size, the minimum interspersing and sizes of gates located in such fence lines, and the removal of boundary line fences or damages to them. Tex. Agric. Code ch. 143.

The Texas Transportation Code regulates fence setback, height, and visibility requirements for fences located on land adjacent to a road or highway in the state highway system and in certain municipalities. Tex. Transp. Code § 250.001.

The Texas Local Government Code requires emergency gate access in multiunit housing complexes located outside municipal boundaries. Tex. Loc. Gov't Code §§ 352.1145–.115. A county may also require a multiunit housing project within its jurisdiction to have easily identifiable addresses on each building. Tex. Loc. Gov't Code § 352.116.

§ 2.102 Financing Statement, Fraudulent Filing

The circumstances under which a party is considered to have fraudulently filed a financing statement and the penalties for doing so are addressed in Tex. Bus. & Com. Code § 9.5185. See also section 2.113 below.

Certain financing statements filed by an inmate or inmate's representative are presumptively fraudulent. For restrictions on filing financing statements by such parties, refer to Tex. Civ. Prac. & Rem. Code §§ 12.001–.007 and Tex. Gov't Code §§ 51.901, 405.021.

§ 2.103 Fixtures

A record of a mortgage or other interest in real property is effective as a financing statement against fixtures if the requirements of Tex. Bus. & Com. Code § 9.502(c) are met. The priority of fixture filings is addressed in Tex. Bus. & Com. Code § 9.334. There is also an interaction between personal property leases and fixtures that should be noted. *See* Tex. Bus. & Com. Code § 2A.309. Mechanic's and materialman's liens on removable improvements, including fixtures, take priority over a deed-of-trust lien even if the deed of trust was recorded before the inception of such liens. *See* Tex. Prop. Code § 53.123; *see also First National Bank v. Whirlpool Corp.*, 517 S.W.2d 262, 269 (Tex. 1974).

§ 2.104 Flood Insurance

The National Flood Insurance Act of 1968, the Flood Disaster Protection Act of 1973, and the National Flood Insurance Reform Act of 1994, 42 U.S.C. §§ 4001–4129, provide flood, mudslide, and flood-related erosion insurance protection to property owners. In specified flood-prone areas, local governments are required to enforce special land use and building restrictions to minimize flood damage. If a loan secured by improved real estate in such an area is made, increased, extended, or renewed by a federally insured or federally regulated lender, the buyer must be notified in writing of the flood hazards a reasonable time before closing. 42 U.S.C. § 4104a. Regulations implementing the flood insurance program are found at 44 C.F.R. pts. 59–78. *See also* Tex. Loc. Gov't Code § 561.001 (county's power affecting flood control); Tex. Loc. Gov't Code § 240.901 (participation in federal flood insurance policy); Tex. Water Code ch. 16, subch. I (Flood Control and Insurance Act).

§ 2.105 Forced Sale of Co-Owner's Interest

The forced sale of a co-owner's interest in real property for reimbursement of property taxes is subject to the provisions of Tex. Prop. Code ch. 29.

§ 2.106 Forcible Entry and Detainer

See section 2.90 above.

§ 2.107 Foreclosure

Nonjudicial foreclosure sales of real property are governed by Tex. Prop. Code §§ 51.001–.002, 51.0021, 51.0025, 51.0075, 51.009 and Tex. Bus. & Com. Code ch. 22 (applicable to residential real property). If a security agreement covers both real and personal property, the personal property may be foreclosed under the Uniform Commercial Code, or both the real and personal property may be foreclosed in accordance with the procedures applicable to the real property. Tex. Bus. & Com. Code § 9.604(a). Certain redemption rights apply to the foreclosure of a condominium unit for failure to pay assessments (*see* Tex. Prop. Code § 82.113(g)), to foreclosures by a property owners' association (Tex. Prop. Code ch. 209), to tax foreclosures (Tex. Tax Code §§ 32.06, 34.21), and to foreclosures of property subject to a federal tax lien (26 U.S.C. § 7425(d)). See section 2.100 above.

A trustee or substitute trustee conducting a sale of residential real property may contract with an attorney to administer or perform the trustee's or substitute trustee's functions, or with an auction company to arrange, manage, sponsor, or advertise a public sale. Tex. Bus. & Com. Code § 22.003.

Deficiency litigation brought after a nonjudicial foreclosure sale must be filed within two years and is governed by the provisions of Tex. Prop. Code § 51.003. Deficiency litigation brought after a judicial foreclosure sale must be filed within ninety days and is governed by the provisions of Tex. Prop. Code § 51.004. A guarantor may institute litigation to contest the deficiency amount remaining after a judicial or nonjudicial foreclosure sale within ninety days after the later of the date of the foreclosure sale or receipt of actual notice of the foreclosure sale. Tex. Prop. Code § 51.005. Evictions after a foreclosure sale should be instituted in accordance with Tex. Prop. Code §§ 24.005, 24.0051 and Tex. R. Civ. P. 500–507, 510.1–.13.

A deed-of-trust foreclosure may also be permitted under limited circumstances after a deed in lieu of foreclosure has been accepted by the lienholder. Tex. Prop. Code § 51.006.

Litigation against the trustee named in a deed of trust, contract lien, or security instrument is subject to the procedures and defenses in Tex. Prop. Code § 51.007.

Home equity loan foreclosures are governed by Tex. R. Civ. P. 735, 736. The Texas Supreme Court has issued model forms for these foreclosures. See section 14.2:9 in this manual. Expedited foreclosure proceedings may be available to allow the foreclosure of a contract lien under Tex. R. Civ. P. 736. *See* Tex. Civ. Prac. & Rem. Code § 17.031. In these expedited proceedings, the court has the ability to order mediation before foreclosure. *See* Tex. Civ. Prac. & Rem. Code § 154.028.

A foreclosure may be subject to the preference provisions of federal bankruptcy law. *See* 11 U.S.C. § 547(b).

See also sections 2.41, 2.43, 2.65, 2.99, and 2.100 above and 2.125 and 2.141 below.

§ 2.108 Foreclosure Limitations Concerning FDIC Interests

If the Federal Deposit Insurance Corporation (FDIC) has a property interest, including a security interest, lien, or mortgage interest, in property that would be extinguished through foreclosure, condemnation, partition, or suit to quiet title, foreclosure must be by judicial sale if the United States is to be a named party or, if the sale is under a junior lien, the government's consent is required to eliminate that interest, with the government having a one-year right of redemption for certain liens eliminated by foreclosure of a superior lien. *See* 12 U.S.C. § 1825(b)(2); 28 U.S.C. § 2410(c). The holder of a superior lien may make a written request to have a junior lien, other than a tax lien, in favor of the United States extinguished if it appears that the sale proceeds will be insufficient to satisfy the government's lien or that the lien has been satisfied by lapse of time or has otherwise become unenforceable. 28 U.S.C. § 2410(e).

§ 2.109 Foreign Entities

Foreign entities are governed by the Texas Business Organizations Code.

§ 2.110 Foreign Ownership of Real Property

Numerous federal and state laws affect real estate conveyances involving foreigners. Tex. Prop. Code § 5.005 provides that aliens have the same real and personal property rights as United States citizens. Land owned by nonresident aliens or foreign governments may not be eligible under some circumstances for appraisal as open-space land or qualified timberland. Tex. Tax Code §§ 23.56, 23.77. The International Investment and Trade in Services Survey Act (22 U.S.C. §§ 3101–3108) and the Agricultural Foreign Investment Disclosure Act of 1978 (7 U.S.C. §§ 3501–3508) also affect these types of transactions. The Committee on Foreign Investment in the United States (CFIUS), formed in 1975, was given the power to review and block acquisitions of controlling interests in U.S. businesses by foreigners. CFIUS was amended by the Foreign Investment Risk Review Modernization Act of 2018 (FIRRMA) to greatly expand CFIUS's jurisdiction. Among other things, FIRRMA gives CFIUS the power to review and block leases and acquisitions by foreigners of U.S. real estate located near air and maritime ports, military facilities, and other sensitive government properties. *See* FIRRMA, Pub. L. No. 115-232, 132 Stat. 1636 (2018). Statutes requiring financial institutions to keep records and reports on monetary transactions are at 31 U.S.C. §§ 5311–5332. Internal Revenue Service requirements for submitting returns, as applied to foreigners with "direct investments" in real property interests in the United States, are at 26 U.S.C. § 6039C. Anyone purchasing realty in the United States from a foreign individual or entity must, with few exceptions, withhold 10 percent of the sales price and report and pay it over to the IRS within twenty days of the date of transfer. *See* 26 U.S.C. § 1445; 26 C.F.R. §§ 1.1445–1 to –11T. Nonforeign affidavits addressing the requirements of section 1445 are included as forms 26-19 and 26-20 in this manual. These affidavits are suggested for use in all transactions. See also sections 2.183 and 2.278 below.

§ 2.111 Forfeiture Laws

Real property may be subject to forfeiture if associated with criminal activities under the

Controlled Substances Act. *See* 21 U.S.C. § 881(7). The Texas Controlled Substances Act (Tex. Health & Safety Code §§ 481.001–.205) and the Code of Criminal Procedure provisions relating to forfeiture of contraband (Tex. Code Crim. Proc. arts. 59.01–.14) may also apply to such cases. Real property is also subject to forfeiture under the Racketeer Influenced and Corrupt Organizations Act. *See* 18 U.S.C. § 1963(b)(1).

§ 2.112 Franchising

The Business Opportunity Act applies to the sale of franchises. Tex. Bus. & Com. Code ch. 51.

§ 2.113 Fraudulent Filings

A person commits a criminal offense if, with intent to harm or defraud, he holds a purported lien against real or personal property that is fraudulent and fails to release the lien. Tex. Penal Code § 32.49. Knowingly presenting for filing a financing statement that is forged, contains a material false statement, or is groundless is also a criminal offense. Tex. Penal Code § 37.101. Actions on fraudulent liens can be found in Tex. Gov't Code §§ 51.902, 51.903. Liability and causes of action for fraudulent liens can be found in Tex. Civ. Prac. & Rem. Code ch. 12. Tex. Civ. Prac. & Rem. Code § 12.002(c) provides that mechanic's lien claimants under chapter 53 of the Texas Property Code are not liable under this section unless they act with intent to defraud.

A person commits a criminal offense if he knowingly or intentionally signs and presents for filing or causes to be presented for filing an assumed name certificate if the document indicates that the person signing the document has the authority to act on behalf of the entity for which the document is presented and the person does not have that authority, if the document contains a materially false statement, or if the document is forged. Tex. Bus. & Com. Code § 71.203. See also section 2.23 above.

Certain filings by inmates and their representatives are presumptively fraudulent. For restrictions on filings by such parties, refer to Tex. Civ. Prac. & Rem. Code §§ 12.001–.007 and Tex. Gov't Code §§ 51.901, 405.022.

§ 2.114 Fraudulent Representations and Promises

A person who makes a material false representation or false promise in a transaction involving real property is liable to the person defrauded for actual (and perhaps punitive) damages, attorney's fees, and court and other costs. Tex. Bus. & Com. Code § 27.01. A violation of section 27.01 that relates to the transfer of title to real estate is a false, misleading, or deceptive act or practice as defined by Tex. Bus. & Com. Code § 17.46(b), and any public remedy under Tex. Bus. & Com. Code ch. 17, subch. E, is available for a violation of that section.

§ 2.115 Fraudulent Transfers

Texas has adopted the Uniform Fraudulent Transfer Act in Tex. Bus. & Com. Code ch. 24. The fraudulent conveyance section of federal bankruptcy law is found at 11 U.S.C. § 548.

§ 2.116 FTC Anti-Holder-in-Due-Course Rule

Certain consumer credit contracts must comply with the notice requirements of 16 C.F.R. pt. 433. A copy of the relevant notice is included in chapter 20 in this manual.

§ 2.117 Future Estates

Future estates are governed by Tex. Prop. Code §§ 5.041–.043.

§ 2.118 Gifts to Minors Act

See section 2.275 below.

§ 2.119 Good Faith and Fair Dealing

No statute or common law imposes a duty of good faith and fair dealing in contracts in Texas, *English v. Fischer*, 660 S.W.2d 521 (Tex. 1983), but contracts governed by the Uniform Commercial Code (UCC) must comply with the good-faith obligation of Tex. Bus. & Com. Code § 1.304. In addition, the obligation of good faith under the UCC cannot be disclaimed by agreement, but contracting parties can define the standards by which the performance of good faith is to be measured, as long as the standards are not manifestly unreasonable. Tex. Bus. & Com. Code § 1.302(b).

§ 2.120 Grantee's Address

No instrument may be recorded unless the mailing address of each grantee appears in the instrument or in a separate writing attached to the instrument or a penalty is paid. Tex. Prop. Code § 11.003(a). However, the failure to comply with this provision will not invalidate the instrument as between the parties, and acceptance by the clerk creates a presumption that the law was satisfied. Tex. Prop. Code § 11.003(b), (c). See section 2.210 below.

§ 2.121 Group Homes

See section 2.45 above.

§ 2.122 Handguns

Persons at least twenty-one years of age who can legally possess a firearm are able to carry a handgun, concealed, or openly in a holster, in nonprohibited public places. Enacted as the Firearm Carry Act of 2021, 87(R) HB 1927 (2021). An individual may obtain a license to carry a handgun. Tex. Gov't Code ch. 411, subch. H. Handguns are prohibited as a matter of law for certain types of private and public properties, including schools (except for licensed holders at institutions of higher education), polling places, courts, government offices, racetracks, and secured areas of airports. Tex. Penal Code § 46.03. The statute does not affect the right of an employer to prohibit handguns on the premises of the business (Tex. Gov't Code § 411.203). Property owners' associations are not allowed to include or enforce any policy that would prohibit or restrict any person who is otherwise authorized from lawfully possessing, transporting, or storing a firearm, any part of a firearm, or firearm ammunition, or prohibit or restrict the otherwise lawful discharge of a firearm. Tex. Prop. Code § 202.020. Signs indicating that handguns are prohibited on site are required for certain alcoholic beverage establishments, hospitals, and nursing homes. Tex. Gov't Code § 411.204. The signs required by this section must meet specific requirements of size, language, and location. Private property owners are allowed to prohibit the carrying of concealed or openly carried handguns on their property if they provide proper legal notice that entry on the property by a license holder with a concealed or openly carried handgun is forbidden. Notice may be given orally, in writing with a statutory warning, or by signage with the statutory warning in English and Spanish in block letters at least one inch in height displayed in a conspicuous manner clearly visible to the public. A person with a license to carry a handgun who enters a property with a firearm after receiving oral or written notice to leave or where the required signage is posted commits a criminal trespass. Exceptions and defenses to prosecution are contained in the statutes criminalizing the conduct. Tex. Penal Code §§ 30.06, 30.07. An instrument granting an access easement may not restrict or prohibit an easement holder or an easement holder's guest from possessing, carrying, or transporting a firearm over the servient estate while using the easement for the easement's purpose. This does not apply to a pipeline, electric transmission, or utility easement. The owner of a servient estate may not enforce a restrictive covenant in an instrument granting an access easement over the servient estate that restricts or prohibits the easement holder or the easement holder's guest from possessing, carrying, or transporting a firearm over the servient estate while using the easement for the easement's purpose. Tex. Prop. Code § 5.020.

§ 2.123 Handicapped Parking

See section 2.15 above.

§ 2.124 Hart-Scott-Rodino Antitrust Improvements Act

Certain large transactions may require advance approval from the Federal Trade Commission under the terms of the Hart-Scott-Rodino Antitrust Improvements Act, 15 U.S.C. § 18a.

§ 2.125 Hazardous Waste Liens

A lien is created in favor of the state under Tex. Health & Safety Code § 361.194 on real property that is the subject of hazardous waste cleanup actions by the state. A federal lien also arises under the Comprehensive Environmental Response, Compensation, and Liability Act of 1980. *See* 42 U.S.C. § 9607(*l*).

§ 2.126 Historic Landmarks or Districts

A municipality may regulate designated places and areas of historical, cultural, or architectural significance. Tex. Loc. Gov't Code § 211.003. A municipality that has established a process for designating such places may not designate a property as a local historic landmark or include the property within a local historic district unless the owner of the property consents or, if the owner does not consent, the designation or inclusion is approved by a three-fourths vote of the municipality's governing body and the zoning, planning, or historical commission of the municipality. Tex. Loc. Gov't Code § 211.0165(a).

§ 2.127 Historic Structures

The Texas Historical Commission regulates the listing and preservation of historic structures in the state under the provisions of Tex. Gov't Code ch. 442. Counties also have certain rights and responsibilities regarding historic structures, sites, and resources. Tex. Loc. Gov't Code ch. 318. Liability for adversely affecting historic structures is addressed in Tex. Gov't Code § 442.016. Many counties and local municipalities also have historic or landmark commissions that regulate historic structures in their jurisdiction.

§ 2.128 Home Equity Lending

The homestead may be used to secure "equity" loans, including equity loans with line-of-credit terms, reverse mortgages, and the conversion and refinancing of a personal property lien on a manufactured home. Tex. Const. art. XVI, § 50. Section 50(f) permits the refinancing of a home equity loan only with another equity loan, a reverse mortgage, or a new loan that satisfies the requirements of section 50(f)(2). Section 50(a)(6)(F) allows for a home equity line of credit with certain limitations. Equity loans may be made for any purpose and must meet a number of constitutional and statutory requirements. A lien that does not satisfy a definition under section 50 is not valid against the homestead, and there is no statute of limitations for bringing an action against a void lien. *Wood v. HSBC Bank USA, N.A.*, 505 S.W.3d 542 (Tex. 2016). Home equity documents for secondary mortgage loans are regulated by the Office of Consumer Credit Commissioner and must be in plain language. Tex. Fin. Code § 341.502. See also section 2.160 below.

For a more extensive discussion of the issues in home equity lending, see chapter 11 in this manual.

§ 2.129 Home Improvement Contracts

There are notice requirements for home improvement contracts on homestead property (Tex. Prop. Code §§ 53.255, 53.256) and for liens claimed under these contracts (Tex. Prop. Code § 53.254). See sections 2.166 and 2.218 below.

§ 2.130 Home Mortgage Disclosure Act of 1975

Financial institutions that make federally related home mortgage loans must compile and make available information to enable citizens and government agencies to determine whether the institutions are fulfilling their obligations to serve the housing needs of the communities and neighborhoods in which they are located. *See* 12 U.S.C. §§ 2801–2810; 12 C.F.R. pt. 203.

§ 2.131 Home Solicitations

The Texas Home Solicitations Transaction Act may apply if the consumer's obligation is entered into at a location other than the contractor's place of business. If the Act applies, certain notices are required. Tex. Bus. & Com. Code ch. 601. See form 4-5 in this manual.

§ 2.132 Homesteads

Homestead rights are generally addressed in Tex. Prop. Code ch. 41, § 53.254, and Tex. Const. art. XVI, §§ 50, 51. A homestead is protected from forced sale for all debts except for liens securing the following: some or all of the purchase money, the taxes due thereon, an owelty of partition, new construction or home improvements, home equity, a reverse mortgage, and the conversion and refinancing of a personal property lien on a manufactured home to a lien on real property. Tex. Const. art. XVI, § 50(a). The amount of land that may be claimed as homestead depends on whether it is urban or rural and, if rural, whether it is claimed by a family or a single person. *See* Tex. Prop. Code § 41.002. Absent unusual circumstances or a judicial declaration that one spouse is incapacitated, the consent of both spouses is required if a homestead is sold or encumbered, regardless of whether it is characterized as community or separate property. Tex. Fam. Code §§ 5.001–.102.

Tex. Prop. Code § 41.005 provides for the voluntary designation of a homestead. This section and Tex. Tax Code §§ 11.13, 11.131, 11.135, 11.41, 11.43(j) set forth the requirements for making such a designation.

Under certain circumstances a lien to recover remediation costs may attach to a homestead. Tex. Health & Safety Code §§ 361.194, 361.197.

The state may be able to recover the costs of nursing home care paid by Medicaid from the homestead of the patient unless certain criteria are met. Tex. Gov't Code § 531.077.

Federal laws may preempt these statutes.

See also sections 2.2 and 2.128 above, chapter 11 in this manual, and section 20.1:2.

§ 2.133 Hotel Occupancy Taxes

The requirements and parameters of hotel occupancy taxes in the state are described in Tex. Tax Code chs. 156, 351, 352 and Tex. Loc. Gov't Code chs. 334, 335.

§ 2.134 House Trailers

See section 2.164 below.

§ 2.135 Impact Fees

The imposition of impact fees is governed by Tex. Loc. Gov't Code ch. 395.

§ 2.136 Implied Title Covenants

Unless the deed expressly provides otherwise, use of the word *grant* or *convey* in a deed implies only that the grantor covenants (a) that before the execution of the conveyance the grantor has not conveyed the estate or any interest in the estate to a person other than the grantee and (b) that at the time of the execution of the conveyance the estate is free from encumbrances. An implied covenant may be the basis for a lawsuit as if it had been expressed in the conveyance. Tex. Prop. Code § 5.023.

§ 2.137 Indemnity Agreements

Texas law limits the validity of indemnity agreements in certain situations, including in construction contracts and certain indemnities by a contractor with respect to an architect's negligence and by an architect with respect to an owner's negligence. See section 17.2:4 in this manual.

§ 2.138 Innocent-Purchaser Defense

The federal Comprehensive Environmental Response, Compensation, and Liability Act of 1980 establishes an innocent-landowner defense to environmental liability under certain circumstances, provided a purchaser has exercised "all appropriate inquiry" in its investigation of the property. *See* 42 U.S.C. §§ 9601(35), 9607(b).

§ 2.139 Insurance Claims

A lender must either endorse an insurance claim payment concerning personal property or provide a written statement of the reason it refuses to endorse within fourteen business days after receiving a request for the endorsement. Tex. Ins. Code ch. 557. Tex. Ins. Code §§ 551.051–.056 address restrictions against cancellation and nonrenewal of commercial liability policies. Sellers of goods or services who reasonably expect to be paid wholly or partly from the proceeds of property insurance claims are prohibited from allowing or assisting the insured person's failure to pay the applicable insurance deductible. Tex. Bus. & Com. Code § 27.02. Insurers must provide disclosures on flood coverage to commercial and residential property insurance policyholders. Tex. Ins. Code § 2002.103. The Texas Windstorm Insurance Association (TWIA) has been extended until 2031 and Tex. Ins. Code § 2210.107(b), relating to a reporting requirement by TWIA to the Texas Department of Insurance, has been repealed.

§ 2.140 Interstate Land Sales Full Disclosure Act

The Interstate Land Sales Full Disclosure Act requires filings and disclosures in some circumstances if there are sales or leases of twenty-five or more lots as part of a common promotional plan in interstate commerce or by use of the mail. *See* 15 U.S.C. §§ 1701–1720. Regulations promulgated under the Act can be found at 24 C.F.R. pts. 1710–1720.

§ 2.141 IRS Information Return (Foreclosures)

Under certain circumstances persons who lend money secured by property and who later acquire an interest in the property in satisfaction of the debt or have reason to know that the property has been abandoned must file an information return with the Internal Revenue Service and send a statement to the debtor. The information return must be filed by February 28, and the statement to the debtor provided by January 31, of the year following the calendar year in which the lender acquires the property or knows or has reason to know of the abandonment. *See* 26 U.S.C. § 6050J; 26 C.F.R. § 1.6050J–1T.

§ 2.142 Joint Tenancy with Right of Survivorship

A joint tenancy with the right of survivorship may be created by written agreement of property owners. Tex. Est. Code § 111.001. However, a joint tenancy between spouses concerning community property is governed by different statutory requirements. See section 2.46 above. For both types of property on the death of any cotenant, the practitioner should determine if title companies will accept the result of the joint tenancy agreement or if court adjudication and confirmation of the result is necessary. Adjudication or confirmation of joint tenancy with right of survivorship in community property is discussed at Tex. Est. Code §§ 112.101–.106.

§ 2.143 Judgment Liens

A recorded and properly indexed abstract of judgment constitutes a lien on the defendant's real property (including after-acquired property) located in the county in which the abstract is recorded and indexed. Tex. Prop. Code § 52.001. The lien continues for ten years after the abstract is recorded and indexed, but if the judgment becomes dormant during that period for lack of a writ of execution, the lien ceases to exist. Tex. Prop. Code § 52.006. Dormancy and revival of judgments are controlled by Tex. Civ. Prac. & Rem. Code § 34.001. But see the special provisions for the duration and revival of judgment liens in favor of the state or a state agency at Tex. Prop. Code § 52.006.

Texas has adopted the Uniform Enforcement of Foreign Judgments Act (Tex. Civ. Prac. & Rem. Code ch. 35) and the Uniform Federal Lien Registration Act (Tex. Prop. Code ch. 14). Generally, federal judgments and those of other states are treated like Texas judgments. *See* Tex. Civ. Prac. & Rem. Code ch. 35; Tex. Prop. Code §§ 14.002, 52.007; 28 U.S.C. § 1962. Texas has also adopted the Uniform Foreign Country Money-Judgment Recognition Act, Tex. Civ. Prac. & Rem. Code ch. 36.

An abstract of judgment generally does not constitute a lien against a homestead at the time the abstract is recorded and indexed. Tex. Const. art. XVI, § 50. For special procedures for effecting a release of a judgment lien against the homestead by statutory affidavit by the judgment debtor, refer to Tex. Prop. Code § 52.0012. Tex. Prop. Code § 52.0012 provides that a homestead affidavit and a certificate of mailing (both in the form prescribed by the statute) may be filed by a judgment debtor as a release of a judgment lien on homestead property.

For special restrictions on the filing of abstracts of judgment by inmates or their representatives, refer to Tex. Civ. Prac. & Rem. Code §§ 12.001–.007.

§ 2.144 Landfills

An owner or lessee must obtain a permit before development of a tract located over a closed municipal solid waste landfill, file a notice of the former use in the real property records, and give notice to prospective buyers or lessees. Tex. Health & Safety Code §§ 361.531–.539. The statute also requires that certain soil testing be conducted of any tract of one acre or more to determine whether it is located over a closed landfill. Tex. Health & Safety Code § 361.538.

§ 2.145 Landlord-Tenant Liens

There are two types of commercial landlord's liens. One is statutory, arising by operation of law. The other is contractual, created by agreement of the parties as a provision of the lease. The contractual landlord's lien constitutes a security agreement under article 9 of the Uniform Commercial Code. Tex. Bus. & Com. Code § 9.109(a)(1). The statutory landlord's lien gives the landlord a preference lien on the property of the tenant or subtenant in the building for rent that is due and for rent that is to become due during the current twelve-month period succeeding the date of the beginning of the rental agreement or an anniversary of that date. Tex. Prop. Code § 54.021. The lien is unenforceable for rent on a commercial building that is more than six months past due unless a lien statement is filed with the county clerk. Tex. Prop. Code § 54.022. The statutory lien can be foreclosed only through judicial proceedings; the contractual lien, depending on its terms, may be foreclosed through either judicial or nonjudicial proceedings.

A residential landlord's lien against a tenant's nonexempt personal property is provided in Tex. Prop. Code §§ 54.041–.048. An agricultural landlord's lien is available in Tex. Prop. Code §§ 54.001–.007.

§ 2.146 Landlord-Tenant Relationship

The landlord-tenant relationship is subject to the Texas Property Code. Chapter 91 contains provisions generally applicable to landlords and tenants. Chapter 92 covers residential tenancies. Chapter 93 covers commercial tenancies. Chapter 94 covers manufactured home community tenancies. If a tenant holds over after termination of a lease, the landlord's remedies include, among others, filing a forcible detainer action (Tex. Prop. Code ch. 24) and enforcing a lien against the tenant's property (Tex. Prop. Code chs. 54, 59). Other landlord-tenant related provisions to note are the prohibition against subletting and assignment (Tex. Prop. Code §§ 91.005, 94.057); landlord's duty to mitigate damages (Tex. Prop. Code §§ 91.006, 94.202); repair provisions (Tex. Prop. Code §§ 92.051–.061, 94.153–.154); landlord's duty to provide a complete copy of the lease (Tex. Prop. Code §§ 92.024, 94.053(b)); security deposits (Tex. Prop. Code §§ 92.101–.110, 93.004–.009, 94.101–.107); late fees (Tex. Prop. Code §§ 92.019, 94.054); rental applications (Tex. Prop. Code §§ 92.351–.355); lockout (Tex. Prop. Code §§ 92.0081, 92.009, 93.002–.003); and utility interruptions (Tex. Prop. Code §§ 92.008, 92.0091, 93.002).

The Texas Property Code addresses the liability of a residential landlord for failure to install smoke alarms (Tex. Prop. Code §§ 92.251–.262) and security devices (Tex. Prop. Code §§ 92.151–.170).

See sections 2.1, 2.5, 2.61, and 2.145 above and 2.161 and 2.239 below. See also chapter 25 in this manual.

§ 2.147 Landowner Liability

Several statutory provisions address landowner liability in different contexts. The Comprehensive Environmental Response, Compensation, and Liability Act governs owner liability for hazardous substances. *See* 42 U.S.C. § 9607. Other state and federal statutes have similar provisions. Statutes concerning limitations on a landowner's liability include Tex. Civ. Prac. & Rem. Code ch. 75 (liability for recreational use, such as hunting and community gardens); Tex. Civ. Prac. & Rem. Code ch. 95 (liability to a contractor); and Tex. Civ. Prac. & Rem. Code § 101.022 (liability of governmental units).

§ 2.148 Landowner's Bill of Rights

The Landowner's Bill of Rights, prepared by the Office of the Attorney General of Texas, is a statement of the rights a real property owner has if condemnation of his real property is sought. The statement may be viewed at the Attorney General's website at **www.texasattorneygeneral.gov/sites/default/files/files/divisions/general-oag/landowners-bill-of-rights.pdf.** The Texas Property Code requires a governmental or private entity with eminent domain authority to provide the Landowner's Bill of Rights statement to the property owner as part of the condemnation process. Tex. Prop. Code § 21.0112. See also section 2.47 above.

§ 2.149 Landscape Architecture

The business of landscape architecture is regulated under Tex. Occ. Code ch. 1052. The lien of a person who provides landscaping services is addressed in Tex. Prop. Code § 53.021(4).

§ 2.150 Lead-Based Paint Disclosures

In 1992, Congress adopted the Residential Lead-Based Paint Hazard Reduction Act, also known as Title X of the Housing and Community Development Act. The lead-based paint provisions are codified at 42 U.S.C. §§ 4851–4856 (the regulations are published in 40 C.F.R. pt. 745). Sellers and landlords must provide purchasers and tenants of residential properties constructed before 1978 with a "Lead Warning Statement," in the form provided in 42 U.S.C. § 4852d, in large type and on a separate sheet of paper from the contract. The required warning statements, prescribed in 40 C.F.R. § 745.113, are included in chapters 4 (for sales) and 25 (for leases) in this manual. The related state statute is found at Tex. Occ. Code ch. 1955. This law applies to all "child-occupied facilities," including day-care centers and preschool and kindergarten classrooms, occupied by the same child, six years of age or younger, for three hours or more, twice a week.

§ 2.151 Legal Incapacity

A person may lack legal capacity to contract for and deal with real property without the supervision of a guardian appointed under the Texas guardianship statutes, Texas Estates Code title 3, sections 1001.001 to 1356.056. In dealing with a guardian in a real estate transaction, the attorney should carefully review the guardianship order. "An incapacitated person for whom a guardian is appointed retains all legal and civil rights and powers except those designated by court order as legal disabilities by virtue of having been specifically granted to the guardian." Tex. Est. Code § 1151.001. Additionally, there must be an annual determination whether the guardianship should be continued, modified, or terminated. Tex. Est. Code §§ 1201.051–.054. Tex. Prop. Code ch. 142 addresses the management of property recovered on behalf of a minor or incapacitated person through a suit by a next friend. See also section 2.171 below.

§ 2.152 Letters of Credit

Letters of credit are governed by the provisions of Tex. Bus. & Com. Code ch. 5.

§ 2.153 Libraries

Public libraries are exempt from attachment, execution, or forced sale. Tex. Prop. Code § 43.001.

§ 2.154 Life Tenants

The duties of a life tenant of real property are set out in Tex. Prop. Code § 5.009.

§ 2.155 Limitations

An action to recover real property conveyed by an instrument containing certain technical defects must be brought within two years of the recordation of the instrument. Tex. Civ. Prac. & Rem. Code § 16.033(a). An action to foreclose a real property vendor's lien or deed-of-trust lien must be brought and a nonjudicial sale must be completed within four years after the cause of action accrues. Tex. Civ. Prac. & Rem. Code § 16.035. A suit to foreclose a mechanic's lien must be commenced not later than the first anniversary of the last day the claimant may file its lien affidavit, unless the claimant and owner enter into and file of record an agreement to extend limitations, in which case they can agree to extend for up to two years. For a claim arising from a residential construction project, suit must be commenced within one year after the last day for filing the lien affidavit or within one year after completion, termination, or abandonment of the work under the original contract, whichever is later. Tex. Prop. Code § 53.158. A suit on a deficiency judgment after a real property foreclosure must be brought within two years of the foreclosure sale. Tex. Prop. Code § 51.003. A contractual limitations period shorter than two years is void, except in a contract relating to the sale or purchase of a business entity if the consideration involved is greater than $500,000. Tex. Civ. Prac. & Rem. Code § 16.070.

The limitations periods on actions on negotiable instruments are governed by Tex. Bus. & Com. Code § 3.118. The limitations periods on actions on nonnegotiable instruments are governed by Tex. Civ. Prac. & Rem. Code §§ 16.003(a), 16.004(a)(3).

See also section 2.6 above.

§ 2.156 Limited Liability Companies

Limited liability companies are governed by the Texas Business Organizations Code generally and by title 3 more specifically. Tex. Bus. Orgs. Code §§ 101.001–.622. See also sections 2.34, 2.59, and 2.109 above and 2.181 and 2.193 below. The company agreement for a limited liability company may establish one or more designated series of members, managers, membership interests, or assets that (a) have separate rights, powers, or duties with respect to specified property or obligations of the limited liability company or profits and losses associated with specified property or obligations or (b) have separate business purposes or investment objectives. A limited liability company may establish a protected series or registered series and has certain powers to act in the name of the protected series or registered series. Specific provisions in the Code deal with distributions, allocations, liabilities of members, and other matters relating to a protected series or registered series. Tex. Bus. Orgs. Code §§ 101.601–.622.

§ 2.157 Limited Liability Partnerships

Limited liability partnerships are governed by the Texas Business Organizations Code generally and by title 4 more specifically. *See* Tex. Bus. Orgs. Code §§ 152.801, 153.351. In Texas, a limited liability partnership is either a preexisting general partnership or a preexisting limited partnership that registers with the secretary of state as a limited liability partnership and complies with other statutory requirements.

Foreign limited liability partnerships are governed by Tex. Bus. Orgs. Code § 152.901 and are subject to Tex. Bus. Orgs. Code § 2.101. Texas law does not define what constitutes "transacting business in Texas" for the purposes of the requirement of Tex. Bus. Orgs. Code § 152.905 that "[b]efore transacting business in this state, a foreign limited liability partnership must file an application for registration in accordance with this section and Chapters 4 and 9." Tex. Bus. Orgs. Code § 9.251, however, does contain a list of activities not constituting transacting business in Texas. *See also* Tex. Bus. Orgs. Code § 153.103. See section 2.109 above.

§ 2.158 Liquidated Damages Clauses

Liquidated damages provisions regarding the sale of goods must comply with the requirements of Tex. Bus. & Com. Code § 2.718.

§ 2.159 Lis Pendens

A party seeking affirmative relief in an action involving title to real property, the establishment of an interest in real property, or the enforcement of an encumbrance against real property may file notice of the pending action with the clerk of the county in which the land is located.

A form of lis pendens is available as form 26-35 in this manual. The person filing such a notice must serve a copy of the notice on each party to the action who has an interest in the real property affected by the notice no later than three days after the notice is filed. Tex. Prop. Code § 12.007(d). Under certain conditions and on motion of a party, the court may cancel the lis pendens anytime during the proceeding. Tex. Prop. Code § 12.008. Under certain other conditions for lis pendens filed after September 1, 2009, and on motion of a party, the court must expunge the notice of lis pendens. Tex. Prop. Code § 12.0071. A recorded lis pendens for which no certified copy of an order expunging the notice of lis pendens has been recorded constitutes notice of the litigation. Tex. Prop. Code § 13.004.

For a certified copy of an order expunging a notice of lis pendens that is recorded on or after September 1, 2017, after such certified copy of the order has been recorded, an interest in the real property covered by the notice of lis pendens may be transferred or encumbered free of all matters asserted or disclosed in the notice and all claims or other matters asserted or disclosed in the action in connection with which the notice was filed. Tex. Prop. Code § 12.0071(f).

§ 2.160 Loan Documents

Tex. Bus. & Com. Code § 26.02 requires a financial institution to give a statute-of-frauds type of notice for loans exceeding $50,000 and to post notices informing borrowers of the provisions of section 26.02. Construction mortgages should clearly identify that they are securing a construction loan to take advantage of the priority provisions of Tex. Bus. & Com. Code § 9.334(h). See also Tex. Gov't Code ch. 83, which prohibits the preparation of deeds, deeds of trust, notes, mortgages, and other documents affecting title to real property for compensation unless the preparer is an attorney licensed in Texas or is qualified under one of the other listed exemptions. See also section 2.268 below.

The Texas Finance Code provides rules relating to loan documents used in home equity loans, which are administered by the Office of Consumer Credit Commissioner. Tex. Fin. Code § 341.502. For a more extensive discussion of the issues in home equity lending, see chapter 11 in this manual.

The Texas Tax Code prohibits a lender from requiring a borrower to waive its right to an agricultural or open-space tax exemption as a condition to a loan or to agree to pay the lender for any losses suffered by the lender due to change of use and loss of this exemption. Tex. Tax Code §§ 23.47, 23.58.

Certain loan documents transferring an interest in real property to or from an individual are required to include the confidentiality notice set out in Tex. Prop. Code § 11.008. See section 3.17 in this manual.

Several other sections also address the preparation of loan documents, including 2.64 and 2.107 above and 2.165, 2.166, 2.267, and 2.279 below.

§ 2.161 Lockouts

Lockouts of residential tenants are governed by Tex. Prop. Code §§ 92.0081, 92.009. Commercial tenant lockouts are governed by Tex. Prop. Code §§ 93.002–.003.

§ 2.162 Lost or Found Property

See sections 2.1 and 2.88 above.

§ 2.163 Low-Income Affordable Housing Tax Credits

See section 2.8 above.

§ 2.164 Manufactured Housing

The Texas Manufactured Housing Standards Act (TMHSA) regulates manufactured housing through the Texas Department of Housing and Community Affairs. Tex. Occ. Code ch. 1201. Title to manufactured homes, the perfection and release of manufactured housing liens, and the cancellation of manufactured housing titles are governed by the TMHSA. Both the TMHSA and the Texas Property Code address the question of when a manufactured home is personal property and when it is real property. Tex. Prop. Code § 2.001; Tex. Occ. Code §§ 1201.2055, 1201.2075, 1201.222. For a more extensive discussion of manufactured housing, see section 5.15:6 in this manual.

Property Code chapter 63 clarifies the status of a lien on a manufactured home when the manufactured home is converted to real property. Tex. Prop. Code ch. 63. Property Code chapter 94 regulates lease agreements in manufactured-home communities entered into on or after April 1, 2002. Tex. Prop. Code ch. 94.

§ 2.165 Master Form Mortgage

Texas permits the filing of a master form mortgage under Tex. Prop. Code § 12.009. A master assignment of financing statements is permitted under the terms of Tex. Bus. & Com. Code § 9.514(d).

§ 2.166 Mechanic's Liens

Mechanic's liens, which may arise in favor of a variety of contractors, workers, and those providing material for construction or for improvements to property, may be either constitutional or statutory. The constitutional lien derives from Tex. Const. art. XVI, § 37. Statutory liens derive from Tex. Prop. Code ch. 53. See chapters 20 and 21 in this manual.

The mechanic's lien procedures and rights may also apply to persons who perform labor or materials for the demolition of a structure under a written contract. Tex. Prop. Code § 53.021(5).

On public construction projects, a mechanic's lien cannot be established against public buildings, structures, or grounds, but subcontractors may have a lien on money, bonds, or warrants due the contractor for the improvements if the prime contract does not exceed $25,000 if with a governmental entity other than a municipality or joint board created under the Transportation Code or $50,000 if with a municipality or joint board. Tex. Prop. Code § 53.231. The McGregor Act, Tex. Gov't Code ch. 2253, establishes procedures for the protection of performance- and payment-bond beneficiaries who have a direct contractual relationship with the prime contractor or a subcontractor on a public construction project. The Miller Act, as amended by the Construction Industry Payment Act of 1999, pertains to bonding requirements for construction, alteration, or repair of federal works. 40 U.S.C. §§ 3131–3134.

Certain mechanic's lien documents transferring an interest in real property to or from an individual must contain the confidentiality notice set out in Tex. Prop. Code § 11.008. See section 3.17 in this manual.

§ 2.167 Military Installations

See section 2.188 below.

§ 2.168 Military Personnel

The Servicemembers Civil Relief Act (formerly the Soldiers' and Sailors' Civil Relief Act) requires that, under some circumstances, enforcement of certain civil liabilities and legal proceedings, including foreclosures, be suspended while armed forces personnel are on active duty. 50 U.S.C. §§ 3901–4043. Delinquency dates for property taxes may also be extended. Tex. Tax Code § 31.02. Deferred delinquent tax that is not paid on or before the date the deferral period expires accrues interest and does not incur a penalty. Tex. Tax Code § 33.01(f).

Texas Property Code section 51.015 also affords certain protections to military servicemembers—during active duty military service and during the nine months thereafter—against collection actions for enforcement of real estate loans secured by the servicemember's dwelling and made to that servicemember before his or her active duty military service commenced. Tex. Prop. Code § 51.015.

Notices of special rights afforded servicemembers are required in suits to evict (Tex. Prop. Code § 24.0051(d)), in the sale of real property under a power of sale or other contractual lien (Tex. Prop. Code § 51.002(i)), and in the notice that must be provided before certain enforcement actions by property owners' associations (Tex. Prop. Code § 209.006(b)). Leases that do not contain notice of a servicemember's right to terminate may lead to the release of liability for unpaid rent. Tex. Prop. Code § 92.017(g).

§ 2.169 Mineral Rights

Chapter 92 of the Texas Natural Resources Code provides procedures to designate drill sites on land proposed to be subdivided. Tex. Nat. Res. Code §§ 92.001–.007. Tex. Nat. Res. Code § 81.0523 preempts the regulation of oil and gas operations by municipalities and other political subdivisions. A municipality or other political subdivision may not enact or enforce an ordinance that bans, limits, or otherwise regulates oil and gas operations within the boundaries or extraterritorial jurisdiction of the municipality or other political subdivision, except for an ordinance that (1) regulates only aboveground activities, (2) is commercially reasonable, (3) does not effectively prohibit an oil and gas operation conducted by a reasonably prudent operator, and (4) is not otherwise preempted by state or federal law. Tex. Nat. Res. Code § 81.0523(b), (c). An ordinance is considered prima facie to be commercially reasonable if the ordinance has been in effect for at least five years and has allowed oil and gas operations to continue during that time period. Tex. Nat. Res. Code § 81.0523(d).

§ 2.170 Mini-Storage Warehouses

See section 2.231 below.

§ 2.171 Minors

Minors do not have the legal capacity to enter into contracts. The age of majority is eighteen years. Tex. Civ. Prac. & Rem. Code §§ 129.001, 129.002. Marriage removes the disabilities of minority. Tex. Fam. Code § 1.104. Under certain circumstances, the disabilities can be judicially removed. Tex. Fam. Code ch. 31. Unless the disability is removed by marriage or by court decree, a guardian must be appointed under terms of the Texas Estates Code to administer real property owned by the minor. Tex. Est. Code §§ 1001.001–.056. Under certain conditions, a parent may petition the court for an order to sell the minor's property instead of having a guardian appointed. Tex. Est. Code § 1351.001. A next friend may also manage property of a minor recovered in a lawsuit if the minor has no guardian. Tex. Prop. Code § 142.001. See also sections 2.151 above and 2.275 below.

§ 2.172 Mobile Homes

See section 2.164 above.

§ 2.173 Mold Assessors and Remediators

Mold remediation and other activities that affect indoor air quality, such as mold assessments, are governed by chapter 1958 of the Texas Occupations Code. Tex. Occ. Code ch. 1958.

Sections 544.301–.305 of the Insurance Code prohibit certain underwriting decisions based on previous mold claims or damages and applies to any insurer that writes residential property insurance in Texas. Tex. Ins. Code §§ 544.301–.305. An insurer may not make an underwriting decision based on previous mold claims or damages if mold remediation was performed on the property and either a certificate of mold remediation was issued or a subsequent inspection by an independent assessor or adjustor revealed no evidence of mold damage. Tex. Ins. Code § 544.303.

§ 2.174 Money Laundering

See section 2.36 above.

§ 2.175 Mortgage Electronic Registration Systems (MERS)

For all practical purposes, Mortgage Electronic Registration Systems, Inc. (MERS) is nothing more than a "book entry system" or "utility" for the real estate finance industry that is intended to eliminate the need for executing and recording assignments when mortgage loans and related servicing rights are sold in the secondary market. MERS is an electronic registration system that tracks the bundle of rights that are transferred when the various beneficial interests associated with real estate loans are bought and sold on the secondary market like stocks and bonds and commodities like coffee, gold, and oil futures.

To invoke the protections of the real property recording statutes in the official land title records, MERS acts as the mortgagee of record for each security instrument that secures a loan registered on the MERS System. Security instruments must contain particular language naming MERS as original mortgagee. MERS maintains a web-based, electronic book entry registration system that tracks the beneficial ownership and servicing rights associated with any registered real estate loan. The mortgage servicer, who is responsible for all the daily administrative details required to service a borrower's loan, inputs all loan level data and changes into MERS.

MERS does not buy, sell, transfer, or assign real estate loans and is not the owner, holder, or servicer of the beneficial ownership and servicing rights associated with loans registered on MERS. As long as a loan is registered on the MERS System, MERS is the mortgagee of record in the real property records, and no assignment or transfer of lien is necessary, regardless of the number of times a registered loan is bought or sold.

MERSCORP, Inc., is a private corporation owned and sponsored by the Mortgage Bankers Association of America; the American Land Title Association; the Federal National Mortgage Association; the Federal Home Loan Mortgage Corporation; the Department of Veterans Affairs; the U.S. Department of Housing and Urban Development; nearly every Tier-1 lender; the major title insurance underwriters; and the three major rating agencies for mortgage-backed securities, Standard & Poor's, Moody's Investors Service, and Fitch Ratings.

§ 2.176 Mortgage Fraud

Intentionally or knowingly making a materially false or misleading written statement to obtain a mortgage loan is a violation of section 32.32 of the Texas Penal Code. Punishment ranges from a class C misdemeanor to a first-degree felony. Intentionally or knowingly making a materially false or misleading written statement in providing an appraisal of real property for compensation also violates section 32.32 of the Texas Penal Code and is subject to the same range of punishment. Tex. Penal Code § 32.32(b–1). Venue for prosecution for mortgage fraud is governed by Tex. Code Crim. Proc. art. 13.271.

Lenders, mortgage bankers, and licensed mortgage brokers must provide all applicants for a home loan a written notice of penalties for making false or misleading written statements containing the promulgated language set out in section 343.105 of the Texas Finance Code, or substantially similar language, at the time of loan closing. *See* Tex. Fin. Code § 343.105. Also see form 10-19 in this manual. The notice must be a separate document in at least a fourteen-point typeface. Borrowers must sign the notice and verify that all statements and representations contained in their written loan applications regarding their identity, employment, annual income, and intent to occupy the residential real property securing the home loan are true and correct as of the date of loan closing. The failure to provide the notice in compliance with the statute expressly does not affect the validity of the home loan or its enforceability by any holder.

§ 2.177 Mortgage Loan Originators

Use of the term *mortgage broker* has been discontinued for purposes of state licensing and registration of mortgage loan originators to conform to terminology established by the Texas Secure and Fair Enforcement for Mortgage Licensing Act of 2009. Tex. Fin. Code ch. 180. Companies engaged in or conducting the business of originating residential mortgage loans (mortgage companies) must be licensed under and comply with the Residential Mortgage Loan Company Licensing and Registration Act while individuals must be licensed under and comply with the Mortgage Banker Registration and Residential Mortgage Loan Originator License Act, administered by the Department of Savings and Mortgage Lending. Tex. Fin. Code chs. 156, 157. An applicant must designate an individual licensed as a residential mortgage loan originator under chapter 157 of the Texas Finance Code as the company's qualifying individual as required by sections 156.2041 through 156.2044 of the Texas Finance Code. A registered mortgage loan originator who does not hold certain listed licenses or a person licensed as a mortgage loan originator in another state may have the temporary authority to act as a mortgage loan originator for up to 120 days upon satisfaction of a number of requirements. Tex. Fin. Code § 180.0511; *see* Tex. Fin. Code § 180.051(a)(1).

An individual licensed under chapter 157 may not be licensed or act as a residential loan originator unless the individual enrolls in the Nationwide Mortgage Licensing System and Registry (or is sponsored by an appropriate entity), obtains a valid unique identifier under that system, and otherwise complies with the applicable requirements of chapter 180 of the Texas Finance Code and rules adopted thereunder by the Texas Finance Commission to carry out the intent of the federal Secure and Fair Enforcement for Mortgage Licensing Act of 2008, 12 U.S.C. §§ 5101–5116.

A licensed residential mortgage loan originator is not required to obtain a regulated loan license under chapter 342 of the Texas Finance Code to make, negotiate, or transact a secondary mortgage loan subject to that chapter. Tex. Fin. Code § 342.051. Mortgage bankers, as defined in section 156.002(8) of the Texas Finance Code, are exempt from chapter 156 if registered under chapter 157. Depository institutions, their regulated subsidiaries, and entities regulated by the Farm Credit Administration are exempt from chapter 156. Tex. Fin. Code § 156.202.

Residential mortgage loan originator compensation, including the practice by creditors of paying mortgage loan originators a yield-spread premium based on the interest rate of a residential mortgage loan or paying compensation based on loan terms other than the principal loan amount, is restricted under amendments to Regulation Z, 12 C.F.R. § 226.36 (Truth in Lending).

Entities and individuals exempt from the licensing requirement are listed in Tex. Fin. Code §§ 156.202(a–1), 157.0121, 180.003(a).

Residential mortgage companies and loan originators must comply with rules and regulations adopted by the Finance Commission. 7 Tex. Admin. Code ch. 80. The commissioner is authorized to enforce compliance with the subject licensing regulations through powers granted under chapters 156 and 157 of the Texas Finance Code. Unlicensed activity is punishable as a class B misdemeanor.

§ 2.178 Municipal Utility Districts (MUDs)

Municipal utility districts are governed by the provisions of Tex. Water Code chs. 49, 54, 59. See also section 2.280 below.

§ 2.179 Naturally Occurring Radioactive Materials (NORM)

The Texas Railroad Commission regulates NORM waste resulting from oil and gas operations. Tex. Health & Safety Code § 401.415.

§ 2.180 Navigable Streams

Survey lines may not cross navigable streams, which are defined as those retaining "an average width of 30 feet from the mouth up." Tex. Nat. Res. Code §§ 21.001(3), 21.012(b). See also Tex. Rev. Civ. Stat. art. 5414a, which controls the validity of patents to and awards of land lying across or partly across watercourses, navigable streams, beds, and abandoned beds of watercourses. See also section 2.291 below.

§ 2.181 Nonprofit Corporations

Nonprofit corporations are governed by the Texas Business Organizations Code generally and by chapter 22 more specifically. Tex. Bus. Orgs. Code §§ 22.001–.409. The sale, lease, exchange, or mortgage of property belonging to a domestic entity is controlled by Tex. Bus. Orgs. Code § 10.251. Most property owners' associations that are incorporated are organized as nonprofit organizations. *See* Tex. Prop. Code chs. 81, 82. See also sections 2.34, 2.59, 2.109, and 2.156 above and 2.193 and 2.276 below.

§ 2.182 Non–Real Estate Taxes Affecting Real Estate

The purchaser of a business or stock of goods must withhold from the purchase price adequate funds to pay taxes that may be owed by the seller (for example, unpaid hotel, parking revenue, sales, and corporate franchise taxes of the seller) until the seller provides a receipt of payment from the comptroller. Tex. Tax Code § 111.020. See also section 2.133 above.

§ 2.183 North American Free Trade Agreement (NAFTA)

In September 2018, the United States, Mexico, and Canada reached an agreement to replace the North American Free Trade Agreement (NAFTA) with the United States–Mexico–Canada Agreement (USMCA). NAFTA remained in force pending the ratification of the USMCA by all three governments. The USMCA entered into force on July 1, 2020, replacing NAFTA. Certain provisions of the USMCA may affect real property and finance transactions. The text of the USMCA is available on the Office of the United States Trade Representative website at

https://ustr.gov/usmca. The USMCA has curtailed NAFTA's protections for investors engaging in cross-border investment with party countries. Certain investments made while NAFTA was still in effect and that remained in existence on July 1, 2020, are eligible to raise dispute claims under NAFTA until July 1, 2023. See also section 2.110 above and section 2.278 below.

§ 2.184 Notarial Seals, Out-of-State

The failure of a non-Texas notary public to attach an official seal to a document will not render the document invalid if a seal is not required in the jurisdiction in which the document is acknowledged. Tex. Prop. Code § 12.001; Tex. Civ. Prac. & Rem. Code § 121.004. The secretary of state annually compiles a list of states that require notarial seals to validate the certificate of acknowledgment and will make the list available to all county clerks by January 1 of each year. Tex. Gov't Code § 405.019. See also section 2.4 above.

§ 2.185 Notaries Public

Notary qualifications and requirements are found in Tex. Gov't Code ch. 406. Notaries may not represent or imply that they are attorneys. Tex. Gov't Code § 406.017. The notary's book is public information and must be available for inspection at reasonable times. Tex. Gov't Code § 406.014(b). By administrative rule, however, notaries public may not record in the public record the identification number on the signer's identification card used. 1 Tex. Admin. Code § 87.40. Notaries may certify copies of documents not recordable in the public records and may take depositions. Tex. Gov't Code § 406.016. Notaries may authenticate a paper or tangible copy of an electronic record to enable recording. Tex. Prop. Code § 12.0013. The form of declaration of authenticity is set out in Tex. Prop. Code § 12.0013(e). Application of a printed seal by a notary public is not required on an electronically transmitted certificate of acknowledgment if the same information as contained in the seal is set forth. Tex. Civ. Prac. & Rem. Code § 121.004(d); Tex. Gov't Code § 406.013(d). See section 2.4 above.

§ 2.186 Nuisance

Statutory provisions relating to common and public nuisances are in Tex. Civ. Prac. & Rem. Code ch. 125, Tex. Loc. Gov't Code ch. 214, and Tex. Health & Safety Code chs. 342, 343. Many municipalities have local ordinances relating to nuisances.

§ 2.187 Open-Space Exemption

The law governing the appraisal of "qualified open-space land" for ad valorem taxes is found in Tex. Tax Code §§ 23.51–.59. The Texas Tax Code prohibits a lender from requiring a borrower to waive its right to an agricultural or open-space tax exemption as a condition to a loan or to agree to pay the lender for any losses suffered by the lender due to change of use and loss of this exemption. Tex. Tax Code §§ 23.47, 23.58. See also section 2.5 above.

§ 2.188 Outdoor Lighting

Astronomical Observatories: The commissioners court of a county within fifty-seven miles of the McDonald Observatory must adopt orders regulating the installation and use of outdoor lighting in any unincorporated territory and adopt orders establishing standards relating to outdoor lighting in proposed subdivisions to minimize the interference with observatory activities. The commissioners court of a county within five miles of the George Observatory or the Stephen F. Austin Observatory may restrict artificial outdoor lighting in any unincorporated territory of the county and establish standards relating to artificial outdoor lighting in proposed subdivisions to minimize the interference with observatory activities. Tex. Loc. Gov't Code

§§ 240.031–.035. A municipality must regulate by ordinance the installation and use of outdoor lighting to protect against its use in a way that interferes with scientific astronomical research of an observatory. Tex. Loc. Gov't Code §§ 229.051–.053. A municipality must by ordinance establish standards relating to proposed subdivisions to minimize interference with observatory activities. Tex. Loc. Gov't Code §§ 229.054–.055.

Military Installations: Sections 240.032 and 240.0325 of the Texas Local Government Code authorize the commissioners court of a county with a population of more than one million that has at least five United States military bases and any county adjacent to that county that is within five miles of a United States Army installation, base, or camp, on request of the commanding officer, to adopt orders regulating the installation and use of outdoor lighting within five miles of the installation, base, or camp in unincorporated territory of the county. There are exceptions for installations in place before the effective date of the order for electric utilities, electric cooperatives, gas utilities, surface coal mining, telecommunications providers, and manufacturing facilities required by the Texas Commission on Environmental Quality to hold a permit and for tracts of land used as a single residence outside the boundaries of a private subdivision, tracts of land maintained for agricultural use, activity that takes place on a tract of land maintained for agricultural use, structures or related improvements located on a tract of land maintained for agricultural use, or a correctional facility operated by or under a contract with the Texas Department of Criminal Justice. Tex. Loc. Gov't Code §§ 240.032, 240.0325.

§ 2.189 Outdoor Signs

The Texas Civil Practice and Remedies Code addresses the subject of trespass by outdoor signs in Tex. Civ. Prac. & Rem. Code §§ 80.001–.003. Municipalities are authorized to relocate, reconstruct, and remove signs under Tex. Loc. Gov't Code ch. 216. The owner of a sign may be entitled to be compensated for the costs associated with the relocation, reconstruction, or removal. Tex. Loc. Gov't Code § 216.003. However, a municipality cannot regulate a private landowner's right to put political signage on the landowner's property. Tex. Elec. Code § 259.003. The Texas Highway Commission regulates highway signs under Tex. Transp. Code chs. 391–395, while recognizing the authority of cities and counties to regulate highway signs in certain circumstances.

§ 2.190 Parking

A landlord who issues a parking permit to a residential tenant must issue the permit for a term that is coterminous with the tenant's lease term and may not terminate or suspend the permit until the date the tenant's right of possession ends. Tex. Prop. Code § 92.0132. A neighborhood may petition a county or municipality to post signs prohibiting the overnight parking of commercial vehicles by complying with Tex. Transp. Code § 545.307. See section 2.261 below.

§ 2.191 Parks and Recreational Projects

Cities and towns are restricted in certain instances from selling or encumbering parks and other recreational projects without authorization by a majority vote of qualified voters. Tex. Gov't Code §§ 1508.001–.010.

§ 2.192 Partition

A joint owner or claimant of real property or an interest in real property or a joint owner of personal property may compel a partition of the interest or the property among the joint owners or claimants. Tex. Prop. Code ch. 23 and Tex. R. Civ. P. 756–771. Tex. Prop. Code ch. 23A addresses the partition of heirship property.

Unless waived by the parties, a nonexclusive access easement shall be granted on partition of property under chapter 23. Tex. Prop. Code § 23.006.

§ 2.193 Partnerships

Partnerships are governed generally by title 4 of the Texas Business Organizations Code. Chapters 151 and 154 apply to both general and limited partnerships. Chapter 152 applies to general partnerships, and chapter 153 applies to limited partnerships.

The sale, lease, exchange, or mortgage of property belonging to a domestic entity is controlled by Tex. Bus. Orgs. Code § 10.251. Every partner is an agent for the partnership, and any act done in the usual course of business, including the execution of instruments, binds the partnership and the partners. Tex. Bus. Orgs. Code §§ 152.301–.302.

If a partner conveys partnership real property without authority and the transaction is not in the usual course of business, the partnership may recover the property from the grantee but not from a bona fide purchaser from the grantee for value without knowledge of the lack of authority. Tex. Bus. Orgs. Code § 152.302(c).

Title to partnership property for general partnerships is governed by Tex. Bus. Orgs. Code § 152.102.

See also sections 2.34, 2.59, 2.109, 2.156, and 2.181 above.

§ 2.194 Personal Property Leases

Personal property leases are governed by the provisions of Tex. Bus. & Com. Code ch. 2A. In addition, Tex. Bus. & Com. Code ch. 92 addresses rental-purchase agreements of consumer personal property.

§ 2.195 Pest Control

The Texas Structural Pest Control Act is found in Tex. Occ. Code ch. 1951.

§ 2.196 Pipeline Easements

See section 2.76 above.

§ 2.197 Plats

See section 2.245 below.

§ 2.198 Powers of Attorney

See section 2.75 above.

§ 2.199 Private Mortgage Insurance Notice

Lenders that require borrowers to purchase mortgage guaranty insurance must provide annually a prescribed statutory notice about the right to cancel. Tex. Ins. Code § 3502.201.

§ 2.200 Private Property Rights

Private real property owners have certain rights under state law to challenge state and local regulations and governmental actions that result in a taking of their property. Tex. Gov't Code ch. 2007. Governmental entities are required to prepare a written takings impact assessment of proposed governmental action that may result in a taking. Failure to do so may render the action void. Tex. Gov't Code ch. 2007. Private real property owners have certain rights to reacquire property taken through eminent domain. Tex. Prop. Code § 21.023. Before a governmental entity with eminent domain authority begins negotiating with a property owner to acquire real property, the entity must provide a landowner's bill of rights statement provided by Tex. Gov't Code § 402.031. Tex. Prop. Code § 21.0112.

See also sections 2.47 and 2.148 above and 2.285 below.

§ 2.201 Property Inspection

The licensing of property inspectors is addressed in the Real Estate License Act. Tex. Occ. Code ch. 1102. Property inspections may be conducted, in part, by electricians, plumbers, carpenters, and others, such as engineers, in their respective fields.

§ 2.202 Property Owners' Associations

The Texas Residential Property Owners Protection Act applies to residential subdivisions that are subject to restrictions that authorize a property owners' association to collect regular or special assessments and that require mandatory membership in the association. Tex. Prop. Code ch. 209. The Act also regulates the foreclosure of an assessment lien and provides a right of redemption after foreclosure. Tex. Prop. Code §§ 209.009–.011. In addition, the Property Code affords certain rights to property owners' associations in cities or counties that meet various specified minimum population requirements to amend, extend, or supplement deed restrictions and to establish assessment lien mechanisms. Tex. Prop. Code chs. 201, 204–206. The statute also sets out certain other statutory powers of property owners' associations. Property owners' associations are subject to the state open meetings and open records laws in very limited circumstances. Tex. Gov't Code §§ 551.0015, 552.0036. Property owners' associations are required to deliver a resale certificate to owners, purchasers of a property in a subdivision, or title companies on demand. The resale certificate must include information relevant to the specific property as well as to the subdivision as a whole. Tex. Prop. Code ch. 207. Property owners' associations are prohibited from adopting or enforcing a restriction that would prohibit or regulate the occasional sale of lemonade or other nonalcoholic beverages by a person under the age of eighteen. Tex. Prop. Code § 202.020. Property owners' associations are also not allowed to adopt or enforce a policy that would prohibit or restrict any person who is otherwise authorized from lawfully possessing, transporting, or storing a firearm, any part of a firearm, or firearm ammunition, or prohibit or restrict the otherwise lawful discharge of a firearm. Tex. Prop. Code § 202.020. (Note that the 86th legislature adopted two sections numbered as Tex. Prop. Code § 202.020.)

Condominium property owners' associations are not governed by chapters 207 and 209; rather, condominiums formed after December 31, 1993, are governed by Texas Property Code chapter 82. Condominiums formed before January 1, 1994, are generally governed by Texas Property Code chapter 81 and selected provisions of chapter 82 set forth in section 82.002(c), unless they amend the condominium declaration and elect to be governed solely by all of chapter 82.

§ 2.203 Property Tax Consultants

Chapter 1152 of the Texas Occupations Code provides for the registration of property tax consultants. A property tax consultant is a person who performs or supervises the performance of property tax consulting services for compensation. Property tax consulting services means preparing for another person a rendition statement or property record, representing another person in a property tax protest, consulting or advising another person concerning the preparation of a rendition statement or property report or acting on behalf of another person in a protest under the Tax Code, negotiating or entering into an agreement with an appraisal district on behalf of another person, or acting as the agent of a property owner in connection with certain property tax matters. Tex. Occ. Code §§ 1152.001–.251.

§ 2.204 Property Tax Loans

With certain exceptions, a person engaging in the business of making, transacting, or negotiating property tax loans, or a person making property tax loans who contracts for, charges, or receives, directly or indirectly, a charge, including interest, compensation, consideration, or any other amount authorized under the statute, must be licensed by the Texas Consumer Credit Commissioner. Tex. Fin. Code ch. 351. The lender must provide the commission records to investigate compliance with the laws, an audit of net assets, and access to the lender's place of business for inspection. The commission is also authorized to prescribe filing documents necessary when a property tax lender pays property taxes for another person. Tex. Tax Code § 32.06.

§ 2.205 Quitclaim Deeds

After the fourth anniversary of the date a quitclaim deed for real property is recorded in the deed records of the county in which the real property is located, the quitclaim deed (1) does not affect the question of the good faith of a subsequent purchaser or creditor and (2) is not notice to a subsequent purchaser or creditor of any unrecorded conveyance of, transfer of, or encumbrance on the real property. Tex. Prop. Code § 13.006, effective for quitclaim deeds recorded on or after September 1, 2021.

§ 2.206 Real Estate Appraisers

See section 2.18 above.

§ 2.207 Real Estate Investment Trusts (REITs)

Real estate investment trusts are governed by the Texas Business Organizations Code generally and by title 5 more specifically. Tex. Bus. Orgs. Code §§ 200.001–.503.

§ 2.208 Real Estate License Act

The Real Estate License Act, Tex. Occ. Code ch. 1101, authorizes the Texas Real Estate Commission to regulate the actions of brokers, salespersons, real estate inspectors and appraisers, and others. It also contains numerous other provisions relating to real estate transactions involving brokers or salespersons.

§ 2.209 Real Estate Settlement Procedures Act (RESPA)

The Real Estate Settlement Procedures Act (RESPA), 12 U.S.C. §§ 2601–2617, and its implementing Regulation X, 12 C.F.R. pt. 1024, apply to mortgage loan transactions that are secured by a lien on residential real property designed principally for occupancy by one to four families and that otherwise meet the definition of a "federally related mortgage loan" set out in 12 C.F.R. § 1024.2. Certain loans, such as business purpose loans and various construction loans with a term of less than two years, are exempt from coverage. 12 C.F.R. § 1024.5. The Bureau of Consumer Financial Protection (BCFP) has rulemaking and enforcement authority for RESPA and sets forth the requirements for the provision of clear and accurate disclosures to consumers. For most transactions subject to RESPA, The BCFP combined the disclosure requirements of RESPA and the Truth in Lending Act and its implementing Regulation Z into new forms (TILA-RESPA Integrated Disclosures or "TRID"). Under TRID, a loan estimate form must be provided at the time of application, and a closing disclosure form must be provided before and at consummation.

For home equity lines of credit or reverse mortgages, a good-faith estimate (GFE) must be provided at the time of application, and a HUD-1 settlement statement must be provided at consummation.

Section 8 of RESPA prohibits kickbacks, referral fees, and unearned fees in connection with federally related mortgage loans. Violators of section 8 may be found civilly liable for treble damages to persons charged for settlement services involved in the violation and criminally liable for both a statutory fine and imprisonment. Referrals of settlement services to affiliates are permitted as an exception to the section 8 prohibitions under strict guidelines for affiliated business arrangements set out in 12 C.F.R. § 1024.15. Sample forms of required consumer disclosures are illustrated in appendix H to Regulation Z, in public guidance documents published in the Federal Register from time to time by the Department of Housing and Urban Development, and as published by the BCFP. See also the discussion in chapter 12 in this manual.

§ 2.210 Recording

The Texas Property Code addresses the recording of instruments used in property transactions. *See* Tex. Prop. Code chs. 11–13. A document to be recorded may be either a paper document or a tangible copy of an electronic record that has been declared true and correct as provided in Tex. Prop. Code §§ 12.0011(b), 12.0013. A form of declaration of authenticity for recording an electronic record is provided in Tex. Prop. Code § 12.0013(e). The rerecording of instruments is permitted under the terms of Tex. Civ. Prac. & Rem. Code § 19.008 if the record was lost, destroyed, or removed and is effective from the date of original recordation. See also section 2.63 above.

§ 2.211 Record Retention

Various federal laws and regulations, including Internal Revenue Service regulations, require the retention of records that affect or involve realty. Records that must be retained under state law may be destroyed after three years, unless otherwise provided. Tex. Bus. & Com. Code § 72.002.

§ 2.212 Recreational Projects and Recreational Use

See sections 2.35, 2.147, and 2.191 above and 2.259 below.

§ 2.213 Redemption Rights

After foreclosure of an assessment lien, condominium unit owners and residential property owners have rights of redemption. *See* Tex. Prop. Code § 82.113(g) (condominium unit owners); Tex. Prop. Code ch. 209 (residential property owners). Redemption rights after a tax foreclosure sale are governed by Tex. Tax Code §§ 34.21–.23. A certificate of redemption properly issued by the United States may be recorded. Tex. Prop. Code § 12.011.

§ 2.214 Registered Mail

If a contract or statute requires that notice be delivered by registered mail, certified mail will also suffice unless registered mail is required by law to provide insurance against loss. Tex. Civ. Prac. & Rem. Code § 136.001.

§ 2.215 Release of Lien by Affidavit

If a mortgagee holds a mortgage on one-to-four-family residential property, or on other real property where the original face amount of the debt is less than $1.5 million, and the mortgagee or its mortgage servicer fails to execute a release of the mortgage, an authorized officer of a title insurance company or a title insurance agent may execute and record an affidavit in a form substantially similar to the affidavit prescribed by Tex. Prop. Code § 12.017. An uncontroverted affidavit, executed and recorded as provided in the statute, operates as a release of the mortgage. Tex. Prop. Code § 12.017.

§ 2.216 Release of Lien by Attorney or Others

Tex. Prop. Code § 52.005 allows the agent or attorney of record to release an abstract of judgment by recording a return or copy of the return on an execution issued on the judgment that is certified by the officer making the return and that complies with the requirements of section 52.005 or a receipt, acknowledgement, or release signed by the party (or his agent or attorney of record) entitled to receive payment of the judgment and that is acknowledged or otherwise proven for record. Tex. Prop. Code § 52.021 allows a release by discharge under bankruptcy laws. Tex. Civ. Prac. & Rem. Code § 31.008 authorizes judges to release liens when the amount due is paid to the court. If a judgment creditor refuses to accept payment of a judgment or refuses to execute a release of judgment after accepting payment, the court may hold a hearing to determine whether a release should be issued. Tex. Civ. Prac. & Rem. Code § 31.008(g). Tex. Prop. Code § 12.017 permits authorized title insurance companies and title insurance agents to file affidavits of record as a substitute for an executed release by the lienholder under certain circumstances. See also sections 2.2 and 2.143 above.

§ 2.217 Republic of Texas Liens

See section 2.113 above.

§ 2.218 Residential Construction Liability

Liability for damages arising out of defects in residential construction projects is addressed in the Residential Construction Liability Act (Tex. Prop. Code ch. 27).

§ 2.219 Residential Rental Locators

The Real Estate License Act requires that residential rental locators be licensed as brokers or salespersons, with certain exceptions. Tex. Occ. Code §§ 1101.002, 1101.151, 1101.351, 1101.553, 1101.757.

§ 2.220 Restrictive Covenants

Any clause not in contravention of law may be inserted into an instrument of conveyance. Tex. Prop. Code § 5.022(c). Restrictive covenants that require the use of wood shingles for structures on residential properties or that are discriminatory on the basis of race, color, religion, or national origin are void. Tex. Prop. Code §§ 5.025, 5.026. Restrictive covenants that are at odds with certain water conservation initiatives are void. Tex. Prop. Code § 202.007. In an action based on breach of a restrictive covenant, the prevailing party who asserted the action may recover attorney's fees in addition to the party's costs and claim. Tex. Prop. Code § 5.006.

The governing body of a municipality that does not have zoning ordinances or that has a population of 1.5 million or more may elect application of Tex. Loc. Gov't Code §§ 212.151–.157 ("Enforcement of Land Use Restrictions Contained in Plats and Other Instruments") for enforcement of restrictive covenants. The municipality may require any person who sells or conveys restricted property located within the municipality first to give the purchaser written notice of the restrictions and of the municipality's right to enforce them. Tex. Loc. Gov't Code § 212.155. A municipal utility district may enforce restrictive covenants. Tex. Water Code § 54.237.

Tex. Gov't Code § 27.034 permits enforcement of certain restrictive covenants in a justice court, although a justice court is prohibited from granting a writ of injunction.

See also sections 2.45, 2.70, and 2.202 above.

§ 2.221 Reverse Mortgages

A reverse mortgage is a type of home equity loan authorized by the Texas Constitution that permits homeowners, age sixty-two or older, to borrow without recourse, based on the equity in their homesteads. Tex. Const. art. XVI, § 50(a)(7), (k)–(p), (v).

See section 2.128 above.

§ 2.222 Right of Rescission

In a credit transaction that involves a principal residence and that is subject to the Truth in Lending Act, the consumer may have a right to rescind the transaction within a certain period. The consumer must be notified of this right. 12 C.F.R. § 1026.23.

§ 2.223 Risk of Loss

See section 2.277 below.

§ 2.224 Roadway Forming County Boundary

Tex. Civ. Prac. & Rem. Code § 15.065 confers concurrent jurisdiction over roadways forming a common county boundary.

§ 2.225 Rule against Perpetuities

Tex. Const. art. I, § 26, provides that perpetuities are not allowed. The principal statutory provision incorporating the rule against perpetuities is found in Tex. Prop. Code § 5.043. The rule as applied to trusts is addressed in Tex. Prop. Code § 112.036, which was amended in 2021 to provide that an interest in the trust must vest (a) for an irrevocable trust with an effective date on or after September 1, 2021, not later than three hundred years after the effective date of the trust, and (b) for an irrevocable trust with an effective date before September 1, 2021, not later than twenty-one years after some life in being at the time of the creation of the interest, plus a period of gestation. The period in clause (a) above may apply if the trust instrument provides that the interest vests under the provisions of the statute applicable as of the date the interest vests.

§ 2.226 Sale of Trust Property to Governmental Entities

A governmental entity may not purchase real property held in trust unless the trustee submits to the governing body of the governmental entity a copy of the trust agreement identifying the true owner of the property. Tex. Gov't Code § 2252.092. See also section 2.68 above.

§ 2.227 Sculptures

See section 2.58 above.

§ 2.228 Securities Acts

The Securities Act of 1933 (15 U.S.C. §§ 77a–77aa) and the Texas Securities Act (Tex. Rev. Civ. Stat. arts. 581–1 to –43) may apply to group ownership of real estate in which passive investors furnish capital and rely on a promoter to make the investment successful. These statutes generally require certain disclosures to the passive investors and prohibit the use of fraudulent devices or schemes in connection with the sale of securities.

§ 2.229 Security Deposits

The Texas Property Code addresses the rights and requirements associated with security deposits in residential leases (Tex. Prop. Code §§ 92.101–.111) and in commercial leases (Tex. Prop. Code §§ 93.004–.012). Tex. Prop. Code § 92.111 creates an alternative fee in lieu of a security deposit for residential leases.

§ 2.230 Security Interests

Security interests in many categories of personal property are governed by Tex. Bus. & Com. Code ch. 9. For a more extensive discussion of security interests, see chapter 9 in this manual.

§ 2.231 Self-Service Storage Facilities

The Texas Property Code governs the creation and perfection of liens against property held in self-service storage facilities or mini-warehouse facilities. Tex. Prop. Code §§ 59.001–.046.

§ 2.232 Seller's Disclosure of Property Condition

See section 2.69 above.

§ 2.233 Sewer Service

The sale of sewer service to the public is regulated under Tex. Water Code ch. 13. No retail utility may provide sewer service to the public without first receiving a certificate of convenience and necessity (CCN) from the Texas Commission on Environmental Quality (TCEQ), with the exception of municipalities (which may provide retail service to areas within their corporate limits without a CCN, provided such areas are not within the certificated area of another retail utility provider). Tex. Water Code § 13.242.

Certain owners with property within a proposed service area will receive notice of new applications for certificates and amendments to existing certificate applications. Tex. Water Code § 13.246. Certain owners may "opt out" or exclude their property from the CCN application. Tex. Water Code § 13.246. Certain owners may petition the TCEQ for a release from a CCN if they can demonstrate that the certificate holder conditions the provision of service on the payment of costs not properly allocable directly to the petitioner's service request. Tex. Water Code § 13.254. Each certificate holder must record a map and a boundary description of the certificated area in the real property records of each applicable county. Tex. Water Code § 13.257.

§ 2.234 Sex Offenders

Convicted sex offenders must register their residences with, and certain notices must be provided to, law enforcement authorities. Tex. Code Crim. Proc. ch. 62.

A convicted sex offender may not own an interest in, be employed by, be an independent contractor for, or be an officer or director of a sexually oriented business. Tex. Bus. & Com. Code ch. 102.

§ 2.235 Shopping Center Stores, Open on Sundays

A clause in a shopping center lease that requires a store to be open when another store in the center is open does not apply on Sundays unless the lease expressly states that it applies on Sundays. Tex. Bus. & Com. Code § 53.001.

§ 2.236 Smoke Alarms

A landlord's obligation to install smoke alarms in residential leased premises is governed by Tex. Prop. Code §§ 92.251–.262.

§ 2.237 Soldiers' and Sailors' Civil Relief Act

The Soldiers' and Sailors' Civil Relief Act has been renamed the Servicemembers Civil Relief Act. See section 2.168 above.

§ 2.238 Special Districts

Numerous special districts created by state statutes affect real estate transactions. Among the most important are conservation districts, drainage districts, fresh water supply districts, hospital districts, irrigation districts, levee improvement districts, municipal management districts, municipal utility districts, navigation districts, utility and reclamation districts, and water control and improvement districts. Statutes creating and governing special districts can be found in the Texas Local Government Code, Texas Health & Safety Code, and the Texas Water Code. The 2003 Texas legislature created a Special District Local Laws Code, organized so that each special district's local law is contained in a single, separate chapter. The Code is a revision of Texas statutes compiled only to make special district laws more accessible and understandable.

§ 2.239 State of Texas Leases

Real property leases between state entities and private parties are governed by the requirements of Tex. Gov't Code chs. 2165, 2167 and 1 Tex. Admin. Code ch. 115.

§ 2.240 Statute of Frauds

To be enforceable, the following types of transactions, among others, must be in writing: contracts for the sale of real estate; conveyances of an interest in land, including an estate of inheritance, a freehold interest, and an estate for a term longer than one year; agreements to pay a commission for certain real property transactions; and agreements that will not be performed within one year from the date they are made. Tex. Prop. Code § 5.021; Tex. Bus. & Com. Code § 26.01. See also section 2.160 above, relating to a notice that must be given to claim a statute-of-frauds defense in connection with a loan.

See chapter 3 in this manual for comments and suggestions relating to the preparation of documents used in any conveyance of real property.

§ 2.241 Statute of Limitations

See section 2.155 above.

§ 2.242 Statutes of Repose

The ten-year statute of repose for registered or licensed architects, engineers, interior designers, and landscape architects is found at Tex. Civ. Prac. & Rem. Code § 16.008(a); for persons who construct or repair improvements to real property, at Tex. Civ. Prac. & Rem. Code § 16.009(a); and for surveyors, at Tex. Civ. Prac. & Rem. Code § 16.011. Except for claims arising out of contracts with the Texas Department of Transportation, a project that receives state or federal funds for designated highway or mass transit spending, or certain civil works projects, a governmental entity must bring a suit against registered or licensed architects, engineers, interior designers, and landscape architects and against persons who construct or repair improvements to real property within eight years after substantial completion of the project. Tex. Civ. Prac. & Rem. Code §§ 16.008(a–1), 16.009(a–1).

§ 2.243 Stormwater Permits

Construction sites of five acres or more must comply with the general stormwater permit requirements found in 57 Fed. Reg. 41,176–41,190 (1992). *See* 40 C.F.R. pt. 122. Construction sites of between one and five acres are addressed by the rules published in 64 Fed. Reg. 68,722 (1999). The general permits for industrial activities were published in 57 Fed. Reg. 41,236 (1992). A new multisector permit for industrial activities was published in 65 Fed. Reg. 64,746 (2000) as corrected in 66 Fed. Reg. 1675 and 16,233 (2001). Certain industrial and other uses may have other stormwater permit requirements under the National Pollutant Discharge Elimination System permit program under the Clean Water Act. Certain large metropolitan areas may implement stormwater permitting programs in compliance with the Clean Water Act. Tex. Loc. Gov't Code ch. 573. See section 2.85 above.

§ 2.244 Streets and Roads

Cities have the authority to assess landowners for the costs to improve streets and sidewalks. Tex. Transp. Code §§ 311.091–.096. Cities may grant the use of streets for private purposes under the provisions of Tex. Transp. Code ch. 316. Suits for relief from street closings are regulated by Tex. Civ. Prac. & Rem. Code §§ 16.005, 65.015. Tex. Transp. Code ch. 203 authorizes the Texas Transportation Commission to construct and maintain state highways. Tex. Transp. Code ch. 311 applies to municipalities. Tex. Transp. Code chs. 251–286 address various aspects of county roads, including the ability of a county road supervisor to limit or prohibit the use of certain county roads by vehicles that may damage the road. Tex. Transp. Code § 251.157. County roads may be abandoned in some cases in which the use becomes infrequent and one of the adjoining property owners has fenced the property for a continuous period of more than twenty years. Tex. Transp. Code § 251.057.

§ 2.245 Subdivisions

Counties may establish substantive requirements for subdivision plats for tracts outside the extraterritorial jurisdiction of municipalities. Tex. Loc. Gov't Code §§ 232.001–.010, 232.0034, 242.001. Cities have the same power over subdivisions within their corporate limits. Tex. Loc. Gov't Code §§ 212.001–.018. Generally, counties and cities are required to enter into a written agreement that identifies the entity authorized to regulate subdivision plats in the city's extraterritorial jurisdiction. Tex. Loc. Gov't Code § 242.001. If counties and cities do not enter into a written agreement before the dates specified in Tex. Loc. Gov't Code § 242.0015(a), the parties must arbitrate the disputed issues. Tex. Loc. Gov't Code § 242.0015.

Special subdivision requirements apply to populous counties (Tex. Loc. Gov't Code §§ 212.0146, 232.006, 242.002), counties near the Mexican border (Tex. Loc. Gov't Code §§ 232.021–.043), and to certain economically distressed counties (Tex. Loc. Gov't Code §§ 232.071–.080). See also sections 2.44 and 2.57 above.

Special subdivision requirements also apply to replats of golf courses in certain counties. Tex. Loc. Gov't Code § 212.0155.

A subdivision plat, replat, or amended plat or replat may not be recorded unless (1) it is approved by the entity authorized to regulate subdivisions, (2) it has attached to it an original tax certificate from each taxing unit with jurisdiction over the tract indicating that no delinquent ad valorem taxes are owed on the tract, and (3) it has attached to it the documents required by Tex. Loc. Gov't Code § 212.0105 or Tex. Loc. Gov't Code § 232.023, if applicable. Tex. Prop. Code § 12.002. If the subdivision plat, replat, or amended plat or replat is filed after September 1 of a year, the plat, replat, or amended plat or replat must also have attached to it a tax receipt from each taxing unit with jurisdiction over the tract indicating that taxes for the current year have been paid or a statement from the collector indicating that taxes for the current year have not been calculated. Tex. Prop. Code § 12.002(e). The tax collector is required, on request, to give the property owner or his agent a statement indicating that taxes for the current year have not been calculated. Tex. Tax Code § 31.075.

Note that tracts within the extraterritorial jurisdiction of a city may require approval from both the city and the county. *See* Tex. Loc. Gov't Code § 242.001. The cancellation and revision of certain subdivision plats are governed by Tex. Loc. Gov't Code §§ 212.013–.016, 232.008–

.009. County-approved subdivision plats terminate on January 1 of the fifty-first year after the year approved if none of the platted land has been sold by that date. Tex. Loc. Gov't Code § 232.002(c).

A property description based on a pending but unrecorded subdivision plat may be used in a sales contract, contract for deed, or deed only if certain conditions are met. Tex. Prop. Code § 12.002.

In counties with populations of 65,000 or more, if all or part of a subdivision plat is revised to provide for another subdivision within all or part of the earlier subdivision, the restrictions that apply to the earlier subdivision apply to the newly created subdivision. Tex. Prop. Code § 205.003.

Municipalities and counties are authorized to require as a condition of platting that a registered engineer certify the adequacy of groundwater. Tex. Loc. Gov't Code §§ 212.0101, 232.0032.

Counties may require that plat applications include a digital map that meets certain criteria, provided that the necessary "digital mapping technology" is "reasonably accessible." Tex. Loc. Gov't Code §§ 232.001, 232.023, 232.072.

§ 2.246 Subletting or Assignment

Subletting or assignment of leased premises is prohibited without the prior consent of a landlord. Tex. Prop. Code § 91.005.

§ 2.247 Submetering

See section 2.281 below.

§ 2.248 Surety

Legal obligations between principals and sureties are governed by the provisions of Tex. Civ. Prac. & Rem. Code ch. 43. The Insurance Code governs construction payment bonds issued by surety companies. *See* Tex. Ins. Code §§ 3503.051–.057. Performance and payment bonds are governed by Tex. Gov't Code ch. 2253 and Tex. Prop. Code §§ 53.201–.239.

§ 2.249 Surveyors

Regulation and licensing of land surveyors are provided by the Board of Professional Engineers and Land Surveyors. Tex. Occ. Code ch. 1001. The Professional Land Surveying Practices Act is contained in Tex. Occ. Code ch. 1071.

The circumstances under which a surveyor's lien attaches to real estate are addressed in Tex. Prop. Code § 53.021(3).

§ 2.250 Survival of Representations and Warranties

The four-year statute of limitations applies to suits for misrepresentations and breaches of warranties. Tex. Civ. Prac. & Rem. Code § 16.004. Contracts that purport to limit the time in which to bring suit on the contract to less than two years are void. The provision does not apply to transactions relating to the sale or purchase of a business entity of more than $500,000. Tex. Civ. Prac. & Rem. Code § 16.070.

§ 2.251 Surviving Spouse of Mortgagor

Chapter 343 of the Texas Finance Code requires a residential mortgage servicer to provide to the surviving spouse of the mortgagor the loan number, the current balance, whether any amounts are delinquent, and what amount, if any, is held in escrow, within thirty days of receiving a request for the loan information. A request from a surviving spouse must include statutory language, a death certificate of the mortgagor, an affidavit from a disinterested party in a form similar to an affidavit of heirship as set forth in

Tex. Est. Code § 203.002, and an affidavit from the surviving spouse stating the property is the surviving spouse's primary residence.

§ 2.252 Swimming Pools and Spas

Pools in multifamily residential projects must have enclosures that comply with Tex. Health & Safety Code ch. 757. Municipalities also may adopt ordinances governing pool enclosures. Tex. Loc. Gov't Code § 214.101. Effective September 1, 2020, the International Swimming Pool and Spa Code, as it existed on May 1, 2019, has been adopted as a uniform code for use in municipalities in the state. The Code applies to all construction, alteration, remodeling, enlargement, and repair of swimming pools and spas in a municipality that elects to regulate pools or spas. A municipality may establish procedures for the adoption of local amendments to the Code. Tex. Loc. Gov't Code § 214.103.

§ 2.253 Taxes

The Property Redevelopment and Tax Abatement Act permits tax abatements in reinvestment zones. Tex. Tax Code ch. 312. See also sections 2.5, 2.133, 2.182, and 2.187 above.

§ 2.254 Telecommunications

Telecommunications companies have certain rights of access to private commercial buildings under the Texas Utilities Code. See especially Tex. Util. Code chs. 51, 54. A telecommunications provider is defined as a person who has been issued a certificate of convenience and necessity or certificate of operating authority by the Public Utility Commission. Tex. Util. Code § 51.002(10).

§ 2.255 Terrorism Regulation

Federal law prohibits transactions with persons who commit, threaten to commit, or support terrorism. *See* Exec. Order No. 13,224, 66 Fed. Reg. 49,079 (Sept. 25, 2001). Additional terrorism regulations are governed by the Office of Foreign Assets Control (OFAC) of the Department of the Treasury. 31 C.F.R. pts. 595–597. Prohibited transactions include those with specially designated terrorists (31 C.F.R. pt. 595), terrorism list governments (31 C.F.R. pt. 596), and foreign terrorist organizations (31 C.F.R. pt. 597). A list of "Specially Designated Nationals and Blocked Persons" is administered by OFAC and is accessible online at **https://home.treasury.gov/policy-issues/financial-sanctions/specially-designated-nationals-and-blocked-persons-list-sdn-human-readable-lists**.

§ 2.256 Texas Department of Housing and Community Affairs

The Texas Department of Housing and Community Affairs is the principal agency in the state that administers programs of housing assistance and development for individuals and families of low, very low, and extremely low income and families with moderate income. Its general enabling statute can be found at Tex. Gov't Code ch. 2306.

§ 2.257 Texas General Land Office

Use of evidence to demonstrate superior title to land based on records filed in the General Land Office is addressed in Tex. Prop. Code § 12.003.

§ 2.258 Timber Production

See section 2.5 above.

§ 2.259 Timeshares

Timeshare projects coming into existence on or after August 26, 1985, must comply with the terms of the Texas Timeshare Act, Tex. Prop. Code ch. 221.

§ 2.260 Title Insurance

The business of title insurance is governed by the Texas Title Insurance Act, Tex. Ins. Code chs. 2501–2704. Insuring forms, rate rules, procedural rules, administrative rules, and claims handling principles and procedures are set out in the "Basic Manual of Rules, Rates and Forms for the Writing of Title Insurance in the State of Texas" promulgated by the Texas Department of Insurance in accordance with Tex. Ins. Code tit. 11.

§ 2.261 Towing of Motor Vehicles

Tex. Occ. Code ch. 2308 governs the removal of unauthorized vehicles from a parking facility or public roadway, the establishment of reserved parking spaces, the enforcement of parking restrictions in parking lots and garages, the towing of unauthorized vehicles from private property, and the regulation of towing companies and parking-facility owners.

§ 2.262 Trademark and Trade-Name Rights

Trademark and trade-name rights are addressed in the provisions of Tex. Bus. & Com. Code ch. 16. The Lanham Act, 15 U.S.C. §§ 1051–1127, is the primary federal trademark statute.

§ 2.263 Transfer on Death Deed

The Texas Real Property Transfer on Death Act, Tex. Est. Code ch. 114, authorizes an individual to make a revocable transfer to one or more designated beneficiaries, including alternate beneficiaries, effective at the transferor's death, by executing and recording a transfer on death deed. During the transferor's lifetime, a transfer on death deed does not affect any right, title, or interest of the transferor in the property; vest any legal or equitable title in a designated beneficiary; or subject the property to the claims of creditors of any designated beneficiary. Notwithstanding the recording of a transfer on death deed, the transferor retains the right to transfer or encumber the property, any present or future homestead rights, and any present or future ad valorem tax exemptions to which the transferor is entitled. A transfer on death deed does not affect the rights of creditors of the transferor, secured or unsecured, nor does it trigger any due-on-sale clause. A transfer on death deed does not affect the eligibility for public assistance of either the transferor or any designated beneficiary. In the 86th legislative session, the statutory forms for the transfer on death deed and the revocation of transfer on death deed were removed from chapter 114 of the Texas Estates Code. Acts 2019, 86th Leg., R.S., ch. 337, § 3.2 (S.B. 874), eff. Sept. 1, 2019. Tex. Gov't Code § 22.020 directs the Texas Supreme Court to promulgate forms for creating and revoking a transfer on death deed. The forms have yet to be promulgated. The Estates Code continues to authorize use of transfer on death deeds and revocation of transfer on death deeds but no longer prescribes statutory language. See section 5.11 in this manual.

§ 2.264 Transportation

Certain adjacent counties are authorized to create a regional county transportation authority. Tex. Transp. Code ch. 460.

§ 2.265 Trespass to Try Title

Trespass to try title is a statutory action to establish title to real property. Tex. Prop. Code ch. 22; Tex. R. Civ. P. 783–809. A declaratory judgment action can be maintained if the sole title issue is the determination of the boundary between adjoining properties. Tex. Civ. Prac. & Rem. Code § 37.004(c).

§ 2.266 Trust Code

The Texas Trust Code, Tex. Prop. Code §§ 111.001–115.017, governs express trusts.

Trustees have certain management rights if environmental problems arise on properties held in trust under Tex. Prop. Code §§ 113.025, 114.001 even if the trust instrument does not expressly authorize such actions. A trustee may grant an agent authority to act for the trustee with respect to real property transactions unless the governing instrument prohibits the trustee from hiring agents. Tex. Prop. Code § 113.018. See also section 2.30 above.

§ 2.267 Truth in Lending

The Truth in Lending Act, 15 U.S.C. §§ 1601–1667f, and its implementing Regulation Z, 12 C.F.R. pt. 1026, promote the informed use of consumer credit by requiring disclosures about the terms and cost of credit transactions. The Act applies to individuals or businesses that regularly offer or extend credit to consumers, including mortgage credit secured by a lien on real property, if the credit is primarily for personal, family, or household purposes and is subject to a finance charge or payable by a written agreement in more than four installments. The Bureau of Consumer Financial Protection (BCFP) is the government agency with rulemaking and enforcement authority for the Act.

Creditors subject to the Act generally are persons who regularly extend consumer credit that is subject to a finance charge and to whom the credit obligation is initially payable. *See* 12 C.F.R. § 1026.2(a)(17). Creditors must make written disclosures for each credit transaction at the time of application, before consummation, and at consummation that reflect the terms of the actual legal obligation between the parties and show the calculated annual percentage rate, finance charge, and other material disclosures of the cost of credit within permitted tolerances for accuracy. Additional written disclosures are required at the time of application for variable rate transactions in which the annual percentage rate may increase after loan consummation. Certain credit transactions secured by a lien on a consumer's principal dwelling are subject to rescission, and creditors must provide consumers written notices of their rights of rescission of those transactions at consummation. Special disclosure rules and limitations on permitted terms apply to certain home mortgage transactions secured by a consumer's principal dwelling in which the annual percentage rate or total points and fees charged the consumer exceed standards set out in the Act. Advertising rules intended to ensure that advertisements promoting credit provide accurate and balanced information about rates, payments, and other loan features apply to all home mortgage loans subject to the Act. Sample forms of various required consumer disclosures are illustrated in appendix H to Regulation Z. Creditors failing to comply with requirements of the Act may be subject to civil liability, administrative penalties, and, in the case of willful and knowing violations, criminal liability.

§ 2.268 Unauthorized Preparation of Real Estate Documents

The Texas Government Code prohibits the preparation of deeds, deeds of trust, notes, mortgages, and other instruments affecting title to real property for compensation unless the preparer is an attorney licensed in Texas or qualifies under one of the other listed exemptions. Tex. Gov't Code ch. 83. Texas law broadly construes the meaning of a charge of compensation for this purpose. *See Hexter Title & Abstract Co. v. Grievance Committee*, 179 S.W.2d 946, 952 (Tex. 1944); Tex. Att'y Gen. Op. No. JM-943 (1988). Written materials, books, printed forms, Internet sites, computer software, and similar products are excluded from the definition of the unauthorized practice of law if the items clearly and conspicuously state that the products are not a substitute for the advice of an attorney licensed to practice law in Texas. Tex. Gov't Code § 81.101(c). However, this exclusion does not affect the applicability or enforceability of chapter 83 and such products or similar media expressly cannot be used in violation of the prohibitions of that chapter against the unauthorized preparation of real estate documents.

§ 2.269 Unclaimed Property

See sections 2.1 and 2.88 above.

§ 2.270 Underground and Aboveground Storage Tanks

Underground storage tanks and certain aboveground tanks must be registered with the Texas Commission on Environmental Quality. *See* 30 Tex. Admin. Code § 334.7; Tex. Water Code §§ 26.341–.367. Underground tanks must also meet certain technical specifications under the provisions of 40 C.F.R. pt. 280. In Texas, an owner of land having an underground storage tank must disclose the existence of the tank to prospective purchasers. 30 Tex. Admin. Code § 334.9. Section 26.342 of the Water Code defines the owner of an underground storage tank for liability purposes. Tex. Water Code § 26.342.

§ 2.271 Underground Facility Damage Prevention and Safety Act

The Underground Facility Damage Prevention and Safety Act, Tex. Util. Code ch. 251, provides for a "one-call" statewide notification service for the location of underground facilities. All excavators in Texas must notify the notification center of their intention to excavate or be subject to penalties.

§ 2.272 Uniform Commercial Code

The Texas version of the Uniform Commercial Code can be found in chapters 1 through 9 of the Texas Business and Commerce Code.

§ 2.273 Uniform Electronic Transactions Act

The Uniform Electronic Transactions Act, Tex. Bus. & Com. Code ch. 322, establishes the enforceability of electronic records and signatures in electronic transactions.

§ 2.274 Uniform Principal and Income Act

The Uniform Principal and Income Act, Tex. Prop. Code ch. 116, determines the allocation of principal and income for trusts.

§ 2.275 Uniform Transfers to Minors Act

Texas has adopted the Uniform Transfers to Minors Act, Tex. Prop. Code §§ 141.001–.025. The Act establishes the terms, conditions, manner, and effect of making transfers to minors.

§ 2.276 Uniform Unincorporated Nonprofit Association Act

Unincorporated nonprofit organizations in Texas are governed by the Texas Business Organizations Code generally and chapter 252 of that code more specifically. *See* Tex. Bus. Orgs. Code §§ 252.001–.017.

An "association" is defined as an entity governed as a cooperative association, an unincorporated nonprofit association, or a for-profit professional association. Tex. Bus. Orgs. Code § 1.002(3).

A "nonprofit association" is defined as an unincorporated organization, other than one created by a trust, consisting of three or more members joined by mutual consent for a common, nonprofit purpose. A form of joint tenancy, tenancy in common, or tenancy by the entirety does not by itself establish a nonprofit association, regardless of whether the co-owners share use of the property for a nonprofit purpose. Tex. Bus. Orgs. Code § 252.001(2).

§ 2.277 Uniform Vendor and Purchaser Risk Act

Tex. Prop. Code § 5.007 adopts the Uniform Vendor and Purchaser Risk Act and allocates responsibility for risk of loss between buyers and sellers, depending on whether legal title and possession have been transferred. However, the parties may by contract allocate the risk differently. Tex. Prop. Code § 5.007(a).

§ 2.278 United States–Mexico–Canada Agreement (USMCA)

In September 2018, the United States, Mexico, and Canada reached an agreement to replace the North American Free Trade Agreement (NAFTA) with the United States–Mexico–Canada Agreement (USMCA). NAFTA remained in force pending the ratification of the USMCA by all three governments. The USMCA entered into force on July 1, 2020, replacing NAFTA. Certain provisions of the USMCA may affect real property and finance transactions. The text of the USMCA is available on the Office of the United States Trade Representative website at **https://ustr.gov/usmca**. The USMCA has curtailed NAFTA's protections for investors engaging in cross-border investment with party countries. Certain investments made while NAFTA was still in effect and that remained in existence on July 1, 2020, are eligible to raise dispute claims under NAFTA until July 1, 2023. See also sections 2.110 and 2.183 above.

§ 2.279 Usury

When using any document that extends credit, attorneys should consider the implications of state and federal usury laws. *See* 12 U.S.C. § 1735f–7; Tex. Fin. Code chs. 301–349. See section 2.282 below.

§ 2.280 Utility District Disclosures

Any person selling or transferring property located in a water, sewer, or other district with taxing authority must give a prospective purchaser notice of the current tax rate and amount of authorized bonded indebtedness and whether the property is located in a municipality's extraterritorial jurisdiction before or at the time of the execution of the contract. A separate copy of the notice must be executed at closing and recorded. Tex. Water Code § 49.452. See the form of utility district disclosure in chapter 4 in this manual. See also sections 2.69 and 2.178 above.

§ 2.281 Utility Submetering and Nonmetering

The Texas Water Code requires that multiunit facilities built after January 1, 2003, be submetered or individually metered and imposes certain requirements before conversion of an existing facility to submetering or allocated billing. Tex. Water Code §§ 13.502, 13.506. The Water Code also limits the right of certain condominium managers and landlords of apartments, manufactured-home rental communities, and commercial multiple-use facilities to charge tenants for utility expenses without proper evidence to show how the utility expenses were calculated. These provisions also limit rent increases before the installation of submeters and provide tenants means of enforcement. Tex. Water Code §§ 13.501–.506.

Buildings with five or more dwelling units, including apartments and condominium units, constructed after 1997 must be separately metered or submetered for electricity. Tex. Util. Code § 184.012.

Utility disconnections by landlords are also limited under the provisions of Tex. Prop. Code § 92.008 (for residential tenancies) and Tex. Prop. Code § 93.002 (for commercial tenancies).

§ 2.282 Variable Interest Rates

The Alternative Mortgage Transaction Parity Act of 1982, 12 U.S.C. §§ 3801–3806, was enacted to give nonfederally chartered housing creditors the same ability to devise alternatives to fixed-rate financing as federal institutions have. It permits nonfederally chartered lenders to make, purchase, and enforce certain mortgage transactions in which the interest rate can change as long as the transactions comply with federal regulations. See also section 2.279 above.

§ 2.283 Vendor and Purchaser Risk Act

See section 2.277 above.

§ 2.284 Venue

Venue for "major transactions" (in which the consideration is more than $1 million) may be determined by the parties. Tex. Civ. Prac. & Rem. Code § 15.020. Venue for actions for the recovery of real property or an estate or interest in real property, for partition of real property, to remove encumbrances from the title to real property, for recovery of damages to real property, or to quiet title to real property is in the county in which all or a part of the property is located. Tex. Civ. Prac. & Rem. Code § 15.011. See also Tex. Prop. Code §§ 23.002, 23A.003 regarding partition actions. Venue for most suits between landlord and tenant is in the county in which all or part of the property is located. Tex. Civ. Prac. & Rem. Code § 15.0115. Venue for trust-related actions is governed by Tex. Prop. Code § 115.002. Venue provisions are addressed generally in chapter 15 of the Civil Practice and Remedies Code. The Property Code contains venue provisions for suits alleging a breach of fiduciary duty by a fiduciary or managerial agent of a charitable trust (Tex. Prop. Code § 123.005); actions to enforce rights or obligations under condominium association declarations, bylaws, or rules (Tex. Prop. Code § 82.008); condemnation proceedings (Tex. Prop. Code § 21.013); and partition actions (Tex. Prop. Code § 23.002).

§ 2.285 Vested Land Use Rights

Chapter 245 of the Local Government Code regulates the issuance of local permits and provides that, if a series of permits is required for a project, the rules, regulations, and other requirements in effect at the time the application for the first permit is filed shall be the sole basis for considering all subsequent permits to complete the project. Tex. Loc. Gov't Code § 245.002(b). Permit holders may take advantage of new rules or changes to the law that enhance a project. Tex. Loc. Gov't Code § 245.002(d). A municipality may adopt a moratorium on the development of residential or commercial property only if it finds a need to prevent a shortage of essential public facilities or that the moratorium is justified because existing commercial development laws are inadequate to protect the public health, safety, or welfare of its residents. Notice and hearing procedures are required. Tex. Loc. Gov't Code §§ 212.131–.136. Certain types of regulations are exempt from the application of chapter 245. *See* Tex. Loc. Gov't Code § 245.004.

After annexing an area, a municipality may not prohibit a person from (1) continuing to use land in the area in the manner in which the land was being used on the date the annexation proceedings were instituted if the land use was legal at that time or (2) beginning to use land in the area in the manner that was planned for the land before the ninetieth day before the effective date of the annexation if certain conditions are met. Tex. Loc. Gov't Code § 43.002. These prohibitions also apply to municipalities incorporated after September 1, 2003. Tex. Loc. Gov't Code § 211.016. See also section 2.200 above.

§ 2.286 Visual Arts

The Visual Artists Rights Act of 1990 (VARA), 17 U.S.C. § 106A, protects the reputations of certain visual artists and the works of art they create. With numerous exceptions, VARA grants three rights: the right of attribution; the right of integrity; and in the case of works of visual art of "recognized stature," the right to prevent destruction. 17 U.S.C. § 106A.

§ 2.287 Voluntary Cleanup Program

Texas has a voluntary cleanup statute, also known as a Brownfields statute, in Tex. Health & Safety Code §§ 361.601–.613. Regulations for the voluntary cleanup program are published at 30 Tex. Admin. Code ch. 333.

§ 2.288 Wage Liens

Under chapter 61 of the Texas Labor Code and chapter 113 of the Texas Tax Code, if the Texas Workforce Commission (TWC) determines that an employer owes unpaid wages to an employee, the TWC is authorized to file an administrative lien against the employer's property to secure the payment of the unpaid wages. *See* Tex. Lab. Code §§ 61.081–.085. Section 61.0825 of the Texas Labor Code provides that such wage liens have priority over all other liens against the same property, except for a lien securing the payment of ad valorem taxes. *See* Tex. Lab. Code § 61.0825.

§ 2.289 Warehouseman's Liens

A warehouseman's lien for property removed from a tenant's premises is governed by Tex. Prop. Code § 24.0062. See also section 2.231 above.

§ 2.290 Water

Groundwater districts and water rights are subject to the Texas Water Code. A district has the authority to collect assessments, pursuant to Tex. Water Code ch. 51, including the ability to place a lien on real and personal property. Tex. Water Code § 51.309. As a condition of service, a water district may require a service applicant or developer to grant permanent recorded easements for the construction and maintenance of the facilities necessary for service. Tex. Water Code § 49.218. Under certain circumstances, a landowner can petition a water district board to have his property deannexed from a water district. Tex. Water Code §§ 49.3075–.3077. See also section 2.280 above.

§ 2.291 Watercourse Forming County Boundary

Tex. Civ. Prac. & Rem. Code § 15.065 provides concurrent jurisdiction over a watercourse that forms a county boundary.

§ 2.292 Water Service

The sale of potable water to the public is regulated under Tex. Water Code ch. 13. See also section 2.233 above.

§ 2.293 Water Wells

Water-well drillers are regulated under Tex. Occ. Code ch. 1901, and water-well pump installers are regulated under Tex. Occ. Code ch. 1902.

Counties with populations of 1.8 million or more may adopt rules to regulate the placement of private water wells in unincorporated areas of the county. *See* Tex. Loc. Gov't Code §§ 240.041–.048.

§ 2.294 Weeds

It is a public nuisance in the unincorporated area of a county to allow weeds to grow within three hundred feet of another residence or commercial establishment. Tex. Health & Safety Code

§ 343.011. Municipalities may require property owners to keep property free from weeds. Tex. Health & Safety Code §§ 342.004, 342.008.

§ 2.295 Wetlands

Wetlands are regulated under section 404 of the Clean Water Act, codified at 33 U.S.C. § 1344. Under section 1344, dredging and filling activities in wetlands are prohibited unless a permit is obtained from the Army Corps of Engineers or other statutory exceptions apply.

§ 2.296 Wills and Estates

A will may be admitted to probate as a muniment of title if the court is satisfied that there are no unpaid debts, excluding debts secured by liens on real estate. Tex. Est. Code § 257.001. Title to real estate can be transferred by a duly probated will. Tex. Est. Code §§ 251.002, 256.001. Subject to the payment of certain debts, the estate devised or bequeathed in a lawful will vests immediately in the devisees or legatees when the testator dies. Tex. Est. Code § 101.001. See also section 2.7 above.

§ 2.297 Windstorm Inspection

Completed structures in coastal counties are required to comply with the state windstorm building specifications and inspection program to qualify for windstorm and hail insurance through the Texas Windstorm Insurance Association. This program is administered by the State Board of Insurance. See also section 2.33 above.

§ 2.298 Wood Shingles

A restrictive covenant that requires the use of wood shingles on a residential building is void under Texas law. Tex. Prop. Code § 5.025.

§ 2.299 Zoning

The authority of municipalities to establish and regulate zoning in their territorial jurisdictions is governed by the provisions of Tex. Loc. Gov't Code ch. 211. Certain counties also have limited authority to impose zoning regulations in unincorporated areas. Tex. Loc. Gov't Code ch. 231.

The authority of municipalities and other political subdivisions to regulate oil and gas operations within the state is expressly preempted in favor of the state's authority to regulate all such operations. Such operations include exploration and production, processing, drilling, hydraulic fracturing, transporting (including by pipelines), disposal, plugging of wells, and remediation activities. Commercially reasonable regulation by municipalities and other political subdivisions of aboveground activities, such as fire safety regulations, emergency response, and traffic control measures that would not prohibit operations by a reasonably prudent operator are permitted. Tex. Nat. Res. Code § 81.0523.

§ 2.300 Additional Resources

Alcantara, Ramona Kantack, David H. Brock, Fred D. Cawyer, and Jack W. Hawthorne, III. "ADA Issues in Real Estate." In *Advanced Real Estate Law Course, 2017*. Austin: State Bar of Texas, 2017.

Alsup, J. Alton. "Preparation of Documents Affecting Title to Texas Real Property as the Unauthorized Practice of Law." In *Advanced Real Estate Law Course, 2008*. Austin: State Bar of Texas, 2008.

Anderson, Arthur J. "Government Takings: What the Government Can Do to Your Client." In *Advanced Real Estate Law Course, 2005*. Austin: State Bar of Texas, 2005.

———. "Zoning and Property Rights: When Does Zoning Become a Protected Property

Interest?" In *Advanced Real Estate Law Course, 2001*. Austin: State Bar of Texas, 2001.

Barron, Paul, and Michael A. Berenson. *Federal Regulation of Real Estate and Mortgage Lending*. 4th ed. 3 vols. St. Paul, MN: West, 2004. Supplement 2016.

Craddock, Daniel K. "Construction Liens, Mechanics Liens, and Bonds: A Guide for Lenders and Developers." In *Mortgage Lending Institute, 2005*. Austin: University of Texas School of Law, 2005.

Dougherty, James L., Jr. "Overview of Local Land Use Regulation." In *Advanced Real Estate Strategies Course, 2008*. Austin: State Bar of Texas, 2008.

Haley, Steven C. "Texas Homestead Law." In *Advanced Real Estate Law Course, 2016*. Austin: State Bar of Texas, 2016.

Howell, Jay D., Jr., and David B. Brooks. *Property Taxes*. 4th ed. Texas Practice Series 21–21A. St. Paul, MN: West, 2001. Supplement 2016.

Jacobus, Charles J. *Texas Real Estate Law*. 11th ed. Cengage Learning, 2012.

Kurtz, Sheldon F., Herbert Hovenkamp, and Carol Necole Brown. *Cases and Materials on American Property Law*. 6th ed. American Casebook Series. St. Paul, MN: West 2012.

Leopold, Aloysius A. *Land Titles and Title Examination*. 3rd ed. Texas Practice Series 3–5A. St. Paul, MN: West, 2005. Supplement 2016.

———. *Marital Property and Homesteads*. Texas Practice Series 38–39. St. Paul, MN: West, 1993. Supplement 2016.

Lipstet, Ira A. "Texas Sales & Property Tax." In *Advanced Real Estate Law Course, 2007*. Austin: State Bar of Texas, 2007.

Malone, Linda A. *Environmental Regulation of Land Use*. St. Paul, MN: West, 2013. Supplement 2015.

McCarthy, Misty. "Rules and Regulations of Title XIV of the Dodd-Frank Act." In *Mortgage Lending Institute, 2013*. Austin: University of Texas School of Law, 2013.

Melamed, Richard. "A Selection of State and Federal Statutes Affecting Real Estate That Are Not in the Property Code." In *Advanced Real Estate Law Course, 2021*. Austin: State Bar of Texas, 2021.

Miller, Walter D. "Statutory Notices for Texas Contracts of Sale." In *Real Estate Law 101, 2018*. Austin: State Bar of Texas, 2018.

Saegert, Jerry C. "Annotated Due Diligence Checklist with Sample Consultant Forms and Glossary of Terms." In *Advanced Real Estate Strategies Course, 2007*. Austin: State Bar of Texas, 2007.

Shelton, R. Walton. "Environmental Law 101." In *Advanced Real Estate Law Course, 2007*. Austin: State Bar of Texas, 2007.

Wolf, Michael Allan, ed. *Powell on Real Property*. Rev. ed. 17 vols. New York: Matthew Bender & Co., 2002. Supplemented.

Wren, Michael A. "Basics of Property Taxes for the Real Estate Lawyer." In *Real Estate Law 101, 2018*. Austin: State Bar of Texas, 2018.

Chapter 3
Preparation, Execution, Proof, and Recording of Documents

Forms

Chapter 3

Preparation, Execution, Proof, and Recording of Documents

§ 3.1 Conveyance Documents Generally

Texas statutes require that a real property conveyance of an estate of more than one year must be in writing, subscribed, and delivered by the grantor or by the grantor's agent authorized in writing. Tex. Prop. Code § 5.021. The following comments and suggestions relate to the preparation of instruments and documents used in any conveyance of real property. The term *instrument* is used throughout this chapter in the dual contexts of its statutory definitions and references and also generically as other documents.

§ 3.2 Monetary Amount

No particular form is required for writing a monetary amount; it may be spelled out, written numerically, or both. Many attorneys prefer to write the amount in capital letters immediately followed by the numerical amount in parentheses—for example, ONE THOUSAND AND NO/100 DOLLARS ($1,000.00) or ONE THOUSAND, TWO HUNDRED FIFTY AND 10/100 DOLLARS ($1,250.10). If there is a variance between unambiguous written words and numbers, the written words control. *Guthrie v. National Homes Corp.*, 394 S.W.2d 494, 495 (Tex. 1965). *See also* Tex. Bus. & Com. Code § 3.114.

§ 3.3 Captions

Instruments have traditionally commenced with these captions, to indicate the county in which the instrument is to be recorded:

THE STATE OF TEXAS)
) KNOW ALL MEN BY THESE PRESENTS:
COUNTY OF ______) (OR INSTRUMENT HEADING)

These captions are not required in modern conveyancing documents and are omitted from the forms in this manual. Even though instruments no longer need a caption, certificates of acknowledgment, which are the written record of the acknowledgment ceremony made by the presiding officer and appended to many real estate instruments, require a caption showing where the acknowledgment ceremony occurred. Captions are therefore included in the certificate of acknowledgment forms contained in this manual. *See* Tex. Civ. Prac. & Rem. Code § 121.007.

§ 3.4 Dates in Instruments

When a transaction requires more than one instrument (such as a deed, a note, and a deed of trust, or a note and a mechanic's lien contract), all instruments should bear the same date. Conveyances can commence on a future date (Tex. Prop. Code § 5.041); thus, the effective date of an instrument can be different from the date of signing. Because instruments are adequately referred to by date, the expression "Executed this _____ day of _____" is unnecessary. Also, as a practical matter, all file copies should show the actual date of the original instrument to facilitate the subsequent amendment of the instrument or reference to it in other instruments relating to the transaction. When the deed has been dated one date and acknowledged on another, absent evidence regarding the actual date of delivery of the deed, the presumption arises that delivery occurred on the date of the deed, not the date of the acknowledgment. *Bell v. Smith*, 532 S.W.2d 680, 685 (Tex. App.—Fort Worth 1976, no writ).

§ 3.5 Headings

Each instrument to be recorded should have a heading clearly identifying it at the top of the first page, below the notice of confidentiality required by Tex. Prop. Code § 11.008. Tex. Loc. Gov't Code § 191.007(c).

§ 3.6 Mailing Address of Grantee

The grantee's mailing address should be shown on instruments conveying an interest in real property, such as deeds, deeds of trust, assignments of leases, and transfers of liens. Preferably, the address should appear in the instrument; it may also be given in a separate, signed writing attached to the instrument. For failure to show the address, the county clerk may assess a penalty filing fee equal to the greater of $25 or twice the statutory recording fee. Tex. Prop. Code § 11.003.

Forms in this manual that are considered to be conveyances provide for the grantee's address. Some county clerks may require the grantee's address on other instruments as well.

§ 3.7 Preparer of Instrument

Although not required, including the preparer's name and address may be useful for the parties and the public generally. Additionally, any instrument being traditionally recorded by the original paper being physically presented to the county clerk's office should be labeled "Record and return to:" with the address of the designated recipient added. There is no need for that return instruction if the instrument is electronically filed in a county clerk's office with that capability.

§ 3.8 Property Description

§ 3.8:1 Specificity of Description

An accurate property description is essential to a valid conveyance. The property must be described with enough certainty that it can be readily identified from the description. The description should include the city, county, and state in which the property is located, and courses and distances in metes-and-bounds descriptions must be unambiguous. If a deed conveys only part of a tract of land and does not designate which part, for example, the description may be insufficient to convey title. *See De Martinez v. De Vidaurri*, 219 S.W.2d 823, 826 (Tex. App.—San Antonio 1949, writ ref'd n.r.e.). If the property has been depicted in a filed plat, the plat reference to the lot and block of the property should be used, along with the recording number of the plat.

§ 3.8:2 General Instructions

The property description can include references to other recorded instruments, such as other deeds, but to depend solely on this reference as the entire description poses the danger that it may not match the intended description exactly or that it may be inaccurate or invalid. Conversely, if the metes-and-bounds description of the property is defective, but reference is made to another recorded instrument that contains a proper legal description of the property, the conveyance will probably be enforceable. *Sorsby v. State*, 624 S.W.2d 227, 232 (Tex. App.—Houston [1st Dist.] 1981, no writ).

The property description should be identical in all instruments relating to the same transaction, such as a deed and a deed of trust.

If the description is too long to fit the space provided in the form, it may be attached to the instrument and incorporated in it by a simple statement in the space provided for the description. An example of typical language for this purpose is "Two hundred acres of the Travis tract, out of the Domingo Losoya Survey No. 4, Abstract No. 10, Sunshine County, Texas, more particularly described in Exhibit A attached to this deed and by this reference incorporated in it." This should be the identical language used as the caption or "lead-in" on the description attached as an exhibit. In this case, the attorney must make certain that the exhibit is actually attached and properly identified as the referenced exhibit.

The attorney should consider adding the phrase *more or less* to references to the quantity of property being conveyed. By doing this, the grantor may be relieved of liability arising from minor shortages. *See Wooten v. State*, 177 S.W.2d 56, 58 (Tex. 1944). This is the case whether the property has recently been surveyed or not because there typically are minor variations between surveys concerning measurements and area computations.

If included in the body of the form, the description should be indented and set out in block form, to make it easily identifiable in the instrument.

§ 3.8:3 Description of Platted Property

Traditionally the lot, block, addition or subdivision numbers, and recording number of the plat designating the property are used for describing the platted property. A typical description using the lot, block, and addition numbers takes the following form:

> Lot _____, Block _____, _____ Addition, [**city**], [**county**] County, Texas, according to the map or plat thereof recorded in Volume _____, Page _____, of the [Real Property Records/[**insert other words of similar import**]] of [**county**] County, Texas.

§ 3.8:4 Description by Metes and Bounds

Metes-and-bounds descriptions are the most common type used for property outside urban areas and for unplatted urban land. These descriptions have been a steady source of litigation. Metes-and-bounds descriptions, as well as other types of property descriptions, have been liberally construed by the courts. When obvious errors have occurred in a property description, courts will generally attempt to find and correct the error to give effect to the conveyance. *See Poitevent v. Scarborough*, 124 S.W. 87 (Tex. 1910). Calls of distance have been held to be the weakest, and calls of distance and quantity must yield to well-established corners. *Warren v. Swanzy*, 361 S.W.2d 479, 484 (Tex. App.—Beaumont 1962, writ ref'd n.r.e.). A missing call in a metes-and-bounds description may be supplied when the omitted call was the only logical one that would make the description close. *See Mansel v. Castles*, 55 S.W. 559 (Tex. 1900).

§ 3.8:5 Recording Reference

It is common to refer to recorded instruments in descriptions, subrogation clauses, releases, transfers, and the like. The reference consists of volume and page recording information or another particular numbering sequence of the appropriate county. From the earliest days, the particular records were named after the instruments themselves—that is, deed records, deed-of-trust records, mechanic's lien records, and so on—and the reference would be, for example, the following:

> recorded in Volume _____, Page _____, Deed of Trust Records of _____ County, Texas

The Texas Local Government Code authorizes microfilming and electronic storage of public records by county clerks. *See* Tex. Loc. Gov't Code §§ 204.002, 205.002. Records are referred to by volume and page numbers in some counties, by film code numbers in other counties, and by county clerk file numbers or other means particular to specific microfilming or electronic storage systems in other counties. In counties employing microfilming, the clerk may consolidate the records (1) relating to real property and (2) relating to an individual, a business entity, or a governmental agency other than a property record or court record into a single class known as "Official Public Records." *See* Tex. Loc. Gov't Code § 193.008.

An instrument recorded under the microfilm system may be referred to as the following:

> recorded in Film Code No. _____ through _____ (or Volume _____, Page _____ or County Clerk File No. _____ or Instrument No. _____), Official Public Records of _____ County, Texas

Section 11.007 of the Texas Property Code provides a uniform system of references to be used in every county whether a microfilm system is in effect or not. A reference in an instrument to the volume and page number, film code number, or county clerk file number of the "real property records" (or words of similar import) for a particular county is equivalent to a reference to deed records, deed-of-trust records, or other specific records to provide effective notice to all persons of the existence of the referenced instrument. Tex. Prop. Code § 11.007. Uniform references for all recorded instruments can be in the following manner:

> recorded in Film Code No._____ through _____ (or Volume _____, Page _____ or County Clerk File No. _____ or Instrument No. _____) of the Official Public Records of _____ County, Texas

In various Texas counties, there may be nonstatutory variations in indexing real property records, which the practitioner should identify before referring back to a previously recorded instrument in a new instrument.

§ 3.9 Signatures

§ 3.9:1 Beneath Signature Lines

If names are not legibly typed or printed under each signature, the county clerk may double the filing fee for every nonconforming page. Tex. Loc. Gov't Code § 191.007(e), (h). If there are no printed signature lines, they should be added below the text of the instrument, unless an instrument is promulgated by the Texas legislature and contains text below the proposed signature space. See, for example, the statutory durable power of attorney (Tex. Est. Code § 752.051) and the directive to physicians (Tex. Health & Safety Code § 166.032).

§ 3.9:2 Person with Physical Disability

If an individual who is physically unable to sign or to make a mark on an instrument presented for notarization so directs, a notary public may sign the individual's name, in the presence of a witness who has no legal or equitable interest in any property that is the subject of the document. The notary public must require identification of the witness in the same manner as from an acknowledging person under section 121.005 of the Texas Civil Practice and Remedies Code. The notary should then write the following beneath the signature: "Signature affixed by notary in the presence of (name of witness), a disinterested witness, under section 406.0165, Government Code." Tex. Gov't Code § 406.0165(b).

§ 3.9:3 Signing with Mark

If the person signing cannot sign the person's name, but can only make a mark, an "X" should be marked in place of the signature, with the signatory's name typed beneath the mark, followed by ", the person's mark."

§ 3.9:4 Original Signatures for Paper Instruments

A paper instrument concerning real or personal property may not be recorded or serve as notice of the paper document unless the paper document contains an original signature or signatures that are acknowledged, sworn to with a proper jurat, or proved according to law. A paper document or instrument can instead be attached as an exhibit to a paper affidavit or other instrument that has an original signature or signatures that are acknowledged, sworn to with a proper jurat, or proved according to law. An original signature is not required for an electronic instrument or other document that complies with chapter 15 of the Texas Property Code, chapter 195 of the Texas Local Government Code, chapter 43 of the Texas Business and Commerce Code, or other applicable law. A "paper document" means a document that is not electronically received by a county clerk. *See* Tex. Prop. Code § 12.0011.

§ 3.9:5 Electronic/Digital Signatures

Contracts are routinely signed electronically, a method both convenient and efficient. The recodified Texas Uniform Electronic Transactions Act applies to any electronic record or electronic signature created, generated, sent, communicated, received, or stored on or after January 1, 2002. Tex. Bus. & Com. Code § 322.004.

One likely exception, however, is Texas home equity loans, which the Texas Constitution requires to be closed only at the office of the lender, a title company, or an attorney. Tex. Const. art. XVI, § 50(a)(6)(N); 7 Tex. Admin. Code § 153.15. Such loans may not be closed at a borrower's home or office. In 2013, the Texas Supreme Court clarified that if a power of attorney is used to close a home equity loan, the power of attorney must have been executed at the office of the lender, a title company, or an attorney. *Finance Commission of Texas v. Norwood*, 418 S.W.3d 566 (Tex. 2013).

Other exceptions to the Act are electronic records and signatures related to wills, codicils, or testamentary trusts and UCC transactions under Texas Business and Commerce Code (1) section 1.108 (related to modification of the Electronic Signatures in Global and National Commerce Act (15 U.S.C. §§ 7001–7031)), (2) section 1.206 ("Presumptions"), and (3) chapters 2 and 2A ("Sales" and "Leases," respectively). *See* Tex. Bus. & Com. Code § 322.003(b) ("1.107" corrected to "1.108" in item 1 above).

The Act also applies only if each party has agreed to conduct transactions by electronic means. Whether the parties agree to conduct a transaction by electronic means is determined from the context and surrounding circumstances, including the parties' conduct. Tex. Bus. & Com. Code § 322.005. Proof of consent is required to establish the validity of the signature.

The Act defines an electronic signature as "an electronic sound, symbol, or process attached to or logically associated with a record and executed or adopted by a person with the intent to sign the record." Tex. Bus. & Com. Code § 322.002(8). An electronic record is "a record created, generated, sent, communicated, received, or stored by electronic means." Tex. Bus. & Com. Code § 322.002(7). A record or signature may not be denied legal effect or enforceability solely because it is in electronic form. A contract may not be denied legal effect or enforceability solely because an electronic record was used in its formation. If a law requires a record to be in writing, an electronic record satisfies the law. If a law requires a signature, an electronic signature satisfies the law. Tex. Bus. & Com. Code § 322.007. If a sender inhibits the ability of a recipient to store or print an electronic record, the electronic record is not enforceable against the recipient. Tex. Bus. & Com. Code § 322.008.

The benefits of having documents signed electronically depend on their enforceability. Electronic signatures can present several issues when a dispute arises between the parties to the contract. For a paper document with a handwritten, wet-ink signature, the genuineness of the signature can be proved by direct evidence like testimony by (1) an eyewitness, (2) a witness familiar with the signatory's handwriting, or (3) an expert who has compared the signature against a genuine specimen. That type of testimony is seldom available or valid when electronic signatures are used.

As with paper documents, an electronic record or electronic signature is attributable to a person if it was the act of the person. The act of the person may be shown in any manner, including a showing of the efficacy of any security procedure applied to attribute the electronic record or electronic signature to the person. The effect of an electronic record or electronic signature attributed to a person is determined from the context and surrounding circumstances at the time of its creation, execution, or adoption, including the parties' agreement, if any, and otherwise as provided by law. Tex. Bus. & Com. Code § 322.009. *See Aeroteck, Inc. v. Boyd*, 624 S.W.3d 199 (Tex. 2021) (concerning validity and enforceability of documents presented for signature in electronic onboarding system to new hire who later denied signing one of presented documents).

The practitioner should not engage in electronic transactions or attempt to obtain an electronic signature without the use of commercially available electronic transaction software. Whenever an electronic document is called into question, the party trying to rely on the document must prove or authenticate the document much in the same manner as a nonelectronic document, by proving that the document was signed by the person it is being used against, that is, that the signature was valid and the document is a true and correct copy.

An electronic signature must be properly authenticated and verified, and so must employ security and verification systems. A security procedure is a "procedure employed for the purpose of verifying that an electronic signature, record, or performance is that of a specific person or for detecting changes or errors in the information in an electronic record," including "the use of algorithms or other codes, identifying words or numbers, encryption, or callback or other acknowledgment procedures." Tex. Bus. & Com. Code § 322.002(13). Security procedures may include requiring personal identifying information—such as a Social Security number or an address—to register for an account; assigning a unique identifier to a user and then tying that identifier to the user's actions; maintaining a single, secure system for tracking user activities that prevents unauthorized access to electronic records; business rules that require users to complete all steps in a program before moving on or completing it; and time stamps showing when users completed certain actions.

§ 3.10 Names

The parties' names in the text of an instrument should be followed by their status—for example, "John J. Doe and Jane R. Doe, spouses." Use an individual's middle name or middle initial to help avoid confusion with other individuals with similar names. For a married woman or widow, a name such as "Mrs. John Doe" should never be used.

Ordinarily, titles showing a person's rank or profession, such as "Captain John J. Doe" or "John

J. Doe, M.D.," should not be used unless they are part of the legal name. Use the labels "Sr." and "Jr." in appropriate instances to distinguish between the ancestor and the legally named "Jr."

Whenever possible, to maintain uniformity of names in the chain of title, all legal instruments to be filed should use precisely the same name for an individual as that used in instruments already recorded, or, if a name is incorrect, the correct name should be used and the correction should be explained in a note following the name. If the party's legal name changes between conveyances, the change should be explained in a note following the name. For example, if the title has been conveyed to Helen J. Doe, a single woman, and she later conveys the title as Helen D. Jones, the fact that she was formerly known as Helen J. Doe or was conveyed title as Helen J. Doe should be noted.

If the property being conveyed or encumbered is homestead property, the record title holder's spouse is required to join in any conveyance or encumbrance. *See* Tex. Fam. Code § 5.001; Tex. Const. art. XVI, § 50(a)(5)(A); Tex. Prop. Code §§ 41.001(b)(3), 53.254(c).

If the grantor or grantee is a legal entity rather than a person, it should be specifically identified by the type of entity and state of formation.

A description usually follows the name of a financial institution but may be unnecessary if the name adequately describes the institution—for example, "First National Bank of Sunshine," "Sunshine Federal Credit Union," or "Sunshine Federal Land Bank Association."

A deed by a corporation, if signed by an officer when recorded, constitutes prima facie evidence that execution was authorized by appropriate resolution of the board of directors; if the deed is executed by anyone other than an officer, it should be accompanied by a certified copy of the board of directors' resolution. Before August 28, 1989, the deed had to be executed by the president or a vice-president to constitute that prima facie evidence. Filing a certified copy of the appropriate resolution provides an additional safeguard to establish the validity of the corporate conveyance. Neither a corporate seal nor attestation by the corporate secretary is required in Texas unless required by the bylaws of the corporation.

§ 3.11 Acknowledgments

§ 3.11:1 Necessity for Acknowledgment

Instruments may be recorded only if they have been acknowledged, proved, or sworn to according to law. *See* Tex. Prop. Code §§ 11.004(a)(1), 12.001, 12.0011. County clerks may record an instrument only if it contains original signatures that are duly acknowledged, sworn to with a proper jurat, or otherwise proved in compliance with applicable law. The recordation of an instrument not duly acknowledged, otherwise proved, or sworn is a nullity and is not constructive notice of its contents. *See, e.g., Sanchez v. Telles*, 960 S.W.2d 762, 767 (Tex. App.—El Paso 1997, writ denied); *Reserve Petroleum Co. v. Hutcheson*, 254 S.W.2d 802, 806 (Tex. App.—Amarillo, 1952, writ ref'd n.r.e.).

Instruments may be acknowledged by an online notary public who has been authorized by the Texas secretary of state to perform online notarizations. *See* Tex. Gov't Code ch. 406, subch. C.

An instrument filed after September 1, 2007, containing a defective acknowledgment is considered lawfully recorded and is constructive notice of its contents after it has been of record for two years. Tex. Civ. Prac. & Rem. Code § 16.033(c).

Generally, the absence of an acknowledgment will not affect the validity of a deed, mortgage, or conveyance between the parties or affect the instrument as a conveyance. *See, e.g., Haile v.*

Holtzclaw, 414 S.W.2d 916, 928 (Tex. 1967). However, by statute, certain instruments must include an acknowledgment. These include subdivision plats, powers of attorney, extensions of real estate lien debt, and management certificates by property owners' associations. *See* Tex. Loc. Gov't Code § 212.004(c); Tex. Est. Code § 751.002; Tex. Civ. Prac. & Rem. Code § 16.036; Tex. Prop. Code § 209.004. Failure of the acknowledgment may render the instrument a nullity, even between the parties to the instrument.

§ 3.11:2 Distinguishing Acknowledgment and Certificate of Acknowledgment

Though used interchangeably, the terms *acknowledgment* and *certificate of acknowledgment* refer to two different concepts. An acknowledgment is a statutory ceremony in which a person who has executed an instrument appears before a competent officer and declares the instrument to be that person's act and deed. A certificate of acknowledgment is the written record of that proceeding made by the officer and appended to the instrument. To effect a valid acknowledgment, there must be both a valid ceremony of acknowledgment and a valid certificate of acknowledgment. *See* Tex. Civ. Prac. & Rem. Code § 121.004; *Punchard v. Masterson*, 101 S.W. 204 (Tex. 1907).

§ 3.11:3 Short-Form Certificate of Acknowledgment

Many practitioners prefer to use the short-form certificate of acknowledgment when the acknowledgment is taken in Texas and if the acknowledger is within one of the six categories of persons or entities specified by statute. Those categories are—

1. natural persons;
2. natural persons acting by attorneys-in-fact;
3. partnerships;
4. corporations;
5. public officers, trustees, executors, administrators, guardians, or other representative signers; and
6. limited liability companies.

Tex. Civ. Prac. & Rem. Code § 121.008.

§ 3.11:4 Ordinary (Long-Form) Certificate of Acknowledgment

The ordinary, or long-form, certificate should be used if instruments are to be executed outside Texas or in instances in which the acknowledger does not fall within one of the six categories for which short-form certificates may be used. Some practitioners have adapted various short-form certificates for use in Texas that do not fit the literal definition of the Texas Civil Practice and Remedies Code. *See* Tex. Civ. Prac. & Rem. Code § 121.008. The practitioner should use the long-form certificate in all instances in which the acknowledger is not within one of the classes specified by the statute.

§ 3.11:5 Electronic Certificate of Acknowledgment

The electronic notarial certificate should be used if the instrument acknowledgment is taken by an online notary public in accordance with Tex. Gov't Code ch. 406, subch. C.

§ 3.12 Requirements of Valid Ceremony of Acknowledgment

A valid ceremony of acknowledgment requires—

1. a competent officer to take the acknowledgment (*see* Tex. Civ. Prac. & Rem. Code § 121.001);
2. a personal appearance by the acknowledger before the officer (*see* Tex. Civ. Prac. & Rem. Code § 121.004(a));
3. the identification of the acknowledger by the officer (*see* Tex. Civ. Prac. & Rem. Code § 121.005); and
4. a statement by the acknowledger that the acknowledger has executed the instrument for the purposes and consideration stated in the instrument (*see* Tex. Civ. Prac. & Rem. Code § 121.004(a)).

There are additional requirements for electronic notarial certificates (*see* Tex. Gov't Code ch. 406, subch. C).

§ 3.12:1 Competent Officer to Take Acknowledgment

Acknowledgments Taken within Texas: Acknowledgments taken in Texas may be made before—

1. a notary public;
2. a clerk of a district court (or deputy district clerk);
3. a judge of a county court;
4. a clerk of a county court (or deputy county clerk);
5. a federal judge, justice, or magistrate; or
6. certain other public officers for specific statutory instruments.

28 U.S.C. §§ 459, 636(a)(2); Tex. Civ. Prac. & Rem. Code § 121.001(a).

Acknowledgments Taken outside Texas but inside the United States or Its Territories: Acknowledgments taken outside Texas but inside the United States or its territories may be made before—

1. a notary public;
2. a clerk of a court of record having a seal;
3. a commissioner of deeds appointed under the laws of Texas; or
4. a federal judge, justice, or magistrate.

28 U.S.C. §§ 459, 636(a)(2); Tex. Civ. Prac. & Rem. Code § 121.001(b).

Acknowledgments Taken outside the United States or Its Territories: Acknowledgments taken outside the United States or its territories may be made before—

1. a minister, commissioner, or chargé d'affaires of the United States who is a resident of and is accredited in the country in which the acknowledgment is taken;
2. a consul general, consul, vice-consul, commercial agent, vice-commercial agent, deputy consul, or consular agent of the United States who is a resident of the country in which the acknowledgment is taken; or
3. a notary public or other official authorized to administer oaths in the jurisdiction in which the acknowledgment or proof by affidavit is taken.

Tex. Civ. Prac. & Rem. Code § 121.001(c).

The preferred method of taking an acknowledgment outside the United States is to use a U.S. foreign service officer authorized in item 1 or 2 above. A form for acknowledgment by a foreign service officer of the United States is included as form 3-32 in this chapter.

If an acknowledgment is taken before a foreign notary public or any other official authorized to administer oaths in the jurisdiction in which the acknowledgment is taken as authorized in Texas Civil Practice and Remedies Code section 121.001(c)(3), it is advisable for the attorney to comply with the Hague Convention on Legalization of Foreign Public Documents, if the instrument is executed in a country that has adopted the Hague Convention, and to seek certification and authentication of the document through an embassy or consular office for a country that has not adopted it. For additional information, see **www.hcch.net**, **https://travel.state.gov/content/travel.html**, and, more specifically, **https://travel.state.gov/content/travel/en/records-and-authentications/authenticate-your-document/office-of-authentications.html**.

Acknowledgments Taken of Military Personnel and Their Spouses: A commissioned officer of the United States Armed Forces or of a United States Armed Forces auxiliary may take an acknowledgment of a written instrument of a member of the armed forces, a member of an armed forces auxiliary, or a member's spouse. Tex. Civ. Prac. & Rem. Code § 121.001(d). A form for a military acknowledgment is included as form 3-33.

Territorial Limitations on Officer's Authority: Texas notaries may take an acknowledgment anywhere in the state but not outside the boundaries of Texas. Tex. Gov't Code § 406.003.

Time Limitations on Officer's Authority: The term of a notary's appointment is four years. Tex. Gov't Code § 406.002. Reapplication may be made for successive terms. Tex. Gov't Code § 406.011. Texas law requires that the expiration date of the notary's commission appear as part of the notary's seal. *See* Tex. Gov't Code § 406.013(a).

The authority of other intrastate officers is limited to the terms of their offices.

Interested Officers Disqualified to Take Acknowledgment: A party to an instrument may not take an acknowledgment for that instrument because one who is financially or beneficially interested in a transaction is disqualified from taking an acknowledgment concerning the transaction. *Dyson Descendant Corp. v. Sonat Exploration Co.*, 861 S.W.2d 942, 948 (Tex. App.—Houston [1st Dist.] 1993, no writ).

A beneficiary or trustee of a trust may not take an acknowledgment of an instrument to which the trust is a party. Nor may a trustee of a deed of trust take an acknowledgment for that instrument. *See Rothschild v. Dougher*, 20 S.W. 142 (Tex. 1892).

Generally, an agent of a party to an instrument is also disqualified to take an acknowledgment if that agency appears on the face of the instrument. To be disqualified, however, the agent must have discretionary authority to negotiate the terms of a particular transaction for the principal. *See Sample v. Irwin*, 45 Tex. 567 (1876); *Uvalde Rock Asphalt Co. v. Warren*, 59 S.W.2d 272 (Tex. App.—Galveston 1933), *aff'd*, 91 S.W.2d 321 (Tex. 1936). But if the agent is a mere salaried employee of a party to an instrument, the agent is not disqualified from taking an acknowledgment of that instrument. *Director, Dallas County Child Welfare v. Thompson*, 667 S.W.2d 282 (Tex. App.—Dallas 1984, no writ); *Anderson v. Pioneer Building & Loan Ass'n*, 163 S.W.2d 421, 425 (Tex. App.—Waco 1942, writ ref'd w.o.m.).

An officer or director of a corporation may not take an acknowledgment of an instrument to which the corporation is a party. A shareholder of a corporation is likewise disqualified if the corporation has one thousand or fewer stockholders and the officer taking the acknowledgment owns more than one-tenth of one percent of the issued and outstanding stock. Tex. Civ. Prac. & Rem. Code § 121.002(b).

Generally, an acknowledgment taken by an interested officer is void and may not be reformed or corrected. However, effect will be given to such an acknowledgment to protect an innocent purchaser who relies on the instrument as constructive notice and has no knowledge of the disqualifying interest of the officer. To render an acknowledgment ineffective because of a disqualifying interest of the notary, the officer's financial or beneficial interest must appear on the face of the instrument or be otherwise known to the party relying on the instrument. Constructive notice of the disqualifying interest may come from a prior recorded instrument. *See, e.g., Gulf Production Co. v. Continental Oil Co.*, 164 S.W.2d 488, 493–94 (Tex. 1942); *Dyson Descendant Corp.*, 861 S.W.2d at 948.

§ 3.12:2 Personal Appearance before Officer

An acknowledgment is invalid unless the acknowledger personally appears before the competent officer. Tex. Civ. Prac. & Rem. Code § 121.004(a). An acknowledgment taken over the telephone or otherwise made without personal contact with the acknowledger fails to satisfy the statutory requirements of an acknowledgment ceremony.

The acknowledger's appearance before the officer may be online. *See* Tex. Gov't Code § 406.110(a).

§ 3.12:3 Acknowledger Must Be Identified by Officer

An officer may not take an acknowledgment unless the officer knows the acknowledger or has satisfactory evidence that the acknowledging person is the same person who executed the instrument. Tex. Civ. Prac. & Rem. Code § 121.005(a).

The law does not prescribe the extent of acquaintance necessary for the acknowledger to be known to the officer. The acquaintance may be of one year or one hour. However, mere introduction by another may be insufficient for the acknowledger to be known to the officer.

Satisfactory evidence of the identity of an acknowledger not known to the officer may be made only by the oath of a credible witness personally known to the officer, by a current identification card or other document issued by the federal government or any state government that contains the photograph and signature of the acknowledging person, or, in the case of a deed or other instrument relating to a residential real estate transaction, by a current passport issued by a foreign country. Tex. Civ. Prac. & Rem. Code § 121.005(a). The most common examples seen are driver's licenses and passports. However, the form provided in Texas Civil Practice and Remedies Code section 121.010 provides for identification only by personal knowledge or oath of a witness.

There are specific identity verification requirements in the instance of online notarizations. *See* Tex. Gov't Code § 406.110(b).

§ 3.12:4 Acknowledger Must Acknowledge Signature before Officer

An officer may not take a valid acknowledgment by simply sitting in mute observation of a person signing the instrument. To effect a valid ceremony of acknowledgment, the acknowledger must state to the officer that the acknowledger executed the instrument in the capacity and for the purposes and consideration stated in the instrument. The officer should treat the acknowledgment as a scripted ceremony and obtain from the acknowledger, as applicable, the following declarations.

1. Individual Acknowledgment. A natural person must acknowledge to the officer that the acknowledger executed

the instrument for the purposes and consideration expressed in the instrument.

2. Attorney-in-Fact. An acknowledger executing an instrument as attorney-in-fact for a principal must acknowledge that the acknowledger executed the instrument as the act of the principal for the purposes and consideration expressed in the instrument.

3. Partnership. An acknowledger executing a document on behalf of a partnership must acknowledge that the acknowledger executed the instrument as the act of the partnership for the purposes and consideration expressed in the instrument.

4. Corporate Acknowledgment. A corporate officer or agent must acknowledge that the acknowledger executed the instrument in the capacity stated, as the act of the corporation, for the purposes and consideration expressed in the instrument.

5. Public Officer, Trustee, Executor or Administrator of an Estate, Guardian, or Other Representative Signer. An acknowledger executing a document as a public officer, trustee, executor or administrator of an estate, or guardian or in another representative capacity must acknowledge that the acknowledger executed the instrument by proper authority in the capacity stated and for the purposes and consideration expressed in the instrument.

6. Limited Liability Company Acknowledgment. A member, manager, authorized officer, or agent must acknowledge that the acknowledger executed the instrument in the capacity stated, as the act of the limited liability company, for the purposes and consideration expressed in the instrument.

Tex. Civ. Prac. & Rem. Code § 121.006(b).

§ 3.12:5 Online Notarization

There are now "notaries public" (Tex. Gov't Code ch. 406, subch. A) and "online notaries public" (Tex. Gov't Code ch. 406, subch. C). An online notary public is an officer commissioned as a traditional notary public who is also commissioned and authorized to perform online notarizations by using two-way video and audio conference technology under subchapter C, chapter 406, of the Texas Government Code. To become an online notary public, a notary public must complete a separate electronic application, provide an email address, and further certify that he or she will comply with the standards developed by the Texas secretary of state for online notaries. Tex. Gov't Code § 406.105.

Online Notarization Procedures: A Texas online notary public may perform an online notarization while physically located within the boundaries of Texas at the time of notarization. However, the signing party (or principal) may be located anywhere. Tex. Gov't Code § 406.110(a). Using two-way video and audio conference technology that meets the requirements of subchapter C, chapter 406, of the Texas Government Code, the online notary public shall verify the identity of the principal creating an electronic signature at the time the signature is taken. Tex. Gov't Code § 406.110(b).

In performing an online notarization, an online notary public affixes an electronic signature and electronic seal to an electronic notarial certificate that is capable of independent verification and renders any subsequent modifications evident. Tex. Gov't Code § 406.109(d). The electronic notarial certificate for an online notarization must include a notation that the notarization is an online notarization. Tex. Gov't

Code § 406.110(d). Other requirements for the electronic notarial certificate are contained in Tex. Gov't Code § 406.101(4). An online notary public shall take reasonable steps to ensure that any registered device used to create an electronic signature is current and has not been revoked or terminated by the device's issuing or registering authority. Tex. Gov't Code § 406.109(a). In addition, an online notary public's electronic signature may be used only for performing online notarizations. If performing a notarization for a paper document with a signer who is physically present, the notary public would sign the notarial certificate in the traditional manner. Tex. Gov't Code § 406.109(c).

Fees: The online notary public may charge the same fees as a traditional notary authorized by Tex. Gov't Code § 406.024, and may charge an additional fee not to exceed $25 for performing an online notarization. Tex. Gov't Code § 406.111. The fee must be included in the electronic record for each online notarization. Tex. Gov't Code § 406.108(a).

Recordkeeping and Public Information: Texas also requires an online notary public to maintain a secure electronic record of electronic documents notarized by the officer. An online notary public shall record:

1. the date and time of each notarization;
2. the type of notarial act;
3. the type, the title, or a description of the electronic document or proceeding;
4. the printed name and address of each principal involved in the transaction or proceeding;
5. the evidence of identity of each principal involved in the transaction or proceeding in the form of:
   a. a statement that the person is personally known to the online notary public;
   b. a notation of the type of identification document provided to the online notary public;
   c. a record of the identity verification made under Tex. Gov't Code § 406.110, if applicable; or
   d. the following:
      i. the printed name and address of each credible witness swearing to or affirming the person's identity; and
      ii. for each credible witness not personally known to the online notary public, a description of the type of identification documents provided to the online notary public;
6. a recording of any video and audio conference that is the basis for satisfactory evidence of identity and a notation of the type of identification presented as evidence; and
7. the fee, if any, charged for the notarization.

Tex. Gov't Code § 406.108(a). As an additional requirement, an online notary shall take reasonable steps to maintain a backup for the required electronic record and protect the backup record from unauthorized use. Tex. Gov't Code § 406.108(b). The required electronic record shall be maintained for at least five years after the date of the transaction or proceeding. Tex. Gov't Code § 406.108(c). Finally, entries in the online notary's records are public information. An online notary public shall, on payment of all fees, provide a certified copy of any record in the notary public's records to any person requesting the copy. An online notary public shall keep the online notary public's electronic record, electronic signature, and electronic seal secure and under the online notary's exclusive control at all times. Tex. Gov't Code § 406.109(b).

§ 3.13 Requirements for Valid Certificate of Acknowledgment

A valid certificate of acknowledgment must—

1. be in English;
2. contain a caption showing where the acknowledgment was taken;
3. recite the official capacity of the officer taking the acknowledgment;
4. recite a personal appearance before the officer;
5. recite that the acknowledger was identified by the officer;
6. recite that the acknowledger acknowledged the instrument;
7. identify the acknowledger;
8. recite the date of the acknowledgment;
9. bear the signature of the officer; and
10. bear the official seal of the officer.

See sections 3.13:1 through 3.13:11 below for more detailed information. Online notarizations are controlled by subchapter C, chapter 406 of the Texas Government Code. See section 3.12:5 above.

The legislature has prescribed statutory forms for an ordinary (long-form) certificate of acknowledgment and certain short-form certificates of acknowledgment. *See* Tex. Civ. Prac. & Rem. Code §§ 121.007, 121.008. The short-form certificates of acknowledgment are preferred for acknowledgments taken within Texas. Short-form certificates of acknowledgment should not be used for acknowledgments taken outside the state of Texas. This chapter includes examples of both ordinary and short-form certificates of acknowledgment. Short-form certificates of acknowledgment are shown in this chapter for acknowledgers falling within the classes identified in Texas Civil Practice and Remedies Code section 121.008.

Ordinary (long-form) certificates of acknowledgment are shown in this chapter for all acknowledgers, and a separate form is included as form 3-29 in this chapter. Electronic certificates of acknowledgment that meet minimum statutory requirements for use in online notarizations are included as forms 3-30 and 3-31.

Short-form certificates of acknowledgment do not require that the certificate state how the officer identified the acknowledger. In all other respects, short-form certificates of acknowledgment must contain all essential elements of a certificate of acknowledgment. For an ordinary, or long-form, certificate, it is necessary that the officer state in the certificate either that the officer personally knows the acknowledger or that evidence of a witness or an identification card or other document was used to identify the acknowledger. Tex. Civ. Prac. & Rem. Code § 121.005(b).

The ordinary, or long-form, certificate of acknowledgment has different statutory requirements than the short-form does; in either case, substantial compliance with the statutory forms is all that is required. Literal compliance is not essential as long as, on balance, the certificate shows that substantially all things required by law to be done have been done. *See Williams v. Cruse*, 130 S.W.2d 908 (Tex. App.—Beaumont 1939, writ ref'd) (construing an ordinary certificate of acknowledgment).

On March 13, 2020, Texas Governor Greg Abbott declared a state of disaster for all Texas counties due to the COVID-19 pandemic. On April 27, 2020, the Office of the Governor temporarily suspended section 121.006(c)(1) of the

Texas Civil Practice and Remedies Code to the extent necessary to allow for appearance before a notary public via videoconference to acknowledge real estate instruments such as mortgages, avoiding the need for in-person contact during the pandemic. The temporary suspension was terminated effective September 1, 2021. Documents executed while this suspension was in effect, and under its terms, remain valid after the termination of this suspension. Nothing in the suspension prevented traditional notarization or an online notarization under chapter 406 of the Texas Government Code.

Any document acknowledged while the suspension was in effect, and in accordance with its terms, shall continue to be considered duly acknowledged and fully compliant with Texas law after the termination of the suspension. All county clerks in Texas shall accept for recording in the public records all documents signed and notarized during the suspension by means of the two-way audio-video communication.

> For assistance in determining the validity of a remote-ink acknowledgment during the suspension, it must be determined whether the following conditions were met:

- A notary public used two-way audio-video communication technology that allowed for direct and contemporaneous interaction between a person signing a document and the notary public by sight and sound.
- A notary public verified the identity of a signatory at the time the signature was taken by using two-way audio-video communication technology. A notary public may verify identity by:
  - personal knowledge of the signatory;
  - analysis based on the signatory's remote presentation of a government-issued identification credential, including a passport or driver's license, that contains the signature and a photograph of the signatory, and is of sufficient quality to allow for identification; or
  - an introduction of the signatory by oath of a credible witness who personally knows the signatory, and who is personally known to the notary public.
- During the two-way audio-video communication:
  - the notary public attested to being physically located in Texas;
  - the signatory attested to being physically located in Texas;
  - the signatory affirmatively stated what documents were being signed; and
  - the signatory's act of signing was close enough to the camera for the notary public to observe it clearly.
- A recording of the two-way audio-video communication of the notarial act must be kept by the notary public for two years from the date of the notarial act.
- The signatory sent the original signed documents by courier, U.S. Mail, or overnight carrier directly to the notary public for the notary public to sign and to affix the official stamp or seal.
- The official date and time of the notarization was the date and time when the notary public witnessed the signatory signing the documents during the two-way audio-video communication.

The documents shall include, whether in a notarial certificate, a jurat, or an acknowledgement, language substantially similar to the following: "This notarization involved the use of two-way audio-video communication pursuant to the suspension granted by the Office of the Governor on April 27, 2020, under section 418.016 of the Texas Government Code."

Office of the Tex. Governor, "Office of the Attorney General Guidance," **https://gov.texas.gov/uploads/files/press/Office_of_the_Attorney_General_Guidance.pdf**. Tex, Att'y Gen. Op. No. KP-0423 (2022).

§ 3.13:1 Certificate Must Be in English

The certificate of acknowledgment and the remainder of the instrument may not be recorded unless they are in English or comply with Tex. Prop. Code § 11.002. For those illiterate in English, no special form of a certificate of acknowledgment is specified. However, prudence may dictate that an affidavit of an interpreter be executed and attached to the instrument. An affidavit of an interpreter is included as form 3-38 in this chapter.

An instrument acknowledged outside the United States or its territories in accordance with Texas Civil Practice and Remedies Code section 121.001(c)(3) that contains a certificate, stamp, or seal of a notary public or other official before whom the acknowledgment was taken or an apostille relating to the acknowledgment, any portion of which is not in English, may be recorded and operate as constructive notice from the date of filing if—

1. a correct English translation of any non-English portion of the certificate, stamp, seal, or apostille is recorded with the original instrument;
2. the accuracy of the translation is sworn to before an officer authorized to administer oaths; and
3. any apostille relating to the acknowledgment complies with the Hague Convention dated October 5, 1961, entitled "Convention Abolishing the Requirement of Legalisation for Foreign Public Documents," a copy of which can be obtained online at **www.hcch.net**.

Tex. Prop. Code § 11.002(c).

§ 3.13:2 Certificate Must Identify Location of Acknowledgment

Each separate certificate of acknowledgment must bear a caption or other indication of where the acknowledgment was taken so that it can be determined that the officer taking the acknowledgment acted within the scope of the officer's geographic authority. Each separate certificate of acknowledgment must contain its own caption. *See* Tex. Civ. Prac. & Rem. Code §§ 121.007, 121.008.

§ 3.13:3 Certificate Must Recite Capacity of Officer

It is not enough that the officer taking the acknowledgment take it correctly within the officer's official capacity. The certificate of acknowledgment must recite the official capacity of the officer on the instrument. *See Gulf, Colorado & Santa Fe Railway Co. v. Carter*, 24 S.W. 1083 (Tex. App.—Dallas 1893, no writ).

§ 3.13:4 Certificate Must Recite Personal Appearance by Acknowledger before Officer

The certificate of acknowledgment must state that the acknowledger made a personal appearance before the officer. Statutory short forms for certificates of acknowledgment accomplish this by stating that the acknowledgment was taken "before me." *See* Tex. Civ. Prac. & Rem. Code §§ 121.006–.008.

§ 3.13:5 Certificate Must Recite That Acknowledger Was Identified by Officer

For an ordinary, or long-form, certificate of acknowledgment, the certificate must recite how the officer identified the acknowledger by the accepted statutory methods. The certificate of acknowledgment must state that the acknowledger was—

1. known to the officer;
2. identified to the officer by the oath of a credible witness personally known to the officer;
3. identified by a current identification card or other document issued by the federal government or any state government that contains the photograph and signature of the acknowledging person; or
4. in the case of a deed or other instrument relating to a residential real estate transaction, identified by a current passport issued by a foreign country.

This requirement does not apply to short-form certificates of acknowledgment. Tex. Civ. Prac. & Rem. Code § 121.005.

§ 3.13:6 Certificate Must Recite That Signatory Acknowledged Instrument

The certificate of acknowledgment must recite that the signatory acknowledged the execution of the instrument. Failure to state this essential fact renders the certificate fatally defective. *See* Tex. Civ. Prac. & Rem. Code §§ 121.007, 121.008.

A long-form certificate of acknowledgment should contain all the components required for a valid ceremony of acknowledgment. See section 3.12 above.

Short-form certificates of acknowledgment require only an abbreviated statement of acknowledgment. Generally, each short-form certificate of acknowledgment requires only a statement that the instrument was "acknowledged." However, short-form certificates of acknowledgment for attorneys-in-fact, partnerships, corporations, and limited liability companies must additionally state that the instrument was acknowledged "on behalf of" the principal, partnership, corporation, or limited liability company. The short-form certificate of acknowledgment for a public officer, trustee, executor, administrator, guardian, or other representative signer must state that the instrument was acknowledged by the representative signer "as (title of representative) of (name of entity or person represented)." Tex. Civ. Prac. & Rem. Code § 121.008.

§ 3.13:7 Certificate Must Identify Acknowledger

The certificate of acknowledgment must show that the person acknowledging the instrument is the same person who signed it. A slight variance between the name of the person shown to have signed and the name of the person shown to have acknowledged the instrument may, but will not necessarily, invalidate the certificate. *See, e.g.*, *Cheek v. Herndon*, 17 S.W. 763 (Tex. 1891).

Pronouns may be employed in certificates of acknowledgment as a substitute for the name of the acknowledger given elsewhere in the certificate. As with the names for which they substitute, errors in the use of pronouns may, but will not necessarily, have the effect of invalidating the certificate. *Cheek*, 17 S.W. at 764.

§ 3.13:8 Certificate Must Recite Date of Acknowledgment

All statutory forms for certificates of acknowledgment provide for the certificate to be dated.

The date must be the date on which the instrument was acknowledged. The date of the acknowledgment must not be earlier than the date of execution of the instrument; otherwise, the notary would appear to have taken the acknowledgment before the document was executed, giving rise to an ineffective acknowledgment. However, an instrument may be dated to become effective on some future date while the acknowledgment is taken and dated with a current date.

§ 3.13:9 Certificate Must Bear Signature of Officer

The officer taking the acknowledgment must sign the certificate. Tex. Civ. Prac. & Rem. Code § 121.004(b)(2).

§ 3.13:10 Certificate Must Bear Official Seal of Officer

The officer taking the acknowledgment of an instrument must affix the officer's official seal of office. Tex. Civ. Prac. & Rem. Code § 121.004(b)(3). An acknowledgment without a seal or containing the wrong seal is generally, but not always, fatally defective. *See McDonald v. Stanfield*, 197 S.W. 892, 893–94 (Tex. App.—Beaumont 1917, writ ref'd). *But see* Tex. Civ. Prac. & Rem. Code § 121.001(d) (failure to attach seal does not invalidate acknowledgment taken by an officer of armed forces); Tex. Civ. Prac. & Rem. Code § 121.004(c); Tex. Prop. Code § 12.001(d) (failure to attach seal invalidates acknowledgment only if taken in a jurisdiction that requires seal).

The notary must use a seal of office that clearly shows, when embossed, stamped, or printed on a document, the words "Notary Public, State of Texas" around a star of five points, the notary's name, and the date the notary's commission expires. For notaries commissioned or reappointed on or after January 1, 2016, the seal of office must also show the notary's identification number assigned by the secretary of state. The seal may be in a circular form not more than two inches in diameter or a rectangular form not more than one inch in width and two and one-half inches in length; must have a serrated or milled-edge border; and must be affixed by a seal press or stamp that embosses or prints a seal that legibly reproduces the required elements of a seal under photographic methods. An indelible ink pad must be used for the stamp. Tex. Gov't Code § 406.013.

Documents notarized before September 1, 1989, are valid if the seal used contained the words "Notary Public, State of Texas" or "Notary Public" and the name of the county but did not have the notary's name and commission expiration date. Continued use of previously authorized forms of seals is not authorized after August 31, 1989.

The notary's seal should not cover or obscure signatures or text.

The ordinary, or long-form, certificate of acknowledgment includes the language above the signature of the officer that the certificate is "given under my hand and seal of office." Tex. Civ. Prac. & Rem. Code § 121.007. However, the presence or absence of these words does not affect the validity of the certificate. The phrase has been eliminated from short-form certificates of acknowledgment. *See* Tex. Civ. Prac. & Rem. Code § 121.008.

§ 3.13:11 Officer Required to Keep Record of Acknowledgments Taken

Unless specifically excused by statute, each officer authorized to take acknowledgments of instruments must enter in a "well-bound book" and officially sign a short statement of each acknowledgment taken. There are general requirements of the information to be recorded in the book, such as the date of the instrument, the date the acknowledgment or proof was taken, the name and mailing address of the acknowledger, information about how the acknowledger was identified, the name of the grantee of the land, the county in which the land is located, and a brief description of the instrument. *See* Tex. Civ. Prac. & Rem. Code § 121.012; Tex. Gov't Code § 406.014(a). Books suitable for this purpose are available commercially.

No penalty is prescribed for the failure of an officer to maintain a well-bound book or to make entries of acknowledgments taken. The failure to make the entry does not affect the validity of the instrument or prove that the acknowledgment was not taken. *See Martin v. Bane*, 450 S.W.2d 142, 144 (Tex. App.—Dallas 1969, no writ).

§ 3.14 Alternative Methods of Proving Instruments

Notwithstanding that an instrument may not contain a valid acknowledgment, it may nevertheless be recorded if proved by alternative methods. The alternative methods of proving a document for recordation include proof by jurat, proof by subscribing witness, acknowledgment by handwriting, proof by suit, and proof by an unsworn declaration.

See sections 3.14:1 through 3.14:5 below for more detailed information.

§ 3.14:1 Proof by Jurat

Jurats are ordinarily used only for affidavits. However, since September 1, 1989, instruments that are only sworn to and not acknowledged or otherwise proved are eligible for recordation. *See* Tex. Prop. Code § 12.001. Affidavits recorded before September 1, 1989, must have been accompanied by an acknowledgment. Any affidavit recorded without an acknowledgment before that date may not constitute constructive notice.

As with acknowledgments, an officer cannot take a valid affidavit by simply sitting in mute observation of the affiant signing the instrument. The officer taking the affidavit should place the affiant under oath or receive the affiant's declaration that the statements contained in the affidavit are true and correct. Failure to attend to these formalities may render the affidavit ineffective. *See* Tex. Gov't Code § 312.011(1). A sample oath for the officer to administer to the affiant is: "Do you swear or affirm to tell the truth, the whole truth, and nothing but the truth?" The affiant must answer "yes" before signing the sworn document.

Affidavits in this manual contain a statement similar to the following: "Affiant on oath swears that the following statements are true and are within the personal knowledge of Affiant." Although the statement is not required by statute, the Supreme Court of Texas has held that an affidavit is insufficient unless the allegations contained in it are direct and unequivocal and perjury can be assigned to them. This requires that the affidavit positively and unqualifiedly represent that the facts disclosed in the affidavit are true and within the personal knowledge of the affiant. *Brownlee v. Brownlee*, 665 S.W.2d 111 (Tex. 1984).

The persons before whom oaths, affidavits, and affirmations may be made include—

1. a notary public;
2. a judge, retired judge, or clerk of a municipal court, in a matter pertaining to a duty of the court;
3. a judge, retired judge, senior judge, clerk, or commissioner of a court of record;
4. a justice of the peace or a clerk of a justice court;

5. a member of a board or commission created by a law of this state, in a matter pertaining to a duty of the board or commission;
6. a person employed by the Texas Ethics Commission who has a duty related to a report required by title 15 of the Texas Election Code in a matter pertaining to that duty;
7. a county tax assessor-collector or an employee of the county tax assessor-collector if the oath relates to a document that is required or authorized to be filed in the office of the county tax assessor-collector;
8. the secretary of state or a former secretary of state;
9. an employee of a personal bond office, or an employee of a county, who is employed to obtain information required to be obtained under oath if the oath is required or authorized by article 17.04 or article 26.04(n) or (o) of the Texas Code of Criminal Procedure;
10. the lieutenant governor or a former lieutenant governor;
11. the speaker of the house of representatives or a former speaker of the house of representatives;
12. the governor or a former governor;
13. a legislator or retired legislator;
14. the secretary of the senate or the chief clerk of the house of representatives;
15. the attorney general or a former attorney general;
16. the secretary or clerk of a municipality in a matter pertaining to the official business of the municipality;
17. a peace officer described by article 2.12 of the Texas Code of Criminal Procedure if the oath is administered when the officer is engaged in the performance of the officer's duties and the administration of the oath relates to the officer's duties;
18. an associate judge, magistrate, master, referee, or criminal law hearing officer; or
19. a county treasurer.

Tex. Gov't Code § 602.002.

§ 3.14:2 Proof by Subscribing Witness

In some cases, an instrument cannot be proved by acknowledgment or jurat because a signatory is dead, unavailable, incompetent, or uncooperative. Proof by subscribing witness may be used if there is a credible witness who saw the signatory sign the instrument or in whose presence the signatory acknowledged the signature. The requirements of proof of an instrument by a subscribing witness are set out in Tex. Civ. Prac. & Rem. Code §§ 121.009, 121.010. Proofs of an instrument by a subscribing witness are included in forms 3-34 and 3-35 in this chapter.

§ 3.14:3 Acknowledgment by Handwriting

In certain limited instances in which neither a standard acknowledgment nor an acknowledgment by a witness is available, an instrument may be proved by an acknowledgment by handwriting. The execution of an instrument may be established for recording by proof of the handwriting of persons who signed the instrument only if—

1. the grantor of the instrument and all the witnesses are dead;
2. the grantor and all the witnesses are not residents of Texas;
3. the residences of the grantor and the witnesses are unknown to the person

seeking to prove the instrument and cannot be ascertained;

4. the witnesses have become legally incompetent to testify; or

5. the grantor of the instrument refuses to acknowledge the execution of the instrument and all the witnesses are dead, not residents of Texas, or legally incompetent or their places of residence are unknown.

Tex. Civ. Prac. & Rem. Code § 121.011.

§ 3.14:4 Proof by Suit

Any person having an interest in an instrument may bring an action in state district court for a judgment proving the instrument. Tex. Prop. Code § 11.005(a). Once a judgment in the action is obtained, a certified copy of it may be attached to the instrument; the instrument may then be recorded as if it contained a proper certificate of acknowledgment. Tex. Prop. Code § 11.005(c). This statute provides an alternative for making an instrument recordable; it does not cure those instruments missing an acknowledgment that require an acknowledgment for their validity. *See McCracken v. Sullivan*, 221 S.W. 336 (Tex. App.—San Antonio 1920, no writ).

§ 3.14:5 Proof by Unsworn Declaration

Chapter 132 of the Texas Civil Practices and Remedies Code provides that an unsworn declaration made under penalty of perjury may be used in lieu of some declarations, verifications, certifications, oaths, or affidavits required by law to be taken before a notary public. Tex. Civ. Prac. & Rem. Code § 132.001. Under this statute, it may be possible for an instrument to be proved by an unsworn declaration of either the signatories to the instrument, the subscribing witnesses, or persons authorized to give evidence of handwriting. To be effective, unsworn declarations must substantially comply with the statutory forms. Tex. Civ. Prac. & Rem. Code § 132.001(d)–(f). This statute does not apply to a lien required to be filed with a county clerk, an instrument concerning real or personal property required to be filed with a county clerk, or an oath of office or an oath required to be taken before a specified official other than a notary public. Tex. Civ. Prac. & Rem. Code § 132.001(b).

§ 3.15 Filing of Documents

The recording of the deed is not necessary to pass title. *Noell v. Crow-Billingsley Air Park Ltd. P'ship*, 233 S.W.3d 408, 416 (Tex. App.—Dallas 2007, pet. denied). The recording, however, establishes a prima facie case of delivery and the accompanying presumption that the grantor intended to convey the land according to the terms of the deed. *Stephens County Museum, Inc. v. Swenson*, 517 S.W.2d 257, 261–62 (citing *Thornton v. Rains*, 299 S.W.2d 287 (Tex. 1957)).

Texas is a race-notice state, and all real property conveyance instruments should be filed in the real property records (also referred to as the official public records, deed records, or deed-of-trust records, depending on the county) of the county in which the property is located as soon as possible after the transaction is complete. Powers of attorney and other authority documents requiring recordation used in connection with a sale or loan secured by real estate should be recorded before the conveyance or loan documents so that the proper authority is in place for the conveyance. Powers of attorney used for real property transactions must be recorded no later than thirty days after the recordation of the instrument signed by the agent. Tex. Est. Code § 751.151.

Some county clerks have filing requirements and fees unique to their county. Contacting the clerk for the specific guidelines before sending documents to be filed of record may prevent the return of unrecorded documents.

County clerks are required to record a paper or tangible copy of an electronic record that is otherwise eligible under state law to be recorded in the real property records if the paper or tangible copy of the electronic record—

1. contains an image of an electronic signature or signatures that are acknowledged, sworn to with a jurat, or proved according to law and
2. has been declared by a notary public or other officer who may take an acknowledgment or proof under section 121.001, Civil Practice and Remedies Code, to be a true and correct copy of the electronic record by (a) executing and attaching an official seal to a tangible paper declaration under penalty of perjury and (b) affixing or attaching the declaration to the printed paper or tangible copy of an electronic record.

The form of declaration by a notary public or other officer who may take an acknowledgment or proof under section 121.001, Civil Practice and Remedies Code, must be substantially as follows:

> DECLARATION OF AUTHENTICITY
>
> State of ____________
>
> County of ____________
>
> The attached document, ________________(insert title), dated ____________ and containing __ pages, is a true and correct copy of an electronic record printed by me or under my supervision. At the time of printing, no security features present on the electronic record indicated any changes or errors in an electronic signature or other information in the electronic record after the electronic record's creation or execution. This declaration is made under penalty of perjury.
>
> Signed this ____ day of ________, ____.
>
> ________________(signature of notary public or other officer)
>
> (seal of office)
>
> ______________(printed name of notary public or other officer)
>
> My commission expires: ____________

See Tex. Prop. Code § 12.0013.

Attorneys, licensed lenders, title companies, federal agencies and lenders, and state agencies may file documents electronically with county clerks. Tex. Loc. Gov't Code § 195.003. Rules for electronic filing have been adopted by the Texas State Library and Archives Commission and are found at 13 Tex. Admin. Code §§ 7.141–.145. *See* Tex. Loc. Gov't Code § 191.009. *See generally* Tex. Loc. Gov't Code ch. 195.

§ 3.16 Filing Fees

Filing fees of county clerks are usually computed per page. *See* Tex. Loc. Gov't Code § 118.011. The per-page filing fee is twice the usual amount if the first page of the document has no identifying heading, the page is not legible, any signature on a page appears without having the name legibly typed or printed beneath it, or a page is oversized. A page must be printed in no smaller than eight-point type. However, failure to meet the type-size requirement does not result in a fee increase or invalidate the recordation of the document. *See* Tex. Loc. Gov't Code §§ 118.0525, 191.007.

If a manuscript cover with legible marks (for example, the name of the attorney preparing the document) is affixed to a document delivered for recording, the clerk is authorized to charge the usual recording fee for the page. *See* Tex. Loc. Gov't Code § 118.011(a)(2).

Filing fees for a low- or moderate-income person buying or improving the person's residence with federal or state assistance may be waived on the county clerk's receipt of a commissioners court directive to waive such fees. A county clerk may have a list of approved grant or aid programs issued by that county's commissioners court, which provides the authorization for waiver of these fees. Tex. Loc. Gov't Code § 118.0135.

No additional fee may be charged for electronic filing. Tex. Loc. Gov't Code § 195.006. A county clerk may not impose requirements or fees for filing or recording a legal paper in addition to those prescribed by statute. Tex. Loc. Gov't Code § 191.007(a). Attorneys should consult, in advance, with the county clerk's office or website to determine applicable fee policies for the instrument(s) at issue.

§ 3.17 Confidentiality Notice

Section 11.008 of the Texas Property Code provides that an individual's Social Security number is not required and should not be included in a document presented for recording in the county clerk's office and that the county clerk does not obtain or maintain the Social Security numbers of individuals. *See* Tex. Prop. Code § 11.008(b). An instrument transferring an interest in real property to or from an individual, regardless of whether the document contains an individual's Social Security number or driver's license number, must include a notice that appears on the top of the first page of the instrument in twelve-point bold-faced type or twelve-point uppercase letters and reads substantially as follows:

> **Notice of confidentiality rights: If you are a natural person, you may remove or strike any or all of the following information from any instrument that transfers an interest in real property before it is filed for record in the public records: your Social Security number or your driver's license number.**

Tex. Prop. Code § 11.008(c).

An "instrument" is "a deed, deed of trust, or any other record recorded by a county clerk related to real property, including a mineral lease, a mechanic's lien, and the release of a mechanic's lien." Tex. Prop. Code § 11.008(a).

"The validity of an instrument as between the parties to the instrument and the notice provided by the instrument are not affected by a party's failure to include the notice required under Subsection (c)." Tex. Prop. Code § 11.008(d).

§ 3.18 Additional Resources

Hadaway, Nicole. "Online Notarizations and State Laws—When Can You Close Remotely?" In *Advanced Real Estate Law Course, 2019*. Austin: State Bar of Texas, 2019.

Haley, Steven C. "Material Alteration of Documents." In *Advanced Real Estate Law Course, 2009*. Austin: State Bar of Texas, 2009.

Johnson, James N. "Execution of Documents." In *Real Estate Law 101 Course, 2018*. Austin: State Bar of Texas, 2018.

Lewallen, Dawn. "eSignature Documents and Notarization: Drafting Considerations for eClosing Real Estate Transactions." In *Advanced Real Estate Drafting Course, 2018*. Austin: State Bar of Texas, 2018.

Melamed, Richard. "New Statutory Forms." In *Advanced Real Estate Drafting Course, 2020*. Austin: State Bar of Texas, 2020.

Melamed, Richard. "Plain Drafting of Real Estate Documents." In *Real Estate Law 101 Course, 2018*. Austin: State Bar of Texas, 2018.

Newsome, Kent. "Nine Rules for Drafting Shorter and Better Documents." In *Advanced Real Estate Drafting Course, 2019*. Austin: State Bar of Texas, 2019.

Schiess, Wayne. "Some Things Every Legal Drafter Should Know." In *Advanced Real Estate Drafting Course, 2007*. Austin: State Bar of Texas, 2007.

Tarver, Lewis T., Jr. "Writing for the Times." In *Advanced Real Estate Drafting Course, 2001*. Austin: State Bar of Texas, 2001.

Weller, Philip D. "Drafting 1.01." In *Advanced Real Estate Drafting Course, 2002*. Austin: State Bar of Texas, 2002.

———. "Perfect Notice." In *Advanced Real Estate Drafting Course, 2007*. Austin: State Bar of Texas, 2007.

Form 3-1

Document Components: Single Person

1. Party Designation

[**Name**], a single person,

2. Signature Block

____
[**Name**]

3. Certificate of Acknowledgment

3.A. Short-Form Certificate of Acknowledgment

STATE OF TEXAS

COUNTY OF [**county**]

This instrument was acknowledged before me on [**date**] by [**name**].

[SEAL]

____
[**Title of officer**]
My commission expires: [**date**]

3.B. Ordinary Certificate of Acknowledgment

STATE OF TEXAS

COUNTY OF [**county**]

Before me, [**name and title of officer**], on this day personally appeared [**name of acknowledger**], [known to me/proved to me on the oath of [**name of witness**]/proved to me through [**description of identity card or other document**]] to be the person whose name is subscribed to the foregoing instrument

and acknowledged to me that [he/she] executed the same for the purposes and consideration therein expressed.

Given under my hand and seal of office this [**specify**] day of [**month**], [**year**].

[SEAL]

____
[**Title of officer**]
My commission expires: [**date**]

Form 3-2

Document Components: Spouses

1. Party Designation

[**Name of spouse A**] and [**name of spouse B**], spouses,

2. Signature Block

____
[**Name of spouse A**]

____
[**Name of spouse B**]

3. Certificate of Acknowledgment

3.A. Short-Form Certificate of Acknowledgment

STATE OF TEXAS

COUNTY OF [**county**]

This instrument was acknowledged before me on [**date**] by [**name of spouse A**] and [**name of spouse B**].

[SEAL]

____
[**Title of officer**]
My commission expires: [**date**]

3.B. Ordinary Certificate of Acknowledgment

STATE OF TEXAS

COUNTY OF [**county**]

Before me, [**name and title of officer**], on this day personally appeared [**name of spouse A**] and [**name of spouse B**], [known to me/proved to me on the oath of [**name of witness**]/proved to me through [**description of identity card[s] or other document[s]**]] to be the persons whose names are subscribed to the foregoing instrument and acknowledged to me that they executed the same for the purposes and consideration therein expressed.

Given under my hand and seal of office this [**specify**] day of [**month**], [**year**].

[SEAL]

____

[**Title of officer**]
My commission expires: [**date**]

Form 3-3

Document Components: Natural Person—Nonhomestead

1. Party Designation

[**Name**], owning, occupying, and claiming other property as homestead,

2. Signature Block

____
[**Name**]

3. Certificate of Acknowledgment

3.A. Short-Form Certificate of Acknowledgment

STATE OF TEXAS

COUNTY OF [**county**]

This instrument was acknowledged before me on [**date**] by [**name**].

____

[SEAL] [**Title of officer**]
My commission expires: [**date**]

3.B. Ordinary Certificate of Acknowledgment

STATE OF TEXAS

COUNTY OF [**county**]

Before me, [**name and title of officer**], on this day personally appeared [**name of acknowledger**], [known to me/proved to me on the oath of [**name of witness**]/proved to me through [**description of identity card or other docu-ment**]] to be the person whose name is subscribed to the foregoing instrument

and acknowledged to me that [he/she] executed the same for the purposes and consideration therein expressed.

Given under my hand and seal of office this **[specify]** day of **[month]**, **[year]**.

[SEAL]

____

[Title of officer]
My commission expires: **[date]**

Form 3-4

Document Components: Multiple Persons—Nonhomestead

1. Party Designation

[Name] and **[name]**, each owning, occupying, and claiming other property as homestead,

2. Signature Block

____
[Name]

____
[Name]

3. Certificate of Acknowledgment

3.A. Short-Form Certificate of Acknowledgment

STATE OF TEXAS

COUNTY OF **[county]**

This instrument was acknowledged before me on **[date]** by **[name[s]]**.

[SEAL]

____
[Title of officer]
My commission expires: **[date]**

3.B. Ordinary Certificate of Acknowledgment

STATE OF TEXAS

COUNTY OF **[county]**

Before me, **[name and title of officer]**, on this day personally appeared **[name[s] of acknowledger[s]]**, [known to me/proved to me on the oath of [**name of witness**]/proved to me through [**description of identity card[s] or other document[s]**]] to be the persons whose names are subscribed to the foregoing instrument and acknowledged to me that they executed the same for the purposes and consideration therein expressed.

Given under my hand and seal of office this [**specify**] day of [**month**], [**year**].

[SEAL]

____
[**Title of officer**]
My commission expires: [**date**]

Form 3-5

Document Components: Spouses—Nonhomestead

1. Party Designation

[Name of spouse A] and **[name of spouse B]**, spouses, owning, occupying, and claiming other property as homestead,

2. Signature Block

____
[Name of spouse A]

____
[Name of spouse B]

3. Certificate of Acknowledgment

3.A. Short-Form Certificate of Acknowledgment

STATE OF TEXAS

COUNTY OF **[county]**

This instrument was acknowledged before me on **[date]** by **[name of spouse A]** and **[name of spouse B]**.

[SEAL]

____
[Title of officer]
My commission expires: **[date]**

3.B. Ordinary Certificate of Acknowledgment

STATE OF TEXAS

COUNTY OF **[county]**

Before me, **[name and title of officer]**, on this day personally appeared **[name of spouse A]** and **[name of spouse B]**, [known to me/proved to me on the oath of **[name of witness]**/proved to me through **[description of identity card[s] or other document[s]]**] to be the persons whose names are subscribed to the foregoing instrument and acknowledged to me that they executed the same for the purposes and consideration therein expressed.

Given under my hand and seal of office this **[specify]** day of **[month]**, **[year]**.

[SEAL]

____
[Title of officer]
My commission expires: **[date]**

Form 3-6

Document Components: Married Person—Separate Property

1. ***Party Designation***

[**Name**], spouse of [**name**], dealing with [**include if applicable:** nonhomestead] separate property,

2. ***Signature Block***

____
[**Name**]

3. ***Certificate of Acknowledgment***

3.A. ***Short-Form Certificate of Acknowledgment***

STATE OF TEXAS

COUNTY OF [**county**]

This instrument was acknowledged before me on [**date**] by [**name**].

[SEAL]

____
[**Title of officer**]
My commission expires: [**date**]

3.B. ***Ordinary Certificate of Acknowledgment***

STATE OF TEXAS

COUNTY OF [**county**]

Before me, [**name and title of officer**], on this day personally appeared [**name of acknowledger**], [known to me/proved to me on the oath of [**name of witness**]/proved to me through [**description of identity card or other document**]] to be the person whose name is subscribed to the foregoing instrument

and acknowledged to me that [he/she] executed the same for the purposes and consideration therein expressed.

Given under my hand and seal of office this [**specify**] day of [**month**], [**year**].

[SEAL]

____
[**Title of officer**]
My commission expires: [**date**]

Form 3-7

Document Components: Natural Person—Assumed Name

1. Party Designation

[**Name**], d/b/a [**assumed name**],

2. Signature Block

____
[**Name**]

3. Certificate of Acknowledgment

3.A. Short-Form Certificate of Acknowledgment

STATE OF TEXAS

COUNTY OF [**county**]

This instrument was acknowledged before me on [**date**] by [**name**] doing business as [**assumed name**].

[SEAL]

____
[**Title of officer**]
My commission expires: [**date**]

3.B. Ordinary Certificate of Acknowledgment

STATE OF TEXAS

COUNTY OF [**county**]

Before me, [**name and title of officer**], on this day personally appeared [**name of acknowledger**], [known to me/proved to me on the oath of [**name of witness**]/proved to me through [**description of identity card or other docu-ment**]] to be the person whose name is subscribed to the foregoing instrument and acknowledged to me that [he/she] does business as [**assumed name**] and executed the same for the purposes and consideration therein expressed.

Given under my hand and seal of office this [**specify**] day of [**month**], [**year**].

[SEAL]

____
[**Title of officer**]
My commission expires: [**date**]

Form 3-8

Document Components: Natural Person by Attorney-in-Fact

1. Party Designation

[**Name of principal**], acting by [**name of attorney-in-fact**], attorney-in-fact,

2. Signature Block

[**Name of principal**]

____

[**Name of attorney-in-fact**], attorney-in-fact

3. Certificate of Acknowledgment

3.A. Short-Form Certificate of Acknowledgment

STATE OF TEXAS

COUNTY OF [**county**]

This instrument was acknowledged before me on [**date**] by [**name of attorney-in-fact**] as attorney-in-fact on behalf of [**name of principal**].

[SEAL]

____

[**Title of officer**]
My commission expires: [**date**]

3.B. Ordinary Certificate of Acknowledgment

STATE OF TEXAS

COUNTY OF [**county**]

Before me, [**name and title of officer**], on this day personally appeared [**name of attorney-in-fact**], [known to me/proved to me on the oath of [**name of**

witness]/proved to me through [**description of identity card or other document**]] to be the person whose name is subscribed to the foregoing instrument and acknowledged to me that [he/she] executed the same on behalf of [**name of principal**] as attorney-in-fact of [**name of principal**] for the purposes and consideration therein expressed.

Given under my hand and seal of office this [**specify**] day of [**month**], [**year**].

[SEAL]

____
[**Title of officer**]
My commission expires: [**date**]

Form 3-9

Document Components: General Partnership—Individual Partner

1. Party Designation

[**Name of partnership**], a [**state of formation**] general partnership,

2. Signature Block

[**Name of partnership**]

By:______________________________
[**Name of partner**], partner

3. Certificate of Acknowledgment

3.A. Short-Form Certificate of Acknowledgment

STATE OF TEXAS

COUNTY OF [**county**]

This instrument was acknowledged before me on [**date**] by [**name of acknowledging partner**], partner, on behalf of [**name of partnership**], a [**state of formation**] general partnership.

[SEAL]

____
[**Title of officer**]
My commission expires: [**date**]

3.B. Ordinary Certificate of Acknowledgment

STATE OF TEXAS

COUNTY OF [**county**]

Before me, [**name and title of officer**], on this day personally appeared [**name of acknowledging partner**], [known to me/proved to me on the oath of [**name of witness**]/proved to me through [**description of identity card or other document**]] to be the person whose name is subscribed to the foregoing instrument and acknowledged to me that [he/she] executed the same as the act of [**name of partnership**], a [**state of formation**] general partnership, as partner, for the purposes and consideration therein expressed.

Given under my hand and seal of office this [**specify**] day of [**month**], [**year**].

[SEAL]

____
[**Title of officer**]
My commission expires: [**date**]

Form 3-10

Document Components: General Partnership—Composition of Partners

1. Party Designation

[Name of partnership], a **[state of formation]** general partnership composed of **[names]**,

2. Signature Block

[Name of partnership]

By:_____________________________
[Name of partner], partner

By:_____________________________
[Name of partner], partner

3. Certificate of Acknowledgment

3.A. Short-Form Certificate of Acknowledgment

STATE OF TEXAS

COUNTY OF **[county]**

This instrument was acknowledged before me on **[date]** by **[name[s] of acknowledging partner[s]]**, partner[s], on behalf of **[name of partnership]**, a **[state of formation]** general partnership.

____

[SEAL] **[Title of officer]**
My commission expires: **[date]**

3.B. Ordinary Certificate of Acknowledgment

STATE OF TEXAS

COUNTY OF **[county]**

Before me, **[name and title of officer]**, on this day personally appeared **[name[s] of acknowledging partner[s]]**, [known to me/proved to me on the oath of [**name of witness**]/proved to me through **[description of identity card[s] or other document[s]]**] to be the person[s] whose name[s] [is/are] subscribed to the foregoing instrument and acknowledged to me that [he/she/they] executed the same as partner[s] as the act of **[name of partnership]**, a **[state of formation]** general partnership, for the purposes and consideration therein expressed.

Given under my hand and seal of office this **[specify]** day of **[month]**, **[year]**.

[SEAL]

____
[Title of officer]
My commission expires: **[date]**

Form 3-11

Document Components: Limited Partnership—Individual General Partner

1. Party Designation

[**Name of limited partnership**], a [**state of formation**] limited partnership,

2. Signature Block

[**Name of limited partnership**]

By:______________________________
[**Name of partner**], general partner of
[**name of limited partnership**]

3. Certificate of Acknowledgment

3.A. Short-Form Certificate of Acknowledgment

STATE OF TEXAS

COUNTY OF [**county**]

This instrument was acknowledged before me on [**date**] by [**name of general partner**], general partner, on behalf of [**name of limited partnership**], a [**state of formation**] limited partnership.

[SEAL]

____
[**Title of officer**]
My commission expires: [**date**]

3.B. Ordinary Certificate of Acknowledgment

STATE OF TEXAS

COUNTY OF [**county**]

Before me, [**name and title of officer**], on this day personally appeared [**name of general partner**], [known to me/proved to me on the oath of [**name of witness**]/proved to me through [**description of identity card or other document**]] to be the person whose name is subscribed to the foregoing instrument and acknowledged to me that [he/she] executed the same as the act of [**name of limited partnership**], a [**state of formation**] limited partnership, as its general partner, for the purposes and consideration therein expressed.

Given under my hand and seal of office this [**specify**] day of [**month**], [**year**].

[SEAL]

____

[**Title of officer**]
My commission expires: [**date**]

Form 3-12

Document Components: Limited Partnership—Entity General Partner

1. Party Designation

[**Name of limited partnership**], a [**state of formation**] limited partnership,

2. Signature Block

[**Name of limited partnership**]

By:______________________________
[**Name and title of officer or agent for general partner**]

3. Certificate of Acknowledgment

3.A. Short-Form Certificate of Acknowledgment

STATE OF TEXAS

COUNTY OF [**county**]

This instrument was acknowledged before me on [**date**] by [**name of acknowledger**], [**title**] of [**name of general partner**], a [**state of formation**] [**type of entity**] general partner, on behalf of [**name of limited partnership**], a [**state of formation**] limited partnership.

[SEAL]

____
[**Title of officer**]
My commission expires: [**date**]

3.B. Ordinary Certificate of Acknowledgment

STATE OF TEXAS

COUNTY OF **[county]**

Before me, **[name and title of officer]**, on this day personally appeared **[name of acknowledger]**, [known to me/proved to me on the oath of **[name of witness]**/proved to me through **[description of identity card or other document]**] to be the person whose name is subscribed to the foregoing instrument and acknowledged to me that [he/she] executed the same as **[title]** of **[name of general partner]**, a **[state of formation]** **[type of entity]** general partner, as the act of **[name of limited partnership]**, a **[state of formation]** limited partnership, for the purposes and consideration therein expressed.

Given under my hand and seal of office this **[specify]** day of **[month]**, **[year]**.

[SEAL]

____
[Title of officer]
My commission expires: **[date]**

Form 3-13

Document Components: Joint Venture—Individual Venturer

1. Party Designation

[**Name of venture**], a [**state of formation**] joint venture,

2. Signature Block

[**Name of venture**]

By:______________________________
[**Name of venturer**], joint venturer

3. Certificate of Acknowledgment

3.A. Short-Form Certificate of Acknowledgment

STATE OF TEXAS

COUNTY OF [**county**]

This instrument was acknowledged before me on [**date**] by [**name of acknowledging venturer**], joint venturer, on behalf of [**name of venture**], a [**state of formation**] joint venture.

[SEAL]

____
[**Title of officer**]
My commission expires: [**date**]

3.B. Ordinary Certificate of Acknowledgment

STATE OF TEXAS

COUNTY OF [**county**]

Before me, [**name and title of officer**], on this day personally appeared [**name of acknowledging venturer**], [known to me/proved to me on the oath of [**name of witness**]/proved to me through [**description of identity card or other document**]] to be the person whose name is subscribed to the foregoing instrument and acknowledged to me that [he/she] executed the same as the act of [**name of venture**], a [**state of formation**] joint venture, as joint venturer, for the purposes and consideration therein expressed.

Given under my hand and seal of office this [**specify**] day of [**month**], [**year**].

[SEAL]

____
[**Title of officer**]
My commission expires: [**date**]

Form 3-14

Document Components: Joint Venture—Composition of Venturers

1. *Party Designation*

[**Name of venture**], a [**state of formation**] joint venture composed of [**names of joint venturers**],

2. *Signature Block*

[**Name of venture**]

By:______________________________
[**Name of joint venturer**], joint venturer

By:______________________________
[**Name of joint venturer**], joint venturer

3. *Certificate of Acknowledgment*

3.A. *Short-Form Certificate of Acknowledgment*

STATE OF TEXAS

COUNTY OF [**county**]

This instrument was acknowledged before me on [**date**] by [**name[s] of venturer[s]**], joint venturer[s], on behalf of [**name of venture**], a [**state of formation**] joint venture.

[SEAL]

____
[**Title of officer**]
My commission expires: [**date**]

3.B. *Ordinary Certificate of Acknowledgment*

STATE OF TEXAS

COUNTY OF [**county**]

Before me, [**name and title of officer**], on this day personally appeared [**name[s] of joint venturer[s]**], [known to me/proved to me on the oath of [**name of witness**]/proved to me through [**description of identity card[s] or other document[s]**]] to be the person[s] whose name[s] [is/are] subscribed to the foregoing instrument and acknowledged to me that [he/she/they] executed the same as the act of [**name of venture**], a [**state of formation**] joint venture, as joint venturer[s], for the purposes and consideration therein expressed.

Given under my hand and seal of office this [**specify**] day of [**month**], [**year**].

[SEAL]

____
[**Title of officer**]
My commission expires: [**date**]

Form 3-15

Document Components: Corporation

1. Party Designation

[**Name of corporation**], a [**state of formation**] corporation,

2. Signature Block

[**Name of corporation**]

By:______________________________

[**Name and title of corporate officer or agent**]

3. Certificate of Acknowledgment

3.A. Short-Form Certificate of Acknowledgment

STATE OF TEXAS

COUNTY OF [**county**]

This instrument was acknowledged before me on [**date**] by [**name of corporate officer or agent**], as the [**title of corporate officer or agent**] of [**name of corporation**], a [**state of formation**] corporation, on behalf of said corporation.

[SEAL]

____
[**Title of officer**]
My commission expires: [**date**]

3.B. Ordinary Certificate of Acknowledgment

STATE OF TEXAS

COUNTY OF [**county**]

Before me, [**name and title of officer**], on this day personally appeared [**name of corporate officer or agent**], [known to me/proved to me on the oath of [**name of witness**]/proved to me through [**description of identity card or other document**]] to be the person whose name is subscribed to the foregoing instrument and acknowledged to me that [he/she] executed the same as the act of [**name of corporation**], a [**state of formation**] corporation, as its [**title of corporate officer or agent**], for the purposes and consideration therein expressed.

Given under my hand and seal of office this [**specify**] day of [**month**], [**year**].

[SEAL]

____
[**Title of officer**]
My commission expires: [**date**]

Form 3-16

Document Components: Nonprofit Corporation

1. Party Designation

[**Name of corporation**], a [**state of formation**] nonprofit corporation,

2. Signature Block

[**Name of corporation**]

By:______________________________
[**Name and title of corporate officer or agent**]

3. Certificate of Acknowledgment

3.A. Short-Form Certificate of Acknowledgment

STATE OF TEXAS

COUNTY OF [**county**]

This instrument was acknowledged before me on [**date**] by [**name and title of corporate officer or agent**], of [**name of corporation**], a [**state of formation**] nonprofit corporation, on behalf of said nonprofit corporation.

[SEAL]

____
[**Title of officer**]
My commission expires: [**date**]

3.B. Ordinary Certificate of Acknowledgment

STATE OF TEXAS

COUNTY OF [**county**]

Before me, [**name and title of officer**], on this day personally appeared [**name of corporate officer or agent**], [known to me/proved to me on the oath of [**name of witness**]/proved to me through [**description of identity card or other document**]] to be the person whose name is subscribed to the foregoing instrument and acknowledged to me that [he/she] executed the same as the act of [**name of corporation**], a [**state of formation**] nonprofit corporation, as its [**title of corporate officer or agent**], for the purposes and consideration therein expressed.

Given under my hand and seal of office this [**specify**] day of [**month**], [**year**].

____

[SEAL] [**Title of officer**]
My commission expires: [**date**]

Form 3-17

Document Components: Trustee—Individual

1. Party Designation

[Name of trustee], trustee of the **[name of trust]** trust under an instrument dated **[date]**, recorded in **[recording data of trust]** of the real property records of **[county]** County, Texas,

2. Signature Block

____

[Name of trustee], trustee of the **[name of trust]** trust

3. Certificate of Acknowledgment

3.A. Short-Form Certificate of Acknowledgment

STATE OF TEXAS

COUNTY OF **[county]**

This instrument was acknowledged before me on **[date]** by **[name of trustee]**, as trustee of **[name of trust]**.

____

[SEAL]

[Title of officer]
My commission expires: **[date]**

3.B. Ordinary Certificate of Acknowledgment

STATE OF TEXAS

COUNTY OF [**county**]

Before me, [**name and title of officer**], on this day personally appeared [**name of trustee**], [known to me/proved to me on the oath of [**name of witness**]/proved to me through [**description of identity card or other document**]] to be the person whose name is subscribed to the foregoing instrument and acknowledged to me that [he/she] executed the same by proper authority as trustee of [**name of trust**], on behalf of said trust, for the purposes and consideration therein expressed.

Given under my hand and seal of office this [**specify**] day of [**month**], [**year**].

[SEAL]

____
[**Title of officer**]
My commission expires: [**date**]

Form 3-18

Document Components: Trustee—Entity

1. *Party Designation*

[Name of trustee], a **[state of formation]** **[type of entity]**, as trustee for the **[name of trust]** trust under an instrument dated **[date]**, recorded in **[recording data of trust]** of the real property records of **[county]** County, Texas,

2. *Signature Block*

[Name of trust]

By:______________________________
[Name and title of trustee's agent]

3. *Certificate of Acknowledgment*

3.A. *Short-Form Certificate of Acknowledgment*

STATE OF TEXAS

COUNTY OF **[county]**

This instrument was acknowledged before me on **[date]** by **[name of trustee's agent]**, as **[title of trustee's agent]** of **[name of trustee]**, a **[state of formation]** **[type of entity]**, as the trustee of **[name of trust]**.

____

[SEAL] **[Title of officer]**
My commission expires: **[date]**

3.B. Ordinary Certificate of Acknowledgment

STATE OF TEXAS

COUNTY OF [**county**]

Before me, [**name and title of officer**], on this day personally appeared [**name of trustee's agent**], [known to me/proved to me on the oath of [**name of witness**]/proved to me through [**description of identity card or other document**]] to be the person whose name is subscribed to the foregoing instrument and acknowledged to me that [he/she] executed the same as [**title of trustee's agent**] of [**name of trustee**], a [**state of formation**] [**type of entity**], by proper authority as the trustee of [**name of trust**], on behalf of said trust, for the purposes and consideration therein expressed.

Given under my hand and seal of office this [**specify**] day of [**month**], [**year**].

[SEAL]

____
[**Title of officer**]
My commission expires: [**date**]

Form 3-19

Document Components: Trustee—Testamentary

1. *Party Designation*

[Name of individual trustee] and **[name of bank trustee]**, testamentary trustees under the will of **[name of decedent]**, probated in **[county]** County, Texas,

2. *Signature Block*

____

[Name of individual trustee], testamentary trustee under the will of **[name of decedent]**, probated in **[county]** County, Texas

____

[Name of bank officer], as **[title of bank officer]** of **[name of bank trustee]**, testamentary trustee under the will of **[name of decedent]**, probated in **[county]** County, Texas

3. *Certificate of Acknowledgment*

3.A. *Short-Form Certificate of Acknowledgment*

STATE OF TEXAS

COUNTY OF **[county]**

This instrument was acknowledged before me on **[date]** by **[name of individual trustee]** and **[name of bank officer]**, as **[title of bank officer]** of **[name of bank trustee]**, the testamentary trustees under the will of **[name of decedent]**, probated in **[county]** County, Texas.

____

[SEAL] **[Title of officer]**
My commission expires: **[date]**

3.B. Ordinary Certificate of Acknowledgment

STATE OF TEXAS

COUNTY OF **[county]**

Before me, **[name and title of officer]**, on this day personally appeared **[name of individual trustee]** and **[name of bank officer]**, as **[title of bank officer]** of **[name of bank trustee]**, [known to me/proved to me on the oath of **[name of witness]**/proved to me through **[description of identity card[s] or other document[s]]**] to be the persons whose names are subscribed to the foregoing instrument and acknowledged to me that they executed the same by proper authority as testamentary trustees under the will of **[name of decedent]**, probated in **[county]** County, Texas, on behalf of said testamentary trust, for the purposes and consideration therein expressed.

Given under my hand and seal of office this **[specify]** day of **[month]**, **[year]**.

____

[SEAL] **[Title of officer]**
My commission expires: **[date]**

Form 3-20

Document Components: Decedent's Estate—Personal Representative

1. Party Designation

[**Name of personal representative**], [**title of personal representative**] of the estate of [**name of decedent**], deceased,

2. Signature Block

____
[**Name of personal representative**], [**title of personal representative**] of the estate of [**name of decedent**], deceased

3. Certificate of Acknowledgment

3.A. Short-Form Certificate of Acknowledgment

STATE OF TEXAS

COUNTY OF [**county**]

This instrument was acknowledged before me on [**date**] by [**name of personal representative**], as [**title of personal representative**] of the estate of [**name of decedent**], deceased.

[SEAL]

____
[**Title of officer**]
My commission expires: [**date**]

3.B. Ordinary Certificate of Acknowledgment

STATE OF TEXAS

COUNTY OF **[county]**

Before me, **[name and title of officer]**, on this day personally appeared **[name of personal representative]**, [known to me/proved to me on the oath of **[name of witness]**/proved to me through **[description of identity card or other document]**] to be the person whose name is subscribed to the foregoing instrument and acknowledged to me that [he/she] executed the same by proper authority as **[title of personal representative]**, on behalf of the estate of **[name of decedent]**, deceased, for the purposes and consideration therein expressed.

Given under my hand and seal of office this **[specify]** day of **[month]**, **[year]**.

[SEAL]

____
[Title of officer]
My commission expires: **[date]**

Form 3-21

Document Components: Decedent's Estate by Personal Representative Also Signing Individually

1. *Party Designation*

[**Name of personal representative**], individually and as [**title of personal representative**] of the estate of [**name of decedent**], deceased,

2. *Signature Block*

____

[**Name of personal representative**],
individually and as [**title of personal representative**] of the estate of [**name of decedent**], deceased

3. *Certificate of Acknowledgment*

3.A. *Short-Form Certificate of Acknowledgment*

STATE OF TEXAS

COUNTY OF [**county**]

This instrument was acknowledged before me on [**date**] by [**name of personal representative**], individually and as [**title of personal representative**] for the estate of [**name of decedent**], deceased.

[SEAL]

____

[**Title of officer**]
My commission expires: [**date**]

3.B. Ordinary Certificate of Acknowledgment

STATE OF TEXAS

COUNTY OF [**county**]

Before me, [**name and title of officer**], on this day personally appeared [**name of personal representative**], [known to me/proved to me on the oath of [**name of witness**]/proved to me through [**description of identity card or other document**]] to be the person whose name is subscribed to the foregoing instrument and acknowledged to me that [he/she] executed the same individually and by proper authority as [**title of personal representative**], on behalf of the estate of [**name of decedent**], deceased, for the purposes and consideration therein expressed.

Given under my hand and seal of office this [**specify**] day of [**month**], [**year**].

[SEAL]

____
[**Title of officer**]
My commission expires: [**date**]

Form 3-22

Document Components: Guardian for Ward

1. Party Designation

[Name of guardian], guardian of the **[include if applicable:** person and] estate of **[name of ward]**, an incapacitated person,

2. Signature Block

____
[Name of guardian], guardian of the **[include if applicable:** person and] estate of **[name of ward]**, an incapacitated person

3. Certificate of Acknowledgment

3.A. Short-Form Certificate of Acknowledgment

STATE OF TEXAS

COUNTY OF **[county]**

This instrument was acknowledged before me on **[date]** by **[name of guardian]** as guardian of the **[include if applicable:** person and] estate of **[name of ward]**, an incapacitated person.

[SEAL]

____
[Title of officer]
My commission expires: **[date]**

3.B. Ordinary Certificate of Acknowledgment

STATE OF TEXAS

COUNTY OF [**county**]

Before me, [**name and title of officer**], on this day personally appeared [**name of guardian**], [known to me/proved to me on the oath of [**name of witness**]/proved to me through [**description of identity card or other document**]] to be the person whose name is subscribed to the foregoing instrument and acknowledged to me that [he/she] executed the same on behalf of [**name of ward**], an incapacitated person, as guardian of the [**include if applicable:** person and] estate of [**name of ward**], for the purposes and consideration therein expressed.

Given under my hand and seal of office this [**specify**] day of [**month**], [**year**].

[SEAL]

____
[**Title of officer**]
My commission expires: [**date**]

Form 3-23

Document Components: Custodian for Minor under Uniform Transfers to Minors Act

1. Party Designation

[**Name of custodian**], custodian for [**name of minor**], a minor, under the Texas Uniform Transfers to Minors Act,

2. Signature Block

____
[**Name of custodian**], custodian for
[**name of minor**]

3. Certificate of Acknowledgment

3.A. Short-Form Certificate of Acknowledgment

STATE OF TEXAS

COUNTY OF [**county**]

This instrument was acknowledged before me on [**date**] by [**name of custodian**] as custodian for [**name of minor**], a minor, under the Texas Uniform Transfers to Minors Act.

[SEAL]

____
[**Title of officer**]
My commission expires: [**date**]

3.B. Ordinary Certificate of Acknowledgment

STATE OF TEXAS

COUNTY OF [**county**]

Before me, [**name and title of officer**], on this day personally appeared [**name of custodian**], [known to me/proved to me on the oath of [**name of witness**]/proved to me through [**description of identity card or other document**]] to be the person whose name is subscribed to the foregoing instrument and acknowledged to me that [he/she] executed the same on behalf of [**name of minor**], a minor, as custodian under the Texas Uniform Transfers to Minors Act, for the purposes and consideration therein expressed.

Given under my hand and seal of office this [**specify**] day of [**month**], [**year**].

[SEAL]

____
[**Title of officer**]
My commission expires: [**date**]

Form 3-24

Document Components: Entity

1. Party Designation

[**Name of entity**], a [**state of formation**] [**type of entity**],

2. Signature Block

[**Name of entity**]

By:______________________________
[**Name and title of officer or agent**]

3. Certificate of Acknowledgment

> No short-form certificate of acknowledgment is provided by statute for entities other than corporations or partnerships. The following is the ordinary certificate of acknowledgment modified for other types of entities.

STATE OF TEXAS

COUNTY OF [**county**]

Before me, [**name and title of officer**], on this day personally appeared [**name of entity's officer or agent**], [known to me/proved to me on the oath of [**name of witness**]/proved to me through [**description of identity card or other document**]] to be the person whose name is subscribed to the foregoing instrument and acknowledged to me that [he/she] executed the same as the act of [**name of entity**], a [**state of formation**] [**type of entity**], as its [**title of entity's officer or agent**], for the purposes and consideration therein expressed.

Given under my hand and seal of office this [**specify**] day of [**month**], [**year**].

[SEAL]

____
[Title of officer]
My commission expires: **[date]**

Form 3-25

Document Components: Entity with Assumed Name

1. Party Designation

[Name of entity], a **[state of formation]** **[type of entity]**, d/b/a **[assumed name]**,

2. Signature Block

[Name of entity]

By:______________________________
[Name and title of entity's officer or agent]

3. Certificate of Acknowledgment

3.A. Short-Form Certificate of Acknowledgment

> By statute, a short-form certificate of acknowledgment can be used only if the entity is a corporation or partnership.

STATE OF TEXAS

COUNTY OF **[county]**

This instrument was acknowledged before me on **[date]** by **[name of entity's officer or agent]** as **[title of entity's officer or agent]** of **[name of entity]**, a **[state of formation]** [corporation/partnership], d/b/a **[assumed name]**, on behalf of said [corporation/partnership].

[SEAL]

____
[Title of officer]
My commission expires: **[date]**

3.B. Ordinary Certificate of Acknowledgment

STATE OF TEXAS

COUNTY OF **[county]**

Before me, **[name and title of officer]**, on this day personally appeared **[name of entity's officer or agent]**, [known to me/proved to me on the oath of **[name of witness]**/proved to me through **[description of identity card or other document]**] to be the person whose name is subscribed to the foregoing instrument and acknowledged to me that [he/she] executed the same as the act of **[name of entity]**, a **[state of formation]** **[type of entity]**, d/b/a **[assumed name]**, as its **[title of entity's officer or agent]**, for the purposes and consideration therein expressed.

Given under my hand and seal of office this **[specify]** day of **[month]**, **[year]**.

[SEAL]

____
[Title of officer]
My commission expires: **[date]**

Form 3-26

Document Components: Cooperative

1. ***Party Designation***

[**Name of cooperative**], a [**state of formation**] cooperative association,

2. ***Signature Block***

[**Name of cooperative**]

By:______________________________
[**Name and title of officer**]

3. ***Certificate of Acknowledgment***

No short-form certificate of acknowledgment is provided by statute for a cooperative. The following is the ordinary certificate of acknowledgment modified for a cooperative.

STATE OF TEXAS

COUNTY OF [**county**]

Before me, [**name and title of officer**], on this day personally appeared [**name of officer of cooperative**], [known to me/proved to me on the oath of [**name of witness**]/proved to me through [**description of identity card or other document**]] to be the person whose name is subscribed to the foregoing instrument and acknowledged to me that [he/she] executed the same as the act of [**name of cooperative**], a [**state of formation**] cooperative association, as its [**title of officer of cooperative**], for the purposes and consideration therein expressed.

Given under my hand and seal of office this [**specify**] day of [**month**], [**year**].

____

[SEAL] **[Title of officer]**
My commission expires: **[date]**

Form 3-27

Document Components: Unincorporated Association—Statement of Authority

1. *Party Designation*

[Name of association], an unincorporated association, by and through **[name of authorized person]**, acting under the statement of authority recorded in **[recording data]** of the real property records of **[county]** County, Texas,

2. *Signature Block*

[Name of association]

By:______________________________
[Name of authorized person], acting under the statement of authority recorded in **[recording data]** of the real property records of **[county]** County,Texas

3. *Signature Block*

[Name of association], an unincorporated association,

____

4. *Certificate of Acknowledgment*

No short-form certificate of acknowledgment is provided by statute for an unincorporated association. The following is the ordinary certificate of acknowledgment modified for an unincorporated association.

STATE OF TEXAS

COUNTY OF **[county]**

Before me, **[name and title of officer]**, on this day personally appeared **[name of authorized person]**, [known to me/proved to me on the oath of **[name of witness]**/proved to me through **[description of identity card or other document]**] to be the person whose name is subscribed to the foregoing instrument and acknowledged to me that [he/she] executed the same as the act of **[name of association]**, an unincorporated association, under the statement of authority recorded in **[recording data]** of the real property records of **[county]** County, Texas, for the purposes and consideration therein expressed.

Given under my hand and seal of office this **[specify]** day of **[month]**, **[year]**.

[SEAL]

____
[Title of officer]
My commission expires: **[date]**

Form 3-28

Document Components: Unincorporated Association—Trustees

1. *Party Designation*

[**Names of trustees**], trustees for [**name of association**], an unincorporated association,

2. *Signature Block*

[**Name of association**], an unincorporated association,

____
[**Name of trustee**], trustee

____
[**Name of trustee**], trustee

3. *Certificate of Acknowledgment*

> No short-form certificate of acknowledgment is provided by statute for an unincorporated association. The following is the ordinary certificate of acknowledgment modified for an unincorporated association.

STATE OF TEXAS

COUNTY OF [**county**]

Before me, [**name and title of officer**], on this day personally appeared [**names of trustees**], [known to me/proved to me on the oath of [**name of witness**]/proved to me through [**description of identity card[s] or other document[s]**]] to be the persons whose names are subscribed to the foregoing instrument and acknowledged to me that they executed the same as the act of [**name of association**], an unincorporated association, as its trustees, for the purposes and consideration therein expressed.

Given under my hand and seal of office this [**specify**] day of [**month**], [**year**].

____

[SEAL]

[**Title of officer**]
My commission expires: [**date**]

Form 3-29

Statutory Form for Ordinary Certificate of Acknowledgment

STATE OF TEXAS

COUNTY OF [**county**]

Before me, [**name and title of officer**], on this day personally appeared [**name of acknowledger**], [known to me/proved to me on the oath of [**name of witness**]/proved to me through [**description of identity card or other document**]] to be the person whose name is subscribed to the foregoing instrument and acknowledged to me that [he/she] executed the same for the purposes and consideration therein expressed.

Given under my hand and seal of office this [**specify**] day of [**month**], [**year**].

[SEAL]

____
[**Title of officer**]
My commission expires: [**date**]

Form 3-30

This form is based on sample language containing minimum statutory requirements provided by the Texas secretary of state at **www.sos.state.tx.us/statdoc/online-np-educational.shtml#sample**.

Electronic Certificate of Acknowledgment

[Long Form]

STATE OF TEXAS

COUNTY OF [**county**]

Before me, [**name of notary or other officer taking acknowledgment**], on this day personally appeared by means of an interactive two-way audio and video communication [**name of acknowledging party**], who [is known to me/proved to me on the oath of [**name of witness**]/has provided satisfactory evidence of identity in accordance with chapter 406, Texas Government Code] to be the person whose name is subscribed to the foregoing instrument and acknowledged to me that [he/she] executed the same for the purposes and consideration therein expressed. This notarial act was an online notarization.

Given under my hand and seal of office this [**specify**] day of [**month**], [**year**].

[SEAL]

[Digital Certificate]

____
[**Title of officer**]
My commission expires: [**date**]

Form 3-31

This form is based on sample language containing minimum statutory requirements provided by the Texas secretary of state at **www.sos.state.tx.us/statdoc/online-np-educational.shtml#sample**.

Electronic Certificate of Acknowledgment

[Short Form]

STATE OF TEXAS

COUNTY OF **[county]**

This instrument was acknowledged before me by means of an interactive two-way audio and video communication on **[date]** by **[name[s] of person[s] acknowledging]**. This notarial act was an online notarization.

[SEAL]

[Digital Certificate]

____
[Title of officer]
My commission expires: **[date]**

Form 3-32

Acknowledgment by Foreign Service Officer

[**Name of country**]

[**County and/or other political subdivision**]

[**City and/or other political subdivision**]

[**Name of foreign service office**]

Before me, [**name, rank, and title of foreign service officer**], of the United States of America at [**city and country**], duly commissioned and qualified and a resident of [**city and country**], on this day personally appeared [**name of acknowledger**], [known to me/proved to me on the oath of [**name of witness**]/proved to me through [**description of identity card or other document**]] to be the person whose name is subscribed to the foregoing instrument and acknowledged to me that [he/she] executed the same for the purposes and consideration therein expressed.

Given under my hand and seal of office this [**specify**] day of [**month**], [**year**].

[SEAL]

____

[**Name, rank, and title of foreign service officer**]

Form 3-33

Military Acknowledgment

IN THE ARMED FORCES OF THE UNITED STATES OF AMERICA with the [**branch of military**] at [**name of base or post**], [**include if applicable: [city and state],**] [**country**].

Before me, [**name, rank, branch, and serial number of officer in U.S. armed forces**], a duly commissioned officer in [the Armed Forces/[**specify auxiliary to armed forces**]] of the United States of America at [**city and country**], on this day personally appeared [**name of acknowledger**], [**include if applicable:** the spouse of [**name, rank, branch, and serial number of military personnel**]], [known to me/proved to me on the oath of [**name, rank, branch, and serial number of witness**], a member of [the Armed Forces/[**specify auxiliary to armed forces**]] of the United States of America/proved to me through [**description of identity card or other document**]] to be the person whose name is subscribed to the foregoing instrument and acknowledged to me that [he/she] executed the same for the purposes and consideration therein expressed.

Given under my hand and seal of office this [**specify**] day of [**month**], [**year**].

[SEAL]

____
[**Name, rank, branch, and serial number of officer**]

Form 3-34

Statement of Subscribing Witness in Presence of Subscriber

STATE OF TEXAS

COUNTY OF [county]

Before me, [name and title of officer taking proof], on this day personally appeared [name of subscribing witness], [known to me/proved to me on the oath of [name of witness]] to be the person whose name is subscribed as a witness to the foregoing instrument of writing, and after being duly sworn by me, stated on oath that [he/she] saw [name], the [grantor/person who executed the foregoing instrument], subscribe the same and that [he/she] had signed the same as a witness at the request of the [grantor/person who executed same].

Given under my hand and seal of office this [specify] day of [month], [year].

[SEAL]

____
[Title of officer]
My commission expires: [date]

Form 3-35

Statement of Subscribing Witness on Acknowledgment by Subscriber

STATE OF TEXAS

COUNTY OF **[county]**

Before me, **[name and title of officer]**, on this day personally appeared **[name of subscribing witness]**, [known to me/proved to me on the oath of **[name of witness]**] to be the person whose name is subscribed as a witness to the foregoing instrument of writing, and after being duly sworn by me, stated on oath that **[name]**, the [grantor/person who executed the foregoing instrument], acknowledged in [his/her] presence that the [grantor/person who executed same] had executed the same for the purposes and consideration expressed therein and that [he/she] had signed the same as a witness at the request of the [grantor/person who executed same].

Given under my hand and seal of office this **[specify]** day of **[month]**, **[year]**.

[SEAL]

____
[Title of officer]
My commission expires: **[date]**

Form 3-36

Acknowledgment of Signature Affixed at Direction of Person with Disability

STATE OF TEXAS

COUNTY OF [**county**]

Before me, [**name and title of officer**], on this day personally appeared [**name of person with disability**], a person having a physical impairment that impedes [his/her] ability to sign the foregoing instrument, [known to me/proved to me on the oath of [**name of witness**]/proved to me through [**description of identity card or other document**]] to be the person whose name is subscribed to the foregoing instrument and directed me to affix [his/her] signature to the foregoing instrument in the presence of [**name of disinterested witness**], a person having no legal or equitable interest in any real or personal property that is the subject of or is affected by the foregoing instrument and whose identity is [known to me/proved to me on the oath of [**name of witness**]/proved to me through [**description of identity card or other document**]], and [**name of person with disability**] directed me to execute the foregoing instrument on [his/her] behalf for the purposes and consideration therein expressed.

Given under my hand and seal of office this [**specify**] day of [**month**], [**year**].

[SEAL]

____
[**Title of officer**]
My commission expires: [**date**]

Form 3-37

Jurat

SUBSCRIBED AND SWORN TO before me on __________________ by [**name of affiant**].

____
Notary Public, State of Texas

Form 3-38

Affidavit of Interpreter

Date:

Affiant: [**name of interpreter**]

Date of Interpretation:

Item Interpreted: [**describe instrument interpreted**]

Affiant on oath swears that the following statements are true and are within the personal knowledge of Affiant:

"I, the undersigned interpreter, am well versed in and competent to speak the [Spanish/[**other language**]] and the English languages, and on the date of interpretation I gave a true and faithful interpretation of the item interpreted in [Spanish/[**other language**]], which is understood by [**name**]."

____

[**Name of interpreter**]

Sworn to and subscribed before me on [**date**] by [**name of interpreter**].

[SEAL]

____

[**Title of officer administering oath**]
My commission expires: [**date**]

Chapter 4
Sales Contracts and Transaction Guide

Forms

Chapter 4

Sales Contracts and Transaction Guide

§ 4.1 General Considerations for Sales Contracts

The real estate sales contract, form 4-2 in this chapter, is drafted as a neutral form of contract, intending to favor neither the buyer nor the seller. While the general terms of the contract may be considered customary in a real estate transaction, all contract terms are subject to negotiation. Terms most likely to vary are in the exhibits. Alternative provisions are provided throughout the contract. Contracts for the purchase and sale of real estate are as diverse as their subject matter, and additional drafting will likely be necessary to tailor the form to the transaction.

§ 4.2 Real Estate Sales Contract

The following sections describe the provisions of the real estate sales contract and include considerations for the attorney in drafting or reviewing a contract, assisting the client during investigation of the property, and closing the transaction. This commentary is organized in the same order as the sections of the contract. The basic information to be filled in throughout the contract is listed in form 4-1.

§ 4.3 Introductory Paragraph: Offer and Acceptance

The introductory paragraph of the contract identifies the seller and buyer and states what the parties must do to form the contract of purchase and sale.

Proper identification of the parties is important, and the seller and the buyer should be identified as fully as possible. Capacity and authority should be considered, especially if a party is not an individual acting on his or her own behalf. See chapter 3 in this manual for a discussion of party designations. The buyer's earnest money must be paid to the title company in good funds for there to be a binding contract.

§ 4.4 Purchase and Sale of Property

§ 4.4:1 Purchase and Sale Agreement

Paragraph A.1. of the contract sets out the agreement of the parties to sell and buy the property. The real and personal property are summarily described in this paragraph and more particularly described in exhibit A. The contract should describe the real and personal property with legal specificity. If the property is not described sufficiently, the contract may be unenforceable because of vagueness. See chapter 3 in this manual for a discussion of property descriptions. Attention should also be given to the conveyance of appurtenant rights, such as permits, licenses, access easements, access to utilities, and similar rights. Exhibit A references clause 4-3-9 to provide a more extensive description of the seller's property rights to be conveyed.

§ 4.4:2 Purchase Price

Two versions of paragraph A.2. are provided, one for a "Purchase Price" that is a stated sum and an alternative for an "Adjusted Purchase Price" that is determined by a formula based on the gross or net area of the land or by other methods devised by the parties. The net area for an adjusted purchase price is typically computed by deducting from the gross area any portion of the land within roadways, floodplains, or other areas where rights are restricted, as shown on the survey. If this method is used, the purchase price cannot be calculated until after the survey is delivered, so applying a minimum and maximum price to the formula should be considered. Clause 4-3-1 sets out additional provisions based on the adjustment of the purchase price.

§ 4.4:3 Payment of Purchase Price

Paragraph A.3. sets forth several payment options: the total consideration may be paid in cash at closing, or all or a portion of the purchase price may be financed.

In the typical seller-financed transaction, at closing, the buyer delivers the cash portion of the purchase price and signs and delivers both a promissory note payable to the seller and a deed of trust encumbering the property as security for the debt. If the seller is providing financing, include exhibit E.

If the transaction is contingent on the buyer obtaining third-party financing, the buyer has two options. The buyer can apply for the financing early enough to confirm before the end of the inspection period if the loan application has been approved. Alternatively, the buyer can negotiate a right to terminate the contract after the end of the financing contingency period if the buyer is unable to obtain third-party financing. The parties may negotiate time limits within which the buyer must separately apply for and obtain third-party financing. The parties may also agree to limit or share the expenses of obtaining the financing. The contract in this manual does not include a financing contingency period.

See chapters 6 and 8 in this manual for further discussion of financing.

§ 4.4:4 Performance

The contract sets deadlines for performance by the seller and buyer and provides two alternate ways to determine most of the deadlines: either a stated date or a specified number of days after the effective date of the contract or another milestone. Paragraph A.4. states that deadlines expire at 5:00 P.M. local time where the property is located; provides for an extension of a deadline when a deadline falls on a Saturday, Sunday, or holiday; and stresses that time is of the essence.

§ 4.5 Earnest Money

§ 4.5:1 Deposit of Earnest Money

Paragraph B.1. provides the amount of the earnest money and the name of the title company that will receipt the earnest money and serve as escrow agent. The escrow agent will be responsible for closing the transaction and receiving and disbursing funds under the terms of the contract. Form 4-4 is the escrow agent receipt and escrow agreement, which defines the rights and duties of the escrow agent and is to be signed by the buyer, the seller, and the escrow agent's representative.

The escrow agent's representative should sign the receipt at the end of the contract and acknowledge the deposit of the earnest money with the escrow agent.

The amount of earnest money is negotiable and depends on several factors, including the purchase price, the type of financing, and the relative financial strengths of the parties. The contract provides that the earnest money will be deposited in one lump sum. The parties alternatively may agree that the buyer is obligated to deposit additional earnest money after agreed conditions have been satisfied—for example, if the buyer decides not to terminate the contract at the end of the inspection period and to proceed to closing.

§ 4.5:2 Interest on Earnest Money

Section B.2. states that the buyer may direct the escrow agent to invest the earnest money in an interest-bearing account in a federally insured financial institution. If the earnest money is to be invested, the escrow agent will require the buyer's tax identification or Social Security number so that accrued interest may be reported to the Internal Revenue Service.

Form 4-4 in this chapter (escrow agent receipt and escrow agreement) provides that the buyer pays the fees charged by the financial institution.

§ 4.5:3 Application of Earnest Money

Paragraph B.3. sets forth that the earnest money will be applied to the purchase price at closing or, if the buyer terminates the contract before closing, applied in accordance with sections D and G of the contract, based on whether the buyer terminates before or after the end of the inspection period.

§ 4.6 Title and Survey

§ 4.6:1 Review of Title

Paragraph C.1. incorporates the statutory notice that the Texas Real Estate License Act requires real estate brokers and real estate salespersons to give to a buyer, advising that the buyer should either have title examined by an attorney or obtain a title insurance policy. Tex. Occ. Code § 1101.652(b)(29). If a broker or salesperson is not involved, the paragraph may be deleted.

§ 4.6:2 Title Commitment; Title Policy; Survey; UCC Search

Paragraphs C.2. through C.4. define the terms "Title Commitment," "Title Policy," "Survey," and "UCC Search."

§ 4.6:3 Delivery of Title Commitment, Survey, and UCC Search

Paragraph C.5. sets the deadlines for the seller to deliver the title commitment, the UCC search, and the seller's existing survey. If the buyer is not satisfied with the seller's survey, this paragraph sets a deadline for the buyer to obtain a current survey. While this process is customary, the designation of a party to deliver the title commitment, UCC search, and survey is negotiable.

§ 4.6:4 Title Objections

Paragraph C.6. provides a typical procedure under which the buyer reviews the title commitment, the survey, and the UCC search and notifies the seller of any objections. After notice, the seller may elect to cure the buyer's objections but is not required to do so. If the seller does not agree to cure, the buyer may either proceed to close the transaction and accept the property subject to the uncured matters or terminate the contract. The seller is obligated to cure title matters that arise by, through, or under the seller after the contract is signed.

§ 4.6:5 Review of Title Commitment

The contract provides that the condition of title will be established by the title commitment and that the seller will pay for an owner title policy for the buyer at closing.

An essential reference on title insurance is the *Basic Manual of Rules, Rates and Forms for the Writing of Title Insurance in the State of Texas*, available from the Texas Department of Insurance at **www.tdi.texas.gov/title/titleman.html**. The manual contains Texas rate and procedural rules; the text of title 11 of the Texas Insurance Code, relating to title insurance; and various bulletins of the Texas State Board of Insurance dealing with title insurance practices.

The attorney should review the signature and effective date of the commitment.

Schedule A: The attorney should confirm that the proposed insured parties are correctly named, the amounts of insurance are correctly stated, and the correct estate is insured—for example, fee simple, easement, or leasehold. Record title should be vested in the seller. The attorney should confirm that the property description is correct and conforms to the description in the survey (if applicable).

Schedule B: The attorney should review the following matters:

- Item 1, relating to covenants and restrictions, should be noted as either "Covenants, conditions, and restrictions (other than any restrictions indicating preference, limitation, or discrimination based on race, color, religion, sex, handicap, familial status, or national origin) as set forth in [**recording data**] of the real property records of [**county**] County, Texas" or "Item 1 of schedule B is hereby deleted in its entirety."
- Item 2, relating to the standard survey exception, may be amended and partially deleted to read "any shortages in area" if a current survey approved by the title company is obtained. An additional 5 percent premium is charged to amend the owner policy for a residential transaction; an additional 15 percent premium is charged to amend the owner policy for a commercial transaction. No additional premium is required to amend the loan policy. The responsibility for paying the extra premium for the survey modification in the owner policy of title insurance is often negotiated between the parties, although the pertinent provision in the contract form provides for the extra premium to be paid by the buyer.
- Item 3, relating to homestead or community property or survivorship rights, and paragraph 4, relating to tidelines, lands comprising the shores and beds of waterways, lands beyond the line of the harbor or bulkhead lines, filled-in lands, artificial islands, statutory water rights, and areas extending from the line of mean low tide to the line of vegetation, apply only to the owner policy and cannot be deleted or amended.
- Paragraph 5, relating to property taxes, should be reviewed for the status of tax payments and the existence of rollback taxes. In the title policy, the exception for taxes should be restricted to taxes for the year in which the closing occurs (unless paid at or before closing), taxes for subsequent years, and rollback taxes for prior years.
- Paragraph 6, relating to the terms and conditions of the documents creating the insured's interest in the land, cannot be revised but will not appear on the title policy. The referenced documents should, however, be reviewed.
- Paragraph 7, relating to materialman's and mechanic's liens, applies only to mortgagee policies on interim construction loans and may be deleted if satisfactory evidence is furnished to the title company.
- Paragraph 8, relating to subordinate liens and leases, applies only to the mortgagee policy.
- Paragraph 9, relating to existing liens, should show only liens permitted by the contract. Copies of all lien documents should be reviewed regarding due-on-sale provisions; dragnet clauses relating to other debt; condemnation provisions; notice,

cure, and default provisions; and subordinate financing. A superior lienholder's estoppel agreement should be obtained from any lienholder whose note and lien are being either assumed or taken "subject to." All other special exceptions, such as easements, mineral interests, leases, or matters shown on a current survey, should be listed specifically and carefully reviewed to determine if they affect the buyer's intended use of the property.

Schedule C: The attorney should ensure that the seller has complied with the contract by curing and effectively removing all matters appearing on schedule C at or before closing. Schedule C matters may require obtaining releases of liens, settling specific claims or lawsuits affecting title to the property, furnishing evidence of good standing and authority (corporate resolution or partnership agreement), and obtaining proof of property settlement and divorce, proof of heirship or probate of a particular estate, or evidence relating to a bankruptcy. From the buyer's perspective, curative matters appearing on schedule C should be attended to by either the seller or the title company. The buyer should object to all schedule C items in the commitment to ensure that they are not added to schedule B of the title policy.

Note: Endorsements providing additional coverage may be available on request, subject to payment of the applicable additional premium. The *Basic Manual of Rules, Rates and Forms for the Writing of Title Insurance in the State of Texas* should be consulted for the eligibility, cost, and use of these endorsements and policy.

§ 4.6:6 Review of Survey

The contract requires that the seller provide a current survey of the property. Different types of surveys and survey certifications are available, depending on the nature of the property and the requirements of the parties. An excellent resource on surveys is the *Manual of Practice for Land Surveying in the State of Texas* ("Texas Standards"), published by the Texas Society of Professional Surveyors. It describes the various categories and conditions for surveys in Texas, the level of accuracy required for each category of survey, matters to be depicted on the survey, and the nature of certificates. In some cases the lender or buyer may require the surveyor to comply with the most recent Minimum Standard Detail Requirements and Accuracy Standards for ALTA/NSPS Land Title Surveys ("ALTA"), as adopted by the American Land Title Association and the National Society of Professional Surveyors. See **www.alta.org/policy-forms**.

The attorney should keep the following points in mind when reviewing the survey:

- The survey should bear a recent date and should conform to, as applicable, ALTA or the required category and condition under the Texas Standards for the type of survey specified in the contract and location of the property.
- The certificate should be sealed and signed and should conform to any certificate specified in the contract.
- There should be a north compass bearing on the survey.
- The attorney should observe the system of reference used for the survey, locate the beginning point, and determine that it is monumented and locatable.
- The survey, particularly all course and distance notations, should be compared to the legal description either appearing on or attached to the survey. This description then should be compared to the one appearing in the contract and the title commitment or title opinion.
- All recorded easements appearing in the title commitment should be located and noted on the survey with the appropriate recording data. Conversely, the attorney

should examine the survey for any matters (such as easements) not appearing in the title commitment.

- The survey should be examined for the location of improvements: Do improvements protrude onto adjoining property or easement areas; are there encroachments of improvements from adjoining property onto the property; are there building setback line violations?
- Any written notations on the survey, such as those relating to rights of parties in possession, should be reviewed to determine their effect on the property and its anticipated use.
- The property should have legal and adequate access to public streets or roads.
- The survey should show the existence and location of utilities.
- The surveyor's certificate should indicate the location of the floodplain, if applicable.

§ 4.6:7 Review of UCC Search

The contract includes provisions for personal property and requires that the seller furnish UCC searches of appropriate records. The scope of the search would depend on the nature of the collateral. See sections 9.2 through 9.6 in this manual.

§ 4.7 Inspection Period and Buyer's Right to Terminate

§ 4.7:1 Inspection Period

Paragraph D.1. sets the period during which the buyer has the opportunity to investigate the property and decide whether to close the transaction.

§ 4.7:2 Buyer's Right to Terminate

Paragraph D.2. provides that the buyer may terminate the contract at any time before the end of the inspection period for any reason and have the earnest money returned, except for the $100 independent consideration for the buyer's right to terminate the contract. Although this contract provides for a nominal $100 independent consideration, the amount is subject to negotiation.

§ 4.7:3 Review of Seller's Records

Paragraph D.3. sets the deadline for the seller to deliver its records as listed on exhibit C to the buyer for its review.

§ 4.7:4 Entry onto Property

Paragraph D.4. provides for reasonable rules of entry by the buyer onto the property, including delivering evidence of commercial general liability insurance.

§ 4.7:5 Environmental Assessment

Paragraph D.5. provides for cooperation by the seller with the buyer's right to conduct environmental assessments of the property.

§ 4.7:6 Buyer's Indemnity and Release of Seller

Paragraph D.6. states that the buyer will indemnify the seller for claims resulting from the buyer's inspection of the property. Except for the environmental indemnity stated in exhibit B in the contract, the indemnity provisions of the contract are not intended to shift risk from the indemnified party to the indemnitor for the indemnified party's own negligence. One consequence of this allocation of risk is that the indemnified party may not be able to recover the costs of defense from the indemnitor if the indemnified party is sued for the consequences of its alleged negligence. *See Fisk Electric Co. v.*

Constructors & Associates, 888 S.W.2d 813 (Tex. 1994). The environmental indemnity shifts risk for the seller's own negligence from the seller to the buyer. It is unlikely, however, that the environmental indemnity will be effective to shift risk in the event of misrepresentation or fraud.

§ 4.8 Representations

Section E sets forth suggested seller's representations and related limitations. Representations are negotiated by the parties with specific reference to the transaction. Representations may include such matters as ownership of the property; organization of the parties; authority to execute the contract and close the transaction; condition of title; parties in possession; pending litigation and claims that may ripen into litigation; pending or threatened condemnation or other taking; use restrictions, such as zoning and restrictive covenants; condition of the property or disclaimer of representations—for example, "as is"; presence of landfills or hazardous and toxic wastes; floodplain location; utility availability and capacity; compliance with all laws; effectiveness of required licenses and permits; status of leases; operation and maintenance of property before closing; accuracy of books and records; agricultural or other special-use tax assessment; payment of ad valorem taxes; and status of debt to be assumed or taken "subject to."

In negotiating representations, the parties often consider issues such as whether the representations will be absolute or based on the seller's knowledge and belief; whether the representations will be based on the knowledge of the entity that is the seller or on the knowledge of specified individuals; whether the seller must perform further investigation to make the representations or may rely on its current knowledge, without further investigation; and whether and to what extent the representations will survive closing.

As set out in exhibit B of the contract, the approach used limits the seller's representations, but it is not intended to insulate the seller from liability for fraud or misrepresentation.

- The seller represents only facts, not opinions. For example, the seller does not represent whether, in the seller's opinion, the property complies with applicable laws and regulations. Instead, the seller represents that it has not received notice of violation of any law, ordinance, regulation, or requirement affecting the property or use of the property, except as stated in the contract.
- The seller makes no representation that is not stated in the contract, including exhibit D (notices, statements, and certificates required by law and regulation).

The following optional clauses are also provided:

- The buyer agrees to accept the property in its "as is, where is" condition, investigate the property on the buyer's own behalf, and not rely on information or representations attributable to the seller, except to the extent stated in the contract.
- The buyer assumes responsibility after closing for all environmental matters relating to the property.

If the parties negotiate different representations, exhibit B must be revised accordingly.

The contract provides that the parties' representations are true and accurate when made and must be true and accurate at closing, or the buyer may terminate the contract.

It is common practice to include representations regarding the organization and authority of the parties in contracts but to defer the obligation to deliver documentary evidence confirming those representations until the closing of the transaction. That evidence customarily consists of certificates of existence and good standing from public officials, certified copies of organizational documents, certified corporate resolutions or partnership consents, and certificates of incumbency. The attorney may consider requiring such documentary evidence at the execution of the contract to avoid encountering a claim after substantial obligations have been paid or incurred that the other party is not authorized to consummate the transaction. While the seller's organizational documents should be available at the time of execution of the contract, the buyer's organizational documents are often not prepared until before closing.

§ 4.9 Condition of Property until Closing; Cooperation; No Recording of Contract

Section F provides for the parties' obligations after signing the contract concerning maintenance and operation of the property, casualty damage, condemnation, claims, governmental proceedings, permits, licenses, and inspections. The contract also sets out the parties' agreement not to record the contract.

§ 4.10 Termination

Section G provides for disposition of the earnest money after termination and for post-termination obligations in certain events.

§ 4.11 Closing

Section H addresses the closing process. Paragraph H.1. sets the closing date. Paragraph H.2. sets out the conditions to closing. Paragraph H.3. lists the closing documents to be delivered by the seller and buyer. The contract provides that, unless the parties agree otherwise before closing, certain closing documents will be on the forms contained in the current edition of the *Texas Real Estate Forms Manual* (State Bar of Texas). This approach defers the time and expense of negotiating the closing documents until after the contract is signed, while providing certainty if the parties do not otherwise negotiate closing documents. Alternately, the closing documents can be negotiated before the contract is signed and, if so, should be attached as exhibits to the contract. When determining whether to contract for a general warranty deed or a special warranty deed, the attorney should refer to section 5.4 in this manual for its discussion of *Chicago Title Insurance Co. v. Cochran Investments, Inc.*, 602 S.W.3d 895, 901 (Tex. 2020).

Paragraph H.3.f. provides that the buyer acquires possession of the property at closing. The parties may agree, however, on earlier or later possession by the buyer. If the buyer takes possession before closing or the seller remains in possession after closing, a lease may be appropriate. See chapter 25 in this manual.

Paragraph H.4. allocates closing obligations and transaction costs between the parties and provides for proration of ad valorem taxes, income, and expenses and for postclosing adjustments.

Paragraph H.4.f. addresses the payment of real estate commissions. Real estate brokers and real estate salespersons must have a written commission agreement to enforce payment of a real estate commission. The commission may be payable on contract execution, when the contract closes, or as otherwise agreed by the parties. The contract provides that the commission agreement is a separate document between the broker and the party responsible for paying the commission. For applicable forms, see forms 26-29 through 26-31 in this manual. Alternately, the contract may include the commission agreement or restate its key terms. The parties indemnify each other against claims by brokers and finders arising by, through, or under the indemnifying party. The contract may state that there are no brokers, but there is no requirement to do so.

If either buyer or seller is licensed as a real estate salesperson or real estate broker and is acting as a broker in the transaction, a disclosure to that effect is required under the Real Estate License Act. Tex. Occ. Code § 1101.652(b)(16).

§ 4.12 Default and Remedies

Paragraph I.1. provides that if the seller fails to perform its obligations under the contract or if the seller's representations are not true and correct as of the closing date, the buyer may elect one of the following remedies: termination (with disposition of the earnest money and payment of additional liquidated damages) or specific performance. In addition, if the seller conveys or encumbers the property before closing so that the buyer cannot enforce specific performance, the buyer may seek recovery of its actual damages caused by the seller's default. The parties may agree to limit the amount of actual damages to be recovered.

Paragraph I.3. provides that if the buyer fails to perform its obligations under the contract, the seller may terminate the contract and have the earnest money paid to the seller. Clause 4-3-6 provides an optional provision that allows the seller to seek additional liquidated damages.

The contract is drafted to limit the parties' remedies, but remedies are often negotiated.

The contract provides that the party prevailing in litigation is entitled to recover attorney's fees and court and other costs.

§ 4.13 Miscellaneous Provisions

Section J sets out a number of provisions integral to a real estate sales contract, including notice, entirety of agreement, amendment, assignment, survival, choice of law and venue, waiver of default, no third-party beneficiaries, severability, ambiguities not construed against the drafting party, no special relationship, counterparts, confidentiality, and binding effect.

There are optional provisions for waiver of consumer rights under the Texas Deceptive Trade Practices–Consumer Protection Act and waiver of a right to trial by jury.

§ 4.13:1 Assignment

Paragraph J.4. contains alternate clauses concerning assignment. The buyer either may not assign the contract without the seller's prior written consent or may assign the contract to only an entity controlled by the buyer.

If the contract provides that the buyer has the right to assign, the assignment provision should state whether the buyer is relieved from obligations under the contract after assignment.

Included in this chapter are four forms related to the assignment process. Form 4-29 is a short-form assignment by a buyer of its rights and obligations under the contract and is typically used as an assignment by the buyer to an entity controlled by the buyer. It can also be used in transactions not involving representations, warranties, and covenants between the buyer and the assignee. Form 4-30 is a long-form assignment that contains representations, warranties, and covenants between the buyer and the assignee. Form 4-31 is a form for consent by the seller if consent is required by the contract. Form 4-32 is a contract for the sale by a buyer to an assignee of the buyer's rights under the contract. It allows the assignee time to investigate the property before paying the buyer for the assignment and before unconditionally depositing substitute earnest money with the title company. The inspection period under the contract should be long enough to allow the assignor or buyer to step back in if the assignee elects to terminate its right to purchase the property.

§ 4.13:2 Exhibits

Section K is a list of exhibits referenced in the contract that should be attached to the contract, as applicable.

Exhibit A—Legal Description of Land: See section 4.4:1 above.

Exhibit B—Representations; Environmental Matters: Party representations are always negotiated by the parties and will vary from transaction to transaction.

Exhibit C—Seller's Records: This exhibit lists the seller's records of the property that will be delivered or made available to the buyer for review during the inspection period and delivered to the buyer at closing.

Exhibit D—Notices, Statements, and Certificates: Federal and state laws and regulations require delivery of certain notices, statements, and certificates when common real estate contracts are executed. The items applicable to the transaction should be included in this exhibit. See the commentary at the tops of forms 4-5 through 4-23 in this chapter addressing those particular notices, and see chapter 2 in this manual for a brief discussion of each law and regulation and for references to other laws and regulations that require notices, statements, and certificates for less common transactions.

Exhibit E—Seller Financing Addendum: This addendum is for use only in situations in which the seller is providing the financing. If obtaining third-party financing is a condition to the buyer's obligations, that fact and the terms of the complying financing may need to be addressed in the contract.

§ 4.14 Closing Functions

The party handling the closing (in this instance, the escrow agent) commonly attends to the following matters.

§ 4.14:1 Payoff Information and Other Closing Expenses

The escrow agent should send a written request to each lienholder for the lienholder's written payoff statement and to sign a release of lien. The authorized representative of the lienholder should be requested to state the remaining principal balance due on the note; the accrued interest as of a certain date; a per diem amount of interest; and whether the lienholder will credit the amount held in the escrow account, if one exists, to the total due or, alternatively, refund the amount directly to the borrower. Closing must occur, resulting in the escrow agent having the funds to pay the lienholder, before the escrow agent records the signed release of lien delivered by the lienholder. Some lienholders will not deliver a signed release of lien until the escrow agent has the funds or has delivered the funds to the lienholder.

Additionally, information concerning other matters requiring payment at closing should be obtained, such as payoff amounts for mechanic's lien claims, federal or state tax liens, property taxes, paving assessments, and abstracted judgments that affect the property. The escrow agent must have the funds required by and a signed release of lien from these lien claimants to satisfy requirements set out in schedule C of the title commitment.

The closing agent must also determine the amounts of closing costs, such as surveying expenses, attorney's fees, brokers' commissions, and loan fees.

§ 4.14:2 Prorations and Deposits

Unless otherwise provided in the contract, the buyer acquires both the monetary benefits and burdens of the property. Prorations are generally based on the settlement or closing date.

Tax Prorations: Tax prorations may be based on the most current property tax information available to the closing agent. The tax proration serves as a bookkeeping adjustment on the closing statement between the seller and the buyer relating to taxes. If taxes have not been paid for the current year, this adjustment involves the seller's being charged on the closing statement with property taxes for the period the seller owned the property. The buyer is then responsible for actual payment of taxes. The buyer receives a corresponding credit of the seller's prorated amount. The contract requires that the seller and the buyer reprorate taxes when actual tax statements become available after closing.

Insurance Prorations: If the seller assigns its fire and extended coverage to the buyer, the buyer should be charged the unearned portion of the prepaid premium. The seller should receive a corresponding credit.

Rent Prorations: If the property is income-producing, rents already received by the seller for the current rental period should be prorated. The seller should be charged the amount for the prorated period, and the buyer should receive a corresponding credit.

Interest Prorations: If the sale is being financed through an assumption or "subject to" transaction, interest becoming due at the next regular payment period should be prorated between the seller and the buyer, usually as of the closing date.

Security Deposits: Tenant security deposits that the seller is holding should be charged to the seller and credited to the buyer, because the buyer ultimately should be responsible for the refund of the deposits. The seller will remain liable to the tenants for security deposits received while the seller was the owner of the property, until the buyer delivers to the tenants a signed statement acknowledging that the buyer of the property has received and is responsible for the tenants' security deposits and setting forth the amount of each deposit. *See* Tex. Prop. Code §§ 92.105(b), 93.007. Additional drafting is required to obligate the buyer to deliver the signed statements.

§ 4.14:3 Preparation of Closing Documents

The closing agent may be expected to prepare several documents.

Closing Statements: Closing statements may be on either the federally prescribed HUD-1 settlement statement, the State Board of Insurance settlement statement, or a separate seller's, buyer's, or borrower's statement, depending on the nature of the transaction. The purpose of a closing statement is to assemble in one document all the pertinent financial features of the contract, including purchase price, loan amounts, costs, expenses of closing the transaction, and prorations. Execution of the statement evidences the parties' agreement with the numbers and computations appearing on the statement.

Affidavits: Affidavits concerning debts and liens, parties in possession, identity of the parties, leases, and marital status will likely be required at closing by the escrow agent.

Financing documents are typically prepared by the lender's attorney. Conveyancing and other closing documents may be prepared by the parties to the transaction, by their attorneys, or by an attorney for the closing agent.

§ 4.14:4 Funding

The closing agent typically disburses funds in connection with closing. Disbursements are made according to the closing statement, usually from funds paid by the buyer and its lenders.

Except in the case of certain nontaxable sales of principal residences, the person responsible for closing a real estate transaction is required to file an information return with the Internal Revenue Service relating to the transaction and is subject to penalties for failing to report. *See* 26 U.S.C. § 6045. This reporting requirement is often satisfied by the responsible person by delivering the seller's closing statement, together with an attachment of additional required information, to the IRS.

If funds will be disbursed at closing, payments must be made to the closing agent with "good funds" as defined by the regulations of the Texas State Board of Insurance. *See* Procedural Rule P-27, *Basic Manual of Rules, Rates and Forms for the Writing of Title Insurance in the State of Texas*.

If it is not necessary to disburse funds at closing, the parties need not comply with the "good funds" rule, and payment may be made in other ways.

The attorney for each buyer and lender should consider obtaining an insured closing service letter from the title insurance underwriter whose policies are to be issued. This letter indemnifies the lender for any fraudulent acts of the closing title insurance company or agency relating to the handling of closing funds. *See* forms T-50 and T-51, *Basic Manual of Rules, Rates and Forms for the Writing of Title Insurance in the State of Texas*. See **www.tdi.texas.gov/title/titlemm5.html**.

§ 4.14:5 Recording Documents

The closing agent is responsible for recording documents intended to be recorded. This responsibility extends to the recording of releases or transfers of liens for notes paid at closing. Each document should be checked before recording to ensure that exhibits referred to in the document are attached and the name and address of the person to whom the document is to be returned after recording is included.

§ 4.14:6 Closing Instructions

Attorneys for the buyer, the seller, and the lender may each prepare closing instructions for the closing agent. For applicable forms, see forms 26-15 through 26-18 in this manual. These instructions relate to the conditions precedent to closing, including the status of the title after closing, the title insurance policies to be issued, disposition of funds, and distribution of documents received by the closing agent.

§ 4.15 Additional Considerations

§ 4.15:1 Transactions Involving Foreign Persons

Buyer: If the buyer is a foreign person, certain disclosures and reports may be required under the Foreign Investment in Real Property Tax Act of 1980. *See* 26 U.S.C. § 6039C.

Seller: With certain exceptions, if the seller of real property located in the United States is a foreign person, the buyer must withhold 15 percent of the purchase price and remit the funds to the Internal Revenue Service within twenty days of the date of transfer. *See* 26 U.S.C. § 1445(a), (b). The buyer should assume that the seller is a foreign person until the contrary is established, because buyers act at their own peril until they obtain a nonforeign affidavit. *See* 26 U.S.C. § 1445(b)(2). Forms 26-19 and 26-20 in this manual are suggested for use in all transactions.

§ 4.15:2 Other Requirements

Before closing, the buyer should arrange for Causes of Loss—Special Form property insurance coverage, liability, flood, and similar types of insurance for any required mortgagee endorsements. The buyer and seller should arrange for payment out of the closing proceeds of any accrued taxes even if the taxes will not be delinquent until after closing. The buyer should notify the tax appraisal district of any change in ownership.

§ 4.15:3 Closing Checklist

The attorney should prepare a closing checklist, itemizing the documents that will be required to close the transaction, including curative documents. The checklist should also refer to all other preclosing considerations relating to the transaction. The closing checklist can be added to form 4-1.

§ 4.15:4 Postclosing Considerations

After closing, recorded documents and relevant title insurance policies issued after closing should be reviewed for accuracy and compliance with the title commitment. The owner policy should be dated on or after the recording date of the deed conveying title to the buyer, and the mortgagee policy should be dated on or after the recording date of the deed of trust of the insured lien.

An original or escrow agent's certified copy of each executed document relating to the closing should be provided to the seller and the buyer or the borrower by their attorneys. Generally, the party benefiting from a document receives the original, and the other parties receive copies.

§ 4.16 Additional Resources

Barton, J. Cary. "Pitfalls of Statutory Notices—Or Lack Thereof." In *Advanced Real Estate Drafting Course, 2013*. Austin: State Bar of Texas, 2013.

Baucum, Michael, and Kathryn E. Allen. "As-Is Update: 'Prudential 2012.'" In *Advanced Real Estate Law Course, 2012*. Austin: State Bar of Texas, 2012.

Becker, Douglas W., and Arturo Machado. "Thorny FIRPTA Withholding Issues Involving Foreign Sellers of Real Estate." In *Advanced Real Estate Drafting Course, 2016*. Austin: State Bar of Texas, 2016.

Beyer, Gerry W. *Real Property*. 2nd ed. West's Texas Forms 13–15. St. Paul, MN: West, 2001. Supplement 2016.

Dysart, Sara E. "Contract Drafting—A Skill to Be Developed!" In *Advanced Real Estate Drafting Course, 2023*. Austin: State Bar of Texas, 2023.

———. "Seller Should Provide Accurate Statutory Notices Incident to the Sale of Real Property." In *Advanced Real Estate Law Course, 2015*. Austin: State Bar of Texas, 2015.

Dysart, Sara E., Mia Lorick, and David A. Weatherbie. "Drafting Clearly Is Important—Texas Cases Where It Made a Difference [Part II]." In *Advanced Real Estate Strategies Course, 2022*. Austin: State Bar of Texas, 2022.

Howard, C. Elaine. "Miscellaneous Sections of a Contract." In *Advanced Real Estate Law Course, 2016*. Austin: State Bar of Texas, 2016.

Love, G. Roland. "Title and Survey Objection Letter, Instruction Letter: Guidelines and Solutions." In *Advanced Real Estate Law Course, 2019*. Austin: State Bar of Texas, 2019.

McPherson, Mark. "Mandatory Statutory Notices for Texas Real Estate Transactions circa 2022." In *Advanced Real Estate Drafting Course, 2022*. Austin: State Bar of Texas, 2022.

———. "Statutory Notices: Incorporating a CLE Paper into Real Estate Sales Forms." In *Advanced Real Estate Drafting Course, 2018*. Austin: State Bar of Texas, 2018.

Mills, Ken. "Top Ten Issues When Negotiating Earnest Money Contracts." In *Advanced Real Estate Law Course, 2015*. Austin: State Bar of Texas, 2015.

Newsome, Kent. "Drafting ROFO/Option Agreements: Key Issues and Sample Forms." In *Advanced Real Estate Drafting Course, 2016*. Austin: State Bar of Texas, 2016.

———. "Rights of First Refusal: What They Are, What They Aren't, and What They Can Do to Your Deal." In *Advanced Real Estate Law Course, 2013*. Austin: State Bar of Texas, 2013.

Newsome, Kent, and Kristen E. Bollinger. "Words and Phrases: An Explanation of Real Estate Legal Terminolgy." In *Advanced Real Estate Law Course, 2021*. Austin: State Bar of Texas, 2021.

Rider, Brian. "Allocation of Risks in Purchase Contracts for Improved Property (Risk Avoidance and Allocation Pre-Closing)." In *Advanced Real Estate Law Course, 2016*. Austin: State Bar of Texas, 2016.

Tomek, David W. "Drafting Clearly Is Important—Texas Cases Where It Made a Difference." In *Advanced Real Estate Drafting Course, 2021*. Austin: State Bar of Texas, 2021.

———. "From Ridiculous 'Asks' to Meaningful Compromise: Drafting and Negotiating Selected Aspects of Earnest Money Contracts for Income-Producing Commercial Properties." In *Advanced Real Estate Drafting Course, 2013*. Austin: State Bar of Texas, 2013.

Weller, Philip D. "Drafting Confidentiality Agreements and Access Agreements." In *Advanced Real Estate Drafting Course, 2014*. Austin: State Bar of Texas, 2014.

Whelan, Thomas M. "Scattershooting at Contracts and Deeds Down at the Courthouse." In *Advanced Real Estate Drafting Course, 2019*. Austin: State Bar of Texas, 2019.

———. "Scattershooting While Wondering Whatever Happened at the Courthouse to Frequently Litigated Provisions in My Favorite Real Estate Sales Forms." In *Advanced Real Estate Drafting Course, 2015*. Austin: State Bar of Texas, 2015.

Form 4-1

This form lists information required to complete the real estate sales contract, form 4-2 in this chapter.

Checklist

[For Use with Real Estate Sales Contract]

1. General description of property: **[address or description, e.g.,** property known as **[specify]**, consisting of **[specify]** acres]

2. Seller: **[name of seller]**

3. Buyer: **[name of buyer]**

4. Where property is located: **[city, county]**

5. Purchase Price: **[amount]** AND NO/100 DOLLARS ($**[amount]**)

6. Amount of Earnest Money: **[amount]** AND NO/100 DOLLARS ($**[amount]**)

7. Title Company: **[name of title company]**

8. Contact information for Title Company: **[address and contact information for title company]**

9. Number of days after the Effective Date for Seller to have Title Commitment and UCC search delivered to Buyer: **[number]**

10. Number of days after the Effective Date for Buyer or Seller (as applicable) to deliver updated Survey: **[number]**

11. Number of days for Buyer to deliver title objections, to run after Buyer has received all of the following: Title Commitment, UCC search, and Seller's survey or current survey: **[number]**

12. Number of days after Buyer sends notice of title objections that Seller has to respond to Buyer's title objections: **[number]**

13. Number of days after Seller's deadline to respond to Buyer's title objections for Buyer to waive its objections or terminate the Contract based on Seller's failure to cure title objections to Buyer's satisfaction: **[number]**

14. Number of days after the Effective Date for Buyer to inspect the Property: **[number]**

15. Number of days after the Effective Date for Seller to deliver Seller's records to Buyer: **[number]**

16. Percentage of Purchase Price for casualty damage to be material: **[percent]**

17. Closing Date: **[actual date, written in the format MM/DD/YYYY, or number of days after the end of the inspection period for the transaction to close]**

18. Maximum amount of Buyer's Liquidated Damages that Seller owes Buyer upon Seller's Default and Buyer does not elect to enforce specific performance: **[amount]** AND NO/100 DOLLARS ($**[amount]**)

19. Number of days after Seller's breach of Contract that Buyer must initiate action for specific performance: **[number]**

20. Contact information for Buyer and any additional parties to notify in the following format:

[Name]
[Address]
[Telephone]
[Email address]

With copy to:

[Name]
[Address]
[Telephone]
[Email address]

21. Contact information for Seller and any additional parties to notify in the following format:

[Name]
[Address]
[Telephone]
[Email address]

With copy to:

[Name]
[Address]
[Telephone]
[Email address]

Form 4-2

Before completing this form, the attorney should complete the real estate sales contract checklist, form 4-1 in this chapter. Information called for in this form by item numbers corresponds with the same-numbered items on that checklist.

Real Estate Sales Contract

[**Checklist item 1**]

This Contract to buy and sell real property between [**item 2**] ("Seller") and [**item 3**] ("Buyer") is effective on the date of the last of the signatures by Seller and Buyer and by the Title Company as escrow agent as defined below to acknowledge receipt of the Contract and the Earnest Money in good funds ("Effective Date").

A. Purchase and Sale of Property

A.1. Purchase and Sale Agreement. Subject to the terms and provisions of this Real Estate Sales Contract (the "Contract"), Seller agrees to sell and convey to Buyer and Buyer agrees to buy and pay Seller for the property [**item 1**] located at [**item 4**], state of Texas, and more fully described in Exhibit A ("Land") [**include the following phrases that are applicable, tailoring punctuation and conjunctions as necessary:** , together with improvements to the Land ("Improvements"), the leases associated with the Land and Improvements ("Leases"), and the personal property described in Exhibit A], all collectively referred to as the "Property."

Select one of the following.

A.2. Purchase Price. The purchase price is [**item 5**] (the "Purchase Price") to be paid by Buyer to Seller for the sale and conveyance of the Property and will be payable in cash at the Closing.

Or

A.2. Adjusted Purchase Price. The purchase price is an adjusted purchase price when it is adjusted based on a current Survey as described in paragraph C.3. below. The purchase price will be adjusted on the basis of the Survey to equal the product of [**item 5**] multiplied by the number of [net/gross] [square feet/acres] of surface area of the Land disclosed by the Survey (the "Purchase Price") [**include if applicable:** subject to the following provisions].

If the purchase price is adjusted based on a survey, include clause 4-3-1 in this chapter if the parties have the right to terminate based on maximum and minimum square footage or acreage.

Select one of the following.

A.3. Payment of the Purchase Price. The Purchase Price will be paid in cash or certified funds, as required by the Title Company.

Or

A.3. Payment of the Purchase Price. A portion of the Purchase Price will be paid in cash or certified funds as required by the Title Company, and the balance of the Purchase Price will be paid by Seller financing as set forth in Exhibit E—Seller Financing Addendum.

Continue with the following.

A.4. Performance. All deadlines in this Contract expire at 5:00 P.M. local time where the Property is located. If a deadline falls on a Saturday, Sunday, or holiday, the deadline will be extended to the next day that is not a Saturday, Sunday, or holiday. A holiday is a day, other than a Saturday or Sunday, on which state or local governmental agencies and financial institutions are not generally open for business where the Property is located. Time is of the essence.

B. Earnest Money

B.1. Deposit of Earnest Money. Upon execution of this Contract, Buyer will deposit Earnest Money in good funds in the amount of [**item 6**], along with this fully executed Contract by Seller and Buyer with [**item 7**] (the "Title Company"), as escrow agent, located at [**item 8**], which sum may be invested by the Title Company in a federally insured, interest-bearing account pending disposition thereof in accordance with this Contract (such sum and the interest accrued thereon being hereinafter referred to collectively as the "Earnest Money") and applied according to the terms of this Contract. The Title Company will acknowledge receipt of the Earnest Money by signing Title Company's "Receipt for Earnest Money Deposit" at the end of this Contract and send copies thereof to Seller and Buyer.

B.2. Interest on Earnest Money. Buyer may direct the Title Company to invest the Earnest Money in an interest-bearing account in a federally insured financial institution by giving notice to the Title Company and satisfying the Title Company's requirements for investing the Earnest Money in an interest-bearing account. Any interest earned on the Earnest Money will become part of the Earnest Money.

B.3. Application of Earnest Money. If the sale of the Property is consummated as contemplated in this Contract, then the Earnest Money will be applied to the Purchase Price at Closing. If this Contract is terminated prior to consummation of the sale of the Property in accordance with this Contract, then the Earnest Money will be applied in accordance with sections D. and G. below.

C. Title and Survey

C.1. Review of Title. The following statutory notice is provided to Buyer on behalf of the real estate licensees, if any, involved in this transaction: Buyer is advised that it should either have the abstract covering the Property examined by an attorney of Buyer's own selection or be furnished with or obtain a policy of title insurance.

C.2. Title Commitment; Title Policy. "Title Commitment" means a Commitment for Issuance of an Owner Policy of Title Insurance by Title Company stating the condition of title to the Land. The "effective date" stated in the Title Commitment must be after the Effective Date of this Contract. "Title Policy" means an Owner Policy of Title Insurance issued by the Title Company in conformity with the last Title Commitment delivered to and approved by Buyer.

C.3. Survey. To be obtained by [Buyer/Seller], at [Buyer's/Seller's] expense:

Select one of the following.

"Survey" means an on-the-ground, staked plat of survey and metes-and-bounds description of the Land, prepared by a Registered Professional Land Surveyor licensed by the state of Texas and acceptable to Buyer, Seller, and the Title Company, dated after the Effective Date, and certified [**include as applicable:** to Seller, Buyer, Title Company, and any other person specified by Buyer] to comply with the most recent Minimum Standard Detail Requirements and Accuracy Standards for ALTA/NSPS Land Title Surveys ("ALTA"), as published by the American Land Title Association and the National Society of Professional Surveyors for the Survey Category.

Or

"Survey" means an on-the-ground, staked plat of survey and metes-and-bounds description of the Land, prepared by a Registered Professional Land Surveyor licensed by the state of Texas and acceptable to Buyer, Seller, and the Title Company. Any existing survey delivered by Seller must be accompanied by an affidavit detailing any changes to the Land and Improvements since the date of the Survey.

Continue with the following.

For purposes of the legal description for the Land to be included in the Title Policy and the Deed and other documents to be delivered at Closing, the field notes prepared by the surveyor will control any conflicts or inconsistencies with the legal description contained on Exhibit A herein or in the Title Commitment and such field notes will be incorporated herein by this reference upon completion and substituted on Exhibit A herein and included as the legal description for the Land in the Deed and the Title Commitment and Owner's and Loan policies.

Select the following if personal property is involved in the sale.

C.4. UCC Search. "UCC Search" means written reports stating the instruments that are on file in the Texas secretary of state's UCC records, the UCC records of any other appropriate state, and the UCC records in the jurisdiction in which Seller is organized, showing as debtor Seller and all other owners of the Personal Property during the five years before the Effective Date of this Contract.

Continue with the following.

C.5. Delivery of Title Commitment, Survey, UCC Search, and Legible Copies. Seller must deliver the Title Commitment, the UCC Search, and legible copies of the instruments referenced in the Title Commitment within **[item 9]** days from the Effective Date of this Contract. If Seller's existing survey is not satisfactory to Buyer or the Title Company, Buyer must obtain a current Survey within **[item 10]** days from the Effective Date of this Contract.

C.6. Title Objections. Buyer has [**item 11**] days after delivery of the last of the Title Commitment, legible copies of the instruments referenced in the Title Commitment, the UCC Search, and the Survey if a new Survey is required by Buyer or Title Company ("Title Objection Deadline") to review the Survey, Title Commitment, UCC Search, and legible copies of the title instruments referenced in them and notify Seller of Buyer's objections to any of them ("Title Objections"). Buyer will be deemed to have approved all matters reflected by the Survey, Title Commitment, and UCC Search to which Buyer has made no Title Objection by the Title Objection Deadline. The matters that Buyer either approves or is deemed to have approved are "Permitted Exceptions." If Buyer notifies Seller of any Title Objections, Seller has [**item 12**] days from receipt of Buyer's notice to notify Buyer whether Seller agrees to cure the Title Objections before Closing ("Cure Notice"). If Seller does not timely give its Cure Notice or timely gives its Cure Notice but does not agree to cure all the Title Objections before Closing, Buyer may, within [**item 13**] days after the deadline for the giving of Seller's Cure Notice, notify Seller that either this Contract is terminated or Buyer will proceed to close, subject to Seller's obligations, at or before Closing, to remove all liquidated liens; remove all exceptions that arise by, through, or under Seller after the Effective Date; and cure any other Title Objections that Seller has agreed to cure in the Cure Notice.

If the property is subject to any lien securing indebtedness in excess of the net purchase price, include clause 4-3-2.

D. Inspection Period and Buyer's Right to Terminate

D.1. Inspection Period. Buyer's inspection of the Property may be conducted commencing on the Effective Date of the Contract and ending at 5:00 P.M. local time where the Property is located, [**item 14**] days after the Effective Date (the "Inspection Period").

D.2. Buyer's Right to Terminate. Buyer may terminate this Contract for any reason by notifying Seller of the termination in writing before the end of the Inspection Period. Upon

Buyer's delivery of written notice of termination to the Seller, the Title Company is hereby authorized to deliver the Earnest Money to Buyer, less $100, which will be paid to Seller as consideration for the right granted by Seller to Buyer to terminate this Contract. Upon written request by Seller, Buyer will provide to Seller copies of the following reports related to the Property in Buyer's possession: environmental reports, physical inspection reports, and surveys.

If Buyer does not deliver written notice to Seller of Buyer's termination of the Contract before the end of the Inspection Period, Buyer waives the right to terminate this Contract pursuant to this provision.

> If additional earnest money is required prior to the end of the inspection period, include clause 4-3-3.

D.3. Review of Seller's Records. Seller will make available to Buyer copies of Seller's records specified in Exhibit C ("Seller's Records"), or otherwise make Seller's Records available for Buyer's review (for instance, through an online file sharing service), within [**item 15**] days from the Effective Date of this Contract.

D.4. Entry onto the Property. Buyer and its duly authorized agents and representatives may enter the Property before Closing, at Buyer's cost and risk, subject to the following:

D.4.a. Buyer must deliver evidence to Seller that Buyer has commercial general liability insurance, with coverages and in amounts that are substantially the same as those maintained by Seller or with such lesser coverages and in such lesser amounts as are reasonably satisfactory to Seller.

D.4.b. Buyer may not interfere in any material manner with existing operations or occupants of the Property.

D.4.c. Buyer must notify Seller in advance of Buyer's plans to conduct tests so that Seller or Seller's representatives may be present during the tests.

D.4.d. If the Property is physically altered because of Buyer's inspections, Buyer must return the Property to its preinspection condition [promptly/within [**number**] days] after the alteration occurs.

D.4.e. Buyer must abide by any other reasonable entry rules imposed by Seller.

D.5. Environmental Assessment. Prior to the end of the Inspection Period, Buyer has the right to conduct environmental assessments of the Property. Seller will provide, or will designate a person with knowledge of the use and condition of the Property to provide, information requested by Buyer or Buyer's agent or representative regarding the use and condition of the Property during the period of Seller's ownership of the Property. Seller will cooperate with Buyer in obtaining and providing to Buyer or its agent or representative information regarding the use and condition of the Property before Seller's period of ownership to the extent that the information is within Seller's possession or control.

D.6. Buyer's Indemnity and Release of Seller

D.6.a. Indemnity. Buyer will indemnify, defend, and hold Seller harmless from any loss, attorney's fees, expenses, or claims arising out of Buyer's inspection of the Property, except those arising out of the acts or omissions of Seller and those for repair or remediation of existing conditions discovered by Buyer's inspection. The obligations of Buyer under this provision will survive termination of this Contract and Closing, any other provision of this Contract to the contrary notwithstanding.

D.6.b. Release. **Buyer releases Seller and those persons acting on Seller's behalf from all claims and causes of action (including claims for attorney's fees and court and other costs) resulting from Buyer's inspection of the Property** [**include if applicable: ,**

including claims arising out of Seller's negligence, but not Seller's gross negligence or intentional misconduct].

E. Representations [; As Is, Where Is Provision; Environmental Matters]

The parties' representations stated in sections A. and D. of Exhibit B are true and correct as of the Effective Date and must be true and correct on the Closing Date. A party who becomes aware that any of the representations of either party are not true and correct will promptly notify the other party. Unless a party notifies the other party to the contrary on or before the Closing Date, or a party has actual knowledge to the contrary as of the Closing Date, each party is entitled to presume that the representations of the other party in Exhibit B are true and correct as of the Closing Date.

Include the following if applicable.

The parties agree to the terms of section B. (As Is, Where Is) and section C. (Environmental Matters) in Exhibit B.

F. Condition of the Property until Closing; Cooperation; No Recording of Contract

F.1. Maintenance and Operation. Until Closing, Seller will (a) maintain the Property as it existed on the Effective Date, except for reasonable wear and tear and casualty damage; (b) use the Property in the same manner as it was used on the Effective Date; (c) comply with all Leases and other contracts of Seller pertaining to the Property in effect on the Effective Date and all laws and all governmental regulations affecting the Property; and (d) not encumber, transfer, or dispose of any of the Property [**include if applicable:** or Personal Property], except to sell inventory, replace equipment, and use supplies in the normal course of operating the Property. Until the end of the Inspection Period, Seller will not enter into, amend, or terminate any Lease or other contract that affects the Property other than in the ordinary course of operating the Property and will promptly give notice to Buyer of each new, amended, or terminated Lease or other contract, including a copy of the Lease or other contract, in sufficient time so that Buyer may consider the new information before the end of the Inspection Period. If Seller's notice is given within three days before the end of the Inspection Period, the Inspection Period will be extended for three days. After the end of the Inspection Period, Seller may not enter into, amend, or terminate any Lease or other contract that affects the Property without first obtaining Buyer's written consent, which Buyer will have no obligation to grant and, if granted, may be conditioned in any manner Buyer in its sole discretion deems appropriate.

F.2. *Casualty Damage.* Seller will notify Buyer promptly after discovery of any casualty damage to the Property. Seller will have no obligation to repair or replace the Property if it is damaged by casualty before Closing. Buyer may terminate this Contract if the casualty damage that occurs before Closing would materially affect Buyer's intended use of the Property, by giving notice to Seller within fifteen days after receipt of Seller's notice of the casualty (or before Closing if Seller's notice of the casualty is received less than fifteen days before Closing). [**Include if applicable**: The casualty damage will be deemed to materially affect Buyer's intended use if the estimated amount of the damage exceeds [**item 16**] percent of the Purchase Price.] If Buyer does not terminate this Contract, Seller will (a) convey the Property to Buyer in its damaged condition, (b) assign to Buyer all of Seller's rights under any property insurance policies covering the Property, and (c) credit to Buyer the amount of the deductibles and coinsurance provisions under any insurance policies covering the Property, but not in excess of the cost to repair the casualty damage and less any amounts previously paid or incurred by Seller to repair the Property. If Seller has not insured the Property and Buyer does not elect to terminate this Contract in accordance with this section, the Purchase Price will be reduced by the cost to repair the casualty damage less any amounts previously paid or incurred by Seller to repair the Property.

F.3. *Condemnation.* Seller will notify Buyer promptly after Seller receives notice that any part of the Property has been or is threatened to be condemned or otherwise taken by a governmental or quasi-governmental authority. Buyer may terminate this Contract if the condemnation would materially affect Buyer's intended use of the Property by giving notice to Seller within fifteen days after receipt of Seller's notice to Buyer (or before Closing if Seller's notice is received less than fifteen days before Closing). The condemnation will be deemed to materially affect Buyer's intended use if [**specify reason, e.g.,** the condemnation would eliminate all curb cuts on Main Street]. If Buyer does not terminate this Contract, (a) Buyer and Seller will each have the right to appear and defend their respective interests in the Property in the condemnation proceedings, (b) any award in condemnation will be assigned to Buyer, (c) if the taking occurs before Closing, the description of the Property will be revised to delete the portion taken, and (d) no change in the Purchase Price will be made.

F.4. *Claims; Hearings.* Seller will notify Buyer promptly after Seller receives notice of any claim or administrative hearing that is threatened, filed, or initiated before Closing that involves or directly affects the Property.

F.5. *Cooperation.* Seller will cooperate with Buyer, (a) before and after Closing, to transfer the applications, permits, and licenses held by Seller and used in the operation of the Property and to obtain any consents necessary for Buyer to operate the Property after Closing, and (b) before Closing, with any reasonable evaluation, inspection, audit, or study of the Property prepared by, for, or at the request of Buyer.

F.6. *No Recording.* Buyer may not file this Contract or any memorandum or notice of this Contract in the real property records of any county. If, however, Buyer records this Contract or a memorandum or notice, Seller may terminate this Contract and record a notice of termination.

F.7. Cessation of Marketing and Other Activities. During the term of this Contract, Seller (a) will not contract to sell or lease the Property or grant any easement or other rights to the Property to any other person (whether or not such contract is denominated as a "back-up" contract); (b) will cease all efforts to market the Property to any other prospective buyer or lessee thereof; and (c) will inform any such prospective buyer or lessee inquiring as to the status of the Property that it is under contract of sale.

G. Termination

G.1. Disposition of Earnest Money after Termination

G.1.a. To Buyer. If Buyer terminates this Contract in accordance with Buyer's rights to terminate, Buyer will send a request for release of the Earnest Money to Seller, with a copy to the Title Company, to be signed by Seller. If Seller fails to deliver a signed release to the Title Company within fifteen days after delivery of the request for release, Buyer may make a written demand on the Title Company for the Earnest Money, and Title Company will promptly deliver a copy of the demand to Seller. Unless Seller delivers a written objection to the Title Company, within fifteen days after the Title Company delivers Buyer's written demand for the Earnest Money, the Title Company will, without any further authorization from Seller, deliver the Earnest Money to Buyer, less $100, which will be paid to Seller as consideration for the right granted by Seller to Buyer to terminate this Contract.

G.1.b. To Seller. If Seller terminates this Contract in accordance with Seller's rights to terminate, Seller will send a request for release of the Earnest Money to Buyer, with a copy to the Title Company, to be signed by Buyer. If Buyer fails to deliver a signed release to the Title Company within fifteen days after delivery of the request for release, Seller may make a written demand on the Title Company for the Earnest Money, and the Title Company will promptly deliver a copy of the demand to Buyer. Unless Buyer delivers a written objection to the Title Company, within fifteen days after the Title Company delivers Seller's written demand for the Earnest Money, the Title Company will, without any further authorization from Buyer, deliver the Earnest Money to Seller.

G.2. Duties after Termination. If this Contract is terminated after the expiration of the Inspection Period, Buyer will promptly return to Seller or destroy as directed by Seller all of Seller's records in Buyer's possession or control. After return of the records, neither party will have further duties or obligations to the other under this Contract, except for those obligations that cannot be or were not performed before termination of this Contract or that expressly survive termination of this Contract.

H. Closing

H.1. Closing. This transaction will close ("Closing") at the Title Company's offices on [**item 17**] (the "Closing Date").

H.2. Conditions of Closing. Neither party will be obligated to close the sale and purchase of the Property unless the other party has satisfied the following conditions, any of which may be waived by the first party in its discretion:

H.2.a. Representations and Warranties. The representations and warranties of the other party must be true and correct at Closing.

H.2.b. Performance of Covenants and Agreements. The other party must have performed all covenants and agreements required to be performed at or before Closing by that party.

H.2.c. No Bankruptcy. No voluntary or involuntary proceeding in bankruptcy shall be pending with respect to that party.

H.3. Closing Documents; Title Company Documents. The parties will execute and deliver the following closing documents and any documents required by the Title Company.

H.3.a. At Closing, Seller will deliver the following items:

Select one of the following.

General Warranty Deed [**include if applicable:** with Vendor's Lien at Buyer's option]

Or

Special Warranty Deed [**include if applicable:** with Vendor's Lien at Buyer's option]

Continue with the following as applicable.

Bill of Sale and Assignment

IRS Nonforeign Person Affidavit

Evidence of Seller's authority to close this transaction

Notices, statements, and certificates as specified in Exhibit D

Assignment and Assumption of Leases

Assignment and Assumption of Contracts

Tenant Estoppel Certificate

H.3.b. At Closing, Buyer will deliver the following items:

Include all applicable items.

Balance of Purchase Price

Evidence of Buyer's authority to close this transaction

Deceptive Trade Practices Act waiver

Assignment and Assumption of Leases

Assignment and Assumption of Contracts

Acknowledgment(s) of receipt of notices, statements, and certificates as specified in Exhibit D

Seller-financing documents

Promissory Note

Deed of Trust

Deed of Trust to Secure Assumption

Security Agreement

Financing Statement

Loan Documents required by third-party lender

The documents listed in these paragraphs H.3.a. and H.3.b. are collectively known as the "Closing Documents." Unless otherwise agreed by the parties before Closing, the Closing Documents for which forms exist in the current edition of the *Texas Real Estate Forms Manual* (State Bar of Texas) will be prepared using those forms.

H.3.c. Payment of Purchase Price. Buyer will deliver the Purchase Price and other amounts that Buyer is obligated to pay under this Contract to the Title Company in funds acceptable to the Title Company. The Earnest Money will be applied to the Purchase Price.

H.3.d. Disbursement of Funds; Recording; Copies. The Title Company will be instructed to disburse the Purchase Price and other funds in accordance with this Contract, record the deed and the other Closing Documents directed to be recorded, and distribute documents and copies in accordance with the parties' written instructions.

H.3.e. Delivery of Originals. Seller will deliver to Buyer the originals of Seller's Records.

H.3.f. Possession. Seller will deliver possession of the Property to Buyer, subject to the Permitted Exceptions existing at Closing and any liens and security interests created at Closing to secure financing for the Purchase Price.

H.4. Transaction Costs

H.4.a. Seller's Costs. Seller will pay the basic charge for the Title Policy; one-half of the escrow fee; the costs to prepare the deed; the costs to obtain, deliver, and record releases of any liens required to be released in connection with the sale; the costs to record documents to cure Title Objections agreed or required to be cured by Seller and to resolve matters shown in Schedule C of the Title Commitment; [**include if applicable:** the Title Company's inspection fee to delete from the Title Policy the customary exception for rights of parties in possession;] the costs to obtain the [Survey, UCC Search, and] certificates or reports of ad valorem taxes; the costs to deliver copies of the instruments described in paragraph C.5. and Seller's records; any other costs expressly required to be paid by Seller in this Contract; and Seller's attorney's fees and expenses.

H.4.b. Buyer's Costs. Buyer will pay one-half of the escrow fee; the costs to obtain, deliver, and record all documents other than those to be obtained or recorded at Seller's expense; [**include if applicable:** the additional premium for the "survey/area and boundary deletion" in the Title Policy, if the deletion is requested by Buyer, as well as the cost of any other endorsements or modifications of the standard form of Title Policy requested by Buyer; the costs of work required by Buyer to have the Survey reflect matters other than those required under this Contract except changes required for curative purposes;] the costs to obtain financing of the Purchase Price, including the incremental premium costs of the loan title policies and endorsements and deletions required by Buyer's lender; any other costs expressly required to be paid by Buyer in this Contract; and Buyer's attorney's fees and expenses.

H.4.c. Ad Valorem Taxes. Ad valorem taxes on the Property for all years before the calendar year of Closing must be paid by Seller at or before Closing. Ad valorem taxes for the Property for the calendar year of Closing will be prorated between Buyer and Seller as of the Closing Date. If the ad valorem taxes for the current year are assessed, the Title Company will pay the current year's ad valorem taxes at Closing. If the ad valorem taxes for the current year are not assessed, Seller's portion of the prorated taxes will be paid to Buyer at Closing as a credit to the Purchase Price. Buyer will assume the obligation to pay, and will pay in full, such taxes for the year of Closing before delinquency. If the assessment for the calendar year of Closing is not known at the Closing Date, the proration will be based on tax rates for the previous tax year applied to the most current assessed value, and Buyer and Seller will adjust the prorations in cash within thirty days after the actual assessment and taxes are known. Seller will promptly notify Buyer of all notices of proposed or final tax valuations and assessments that Seller receives after the Effective Date and after Closing.

If the property is subject to more than one tax parcel, include clause 4-3-4.

If the property is subject to reduced valuations and reduced tax assessments, include clause 4-3-5.

H.4.d. Income and Expenses. Income and expenses, including service contracts assumed by Buyer, general and special assessments, and sewer, water and other utility costs pertaining to the Property will be prorated as of the Closing Date on an accrual basis and paid at Closing as a credit or debit adjustment to the Purchase Price. Invoices that are received after Closing for operating expenses incurred on or before the Closing Date and not adjusted at

Closing will be prorated between the parties as of the Closing Date, and Seller will pay its share within ten days after receipt of Buyer's notice of the deficiency.

H.4.e. Postclosing Adjustments. If errors in the prorations made at Closing are identified within ninety days after Closing, Seller and Buyer will make post-closing adjustments to correct the errors within fifteen days after receipt of notice of the errors.

H.4.f. Brokers' Commissions. Other than the real estate broker disclosed in writing to the other party and the responsibility for the payment thereof set forth in such written disclosure, Buyer and Seller represent that there are no other real estate agents or brokers involved in this transaction and each indemnify and agree to defend and hold the other party harmless from any loss, attorney's fees, and court and other costs arising out of a claim by any person or entity claiming by, through, or under the indemnitor for a broker's or finder's fee or commission because of this transaction or this Contract, whether the claimant is disclosed to the indemnitee or not.

H.5. Issuance of Title Policy. Seller will cause the Title Company to issue the Title Policy to Buyer promptly after Closing.

I. Default and Remedies

I.1. Seller's Default; Remedies before Closing. If Seller fails to perform its obligations under this Contract or if Seller's representations are not true and correct as of the Closing Date ("Seller's Default"), Buyer may elect one of the following as its sole and exclusive remedy before Closing:

> If the buyer's liquidated damages equal $0, modify paragraph I.1.a. as appropriate.

I.1.a. Termination; Liquidated Damages. Buyer may terminate this Contract by giving notice to Seller on or before the Closing Date and have the Earnest Money, less $100 as described above, returned to Buyer. Unless Seller's Default relates to the untruth or incorrectness of Seller's representations for reasons not reasonably within Seller's control, if Seller's Default occurs after Buyer has incurred costs to inspect the Property after the Effective Date and Buyer terminates this Contract in accordance with the previous sentence, Seller will also pay to Buyer as liquidated damages Buyer's actual out-of-pocket expenses incurred to inspect the Property after the Effective Date ("Buyer's Expenses"), not to exceed the amount of [**item 18**] ("Buyer's Liquidated Damages"), within ten days after Seller's receipt of Buyer's itemization of Buyer's Expenses accompanied by reasonable evidence thereof.

I.1.b. Specific Performance. Unless Seller's Default relates to the untruth or incorrectness of Seller's representations for reasons not reasonably within Seller's control, Buyer may enforce specific performance of Seller's obligations under this Contract, but any such action must be initiated, if at all, within [**item 19**] days after the breach or alleged breach of this Contract. If such action is not initiated within that period and this Contract has not previously been terminated, Buyer will be deemed to have elected to terminate this Contract as of the expiration of that period. If title to the Property is awarded to Buyer, the conveyance will be subject to the matters stated in the Title Commitment.

I.1.c. Actual Damages. If Seller conveys or encumbers any portion of the Property before Closing so that Buyer's ability to enforce specific performance of Seller's obligations under this Contract is precluded or impaired, Buyer will be entitled to seek recovery from Seller for the actual damages sustained by Buyer by reason of Seller's Default, including attorney's fees and expenses and court costs.

I.2. Seller's Default; Remedies after Closing. If Seller's representations are not true and correct at Closing due to circumstances reasonably within Seller's control and Buyer does not become aware of the untruth or incorrectness of such representations until after Closing, Buyer will have all the rights and remedies available at law or in equity. If Seller fails to perform any of its obligations under this Contract that survive Closing, Buyer will have all rights and remedies available at law or in equity unless otherwise provided by the Closing Documents.

I.3. *Buyer's Default; Remedies before Closing.* If Buyer fails to perform any of its obligations under this Contract ("Buyer's Default"), Seller may terminate this Contract by giving notice to Buyer on or before Closing and have the Earnest Money paid to Seller.

> If the buyer agrees to pay the seller additional liquidated damages, include clause 4-3-6.

I.4. *Buyer's Default; Remedies after Closing.* If Buyer fails to perform any of its obligations under this Contract that survive Closing, Seller will have all rights and remedies available at law or in equity unless otherwise provided by the Closing Documents.

I.5. *Liquidated Damages.* The parties agree that just compensation for the harm that would be caused by a default by either party cannot be accurately estimated or would be very difficult to accurately estimate and that Buyer's Liquidated Damages or the Earnest Money [**include if applicable:** and Seller's Additional Liquidated Damages] are reasonable forecasts of just compensation to the nondefaulting party for the harm that would be caused by a default.

I.6. *Attorney's Fees.* If either party retains an attorney to enforce this Contract, the party prevailing in litigation is entitled to recover reasonable attorney's fees and court and other costs.

J. Miscellaneous Provisions

J.1. *Notices.* Any notice required by or permitted under this Contract must be in writing. Any notice required by this Contract will be deemed to be given (whether received or not) the earlier of receipt or three business days after being deposited with the United States Postal Service, postage prepaid, certified mail, return receipt requested, and addressed to the intended recipient at the address shown in this Contract. Notice may also be given by regular mail, personal delivery, courier delivery, or email and will be effective when received, provided that (a) any notice received on a Saturday, Sunday, or holiday will be deemed to have been received on the next day that is not a Saturday, Sunday, or holiday and (b) any notice received after 5:00 P.M. local time at the place of delivery on a day that is not a Saturday, Sunday, or holiday will be deemed to have been received on the next day that is not a Saturday, Sunday, or holiday. Any address for notice may be changed by not less than ten days' prior written notice given as provided herein. Copies of each notice must be given by one of these methods to the attorney of the party to whom notice is given.

To Buyer: **[item 20]**

To Seller: **[item 21]**

J.2. Entire Agreement. This Contract, its exhibits, and any Closing Documents are the entire agreement of the parties concerning the sale of the Property by Seller to Buyer. There are no representations, warranties, agreements, or promises pertaining to the Property or the sale of the Property by Seller to Buyer, and Buyer is not relying on any statements or representations of Seller or any agent of Seller, that are not in this Contract, its exhibits, and any Closing Documents.

J.3. Amendment. This Contract may be amended only by an instrument in writing signed by the parties.

Select one of the following.

J.4. Prohibition of Assignment. Buyer may not assign this Contract or Buyer's rights under it without Seller's prior written consent, which Seller has no obligation to grant and which, if granted, may be conditioned in any manner Seller deems appropriate, and any attempted assignment without Seller's consent is void. The consent by Seller to any assignment by Buyer will not release Buyer of its obligations under this Contract, and Buyer and the assignee will be jointly and severally liable for the performance of those obligations after any such assignment.

Or

J.4. *Assignment.* Buyer may assign this Contract and Buyer's rights under it only to an entity in which Buyer possesses, directly or indirectly, the power to direct or cause the direction of its management and policies, whether through the ownership of voting securities or otherwise, and any other assignment is void. No such assignment will release Buyer of its obligations under this Contract, and Buyer and the assignee will be jointly and severally liable for the performance of such obligations after any such assignment.

Continue with the following.

J.5. *Survival.* The provisions of this Contract that expressly survive termination or Closing and other obligations of this Contract that cannot be performed before termination of this Contract or before Closing survive termination of this Contract or Closing, and the legal doctrine of merger does not apply to these matters. If there is any conflict between the Closing Documents and this Contract, the Closing Documents control. The representations made by the parties as of Closing survive Closing.

J.6. *Choice of Law; Venue.* THIS CONTRACT IS TO BE CONSTRUED UNDER THE LAWS OF THE STATE OF TEXAS, WITHOUT REGARD TO CHOICE-OF-LAW RULES OF ANY JURISDICTION. VENUE IS IN THE COUNTY WHERE THE PROPERTY IS LOCATED.

J.7. *Waiver of Default.* Default is not waived if the nondefaulting party fails to declare a default immediately or delays taking any action with respect to the default.

J.8. *No Third-Party Beneficiaries.* There are no third-party beneficiaries of this Contract.

J.9. *Severability.* If a provision in this Contract is unenforceable for any reason, to the extent the unenforceability does not destroy the basis of the bargain among the parties, the unenforceability does not affect any other provision of this Contract, and this Contract is to be construed as if the unenforceable provision is not a part of the Contract.

J.10. *Ambiguities Not to Be Construed against Party Who Drafted Contract.* The rule of construction that ambiguities in a document are construed against the party who drafted it does not apply in interpreting this Contract.

J.11. *No Special Relationship.* The parties' relationship is an ordinary commercial relationship, and the parties do not intend to create the relationship of principal and agent, partners, joint venturers, or any other special relationship.

J.12. *Counterparts.* If this Contract is executed in multiple counterparts, all counterparts taken together constitute this Contract. Copies of signatures to this Contract are effective as original signatures.

J.13. *Confidentiality.* This Contract, this transaction, and all information learned in the course of this transaction will be kept confidential, except to the extent disclosure is required by law or court order or to enable third parties to advise or assist Buyer to inspect the Property or Seller or Buyer to close this transaction. Remedies for violations of this provision are limited to injunctions, and no damages or rescission may be sought or recovered as a result of any such violations.

J.14. *Binding Effect.* This Contract binds, benefits, and may be enforced by the parties and their respective heirs, successors, and permitted assigns.

> If the DTPA is applicable and the buyer is a consumer and has agreed to waive its rights under the DTPA, include clause 4-3-7. Alternatively, include form 4-22 in exhibit D.

> If the parties have agreed to waive their right to trial by jury, include clause 4-3-8.

K. Exhibits

The following are attached to and are a part of this Contract:

Exhibit A—Legal Description of Land [and Personal Property]

Exhibit B—Representations; Environmental Matters

Exhibit C—Seller's Records

Exhibit D—Notices, Statements, and Certificates

[**Include if applicable:** Exhibit E—Seller Financing Addendum]

____
[Name and title of seller]
Date:

____
[Name and title of buyer]
Date:

Title Company's Acceptance of Contract

Title Company, by its execution and delivery of this Real Estate Sales Contract, acknowledges it is "the person responsible for closing" the transaction that is the subject of this Contract pursuant to section 6045(e) of the Internal Revenue Code and to prepare and file all informational returns, including, without limitation, IRS Form 1099S, and to otherwise comply with the provisions of section 6045(e) of the Internal Revenue Code, and acknowledges receipt of a fully executed counterpart of this Real Estate Sales Contract on this ____ day of _________, 20__.

[Item 7]

By:______________________________
Name:
Title:

Receipt for Earnest Money Deposit

Title Company acknowledges receipt of the Earnest Money deposit of [**item 6**] required under this Real Estate Sales Contract on this ____ day of _________, 20__.

[**Item 7**]

By:______________________________
Name:
Title:

> If additional earnest money is required prior to the end of the inspection period, include the following.

Receipt for Additional Earnest Money Deposit

Title Company acknowledges receipt of the Additional Earnest Money deposit of [**amount**] AND NO/100 DOLLARS ($[**amount**]) required under this Real Estate Sales Contract on this ____ day of _________, 20__.

[**Item 7**]

By:______________________________
Name:
Title:

Exhibit A

Legal Description of Land [and Personal Property]

Include legal description of the land.

If the legal description should include a more extensive description of the seller's property interests to be conveyed to the buyer, add the words "together with" at the end of the metes-and-bounds description and include clause 4-3-9.

Include one of the following if the transaction involves some personal property.

All personal property associated with the Land and Improvements, except the following: [**list exceptions**].

Or

The following described personal property: [**describe property**].

Exhibit B

Representations; Environmental Matters

A. Seller's Representations to Buyer

Seller represents to Buyer that the following are true and correct as of the Effective Date and will be true and correct on the Closing Date, unless Seller has given Buyer notice of any changes prior to the Closing Date that such circumstances have changed due to causes not reasonably within Seller's control.

> If the seller is an individual or is acting in a representative capacity, some of the items should be modified.

A.1. Authority. Seller is a [**specify type of organization**] duly organized, validly existing, and in good standing under the laws of the state of [Texas/[**state**]] with authority to perform its obligations under this Contract. This Contract is binding on Seller. This Contract is, and all documents required by this Contract to be executed and delivered to Buyer at Closing will be, duly authorized, executed, and delivered by Seller.

A.2. Litigation. Seller has not received written notice and has no actual knowledge of any litigation pending or threatened against the Property or Seller that might adversely affect the Property or Seller's ability to perform its obligations under this Contract [**include if applicable:** , except: [**specify**]].

A.3. Violation of Governmental Requirements. Seller has not received written notice and has no actual knowledge of violation of any law, ordinance, regulation, restriction, or legal requirements affecting the Property or Seller's use of the Property [**include if applicable:** , except: [**specify**]].

A.4. Licenses, Permits, and Approvals. Seller has not received written notice and has no actual knowledge that any license, permit, or approval necessary to use the Property in the manner in which it is currently being used has expired or will not be renewed on expiration or that any material condition will be imposed to use or renew the same [**include if applicable:** , except: [**specify**]].

A.5. Condemnation; Zoning; Land Use; Hazardous Materials. Seller has not received written notice and has no actual knowledge of any condemnation, zoning, land-use, hazardous materials, or other proceedings affecting the Property or any written inquiries or notices by any governmental authority or third party with respect to condemnation, zoning, or other land-use regulations or the presence of hazardous materials affecting the Property [**include if applicable:** , except: [**specify**]].

A.6. Terrorist Organizations Lists. Seller is not and Seller has no actual knowledge that any of its partners, members, shareholders, owners, employees, officers, directors, representatives, or agents is a person or entity with whom U.S. persons or entities are restricted from doing business under regulations of the Office of Foreign Asset Control of the Department of the Treasury or under any statute, executive order, or other governmental action.

A.7. No Other Obligation to Sell Property or Restriction against Sale. Seller is not obligated to sell any of the Property to any person other than Buyer. Seller's performance of this Contract will not cause a breach of any other agreement or obligation to which Seller is a party or by which Seller or the Property is bound.

A.8. No Liens. On the Closing Date, the Property will be free and clear of all mechanic's and materialman's liens and other liens and encumbrances of any nature not arising by, through, or under Buyer except the Permitted Exceptions or liens to which Buyer has given its consent in writing, and no work or materials will have been furnished to the Property by Seller that might give rise to mechanic's, materialman's, or other liens against the Property other than work or materials to which Buyer has given its consent in writing.

A.9. Seller's Records. The records provided by Seller to Buyer for Buyer's inspections will be true, correct, and complete copies of the records in Seller's possession or control. The records that were prepared by or under Seller's supervision and control will be true, correct, and complete in all material respects. Unless Seller notifies Buyer to the contrary at the time of delivery of records provided by Seller to Buyer that were not prepared by or under Seller's supervision and control, Seller has no actual knowledge that such records are not true, correct, and complete in any material respect.

A.10. No Other Representation. Except as stated above or in the notices, statements, and certificates set forth in Exhibit D, Seller makes no representation with respect to the Property.

A.11. No Warranty. Except as set forth in this Contract and in the Closing Documents, Seller has made no warranty in connection with this transaction.

Include the following if the conveyance is on an "as is" basis.

B. "As Is, Where Is"

THIS CONTRACT IS AN ARM'S-LENGTH AGREEMENT BETWEEN THE PARTIES. THE PURCHASE PRICE WAS BARGAINED ON THE BASIS OF AN "AS IS, WHERE IS" TRANSACTION AND REFLECTS THE AGREEMENT OF THE PARTIES THAT THERE ARE NO REPRESENTATIONS, DISCLOSURES, OR EXPRESS OR IMPLIED WARRANTIES, EXCEPT THOSE IN THIS CONTRACT AND THE CLOSING DOCUMENTS.

BUYER IS NOT RELYING ON ANY REPRESENTATIONS, DISCLOSURES, OR EXPRESS OR IMPLIED WARRANTIES OTHER THAN THOSE EXPRESSLY CONTAINED IN THIS CONTRACT AND THE CLOSING DOCUMENTS. BUYER IS NOT RELYING ON ANY INFORMATION REGARDING THE PROPERTY PROVIDED BY ANY PERSON, OTHER THAN BUYER'S OWN INSPECTION AND THE REP-

RESENTATIONS AND WARRANTIES CONTAINED IN THIS CONTRACT AND THE CLOSING DOCUMENTS.

The provisions of this section B. regarding the Property [will/will not] be included in the deed [**include if applicable:** and bill of sale] with appropriate modification of terms as the context requires.

> Include the following if the seller retains no liability for environmental matters after closing.

C. Environmental Matters

AFTER CLOSING, BUYER RELEASES SELLER FROM LIABILITY FOR ENVIRONMENTAL PROBLEMS AFFECTING THE PROPERTY, INCLUDING LIABILITY (1) UNDER THE COMPREHENSIVE ENVIRONMENTAL RESPONSE, COMPENSATION, AND LIABILITY ACT (CERCLA), THE RESOURCE CONSERVATION AND RECOVERY ACT (RCRA), THE TEXAS SOLID WASTE DISPOSAL ACT, OR THE TEXAS WATER CODE; OR (2) ARISING AS THE RESULT OF THEORIES OF PRODUCTS LIABILITY AND STRICT LIABILITY, OR UNDER NEW LAWS OR CHANGES TO EXISTING LAWS ENACTED AFTER THE EFFECTIVE DATE THAT WOULD OTHERWISE IMPOSE ON SELLERS IN THIS TYPE OF TRANSACTION NEW LIABILITIES FOR ENVIRONMENTAL PROBLEMS AFFECTING THE PROPERTY. **THIS RELEASE APPLIES EVEN WHEN THE ENVIRONMENTAL PROBLEMS AFFECTING THE PROPERTY RESULT FROM SELLER'S OWN NEGLIGENCE OR THE NEGLIGENCE OF SELLER'S REPRESENTATIVE.**

The provisions of this section C. regarding the Property [will/will not] be included in the deed [**include if applicable:** and bill of sale] with appropriate modification of terms as the context requires.

D. Buyer's Representations to Seller

Buyer represents to Seller that the following are true and correct as of the Effective Date and will be true and correct on the Closing Date, unless Buyer has given Seller notice of any changes prior to the Closing Date that such circumstances have changed due to causes not reasonably within Buyer's control.

> If the buyer is an individual or is acting in a representative capacity, some of the items should be modified.

D.1. Authority. Buyer is a [**specify type of organization**] duly organized, validly existing, and in good standing under the laws of the state of [Texas/[**state**]] with authority to perform its obligations under this Contract. This Contract is binding on Buyer. This Contract is, and all documents required by this Contract to be executed and delivered to Seller at Closing will be, duly authorized, executed, and delivered by Buyer.

D.2. Terrorist Organizations Lists. Buyer is not and Buyer has no actual knowledge that any of its partners, members, shareholders, owners, employees, officers, directors, representatives, or agents is a person or entity with whom U.S. persons or entities are restricted from doing business under regulations of the Office of Foreign Asset Control of the Department of the Treasury or under any statute, executive order, or other governmental action.

> Include other representations from the buyer to the seller as needed.

Exhibit C

Seller's Records

To the extent that Seller has possession or control of the following items pertaining to and currently impacting the Property, Seller will deliver or make the items or copies of them available to Buyer by the deadline stated in paragraph D.3.:

Select items as agreed by the parties.

Governmental

governmental licenses, certificates, permits, and approvals

tax statements for the current year and the last [**number**] years

notices of appraised value for the current year and the last [**number**] years

records of any tax exemption, special use, or other valuation or exemption applicable to the Property

records of regulatory proceedings or violations (for example, condemnation, environmental)

other: [**specify**]

Land

soil reports

environmental reports and other information regarding the environmental condition of the Property

water rights

engineering reports

prior surveys

site plans

other: [**specify**]

Facilities

as-built plans, specifications, and mechanical drawings for improvements

warranty agreements

management, employment, labor, service, equipment, supply, and maintenance agreements

insurance policies and loss runs

ADA and other building inspection reports

engineering reports

environmental reports

incident reports

operating and maintenance plans (for example, asbestos maintenance plans)

life-safety plans

other: [**specify**]

Financial

annual operating statements for the most recent [**number**] years of operation

monthly operating statements since the close of the last fiscal year balance sheet as of [**date**]

books and records for the Property

utility bills for the most recent [**number**] months of operation

other: [**specify**]

Leases

commission and leasing agent agreements

rent roll setting forth for each Lease:

tenant's name

square footage leased

date of expiration of current and renewal terms

renewal options

basic rent and formula for any additional rents

amount of additional rent paid during the last [**number**] [months/years]

prepaid rent

delinquent rent

security deposit

current tenant or landlord defaults

options to purchase any portion of the Property

rights of first refusal to lease other space

rights to rent concessions, tenant improvements, or other allowances

unpaid or contingent brokerage commissions (including commission on renewals)

estoppel letters and/or subordination agreements

other: [**specify**]

Licenses, Agreements, and Encumbrances

all licenses, agreements, and encumbrances (including all amendments and exhibits) affecting title to or use of the Property that have not been recorded in the real property records of the county or counties in which the Property is located

Exhibit D

Notices, Statements, and Certificates

Certain notices must be contained in the contract and others must be provided as separate notices. Please refer to the statutory requirements for each notice.

The notices, statements, and certificates (arranged by their application to particular transactions) that are listed below are [included in the sales contract] [and] [attached for delivery to Buyer], and Buyer acknowledges receipt of the notices, statements, and certificates by executing this contract:

Include one or more of the following paragraphs as applicable and modify section headers and paragraph numbers as appropriate.

A. Consumer Notices

Notice of Cancellation. Notice concerning the purchaser's three-day right of rescission under a contract to purchase real property if (1) the seller or the seller's agent solicits the sale at a place other than the seller's place of business; (2) the purchaser submits the purchase contract to the seller or the seller's agent at a place other than the seller's place of business; and (3) the consideration payable under the purchase contract exceeds $100; unless either (1) the purchaser is represented by a licensed attorney; (2) the transaction is negotiated by a licensed real estate broker; or (3) the transaction is negotiated at a place other than the purchaser's residence by the person who owns the property, as described in chapter 601 of the Texas Business and Commerce Code.

If applicable, attach form 4-5 in this chapter to the end of this exhibit D.

And/Or

B. Residential Transaction Notices

B.1. Seller's Disclosure of Property Condition. Seller's disclosure of the condition of residential property, described in section 5.008 of the Texas Property Code.

> If applicable, attach form 4-23, with all relevant information filled in, to the end of this exhibit D.

And/Or

B.2. Notice of Membership in Property Owners' Association. Notice concerning the sale of single-family residential property that is subject to membership in a property owners' association, described in section 5.012 of the Texas Property Code.

> If applicable, attach form 23-9 in this manual to the end of this exhibit D.

And/Or

B.3. Seller's Disclosure of Location of Conditions under Surface of Unimproved Real Property. Seller's disclosure of the location of pipelines under the surface of unimproved property to be used for residential purposes, described in section 5.013 of the Texas Property Code. A seller of unimproved property to be used for residential purposes shall provide the purchaser written notice disclosing the location of any transportation pipeline to the best of the seller's belief and knowledge as of the date the notice is completed and signed by the seller. If the information required to be disclosed is not known by the seller, the seller shall indicate that fact in the notice. A seller is not required to give this notice if (a) the seller is obligated under the terms of the contract to furnish a title insurance commitment to the buyer before Closing and (b) the buyer is entitled to terminate the contract if the buyer's objections to title as permitted by the contract are not cured by the seller before Closing.

> No form is provided, because the real estate sales contract portion of this form 4-2 satisfies the provisions for exemption from disclosure.

And/Or

B.4. *Notice of Obligation to Pay Public Improvement District Assessment.* Seller's disclosure that a single-family residential property is located within a public improvement district, described in section 5.014 of the Texas Property Code.

If applicable, attach form 4-6 to the end of this exhibit D.

And/Or

B.5. *Residential Contracts for Deed.* Notice regarding the sale of property used or to be used as the purchaser's residence if the contract does not provide for delivery of a deed from the seller to the purchaser within 180 days after the final execution of the contract.

See Tex. Prop. Code §§ 5.069–.074.

And/Or

B.6. *Notice Regarding Insulation to Buyer of New Home.* Notice concerning insulation to be installed in a new home, described in section 460.16 of title 16 of the Code of Federal Regulations.

If applicable, attach form 4-7 to the end of this exhibit D.

And/Or

B.7. *Disclosure of Information on Lead-Based Paint and/or Lead-Based Paint Hazards.* Lead-based paint warning statement, described in section 745.100 *et seq.* of title 40 of the Code of Federal Regulations.

If applicable, attach form 4-8 to the end of this exhibit D.

And/Or

B.8. *Asbestos Disclosure Notice.* Notice concerning asbestos, described in sections 1910.1001 and 1926.1101 of title 29 of the Code of Federal Regulations.

If applicable, attach form 4-9 to the end of this exhibit D.

And/Or

B.9. Notice Regarding Sale Subject to a Recorded Lien. Notice to the purchaser and each lienholder required under Texas Property Code section 5.016 that property being sold will be conveyed subject to a lien.

If applicable, attach form 4-10 to the end of this exhibit D.

And/Or

C. Condominium Transaction Notices

C.1. Acknowledgment of Receipt of Condominium Documents. Condominium declaration, bylaws, and association rules, described in section 82.156 of the Texas Property Code.

If applicable, attach form 24-8 to the end of this exhibit D.

And/Or

C.2. Condominium Resale Certificate. Resale certificate from the condominium owners' association or waiver of resale certificate, described in section 82.157 of the Texas Property Code.

If applicable, attach condominium resale certificate promulgated by the Texas Real Estate Commission, available at **www.trec.texas.gov/forms/condominium-resale-certificate**, or form 24-7 (waiver of condominium resale certificate) to the end of this exhibit D.

And/Or

D. All Real Property Transaction Notices

D.1. Storage Tanks Disclosure Provider. Notice concerning underground storage tanks, described in section 334.9 of title 30 of the Texas Administrative Code.

If applicable, attach form 4-11 to the end of this exhibit D.

And/Or

D.2. *Notice to Purchaser Regarding Restrictive Covenants.* Notice of deed restrictions, described in section 212.155 of the Texas Local Government Code.

If applicable, attach form 4-12 to the end of this exhibit D.

And/Or

D.3. *Notice to Purchaser Regarding Coastal Area Property.* Notice regarding real property located adjacent to tidally influenced, submerged lands of Texas, described in section 33.135 of the Texas Natural Resources Code.

If applicable, attach form 4-13 to the end of this exhibit D.

And/Or

D.4. *Notice to Purchaser of Property Seaward of Gulf Intracoastal Waterway.* Notice concerning public easements to the public beach, described in section 61.025 of the Texas Natural Resources Code.

If applicable, attach form 4-14 to the end of this exhibit D.

And/Or

D.5. *Notice Regarding Possible Liability for Additional Taxes.* Notice of additional tax liability for vacant land that has been subject to a special tax appraisal method, described in section 5.010 of the Texas Property Code.

If applicable, attach form 4-15 to the end of this exhibit D.

And/Or

D.6. Notice Regarding Possible Annexation. Notice concerning the sale of property located outside the limits of a municipality that may now or later be included in the extraterritorial jurisdiction of a municipality and may now or later be subject to annexation by the municipality, described in section 5.011 of the Texas Property Code.

If applicable, attach form 4-16 to the end of this exhibit D.

And/Or

D.7. Notice for Unimproved Property in a Certificated Service Area of a Utility Service Provider. Notice for property in a certificated service area of a utility service provider, described in section 13.257 of the Texas Water Code.

If applicable, attach form 4-17 to the end of this exhibit D.

And/Or

D.8. Utility District Notice. Notice concerning the bonded indebtedness of, or rates to be charged by, a utility or other special district, described in section 49.452 of the Texas Water Code, with the form of notice to be used being dependent on whether the property (a) is located in whole or in part within the extraterritorial jurisdiction of one or more home-rule municipalities but is not located within the corporate boundaries of a municipality, (b) is located in whole or in part within the corporate boundaries of a municipality, or (c) is not located in whole or in part within the corporate boundaries of a municipality or the extraterritorial jurisdiction of one or more home-rule municipalities.

If applicable, attach form 4-18 to the end of this exhibit D.

And/Or

D.9. Notice to Purchaser of Property Located in Certain Annexed Water Districts. Notice required by section 54.016(h)(4)(A) of the Texas Water Code when property being sold is in a water or sanitary sewer district that entered a contract with a city with a population of 1.18 million or less under which the city is permitted to set rates in the district after annexation that are different from rates charged other residents of the city.

If applicable, attach form 4-19 to the end of this exhibit D.

And/Or

D.10. Notice to Purchaser that Property Is Located within the Area of the Alignment of a Transportation Project. Notice required under Texas Local Government Code section 232.0033 that all or part of the subdivision in which the property being sold is located is within the area of the alignment of a transportation project as shown in the final environmental decision document that is applicable to a future transportation corridor identified in a contract between the Texas Department of Transportation and a county under Texas Transportation Code section 201.619.

If applicable, attach form 4-20 to the end of this exhibit D.

And/Or

D.11. Certificates of Mold Remediation. Notice pursuant to section 1958.154 of the Texas Occupations Code, titled "Certificate of Mold Remediation; Duty of Property Owner," requiring a property owner who sells property that has been issued a certificate of mold remediation pursuant to this section to deliver copies to the purchaser of each certificate of mold remediation issued for the property within the preceding five years.

And/Or

D.12. Notice of Water Level Fluctuations. Notice to purchasers of real property adjoining an impoundment of water, including a reservoir or lake, constructed and maintained under Texas Water Code chapter 11, that has storage capacity of at least 5,000 acre-feet at the impoundment's normal operating level, provided pursuant to section 5.019 of the Texas Property Code.

If applicable, attach form 4-21 to the end of this exhibit D.

And/Or

E. Property Owners' Association Disclosures

E.1. Resale Certificate. Resale certificate from a property owners' association that is entitled to levy regular or special assessments as described in sections 207.002–.003 of the Texas Property Code. In contrast to the obligation of a condominium seller to provide the condominium governing documents and resale certificate under section 82.157 of the Texas Property Code, the obligation in chapter 207 is an obligation of the property owners' association upon a request from an owner, purchaser, agent, title insurance company, or other interested party.

If applicable, attach form 23-10 to the end of this exhibit D.

Exhibit E

Seller Financing Addendum

A. Promissory Note. The promissory note ("Note") will be payable by Buyer ("Maker") to the order of Seller ("Payee") at the place designated by Payee. The Note may be prepaid in whole or in part at any time without penalty, premium, or restriction of any kind. Any prepayments are to be applied to the payment of the installments of principal last maturing, and interest will immediately cease on the prepaid principal. The lien securing payment of the Note will be inferior to any lien securing any superior note described in the contract. The Note will be payable as follows:

Select one of the following.

In one payment due [**number**] days after the date of the Note with interest payable [at maturity/monthly/quarterly/annually].

Or

In [**number**] installments of $[**amount**] each [including interest/plus interest] beginning [**number**] days after the date of the Note and continuing at [monthly/quarterly/annual] intervals thereafter until [**date**], when the entire balance of the Note will be due and payable.

Or

Interest only in [**number**] installments for the first [**number**] year[s] and thereafter in [**number**] installments of $[**amount**] each [including interest/plus interest] beginning [**number**] days after the date of the Note and continuing at [monthly/quarterly/annual] intervals thereafter until [**date**], when the entire balance of the Note will be due and payable.

Or

Other: [**specify**].

Continue with the following.

B. Deed of Trust. The deed of trust ("Deed of Trust") securing the Note will provide for the following:

Select one of the following.

B.1. Assumption without Consent. The Property may be sold, transferred, or conveyed without the consent of Payee, provided any subsequent buyer or transferee assumes in writing for the benefit of Payee the obligation to pay the Note and to perform the covenants and agreements in the Deed of Trust in accordance with the terms of those instruments. No such assumption will release Maker from any liabilities or obligations arising under the Note or Deed of Trust. Neither the creation of a subordinate lien nor a sale thereunder will be construed as a sale or conveyance of the Property.

Or

B.1. Prohibition on Transfer

Include the following for a residential deed of trust if a due-on-sale clause is desired.

If Maker transfers any part of the Property without Payee's prior written consent, Payee may declare the Obligation immediately payable and invoke any remedies provided in the deed of trust for default. If the Property is residential real property containing fewer than five dwelling units or a residential manufactured home, this provision does not apply to (a) a subordinate lien or encumbrance that does not transfer rights of occupancy of the Property; (b) creation of a purchase-money security interest for household appliances; (c) transfer by devise, descent, or operation of law on the death of a co-Maker; (d) grant of a leasehold interest of three years or less without an option to purchase; (e) transfer to a spouse or children of Maker or between co-Makers; (f) transfer to a relative of Maker on Maker's death; (g) a transfer resulting from a decree of a dissolution of marriage, a legal separation agreement, or an incidental property settlement agreement by which the spouse of Maker becomes an owner of the Property; or (h) transfer to an inter vivos trust in which Maker is and remains a beneficiary and occupant of the Property.

> Include the following for a commercial deed of trust if a due-on-sale clause is desired.

Maker may not sell, transfer, or otherwise dispose of any Property, whether voluntarily or by operation of law, without the prior written consent of Payee. If granted, consent may be conditioned upon (a) the grantee's integrity, reputation, character, creditworthiness, and management ability being satisfactory to Payee; and (b) the grantee's executing, before such sale, transfer, or other disposition, a written assumption agreement containing any terms Payee may require, such as a principal pay down on the Obligation, an increase in the rate of interest payable with respect to the Obligation, a transfer fee, or any other modification of the Note, the Deed of Trust, or any other instruments evidencing or securing the Obligation.

> Continue with the following.

B.2. Prohibition on Further Encumbrances. Maker may not cause or permit any Property to be encumbered by any liens, security interests, or encumbrances other than the liens securing the Obligation and the liens securing ad valorem taxes not yet due and payable without the prior written consent of Payee. If granted, consent may be conditioned upon Maker's executing, before granting such lien, a written modification agreement containing any terms Payee may require, such as a principal pay down on the Obligation, an increase in the rate of interest payable with respect to the Obligation, an approval fee, or any other modification of the Note, the Deed of Trust, or any other instruments evidencing or securing the Obligation.

Maker may not grant any lien, security interest, or other encumbrance ("Subordinate Instrument") covering the Property that is subordinate to the liens created by the Deed of

Trust without the prior written consent of Payee. If granted, consent may be conditioned upon the Subordinate Instrument's containing express covenants to the effect that—

a. the Subordinate Instrument is unconditionally subordinate to the Deed of Trust;

b. if any action is instituted to foreclose or otherwise enforce the Subordinate Instrument, no action may be taken that would terminate any occupancy or tenancy without the prior written consent of Payee, and that consent, if granted, may be conditioned in any manner Payee determines;

c. rents, if collected by or for the holder of the Subordinate Instrument, will be applied first to the payment of the Obligation then due and to expenses incurred in the ownership, operation, and maintenance of the Property in any order Payee may determine, before being applied to any indebtedness secured by the Subordinate Instrument;

d. written notice of default under the Subordinate Instrument and written notice of the commencement of any action to foreclose or otherwise enforce the Subordinate Instrument must be given to Payee concurrently with or immediately after the occurrence of any such default or commencement; and

e. in the event of the bankruptcy of Maker, all amounts due on or with respect to the Obligation and the Deed of Trust will be payable in full before any payments on the indebtedness secured by the Subordinate Instrument and all decisions or elections in such proceedings affecting the Property will be made and controlled by Payee.

B.3. Prohibition on Transfer of Interests in Borrower. Maker may not cause or permit any of the following events to occur without the prior written consent of Payee: if

Maker is (a) a corporation, the termination of the corporation or the sale, pledge, encumbrance, or assignment of any shares of its stock; (b) a limited liability company, the termination of the company or the sale, pledge, encumbrance, or assignment of any of its membership interests; (c) a general partnership or joint venture, the termination of the partnership or venture or the sale, pledge, encumbrance, or assignment of any of its partnership or joint venture interests, or the withdrawal from or admission into it of any general partner or joint venturer; or (d) a limited partnership, (i) the termination of the partnership; (ii) the sale, pledge, encumbrance, or assignment of any of its general partnership interests, or the withdrawal from or admission into it of any general partner; (iii) the sale, pledge, encumbrance, or assignment of a controlling portion of its limited partnership interests; or (iv) the withdrawal from or admission into it of any controlling limited partner or partners. If granted, consent may be conditioned upon (a) the integrity, reputation, character, creditworthiness, and management ability of the person succeeding to the ownership interest in Maker (or security interest in such ownership) being satisfactory to Payee; and (b) the execution, before such event, by the person succeeding to the interest of Maker in the Property or ownership interest in Maker (or security interest in such ownership) of a written modification or assumption agreement containing such terms as Payee may require, such as a principal pay down on the Obligation, an increase in the rate of interest payable with respect to the Obligation, a transfer fee, or any other modification of the Note, the Deed of Trust, or any other instruments evidencing or securing the Obligation.

Select one of the following.

B.4. Without Escrow. Maker will furnish to Payee annually, before the taxes become delinquent, copies of tax receipts showing that all taxes on the Property have been paid. Maker will furnish to Payee annually evidence of current paid-up insurance naming Payee as an insured.

Or

B.4. With Escrow. Maker will, in addition to the principal and interest installments, deposit with Payee a pro rata part of the estimated annual ad valorem taxes on the Property and a pro rata part of the estimated annual insurance premiums for the improvements on the Property. These tax and insurance deposits are only estimates and may be insufficient to pay total taxes and insurance premiums. Maker must pay any deficiency within thirty days after notice from Payee. Maker's failure to pay the deficiency will constitute a default under the Deed of Trust. If any superior lienholder on the Property is collecting escrow payments for taxes and insurance, this paragraph will be inoperative as long as payments are being made to the superior lienholder.

Continue with the following.

B.5. Cross-Default. Any act or occurrence that would constitute default under the terms of any lien superior to the lien securing the Note will constitute a default under the Deed of Trust securing the Note.

C. Recourse Provisions. The Note and Deed of Trust are subject to the following provisions:

Select one of the following.

Full Recourse. Maker will have full recourse liability for repayment of the principal and interest of the Note and the performance of all covenants and agreements of Maker in the Deed of Trust.

Or

No Recourse. Maker will not have any recourse liability for repayment of the principal and interest of the Note or the performance of any covenants and agreements of Maker in the Deed of Trust. The sole remedy of Payee or other holder of the Note in the event of a default by Maker under the Note or Deed of Trust will be to foreclose the liens and security interests granted in the Deed of Trust, and Payee or other holder of the Note will not be entitled to any deficiency judgment against Maker.

Or

Partial Recourse. Except as set forth below, Maker will not have any recourse liability for repayment of the principal and interest of the Note or the performance of any covenants and agreements of Maker in the Deed of Trust. Except as set forth below, the sole remedy of Payee or other holder of the Note in the event of a default by Maker under the Note or Deed of Trust will be to foreclose the liens and security interests granted in the Deed of Trust, and Payee or other holder of the Note will not be entitled to any personal judgment against Maker. Maker will have full recourse liability for any loss or damage actually suffered or incurred by Payee or other holder of the Note by reason of the following matters:

1. taxes, assessments, and charges for labor, materials, or other amounts that if unpaid may create an encumbrance against the Property that accrue before foreclosure;

2. unpaid premiums for insurance required hereunder that accrue before foreclosure;

3. damage to the Property to the extent such damage would be otherwise covered by insurance required hereunder that was not maintained;

4. all rents, issues, profits, and income derived from the Property, including forfeited security deposits, after a default occurs and not expended for debt service or operating expenses of the Property before foreclosure;

5. tenant security deposits for leases of the Property not forfeited by or refunded to the tenants;

6. any condemnation or insurance proceeds not paid or applied as required in the Deed of Trust;

7. damage to and depreciation of the Property beyond normal wear and tear caused by the negligence of Maker or the failure of Maker to keep the Property in good repair and condition;

8. the return of or reimbursement for personal property taken from the Property by or on behalf of Maker and not replaced with personal property of equal utility and value;

9. damages resulting from fraud or misrepresentation by Maker;

10. damages resulting from breach of any warranty of title by Maker;

11. interest on the Note from the date of default through foreclosure, payment, or settlement of the debt;

12. all interest on the Note during any bankruptcy proceeding of Maker and all reasonable attorney's fees and expenses incurred as a result of Maker's bankruptcy; and

13. all attorney's fees and expenses incurred by Payee to collect any of the foregoing amounts.

Continue with the following.

____
Buyer/Maker

____
Seller/Payee

Form 4-3

Additional Clauses for Sales Contract

Adjusted Purchase Price

Clause 4-3-1

> If the purchase price is adjusted based on a survey, include the following provisions after the paragraph A.2. titled "Adjusted Purchase Price" in form 4-2 in this chapter.

A.2.a. If the Purchase Price based on the Survey exceeds an amount ("Maximum Purchase Price") that is equal to **[percent]** percent of the Purchase Price, Buyer may terminate this Contract and recover the Earnest Money by giving Seller Buyer's calculation of the Purchase Price and notice of termination within ten days after the Survey was delivered to both parties; provided, however, that Buyer's notice of termination will be automatically rescinded and the Purchase Price will be equal to the Maximum Purchase Price if Seller gives Buyer notice within ten days after receiving Buyer's notice of termination that Seller has waived the right to receive the portion of the Purchase Price in excess of the Maximum Purchase Price.

A.2.b. If the Purchase Price based on the Survey is less than an amount ("Minimum Purchase Price") that is equal to **[percent]** percent of the Purchase Price, Seller may terminate this Contract by giving Buyer Seller's calculation of the Purchase Price and notice of termination within ten days after the Survey was delivered to both parties; provided, however, that Seller's notice of termination will be automatically rescinded if Buyer gives Seller notice within ten days after receiving Seller's notice of termination that Buyer has waived the right to purchase the Property for a Purchase Price that is less than the Minimum Purchase Price.

A.2.c. If the calculation of the Purchase Price is to be made on the basis of the net square feet of surface area disclosed by the Survey, the net square feet of surface area will be the gross square feet of surface area within the Land less any portion of the surface area of the Land that is within a flood plain as specified on the applicable current FEMA map and any portion of the surface area of the Land that is subject to a right-of-way or easement that serves any land other than the Land.

Property Subject to Lien Securing Indebtedness in Excess of Net Purchase Price

Clause 4-3-2

Add this provision when the property is subject to any lien securing indebtedness in excess of the net purchase price.

C.7. *Partial Release of Liens.* If, as of the Effective Date, the Property is subject to any liens that secure indebtedness in excess of the estimated net proceeds of the Purchase Price after the satisfaction of brokers' commissions and other transaction costs for which Seller is responsible, then Seller promptly must obtain a written agreement or agreements (collectively, the "Partial Release Agreement") binding and enforceable against the holders of such liens ("Holders") for the benefit of Seller. The Partial Release Agreement must constitute an agreement to release all of such liens with respect to the Property on the payment to the Holders of an amount that does not exceed the net proceeds of the Purchase Price after the satisfaction of brokers' commissions and other transaction costs for which Seller is responsible. If Seller is required to provide a Partial Release Agreement, the Inspection Period will not commence until the executed Partial Release Agreement, in a form reasonably satisfactory to Buyer, is delivered to Buyer.

Additional Earnest Money

Clause 4-3-3

> Add this provision to the end of paragraph D.2. in form 4-2 if additional earnest money is required prior to the end of the inspection period.

Additional Earnest Money. If Buyer does not terminate this Contract pursuant to this provision, Buyer must deposit the additional Earnest Money in the amount of [**amount**] AND NO/100 DOLLARS ($[**amount**]) with [**checklist item 7**] on or before the end of the Inspection Period (the "Additional Earnest Money") to be applied to the Purchase Price or distributed in accordance with the terms of the Contract.

Property Subject to More Than One Tax Parcel

Clause 4-3-4

> Add this provision after paragraph H.4.c. in form 4-2 when the property is subject to more than one tax parcel.

Partial Tax Parcels. If the Property contains more than one unimproved partial tax parcel for the year of Closing, then the taxes and other assessments attributable to any such tax parcel for the year of Closing shall be allocated between the portion of such tax parcel that is within the Property and the portion of such tax parcel that is outside the Property on the basis of the respective percentages that the gross surface area of the portion of such tax parcel that is within the Property and the gross surface area of the portion of such tax parcel that is outside the Property represent of the total gross surface area of such tax parcel; provided, however, that the result of the foregoing computation shall be adjusted as applicable in order to reflect the taxable value of any improvements that have been constructed on either or both of the portions of such tax parcel. If the Property contains one or more partial tax parcels for the year of Closing, and all taxes and other assessments attributable to such tax parcel have not been paid in full at or prior to Closing, each of Seller and Buyer shall be obligated to pay the taxes and other assessments due with respect to their respective portions of such tax parcel for the entire year of Closing on or before the due date thereof and to indemnify, defend, and hold the other party harmless from and against any loss resulting from a failure to pay such taxes and assessments when they become due and payable.

Property Subject to Special Valuations and Reduced Tax Valuations

Clause 4-3-5

> Add this provision after paragraph H.4.c. in form 4-2 when the property is subject to special valuations and reduced tax valuations.

Special Valuations and Reduced Tax Valuations. If the Property has been the subject of special valuation and reduced tax assessments pursuant to the provisions of chapter 23, subchapter D, of the Texas Tax Code or under any other provision of law with respect to any period before the Closing, and if additional taxes, penalties, or interest are assessed pursuant to Code section 23.55 or under the other provision of law, the following will apply:

i. If Seller changes the use of the Property before Closing, resulting in the assessment of additional taxes for periods before Closing, Seller will pay the additional taxes.

> Select one of the following.

ii. If this sale or Buyer's use of the Property results in the assessment of additional taxes for periods before Closing, Buyer will pay the additional taxes

Or

ii. At Closing, the parties will determine the amount of deferred taxes payable if the sale of the Property as herein contemplated were deemed as of the Closing Date to constitute a change in the use of the Property that would result in the "roll-back" or recapture of deferred taxes for the current year and all preceding tax years for which the "roll-back" or recapture could be imposed ("Potential Roll-Back Amount"). Seller will pay at Closing an amount equal to the Potential Roll-Back Amount to all applicable taxing jurisdictions. On such payment, Seller will have no further liability for any further roll-back amounts and Buyer will assume any and all obligations for, and indemnify, defend, and hold Seller harmless from and against, any liability for any further roll-back amounts.

Or

ii. At Closing, the parties will determine the amount of deferred taxes payable if the sale of the Property as herein contemplated were deemed as of the Closing Date to constitute a change in the use of the Property that would result in the "roll-back" or recapture of deferred taxes for the current year and all preceding tax years for which the "roll-back" or recapture could be imposed ("Potential Roll-Back Amount") as of the Closing Date. Seller will deposit at Closing an amount equal to the Potential Roll-Back Amount with Title Company, to be held in an interest-bearing escrow account in accordance with the terms and conditions hereinafter set forth ("Roll-Back Escrow Account"). If a subsequent change in the use of the Property results in a roll-back of deferred taxes, the portion of recaptured deferred taxes attributable to the period before the Closing, if any, will be paid from the Roll-Back Escrow Account and the portion of deferred taxes attributable to the period from and after the Closing, if any, will be paid by Buyer (or its successors or assigns). On the earlier of (a) the date on which there is no longer any statutory basis for recapturing any deferred taxes attributable to the period before the Closing or (b) the date on which all taxes that may then potentially be recaptured for any period before the Closing have been recaptured, the remaining balance in the Roll-Back Escrow Account, if any, will be distributed to Seller.

Additional Liquidated Damages

Clause 4-3-6

> If the buyer agrees to pay the seller additional liquidated damages, add this provision after paragraph I.3. in form 4-2.

Seller's Additional Liquidated Damages. Buyer's Default occurs after Seller has incurred costs to perform its obligations under this Contract and Seller terminates this Contract in accordance with the previous sentence. Buyer will also reimburse Seller for the lesser of Seller's actual out-of-pocket expenses incurred after the Effective Date to perform its obligations under this Contract ("Seller's Expenses") in an amount not to exceed [**amount**] AND NO/100 DOLLARS ($[**amount**]) as Seller's Additional Liquidated Damages, within ten days after Buyer's receipt of an invoice from Seller stating the amount of Seller's Expenses accompanied by reasonable evidence of Seller's

Expenses. The foregoing constitutes Seller's sole and exclusive remedies for a default by Buyer before Closing.

Waiver of Consumer Rights

Clause 4-3-7

> Add this provision to the end of section J. in form 4-2 if the DTPA is applicable and the buyer is a consumer and has agreed to waive its rights under the DTPA. Alternatively, include form 4-22 in exhibit D.

Waiver of Consumer Rights. **BUYER WAIVES ITS RIGHTS UNDER THE TEXAS DECEPTIVE TRADE PRACTICES–CONSUMER PROTECTION ACT, SECTION 17.41 *ET SEQ.* OF THE TEXAS BUSINESS AND COMMERCE CODE, A LAW THAT GIVES CONSUMERS SPECIAL RIGHTS AND PROTECTIONS. AFTER CONSULTATION WITH AN ATTORNEY OF ITS OWN SELECTION, BUYER VOLUNTARILY CONSENTS TO THIS WAIVER.**

Waiver of Jury Trial

Clause 4-3-8

> Add this provision to the end of section J. in form 4-2 if the parties have agreed to waive their right to trial by jury.

Waiver of Jury Trial. **BUYER AND SELLER, EACH AFTER CONSULTATION WITH AN ATTORNEY OF ITS OWN SELECTION (WHICH COUNSEL WAS NOT DIRECTLY OR INDIRECTLY IDENTIFIED, SUGGESTED, OR SELECTED BY THE OTHER PARTY), BOTH VOLUNTARILY WAIVE A TRIAL BY JURY OF ANY ISSUE ARISING IN AN ACTION OR PROCEEDING BETWEEN THE PARTIES OR THEIR SUCCESSORS, UNDER OR CONNECTED WITH THIS CONTRACT OR ITS PROVISIONS. BUYER AND SELLER ACKNOWLEDGE TO EACH OTHER THAT BUYER AND SELLER ARE NOT IN SIGNIFICANTLY DISPARATE BARGAINING POSITIONS.**

Additional Seller's Property Rights

Clause 4-3-9

> Add this provision to exhibit A in form 4-2 as part of the legal description following the metes-and-bounds description if the legal description should include a more extensive description of the seller's property rights to be conveyed to the buyer.

a. all of Seller's right, title, and interest in and to any alleys, strips, or gores adjoining the Land and all of Seller's rights of ingress and egress to the Land, including, without limitation, any easements, rights-of-way, rights, or other interests in, on, under, or to any land, highway, street, road, right-of-way, or avenue, open or proposed, in, on, under, across, in front of, abutting, or adjoining the Land; and all of Seller's right, title, and interest in and to any awards made, or to be made in lieu thereof, and in and to any unpaid awards for damage to the Land by reason of a change of grade thereof;

b. all development or vested rights, utility capacity, governmental approvals, licenses, and permits (including all water, sewer, and drainage capacity currently held by or for Seller, if any, for the Land on the Closing Date), to the extent they relate to the ownership, use, leasing, maintenance, service, or operation of the Land;

c. all of Seller's right, title, and interest in and to any oil, gas, and other minerals in, under, and that may be produced from the Land, regardless of whether or not the minerals are considered part of the surface estate or part of the mineral estate;

d. all of Seller's right, title, and interest in and to all groundwater under the Land and all dedicated or adjudicated surface water on, belonging to or adjacent to the Land;

e. all of Seller's right, title, and interest in and to all site plans, surveys, environmental studies, soil studies, substrata studies, architectural drawings, plans and specifications, engineering plans and studies, floor plans, landscape plans, and other plans or studies of any kind that relate to the Land in the possession of or under the control of Seller; and

f. all other rights, privileges, and appurtenances owned by Seller that relate in any way to the above-described properties.

Form 4-4

Escrow Agent Receipt and Escrow Agreement

Seller:

Buyer:

Date of Contract:

Property:

Earnest Money:

Underwriter:

Escrow Agent:

Escrow Agent Fee:

GF Number:

Escrow Agent acknowledges receipt of one or more fully executed counterparts of the Contract and the Earnest Money. All capitalized terms used in this Escrow Agent Receipt and Escrow Agreement and not otherwise defined herein have the same meanings as in the Contract.

1. *Duties.* Escrow Agent will—

    a. hold and disburse all funds that it receives, as directed in the Contract;

    b. if directed by Buyer, and after Buyer's compliance with Escrow Agent's requirements for investing the Earnest Money and agreement to pay the fees reasonably required for investing the Earnest Money, invest the Earnest

Money in an interest-bearing account in a federally insured financial institution, with Escrow Agent having sole signature authority over the account;

c. use its best efforts to obtain from Underwriter the title commitment by the deadline stated in the Contract;

d. obtain tax and other certificates as directed by the parties, at their expense;

e. prepare the closing statement;

f. if closing occurs, use its best efforts to obtain from Underwriter the Title Policy not more than fifteen days after closing, in accordance with the last title commitment delivered to and approved by the parties at or before closing;

g. file for record the deed and other documents requested by the parties to be recorded;

h. be the party responsible for complying with reporting requirements, if any, of the Internal Revenue Service, the U.S. Department of Housing and Urban Development, and any other governmental agencies, relying on information provided by Buyer and Seller; and

i. except as required by law or court order, keep confidential the terms of the Contract and this transaction generally and not disclose information about them to anyone except its employees and agents who need to know the information to perform their assigned duties in connection with this transaction.

2. *Loss or Impairment of Earnest Money.* Buyer and Seller release Escrow Agent from liability for any loss or impairment of the Earnest Money when deposited in an account of a federally insured financial institution, if the loss or impairment results from the failure,

insolvency, or receivership of the financial institution in which the Earnest Money is deposited.

3. *Return of Earnest Money.* If either Buyer or Seller demands payment of the Earnest Money, Escrow Agent may either require, as a condition of disbursement, that all parties sign a directive to Escrow Agent to disburse the Earnest Money or notify the other party of the demand. If the other party does not object by notice to Escrow Agent within five days, Escrow Agent is authorized to disburse the Earnest Money to the party making the demand. Escrow Agent may, however, reimburse itself for its out-of-pocket expenses for long-distance calls, courier and delivery services, tax certificates, UCC searches, certified copies, the cost to obtain the survey, and other fees incurred in fulfilling its obligations as Escrow Agent and closing agent (collectively, "Escrow Agent Expenses"). If Escrow Agent determines that a dispute concerning the right to receive the Earnest Money is unlikely to be resolved within sixty days, Escrow Agent may interplead the Earnest Money into the registry of a court of competent jurisdiction in the county in which Escrow Agent is located and petition the court to assess its attorney's fees and court and other costs against the parties.

4. *Termination of Escrow Agent's Participation.* Buyer and Seller, acting together, may terminate Escrow Agent's role in this transaction by notice to Escrow Agent and payment of Escrow Agent Expenses. Escrow Agent may resign on ten days' notice to Buyer and Seller. Within five days after termination or on resignation, Escrow Agent will deliver to Seller all items Escrow Agent obtained from third parties in connection with this transaction, charge Escrow Agent Expenses against the Earnest Money, and disburse the remainder of the Earnest Money to the party jointly designated by Buyer and Seller.

5. *Fee and Expenses.* Escrow Agent's fee for acting as closing and escrow agent may not exceed the Escrow Agent Fee. In addition to the Escrow Agent Fee, Escrow Agent will be reimbursed for Escrow Agent Expenses. Buyer and Seller will pay the Escrow Agent Fee and Escrow Agent Expenses in accordance with the terms of the Contract. The Escrow

Agent Fee and Escrow Agent Expenses will be paid at closing or after termination or resignation as described above.

6. *Notices.* All notices must be in writing and delivered to Buyer, Seller, their respective attorneys, and Escrow Agent in the manner and at the addresses stated in the Contract. Each party may change its address for notice purposes by not less than ten days' prior notice to the other parties.

____
[**Name and title of seller**]
Date:

____
[**Name and title of buyer**]
Date:

____
[**Name and title of escrow agent**]
Date:

Form 4-5

A notice concerning the purchaser's three-day right of rescission under a contract to purchase real property must be given if (1) the seller or the seller's agent solicits the sale at a place other than the seller's place of business; (2) the purchaser submits the purchase contract to the seller or the seller's agent at a place other than the seller's place of business; and (3) the consideration payable under the purchase contract exceeds $100; unless either (1) the purchaser is represented by a licensed attorney; (2) the transaction is negotiated by a licensed real estate broker; or (3) the transaction is negotiated at a place other than the purchaser's residence by the person who owns the property. Tex. Bus. & Com. Code § 601.002.

The notice of cancellation form must be easily detachable from the contract to which it is attached, must be in the same language as the contract, and must contain the following information and statements in ten-point bold-faced type. Tex. Bus. & Com. Code § 601.053.

Notice of Cancellation

[Date]

YOU MAY CANCEL THIS TRANSACTION, WITHOUT ANY PENALTY OR OBLIGATION, WITHIN THREE BUSINESS DAYS FROM THE ABOVE DATE.

IF YOU CANCEL, ANY PROPERTY TRADED IN, ANY PAYMENTS MADE BY YOU UNDER THE CONTRACT OR SALE, AND ANY NEGOTIABLE INSTRUMENT EXECUTED BY YOU WILL BE RETURNED WITHIN 10 BUSINESS DAYS FOLLOWING RECEIPT BY THE MERCHANT OF YOUR CANCELLATION NOTICE, AND ANY SECURITY INTEREST ARISING OUT OF THE TRANSACTION WILL BE CANCELED.

IF YOU CANCEL YOU MUST MAKE AVAILABLE TO THE MERCHANT AT YOUR RESIDENCE, IN SUBSTANTIALLY AS GOOD CONDITION AS WHEN RECEIVED, ANY GOODS DELIVERED TO YOU UNDER THIS CONTRACT OR SALE; OR YOU MAY IF YOU WISH, COMPLY WITH THE INSTRUCTIONS OF THE MERCHANT REGARDING THE RETURN SHIPMENT OF THE GOODS AT THE MERCHANT'S EXPENSE AND RISK.

IF YOU DO NOT AGREE TO RETURN THE GOODS TO THE MERCHANT OR IF THE MERCHANT DOES NOT PICK THEM UP WITHIN 20 DAYS OF THE DATE OF YOUR NOTICE OF CAN-

CELLATION, YOU MAY RETAIN OR DISPOSE OF THE GOODS WITHOUT ANY FURTHER OBLIGATION.

TO CANCEL THIS TRANSACTION, MAIL OR DELIVER A SIGNED AND DATED COPY OF THIS CANCELLATION NOTICE OR ANY OTHER WRITTEN NOTICE, OR SEND A TELEGRAM, TO [name of merchant], AT [address of merchant's place of business] NOT LATER THAN MIDNIGHT OF [date].

I HEREBY CANCEL THIS TRANSACTION.

Dated: ______________________________.

____

[Name of purchaser]

> In addition to giving the notice of cancellation separately, the seller must insert the following at the end of the contract to purchase above the buyer's signature. This must be in a minimum of ten-point bold-faced type.

YOU, THE BUYER, MAY CANCEL THIS TRANSACTION AT ANY TIME PRIOR TO MIDNIGHT OF THE THIRD BUSINESS DAY AFTER THE DATE OF THIS TRANSACTION. SEE THE ATTACHED NOTICE OF CANCELLATION FORM FOR AN EXPLANATION OF THIS RIGHT.

____

[Name of buyer]

Form 4-6

A person who proposes to sell or otherwise convey real property that is located in a public improvement district established under Texas Local Government Code chapter 372, subchapter A, or chapter 382 shall first give to the purchaser of the property the notice set forth below. Tex. Prop. Code § 5.014(a). Certain transactions are exempted. The notice must be given before the effective date of the executory contract. Notice may be given separately or as an addendum or paragraph of the contract. If an executory contract is entered into without the notice having been given, the purchaser is entitled to terminate the contract. If, however, the seller furnishes the notice at or before the closing of the contract and the purchaser elects to close even though the notice was not timely furnished before execution of the contract, it shall be conclusively presumed that the purchaser has waived all rights to terminate the contract, recover damages, or seek other remedies or rights under Tex. Prop. Code § 5.0145.

Tex. Prop. Code § 5.014(a–2) sets forth the notice required by Tex. Prop. Code § 5.014(a) for districts described by Tex. Loc. Gov't Code § 372.0035, which are composed of territory where the only businesses are hotels, as described therein. In these districts, the seller must deliver this notice in compliance with Tex. Prop. Code § 5.014(a).

The seller or the municipality or county that created the public improvement district may provide additional information regarding the district in the notice, including whether the assessment has been levied, the amount of the assessment, and the payment schedule for assessments.Tex. Prop. Code § 5.014(b).

Notice of Obligation to Pay Improvement District Assessment to **[name of municipality or county levying assessment]**, Texas, Concerning the Following [Hotel] Property **[street address]**

Seller[s]:

Purchaser[s]:

Real Property:

Date:

As the purchaser of the real property described above, you are obligated to pay assessments to **[name of municipality or county]**, Texas, for the costs of a portion of a public improvement or services project (the "Authorized [Improvements/Services]") undertaken for the benefit of the property within **[name of public improvement district]** (the "District") created under [Subchapter A, Chapter 372, Local Government Code/Chapter 382, Local Government Code].

> If an assessment has been levied against real property, other than a hotel property in a territory where the only businesses are hotels, include the following.

AN ASSESSMENT HAS BEEN LEVIED AGAINST YOUR PROPERTY FOR THE AUTHORIZED IMPROVEMENTS, WHICH MAY BE PAID IN FULL AT ANY TIME. IF THE ASSESSMENT IS NOT PAID IN FULL, IT WILL BE DUE AND PAYABLE IN ANNUAL INSTALLMENTS THAT WILL VARY FROM YEAR TO YEAR DEPENDING ON THE AMOUNT OF INTEREST PAID, COLLECTION COSTS, ADMINISTRATIVE COSTS, AND DELNQUENCY COSTS.

The exact amount of the assessment may be obtained from [**name of municipality or county**]. The exact amount of each annual installment will be approved each year by [**name of city council or county commissioners court**] in the annual service plan update for the district. More information about the assessments, including the amounts and due dates, may be obtained from [**name of municipality or county**].

Your failure to pay any assessment or any annual installment may result in penalties and interest being added to what you owe or in a lien on and the foreclosure of your property.

> If an assessment has been levied against a hotel property in a territory where the only businesses are hotels, include the following.

AN ASSESSMENT HAS BEEN LEVIED AGAINST YOUR PROPERTY FOR THE AUTHORIZED SERVICES, WHICH MUST BE PAID IN FULL WITH EVERY PAYMENT BY THE HOTEL OF LOCAL HOTEL OCCUPANCY TAX REMITTANCES TO THE MUNICIPALITY. YOUR FAILURE TO PAY THE ASSESSMENT MAY RESULT IN PENALITIES AND INTEREST BEING ADDED TO WHAT YOU OWE, AND MAY

INCLUDE THE PURSUIT OF ANY OTHER REMEDY THAT IS AUTHORIZED UNDER SECTION 372.0035(d), LOCAL GOVERNMENT CODE.

Information about the calculation of the assessment may be obtained from [**name of municipality**]. The exact assessment rate will be approved each year by [**name of city council**] in the annual service plan update for the district. More information about the assessments, including the assessment rate and due dates, may be obtained from [**name of municipality**].

Continue with the following.

The undersigned purchaser acknowledges receipt of this notice before the effective date of a binding contract for the purchase of the real property at the address described above.

____
[**Name of purchaser**]
Date:

Form 4-7

This form sets out the mandatory notice under 16 C.F.R. § 460.16. A new home seller must include in every sales contract the type, thickness, and R-value of the insulation that will be installed in each part of the house. The exception to this rule is that if the buyer signs a sales contract before the seller knows what type of insulation will be put in the house, or if there is a change in the contract, the seller can give the buyer a receipt stating this information as soon as the seller finds out the information. This regulation is enforceable by the Federal Trade Commission. The failure of the seller to provide this information does not appear to invalidate the contract or render the sale voidable but may subject the seller to a claim for damages.

Use this form when the information was not available to be included in the sales contract or the relevant information changed after the execution of the sales contract.

Notice Regarding Insulation to Buyer of New Home

Seller:

Address:

Buyer:

Address of Buyer's new home:

Description of type, thickness, and R-value of the insulation that will be installed in each part of the new house:

____
[Name of seller]
Date:

Form 4-8

This disclosure is used to warn a buyer about potential risks associated with lead-based paint. The form is based on the notice requirements of 40 C.F.R. § 745.113 and the disclosure form suggested by the Department of Housing and Urban Development; the language should not be altered without a review of the applicable regulations. The heading and text of the notice are required by the regulations to be in bold-faced type.

Disclosure of Information on Lead-Based Paint and/or Lead-Based Paint Hazards

[Sales]

Seller's Name and Address:

Buyer's Name and Address:

Description of Property:

Lead Warning Statement

Every purchaser of any interest in residential real property on which a residential dwelling was built prior to 1978 is notified that such property may present exposure to lead from lead-based paint that may place young children at risk of developing lead poisoning. Lead poisoning in young children may produce permanent neurological damage, including learning disabilities, reduced intelligence quotient, behavioral problems, and impaired memory. Lead poisoning also poses a particular risk to pregnant women. The seller of any interest in residential real property is required to provide the buyer with any information on lead-based paint hazards from risk assessments or inspections in the seller's possession and notify the buyer of

any known lead-based paint hazards. A risk assessment or inspection for possible lead-based paint hazards is recommended prior to purchase.

Seller's Disclosure

(a) Presence of lead-based paint and/or lead-based paint hazards (check (i) or (ii) below):

☐ (i) Known lead-based paint and/or lead-based paint hazards are present in the housing [**explain, providing the basis for the determination that lead-based paint and/or lead-based paint hazards exist, its/their location[s] and condition[s], and any additional information about the lead-based paint or lead-based paint hazards (if known)**].

☐ (ii) Seller has no knowledge of lead-based paint and/or lead-based paint hazards in the housing.

(b) Records and reports available to Seller (check (i) or (ii) below):

☐ (i) Seller has provided Buyer with all available records and reports pertaining to lead-based paint and/or lead-based paint hazards in the housing (list documents below).

____

☐ (ii) Seller has no reports or records pertaining to lead-based paint and/or lead-based paint hazards in the housing.

Buyer's Acknowledgment (initial)

____ (c) Buyer has received copies of all information listed above.

____ (d) Buyer has received the lead hazard information pamphlet described in 15 U.S.C. section 2686.

____ (e) Buyer has (check (i) or (ii) below):

☐ (i) received a ten-day opportunity (or mutually agreed upon period) to conduct a risk assessment or inspection for the presence of lead-based paint and/or lead-based paint hazards; or

☐ (ii) waived the opportunity to conduct a risk assessment or inspection for the presence of lead-based paint and/or lead-based paint hazards.

Agent's Acknowledgment (initial)

____ (f) Agent has informed Seller of Seller's obligations under 42 U.S.C. section 4852d and is aware of his/her responsibility to ensure compliance.

Certification of Accuracy

The following parties have reviewed the information above and certify, to the best of their knowledge, that the information they have provided is true and accurate.

____
Seller Date

____
Buyer Date

____
Agent Date

Form 4-9

This form is used to confirm a seller's knowledge of the presence or absence of asbestos in the property being sold, as required by 29 C.F.R. §§ 1910.1001 *et seq.*, 1926.1101 *et seq.*

Asbestos Disclosure Notice

[Sales]

Date:

Seller's Name and Address:

Buyer's Name and Address:

Description of Property:

THIS ASBESTOS DISCLOSURE NOTICE ("NOTICE") IS A DISCLOSURE OF KNOWLEDGE OF THE CONDITION OF THE PROPERTY AS OF THE DATE SIGNED AND IS NOT A SUBSTITUTE FOR ANY INSPECTIONS OR WARRANTIES THAT MAY BE DESIRED. THIS NOTICE IS NOT A WARRANTY OF ANY KIND.

Seller's Disclosure

1. Presence of asbestos-containing or presumed asbestos-containing material (check one):

☐ Known asbestos-containing material is present in the Property (explain).

____

☐ The Property was constructed before 1981, and presumed asbestos-containing material is present in the Property (explain).

____

☐ The Property was constructed after 1980, and Seller has no knowledge of asbestos-containing material in the Property.

2. Records and reports available to Buyer (check one):

☐ Seller has provided Buyer with all available records and reports pertaining to asbestos-containing material in the Property (list documents below).

____

☐ Seller has no records or reports pertaining to asbestos-containing material in the Property.

3. Seller has no knowledge of other facts or records concerning the presence, location, or quantity of asbestos-containing or presumed asbestos-containing material in the property (including any data supporting any rebuttal of the presumption that a material contains asbestos).

Buyer's Acknowledgment

Buyer has received copies of all information listed above. Buyer is aware of Buyer's responsibility to ensure compliance with 15 U.S.C. sections 2641 through 2656 and 29 C.F.R. sections 1910.1001 *et seq.* and 1926.1101 *et seq.*

____
Seller Date

____
Buyer Date

Form 4-10

Under Tex. Prop. Code § 5.016, a person may not convey an interest in or enter into a contract to convey an interest in residential real property that will be encumbered by a recorded lien at the time the interest is conveyed unless, on or before the seventh day before the earlier of the effective date of the conveyance or the execution of an executory contract binding the purchaser to purchase the property, an option contract, or other contract, the person provides the purchaser and each lienholder a separate written disclosure statement in at least twelve-point type that provides the information set out in the form below.

A violation of this section does not invalidate a conveyance. Except for certain transactions exempted from the disclosure requirements, if a contract is entered into without the seller providing the notice, the purchaser may terminate the contract for any reason on or before the seventh day after the date the purchaser receives the notice in addition to other remedies provided by this section or other law. Tex. Prop. Code § 5.016(c) exempts a number of transfers from the disclosure requirements, including transfers in which the purchaser obtains a title insurance policy insuring the transfer of title to the real property and transfers to a person who has purchased, conveyed, or entered into contracts to purchase or convey an interest in real property four or more times in the preceding twelve months.

Under Tex. Prop. Code § 5.016(d), a violation of this section is not actionable if the person required to give notice reasonably believes and takes any necessary action to ensure that each lien for which notice was not provided will be released on or before the thirtieth day after the date on which title to the property is transferred.

WARNING: ONE OR MORE RECORDED LIENS HAVE BEEN FILED THAT MAKE A CLAIM AGAINST THIS PROPERTY AS LISTED BELOW. IF A LIEN IS NOT RELEASED AND THE PROPERTY IS CONVEYED WITHOUT THE CONSENT OF THE LIENHOLDER, IT IS POSSIBLE THE LIENHOLDER COULD DEMAND FULL PAYMENT OF THE OUTSTANDING BALANCE OF THE LIEN IMMEDIATELY. YOU MAY WISH TO CONTACT EACH LIENHOLDER FOR FURTHER INFORMATION AND DISCUSS THIS MATTER WITH AN ATTORNEY.

Notice Regarding Sale Subject to a Recorded Lien

This notice is being provided pursuant to section 5.016 of the Texas Property Code.

Property: [**identify the property**]

Seller:

Seller's Address:

Buyer:

Buyer's Address:

[First] Recorded Lien

Lienholder:

Lienholder's address:

Lienholder's telephone number:

Amount of debt secured by this lien:

Interest rate:

Required periodic installments:

Account number:

Other terms:

Has lienholder consented to sale by Seller to Purchaser? ____Yes ____No

> If there is more than one lien, repeat above information for each additional lien and designate as "First Recorded Lien," "Second Recorded Lien," etc., as applicable.

[First] Insurance Policy

Insurer:

Insured:

Amount for which property is insured:

Property insured:

If there is more than one insurance policy, repeat above information for each additional policy and designate as "First Insurance Policy," "Second Insurance Policy," etc., as applicable.

Amount of Any Property Taxes Due on Property:

____

[Name of seller]
Date:

____

[Name of buyer]
Date:

Form 4-11

If the property contains an underground storage tank or tank system or an aboveground tank or tank system subject to regulation by the Texas Commission on Environmental Quality, the following notice is given by the seller to the purchaser pursuant to 30 Tex. Admin. Code § 334.9.

Storage Tanks Disclosure Provider

Seller:

Seller's Address:

Buyer:

Buyer's Address:

Description of Property:

The number of tanks involved is [**number**].

Attached is a description of each tank (capacity, tank material, and product stored, if applicable).

The designated facility identification number (if the entire facility is being conveyed) is [**number**].

Include one or both of the following if applicable.

The underground storage tank[s] included in this conveyance [is/are] presumed to be regulated by the Texas Commission on Environmental Quality and may be subject to certain registration, compliance self-certification, construction notification, and other requirements found in chapter 334 of title 30 of the Texas Administrative Code.

And/Or

The aboveground storage tank[s] included in this conveyance [is/are] presumed to be regulated by the Texas Commission on Environmental Quality and may be subject to certain registration, delivery prohibition, installation notification, and other requirements found in chapter 334 of title 30 of the Texas Administrative Code.

____

[Name of seller]
Date:

____

[Name of buyer]
Date:

Form 4-12

Pursuant to Tex. Loc. Gov't Code § 212.155, if the governing body of a municipality has required any person who sells or conveys restricted property located within its jurisdiction to first give written notice to the purchaser of (1) the restrictions and (2) the municipality's right to enforce compliance with the restrictions, the following written notice must be given to the purchaser on or before the final closing, signed and acknowledged by both seller and purchaser, and recorded in the real property records in the county where the real property is located.

Notice to Purchaser Regarding Restrictive Covenants

STATE OF TEXAS)

COUNTY OF)

Buyer:

Seller:

Property: **[include legal description and street address]**

The Property is being purchased by Buyer and is subject to deed restrictions recorded in **[recording data]** of the Official Public Records of **[county]** County, Texas. THE RESTRICTIONS LIMIT THE BUYER'S USE OF THE PROPERTY. THE CITY OF **[city]** IS AUTHORIZED BY STATUTE TO ENFORCE COMPLIANCE WITH CERTAIN DEED RESTRICTIONS. ANY PROVISIONS THAT RESTRICT THE SALE, RENTAL, OR USE OF THE REAL PROPERTY ON THE BASIS OF RACE, COLOR, RELIGION, SEX, OR NATIONAL ORIGIN ARE UNENFORCEABLE; however, the inclusion of such provisions does not render the remainder of the deed restrictions invalid.

Seller:

____
[Name of seller]
Date:

Include acknowledgment.

The undersigned hereby acknowledges receipt of the Notice to Purchaser Regarding Restrictive Covenants at or before closing the purchase of the Property.

Buyer:

____
[Name of buyer]
Date:

Include acknowledgment.

Form 4-13

This form sets out the mandatory notice under Tex. Nat. Res. Code § 33.135. The notice must be placed in a written executory contract for the sale, transfer, or conveyance of real property (other than a mineral, leasehold, or security interest) adjoining and abutting the tidally influenced waters of the State of Texas. Tex. Nat. Res. Code § 33.135(a). If the real property described in this section is sold, transferred, or conveyed without a written executory contract, this notice must be delivered to the grantee for execution and acknowledgment of receipt before the conveyance is recorded. Tex. Nat. Res. Code § 33.135(b). Failure to include this notice in a written executory contract is grounds for the purchaser to terminate the contract and have its earnest money returned. Tex. Nat. Res. Code § 33.135(c). Failure to provide this notice before closing, either in a written executory contract or in a separate written statement, is a deceptive act under Tex. Bus. & Com. Code § 17.46. Tex. Nat. Res. Code § 33.135(d).

Notice to Purchaser Regarding Coastal Area Property

(1) The real property described in and subject to this contract adjoins and shares a common boundary with the tidally influenced submerged lands of the state. The boundary is subject to change and can be determined accurately only by a survey on the ground made by a licensed state land surveyor in accordance with the original grant from the sovereign. The owner of the property described in this contract may gain or lose portions of the tract because of changes in the boundary.

NOTICE REGARDING COASTAL AREA PROPERTY

(2) The seller, transferor, or grantor has no knowledge of any prior fill as it relates to the property described in and subject to this contract.

(3) State law prohibits the use, encumbrance, construction, or placing of any structure in, on, or over state-owned submerged lands below the applicable tide line, without proper permission.

(4) The purchaser or grantee is hereby advised to seek the advice of an attorney or other qualified person as to the legal nature and effect of the facts set forth in this notice on the property described in and subject to this contract. Information regarding the location of the

applicable tide line as to the property described in and subject to this contract may be obtained from the surveying division of the General Land Office in Austin.

Form 4-14

This form sets out the mandatory notice under Tex. Nat. Res. Code § 61.025. The following notice must be placed in a written executory contract for the sale, transfer, or conveyance of real property (other than a mineral, leasehold, or security interest) located seaward of the Gulf Intracoastal Waterway to its southernmost point and then seaward of the longitudinal line also known as 97 degrees, 12', 19" which runs southerly to the international boundary from the intersection of the centerline of the Gulf Intracoastal Waterway and the Brownsville Ship Channel. Tex. Nat. Res. Code § 61.025(a). If the real property described in this section is sold, transferred, or conveyed without a written executory contract, this notice must be delivered to the grantee for execution and acknowledgment of receipt not later than ten calendar days before closing of the transaction. Tex. Nat. Res. Code § 61.025(b). Failure to include this notice in a written executory contract is grounds for the purchaser to terminate the contract and have its earnest money returned. Tex. Nat. Res. Code § 61.025(c). Failure to provide this notice before closing, either in a written executory contract or in a separate written statement, is a deceptive act under Tex. Bus. & Com. Code § 17.46. Tex. Nat. Res. Code § 61.025(d).

Notice to Purchaser of Property Seaward of Gulf Intracoastal Waterway

CONCERNING THE PROPERTY AT ______________________________

DISCLOSURE NOTICE CONCERNING LEGAL AND ECONOMIC RISKS OF PURCHASING COASTAL REAL PROPERTY NEAR A BEACH

WARNING: THE FOLLOWING NOTICE OF POTENTIAL RISKS OF ECONOMIC LOSS TO YOU AS THE PURCHASER OF COASTAL REAL PROPERTY IS REQUIRED BY STATE LAW.

- READ THIS NOTICE CAREFULLY. DO NOT SIGN THIS CONTRACT UNTIL YOU FULLY UNDERSTAND THE RISKS YOU ARE ASSUMING.

- BY PURCHASING THIS PROPERTY, YOU MAY BE ASSUMING ECONOMIC RISKS OVER AND ABOVE THE RISKS INVOLVED IN PURCHASING INLAND REAL PROPERTY.

- IF YOU OWN A STRUCTURE LOCATED ON COASTAL REAL PROPERTY NEAR A GULF COAST BEACH, IT MAY COME TO BE LOCATED ON THE PUBLIC BEACH BECAUSE OF COASTAL EROSION AND STORM EVENTS.

- AS THE OWNER OF A STRUCTURE LOCATED ON THE PUBLIC BEACH, YOU COULD BE SUED BY THE STATE OF TEXAS AND ORDERED TO REMOVE THE STRUCTURE.

- THE COSTS OF REMOVING A STRUCTURE FROM THE PUBLIC BEACH AND ANY OTHER ECONOMIC LOSS INCURRED BECAUSE OF A REMOVAL ORDER WOULD BE SOLELY YOUR RESPONSIBILITY.

The real property described in this contract is located seaward of the Gulf Intracoastal Waterway to its southernmost point and then seaward of the longitudinal line also known as 97 degrees, 12', 19" which runs southerly to the international boundary from the intersection of the centerline of the Gulf Intracoastal Waterway and the Brownsville Ship Channel. If the property is in close proximity to a beach fronting the Gulf of Mexico, the purchaser is hereby advised that the public has acquired a right of use or easement to or over the area of any public beach by prescription, dedication, or presumption, or has retained a right by virtue of continuous right in the public since time immemorial, as recognized in law and custom.

The extreme seaward boundary of natural vegetation that spreads continuously inland customarily marks the landward boundary of the public easement. If there is no clearly marked natural vegetation line, the landward boundary of the easement is as provided by sections 61.016 and 61.017, Natural Resources Code.

Much of the Gulf of Mexico coastline is eroding at rates of more than five feet per year. Erosion rates for all Texas Gulf property subject to the open beaches act are available from the Texas General Land Office.

State law prohibits any obstruction, barrier, restraint, or interference with the use of the public easement, including the placement of structures seaward of the landward boundary of the easement. OWNERS OF STRUCTURES ERECTED SEAWARD OF THE VEGETATION LINE (OR OTHER APPLICABLE EASEMENT BOUNDARY) OR THAT BECOME SEAWARD OF THE VEGETATION LINE AS A RESULT OF PROCESSES SUCH AS SHORELINE EROSION ARE SUBJECT TO A LAWSUIT BY THE STATE OF TEXAS TO REMOVE THE STRUCTURES.

The purchaser is hereby notified that the purchaser should:

(1) determine the rate of shoreline erosion in the vicinity of the real property; and

(2) seek the advice of an attorney or other qualified person before executing this contract or instrument of conveyance as to the relevance of these statutes and facts to the value of the property the purchaser is hereby purchasing or contracting to purchase.

Form 4-15

The following is the mandatory notice to be placed in bold-faced type in a contract for the sale and purchase of vacant land pursuant to Tex. Prop. Code § 5.010. This notice requirement does not apply to certain sellers or buyers, Tex. Prop. Code § 5.010(b), (c), or if the contract contains a separate paragraph providing for the payment of any additional ad valorem taxes and interest that become due as a penalty because of the transfer of the property or a subsequent change in use of the property. Tex. Prop. Code § 5.010(d). If the seller fails to include this notice in the contract, the purchaser is entitled to recover from the seller an amount equal to the amount of any additional taxes and interest incurred as a penalty because of the transfer of the land or a subsequent change in use of the land that occurs before the fifth anniversary of the date of the transfer. Tex. Prop. Code § 5.010(e).

NOTICE REGARDING POSSIBLE LIABILITY FOR ADDITIONAL TAXES

If for the current ad valorem tax year the taxable value of the land that is the subject of this contract is determined by a special appraisal method that allows for appraisal of the land at less than its market value, the person to whom the land is transferred may not be allowed to qualify the land for that special appraisal in a subsequent tax year and the land may then be appraised at its full market value. In addition, the transfer of the land or a subsequent change in the use of the land may result in the imposition of an additional tax plus interest as a penalty for the transfer or the change in the use of the land. The taxable value of the land and the applicable method of appraisal for the current tax year is public information and may be obtained from the tax appraisal district established for the county in which the land is located.

Form 4-16

A person who sells an interest in real property must give the purchaser a written notice substantially similar to the following unless the property is located wholly within a municipality's corporate boundaries. Exceptions exist for some types of transactions. Tex. Prop. Code § 5.011.

Notice Regarding Possible Annexation

If the property that is the subject of this contract is located outside the limits of a municipality, the property may now or later be included in the extraterritorial jurisdiction of a municipality and may now or later be subject to annexation by the municipality. Each municipality maintains a map that depicts its boundaries and extraterritorial jurisdiction. To determine if the property is located within a municipality's extraterritorial jurisdiction or is likely to be located within a municipality's extraterritorial jurisdiction, contact all municipalities located in the general proximity of the property for further information.

Dated: ______________________________.

____

[Name of purchaser]

Form 4-17

This notice must be given to the purchaser of an unimproved property that has no existing water facilities and that is located in a certificated service area of a utility service provider. Tex. Water Code § 13.257. Refer to Tex. Water Code § 13.257(c) for types of sales that are excepted from the notice requirement. The seller must give a prospective purchaser this notice before or at the same time as the execution of the contract. At closing, the purchaser and seller must sign and acknowledge a separate copy of the notice with current information; that copy must be recorded. Tex. Water Code § 13.257(g). Each special utility district keeps a map of its service area; this information is also available from the Texas Commission on Environmental Quality.

Notice for Unimproved Property in a Certificated Service Area of a Utility Service Provider

The real property, described below, that you are about to purchase may be located in a certificated water or sewer service area, which is authorized by law to provide water or sewer service to the properties in the certificated area. If your property is located in a certificated area there may be special costs or charges that you will be required to pay before you can receive water or sewer service. There may be a period required to construct lines or other facilities necessary to provide water or sewer service to your property. You are advised to determine if the property is in a certificated area and contact the utility service provider to determine the cost that you will be required to pay and the period, if any, that is required to provide water or sewer service to your property.

The undersigned purchaser hereby acknowledges receipt of the foregoing notice at or before the execution of a binding contract for the purchase of the real property described in the notice or at closing of purchase of the real property.

Insert property description.

____

[Name of purchaser]
Date:

No signatures are required if the notice is an addendum to a signed purchase and sale contract. If the notice is separate from the purchase and sale contract, only the purchaser's signature is required. Both the purchaser and seller must sign the copy executed at the time of closing. Tex. Water Code § 13.257(g).

____

[Name of seller]

Date:

Except for notices included as an addendum to or paragraph of a purchase contract, the notice must be executed by the seller and purchaser, as indicated.

Include acknowledgments if the notice is signed at the time of closing.

Form 4-18

This form sets out the mandatory notice under Tex. Water Code § 49.452. The seller must give a prospective purchaser the notice before or at the same time as the execution of the contract. If the seller fails to provide the notice, the purchaser may cancel the contract. By accepting the notice, the purchaser waives its rights under section 49.452. Tex. Water Code § 49.452(f). A separate copy of the notice must be executed by the seller and the purchaser, acknowledged, and recorded with the deed for the transaction. Tex. Water Code § 49.452(h). This form does not detail the permissible modifications that may be necessary under different circumstances. See section 2.280 in this manual.

Utility District Notice

Seller[s]:

Purchaser[s]:

The real property, described below, that you are about to purchase is located in the [**district**] District. The district has taxing authority separate from any other taxing authority and may, subject to voter approval, issue an unlimited amount of bonds and levy an unlimited rate of tax in payment of such bonds. As of [this date/January 1, [**year**]], the rate of taxes levied by the district on real property located in the district is $[**amount**] on each $100 of assessed valuation. If the district has not yet levied taxes, the most recent projected rate of tax, as of [this date/January 1, [**year**]], is $[**amount**] on each $100 of assessed valuation. The total amount of bonds, excluding refunding bonds and any bonds or any portion of bonds issued that are payable solely from revenues received or expected to be received under a contract with a governmental entity, approved by the voters and which have been or may, at [this date/January 1, [**year**]], be issued is $[**amount**], and the aggregate initial principal amounts of all bonds issued for one or more of the specified facilities of the district and payable in whole or in part from property taxes is $[**amount**].

The district has the authority to adopt and impose a standby fee on property in the district that has water, sanitary sewer, or drainage facilities and services available but not connected and which does not have a house, building, or other improvement located thereon and does not substantially utilize the utility capacity available to the property. The district may exercise the authority without holding an election on the matter. As of [this date/January 1, [**year**]], the most recent amount of the standby fee is $[**amount**]. An unpaid standby fee is a personal obligation of the person that owned the property at the time of imposition and is secured by a lien on the property. Any person may request a certificate from the district stating the amount, if any, of unpaid standby fees on a tract of property in the district.

> Select one of the following paragraphs if appropriate. Include the first paragraph if the property is in a district located in whole or in part in the extraterritorial jurisdiction of one or more home-rule municipalities and not located within the corporate boundaries of a municipality as defined by Tex. Water Code § 49.452(b). Include the second paragraph if the property is in a district located in whole or in part within the corporate boundaries of a municipality as defined by Tex. Water Code § 49.452(c). Do not include either paragraph if the property is in a district that is not located in whole or in part within the corporate boundaries of a municipality or the extraterritorial jurisdiction of one or more home-rule municipalities as defined by Tex. Water Code § 49.452(d).

The district is located in whole or in part in the extraterritorial jurisdiction of the city of [**city**]. By law, a district located in the extraterritorial jurisdiction of a municipality may be annexed without the consent of the district or the voters of the district. When a district is annexed, the district is dissolved.

> Or

The district is located in whole or in part within the corporate boundaries of the city of [**city**]. The taxpayers of the district are subject to the taxes imposed by the municipality and by the district until the district is dissolved. By law, a district located within the corporate boundaries of a municipality may be dissolved by municipal ordinance without the consent of the district or the voters of the district.

> Continue with the following.

The purpose of this district is to provide water, sewer, drainage, or flood control facilities and services within the district through the issuance of bonds payable in whole or in part from property taxes. The cost of these utility facilities is not included in the purchase price of your property, and these utility facilities are owned or to be owned by the district. The legal description of the property you are acquiring is as follows: [**legal description**].

____
[**Name of seller**]
Date:

Include acknowledgment.

PURCHASER IS ADVISED THAT THE INFORMATION SHOWN ON THIS FORM IS SUBJECT TO CHANGE BY THE DISTRICT AT ANY TIME. THE DISTRICT ROUTINELY ESTABLISHES TAX RATES DURING THE MONTHS OF SEPTEMBER THROUGH DECEMBER OF EACH YEAR, EFFECTIVE FOR THE YEAR IN WHICH THE TAX RATES ARE APPROVED BY THE DISTRICT. PURCHASER IS ADVISED TO CONTACT THE DISTRICT TO DETERMINE THE STATUS OF ANY CURRENT OR PROPOSED CHANGES TO THE INFORMATION SHOWN ON THIS FORM.

The undersigned purchaser[s] hereby acknowledge[s] receipt of the foregoing notice at or prior to execution of a binding contract for the purchase of the real property described in such notice or at closing of purchase of the real property.

____
[**Name of purchaser**]
Date:

Include acknowledgment.

Form 4-19

This form sets out the mandatory notice under Tex. Water Code § 54.016(h)(4). If the real property is located in a water or sanitary sewer district that entered into a contract with a city, other than a city with a population of more than one million in a county of more than two million, that allows the city to set rates in the district after annexation that are different from rates charged to other residents of the city, the seller at or before closing must deliver a separate written notice, executed and acknowledged by the seller, containing the information in this notice. The purchaser must sign the notice to evidence receipt. Tex. Water Code § 49.452(g)–(p) applies to this notice provision, including the purchaser's right to seek damages if the sale or conveyance of the property is not made in compliance with this statute.

Notice to Purchaser of Property Located in Certain Annexed Water Districts

The real property that is being conveyed is subject to the following [water/sewer/water and sewer] rates and adjustments:

1. the basis on which the monthly [water/sewer/water and sewer] rate is to be charged under the contract stated as a percentage of the [water/sewer/water and sewer] rates of the city is [**percent**] percent;

2. length of time such rates will be in effect is [**time period**]; and

3. the time or conditions of annexation by the city implementing such rates are [**describe conditions and period of annexation**].

____
[**Name of seller**]
Date:

____
[**Name of purchaser**]
Date:

Include acknowledgment.

Form 4-20

Pursuant to Tex. Loc. Gov't Code § 232.0033, a seller and subdivider of land located within the area of the alignment of a transportation project, as shown on the final environmental decision document applicable to the future transportation corridor identified in an agreement between the Texas Department of Transportation and the county under Tex. Transp. Code § 201.619, must provide the following conspicuous statement in the contract.

Notice to Purchaser That Property Is Located within the Area of the Alignment of a Transportation Project

Property: [**describe property**]

THE PROPERTY IS LOCATED WITHIN THE AREA OF THE ALIGNMENT OF A TRANSPORTATION PROJECT AS SHOWN ON A FINAL ENVIRONMENTAL DECISION DOCUMENT THAT IS APPLICABLE TO THE FUTURE TRANSPORTATION CORRIDOR IDENTIFIED IN AN AGREEMENT UNDER SECTION 201.619 OF THE TEXAS TRANSPORTATION CODE.

Form 4-21

A seller of residential or commercial property adjoining an impoundment of water, including a reservoir or lake, constructed and maintained under chapter 11 of the Texas Water Code, that has a storage capacity of at least 5,000 acre-feet at the impoundment's normal operating level, must give the purchaser written notice in substantially the form prescribed by statute and as set forth below. The notice must be given on or before the effective date of the executory contract. If a contract is entered into without the seller giving the notice, the purchaser may terminate the contract for any reason within seven days after the purchaser receives the notice from the seller or a third party. After the date of the conveyance, the purchaser may bring an action for misrepresentation against the seller if the seller failed to give the notice prior to closing and had actual knowledge that the water level described in the statute fluctuates for various reasons, including the two reasons set out in the notice. The requirement applies to an executory contract entered into on or after September 1, 2015. Tex. Prop. Code § 5.019.

Notice of Water Level Fluctuations

Seller[s]:

Purchaser[s]:

Property: **[street address and city or legal description]**

The water level of the impoundment of water adjoining the Property fluctuates for various reasons, including as a result of

(1) an entity lawfully exercising its right to use the water stored in the impoundment, or

(2) drought or flood conditions.

____

[Name of purchaser[s]]

Form 4-22

This form is used by a purchaser of real property to waive the consumer protection rights afforded by the Deceptive Trade Practices–Consumer Protection Act, Tex. Bus. & Com. Code §§ 17.41–.63. The language of the waiver is based on that suggested in the statute and must be in at least ten-point, boldfaced type. *See* Tex. Bus. & Com. Code § 17.42.

Waiver of Consumer Rights

Date:

Contract

Date:

Seller:

Seller's Address:

Buyer:

Buyer's Address:

Property:

WAIVER OF CONSUMER RIGHTS: IN CONNECTION WITH THE FOREGOING EARNEST MONEY CONTRACT, BUYER WAIVES BUYER'S RIGHTS UNDER THE DECEPTIVE TRADE PRACTICES–CONSUMER PROTECTION ACT, SECTION 17.41 *ET SEQ.*, TEXAS BUSINESS & COMMERCE CODE, A LAW THAT GIVES CONSUMERS SPECIAL RIGHTS AND PROTECTIONS. AFTER CONSULTATION WITH AN ATTORNEY OF BUYER'S OWN SELECTION, BUYER VOLUNTARILY CONSENTS TO THIS WAIVER.

____
[Name of buyer]

Form 4-23

This form is based on the form found in Tex. Prop. Code § 5.008. Under section 5.008, a seller of not more than one dwelling unit of residential real property must provide a written notice substantially similar to this form.

Seller's Disclosure of Property Condition

Seller: ____

Property (address and city): ______________________________

THIS NOTICE IS A DISCLOSURE OF SELLER'S KNOWLEDGE OF THE CONDITION OF THE PROPERTY AS OF THE DATE SIGNED BY SELLER AND IS NOT A SUBSTITUTE FOR ANY INSPECTIONS OR WARRANTIES THE PURCHASER MAY WISH TO OBTAIN. IT IS NOT A WARRANTY OF ANY KIND BY SELLER OR SELLER'S AGENTS.

Seller ___ is ___ is not occupying the Property.

If unoccupied, how long since Seller has occupied the Property? ____________________

1. The Property has the items checked below:

   Write Yes (Y), No (N), or Unknown (U).

____ Range	____ Oven	____ Microwave
____ Dishwasher	____ Trash Compactor	____ Disposal
____ Washer/Dryer Hookups	____ Window Screens	____ Rain Gutters
____ Security System	____ Fire Detection Equipment	____ Intercom System
	____ Smoke Detector	

	____ Smoke Detector-Hearing Impaired	
	____ Carbon Monoxide Alarm	
	____ Emergency Escape Ladder(s)	
____ TV Antenna	____ Cable TV Wiring	____ Satellite Dish
____ Ceiling Fan(s)	____ Attic Fan(s)	____ Exhaust Fan(s)
____ Central A/C	____ Central Heating	____ Wall/Window Air Conditioning
____ Plumbing System	____ Septic System	____ Public Sewer System
____ Patio/Decking	____ Outdoor Grill	____ Fences
____ Pool	____ Sauna	____ Spa ____ Hot Tub
____ Pool Equipment	____ Pool Heater	____ Automatic Lawn Sprinkler System
____ Fireplace(s) & Chimney (Woodburning)		____ Fireplace(s) & Chimney (Mock)
____ Natural Gas Lines		____ Gas Fixtures
____ Liquid Propane Gas:	____ LP Community (Captive)	____ LP on Property
Garage: ____ Attached	____ Not Attached	____ Carport
Garage Door Opener(s):	____ Electronic	____ Control(s)
Water Heater:	____ Gas	____ Electric
Water Supply: ____ City	____ Well ____ MUD	____ Co-op

Roof Type: ____________________________________ Age: ____________
(approx)

Are you (Seller) aware of any of the above items that are not in working condition, that have known defects or that are in need of repair? ___ Yes ___ No ___ Unknown. If yes, then describe. (Attach additional sheets if necessary):______________________________

____

____

____

2. Does the property have working smoke detectors installed in accordance with the smoke detector requirements of chapter 766, Health and Safety Code?*

___ Yes ___ No ___ Unknown. If the answer to this question is no or unknown, explain. (Attach additional sheets if necessary): ______________________

____

____

* Chapter 766 of the Health and Safety Code requires one-family or two-family dwellings to have working smoke detectors installed in accordance with the requirements of the building code in effect in the area in which the dwelling is located, including performance, location, and power source requirements. If you do not know the building code requirements in effect in your area, you may check unknown above or contact your local building official for more information. A buyer may require a seller to install smoke detectors for the hearing impaired if: (1) the buyer or a member of the buyer's family who will reside in the dwelling is hearing impaired; (2) the buyer gives the seller written evidence of the hearing impairment from a licensed physician; and (3) within ten days after the effective date, the buyer makes a written request for the seller to install smoke detectors for the hearing impaired and specifies the locations for installation. The parties may agree who will bear the cost of installing the smoke detectors and which brand of smoke detectors to install.

3. Are you (Seller) aware of any known defects/malfunctions in any of the following? Write Yes (Y) if you are aware; write No (N) if you are not aware.

____ Interior Walls	____ Ceilings	____ Floors
____ Exterior Walls	____ Doors	____ Windows

____ Roof ____ Foundation/Slab(s) ____ Basement

____ Walls/Fences ____ Driveways ____ Sidewalks

____ Plumbing/Sewers/ Septics ____ Electrical Systems ____ Lighting Fixtures

____ Other Structural Components (Describe): ______________________________

____

____

If the answer to any of the above is yes, explain. (Attach additional sheets if necessary):

____

____

____

4. Are you (Seller) aware of any of the following conditions?

Write Yes (Y) if you are aware; write No (N) if you are not aware.

____ Active Termites (includes wood-destroying insects)

____ Termite or Wood Rot Damage Needing Repair

____ Previous Termite Damage

____ Previous Termite Treatment

____ Improper Drainage

____ Water Damage Not Due to a Flood Event

____ Landfill, Settling, Soil Movement, Fault Lines

____ Single Blockable Main Drain in Pool/Hot Tub/Spa*

____ Previous Structural or Roof Repair

____ Hazardous or Toxic Waste

____ Asbestos Components

____ Urea-Formaldehyde Insulation

____ Radon Gas

____ Lead Based Paint

____ Aluminum Wiring

____ Previous Fires

____ Unplatted Easements

____ Subsurface Structure or Pits

____ Previous Use of Premises for Manufacture of Methamphetamine

If the answer to any of the above is yes, explain. (Attach additional sheets if necessary):

____

____

____

* A single blockable main drain may cause a suction entrapment hazard for an individual.

5. Are you (Seller) aware of any item, equipment, or system in or on the Property that is in need of repair? ___ Yes (if you are aware) ___ No (if you are not aware). If yes, explain. (Attach additional sheets if necessary): ______________________

____

____

6. Are you (Seller) aware of any of the following conditions?*

Write Yes (Y) if you are aware; write No (N) if you are not aware.

____ Present flood insurance coverage

____ Previous flooding due to a failure or breach of a reservoir or a controlled or emergency release of water from a reservoir

____ Previous water penetration into a structure on the property due to a natural flood event

Write Yes (Y) if you are aware and check "wholly" or "partly" as applicable; write No (N) if you are not aware.

____ Located ( ) wholly ( ) partly in a 100-year floodplain (Special Flood Hazard Area–Zone A, V, A99, AE, AO, AH, VE, or AR)

____ Located ( ) wholly ( ) partly in a 500-year floodplain (Moderate Flood Hazard Area–Zone X (shaded))

____ Located ( ) wholly ( ) partly in a floodway

____ Located ( ) wholly ( ) partly in a flood pool

____ Located ( ) wholly ( ) partly in reservoir

If the answer to any of the above is yes, explain. (Attach additional sheets if necessary):

____

____

*For purposes of this notice:

"100-year floodplain" means any area of land that (1) is identified on the flood insurance rate map as a special hazard area, which is designated as Zone A, V, A99, AE, AO, VE, or AR on the map; (2) has a 1 percent annual chance of flooding, which is considered to be a high risk of flooding; and (3) may include a regulatory floodway, flood pool, or reservoir.

"500-year floodplain" means any area of land that (1) is identified on the flood insurance rate map as a moderate flood hazard area, which is designated on the map as Zone X (shaded); and (2) has a two-tenths of 1 percent annual chance of flooding, which is considered to be a moderate risk of flooding.

"Flood pool" means the area adjacent to a reservoir that lies above the normal maximum operating level of the reservoir and that is subject to controlled inundation under the management of the U.S. Army Corps of Engineers.

"Flood insurance rate map" means the most recent flood hazard map published by the Federal Emergency Management Agency under the National Flood Insurance Act of 1968 (42 U.S.C. §§ 4001–4131).

"Floodway" means an area that is identified on the flood insurance rate map as a regulatory floodway, which includes the channel of a river or other watercourse and the adjacent land areas that must be reserved for the discharge of a base flood, also referred to as a 100-year flood, without cumulatively increasing the water surface elevation more than a designated height.

"Reservoir" means a water impoundment project operated by the U.S. Army Corps of Engineers that is intended to retain water or delay the runoff of water in a designated surface area of land.

Have you (Seller) ever filed a claim for flood damage to the property with any insurance provider, including the National Flood Insurance Program (NFIP)?*
__ Yes __ No. If yes, explain. (Attach additional sheets if necessary): ______________
____
____

*Homes in high-risk flood zones with mortgages from federally regulated or insured lenders are required to have flood insurance. Even when not required, the Federal Emergency Management Agency (FEMA) encourages homeowners in high-risk, moderate-risk, and low-risk flood zones to purchase flood insurance that covers the structure(s) and the personal property within the structure(s).

Have you (Seller) ever received assistance from FEMA or the U.S. Small Business Administration (SBA) for flood damage to the property? __ Yes __ No. If yes, explain. (Attach additional sheets if necessary): ______________________________
____
____

7. Are you (Seller) aware of any of the following conditions?

Write Yes (Y) if you are aware; write No (N) if you are not aware.

____ Room additions, structural modifications, or other alterations or repairs made without necessary permits or not in compliance with building codes in effect at that time.

____ Homeowners' Association or maintenance fees or assessments.

____ Any "common area" (facilities such as pools, tennis courts, walkways, or other areas) co-owned in undivided interest with others.

____ Any notices of violations of deed restrictions or governmental ordinances affecting the condition or use of the Property.

____ Any lawsuits directly or indirectly affecting the Property.

____ Any condition on the Property which materially affects the physical health or safety of an individual.

____ Any rainwater harvesting system located on the property that is larger than 500 gallons and that uses a public water supply as an auxiliary water source.

____ Any portion of the Property that is located in a groundwater conservation district or a subsidence district.

If the answer to any of the above is yes, explain. (Attach additional sheets if necessary):

____

____

8. If the property is located in a coastal area that is seaward of the Gulf Intracoastal Waterway or within 1,000 feet of the mean high tide bordering the Gulf of Mexico, the property may be subject to the Open Beaches Act or the Dune Protection Act (chapter 61 or 63, Natural Resources Code, respectively) and a beachfront construction certificate or dune protection permit may be required for repairs or improvements. Contact the local government with ordinance authority over construction adjacent to public beaches for more information.

9. This property may be located near a military installation and may be affected by high noise or air installation compatible use zones or other operations. Information relating to high noise and compatible use zones is available in the most recent Air Installation Compatible Use Zone Study or Joint Land Use Study prepared for a military installation and may be accessed on the website of the military installation and of the county and any municipality in which the military installation is located.

____

Signature of Seller

Date

The undersigned purchaser hereby acknowledges receipt of the foregoing notice.

Signature of Buyer

Date

Form 4-24

Access and Due Diligence Agreement

Basic Information

Date:

Seller:

Seller's Mailing Address:

Buyer:

Buyer's Mailing Address:

Property:

A. Recitals

A.1. Seller is the owner of the Property.

A.2. Buyer is considering buying the Property from Seller, and Buyer and Seller are currently negotiating the terms of a possible purchase ("Possible Transaction").

A.3. In connection with the Possible Transaction, Buyer wants a license to enter the Property to examine, inspect, and perform tests on the Property to evaluate the physical and environmental condition of the Property and to perform other tests and inspections related to the Possible Transaction. Seller has agreed to grant Buyer the license to enter the Property for that purpose in accordance with the terms and conditions of this Agreement.

B. Agreement

For valuable consideration, the receipt and sufficiency of which is acknowledged, Buyer and Seller agree as follows:

B.1. Investigation Period. The "Investigation Period" means the period from the date of this Agreement until the earliest of (a) 5:00 P.M. local time where the Property is located on [**date**]; (b) receipt by Buyer of written notice from Seller terminating this Agreement, which termination may be made at Seller's sole discretion; or (c) the execution and delivery by Seller and Buyer of a purchase and sale agreement ("Sales Contract") for the Property.

B.2. Entry onto the Property. Buyer may enter the Property during the Investigation Period to inspect it at Buyer's cost and risk, subject to the following:

B.2.a. Buyer must deliver evidence to Seller that Buyer has liability insurance for its proposed inspection activities, with coverages and in amounts that are substantially the same as those maintained by Seller or with such lesser coverages and in such lesser amounts as are reasonably satisfactory to Seller.

B.2.b. Buyer may not interfere in any material manner with existing operations or occupants of the Property.

B.2.c. Buyer must notify Seller in advance of Buyer's plans to conduct tests so that Seller may be present during the tests.

B.2.d. If the Property is physically altered because of Buyer's inspections, Buyer must return the Property to its preinspection condition promptly after the alteration occurs.

B.2.e. Buyer must deliver to Seller copies of all inspection reports that Buyer prepares or receives from third-party consultants or contractors within three days after their preparation or receipt.

B.2.f. Buyer must abide by any other reasonable entry rules imposed by Seller.

B.3. *Environmental Assessment.* Buyer has the right to conduct environmental assessments of the Property. Seller will provide, or will designate a person with knowledge of the use and condition of the Property to provide, information requested by Buyer or Buyer's agent or representative regarding the use and condition of the Property during the period of Seller's ownership of the Property. Seller will cooperate with Buyer in obtaining and providing to Buyer or its agent or representative information regarding the Property.

B.4. *Property Documents.* Seller has previously made, or will make, available to Buyer and Buyer's representatives for their review, certain items and information pertaining to the Property with the exception of any financially privileged documents pertaining to Seller (collectively referred to as the "Property Documents"). The Property Documents have been or will be made available to Buyer without representation or warranty by, or recourse against, Seller. Buyer will not rely on the Property Documents and will independently verify the truth, accuracy, and completeness of any information or items contained therein.

B.5. *Buyer's Indemnity and Release of Seller.* Buyer will indemnify, defend, and hold Seller harmless from any loss, attorney's fees, expenses, or claims arising out of Buyer's investigation of the Property, except those arising out of the acts or omissions of Seller and those for repair or remediation of existing conditions discovered by Buyer's inspection. The obligations of Buyer under this provision will survive termination of this Agreement, the execution or termination of the Sales Contract, and closing. Buyer releases Seller and those persons acting on Seller's behalf from all claims and causes of action (including claims for attorney's fees and court and other costs) resulting from Buyer's investigation of the Property.

B.6. No Waiver. No waiver of default by any party to this Agreement may be implied from failure to take action by any other party to the Agreement, regardless of whether the default continues or is repeated. No express waiver of a default will affect any other default or cover any other period not specified in the express waiver. A waiver of any default in the performance of any provision contained in this Agreement will not be deemed to be a waiver of any subsequent default in the performance of the same provision or any other provision contained in this Agreement.

B.7. Assignment. The license granted to Buyer under the terms of this Agreement is personal to Buyer, and neither this Agreement nor the license may be transferred or assigned by Buyer.

B.8. Notices. Any notice required by or permitted under this Agreement must be in writing. Any notice required by this Agreement will be deemed to be given (whether received or not) the earlier of receipt or three business days after being deposited with the United States Postal Service, postage prepaid, certified mail, return receipt requested, and addressed to the intended recipient at the address shown in this Agreement. Notice may also be given by regular mail, personal delivery, courier delivery, or email and will be effective when received, provided that (a) any notice received on a Saturday, Sunday, or holiday will be deemed to have been received on the next day that is not a Saturday, Sunday, or holiday and (b) any notice received after 5:00 P.M. local time at the place of delivery on a day that is not a Saturday, Sunday, or holiday will be deemed to have been received on the next day that is not a Saturday, Sunday, or holiday. Any address for notice may be changed by not less than ten days' prior written notice given as provided herein. Copies of each notice must be given by one of these methods to the attorney of the party to whom notice is given.

B.9. Amendment. This Agreement may be amended only by an instrument in writing signed by the parties.

B.10. Revocation. The license granted under this Agreement is revocable by Seller, at any time, for any reason or no reason, on receipt by Buyer from Seller of written notice of revocation.

B.11. Business Days; Holidays; Weekends. As used in this Agreement, the term *business day* means any day, other than a Saturday or Sunday, on which banks located in [**city, state**] are not required or authorized to close. If any notice or action required or permitted by this Agreement falls on a date that is not a business day, the date will be extended to the next business day.

B.12. Entire Agreement. This Agreement is the entire agreement between Seller and Buyer concerning Buyer's investigations, and no modification or subsequent agreement relative to the subject matter of this Agreement will be binding on either party unless reduced to writing and signed by the party to be bound.

B.13. No Third-Party Beneficiaries. There are no third-party beneficiaries of this Agreement.

B.14. Severability. If a provision in this Agreement is unenforceable for any reason, to the extent the unenforceability does not destroy the basis of the bargain among the parties, the unenforceability does not affect any other provision of this Agreement, and this Agreement is to be construed as if the unenforceable provision is not a part of the Agreement.

B.15. Ambiguities Not to Be Construed against Party Who Drafted Agreement. The rule of construction that ambiguities in a document are construed against the party who drafted it does not apply in interpreting this Agreement.

B.16. No Special Relationship. The parties' relationship is an ordinary commercial relationship, and the parties do not intend to create the relationship of principal and agent, partners, joint venturers, or any other special relationship.

B.17. Counterparts. If this Agreement is executed in multiple counterparts, all counterparts taken together constitute this Agreement. Copies of signatures to this Agreement are effective as original signatures.

B.18. Confidentiality. This Agreement, this transaction, and all information learned in the course of this transaction will be kept confidential, except to the extent disclosure is required by law or court order or to enable third parties to advise or assist Buyer to investigate the Property or either party to close this transaction. Remedies for violations of this provision are limited to injunctions, and no damages or rescission may be sought or recovered as a result of any such violations.

B.19. Binding Effect. This Agreement binds, benefits, and may be enforced by the parties and their respective heirs, successors, and permitted assigns.

B.20. Time. Time is of the essence with respect to this Agreement.

B.21. Governing Law. This Agreement is to be construed and enforced in accordance with the laws of the state in which the Property is located.

B.22. No Obligation Regarding Possible Transaction. Notwithstanding the rights granted to Buyer under this Agreement, and notwithstanding any negotiations or other communications between Seller and Buyer, neither Seller nor Buyer has any obligation whatsoever to proceed with the Possible Transaction or otherwise enter into a Sales Contract or any other agreement concerning Seller's sale or Buyer's purchase of the Property or any portion thereof, or to otherwise negotiate for or consummate any transaction of any kind concerning the Property or any portion thereof. Neither Seller nor Buyer has any obligations whatsoever regarding the purchase and sale of the Property unless and until Seller and Buyer execute and enter into a binding Sales Contract, which either party may or may not do in its sole discretion.

Seller:

[Name of seller]

By:________________________________
Name:
Title:

Buyer:

[Name of buyer]

By:________________________________
Name:
Title:

Form 4-25

Option to Purchase

[For Use with Real Estate Sales Contract]

Date:

Seller:

Seller's Address:

Buyer:

Buyer's Address:

Property:

Option Fee:

Expiration Date:

Contract: The Real Estate Sales Contract attached as Exhibit [**exhibit number/letter**]

Purchase Price:

Underwriter:

Escrow Agent:

Escrow Agent's Address:

In consideration of the Option Fee, Seller grants to Buyer the exclusive and irrevocable option to purchase the Property on the following terms and conditions:

1. *Application of Option Fee.* The Option Fee [will/will not] be applied to the Purchase Price.

2. *Exercise of Option.* To exercise the option, Buyer must execute and deliver to Seller the Contract by the Expiration Date. Within three business days of receiving Buyer's signed Contract, Seller must execute and deliver the Contract to Escrow Agent.

3. *Termination of Option.* If Buyer does not exercise the option by the Expiration Date, the option terminates, Seller retains the Option Fee, and Buyer will execute and deliver to Seller a recordable release of the option.

4. *Seller's Default.* If Buyer exercises the option but Seller does not timely execute and deliver the Contract, Buyer has all applicable remedies, including specific performance.

Optionor/Seller:

____

[Name of seller]

Optionee/Buyer:

____

[Name of buyer]

Include acknowledgments at the election of the parties or if the buyer intends to file this option agreement in the public records.

Attach exhibit.

Form 4-26

Memorandum of Option

Date:

Seller:

Seller's Address:

Buyer:

Buyer's Address:

Property:

Expiration Date:

Seller has granted Buyer an option to purchase the Property. The option must be exercised by the Expiration Date.

Optionor/Seller:

____

[Name of seller]

Optionee/Buyer:

____

[Name of buyer]

Include acknowledgments.

Form 4-27

Right of First Refusal Agreement

Basic Information

Date:

Grantor:

Grantor's Address:

Grantee:

Grantee's Address:

Property:

Term:

A. Grant

A.1. Grantor grants to Grantee a right of first refusal to acquire the Property.

A.2. During the Term, if Grantor receives an offer for the sale or other transfer of the Property or any portion thereof or interest therein for any form of consideration that Grantor wishes to accept, Grantor agrees to notify Grantee in writing before accepting the offer. The notice will state the identity of the proposed transferee and the complete terms of the proposed transfer. If the proposed consideration for the transfer is other than cash, the notice will also state the cash equivalent reasonably determined by the Grantor for the noncash consideration.

A.3. Grantee will have the right to purchase the Property on the terms set forth in Grantor's notice by giving written notice to Grantor within [thirty/[**number**]] days following the receipt of Grantor's notice. If Grantee affirmatively exercises such right, the Property will be transferred to Grantee, and Grantee will pay to Grantor the consideration on the terms set forth in the notice from Grantor.

A.4. If Grantee does not affirmatively exercise its right within the [thirty/[**number**]]-day period, Grantor may transfer the Property to the party and on the terms described in Grantor's notice to Grantee within the [180/[**number**]]-day period following the expiration of the [thirty/[**number**]]-day period. If a transfer is not consummated within the [180/[**number**]]-day period, Grantor may not transfer the Property without again complying with the provisions of this Agreement. If Grantor wishes to effect a transfer on terms that are less favorable to Grantor than those described in Grantor's notice, Grantor must repeat the process set forth in this Agreement by giving a new notice to Grantee setting forth the new terms. If Grantor timely consummates a transfer, this Agreement will automatically terminate when the Property is conveyed to the party named in Grantor's notice to Grantee.

A.5. If an offer received by Grantor calls for delivery of a promissory note or other deferred payment obligation, the promissory note or other deferred payment obligation of Grantee will be deemed equivalent to those offered.

A.6. If any offer provides for noncash consideration, Grantee disputes Grantor's determination of the value of the noncash consideration set forth in Grantor's notice, and Grantor and Grantee cannot resolve the dispute within five business days after Grantee gives notice of the dispute to Grantor, the matter will be submitted to binding arbitration in [**city**], Texas, under the Commercial Arbitration Rules of the American Arbitration Association by a single arbitrator, and the determination of such arbitrator shall be binding on both parties. The [thirty/[**number**]]-day period for exercise of Grantee's rights will be tolled during the period the arbitration proceeding is pending.

A.7. The rights granted in this Agreement expire at the end of the Term.

B. Transfers by Gift, Devise, Descent, or Otherwise without Consideration

If the Property is transferred by gift, devise, descent, or another transaction that does not involve the payment of consideration in any form, the provisions of this Agreement will be fully binding on the person acquiring title to the Property in that transaction.

C. Recordation

Grantee may record this Agreement or a memorandum of this Agreement in the real property records of [**county**] County, Texas. Grantee will, on request, execute and record a release of this Agreement following its expiration or termination.

D. Assignment

Grantee [may/may not] assign its rights under this Agreement.

E. Notices

Any notice required or permitted under this Agreement must be in writing. Any notice required by this Agreement will be deemed to be given (whether received or not) the earlier of receipt or three business days after being deposited with the United States Postal Service, postage prepaid, certified mail, return receipt requested, and addressed to the intended recipient at the address shown in this Agreement. Notice may be also given by regular mail, personal delivery, courier delivery, or email and will be effective when received. Any address for notice may be changed by written notice given as provided herein.

____
[**Name of grantor**]

____
[**Name of grantee**]

Form 4-28

Right of First Offer Agreement

Basic Information

Date:

Grantor:

Grantor's Address:

Grantee:

Grantee's Address:

Property:

Term:

A. Grant

A.1. Grantor grants to Grantee a right of first offer to acquire the Property.

A.2. During the Term, if Grantor wishes to sell the Property or any portion thereof or interest therein for any form of consideration, Grantor must give written notice to Grantee stating the complete terms of the proposed transfer, including the consideration, which must be stated as a cash purchase price.

A.3. Grantee will have the right to purchase the Property on the terms set forth in Grantor's notice by giving written notice to Grantor within [thirty/[**number**]] days following the receipt of Grantor's notice. If Grantee affirmatively exercises that right, the Property will be transferred to Grantee, and Grantee will pay to Grantor the consideration on the terms set forth in the notice from Grantor.

A.4. If Grantee does not affirmatively exercise its right within the [thirty/[**number**]]-day period, Grantor may transfer the Property to another party on the terms described in Grantor's notice to Grantee within the [270/[**number**]]-day period following the expiration of the [thirty/[**number**]]-day period. If a transfer is not consummated within the [270/[**number**]]-day period, Grantor may not transfer the Property without again complying with the provisions of this Agreement. If Grantor wishes to effect a transfer on terms that are less favorable to Grantor than those described in Grantor's notice, Grantor must repeat the process set forth in this Agreement by giving a new notice to Grantee setting forth the new terms. If Grantor timely consummates a transfer, this Agreement will automatically terminate when the Property is conveyed to another party.

A.5. The rights granted in this Agreement expire at the end of the Term.

B. Transfers by Gift, Devise, Descent, or Otherwise without Consideration

If the Property is transferred by gift, devise, descent, or another transaction that does not involve the payment of consideration in any form, the provisions of this Agreement will be fully binding on the person acquiring title to the Property in that transaction.

C. Recordation

Grantee may record this Agreement or a memorandum of this Agreement in the real property records of [**county**] County, Texas. Grantee will, on request, execute and record a release of this Agreement following its expiration or termination.

D. Assignment

Grantee [may/may not] assign its rights under this Agreement.

E. Notices

Any notice required or permitted under this Agreement must be in writing. Any notice required by this Agreement will be deemed to be given (whether received or not) the earlier of receipt or three business days after being deposited with the United States Postal Service, postage prepaid, certified mail, return receipt requested, and addressed to the intended recipient at the address shown in this Agreement. Notice may be also given by regular mail, personal delivery, courier delivery, or email and will be effective when received. Any address for notice may be changed by written notice given as provided herein.

____
[Name of grantor]

____
[Name of grantee]

Form 4-29

Assignment of Real Estate Sales Contract
[Short Form]

Date:

Assignor:

Address:

Phone:

Email:

Type of entity:

Assignee:

Address:

Phone:

Email:

Type of entity:

Contract: Real Estate Sales Contract between [**name of seller**] ("Seller") and Assignee, as Buyer, escrowed under GF #[**number**] at the title company [**name of company**] as Escrow Agent.

Assignment: Assignor assigns to Assignee all of Assignor's right, title, and interest as Buyer in and to the Contract including the Earnest Money deposited in escrow with

Escrow Agent. Assignee assumes and agrees to perform Buyer's obligations under the Contract.

____
[Name and title of assignor]

____
[Name and title of assignee]

Form 4-30

Assignment of Real Estate Sales Contract
[Long Form]

Date:

Assignor:

Address:

Phone:

Email:

Type of entity:

Assignee:

Address:

Phone:

Email:

Type of entity:

Contract: Real Estate Sales Contract between Seller and Buyer, the Assignor, for sale of the Property to Buyer involving—

Seller:

Property: The land commonly known as [**describe property**] and more fully described in Exhibit A ("Land") [**include the following phrases as applicable:** , together with improvements to the Land ("Improvements"), the leases associated with the Land

and Improvements ("Leases"), and the personal property described in Exhibit A ("Personal Property")].

Earnest Money:

Escrow: [**title company name, GF #, address, and escrow officer contact information**]

Consideration:

[**Include if applicable:** Consent: This Assignment is conditioned on the consent of Seller.]

For the Consideration, Assignor and Assignee agree as follows:

A. Exhibits

The following are attached to and are a part of this Assignment:

Exhibit A—Real Estate Sales Contract

Exhibit B—Representations

Exhibit C—Records

B. Assignment and Assumption

B.1. Assignment. Assignor for the Consideration assigns to Assignee all of Assignor's right, title, and interest as Buyer in and to the Contract including the Earnest Money deposited in escrow with Escrow Agent.

B.2. Assumption. Assignee assumes and agrees to perform Buyer's obligations under the Contract [**include if applicable:** arising after the Date of this Assignment]. [**Include if applicable:** Assignee will indemnify, defend, and hold Assignor harmless from any loss, attorney's fees, expenses, or claims arising out of or related to Assignee's failure to perform any of the obligations of Buyer under the Contract after the Date of this Assignment. Assignor will indemnify, defend, and hold Assignee harmless from any loss, attorney's fees, expenses, or claims arising out of or related to Assignor's failure to perform any of the obligations of Buyer under the Contract before the Date of this Assignment.] [**Include if applicable:** Assignee has reimbursed Assignor for an amount equal to the assigned Earnest Money.]

B.3. Records. To the extent that Assignor has possession or control of the items listed in Exhibit C, Assignor will deliver or make the items or copies of them available to Buyer within three business days after the Date.

C. Representations

C.1. Contract. Attached as Exhibit A is a true and correct copy of the Contract.

C.2. Representations. The representations stated in sections A. and C. of Exhibit B to this Assignment are true and correct as of the Date. A party to this Assignment who becomes aware that any of the representations of either party are not true and correct will promptly notify the other party. Unless a party notifies the other party to the contrary on or before the Closing Date, or a party has actual knowledge to the contrary as of the Closing Date, each party to this Assignment is entitled to presume that the representations of the other party in Exhibit B are true and correct as of the Closing Date under the Contract.

C.3. As Is, Where Is. The parties agree to the terms of section B. (As Is, Where Is) in Exhibit B.

D. Miscellaneous

D.1. Notices. Any notice required by or permitted under this Assignment must be in writing. Any notice required by this Assignment will be deemed to be given (whether received or not) the earlier of receipt or three business days after being deposited with the United States Postal Service, postage prepaid, certified mail, return receipt requested, and addressed to the intended recipient at the address shown in this Assignment. Notice may also be given by regular mail, personal delivery, courier delivery, or email and will be effective when received, provided that (a) any notice received on a Saturday, Sunday, or holiday will be deemed to have been received on the next day that is not a Saturday, Sunday, or holiday and (b) any notice received after 5:00 P.M. local time at the place of delivery on a day that is not a Saturday, Sunday, or holiday will be deemed to have been received on the next day that is not a Saturday, Sunday, or holiday. Any address for notice may be changed by not less than ten days' prior written notice given as provided herein. Copies of each notice must be given by one of these methods to the attorney of the party to whom notice is given.

D.2. *Entire Agreement.* This Assignment is the entire agreement of the parties concerning the assignment by Assignor of the sale of the Property by Seller. There are no representations, warranties, agreements, or promises of Assignor pertaining to the Property or the sale of the Property, and Assignee is not relying on any statements or representations of Assignor or any agent of Assignor that are not in this Assignment.

D.3. *Amendment.* This Assignment may be amended only by an instrument in writing signed by the parties.

D.4. *Prohibition of Assignment.* Assignee may not assign this Assignment, the Contract, Assignee's rights under this Assignment, or Buyer's rights under the Contract without Assignor's prior written consent, which Assignor has no obligation to grant and which, if granted, may be conditioned in any manner Assignor deems appropriate, and any attempted assignment without Assignor's consent is void. The consent by Assignor to any assignment by Assignee will not release Assignee of its obligations under this Assignment, and Assignee and its assignee will be jointly and severally liable for the performance of those obligations after any such assignment.

D.5. *Survival.* The provisions of this Assignment that expressly survive termination or Closing and other obligations of this Assignment that cannot be performed before termination of this Assignment or before Closing survive termination of this Assignment or Closing, and the legal doctrine of merger does not apply to these matters. The representations made by the parties as of Closing survive Closing.

D.6. Choice of Law; Venue. THIS ASSIGNMENT IS TO BE CONSTRUED UNDER THE LAWS OF THE STATE OF TEXAS, WITHOUT REGARD TO CHOICE-OF-LAW RULES OF ANY JURISDICTION. VENUE IS IN THE COUNTY FOR PERFORMANCE.

D.7. Waiver of Default. Default is not waived if the nondefaulting party fails to declare a default immediately or delays taking any action with respect to the default.

D.8. No Third-Party Beneficiaries. There are no third-party beneficiaries of this Assignment.

D.9. Severability. If a provision in this Assignment is unenforceable for any reason, to the extent the unenforceability does not destroy the basis of the bargain among the parties, the unenforceability does not affect any other provision of this Assignment, and this Assignment is to be construed as if the unenforceable provision is not a part of the Assignment.

D.10. Ambiguities Not to Be Construed against Party Who Drafted Assignment. The rule of construction that ambiguities in a document are construed against the party who drafted it does not apply in interpreting this Assignment.

D.11. No Special Relationship. The parties' relationship is an ordinary commercial relationship, and the parties do not intend to create the relationship of principal and agent, partners, joint venturers, or any other special relationship.

D.12. Counterparts. If this Assignment is executed in multiple counterparts, all counterparts taken together constitute this Assignment. Copies of signatures to this Assignment are effective as original signatures.

D.13. Confidentiality. This Assignment, this transaction, and all information learned in the course of this transaction shall be kept confidential, except to the extent disclosure is required by law or court order or to enable third parties to advise or assist Assignee to investigate the Property or either party to close this transaction. Remedies for violations of this provision are limited to injunctions, and no damages or rescission may be sought or recovered as a result of any such violations.

D.14. Binding Effect. This Assignment binds, benefits, and may be enforced by the parties and their respective heirs, successors, and permitted assigns.

D.15. Waiver of Consumer Rights. ASSIGNEE WAIVES ITS RIGHTS UNDER THE TEXAS DECEPTIVE TRADE PRACTICES–CONSUMER PROTECTION ACT, SECTION 17.41 *ET SEQ.* OF THE TEXAS BUSINESS AND COMMERCE CODE, A LAW THAT GIVES CONSUMERS SPECIAL RIGHTS AND PROTECTIONS. AFTER CONSULTATION WITH AN ATTORNEY OF ITS OWN SELECTION, ASSIGNEE VOLUNTARILY CONSENTS TO THIS WAIVER.

D.16. Waiver of Jury Trial. Assignor and Assignee, each after consultation with an attorney of its own selection (which counsel was not directly or indirectly identified, suggested, or selected by the other party), both voluntarily waive a trial by jury of any issue arising in an action or proceeding between the parties or their successors, under or connected with this Assignment or its provisions. Assignor and Assignee acknowledge to each other that Assignor and Assignee are not in significantly disparate bargaining positions.

____
[Name and title of assignor]
Date:

____
[Name and title of assignee]
Date:

Exhibit A

Real Estate Sales Contract

Attach real estate sales contract.
See form 4-2 in this chapter.

Exhibit B

Representations

A. Assignor's Representations to Assignee

Assignor represents to Assignee that the following are true and correct as of the Date and will be true and correct on the Closing Date, unless Assignor has given Assignee notice of any changes before the Closing Date that such circumstances have changed due to causes not reasonably within Assignor's control.

A.1. *Authority.* Assignor is a [**specify type of organization**] duly organized, validly existing, and in good standing under the laws of the state of [Texas/[**state**]] with authority to perform its obligations under this Assignment. This Assignment is binding on Assignor.

A.2. *Litigation.* Assignor has not received written notice and has no actual knowledge of any litigation pending or threatened against the Property or Assignor that might adversely affect the Property or Assignor's ability to perform its obligations under this assignment [**include if applicable:** , except: [**specify**]].

A.3. *Violation of Governmental Requirements.* Assignor has not received written notice and has no actual knowledge of violation of any law, ordinance, regulation, restriction, or legal requirements affecting the Property or Seller's use of the Property [**include if applicable:** , except: [**specify**]].

A.4. *Licenses, Permits, and Approvals.* Assignor has not received written notice and has no actual knowledge that any license, permit, or approval necessary to use the Property in the manner in which it is currently being used has expired or will not be renewed on expiration or that any material condition will be imposed to use or renew the same [**include if applicable:** , except: [**specify**]].

A.5. Condemnation; Zoning; Land Use; Hazardous Materials. Assignor has not received written notice and has no actual knowledge of any condemnation, zoning, land-use, hazardous materials, or other proceedings affecting the Property or any written inquiries or notices by any governmental authority or third party with respect to condemnation, zoning, or other land-use regulations or the presence of hazardous materials affecting the Property [**include if applicable:** , except: [**specify**]].

A.6. Terrorist Organizations Lists. Assignor is not and Assignor has no actual knowledge that any of its partners, members, shareholders, owners, employees, officers, directors, representatives, or agents is a person or entity with whom U.S. persons or entities are restricted from doing business under regulations of the Office of Foreign Asset Control of the Department of the Treasury or under any statute, executive order, or other governmental action.

A.7. No Other Obligation to Sell Property or Restriction against Sale. Assignor is not obligated to sell any of the Property to any person other than Assignee. Assignor's performance of this Assignment will not cause a breach of any other agreement or obligation to which Assignor is a party or by which Assignor or the Property is bound.

A.8. No Liens. On the Closing Date, the Property will be free and clear of all mechanic's and materialman's liens and other liens and encumbrances of any nature arising through Assignor.

A.9. Assignor's Records. Assignor's Records provided by Assignor to Assignee as provided in Exhibit C for Assignee's inspections will be true, correct, and complete copies of the records in Assignor's possession or control. Assignor's Records that were prepared by or under Assignor's supervision and control will be true, correct, and complete in all material respects. Unless Assignor notifies Assignee to the contrary at the time of delivery of Records provided by Assignor to Assignee that were not prepared by or under Assignor's supervision and control, Assignor has no actual knowledge that such Records are not true, correct, and complete in any material respect.

A.10. No Other Representation. Except as stated above, Assignor makes no representation with respect to the Property.

A.11. No Warranty. Assignor has made no warranty in connection with this transaction.

B. "As Is, Where Is"

THIS ASSIGNMENT IS AN ARM'S-LENGTH AGREEMENT BETWEEN THE PARTIES. THE CONSIDERATION WAS BARGAINED ON THE BASIS OF AN "AS IS, WHERE IS" TRANSACTION AND REFLECTS THE AGREEMENT OF THE PARTIES THAT THERE ARE NO REPRESENTATIONS, DISCLOSURES, OR EXPRESS OR IMPLIED WARRANTIES, EXCEPT THE REPRESENTATIONS IN THIS ASSIGNMENT.

ASSIGNEE IS NOT RELYING ON ANY REPRESENTATIONS, DISCLOSURES, OR EXPRESS OR IMPLIED WARRANTIES OTHER THAN THOSE EXPRESSLY CONTAINED IN THIS ASSIGNMENT. ASSIGNEE IS NOT RELYING ON ANY INFORMATION REGARDING THE PROPERTY PROVIDED BY ANY PERSON, OTHER THAN ASSIGNEE'S OWN INSPECTION AND THE REPRESENTATIONS CONTAINED IN THIS ASSIGNMENT.

C. Assignee's Representations to Assignor

Assignee represents to Assignor that the following are true and correct as of the Date and will be true and correct on the Closing Date, unless Assignee has given Assignor notice of any changes before the Closing Date that such circumstances have changed due to causes not reasonably within Assignee's control.

C.1. Authority. Assignee is a [**specify type of organization**] duly organized, validly existing, and in good standing under the laws of the state of [Texas/[**state**]] with authority to perform its obligations under this Assignment. This Assignment is binding on Assignee. This Assignment is, and all documents required by this Assignment to be executed and delivered to Seller at Closing will be, duly authorized, executed, and delivered by Assignee.

C.2. Terrorist Organizations Lists. Assignee is not and Assignee has no actual knowledge that any of its partners, members, shareholders, owners, employees, officers, directors, representatives, or agents is a person or entity with whom U.S. persons or entities are restricted from doing business under regulations of the Office of Foreign Asset Control of the Department of the Treasury or under any statute, executive order, or other governmental action.

Exhibit C

Records

A. Seller's Records. The following records delivered by Seller to Assignor ("Seller's Records"):

List applicable seller's records.

B. Title and Survey Information. The following title and survey information delivered to Assignor ("Title and Survey Information"):

List applicable title and survey information.

C. Assignor's Records and Studies. The following records and studies obtained by Assignor other than those listed in paragraph A. ("Assignor's Records and Studies"):

List applicable records and studies.

Form 4-31

Seller's Consent to Assignment

Date:

Seller:

Address:

Phone:

Email:

Type of entity:

Assignor:

Address:

Phone:

Email:

Type of entity:

Assignee:

Address:

Phone:

Email:

Type of entity:

Contract: Real Estate Sales Contract between Seller and Buyer for sale of the Property to Buyer involving—

Earnest Money:

Escrow: [**title company name, GF #, address, and escrow officer contact information**].

Consideration:

For the Consideration, Seller, Assignor, and Assignee agree as follows:

A. Exhibits

The following are attached to and are a part of this Assignment:

Exhibit A—Assignment of Real Estate Sales Contract

Exhibit B—Representations

Exhibit C—Records

B. Assignment, Assumption, and Consent

B.1. Assignment. Assignor and Assignee represent to Seller that a true, correct, and complete copy of the Assignment of Real Estate Sales Contract ("Assignment") executed by Assignor and Assignee is attached as Exhibit A. The Assignment sets forth the entire agreement between Assignor and Assignee.

B.2. Assumption. Assignee assumes and agrees to perform Buyer's obligations under the Contract.

B.3. Consent. Seller consents to the Assignment on the terms of this Consent. Seller's consent to the Assignment is not a consent to any other assignment. In addition to the Conditions of Closing set out in paragraph K.1. of the Contract, Seller will not be obligated to close the sale of the Property to Assignee unless Assignee has satisfied the following conditions, any of which may be waived by Seller in its discretion:

B.3.a. The representations of Assignee to Seller in this Consent are true and correct at Closing.

B.3.b. The representations of Assignor to Seller in this Consent are true and correct at Closing.

B.3.c. Assignee must have performed all covenants and agreements required to be performed by it at or before Closing.

Select one of the following.

The consent by Seller to this assignment by Assignor to Assignee does not release Assignor of its obligations under the Contract. Assignor and Assignee are jointly and severally liable to Seller for the performance of the obligations of Buyer under the Contract.

Or

The consent by Seller to this assignment by Assignor to Assignee releases Assignor of its obligations under the Contract except for Assignor's representations to Seller in this Consent.

Continue with the following.

C. Representations

C.1. Representations

C.1.a. Assignor. Assignor represents to Seller that its representations stated in sections A. and D. of Exhibit B to the Contract are true and correct as of the Date and will be true and correct on the Closing Date.

Assignor represents to Seller that the Records listed in Exhibit C and provided by Assignor to Assignee for Assignee's inspections are true, correct, and complete copies of the Records in Assignor's possession or control. Assignor's Records and Studies that were prepared by or under Assignor's supervision and control are true, correct, and complete in all material respects.

C.1.b. Assignee. Assignee represents to Seller that its representations stated in section A. of Exhibit B to this Consent are true and correct as of the Date and will be true and correct on the Closing Date.

C.1.c. Subsequent Notice. If Assignor or Assignee becomes aware that any of the representations of either Assignor or Assignee to Seller are not true and correct, it will promptly notify Seller. Unless Assignor or Assignee notifies Seller to the contrary on or before the Closing Date, or Seller has actual knowledge to the contrary as of the Closing Date, Seller is entitled to presume that the representations in this Consent are true and correct as of the Closing Date.

C.2. As Is, Where Is. Assignee agrees to the terms of section B. (As Is, Where Is) in Exhibit B to this Consent and in section B. to the Contract.

D. Insurance and Indemnity

D.1. Insurance. Assignee agrees to maintain the insurance set out in Exhibit C to the Contract through Closing.

D.2. Indemnity. ASSIGNEE WILL INDEMNIFY, DEFEND, AND HOLD SELLER HARMLESS FROM ANY LOSS, ATTORNEY'S FEES, EXPENSES, OR CLAIMS ("INDEMNIFIED LIABILITIES") ARISING OUT OF ASSIGNEE'S ACTS OR OMISSIONS AFTER THE DATE, INCLUDING INDEMNIFIED LIABILITIES CAUSED IN WHOLE OR IN PART BY THE NEGLIGENCE OF ASSIGNEE OR ITS EMPLOYEES OR CONTRACTORS, INCLUDING IF THE INDEMNIFIED LIABILITIES ARISE IN PART FROM THE

NEGLIGENCE OF ASSIGNOR OR ITS EMPLOYEES. THIS INDEMNITY IS (a) INDEPENDENT OF A PARTY'S INSURANCE, (b) WILL NOT BE LIMITED BY DAMAGES PAID UNDER THE WORKERS' COMPENSATION ACT, AND (c) WILL SURVIVE THE CLOSING OR THE TERMINATION OF THE CONTRACT.

E. Miscellaneous

E.1. Notices. Any notice required by or permitted under this Consent must be in writing. Any notice required by this Consent will be deemed to be given (whether received or not) the earlier of receipt or three business days after being deposited with the United States Postal Service, postage prepaid, certified mail, return receipt requested, and addressed to the intended recipient at the address shown in this Consent. Notice may also be given by regular mail, personal delivery, courier delivery, or email and will be effective when received, provided that (a) any notice received on a Saturday, Sunday, or holiday will be deemed to have been received on the next day that is not a Saturday, Sunday, or holiday and (b) any notice received after 5:00 P.M. local time at the place of delivery on a day that is not a Saturday, Sunday, or holiday will be deemed to have been received on the next day that is not a Saturday, Sunday, or holiday. Any address for notice may be changed by not less than ten days' prior written notice given as provided herein. Copies of each notice must be given by one of these methods to the attorney of the party to whom notice is given.

E.2. Entire Agreement. This Consent is the entire agreement of the parties concerning consent by Seller to the assignment by Assignor to Assignee. There are no representations, warranties, agreements, or promises pertaining to the Property or the sale of the Property by Seller to Buyer, and Assignee is not relying on any statements or representations of Assignor, Seller, or any agent of Assignor or Seller that are not in the Contract, this Consent, or the Assignment.

E.3. Amendment. This Consent may be amended only by an instrument in writing signed by the parties.

E.4. Prohibition of Assignment. Assignee may not assign this Consent or the Contract or Assignee's rights under this Agreement or Buyer's rights under the Contract without Seller's prior written consent, which Seller has no obligation to grant and which, if granted, may be conditioned in any manner Seller deems appropriate, and any attempted assignment without Seller's consent is void. The consent by Seller to any assignment by Assignee will not release Assignor or Assignee of its obligations under this Consent, and Assignor, Assignee, and Assignee's assignee will be jointly and severally liable for the performance of Buyer's obligations after any such assignment.

E.5. Survival. The provisions of this Consent that expressly survive termination or Closing and other obligations of this Consent that cannot be performed before termination of this Consent or before Closing survive termination of this Consent or Closing, and the legal doctrine of merger does not apply to these matters. The representations made by the parties as of Closing survive Closing.

E.6. Choice of Law; Venue. THIS CONSENT IS TO BE CONSTRUED UNDER THE LAWS OF THE STATE OF TEXAS, WITHOUT REGARD TO CHOICE-OF-LAW RULES OF ANY JURISDICTION. VENUE IS IN THE COUNTY FOR PERFORMANCE.

E.7. Waiver of Default. Default is not waived if the nondefaulting party fails to declare a default immediately or delays taking any action with respect to the default.

E.8. No Third-Party Beneficiaries. There are no third-party beneficiaries of this Consent.

E.9. Severability. If a provision in this Consent is unenforceable for any reason, to the extent the unenforceability does not destroy the basis of the bargain among the parties, the unenforceability does not affect any other provision of this Consent, and this Consent is to be construed as if the unenforceable provision is not a part of the Consent.

E.10. Ambiguities Not to Be Construed against Party Who Drafted Consent. The rule of construction that ambiguities in a document are construed against the party who drafted it does not apply in interpreting this Consent.

E.11. No Special Relationship. The parties' relationship is an ordinary commercial relationship, and the parties do not intend to create the relationship of principal and agent, partners, joint venturers, or any other special relationship.

E.12. Counterparts. If this Consent is executed in multiple counterparts, all counterparts taken together constitute this Consent. Copies of signatures to this Consent are effective as original signatures.

E.13. Confidentiality. This Consent, this transaction, and all information learned in the course of this transaction shall be kept confidential, except to the extent disclosure is required by law or court order or to enable third parties to advise or assist Assignee to investigate the Property or either party to close this transaction. Remedies for violations of this provision are limited to injunctions, and no damages or rescission may be sought or recovered as a result of any such violations.

E.14. Binding Effect. This Consent binds, benefits, and may be enforced by the parties and their respective heirs, successors, and permitted assigns.

E.15. Waiver of Consumer Rights. ASSIGNEE WAIVES ITS RIGHTS UNDER THE TEXAS DECEPTIVE TRADE PRACTICES–CONSUMER PROTECTION ACT, SECTION 17.41 *ET SEQ.* OF THE TEXAS BUSINESS AND COMMERCE CODE, A LAW THAT GIVES CONSUMERS SPECIAL RIGHTS AND PROTECTIONS. AFTER CONSULTATION WITH AN ATTORNEY OF ITS OWN SELECTION, ASSIGNEE VOLUNTARILY CONSENTS TO THIS WAIVER.

E.16. Waiver of Jury Trial. Assignor and Assignee, each after consultation with an attorney of its own selection (which counsel was not directly or indirectly identified, suggested, or selected by the other party), both voluntarily waive a trial by jury of any issue arising in an action or proceeding between the parties or their successors, under or connected with this Consent or its provisions. Assignor and Assignee acknowledge to each other that Assignor and Assignee are not in significantly disparate bargaining positions.

____
[Name and title of seller]
Date:

____
[Name and title of assignor]
Date:

____
[Name and title of assignee]
Date:

Exhibit A

Assignment of Real Estate Sales Contract

Attach assignment of real estate sales contract. See forms 4-29 and 4-30 in this chapter.

Exhibit B

Representations

A. Assignee's Representations to Seller

Assignee represents to Seller that the following are true and correct as of the Date and will be true and correct on the Closing Date, unless Seller has given Assignee notice of any changes before the Closing Date that such circumstances have changed due to causes not reasonably within Assignee's control.

A.1. Authority. Assignee is a [**specify type of organization**] duly organized, validly existing, and in good standing under the laws of the state of [Texas/[**state**]] with authority to perform its obligations under this Assignment. This Consent and the Assignment are binding on Assignee.

A.2. Litigation. Assignee has not received written notice and has no actual knowledge of any litigation pending or threatened against the Property or Assignee that might adversely affect the Property or Assignee's ability to perform its obligations under this Assignment [**include if applicable:** , except: [**specify**]].

A.3. Violation of Governmental Requirements. Assignee has not received written notice and has no actual knowledge of violation of any law, ordinance, regulation, restriction, or legal requirements affecting the Property or Seller's use of the Property [**include if applicable:** , except: [**specify**]].

A.4. Licenses, Permits, and Approvals. Assignee has not received written notice and has no actual knowledge that any license, permit, or approval necessary to use the Property in the manner in which it is currently being used has expired or will not be renewed on expiration or that any material condition will be imposed to use or renew the same [**include if applicable:** , except: [**specify**]].

A.5. Condemnation; Zoning; Land Use; Hazardous Materials. Assignee has not received written notice and has no actual knowledge of any condemnation, zoning, land-use, hazardous materials, or other proceedings affecting the Property or any written inquiries or notices by any governmental authority or third party with respect to condemnation, zoning, or other land-use regulations or the presence of hazardous materials affecting the Property [**include if applicable:** , except: [**specify**]].

A.6. Terrorist Organizations Lists. Assignee is not and Assignee has no actual knowledge that any of its partners, members, shareholders, owners, employees, officers, directors, representatives, or agents is a person or entity with whom U.S. persons or entities are restricted from doing business under regulations of the Office of Foreign Asset Control of the Department of the Treasury or under any statute, executive order, or other governmental action.

A.7. No Other Obligation to Sell Property or Restriction against Sale. Assignee is not obligated to sell any of the Property to any person other than Assignee. Assignee's performance of this agreement will not cause a breach of any other agreement or obligation to which Assignee is a party or by which Assignee or the Property is bound.

A.8. No Liens. On the Closing Date, the Property will be free and clear of all mechanic's and materialman's liens and other liens and encumbrances of any nature arising through Assignee.

A.9. No Other Representation. Except as stated above or in the notices, statements, and certificates set forth in Exhibit D to the Contract, Seller makes no representation with respect to the Property.

A.10. No Warranty. Seller has made no warranty in connection with this transaction.

B. "As Is, Where Is"

THIS CONSENT, THE ASSIGNMENT, AND THE CONTRACT ARE AN ARM'S-LENGTH AGREEMENT BETWEEN THE PARTIES. THE CONSIDERATION WAS BARGAINED ON THE BASIS OF AN "AS IS, WHERE IS" TRANSACTION AND REFLECTS THE AGREEMENT OF THE PARTIES THAT THERE ARE NO REPRESENTATIONS, DISCLOSURES, OR EXPRESS OR IMPLIED WARRANTIES, EXCEPT THOSE IN THIS CONSENT OR THE CONTRACT.

ASSIGNEE IS NOT RELYING ON ANY REPRESENTATIONS, DISCLOSURES, OR EXPRESS OR IMPLIED WARRANTIES OTHER THAN THOSE EXPRESSLY CONTAINED IN THIS CONSENT. ASSIGNEE IS NOT RELYING ON ANY INFORMATION REGARDING THE PROPERTY PROVIDED BY ANY PERSON, OTHER THAN ASSIGNEE'S OWN INSPECTION AND THE REPRESENTATIONS AND WARRANTIES OF SELLER CONTAINED IN THIS CONSENT OR THE CONTRACT.

Exhibit C

Records

A. Seller's Records. Assignee acknowledges that the following records of Seller ("Seller's Records") have been delivered to Assignee:

List applicable seller's records.

B. Title and Survey Information. Assignee acknowledges that the following title and survey information have been delivered to Assignee ("Title and Survey Information"):

List applicable title and survey information.

C. Assignor's Records and Studies. Assignee acknowledges that the following records and studies ("Assignor's Records and Studies") have been delivered to Assignee:

List applicable records and studies.

Form 4-32

Contract for Assignment of Real Estate Sales Contract

Execution by the first party to execute this Contract for Assignment of Real Estate Sales Contract ("Contract for Assignment") and delivery to the other party constitutes an offer to buy or sell Buyer's rights under the Real Estate Sales Contract ("Contract"). Unless accepted by the other party by execution of this Contract for Assignment and escrowed with the Title Company by the Deposit Deadline, the offer lapses and is void. This Contract for Assignment is effective upon escrow with the Title Company of this Contract for Assignment executed by Assignor and Assignee ("Date").

Deposit Deadline:

Assignor:

Address:

Phone:

Email:

Type of entity:

Assignor's Attorney:

Law firm:

Address:

Phone:

Email:

Assignee:

Address:

Phone:

Email:

Type of entity:

Assignee's Attorney:

Law firm:

Address:

Phone:

Email:

Assignee's Sales Agent:

Brokerage firm:

Address:

Phone:

Email:

Contract: Real Estate Sales Contract between Seller and Buyer, the Assignor, for sale of the Property to Buyer, a true, correct, and complete copy of which is attached hereto as Exhibit A, involving—

Seller:

Property: The land commonly known as [**describe property**] and more fully described in Exhibit A ("Land") [**include the following phrases that are applicable, tailoring punctuation and conjunctions as necessary:** , together with improvements to the Land ("Improvements"), the leases associated with the Land and Improvements ("Leases"), and the personal property described in Exhibit A ("Personal Property")].

Earnest Money:

Escrow: [**title company name, GF #, address, and escrow officer contact information**] ("Title Company")

Consideration:

Independent Consideration: Assignee is to pay $100 ("Independent Consideration") to Assignor within three business days of the execution by Assignor and Assignee and escrow of this Contract for Assignment with the Title Company as Escrow Agent for Assignor and Assignee. The Independent Consideration is consideration for Assignee's Termination Option.

Substitute Earnest Money: An amount equal to the Earnest Money under the Contract.

Assignment Fee:

Assignee's Liquidated Damages:

Assignor's Additional Liquidated Damages:

Consent: This Assignment is conditioned on the consent of Seller.

For the Consideration, Assignor and Assignee agree as follows:

A. Exhibits

The following are attached to and are a part of this Contract for Assignment:

Exhibit A—Real Estate Sales Contract

Exhibit B—Representations

Exhibit C—Records

Exhibit D—Assignment of Real Estate Sales Contract

Exhibit E—Assignee's Insurance

B. Assignment in Escrow

B.1. Assignment of Contract. Within five business days of the escrow by the parties of this Contract for Assignment, Assignor and Assignee are to execute and deliver to the Title Company the Assignment of Real Estate Sales Contract ("Assignment"), a form of which is attached as Exhibit D.

B.2. Substitute Earnest Money. Assignee is to deposit with Escrow Agent the Substitute Earnest Money within three business days of the escrow of this Contract for Assignment with Escrow Agent.

B.3. Assignment Fee. Assignee is to deposit with Escrow Agent the Assignment Fee within three business days of the escrow of this Contract for Assignment with Escrow Agent.

B.4. Escrow. The Assignment, Substitute Earnest Money, and Assignment Fee are to be held by Escrow Agent pending determination by Assignee of whether to exercise Assignee's Termination Option.

B.4.a. Assignment Effective Date. The "Assignment Effective Date" is the day after the expiration of the Inspection Period without Assignee having exercised the Termination Option. On the Assignment Effective Date, Escrow Agent is to do the following:

i. Deliver to Assignee the escrowed Assignment.

ii. Deliver to Assignor the Assignment Fee.

iii. Substitute the Substitute Earnest Money for the Earnest Money deposited by Assignor as Buyer under the Contract and send the monies deposited by Assignor as the Earnest Money to Assignor.

B.4.b. Termination. If Assignee exercises the Termination Option, Escrow Agent is to do the following:

i. Deliver to Assignor the escrowed Assignment.

ii. Send to Assignee the Assignment Fee and Substitute Earnest Money.

C. Inspection Period

C.1. Review of Records. Assignor will deliver to Assignee copies of the Records specified in Exhibit C, or otherwise make those records available for Assignee's review, within five business days of the deposit with Escrow Agent of the fully executed Contract for Assignment, the Substitute Earnest Money, and the Assignment Fee.

C.2. Entry onto Property. Assignee may enter the Property before expiration of the Inspection Period to inspect it at Assignee's cost and risk, subject to the following:

C.2.a. Insurance. Assignee must deliver evidence to Assignor that Assignee has commercial general liability insurance, with coverages specified in Exhibit E. Assignee must deliver evidence to Seller that Assignee has insurance with coverages as required by the Contract.

C.2.b. Operations at Property. Assignee may not interfere in any material manner with existing operations or occupants of the Property.

C.2.c. Notice of Testing. Assignee must notify Assignor in advance of Assignee's plans to conduct tests so that Assignor may be present during the tests.

C.2.d. Restoration. If the Property is physically altered because of Assignee's inspections, Assignee must return the Property to its preinspection condition promptly after the alteration occurs.

C.2.e. Third-Party Reports. Assignee must deliver to Assignor copies of all inspection reports that Assignee prepares or receives from third-party consultants or contractors within three days after their preparation or receipt.

C.2.f. Rules. Assignee must abide by any other reasonable entry rules imposed by Seller, Assignor, or both.

C.2.g. Contract Protocols. Assignee must abide by the requirements of the Contract regarding entry on the Property.

C.3. Environmental Assessment. Assignee has the right to conduct environmental assessments of the Property. Assignor will provide, or will designate a person with knowledge of the use and condition of the Property to provide, information requested by Assignee or Assignee's agent or representative regarding the use and condition of the Property. Assignor will cooperate with Assignee in obtaining and providing to Assignee or its agent or representative information regarding the use and condition of the Property before Assignor's period of ownership to the extent that the information is within Assignor's possession or control.

C.4. Assignee's Right to Terminate. Assignee may terminate this Contract for Assignment for any reason by notifying Assignor of the termination before the end of the Inspection Period ("Termination Option"). If Assignee does not notify Assignor of Assignee's termination of the contract before the end of the Inspection Period, Assignee waives the right to terminate this Contract for Assignment pursuant to this provision.

C.5. Release. ASSIGNEE RELEASES SELLER AND ASSIGNOR AND THOSE PERSONS ACTING ON SELLER'S OR ASSIGNOR'S BEHALF FROM ALL CLAIMS AND CAUSES OF ACTION (INCLUDING CLAIMS FOR ATTORNEY'S FEES AND COURT AND OTHER COSTS) RESULTING FROM ASSIGNEE'S INVESTIGATION OF THE PROPERTY [**include if applicable:** , INCLUDING CLAIMS ARISING OUT OF SELLER'S OR ASSIGNOR'S NEGLIGENCE, BUT NOT SELLER'S OR ASSIGNOR'S GROSS NEGLIGENCE OR INTENTIONAL MISCONDUCT].

C.6. Performance of Contract

C.6.a. Assignor to Assignee

i. *Modifications to Contract.* Assignor agrees not to modify or in any way alter the terms of the Contract without the prior written consent of Assignee.

ii. *Release of Seller.* Assignor agrees not to waive, excuse, condone, or in any manner release or discharge Seller from the obligations, covenants, conditions, and agreements of Seller to be performed under the Contract.

iii. *Termination of Contract.* Assignor agrees not to terminate the Contract.

iv. *Performance of Contract.* Assignor agrees to abide faithfully by, perform, and discharge every material obligation, covenant, and agreement of the Contract to be performed by Buyer before the expiration of the Inspection Period and shall obtain Assignee's consent before exercising any elections or taking any actions.

v. *Forwarding Notices.* Assignor agrees to promptly send Assignee any notice or demand that Assignor receives from Seller.

vi. *Enforcement of Seller's Obligations.* Assignor agrees to vigorously enforce the obligations of Seller under the Contract.

vii. *Notice of Default by Assignor.* Assignor agrees to promptly notify Assignee of any notice of default by Assignor that Assignor receives.

viii. *Assignee Cure Rights.* Assignee is hereby given the right to undertake to cure any default by Assignor on the Contract.

ix. *Assignee's Dealing with Seller.* Assignor authorizes Assignee to contact Seller and the Title Company and obtain Seller's Records and Title and Survey Information. Assignee shall furnish Assignor a copy of any Seller's Records and Title and Survey Information it receives from Seller or the Title Company that have not already been furnished to Assignor.

C.6.b. Assignee to Assignor. Assignee agrees not to take actions or omit to take actions that will cause Assignor to default on the Contract.

C.7. Consent by Assignor to Assignment. Assignor and Assignee are to cooperate in seeking Seller's consent for Assignor to assign Buyer's rights under the Contract to Assignee.

D. Representations

D.1. Contract. Attached as Exhibit A is a true and correct copy of the Contract.

D.2. Representations. The representations stated in sections A. and C. of Exhibit B to this Contract for Assignment are true and correct as of the Date and must be true and correct as of the Assignment Effective Date. A party to this Consent for Assignment who becomes aware that any of the representations of either party are not true and correct will promptly notify the other party. Unless a party notifies the other party to the contrary on or before the Assignment Effective Date, or a party has actual knowledge to the contrary as of the Assignment Effective Date, each party to this Contract for Assignment is entitled to presume that the representations of the other party in Exhibit B are true and correct as of the Assignment Effective Date.

D.3. As Is, Where Is. The parties agree to the terms of section B. (As Is, Where Is) in Exhibit B.

E. Insurance and Indemnity

E.1. Insurance. Assignee agrees to maintain the insurance set out in Exhibit E through Closing.

E.2. Indemnity. ASSIGNEE WILL INDEMNIFY, DEFEND, AND HOLD ASSIGNOR HARMLESS FROM ANY LOSS, ATTORNEY'S FEES, EXPENSES, OR CLAIMS ("INDEMNIFIED LIABILITIES") ARISING OUT OF ASSIGNEE'S ACTS OR OMISSIONS AFTER THE DATE, INCLUDING INDEMNIFIED LIABILITIES CAUSED IN WHOLE OR IN PART BY THE NEGLIGENCE OF ASSIGNEE OR ITS EMPLOYEES OR CONTRACTORS, INCLUDING IF THE INDEMNIFIED LIABILITIES ARISE IN PART FROM THE NEGLIGENCE OF ASSIGNOR OR ITS EMPLOYEES. THIS INDEMNITY IS (a) INDEPENDENT OF A PARTY'S INSURANCE, (b) WILL NOT BE LIMITED BY DAMAGES PAID UNDER THE WORKERS' COMPENSATION ACT, AND (c) WILL SURVIVE THE CLOSING OR THE TERMINATION OF THE CONTRACT.

F. Default and Remedies

F.1. Assignor's Defaults. If Assignor fails to perform its obligations under this Contract for Assignment or if Assignor's representations are not true and correct as of the Assignment Effective Date ("Assignor's Default"), Assignee's sole and exclusive remedy is to terminate this Contract for Assignment by giving notice to Assignor and Escrow Agent on or before [**number**] days after the Inspection Period and have the Substitute Earnest Money and Assignment Fee returned to Assignee. If Assignor's Default occurs after Assignee has incurred costs to investigate the Property and Assignee terminates this Contract for Assignment in accordance with the previous sentence, Assignor will also pay to Assignee as liquidated damages the lesser of Assignee's actual out-of-pocket expenses incurred to investigate the Property after the Effective Date ("Assignee's Expenses") or the amount of Assignee's Liquidated Damages, within ten days after Assignor's receipt of an invoice from Assignee stating the amount of Assignee's Expenses accompanied by reasonable evidence of Assignee's Expenses.

F.2. Assignee's Default. If Assignee fails to perform any of its obligations under this Contract for Assignment ("Assignee's Default"), Assignor's sole and exclusive remedy is to terminate this Contract for Assignment by giving notice to Assignee and Escrow Agent and have the Assignment Fee, if not previously delivered by Escrow Agent to Assignor as provided in this Contract for Assignment, as liquidated damages. If Assignee's Default occurs after Assignor has incurred costs to perform its obligations under this Contract for Assignment and Assignor terminates this Contract for Assignment in accordance with the previous sentence, Assignee will also reimburse Assignor for the lesser of Assignor's actual out-of-pocket expenses incurred after the Effective Date to perform its obligations under this Contract for Assignment ("Assignor's Expenses") or the amount of Assignor's Additional Liquidated Damages, within ten days after Assignee's receipt of an invoice from Assignor stating the amount of Assignor's Expenses accompanied by reasonable evidence of Assignor's Expenses.

F.3. Assignee's Default; Remedies after Closing. If Assignee fails to perform any of its obligations under this Contract for Assignment that survive Closing, Assignor will have all rights and remedies available at law or in equity unless otherwise provided by the Closing Documents.

F.4. Liquidated Damages. The parties agree that just compensation for the harm that would be caused by a default by either party cannot be accurately estimated or would be very difficult to accurately estimate and that Assignee's Liquidated Damages and Assumption Fee and Assignor's Additional Liquidated Damages are reasonable forecasts of just compensation to the nondefaulting party for the harm that would be caused by a default.

F.5. Attorney's Fees. If either party retains an attorney to enforce this Contract for Assignment, the party prevailing in litigation is entitled to recover reasonable attorney's fees and court and other costs.

G. Miscellaneous

G.1. Notices. Any notice required by or permitted under this Contract for Assignment must be in writing. Any notice required by this Contract for Assignment will be deemed to be given (whether received or not) the earlier of receipt or three business days after being deposited with the United States Postal Service, postage prepaid, certified mail, return receipt requested, and addressed to the intended recipient at the address shown in this contract. Notice may also be given by regular mail, personal delivery, courier delivery, or email and will be effective when received, provided that (a) any notice received on a Saturday, Sunday, or holiday will be deemed to have been received on the next day that is not a Saturday, Sunday, or holiday and (b) any notice received after 5:00 P.M. local time at the place of delivery on a day that is not a Saturday, Sunday, or holiday will be deemed to have been received on the next day that is not a Saturday, Sunday, or holiday. Any address for notice may be changed by not less than ten days' prior written notice given as provided herein. Copies of each notice must be given by one of these methods to the attorney of the party to whom notice is given.

G.2. *Entire Agreement.* This Contract for Assignment is the entire agreement of the parties concerning the assignment by Assignee. There are no representations, warranties, agreements, or promises pertaining to the Property or the sale of the Property by Assignor to Buyer, and Assignee is not relying on any statements or representations of Buyer, Assignor, or any agent of Buyer or Seller that are not in the Contract or this Contract for Assignment.

G.3. *Amendment.* This Contract for Assignment may be amended only by an instrument in writing signed by the parties.

G.4. *Prohibition of Assignment.* Assignee may not assign this Contract for Assignment or the Contract or Assignee's rights under this Contract for Assignment or Buyer's rights under the Contract without Assignor's prior written consent, which Assignor has no obligation to grant and which, if granted, may be conditioned in any manner Assignor deems appropriate, and any attempted assignment without Assignor's consent is void. The consent by Assignor to any assignment by Assignee will not release Assignee of its obligations under this Agreement, and Assignee and its assignee will be jointly and severally liable for the performance of those obligations after any such assignment.

G.5. *Survival.* The provisions of this Contract for Assignment that expressly survive termination or Closing and other obligations of this Contract for Assignment that cannot be performed before termination of this Contract for Assignment or before Closing survive termination of this Contract for Assignment or Closing, and the legal doctrine of merger does not apply to these matters. The representations made by the parties as of Closing survive Closing.

G.6. *Choice of Law; Venue.* THIS CONTRACT FOR ASSIGNMENT IS TO BE CONSTRUED UNDER THE LAWS OF THE STATE OF TEXAS, WITHOUT REGARD TO CHOICE-OF-LAW RULES OF ANY JURISDICTION. VENUE IS IN THE COUNTY FOR PERFORMANCE.

G.7. Waiver of Default. Default is not waived if the nondefaulting party fails to declare a default immediately or delays taking any action with respect to the default.

G.8. No Third-Party Beneficiaries. There are no third-party beneficiaries of this Contract for Assignment.

G.9. Severability. If a provision in this Contract for Assignment is unenforceable for any reason, to the extent the unenforceability does not destroy the basis of the bargain among the parties, the unenforceability does not affect any other provision of this Contract for Assignment, and this Contract for Assignment is to be construed as if the unenforceable provision is not a part of the Contract for Assignment.

G.10. Ambiguities Not to Be Construed against Party Who Drafted Assignment. The rule of construction that ambiguities in a document are construed against the party who drafted it does not apply in interpreting this Contract for Assignment.

G.11. No Special Relationship. The parties' relationship is an ordinary commercial relationship, and the parties do not intend to create the relationship of principal and agent, partners, joint venturers, or any other special relationship.

G.12. Counterparts. If this Contract for Assignment is executed in multiple counterparts, all counterparts taken together constitute this Contract for Assignment. Copies of signatures to this Contract for Assignment are effective as original signatures.

G.13. Confidentiality. This Contract for Assignment, this transaction, and all information learned in the course of this transaction shall be kept confidential, except to the extent disclosure is required by law or court order or to enable third parties to advise or assist Assignee to investigate the Property or either party to close this transaction. Remedies for violations of this provision are limited to injunctions, and no damages or rescission may be sought or recovered as a result of any such violations.

G.14. Binding Effect. This Contract for Assignment binds, benefits, and may be enforced by the parties and their respective heirs, successors, and permitted assigns.

G.15. Waiver of Consumer Rights. ASSIGNEE WAIVES ITS RIGHTS UNDER THE TEXAS DECEPTIVE TRADE PRACTICES–CONSUMER PROTECTION ACT, SECTION 17.41 *ET SEQ.* OF THE TEXAS BUSINESS AND COMMERCE CODE, A LAW THAT GIVES CONSUMERS SPECIAL RIGHTS AND PROTECTIONS. AFTER CONSULTATION WITH AN ATTORNEY OF ITS OWN SELECTION, ASSIGNEE VOLUNTARILY CONSENTS TO THIS WAIVER.

G.16. Waiver of Jury Trial. Assignor and Assignee, each after consultation with an attorney of its own selection (which counsel was not directly or indirectly identified, suggested, or selected by the other party), both voluntarily waive a trial by jury of any issue arising in an action or proceeding between the parties or their successors, under or connected with this Contract for Assignment or its provisions. Assignor and Assignee acknowledge to each other that Assignor and Assignee are not in significantly disparate bargaining positions.

G.17. Broker's Commissions. Assignor and Assignee each indemnify and agree to defend and hold the other party harmless from any loss, attorney's fees, and court and other costs arising out of a claim by any person or entity claiming by, through, or under the indemnitor for a broker's or finder's fee or commission because of this transaction or this Contract for Assignment or the Contract, whether the claimant is disclosed to the indemnitee or not. At Closing under the Contract, each party will provide the other party with a release of broker's or appraiser's liens from all brokers or appraisers for which such party is responsible.

____

[Name and title of assignor]
Date:

____

[Name and title of assignee]
Date:

Exhibit A

Real Estate Sales Contract

Attach real estate sales contract. See form 4-2 in this chapter.

Exhibit B

Representations

A. Assignor's Representations to Assignee

Assignor represents to Assignee that the following are true and correct as of the Date and will be true and correct on the Assignment Effective Date, unless Assignor has given Assignee notice of any changes before the Assignment Effective Date that such circumstances have changed due to causes not reasonably within Assignor's control.

A.1. Authority. Assignor is a [**specify type of organization**] duly organized, validly existing, and in good standing under the laws of the state of [Texas/[**state**]] with authority to perform its obligations under this Assignment. This Assignment is binding on Assignor.

A.2. Litigation. Assignor has not received written notice and has no actual knowledge of any litigation pending or threatened against the Property or Assignor that might adversely affect the Property or Assignor's ability to perform its obligations under this Assignment [**include if applicable:** , except: [**specify**]].

A.3. Violation of Governmental Requirements. Assignor has not received written notice and has no actual knowledge of violation of any law, ordinance, regulation, restriction, or legal requirements affecting the Property or Seller's use of the Property [**include if applicable:** , except: [**specify**]].

A.4. Licenses, Permits, and Approvals. Assignor has not received written notice and has no actual knowledge that any license, permit, or approval necessary to use the Property in the manner in which it is currently being used has expired or will not be renewed on expiration or that any material condition will be imposed to use or renew the same [**include if applicable:** , except: [**specify**]].

A.5. Condemnation; Zoning; Land Use; Hazardous Materials. Assignor has not received written notice and has no actual knowledge of any condemnation, zoning, land-use, hazardous materials, or other proceedings affecting the Property or any written inquiries or notices by any governmental authority or third party with respect to condemnation, zoning, or other land-use regulations or the presence of hazardous materials affecting the Property [**include if applicable:** , except: [**specify**]].

A.6. Terrorist Organizations Lists. Assignor is not and Assignor has no actual knowledge that any of its partners, members, shareholders, owners, employees, officers, directors, representatives, or agents is a person or entity with whom U.S. persons or entities are restricted from doing business under regulations of the Office of Foreign Asset Control of the Department of the Treasury or under any statute, executive order, or other governmental action.

A.7. No Other Obligation to Sell Property or Restriction against Sale. Assignor is not obligated to sell any of the Property to any person other than Assignee. Assignor's performance of this Assignment will not cause a breach of any other agreement or obligation to which Assignor is a party or by which Assignor or the Property is bound.

A.8. No Liens. On the Assignment Effective Date, the Property will be free and clear of all mechanic's and materialman's liens and other liens and encumbrances of any nature arising through Assignor.

A.9. Assignor's Records. The records provided by Assignor to Assignee for Assignee's inspections will be true, correct, and complete copies of the records in Assignor's possession or control. The records that were prepared by or under Assignor's supervision and control will be true, correct, and complete in all material respects. Unless Assignor notifies Assignee to the contrary at the time of delivery of records provided by Assignor to Assignee that were not prepared by or under Assignor's supervision and control, Assignor has no actual knowledge that such records are not true, correct, and complete in any material respect.

A.10. No Other Representation. Except as stated above or in the notices, statements, and certificates set forth in Exhibit D to the Contract, Assignor makes no representation with respect to the Property.

A.11. No Warranty. Assignor has made no warranty in connection with this transaction.

B. "As Is, Where Is"

THIS ASSIGNMENT IS AN ARM'S-LENGTH AGREEMENT BETWEEN THE PARTIES. THE CONSIDERATION WAS BARGAINED ON THE BASIS OF AN "AS IS, WHERE IS" TRANSACTION AND REFLECTS THE AGREEMENT OF THE PARTIES THAT THERE ARE NO REPRESENTATIONS, DISCLOSURES, OR EXPRESS OR IMPLIED WARRANTIES, EXCEPT THOSE IN THIS ASSIGNMENT.

ASSIGNEE IS NOT RELYING ON ANY REPRESENTATIONS, DISCLOSURES, OR EXPRESS OR IMPLIED WARRANTIES OTHER THAN THOSE EXPRESSLY CONTAINED IN THIS ASSIGNMENT. ASSIGNEE IS NOT RELYING ON ANY INFORMATION REGARDING THE PROPERTY PROVIDED BY ANY PERSON, OTHER THAN ASSIGNEE'S OWN INSPECTION AND THE REPRESENTATIONS AND WARRANTIES CONTAINED IN THIS ASSIGNMENT.

C. Assignee's Representations to Assignor

Assignee represents to Assignor that the following are true and correct as of the Date and will be true and correct on the Assignment Effective Date, unless Assignee has given Assignor notice of any changes before the Assignment Effective Date that such circumstances have changed due to causes not reasonably within Assignee's control.

C.1. Authority. Assignee is a [**specify type of organization**] duly organized, validly existing, and in good standing under the laws of the state of [Texas/[**state**]] with authority to perform its obligations under this Assignment. This Contract for Assignment is binding on Assignee. This Contract for Assignment is, and all documents required by this Contract for Assignment to be executed and delivered to Seller at Closing will be, duly authorized, executed, and delivered by Assignee.

C.2. Terrorist Organizations Lists. Assignee is not and Assignee has no actual knowledge that any of its partners, members, shareholders, owners, employees, officers, directors, representatives, or agents is a person or entity with whom U.S. persons or entities are restricted from doing business under regulations of the Office of Foreign Asset Control of the Department of the Treasury or under any statute, executive order, or other governmental action.

Exhibit C

Records

To the extent that Assignor has possession or control of the following items pertaining to and currently impacting the Property, Assignor will deliver or make the items or copies of them available to Buyer by [**date**]:

A. Seller's Records. The following records delivered by Seller to Assignor ("Seller's Records"):

List applicable seller's records.

B. Title and Survey Information. The following title and survey information delivered to Assignor:

List applicable title and survey information.

C. Assignor's Records and Studies. The following records and studies obtained by Seller other than those listed in A.:

List applicable records and studies.

Exhibit D

Assignment of Real Estate Sales Contract

Attach assignment of real estate sales contract. See forms 4-29 and 4-30 in this chapter.

Exhibit E

Assignee's Insurance

> Specify insurance the assignee must maintain through the closing.

Form 4-33

Letter of Intent

[**Date**]

[**Name and address of seller**]

Re: Letter of intent [**describe transaction**]
[**describe property by address or lot and block number, city, county, state**]

[**Salutation**]

The attached exhibits and this letter of intent (collectively, this "Letter") outline the business points under which [**name of buyer**] ("Buyer") will consider acquiring the property described above (the "Property") from [**name of seller**] ("Seller"). Buyer is interested in purchasing the Property on the general terms referenced in this Letter.

1. *Contract*. No right or obligation of either party, except those specifically set forth in the binding agreements relating to the proposed transaction listed in the attached Exhibit A, will arise until the execution of a real estate sales contract (the "Contract") incorporating the essential terms of this Letter and other terms and conditions satisfactory to both parties. Except as otherwise agreed by the parties, the Contract will be prepared on the most current form of real estate sales contract published by the State Bar of Texas in its *Texas Real Estate Forms Manual*. The initial draft of the Contract will be prepared by Seller's attorney within [**number**] days after the effective date of this Letter and distributed contemporaneously to all parties by [**describe method of delivery**].

2. *Payment of the Purchase Price*. The purchase price will be paid by wire transfer of immediately available funds to the escrow agent at closing.

3. *Title.* Title will be conveyed free and clear of all defects, liens, encumbrances, and easements, except as approved by Buyer during the title review period specified in the Contract.

4. *Effect.* Each party agrees that this Letter is intended only to set forth the discussions of the parties and will not constitute a complete statement of the agreement or be a legally binding or enforceable agreement or commitment on the part of either party with respect to the matters described herein (except with respect to the binding agreements relating to the proposed transaction listed in Exhibit A, which will be fully enforceable and will survive the termination of this Letter, the termination of the Contract, and the closing of any transaction). This Letter is not intended to impose on either party an enforceable duty or obligation to negotiate toward or conclude any such agreement or commitment. Each party acknowledges that, except with respect to the binding agreements relating to the proposed transaction listed in Exhibit A, in no event will any discussions, negotiations, or other communications between the parties regarding this Letter or the terms contained herein rise to the level of an oral or written agreement. The parties have no obligation of good faith and fair dealing. The parties' respective legal obligations will otherwise arise, if at all, solely from a fully executed Contract.

5. *Counterparts.* If this Letter is executed in multiple counterparts, all counterparts taken together will constitute this Letter.

6. *Exclusive Negotiations.* Until 5:00 P.M. on [**date**], Seller will negotiate only with Buyer for the sale of the Property.

Binding/Nonbinding Nature

SELLER AND BUYER ARE NOT LEGALLY BOUND TO ENTER INTO THE TRANSACTION DESCRIBED HEREIN UNLESS AND UNTIL THE CONTRACT IS EXECUTED BY BUYER. SELLER AND BUYER ARE BOUND TO COMPLY WITH THE PROVISIONS SPECIFICALLY LISTED AS BINDING

AGREEMENTS. SELLER AND BUYER EACH ACKNOWLEDGE RECEIPT OF $10.00 AND OTHER VALUABLE CONSIDERATION, WHICH EACH SUCH PARTY ACCEPTS AS LEGALLY SUFFICIENT TO BIND SUCH PARTY TO PERFORM THE BINDING AGREEMENTS.

If the foregoing meets with your approval, please sign and return the enclosed duplicate copy of this Letter on or before 5:00 P.M. central [standard/daylight saving] time on [**date**]. An electronic copy of this Letter executed by you will be considered an original. This Letter is effective on the date of the last of the signatures by Seller and Buyer. We look forward to receiving your prompt response.

Sincerely,

____

[**Name of buyer**]
[a/an] [individual/partnership/limited partnership/corporation]

Include the following if applicable.

By:

____

[**Name of representative**]
[**Title**]

Continue with the following.

Agreed to and accepted on [**date**].

____

[**Name of seller**],
[a/an] [individual/partnership/limited partnership/corporation]

Include the following if applicable.

By:

____

Name of representative

____

Title

Attach exhibits.

Exhibit A

Nonbinding Terms of Proposed Transaction

Seller:

Address:

Phone:

Email:

Type of entity:

Seller's Attorney:

Law Firm:

Address:

Phone:

Email:

Seller's Sales Agent:

Brokerage Firm:

Address:

Phone:

Email:

Buyer:

Address:

Phone:

Email:

Type of entity:

Buyer's Attorney:

Law Firm:

Address:

Phone:

Email:

Buyer's Sales Agent:

Brokerage Firm:

Address:

Phone:

Email:

Property: The land commonly known as [**describe property**] and more fully described in Exhibit B ("Land") [**include the following phrases that are applicable, tailoring punctuation and conjunctions as necessary:** , together with improvements to the Land ("Improvements"), the leases associated with the Land and Improvements ("Leases"), and the personal property described in Exhibit B ("Personal Property")].

Underwriter:

Escrow Agent:

Address:

Phone:

Email:

[**Include if applicable:** Estimated] Purchase Price

Cash portion:

Seller-financed portion (principal amount of note):

Third-party-financed portion:

Total purchase price:

Earnest Money

[Initial] Earnest Money:

[Additional Earnest Money:]

Deadlines and Closing Date

1. [Initial] Earnest Money deadline: [**date**]

2. Delivery of Title Commitment: [[**date**]/[**number**] days after the Contract effective date]

3. Delivery of Survey: [[**date**]/[**number**] days after the Contract effective date]

4. Delivery of UCC Search: [[**date**]/[**number**] days after the Contract effective date]

5. Delivery of legible copies of instruments referenced in the Title Commitment, Survey, and UCC Search: [[**date**]/[**number**] days after the Contract effective date]

6. Delivery of Title Objections: [[**date**]/[**number**] days after delivery of items 1.–5.]

7. Delivery of Seller's records as specified in the Contract: [[**date**]/[**number**] days after the Contract effective date]

8. End of Inspection Period: [[**date**]/[**number**] days after the Contract effective date]

Include the following if applicable.

9. Additional Earnest Money Deadline: [[**date**]/[**number**] days after the end of the Inspection Period]

Continue with the following.

[9./10.] Closing Date: [[**date**]/[**number**] days after the end of the Inspection Period]

[10./11.] Closing Time: [**time**]

Binding Agreements Relating to Proposed Transaction

1. If the Contract is not finally negotiated, signed by all parties, and tendered to Escrow Agent with the earnest money within [**number**] days of the effective date of this Letter, this Letter will terminate.

2. Seller agrees to abate all marketing efforts for the Property during the term of this Letter. Any existing signs may remain. Any ordered advertising will be canceled, if cancelable without penalty; otherwise ordered advertising may proceed, but no additional advertising may occur. Brokers and prospective buyers will not be shown the Property and may be given only currently available printed information about the Property prepared by Seller's Sales Agent.

3. Except as may be required by law or to its own attorney, advisors, and existing or prospective lenders or investors, no party to this Letter nor any affiliate will disclose the existence of this Letter, names of the parties, or the transaction contemplated herein; or issue any press release or make any other disclosure to a nonaffiliated third person concerning the existence of this Letter or the matters contained herein without the written consent of each party.

4. Each party will pay its own expenses related to this Letter and the Contract.

Insert any other applicable agreements.

5. Unless Seller agrees otherwise, Buyer is not permitted to enter into the Property for the purpose of inspecting it before the execution of the Contract. If Buyer is permitted by Seller to enter the Property for the purpose of inspecting it before the execution of the Contract, Buyer will indemnify, defend, and hold Seller harmless from and against any losses, damages, costs, expenses, or claims arising in connection with or out of such entry and inspection by Buyer.

Exhibit B

Description of the Land [and Personal Property]

Include legal description of the land.

That certain tract of land more particularly described as [**property**].

Include one of the following if the transaction involves some personal property.

All personal property associated with the Land and Improvements, except the following: [**list exceptions**].

Or

The following described personal property: [**describe property**].

Chapter 5

Deeds, Bills of Sale, and Other Transfers

Forms

Chapter 5

Deeds, Bills of Sale, and Other Transfers

§ 5.1 General Considerations for Deeds

Form 5-1 in this chapter, a general warranty deed, conveys to a grantee a fee simple estate in real property with a covenant of general warranty, subject to the reservations and exceptions stated in the deed.

The traditional deed clauses include the granting clause, the habendum clause, and the warranty clause. The customary granting clause includes the grant of the property with its related rights and appurtenances and begins with "grants, sells, and conveys." The customary habendum clause defines the extent of property ownership to be held by the grantee and begins with "to have and to hold." The customary warranty clause describes the warranty of title made by the grantor and begins with "Grantor binds."

Two implied covenants, often called "warranties," are given by stating that the deed "grants" or "conveys." By using either of those words, the grantor covenants that—

1. before the execution of the conveyance, the grantor has not conveyed the estate or any interest in the estate to a person other than the grantee; and

2. at the time of the execution of the conveyance, the estate is free from encumbrances.

Tex. Prop. Code § 5.023.

Taxes, assessments, and liens on real property are included in the term *encumbrance*. Tex. Prop. Code § 5.024.

The general warranty of title obligates the grantor to indemnify the grantee against any loss resulting from a title defect or from any encumbrances that arose before the conveyance. The grantor warrants that he will restore the purchase price to the grantee if the property is lost. *City of Beaumont v. Moore*, 202 S.W.2d 448, 453 (Tex. 1947). However, the express covenant of warranty and the implied covenants are limited if exceptions, reservations, and encumbrances are excepted from those warranties by the terms of the deed. A reliable title examination is important to determine if title defects or encumbrances exist.

A deed must identify a grantor and a grantee, contain operative words or words of grant showing the intent of the grantor to convey title to a real property interest to the grantee, and contain an adequate description of the property that is sufficient to identify the subject matter of the grant. *Harlan v. Vetter*, 732 S.W.2d 390 (Tex. App.—Eastland 1987, writ ref'd n.r.e.). A description in a deed must furnish within itself or by reference to some other existing writing the means by which the land to be conveyed may be identified with reasonable certainty. *Morrow v. Shotwell*, 477 S.W.2d 538 (Tex. 1972). See section 3.8 in this manual for a discussion of property descriptions.

§ 5.1:1 Statutory Requirements

Although no particular form of warranty deed is required by statute, the Texas Property Code suggests a form and states that any form substantially the same "conveys a fee simple estate in real property with a covenant of general warranty." Tex. Prop. Code § 5.022. The conveyance and warranty clauses in form 5-1 in this chapter are substantially the same as the statutory language. A deed does not have to include a warranty, and the parties may insert any clause or use any form not in contravention of law. Tex. Prop. Code § 5.022.

A deed must be in writing and must be subscribed and delivered by the grantor. Tex. Prop. Code § 5.021. A corporation may convey real property by a deed with or without its seal (subject to any approval required by the Texas Business Organizations Code or the governing documents of the corporation). Tex. Bus. Orgs. Code § 10.251. An unrecorded deed is binding on a party to the instrument, the party's heirs, and a subsequent purchaser who does not pay a valuable consideration or who has notice of the unrecorded deed, but it is void as to a creditor or subsequent purchaser for value without notice. Tex. Prop. Code § 13.001. If a party to a deed is an individual, the deed must contain the confidentiality rights notice required by Tex. Prop. Code § 11.008(c). See section 3.17 in this manual.

§ 5.1:2 Characterization of Marital Property

Texas follows the community system of property rights of spouses. Under the inception of title doctrine, the character of property, whether separate or community, is fixed at the time of acquisition. *Henry S. Miller Co. v. Evans*, 452 S.W.2d 426, 430 (Tex. 1970).

Separate property consists of the property owned or claimed by a spouse before marriage; the property acquired by the spouse during marriage by gift, devise, or descent; and the recovery for personal injuries sustained by the spouse during the marriage, except any recovery for loss of earning capacity during marriage. Tex. Fam. Code § 3.001. Spouses may also set aside all or part of their community property as separate property by partition or exchange agreement. *See* Tex. Const. art. XVI, § 15; Tex. Fam. Code §§ 4.102–.106. Although such property may undergo changes or mutations, as long as it can be traced and properly identified it will remain separate property. *McKinley v. McKinley*, 496 S.W.2d 540 (Tex. 1973).

Community property consists of the property, other than separate property, acquired by either spouse during marriage. Tex. Fam. Code § 3.002.

Property possessed by either spouse during or on dissolution of marriage is presumed to be community property unless there is clear and convincing evidence that it is separate property. Tex. Fam. Code § 3.003. The presumption of community property may be rebutted and a separate-property presumption may arise if (1) one spouse is the grantor and the other spouse is the grantee (*Story v. Marshall*, 24 Tex. 305, 308 (1859)), (2) one spouse furnishes separate-property consideration and title is taken in the name of the other spouse (*Smith v. Strahan*, 16 Tex. 314 (1856)), or (3) the instrument of conveyance contains a "separate property recital" (for example, a statement that the property is conveyed to a spouse as that spouse's separate property) (*Henry S. Miller Co.*, 452 S.W.2d at 431).

Control of marital property is a separate matter from ownership; it relates to who may sell and convey marital property. A spouse has sole control of his or her own separate property. Tex. Fam. Code § 3.101. However, if the property is homestead, both spouses must execute the conveyance. Tex. Const. art. XVI, § 50. The general rules governing control of community property are statutory. *See* Tex. Fam. Code § 3.102. Third parties are entitled to rely on certain evidence concerning control. *See* Tex. Fam. Code § 3.104. Rules of marital property liability are also governed by statute. *See* Tex. Fam. Code § 3.202.

§ 5.2 General Warranty Deed

§ 5.2:1 General Information about Parties, Addresses, and Property Descriptions

See chapter 3 in this manual for general information about designations of parties, addresses, and property descriptions.

§ 5.2:2 Consideration—Cash Sale

If the parties wish to show the actual amount of the consideration, they may use a description like the one in clause 5-6-6 in this chapter. If the parties prefer not to show the amount of cash paid in a document that will become a public record, the deed may recite as consideration "cash" or a nominal amount and "other consideration." Suitable descriptions for this purpose are set out in clauses 5-6-4 and 5-6-5. Note, however, that the fictional recitation of a nominal amount may create rights in the grantee or other consequences that the parties do not intend. *See 1464–Eight, Ltd. v. Joppich*, 154 S.W.3d 101 (Tex. 2004).

§ 5.2:3 Consideration—Assumption of Note

If the grantee assumes a note secured by one or more liens, the consideration description in the warranty deed should contain a recitation of any actual or nominal cash paid, a promise to assume and pay the unpaid principal and earned interest of the note, a promise to abide by all terms in all instruments securing the note, and an indemnity to protect the grantor from a breach by the grantee. For an example of such a clause, see clause 5-6-2 in this chapter.

Clause 5-6-2 can be adapted to fit any existing lien. This clause assigns to the grantee any escrow fund for payment of taxes and insurance. Because insurance is often not assumed, an assignment of it to the grantee might prevent the grantor from receiving unearned premiums on cancellation. The clause also states the unpaid principal balance. If the parties do not want to state the unpaid principal balance, the recitation of that balance should be omitted. Most deeds with assumptions provide for a vendor's lien and a deed of trust to secure assumption. It is important for the grantee to accept a deed with an assumption by signing either the deed or a separate acceptance document because the promises to pay the note and to perform the obligations under the deed of trust and the indemnity benefiting the grantor are contractual obligations of the grantee.

If the grantee assumes a note and the grantor wants to secure payment of the note with both a vendor's lien in the deed and a deed of trust to secure assumption, the deed should provide for the vendor's lien in the reservations description and refer to the deed of trust to secure assumption at the end of the deed. See clause 5-9-23. The deed should recite the assumption of the note in the consideration description. Of course, if only a vendor's lien is retained, references to the deed of trust to secure assumption should be omitted.

§ 5.2:4 Consideration—Subject to Note That Grantee Does Not Assume

If the consideration is cash but the property is encumbered by a lien securing a note that the grantee does not assume, the deed should show that the conveyance is subject to that encumbrance. In this instance the consideration description in the deed will recite the cash consideration, and the exceptions description should show that the conveyance is subject to one or more liens and that the grantee does not assume the debt. See clause 5-8-39 in this chapter.

§ 5.2:5 Consideration—Separate Property of Grantee

If the property is conveyed as the grantee's separate property, that fact should be recited in the deed. There are two opportunities to characterize the property as separate. First, the description of consideration may state that it was paid from the grantee's separate property. See clauses 5-6-11 and 5-6-12 in this chapter. Second, the parties should insert a reference to the separate nature of the property in the space provided for miscellaneous clauses following the conveyance and warranty clause. For an example, see clause 5-9-16.

§ 5.2:6 Reservations from Conveyance

Properly used, a reservation creates a new severance in favor of the grantor. *Donnell v. Otts*, 230 S.W. 864, 865 (Tex. App.—Fort Worth 1921, no writ); *Klein v. Humble Oil & Refining Co.*, 67 S.W.2d 911, 915 (Tex. App.—Beaumont 1934), *aff'd*, 86 S.W.2d 1077 (Tex. 1935).

If the grantor wishes to reserve a property right from the conveyance, the reservation should be described under that heading in the deed. A reservation in favor of a third party is inoperative. *Little v. Linder*, 651 S.W.2d 895, 900–901 (Tex. App.—Tyler 1983, writ ref'd n.r.e.).

Examples of common reservations are found in form 5-7 in this chapter.

§ 5.2:7 Exceptions to Conveyance and Warranty

All encumbrances affecting the property, whether recorded or not, must be excepted to, or the grantor will breach the general warranty clause immediately on execution of the warranty deed. The items may be excepted to in broad, general terms or specifically itemized. The broad exceptions are more commonly preferred by sellers and the specific exceptions by buyers.

If specific exceptions are used, those suggested in form 5-8 in this chapter may be appropriate, depending on the condition of title. If the parties have agreed not to examine title, the broadest possible exception will be appropriate. See clauses 5-8-1 and 5-8-2.

Properly used, an exception excludes an existing outstanding interest from the conveyance. *Donnell v. Otts*, 230 S.W. 864, 865 (Tex. App.—Fort Worth 1921, no writ). Exceptions should be drafted so as not to validate an instrument that is no longer in effect. *Morgan v. Fox*, 536 S.W.2d 644, 649–50 (Tex. App.—Corpus Christi–Edinburg 1976, writ ref'd n.r.e.).

§ 5.3 General Warranty Deed with Vendor's Lien

The warranty deed with vendor's lien is designed for use anytime a portion of the purchase price is financed. This usually occurs when the note is to be executed either in favor of the grantor or a third-party mortgagee financing the grantee's purchase of the property. Other circumstances in which use of a warranty deed with vendor's lien is appropriate include the assumption of an existing first-lien note together with execution of a new second-lien note to the grantor or a third party, or execution of new first- and second-lien notes. See form 5-2 in this chapter.

§ 5.3:1 General Considerations for Vendor's Lien

Anytime the entire purchase price is not paid to the grantor of real property, an implied vendor's lien arises in favor of the grantor, whether stated in the deed or not. *Briscoe v. Bronaugh*, 1 Tex. 326, 330 (1846); *Delley v. Unknown Stockholders of the Brotherly & Sisterly Club of Christ, Inc.*, 509 S.W.2d 709, 714 (Tex. App.—Tyler

1974, writ ref'd n.r.e.). A bona fide purchaser for value and without notice of the implied vendor's lien, however, takes title free from the implied lien. *Smith v. Price*, 230 S.W. 836, 838 (Tex. App.—Austin 1921, no writ). Implied vendor's liens may arise in the following instances:

1. Seller Financing. An implied vendor's lien may arise in favor of a grantor who finances a portion of the conveyed property's purchase price. *Manz v. Johnson*, 531 S.W.2d 934, 936 (Tex. App.—Fort Worth 1976, no writ).

2. Third-Party Lender—Assumption. An implied vendor's lien may arise in favor of a third-party lender if part of the purchase price is the assumption of lien debt due the lender. *Etter v. Tuck*, 101 S.W.2d 843, 844 (Tex. App.—Dallas 1937, no writ).

3. Exchange. An implied vendor's lien may arise in the land conveyed and for the benefit of the party who received exchange property with a defective title. *White v. Street*, 2 S.W. 529, 531 (Tex. 1886); *Price*, 230 S.W. at 838.

4. Spreading. If a grantor conveys two tracts of land and receives the full purchase price for one but takes a note for the other, the grantor is entitled to an implied vendor's lien on both tracts. *Bielss v. Moeller*, 83 S.W.2d 1098, 1101 (Tex. App.—Austin 1935, no writ). Similarly, if one of the two tracts is encumbered by a lien that is assumed, the holder of the assumed debt is entitled to an implied vendor's lien on both tracts. *Fidelity Union Fire Insurance Co. v. Cain*, 28 S.W.2d 833, 836 (Tex. App.—Dallas 1930, no writ).

Although an express vendor's lien may be reserved in documents other than the deed, reserving it in the deed has the advantage of its being recorded for notice purposes. *See Simms v. Espindola*, 310 S.W.2d 364, 366–67 (Tex. App.—San Antonio 1958, writ ref'd n.r.e.). Texas courts have consistently held that a deed expressly retaining a vendor's lien is an executory contract as it applies to the grantor and grantee and those in privity with them, but it is executory only to the extent that superior title remains in the grantor and will be vested automatically in the grantee on payment of the purchase money. *See Zapata v. Torres*, 464 S.W.2d 926, 928–29 (Tex. App.—Dallas 1971, no writ). In all other respects affecting the parties and strangers to the transaction, the deed is an executed contract rather than an executory one. *See Babb v. McGee*, 507 S.W.2d 821, 823 (Tex. App.—Dallas 1974, writ ref'd n.r.e.).

The phrase *vendor's lien and superior title* is the conventional means of expressing the intention of the parties to make rescission available to the vendor's lien holder.

§ 5.3:2 Execution of Note to Grantor or Third Party

If the grantee in the deed gives the grantor a note for consideration, both a note and a deed of trust are ordinarily required. The note should contain a security clause such as clauses 6-5-1 through 6-5-4 in this manual. The deed of trust should contain a vendor's lien clause, such as clause 8-3-1.

The same documents are required when the note is to a third party, and the note should also have a security clause like that suggested for a note payable to the grantor. The deed of trust, however, should instead have a clause like clause 8-3-2. In this case, the vendor's lien is reserved in the deed and transferred to the third-party lender.

§ 5.3:3 Execution of First-Lien Note and Second-Lien Note

Two separate notes and two deeds of trust are necessary if the grantee in the deed is to execute a first-lien note payable to the grantor or a third party and a second-lien note payable to the grantor or a third party. Each note is secured by a deed of trust in which each respective payee is the beneficiary. Each of the four documents should be identified as "first-lien" or "second-lien," both in its title and in additional language.

§ 5.3:4 Assumption of First-Lien Note and Execution of Second-Lien Note

The grantee's assumption of a first-lien note is ordinarily accompanied by a deed of trust to secure assumption. The simultaneous execution of a second-lien note requires a note payable to the grantor or a third party and a deed of trust naming the grantor or the third party as beneficiary. These two documents should be identified as second-lien instruments both in their titles and in additional language. See the discussion at sections 5.2:3 above and 5.3:5 below and sections 8.6 and 8.7 in this manual.

§ 5.3:5 Consideration and Miscellaneous Clauses

Clauses 5-6-1, 5-6-2, 5-6-8, 5-6-13, and 5-6-14 in this chapter describe a variety of financing choices if the consideration involves a note, an assumption, or both.

Execution of Note to Grantor: A common transaction involving the warranty deed with vendor's lien is one in which the grantee executes a note in favor of the grantor. See clause 5-6-13. In addition to the deed provisions, the note should contain a security clause, such as clauses 6-5-1 through 6-5-4 in this manual. The deed of trust should contain a clause like clause 8-3-1.

Execution of Note to Third Party: If the note is in favor of a third party financing the grantee's purchase, the warranty deed with vendor's lien should contain both a consideration clause like clause 5-6-13 and another clause noting that the lien is retained in favor of the third party. The second clause should appear in the space provided for additional clauses. See clause 5-9-8. Also, the note should contain a security clause like clauses 6-5-1 through 6-5-4, and the deed of trust should contain a clause like clause 8-3-2.

Execution of First-Lien Note to Third Party and Second-Lien Note to Grantor: If the grantee executes a first-lien note to a third party and a second-lien note to the grantor, appropriate clauses must be added to the consideration description and to the clause that retains the lien, as suggested at clause 5-6-8 and clause 5-9-9.

Assumption of First-Lien Note and Execution of Second-Lien Note to Grantor: If the grantee assumes an existing first-lien note and executes a second-lien note to the grantor, the grantor should provide that the vendor's lien secures both the second-lien note and the assumption. Clause 5-6-1 and clause 5-9-10 provide for this. When used with the second-lien clause in the note, which appears as clauses 6-6-1 and 6-6-2, they authorize maturity of the second-lien note if the grantee defaults on the note assumed. If the grantor is not released from liability for the assumed debt, the assumption is generally also secured by a deed of trust to secure assumption, form 8-2.

Assumption of First-Lien Note and Execution of Second-Lien Note to Third Party: If the grantee assumes an existing first-lien note and executes a second-lien note to a third party, the deed should provide that the vendor's lien secures both the second-lien note and the assumption. For this use clause 5-6-1 and clause 5-9-11. The assumption is generally also secured by a deed of trust to secure assumption, form 8-2.

§ 5.4 Special Warranty Deed

By converting the general warranty to a special warranty, the grantor warrants to defend the title conveyed to the grantee only to the extent that claims are made by, through, or under the grantor. The special warranty covers only title defects caused by the grantor, not those caused by the grantor's predecessors in title. Title insurance coverage for covenants of warranty on the insured's conveyance of title is available under an owner policy of title insurance; however, this coverage is limited to title defects that are covered by both the covenants of warranty and the title insurance policy. Because the owner policy purchased on acquisition of property covers only title defects caused before the purchase, and the special warranty warrants only against title defects caused after the purchase, the title insurance coverage for covenants of warranty provides no benefit under these circumstances.

In *Cochran Investments, Inc. v. Chicago Title Insurance Co.*, 550 S.W.3d 196, 205 (Tex. App.—Houston [14th Dist.] 2018), *aff'd*, 602 S.W.3d 895 (Tex. 2020), the Fourteenth Court of Appeals held that the special warranty deed in that case did not imply a covenant of seisin. A covenant of seisin is "an assurance to the grantee that the grantor actually owns the property being conveyed, in the quantity and quality which he purports to convey, and it is breached if the grantor does not own the estate that he undertakes to convey." *Cochran Investments*, 550 S.W.3d at 202 (citing *Jackson v. Wildflower Production Co.*, 505 S.W.3d 80, 89 n.12 (Tex. App.—Amarillo 2016, pet. denied). The case was appealed to the Texas Supreme Court, which decided the case on the basis of the special warranty, leaving open the question whether a special warranty deed includes an implied covenant of seisin. *Chicago Title Insurance*, 602 S.W.3d at 901. The court held that, whether or not the special warranty deed contained a covenant of seisin, the grantor's liability under the deed was limited by the special warranty, which limited the circumstances under which the grantee can recover. *Chicago Title Insurance*, 602 S.W.3d at 908.

Because the supreme court did not rule on whether the special warranty deed in that case included an implied covenant of seisin, concern remains over whether it does. Clause 5-9-27 in this chapter may be used to include an express covenant of seisin.

§ 5.5 Deed without Warranty

A covenant of warranty is not required in a conveyance. Tex. Prop. Code § 5.022(b). The deed without warranty passes the grantor's title to the grantee with an express exclusion of warranties. This deed relieves the grantor of any warranty responsibility for title defects yet provides the grantee a true deed, as opposed to a mere quitclaim. See form 5-4 in this chapter.

§ 5.6 Quitclaim

A quitclaim conveys only the right, title, and interest that the grantor has in the property at the time the instrument is executed and delivered. It will not convey "after-acquired" title—that is, title acquired after the date of the execution and delivery of the quitclaim deed. There is no recourse by the grantee or any subsequent owner of the property against the grantor. See form 5-5 in this chapter for an example of a quitclaim.

A quitclaim gives notice to the grantee that title to the property may not be clear, so the grantee is not a bona fide purchaser for value. Thus, if the grantor has title to the property but will not warrant title, a deed without warranty is preferable to a quitclaim. An adverse possessor cannot rely on a quitclaim as a basis for claiming title to property under the Texas five-year limitations statute, Tex. Civ. Prac. & Rem. Code § 16.025;

Porter v. Wilson, 389 S.W.2d 650 (Tex. 1965). After the fourth anniversary of the date a quitclaim is recorded in the county where the property is located, the quitclaim does not affect the question of the good faith of a subsequent purchaser or creditor and is not notice to a subsequent purchaser or creditor of any unrecorded conveyance of, transfer of, or encumbrance on the real property. Tex. Prop. Code § 13.006.

§ 5.7 Bill of Sale

§ 5.7:1 Purpose and Effect

Some types of personal property are subject to statutory requirements for a bill of sale on transfer of title. A nonexclusive list includes (1) livestock (Tex. Agric. Code § 146.001), (2) trees or timber (Tex. Nat. Res. Code §§ 151.001–.006), and (3) used pipeline and oil and gas equipment (Tex. Nat. Res. Code §§ 112.011–.012).

For other types of property, recording is optional but useful for notifying third parties of the buyer's rights under a contract for sale. *See* Tex. Bus. & Com. Code § 2.107(c) (contract for sale of goods to be severed from realty).

The sale of a motor vehicle cannot occur unless the owner designated on the title submits a transfer of ownership of the title. Tex. Transp. Code § 501.071.

Caution: A transaction involving appliance warranties may be subject to the Magnuson-Moss Warranty–Federal Trade Commission Improvement Act, 15 U.S.C. §§ 2301–2312.

§ 5.7:2 Instructions for Completing Forms

The bill of sale, form 5-16 in this chapter, may be used to transfer title to most personal property. This form makes an express warranty of title, but that warranty and implied warranties may be excluded.

The blanket bill of sale, form 5-15, is used to ensure that the buyer has acquired ownership of the personal property assets that may be involved in a transaction if a specific listing of items is impractical.

If a blanket bill of sale is used, it is important that the seller specifically identify as excluded property anything that will not be transferred.

Generally, the description of the property should clearly identify the personal property sold and, if possible, should include a specific description, make, model, and identifying number.

See the discussion at section 5.12:2 below about the possibility of including the bill of sale in the deed itself.

§ 5.7:3 Warranties

The sale of goods creates three implied warranties under the Texas Uniform Commercial Code:

1. Warranty of Title. The seller warrants that at the time of conveyance the title conveyed is good, that its transfer is lawful, and that the title is free from encumbrances other than those known to the buyer. Tex. Bus. & Com. Code § 2.312. In addition to the implied warranty of title, the bill of sale forms (forms 5-15 and 5-16 in this chapter) contain an express warranty of title.
2. Warranty of Merchantability. If the seller is a merchant of goods of the kind sold, the sale creates an implied warranty of merchantability for the goods. Tex. Bus. & Com. Code § 2.314(a). The UCC defines minimum standards of merchantability. Course of dealing or usage may imply other minimum standards.
3. Warranty of Fitness. If the seller has reason to know that the buyer is relying on the seller's skill or judgment in

furnishing goods suitable for a particular purpose, a warranty of fitness for that purpose arises. Tex. Bus. & Com. Code § 2.315.

These warranties may be excluded or modified through revisions to the bill of sale. Any exclusion is subject to the provisions of Tex. Bus. & Com. Code § 2.316.

§ 5.8 Correction Deed

Correction deeds are generally used to accomplish amicably what would otherwise be done through a suit for reformation. Reformation is the equitable power of courts to correct a written instrument that due to mutual mistake fails to embody the actual agreement reached by the parties. *National Resort Communities, Inc. v. Cain*, 526 S.W.2d 510, 513–14 (Tex. 1975). Reformation will not go beyond the original agreement. *Southwest Savings Ass'n v. Dunagan*, 392 S.W.2d 761, 768 (Tex. App.—Dallas 1965, writ ref'd n.r.e.).

Types of mistakes subject to reformation include mistakes in descriptions (*Wilson v. Dearing, Inc.*, 415 S.W.2d 475, 476 (Tex. App.—Eastland 1967, no writ)); omissions and inclusions (*Parker v. McKinnon*, 353 S.W.2d 954, 955 (Tex. App.—Amarillo 1962, writ ref'd n.r.e.)); scrivener's errors (*Fenn v. Boxwell*, 312 S.W.2d 536, 541 (Tex. App.—Amarillo 1958, writ ref'd n.r.e.)); and mistakes of law (*Martin v. Snuggs*, 302 S.W.2d 676, 680 (Tex. App.—Fort Worth 1957, writ ref'd n.r.e.)). A grantor may not use a correction deed as a unilateral attempt to add restrictive covenants to a deed. *Joe T. Garcia's Enterprises v. Snadon*, 751 S.W.2d 914, 916 (Tex. App.—Dallas 1988, writ denied).

As between the parties, a correction deed generally relates back to the date of the original incorrect deed. *Parker*, 353 S.W.2d at 956; *Buccaneer's Cove, Inc. v. Mainland Bank*, 831 S.W.2d 582, 584 (Tex. App.—Corpus Christi–Edinburg 1992, no writ). However, bankruptcy of an intervening bona fide purchaser for value will prevent the relation back. *See In re Jones*, 37 B.R. 969 (Bankr. N.D. Tex. 1984).

The consideration for the correction deed is the correction. *Tatum v. Blackstock*, 418 S.W.2d 269, 274 (Tex. App.—Waco 1967, writ ref'd n.r.e.). Although the correction deed is considered a replacement for the original deed, the original deed will be used to determine the intention of the parties; further, the original deed may continue to be controlling with respect to matters outside of the stated purpose of the correction deed. *Parker*, 353 S.W.2d at 956.

A party to a deed who knows of a mistake should immediately request a correction deed. *Barker v. Coastal Builders, Inc.*, 271 S.W.2d 798, 804 (Tex. 1954). Suits for reformation are subject to the four-year limitations period. Tex. Civ. Prac. & Rem. Code § 16.051; *Brown v. Havard*, 593 S.W.2d 939, 943 (Tex. 1980). The discovery rule, which might toll limitations, does not apply to a plainly evident mistake in an unambiguous deed. *Cosgrove v. Cade*, 468 S.W.3d 32, 36 (Tex. 2015). Certain technical defects in instruments will be cured by statute unless suit is brought within two years of recording. Tex. Civ. Prac. & Rem. Code § 16.033.

While a correction deed replaces and is a substitute for the original instrument, a correction deed is subject to the property interest of a creditor or a subsequent purchaser for valuable consideration without notice after the original instrument was properly recorded and before the correction deed is properly recorded. Tex. Prop. Code § 5.030(b), (c). A title search is suggested to determine whether any intervening creditors or bona fide purchasers exist.

Instruments that correct a conveyance of real property should comply with sections 5.027 through 5.031 of the Texas Property Code. Nonmaterial corrections are subject to section 5.028, and material corrections are subject to section 5.029.

Instruments that correct a material error must be, and instruments that correct a nonmaterial error may be, executed by each party to the conveyance or, if applicable, the parties' heirs, successors, or assigns. The Texas Supreme Court has held that if the original signatories to the instrument are available to execute the correction, they can correct the instrument without joinder of a subsequent or current owner of the real property. *Broadway National Bank v. Yates Energy Corp.*, 631 S.W.3d 16 (Tex. 2021), *reh'g denied* (Sept. 24, 2021). Tex. Prop. Code § 5.029(a). These instruments must be recorded. Tex. Prop. Code §§ 5.028(d)(1), 5.029(b)(2). Clause 5-9-5 may be inserted as the last paragraph in a restated deed executed by the original parties to the conveyance, or by their heirs, successors, or assigns, to correct a material or nonmaterial error.

A person who has personal knowledge of the relevant facts is authorized to execute a correction instrument to make a nonmaterial change that resulted from a clerical error, without the joinder of the original parties to the conveyance or their heirs, successors, or assigns. These changes include correction of an inaccurate or incorrect element in a legal description, including a distance, angle, direction, bearing, or chord, a reference to a plat or other plat information, and other matters set forth in the statute; an addition, correction, or clarification of a party's name or marital status; the date on which the conveyance was executed; the recording data for an instrument referenced in the correction instrument; or a fact relating to the acknowledgment or authentication of the original conveyance. Tex. Prop. Code § 5.028(a). A correction instrument executed by a person with knowledge of the relevant facts may also provide an acknowledgment or authentication that was not included in the original conveyance.

A person who has personal knowledge of the relevant facts is authorized to execute a correction instrument to make a nonmaterial change that resulted from an inadvertent error, without the joinder of the original parties to the conveyance or their heirs, successors, or assigns. These changes include the addition, correction, or clarification of a legal description prepared in connection with the preparation of the original instrument but inadvertently omitted or an omitted call in a metes-and-bounds description that completes the legal description of the property. Tex. Prop. Code § 5.028(a–1).

The person executing the correction instrument must disclose in the instrument the basis for his knowledge of the relevant facts; send a copy of the correction instrument and notice by first class mail, email, or other reasonable means to each party to the original conveyance and, if applicable, the parties' heirs, successors, and assigns; and record the correction instrument and evidence of notice. Tex. Prop. Code § 5.028(d)(2). Form 5-24 in this chapter is a form for making a nonmaterial correction by a person with knowledge of relevant facts.

In addition to nonmaterial corrections, including the corrections described by section 5.028 of the Property Code, the parties to the original transaction or their successors or assigns may execute a correction instrument to make a material correction to the recorded original instrument of conveyance. These material changes include adding a buyer's disclaimer of an interest in the property, a mortgagee's consent to or subordination to a recorded document, or land to a conveyance that correctly conveys other land; removing land from a conveyance that correctly conveys other land; and correcting a description of a lot or unit number or letter of property that is inaccurately identified as another lot or unit number or letter. Tex. Prop. Code § 5.029.

A correction instrument that complies with section 5.028 or 5.029 of the Property Code is (1) effective as of the effective date of the conveyance, (2) prima facie evidence of the facts stated in the correction instrument, and (3) notice to a subsequent buyer of the facts stated in the correction instrument. Tex. Prop. Code § 5.030.

Title companies may require a jurat as a prerequisite to acceptance.

See clause 5-9-5 and form 5-24 for correction deed language.

§ 5.9 Gift Deed

The essential elements of a gift made during a grantor's life are donative intent, delivery, and acceptance. *Gannon v. Baker*, 830 S.W.2d 706, 710 (Tex. App.—Houston [1st Dist.] 1992, writ denied).

If the grantor desires to make a gift, the commonly understood terminology to evidence the donative interest, although not true consideration, is a recitation of "love and affection" as the consideration. However, other words and phrases that accomplish the same purpose are appropriate, especially when "love and affection" are not the grantor's motivation to make the gift. See clauses 5-6-9 and 5-6-10 in this chapter. Further, the deed should be titled "Gift Deed."

An essential characteristic of a gift is the absence of consideration paid by the donee to the donor. A deed by gift that otherwise satisfies the requirements for an effective conveyance will vest title in the grantee to the same extent as a deed with valuable consideration. *Woodworth v. Cortez*, 660 S.W.2d 561, 564 (Tex. App.—San Antonio 1983, writ ref'd n.r.e.).

A gift is presumed if a parent purchases property in the name of a child. *Woodworth*, 660 S.W.2d at 564.

§ 5.10 Partition Deed

A partition is the act of dividing the undivided interests in property held by joint owners so each owns full title to a separate tract. The term *joint owner* includes ownership arrangements also sometimes known as tenants in common, cotenants, or joint tenants. Partitions may be either voluntary or involuntary. A voluntary partition is accomplished by a written instrument or deed. *Houston Oil Co. of Texas v. Kirkindall*, 145 S.W.2d 1074, 1077 (Tex. 1941); *Chandler v. Hartt*, 467 S.W.2d 629, 634 (Tex. App.—Tyler 1971, writ ref'd n.r.e.). An involuntary partition arises when a cotenant exercises the statutory right to compel a partition. *See* Tex. Prop. Code §§ 23.001–.004. If property is partitioned involuntarily, a nonexclusive access easement may be required in limited circumstances. *See* Tex. Prop. Code § 23.006. An express agreement among joint owners not to partition is enforceable. *Lichtenstein v. Lichtenstein Building Corp.*, 442 S.W.2d 765, 769 (Tex. App.—Corpus Christi–Edinburg 1969, no writ).

Form 5-23 in this chapter is a partition deed for effectuating a voluntary partition. Often partition deeds are executed by family members who have inherited the co-owned properties. In this situation, a special warranty of title ordinarily will be preferred by the parties. Often no title search is obtained, and a party usually will not want to be responsible for warranting title to the land partitioned to the other family members (except as to that party's own acts). Accordingly, form 5-23 contains a special warranty of title. If a general warranty of title or deed without warranty is desired, form 5-23 may be adapted to provide for this. If no title search is performed in connection with a partition deed, the other parties may be unaware that one party's acts have given rise to a lien, such as a federal tax lien or child support lien. Knowledge of the existence of a lien before the partition deed is executed is desirable so that the lien may be addressed, as this is preferable to a claim for breach of warranty of title, whether special or general.

Partitions are not subject to the statute of frauds, making oral partitions enforceable (*Houston Oil Co. of Texas*, 145 S.W.2d at 1077), and partitions do not alter the character of property as either separate or community (*Westhoff v. Reitz*, 554 S.W.2d 1 (Tex. App.—Fort Worth 1977, writ ref'd n.r.e.).

Owelty is the difference that is paid by one joint owner to another or a lien that arises for the purpose of equalizing the partition. In instances in which one joint owner is to receive owelty from another, see the discussion of owelty of partition in section 5.13:5 below.

If suit is filed to foreclose a tax lien, joint owners are entitled to partition their property and have the taxes apportioned pro rata. Tex. Tax Code § 33.46.

§ 5.11 Transfer on Death Deed

The Texas Real Property Transfer on Death Act authorizes an individual to execute and record a transfer on death deed to make a revocable transfer of the transferor's interest in real property to one or more designated beneficiaries, including alternate beneficiaries, effective at the transferor's death. *See* Tex. Est. Code ch. 114. In the 86th legislative session, the statutory forms for the transfer on death deed and the revocation of transfer on death deed were removed from chapter 114 of the Texas Estates Code. Acts 2019, 86th Leg., R.S., ch. 337, § 3.2 (S.B. 874), eff. Sept. 1, 2019. Tex. Gov't Code § 22.020 directs the Texas Supreme Court to promulgate forms for creating and revoking a transfer on death deed. As of the publication date of this edition, the forms are not yet complete. The Estates Code continues to authorize use of transfer on death deeds and revocation of transfer on death deeds but no longer prescribes statutory language.

§ 5.11:1 Purpose and Effect

A transfer on death deed transfers a transferor's interest in real property to designated beneficiaries effective at the transferor's death. Tex. Est. Code § 114.051. As a transfer on death deed is nontestamentary, probate proceedings are not necessary to transfer the transferor's interest in the described real property to the designated beneficiaries. Tex. Est. Code § 114.053.

During the transferor's lifetime, a transfer on death deed does not affect any right, title, or interest of the transferor in the property, vest any legal or equitable title in a designated beneficiary, or subject the property to the claims of creditors of any designated beneficiary. Notwithstanding the recordation of a transfer on death deed, the transferor retains the right to transfer or encumber the property, any present or future homestead rights, and any present or future ad valorem tax exemptions to which the transferor is entitled. During the transferor's lifetime, a transfer on death deed does not affect the rights of creditors of the transferor, secured or unsecured, and does not trigger any "due on sale" clause. Upon the death of the transferor a secured creditor's rights are subject to the Texas Estates Code. A transfer on death deed does not affect the eligibility for public assistance of either the transferor or any designated beneficiary. Tex. Est. Code § 114.101.

At the death of the transferor, the transferor's interest in the property is transferred to the designated beneficiaries in accordance with the deed. Tex. Est. Code § 114.103(a). A transfer under a transfer on death deed lapses as to a designated beneficiary that disclaims in the manner provided in chapter 122 of the Estates Code. Tex. Est. Code § 114.105. A transfer also lapses as to a designated beneficiary that does not survive the transferor by 120 hours. Lapsed transfers of concurrent interests pass in accordance with subchapter D of chapter 255 of the Estates Code. Except where chapter 255 applies, concurrent interests are transferred in equal, undivided interests with no right of survivorship, subject to the transferor's option to provide alternative disposition of lapsed transfers. Tex. Est. Code § 114.103(a).

Even if the transfer on death deed provides otherwise, a transfer on death deed transfers title to a beneficiary without warranty of title. Tex. Est. Code § 114.103(d). A beneficiary under a transfer on death deed takes title to the property subject to all conveyances, liens, encumbrances and other rights enforceable against the property at the transferor's death. Tex. Est. Code § 114.104. Although not considered a probate asset, claims against the transferor's estate, expenses of administration, estate taxes, allowances in lieu of exempt property, and family allowances are enforceable against property transferred by a transfer on death deed. Tex. Est. Code § 114.106.

§ 5.11:2 Requirements Generally; Exceptions

A transfer on death deed must state that the transfer occurs at the transferor's death, be properly executed by the transferor, be properly recorded before the transferor's death, and contain the essential elements and formalities of deeds, except consideration, notice, delivery, or acceptance. Tex. Est. Code §§ 114.055, 114.056. No statutorily required notice or disclosure need be given in connection with a transfer on death deed. Tex. Est. Code § 114.101(6).

§ 5.11:3 Transferor Considerations

A transferor must have capacity to contract to make or revoke a transfer on death deed. Tex. Est. Code § 114.054(a). A transfer on death deed cannot be created under a power of attorney. Tex. Est. Code § 114.054(b).

§ 5.11:4 Proper Recordation

To be effective, a transfer on death deed must be recorded before the transferor's death in the county where the property is located. Tex. Est. Code § 114.003. Likewise, an instrument revoking a transfer on death deed must be recorded before the transferor's death. Tex. Est. Code § 114.057(a).

§ 5.11:5 Caution—Existing Rights of Survivorship

If a transferor is a joint owner with right of survivorship, a transfer on death deed will not be effective unless the transferor is the surviving joint owner. Tex. Est. Code § 114.103(b). A transfer on death deed made by joint owners with the right of survivorship can be revoked only by all living joint owners. Tex. Est. Code § 114.057(e).

§ 5.11:6 Revocation Generally

Even if the transfer on death deed provides otherwise, a transfer on death deed is revocable. Tex. Est. Code § 114.052. Revocation, in whole or in part, is effective upon the proper recordation before the transferor's death of a subsequent, inconsistent transfer on death deed, a subsequent instrument of revocation, a divorce decree dissolving the marital relationship between the transferor and a designated beneficiary, or a subsequent conveyance by the transferor. If the transfer on death deed is made by more than one transferor, a revocation is only effective as to the interest of the revoking transferor and does not affect the interests of the nonrevoking transferors. Tex. Est. Code § 114.057.

§ 5.11:7 Revocation—Subsequent Transfer on Death Deed

A prior transfer on death deed is revoked on the recordation of a subsequently acknowledged transfer on death deed as to the interests that are expressly stated or are inconsistent with the subsequent deed. Tex. Est. Code § 114.057(a). Form 5-25 in this chapter provides optional clauses for revoking all or part of a prior transfer on death deed. Alternatively, form 5-26 or form 5-27 can be used to document the revocation of the prior transfer on death deed in whole or in part.

§ 5.11:8 Revocation—Subsequent Instrument of Revocation

A prior transfer on death deed is revoked upon the recordation of a subsequently acknowledged instrument of revocation, other than a will, that expressly revokes the prior deed, as to the beneficiaries and property designated in the instrument. Tex. Est. Code § 114.057(a). A subsequent will made by the transferor does not revoke nor supersede a transfer on death deed. Tex. Est. Code § 114.057(b).

Form 5-26 or form 5-27 in this chapter can be used to revoke a prior transfer on death deed in whole or in part.

§ 5.11:9 Revocation—Divorce

The recordation of a notice of a final decree of divorce dissolving the marital relationship between a transferor and a designated beneficiary revokes a transfer on death deed as to the divorced, designated beneficiary. Tex. Est. Code § 114.057(c).

§ 5.11:10 Revocation—Subsequent Conveyance; Protection of Purchasers

A subsequent, valid conveyance by the transferor during the transferor's lifetime renders a prior transfer on death deed void as to any interest in the property conveyed if the conveyancing instrument is properly recorded before the death of the transferor. Tex. Est. Code § 114.102.

Form 5-26 or form 5-27 in this chapter, as the circumstances dictate, will document the revocation of a prior transfer on death deed.

§ 5.11:11 Instructions for Completing Form

Form 5-25 in this chapter can be used to transfer to one or more designated beneficiaries, including alternative beneficiaries, the transferor's interest in real property effective at death of the transferor.

Although the transferor can rely upon the presumed anti-lapse provisions in chapter 114 of the Texas Estates Code, if the transferor intends to transfer the transferor's community property interest in property to a surviving spouse, or to the transferor's children if the transferor's spouse predeceases the transferor, it is recommended that the transferor's spouse be designated as the primary beneficiary and the children designated as the alternate beneficiaries.

Caution should be employed in selecting the alternative clauses for disposition of the property where a named primary beneficiary does not survive the transferor as the alternative clause selected will determine whether the deceased primary beneficiary's share will pass to the other primary beneficiaries, the descendants of the deceased primary beneficiary, or named alternative beneficiaries. Alternative clauses are provided for the disposition of the property to the descendants of a deceased beneficiary or to the other named beneficiaries.

As consideration is not required for the validity of a transfer on death deed, and to avoid uncertainty about whether consideration was exchanged, references to recitations and confessions of consideration are intentionally omitted in form 5-25.

As there are no warranties of title under a transfer on death deed and, at the death of the transferor, title passes subject to all present and subsequent conveyances, liens, and other encumbrances, references to exceptions to conveyance and warranties are intentionally omitted in form 5-25.

Any interest that the transferor intends to reserve from the transfer on death deed should be properly described in the heading "Reservations from Transfer." See section 5.2:6 above for a discussion of reservations. Examples of common reservations are found in form 5-7.

Form 5-26 revokes a prior transfer on death deed in its entirety.

Form 5-27, depending on the options clause selected, partially revokes a prior transfer on death deed as to the property described either to all beneficiaries or only as to specifically named beneficiaries.

§ 5.12 Additional Clauses

Provisions other than the consideration clause, property description, reservations, and exceptions may be called for in some deeds. These clauses may be located in several different places in the deed. Use of some of these provisions is discussed in this section, and sample language is found in form 5-9 in this chapter.

§ 5.12:1 Waiver of Implied Liens

The implied vendor's lien should be negated if its existence is not intended by the parties. If the grantor who receives the full price for one parcel is to waive the implied lien on that parcel, the waiver in clause 5-9-24 in this chapter may be used. If an existing lien affects only a portion of the property conveyed by an assumption deed, the deed should contain an express waiver to avoid spreading the lien. Clause 5-9-25 is an example of an appropriate waiver for this purpose. If the parties exchanging property wish to waive the implied lien, the waiver in clause 5-6-7 may be used in the description of the consideration.

§ 5.12:2 Bill of Sale Combined

Many kinds of personal property, including items used in operating the improvements that can be removed without materially damaging the improvements, are often transferred as part of the sale of real property.

Personal property is not included in the real property description and thus is not transferred by the deed. Instead, personal property is transferred by bill of sale. The personal property transfer can be accomplished in a separate bill of sale or by including the bill of sale in the deed itself. A combined instrument has the benefit of reducing the number of documents to be signed at closing.

To add the personal property transfer to the deed, the drafter may use the clauses provided. See clauses 5-9-12 and 5-9-13 in this chapter.

§ 5.12:3 "As Is" Conveyance

If the conveyance is on an "as is" basis, the parties may evidence the basis of the bargain in the deed. See clause 5-9-1 in this chapter.

For a separate disclaimer form, see form 26-33 in this manual.

§ 5.12:4 Fee Simple Determinable

A fee simple determinable exists if a fee simple estate will terminate automatically and revert to the grantor on the occurrence of a stated event.

The phrase "as long as" has been recognized as evidencing a fee simple determinable estate. *See Clark v. Perez*, 679 S.W.2d 710, 712 (Tex. App.—San Antonio 1984, no writ). In addition, it is prudent practice to state an intent to create a fee simple determinable because of the presumption that a conveyance is a fee simple absolute (*see* Tex. Prop. Code § 5.001(a)) and the rule of interpretation construing provisions as covenants rather than conditions. *Schwarz-Jordan, Inc. v. Delisle Construction Co.*, 569 S.W.2d 878, 881 (Tex. 1978). See clause 5-9-7 in this chapter.

In some cases the event that would cause the fee simple determinable condition to be satisfied is not evident from an inspection of the property, which creates uncertainty concerning title. In those situations, it is suggested that the condition language include a provision for recording a document that establishes with certainty the satisfaction of the condition. For example, the suggested clause at 5-9-6 includes a provision allowing an affidavit to serve as evidence of the satisfaction of the condition, unless contradicted by another affidavit.

§ 5.12:5 Strips and Gores

For public policy reasons, a deed may be construed as including a small parcel of land in the conveyance of the larger tract if it is shown that the small parcel to be included (1) is small in comparison to the land conveyed, (2) is adjacent to or surrounded by the land conveyed, (3) belonged to the grantor at the time of the conveyance, and (4) was of no benefit or importance to the grantor. *Alkas v. United Savings Ass'n of Texas*, 672 S.W.2d 852, 857 (Tex. App.—Corpus Christi–Edinburg 1984, writ ref'd n.r.e.). This doctrine is called the "strip and gore doctrine." Including a strips-and-gores provision in the deed is intended to ensure that the principle is applied in the transaction without the necessity of supplying proof of these elements. See clause 5-9-17 in this chapter for an example.

Because of the strip and gore doctrine, a conveyance of land bounded by a public highway carries with it the fee to the center of the road as part and parcel of the grant, even if the deed describes the abutting land by metes and bounds extending only to the edge of the highway. *State v. Williams*, 335 S.W.2d 834, 836 (Tex. 1960); *Krenek v. Texstar North America, Inc.*, 787 S.W.2d 566, 568–69 (Tex. App.—Corpus Christi–Edinburg 1990, writ denied). The doctrine does not apply if the grantor owns land on both sides of the strip. *Rio Bravo Oil Co. v. Weed*, 50 S.W.2d 1080, 1086 (Tex. 1932). Nor does the doctrine apply if the strip is larger and more valuable than the conveyed tract. *Angelo v. Biscamp*, 441 S.W.2d 524, 527 (Tex. 1969).

The strips-and-gores provision should be included in a deed conveyance form rather than a quitclaim to avoid the concerns about quitclaims stated in the commentary at section 5.6 above; however, the warranties should be eliminated in case no strips or gores exist.

When using the strips-and-gores provision, the attorney should review other provisions of the deed that describe the property, because the strips and gores are discussed separately from the property. One suggestion is to add "and all strips and gores and appurtenances thereto" to the references to the property, other than in the warranty clause. Another option is to include strips and gores as a defined term within the definition of the property, then except the strips and gores out of the warranty in the express exclusion of warranties provisions.

§ 5.12:6 Wraparound Lien

If the seller agrees to continue to service an existing lien debt while the buyer executes a new note that is not reduced by the amount of the preexisting lien debt (commonly known as a wraparound transaction), the deed should be written to take exception to the preexisting lien to avoid breaching the warranty concerning encumbrances. The buyer should take title "subject to," and without assuming, the preexisting lien debt.

See clause 5-9-26 in this chapter. See also section 6.4:2 in this manual and sections 8.3 through 8.5:4.

§ 5.12:7 Transfer of Escrow and Insurance Policy

Lenders often establish an escrow for the payment of taxes and insurance relating to the property securing the loan. The escrow arrangement generally seeks to ensure that sufficient funds exist in the escrow to pay all real property ad valorem taxes when they come due and to pay the annual hazard insurance premium on its anniversary date.

If real property is transferred with the assumption of an existing lien debt or subject to a preexisting lien debt, regardless of whether the insurance and taxes are being prorated to the date of closing, it is customary for the seller to transfer the entire escrow fund to the buyer. It is generally considered simpler to prorate the escrow balance to the date of closing through the closing settlement statement, rather than have the buyer send money to the lender and expect the lender to reimburse the seller for that exact amount out of the escrow. The transfer of the escrow fund is usually included in the deed, although this is not required. Additionally, some lenders require the signing of a separate transfer form before the escrow will be transferred to the buyer. The more cautious approach would be to include the transfer both in the deed and in a separate document.

The transfer of escrow often includes a transfer of the insurance policy to the buyer, if the seller has agreed that the policy will be transferred. If the buyer will not assume the existing coverage, the seller should keep the policy in order to be entitled to the refund of unearned premiums when the buyer's replacement policy is substituted for the seller's policy coverage. Several aspects of insurance are regulated by statute, such as the fee for substitution of coverage and the kind of insurance binder a mortgage company must accept. The statutes governing prohibited practices relating to property insurance are found in chapter 549 of the Texas Insurance Code. *See* Tex. Ins. Code ch. 549. Unless the drafting attorney knows the agreement concerning the transfer of the insurance policy, it is suggested the deed include either nothing concerning the insurance or a statement that any transfer of insurance will be handled between the buyer and seller by separate instrument.

Form 5-17 in this chapter is provided to accomplish the transfer of escrow by separate instrument. Clause 5-9-22 may be used to incorporate the transfer of escrow in the deed.

§ 5.12:8 Assumption of Liability Agreements for VA-Guaranteed Loans

If a loan guaranteed by the Department of Veterans Affairs (VA) is assumed, the VA has a number of requirements for the new loan. *See* 38 U.S.C. § 3714; 38 C.F.R. §§ 36.4300–.4393; U.S. Dep't of Veterans Affairs, Veterans Benefits Administration, Lender's Handbook: VA Pamphlet 26-7, available at **www.benefits.va.gov/warms/pam26_7.asp**. Clause 5-9-2 in this chapter is based on the sample indemnity liability assumption clause in chapter 9 of VA Pamphlet 26-7.

§ 5.12:9 Restrictive Covenants

To be enforceable, restrictive covenants imposed by grant must satisfy certain requirements: (1) there must be privity of estate between the parties to the contract; (2) the restrictive covenants must relate to something in existence, or assignees must be named if they are to be bound by the restrictive covenants; (3) the restrictive covenants must touch or concern the land (that is, enhance or benefit it) (*see Homsey v. University Gardens Racquet Club*, 730 S.W.2d 763, 764 (Tex. App.—El Paso 1987, writ ref'd n.r.e.)); and (4) the original contracting parties must intend that the restrictive covenant run with the land. *Billington v. Riffe*, 492 S.W.2d 343, 346 (Tex. App.—Amarillo 1973, no writ). Further, the restrictive covenant must furnish adequate notice to the property owner of the specific restriction sought to be enforced. *Davis v. Huey*, 620 S.W.2d 561, 566 (Tex. 1981).

The restrictive covenants should make clear which lands are benefited by the covenants and that the owners thereby have standing to enforce the restrictive covenants. See clauses 5-9-14 and 5-9-15 in this chapter.

§ 5.13 Additional Documents

§ 5.13:1 Acceptance of Deed

Acceptance is necessary for a deed to be effective. *Robert Burns Concrete Contractors, Inc. v. Norman*, 561 S.W.2d 614, 618 (Tex. App.—Tyler 1978, writ ref'd n.r.e.). Traditionally, the grantee's acceptance is implied. *Martin v. Uvalde Savings & Loan Ass'n*, 773 S.W.2d 808 (Tex. App.—San Antonio 1989, no writ). However, the parties may want written confirmation of the grantee's acceptance of the deed as to matters of form, substance, or both. Evidence of the grantee's acceptance may be needed to enforce the grantor's obligations under a deed, such as the promise to pay and the indemnity in the assumption or warranty deed. Confirmation can best be achieved by the grantee's signature on the deed, although a separate instrument may be used. See form 5-10 in this chapter.

§ 5.13:2 Deed in Lieu of Foreclosure

The term *deed in lieu of foreclosure* (or *deed in lieu*) describes a conveyance in which the consideration given by the grantee typically is the cancellation of the debt owed by the borrower, the release of the borrower from liability on the secured debt, and, in some cases, the release and discharge of the liens securing the debt. The deed in lieu does not have the same effect on title as a trustee's deed in a nonjudicial foreclosure because the deed in lieu does not relate back to the date the deed of trust was filed for record to extinguish exceptions or encumbrances filed after the deed of trust. Instead, the grantee takes the property subject to whatever encumbrances and other exceptions have been imposed on the property before the deed in lieu is recorded, as is the case with any other deed. *Flag-Redfern Oil Co. v. Humble Exploration Co.*, 744 S.W.2d 6, 9 (Tex. 1987).

If a holder of a debt secured by a deed of trust accepts title by a deed in lieu and later discovers that an encumbrance that was unknown to the holder and not disclosed by the debtor existed before the deed in lieu, the holder has four years to void the deed in lieu; further, the lien is restored to its former priority, and the holder may proceed with a foreclosure under the deed of trust. *See* Tex. Prop. Code § 51.006.

See form 5-13 in this chapter for an example of a deed in lieu of foreclosure.

§ 5.13:3 Trustee's Deed in Nonjudicial Foreclosure

For commentary and a form, see section 14.6:4 and form 14-15 in this manual.

§ 5.13:4 Administration or Guardianship Deed

The Texas Estates Code governs the sale of property held by an estate. *See* Tex. Est. Code chs. 356, 1158. A court order is required for any sale of estate property unless otherwise provided by law. Tex. Est. Code §§ 356.001, 1158.001. Sales authorized by a will may be carried out by the executor without the need for a court order.

Tex. Est. Code § 356.002. The administration or guardianship deed, form 5-14 in this chapter, is drafted to follow the format required by the Estates Code. *See* Tex. Est. Code §§ 356.557, 1158.557.

§ 5.13:5 Owelty of Partition Deed and Agreement

Owelty results from an unequal partition between joint owners of real property whether by court decree or contract. Because the tract partitioned does not lend itself to an equal division, the difference in value between the partitioned tracts is adjusted by payment from one joint owner to the other. This difference is known as owelty. Because owelty payments are in the nature of purchase money, a lien to secure a payment arises. Such a lien is a purchase-money lien and is valid against the homestead. *Sayers v. Pyland*, 161 S.W.2d 769, 772 (Tex. 1942).

In transactions in which one joint owner simply buys all of the interest of a fellow joint owner, the issue is less clear. Some decisions have determined that such a sale does not involve a true partition; therefore a lien securing the purchase may not encumber the entirety of the homestead. *In re Shults*, 97 B.R. 874 (Bankr. N.D. Tex. 1989). The Texas Constitution and the Texas Property Code provide that the homestead may be encumbered by "an owelty of partition imposed against the entirety of the property by a court order or by a written agreement of the parties to the partition, including a debt of one spouse in favor of the other spouse resulting from a division or an award of a family homestead in a divorce proceeding." Tex. Const. art. XVI, § 50(a)(3); Tex. Prop. Code § 41.001(b)(4). Even after this constitutional amendment, there has been question about whether the entirety of the homestead may be encumbered by an owelty lien in the absence of an actual partition in kind. Opinion predominates in favor of the validity of these liens to the extent that such liens are generally insurable encumbrances.

An owelty of partition transaction that is not based on a court order should be documented by both a deed and a separate written partition agreement (not by a purchase and sale agreement).

The owelty of partition deed, form 5-11 in this chapter, should refer either to the court order or to the separate agreement on which it is based. See form 5-12 for an owelty of partition agreement.

§ 5.13:6 Survivorship Agreement for Community and Noncommunity Property

Rights of survivorship will not be inferred from a joint tenancy in property that is not the community property of the tenants. Tex. Est. Code § 101.002. However, the joint tenants may agree in writing to implement rights of survivorship. Tex. Est. Code § 111.001. Spouses may agree between themselves that all or part of their community property, then existing or to be acquired, will be owned with rights of survivorship. Tex. Est. Code § 112.051.

Rights of survivorship in community property are treated differently from rights of survivorship in other property. *See* Tex. Est. Code §§ 111.002, 112.052. However, whether the property is community or not, the agreement must be in writing. In the case of community property, both spouses must sign the agreement. Tex. Est. Code § 112.052. For property that is not community, it is suggested that all joint tenants sign the writing for it to qualify as an agreement that satisfies the statute. *See* Tex. Est. Code § 111.001(a). The phrases *with right of survivorship, will become the property of the survivor, will vest in and belong to the surviving spouse*, or *will pass to the surviving spouse* are suggested for inclusion in the agreement.

Rights of survivorship do not affect the community status of property or the rights of the spouses concerning management, control, and disposition, unless the agreement so provides. Tex. Est. Code § 112.151. On the death of a spouse, a transfer resulting from the right of survivorship is not considered a testamentary transfer. Tex. Est. Code § 112.052. An agreement between spouses may be revoked in accordance with the agreement's terms. If no provision is made for revocation, the agreement may be revoked by a written instrument signed by both spouses or by a written instrument signed by one spouse and delivered to the other spouse. Tex. Est. Code § 112.054(b). The disposition of property by one or both spouses will also revoke the agreement as to that property if the disposition is not inconsistent with the terms of the agreement and applicable law. Tex. Est. Code § 112.054(c). Although an agreement between spouses creating rights of survivorship is effective without court adjudication, the surviving spouse may obtain such an adjudication by application to the court. *See* Tex. Est. Code §§ 112.053, 112.101. The agreement between spouses and any revocation should be recorded, and a copy provided to the personal representative of the deceased spouse's estate, to avoid the acquisition of good title by a buyer without actual notice of the agreement or the revocation under Tex. Est. Code §§ 112.201–.208. Community property subject to the sole or joint management, control, and disposition of a spouse during marriage continues to be subject to the liabilities of that spouse on death, regardless of the right of survivorship. *See* Tex. Est. Code §§ 112.251–.253.

See form 5-18 in this chapter for a survivorship agreement and form 5-19 for a survivorship agreement for community property.

§ 5.13:7 Community Interest Special Warranty Deed

The Texas Constitution and the Texas Family Code provide a method of converting title of real and personal property from separate to community property. *See* Tex. Const. art. XVI, § 15; Tex. Fam. Code §§ 4.201–.206. Before January 1, 2000, the effective date of these provisions, separate property could not be converted to community property because Texas is an inception of title state. The primary purpose of the community interest special warranty deed is to allow a surviving spouse, at the time of the other spouse's death, to obtain a nontaxable increase in the basis of the property for federal estate tax purposes. According to the Internal Revenue Code, all community property receives an increase in basis to the current market value at the death of the first spouse. *See* 26 U.S.C. § 1014(b)(6). Strict compliance with the provisions of the Family Code, including the use of bold-faced type, capital letters, or underlined warnings that must appear in the document, is necessary to convert the property to community property. *See* Tex. Fam. Code §§ 4.201–.206.

There are implications in this type of transaction for divorce, property management rights, and creditor claims, as described in section 4.205 of the Family Code. A separate agreement may be used to address personal-property or family-law issues. The form in this manual deals only with creating an effective conveyance of real property rights. See form 5-20 in this chapter for a community interest special warranty deed.

§ 5.13:8 Assignment and Assumption of Leases

The right to receive rent passes with title to real property, and the seller's tenant becomes the buyer's tenant as a matter of law. *Arredondo v. Mora*, 340 S.W.2d 322, 325 (Tex. App.—El Paso 1960, writ ref'd n.r.e.). Nevertheless, parties to a real estate sales contract often provide for a separate assignment and assumption agreement in which the seller assigns its rights in leases affecting the property and the buyer assumes the landlord's obligations under some or all of those leases. The assignment and assumption often contains indemnities by the parties covering their respective periods of responsibility for the landlord's obligations under the leases, including those for tenant improvements and brokerage commissions. The assignment and assumption of leases can be modified to include a general or special warranty of title. See form 5-21 in this chapter for an assignment and assumption of leases and form 5-22 for a notice of transfer of security deposit.

§ 5.14 General Considerations for Minerals

§ 5.14:1 Surface and Mineral Estates Generally

Texas mineral law is complex and extensive, and a comprehensive review is beyond the scope of this manual. This commentary is intended to identify common conveyancing issues that arise in transactions in which the primary focus is the surface estate, not the mineral estate. Attorneys who are not experienced in mineral law are urged to exercise caution and seek appropriate counsel when mineral law issues arise.

In Texas, the mineral estate may be severed from the surface estate. The mineral estate is the dominant estate and has five essential attributes: the right to explore and develop (ingress and egress); the right to lease (the executive right); the right to receive bonus payments; the right to receive delay rentals; and the right to receive royalty. *Day & Co. v. Texland Petroleum, Inc.*, 786 S.W.2d 667 (Tex. 1990); *Altman v. Blake*, 712 S.W.2d 117, 118 (Tex. 1986). The mineral estate, and each of its five separate attributes, may be held in undivided interests.

Grants and reservations in Texas are commonly styled "oil, gas, and other minerals" or "all minerals in and under the land." Although the meanings of "oil" and "gas" are usually clear, adjudication has been required to determine what minerals are included in a conveyance of "minerals." The Supreme Court of Texas has held that "a severance of minerals in an oil, gas and other minerals clause includes all substances within the ordinary and natural meaning of that word, whether their presence or value is known at the time of severance." *Moser v. U.S. Steel Corp.*, 676 S.W.2d 99, 102 (Tex. 1984). The *Moser* decision confirmed the court's previous holdings that, as a matter of law, certain substances belong to the surface estate: building stone, limestone, caliche, surface shale, water, sand, gravel, and near-surface lignite, iron, and coal. *Moser*, 676 S.W.2d at 102.

According to the common-law "greatest possible estate" rule, a conveyance will pass all of the estate owned by the grantor at the time of the conveyance unless the instrument states reservations that limit the estate being conveyed. *Cockrell v. Texas Gulf Sulphur Co.*, 299 S.W.2d 672, 675 (Tex. 1956). Thus, a conveyance without a specific reservation of the minerals will convey the grantor's entire mineral estate. *Harris v. Currie*, 176 S.W.2d 302, 304 (Tex. 1943). A result of the "greatest possible estate" rule is found in the *Duhig* rule, which provides that an outstanding right in the mineral estate will be charged to the grantor's mineral estate reservation, unless a contrary intent is stated in the instrument. *See Duhig v. Peavy-Moore Lumber Co.*, 144 S.W.2d 878, 880 (Tex. 1940).

§ 5.14:2 Royalty

Royalty is the nonpossessory right to receive a cost-free share of production. It may be reserved in a lease or severed from the fee in a grant or reservation in a deed. An "overriding royalty" or "override" is carved out of the lessee's interest in the leasehold estate and, absent fraud, breach of fiduciary duty, or similar wrongdoing, terminates when the lease from which it was created terminates.

A royalty clause must be drafted carefully. For example, each of the following may have a different result: an undivided 1/8 royalty; an undivided 1/8 of the royalty; and an undivided 1/8 in a 1/8 royalty. *See, e.g., Winslow v. Acker*, 781 S.W.2d 322, 326–27 (Tex. App.—San Antonio 1989, writ denied); *Ray v. Truitt*, 751 S.W.2d 205, 207 (Tex. App.—El Paso 1988, no writ); *Tiller v. Tiller*, 685 S.W.2d 456, 458 (Tex. App.—Austin 1985, no writ); *Lane v. Elkins*, 441 S.W.2d 871, 874–75 (Tex. App.— Eastland 1969, writ ref'd n.r.e.).

§ 5.14:3 Surface Use

The right to develop the mineral estate includes the right to use the surface to the extent reasonably necessary for development purposes. *Sun Oil Co. v. Whitaker*, 483 S.W.2d 808, 810 (Tex. 1972).

The surface owner whose land is to be developed for mineral purposes should be aware of the line of Texas cases concerning surface damages that includes *Acker v. Guinn*, 464 S.W.2d 348 (Tex. 1971), *Reed v. Wylie*, 597 S.W.2d 743 (Tex. 1980), and *Moser v. U.S. Steel Corp.*, 676 S.W.2d 99 (Tex. 1984). In *Moser*, the Supreme Court of Texas confirmed that the mineral owner has the right to use the surface to develop the minerals, but within certain guidelines. For instruments executed before June 8, 1983, the mineral owner is liable for destruction of the surface only if the destruction is negligently inflicted, regardless of how the mineral is described in the severance. For instruments executed on or after June 8, 1983, however, the negligence rule applies only to minerals that are specifically conveyed or named in the instrument. If the mineral is not specifically conveyed or named in the instrument, the mineral owner must compensate the surface owner for surface destruction, whether the result of negligence or not. *Moser*, 676 S.W.2d at 103. In addition, the mineral owner must accommodate the surface owner's use of the land to the extent described in *Getty Oil Co. v. Jones*, 470 S.W.2d 618 (Tex. 1971), and *Sun Oil Co.*, 483 S.W.2d at 810–11.

The surface owner may want to protect the surface by contractual restrictions on mineral operations. Such protections may include limitations on areas that may be used for mineral operations, such as designation of drill sites and pipeline and access easements; alternatively, the surface owner may contract with the mineral owner for a complete prohibition of use of the surface by the mineral owner (a surface-use waiver by the mineral owner).

§ 5.14:4 Existing Mineral Lease

There are special drafting considerations if the land being conveyed is subject to an existing mineral lease. For example, the grantor and the grantee should include in the deed their agreement on how to allocate the benefits of an undisputed existing lease between them.

§ 5.14:5 Life Tenant's Right to Consume Royalty

Whether the life tenant, as the owner of a life estate, is entitled to consume the royalty from mineral production on the property depends on the circumstances. If, at the inception of the life estate, there exists either mineral production or a mineral lease, the "open mine" doctrine entitles the life tenant to consume the royalties. *Thompson v. Thompson*, 236 S.W.2d 779, 786–87 (Tex. 1951); *Youngman v. Shular*, 281 S.W.2d 373, 375 (Tex. App.—San Antonio 1955), *aff'd*, 288 S.W.2d 495 (Tex. 1956). Otherwise, the life tenant is not entitled to consume the royalty and must account for it to the remainderman. *Swayne v. Lone Acre Oil Co.*, 86 S.W. 740, 742 (Tex. 1905).

§ 5.14:6 Special Problem Areas

Although a discussion of all areas of concern encountered with mineral interests is beyond the scope of this manual, special consideration should be given to—

- land subject to the Texas Relinquishment Act, where the minerals are owned by the state of Texas and the surface owner acts as the agent for the state in leasing them (*see* Tex. Nat. Res. Code §§ 52.171–.190);
- exploration by the owners of the right to develop the minerals without executing a mineral lease;
- discrimination by the owner of the executive right (right to lease) among the owners of the right to royalty, the right to delay rentals, and the right to bonus payments;
- ownership of mineral rights by more than one party; and
- severance of the mineral estate, limited by depth of the minerals or duration of the severance.

See clauses 5-7-8 through 5-7-14 in this chapter for reservation of minerals and clauses 5-8-34 through 5-8-36 for exceptions of minerals.

§ 5.15 General Considerations for Other Forms of Real Property

§ 5.15:1 Timber

The right to harvest growing timber with the accompanying ingress and egress rights together constitutes an interest in real property, which must be conveyed by deed. *Burkitt v. Wynne*, 132 S.W. 816 (Tex. App. 1910, writ ref'd). See clause 5-9-18 in this chapter.

§ 5.15:2 Easements

An easement is an interest in real property. *Settegast v. Foley Bros. Dry Goods Co.*, 270 S.W. 1014, 1016 (Tex. 1925). It gives the holder the right to use another's land for a specific purpose. *Lakeside Launches, Inc. v. Austin Yacht Club, Inc.*, 750 S.W.2d 868, 871 (Tex. App.—Austin 1988, writ denied). See clauses 5-7-1 through 5-7-4 and 5-8-14 through 5-8-25 in this chapter.

§ 5.15:3 Condominiums

A description of a condominium unit constitutes a sufficient legal description of the unit and all rights, obligations, and interests appurtenant to the unit if the description contains (1) the name of the condominium; (2) the recording data for the declaration, including any amendments, plats, and plans; (3) the county in which the condominium is located; and (4) the identifying number of the unit. Tex. Prop. Code § 82.054. This requirement from the Texas Uniform Condominium Act (Texas Property Code chapter 82) applies to all condominiums. Tex. Prop. Code § 82.002(c).

Some pre-1994 condominium regimes describe apartments by reference to a unit number and building letter. *See* Tex. Prop. Code § 81.102(a)(2). It is suggested that condominiums operating under the prior Condominium Act (Texas Property Code chapter 81) continue to include the building letter for description. As a practical matter, if condominiums recorded before January 1, 1994, use identifying numbers for apartments that are repeated in each of the buildings (for example, each building includes apartments 1 through 10), a reference to the building letter will be needed to distinguish between like-numbered apartments. See clause 5-8-13 in this chapter for an exception for use in a condominium deed and clause 5-9-3 for a condominium deed property description. See also chapter 24 in this manual for additional information on condominiums.

§ 5.15:4 Townhouse and Planned Unit Development Properties

The traditional townhouse project and planned unit developments (PUD) are similar in that both involve privately owned building sites with the common area owned by a separate association (usually a nonprofit corporation) whose members are the owners of the building sites. Easements are provided for access and utilities over the common area in both types of projects.

The description for a typical townhouse or lot within a PUD need not refer specifically to the common area if, as is customary, the common area is owned by the separate community association and ownership of the townhouses or lots in the PUD necessarily includes membership in the association and a pro rata ownership interest in the common area.

Deeds for either townhouses or PUD properties should except to the association restrictive covenants and the assessment lien. See clause 5-9-20 in this chapter for a property description and clause 5-9-21 for exceptions typical of a townhouse deed.

Townhouses generally involve building sites that are the outline or footprint of the separately owned townhouse unit's perimeter walls, whereas PUDs usually involve one conventional city lot per unit, including a yard and other city lot features. Because townhouses are usually more limited in space, the concept of limited common area is popular for townhouses. Limited common area involves limited access areas, such as screened patios, that are part of the common area but that usually no other owners may trespass on.

§ 5.15:5 Timeshare

A "timeshare estate" is an arrangement under which the purchaser receives the right to occupy a timeshare property and an estate interest in the real property. Tex. Prop. Code § 221.002(24). Once the timeshare plan is established, each timeshare interest may be separately conveyed or encumbered, and the title is recordable. Tex. Prop. Code § 221.012.

§ 5.15:6 Manufactured Housing

The Texas Department of Housing and Community Affairs (TDHCA) administers manufactured housing according to the Texas Manufactured Housing Standards Act. Tex. Occ. Code ch. 1201. Forms pertaining to manufactured housing can be obtained from the TDHCA. Regulations have been promulgated to administer and enforce the Act in title 10, chapter 80, of the Texas Administrative Code. Ownership of a manufactured home is evidenced by the filing of a statement of ownership issued by the TDHCA. Tex. Occ. Code §§ 1201.003(30)(A), 1201.205. At the sale or transfer of manufactured home, ownership does not pass or vest until a completed application for the issuance of a statement of ownership is filed with the TDHCA. Tex. Occ. Code § 1201.206(e).

A process exists that allows the owner of a manufactured home to elect to treat the home as real estate, making it a part of the real property. *See* Tex. Occ. Code §§ 1201.2055, 1201.2075, 1201.222; Tex. Prop. Code § 2.001(b).

The TDHCA is required to make available to the public through the department's website searchable and downloadable records regarding the ownership, liens, and installation of manufactured homes. Tex. Occ. Code §§ 1201.010, 1201.207(b).

The Texas Certificate of Title Act (Tex. Transp. Code ch. 501) governs "house trailers." The Act does not contain a mechanism for converting house trailers to real estate by affixing them to the real estate. House trailers are generally defined as trailers designed for human habitation, and they are treated differently from manufactured housing. *See* Tex. Transp. Code § 501.002(9); Tex. Occ. Code § 1201.003(12), (18), (20).

If the owner of the manufactured home has elected to treat the home as real property, a copy of the statement of ownership must be recorded in the real property records of the county where the manufactured home is located. Tex. Occ. Code § 1201.222; Tex. Prop. Code § 2.001(b).

Texas statutes address when a manufactured home is personal property and when it is real property. *See* Tex. Occ. Code § 1201.222; Tex. Prop. Code § 2.001(b). Ordinarily, a manufactured home is personal property. However, if the statement of ownership issued by the TDHCA reflects that the owner had elected to treat the home as real property and a certified copy of the statement of ownership has been recorded in the real property records of the county where the home is located, the manufactured home will be real property. Property Code chapter 63 clarifies the status of a lien on a manufactured home when it converts to real property. *See* Tex. Prop. Code ch. 63.

§ 5.16 Additional Resources

Baucum, Michael. "Special Warranty Deed Section." In *Advanced Real Estate Law Course, 2010*. Austin: State Bar of Texas, 2010.

Beitel, Jay G. "Owelty Liens and Deed Reservations and Exceptions." In *Advanced Real Estate Drafting Course, 2015*. Austin: State Bar of Texas, 2015.

Beyer, Gerry W. *Real Property*. 2nd ed. West's Texas Forms 13–15. St. Paul, MN: West, 2001. Supplement 2016.

Boykin, Stephen A. "So You Don't Own the Minerals." In *Advanced Real Estate Law Course, 2008*. Austin: State Bar of Texas, 2008.

———. "Texas Oil and Gas Leasing: A Primer." In *Advanced Real Estate Law Course, 2009*. Austin: State Bar of Texas, 2009.

Dysart, Sara E. "Reservation or Exception, What Is It Going to Be?" In *Advanced Real Estate Law Course, 2017*. Austin: State Bar of Texas, 2017.

———. "A Walk Down 'Bad Deed Lane.'" In *Advanced Real Estate Law Course, 2020*. Austin: State Bar of Texas, 2020.

Johnson, James N. "Modifying and Terminating Easements." In *Advanced Real Estate Drafting Course, 2008*. Austin: State Bar of Texas, 2008.

Johnson, Leslie S. "A Detailed Review of *Cochran Investments, Inc. v. Chicago Title Insurance Company*." In *Advanced Real Estate Law Course, 2020*. Austin: State Bar of Texas, 2020.

Jones, Jerry Frank. "Transfer on Death Deeds (TODDs)." In *Advanced Real Estate Drafting Course, 2016*. Austin: State Bar of Texas, 2016.

Koppenheffer, Julie, and Grant Ellis. "Conservation Easements." In *Advanced Real Estate Law Course, 2008*. Austin: State Bar of Texas, 2008.

Love, G. Roland. "Quitclaims—Texas and Beyond." In *Advanced Oil, Gas, & Energy Resources Law Course, 2016*. Austin: State Bar of Texas, 2016.

Lucksinger, Michael J. "Transfer on Death Deed, Lady Bird Deed, Survivorship Agreements." In *Advanced Real Estate Law Course, 2016*. Austin: State Bar of Texas, 2016.

Nickum, Ronald D. "The Role of Minerals in Real Estate Drafting: Ten Common Pitfalls Created by Mineral and Royalty Case Law." In *Advanced Real Estate Drafting Course, 2009*. Austin: State Bar of Texas, 2009.

Sheehan, Ty Hunter and Wesley Williams. "Conveyances—Recent Developments, Deeds, Reservations and Exceptions, and Things I Have to Look Up Every Four Years." In *Advanced Real Estate Law Course, 2019*. Austin: State Bar of Texas, 2019.

St. Claire, Frank A., and William V. Dorsaneo III. *Texas Real Estate Guide*. New York: Matthew Bender & Co., 2001.

Whelan, Thomas M. "Scattershooting While Wondering Whatever Happened at the Courthouse to Frequently Litigated Provisions in My Favorite Real Estate Sales Forms." In *Advanced Real Estate Drafting Course, 2015*. Austin: State Bar of Texas, 2015.

Form 5-1

General Warranty Deed

Notice of confidentiality rights: If you are a natural person, you may remove or strike any or all of the following information from any instrument that transfers an interest in real property before it is filed for record in the public records: your Social Security number or your driver's license number.

Date:

Grantor:

Grantor's Mailing Address:

Grantee:

Grantee's Mailing Address:

Consideration:

> See form 5-6 in this chapter for consideration clauses.

Property (including any improvements):

> If the conveyance includes personal property, include the defined term from clause 5-9-12.

Reservations from Conveyance:

> State "None" or, to create reservations of title, include the appropriate clauses from form 5-7.

Exceptions to Conveyance and Warranty:

> State "None" or, to create exceptions to conveyance and warranty, include the appropriate clauses from form 5-8.

Grantor, for the Consideration and subject to the Reservations from Conveyance and the Exceptions to Conveyance and Warranty, grants, sells, and conveys to Grantee the Property, together with all and singular the rights and appurtenances thereto in any way belonging, to have and to hold it to Grantee and Grantee's heirs, successors, and assigns forever. Grantor binds Grantor and Grantor's heirs and successors to warrant and forever defend all and singular the Property to Grantee and Grantee's heirs, successors, and assigns against every person whomsoever lawfully claiming or to claim the same or any part thereof, except as to the Reservations from Conveyance and the Exceptions to Conveyance and Warranty.

> If the conveyance includes personal property, include clause 5-9-13.

> If appropriate, include additional clauses like those suggested in form 5-9.

When the context requires, singular nouns and pronouns include the plural.

____

[Name of grantor]

> If the deed imposes contractual obligations on the grantee, include the following signature line.

____

[Name of grantee]

> Include acknowledgments.

Form 5-2

Warranty Deed with Vendor's Lien

Notice of confidentiality rights: If you are a natural person, you may remove or strike any or all of the following information from any instrument that transfers an interest in real property before it is filed for record in the public records: your Social Security number or your driver's license number.

Date:

Grantor:

Grantor's Mailing Address:

Grantee:

Grantee's Mailing Address:

Consideration:

See form 5-6 in this chapter for consideration clauses.

Property (including any improvements):

If the conveyance includes personal property, include the defined term from clause 5-9-12.

Reservations from Conveyance:

State "None" or, to create reservations of title, include the appropriate clauses from form 5-7.

Exceptions to Conveyance and Warranty:

State "None" or, to create exceptions to conveyance and warranty, include the appropriate clauses from form 5-8.

Grantor, for the Consideration and subject to the Reservations from Conveyance and the Exceptions to Conveyance and Warranty, grants, sells, and conveys to Grantee the Property, together with all and singular the rights and appurtenances thereto in any way belonging, to have and to hold it to Grantee and Grantee's heirs, successors, and assigns forever. Grantor binds Grantor and Grantor's heirs and successors to warrant and forever defend all and singular the Property to Grantee and Grantee's heirs, successors, and assigns against every person whomsoever lawfully claiming or to claim the same or any part thereof, except as to the Reservations from Conveyance and the Exceptions to Conveyance and Warranty.

The vendor's lien against and superior title to the Property are retained until each note described is fully paid according to its terms, at which time this deed will become absolute.

If the conveyance includes personal property, include clause 5-9-13.

If appropriate, include additional clauses like those suggested in form 5-9.

When the context requires, singular nouns and pronouns include the plural.

____

[Name of grantor]

If the deed imposes contractual obligations on the grantee, include the following signature line.

____

[Name of grantee]

Include acknowledgments.

Form 5-3

Special Warranty Deed

Notice of confidentiality rights: If you are a natural person, you may remove or strike any or all of the following information from any instrument that transfers an interest in real property before it is filed for record in the public records: your Social Security number or your driver's license number.

Date:

Grantor:

Grantor's Mailing Address:

Grantee:

Grantee's Mailing Address:

Consideration:

> See form 5-6 in this chapter for consideration clauses.

Property (including any improvements):

> If the conveyance includes personal property, include the defined term from clause 5-9-12.

Reservations from Conveyance:

> State "None" or, to create reservations of title, include the appropriate clauses from form 5-7.

Exceptions to Conveyance and Warranty:

> State "None" or, to create exceptions to conveyance and warranty, include the appropriate clauses from form 5-8.

To include express language indicating the intent of the parties to convey the property with the covenant of seisin, include clause 5-9-27.

Grantor, for the Consideration and subject to the Reservations from Conveyance and the Exceptions to Conveyance and Warranty, grants, sells, and conveys to Grantee the Property, together with all and singular the rights and appurtenances thereto in any way belonging, to have and to hold it to Grantee and Grantee's heirs, successors, and assigns forever. Grantor binds Grantor and Grantor's heirs and successors to warrant and forever defend all and singular the Property to Grantee and Grantee's heirs, successors, and assigns against every person whomsoever lawfully claiming or to claim the same or any part thereof when the claim is by, through, or under Grantor but not otherwise, except as to the Reservations from Conveyance and the Exceptions to Conveyance and Warranty.

If the conveyance includes personal property, include clause 5-9-13.

If appropriate, include additional clauses like those suggested in form 5-9.

When the context requires, singular nouns and pronouns include the plural.

____

[Name of grantor]

If the deed imposes contractual obligations on the grantee, include the following signature line.

____

[Name of grantee]

Include acknowledgments.

Form 5-4

Deed without Warranty

Notice of confidentiality rights: If you are a natural person, you may remove or strike any or all of the following information from any instrument that transfers an interest in real property before it is filed for record in the public records: your Social Security number or your driver's license number.

Date:

Grantor:

Grantor's Mailing Address:

Grantee:

Grantee's Mailing Address:

Consideration:

> See form 5-6 in this chapter for consideration clauses.

Property (including any improvements):

> If the conveyance includes personal property, include the defined term from clause 5-9-12.

Reservations from Conveyance:

> State "None" or, to create reservations of title, include the appropriate clauses from form 5-7.

Exceptions to Conveyance:

> State "None" or, to create exceptions to conveyance, include the appropriate clauses from form 5-8.

Grantor, for the Consideration and subject to the Reservations from Conveyance and the Exceptions to Conveyance, grants, sells, and conveys to Grantee the Property, together with all and singular the rights and appurtenances thereto in any way belonging, to have and to hold it to Grantee and Grantee's heirs, successors, and assigns forever, without express or implied warranty. All warranties that might arise by common law as well as the warranties in section 5.023 of the Texas Property Code (or its successor) are excluded.

Include the following paragraph if applicable.

This conveyance is intended to include any property interests obtained by after-acquired title.

If the conveyance includes personal property, include clause 5-9-13, omitting the warranty in the first paragraph.

If appropriate, include additional clauses like those suggested in form 5-9.

Continue with the following.

When the context requires, singular nouns and pronouns include the plural.

____

[Name of grantor]

If the deed imposes contractual obligations on the grantee, include the following signature line.

____

[Name of grantee]

Include acknowledgments.

Form 5-5

Quitclaim

Notice of confidentiality rights: If you are a natural person, you may remove or strike any or all of the following information from any instrument that transfers an interest in real property before it is filed for record in the public records: your Social Security number or your driver's license number.

Date:

Grantor:

Grantor's Mailing Address:

Grantee:

Grantee's Mailing Address:

Consideration:

See form 5-6 in this chapter for consideration clauses.

Property (including any improvements):

For the Consideration, Grantor quitclaims to Grantee all of Grantor's right, title, and interest in and to the Property, to have and to hold it to Grantee and Grantee's heirs, successors, and assigns forever. Neither Grantor nor Grantor's heirs, successors, or assigns will have, claim, or demand any right or title to the Property or any part of it.

When the context requires, singular nouns and pronouns include the plural.

____

[Name of grantor]

If the quitclaim imposes contractual obligations on the grantee, include the following signature line.

____
[Name of grantee]

Include acknowledgments.

Form 5-6

Consideration Clauses

Select only one consideration clause.

Assumption of First-Lien Note and Execution of Second-Lien Note to Grantor or Third Party

Clause 5-6-1

Use the following with the warranty deed with vendor's lien; also use clause 5-9-10 in this chapter if the second-lien note is payable to the grantor or clause 5-9-11 if the second-lien note is payable to a third party.

[**Include if applicable:** Cash and] Grantee's assumption and agreement to pay, according to the terms of the first-lien note, the unpaid principal and earned interest of [**amount**] DOLLARS ($[**amount**]) with interest from [**date**] on the first-lien note, and a second-lien note of even date executed by Grantee. The first-lien note is dated [**date**], is executed by [**name**], and is payable to the order of [**name**] in the principal amount of [**amount**] DOLLARS ($[**amount**]). The first-lien note is secured by the first and superior vendor's lien against, and superior title to, the Property retained in a deed dated [**date**] and recorded in [**recording data**] of the real property records of [**county**] County, Texas. The first-lien note is also secured by a first-lien deed of trust of even date to [**name**], trustee, recorded in [**recording data**] of the real property records of [**county**] County, Texas. As further consideration Grantee promises to keep and perform all the covenants and obligations of the grantor[s] named in that deed of trust and to indemnify, defend, and hold Grantor harmless from any loss, attorney's fees, expenses, or claims attributable to breach or default of any provision of this assumption by Grantee. The second-lien note is payable to the order of [Grantor/[**name of third party**]] in the principal amount of

[amount] DOLLARS ($**[amount]**). The second-lien note is secured by a second and inferior vendor's lien against, and superior title to, the Property retained in this deed [**include if applicable:** for the benefit of [**name of third party**]] and is also secured by a second-lien deed of trust of even date from Grantee to [**name**], trustee.

Assumption of Note Secured by Vendor's Lien and Deed of Trust

Clause 5-6-2

Use the following with clause 5-9-23.

[**Include if applicable:** Cash and] Grantee's assumption of and agreement to pay, according to the note's terms, the unpaid principal and earned interest of [**amount**] DOLLARS ($[**amount**]) on the note in the original principal sum of [**amount**] DOLLARS ($[**amount**]) dated [**date**], executed by [**name**], and payable to the order of [**name**]. The note is secured by an express vendor's lien and superior title retained in a deed dated [**date**], recorded in [**recording data**] of the real property records of [**county**] County, Texas, and additionally secured by a deed of trust dated [**date**], from [**name**] to [**name**], trustee, recorded in [**recording data**] of the real property records of [**county**] County, Texas. As further consideration Grantee promises to keep and perform all the covenants and obligations of the grantor[s] named in that deed of trust and to indemnify, defend, and hold Grantor harmless from any loss, attorney's fees, expenses, or claims attributable to a breach or default of any provision of this assumption by Grantee. Grantor assigns to Grantee any funds on deposit for payment of taxes and insurance premiums.

Capital Contribution

Clause 5-6-3

Use the following if the property is serving as a contribution to a legal entity.

[[**Number**] shares/[**describe other ownership interest**]] in [**name of legal entity**] [**include if applicable:** with a value of $[**amount**]]. The Property is conveyed to Grantee for the purpose of contributing to the capital of [**name of entity**].

Cash

Clause 5-6-4

Cash and other good and valuable consideration, the receipt and sufficiency of which are hereby acknowledged.

Or

Clause 5-6-5

[**amount**] DOLLARS ($[**amount**]) and other good and valuable consideration, the receipt and sufficiency of which are hereby acknowledged.

Or

Clause 5-6-6

[**amount**] DOLLARS ($[**amount**]).

Exchange of Property

Clause 5-6-7

[Part cash and the/The] exchange of property, title to which is accepted by Grantor the same as if the consideration represented by the exchange were paid in cash. [**Include if applicable:** There is no lien, either expressed or implied, created by the exchange of property. Any such lien is waived and released by Grantor.]

First-Lien Note to Third Party and Second-Lien Note to Grantor

Clause 5-6-8

> Use the following in the warranty deed with vendor's lien with clause 5-9-9.

[Cash and two/Two] notes of even date executed by Grantee and referred to as the first-lien note and the second-lien note. The first-lien note is payable to the order of [**name of third party**] in the principal amount of [**amount**] DOLLARS ($[**amount**]). The first-lien note is secured by the first and superior vendor's lien against, and superior title to, the Property retained in this deed in favor of [**name of third party**] and is also secured by a first-lien deed of trust of even date from Grantee to [**name**], trustee. The second-lien note is payable to the order of Grantor in the principal amount of [**amount**] DOLLARS ($[**amount**]). The second-lien note is secured by a second and inferior vendor's lien against, and superior title to, the Property retained in this deed and is also secured by a second-lien deed of trust of even date from Grantee to [**name**], trustee.

Gift

Clause 5-6-9

Love of, and affection for, Grantee.

Or

Clause 5-6-10

Grantor's intention to make a gift as a charitable contribution under applicable income tax laws and regulations.

Grantee's Separate Property

Clause 5-6-11

Cash and other good and valuable consideration, the receipt and sufficiency of which are hereby acknowledged, paid from Grantee's separate property.

Or

Clause 5-6-12

[**describe consideration**] and other good and valuable consideration paid from Grantee's separate property.

Note to Grantor or Third Party

Clause 5-6-13

Use the following in the warranty deed with vendor's lien; also use clause 5-9-8 if the note is executed in favor of a third party.

[Cash and a/A] note of even date executed by Grantee and payable to the order of [Grantor/[**name of third party**]] in the principal amount of [**amount**]

DOLLARS ($[**amount**]). The note is secured by a first and superior vendor's lien and superior title retained in this deed [**include if applicable:** in favor of [**name of third party**]] and by a first-lien deed of trust of even date from Grantee to [**name**], trustee.

Wraparound Lien [Deed Subject to]

Clause 5-6-14

Use the following with clauses 5-8-51 and 5-9-26.

[Cash and a/A] wraparound note ("Wraparound Lien Debt") of even date in the principal amount of [**amount**] DOLLARS ($[**amount**]) executed by Grantee, payable to the order of Grantor. The note is secured by a vendor's lien retained in this deed and by a deed of trust of even date from Grantee to [**name**], trustee (collectively, the "Wraparound Lien").

Form 5-7

If no reservations are to be made, as is most often the case, the word "None" should be inserted in the deed; otherwise, use a specific reservation such as one of those set forth below.

Reservations from Conveyance

Easement

Clause 5-7-1

For Grantor and Grantor's heirs, successors, and assigns forever, a reservation of the free, uninterrupted, and perpetual use of, and a separate right to maintain, a nonexclusive easement over the passageway described in this paragraph and located on the Property. This easement is located [**describe, e.g.,** along the entire northern boundary of the Property as it exists at this time and is fifty feet in width].

Easement—Access

Clause 5-7-2

Include the following defined terms.

Dominant Estate Property (including any improvements):

Easement Property: [**Describe by metes and bounds the property serving as the easement, and include a drawing as an exhibit, if available.**]

Easement Purpose: To provide free and uninterrupted pedestrian and vehicular ingress and egress to and from the Dominant Estate Property, and portions thereof, to and from [**describe public thoroughfare**].

Clause 5-7-3

Include the following under reservations from conveyance.

For Grantor and Grantor's heirs, successors, and assigns, in common with Grantee and Grantee's heirs, successors, and assigns, a reservation of an easement over, on, and across the Easement Property for the Easement Purpose and for the benefit of the Dominant Estate Property, and portions thereof, together with all and singular the rights and appurtenances thereto in any way belonging, in accordance with the terms and conditions set forth below.

Clause 5-7-4

Include the following at the end of the deed, immediately above the last paragraph, which states: "When the context requires, singular nouns and pronouns include the plural."

The following terms and conditions apply to the easement:

1. *Character of Easement.* The easement is appurtenant to and runs with the Dominant Estate Property and all portions of it, whether or not the easement is referenced in any conveyance of the Dominant Estate Property or any portion of it. The easement binds and inures to the benefit of Grantor and Grantee and their respective heirs, successors, and assigns.

2. *Duration of Easement.* The easement is [perpetual/[**state limitation**]].

3. *Exclusiveness of Easement.* The easement is nonexclusive, and Grantor reserves for Grantor and Grantor's heirs, successors, and assigns the right to convey the easement or other rights or easements to others.

4. *Secondary Easement.* In addition, the holder of the easement has the right to use as much of the surface of the property adjacent to the Easement

Property as may be reasonably necessary to construct and maintain a road reasonably suited for the Easement Purpose. However, the holder must promptly restore any adjacent property to its previous physical condition if changed by the use of the rights granted by this secondary easement.

5. *Maintenance.* Improvement and maintenance of the Easement Property will be at the sole expense of the holder of the easement. The holder has the right to eliminate any encroachments into the Easement Property. The holder of the easement will maintain the Easement Property in a neat and clean condition.

6. *Grantee's Rights.* Grantee and Grantee's heirs, successors, and assigns have the right to use the surface of the Easement Property for all purposes that do not unreasonably interfere with or interrupt the use of the easement.

7. *Indemnity by Easement Holder.* The holder of the easement agrees to indemnify, defend, and hold Grantee and Grantee's successors in interest harmless from any loss, attorney's fees, court and other costs, expenses, or claims attributable to breach or default of any provision of this easement by the holder.

Life Estate

Clause 5-7-5

For Grantor and Grantor's assigns, a reservation of the full possession, benefit, and use of the Property for the remainder of the life of Grantor, as a life estate.

Life Estate with Power of Sale

Clause 5-7-6

For Grantor and Grantor's assigns, a reservation of the full possession, benefit, and use of the Property for the remainder of the life of Grantor, as a life estate. Grantor retains complete power, without the joinder of any person, to mortgage, sell, and convey the Property and to spend any proceeds; to exchange it for other property; to lease the surface and subsurface of the Property; to execute and deliver oil, gas, and other mineral leases for any term of years and for a term based on the continuing production of oil, gas, or other minerals from the Property, ending either before or after Grantor's death; and to invest and reinvest all proceeds from the sale or other disposition of the Property. This life estate carries with it the right to possess and consume all bonuses, delay rentals, royalties, and other benefits payable on any mortgage, sale, or conveyance under oil, gas, and other mineral leases covering the Property at the inception of this life estate without any duty to the remainderman and without liability for waste.

Life Estate with Right to Consume Corpus

Clause 5-7-7

For Grantor and Grantor's assigns, a reservation of the full possession, benefit, and use of the Property for the remainder of the life of Grantor, including the right to consume the corpus, whether by sale, conveyance, mortgage, mineral lease, or otherwise, without any duty to the remainderman and without liability for waste.

Mineral Estate—Entirety

Clause 5-7-8

For Grantor and Grantor's heirs, successors, and assigns forever, a reservation of all oil, gas, and other minerals in and under and that may be produced from the Property. If the mineral estate is subject to existing production or an existing lease, this reservation includes the production, the lease, and all benefits from it.

Mineral Estate—Fraction of Entirety

Clause 5-7-9

For Grantor and Grantor's heirs, successors, and assigns forever, a reservation of an undivided [**fraction**] of all oil, gas, and other minerals in and under and that may be produced from the Property.

Mineral Estate—Term Mineral Interest

Clause 5-7-10

For Grantor and Grantor's heirs, successors, and assigns for the limited term described, a reservation of all oil, gas, and other minerals in and under and that may be produced from the Property [**include specific terms plus production tail, e.g.,** for a term of [**number**] years from this date, at which time this reservation will automatically terminate; except, however, if oil, gas, or other minerals are being produced from the Property at the end of the term of years, the term will extend for as long thereafter as oil, gas, or other minerals are being produced in paying quantities from the Property or land pooled with it].

Mineral Estate—Royalty

Clause 5-7-11

For Grantor and Grantor's heirs, successors, and assigns forever, a reservation of an undivided [**fraction**] of the royalty under any any oil, gas, and mineral lease now or hereafter covering the Property or any portion of it; and the right to receive as a royalty an undivided [**fraction (ordinarily should not exceed one-fourth)**] [**include one of the following:** of all oil, gas, or other minerals now or hereafter produced from the Property without an oil, gas, or mineral lease/ royalty on the oil, gas, and other minerals in and under and that may be produced from the Property].

Mineral Estate—Prohibition against Exploration by Minerals' Owner

Clause 5-7-12

As long as Grantor or Grantor's heirs, successors, and assigns own a fraction of the royalty that is severed from the ownership of the minerals, Grantee and Grantee's heirs, successors, and assigns are prohibited from exploring for, developing, or producing the oil, gas, and other minerals in and under, and that may be produced from, the Property; instead, these activities may be conducted only by a bona fide unrelated party, through a lease providing for a royalty equal to or greater than the customary royalty prevailing in the area at the time of the lease.

Mineral Estate—Waiver of Surface Rights

Clause 5-7-13

Grantor waives the right of ingress and egress to and from the surface of the Property relating to the portion of the mineral estate owned by Grantor.

Nothing herein, however, restricts or prohibits the pooling or unitization of the portion of the mineral estate owned by Grantor with land other than the Property; or the exploration or production of the oil, gas, and other minerals by means of wells that are drilled or mines that open on land other than the Property but enter or bottom under the Property, provided that these operations in no manner interfere with the surface or subsurface support of any improvements constructed or to be constructed on the Property.

Mineral Estate—Waiver of Surface Rights; Reservation of Drill Site

Clause 5-7-14

Include the following defined terms.

Drill Site:

Access Routes:

Include the following under reservations from conveyance.

For Grantor and Grantor's heirs, successors, and assigns forever, a reservation of a perpetual, exclusive easement in and to the free and uninterrupted use of the Drill Site to explore and produce the oil, gas, and other minerals in and under and that may be produced from the Property, together with access to and from the Drill Site over the Access Routes. Grantor waives the right to explore and develop from the surface of the Property the portion of the mineral estate owned by Grantor, other than on or from the Drill Site.

Form 5-8

Exceptions to Conveyance and Warranty

Broad Exceptions

Clause 5-8-1

Liens described as part of the Consideration and any other liens described in this deed as being either assumed or subject to which title is taken; validly existing easements, rights-of-way, and prescriptive rights, whether of record or not; all presently recorded and validly existing restrictions, reservations, covenants, conditions, oil and gas leases, mineral interests, and water interests outstanding in persons other than Grantor, and other instruments, other than conveyances of the surface fee estate, that affect the Property; validly existing rights of adjoining owners in any walls and fences situated on a common boundary; any discrepancies, conflicts, or shortages in area or boundary lines; any encroachments or overlapping of improvements; all rights, obligations, and other matters arising from and existing by reason of the [**county**] County [**specify water improvement or other applicable governmental district, agency, authority, etc.**]; and taxes for [**current year**], which Grantee assumes and agrees to pay [, and subsequent assessments for that and prior years due to change in land usage, ownership, or both, the payment of which Grantee assumes/but not subsequent assessments for that and prior years due to change in land usage, ownership, or both, the payment of which Grantor assumes].

Or

Clause 5-8-2

Liens described as part of the Consideration and any other liens described in this deed as being either assumed or subject to which title is taken; validly existing easements, rights-of-way, and prescriptive rights, whether of record or not; all presently recorded and validly existing instruments, other than conveyances of the surface fee estate, that affect the Property; and taxes for [**current year**], which Grantee assumes and agrees to pay [, and subsequent assessments for that and prior years due to change in land usage, ownership, or both, the payment of which Grantee assumes/but not subsequent assessments for that and prior years due to change in land usage, ownership, or both, the payment of which Grantor assumes].

Or

Clause 5-8-3

The following paragraph follows the exceptions called for by TREC no. 20-13 Rev. 11/15, "One to Four Family Residential Contract (Resale)," in conjunction with the title insurance forms, and it should be used when the contract for the transaction so provides. Always compare the contract and title insurance forms to confirm that changes have not been made since this clause was published.

Liens described as part of the Consideration and any other liens described in this deed as being either assumed by Grantee or subject to which title is taken by Grantee; validly existing restrictive covenants common to the platted subdivision in which the Property is located; standby fees, taxes, and assessments by any taxing authority for the year [**the first year for which taxes are not paid as part of the closing**] and subsequent years, and subsequent taxes and assessments by any taxing authority for prior years due to change in land usage or ownership; validly existing utility easements created by the dedication deed or plat of the subdivision in which the Property is located; [**describe**

validly existing reservations or exceptions approved in writing by the grantee and other matters waived by the grantee under the terms of the contract and described in schedule B of the owner policy of title insurance issued to the grantee as part of the transaction; if they are numerous or lengthy, reference to an exhibit is appropriate], recorded in [**recording data**] of the real property records of [**county**] County, Texas; any discrepancies, conflicts, or shortages in area or boundary lines, or any encroachments or protrusions, or any overlapping of improvements; homestead or community property or survivorship rights, if any, of any spouse of Grantee; and any validly existing titles or rights asserted by anyone, including but not limited to persons, the public, corporations, governments, or other entities, to (1) tidelands or lands comprising the shores or beds of navigable or perennial rivers and streams, lakes, bays, gulfs, or oceans, (2) lands beyond the line of the harbor or bulkhead lines as established or changed by any government, (3) filled-in lands or artificial islands, (4) water rights, including riparian rights, or (5) the area extending from the line of mean low tide to the line of vegetation or the right of access to that area or easement along and across that area.

Specific Exceptions

> To create specific exceptions, include each of the following that applies. This is typically done with an introductory phrase such as "To the extent they validly exist:" followed by numbered paragraphs.

Abstract of Judgment

Clause 5-8-4

Abstract of judgment dated [**date**], styled "[**style of judgment**]," filed for record, recorded in [**recording data**] of the real property records of [**county**]

County, Texas, in the amount of $[**amount**], plus costs, interest, and attorney's fees.

Access Restrictions on Subdivision Plat

Clause 5-8-5

Limited, restricted, or nonaccess restrictions as shown on subdivision plat recorded in [**recording data**] of the real property records of [**county**] County, Texas.

Access Unavailable

Clause 5-8-6

Failure of the Property to have rights of ingress to and egress from a public thoroughfare.

Or

Clause 5-8-7

Failure of the Property to have the right of access to [**specify thoroughfare**].

Accretion

Clause 5-8-8

The rights of adjoining land owners in and to that part of the Property that may constitute accretion.

Areas and Boundaries

Clause 5-8-9

Any discrepancies, conflicts, or shortages in area or boundary lines, or any encroachments or protrusions or any overlapping of improvements.

Assignment of Lien

Clause 5-8-10

The note and deed of trust assigned to [**name**] by assignment of lien dated [**date**], recorded in [**recording data**] of the real property records of [**county**] County, Texas.

Building Setback Line

Clause 5-8-11

Building setback line [**number**] feet wide along [**describe**] property line as shown on [**include if applicable:** subdivision] plat recorded in [**recording data**] of the real property records of [**county**] County, Texas.

Cemetery

Clause 5-8-12

The dedication of a portion of the Property to and for use as a cemetery; the easements, privileges, and licenses existing in plot owners and their relatives in and to the cemetery portion, including the rights of burial, upkeep, ornamentation, and visitation; and the regulations and rules as established and amended by all cemetery owners covering the cemetery portion.

Implied easement for ingress and egress across the Property to and from the cemetery tract.

Condominiums

Clause 5-8-13

See also clause 5-8-31.

Terms, conditions, covenants, options, restrictions, bylaws, and easements contained in the declaration of condominium and bylaws executed by [**name**], dated [**date**], recorded in [**recording data**] of the real property records of [**county**] County, Texas, as the same have been amended, supplemented, and restated in the real property records of [**county**] County, Texas.

Contract for Deed

Clause 5-8-14

Terms of [**include if applicable:** unrecorded] contract for deed between [**name**] and [**name**], dated [**date**] [**include if applicable:** , recorded in [**recording data**] of the real property records of [**county**] County, Texas].

Cotenant Rights

Clause 5-8-15

Rights and claims of and against any and all cotenants in the Property such as partition, owelty, and contribution.

Deed of Trust

Clause 5-8-16

Deed of trust dated [**date**], executed by [**name**] to [**name**], trustee, recorded in [**recording data**] of the real property records of [**county**] County, Texas, securing the payment of a note of even date in the principal amount of $[**amount**].

Deed of Trust to Secure Assumption

Clause 5-8-17

Deed of trust to secure assumption dated [**date**], executed by [**name**] to [**name**], trustee, recorded in [**recording data**] of the real property records of [**county**] County, Texas, securing the assumption of the $[**amount**] note described in the deed of trust recorded in [**recording data**] of the real property records of [**county**] County, Texas.

Easement—Aerial

Clause 5-8-18

An unobstructed aerial easement [**number**] feet wide from a plane [**number**] feet above the ground upward, along the property line[s], shown on subdivision plat recorded in [**recording data**] of the real property records of [**county**] County, Texas.

Easement—Common Area Utility

Clause 5-8-19

Easements affecting common areas for utility [**include if applicable:** or other] purposes such as public utilities and drainage, as shown on subdivision plat recorded in [**recording data**] of the real property records of [**county**] County, Texas.

Easement—Flood Control

Clause 5-8-20

[**County**] County flood control drainage easement, as shown on subdivision plat recorded in [**recording data**] of the real property records of [**county**] County, Texas.

Easement—Pipeline

Clause 5-8-21

Pipeline easement granted [across a specified area/as a blanket easement] to [**name**], executed by [**name**], in instrument dated [**date**], recorded in [**recording data**] of the real property records of [**county**] County, Texas.

Easement—Reciprocal

Clause 5-8-22

Reciprocal easement for [**specify**] in instrument dated [**date**] and recorded in [**recording data**] of the real property records of [**county**] County, Texas.

Easement—Specific

Clause 5-8-23

[**Type**] easement to [**name**], dated [**date**], executed by [**name**], recorded in [**recording data**] of the real property records of [**county**] County, Texas.

Easement—Zero Lot Line on Subdivision Plat

Clause 5-8-24

Easement [**number**] feet wide along side lot line[s] for encroachments caused by settling and overhang of adjacent structures and for construction, maintenance, and repair, as shown on subdivision plat recorded in [**recording data**] of the real property records of [**county**] County, Texas.

Easements—Unrecorded

Clause 5-8-25

Visible and apparent easements on or across the Property.

Electric Service Agreements

Clause 5-8-26

[**Name of authority**] agreement for underground extension of electrical service dated [**date**], recorded in [**recording data**] of the real property records of [**county**] County, Texas.

Financing Statement (County Records)

Clause 5-8-27

UCC1 financing statement executed by [**name**], debtor, to [**name**], secured party, recorded in [**recording data**] of the [**specify**] records of [**county**] County, Texas, on [**date**].

General Restrictions

Clause 5-8-28

Restrictions recorded in [**recording data**] of the real property records of [**county**] County, Texas.

Lease Agreement

Clause 5-8-29

[Unrecorded lease/Lease] agreement between [**name**], as lessor, and [**name**], as lessee, dated [**date**] [**include if applicable:** , recorded in [**recording data**] of the real property records of [**county**] County, Texas] [**include if applicable:** and assigned to [**name**] by instrument dated [**date**], recorded in [**recording data**] of the real property records of [**county**] County, Texas].

Loan Modification

Clause 5-8-30

The note and deed of trust modified by a modification agreement dated [**date**], executed by [**name**], owner, and [**name**], lender, recorded in [**recording data**] of the real property records of [**county**] County, Texas.

Maintenance Assessment Exception (Property Owners' Association)

Clause 5-8-31

See also clause 5-8-13.

[Annual assessments/Current maintenance charges] for the year [**year**] and subsequent years not yet due and payable, secured by an inchoate lien, as set forth in the instrument dated [**date**] and recorded in [**recording data**] of the real property records of [**county**] County, Texas.

Mechanic's Lien by Affidavit

Clause 5-8-32

Claim of mechanic's lien by affidavit dated [**date**], executed by [**name**], recorded in [**recording data**] of the real property records of [**county**] County, Texas, claiming a lien in the amount of $[**amount**].

Mechanic's Lien Contract with Deed-of-Trust Provision

Clause 5-8-33

Mechanic's lien contract dated [**date**], executed by [**name**] to [**name**], securing [**name**], payee, in the payment of one note of even date in the original principal amount of $[**amount**], with a deed of trust to [**name**], trustee, incorporated therein, and assigned to [**name**] by assignment incorporated therein, recorded in [**recording data**] of the real property records of [**county**] County, Texas.

Mineral Estate or Royalty Conveyed or Reserved

Clause 5-8-34

A [mineral estate/right to royalty], together with all related rights, express or implied, as described in instrument executed by [**name**] to [**name**], dated [**date**], recorded in [**recording data**] of the real property records of [**county**] County, Texas [**include if applicable:** , as modified by waiver of surface rights in instrument dated [**date**], executed by [**name**], and recorded in [**recording data**] of the real property records of [**county**] County, Texas].

Mineral Lease

Clause 5-8-35

Oil, gas, or mineral lease dated [**date**], between [**name**] and [**name**], recorded in [**recording data**] of the real property records of [**county**] County, Texas.

Mineral Reservation by Predecessor

Clause 5-8-36

Reservation by [**name**] of the subsurface mineral estate, including oil, gas, and other minerals in and under the Property, including all easements owned or held by any lessee or mineral owner on, over, or across the Property for the purpose of producing or transporting any of the minerals together with the right of ingress and egress, in a deed recorded in [**recording data**] of the real property records of [**county**] County, Texas.

Notice of Assessment

Clause 5-8-37

Notice of assessment by [city of [**city**]/[**county**] County, Texas,] for [**purpose**] in the amount of $[**amount**], and related charges, dated [**date**], recorded in [**recording data**] of the real property records of [**county**] County, Texas.

Party Wall

Clause 5-8-38

Party wall agreement dated [**date**] between [**name**] and [**name**], recorded in [**recording data**] of the real property records of [**county**] County, Texas.

Property Encumbered by Lien Securing Note That Grantee Does Not Assume

Clause 5-8-39

A lien securing a promissory note in the original principal amount of [**amount**] DOLLARS ($[**amount**]), described in and secured by a deed of trust recorded in [**recording data**] of the real property records of [**county**] County, Texas. Grantee does not assume payment of the note or liability under any instrument securing the note.

Reinstatement of Accelerated Loan

Clause 5-8-40

The note and deed of trust reinstated by reinstatement agreement dated [**date**], executed by [**name**], owner, and [**name**], lender, recorded in [**recording data**] of the real property records of [**county**] County, Texas.

Riparian Rights

Clause 5-8-41

Any title or rights asserted by anyone, including but not limited to persons, the public, corporations, governments, or other entities, to any portions of the Property that may be within the bed of [**specify**].

River Exception

Clause 5-8-42

Past and future action of the [**name of river**] by means of accretion, erosion, or avulsion.

Roadway

Clause 5-8-43

Any portion of the Property within the limits or boundaries of any public or private roadway or highway.

Taxes

Clause 5-8-44

Standby fees, taxes, and assessments by any taxing authority for the year [**year**] and subsequent years, and subsequent taxes and assessments by any taxing authority for prior years due to change in land usage or ownership.

Or

Clause 5-8-45

Taxes for [**current year**], which Grantee assumes and agrees to pay, [and subsequent assessments for that and prior years due to change in land usage, ownership, or both, the payment of which Grantee assumes/but not subsequent assessments for that and prior years due to change in land usage, ownership, or both, the payment of which Grantor assumes].

Tax Lien—Federal

Clause 5-8-46

Federal tax lien against [**name**], recorded in [**recording data**] of the real property records of [**county**] County, Texas, in the amount of $[**amount**], plus penalty and interest.

Tax Lien—State

Clause 5-8-47

State tax lien against [**name**], recorded in [**recording data**] of the real property records of [**county**] County, Texas, in the amount of $[**amount**], plus penalty and interest.

Tenant Possession Rights

Clause 5-8-48

Rights of tenants in possession under unrecorded leases.

Tideland

Clause 5-8-49

Any titles or rights asserted by anyone, including but not limited to persons, the public, corporations, governments, or other entities, to (1) tidelands or lands comprising the shores or beds of navigable or perennial rivers and streams, lakes, bays, gulfs, or oceans, (2) lands beyond the line of the harbor or bulkhead lines as established or changed by any government, (3) filled-in lands or artificial islands, (4) water rights, including riparian rights, or (5) the area extending from the line of mean low tide to the line of vegetation or the right of access to that area or easement along and across that area.

Title Insurance Concurrent Exceptions

Clause 5-8-50

> Use the following clause to avoid warranty liability that is not covered by the owner policy of title insurance issued to the grantee.

Any law, ordinance, or governmental regulation (including but not limited to building and zoning laws, ordinances, or regulations) restricting, regulating, prohibiting, or relating to—

1. the occupancy, use, or enjoyment of the Property;

2. the character, dimensions, or location of any improvement now or hereafter erected on the Property;

3. a separation in ownership or a change in the dimensions or area of the Property or any parcel of which the Property is or was a part; or

4. environmental protection or the effect of any violation of these laws, ordinances, or governmental regulations, except to the extent that a notice of the enforcement thereof or a notice of a defect, lien, or encumbrance resulting from a violation or alleged violation affecting the Property has been recorded in the public records on or before this date.

Any governmental police power, except to the extent that a notice of the exercise thereof or a notice of defect, lien, or encumbrance resulting from a violation or alleged violation affecting the Property has been recorded in the public records on or before this date.

Rights of eminent domain unless notice of its exercise has been recorded in the public records on or before this date, but not excluding any taking that has occurred before this date that would be binding on the rights of a purchaser for value without knowledge.

The refusal of any person to purchase, lease, or lend money on the estate or property interest conveyed by this deed because of unmarketability of title.

Any claim that arises out of the transaction vesting in Grantee the estate or interest conveyed by this deed, by reason of the operation of federal bankruptcy, state insolvency, or other state or federal creditors' rights laws that is based on either (1) the transaction creating the estate or interest conveyed by this deed being deemed a fraudulent conveyance or fraudulent transfer or a voidable distribution or voidable dividend, (2) the subordination or recharacterization of the estate or interest conveyed by this deed as a result of the application of the doctrine of equitable subordination, or (3) the transaction creating the estate or property interest conveyed by this deed being deemed a preferential transfer.

Vendor's Lien and Deed of Trust

Clause 5-8-51

Vendor's lien and superior title retained in deed dated [**date**], executed by [**name**] to [**name**], recorded in [**recording data**] of the real property records of [**county**] County, Texas, securing the payment of a note of even date in the principal amount of $[**amount**], additionally secured by a deed of trust of even date to [**name**], trustee, recorded in [**recording data**] of the real property records of [**county**] County, Texas.

Form 5-9

Additional Clauses for Deeds

"As Is" Conveyance

Clause 5-9-1

GRANTEE IS TAKING THE PROPERTY IN AN ARM'S-LENGTH AGREEMENT BETWEEN THE PARTIES. THE CONSIDERATION WAS BARGAINED ON THE BASIS OF AN "AS IS, WHERE IS" TRANSACTION AND REFLECTS THE AGREEMENT OF THE PARTIES THAT THERE ARE NO REPRESENTATIONS OR EXPRESS OR IMPLIED WARRANTIES [**include if applicable:** , EXCEPT THOSE CONTAINED IN THE PURCHASE CONTRACT, THIS DEED, AND THE OTHER CLOSING DOCUMENTS]. GRANTEE HAS NOT RELIED ON ANY INFORMATION OTHER THAN GRANTEE'S INSPECTION [**include if applicable:** AND THE REPRESENTATIONS AND WARRANTIES EXPRESSLY CONTAINED IN THE PURCHASE CONTRACT, THIS DEED, AND THE OTHER CLOSING DOCUMENTS].

> Include the following if the grantor retains no liability for environmental matters after conveyance.

GRANTEE RELEASES GRANTOR FROM LIABILITY FOR ENVIRONMENTAL PROBLEMS AFFECTING THE PROPERTY, INCLUDING LIABILITY (1) UNDER THE COMPREHENSIVE ENVIRONMENTAL RESPONSE, COMPENSATION, AND LIABILITY ACT (CERCLA), THE RESOURCE CONSERVATION AND RECOVERY ACT (RCRA), THE TEXAS SOLID WASTE DISPOSAL ACT, AND THE TEXAS WATER CODE; OR (2) ARISING AS THE RESULT OF THEORIES OF PRODUCT

LIABILITY AND STRICT LIABILITY, OR UNDER NEW LAWS OR CHANGES TO EXISTING LAWS ENACTED AFTER THE EFFECTIVE DATE OF THE PURCHASE CONTRACT THAT WOULD OTHERWISE IMPOSE ON GRANTORS IN THIS TYPE OF TRANSACTION NEW LIABILITIES FOR ENVIRONMENTAL PROBLEMS AFFECTING THE PROPERTY. [**Include if applicable: THIS RELEASE APPLIES EVEN WHEN THE ENVIRONMENTAL PROBLEMS AFFECTING THE PROPERTY RESULT FROM GRANTOR'S OWN NEGLIGENCE OR THE NEGLIGENCE OF GRANTOR'S REPRESENTATIVE.**]

Assumption of Liability for VA-Guaranteed Loans

Clause 5-9-2

As part of the Consideration for this conveyance Grantee herein expressly assumes and agrees to pay the balance owing on the promissory note dated [**date**], in the original principal amount of $[**amount**], secured by and fully described in the deed of trust of the same date recorded in [**recording data**] of the real property records of [**county**] County, Texas. Grantee hereby agrees to assume all of the obligations of [**name of the veteran and spouse if applicable**] under the terms of the instruments creating that loan. Grantee further agrees to indemnify the Department of Veterans Affairs to the extent of any claim payment arising from the guaranty or insurance of the indebtedness created by such instruments. This agreement of assumption is evidenced by Grantee's acceptance of this deed.

Condominium Deed—Property Description

Clause 5-9-3

Unit [**identifying number**] [**include if applicable:** building [**building letter**]], [**name of condominium**], a condominium regime located in [**county**] County, Texas, according to the [**title of declaration**], including any amendments, plats, and plans, dated [**date**], recorded [**recording data for declaration, including any amendments, plats, and plans**] (collectively, the "Declaration"), together with the appurtenant common elements described in the Declaration.

Clause 5-9-4 ***reserved***

Correction Deed—New Document

Clause 5-9-5

> An instrument correcting a material error should comply with the requirements of Tex. Prop. Code § 5.029. The correction instrument can be a restatement of the deed titled "Correction Instrument," and the instrument must be executed by each party to the deed or, if applicable, the parties' heirs, successors, or assigns. The following paragraph should be included at the end of the restated text from the deed.

This deed is made as a correction deed in substitution of the deed titled "[**title of original deed**]" ("Corrected Deed") dated [**date**] and recorded in [**recording data**] of the real property records of [**county**] County, Texas, to correct the following incorrect information: [**state the incorrect information and the correction[s], e.g.,** the legal description incorrectly stated the acreage as "32 acres," when it should have stated the acreage as "23 acres"]. Other than the stated correction, this deed is intended to restate in all respects the Corrected Deed, and the effective date of this correction deed relates back to the effective date of the Corrected Deed.

Fee Simple Determinable

Clause 5-9-6

Include the following defined term.

Fee Simple Determinable Condition: [**State the condition that will prevent reversion, e.g.,** The Property will be used as a motel with between fifty and one hundred separate operating motel rooms for a minimum of five years from the date of conveyance. An affidavit stating that the condition has been fulfilled, filed during the first six months of the sixth year, if not contradicted by a recorded statement filed within the same six months, is conclusive evidence that the condition has been satisfied, and Grantee and third parties may rely on it.]

Clause 5-9-7

Include the following provision with the granting provision of the deed in place of the word "forever."

for as long as the Fee Simple Determinable Condition is satisfied, and if the Fee Simple Determinable Condition is not satisfied, the Property will automatically revert to and be owned by Grantor without the necessity of any further act on the part of Grantor, it being Grantor's intent to convey a fee simple determinable estate to Grantee.

For Use with Warranty Deed with Vendor's Lien

Clause 5-9-8

Use the following with clause 5-6-13 in this chapter if the payee is a third party.

[**Name of third party**], at Grantee's request, has paid in cash to Grantor that portion of the purchase price of the Property that is evidenced by the note. The first and superior vendor's lien against and superior title to the Property are retained for the benefit of [**name of third party**] and are transferred to [**name of third party**] without recourse against Grantor.

Clause 5-9-9

Use the following with clause 5-6-8.

[**Name of third party**], at Grantee's request, has paid in cash to Grantor that portion of the purchase price of the Property that is evidenced by the first-lien note. The first and superior vendor's lien against and superior title to the Property are retained for the benefit of [**name of third party**] and are transferred to [**name of third party**] without recourse on Grantor to secure the first-lien note. The second and inferior vendor's lien against and superior title to the Property are retained for the benefit of Grantor to secure the second-lien note. Grantor agrees that this second and inferior vendor's lien against and superior title to the Property are and will remain subordinate and inferior to all liens securing the first-lien note, regardless of the frequency or manner of renewal, extension, or alteration of any part of the first-lien note or the liens securing it.

Clause 5-9-10

Use the following with clause 5-6-1 if the second-lien note is payable to the grantor.

The second and inferior vendor's lien against and superior title to the Property are retained for the benefit of Grantor to secure both Grantee's assumption of the first-lien note and payment of the second-lien note to Grantor. Grantee's assumption of the first-lien note is also secured by a deed of trust to secure assumption of even date, from Grantee to [**name**], trustee. If Grantee defaults in payment of the assumed note or the second-lien note or in observance of any covenant or condition of any instrument securing their payment, Grantor will have the right to foreclose the vendor's lien reserved in this deed. Grantor assigns to Grantee all funds on deposit for payment of taxes and insurance premiums.

Clause 5-9-11

Use the following with clause 5-6-1 if the second-lien note is payable to a third party.

The first and superior vendor's lien against and superior title to the Property are retained in this deed for the benefit of the holders of the first-lien note and the second-lien note, to secure both Grantee's assumption of the first-lien note and payment of the second-lien note. Grantee's assumption of the first-lien note is also secured by a deed of trust to secure assumption of even date, from Grantee to [**name**], trustee. The inferior vendor's lien is transferred to [**name of third party**] without recourse on Grantor. If Grantee defaults in payment of the assumed note or the second-lien note or in observance of any covenant or condition of any instrument securing their payment, both Grantor and [**name of third party**] will have the independent right to foreclose the vendor's lien. However, as between the two parties holding the vendor's lien retained in this deed, the rights, title, and interest of [**name of third party**] are subordinate to the rights, title, and interest of Grantor. Cancellation of the assumed note and release of the liens securing it will release the liens securing the assumption, including the vendor's lien and deed of trust to secure assumption, without specific reference to them or the joinder of Grantor. Grantor assigns to Grantee all funds on deposit for payment of taxes and insurance premiums.

Personal Property

Clause 5-9-12

Include the following defined term.

Personal Property: The property constituting personal property located in or on and used in the enjoyment of the Property [**include if applicable:** , including the items identified on the attached Personal Property Schedule, incorporated in this deed by reference].

Clause 5-9-13

Include the following paragraph after the granting, habendum, and warranty clauses.

For the same Consideration, Grantor sells, transfers, and delivers the Personal Property to Grantee and warrants and agrees to defend title to the Personal Property to Grantee and Grantee's successors and assigns against all lawful claims. Title in the Personal Property passes at the time this deed is delivered.

Include the following if applicable.

THE PERSONAL PROPERTY TRANSFERRED TO GRANTEE IS SOLD, TRANSFERRED, AND DELIVERED "AS IS" AND "WITH ALL FAULTS"; FURTHER, GRANTOR EXCLUDES ALL WARRANTIES AND REPRESENTATIONS, EXPRESS OR IMPLIED, INCLUDING, WITHOUT LIMITATION, ANY WARRANTY OF MERCHANTABILITY OR FITNESS FOR A PARTICULAR PURPOSE.

Restrictive Covenants

Clause 5-9-14

Include the following defined terms.

Affected Property Owners: [**e.g.,** All the owners of land in the Ranchette Estates Subdivision, as shown by plat recorded in [**recording data**] of the real property records of [**county**] County, Texas.]

Restrictions: [**State enumerated restrictions.**]

Clause 5-9-15

> Include the following paragraph after the granting, habendum, and warranty clauses.

Grantor, as the fee simple owner of the Property, establishes the Restrictions as covenants, conditions, and restrictions, whether mandatory, prohibitive, permissive, or administrative, to regulate the structural integrity, appearance, and uses of the Property and the improvements placed on it. Grantor and Grantee stipulate that (1) the Restrictions touch and concern the Property; (2) privity of estate exists by reason of the ownership of the Property; (3) notice is given by filing this instrument in the real property records of the county in which the Property is situated; and (4) the Restrictions are reasonable, their purposes being for the common benefit of Grantor, Grantee, and the Affected Property Owners, who are affected by the structural integrity, appearance, and uses of the Property. The Restrictions run with the land making up the Property, are binding on Grantee and Grantee's successors and assigns forever, and inure to the benefit of Grantor, Grantee, Affected Property Owners, and their successors and assigns forever.

Separate Property

Clause 5-9-16

Grantor grants and conveys the Property to Grantee as separate property.

Strips and Gores

Clause 5-9-17

Grantor, for the same Consideration and subject to the Reservations from Conveyance and the Exceptions to Conveyance [**include if applicable:** and Warranty], grants, sells, and conveys to Grantee, without express or implied warranty, the strips or gores, if any, between the Property and abutting properties and land lying in or under any public thoroughfare, opened or proposed, abutting or adjacent to the Property, together with all and singular the rights and appurtenances thereto in any way belonging, to have and to hold it to Grantee and Grantee's heirs, successors, and assigns forever. All warranties that might arise by common law as well as the warranties in section 5.023 of the Texas Property Code (or its successor) are excluded as to the property conveyed by this paragraph.

Timber Deed—Property Description

Clause 5-9-18

Easement for the purpose of cutting and removing timber from the Property created by easement agreement dated [**date**], between [**name**] and [**name**], recorded in [**recording data**] of the real property records of [**county**] County, Texas.

Townhouse Deed

Clause 5-9-19

Include the following defined term.

Building Site:

Clause 5-9-20

> The common area is typically described as all lots in the subdivision, "SAVE AND EXCEPT the building sites within the lots." The following paragraph is an example of a legal description for a townhouse.

Building Site number [**identifying number**] in lot [**number**], block [**number**], [**subdivision name**], a subdivision recorded in volume [**number**], page [**number**], Map Records, [**county**] County, Texas, together with the easements, undivided interest in common area, and other rights, title, and interest that are appurtenant to ownership of the townhouse Property under the terms of the [**describe declaration**], as amended from time to time [**include if applicable:** , and the plat of the subdivision].

Clause 5-9-21

> Include the following with the exceptions section of the deed.

1. The rights of other townhouse owners within the common building of which this townhouse is a part, including reasonable rights of access for maintenance and repair in and to all structural elements that comprise any part of the overall structural unit of the building and all utility lines and facilities that comprise any part of the utility service to the entire building.

2. The rights given to, and obligations imposed on, each Building Site owner under the terms of the [**describe declaration**], as amended from time to time, such as assessments for maintenance of the common area secured by an inchoate lien against the townhouses, all of which are covenants running with the land and binding on any townhouse owner.

Transfer of Escrow and Insurance Policy

Clause 5-9-22

Include the following to incorporate the transfer of escrow in the deed.

Grantor assigns to Grantee all funds held in escrow for payment of taxes and insurance premiums. If the casualty insurance policy is to be assigned to Grantee, the transfer will be handled by separate instrument.

Vendor's Lien and Deed of Trust to Secure Assumption

Clause 5-9-23

Use the following with clause 5-6-2.

The first and superior vendor's lien against and superior title to the Property are retained in this deed to secure Grantee's assumption of the note. Grantee's assumption of the note is also secured by a deed of trust to secure assumption of even date, from Grantee to [**name**], trustee. If default occurs in payment of the assumed note or in observance of any covenant or condition of any instrument securing the assumed note, Grantor and the holder of the assumed note each have the independent right to foreclose the vendor's lien. However, as between the two holders of the vendor's lien, Grantor's rights, title, and interest are subordinate to the rights, title, and interest of the holder of the assumed note. Cancellation of the assumed note and release of the liens securing it will release the liens securing the assumption, including the vendor's lien and deed of trust to secure assumption, without specific reference to them or the joinder of Grantor.

Waiver of Implied Liens

Clause 5-9-24

Grantor has been paid in full for [**describe property, e.g.,** Parcel One], and any lien, expressed or implied, in favor of Grantor against [**describe property, e.g.,** Parcel One] is waived. Grantor's liens are against [**describe property, e.g.,** Parcel Two] only.

Or

Clause 5-9-25

Grantor waives any expressed or implied lien on [**describe property, e.g.,** Parcel One] arising by reason of Grantee's assumption of the note in the original principal amount of [**amount**] DOLLARS ($[**amount**]).

Wraparound Lien [Deed Subject to]

Clause 5-9-26

Use the following with clauses 5-6-14 and 5-8-51.

This conveyance is made subject to the prior lien ("Underlying Lien") of a deed of trust recorded in [**recording data**] of the real property records of [**county**] County, Texas, to [**name**], trustee, which secures payment of a promissory note ("Underlying Lien Debt") in the principal amount of [**amount**] DOLLARS ($[**amount**]). Grantee in this deed does not assume payment of that Underlying Lien Debt. As further consideration Grantor promises to keep and perform all the covenants and obligations of the grantor named in the Underlying Lien deed of trust and to indemnify, defend, and hold Grantee harmless against any damages caused by Grantor's breach of its obligations under the

Underlying Lien Debt and related documents, as long as Grantee is not in default on the Wraparound Lien Debt and documents relating to it.

Covenant of Seisin

Clause 5-9-27

Grantor warrants that Grantor is lawfully seized of good and indefeasible title to the Property and has the right to convey title to the Property subject to any Reservations or Exceptions from Conveyance contained herein.

Form 5-10

Grantee's Acceptance of Deed

[Name], Grantee, accepts the attached deed and consents to its form and substance. Grantee acknowledges that the terms of the deed conform with Grantee's intent and that they will control in the event of any conflict with the contract Grantee signed regarding the Property described in the deed.

Include the following for an assumption transaction.

Grantee agrees to the obligations imposed on Grantee by the terms of the deed.

Continue with the following.

____
[Name of grantee]
Date:

Form 5-11

The owelty lien created in this form is against the entire property, including the share owned by the grantee before the partition.

Owelty of Partition Deed

Notice of confidentiality rights: If you are a natural person, you may remove or strike any or all of the following information from any instrument that transfers an interest in real property before it is filed for record in the public records: your Social Security number or your driver's license number.

Date:

Grantor:

Grantor's Mailing Address:

Grantee:

Grantee's Mailing Address:

Consideration: [Cash and a/A] note of even date executed by Grantee and payable to the order of [**name of third party or grantor**] in the principal amount of [**amount**] DOLLARS ($[**amount**]). The note is secured by a first and superior vendor's lien, an owelty lien, and superior title retained in this deed in favor of [**name of third party or grantor**] and by a first-lien deed of trust of even date from Grantee to [**name**], trustee.

Property (including any improvements): [**Describe the entire property being partitioned.**]

Property Portion Conveyed (including any improvements): [**Describe the property being conveyed by this deed.**]

Reservations from Conveyance:

> State "None" or, to create reservations of title, include the appropriate clauses from form 5-7 in this chapter.

Exceptions to Conveyance and Warranty:

> State "None" or, to create exceptions to conveyance and warranty, include the appropriate clauses from form 5-8.

Grantor, for the Consideration and subject to the Reservations from Conveyance and the Exceptions to Conveyance and Warranty, grants, sells, and conveys to Grantee the Property, together with all and singular the rights and appurtenances thereto in any way belonging, to have and to hold it to Grantee and Grantee's heirs, successors, and assigns forever. Grantor binds Grantor and Grantor's heirs and successors to warrant and forever defend all and singular the Property to Grantee and Grantee's heirs, successors, and assigns against every person whomsoever lawfully claiming or to claim the same or any part thereof, except as to the Reservations from Conveyance and the Exceptions to Conveyance and Warranty.

The vendor's lien and owelty lien against, and superior title to, the Property are retained until the note described is fully paid according to its terms, at which time this deed becomes absolute.

> Include the following if applicable.

[**Name of third party**], at Grantee's request, has paid in cash to Grantor that portion of the purchase price of the Property Portion Conveyed that is evidenced by the note described. The vendor's lien, owelty lien, and superior title to the Property are retained for the benefit of, and are transferred to, [**name of third party**] without recourse on Grantor.

Continue with the following.

Owelty Recitals

For transactions as a consequence of divorce, choose the first alternative paragraph below. For transactions based on a separate agreement between the parties, choose the second alternative paragraph.

First. A divorce was granted terminating the marriage between Grantor and Grantee by divorce decree dated [**date**], rendered in Cause No. [**number**] in the [**designation**] Court of [**county**] County, Texas. An order partitioning the Property was entered [**date**] in the same cause and Court.

Or

First. Grantor and Grantee have agreed to the transfer of ownership and owelty of partition effected by this deed by separate Owelty of Partition Agreement dated [**date**], between Grantor and Grantee, as cotenants of the Property.

Continue with the following.

Second. Grantor and Grantee, owning the Property as tenants in common, desire to effect a partition of the Property in order that Grantee own 100 percent of the Property in fee simple. [**Include if applicable:** Grantee has arranged to borrow the amount of $[**amount**] from [**name of lender**] ("Lender"), in order to acquire the Property Portion Conveyed in fee simple. Lender is willing to advance that amount provided that the indebtedness is secured by a first and superior vendor's lien, owelty lien, superior title, and a deed-of-trust lien, all on the full fee simple title in and to 100 percent of the Property.]

Third. The Property is not susceptible to partition in kind and, for Grantee to acquire the full fee simple title in and to the Property Portion Conveyed, it is necessary to fix a lien on the entirety of the Property in the amount of $[**amount**]. The lien represents an owelty of partition and the necessary adjustment between the parties to carry out the purposes of the partition. Grantee acknowledges that the vendor's lien, owelty lien or owelty of partition, and superior title are superior to Grantee's rights to use and occupy the Property as Grantee's homestead or otherwise as fully and completely as if the liens or owelty of partition were fixed and judicially decreed in a partition suit between Grantor and Grantee.

Grantee joins in the execution of this deed and binds Grantee's heirs, successors, and assigns in acceptance of the delivery of the deed. Grantee stipulates to [Grantor and Grantor's/ Lender and Grantor and each of their respective] heirs, successors, and assigns the following: (1) the truth and correctness of the Recitals and the validity of the vendor's lien, owelty lien, superior title, and deed-of-trust lien securing the payment of the indebtedness, on the entirety of the full fee simple title to the Property; (2) the vendor's lien, owelty lien, superior title, and deed-of-trust lien are prior and superior to any right of use, occupancy, and homestead that Grantee may have or claim in and to the Property; [and] (3) the whole fee simple title to the Property is vested in Grantee under this deed [**include if applicable:** ; and (4) Lender has advanced funds to Grantee in reliance on the stipulations and representations made and the facts stated in this deed].

____
[Name of grantor]

____
[Name of grantee]

Include acknowledgments.

Form 5-12

This form may be used with the owelty of partition deed in fixing a lien on homestead property if appropriate under Tex. Prop. Code § 41.001(b)(4).

Owelty of Partition Agreement

Date:

Selling Cotenant: [**include address**]

Purchasing Cotenant: [**include address**]

Property:

Consideration: Cash and the mutual covenants and agreements between the parties, the receipt and sufficiency of which are acknowledged and stipulated.

Selling Cotenant and Purchasing Cotenant are the owners, as tenants in common, of the Property. By this agreement, Selling Cotenant and Purchasing Cotenant (collectively, the "Parties") evidence an owelty of partition by written agreement, including the creation of a debt of the Purchasing Cotenant in favor of the Selling Cotenant [**include if applicable:** as the result of the division or award of a family homestead in a divorce proceeding].

The Parties stipulate that the Property is not susceptible to partition in kind and, for Purchasing Cotenant to acquire the full fee simple title in the Property, it is necessary to fix a lien on the entirety of the Property in the amount of $[**amount**].

To effectuate this agreement, Selling Cotenant will execute an owelty of partition deed to Purchasing Cotenant in which a vendor's lien and owelty lien in the above amount are reserved, and Purchasing Cotenant will execute a promissory note in the above amount secured by a vendor's lien, superior title, an owelty lien, and a deed-of-trust lien describing the entirety of the Property.

____

[Name of selling cotenant]

____

[Name of purchasing cotenant]

Include acknowledgments.

Form 5-13

Deed in Lieu of Foreclosure

Notice of confidentiality rights: If you are a natural person, you may remove or strike any or all of the following information from any instrument that transfers an interest in real property before it is filed for record in the public records: your Social Security number or your driver's license number.

Date:

Grantor:

Grantor's Mailing Address:

Grantee:

Grantee's Mailing Address:

Note:

Deed of Trust:

Consideration: **[amount]** DOLLARS ($**[amount]**), the receipt and sufficiency of which are hereby acknowledged, and further the release of Grantor from all liability for the indebtedness and obligations under the Note and Deed of Trust, except that no release is given of any liens or warranties of title and further except that the indebtedness under the Note is not canceled or extinguished.

Property (including any improvements):

Exceptions to Conveyance and Warranty: The liens described in this deed and the exceptions to conveyance and warranty in the Deed of Trust.

Grantor, for the Consideration and subject to the Exceptions to Conveyance and Warranty, grants, sells, and conveys to Grantee the Property, together with all and singular the rights and appurtenances thereto in any way belonging, to have and to hold it to Grantee and Grantee's heirs, successors, and assigns forever. Grantor binds Grantor and Grantor's heirs and successors to warrant and forever defend all and singular the Property to Grantee and Grantee's heirs, successors, and assigns against every person whomsoever lawfully claiming or to claim the same or any part thereof, except as to the Exceptions to Conveyance and Warranty.

Conveyance in Lieu of Foreclosure

This deed and the conveyances being made are executed, delivered, and accepted in lieu of foreclosure and will be interpreted and construed the same as a foreclosure of the liens and as an absolute conveyance to Grantee of all right, title, and interest in and to the Property, including specifically but without limitation any equity or rights of redemption of Grantor in or to the Property.

Continuing Nature of Lien

Notwithstanding the release of Grantor from all liability for the indebtedness and obligations under the Note and Deed of Trust, the indebtedness has not been canceled or extinguished and the Property continues to be subject to the performance of the obligations under the Deed of Trust. The Deed of Trust lien is not released or relinquished in any manner, and the indebtedness, obligations, and lien will remain valid and continuous and in full force and effect, unless and until the indebtedness, obligations, and liens are expressly released by written instrument executed and delivered by the holder thereof, at the holder's sole discretion.

Nonmerger

Neither Grantor nor Grantee intend that there be, and there will never be, a merger of the Deed of Trust lien with the fee simple title or any other interest of Grantee in the Property by virtue of this conveyance, and the parties expressly provide that any interest in the Deed of Trust lien and fee simple title will be and remain at all times separate and distinct.

____
[Name of grantor]

____
[Name of grantee]

Include acknowledgments.

Form 5-14

[Administration/Guardianship] Deed

Notice of confidentiality rights: If you are a natural person, you may remove or strike any or all of the following information from any instrument that transfers an interest in real property before it is filed for record in the public records: your Social Security number or your driver's license number.

Date:

Grantor: The estate of [**name of deceased or ward**], [deceased/an incapacitated person].

Grantor's Mailing Address:

Grantee:

Grantee's Mailing Address:

Consideration:

Property (including any improvements):

> If the conveyance includes personal property, include the defined term from clause 5-9-12 in this chapter.

Reservations from Conveyance:

> State "None" or, to create reservations of title, include the appropriate clauses from form 5-7.

Exceptions to Conveyance and Warranty:

> State "None" or, to create exceptions to conveyance and warranty, include the appropriate clauses from form 5-8.

By an order of the [**designation**] Court of [**county**] County, Texas, made on [**date**], directing the sale of the Property belonging to Grantor, which estate was then and is now pending in that court, I, [**name**], [executor/guardian] of the estate of [**name of deceased or**

ward], [deceased/an incapacitated person], sold on [**date**], by private sale in [**city**], [**county**] County, Texas, the Property to Grantee for the Consideration.

The report of the sale was filed on [**date**] and made to the Court, and the sale was confirmed by the decree of the Court by its Order Confirming Sale of Real Property, which is attached and incorporated herein by reference as Exhibit A.

Grantor, for the Consideration and subject to the Reservations from Conveyance and the Exceptions to Conveyance and Warranty, grants, sells, and conveys to Grantee the Property, together with all and singular the rights and appurtenances thereto in any way belonging, to have and to hold it to Grantee and Grantee's heirs, successors, and assigns forever. Grantor binds Grantor and Grantor's heirs and successors to warrant and forever defend all and singular the Property to Grantee and Grantee's heirs, successors, and assigns against every person whomsoever lawfully claiming or to claim the same or any part thereof, except as to the Reservations from Conveyance and the Exceptions to Conveyance and Warranty.

> If the conveyance includes personal property, include clause 5-9-13.

> If appropriate, include additional clauses like those suggested in form 5-9.

When the context requires, singular nouns and pronouns include the plural.

____

[**Name of grantor**]

> If the deed imposes contractual obligations on the grantee, include the following signature line.

____

[**Name of grantee**]

> Include acknowledgments.

Form 5-15

Blanket Bill of Sale

Date:

Seller:

Seller's Mailing Address:

Buyer:

Buyer's Mailing Address:

Real Property (including improvements):

Transferred Properties:

All items of personal property, both tangible and intangible (excluding cash), affixed or attached to, or placed or situated on, or used or acquired in any way whatever in connection with the completion and comfortable use, enjoyment, occupancy, or operation of the Real Property, including, without limitation, the following:

1. All equipment, furniture, building supplies, appliances, and fixtures owned by Seller and located in or on or used in connection with the Real Property or the operations thereon.

2. All of Seller's interest in all use, occupancy, building, and operating permits, if any, and all licenses and approvals issued from time to time with respect to the Real Property or the Transferred Properties.

3. All of Seller's interest in all management, maintenance, service, supply, employment, and vending machine contracts, if any, relating to the Real Property or the Transferred Properties.

4. All of Seller's interest in and to all existing and assignable guarantees and warranties, express or implied, if any, issued in connection with the construction, alteration, and repair of the Real Property and the purchase, installation, and repair of the Transferred Properties, to the extent that such guarantees and warranties are known to and in the possession of Seller.

5. All rights Seller may have to use the trade name, or any similar name, it being understood that Seller covenants not to use the name.

6. All rights Seller may have, if any, to any trademarks, promotional material, tenant data, telephone numbers and listings, post office boxes, all master keys and keys to common areas, all goodwill, if any, and all other rights, privileges, and appurtenances owned by Seller and in any way related to or used in connection with the existing business operation of the Real Property.

7. All funds or reserve accounts deposited with any lienholder of the Real Property as an escrow fund or impound for the payment of taxes, assessments, and premiums for insurance pertaining to the Real Property.

8. All of Seller's right, title, and interest in and to the hazard insurance policy carried by Seller on the Transferred Properties.

Include the following if applicable.

9. All items identified on the itemized properties schedule attached and incorporated herein by reference as Exhibit [**exhibit number/letter**].

Continue with the following.

Exceptions to Transfer and Warranty:

[The Existing Lien and those/Those] exceptions contained in the warranty deed of even date conveying the Real Property from Seller to Buyer.

Trade Name:

Excluded Properties:

Consideration:

[Existing Lien:]

Seller is conveying the Real Property to Buyer by warranty deed. As part of this transaction, Seller desires to transfer all the Transferred Properties to Buyer.

For the Consideration, Seller transfers to Buyer the Transferred Properties, save and except the Excluded Properties, and subject to the Exceptions to Transfer and Warranty.

As a material part of the Consideration for this sale, Seller and Buyer agree that Buyer is taking the Transferred Properties "AS IS" and that there are no representations, disclosures, or express or implied warranties except those contained in the purchase contract and this bill of sale. Buyer has not relied on any information other than Buyer's inspection and the representations and warranties expressly contained in the purchase contract and this bill of sale.

To have and to hold the Transferred Properties to Buyer and Buyer's heirs, successors, and assigns forever. Seller binds Seller and Seller's heirs and successors to warrant and forever defend all and singular the Transferred Properties to Buyer and Buyer's heirs, successors, and assigns against every person whomsoever lawfully claiming or to claim the same or any part thereof when the claim is by, through, or under Seller but not otherwise, subject to the Exceptions to Transfer and Warranty.

Seller appoints Buyer and Buyer's heirs, successors, and assigns as Seller's agent and attorney-in-fact to act for Seller in any lawful way in the exercise of the claims and litigation powers described in section 752.110 of the Texas Estates Code, or its successor, as amended, with respect to the Transferred Properties or the properties intended to be transferred by this bill of sale. This is a special power coupled with an interest and is irrevocable.

Seller agrees to execute and deliver any additional documents and to perform any additional acts reasonably necessary or appropriate to carry out the intent of this bill of sale in transferring the Transferred Properties to Buyer.

When the context requires, singular nouns and pronouns include the plural.

____
[Name of seller]

____
[Name of buyer]

Include acknowledgments. If applicable, attach the properties schedule as an exhibit.

Form 5-16

Bill of Sale

Date:

Seller:

Seller's Mailing Address:

Buyer:

Buyer's Mailing Address:

Consideration:

Transferred Properties:

Reservations from Transfer:

Exceptions to Transfer and Warranty:

Seller, for the Consideration and subject to the Reservations from Transfer and the Exceptions to Transfer and Warranty, sells, transfers, and delivers the Transferred Properties to Buyer, together with all and singular the rights and appurtenances thereto in any way belonging, to have and to hold it to Buyer and Buyer's heirs, successors, and assigns forever. Seller binds Seller and Seller's heirs and successors to warrant and forever defend all and singular the Transferred Properties to Buyer and Buyer's heirs, successors, and assigns against every person whomsoever lawfully claiming or to claim the same or any part thereof when the claim is by, through, or under Seller but not otherwise, except as to the Reservations from Transfer and the Exceptions to Transfer and Warranty.

As a material part of the Consideration for this sale, Seller and Buyer agree that Buyer is taking the Transferred Properties "AS IS" and that there are no representations, disclosures, or express or implied warranties except those contained in the purchase contract and this bill of sale. Buyer has not relied on any information other than Buyer's inspection and the representations and warranties expressly contained in the purchase contract and this bill of sale.

When the context requires, singular nouns and pronouns include the plural.

____
[Name of seller]

____
[Name of buyer]

Include acknowledgments.

Form 5-17

Transfer of Escrow Funds [and Hazard Insurance Policy]

Date:

Loan: Loan Number [**number**] held by [**name**] ("Lender"), under Seller's name as the current debtor.

Seller:

Seller's Mailing Address:

Buyer:

Buyer's Mailing Address:

For the sale consideration, Seller assigns and transfers to Buyer all the accumulated escrow deposits made under the provisions of the deed of trust securing the Loan [**include if applicable:** along with all of Seller's interest in and to the existing hazard insurance policy covering the improvements located on the real property securing the Loan. Seller authorizes and directs Lender and the hazard insurer to endorse and transfer the existing policy from Seller to Buyer].

____

[**Name of seller**]

Form 5-18

A joint tenancy may be created by written agreement of property owners in compliance with statutory requirements. *See* Tex. Est. Code § 111.001. This agreement may be used to evidence a joint tenancy with right of survivorship. Caution: This form should not be used between spouses regarding community property. See form 5-19 in this chapter.

Survivorship Agreement

Notice of confidentiality rights: If you are a natural person, you may remove or strike any or all of the following information from any instrument that transfers an interest in real property before it is filed for record in the public records: your Social Security number or your driver's license number.

Date:

Owners:

Property:

Owners own the Property jointly and for valuable consideration agree with each other as follows:

1. If no severance occurs before the death of [either/any] Owner, then on the death of [either/any] Owner, the interest of the joint Owner who dies will survive to the surviving joint Owner[s].

2. Owners will after this date own the Property in the same manner as joint tenants with right of survivorship.

3. This agreement may be revoked, and the joint tenancy of Owners in the Property may be severed, only by a written instrument signed by all Owners.

4. This agreement is binding on Owners and Owners' respective heirs and successors.

____
[Name of owner]

____
[Name of owner]

Include acknowledgments.

Form 5-19

This form is used to create a right of survivorship in community property as provided for by Tex. Est. Code §§ 112.051–.054. See section 2.46 in this manual. When using this form, the attorney should review any wills or other estate planning instruments to avoid unintentional effects on the family's estate plan.

Survivorship Agreement for Community Property

Notice of confidentiality rights: If you are a natural person, you may remove or strike any or all of the following information from any instrument that transfers an interest in real property before it is filed for record in the public records: your Social Security number or your driver's license number.

Date:

Spouses:

Property:

Spouses own the Property jointly and for valuable consideration agree with each other as follows:

1. As long as the Property remains community property, on the death of either Spouse, the Property interest of the Spouse who dies will become the Property of the surviving Spouse and will not descend to or be vested in the heirs or devisees of the deceased Spouse.

2. Spouses will after this date own the Property in the same manner as joint tenants with right of survivorship.

3. This agreement may be revoked, and the joint tenancy of the Spouses may be severed, only by a written instrument signed by both Spouses [**include if applicable:** or by a written instrument signed by one Spouse and delivered to the other Spouse].

____
[Name of spouse A]

____
[Name of spouse B]

Include acknowledgments.

Form 5-20

Note that an agreement to convert separate property to community property is enforceable without consideration. Tex. Fam. Code § 4.203.

Community Interest Special Warranty Deed

Notice of confidentiality rights: If you are a natural person, you may remove or strike any or all of the following information from any instrument that transfers an interest in real property before it is filed for record in the public records: your Social Security number or your driver's license number.

Date:

Grantor: [**name exactly as shown on prior deed**]

Grantor's Mailing Address:

Grantee: [**names of grantor and grantor's spouse**], a married couple

Grantee's Mailing Address:

Consideration:

> See form 5-6 in this chapter for consideration clauses.

Property (including any improvements):

> If the conveyance includes personal property, include the defined term from clause 5-9-12.

Exceptions to Conveyance and Warranty:

> State "None" or, to create exceptions to conveyance and warranty, include the appropriate clauses from form 5-8.

> The following statements or substantially similar words must be prominently displayed in bold-faced type, capital letters, or underlined.

THIS INSTRUMENT CHANGES SEPARATE PROPERTY TO COMMUNITY PROPERTY. THIS MAY HAVE ADVERSE CONSEQUENCES DURING MARRIAGE AND ON TERMINATION OF THE MARRIAGE BY DEATH OR DIVORCE. FOR EXAMPLE:

EXPOSURE TO CREDITORS. IF YOU SIGN THIS AGREEMENT, ALL OR PART OF THE SEPARATE PROPERTY BEING CONVERTED TO COMMUNITY PROPERTY MAY BECOME SUBJECT TO THE LIABILITIES OF YOUR SPOUSE. IF YOU DO NOT SIGN THIS AGREEMENT, YOUR SEPARATE PROPERTY IS GENERALLY NOT SUBJECT TO THE LIABILITIES OF YOUR SPOUSE UNLESS YOU ARE PERSONALLY LIABLE UNDER ANOTHER RULE OF LAW.

LOSS OF MANAGEMENT RIGHTS. IF YOU SIGN THIS AGREEMENT, ALL OR PART OF THE SEPARATE PROPERTY BEING CONVERTED TO COMMUNITY PROPERTY MAY BECOME SUBJECT TO EITHER THE JOINT MANAGEMENT, CONTROL, AND DISPOSITION OF YOU AND YOUR SPOUSE OR THE SOLE MANAGEMENT, CONTROL, AND DISPOSITION OF YOUR SPOUSE ALONE. IN THAT EVENT, YOU WILL LOSE YOUR MANAGEMENT RIGHTS OVER THE PROPERTY. IF YOU DO NOT SIGN THIS AGREEMENT, YOU WILL GENERALLY RETAIN THOSE RIGHTS.

LOSS OF PROPERTY OWNERSHIP. IF YOU SIGN THIS AGREEMENT AND YOUR MARRIAGE IS SUBSEQUENTLY TERMINATED BY THE DEATH OF EITHER SPOUSE OR BY DIVORCE, ALL OR PART OF THE SEPARATE PROPERTY BEING CONVERTED TO COMMUNITY PROPERTY MAY BECOME THE SOLE PROPERTY OF YOUR SPOUSE OR YOUR SPOUSE'S HEIRS. IF YOU DO NOT SIGN THIS AGREEMENT, YOU GENERALLY CANNOT BE DEPRIVED OF OWNERSHIP OF YOUR SEPARATE PROPERTY ON TERMINATION OF YOUR MARRIAGE, WHETHER BY DEATH OR DIVORCE.

Grantor, for the Consideration [**include if applicable:** and subject to the Exceptions to Conveyance and Warranty], grants, sells, and conveys to Grantee the Property, together with all and singular the rights and appurtenances thereto in any way belonging, with the intent that the Property be converted to community property, to have and to hold it to Grantee and Grantee's heirs, executors, administrators, and assigns against every person whomsoever lawfully claiming or to claim the same or any part thereof, by, through, or under Grantor, but not otherwise.

When the context requires, singular nouns and pronouns include the plural.

____

[Name of grantor]

This deed must include signature lines for both spouses.

____

[Name of grantee]

____

[Name of grantee]

Include acknowledgments.

Form 5-21

Assignment and Assumption of Leases

Date:

Assignor:

Assignor's Mailing Address:

Assignee:

Assignee's Mailing Address:

Property (including any improvements):

Leases: All agreements under which any portion of the Property is used or occupied by anyone, other than Assignor, including those described as follows: [**describe leases or reference attached rent roll**].

Assumed Leases: The Leases described as follows: [**describe assumed leases or reference attached exhibit**].

Consideration:

Assignor is conveying the Property to Assignee by warranty deed dated this date.

Assignor, for the Consideration and subject to the Reservations from Conveyance and the Exceptions to Conveyance and Warranty in the warranty deed, to the extent they affect the Leases, assigns to Assignee all of Assignor's right, title, and interest in and to the Leases. Assignor binds Assignor and Assignor's heirs and successors to warrant and forever defend all and singular the Leases to Assignee and Assignee's heirs, successors, and assigns against every person whomsoever lawfully claiming or to claim the same or any part thereof [**include**

if applicable: when the claim is by, through, or under Assignor but not otherwise], except as to the Reservations from Conveyance and the Exceptions to Conveyance and Warranty in the warranty deed, to the extent they affect the Leases.

Assignee assumes and agrees to perform the landlord's obligations under the Assumed Leases arising after this date. The obligation to repay security and prepaid rental deposits to tenants under the Assumed Leases is limited to the amount of cash delivered or credited by Assignor to Assignee with respect to security and prepaid rental deposits. Assignee will indemnify, defend, and hold Assignor harmless from any loss, attorney's fees, expenses, or claims arising out of or related to Assignee's failure to perform any of the obligations of the landlord under the Assumed Leases after this date.

Assignor will indemnify, defend, and hold Assignee harmless from any loss, attorney's fees, expenses, or claims arising out of or related to Assignor's failure to perform any of the obligations of the landlord under the Leases before this date.

When the context requires, singular nouns and pronouns include the plural.

____
[**Name of assignor**]

____
[**Name of assignee**]

Include acknowledgments. Attach exhibits.

Form 5-22

This form is to be used to notify a residential or commercial tenant that its security deposit has been transferred to a new owner in connection with a sale of the property, thereby releasing the former owner from liability to the tenant for the security deposit. *See* Tex. Prop. Code §§ 92.105, 93.007.

Notice of Transfer of Security Deposit

Date:

Lease

Date:

Former Landlord:

Tenant:

Tenant's Address:

Premises:

Security Deposit: $[**amount**]

New Landlord:

New Landlord's Address:

Former Landlord sold the [Premises/the property in which the Premises are located] to New Landlord and assigned the Lease to New Landlord. Former Landlord also transferred or credited the Security Deposit to New Landlord. New Landlord has received the Security Deposit or a credit for the amount of the Security Deposit and is liable for the return of the Security Deposit.

Include the following if applicable.

All rent and other amounts payable by Tenant under the Lease after Tenant's receipt of this letter should be paid to or for the account of New Landlord at New Landlord's Address.

Continue with the following.

____
[Name of new landlord]

____
[Name of former landlord]

Form 5-23

Partition Deed

Notice of confidentiality rights: If you are a natural person, you may remove or strike any or all of the following information from any instrument that transfers an interest in real property before it is filed for record in the public records: your Social Security number or your driver's license number.

Date:

First Party:

First Party's Mailing Address:

Second Party:

Second Party's Mailing Address:

Consideration: The partition effected hereby.

Partition of Share Number One

Share Number One Property (including any improvements):

> If the conveyance includes personal property, include the defined term from clause 5-9-12 in this chapter.

Reservations from Share Number One Conveyance:

> State "None" or, to create reservations of title, include the appropriate clauses from form 5-7.

Exceptions to Share Number One Conveyance and Warranty:

> State "None" or, to create exceptions to conveyance and warranty, include the appropriate clauses from form 5-8.

First Party shall have and possess in severalty the Share Number One Property, and Second Party, for the Consideration and subject to the Reservations from Share Number One Conveyance and the Exceptions to Share Number One Conveyance and Warranty, grants and conveys to First Party the Share Number One Property, together with all and singular the rights and appurtenances thereto in any way belonging, to have and to hold it to First Party and First Party's heirs, successors, and assigns forever. Second Party binds Second Party and Second Party's heirs and successors to warrant and forever defend all and singular the Share Number One Property to First Party and First Party's heirs, successors, and assigns against every person whomsoever lawfully claiming or to claim the same or any part thereof, except as to the Reservations from Share Number One Conveyance and the Exceptions to Share Number One Conveyance and Warranty.

Select one of the following.

First Party releases Second Party from any claim or lien for owelty.

Or

Inequality in the value of the shares partitioned hereby is being equalized by adjustment in the division of cash or other property from the estate of [**name**], deceased, in accordance with an agreement between First Party and Second Party; accordingly no lien on any of the property partitioned hereby arises.

Continue with the following.

Partition of Share Number Two

Share Number Two Property (including any improvements):

If the conveyance includes personal property, include the defined term from clause 5-9-12.

Reservations from Share Number Two Conveyance:

State "None" or, to create reservations of title, include the appropriate clauses from form 5-7.

Exceptions to Share Number Two Conveyance and Warranty:

State "None" or, to create exceptions to conveyance and warranty, include the appropriate clauses from form 5-8.

Second Party shall have and possess in severalty the Share Number Two Property, and First Party, for the Consideration and subject to the Reservations from Share Number Two Conveyance and the Exceptions to Share Number Two Conveyance and Warranty, grants and conveys to Second Party the Share Number Two Property, together with all and singular the rights and appurtenances thereto in any way belonging, to have and to hold it to Second Party and Second Party's heirs, successors, and assigns forever. First Party binds First Party and First Party's heirs and successors to warrant and forever defend all and singular the Share Number Two Property to Second Party and Second Party's heirs, successors, and assigns against every person whomsoever lawfully claiming or to claim the same or any part thereof, except as to the Reservations from Share Number Two Conveyance and the Exceptions to Share Number Two Conveyance and Warranty.

Select one of the following.

Second Party releases First Party from any claim or lien for owelty.

Or

Inequality in the value of the shares partitioned hereby is being equalized by adjustment in the division of cash or other property from the estate of [**name**], deceased, in accordance with an agreement between First Party and Second Party; accordingly no lien on any of the property partitioned hereby arises.

Continue with the following.

When the context requires, singular nouns and pronouns include the plural.

____
[Name of first party]

____
[Name of second party]

Include acknowledgments.

Form 5-24

Correction Instrument
[Nonmaterial Correction]

Notice of confidentiality rights: If you are a natural person, you may remove or strike any or all of the following information from any instrument that transfers an interest in real property before it is filed for record in the public records: your Social Security number or your driver's license number.

Date:

Person Executing Correction Instrument:

Mailing Address of Person Executing Correction Instrument:

Conveyance Being Corrected

Date:

Grantor:

Grantee:

Recording information:

Error Being Corrected:

Correction:

Facts Relevant to the Correction:

Basis for Personal Knowledge of Facts Relevant to the Correction:

Person Executing Correction Instrument changes the Conveyance by this Correction Instrument.

Person Executing Correction Instrument has personal knowledge of the Facts Relevant to the Correction.

I certify that I have given notice of this Correction Instrument to each party to the original instrument in accordance with provisions of section 5.028(d)(2) of the Texas Property Code.

Attach copies of transmittal letters and proof of mailing, copies of emails, or copies of other reasonable means of giving notice.

____

[Name]

Include acknowledgments.

Form 5-25

The Texas Real Property Transfer on Death Act authorizes an individual to transfer the individual's interest in real property to one or more beneficiaries effective at the transferor's death by a transfer on death deed. Tex. Est. Code § 114.051. To be effective, a transfer on death deed must be recorded before the transferor's death. Tex. Est. Code § 114.055. In the 86th legislative session, the statutory forms for the transfer on death deed and the revocation of transfer on death deed were removed from chapter 114 of the Texas Estates Code. Acts 2019, 86th Leg., R.S., ch. 337, § 3.2 (S.B. 874), eff. Sept. 1, 2019. Tex. Gov't Code § 22.020 directs the Texas Supreme Court to promulgate forms for creating and revoking a transfer on death deed. At the time of this publication, the forms are not yet complete. The Estates Code continues to authorize use of transfer on death deeds and revocation of transfer on death deeds but no longer prescribes statutory language.

Revocable Transfer on Death Deed

Notice of confidentiality rights: If you are a natural person, you may remove or strike any or all of the following information from any instrument that transfers an interest in real property before it is filed for record in the public records: your Social Security number or your driver's license number.

Date:

Transferor:

Transferor's Mailing Address:

Designated Beneficiary

Primary Beneficiary:

Primary Beneficiary's Mailing Address:

Include the following if applicable.

Designated Alternate Beneficiary

Alternate Beneficiary:

Alternate Beneficiary's Mailing Address:

Include the following if a prior transfer on death deed is being revoked in whole or in part.

Prior Transfer on Death Deed

Date:

Transferor:

Primary Beneficiary:

Alternate Beneficiary:

Recording Information:

Continue with the following.

Property (including any improvements):

Reservations from Transfer:

State "None" or, to create reservations of title, include the appropriate clauses from form 5-7.

Select one of the following alternative clauses.

Surviving Primary Beneficiary

Transferor, subject to the Reservations from Transfer, at Transferor's death, grants and conveys the Property to Primary Beneficiary, to have and hold forever, but if any Primary Beneficiary predeceases Transferor, Transferor, subject to the Reservations from Transfer, at Transferor's death, grants and conveys that deceased Primary Beneficiary's share in the Property to surviving Primary Beneficiary, to have and hold forever.

Or

Anti-Lapse, Descendants of Deceased Primary Beneficiary

Transferor, subject to the Reservations from Transfer, at Transferor's death, grants and conveys the Property to Primary Beneficiary, to have and hold forever, but if any Primary Beneficiary predeceases Transferor and was a descendant of either of Transferor's parents, Transferor, subject to the Reservations from Transfer, at Transferor's death, grants and conveys that deceased Primary Beneficiary's share to the surviving descendants of that Primary Beneficiary, to have and hold forever.

Continue with the following.

Select one of the following alternative clauses.

Anti-Lapse, Surviving Descendants of Primary Beneficiary

If Transferor is not survived by any Primary Beneficiary, Transferor, subject to the Reservations from Transfer, at Transferor's death, grants and conveys the Property to the surviving descendants of the deceased Primary Beneficiary if the deceased Primary Beneficiary is a descendant of the Transferor or either of Transferor's parents or to Alternate Beneficiary if the deceased Primary Beneficiary is not a descendant of the Transferor or either of Transferor's parents, to have and hold forever.

Or

Alternate Beneficiaries

If Transferor is not survived by any Primary Beneficiary, Transferor, subject to the Reservations from Transfer, at Transferor's death, grants and conveys the Property to Alternate Beneficiary, to have and hold forever.

If one or more alternate beneficiaries are designated, select one of the following alternative clauses.

Surviving Alternate Beneficiary

If any Alternate Beneficiary predeceases Transferor, Transferor, subject to the Reservations from Transfer, at Transferor's death, grants and conveys that deceased Primary Beneficiary's share in the Property to surviving Alternate Beneficiary.

Or

Anti-Lapse, Descendants of Deceased Alternate Beneficiary

If any Alternate Beneficiary predeceases Transferor and that deceased Alternate Beneficiary was a descendant of either of Transferor's parents, Transferor, subject to the Reservations from Transfer, at Transferor's death, grants and conveys that deceased Alternate Beneficiary's share in the Property to the surviving descendants of the deceased Alternate Beneficiary.

If a prior transfer on death deed is being revoked in whole or in part, select one of the following alternative clauses.

Revocation of Prior Transfer on Death Deed

Transferor revokes the Prior Transfer on Death Deed.

Or

Partial Revocation of Prior Transfer on Death Deed

Transferor revokes the Prior Transfer on Death Deed as to all Beneficiaries but only to the Property.

Continue with the following.

When the context requires, singular nouns and pronouns include the plural.

____
[Name of transferor]

Include acknowledgment.

Form 5-26

In the 86th legislative session, the statutory forms for the transfer on death deed and the revocation of transfer on death deed were removed from chapter 114 of the Texas Estates Code. Acts 2019, 86th Leg., R.S., ch. 337, § 3.2 (S.B. 874), eff. Sept. 1, 2019. Tex. Gov't Code § 22.020 directs the Texas Supreme Court to promulgate forms for creating and revoking a transfer on death deed. At the time of this publication, the forms are not yet complete. The Estates Code continues to authorize use of transfer on death deeds and revocation of transfer on death deeds but no longer prescribes statutory language.

Revocation of Transfer on Death Deed

Notice of confidentiality rights: If you are a natural person, you may remove or strike any or all of the following information from any instrument that transfers an interest in real property before it is filed for record in the public records: your Social Security number or your driver's license number.

Date:

Transferor:

Transferor's Mailing Address:

Prior Transfer on Death Deed

Date:

Transferor:

Primary Beneficiary:

Alternate Beneficiary:

Property:

Recording Information:

Transferor revokes the Prior Transfer on Death Deed in its entirety.

____

[**Name of transferor**]

Include acknowledgment.

Form 5-27

In the 86th legislative session, the statutory forms for the transfer on death deed and the revocation of transfer on death deed were removed from chapter 114 of the Texas Estates Code. Acts 2019, 86th Leg., R.S., ch. 337, § 3.2 (S.B. 874), eff. Sept. 1, 2019. Tex. Gov't Code § 22.020 directs the Texas Supreme Court to promulgate forms for creating and revoking a transfer on death deed. At the time of this publication, the forms are not yet complete. The Estates Code continues to authorize use of transfer on death deeds and revocation of transfer on death deeds but no longer prescribes statutory language.

Partial Revocation of Transfer on Death Deed

Notice of confidentiality rights: If you are a natural person, you may remove or strike any or all of the following information from any instrument that transfers an interest in real property before it is filed for record in the public records: your Social Security number or your driver's license number.

Date:

Transferor:

Transferor's Mailing Address:

Prior Transfer on Death Deed

Date:

Transferor:

Primary Beneficiary:

Alternate Beneficiary:

Recording Information:

Revoked Property (including improvements):

Select one of the following. If revocation is to some designated beneficiaries, choose the first alternative clause below. If revocation is only of the described property, choose the second alternative clause.

Transferor revokes the Prior Transfer on Death Deed as to the transfer of the Revoked Property to [**names of revoked designated beneficiaries**].

Or

Transferor revokes the Prior Transfer on Death Deed as to the transfer of the Revoked Property to all Beneficiaries in the Prior Transfer on Death Deed.

____
[**Name of transferor**]

Include acknowledgment.

Chapter 6

Promissory Notes

Chapter 6

Promissory Notes

§ 6.1 General Considerations Concerning Loan Transactions

In many of the loan transactions that are the subject of this manual, a seller or third party (lender) lends a buyer (borrower) all or a portion of the purchase money for real or personal property. The borrower usually executes a note promising to pay the lender. In the case of real property, the borrower usually executes a deed of trust encumbering the real property to secure the loan. If the loan is secured by personal property only, a security agreement and financing statement typically are also executed. If the real estate includes fixtures and personal property, the lender may include a security agreement and financing statement in the deed of trust to protect its interest in all the property related to the real estate. The forms in this chapter are intended for transactions such as these, but they may be modified as appropriate to fit other types of loans.

For mechanic's lien transactions, the mechanic's lien note (form 20-2 in this manual) should be used. The mechanic's lien note is discussed in section 20.4:3.

For home equity loans, the home equity extension of credit (form 11-2) should be used instead of the note in this chapter.

The deed of trust to encumber real estate is discussed in chapter 8. The security agreement and financing statement are discussed in chapter 9, and modifications that may be made to the deed of trust to include a security agreement and financing statement are discussed in sections 8.11 through 8.11:2 and clause 8-9-10. In many loan transactions, in addition to the promissory note, there will be a separate loan agreement that includes details of the transaction. Promissory notes frequently refer to a separate loan agreement. See clauses 6-6-10 and 6-6-11. A separate loan agreement is included in this manual. See form 10-17.

§ 6.1:1 Promissory Note

The standard form (form 6-1 in this chapter) contains provisions most commonly used in promissory notes: the borrower's unconditional promise to pay a sum certain to the lender; a description of events constituting defaults under the note and the lender's right to accelerate the balance of the note on the occurrence of a default; the borrower's waiver of the right to require the lender to give notices and demands otherwise required by law; a usury savings clause; and the borrower's agreement to pay costs and reasonable attorney's fees resulting from legal action seeking enforcement or payment. *See F.R. Hernandez Construction & Supply Co. v. National Bank of Commerce*, 578 S.W.2d 675, 677 (Tex. 1979) (contractual attorney's fees).

Texas law has long "held that an installment of interest past due becomes principal, and bears interest, without any express stipulation to that effect." *Bothwell v. Farmers' & Merchants' State Bank & Trust Co.*, 30 S.W.2d 289, 291 (Tex. 1930); *see Bair Chase Property Co. v. S&K Development Co.*, 260 S.W.3d 133, 142 n.5 (Tex. App.—Austin 2008, pet. denied). The language in form 6-1 matches the common law of Texas and provides that interest commences and continues on any part of an installment that is not timely paid when due.

In a Chapter 13 bankruptcy, the word *maturity* may be limited to meaning only the last date to pay the entire obligation. *See Indian Cave Park Partnership v. Hence*, 255 F. App'x 28 (5th Cir. 2007). As a result, for a Chapter 13 debtor, a bankruptcy court may permit the debtor to stretch out (perhaps over the full five years of a plan) payment of the arrearage amount due on the date the bankruptcy case is filed. (The arrearage is the due and unpaid amount at the bankruptcy filing, other than that due because of acceleration.)

Although form 6-1 contains an express waiver of the borrower's right to notices and demands that might accompany default proceedings, many attorneys attempting to enforce or collect on notes choose to give written notice to borrowers of certain actions and intentions—for example, notice of default, notice of intention to accelerate maturity, and notice of acceleration of maturity. Even though they obtain a waiver, these attorneys do not rely on the waiver and instead view it more as a safeguard to protect lenders from the complications of minor technicalities than as a license to foreclose without notice or demand on borrowers who might be unaware of default proceedings. Notwithstanding any express waiver in the note or other security instruments, certain notices regarding foreclosure under a power of sale conferred by a deed of trust or other contractual lien must be served on the debtor. *See* Tex. Prop. Code § 51.002; Tex. Bus. & Com. Code §§ 9.601, 9.602, 9.604(c). The statute of limitations for enforcing the obligation to pay the note runs from the due date of any such payment or, if the due date is accelerated, from the accelerated due date. Tex. Bus. & Com. Code § 3.118.

A notice-of-default clause may be added to require the lender to give the borrower notice of default and allow the borrower a period of time to cure the default. See clause 6-6-8 for an example of a notice-of-default clause.

Promises to pay, such as the standard promissory note, may constitute "negotiable instruments" as defined by the Texas Uniform Commercial Code. *See* Tex. Bus. & Com. Code § 3.104. Transferees of negotiable instruments enjoy many benefits, including the possibility of being deemed a "holder in due course." *See* Tex. Bus. & Com. Code § 3.302. Certain terms added to the note may render it nonnegotiable. Determining negotiability is beyond the scope of this manual. For provisions of the Texas Uniform Commercial Code affecting negotiability, see Tex. Bus. & Com. Code §§ 3.101–.207.

A promissory note is a component of a "loan agreement" as defined in the Texas Business and Commerce Code statute of frauds for loan documents and requires the notice prescribed therein. *See* Tex. Bus. & Com. Code § 26.02. The notice of final agreement, form 10-14, may be used to satisfy the statutory requirements.

§ 6.1:2 Note Secured by Real Property

Parties may wish to secure a loan with real estate, such as a loan to purchase real estate or a refinance of a real estate secured loan. In these instances the promissory note not only serves as evidence of the debt but also defines the terms of payment and, with the deed of trust, the rights and responsibilities of the parties. A deed of trust is usually used to document the lien on the real estate that secures the note. Security-for-payment clauses, used to describe the deed of trust, are found in form 6-5 in this chapter.

§ 6.1:3 Unsecured Note

An unsecured promissory note evidences a debt and the borrower's promise to pay the debt according to stated terms without collateral to secure the debt.

§ 6.1:4 Note Secured by Personal Property

If the note is secured by personal property only, a security agreement and financing statement usually are used to document and perfect the lien that secures the note. If the note is secured by a lien on real and personal property, the deed of trust may include a security agreement and financing statement. Security-for-payment clauses, used to describe the security agreement, are found in form 6-5 in this chapter.

§ 6.2 Cautions

§ 6.2:1 Usury

Texas usury law is complicated, technical, and beyond the scope of this manual. Most promissory notes contain a "usury savings clause," and one is included in form 6-1 in this chapter. Such a clause is intended to protect against unintentional violations of usury law. However, a usury savings clause may not protect against all usury claims, such as where a note is usurious "on its face." *See Nevels v. Harris*, 102 S.W.2d 1046 (Tex. 1937).

§ 6.2:2 Truth in Lending

An extension of credit may be subject to the Truth in Lending Act and its accompanying Regulation Z. See the discussion of this subject in chapter 12 in this manual. No forms are provided in the manual for variable-interest-rate loans.

§ 6.2:3 Imputed Interest

Interest may be imputed to a loan under provisions in the Internal Revenue Code if the interest rate chosen by the parties is lower than the minimum rate required by applicable provisions of the Code. *See* 26 U.S.C. § 7872.

§ 6.2:4 Negotiability

Certain terms added to the note may render it nonnegotiable. Determining negotiability is beyond the scope of this manual. For provisions of the Texas Uniform Commercial Code affecting negotiability, see Tex. Bus. & Com. Code §§ 3.101–.207.

§ 6.2:5 Unsecured Note

The borrower wishing to borrow under an unsecured note should be wary of future or other indebtedness clauses commonly used in deeds of trust, security agreements, and other collateral documents. If the borrower has executed loan documents with the same lender in the past, the lender might rely on any future and other indebtedness clauses in prior loan documents to secure a subsequent note.

§ 6.2:6 Consistency among Documents

Because several documents may be required for a loan transaction, provisions among the various documents must be consistent. *See, e.g., Mathis v. DCR Mortgage III Sub 1, LLC*, 389 S.W.3d 494 (Tex. App.—El Paso 2012, no pet.). For example, the promissory note and the deed of trust may both have an express waiver of notice of default, or a loan agreement and a promissory note may both address prepayment rights. The attorney should review all documents carefully to be sure the provisions are consistent. A "conflicts" clause may be added to state which document will control if a conflict between provisions arises. See clause 6-6-12 in this chapter for an example of a conflicts clause.

§ 6.2:7 Consumer Loans under Texas Finance Code Chapter 342

Texas Finance Code chapter 342 regulates loans made by lenders in the business of making, arranging, or negotiating loans subject to the chapter if the interest exceeds 10 percent per year; the loan is extended primarily for personal, family, or household use to a person located in the state at the time the loan is made; and the loan either is not secured by a lien on real property or is a secondary mortgage loan secured by a lien on real property improved by a dwelling designed for occupancy by four or fewer families and is subject to one or more prior liens. Tex. Fin. Code § 342.005. A lender in the business of making, arranging, or negotiating loans regulated by chapter 342 must obtain a license from the Texas Office of Consumer Credit Commissioner (the OCCC) unless the lender is a bank, savings bank, savings and loan association, credit union, or a residential mortgage loan originator licensed under Finance Code chapter 156. Tex. Fin. Code §§ 124.005, 339.004, 341.103–.104, 342.051. Unless exempt under Finance Code section 180.003, an individual who acts as a residential mortgage loan originator in the making, transacting, or negotiating of a secondary mortgage loan subject to chapter 342 must be individually licensed under chapter 342, be enrolled with the Nationwide Mortgage Licensing System and Registry as required by section 180.052, and comply with other applicable requirements of the Texas Secure and Fair Enforcement of Mortgage Licensing Act of 2009. Tex. Fin. Code ch. 180.

Finance Code section 341.502 provides that "[a] contract for a loan under Chapter 342, a retail installment transaction under Chapter 348, or a home equity loan regulated by the Office of Consumer Credit Commissioner must be . . . written in plain language designed to be easily understood by the average consumer." *See* Tex. Fin. Code § 341.502(a). The Finance Commission of Texas is authorized to adopt model contracts for loans subject to that section. A lender may not use a contract other than a model contract unless the lender has submitted the contract to the OCCC for its approval. If the OCCC issues an order disapproving a submitted contract, the lender may not use the contract after the order takes effect. Tex. Fin. Code § 341.502(c). Plain-language model contracts and related rules for second-lien home improvement loans are codified at 7 Tex. Admin. Code §§ 90.601–.604.

The Texas attorney general has determined that section 341.502(a) is applicable only to those loan transactions for which the consumer credit commissioner is the appointed regulating official and has no application to loan transactions subject to the regulatory authority of the banking commissioner, the savings and mortgage lending commissioner, the credit union commissioner, and federal regulatory officials. Tex. Att'y Gen. Op. No. JC-0513 (2002). Banks, savings and loan associations, and credit unions accordingly are not required to comply with the section 341.502 "plain language" contract requirements or to obtain a license to engage in the business of making subordinate lien loans subject to chapter 342. Tex. Fin. Code § 342.051(c)(1). These institutional lenders nevertheless are thought to be subject to other substantive law provisions of chapter 342, including, for example, the limitations of that chapter on the collection of authorized fees and charges, as enforced policies of their respective regulatory agencies. *See* Tex. Fin. Code §§ 342.308, 342.502.

Before using the promissory note forms contained in this chapter of the manual for a loan subject to chapter 342 of the Finance Code, the attorney should determine whether the lender is subject to the plain-language model contract provisions of Finance Code section 341.502. The forms contained in this chapter have not been submitted to or approved by the OCCC.

If the attorney decides that the forms contained in this chapter may nevertheless be used for a loan regulated by chapter 342 of the Finance Code, the forms still must be modified to comply with the requirements of that chapter. For example, there are limits on the enforcement fees that may be collected from a borrower. *See* Tex. Fin. Code §§ 342.307, 342.502. The third paragraph of the note form, form 6-1 in this chapter, concerning attorney's fees should be replaced in its entirety with clause 6-6-14 for a loan under subchapter E of chapter 342 (that is, an installment loan not secured by a lien on real property) and replaced by clause 6-6-15 for a secondary mortgage loan subject to subchapter G of chapter 342.

§ 6.2:8 Cosigners

When the promissory note is signed by more than one party, the nature of the liability of the signers may be an issue. For example, a party who cosigns the promissory note as a maker but does not receive any of the proceeds of the loan is an "accommodation party" and is primarily liable on the note as a borrower. *See* Tex. Bus. & Com. Code § 3.419(a), (b). The rights of an accommodation party, however, differ from those of a true comaker. *See, e.g.*, Tex. Bus. & Com. Code § 3.419(f). If a party signing the promissory note does not intend to have full liability as a comaker, the note should specifically so indicate. See section 6.4:4 below for language indicating an intent to be a guarantor.

§ 6.3 Instructions for Completing Form

§ 6.3:1 Borrower's Mailing Address

Under certain circumstances, the lender may be required to give certain notices to the borrower. As a result, the parties should confirm the exact address for mailing. This will eliminate the possibility that the borrower may not receive any notices and avoid questions about whether the lender properly gave any required notice.

§ 6.3:2 Place for Payment

The attorney may want to provide under "Place for Payment" not only the address, city, county, and state stipulated by the lender but also the phrase "or any other place that Lender may designate in writing." This phrase permits the lender to change the place of payment.

§ 6.3:3 Annual Interest Rate

If the parties intend that interest will begin accruing at a time different from the date of the note, they should modify the form accordingly. If, for example, the note will be funded after it has been signed, the heading "Annual Interest Rate" could be modified to read "Annual Interest Rate on Unpaid Principal from Date of Funding, which is [**date**]."

Descriptions of variable interest rates necessarily include terms of payment that govern the conditions for changing the rates. Variable interest rate provisions usually relate to an index rate, such as the prime rate of interest as published by the *Wall Street Journal* on a particular date; however, other indexes are commonly used. An index rate should be well defined in the note and a provision for a replacement rate's selection should be included. The use of variable rates may require some modification of the note form. One suitable alteration for this purpose is to delete the heading for interest and modify the heading "Terms of Payment" to read "Terms of Payment, Including Variable Interest Rate on Unpaid Principal." Examples of variable rates appear as clauses 6-2-17 and 6-2-18 in this chapter.

A conspicuous variable-rate disclosure must be made if credit extended primarily for personal, family, or household use includes a variable interest rate and if federal truth-in-lending disclosures are not made because the amount of the credit exceeds $25,000 and the credit is not secured either by personal property (for example, a manufactured home) used as the principal residence of the debtor or by real property. *See* Tex. Fin. Code § 303.015(c). See clause 6-6-16 for an example of the statutorily required variable-rate disclosure.

§ 6.3:4 Payment Clauses

The promissory note form may be adapted to variable-interest-rate loans, although only clauses 6-2-17 and 6-2-18 in this chapter are drafted for variable rates.

§ 6.3:5 Prepayment and Application of Prepayment Clauses

If the borrower will have the right to make prepayments on the note, a clause from form 6-3 in this chapter should be added to the note, and a clause from form 6-4 should be added to govern application of that prepayment. If the borrower will not have a right of prepayment at any time, clause 6-3-10 may be added after the payment clause to avoid controversy.

The purpose of the yield maintenance clause, clause 6-3-9, is to allow the lender or holder of the note, on prepayment of the note, to receive the same yield as provided in the note.

§ 6.3:6 Security for Payment

If security for the note consists of real property with an express vendor's lien retained in the deed and a deed of trust, the security clause should identify the relevant documents, name the trustee, and describe the property. An abbreviated legal description or the full legal description from the deed and deed of trust may be used. A suitable clause is a straightforward statement followed by the property description. See clause 6-5-1 in this chapter.

If the note is secured only by real property without a vendor's lien, the security clause should identify the deed of trust, name the trustee, and describe the property. See clause 6-5-2. If the borrower does not own the property, the security clause should not recite that "Borrower" has executed the deed of trust; rather it should identify by name the parties who are to sign that document. See also the discussion in section 8.2:1 in this manual.

If the note is secured by both real property and personal property, the security clause should describe both types of security. If the deed of trust and security agreement are in separate documents, clause 6-5-4 should be used. If any borrowers shown on the note did not also execute the deed of trust or any separate security agreement, clause 6-5-4 should be modified as suggested in the preceding paragraph.

Clause 6-5-3 is appropriate if the deed of trust also includes the security agreement and the collateral consists of real property and other property, such as fixtures or personalty. If the deed of trust covers both real property and personal property, the lender may proceed against both the real and personal property by foreclosing on the deed of trust. Tex. Bus. & Com. Code § 9.604(a). For a discussion of corresponding provisions to be inserted in the deed of trust in this event, see sections 8.11 and 8.11:2 and the related clauses in form 8-9.

Clause 6-5-5 is appropriate if the security interest is created not in the deed of trust but in a separate security agreement. If the borrower defaults, the personal property collateral covered by the separate security agreement must be sold according to the terms of the security agreement and the Uniform Commercial Code rather than as part of the realty foreclosure sale administered by the trustee.

If another note serves as security, the clause should indicate whether that note is unsecured or secured by other liens described in the clause.

Caution: There is no requirement that the note include a description of the collateral securing the note. The practitioner should remember that the security-for-payment clauses do not, by themselves, create or perfect a lien or security interest. A lien must be created in a separate document, such as a deed of trust or a security agreement.

Practitioners should also take care to use security-for-payment clauses consistently. The use of the clause in one transaction and the failure to use the clause in another transaction, both of which are intended to be secured, may cause an ambiguity or a conflict between the documents.

§ 6.4 Additional Clauses

Additional clauses that may be useful in the promissory note, such as second lien, wraparound loan, late charge, guaranty, notice of default, nonrecourse, reamortization, conflicts, and choice-of-law clauses, appear in form 6-6 in this chapter.

§ 6.4:1 Second Lien

If the lien securing the note is subordinate to a lien in the real or personal property securing an earlier note, insert one of the optional clauses 6-6-1, 6-6-2, or 6-6-3 in this chapter. Additionally, if the loan is a secondary mortgage loan, the attorney's fee clause should be modified. See section 6.2:7 above and section 8.4 in this manual for a discussion of issues related to second liens.

§ 6.4:2 Wraparound Note

If the promissory note is part of a wraparound loan transaction, insert clause 6-6-4 in this chapter. The principal amount of the promissory note for a wraparound loan transaction will include the amount due under a prior note that will remain outstanding and secured by a first-lien mortgage. The borrower under the wraparound note makes one payment to the lender or the holder of the wraparound note. The lender or holder of the wraparound note continues to make the payments on the prior note, using part of the payments received from the wraparound note.

The wraparound note should be structured so that the payments are due before payments are due on the prior note. The maturity date of the prior note should be before the maturity date of the wraparound note, so as to afford the borrower some degree of assurance that by the time the wraparound note is paid, the prior note will be paid and the lien securing the note will be released.

Caution: The borrower should be advised of risks associated with wraparound notes. Generally the borrower will not receive notice of a default under the first-lien mortgage before foreclosure by the lender or holder of the prior note.

A more detailed discussion of wraparound notes is beyond the scope of this manual. For a general discussion of wraparound loan transactions, see sections 8.3 through 8.5:4 in this manual.

§ 6.4:3 Late Charge

A late charge may be included, but it should be determined that it is not usurious. See Texas Finance Code chapters 302, 342, and 347 for usury provisions.

Texas courts have consistently held that whether a charge is actually interest is a fact question to be determined from all the circumstances. A late payment charge is generally considered interest, because it is a charge for "detention" of money. *See* Tex. Fin. Code § 301.002(a)(4); *see also Dixon v. Brooks*, 604 S.W.2d 330, 333 (Tex. App.—Houston [14th Dist.] 1980, writ ref'd n.r.e.). *But see RIMCO Enterprises, Inc. v. Texas Electric Service Co.*, 599 S.W.2d 362, 366 (Tex. App.—Fort Worth 1980, writ ref'd n.r.e.). A loan primarily for business, commercial, investment, agricultural, or other similar purposes is a commercial loan. Tex. Fin. Code § 306.001(5). For a commercial loan, a late charge of up to 5 percent of the amount of an installment that is past due by not less than ten days may be assessed in addition to interest. Tex. Fin. Code § 306.006(1). Late charges for a secondary mortgage loan are authorized by Tex. Fin. Code § 342.302. If a late charge complies with either of these provisions of the Finance Code, the late charge is an authorized additional charge or additional interest that is not added to other interest for usury purposes. If a late charge does not comply with either of these provisions, it generally will be considered interest for usury purposes. *See Butler v. Holt Machinery Co.*, 741 S.W.2d 169 (Tex. App.—San Antonio 1987) (opinion corrected on denial of rehearing, 739 S.W.2d 958); *Talbert v. First National Bank*, 664 S.W.2d 126 (Tex. App.—Tyler 1983, writ ref'd n.r.e.). Late charges for certain secondary mortgage loans may not exceed interest at the maximum contract rate for the period the installment is not paid. *See* Tex. Fin. Code § 342.305. See section 8.4 in this manual for a definition of a secondary mortgage loan and the requirements of such loans. A clause assessing a late charge should, therefore, be used cautiously. See clause 6-6-5. Late charges for first-lien residential real property loans that are subject to the federal preemption of state usury limitations are interest and therefore are also within the federal preemption and thus not subject to state usury limitations. Tex. Fin. Code § 302.103.

§ 6.4:4 Guaranty

If the parties wish to have a third party guarantee the promissory note and do not wish to execute a separate document, use clause 6-6-6 in this chapter. For a stand-alone guaranty form, see section 10.13 and form 10-15 in this manual. As a surety, a guarantor is entitled to certain notices and defenses. *See, e.g.*, Tex. Civ. Prac. & Rem. Code ch. 43. Clause 6-6-6 contains the same kinds of waivers as are found in the stand-alone guaranty form.

§ 6.4:5 Default

Alternative default clauses for secured notes and unsecured notes are found in form 6-1 in this chapter.

A time for cure is not included in the note at form 6-1. If the borrower desires to receive notice and opportunity to cure any default before the lender accelerates the debt, the second paragraph of the default clauses and the section titled "Waivers" in form 6-1 should be replaced with clause 6-6-8.

§ 6.4:6 Nonrecourse

In a nonrecourse transaction, the lender's right to recover judgment against the borrower for the debt evidenced by the note is negated, and the lender may proceed only against the collateral. Notes executed in these transactions must include a nonrecourse provision. A note may also provide for partial recourse. See clauses 6-6-18, 6-6-19, and 6-6-20 in this chapter.

§ 6.4:7 Reamortization

The reamortization clause allows the unpaid principal balance to be reamortized if the proceeds of a casualty or condemnation are applied to prepay a portion of the unpaid principal balance. See clause 6-6-9 in this chapter. A change in the interest rate due to a variation of the index rate may also necessitate a reamortization of the payments due under the note.

§ 6.4:8 Conflicts

When the lender and the borrower execute a promissory note and a loan agreement, additional provisions may be necessary to harmonize the note with the loan agreement. A note may be one of several promissory notes executed under a loan agreement, or it may be desirable simply to recite that the note is executed under the loan agreement. In other cases, a "conflicts" clause may be necessary to address conflicting provisions of the note and loan agreement. This provision gives one instrument effect over the other to the extent of the conflict. See clause 6-6-12 in this chapter.

§ 6.4:9 Choice of Law

A choice-of-law provision is found at clause 6-6-13 in this chapter.

§ 6.4:10 Fair Credit Reporting Act

Any financial institution that extends credit to an individual and regularly and in the ordinary course of business reports negative information to a credit bureau must give its individual customers a clear and conspicuous written notice about reporting negative information. *See* 15 U.S.C. § 6809. A financial institution complies with the notice requirement if the institution uses a model notice promulgated by the Board of Governors of the Federal Reserve System. There are two model notices: one that may be used before reporting negative information to a credit bureau and one that may be used after reporting negative information to a credit bureau. See clauses 14-7-2 and 14-7-3 in this manual for examples of these notices. If the financial institution chooses to give the notice in its initial loan documentation or related communication, the first form of notice should be given. The model form may be included with the note. This form of notice is found in clause 6-6-17. See section 2.95 in this manual.

§ 6.4:11 Spreading

The concept of spreading allows for the calculation of interest for usury purposes to be made over the stated term of the loan, rather than at any particular point in time during the loan. *See, e.g.*, Tex. Fin. Code § 302.001. In certain loans, this can mitigate the effect of fees and charges made or collected at the beginning of the loan term. Spreading is expressly authorized for commercial loans and for consumer loans secured by real property. Tex. Fin. Code §§ 302.101, 306.004. Spreading is not statutorily permitted for consumer loans not secured by real property. A form of spreading provision is included as clause 6-6-21 in this chapter.

§ 6.5 Additional Forms

§ 6.5:1 Deed of Trust and Security Agreement

If the note is secured by a lien on real estate, a deed of trust, described in chapter 8 in this manual, or a security agreement and financing statement, described in chapter 9, or both, will be necessary. The deed of trust creates a lien on real property and enables the holder to enforce the lien by nonjudicial foreclosure. A security agreement is necessary to create or secure a lien against personal property and enable the holder to enforce the lien. See chapter 9 for a discussion of security agreements. The note may also be secured by a mechanic's lien. See form 20-1 for a mechanic's lien contract.

§ 6.5:2 Notice to Cosigner

By using form 6-7 in this chapter the lender discloses to a cosigner of a note the obligations the cosigner is assuming and the resulting potential liability. For consumer loans, banks (excluding savings banks that are members of the Federal Home Loan Bank System) must inform a cosigner of a note of the cosigner's liability on the note before the cosigner becomes obligated. *See* 16 C.F.R. § 444.3. The cosigner's execution of a disclosure statement substantially similar to form 6-7, in a separate document or included in the note, is sufficient to comply with this regulation, which prohibits unfair or deceptive acts or practices. This regulation does not apply to real estate purchase-money loans but applies to other obligations secured by real estate.

§ 6.6 Additional Resources

Nolan, John M., and Edward A. Peterson. 1 *Texas Annotated Real Estate Forms: Promissory Note*. State Bar of Texas, 2015.

St. Claire, Frank A., and William V. Dorsaneo III. *Texas Real Estate Guide*. New York: Matthew Bender & Co., 2001.

Thalheimer, Jonathan. "LIBOR: The Long Life and Untimely Demise of The World's Most Important Number." In *Advanced Real Estate Strategies Course*, 2020. Austin: State Bar of Texas, 2020.

Form 6-1

Promissory Note

Basic Information

Date:

Borrower:

Borrower's Mailing Address:

Lender:

Place for Payment:

Principal Amount:

Annual Interest Rate:

Maturity Date:

Annual Interest Rate on Matured, Unpaid Amounts:

Terms of Payment (principal and interest): [**Insert clause from form 6-2 in this chapter.**]

Security for Payment: [**Insert clause from form 6-5; if note is unsecured, write "None."**]

Other Security for Payment:

Promise to Pay

Borrower promises to pay to the order of Lender the Principal Amount plus interest at the Annual Interest Rate. This note is payable at the Place for Payment and according to the Terms of Payment. All unpaid amounts are due by the Maturity Date. If any amount is not paid either when due under the Terms of Payment or on acceleration of maturity, Borrower promises to pay any unpaid amount plus interest from the date the payment was due to the date of payment at the Annual Interest Rate on Matured, Unpaid Amounts.

Defaults and Remedies

Select one of the following. For an unsecured note, use the first paragraph. For a secured note, use the second paragraph.

A default exists under this note if (1) Borrower defaults in the payment of this note or in the performance of any obligation in any instrument securing or collateral to this note; (2) (a) Borrower or (b) any other person liable on any part of this note (an "Other Obligated Party") fails to timely pay or perform any obligation or covenant in any written agreement between Lender and Borrower or any Other Obligated Party other than as described in (1) above; (3) any representation in this note or in any other written agreement between Lender and Borrower or any Other Obligated Party is materially false when made; (4) a receiver is appointed for Borrower or an Other Obligated Party; (5) a bankruptcy or insolvency proceeding is commenced by Borrower, a partnership of which Borrower is a general partner, or an Other Obligated Party; (6) (a) a bankruptcy or insolvency proceeding is commenced against Borrower, a partnership of which Borrower is a general partner, or an Other Obligated Party and (b) the proceeding continues without dismissal for sixty days, the party against whom the proceeding is commenced admits the material allegations of the petition against it, or an order for relief is entered; or (7) Borrower, a partnership of which Borrower is a general partner, or an Other Obligated Party is terminated, begins to wind up its affairs, or is authorized to terminate or wind up its affairs by its governing body or persons, or any event occurs or condition exists that permits the termination or winding up of the affairs of Borrower, a partnership of which Borrower is a general partner, or an Other Obligated Party.

Or

A default exists under this note if (1) Borrower defaults in the payment of this note or in the performance of any obligation in any instrument securing or collateral to this note; (2) (a) Borrower or (b) any other person liable on any part of this note (an "Other Obligated Party") fails to timely pay or perform any obligation or covenant in any written agreement between Lender and Borrower or any Other Obligated Party other than as described in (1) above; (3) any representation in this note or in any other written agreement between Lender and Borrower or any Other Obligated Party is materially false when made; (4) a receiver is appointed for Borrower or an Other Obligated Party or any property on which a lien or security interest is created as security (the "Collateral Security") for any part of this note; (5) any Collateral Security is assigned for the benefit of creditors; (6) a bankruptcy or insolvency proceeding is commenced by Borrower, a partnership of which Borrower is a general partner, or an Other Obligated Party; (7) (a) a bankruptcy or insolvency proceeding is commenced against Borrower, a partnership of which Borrower is a general partner, or an Other Obligated Party and (b) the proceeding continues without dismissal for sixty days, the party against whom the proceeding is commenced admits the material allegations of the petition against it, or an order for relief is entered; (8) Borrower, a partnership of which Borrower is a general partner, or an Other Obligated Party is terminated, begins to wind up its affairs, or is authorized to terminate or wind up its affairs by its governing body or persons, or any event occurs or condition exists that permits the termination or winding up of the affairs of Borrower, a partnership of which Borrower is a general partner, or an Other Obligated Party; or (9) any Collateral Security is impaired by loss, theft, damage, levy and execution, issuance of an official writ or order of seizure, or destruction, unless it is promptly replaced with collateral security of like kind and quality or restored to its former condition.

> If the borrower desires to receive notice and opportunity to cure any default before the lender accelerates the debt, replace the following two paragraphs with clause 6-6-8. See section 6.4:5 in this chapter.

Upon the occurrence of a default under this note, Lender may declare the unpaid principal balance, earned interest, and any other amounts owed on the note immediately due, and may exercise all other rights and remedies available at law or in equity.

Waivers

Borrower waives, to the extent permitted by law, all (1) demand for payment, (2) presentation for payment, (3) notice of intention to accelerate maturity, (4) notice of acceleration of maturity, (5) protest, [and] (6) notice of protest [**include if applicable:** , and (7) rights under sections 51.003, 51.004, and 51.005 of the Texas Property Code] [**include if applicable:** , and [(7)/(8)] rights under section 17.001 and chapter 43 of the Texas Civil Practice and Remedies Code [and rule 31 of the Texas Rules of Civil Procedure]].

Attorney's Fees

> The following paragraph concerning attorney's fees should be replaced in its entirety with clause 6-6-14 for a loan under subchapter E of chapter 342 and replaced by clause 6-6-15 for a secondary mortgage loan subject to subchapter G of chapter 342. See section 6.2:7.

Borrower also promises to pay reasonable attorney's fees and court and other costs if an attorney is retained to collect or enforce the note. These expenses will bear interest from the date of advance at the Annual Interest Rate on Matured, Unpaid Amounts. Borrower will pay Lender these expenses and interest on demand at the Place for Payment. These expenses and interest will become part of the debt evidenced by the note and will be secured by any security for payment.

> Insert appropriate prepayment clause(s) from form 6-3 and, if appropriate, an application-of-prepayment clause from form 6-4.

Interest Calculation

Select one of the following.

Interest on the debt evidenced by this note is computed on a 365/365 basis; that is, by applying the ratio of the interest rate over a year of 365 days, multiplied by the outstanding Principal Amount, multiplied by the actual number of days the Principal Amount is outstanding, unless such calculation would result in a usurious rate, in which case interest shall be calculated on a per diem basis of a year of 365 or 366 days, as the case may be. All interest payable under this note is computed using this method.

Or

Interest on the debt evidenced by this note is computed on a 365/360 basis; that is, by applying the ratio of the interest rate over a year of 360 days, multiplied by the outstanding Principal Amount, multiplied by the actual number of days the Principal Amount is outstanding, unless such calculation would result in a usurious rate, in which case interest shall be calculated on a per diem basis of a year of 365 or 366 days, as the case may be. All interest payable under this note is computed using this method.

Usury Savings

Interest on the debt evidenced by this note will not exceed the maximum rate or amount of nonusurious interest that may be contracted for, taken, reserved, charged, or received under law. Any interest in excess of that maximum amount will be credited on the Principal Amount or, if the Principal Amount has been paid, refunded. On any acceleration or required or permitted prepayment, any excess interest will be canceled automatically as of the acceleration or prepayment or, if the excess interest has already been paid, credited on the Principal Amount or, if the Principal Amount has been paid, refunded. This provision overrides any conflicting provisions in this note and all other instruments concerning the debt.

If the parties wish to include spreading, insert clause 6-6-21. See section 6.4:11.

Other Clauses

Each Borrower is responsible for all obligations represented by this note.

When the context requires, singular nouns and pronouns include the plural.

If appropriate, include additional clauses, like those suggested in form 6-6.

____

[Name of borrower]

If there is a guarantor and no separate guaranty, include clause 6-6-6 with the signature of the guarantor.

Form 6-2

Payment Clauses

Fixed Maturity—On a Certain Date

Clause 6-2-1

The Principal Amount is due and payable on [**date**], and the interest is due and payable [at maturity/monthly as it accrues/quarterly as it accrues/semiannually as it accrues/annually as it accrues/as follows: [**specify**]]. Payments will be applied first to accrued interest and the remainder to reduction of the Principal Amount.

Or

Clause 6-2-2

The Principal Amount is due and payable [**number**] days after the date of this note, and the interest is due and payable [at maturity/monthly as it accrues/quarterly as it accrues/semiannually as it accrues/annually as it accrues/as follows: [**specify**]]. Payments will be applied first to accrued interest and the remainder to reduction of the Principal Amount.

Monthly Installments, Including Interest, until Fully Paid

Clause 6-2-3

The Principal Amount and interest are due and payable in equal monthly installments of [**amount**] DOLLARS ($[**amount**]), on the [**specify**] day of each month, beginning [**date**] and continuing until the unpaid principal and accrued, unpaid interest have been paid in full. Payments will be applied first to accrued interest and the remainder to reduction of the Principal Amount.

Monthly Installments, Including Interest, with Fixed Maturity and a Balloon Payment

Clause 6-2-4

The Principal Amount and interest are due and payable in equal monthly installments of [**amount**] DOLLARS ($[**amount**]), on the [**specify**] day of each month, beginning [**date**] and continuing until [the expiration of [**number**] years from the date of this note/[**specify date**]], when the entire amount of principal and accrued, unpaid interest will be payable in full. Payments will be applied first to accrued interest and the remainder to reduction of the Principal Amount.

Or

Clause 6-2-5

The Principal Amount and interest are due and payable in equal monthly installments of [**amount**] DOLLARS ($[**amount**]), beginning [**date**], and thereafter on the [**specify**] day of each succeeding month through [**date**], and in one final installment on [**date**] in the amount of the unpaid principal and accrued, unpaid interest as of that date. Payments will be applied first to accrued interest and the remainder to reduction of the Principal Amount.

Monthly Installments, Including Interest, When Amount Changes at Certain Times

Clause 6-2-6

The Principal Amount and interest are due and payable in equal monthly installments of [**amount**] DOLLARS ($[**amount**]), on the [**specify**] day of each month, beginning [**date**] and continuing through [**date**]. After that date the unpaid principal balance and interest are payable in equal monthly installments of [**amount**] DOLLARS ($[**amount**]), on the [**specify**] day of each month, beginning [**date**] and continuing until the Principal Amount and accrued, unpaid interest have been paid in full. Payments will be applied first to accrued interest and the remainder to reduction of the Principal Amount.

Initial Installments of Interest, Followed by Installments of Principal and Interest and a Balloon Payment

Clause 6-2-7

Interest only is due and payable monthly as it accrues on the [**specify**] day of each month, beginning [**date**] and continuing through [**date**]. After that date the unpaid principal balance and interest are due and payable in equal monthly installments of [**amount**] DOLLARS ($[**amount**]), on the [**specify**] day of each month, beginning [**date**] and continuing until the expiration of [**number**] years from the date of this note. At that time the unpaid principal balance and accrued, unpaid interest will be payable in full. Payments will be applied first to accrued interest and the remainder to reduction of the Principal Amount.

Additional Installment to Be Paid on Principal within Certain Time

Clause 6-2-8

> The following sentence should be added before the last sentence of the payment clause if an additional installment will be paid within a specified time.

An additional principal installment of [**amount**] DOLLARS ($[**amount**]) is due and payable [[**specify**] days after the date of this note/on [**date**]].

Monthly Installments of Principal, Plus Interest

Clause 6-2-9

The Principal Amount is due and payable in equal monthly installments of [**amount**] DOLLARS ($[**amount**]), on the [**specify**] day of each month, beginning [**date**] and continuing until the Principal Amount has been paid in full. Interest computed on the unpaid principal balance is due and payable monthly as it accrues, on the same dates as and in addition to the installments of principal. Payments will be applied first to accrued interest and the remainder to reduction of the Principal Amount.

Annual Installments, Including Interest

Clause 6-2-10

The Principal Amount and interest are due and payable in equal annual installments of [**amount**] DOLLARS ($[**amount**]), on [**date**] of each year, beginning [**date**] and continuing annually until the Principal Amount and accrued, unpaid interest have been paid in full. Payments will be applied first to accrued interest and the remainder to reduction of the Principal Amount.

Annual Principal Installments, Plus Interest

Clause 6-2-11

The Principal Amount is due and payable in equal annual installments of [**amount**] DOLLARS ($[**amount**]), on [**date**] of each year, beginning [**date**] and continuing annually until the Principal Amount has been paid in full. Interest on the unpaid principal balance is due and payable annually as it accrues, on the same dates as and in addition to the installments of principal. Payments will be applied first to accrued interest and the remainder to reduction of the Principal Amount.

Or

Clause 6-2-12

The Principal Amount is due and payable in three annual installments, as follows:

the first, in the amount of [**amount**] DOLLARS ($[**amount**]), on [**date**];

the second, in the amount of [**amount**] DOLLARS ($[**amount**]), on [**date**];

the third, in the amount of [**amount**] DOLLARS ($[**amount**]), on [**date**].

Interest on the unpaid principal balance is due and payable annually as it accrues, on the same dates as and in addition to the installments of principal. Payments will be applied first to accrued interest and the remainder to reduction of the Principal Amount.

Semiannual Installments, Including Interest

Clause 6-2-13

The Principal Amount and interest are due and payable in equal semiannual installments of [**amount**] DOLLARS ($[**amount**]). The first installment is payable on [**date**] and the others semiannually on the [**specify**] day of [**month**] and [**month**] of each year until the Principal Amount and accrued, unpaid interest have been paid in full. Payments will be applied first to accrued interest and the remainder to reduction of the Principal Amount.

Semiannual Principal Installments, Plus Interest

Clause 6-2-14

The Principal Amount is due and payable in equal semiannual installments of [**amount**] DOLLARS ($[**amount**]), on the [**specify**] day of [**month**] and [**month**] of each year, beginning [**date**] and continuing semiannually until the Principal Amount has been paid in full. Interest on the unpaid principal balance is due and payable semiannually as it accrues, on the same dates as and in addition to the installments of principal. Payments will be applied first to accrued interest and the remainder to reduction of the Principal Amount.

Quarterly Installments, Including Interest

Clause 6-2-15

The Principal Amount and interest are due and payable in equal quarterly installments of [**amount**] DOLLARS ($[**amount**]). The first installment is payable on [**date**] and the others quarterly on the [**specify**] day of [**month**], [**month**], [**month**], and [**month**] of each year until the Principal Amount and accrued, unpaid interest have been paid in full. Payments will be applied first to accrued interest and the remainder to reduction of the Principal Amount.

Quarterly Installments, Plus Interest

Clause 6-2-16

The Principal Amount is due and payable in equal quarterly installments of [**amount**] DOLLARS ($[**amount**]), on the [**specify**] day of [**month**], [**month**], [**month**], and [**month**] of each year, beginning [**date**] and continuing quarterly until the Principal Amount has been paid in full. Interest on the unpaid principal balance is due and payable quarterly as it accrues, on the same dates as and in addition to the installments of principal. Payments will be applied first to accrued interest and the remainder to reduction of the Principal Amount.

Variable Rates—Commercial Transaction

Clause 6-2-17

Interest will accrue at the rate per year that will be the lesser of [**percent**] percent ([**percent**]%) in excess of the Prime Interest Rate, adjusted [daily/on the first day of each calendar month] based on the Prime Interest Rate then in effect, or the maximum nonusurious rate of interest permitted by applicable law. [**Include if applicable:** At no time will the interest rate be greater than [**percent**] percent ([**percent**]%) or less than [**percent**] percent ([**percent**]%).]

Select one of the following.

The Prime Interest Rate means the annual rate of interest announced from time to time by [**financial institution**] as its base or prime commercial lending rate. If that rate ceases to be available, the Prime Interest Rate will be a reasonably comparable rate to be determined by Lender.

Or

The Prime Interest Rate means the annual rate of interest identified as the "U.S. prime rate" in the "Money Rates" column published in the *Wall Street Journal*. If the published prime rate is expressed on the applicable date as a range, the prime rate for purposes of this note will be the average between the high and low of that range. If the *Wall Street Journal* ceases to publish a prime rate, Lender may refer to another similar source to identify the prime rate on corporate loans at large United States money center commercial banks and apply that rate.

Continue with the following.

Payments will be applied first to accrued interest and the remainder to reduction of the Principal Amount.

Variable Rates—Residential Transaction

Clause 6-2-18

The initial interest rate will be [**percent**] percent ([**percent**]%) per year, and it may change on the [**specify**] day of [**month**] [**year**] and on that day every [**number**] month[s] thereafter. Each date on which the interest rate could change is a "Change Date."

Beginning with the first Change Date, the interest rate will be based on an index, which is [the weekly average yield on United States Treasury Securities adjusted to a constant maturity of one year as made available by the Federal Reserve Board/[**state other index**]].

The most recent index figure available as of the date forty-five days before each Change Date is the "Current Index."

If the index is no longer available, a new index will be chosen by Lender on the basis of comparable information.

Before each Change Date, the new interest rate will be calculated by adding [**number**] percentage point[s] to the Current Index. The result of this addition will be rounded to the nearest one-eighth of 1 percent (0.125%). Subject to the limits stated below, this rounded amount will be the new interest rate until the next Change Date.

The amount of the monthly payment that would be sufficient to pay in full the Principal Amount remaining on the Change Date by the maturity date at the new interest rate, in substantially equal payments, will be calculated and will be the new amount of the monthly payment. Payments will be applied first to accrued interest and the remainder to reduction of the Principal Amount.

The interest will never be increased or decreased on any single Change Date by more than [**number**] percentage point[s] from the highest rate of interest that has been paid during the preceding twelve months.

The interest rate will never be greater than [**percent**] percent ([**percent**]%).

The new interest rate will become effective on each Change Date. The new monthly payment will be paid from the first monthly payment date after the Change Date until the amount of the monthly payment changes again.

Lender will notify Borrower of the new interest rate, new monthly payment amount, and due date of the first new monthly payment at least [**number**] days before the new monthly payment is due.

Form 6-3

A clause from form 6-4 in this chapter should be added to a prepayment clause allowing partial prepayments if the prepayment clause does not specify how the prepayment will be applied. The attorney may wish to add clause 6-3-11 to a prepayment clause that includes a premium payment or a yield maintenance amount.

Prepayment Clauses

Prepayment

Clause 6-3-1

Borrower may prepay this note in any amount at any time before the Maturity Date without penalty or premium.

Or

Clause 6-3-2

Borrower may prepay at any time before the Maturity Date the entire unpaid principal balance of this note with interest to the date of prepayment plus a premium of [**percent**] percent ([**percent**]%) of the amount of the principal balance.

Or

Clause 6-3-3

On or after [**number**] years after the date of this note, Borrower may prepay on any monthly installment date the entire unpaid principal balance, with interest to the date of prepayment, or any part of it in multiples of [**amount**] DOLLARS ($[**amount**]), with interest to the date of prepayment, in addition to the monthly installment then payable.

Or

Clause 6-3-4

Borrower has the option at any time to pay [**amount**] DOLLARS ($[**amount**]) or multiples of that amount on any installment date before the Maturity Date, but the total prepayments in any one year may not exceed [**percent**] percent ([**percent**]%) of the Principal Amount of this note. Before exercising this option, Borrower will give [**number**] days' written notice to Lender.

Or

Clause 6-3-5

Borrower has the option at any time to make prepayments on this note on any installment date before the Maturity Date, subject to these conditions: If the total prepayments during any one year do not exceed [**percent**] percent ([**percent**]%) of the Principal Amount of this note, no premium for prepayment will be due; if total prepayments during any one year exceed that amount, Borrower will pay a premium equal to [**percent**] percent ([**percent**]%) of the amount by which prepayments exceed the amount allowed without premium.

Or

Clause 6-3-6

Borrower may prepay on any monthly installment date before the Maturity Date all or any part of the unpaid principal balance plus accrued interest on the amount of principal prepaid, and Borrower agrees to pay a premium of [**percent**] percent ([**percent**]%) of any amount of principal prepaid.

Or

Clause 6-3-7

Borrower has the option at any time to prepay on any installment date before the Maturity Date all or any part of the unpaid principal balance plus accrued interest on the amount of principal prepaid, and Borrower agrees to pay a premium of [**percent**] percent ([**percent**]%) of the amount of principal prepaid; however, during the first three years of this note, prepayments of unpaid principal must be [**amount**] DOLLARS ($[**amount**]) or multiples of that amount, and in each of those years total prepayments may not exceed [**percent**] percent ([**percent**]%) of the Principal Amount of this note.

Or

Clause 6-3-8

Borrower has the option at any time of doubling the regular principal payment payable on any principal payment date; however, all additional payments will be applied to the final maturing installment or installments of principal.

Yield Maintenance Clause

Clause 6-3-9

On or after [**number**] [years/months] following the date of this note and thirty days following Lender's receipt of written notice of Borrower's election to prepay, Borrower may prepay the entire unpaid principal balance plus all accrued interest plus the greater of the Yield Maintenance Amount or a premium of 1 percent (1%) of the unpaid principal balance.

The Yield Maintenance Amount is an amount, never less than zero, equal to the present value of a series of Monthly Amounts, assumed to be paid at the end of each month remaining from the prepayment date through the Maturity Date, discounted at the U.S. Securities Rate.

The Monthly Amount is the Annual Interest Rate minus the yield (U.S. Securities Rate), as of the prepayment date, as published by the Federal Reserve System in its "Statistical Release H.15(519), Selected Interest Rates" under the caption "U.S. Government Securities/Treasury Constant Maturities," for a U.S. Government Security with a term equal to that remaining on this note on the prepayment date (which term may be obtained by interpolating between the yields published for specific whole years), divided by twelve and the quotient then multiplied by the amount prepaid on the prepayment date.

No Right of Prepayment

Clause 6-3-10

Borrower may not make any prepayments without the prior written consent of Lender.

Prepayment because of Casualty or Condemnation

Clause 6-3-11

If Borrower prepays this note because of a casualty or condemnation the [premium/Yield Maintenance Amount] will not apply.

Form 6-4

If the note allows partial prepayment, the prepayment clause (form 6-3 in this chapter) should specify how the prepayment will be applied. The following clauses suggest three possibilities; the appropriate clause should be added to the prepayment clause if the prepayment clause does not specify how the prepayment will be applied.

Application of Prepayment

Clause 6-4-1

Prepayments will be applied to installments on the last maturing principal, and interest on that prepaid principal will immediately cease to accrue.

Or

Clause 6-4-2

Partial prepayments will be credited to principal; installments will continue as scheduled and interest on that prepaid principal will immediately cease to accrue.

Or

Clause 6-4-3

Prepayments will be applied first to accrued interest and the remainder to installments on principal in the inverse order of maturity so that they will be applied to the last maturing principal installments first. These prepayments will not reduce the amount or time of payment of the remaining installments, which will continue until the Principal Amount and all accrued interest are paid. Interest on the prepaid principal will immediately cease to accrue.

Form 6-5

Security for Payment

Note Secured by Real Property Only

Clause 6-5-1

This note is secured by a vendor's lien [**include if applicable:** and superior title] retained in a deed from [**name**] to Borrower dated [**date**] and by a deed of trust of even date from [Borrower/[**name of grantor in deed of trust**]] to [**name of trustee**], trustee, both of which cover the following real property: [**property description**].

Or

Clause 6-5-2

This note is secured by a deed of trust dated [**date**] from [Borrower/[**name of grantor in deed of trust**]] to [**name of trustee**], trustee, which covers the following real property: [**property description**].

Note Secured by Both Real Property and Personal Property

Clause 6-5-3

This note is secured by a deed of trust and security agreement dated [**date**] from [Borrower/[**name of grantor in deed of trust and security agreement**]] to [**name of trustee**], trustee. The deed of trust contains a security agreement that covers the personal property described in the deed of trust and the following real property: [**property description**].

Security Interest Is Created in a Deed of Trust and a Separate Security Agreement

Clause 6-5-4

This note is secured by a deed of trust dated [**date**] from [Borrower/[**name of grantor in deed of trust**]] to [**name of trustee**], trustee, which covers the following real property: [**property description**]. This note is additionally secured by a security interest created in a security agreement that covers personal property and that is dated [**date**] and executed by [Borrower/[**name of debtor in security agreement**]] as the debtor in favor of Lender as the secured party.

Note Secured by Personal Property Only

Clause 6-5-5

This note is secured by a security interest created in a security agreement that covers [**type of collateral**] and that is dated [**date**] and executed by [Borrower/[**name of debtor in security agreement**]] as the debtor in favor of Lender as the secured party.

Form 6-6

Additional Clauses for Promissory Notes

Second Lien

Clause 6-6-1

The lien[s] securing this note [is/are] subordinate to the lien securing another note in the original principal amount of [**amount**] DOLLARS ($[**amount**]), dated [**date**], and executed by [**name**], payable to the order of [**name**].

Or

Clause 6-6-2

The lien securing this note is subordinate to the lien securing another note in the original principal amount of [**amount**] DOLLARS ($[**amount**]), dated [**date**], and executed by [**name**], payable to the order of [**name**], and described in a deed of trust recorded in [**recording data**] of the real property records of [**county**] County, Texas. If there is a default in payment of any part of principal or interest of that $[**amount**] note or a breach of any covenants contained in any instruments securing it, the debt evidenced by this note will immediately become payable at the option of Lender. If Borrower fails to perform any of Borrower's obligations in that $[**amount**] note or in any instruments securing it, Lender may perform those obligations and be reimbursed by Borrower, on demand, at the Place for Payment for any amounts advanced, including attorney's fees, plus interest on those amounts from the date of payment at the Annual Interest Rate on Matured, Unpaid Amounts. The amount to be reimbursed will be secured by all instruments securing this note.

Or

Clause 6-6-3

This note is the second of two notes that Borrower executed today in favor of Lender, and each lien securing payment of this note is and will remain subordinate to each lien securing payment of the first note in the original principal amount of **[amount]** DOLLARS ($**[amount]**).

Wraparound Lien

Clause 6-6-4

> The following paragraph is to be used for a wraparound loan transaction in conjunction with deed-of-trust forms, if modified as suggested in sections 8.3–8.5:4 in this manual.

The lien[s] securing this note [is/are] subordinate to the lien[s] securing payment of the unpaid balance of a prior note in the original principal amount of **[amount]** DOLLARS ($**[amount]**), dated **[date]**, and executed by **[name]**, described in and secured by a deed of trust recorded in **[recording data]** of the real property records of **[county]** County, Texas. Borrower has not assumed payment of that prior note, but Lender is obligated to pay it according to its terms. If Lender defaults in payment of the prior note, Borrower has the right to cure the default and receive credit on this note. The subordinate lien[s] securing this note [is/are] also provided for in the warranty deed with vendor's lien and deed of trust described above, which this note incorporates and is subject to.

Late Charge

Clause 6-6-5

If any installment becomes overdue for more than [**number**] days, at Lender's option a late payment charge of $[**amount**] may be charged in order to defray the expense of handling the delinquent payment.

Guaranty of Payment

Clause 6-6-6

For value received, [I/we], [**name[s]**], [jointly and severally,] absolutely, irrevocably, and unconditionally guarantee payment of this note according to its terms to the same extent as if [I/we] were Borrower[s] on this note. [I/We] [jointly and severally] waive all demands and all notices, including notice of intention to accelerate maturity, notice of acceleration of maturity, notice of nonpayment or default, presentment for payment, protest, notice of protest, suit, and diligence. [I/We] also [jointly and severally] waive any notice of and defense based on the extension of time of payment or change in methods of payment or the release of any collateral securing this note and consent to all renewals, extensions, and other adjustments in the manner of payment of this note and any transfer of this note to any third party. This is an unconditional guaranty of payment and performance, not of collection, and it is an agreement of guaranty, not of suretyship. [I/We] [jointly and severally] waive defenses based on suretyship or impairment of collateral and all requirements of law, if any, that any collection efforts be made against Borrower or that any action be brought against Borrower before resorting to this guaranty, including rights under section 17.001 and chapter 43 of the Texas Civil Practice and Remedies Code and rule 31 of the Texas Rules of Civil Procedure.

____

[**Name of guarantor**]

Clause 6-6-7 ***reserved***

Notice to Cure Default

Clause 6-6-8

Notwithstanding any other provision of this note, in the event of a default, before exercising any of Lender's remedies under this note or any [deed of trust/security agreement/instrument] securing [**include if applicable:** or collateral to] it, Lender will first give Borrower written notice of default and Borrower will have ten days after notice is given in which to cure the default. If the default is not cured ten days after notice, (1) Borrower and each surety, endorser, and guarantor waive all demand for payment, presentation for payment, notice of intention to accelerate maturity, notice of acceleration of maturity, protest, and notice of protest, to the extent permitted by law [**include if applicable:** , and rights under sections 51.003, 51.004, and 51.005 of the Texas Property Code] [**include if applicable:** , and rights under section 17.001 and chapter 43 of the Texas Civil Practice and Remedies Code [and rule 31 of the Texas Rules of Civil Procedure]]; and (2) Lender may declare the unpaid principal balance, earned interest, and any other amounts owed on the note immediately due and may exercise all other rights and remedies available at law or in equity.

Reamortization

Clause 6-6-9

If the proceeds of a casualty or condemnation are applied to the Principal Amount of this note resulting in prepayment of more than 10 percent of the unpaid principal balance and more than one year remains until the Maturity Date, the unpaid principal balance will be reamortized over the remaining period of this note. The reamortization will be used to calculate the amount of the monthly payment that would be sufficient to pay in full the unpaid principal amount remaining on the prepayment date, plus interest, by the Maturity Date. The reduced payments of principal and interest to be made on this note as the result of the reamortization will be the new monthly amount, and the payments will begin the next month after the prepayment date.

Loan Agreements

Clause 6-6-10

This note is the [**identify defined term from the loan agreement**] note required under [**specific provision**] of a loan agreement of the same date as the note.

Or

Clause 6-6-11

The execution and delivery of this note are required under a loan agreement of the same date as the note.

Conflicts

Clause 6-6-12

If any provision of this note conflicts with any provision of a loan agreement, deed of trust, or security agreement of the same transaction between Lender and Borrower, the provisions of the [loan agreement/deed of trust/security agreement/note] will govern to the extent of the conflict.

Choice of Law

Clause 6-6-13

This note will be construed under the laws of the state of Texas, without regard to choice-of-law rules of any jurisdiction.

Attorney's Fees (Consumer Loan under Texas Finance Code Chapter 342, Not Secured by a Lien on Real Estate)

Clause 6-6-14

Borrower also promises to pay court and other costs and attorney's fees assessed by a court if an attorney is retained to collect or enforce the note. Borrower will pay Lender these expenses on demand at the Place for Payment. These expenses will become part of the debt evidenced by the note and will be secured by any security for payment.

Attorney's Fees (Secondary Mortgage Loan under Texas Finance Code Chapter 342)

Clause 6-6-15

Borrower also promises to pay reasonable attorney's fees and court and other costs and fees incurred if an attorney is retained who is not an employee of Lender to collect or enforce the note. Borrower will pay Lender these expenses on demand at the Place for Payment. These expenses will become part of the debt evidenced by the note and will be secured by any security for payment.

Variable-Rate Disclosure

Clause 6-6-16

NOTICE TO CONSUMER: UNDER TEXAS LAW, IF YOU CONSENT TO THIS AGREEMENT, YOU MAY BE SUBJECT TO A FUTURE RATE AS HIGH AS 24 PERCENT PER YEAR.

Fair Credit Reporting Act Notice

Clause 6-6-17

Lender may report information about Borrower's loan account to credit bureaus. Late payments, missed payments, or other defaults on this note may be reflected in your credit report.

Nonrecourse

Clause 6-6-18

Notwithstanding any other provision of this note, Lender may satisfy the debt evidenced by this note only by the enforcement of Lender's rights in the [**identify collateral**] pursuant to [**identify collateral documents**], and Borrower will not be liable for a money judgment in the event of a default under this note or the [**identify collateral documents**].

Or

Clause 6-6-19

Notwithstanding any other provision of this note, Lender may satisfy the debt evidenced by this note only by the enforcement of Lender's rights in the [**identify collateral**] pursuant to [**identify collateral documents**], and Borrower will not be liable for a money judgment in the event of a default in payment of the debt evidenced by this note; provided, however, Lender may recover against Borrower if Borrower defaults on Borrower's obligation to [**describe obligations, e.g.,** pay ad valorem taxes owed on the collateral].

Partial Recourse

Clause 6-6-20

Borrower has no personal liability for the obligations under this note or under the Deed of Trust, and no personal judgment may be taken and no claim for personal liability may be made against Borrower. Lender's sole remedy for default under this note or the Deed of Trust is the foreclosure of the liens and security interests created hereunder. Exceptions to the foregoing provisions are limited to, and Borrower is liable for, the following: taxes, assessments, and charges for labor, materials, or other amounts that if unpaid may create an encumbrance against the collateral for this note; unpaid premiums for insurance required under the Deed of Trust; damage to the collateral for this note if any insurance required hereunder is not maintained; all rents, issues, profits, and income derived from the collateral for this note after a default occurs and not expended for operating expenses of the collateral for this note; tenant security deposits for leases of the collateral for this note; any condemnation or insurance proceeds not paid or applied as required hereunder; [**include if applicable:** damage to and depreciation of the collateral for this note beyond normal wear and tear caused by the negligence of Borrower or the failure of Borrower to keep the collateral for this note in good repair and condition; the return of or reimbursement for all personal property taken from the collateral for this note by or on behalf of Borrower;] damages resulting from any fraud or misrepresentation by Borrower; damages resulting from any breach of any warranty of title; interest on the note from the date of default through foreclosure, payment, or settlement of the debt; all interest on the note during any bankruptcy proceeding of Borrower and all reasonable attorney's fees and expenses incurred as a result of Borrower's bankruptcy; and all attorney's fees and expenses incurred by Lender or other holder of the note to collect any of the foregoing amounts.

Spreading

Clause 6-6-21

All calculations of the rate of interest contracted for, charged, taken, reserved, or received in connection with this note that are made for the purpose of determining whether such rate exceeds the maximum nonusurious rate of interest permitted by law shall be made, to the extent permitted by applicable laws, by spreading, during the period of the full term of this note, all interest at any time contracted for, charged, taken, reserved, or received by Lender.

Form 6-7

For consumer loans, execution of this disclosure notice before the cosigner becomes obligated will comply with the applicable federal regulation. 12 C.F.R. §§ 227.1–.16.

Notice to Cosigner

You are being asked to guarantee this debt. Think carefully before you do. If the borrower does not pay the debt, you will have to. Be sure you can afford to pay if you have to, and that you want to accept this responsibility.

You may have to pay up to the full amount of the debt if the borrower does not pay. You may also have to pay late fees or collection costs, which increase the amount.

The creditor can collect this debt from you without first trying to collect from the borrower. The creditor can use the same collection methods against you that can be used against the borrower, such as suing you, garnishing your wages, or the like. If this debt is ever in default, that fact may become a part of your credit record.

This notice is not the contract that makes you liable for the debt.

I HAVE READ AND UNDERSTAND THE FOREGOING NOTICE.

____

[Name of cosigner]
Date:

Chapter 7
Letters of Credit

Forms

Chapter 7

Letters of Credit

§ 7.1 General Considerations for Letters of Credit in Real Estate Transactions

Developers, investors, buyers, sellers, lenders, landlords, and tenants may have need for letters of credit in real estate transactions. For instance, a tenant may furnish a letter of credit to its landlord as a portion of its security deposit; a letter of credit may be used to provide assurances that agreed-to joint venture investments will be funded; a letter of credit may be used to fund obligations for the purchase price for the acquisition of large tracts; a seller or landlord may use a letter of credit to secure construction or development obligations to a buyer or tenant; a letter of credit may be used to provide security for payment of bonds issued by tax-exempt entities for construction of low-cost housing or university or hospital facilities; a contractor may provide a letter of credit as security for completion of construction, performance of warranty obligations, and payment of subcontractors and suppliers; several builders party to a joint development agreement may provide letters of credit to an escrow agent to ensure payment of costs of roads, drainage, and other infrastructure; a letter of credit may provide security for the payment of indemnification obligations under a purchase and sale agreement; or the holder of a letter of credit may grant a security interest in the letter's proceeds to secure the holder's own loans for development of real estate projects.

§ 7.2 Definition

A letter of credit, whether documentary or standby, is an irrevocable (unless specifically provided otherwise—see section 7.9:1 below), independent, and binding undertaking of a bank to make a payment to the beneficiary upon the presentation of certain documentation. It is not a guaranty or a surety bond, although in many cases it may serve the same function.

§ 7.3 Types

There are two primary types of letters of credit: the documentary credit and the standby credit.

Documentary letters of credit facilitate commerce within and among countries. For instance, a U.S. seller may be unwilling to ship goods to a buyer in another country based solely on the foreign buyer's agreement to pay. Not only would the seller bear the risk of nonpayment, but it also might be required to enforce its rights in the foreign country. The delivery to the seller of a letter of credit as a condition to shipment relieves the seller of those risks. On the other hand, a U.S. buyer of foreign goods may want assurance that goods nominally fulfilling requirements of a purchase order are shipped before it is obligated to pay for the goods. Typically, the documentary letter of credit is payable only on submission of documentation such as shipping receipts, bills of lading, invoices, freight receipts, evidence of insurance, and inspection certificates evidencing that the seller has complied with the sales contract. The parties expect the letter of credit to be the actual source of payment of the sales transaction. The parties expect to draw upon the letter of credit because it is the method by which the seller is to receive payment for the goods. No default or other action by the buyer is required as a condition for the draw.

Standby letters of credit provide a source of payment for underlying contractual payment or performance obligations, such as a loan, a lease, or an acquisition agreement. It is typical, although not required, that a standby letter of credit is drawn only if there is a problem with the transaction or the account party has in some way breached an obligation. For instance, a letter of credit issued to a regulatory agency to ensure environmental remediation may be called upon if the account party defaults in the payment of its obligations. If a letter of credit backs a bond, the letter of credit may be drawn upon only if the bond is called and the bonding agency is required to pay the obligee.

§ 7.4 Parties to a Letter-of-Credit Transaction

Letters of credit use specific terms to identify the various parties to a transaction.

Issuer: The issuer is the bank that issues the letter of credit and agrees to make the payment upon presentation of specified documents. This is the party upon whose creditworthiness the transaction depends. The issuer's obligation is a simple, unsecured, corporate undertaking and is not insured by the FDIC. In fact, if the issuer is taken over by the FDIC, the FDIC may repudiate the obligations of the letter of credit. *See Lexon Insurance Co. v. FDIC*, 7 F.4th 315 (5th Cir. 2021).

Account Party, Applicant, or Customer: The account party, applicant, or customer is the party who requests the issuance of the letter of credit. In a standby transaction, this is the borrower or other obligor who obtains credit or induces another to enter into a transaction or to take or refrain from taking action based on the letter of credit. The applicant is responsible for reimbursing the issuer if the letter of credit is drawn.

Beneficiary: The beneficiary is the party entitled to receive the benefits of the letter of credit. In a standby transaction, this may be the lender who requires the letter of credit as a condition to making a loan or the landlord who requires a security deposit.

Confirmer: The confirmer is a bank or other person that confirms the obligations of the issuer. This person, which may be known to the beneficiary or located in the beneficiary's jurisdiction, or which may have a stronger credit rating than the issuer, supplies additional credit or security to the beneficiary. The confirmer is independently responsible for honoring presentations under the issuer's letter of credit. The beneficiary essentially has two obligors: the issuer and the confirmer.

§ 7.5 Sources of Letter-of-Credit Law and Practice

Chapter 5 of the Texas Business and Commerce Code governs documentary and standby letters of credit. While this is the law that governs letter-of-credit transactions, additional conventions and practices may also apply to letters of credit. The two most likely to be selected in domestic letter-of-credit transactions are the UCP and the ISP98. For a letter of credit to be governed by one of these conventions, it must specifically state that it is governed by UCP or ISP98.

The International Chamber of Commerce has adopted Uniform Customs and Practice for Documentary Credits (UCP). This was first published in 1933 and was subsequently revised many times. The current revision, ICC Publication No. 600, was adopted in 2006. The UCP memorializes customs and practices of issuers of documentary letters of credit. It was also widely used to govern standby letters of credit before the adoption of ISP98.

The International Chamber of Commerce adopted International Standby Practices (ISP98) in 1998 specifically to standardize practices for standby letters of credit. Even though ISP98 is more closely aligned with standby letter-of-credit practice, some issuers continue to use UCP for standby as well as for documentary letters of credit.

§ 7.6 Differences between ISP98 and UCP

There are many differences between ISP98 and UCP, including the absence of detailed provisions for insurance, shipping documents, and other trade-related concerns that are important in UCP for documentary letters of credit. ISP98, dealing specifically with standby letters of credit, has no need for such provisions.

An important difference between UCP and ISP98 for a beneficiary is the effect on the letter of credit arising from an extended disruption in business because of weather and other force majeure events. ISP98 provides the following:

> If on the last business day for presentation the place for presentation stated in a standby is for any reason closed and presentation is not timely made because of the closure, then the last day for presentation is automatically extended to the day occurring thirty calendar days after the place for presentation re-opens for business, unless the standby otherwise provides.

Int'l Standby Prac. R. 314(a).

UCP articles 29 and 36 address closure in different fashions. Under article 29, if a presentation is due on any day when the bank is closed for any reason other than those set forth in article 36 (which governs force majeure issues), the presentation is extended to the first following banking day. Article 36 provides the following:

> A bank assumes no liability or responsibility for the consequences arising out of the interruption of its business by Acts of God, riots, civil commotions, insurrections, wars, acts of terrorism, or by any strikes or lockouts or any other causes beyond its control. A bank will not, upon resumption of its business, honour or negotiate under a credit that expired during such interruption of its business.

Uniform Customs and Prac. for Documentary Credits art. 36. Although article 36 would relieve the bank of the obligation to honor a draft due to closure for a force majeure event, many issuers routinely modify this rule if requested. A beneficiary who is presented with a letter of credit governed by UCP should check to see if article 36 is waived; if it is not, the beneficiary may wish to request an amendment to the proposed form.

An additional difference between ISP98 and UCP, discussed in greater detail in section 7.9:4 below, is that in the event of death, bankruptcy, and other similar changes in the identity of the beneficiary, ISP98 specifically provides for rights to a successor to make a drawing, while UCP does not.

§ 7.7 The Independence Principle

The essence of the letter-of-credit transaction is the independent undertaking of the issuing bank. This "independence" principle is one of the most cited aspects of letter-of-credit law.

ISP98 provides in rule 1.06(a) that a letter of credit is "an irrevocable, independent, documentary, and binding undertaking." Int'l Standby Prac. R. 1.06(a). Rule 1.06(c) stipulates that enforcement does not depend upon, among other conditions, either the "beneficiary's right to obtain payment from the applicant" or "the issuer's knowledge of performance or breach of any reimbursement agreement or underlying transaction." Int'l Standby Prac. R. 106(c)(ii), (iv). Thus, the existence of a dispute between applicant and beneficiary about whether conditions for payment have actually occurred will not authorize the issuer to refuse to honor a presentation that appears to comply with the requirements of the letter of credit.

UCP provides a similar provision in article 4 and provides the following:

> A credit by its nature is a separate transaction from the sale or other contract on which it may be based. Banks are in no way concerned with or bound by such contract, even if any reference whatsoever to it is included in the credit. Consequently, the undertaking of a bank to honour, to negotiate, or to fulfil any other obligation under the credit is not subject to claims or defences by the applicant resulting from its relationships with the issuing bank or the beneficiary.

Uniform Customs and Prac. for Documentary Credits art. 4.

This independence principle is the primary difference between a letter of credit and a guaranty or surety bond. With a guaranty or surety bond, the guarantor or surety company has no obligation until there is a default, and it would expect to investigate whether the conditions of its obligations had accrued, including whether there had been an actual default or failure of performance under the underlying contract. The opposite is true in the case of the letter of credit. The issuer examines only whether the conditions for draws have been met. It does not investigate any provisions of the underlying contract.

§ 7.8 Reimbursement

The issuer pays drafts drawn under the letter of credit from its assets. An issuer that has honored a presentation is entitled to be reimbursed by the applicant in immediately available funds not later than the date of its payment of funds. Tex. Bus. & Com. Code § 5.108(i)(1). This reimbursement obligation may be evidenced by a reimbursement agreement or a letter-of-credit application, or the applicant may agree that any amounts paid under the letter of credit will be considered advances under an existing credit facility. The issuer may have required a guaranty and security in the property of the account party or guarantor. These requirements are typically made based on the issuer's underwriting of the credit of the account party.

§ 7.9 Drafting Considerations

Form 7-2 in this chapter is an example of a simple standby letter of credit. Other examples of standby letters of credit may be found at the Institute of International Banking Law & Practice website, **https://iiblp.org**. Typically, the issuing bank will prepare the letter of credit based on its internal policies and procedures. However, the applicant and the beneficiary may be able to request changes to address specific concerns or deal points, such as requirements that a letter of credit be furnished substantially in a form attached to a lease or credit agreement. Several basic points are described in this section.

§ 7.9:1 Revocable or Irrevocable

Texas law provides that a letter of credit is revocable only if it specifically states so. Tex. Bus. & Com. Code § 5.106(a). Under UCP, a letter of credit is deemed to be irrevocable unless it provides otherwise. ISP98 specifically provides in rule 1.06(a) that a standby letter of credit is irrevocable. Notwithstanding the strong support for irrevocable letters of credit in the law and banking conventions, letters of credit typically state specifically that they are irrevocable.

§ 7.9:2 Documentary Submissions

A letter of credit is drawn upon the submission of documents and certificates specified in the letter. A standby letter of credit does not provide that the beneficiary may draw upon an event of default under a lease, a credit agreement, or another agreement between the beneficiary and the applicant. Rather, it might provide that a draw would be paid upon submission of documents to the issuing bank, such as a certificate of the beneficiary that the applicant is in default under other agreements. With such a provision, the issuing bank is removed from the underlying transaction and fulfills its obligation upon the receipt of the specified documents.

§ 7.9:3 Transferable

A letter of credit can be transferred only if it so states. Tex. Bus. & Com. Code § 5.112; Int'l Standby Prac. R. 6.02(a); Uniform Customs and Prac. for Documentary Credits art. 48(b). If the beneficiary is the collateral agent for lenders under a secured credit facility or the trustee for bondholders under bonds and the parties wish to provide for transfer to a successor agent, the letter of credit would provide for this right. If a letter of credit is provided as security for a lessee's lease obligations, the lease may provide that if the lessor sells the property the lessee would consent to a transfer or would post a replacement letter of credit in favor of the new owner. If the parties wish to provide in the letter of credit itself for transfer to a subsequent owner, a clause to that effect could be included in the letter of credit.

§ 7.9:4 Successor Beneficiary

The successor of the beneficiary may submit draws. Tex. Bus. & Com. Code § 5.113. "Successor of a beneficiary" is a person "who succeeds to substantially all of the rights of a beneficiary by operation of law, including a corporation with or into which the beneficiary has been merged or consolidated, an administrator, an executor, a personal representative, a trustee in bankruptcy, a debtor in possession, a liquidator, and a receiver." Tex. Bus. & Com. Code § 5.102(a)(15). ISP98 rules 6.11 through 6.14 contain detailed provisions for presentations by "an heir, personal representative, liquidator, trustee, receiver, successor corporation, or similar person who claims to be designated by law to succeed to the interests of a beneficiary." Int'l Standby Prac. R. 6.11; *see* Int'l Standby Prac. R. 6.12–6.14. UCP does not directly address this issue. The beneficiary may not assign a single contract and a letter of credit securing payment and performance under chapter 5 of the Texas Business and Commerce Code and ISP98. However, a successor to the beneficiary may submit a draw that otherwise would have to be submitted by the originally named beneficiary.

§ 7.9:5 Expiration Date

Texas law provides that, unless otherwise stated, a letter of credit will expire one year after its stated date of issuance, and a letter of credit which states that it is perpetual expires five years after its date of issuance. Tex. Bus. & Com. Code § 5.106. Under UCP article 42, all letters of credit must contain expiration dates. Under ISP98 rule 9.01, a standby must either contain an expiration date "or permit the issuer to terminate the standby upon reasonable prior notice or payment." Int'l Standby Prac. R. 9.01. If the events that must be certified in connection with a draw have not occurred before the expiration date, the issuing bank is not obligated to extend the time for a draw.

To comply with their underwriting standards, including the ability to monitor the credit of the applicant, banks may issue letters of credit with a one-year expiration date with an "evergreen" renewal. Under these circumstances, the letter of credit typically provides that it will automatically renew for successive one-year periods unless the issuing bank advises the beneficiary within some period before expiration that the letter of credit will not be renewed for an additional year. In these cases, the letter of credit may provide that the beneficiary may draw down the full amount of the credit upon a certificate stating that the letter of credit is not being extended and that the beneficiary is entitled to draw the full amount. If so, the beneficiary and the applicant may address in the lease, credit agreement, or underlying document what will be done with the proceeds of that draw. The parties may intend that the proceeds be held in escrow, subject to a security interest to secure the obligations, or may be held only until the applicant is able to procure an acceptable alternate letter of credit.

Even in cases such as the evergreen, in which the issuing bank can decline to extend on any anniversary, many banks also prefer to include a final maturity date beyond which there will be no extensions. This allows the issuer to clear the expired letter of credit from its books without having to obtain evidence from the beneficiary that the letter of credit was cancelled or released.

§ 7.9:6 Submission of Certificates; Sight Draft

The types of certificates that may be required in connection with a draw are subject to negotiation between the applicant and the beneficiary to conform to the provisions of the underlying contract. While older letters of credit typically required submission of a sight draft, together with certificates, these are seldomly required in more recent credits. A sight draft is a draft payable on presentation to the bank that issued the letter of credit. Form 7-3 in this chapter is a simple sight draft for use if required under the particular letter of credit.

§ 7.9:7 Submission of Originals or Electronic Copies

The parties may consider whether the beneficiary must submit originally signed certificates or other documents for the draw or whether it would be authorized to submit electronic forms of certificates. Submission of originals can require more advance planning (and potential travel time if personal deliveries are made to reduce errors), particularly if the issuing bank is located in another state. Cases have generally provided that absent specific agreement to the contrary, original documents must be presented.

§ 7.9:8 Partial Draws

ISP98 rule 3.08 provides that a standby may be drawn in partial or successive draws unless it provides to the contrary. UCP article 31 allows partial drawings but does not stipulate whether this is the default rule or if it must be reflected in the terms of the letter of credit itself. Texas law is silent regarding partial draws. If the parties intend to allow the letter of credit to be drawn in successive draws, the letter should provide this right.

§ 7.9:9 Choice of Law

The parties may choose any jurisdiction's law to control a letter of credit, regardless of whether the jurisdiction bears any relation to the transaction. If no other jurisdiction's law is specified, a letter of credit issued by a Texas bank is governed by the Texas Business and Commerce Code and may also be governed by either ISP98 or UCP, if so stated in the letter of credit. Typically, the issuer will select the law of its main office or the law of a state in which it maintains a substantial commercial presence.

§ 7.10 Pitfalls in Draw Process

As indicated at section 7.9 above, many details should be carefully considered in drafting a letter of credit. For example, when drawing on a letter of credit, the beneficiary must submit documents that comply exactly with the requirements of the letter. If the letter of credit calls for documentation the beneficiary cannot furnish, the issuer will not fund the draw. The applicant could agree to an amendment to the letter of credit or could agree that the issuer may pay a nonconforming draw, but that is unlikely if the draw is in connection with a default or other issue with the underlying contract between the beneficiary and the account party. Other potential defects could also result in a draw not being honored.

§ 7.10:1 Draw after Expiration Date of Letter of Credit

If the draw is not submitted before the stated expiration date of the letter of credit, it will not be honored. For that reason, if the letter of credit does not permit electronic submissions, the beneficiary must plan the draw sufficiently in advance to ensure that original certificates or other documentation can be delivered to the issuer before the expiration date. If the expiration date is imminent, a beneficiary may consider sending an officer or agent to the city where the submission must be made rather than relying on couriers or other delivery services.

§ 7.10:2 Inability to Present Exact Documentation Required

If the letter of credit requires specific documents that cannot be supplied, for example, a certificate of a person who is no longer part of the beneficiary or an original letter of credit that cannot be located, the issuer will likely refuse to fund the letter of credit.

§ 7.10:3 Injunction Filed by Account Party

Most issuers will not alert the account party when a draw is presented, and no issuers would ask permission to fund a draw that complies with the terms of the letter of credit. They cite their reputation as the reason: if they do not honor conforming draws, others would be unwilling to accept their letters of credit in the future. However, some letters of credit require as a part of the draw a certificate that the beneficiary has notified the account party of its intent to make the draw. If the account party disputes the draw (such as disputing that a default exists under the operating contract at the source of the letter-of-credit transaction), it may sue to enjoin the issuer from honoring the draw. While the ability of an account party to obtain such an injunction is limited, it remains a possibility. Generally, a draw will be paid unless a required document is forged or "materially fraudulent" or honoring the presentation would facilitate a material fraud by the beneficiary on the issuer or applicant. *See* Tex. Bus. & Com. Code § 5.109.

§ 7.10:4 Force Majeure Issues

As stated at section 7.6 above, whether a letter of credit can be extended due to force majeure or other extended disruptions of business depends on whether it is governed by UCP or by ISP98.

The COVID-19 pandemic raises the question whether any additional or special provisions might enable the beneficiary to obtain delays or extensions in the term of the letter of credit due to force majeure or similar theories. This is highly unlikely—the standard rules and obligations still apply—and the beneficiary should assume it is not available. A letter of credit governed by ISP98 will obtain a thirty-day extension if the issuer's place of business is closed, as discussed at section 7.6 above. A letter of credit governed by UCP article 36 will obtain an extension to the next available banking day if a bank is closed for any reason other than those set forth in article 36, also discussed at section 7.6 above. However, if the issuer's place of business is open but the beneficiary is subject to "stay home" orders or its operations are so impacted by the pandemic that it is delayed in compiling the documents necessary for the draw, it does not seem that either ISP98 or UCP will provide a specific remedy.

In March 2020, the International Chamber of Commerce (ICC) began issuing guidance, including limited emergency guidance regarding the flexibility of ICC rule interpretation for banks and, for issues beyond the ICC's reach, recommended policy and other steps for governments (Int'l Chamber of Commerce, "ICC Memo to Governments and Central Banks on Essential Steps to Safeguard Trade Finance Operations" (Apr. 6, 2020), **https://iccwbo.org/content/uploads/sites/3/2020/04/icc-memo-on-essential-steps-to-safeguard-trade-finance-operations.pdf**), as well as a guidance paper generally addressing the impact of COVID-19 on financial transactions subject to its rules (Int'l Chamber of Commerce, "Guidance Paper on the Impact of COVID-19 on Trade Finance Transactions Issued Subject to ICC Rules" (July 4, 2020), **https://iccwbo.org/content/uploads/sites/3/2020/04/2020-10-the-impact-of-covid-19.pdf**).

§ 7.11 Security Interests in Letters of Credit

Section 9.5:5 in this manual identifies the method by which a creditor may perfect a security interest in a letter of credit. Notwithstanding the ability to obtain a perfected security interest in the proceeds of the letter of credit, the secured creditor will be forced to rely on its debtor's compliance with the terms of the credit, such as submission of drafts and documents, in order to obtain proceeds. As a result, a security interest in this sort of collateral may be less desirable than a security interest in a deposit account or some other collateral that would not be so dependent on the actions of the obligor to realize its value.

§ 7.12 Additional Resources

Bastian-Rodriguez, Allison A. "Letters of Credit: Don't Forget the *Real Estate Forms Manual*!" In *Advanced Real Estate Drafting Course, 2021*. Austin: State Bar of Texas, 2021.

Byrne, James E. *Standby & Demand Guarantee Practice: Understanding UCP600, ISP98 & URDG 758*. Montgomery Village, MD: Institute of International Banking Law & Practice, Inc., 2014.

Institute of International Banking Law & Practice, Inc. *International Standby Practices: ISP98*. New York: ICC Publishing, Inc., 2012.

International Chamber of Commerce. *ICC Uniform Customs and Practice for Documentary Credits: UCP 600*. New York: ICC Publishing, Inc., 2007.

Maloney, Marilyn C. "Letters of Credit in Real Estate Transactions." In *Advanced Real Estate Law Course, 2015*. Austin: State Bar of Texas, 2015.

Form 7-1

This form outlines information to consider when applying for the issuance of a standby letter of credit or accepting a standby letter of credit. Further information regarding items on the checklist is contained in the referenced sections of the practice notes.

Checklist

[For Standby Letter of Credit]

1.	Name of the issuer.	See § 7.4
2.	Name of the confirmer (if any).	See § 7.4
3.	Name of the customer/applicant/account party.	See § 7.4
4.	Name of the beneficiary.	See § 7.4
5.	Expiration date of the letter of credit.	See § 7.9:5
6.	Is the letter of credit revocable or irrevocable?	See § 7.9:1
7.	Is the letter of credit transferable?	See § 7.9:3
8.	Are partial draws permitted?	See § 7.9:8
9.	Conditions to a draw under the letter of credit/what documents must be produced for a draw?	See §§ 7.9:2 and 7.9:6
10.	Location for presentation of documents for a draw under the letter of credit/submission required in person or via electronic means?	See § 7.9:7
11.	Does the original letter of credit have to be submitted with a draw?	See § 7.9:7
12.	Governing law/governed by ISP98 or UCP?	See §§ 7.6 and 7.9:9
13.	If governed by UCP, has the issuer modified the effect of article 36?	See § 7.6

Form 7-2

Standby Letter of Credit

Irrevocable Standby Letter of Credit No. [**number**]

Beneficiary:

Address of Beneficiary:

We hereby issue our Irrevocable Standby Letter of Credit No. [**number**] (this "Letter of Credit") in your favor at the request and for the account of [**name of account party**] in the amount up to but not exceeding the aggregate sum of [**amount in words**] U.S. Dollars (U.S. $[**amount in numerals**]) effective immediately and expiring as set forth below.

Select one of the following.

This Letter of Credit is payable only in a single drawing.

Or

This Letter of Credit is payable in partial and multiple drawings.

Continue with the following.

This Letter of Credit is payable upon presentation of the following:

Select one or more of the following.

1. Your sight draft drawn on us.

2. A written sworn statement signed by a purportedly authorized officer of Beneficiary stating that it is entitled to the amount of U.S. $[**amount**] and that the amount is due and payable as a result of the account party's failure to perform its obligations under the terms of [**identify underlying instrument, e.g.,** the credit agreement].

3. The original of this Letter of Credit.

Include other conditions as applicable.

Continue with the following.

This Letter of Credit shall expire on [**date**].

Include the following if applicable.

It is a condition of this Letter of Credit that it shall be automatically extended without amendment for an additional period of [**extension period, e.g.,** one year] from the present or any future expiration date unless at least [**number**] days before that date we notify Beneficiary in writing at its above address by registered mail or courier services that we elect not to renew this Letter of Credit for the additional period. Upon receipt by Beneficiary of such notice Beneficiary may draw under this Letter of Credit before or on the then-current expiration date by presentation to us of the following:

Select one or more of the following.

1. Your sight draft drawn on us.

2. A written sworn statement signed by a purportedly authorized officer of Beneficiary stating that it is entitled to the amount of U.S. $[**amount**] and that the amount is due and payable as a result of our having given a notice of nonextension of this Letter of Credit.

3. The original of this Letter of Credit.

Include other conditions as applicable.

Select one of the following.

This Letter of Credit may not be transferred or assigned in whole or in part.

Or

This Letter of Credit may be transferred or assigned to [**successor, e.g.,** any successor agent under the credit agreement].

Continue with the following.

This Letter of Credit sets forth in full the terms of our undertaking, which shall not in any way be modified or amplified by reference to any document, instrument, or agreement referred to herein or to which this Letter of Credit relates, and any such reference shall not be deemed to incorporate herein by reference any document, instrument, or agreement.

This Letter of Credit shall be governed by the Uniform Commercial Code as enacted in the State of [Texas/[**state**]] on the date of its issuance and shall also, to the extent not inconsistent with that code, be governed by [International Standby Practices 1998, International Chamber of Commerce Publication No. 590 (ISP98)/Uniform Customs and Practice for Documentary Credits, International Chamber of Commerce Publication No. 600 (UCP)].

Include the following if applicable.

Notwithstanding article 36 of the UCP, if this Letter of Credit expires while we are closed for a reason beyond our control, we will honor a presentation under this Letter of Credit provided the presentation is made within thirty days of the resumption of our business.

Continue with the following.

[**Name of issuer**]

By ____________________________________

[**Name and title of officer or agent**]
Date:

Form 7-3

Sight Draft

$[**Amount**]

[**Date**]

At Sight

Pay to the order of: [**name of beneficiary**]

[**Amount in words**] U.S. dollars (U.S. $[**amount in numerals**])

Value received and charged to the account of: [**name of account party**]

Drawn under Irrevocable Letter of Credit No. [**number**]

To: [**name and address of issuer of the letter of credit**]

[**Name of beneficiary**]

By ______________________________________

[**Name and title of officer or agent**]

Chapter 8
Deeds of Trust

Forms

Chapter 8

Deeds of Trust

§ 8.1 Use and Effect of Deed of Trust

A deed of trust is a mortgage with a power of sale. Although a deed of trust by its literal terms conveys the described property in trust to the trustee, its actual effect under Texas law is to create a lien against the property to secure a debt of the grantor of the lien to the beneficiary of the lien. The deed of trust is often used to establish a lien on property for which a lender has advanced purchase money, but it may also secure a loan or other obligation unrelated to the property. The primary advantage of the deed of trust over the type of mortgage used in many other states is that it provides the default remedy of nonjudicial foreclosure by a trustee's sale without the necessity of a lawsuit.

This chapter provides three basic forms: the deed of trust (form 8-1), the deed of trust to secure assumption (form 8-2), and the leasehold deed of trust (form 8-10). As discussed in this chapter, the forms may be adapted to a variety of situations.

The deed of trust often includes a security agreement and financing statement to cover personal property and fixtures associated with the real estate. For drafting instructions for using a deed of trust with a security agreement, see section 8.11:2 below.

The Texas Trust Code does not apply to a deed of trust. Tex. Prop. Code § 111.003(4).

§ 8.1:1 Terms and Conditions

The deed-of-trust form provided in this manual may be adapted to cover indebtedness other than the note specifically described, such as future advances or overdrafts, and to serve as a security agreement for personal property. Due-on-sale clauses, prohibitions against further encumbrances, and tax and insurance reserve clauses may be added. Clauses for these purposes are suggested in form 8-9 in this chapter.

§ 8.1:2 Precautions for Deed of Trust

The lender's attorney should determine whether the property is the borrower's homestead and, if so, whether a valid lien can be created against it. The Texas Constitution and Property Code allow liens against homesteads only under certain conditions. *See* Tex. Const. art. XVI, § 50; Tex. Prop. Code ch. 41.

Article XVI, section 50, of the Texas Constitution was amended in 1997 to permit home equity lending under certain circumstances. Home equity lending is discussed in chapter 11 in this manual. The attorney is cautioned against using the forms in this chapter for that purpose. In particular, the attorney should be aware that nonjudicial foreclosure is not available in home equity loans.

Trustees foreclosing under a deed of trust must comply exactly with all requirements of Property Code section 51.002, which specifies in detail the procedures for a trustee's sale. *See* Tex. Prop. Code § 51.002. Trustees must also comply with any additional requirements imposed by the deed of trust. Under certain circumstances, a lender, trustee, or substitute trustee may rescind a nonjudicial foreclosure sale involving residential real property. *See* Tex. Prop. Code § 51.016. See section 14.6:8 in this manual. Foreclosures are discussed in chapter 14.

A deed of trust is generally a component of a "loan agreement" as defined in the Texas Business and Commerce Code statute of frauds for loan documents and requires the notice prescribed therein. *See* Tex. Bus. & Com. Code § 26.02. The notice of final agreement, form 10-14 in this manual, may be used to satisfy the statutory requirements.

Texas Finance Code chapter 343 regulates certain types of home loans. For example, "[a] lender may not replace or consolidate a low-rate home loan directly made by a government or nonprofit lender before the seventh anniversary of the date of the loan" unless the transaction meets the requirements of chapter 343 of the Texas Finance Code. Tex. Fin. Code § 343.101(b). See section 10.14 for further discussion.

§ 8.2 Considerations in Drafting Deed of Trust

§ 8.2:1 Parties

For general information about designation of parties, see the remarks at section 3.10 in this manual.

The party granting the deed-of-trust lien and the borrower in the note secured are not necessarily the same party. The attorney drafting the deed of trust must make certain that all parties are properly designated. Paragraph E.14. in the deed-of-trust form (form 8-1 in this chapter) recognizes that the party granting the lien and the party obligated to pay the note may not be the same. This provision is included to add versatility to the form. The attorney dealing with such a situation, however, should consider specifying in greater detail the obligations of the respective parties—for example, that while the borrower in the note is obligated to pay the note, the grantor in the deed of trust is responsible for performance of the other covenants contained in the deed of trust, such as payment of ad valorem taxes. If the attorney elects to add such detail, the deed of trust should make clear that any default by either party is also a default by the other, entitling the lender to exercise the remedies contained in both the note and the deed of trust.

The lender should be identified by full name and, if the lender is a legal entity rather than a natural person, the type of entity. The lender's name should appear exactly as it does in the note.

Individuals, not corporations, are usually named as trustees. Institutional lenders frequently prefer to designate one of their own officers or attorneys to serve in this capacity.

One or more persons may be authorized to exercise the power of sale under a security instrument. *See* Tex. Prop. Code § 51.0074(a).

§ 8.2:2 Description of Note

The deed of trust should provide at least basic information about the note so that the note may be clearly identified. Attorneys have different ideas about how much information the deed of trust should reveal about the note being secured, and some prefer not to disclose the payment terms. Usually, though, the note's date, amount, borrower, lender, and, if desired, final maturity date are shown. If parties prefer not to disclose the payment terms, they may insert in the relevant space on the form a short phrase such as "As provided in the note" or "Monthly installments according to terms provided in the note."

If the final maturity date of the note is stated, it should be possible to avoid any assertion that limitations began to run on execution of the note. Stating the final maturity date should also make limitations available in clearing title of old time-barred deeds of trust. On the other hand, if this information is included in the deed of trust, it is critical that it be accurate and that any extensions granted by the lender be documented in a duly recorded extension agreement to preclude limitations barring a valid deed-of-trust lien against purchasers for value without notice.

§ 8.2:3 Property Description

For remarks and cautions in general about property descriptions, see section 3.8 in this manual. Also, note that the description of the property in the leasehold deed of trust (form 8-10 in this chapter) should be of the leasehold interest of the tenant granting the deed-of-trust lien.

§ 8.2:4 Prior Liens

If the deed of trust creates a first lien on the property, the word *none* is adequate for the space for listing prior liens on the form. If the lien is a second or other subordinate lien, all prior liens should be fully described.

In listing the prior liens, the attorney should not overlook previously recorded deeds of trust to secure assumption that affect the priority of subsequent liens.

§ 8.2:5 Other Exceptions to Conveyance and Warranty

For remarks about reservations from conveyance and exceptions to conveyance and warranty, see sections 5.2:6 and 5.2:7 in this manual.

§ 8.2:6 Vendor's Lien Clauses

If a vendor's lien clause is used it should be added to paragraph 19. of "General Provisions" in the deed of trust. See form 8-3 in this chapter. Clause 8-3-3 may be used if no vendor's lien is expressly retained in the deed and the note evidences money used to purchase the property.

§ 8.2:7 Mechanic's Lien Clauses

If a mechanic's lien contract with power of sale is used (such as that in chapter 20 in this manual), a deed of trust is not necessary but should be used if there is a third-party lender. If a mechanic's lien contract without a power of sale is used and a contractor wants to reserve the right to a nonjudicial foreclosure in a separate deed of trust, a clause like clause 8-9-1 should be added to paragraph 19. of "General Provisions."

§ 8.2:8 Clauses Extending Existing Liens

If an existing lien is extended, the clauses in form 8-4 in this chapter should be added to paragraph 19. of "General Provisions."

Extension of Existing Deed-of-Trust Lien: The bracketed sentences of clauses 8-4-1 through 8-4-4 are appropriate if the renewed and extended note has been assigned to the lender secured by the deed of trust but should not be used if the lender secured by the deed of trust is the original lender in the note.

In the transaction described in clause 8-4-2, the sum of the unpaid balance of the prior note and the amount of cash advanced should equal the amount of the note secured by this deed of trust.

Alternative Renewal and Extension Language: Some attorneys prefer to use more comprehensive language renewing and extending the lien than that in extension clauses 8-4-1 through 8-4-4. The language suggested in clause 8-4-5 extends a deed-of-trust lien, but it can be modified to address other types of liens. If clause 8-4-5 is used, it replaces the sentence in clauses 8-4-1 through 8-4-4 beginning "Grantor acknowledges that the lien(s) . . ."

Extension of Prior Lien to Be Released, Not Assigned: Clause 8-4-6 is drafted for use if a note and a deed of trust are being used to extend a deed-of-trust lien, but it can be modified to extend other types of liens.

Extension of Lien to Only Part of Property: Clause 8-4-7 extends a vendor's lien and a deed-of-trust lien as to only part of the property.

§ 8.2:9 Acknowledging Cash Advanced

Clause 8-3-3 in this chapter acknowledges the receipt of cash and is appropriate if all or part of the cash advanced is applied to the purchase price and no vendor's lien is retained in the deed. If cash is advanced and used for other purposes, one of the clauses in form 8-5 may be suitable or may be adapted, and it should be added to paragraph 19 of "General Provisions."

To Pay Ad Valorem Taxes: If the borrower files a sworn affidavit with the tax office authorizing the lender to pay taxes on the property, the tax office transfers the tax lien to the lender when the lender pays the taxes. The lien must be recorded in the real property records of the county in which the property is located, with a sworn statement and affidavit attesting to the transfer of the tax lien, and foreclosure on the lien may not be initiated for one year after its recording, unless the deed of trust or other agreement between the borrower and the lender provides otherwise. Tex. Tax Code §§ 32.06, 32.065. See clause 8-5-3. See also section 2.5 in this manual.

§ 8.2:10 Due-on-Sale Clause

The deed-of-trust form in this manual includes a due-on-sale clause, that is, a clause accelerating the underlying debt on the transfer of property. The attorney should remove this clause if it is not applicable to the transaction in question. Events triggering acceleration of the debt under the due-on-sale clause include transfer of the property by the owner, granting of subordinate liens on the property, and transfers of equity interest in the owner, with exceptions for transfers to other family members or entities when no change of control results. Because many lenders evaluate the creditworthiness, track record, and management ability of the grantor, as well as the predicted cash flow of the property, during the underwriting process, they require that a deed of trust contain a due-on-sale clause to prevent a change of management or ownership (including current ownership of voting interests in business entities not publicly held) without an opportunity for the lender to reevaluate the security for the loan. Many lenders also require a due-on-sale clause that applies when subordinate liens are granted because historically many bankruptcy proceedings have been funded by subordinate lenders attempting to delay foreclosure proceedings. The Texas Real Estate Commission's Seller Financing Addendum contains an election that includes a due-on-sale clause. Federal law prohibits the enforcement of a due-on-sale clause for owner-occupied residential property under certain circumstances. *See* 12 U.S.C. § 1701j–3(d); 12 C.F.R. § 591.5(b). The exceptions to the due-on-sale clause in the residential deed of trust are derived from these federal restrictions.

Alternative due-on-transfer clauses are found at clauses 8-9-21 through 8-9-23 in this chapter.

§ 8.2:11 Confidentiality Notice

If any party to a deed of trust, including the trustee, is an individual, the deed of trust must contain the confidentiality notice required by Tex. Prop. Code § 11.008. See section 3.17 in this manual.

§ 8.3 Use and Effect of Subordinate Deed of Trust

A subordinate deed of trust is one that is either recorded after a previously recorded deed of trust or, less often, expressly made subordinate to it by agreement of the lender. A deed of trust can also become subordinate by another lien's having a superpriority—for example, ad valorem tax liens. The most common uses of a subordinate deed of trust are in cases involving a borrower whose property is subject to an existing lien and who desires additional financing to be secured by the same property, and in cases involving seller financing.

A wraparound mortgage is a subordinate mortgage secured by real property on which a prior lien remains outstanding and unsatisfied and on which the original obligor remains obligated. The wraparound debt includes within it the balance of the underlying lien debt. In some wraparound mortgages the prior lien may be "wrapped" more than once.

In a wraparound financing transaction, the borrower (usually the buyer) agrees to make payments on the wraparound mortgage to the lender (usually the seller) who, as required by the wraparound mortgage agreement, must in turn make payments on the prior, underlying, or wrapped lien to the prior lienholder. If the lender fails to pay off the first lien, the wraparound agreement normally gives the borrower the right to make the first-lien payments and receive credit on the wraparound note. The two primary reasons for a wraparound transaction are to take advantage of the spread in interest rates between the underlying and wrap notes and to provide the wrap-note lender with the assurances that the underlying note payments are made. Use of the forms provided in this manual for a wraparound transaction requires the use of specific clauses in both the note and the deed of trust. For examples of these, see clauses 6-6-4 and 8-9-11 in this manual.

§ 8.4 Precautions for Subordinate Deed of Trust

Subordinate lien financing involves a number of considerations for all the parties involved: the borrower, the prior lender, and the subordinate lender. The borrower should ascertain that the creation of a subordinate lien will not be a default under the prior deed of trust, because subordinate encumbrances are expressly prohibited in many deeds of trust. The prior lender may have concerns about the ability of the borrower to service both the superior and subordinate lien debts. If the borrower should default on the subordinate lien debt and the subordinate lender should foreclose, the borrower, although still liable on the debt, will no longer be the owner of the property, and the incentive to repay the senior loan will obviously be diminished.

The party at greatest risk in subordinate lien financing transactions is the subordinate lender. Foreclosure of a superior lien extinguishes all subordinate liens. *See Exchange Savings & Loan Ass'n v. Monocrete Proprietary, Ltd.*, 629 S.W.2d 34 (Tex. 1982). In Texas, unlike many other jurisdictions, a subordinate lienholder is not entitled by law to notice of default on the prior lien debt or notice of foreclosure proceedings. The subordinate lienholder is likewise not entitled to share in the foreclosure proceeds, unless there is an excess after payment of costs and expenses in connection with the foreclosure and satisfaction of the prior lien debt. The subordinate lienholder may therefore want to obtain the prior lienholder's agreement to provide notice of any default by the borrower under the first-lien note and deed of trust and the opportunity to cure such default or require the borrower to provide continuing proof that payments on the prior lien debt have been made.

Another concern for the subordinate lender is the potential application of a "dragnet" or "other indebtedness" clause in the prior deed of trust. If the prior deed of trust secures debt of the borrower other than the prior lien note itself, there is a likelihood that the total debt secured by the prior lien will exceed the value of the property, and the subordinate lender's lien may be for all practical purposes worthless. These are issues that the subordinate lender may want to address by an agreement with the prior lender, generally called a lender's "estoppel certificate" or an intercreditor agreement. See form 10-10 in this manual.

A subordinate lien transaction may be subject to chapter 342 of the Texas Finance Code if the property is a dwelling designed for occupancy by four or fewer families and the interest rate exceeds 10 percent per year. *See* Tex. Fin. Code §§ 342.001(4), 342.005. Chapter 342 applies to a secondary mortgage loan made by a person in the business of making, arranging, or negotiating those types of loans. Tex. Fin. Code § 342.005(3). The chapter does not apply to a secondary mortgage loan made by a seller of property to secure all or part of the unpaid purchase price. Tex. Fin. Code § 342.006. If a lender is in the business of making, arranging, or negotiating secondary mortgage loans, the lender must obtain a license from the Office of Consumer Credit Commissioner (the OCCC) unless the lender is a bank, savings bank, savings and loan association, credit union, or a residential mortgage loan originator licensed under chapter 156. *See* Tex. Fin. Code §§ 124.005, 339.004, 341.103–.104, 342.051. Unless exempt under section 180.003, an individual who acts as a residential mortgage loan originator in the making, transacting, or negotiating of a secondary mortgage loan subject to chapter 342 must individually be licensed under chapter 342, be enrolled with the Nationwide Mortgage Licensing System and Registry as required by section 180.52, and comply with other applicable requirements of the Texas Secure and Fair Enforcement of Mortgage Licensing Act of 2009. Tex. Fin. Code ch. 180.

Chapter 342 loans are highly specialized and regulated, and thus if a subordinate lien transaction is subject to chapter 342, the attorney must carefully review the chapter to make sure all requirements have been met. Texas Finance Code section 341.502 provides that "[a] contract for a loan under Chapter 342, a retail installment transaction under Chapter 348, or a home equity loan regulated by the Office of Consumer Credit Commissioner must be . . . written in plain language designed to be easily understood by the average consumer." Tex. Fin. Code § 341.502(a). The Finance Commission of Texas is authorized to adopt model contracts for loans subject to that section. A lender may not use a contract other than a model contract unless the lender has submitted the contract to the OCCC for its approval. If the OCCC issues an order disapproving a submitted contract, the lender may not use the contract after the order takes effect. Tex. Fin. Code § 341.502(b)–(d). Plain-language model contracts and related rules for chapter 342, subchapter G, second-lien home improvement contracts are codified at 7 Tex. Admin. Code §§ 90.601–.604.

The attorney general of Texas determined that section 341.502(a) is applicable only to those loan transactions for which the consumer credit commissioner is the appointed regulating official and has no application to loan transactions subject to the regulatory authority of the banking commissioner, the savings and mortgage lending commissioner, the credit union commissioner, and federal regulatory officials. *See* Tex. Att'y Gen. Op. No. JC-0513 (2002).

Banks, savings and loan associations, and credit unions accordingly are not required to comply with the section 341.502 "plain language" contract requirements or to obtain a license to engage in the business of making subordinate lien loans subject to chapter 342. Tex. Fin. Code § 342.051(c)(1). These institutional lenders nevertheless are thought to be subject to other substantive law provisions of chapter 342, including, for example, the limitations of that chapter on the collection of authorized fees and charges, as enforced by the policies of their respective regulatory agencies. *See* Tex. Fin. Code §§ 342.308, 342.502.

Before using the deed-of-trust forms contained in this chapter of the manual for a loan subject to chapter 342 of the Texas Finance Code, the attorney should determine whether the lender is subject to the plain-language model contract provisions of Texas Finance Code section 341.502. The forms contained in this chapter have not been submitted to or approved by the OCCC.

If the attorney decides that the forms contained in this chapter may nevertheless be used for a loan regulated by chapter 342 of the Texas Finance Code, the forms still must be modified to comply with the requirements of that chapter. For example, the secondary mortgage loan documents for a loan made by a licensed lender must contain the name, mailing address, and telephone number of the OCCC. Tex. Fin. Code § 14.104. See clause 8-9-24 in this chapter. Neither the deed-of-trust forms nor the note forms in this manual contain that information. The attorney should include that information in both the deed-of-trust form and the note form when documenting a secondary mortgage loan if the lender has a license from the OCCC. Additionally, if a subordinate lien transaction is subject to chapter 342, the printed language in the deed of trust must be modified slightly. In paragraph 4. of "Grantor's Obligations," the phrase "issued by insurers and written on policy forms acceptable to Lender" must be struck. This change is necessary because Finance Code sections 342.404 through 342.405 and 342.413 prohibit a lender from approving the selection of insurance. *See* Tex. Fin. Code §§ 342.404–.405, 342.413. Also, Finance Code section 342.404 provides that when insurance is required in connection with a loan made under that chapter, the lender must furnish the borrower a statement like the one in clause 8-9-9, which may be added to the deed of trust as a numbered paragraph under "General Provisions." *See* Tex. Fin. Code § 342.404.

The same chapter imposes other requirements if the lender sells or procures insurance related to the loan at a rate not fixed or approved by the State Board of Insurance. *See* Tex. Fin. Code § 342.405.

Finance Code section 342.307 limits the enforcement fees that may be included in secondary mortgage loan documents. To comply with this section, the attorney's fee provisions in the note, form 6-1, and the deed of trust should be modified if used in transactions subject to chapter 342 of the Finance Code. *See* Tex. Fin. Code § 342.307. In the note, the third paragraph, concerning attorney's fees, should be replaced with clause 6-6-15. See section 6.2:7. To modify the deed of trust, in paragraph E.16., after the words "an attorney" add "who is not an employee of Lender."

An institutional third-party lender may be required to provide the borrower a truth-in-lending disclosure (loan) form. An example of this form is included in chapter 12 in this manual. The clauses in form 8-8 are examples of second-lien clauses.

If the prior deed of trust contains a due-on-sale clause, the wraparound deed-of-trust conveyance, like other subordinate liens, may violate the due-on-sale clause.

The wraparound mortgage has usury implications that are not yet fully settled, centering primarily around the issue of whether the entire principal amount of the wraparound note or merely the difference between the principal amount of the wraparound note and the balance of the underlying note should be used for interest calculations. The attorney is referred to the December 31, 1981, letter from the OCCC, which may be obtained from that office, and to *Summers v. Consolidated Capital Special Trust*, 783 S.W.2d 580 (Tex. 1989), for two analyses of these issues.

The wraparound mortgage, like other subordinate lien mortgages, may be subject to chapter 342 of the Texas Finance Code.

§ 8.5 Considerations in Drafting Subordinate Deed of Trust

It is essential that a subordinate deed of trust contain terms and provisions identifying the prior lien and obligating the borrower to keep the prior note and deed of trust current and not in default. The clauses in form 8-8 in this chapter may be used for this purpose. The parties may wish to attempt to obtain an estoppel letter or intercreditor agreement from the prior lienholder. An example of such an instrument may be found at form 10-10 in this manual.

There are additional considerations in drafting instruments for a wraparound transaction: modification of the warranty deed with vendor's lien (see chapter 5), promissory note (see chapter 6), and deed of trust (see sections 8.2:1 through 8.2:9 above). These forms should be completed according to the instructions in their respective sections of this manual, and then all three documents should be modified further according to the instructions in sections 8.5:1 through 8.5:4 below.

§ 8.5:1 Additional Clauses for Wraparound Deed of Trust

A deed of trust should be drafted according to the comments in sections 8.2:1 through 8.2:9 above and then modified to accommodate a wraparound transaction.

If the transaction is subject to chapter 342 of the Texas Finance Code, see section 8.4 above for a suggested modification of the form.

In the space following "General Provisions," a vendor's lien clause like clause 8-3-1 in this chapter should appear. Also, a wraparound clause similar to clause 8-9-11 should be included in the same part of the deed of trust.

If the deed of trust securing the prior note requires monthly deposits to a reserve account for payment of taxes and insurance premiums, a similar requirement should be inserted in the wraparound deed of trust securing the wraparound note. A clause serving this purpose appears at 8-9-4. Also, language similar to that suggested in the second part of clause 8-9-11 should be added to the wraparound lien clause.

§ 8.5:2 Additional Documents for Use with Wraparound Mortgage

An additional document often used in wraparound transactions is a collection agreement specifying the terms by which the borrower makes payments on the subordinate lien note to an escrow agent, usually a bank, rather than to the lender. This procedure protects the borrower from the possibility that the lender will fail to forward part of the payment to the holder of the prior lien. The lender's failure to make payments on the prior lien would, of course, cause a default that the borrower would have to cure to avoid a foreclosure on the property. A collection agreement usually provides that the agent will use the borrower's subordinate lien payment to pay the prior lienholder and then remit the excess to the lender. A sample of such an agreement is found at form 10-7 in this manual.

§ 8.5:3 Statute Applicable to Wraparound Mortgages for Certain Residential Real Estate Transactions

Subtitle E, title 3, Finance Code, amended effective January 1, 2022, adds chapter 159, "Wrap Mortgage Loan Financing," for residential real estate transactions. Unless exempt, any owner of Texas residential real estate who makes more than three wrap mortgage loans for all or part of the purchase price to purchasers of that property in any twelve-consecutive-month period must comply with certain licensing, transactional, and disclosure requirements. See Tex. Fin. Code §§ 159.001–.108. See section 8.5 above. A chapter 159 wrap mortgage is defined as a loan that is made to finance the purchase of residential real estate that will continue to be subject to an unreleased lien that (a) attached to the residential real estate before the loan was made, (b) secures a debt incurred by a person other than the wrap borrower that was not paid off at the time the loan was made, and (c) obligates the wrap borrower to the wrap lender for payment of the outstanding principal balance of the debt and any remaining amount of the purchase price financed by the wrap lender. See Tex. Fin. Code § 159.001(7). A person may not originate or make a wrap mortgage loan unless the person is licensed or registered to originate or make residential mortgage loans under chapter 156 ("Residential Mortgage Loan Companies"), 157 ("Mortgage Bankers and Residential Mortgage Loan Originators"), or 342 ("Consumer Loans") or is exempt from licensing or registration as provided under an applicable provision of those chapters. Tex. Fin. Code § 159.051.

Wrap mortgages on unimproved property or for the sale of residential real estate that is the wrap lender's homestead are exempt from the requirements of chapter 159. *See* Tex. Fin. Code § 159.002. For a list of exemptions, *see* Tex. Fin. Code § 156.202, 157.0121, 159.003.

In addition to the notice requirements of Tex. Prop. Code § 5.016, Tex. Fin. Code § 159.101 provides that wrap mortgage lenders subject to Tex. Fin. Code ch. 159 must, on or before the seventh day before the wrap mortgage loan agreement is entered into, provide to the wrap borrower a separate written disclosure statement in at least twelve-point type in substantially the following form:

> NOTICE REGARDING PROPERTY INSURANCE: ANY INSURANCE MAINTAINED BY A SELLER, LENDER, OR OTHER PERSON WHO IS NOT THE BUYER OF THIS PROPERTY MAY NOT PROVIDE COVERAGE TO THE BUYER IF THE BUYER SUFFERS A LOSS OR INCURS LIABILITY IN CONNECTION WITH THE PROPERTY. TO ENSURE THE BUYER'S INTERESTS ARE PROTECTED, THE BUYER SHOULD PURCHASE THE BUYER'S OWN PROPERTY INSURANCE. BEFORE PURCHASING THIS PROPERTY, YOU MAY WISH TO CONSULT AN INSURANCE AGENT REGARDING THE INSURANCE COVERAGE AVAILABLE TO YOU AS A BUYER OF THE PROPERTY.

This disclosure statement must be dated and signed by the wrap borrower upon receipt. If the negotiations with the borrower were conducted primarily in a language other than English, the wrap lender must provide the disclosure in that other language. Tex. Fin. Code § 159.102.

Failure to timely provide the wrap mortgage loan disclosure can result in dire consequences for a wrap lender, specifically due to the tolling of limitations and rescission of the wrap mortgage loan agreement and related purchase agreement. If a wrap lender fails to provide the disclosure statement, the statute of limitations period applicable to any cause of action the wrap borrower has against the wrap lender in connection with the wrap mortgage loan is tolled until the 120th day after the date the disclosure is provided. *See* Tex. Fin. Code § 159.103(d). As it relates to rescission, if the disclosure statement and any required foreign language disclosure statement are received by the wrap borrower on or before the closing date of the wrap mortgage loan, the wrap borrower may rescind the loan for up to the seventh day after the date of receipt of the statement, regardless of whether disclosure is timely made. *See* Tex. Fin. Code § 159.101(d). If the wrap borrower receives the required disclosure after closing but before rescinding the loan, the wrap borrower may rescind the loan up to twenty-one days after receipt of the disclosure. *See* Tex. Fin. Code § 159.104(b). If the wrap lender fails to provide the disclosure altogether, the wrap borrower may rescind the loan at any time. *See* Tex. Fin. Code § 159.104(a). No later than thirty days after rescission, the wrap lender must return all principal and interest payments made by the wrap borrower on the wrap mortgage loan; any money or property given as earnest money, down payment, or otherwise in connection with the wrap mortgage loan or related purchase transaction; and any escrow amounts for the wrap mortgage loan or related purchase transaction. Tex. Fin. Code § 159.104(c). The wrap lender may avoid rescission if, no later than thirty days after receiving a notice of rescission, the wrap lender pays the outstanding principal balance on the original obligation as defined in Tex. Fin. Code § 159.001(7), pays due and unpaid taxes or government assessments, pays the wrap borrower noncompliance damages of $1,000 and reasonable attorney's fees, and provides to the wrap borrower evidence of the loan, tax, and assessment payoffs. Tex. Fin. Code § 159.104(e).

Chapter 159 continues with enforcement rights and remedies. Section 159.105 states that a lien securing a wrap mortgage loan is void unless the transaction is closed by an attorney or a title company. Sections 159.151 and 159.152 provide that a person who receives a payment from a wrap borrower holds the payment in trust for the benefit of the wrap borrower and owes a fiduciary duty to the wrap borrower to use the payment to satisfy the obligations of the prior lien and any taxes and insurance for which the wrap lender has received such payments from the wrap borrower. The Texas Finance Commission has the authority to investigate and inspect certain lenders, issue cease and desist orders, and impose administrative penalties of up to $1,000 per day for violation of such orders. See Tex. Fin. Code § 159.252, 159.253, 159.301. Lenders considering making wrap mortgages on residential property should carefully review Tex. Fin. Code ch. 159.

The Texas Finance Commission has adopted a model form that satisfies these requirements, which is accessible at **https://texreg.sos.state.tx.us/fids/202105163-1.pdf**.

§ 8.5:4 Other Comments

The prior note may be secured by liens other than those discussed in sections 8.2:6 through 8.2:9 above. If so, those liens should be described.

The lender sometimes adds to the clauses a provision that, as between the borrower and the lender, the lender is not required to make payments under the prior note or liens if the borrower fails to make payments on the wraparound note.

The borrower often insists on another modification of the clauses to provide compensation beyond the amount tendered to cure a default by the lender in payment of the prior note. A common provision credits the borrower with 110 percent of the payment made to cure the default and characterizes the added 10 percent as liquidated damages to compensate for expenses incurred.

The borrower also will often include in the wraparound note a requirement that the lender must give notice regularly that the prior note payment has been made.

The wraparound note should be structured so that payments are due before payments are due on the prior note.

§ 8.5:5 Confidentiality Notice

If any party to a deed of trust, including the trustee, is an individual, the deed of trust must contain the confidentiality notice required by Tex. Prop. Code § 11.008. See section 3.17 in this manual.

§ 8.6 Use and Effect of Deed of Trust to Secure Assumption

The deed of trust to secure assumption may be used if the buyer assumes payment of a debt for which the seller is liable at the time of sale. If this instrument is used under these circumstances, the seller usually conveys title by deed with a vendor's lien reserved. The assumed debt and lien are evidenced by a note and deed of trust. The deed of trust to secure assumption provides that the lien it creates is released with the release of the prior deed of trust, unless before the release the seller files a notice with the proper county clerk setting forth any amount the seller has advanced to cure a default in payment of the assumed lien.

The primary function of the deed of trust to secure assumption is to give the seller recourse against the property if the buyer defaults in payment of the debt secured by the first lien.

In a transaction involving the deed of trust to secure assumption the buyer is the grantor in the deed of trust to secure assumption and the grantee in the warranty deed. The seller is the grantor in the warranty deed, the lender in the deed of trust to secure assumption, and usually the borrower in the note and grantor in the deed of trust assumed.

Caution: The deed of trust to secure assumption is not appropriate for use in a wraparound mortgage transaction. Also, its use may violate a due-on-sale clause in the prior deed of trust.

§ 8.7 Considerations in Drafting Deed of Trust to Secure Assumption

Chapter 3 in this manual offers useful suggestions for completing the basic information required for this form, such as designation of parties and recording information. The property description should either repeat exactly the description in the deed of trust assumed or incorporate that description by reference. References to the deed of trust should include its recording information.

§ 8.7:1 Additional Clauses for Use with Deed of Trust to Secure Assumption

The assumption provision in the deed includes an indemnity against all damages caused by the assuming party's breach of its obligations. It is likely, considering the election-of-remedies provision of paragraph 3. under section D, "General Provisions," in the deed of trust to secure assumption, that a cause of action for damages would survive action taken under the deed of trust to secure assumption.

§ 8.7:2 Warranty Deed Provisions for Use with Deed of Trust to Secure Assumption

The grantor in the warranty deed accompanying the deed of trust to secure assumption is the beneficiary (lender) of the deed of trust to secure assumption, and the buyer of the property is the grantee in the deed and the borrower (grantor) in the deed of trust to secure assumption.

The deed should contain an assumption clause like clause 5-6-1 in this manual and a clause for vendor's lien and deed of trust to secure assumption like clause 5-9-10 or 5-9-11.

§ 8.8 Use of Leasehold Deed of Trust

The leasehold deed of trust should be used if the grantor is encumbering a leasehold interest instead of a fee interest in real property. The grantor of the leasehold deed of trust must be the tenant under the lease encumbered by the leasehold deed of trust.

The attorney drafting the leasehold deed of trust must first determine if the tenant's interest in the lease may be encumbered. The encumbrance of a tenant's interest in a lease is considered a sublease under Texas law. *See Amco Trust, Inc. v. Naylor*, 317 S.W.2d 47 (Tex. 1958); *American National Bank & Trust Co. v. First Wisconsin Mortgage Trust*, 577 S.W.2d 312 (Tex. App.—Beaumont 1979, writ ref'd n.r.e.), *disapproved on other grounds by Stewart Title Guaranty Co. v. Sterling*, 822 S.W.2d 1, 11 (Tex. 1991). Section 91.005 of the Property Code prohibits subleases without the prior consent of the landlord. Also, many leases in Texas expressly prohibit the subleasing or encumbering of the tenant's interest without the landlord's consent. However, a tenant whose lease gives authorization to sublease any part of the leased premises also has the right to encumber the leasehold estate. *See Menger v. Ward*, 30 S.W. 853 (Tex. 1895).

Therefore, the attorney must find that the lease allows encumbrance of the tenant's interest without the landlord's consent or that any required landlord consent has been obtained before execution of the leasehold deed of trust. See form 8-11 in this chapter for a form of consent by landlord to a leasehold deed of trust that also includes additional representations and agreements by the landlord that a lender will require as a condition to making a loan secured by the leasehold deed of trust, including the opportunity to cure defaults by the tenant under the lease.

In addition to a description of the lease, the leasehold deed of trust contains affirmative and negative covenants and representations by the grantor that relate specifically to the lease that is being encumbered. These covenants are intended generally to cause the grantor to keep the lease in effect during the term of the loan in substantially the same status as the grantor represented it to be when the loan was made.

Certain covenants in the deed of trust (form 8-1) that may be inconsistent with the tenant's obligations under the lease (for example, payment of taxes, maintenance and repair, and insurance) have been deleted from the leasehold deed of trust in favor of the covenants by the grantor to observe and perform all of its obligations and to enforce the landlord's obligations under the lease.

§ 8.8:1 Confidentiality Notice

If any party to a deed of trust, including the trustee, is an individual, the deed of trust must contain the confidentiality notice required by Tex. Prop. Code § 11.008. See section 3.17 in this manual.

§ 8.8:2 Title Insurance for Leasehold Deeds of Trust

A leasehold loan policy endorsement (T-5) is available, at no extra charge, for leasehold deeds of trust.

§ 8.9 Use of Consent to Leasehold Deed of Trust

If the lease does not allow encumbrance of the tenant's interest without the landlord's consent, the lease will also not contain the additional representations and agreements by the landlord that a lender will typically require as a condition to making a loan secured by the leasehold deed of trust. In this case, the lender not only must obtain the written consent of the landlord to the leasehold deed of trust but should also seek from the landlord certain representations about the status of the lease and certain affirmative and negative covenants designed to preserve the lease as viable collateral for the loan. The consent to leasehold deed of trust (form 8-11 in this chapter) may be used for this purpose.

Form 8-11 covers common issues of importance to the lender, including rights to give to the tenant notice and cure of tenant defaults, access to the leased premises to enforce a security interest in the tenant's personalty, free assignability of the lease at foreclosure and to a purchaser from the lender of the tenant's assets after foreclosure, and to demand a new lease on the same terms if the lease is terminated or rejected by a trustee in bankruptcy. The lender that is considering demanding a new lease should also be aware of the effect of the termination of the lease on any subleases in effect as of the termination and may wish to consider adding to form 8-11 a provision that allows the new tenant to reinstate desirable subleases without the landlord's consent.

§ 8.10 Additional Clauses

If used, clauses such as those in form 8-9 in this chapter should appear as numbered paragraphs following paragraph E.12. in the deed of trust (form 8-1), paragraph E.9. in the deed of trust to secure assumption (form 8-2), and paragraph G.11. in the leasehold deed of trust (form 8-10).

Both the deed of trust and the deed of trust to secure assumption may be modified to secure other obligations of the borrower such as guaranties and "subject to" transactions in which the borrower does not assume the underlying debt.

§ 8.10:1 Future Advances

Future advance clauses may be enforceable to the extent that they secure a debt that is within the reasonable contemplation of the parties when the deed of trust is executed. The lien securing a future advance may have priority over an intervening lien if the intervening lienholder has notice that the earlier lien secures future advances. Form 8-6 in this chapter contains several examples of future advance clauses. If the future indebtedness to be secured is that of someone other than the borrower granting the lien, these clauses should be modified accordingly.

Clause 8-6-4, in addition to future advances, also covers present or future debts of other borrowing entities in which the borrower has an interest.

§ 8.10:2 Partial Release

If the parties anticipate circumstances requiring partial release of the lien, such as subdivision of the property, they often include partial release provisions in the deed of trust or, if the terms are complex and lengthy, in a separate agreement referred to in the deed of trust. The partial release clause should specify exactly which part of the property will be released from the lien and what amount of debt must be paid. The terms of release, especially an accurate description of the affected property, must be precise. The clauses in form 8-7 in this chapter are examples of partial release clauses. The first is for use if releases are by acre, the second if the property is subdivided at the time of the granting of the deed of trust, and the third if a separate agreement is used in connection with a seller-financed sale contemplating the buyer's subdivision of the property. Because each situation requiring a partial release is unique, these clauses must be adapted to the particular situation at hand.

For an example of a partial release of lien, see form 10-3 in this manual.

§ 8.10:3 Recordkeeping

If the property covered by the deed of trust is income-producing, the lender will frequently require the grantor to maintain records of operation on the property and make them available for the lender's review. Clause 8-9-14 in this chapter contains such a requirement.

§ 8.10:4 Financial Statements

If the loan is commercial, the lender will frequently require the grantor to prepare and submit to the lender periodic financial statements, either on request or on an annual basis. Such a requirement is also sometimes imposed in connection with residential construction loans, but rarely in connection with residential mortgage loans. Clause 8-9-15 in this chapter requires financial statements from the grantor.

§ 8.10:5 Appraisals

In the aftermath of the banking and thrift crisis of the 1980s, the requirements for appraisals of real property securing loans made by federally insured lenders were greatly strengthened and banking regulatory agencies were required to develop standards for appraisals. *See* 12 U.S.C. §§ 3331, 3335. These standards were codified at 12 C.F.R. §§ 34.41–.47, 225.61–.67, 323.1–.7, 564.1–.8. Appraisals may be required not only in connection with the underwriting of the loan but also during its term. Clause 8-9-16 in this chapter allows the lender to obtain such appraisals at the grantor's expense.

§ 8.10:6 Further Assurances

Institutional lenders commonly require grantors to agree to reexecute documents, modify executed documents, or execute additional documents if the lender determines that it is necessary to secure or perfect the lender's liens or security interests or to correct errors in the loan documents. Such agreements, commonly called agreements for further assurances, may take the form of separate documents, or they may be included as clauses in the loan documents. Clause 8-9-17 in this chapter is a further assurance clause for use in the deed of trust.

§ 8.10:7 Insurance

The attorney may wish to substitute the more detailed insurance provisions found at clause 8-9-18 in this chapter for the existing provisions in the deed-of-trust form, particularly if the deed of trust covers income-producing property or secures a construction loan. If clause 8-9-18 is used, it replaces the clause at paragraph B.1. in the deed of trust. Form 8-12 describes specific endorsements and coverage that the lender may want to include.

If the lender requires contractual indemnity from the borrower independent of insurance, or for damages that would otherwise be the lender's responsibility (for example, arising out of the ordinary negligence or strict liability of the lender), form 8-12 may be used, adapted, or incorporated into the deed of trust. Clauses that indemnify the lender for the lender's negligence or other liability must be in type more conspicuous than the other indemnity language in the document.

§ 8.10:8 Subordinate Liens

In the context of commercial loans, the lender may wish to prohibit junior liens against the property because their foreclosure would divest the grantor of title to the collateral for the loan, even though the foreclosure would not affect the prior lien position. Clause 8-9-19 in this chapter prohibits subordinate liens against the property covered by the deed of trust.

§ 8.10:9 Business Use

The applicability of several Texas statutes depends on whether loan proceeds are used primarily for business, commercial, investment, or similar purposes or are made primarily for personal, family, or household use. Texas Business and Commerce Code section 26.02 provides that the statute-of-frauds provisions for written loan agreements do not apply to certain loans made primarily for personal, family, or household use. *See* Tex. Bus. & Com. Code § 26.02(a)(2). Texas Civil Practice and Remedies Code section 15.020 excludes from the definition of a major transaction one entered into primarily for personal, family, or household purposes. Parties to a major transaction may agree in writing that a suit arising from the transaction may be brought in a specific county of the state. *See* Tex. Civ. Prac. & Rem. Code § 15.020. Texas Finance Code section 303.009(c) provides that credit extended for business, commercial, investment, or similar purposes may take advantage of interest rate ceilings up to 28 percent per year rather than the otherwise applicable 24 percent per year maximum rate ceiling. *See* Tex. Fin. Code § 303.009(c). Finance Code section 306.001(5) defines a commercial loan as a loan made primarily for business, commercial, investment, agricultural, or similar purposes and not including a loan made primarily for personal, family, or household use. *See* Tex. Fin. Code § 306.001(5). The Finance Code includes special provisions for commercial loans. For example, section 342.005 subjects a loan extended primarily for personal, family, or household use to the requirements of Finance Code chapter 342. *See* Tex. Fin. Code § 342.005. If a party is relying on any of these statutes as a basis for terms of a transaction, a statement of the purpose of the loan establishes a basis for that reliance. See clause 8-9-20 in this chapter.

§ 8.10:10 No Personal Liability

If the lender is satisfied that the collateral itself is ample security for the repayment of the loan, the lender may agree that the borrower will have no personal liability for the repayment of the loan and that the lender's sole recourse in the event of default is to foreclose on the collateral. Such agreements generally except from the "no personal liability" conditions certain "bad acts" by the borrower, such as failure to pay taxes, misapplication of insurance proceeds, failure to pay charges for labor and material that could give rise to liens against the property, and diversion of revenues from the operation of the property. See clause 8-9-26 in this chapter.

§ 8.10:11 Due-on-Sale Clause

Institutional lenders often base their willingness to make a loan on the creditworthiness of the borrower, rather than the expected cash flow of the property, and in such cases generally want the original borrower to own the property as long as the loan remains outstanding. See section 8.2:10 above for a discussion of due-on-sale clauses.

§ 8.11 Deed of Trust as Security Agreement and Financing Statement

In addition to creating a lien on the real property conveyed, the deed of trust with a few modifications can serve as a security agreement for personal property collateral related to the real estate and thus give the creditor the benefit of the secured transactions provisions of revised chapter 9 of the Texas Business and Commerce Code (Tex. Bus. & Com. Code §§ 9.101–.709). With other modifications described below, it may also serve as a financing statement for several classifications of collateral, including fixtures.

§ 8.11:1 Legal Considerations

The attorney should refer to revised chapter 9 of the Texas Business and Commerce Code for the requirements for creating and perfecting a security interest. *See* Tex. Bus. & Com. Code §§ 9.203, 9.308–.316, 9.502.

If the deed of trust, as security agreement, covers both personal and real property and the debtor defaults, the creditor may proceed under chapter 9 of the Code as to the personal property without prejudicing any rights with respect to the real property or "may proceed . . . as to both the personal property and the real property in accordance with the rights with respect to the real property," in which case the default provisions of chapter 9 do not apply. Tex. Bus. & Com. Code § 9.604(a). The deed of trust creates a lien on fixtures even without constituting a security agreement because chapter 9 does not prevent creation of an encumbrance on fixtures under real property law. *See* Tex. Bus. & Com. Code § 9.334(b). If the deed of trust, as security agreement, covers goods that are or become fixtures, the creditor may proceed under chapter 9 or may proceed in accordance with the rights with respect to real property, in which case the default provisions of chapter 9 do not apply. Tex. Bus. & Com. Code § 9.604(b).

A properly created and perfected security interest affords the creditor the benefit of the priorities established by chapter 9, which can protect the creditor against other creditors claiming the same collateral. In many cases, a valid security interest may be perfected by the proper filing of a financing statement in the appropriate UCC filing offices. See section 9.5 in this manual for a discussion of the other means of perfecting an attached security interest. Chapter 9 generally requires that financing statements be filed in the office of the secretary of state. The proper place to file a financing statement covering as-extracted collateral (which includes oil, gas, or other minerals), timber to be cut, or fixtures, however, is the real estate recording office for a mortgage on the related real property. Tex. Bus. & Com. Code § 9.501(a). A deed of trust duly recorded in the proper office will be effective as a financing statement covering as-extracted collateral, timber, or fixtures if it—

1. provides the name of the debtor (grantor);
2. provides the name of the secured party (beneficiary) or the secured party's representative;
3. indicates the goods, fixtures, or accounts that it covers;
4. indicates that it covers this type of collateral;
5. indicates that it is to be filed for record in the real property records;
6. provides a legally sufficient description of the real property to which the collateral is related; and
7. provides the name of a record owner if the debtor does not have an interest of record in the real property (for example, a leasehold estate not filed of record).

Tex. Bus. & Com. Code § 9.502(a), (b).

In addition to the foregoing minimum requirements, a real estate filing office may refuse to accept a deed of trust filed as a financing statement unless it also—

8. provides the debtor's mailing address;
9. indicates whether the debtor is an individual or an organization;
10. if the debtor is an individual, indicates the debtor's surname; and
11. provides the mailing address of the secured party or its representative.

Tex. Bus. & Com. Code § 9.516(b)(3)(C), (b)(4), (b)(5).

The difference in legal effect between the absence from the deed of trust of any of the minimum requirements in items 1. through 7. above and the absence from the deed of trust of any of the requirements in items 8. through 11. above is that, in the former case, the deed of trust *will be ineffective* as a financing statement even if it is accepted for filing by the real estate filing office, whereas in the latter case the recorded deed of trust *will be effective* as a financing statement (as long as the requirements in items 1. through 7. are included). *See* Tex. Bus. & Com. Code § 9.520(c). If the deed of trust is to serve as a financing statement, the preparer should note the first boxed instruction in forms 8-1 and 8-2 in this chapter calling for the inclusion of the information set forth in items 8. through 11. above that is not already called for in those forms.

No filing fee is required beyond the regular fee charged for recording the deed of trust with respect to a deed of trust that is effective as a financing statement filed as a fixture filing or as a financing statement covering as-extracted collateral or timber to be cut. Tex. Bus. & Com. Code § 9.525(e). Unlike a regular financing statement (which is effective, if not continued, for only five years from the date of filing), a deed of trust that satisfies the above requirements is effective as a fixture filing, and as a financing statement covering as-extracted collateral or timber to be cut, "until the mortgage is released or satisfied of record or its effectiveness otherwise terminates as to the real property." Tex. Bus. & Com. Code § 9.515(g).

For other documents and commentary relating to security agreements and financing statements, see chapter 9 in this manual.

§ 8.11:2 Modifications and Clauses

If the deed of trust is to serve as a security agreement or as a security agreement and a financing statement, a heading to that effect should be added beneath or beside the "Deed of Trust" heading.

Chapter 9, as effective July 1, 2001, retains the requirement that a security agreement reasonably identify the collateral. *See* Tex. Bus. & Com. Code §§ 9.108(a), 9.203(b)(3)(A). Reasonable identification of collateral may be by specific listing, category, type, quantity, computational formula, or any other method under which the identity of the collateral is objectively determinable. Tex. Bus. & Com. Code § 9.108(b). In a security agreement, an "all assets" or "all personal property" description is, however, insufficient. Tex. Bus. & Com. Code § 9.108(c). Even though an "all assets" or "all personal property" collateral description is insufficient in a security agreement, an indication in a financing statement that the collateral is "all assets or all personal property" is sufficient. Tex. Bus. & Com. Code § 9.504. Accordingly, if a deed of trust is to be used as a security agreement as well as a financing statement, the deed of trust must reasonably identify the collateral. If, however, the deed of trust is to serve only as a financing statement, an "all assets or all personal property" description is sufficient.

If the collateral is not affixed to the real estate conveyed, it may be sufficiently described, for security agreement purposes, by adding to the legal description of the realty a phrase such as "and all inventory, equipment, and consumer goods on the property." If the collateral is affixed to the real estate, it may still be described, for security agreement purposes, by a phrase or sentence added to the legal description of the realty. A description of fixtures, for example, might be "and all goods that are or will be fixtures and that are or will be located on the property."

To serve as a security agreement, the deed of trust must also clearly state that the borrower grants a security interest in the collateral to the lender. A clause such as 8-9-10 in this chapter should appear as a numbered paragraph under "General Provisions."

In addition, if the deed of trust is to secure a construction loan, to take advantage of the priority afforded construction lenders by revised section 9.334, the attorney should add the personal property description and construction mortgage clauses found at clauses 8-9-12 and 8-9-13, respectively. The attorney should also give serious consideration to preparing a construction loan agreement to deal with such issues as retainage, conditions for advances, and storage of supplies and materials.

§ 8.12 Additional Resources

Beyer, Gerry W. *Real Property.* 2nd ed. West's Texas Forms 13–15. St. Paul, MN: West, 2001. Supplement 2014.

Nolan, John M., Michael F. Alessio, and Edward A. Peterson. "Texas Annotated Deed of Trust." In *Advanced Real Estate Strategies Course, 2015*. Austin: State Bar of Texas, 2015.

St. Claire, Frank A., and William V. Dorsaneo III. *Texas Real Estate Guide*. New York: Matthew Bender & Co., 2001.

Form 8-1

Deed of Trust

Notice of confidentiality rights: If you are a natural person, you may remove or strike any or all of the following information from any instrument that transfers an interest in real property before it is filed for record in the public records: your Social Security number or your driver's license number.

Basic Information

Date:

Grantor:

> If the deed of trust is to be filed as a financing statement and if the grantor is an organization, the deed of trust should also indicate the type of organization, the jurisdiction of the organization, and an organizational identification number.

Grantor's Mailing Address:

Trustee[s]:

Trustee's Mailing Address[es]:

Lender:

Lender's Mailing Address:

Obligation

Note

Date:

Original principal amount:

Borrower:

Lender:

Maturity date:

> If there is more than one note, repeat above information for each additional note and change the word *Note* to *Notes* in all applicable instances.

Other Debt: [**include optional clauses from form 8-6 in this chapter or describe other debt**]

Property (including any improvements):

> For construction loans, include clause 8-9-12 immediately following the real property description.

Prior Lien: [**include recording information**]

> If there is more than one prior lien, repeat above information for each additional prior lien and change the words *Prior Lien* to *Prior Liens* in all applicable instances.

Other Exceptions to Conveyance and Warranty:

A. Granting Clause

For value received and to secure payment of the Obligation, Grantor conveys the Property to Trustee in trust. Grantor warrants and agrees to defend the title to the Property, subject to the Other Exceptions to Conveyance and Warranty. On payment of the Obligation and all other amounts secured by this deed of trust, this deed of trust will have no further effect, and Lender will release it at Grantor's expense.

B. Grantor's Obligations

> Consider substituting all or part of clause 8-9-18, as appropriate, for clause B.1. to cover different risks specific to the activities on or regarding the property.

B.1. Grantor agrees to maintain all property and liability insurance coverages with respect to the Property, revenues generated by the Property, and operations on the Property that Lender reasonably requires ("Required Insurance Coverages"), issued by insurers and written on policy forms acceptable to Lender, and as to property loss, that are payable to Lender under policies containing standard mortgagee clauses, and deliver evidence of the Required Insurance Coverages in a form acceptable to Lender before execution of this deed of trust and again at least ten days before the expiration of the Required Insurance Coverages.

B.2. Grantor agrees to—

a. keep the Property in good repair and condition;

b. pay all taxes and assessments on the Property before delinquency, not authorize a taxing entity to transfer its tax lien on the Property to anyone other than Lender, and not request a deferral of the collection of taxes pursuant to section 33.06 of the Texas Tax Code;

c. defend title to the Property subject to the Other Exceptions to Conveyance and Warranty and preserve the lien's priority as it is established in this deed of trust;

d. obey all laws, ordinances, and restrictive covenants applicable to the Property;

e. keep any buildings occupied as required by the Required Insurance Coverages;

f. if the lien of this deed of trust is not a first lien, pay or cause to be paid all prior lien notes and abide by or cause to be abided by all prior lien instruments; and

g. notify Lender of any change of address.

C. Lender's Rights

C.1. Lender or Lender's mortgage servicer may appoint in writing one or more substitute trustees, succeeding to all rights and responsibilities of Trustee.

C.2. If the proceeds of the Obligation are used to pay any debt secured by prior liens, Lender is subrogated to all the rights and liens of the holders of any debt so paid.

C.3. Lender may apply any proceeds received under the property insurance policies covering the Property either to reduce the Obligation or to repair or replace damaged or destroyed improvements covered by the policy. If the Property is Grantor's primary residence and Lender reasonably determines that repairs to the improvements are economically feasible, Lender will make the property insurance proceeds available to Grantor for repairs.

C.4. Notwithstanding the terms of the Note to the contrary, and unless applicable law prohibits, all payments received by Lender from Grantor with respect to the Obligation or this deed of trust may, at Lender's discretion, be applied first to amounts payable under this deed of trust and then to amounts due and payable to Lender with respect to the Obligation, to be applied to late charges, principal, or interest in the order Lender in its discretion determines.

C.5. If Grantor fails to perform any of Grantor's obligations, Lender may perform those obligations and be reimbursed by Grantor on demand for any amounts so paid, including attorney's fees, plus interest on those amounts from the dates of payment at the rate stated in the Note for matured, unpaid amounts. The amount to be reimbursed will be secured by this deed of trust.

C.6. **COLLATERAL PROTECTION INSURANCE NOTICE**

In accordance with the provisions of section 307.052(a) of the Texas Finance Code, the Beneficiary hereby notifies the Grantor as follows:

(A) the Grantor is required to:

(i) keep the collateral insured against damage in the amount the Lender specifies;

(ii) purchase the insurance from an insurer that is authorized to do business in the state of Texas or an eligible surplus lines insurer; and

(iii) name the Lender as the person to be paid under the policy in the event of a loss;

(B) the Grantor must, if required by the Lender, deliver to the Lender a copy of the policy and proof of the payment of premiums; and

(C) if the Grantor fails to meet any requirement listed in Paragraph (A) or (B), the Lender may obtain collateral protection insurance on behalf of the Grantor at the Grantor's expense.

C.7. If a default exists in payment of the Obligation or performance of Grantor's obligations and the default continues after any required notice of the default and the time allowed to cure, Lender may—

a. declare the unpaid principal balance and earned interest on the Obligation immediately due;

b. exercise Lender's rights with respect to rent under the Texas Property Code as then in effect;

c. direct Trustee to foreclose this lien, in which case Lender or Lender's agent will cause notice of the foreclosure sale to be given as provided by the Texas Property Code as then in effect; and

d. purchase the Property at any foreclosure sale by offering the highest bid and then have the bid credited on the Obligation.

C.8. Lender may remedy any default without waiving it and may waive any default without waiving any prior or subsequent default.

D. Trustee's Rights and Duties

If directed by Lender to foreclose this lien, Trustee will—

D.1. either personally or by agent give notice of the foreclosure sale as required by the Texas Property Code as then in effect;

D.2. sell and convey all or part of the Property "AS IS" to the highest bidder for cash with a general warranty binding Grantor, subject to the Prior Lien and to the Other Exceptions to Conveyance and Warranty and without representation or warranty, express or implied, by Trustee;

D.3. from the proceeds of the sale, pay, in this order—

a. expenses of foreclosure, including a reasonable commission to Trustee;

b. to Lender, the full amount of principal, interest, attorney's fees, and other charges due and unpaid;

c. any amounts required by law to be paid before payment to Grantor; and

d. to Grantor, any balance; and

D.4. be indemnified, held harmless, and defended by Lender against all costs, expenses, and liabilities incurred by Trustee for acting in the execution or enforcement of the trust created by this deed of trust, which includes all court and other costs, including attorney's fees, incurred by Trustee in defense of any action or proceeding taken against Trustee in that capacity.

E. General Provisions

E.1. If any of the Property is sold under this deed of trust, Grantor must immediately surrender possession to the purchaser. If Grantor does not, Grantor will be a tenant at sufferance of the purchaser, subject to an action for forcible detainer.

E.2. Recitals in any trustee's deed conveying the Property will be presumed to be true.

E.3. Proceeding under this deed of trust, filing suit for foreclosure, or pursuing any other remedy will not constitute an election of remedies.

E.4. This lien will remain superior to liens later created even if the time of payment of all or part of the Obligation is extended or part of the Property is released.

E.5. If any portion of the Obligation cannot be lawfully secured by this deed of trust, payments will be applied first to discharge that portion.

E.6. Grantor assigns to Lender all amounts payable to or received by Grantor from condemnation of all or part of the Property, from private sale in lieu of condemnation, and from damages caused by public works or construction on or near the Property. After deducting any expenses incurred, including attorney's fees and court and other costs, Lender will either release any remaining amounts to Grantor or apply such amounts to reduce the Obligation. Lender will not be liable for failure to collect or to exercise diligence in collecting any such amounts. Grantor will immediately give Lender notice of any actual or threatened proceedings for condemnation of all or part of the Property.

E.7. Grantor collaterally assigns to Lender all present and future rent from the Property and its proceeds. Grantor warrants the validity and enforceability of the assignment. Grantor will apply all rent to payment of the Obligation and performance of this deed of trust, but if the rent exceeds the amount due with respect to the Obligation and the deed of trust, Grantor may retain the excess. If a default exists in payment of the Obligation or performance of this deed of trust, Lender may exercise Lender's rights with respect to rent under the Texas Property Code as then in effect. Lender neither has nor assumes any obligations as lessor or landlord with respect to any occupant of the Property. Lender may exercise Lender's rights and remedies under this paragraph without taking possession of the Property. Lender will apply all rent collected under this paragraph as required by the Texas Property Code as then in effect. Lender is not required to act under this paragraph, and acting under this paragraph does not waive any of Lender's other rights or remedies.

E.8. Interest on the debt secured by this deed of trust will not exceed the maximum amount of nonusurious interest that may be contracted for, taken, reserved, charged, or received under law. Any interest in excess of that maximum amount will be credited on the principal of the debt or, if that has been paid, refunded. On any acceleration or required or permitted prepayment, any such excess will be canceled automatically as of the acceleration or prepayment or, if already paid, credited on the principal of the debt or, if the principal of the debt has been paid, refunded. This provision overrides any conflicting provisions in this and all other instruments concerning the debt.

E.9. In no event may this deed of trust secure payment of any debt that may not lawfully be secured by a lien on real estate or create a lien otherwise prohibited by law.

If a due-on-sale clause is desired, select one of the following.

Select the following for a residential deed of trust.

E.10. If Grantor transfers any part of the Property without Lender's prior written consent, Lender may declare the Obligation immediately payable and invoke any remedies provided in this deed of trust for default. If the Property is residential real property containing fewer than five dwelling units or a residential manufactured home, this provision does not apply to (a) a subordinate lien or encumbrance that does not transfer rights of occupancy of the Property; (b) creation of a purchase-money security interest for household appliances; (c) transfer by devise, descent, or operation of law on the death of a co-Grantor; (d) grant of a leasehold interest of three years or less without an option to purchase; (e) transfer to a spouse or children of Grantor or between co-Grantors; (f) transfer to a relative of Grantor on Grantor's death; (g) a transfer resulting from a decree of a dissolution of marriage, a legal separation agreement, or an incidental property settlement agreement by which the spouse of Grantor becomes an owner of the Property; or (h) transfer to an inter vivos trust in which Grantor is and remains a beneficiary and occupant of the Property.

Select the following for a commercial deed of trust.

E.10. Grantor may not sell, transfer, or otherwise dispose of any Property, whether voluntarily or by operation of law, without the prior written consent of Lender. If granted, consent may be conditioned upon (a) the grantee's integrity, reputation, character, creditworthiness, and management ability being satisfactory to Lender; and (b) the grantee's executing, before such sale, transfer, or other disposition, a written assumption agreement containing any terms Lender may require, such as a principal pay down on the Obligation, an increase in the rate of interest payable with respect to the Obligation, a transfer fee, or any other modification of the Note, this deed of trust, or any other instruments evidencing or securing the Obligation.

Grantor may not cause or permit any Property to be encumbered by any liens, security interests, or encumbrances other than the liens securing the Obligation and the liens securing ad valorem taxes not yet due and payable without the prior written consent of Lender. If granted, consent may be conditioned upon Grantor's executing, before granting such lien, a written modification agreement containing any terms Lender may require, such as a principal pay down on the Obligation, an increase in the rate of interest payable with respect to the Obligation, an approval fee, or any other modification of the Note, this deed of trust, or any other instruments evidencing or securing the Obligation.

Grantor may not grant any lien, security interest, or other encumbrance (a "Subordinate Instrument") covering the Property that is subordinate to the liens created by this deed of trust without the prior written consent of Lender. If granted, consent may be conditioned upon the Subordinate Instrument's containing express covenants to the effect that—

a. the Subordinate Instrument is unconditionally subordinate to this deed of trust;

b. if any action is instituted to foreclose or otherwise enforce the Subordinate Instrument, no action may be taken that would terminate any occupancy or tenancy without the prior written consent of Lender, and that consent, if granted, may be conditioned in any manner Lender determines;

c. rents, if collected by or for the holder of the Subordinate Instrument, will be applied first to the payment of the Obligation then due and to expenses incurred in the ownership, operation, and maintenance of the Property in any order Lender may determine, before being applied to any indebtedness secured by the Subordinate Instrument;

d. written notice of default under the Subordinate Instrument and written notice of the commencement of any action to foreclose or otherwise enforce the Subordinate Instrument must be given to Lender concurrently with or immediately after the occurrence of any such default or commencement; and

e. in the event of the bankruptcy of Grantor, all amounts due on or with respect to the Obligation and this deed of trust will be payable in full before any payments on the indebtedness secured by the Subordinate Instrument.

Grantor may not cause or permit any of the following events to occur without the prior written consent of Lender: if Grantor is (a) a corporation, the termination of the corporation or the sale, pledge, encumbrance, or assignment of any shares of its stock; (b) a limited liability company, the termination of the company or the sale, pledge, encumbrance, or assignment of any of its membership interests; (c) a general partnership or joint venture, the termination of the partnership or venture or the sale, pledge, encumbrance, or assignment of any of its partnership or joint venture interests, or the withdrawal from or admission into it of any general partner or joint venturer; or (d) a limited partnership, (i) the termination of the partnership, (ii) the sale, pledge, encumbrance, or assignment of any of its general partnership interests, or the withdrawal from or admission into it of any general partner, (iii) the sale, pledge, encumbrance, or assignment of a controlling portion of its limited partnership interests, or (iv) the withdrawal from or admission into it of any controlling limited partner or partners. If granted, consent may be conditioned upon (a) the integrity, reputation, character, creditworthiness, and management ability of the person succeeding to the ownership interest in Grantor (or security interest in such ownership) being satisfactory to Lender; and (b) the execution, before such event, by the person succeeding to the interest of Grantor in the Property or ownership interest in Grantor (or security interest in such ownership) of a written modification or assumption agreement containing such terms as Lender may require, such as a principal pay down on the Obligation, an increase in the rate of interest payable with respect to the Obligation, a transfer fee, or any other modification of the Note, this deed of trust, or any other instruments evidencing or securing the Obligation.

Continue with the following.

E.11. When the context requires, singular nouns and pronouns include the plural.

E.12. The term *Note* includes all extensions, modifications, and renewals of the Note and all amounts secured by this deed of trust.

E.13. This deed of trust binds, benefits, and may be enforced by the successors in interest of all parties.

E.14. If Grantor and Borrower are not the same person, the term *Grantor* includes Borrower.

E.15. Grantor and each surety, endorser, and guarantor of the Obligation waive, to the extent permitted by law, all (a) demand for payment, (b) presentation for payment, (c) notice of intention to accelerate maturity, (d) notice of acceleration of maturity, (e) protest, [and] (f) notice of protest [**include if applicable:** and (g) rights under sections 51.003, 51.004, and 51.005 of the Texas Property Code].

E.16. Grantor agrees to pay reasonable attorney's fees, trustee's fees, and court and other costs of enforcing Lender's rights under this deed of trust if an attorney [**include if the transaction is a secondary mortgage loan:** who is not an employee of Lender] is retained for its enforcement.

E.17. If any provision of this deed of trust is determined to be invalid or unenforceable, the validity or enforceability of any other provision will not be affected.

E.18. The term *Lender* includes any mortgage servicer for Lender.

E.19. Grantor hereby grants Lender a right of first refusal with respect to Grantor's power to authorize any third party (other than Lender pursuant to its rights as set forth in this instrument) to pay ad valorem taxes on the Property and authorize a taxing entity to transfer its tax lien on the Property to that third party. Grantor's authorization to any third party (other than Lender) to pay the ad valorem taxes and receive transfer of a taxing entity's lien for ad valorem taxes shall be null and void and of no force and effect unless Lender, within ten days after receiving written notice from Grantor, fails to pay the ad valorem taxes pursuant to Lender's rights as set forth in this instrument.

E.20. Grantor represents that this deed of trust and the Note are given for the following purposes: [**list specific purposes**].

____
[**Name of grantor**]

Include acknowledgment.

Form 8-2

Deed of Trust to Secure Assumption

Notice of confidentiality rights: If you are a natural person, you may remove or strike any or all of the following information from any instrument that transfers an interest in real property before it is filed for record in the public records: your Social Security number or your driver's license number.

Basic Information

Date:

Grantor:

> If the deed of trust is to be filed as a financing statement and if the grantor is an organization, the deed of trust should also indicate the type of organization, the jurisdiction of the organization, and an organizational identification number.

Grantor's Mailing Address:

Trustee:

Trustee's Mailing Address:

Beneficiary:

Beneficiary's Mailing Address:

Note and Deed of Trust Assumed

Date:

Original principal amount:

Borrower:

Lender:

Recording information:

Property (including any improvements):

Prior Lien: [**include recording information**]

> If there is more than one prior lien, repeat above information for each additional prior lien and change the words *Prior Lien* to *Prior Liens* in all applicable instances.

Other Exceptions to Conveyance and Warranty:

Consideration: Beneficiary has conveyed the Property to Grantor, who as part of the consideration promised to pay the Note Assumed and to be bound by the Deed of Trust Assumed.

A. Granting Clause

For value received and to secure Grantor's assumption, Grantor conveys the Property to Trustee in trust. Grantor warrants and agrees to defend the title to the Property, subject to the Other Exceptions to Conveyance and Warranty. If Grantor performs all the covenants of the Note and Deed of Trust Assumed and if Beneficiary has not filed a notice of advancement, a release of the Deed of Trust Assumed will release this deed of trust to secure assumption and Beneficiary's vendor's lien.

B. Grantor's Obligations

Grantor agrees to—

B.1. perform all the covenants of the Note and Deed of Trust Assumed; and

B.2. notify Beneficiary and Lender of any change of address.

C. Beneficiary's Rights

C.1. Beneficiary may appoint in writing a substitute trustee, succeeding to all rights and responsibilities of Trustee.

C.2. If Grantor fails to perform any of Grantor's obligations under the Note Assumed or Deed of Trust Assumed, Beneficiary may perform those obligations, advance funds required, and then be reimbursed by Grantor on demand for any amounts so advanced, including attorney's fees, plus interest on those amounts from the dates of payment at the highest legal rate. The amount to be reimbursed will be secured by this deed of trust to secure assumption.

C.3. **COLLATERAL PROTECTION INSURANCE NOTICE**

In accordance with the provisions of section 307.052(a) of the Texas Finance Code, the Beneficiary hereby notifies the Grantor as follows:

(A) the Grantor is required to:

(i) keep the collateral insured against damage in the amount the Lender specifies;

(ii) purchase the insurance from an insurer that is authorized to do business in the state of Texas or an eligible surplus lines insurer; and

(iii) name the Lender as the person to be paid under the policy in the event of a loss;

(B) the Grantor must, if required by the Lender, deliver to the Lender a copy of the policy and proof of the payment of premiums; and

(C) if the Grantor fails to meet any requirement listed in Paragraph (A) or (B), the Lender may obtain collateral protection insurance on behalf of the Grantor at the Grantor's expense.

C.4. Beneficiary may file a sworn notice of such advancement in the office of the county clerk in the county in which the Property is located. The notice will detail the dates, amounts, and purposes of the amounts advanced and the legal description of the Property.

C.5. If Grantor fails on demand to reimburse Beneficiary for the amounts advanced and such failure continues after Beneficiary gives Grantor notice of the failure and the time within which it must be cured, to the extent required by law or by written agreement, Beneficiary may—

a. exercise Beneficiary's rights with respect to rent under the Texas Property Code as then in effect;

b. direct Trustee to foreclose this lien, in which case Beneficiary or Beneficiary's agent will cause notice of the foreclosure sale to be given as provided by the Texas Property Code as then in effect; and

c. purchase the Property at any foreclosure sale by offering the highest bid and then have the bid credited to the amount owed to Beneficiary.

D. Trustee's Rights and Duties

If directed by Beneficiary to foreclose this lien, Trustee will—

D.1. either personally or by agent give notice of the foreclosure sale as required by this deed of trust to secure assumption and the Texas Property Code as then in effect;

D.2. sell and convey all or part of the Property "AS IS" to the highest bidder for cash with a general warranty binding Grantor, subject to the Prior Lien and to the Other Exceptions to Conveyance and Warranty and without representation or warranty, express or implied, by Trustee;

D.3. from the proceeds of the sale, pay, in this order—

a. expenses of foreclosure, including a reasonable commission to Trustee;

b. to Beneficiary, the full amount advanced, attorney's fees, and other charges due and unpaid;

c. any amounts required by law to be paid before payment to Grantor; and

d. to Grantor, any balance; and

D.4. be indemnified, held harmless, and defended by Beneficiary against all costs, expenses, and liabilities incurred by Trustee for acting in the execution or enforcement of the trust created by this deed of trust to secure assumption, which includes all court and other costs, including attorney's fees, incurred by Trustee in defense of any action or proceeding taken against Trustee in that capacity.

E. General Provisions

E.1. If any of the Property is sold under this deed of trust to secure assumption, Grantor must immediately surrender possession to the purchaser. If Grantor does not, Grantor will be a tenant at sufferance of the purchaser, subject to an action for forcible detainer.

E.2. Recitals in any trustee's deed conveying the Property will be presumed to be true.

E.3. Proceeding under this deed of trust to secure assumption, filing suit for foreclosure, or pursuing any other remedy will not constitute an election of remedies.

E.4. This lien will be superior to liens later created even if Beneficiary has made no advancements when later liens are created.

E.5. If any portion of the advancements cannot be lawfully secured by this deed of trust to secure assumption, payments will be applied first to discharge that portion.

E.6. A sale of the Property under this deed of trust to secure assumption—

a. is subject to Grantor's continuing obligation to make all payments owing on the Note Assumed and to perform all obligations under the Deed of Trust Assumed; and

b. does not extinguish Trustee's right to conduct subsequent sales of the Property for future Grantor defaults under this deed of trust to secure assumption.

E.7. Grantor collaterally assigns to Beneficiary all present and future rent from the Property and its proceeds. Grantor warrants the validity and enforceability of the assignment. Grantor will apply all rent to payment of the Note Assumed and performance of the Deed of Trust Assumed, but if the rent exceeds the amount due with respect to the Note and Deed of Trust Assumed, Grantor may retain the excess. If a default exists in payment of the Note Assumed or performance of this deed of trust to secure assumption or of the Deed of Trust Assumed, Beneficiary may exercise Beneficiary's rights with respect to rent under the Texas Property Code as then in effect. Beneficiary neither has nor assumes any obligations as lessor or landlord with respect to any occupant of the Property. Beneficiary may exercise Beneficiary's rights and remedies under this paragraph without taking possession of the Property.

Beneficiary will apply all rent collected under this paragraph as required by the Texas Property Code as then in effect. Beneficiary is not required to act under this paragraph, and acting under this paragraph does not waive any of Beneficiary's other rights or remedies.

E.8. Interest on the debt secured by this deed of trust to secure assumption will not exceed the maximum amount of nonusurious interest that may be contracted for, taken, reserved, charged, or received under law. Any interest in excess of that maximum amount will be credited on the principal of the debt or, if that has been paid, refunded. On any acceleration or required or permitted prepayment, any such excess will be canceled automatically as of the acceleration or prepayment or, if already paid, credited on the principal of the debt or, if the principal of the debt has been paid, refunded. This provision overrides any conflicting provisions in this and all other instruments concerning the debt.

E.9. Any action taken under this deed of trust to secure assumption will not extinguish the rights of Beneficiary to proceed against Grantor under the indemnity contained in the deed by which Borrower assumed the Note and Deed of Trust Assumed.

E.10. The term *Beneficiary* includes any mortgage servicer for Beneficiary.

E.11. When the context requires, singular nouns and pronouns include the plural.

E.12. This deed of trust to secure assumption binds, benefits, and may be enforced by the successors in interest of all parties.

E.13. Grantor waives and surrenders to Lender (a) Grantor's power to authorize anyone (other than Lender or Grantor) to pay ad valorem taxes on the Property and (b) Grantor's power to authorize a taxing entity to transfer its tax lien on the Property to anyone other than Lender. Grantor agrees and declares that any authorization from Grantor to another (other than Lender) to pay the taxes and transfer a tax lien on the Property is void.

____
[Name of grantor]

Include acknowledgment.

Form 8-3

Vendor's Lien Clauses

If Vendor's Lien in Favor of Seller Is Retained in Deed

Clause 8-3-1

The debt evidenced by the Note is in [**include if applicable:** part] payment of the purchase price of the Property; the debt is secured both by this deed of trust and by a vendor's lien on the Property, which is expressly retained in a deed [to Grantor of even date/of even date given by [**name**] to [**name**]]. This deed of trust does not waive the vendor's lien, and the two liens and the rights created by this deed of trust are cumulative. Lender may elect to foreclose either of the liens without waiving the other or may foreclose both.

Or

If Vendor's Lien in Favor of Third Party Is Retained in Deed

Clause 8-3-2

The debt evidenced by the Note is in part payment of the purchase price of the Property; the debt is secured by this deed of trust and by a vendor's lien on the Property, which is expressly retained in a deed [to Grantor of even date/of even date given by [**name**] to [**name**]]. The vendor's lien is transferred to Lender by the deed. This deed of trust does not waive the vendor's lien, and the two liens and the rights created by this deed of trust are cumulative. Lender may elect to foreclose either of the liens without waiving the other or may foreclose both.

For Use If Lien Is Not Retained in Deed

Clause 8-3-3

Grantor expressly acknowledges a vendor's lien on the Property as security for the Note secured by this deed of trust, which represents funds advanced by Lender at Grantor's request and used in payment of [**include if applicable:** a portion of] the purchase price of the Property. This deed of trust does not waive the vendor's lien, and the two liens and the rights created by this deed of trust are cumulative. Lender may elect to enforce either of the liens without waiving the other or may enforce both.

Form 8-4

Clauses Extending Existing Liens

Extension of Existing Deed-of-Trust Lien

Clause 8-4-1

The Note renews and extends the balance of **[amount]** DOLLARS (\$**[amount]**) that Grantor owes on a prior note in the original principal amount of **[amount]** DOLLARS (\$**[amount]**), which is dated **[date]**, executed by **[name]**, and payable to the order of **[name]**. The prior note is more fully described in and secured by a deed of trust on the Property, which is dated **[date]** and recorded in **[recording data]** of the real property records of **[county]** County, Texas. [**Include if applicable:** The prior note and the lien securing it have been transferred to Lender.] Grantor acknowledges that the lien securing the prior note is valid, that it subsists against the Property, and that by this deed of trust it is renewed and extended in full force to secure payment of the Note.

Extension of Existing Deed-of-Trust Lien and Security for Cash Advanced

Clause 8-4-2

The Note renews and extends the balance of **[amount]** DOLLARS (\$**[amount]**) that Grantor owes on a prior note in the original principal amount of **[amount]** DOLLARS (\$**[amount]**), which is dated **[date]**, executed by **[name]**, and payable to the order of **[name]**. The prior note is secured by a deed of trust on the Property from **[name]** to **[name]**, Trustee, dated **[date]** and recorded in **[recording data]** of the real property records of **[county]** County, Texas. [**Include if applicable:** The prior note and the lien securing it have been transferred to Lender.] The Note also represents **[amount]** DOLLARS

($[**amount**]) in cash that Lender advanced to Grantor on [**date**] at Grantor's request. Grantor acknowledges receipt of the amount advanced. Grantor acknowledges that the lien securing the prior note is valid, that it subsists against the Property, and that by this deed of trust it is renewed and extended in full force until the Note secured by this deed of trust is paid.

Extension of Existing Vendor's Lien and Deed of Trust

Clause 8-4-3

The Note renews and extends the balance of [**amount**] DOLLARS ($[**amount**]) that Grantor owes on a prior note in the original principal amount of [**amount**] DOLLARS ($[**amount**]), which is dated [**date**], executed by [**name**], and payable to the order of [**name**]. The prior note is secured by two instruments, both of which create liens against the Property: a deed retaining a vendor's lien from [**name**] to [**name**], dated [**date**] and recorded in [**recording data**] of the real property records of [**county**] County, Texas; and a deed of trust from [**name**] to [**name**], Trustee, dated [**date**] and recorded in [**recording data**] of the real property records of [**county**] County, Texas. [**Include if applicable:** The prior note and the liens securing it have been transferred to Lender.] Grantor acknowledges that the liens securing the prior note are valid, that they subsist against the Property, and that by this deed of trust they are renewed and extended in full force until the Note is paid.

Extension of Mechanic's Lien Contract

Clause 8-4-4

The Note renews and extends the balance of [**amount**] DOLLARS ($[**amount**]) that Grantor owes on a prior note in the original principal amount of **[amount]** DOLLARS ($**[amount]**), which is dated **[date]**, executed by **[name]**, and payable to the order of **[name]**. The prior note is secured by a mechanic's lien contract creating a lien on the Property, dated **[date]** and recorded in **[recording data]** of the real property records of **[county]** County, Texas. [**Include if applicable:** The prior note and the lien securing it have been transferred to Lender.] Grantor acknowledges that the lien securing the prior note is valid, that it subsists against the Property, and that by this deed of trust it is renewed and extended in full force until the Note is paid.

Alternative Renewal and Extension Language

Clause 8-4-5

> If clause 8-4-5 is used, its language should replace the last sentence in one of the preceding clauses, which begins "Grantor acknowledges that the lien(s) securing the prior note . . ."

Grantor acknowledges and agrees that this extension and renewal will not be considered a novation of account or a new contract but that all rights, titles, powers, liens, security interests, and estates created by the prior note and deed of trust securing it constitute a valid and subsisting lien against the Property. Grantor also acknowledges that by this deed of trust Lender and Lender's heirs, successors, and assigns are subrogated to all rights, titles, powers, security interests, and liens that accrued to the original holder and owner of the prior note.

Extension of Prior Lien to Be Released, Not Assigned

Clause 8-4-6

The Note represents the amount of **[amount]** DOLLARS ($**[amount]**) in cash that Lender advanced to Grantor and that Grantor used [**include if applica-**

ble: in part] to discharge a prior note in the original principal amount of [**amount**] DOLLARS ($[**amount**]), which is dated [**date**], executed by [**name**], and payable to the order of [**name**]. The prior note is secured by a deed of trust on the Property from [**name**] to [**name**], Trustee, dated [**date**] and recorded in [**recording data**] of the real property records of [**county**] County, Texas. Grantor acknowledges that the lien securing the prior note is valid, that it subsists against the Property, and that by this deed of trust it is renewed and extended in full force until the Note is paid, even though the prior lien is released and not assigned to Lender.

Extension of Lien to Only Part of Property

Clause 8-4-7

The Note represents the amount of [**amount**] DOLLARS ($[**amount**]) in cash that Lender advanced to Grantor and that Grantor used [**include if applicable:** in part] to discharge a prior note in the original principal amount of [**amount**] DOLLARS ($[**amount**]), which is dated [**date**], executed by [**name**], and payable to the order of [**name**]. The prior note is secured by two instruments, both of which create liens against real estate that includes the Property: a deed retaining a vendor's lien executed by [**name**] to [**name**], dated [**date**] and recorded in [**recording data**] of the real property records of [**county**] County, Texas; and a deed of trust from [**name**] to [**name**], Trustee, dated [**date**] and recorded in [**recording data**] of the real property records of [**county**] County, Texas. Grantor acknowledges that, to the extent they cover the Property, the liens securing the prior note are valid, that they subsist against the Property as well as the other real estate, and that by this deed of trust they are renewed and extended in full force until the Note is paid.

Form 8-5

Clauses Acknowledging Cash Advanced

To Individuals

Clause 8-5-1

The Note represents **[amount]** DOLLARS ($**[amount]**) in cash that Lender advanced to Grantor on this day at Grantor's request and that Grantor acknowledges receiving.

To a Corporation

Clause 8-5-2

The Note represents **[amount]** DOLLARS ($**[amount]**) in cash that Lender advanced to Grantor on this day at its request and that it will use under its charter powers to discharge corporate debts. Grantor represents to Lender that its board of directors has authorized its legally elected, qualified, and acting officers to execute the Note and this deed of trust.

To Pay Ad Valorem Taxes

Clause 8-5-3

The Note represents **[amount]** DOLLARS ($**[amount]**) in cash that, at Grantor's request, Lender advanced to pay the following taxes [**include if applicable:** , including penalties, interest, and collection expenses,] assessed and owed on the Property, which Grantor now owns: **[amount]** DOLLARS ($**[amount]**) to **[county]** County in payment of taxes for the years **[specify]**;

and **[amount]** DOLLARS ($**[amount]**) to the city of **[city]** in payment of taxes for the years **[specify]**.

Grantor agrees that Lender is subrogated to the rights, liens, and equities of the tax authorities paid, and the same are renewed and extended by this deed of trust until the Note is paid.

To Pay Income Taxes

Clause 8-5-4

The Note includes **[amount]** DOLLARS ($**[amount]**) that, at Grantor's request, Lender advanced to the United States Internal Revenue Service to discharge federal tax lien number **[number]**, which is recorded in **[recording data]** of the federal tax lien records of **[county]** County, Texas. Grantor agrees that Lender is subrogated to all rights, titles, and liens held by the tax authority under this federal tax lien, which Grantor acknowledges to be valid and subsisting, and the same are renewed and extended by this deed of trust until the Note is fully paid.

Form 8-6

Other Indebtedness Clauses

Clause 8-6-1

This deed of trust also secures payment of any debt that Grantor may subsequently owe to Lender and that arises while Grantor owns the Property.

Or

Clause 8-6-2

This deed of trust also secures payment of any debt that Grantor may subsequently owe to Lender; when it accrues, any such future debt will bear interest at the rates provided in the Note, will be payable to Lender at the same place provided in the Note, and in all respects will be deemed a part of the debt secured by this deed of trust.

Or

Clause 8-6-3

This conveyance is also made in trust to secure payment of all other present and future debts that Grantor may owe to Lender, regardless of how any other such debt is incurred or evidenced. Payment on all present and future debts of Grantor to Lender will be made at [**specify**] in [**county**] County, Texas, and the debts will bear interest as provided in notes or other evidences of debt that Grantor will give to Lender. This conveyance is also made to secure payment of any renewal or extension of any present or future debt that Grantor owes to Lender, including any loans and advancements from Lender to Grantor under the provisions of this deed of trust. When Grantor repays all debts owed to Lender, this deed-of-trust lien will terminate only if Lender releases this deed of trust at the request of Grantor. Until Lender releases it, this deed of trust will remain fully in effect to secure other present and future advances and debts, regardless of any additional security given for any debt and regardless of any modification.

Or

Clause 8-6-4

This deed of trust, to the extent permitted by law, also secures payment of all other present and future debts, obligations, and liabilities owed to Lender by Grantor as a partner, venturer, or member of any partnership, joint venture, association, or other group, regardless of how the other debts, obligations, and liabilities are incurred and regardless of whether they are evidenced by a note, open account, overdraft, endorsement, surety agreement, guarantee, or other document.

Form 8-7

Partial Release Clauses

Clause 8-7-1

If no default exists under any of the terms and conditions of this deed of trust or the Note, and if no event has occurred that, with notice, passage of time, or both, would be an event of default, Grantor is entitled to partial releases of the lien of the deed of trust on the following terms and conditions:

1. Releases will be granted by tracts of not less than [**number**] acre[s] each, successively and contiguously, beginning with the [**specify**] portion of the Property and proceeding [**specify**]. Each tract to be released will be approximately [**specify, e.g.,** rectangular] in shape and will have as its boundary a portion of the Property's frontage on [**specify**], and as its [**specify**] boundary an approximately equal portion of the [**specify**] boundary of the Property. No release will be granted that would deny frontage or disproportionately reduce the frontage on [**specify**] available to the unreleased portion of the Property or cause the unreleased portion of the property to be less than [**specify area**]. Access from the unreleased portion of the Property to [**specify**] must be at least [**number**] ([**number**]) feet wide.

2. To obtain a release, a principal amount of $[**amount**] per [acre/square foot] in cash must be paid on the Note. All payments for partial releases will be applied as a prepayment on the Note.

3. At the time a partial release is requested, the party requesting the release must furnish to the holder of the Note a calculation of area

by field notes and a plat of survey, indicating the area to be released and its relationship to the portion of the Property not to be released. All expenses incident to the granting of partial releases will be borne by the party requesting the release, including but not limited to the cost of the survey, Lender's attorney's fees, and recording costs. Under no circumstances will the unreleased portion be incapable of supporting a building permit.

Or

Clause 8-7-2

If no default exists under the Note or this deed of trust, and if no event has occurred that, with notice, passage of time, or both, would be an event of default, Grantor may have released from all liens securing the Note one or more lots out of the Property by paying to Lender the release price per lot as follows:

1. The release price per lot will be the greater of $[**amount**] or the net proceeds from the sale of that lot. "Net proceeds" is the gross sales price received by Grantor, or any person or entity related to or affiliated with Grantor, less the expenses of sale, including title insurance premiums, survey fees, real estate commissions not to exceed 6 percent of the gross sales price, reasonable attorney's fees, filing fees, recording fees, and other reasonable and customary closing costs in connection with the sale. Only those real estate commissions paid to parties other than Grantor, including persons or entities affiliated with Grantor, may be counted as deductible expenses.

2. The release price paid by Grantor will be applied by Lender as a prepayment on the Note. All payments for partial releases will be applied as a prepayment on the Note.

3. At the time a partial release is requested, the party requesting the release must furnish to the holder of the Note a calculation of area by field notes and a plat of survey, indicating the area to be released and its relationship to the portion of the Property not to be released. All expenses incident to the granting of partial releases will be borne by the party requesting the release, including but not limited to the cost of the survey, Lender's attorney's fees, and recording costs.

Or

Clause 8-7-3

Grantor is entitled to partial releases from the vendor's lien and this deed of trust as provided in an agreement of even date between Grantor and Lender.

Form 8-8

Second-Lien Clauses for Use with Subordinate Deeds of Trust

Clause 8-8-1

The lien created by this deed of trust will be subordinate to the lien securing payment of a note, and any renewals, extensions, and modifications thereof, in the original principal amount of [**amount**] DOLLARS ($[**amount**]), which is dated [**date**], executed by [**name**], payable to the order of [**name**], and more fully described in a deed of trust recorded in [**recording data**] of the real property records of [**county**] County, Texas. If default occurs in payment of any part of principal or interest of that $[**amount**] note or in observance of any covenants of the deed of trust securing it, the entire debt secured by this deed of trust will immediately become payable at the option of Lender.

Or

Clause 8-8-2

If Grantor fails to pay any part of principal or interest secured by a prior lien or liens on the Property when it becomes payable or defaults on any prior lien instrument, the entire debt secured by this deed of trust will immediately become payable at the option of Lender.

Form 8-9

Additional Clauses for Deeds of Trust

Mechanic's Lien Clause

Clause 8-9-1

The Note secured by this deed of trust is given in part payment for improvements on the Property that Lender has agreed to make for Grantor under a mechanic's lien contract of even date between Grantor as owner and Lender as contractor creating a lien against the Property to secure the Note. Grantor acknowledges that the lien created by the mechanic's lien contract is valid, that it subsists against the Property, and that by this deed of trust it is renewed and extended in full force and effect until the Note is fully paid.

Homestead Disclaimer and Designation

Clause 8-9-2

Grantor represents to Lender that no part of the Property is exempt as homestead from forced sale under the Texas Constitution or other laws.

> Include the following paragraph only if there is no separate designation of homestead executed by the grantor. A separate instrument is preferable. See form 10-8 in this manual.

All real estate constituting Grantor's homestead exempt from forced sale under the Texas Constitution or other laws consists of the following: [**include legal description of homestead**].

> Or

Clause 8-9-3

> See comment in clause 8-9-2 concerning desirability of a separate homestead and disclaimer instrument.

Grantor represents to Lender that no part of the Property is either the residential or business homestead of Grantor and that Grantor neither resides nor intends to reside in nor conducts nor intends to conduct business on the Property. Grantor renounces all present and future rights to a homestead exemption for the Property. Grantor's homestead and residence is property in [**county**] County, Texas, known as [**address**], [**city**], Texas. Grantor acknowledges that Lender relies on the truth of representations in this paragraph in making the loan secured by this deed of trust.

Tax and Insurance Reserve or Escrow Account

Clause 8-9-4

Grantor agrees to make an initial deposit in a reasonable amount to be determined by Lender and then make monthly payments to a fund for taxes and insurance premiums on the Property. Monthly payments will be made on the payment dates specified in the Note, and each payment will be one-twelfth of the amount that Lender estimates will be required annually for payment of taxes and insurance premiums. The fund will accrue no interest, and Lender will hold it without bond in escrow and use it to pay the taxes and insurance premiums. If Grantor has complied with the requirements of this paragraph, Lender must pay taxes before [the end of the calendar year/delinquency]. Grantor agrees to make additional deposits on demand if the fund is ever insufficient for its purpose. If an excess accumulates in the fund, Lender may either credit it to future monthly deposits until the excess is exhausted or refund it to Grantor. When Grantor makes the final payment on the Note, Lender will credit to that payment the whole amount then in the fund [**include if applicable:** or, at Lender's option, refund it after the Note is paid]. If this deed of trust is foreclosed, any balance in the fund over that needed to pay taxes, including taxes accruing but not yet payable, and to pay insurance premiums will be paid under section C, "Trustee's Rights and Duties." [**Include if applicable:** If the Property is transferred, any balance then in the fund will still be subject to the provisions of this paragraph and will inure to the benefit of the transferee.] Deposits to the fund described in this paragraph are in addition to the [**include if applicable:** monthly] payments provided for in the Note.

Assignment of Insurance Policies and Unearned Premiums

Clause 8-9-5

If the Property is transferred by foreclosure, the transferee will acquire title to all insurance policies on the Property, including all paid but unearned premiums.

Evidence of Payment of Taxes

Clause 8-9-6

Clause 8-9-6 should not be used if the escrow clause at 8-9-4 is used.

Grantor agrees to furnish on Lender's request evidence satisfactory to Lender that all taxes and assessments on the Property have been paid when due.

Evidence of Payment of Taxes and Insurance

Clause 8-9-7

Grantor will furnish to Lender or other holder of the Note annually, before taxes become delinquent, copies of tax receipts showing that all taxes on the Property have been paid. Grantor will annually furnish to Lender or other holder of the Note evidence of current paid-up insurance naming Lender or other holder of the Note as an insured.

Inspection of Collateral

Clause 8-9-8

Grantor agrees to allow Lender or Lender's agents to enter the Property at reasonable times and inspect it and any personal property in which Lender is granted a security interest by this deed of trust.

Consumer Credit Insurance Notice

Clause 8-9-9

GRANTOR MAY FURNISH ANY INSURANCE REQUIRED BY THIS DEED OF TRUST EITHER THROUGH EXISTING POLICIES OWNED OR CONTROLLED BY GRANTOR OR THROUGH EQUIVALENT COVERAGE FROM ANY INSURANCE COMPANY AUTHORIZED TO TRANSACT BUSINESS IN TEXAS.

Deed of Trust as a Security Agreement

Clause 8-9-10

In addition to creating a deed-of-trust lien on all the real and other property described above, Grantor also grants to Lender a security interest in all of the above-described personal property pursuant to and to the extent permitted by the Texas Uniform Commercial Code.

> If the security agreement covers nonfixtures and other personalty, continue with the following.

In the event of a foreclosure sale under this deed of trust, Grantor agrees that all the Property may be sold as a whole at Lender's option and that the Property need not be present at the place of sale.

Wraparound Lien

Clause 8-9-11

The lien created by this deed of trust is subordinate to the lien securing the unpaid balance of a prior promissory note in the original principal amount of [**amount**] DOLLARS ($[**amount**]), which is described in and secured by a deed of trust recorded in [**recording data**] of the real property records of [**county**] County, Texas. Grantor has not assumed payment of the prior note, but Lender is obligated to pay it according to its terms. Lender agrees to timely pay all installment payments due on the prior note and to deliver to Grantor a good and sufficient release of the prior deed of trust at or before the time Grantor pays the Note secured by this deed of trust to Lender. The warranty deed with vendor's lien referred to above provides that in the event of default in payment of the prior note, Grantor will have the right to cure any such default as long as Grantor is not in default in payment of the Note secured by this deed of trust or in default in performance of the covenants of this deed of trust. If Grantor cures a default in payment of the prior note, Grantor may receive credit on the Note secured by this deed of trust for all amounts so paid as of the date of the payment, in accordance with the terms of the Note.

> If the deed of trust securing the prior note requires monthly deposits to a reserve account for payment of taxes and insurance premiums, continue with the following.

If Lender fails to make when due any deposit to the tax and insurance reserve fund provided for under the deed of trust securing payment of the prior note, Grantor will have the right to make the deposit to the tax and insurance reserve fund as long as Grantor is not in default in payment of the Note secured by this deed of trust or in performance of the covenants of this deed of trust. If Grantor makes such a deposit, Grantor will receive credit on the tax and insurance reserve fund provided for in this deed of trust for all amounts so deposited, as of the date of the deposit.

For Deed of Trust for Construction Loan

> To create a deed of trust for a construction loan, include clauses 8-9-10, 8-9-12, and 8-9-13 in the deed of trust.

Clause 8-9-12

> Include clause 8-9-12 immediately following the real property description.

, together with the following personal property:

All fixtures, supplies, building materials, and other goods of every nature now or hereafter located, used, or intended to be located or used on the Property;

All plans and specifications for development of or construction of improvements on the Property;

All contracts and subcontracts relating to the construction of improvements on the Property;

All accounts, contract rights, instruments, documents, general intangibles, and chattel paper arising from or by virtue of any transactions relating to the Property;

All permits, licenses, franchises, certificates, and other rights and privileges obtained in connection with the Property;

All proceeds payable or to be payable under each policy of insurance relating to the Property; and

All products and proceeds of the foregoing.

Notwithstanding any other provision in this deed of trust, the term "Property" does not include personal effects used primarily for personal, family, or household purposes.

Clause 8-9-13

Include clause 8-9-13 above the signatures. In paragraph 1., select the appropriate Code reference depending on the date of the transaction.

E. Construction Loan Mortgage

1. This deed of trust is a "construction mortgage" within the meaning of section 9.334 of the Texas Business and Commerce Code. The liens and security interests created and granted by this deed of trust secure an obligation incurred for the construction of improvements on land [**include if applicable:** , including the acquisition cost of the land].

2. Grantor agrees to comply with the covenants and conditions of the construction loan agreement, if any, executed in connection with the Note and this deed of trust. All advances made by Lender under the construction loan

agreement will be indebtedness of Grantor secured by the liens created by this deed of trust, and such advances are conditioned as provided in the construction loan agreement.

3. All amounts disbursed by Lender before completion of the improvements to protect the security of this deed of trust up to the principal amount of the Note will be treated as disbursements under the construction loan agreement. All such amounts will bear interest from the date of disbursement at the rate stated in the Note, unless collections from Grantor of interest at that rate would be contrary to applicable law, in which event such amounts will bear interest at the rate stated in the Note for matured, unpaid amounts and will be payable on notice from Lender to Grantor requesting payment.

4. From time to time as Lender deems necessary to protect Lender's interests, Grantor will, on request of Lender, execute and deliver to Lender, in such form as Lender directs, assignments of any and all rights or claims that relate to the construction of improvements on the Property.

5. In case of breach by Grantor of the covenants and conditions of the construction loan agreement, Lender, at its option, with or without entry on the Property, may (a) invoke any of the rights or remedies provided in the construction loan agreement, (b) accelerate the amounts secured by this deed of trust and invoke the remedies provided in this deed of trust, or (c) do both.

6. If, after commencement of amortization of the Note, the Note and this deed of trust are sold by Lender, after the sale the construction loan agreement will cease to be a part of this deed of trust, and Grantor will not assert any right of setoff, counterclaim, or other claim or defense arising out of or in con-

nection with the construction loan agreement against the obligations of the Note and this deed of trust.

> If property is homestead, include the following, which must appear in a minimum of ten-point bold-faced type or equivalent "next to" the grantor's signature line. Tex. Prop. Code § 41.007(a).

IMPORTANT NOTICE: You and your contractor are responsible for meeting the terms and conditions of this contract. If you sign this contract and you fail to meet the terms and conditions of this contract, you may lose your legal ownership rights in your home. KNOW YOUR RIGHTS AND DUTIES UNDER THE LAW.

Recordkeeping

Clause 8-9-14

Grantor agrees to (1) keep at Grantor's address, or such other place as Lender may approve, accounts and records reflecting the operation of the Property and copies of all written contracts, leases, and other instruments that affect the Property; (2) prepare financial accounting records in compliance with [generally accepted/sound/cash basis federal income tax] accounting principles consistently applied; and (3), at Lender's request from time to time, permit Lender to examine and make copies of such books, records, contracts, leases, and other instruments at any reasonable time.

Financial Statements

Clause 8-9-15

Grantor agrees to deliver to Lender, at Lender's request from time to time, [audited/reviewed/compiled/internally prepared] financial statements of

Grantor and each guarantor of the Note prepared in accordance with [generally accepted/sound/cash basis federal income tax] accounting principles consistently applied, in detail reasonably satisfactory to Lender and certified to be true and correct by [**include if applicable:** the chief financial officer of] Grantor [**include if applicable:** and accompanied by an opinion of an independent certified public accountant].

Appraisals

Clause 8-9-16

If Lender orders an appraisal of the Property while a default exists or to comply with legal requirements affecting Lender, Grantor, at Lender's request, agrees to reimburse Lender for the cost of any such appraisal. [**Include if applicable:** Lender agrees to deliver to Grantor a copy of any such appraisal within ten days of receipt of Grantor's reimbursement]. If Grantor fails to reimburse Lender for any such appraisal within ten days of Lender's request, that failure is a default under this deed of trust.

Further Assurances

Clause 8-9-17

Grantor agrees to execute, acknowledge, and deliver to Lender any document requested by Lender, at Lender's request from time to time, to (1) correct any defect, error, omission, or ambiguity in this deed of trust or in any other document executed in connection with the Note or this deed of trust; (2) comply with Grantor's obligations under this deed of trust and other documents; (3) subject to and perfect the liens and security interests of this deed of trust and other documents any property intended to be covered thereby; and (4) protect, perfect, or preserve the liens and the security interests of this deed of trust and other documents against third persons or make any recordings, file any notices, or obtain any consents requested by Lender in connection therewith. Grantor agrees to pay all costs of the foregoing.

Insurance

Clause 8-9-18

B.1. Grantor agrees to maintain, at Grantor's expense, the following insurance plus such other insurance policies with other coverages or increased coverages as Lender may require from time to time ("Required Insurance Coverages"):

B.1.a. Liability Insurance Policies

i. commercial general liability insurance on Insurance Services Office ("ISO") standard occurrence-based form, covering Grantor and Grantor's operations on the Property and containing contractual liability coverage for broad-form indemnities [./, and/;]

> Include one or more of the following paragraphs as applicable and modify paragraph numbers as appropriate.

> Include the following if the grantor uses motor vehicles in its operations.

ii. business automobile liability insurance covering owned, nonowned, or rented automobiles [./; [and]]

> And/Or

Include the following if the grantor is operating the property with its own employees.

iii. workers' compensation insurance and employer's liability insurance covering Grantor [./; [and]]

And/Or

Include the following if the property will be leased to third parties or if the grantor employs a third-party property manager.

iv. for any third party-manager or lessee of the Property (a) commercial general liability insurance equivalent to the ISO standard occurrence-based form, covering the manager or lessee and its operations on the Property and containing contractual liability coverage for broad-form indemnities, (b) business automobile liability insurance covering owned, nonowned, or rented automobiles, and (c) workers' compensation insurance and employer's liability insurance covering the manager or lessee [./; [and]]

And/Or

Include the following if construction will occur at the property.

v. for all contractors and subcontractors performing construction at the Property, (a) commercial general liability insurance equivalent to the ISO standard occurrence-based form, covering the contractor or subcontractor and its operations on the Property and containing contractual liability coverage for broad-form indemnities, (b) business automobile liability insurance covering owned, nonowned, or rented automobiles, and (c) workers' compensation insurance and employer's liability insurance covering the contractor or subcontractor [./; [and]]

And/Or

Include the following if a third-party design professional is employed to design improvements at the property.

vi. for all engineers, architects, and other design professionals performing work with respect to the Property, (a) professional liability insurance, [**include the following if the design professional will be performing part of its duties at the property:** (b) commercial general liability insurance equivalent to the ISO standard occurrence-based form, covering the design professional and its operations on the Property and containing contractual liability coverage for broad-form indemnities,] [(b)/(c)] business automobile liability insurance covering owned, nonowned, or rented automobiles, and [(c)/(d)] workers' compensation insurance and employer's liability insurance covering the design professional.

Continue with the following.

Each commercial general and business automobile liability insurance policy will name Lender as an additional insured on an additional insured endorsement acceptable to Lender.

B.1.b. Property Insurance Policies

Include one or more of the following paragraphs as applicable and modify paragraph numbers as appropriate.

> Include the following if the property includes a completed building or if a building is under construction, for the period after completion of construction.

i. commercial property insurance using ISO form CP 00 10, "Building and Personal Property Coverage Form," and CP 10 30, "Causes of Loss—Special Form," insuring against all direct physical loss or damage to the Property except for exclusions or limitations acceptable to Lender, including optional coverages for agreed value and replacement cost (without deduction for depreciation), and endorsements to cover equipment breakdown (formerly boiler and machinery), higher limits for increased costs to comply with an ordinance or law, higher limits for debris removal, business income and rental value (formerly business interruption), [and] terrorism [**include the following if the property is in a "Special Flood Hazard Area" as defined in the National Flood Insurance Program and flood insurance in excess of the National Flood Insurance Program limits is desired:** , and flood coverage] [./; [and]]

> And/Or

> Include the following if the property is in a "Special Flood Hazard Area" as defined in the National Flood Insurance Program.

ii. flood insurance policy covering the Property issued pursuant to the National Flood Insurance Program [./; [and]]

> And/Or

> Include the following for while any improvements on the property are under construction and in lieu of commercial property insurance.

iii. a builder's risk property insurance policy written on a completed value, nonreporting form and on an all-risks basis, with no exclusions unacceptable to Lender, with coverage extensions, if necessary, to eliminate coinsurance and to cover collapse, debris removal, soft costs such as loan interest, real estate taxes, and additional legal, architectural, and engineering costs, [**include the following if the property is in a "Special Flood Hazard Area" as defined in the National Flood Insurance Program:** floods,] loss of rents, testing of mechanical equipment, and increased costs due to ordinance or law [./; [and]]

And/Or

Include the following if the property will be leased to third parties or if the grantor employs a third-party property manager.

iv. for third-party property managers and lessees, commercial property insurance using CP 10 30, "Causes of Loss—Special Form," insuring against all direct physical loss or damage to the furniture fixtures, equipment, and other business personal property of the property manager or lessee. In addition, lessees' commercial property insurance policies will cover any leasehold improvements or betterments constructed by or for the lessee.

Continue with the following.

Any commercial general or builder's risk policy carried by Grantor will contain standard mortgagee or lender loss payable clauses providing that (i) the insurer will pay the loss or damage directly to Lender, (ii) Lender will have the right to receive payment under the policy even if the insurance company has denied Grantor's claim or Grantor has failed to comply with the terms of the policy, (iii) the insurer will give written notice to Lender of cancellation ten days before its cancellation for nonpayment or thirty days before cancellation for any other reason, and (iv) the insurer will give written notice to Lender if the policy has not been renewed ten days before its expiration.

B.2. General Insurance Policy Requirements

Any reference to an ISO form in this deed of trust is to the most recent edition of the form or equivalent.

The Required Insurance Coverages will (a) be issued by companies reasonably acceptable to Lender, (b) be in a form and with exclusions, endorsements, and amendments acceptable to Lender, and (c) have limits, deductibles, and self-insured retention acceptable to Lender.

Grantor will deliver evidence of the Required Insurance Coverages in a form acceptable to Lender at least ten days before the expiration of the Required Insurance Coverages; the original of each policy, coincident with the execution of this deed of trust; and the original of each renewal policy, not less than ten days before the expiration of the initial policy or each immediately preceding renewal policy. In case of Grantor's failure to keep the Property insured or to provide evidence that the Property is insured, as required herein, Lender, after notice to Grantor, at its option may acquire the Required Insurance Coverages at Grantor's sole expense.

Subordinate Liens

Clause 8-9-19

Grantor agrees not to grant any lien or security interest in the Property or to permit any junior encumbrance to be recorded or any claim to otherwise become an encumbrance against the Property. If an involuntary encumbrance is filed against the Property, Grantor agrees, within thirty days, to either remove the involuntary encumbrance or provide a bond acceptable to Lender against the involuntary encumbrance.

Business Use

Clause 8-9-20

Grantor warrants to Lender and agrees that the proceeds of the Note will be used primarily for business or commercial purposes and not primarily for personal, family, or household purposes.

Due on Transfer—Nonresidential Property

Clause 8-9-21

Lender may declare the debt secured by this deed of trust immediately payable and invoke any remedies provided in this deed of trust for default if Grantor transfers any of the Property to a person who is not a permitted transferee without Lender's consent or, if Grantor is not a natural person, if any person owning a direct or indirect interest in Grantor transfers such interest to a person that is not a "permitted transferee" without Lender's consent. "Permitted transferee" for a natural person means that person's spouse or children, any trust for that person's benefit or the benefit of the person's spouse or children, or any corporation, partnership, or limited liability company in which the direct and beneficial owner of all the equity interest is a natural person or that person's spouse or children or any trust for the benefit of them; and the heirs, beneficiaries, executors, administrators, or personal representatives of a natural person on the death of that person or on the incompetency or disability of that person for purposes of the protection and management of that person's assets; and for a person that is not a natural person, any other person controlling, controlled by, or under common control with that person.

Clause 8-9-22

If all or any part of the Property is sold, transferred, or conveyed without the prior written consent of Lender or other holder of the Note, Lender or other holder of the Note may, at its sole option, declare the outstanding principal balance of the Note plus accrued interest immediately due and payable. Lender or other holder of the Note has no obligation to consent to any such sale or conveyance of the Property, and Lender or other holder of the Note is entitled to condition any consent on a change in the interest rate that will thereafter apply to the Note and any other change in the terms of the Note or Deed of Trust that Lender or other holder of the Note in its sole discretion deems appropriate. A lease for a period longer than three years, a lease with an option to purchase, or a contract for deed will be deemed to be a sale, transfer, or conveyance of the Property for purposes of this provision. Any deed under threat or order of condemnation, any conveyance solely between makers, and the passage of title by reason of death of a maker or by operation of law will not be construed as a sale or conveyance of the Property. The creation of a subordinate lien without the consent of Lender or other holder of the Note will be construed as a sale or conveyance of the Property, but any subsequent sale under a subordinate lien to which Lender or other holder of the Note has consented will not be construed as a sale or conveyance of the Property.

Due-on-Sale Clause (Residential)

Clause 8-9-23

If Grantor transfers any part of the Property without Lender's prior written consent, Lender may declare the debt secured by this deed of trust immediately payable and invoke any remedies provided in this deed of trust for default. If the Property is residential real property containing fewer than five dwelling units or a residential manufactured home occupied by Grantor, exceptions to this provision are limited to (1) a subordinate lien or encumbrance that does not transfer rights of occupancy of the Property; (2) creation of a purchase-money security interest for household appliances; (3) transfer by devise, descent, or operation of law on the death of a co-Grantor; (4) grant of a leasehold interest of three years or less without an option to purchase; (5) transfer to a spouse or children of Grantor or between co-Grantors; (6) transfer to a relative of Grantor on Grantor's death; and (7) transfer to an inter vivos trust in which Grantor is and remains a beneficiary and occupant of the Property.

Office of Consumer Credit Commissioner

Clause 8-9-24

Lender is subject to regulation by the Office of Consumer Credit Commissioner of the state of Texas. The name, mailing address, and telephone numbers of the office are:

Office of Consumer Credit Commissioner
2601 North Lamar Boulevard
Austin, TX 78705-4207
512-936-7600
800-538-1579

No Recourse

Clause 8-9-25

Grantor will not have any recourse liability for repayment of the principal and interest of the Note or the performance of any covenants and agreements of Grantor in this Deed of Trust. The sole remedy of Lender or other holder of the Note in the event of a default by Grantor under the Note or this Deed of Trust will be to foreclose the liens and security interests granted in this Deed of Trust, and Lender or other holder of the Note will not be entitled to any personal judgment against Grantor.

Partial Recourse

Clause 8-9-26

Grantor has no personal liability for the obligations under this deed of trust or under the Note, and no personal judgment may be taken and no claim for personal liability may be made against Grantor. Lender's sole remedy for default under the Note or this deed of trust is the foreclosure of the liens and security interests created hereunder. Exceptions to the foregoing provisions are limited to, and Grantor is liable for, the following: taxes, assessments, and charges for labor, materials, or other amounts that if unpaid may create an encumbrance against the Property; unpaid premiums for insurance required hereunder; damage to the Property if any insurance required hereunder is not maintained; all rents, issues, profits, and income derived from the Property after a default occurs and not expended for operating expenses of the Property; tenant security deposits for leases of the Property; any condemnation or insurance proceeds not paid or applied as required hereunder; [**include if applicable:** damage to and depreciation of the Property beyond normal wear and tear caused by the negligence of Grantor or the failure of Grantor to keep the Property in good repair and condition; the return of or reimbursement for all personal property taken from the Property by or on behalf of Grantor;] damages resulting from any fraud or misrepresentation by Grantor; damages resulting from any breach of any warranty of title; interest on the Note from the date of default through foreclosure, payment, or settlement of the debt; all interest on the Note during any bankruptcy proceeding of Grantor and all reasonable attorney's fees and expenses incurred as a result of Grantor's bankruptcy; and all attorney's fees and expenses incurred by Lender to collect any of the foregoing amounts.

Full Recourse

Clause 8-9-27

Grantor will have full recourse liability for repayment of the principal and interest of the Note and the performance of all covenants and agreements of Grantor in this Deed of Trust.

Assumption without Consent

Clause 8-9-28

The Property may be sold, transferred, or conveyed without the consent of Lender or other holder of the Note, provided any subsequent buyer or transferee assumes in writing for the benefit of Lender or other holder of the Note the obligation to pay the Note and to perform the covenants and agreements in this Deed of Trust in accordance with the terms of those instruments. No such assumption will release Grantor from any liabilities or obligations arising under the Note or Deed of Trust. Neither the creation of a subordinate lien nor a sale thereunder will be construed as a sale or conveyance of the Property.

Assumption with Consent

Clause 8-9-29

The Property may be sold, transferred, or conveyed provided that (1) any subsequent buyer assumes in writing for the benefit of Lender or other holder of the Note the obligation to pay the Note and to perform the covenants and agreements in this Deed of Trust in accordance with the terms of those instruments and (2) Grantor or the subsequent buyer obtains prior written consent to the sale from Lender or other holder of the Note. Consent will be based on the subsequent buyer's credit history, with no change in interest rate or terms, and may not be unreasonably withheld, conditioned, or delayed. No such assumption will release Grantor from any liabilities or obligations arising under the Note or Deed of Trust. If all or any part of the Property is sold, conveyed, leased for a period longer than three years, leased with an option to purchase, otherwise sold (including by contract for deed), or otherwise transferred or conveyed without prior written consent of Lender or other holder of the

Note, Lender or other holder of the Note may, at its sole option, declare the outstanding principal balance of the Note plus accrued interest immediately due and payable. Any deed under threat or order of condemnation, any conveyance solely between Grantors, and the passage of title by reason of death of a Grantor or by operation of law will not be construed as a sale or conveyance of the Property. [**Select one of the following:** Neither the creation of a subordinate lien nor a sale thereunder will be construed as a sale or conveyance of the Property./The creation of a subordinate lien without the consent of Lender will be construed as a sale or conveyance of the Property, but any subsequent sale under a subordinate lien to which Lender or other holder of the Note has consented will not be construed as a sale or conveyance of the Property.]

With Escrow

Clause 8-9-30

Grantor will deposit with Lender or other holder of the Note, in addition to the principal and interest installments, a pro rata part of the estimated annual ad valorem taxes on the Property and a pro rata part of the estimated annual insurance premiums for the improvements on the Property. These tax and insurance deposits are only estimates and may be insufficient to pay total taxes and insurance premiums. Grantor must pay any deficiency within thirty days after notice from Lender or other holder of the Note. Grantor's failure to pay the deficiency will constitute a default under the Deed of Trust. If any superior lienholder on the Property is collecting escrow payments for taxes and insurance, this paragraph will be inoperative as long as payments are being made to the superior lienholder.

Cross-Default

Clause 8-9-31

Any act or occurrence that would constitute default under the terms of any lien superior to the lien securing the Note will constitute a default under this Deed of Trust securing the Note.

Form 8-10

Leasehold Deed of Trust

Notice of confidentiality rights: If you are a natural person, you may remove or strike any or all of the following information from any instrument that transfers an interest in real property before it is filed for record in the public records: your Social Security number or your driver's license number.

Basic Information

Date:

Grantor:

Grantor's Mailing Address:

Trustee:

Trustee's Mailing Address:

Lender:

Lender's Mailing Address:

Obligation

Note

Date:

Original principal amount:

Borrower:

Lender:

Maturity date:

Other Debt: [**include optional clauses from form 8-6 in this chapter or describe other debt**]

Property (including any improvements): The Leasehold Estate.

Lease

Date:

Landlord:

Tenant: Grantor

Premises:

Amendments (if applicable):

Leasehold Estate: All of Tenant's rights under the Lease.

Prior Lien: [**include recording information**]

Other Exceptions to Conveyance and Warranty:

A. Granting Clause

For value received and to secure payment of the Obligation, Grantor conveys the Property to Trustee in trust. Grantor warrants and agrees to defend the title to the Property, subject to the Other Exceptions to Conveyance and Warranty. On payment of the Obligation and all other amounts secured by this deed of trust, this deed of trust will have no further effect, and Lender will release it at Grantor's expense.

B. Grantor agrees to—

B.1. perform all of Tenant's obligations under the Lease and deliver, on Lender's written request, satisfactory evidence of timely payment of all rents and other charges due under the Lease;

B.2. enforce Landlord's obligations under the Lease;

B.3. within [**number**] days after receipt, deliver a copy of each notice received by Grantor from Landlord to Lender;

B.4. timely exercise each option to extend the term of the Lease as long as the Obligation remains unpaid and concurrently deliver to Lender a copy of the notice doing so. If Grantor does not exercise an option to extend the term of the Lease, Lender may, at its option, exercise the option on behalf of Grantor. Grantor appoints Lender its attorney-in-fact to execute and deliver all instruments necessary to extend the term of the Lease or to exercise any other rights, powers, or privileges under the Lease; this power, being coupled with an interest, is irrevocable as long as the Obligation remains unpaid;

B.5. use commercially reasonable efforts to deliver to Lender, within twenty days after written request by Lender, an estoppel certificate from Landlord setting forth (a) that the Lease has not been modified or, if it has been modified, the date of each modification (together with copies of each modification), (b) the date to which all rent has been paid by Tenant under the Lease, and (c) whether there are any defaults of Tenant under the Lease and, if there are, setting forth the nature of the default(s) in reasonable detail;

B.6. execute and deliver on the request of Lender any instruments required to permit Lender to cure any default under the Lease or preserve the interest of Lender in the Leasehold Estate;

B.7. defend title to the Property subject to the Other Exceptions to Conveyance and Warranty and preserve the lien's priority as it is established in this deed of trust;

B.8. obey all laws, ordinances, and restrictive covenants applicable to the Property;

B.9. if the lien of this deed of trust is not a first lien, pay or cause to be paid all prior lien notes and abide by or cause to be abided by all prior lien instruments; and

B.10. notify Lender of any change of address.

C. Grantor agrees not to—

C.1. do or permit anything to be done that will impair the security of this deed of trust or will be grounds for terminating the Lease; or

C.2. consent, without Lender's prior written consent, to (a) any waiver, cancellation, or amendment of any provision of the Lease or (b) the subordination of the Lease to any mortgage of the fee interest of Landlord in the Premises.

D. Grantor represents that—

D.1. the Lease is enforceable;

D.2. except as set forth above, there are no amendments to the Lease; and

D.3. Grantor is not in default under the Lease and, to the best of Grantor's knowledge, Landlord is not in default under the Lease, and no event exists that, with the passage of time or the giving of notice, or both, would constitute a default under the Lease.

E. Lender's Rights

E.1. Lender or Lender's mortgage servicer may appoint in writing a substitute trustee, succeeding to all rights and responsibilities of Trustee.

E.2. If the proceeds of the Obligation are used to pay any debt secured by prior liens, Lender is subrogated to all the rights and liens of the holders of any debt so paid.

E.3. Notwithstanding the terms of the Note to the contrary, and unless applicable law prohibits, all payments received by Lender from Grantor with respect to the Obligation or this deed of trust may, at Lender's discretion, be applied first to amounts payable under this deed of trust and then to amounts due and payable to Lender with respect to the Obligation, to be applied to late charges, principal, or interest in the order Lender in its discretion determines.

E.4. If Grantor fails to perform any of Grantor's obligations, Lender may perform those obligations and be reimbursed by Grantor on demand for any amounts so paid, including attorney's fees, plus interest on those amounts from the dates of payment at the rate stated in the Note for matured, unpaid amounts. The amount to be reimbursed will be secured by this deed of trust.

E.5. **COLLATERAL PROTECTION INSURANCE NOTICE**

In accordance with the provisions of section 307.052(a) of the Texas Finance Code, the Beneficiary hereby notifies the Grantor as follows:

(A) the Grantor is required to:

(i) keep the collateral insured against damage in the amount the Lender specifies;

(ii) purchase the insurance from an insurer that is authorized to do business in the state of Texas or an eligible surplus lines insurer; and

(iii) name the Lender as the person to be paid under the policy in the event of a loss;

(B) the Grantor must, if required by the Lender, deliver to the Lender a copy of the policy and proof of the payment of premiums; and

(C) if the Grantor fails to meet any requirement listed in Paragraph (A) or (B), the Lender may obtain collateral protection insurance on behalf of the Grantor at the Grantor's expense.

E.6. If a default exists in payment of the Obligation or performance of Grantor's obligations and the default continues after any required notice of the default and the time allowed to cure, Lender may—

a. declare the unpaid principal balance and earned interest on the Obligation immediately due;

b. exercise Lender's rights with respect to rent under the Texas Property Code as then in effect;

c. direct Trustee to foreclose this lien, in which case Lender or Lender's agent will cause notice of the foreclosure sale to be given as provided by the Texas Property Code as then in effect; and

d. purchase the Property at any foreclosure sale by offering the highest bid and then have the bid credited on the Obligation.

E.7. Lender may remedy any default without waiving it and may waive any default without waiving any prior or subsequent default.

E.8. If Grantor fails to perform any of its obligations, covenants, or agreements under the Lease, Lender may do any act it deems necessary to cure such failure. Lender may enter the Premises with or without notice and to do anything that Lender deems necessary or prudent to do.

E.9. If Lender elects to make any payments or do any act or thing required to be paid or done by Grantor as Tenant under the Lease, Lender will be fully subrogated to the rights of Landlord, and any sums advanced by Lender are a part of the Obligation.

F. Trustee's Rights and Duties

If directed by Lender to foreclose this lien, Trustee will—

F.1. either personally or by agent give notice of the foreclosure sale as required by the Texas Property Code as then in effect;

F.2. sell and convey all or part of the Property "AS IS" to the highest bidder for cash with a general warranty binding Grantor, subject to the Prior Lien and to the Other Exceptions to Conveyance and Warranty and without representation or warranty, express or implied, by Trustee;

F.3. from the proceeds of the sale, pay, in this order—

a. expenses of foreclosure, including a reasonable commission to Trustee;

b. to Lender, the full amount of principal, interest, attorney's fees, and other charges due and unpaid;

c. any amounts required by law to be paid before payment to Grantor; and

d. to Grantor, any balance; and

F.4. be indemnified, held harmless, and defended by Lender against all costs, expenses, and liabilities incurred by Trustee for acting in the execution or enforcement of the trust created by this deed of trust, which includes all court and other costs, including attorney's fees, incurred by Trustee in defense of any action or proceeding taken against Trustee in that capacity.

G. General Provisions

G.1. If any of the Property is sold under this deed of trust, Grantor must immediately surrender possession to the purchaser. If Grantor fails to do so, Grantor will become a tenant at sufferance of the purchaser, subject to an action for forcible detainer.

G.2. Recitals in any trustee's deed conveying the Property will be presumed to be true.

G.3. Proceeding under this deed of trust, filing suit for foreclosure, or pursuing any other remedy will not constitute an election of remedies.

G.4. This lien will remain superior to liens later created even if the time of payment of all or part of the Obligation is extended or part of the Property is released.

G.5. If any portion of the Obligation cannot be lawfully secured by this deed of trust, payments will be applied first to discharge that portion.

G.6. Grantor assigns to Lender all amounts payable to or received by Grantor from condemnation of all or part of the Property, from private sale in lieu of condemnation, and from damages caused by public works or construction on or near the Property. After deducting any expenses incurred, including attorney's fees and court and other costs, Lender will either release any remaining amounts to Grantor or apply such amounts to reduce the Obligation. Lender will not be liable for failure to collect or to exercise diligence in collecting any such amounts. Grantor will immediately give Lender notice of any actual or threatened proceedings for condemnation of all or part of the Property.

G.7. Grantor collaterally assigns to Lender all present and future rent from the Property and its proceeds. Grantor warrants the validity and enforceability of the assignment. Grantor will apply all rent to payment of the Obligation and performance of this deed of trust, but if the rent exceeds the amount due with respect to the Obligation and the deed of trust,

Grantor may retain the excess. If a default exists in payment of the Obligation or performance of this deed of trust, Lender may exercise Lender's rights with respect to rent under the Texas Property Code as then in effect. Lender neither has nor assumes any obligations as lessor or landlord with respect to any occupant of the Property. Lender may exercise Lender's rights and remedies under this paragraph without taking possession of the Property. Lender will apply all rent collected under this paragraph as required by the Texas Property Code as then in effect. Lender is not required to act under this paragraph, and acting under this paragraph does not waive any of Lender's other rights or remedies.

G.8. Interest on the debt secured by this deed of trust will not exceed the maximum amount of nonusurious interest that may be contracted for, taken, reserved, charged, or received under law. Any interest in excess of that maximum amount will be credited on the principal of the debt or, if that has been paid, refunded. On any acceleration or required or permitted prepayment, any excess will be canceled automatically as of the acceleration or prepayment or, if already paid, credited on the principal of the debt or, if the principal of the debt has been paid, refunded. This provision overrides any conflicting provisions in this and all other instruments concerning the debt.

G.9. In no event may this deed of trust secure payment of any debt that may not lawfully be secured by a lien on real estate or create a lien otherwise prohibited by law.

G.10. When the context requires, singular nouns and pronouns include the plural.

G.11. The term *Note* includes all extensions, modifications, and renewals of the Note and all amounts secured by this deed of trust.

G.12. This deed of trust binds, benefits, and may be enforced by the successors in interest of all parties.

G.13. If Grantor and Borrower are not the same person, the term *Grantor* includes Borrower.

G.14. Grantor and each surety, endorser, and guarantor of the Obligation waive all demand for payment, presentation for payment, notice of intention to accelerate maturity, notice of acceleration of maturity, protest, and notice of protest, to the extent permitted by law.

G.15. Grantor agrees to pay reasonable attorney's fees, trustee's fees, and court and other costs of enforcing Lender's rights under this deed of trust if this deed of trust is placed in the hands of an attorney [**include if the transaction is a secondary mortgage loan:** who is not an employee of Lender] for enforcement.

G.16. If any provision of this deed of trust is determined to be invalid or unenforceable, the validity or enforceability of any other provision will not be affected.

G.17. As long as the Obligation remains unpaid, unless Lender otherwise consents in writing, the fee title to the Premises and the Leasehold Estate will not merge but will always remain separate, notwithstanding a union of the estates.

G.18. This deed of trust does not constitute an assignment of the Lease, and Lender has no liability or obligation under the Lease by reason of its acceptance of this deed of trust. Lender is liable for the obligations of Tenant arising out of the Lease for only that period of time after Lender has acquired, by foreclosure or otherwise, and is holding Grantor's interest in the Leasehold Estate.

G.19. The term *Lender* includes any mortgage servicer for Lender.

G.20. Grantor represents that this deed of trust and the Note are given for the following purposes: [**list specific purposes**].

F.4. If Grantor and Borrower are not the same person, the term Grantor includes ______________________
[Name of grantor]
Borrower.

F.5. Grantor and each surety, endorser, and guarantor of the Obligation waive all demands for payment, presentation for payment, notice of intention to accelerate maturity, notice of acceleration of maturity, protest, and notice of protest, to the extent permitted by law.

F.6. Grantor agrees to pay reasonable attorney's fees, trustee's fees, and court and other costs of enforcing Lender's rights under this deed of trust if this deed of trust is placed in the hands of an attorney for enforcement. [Include if the transaction is a home equity loan: [illegible] of Lender for such [illegible].]

F.7. If any provision of this deed of trust is determined to be invalid or unenforceable, the validity or enforceability of any other provision will not be affected.

F.8. As long as the Obligation remains unpaid, unless Lender otherwise consents in writing, the fee title to and the leasehold estate in the Leasehold Estate will not merge, but will always remain separate and distinct, notwithstanding the union of the same.

F.9. This deed of trust does not constitute an assignment of the Lease, and Lender has no liability or obligation under the Lease by reason of its acceptance of this deed of trust. Lender is liable for the obligations of Tenant arising out of the Lease for only that period of time after Lender has acquired, by foreclosure or otherwise, and is holding Grantor's interest in the Leasehold Estate.

F.10. The term Lender includes any mortgage servicer for Lender.

F.11. Grantor represents that this deed of trust and the Note are given for the following purposes: [list specific purposes]

Form 8-11

Consent to Leasehold Deed of Trust

Basic Information

Date:

Landlord:

Landlord's Mailing Address:

Tenant:

Tenant's Mailing Address:

Lender:

Lender's Mailing Address:

Lease (between Landlord and Tenant)

Date:

Premises:

Recording information (if applicable):

Amendments (if applicable):

Obligation

Note

Date:

Maker: Tenant

Payee: Lender

Original principal amount:

Maturity date:

Deed of Trust

Date:

Trustee:

Recording information (if known):

Other Debt (if any):

A. Landlord's Agreements and Representations

A.1. Landlord consents to the encumbrance by Tenant of Tenant's interest under the Lease pursuant to the Deed of Trust.

A.2. Landlord represents to Lender that (a) the Lease is in effect, (b) except as set forth above, there are no amendments to the Lease, (c) no default under the Lease has occurred by Landlord or by Tenant, and (d) to Landlord's actual knowledge, no event has occurred that, with the passage of time or the giving of notice or both, is a default by Landlord or Tenant under the Lease.

A.3. Until the Obligation is satisfied, Landlord will not (a) take any action to terminate the Lease or exercise any other remedy for default by Tenant under the Lease without first complying with the requirements of this agreement or (b) modify or cancel the Lease without Lender's prior written consent.

A.4. Lender has the right to access and remove from the Premises Tenant's personal property to enforce Lender's security interest, either during the term of the Lease or within [**number**] days after the expiration or termination of the Lease or rejection of the Lease in bankruptcy. If Lender exercises this right after the end of the Lease term, Lender must, for that period, pay all rent and comply with all other requirements of Tenant under the Lease as a condition to exercising this right. Landlord subordinates to Lender's security interest any lien that Landlord has in any of Tenant's personal property located at the Premises.

A.5. Landlord will concurrently send to Lender a copy of any notice of default sent to Tenant. Landlord will accept performance by Lender of any term of the Lease.

A.6. The Lease will not be terminated because of a default by Tenant unless (a) notice of the default is delivered to Lender; (b) Lender has not cured a monetary default within fifteen days after the expiration of any of Tenant's notice and cure periods set forth in the Lease; (c) Lender has not cured a nonmonetary default within thirty days after the expiration of any of Tenant's cure periods in the Lease or, if the default is curable but cannot be cured within the thirty-day period, (i) Lender has not notified Landlord within the thirty-day period that it intends to cure the default, (ii) Lender has not diligently commenced to cure the default, or (iii) Lender does not prosecute the cure to completion within a reasonable period of time after the expiration of any applicable cure periods in the Lease, but not to exceed sixty days; and (d) with respect to a nonmonetary default of such a nature that it is not reasonably susceptible of being cured by Lender (e.g., a nonpermitted assignment by Tenant), Lender is not otherwise paying rent and performing all of Tenant's obligations that, by their nature, Lender may perform.

A.7. If Lender acquires Tenant's interest under the Lease pursuant to foreclosure proceedings or otherwise, Lender is not required to cure any default under the Lease existing prior to such acquisition if the default cannot be cured by the payment of money or is personal to Tenant and, therefore, not susceptible of cure by Lender.

A.8. The following transfers of Tenant's interest under the Lease are permitted and do not require the consent of Landlord as long as the transferee assumes all of Tenant's obligations under the Lease: (a) a transfer resulting from a foreclosure under the Deed of Trust, (b) a deed in lieu of foreclosure of the Deed of Trust, and (c) a subsequent transfer by Lender or its designee if they acquire such interest.

A.9. On request by Lender, Landlord will deliver to Lender estoppel certificates related to the Lease and copies of documents creating or evidencing the Lease, certified by Landlord.

B. General Provisions

B.1. Until the Obligation is satisfied, Landlord and Tenant will not subordinate the Lease to any lien that may be placed on Landlord's interest in the Premises unless the lienholder enters into a subordination and nondisturbance agreement reasonably acceptable to Landlord, Tenant, and Lender.

B.2. If the Lease is terminated for any reason before expiration of its stated term or is rejected in bankruptcy, Landlord will, within fifteen days after Lender requests it, deliver to Lender or its designee a new lease of the Premises on the following terms:

a. The new lease will be for the remainder of the term of the Lease, effective on the date of termination or rejection, and will contain the same terms contained in the Lease.

b. The new lease will be executed by Landlord and Lender or its designee within ten days after receipt by Lender of the new lease.

c. On execution of the new lease, the new tenant will cure all monetary defaults that existed under the Lease upon its termination or rejection.

d. Within thirty days after the execution of the new lease, the new tenant will cure all nonmonetary defaults that existed upon termination or rejection that are curable or, if any nonmonetary default is curable but cannot be cured within the thirty-day period, (i) the new tenant must notify Landlord within the thirty-day period that the new tenant intends to cure the default, (ii) the new tenant must diligently commence to cure the default, and (iii) the new tenant must diligently prosecute the cure to completion within a reasonable period of time after execution of the new lease, but not to exceed sixty days.

e. All noncurable defaults that existed under the Lease on its termination or rejection shall be waived.

f. Any new lease will have the same priority as the Lease.

g. Landlord will hold for the account of the new tenant any moneys then held by or payable to Landlord that Tenant would have been entitled to receive but for the termination or rejection of the Lease.

B.3. To the extent of any inconsistency between the terms contained in the Lease and the terms set forth in this agreement, the terms of this agreement will control.

B.4. If the ownership of the fee and leasehold interests in the Premises become vested in the same person or entity, that occurrence will not result in a merger of title as long as the Deed of Trust remains outstanding.

B.5. Any notice required or permitted under this agreement must be in writing. Any notice required by this agreement will be deemed to be given (whether received or not) the earlier of receipt or three business days after being deposited with the United States Postal Service, postage prepaid, certified mail, return receipt requested, and addressed to the intended recipient at the address shown in this agreement. Notice may also be given by regular mail, personal delivery, courier delivery, or email and will be effective when received. Any address for notice may be changed by written notice given as provided herein.

B.6. This agreement will not be affected by (a) any renewal or modification of the Obligation, (b) the invalidity or unenforceability of any document evidencing or securing the Obligation, (c) the release or other disposition of any collateral for the Obligation, (d) the exercise or nonexercise of any right or remedy with respect to the Obligation, or (e) any waiver, consent, release, delay or other action, inaction, or omission with respect to the Obligation.

____

[Name of landlord]

____

[Name of tenant]

____

[Name of lender]

Form 8-12

Insurance and Indemnity Agreement

Basic Information

Date:

Borrower:

Borrower's Mailing Address:

Lender:

Lender's Mailing Address:

Obligation

Note

Date:

Original principal amount:

Borrower:

Lender:

Maturity date:

Other Debt: **[describe other debt]**

Property (including any improvements):

A. Borrower's Covenants

Borrower agrees to—

A.1. comply with the requirements set forth in the attached Insurance Addendum;

A.2. INDEMNIFY, DEFEND, AND HOLD LENDER AND ITS SHAREHOLDERS, MEMBERS, PARTNERS, AGENTS, CONTRACTORS, OFFICERS, AND EMPLOYEES HARMLESS FROM (a) ANY HARM TO OR IMPAIRMENT OR LOSS OF PROPERTY OR ITS USE, (b) HARM TO OR DEATH OF A PERSON, OR (c) "PERSONAL AND ADVERTISING INJURY" AS DEFINED IN THE FORM OF LIABILITY INSURANCE BORROWER IS REQUIRED TO MAINTAIN (AND ANY RESULTING OR RELATED CLAIM, ACTION, LOSS, LIABILITY, OR REASONABLE EXPENSE, INCLUDING ATTORNEY'S FEES AND OTHER FEES AND COURT AND OTHER COSTS), OCCURRING IN ANY PORTION OF THE PROPERTY DURING THE PERIOD THE OBLIGATION IS OUTSTANDING. **THE INDEMNITY CONTAINED IN THIS PARAGRAPH IS (a) INDEPENDENT OF BORROWER'S INSURANCE, (b) WILL NOT BE LIMITED BY COMPARATIVE NEGLIGENCE STATUTES OR DAMAGES PAID UNDER WORKERS' COMPENSATION OR SIMILAR EMPLOYEE BENEFIT ACTS, (c) WILL SURVIVE REPAYMENT OF THE OBLIGATION OR FORECLOSURE OF THE PROPERTY BY LENDER OR EXECUTION BY BORROWER OF A DEED IN LIEU OF FORECLOSURE WITH RESPECT TO THE PROPERTY, AND (d) WILL APPLY EVEN IF THE HARM, IMPAIRMENT, LOSS, OR INJURY IS CAUSED IN WHOLE OR IN PART BY THE ORDINARY NEGLIGENCE OR STRICT LIABILITY OF THE INTENDED BENEFICIARY OF THE INDEMNITY, BUT WILL NOT APPLY TO THE EXTENT THE HARM, IMPAIRMENT, LOSS, OR INJURY IS CAUSED BY THE SOLE OR GROSS NEGLIGENCE OR WILLFUL MISCONDUCT OF THE INTENDED BENEFICIARY OF THE INDEMNITY.**

B. General Provisions

B.1. When the context requires, singular nouns and pronouns include the plural.

B.2. The term *Note* includes all extensions, modifications, and renewals of the Note.

B.3. This agreement binds, benefits, and may be enforced by the successors in interest of all parties.

B.4. Borrower agrees to pay reasonable attorney's fees, trustee's fees, and court and other costs of enforcing Lender's rights under this agreement if this agreement is placed in the hands of an attorney for enforcement.

B.5. If any provision of this agreement is determined to be invalid or unenforceable, the validity or enforceability of any other provision will not be affected.

____

[Name of borrower]

Addendum to Insurance and Indemnity Agreement

> Texas law prohibits additional insured coverage in a construction contract, or in an agreement collateral to or affecting a construction contract, except that pertaining to a single family house, townhouse, duplex, or directly related land development, or to a public works project of a municipality. Tex. Ins. Code ch. 151. See section 17.2:4 in this manual.

Insurance and Indemnity Agreement

Date:

Borrower:

Lender:

This addendum is part of the Insurance and Indemnity Agreement.

A. Borrower agrees to maintain (or, if applicable, cause Borrower's third-party manager, lessee, general contractor, or third-party design professional to maintain) the property and/or liability insurance policies below (mark applicable boxes) containing contractual liability coverage for broad-form indemnities, plus any other coverages and increased coverages as Lender may reasonably require:

FROM BORROWER AND BORROWER'S THIRD-PARTY MANAGER

Type of Insurance or Endorsement	**Minimum Policy or Endorsement Limit**	

Liability Policies Required of Both Borrower and Borrower's Third-Party Manager in All Situations:

☐	Commercial general liability (occurrence basis)	Per occurrence:	$____________
		General aggregate:	$____________

Or

☐	Business owner's policy or commercial package coverage policy	Per occurrence: General aggregate:	$__________ $__________

Required Endorsements to Both Borrower's and Borrower's Third-Party Manager's Commercial General Liability or Business Owner's Policy:

☐	Designated location(s) general aggregate limit	$__________
☐	____________________	$__________

> Include any other desired endorsements. See chapter 17.

Additional Liability Insurance Policies Required of Borrower or Borrower's Third-Party Manager:

☐	Workers' compensation	$500,000
☐	Employer's liability	$__________
☐	Business automobile liability	$__________
☐	Liquor law or dramshop liability	$__________
☐	Garagekeepers liability	$__________
☐	Hotel safe deposit box legal liability	$__________
☐	Innkeepers liability	$__________
☐	Bailee customer's liability	$__________
☐	Comprehensive crime insurance (or, in the alternative, a fidelity bond)	$__________
☐	Excess liability	$__________
	Or	
☐	Umbrella liability (occurrence basis)	$__________

Additional Liability Insurance Policies Required during Construction Period:

FROM GENERAL CONTRACTOR

Type of Insurance or Endorsement	**Minimum Policy or Endorsement Limit**

General Liability Insurance Policy Required of General Contractor:

☐	Commercial general liability (occurrence basis)	Per occurrence:	$__________
		General aggregate:	$__________

Required Endorsements to General Contractor's Commercial General Liability Policy:

☐	Designated construction project(s) general aggregate limit	$__________
☐	____________________	$__________

Include any other desired endorsements. See chapter 17.

Additional Liability Insurance Policies Required of General Contractor:

☐	Workers' compensation	$500,000
☐	Employer's liability	$__________
☐	Business automobile liability	$__________
☐	Professional liability	$__________
☐	Excess liability	$__________
	Or	
☐	Umbrella liability (occurrence basis)	$__________

FROM DESIGN PROFESSIONAL (ARCHITECT, ENGINEER, ETC.)

Type of Insurance or Endorsement	**Minimum Policy or Endorsement Limit**

Professional Liability Insurance Policy Required:

☐	Professional liability	$__________

Property Insurance Policies If No Construction Is Contemplated or, If Construction Is Contemplated, for the Period After Construction Is Completed:

☐	Causes of loss—special form	100 percent of replacement cost of the Property
	Or	
☐	Business owner's policy	100 percent of replacement cost of the Property

Required Endorsements to Causes of Loss or Business Owner's Policy:

☐	Business income and additional expense	Sufficient limits to address reasonably anticipated business interruption losses for a period of ____ months
☐	Boiler and machinery	$____________
☐	Flood (if Property is located within a 100-year floodplain (FEMA Flood Zone "A" or any subdesignation of Zone "A"))	$____________
☐	Earth movement	$____________
☐	Ordinance or law coverage	$____________
☐	Terrorism coverage (if Property is valued over $____________)	$____________
☐	Glass	Sufficient limits to cover plate glass
☐	Signs	Sufficient limits to cover exterior signage

Include any other desired endorsements. See chapter 17.

Property Insurance Policy during Construction Period:

☐	Builder's risk on a "completed value" basis	100 percent of replacement cost of the improvements to be constructed

Required Endorsements to Builder's Risk Insurance:

☐	Additional expenses due to delay in completion	Sufficient limits to address reasonably anticipated business interruption losses for a period of ____ months

☐	Agreed value	$__________
☐	Agreed penalty	$__________
☐	Damage arising from error, omission, or deficiency in design, specifications, workmanship, or materials, including collapse	$__________
☐	Debris removal additional limit	$__________
☐	Earthquake	$__________
☐	Expediting expenses	$__________
☐	Flood	$__________
☐	Freezing	$__________
☐	Ordinance or law	$__________
☐	Pollutant cleanup and removal	$ 1,000,000
☐	Preservation of property	$__________
☐	Replacement cost	$__________
☐	Testing	$__________

B. Borrower agrees to comply with the following additional insurance requirements:

B.1. The commercial general liability (or business owner's policy or commercial package coverage policy) must be endorsed to name Lender as an "additional insured" and must not be endorsed to exclude the partial, contributory, or comparative negligence of Lender from the definition of "insured contract."

B.2. Additional insured endorsements must not exclude coverage for the sole or contributory ordinary negligence of Lender.

B.3. Property insurance policies must contain waivers of subrogation of claims against Lender.

B.4. Evidence of insurance and copies of any additional insured endorsements with respect to Borrower's insurance must be delivered by Borrower to Lender in a form acceptable to Lender at least ten days before the expiration of the policies; the original of each policy, coincident with the execution of the documents representing the Obligation; and the original of each renewal policy, not less than ten days before the expiration of the initial policy or each immediately preceding renewal policy. In case of Borrower's failure to keep the Property insured or to provide evidence that the Property is insured, as required herein, Lender, after notice to Grantor, at its option may acquire the Required Insurance Coverages at Grantor's sole expense.

B.5. **COLLATERAL PROTECTION INSURANCE NOTICE**

In accordance with the provisions of section 307.052(a) of the Texas Finance Code, the Beneficiary hereby notifies the Grantor as follows:

(A) the Grantor is required to:

(i) keep the collateral insured against damage in the amount the Lender specifies;

(ii) purchase the insurance from an insurer that is authorized to do business in the state of Texas or an eligible surplus lines insurer; and

(iii) name the Lender as the person to be paid under the policy in the event of a loss;

(B) the Grantor must, if required by the Lender, deliver to the Lender a copy of the policy and proof of the payment of premiums; and

(C) if the Grantor fails to meet any requirement listed in Paragraph (A) or (B), the Lender may obtain collateral protection insurance on behalf of the Grantor at the Grantor's expense.

B.6. Certificates of insurance and copies of any additional insured endorsements with respect to a third-party manager's, contractor's, subcontractor's, or design professional's insurance must be delivered by Borrower to Lender before such party enters the Property and thereafter at least ten days before the expiration of the policies.

C. Borrower agrees to obtain the approval of Lender with respect to the following: the forms of Borrower's (or third-party manager's, general contractor's, or design professional's) insurance policies, endorsements, and certificates and other evidence of insurance; the amounts of any deductibles or self-insured retentions amounts under Borrower's (or third-party manager's, general contractor's, or design professional's) insurance; and the creditworthiness and ratings of the insurance companies issuing Borrower's (or third-party manager's, general contractor's, or design professional's) insurance.

Chapter 9
Security Agreements

Forms

Chapter 9

Security Agreements

§ 9.1 Introduction to Security Agreements

Chapter 9 of the Texas Business and Commerce Code, titled "Secured Transactions," governs consensual security interests in personal property and fixtures.

Important Reminder: This chapter presents an overview of chapter 9. It is necessarily limited in scope. It does not address a number of specialized areas of secured transactions within the scope of chapter 9. The rules for creating and perfecting a security interest are complex. Accordingly, in the context of any particular transaction to which chapter 9 is relevant, the practitioner should consult the statutory text, the official comments, secondary sources, and any relevant case law.

§ 9.2 Scope of Chapter 9

§ 9.2:1 Security Agreements Generally

Generally, chapter 9 governs any interest, regardless of its form, in personal property and fixtures created by contract that secures payment or performance of an obligation. Tex. Bus. & Com. Code § 9.109(a)(1). That interest is called a security interest. Tex. Bus. & Com. Code § 1.201(b)(35). The property subject to a security interest is called collateral. Tex. Bus. & Com. Code § 9.102(a)(12). Chapter 9 also generally governs sales of accounts, chattel paper, payment intangibles, and promissory notes. Tex. Bus. & Com. Code § 9.109(a)(3). Chapter 9 also includes agricultural liens and all consignments, even true consignments, within its scope. Tex. Bus. & Com. Code § 9.109(a)(2), (a)(4).

§ 9.2:2 Form of Transaction Irrelevant

The form of the transaction or the label that the parties give to the transaction is irrelevant for determining whether chapter 9 applies. Rather, whether chapter 9 governs a transaction is based on the economic reality of the transaction. The parties may characterize a transaction as a sale or a lease of goods, but if in economic reality a security interest is created, chapter 9 governs. Tex. Bus. & Com. Code § 9.109(a)(1). The parties are not required to provide in their documents that a "security interest" is being created under a "security agreement." The parties may use other terms, such as *assignment*, *hypothecation*, *conditional sale*, *trust deed*, and so forth. Chapter 9 governs if a security interest in personal property is created. Tex. Bus. & Com. Code § 9.109(a)(1) ("regardless of its form"). Similarly, it is generally irrelevant whether title to collateral is in the name of the debtor or the secured party. Tex. Bus. & Com. Code § 9.202.

§ 9.2:3 Exclusions from Scope

Chapter 9 governs most consensual security interests in personal property and fixtures. Certain consensual interests in personal property collateral are not governed by chapter 9. These interests include common-law bailments and true leases of personal property, the latter being governed by Texas UCC chapter 2A (*see* Tex. Bus. & Com. Code ch. 2A). True consignments, with exceptions for small and consumer consignments, are governed by chapter 9. Tex. Bus.

& Com. Code § 9.102(a)(20) (defining "consignment"), § 9.109(a)(4).

Chapter 9 also excludes from its scope certain security interests on personal property collateral.

Federal Preemption: Chapter 9 does not apply to the extent it is preempted by federal law. Tex. Bus. & Com. Code § 9.109(c)(1). *See also* Tex. Bus. & Com. Code § 9.109 cmt. 8.

Landlord's, Statutory, and Common-Law Liens; Agricultural Liens: Landlord's liens and statutory and common-law liens for services or materials, except for agricultural liens, are not governed by chapter 9. Tex. Bus. & Com. Code § 9.109(d)(1), (d)(2). Agricultural liens are governed by chapter 9. Agricultural liens are generally nonpossessory statutory liens on a debtor's farm products in favor of a landlord or supplier of goods or services for the debtor's farming operations. Tex. Bus. & Com. Code § 9.102(a)(5) (defining "agricultural lien"), §§ 9.109(a)(2), 9.109(d)(1), (d)(2).

Security Interest Granted by State or Foreign Government or Governmental Unit: A security interest granted by a state or foreign government or governmental unit is included within the scope of chapter 9 if no other state or foreign statute governs security interests created by that entity. Tex. Bus. & Com. Code § 9.109(c)(2), (c)(3); *see also* Tex. Bus. & Com. Code § 9.102(a)(45) (defining "governmental unit"), § 9.102(a)(77) (defining "state"). Texas Government Code chapter 1208 governs creation, validity, and perfection of security interests granted by Texas governmental subdivisions; security interests granted by Texas political subdivisions are not governed by chapter 9. *See* Tex. Gov't Code ch. 1208.

Certain Sales of Payment Intangibles and Promissory Notes: Chapter 9 govern sales of accounts, chattel paper, payment intangibles, and promissory notes but excludes from its scope sales of these types of collateral for collection or in satisfaction of preexisting debt. Tex. Bus. & Com. Code § 9.109(d)(5), (d)(7).

Insurance Claims; Health-Care Insurance Receivables: With one exception, chapter 9 excludes transfers of insurance claims as original collateral. Chapter 9 governs transfers of insurance claims, as original collateral, arising out of the provision of health-care goods and services. Tex. Bus. & Com. Code § 9.102(a)(46) (defining "health care insurance receivable"), § 9.109(d)(8).

Commercial Tort Claims: Noncommercial tort claims, such as consumer personal injury claims, are excluded from chapter 9. Chapter 9 does govern security interests in commercial tort claims. Tex. Bus. & Com. Code § 9.102(a)(13) (defining "commercial tort claim"), § 9.109(d)(12).

Deposit Accounts: Chapter 9 excludes from its scope an assignment of a deposit account in a consumer transaction. Chapter 9 governs an assignment of a deposit account in a transaction that is not a consumer transaction. Tex. Bus. & Com. Code § 9.102(a)(26) (defining "consumer transaction"), § 9.102(a)(29) (defining "deposit account"), § 9.109(d)(13). Chapter 9 provides rules governing the priority dispute between a depositary bank exercising its right of set-off against a deposit account and a secured party claiming a security interest in the same account, whether as original collateral in a nonconsumer transaction or as proceeds. Tex. Bus. & Com. Code §§ 9.109(d)(10)(A), 9.340.

Real Property Interests: Chapter 9 contains a real property interest exclusion. With an exception for fixtures, the creation or transfer of an interest in or a lien on real property, including a lease or rents (as defined in Tex. Prop. Code § 64.001) thereunder, is not governed by chapter 9. Tex. Bus. & Com. Code § 9.109(d)(11). The Texas UCC contains a nonuniform expansion to this exclusion and also excludes from chapter 9 "the interest of a vendor or vendee in a contract for deed to purchase an interest in real property, or the interest of an optionor or optionee in an option to purchase an interest in real property." Tex. Bus. & Com. Code § 9.109(d)(11). By comparison, however, the definition of "account" under chapter 9 explicitly includes rights to payment for property (real or personal) sold. Tex. Bus. & Com. Code § 9.102(a)(2).

Effect of Exclusion: Even though a type of property may be excluded from chapter 9, a secured party may be able to obtain a security interest in property of that type using other federal or Texas statutes or common law.

§ 9.3 Definitions

§ 9.3:1 Security Interest, Security Agreement, Collateral

Under chapter 9, security interest basically means "an interest in personal property or fixtures which secures payment or performance of an obligation." Tex. Bus. & Com. Code § 1.201(b)(35). Additionally, security interests include "any interest of a consignor and a buyer of accounts, chattel paper, a payment intangible, or a promissory note." Tex. Bus. & Com. Code § 1.201(b)(35).

A security agreement is an "agreement that creates or provides for a security interest." Tex. Bus. & Com. Code § 9.102(a)(74).

Collateral is "the property subject to a security interest." Tex. Bus. & Com. Code § 9.102(a)(12). To conform the scope of the term *collateral* to the scope of the term *security interest*, the definition of the term *collateral* includes "proceeds . . . accounts, chattel paper, payment intangibles, and promissory notes that have been sold; and goods [under] a consignment." Tex. Bus. & Com. Code § 9.102(a)(12).

§ 9.3:2 Parties

Secured Party: The person to whom a security interest is granted is called the "secured party." Tex. Bus. & Com. Code § 9.102(a)(73)(A). A secured party also includes a buyer of accounts, chattel paper, payment intangibles, or promissory notes (Tex. Bus. & Com. Code § 9.102(a)(73)(D)); a holder of an agricultural lien (Tex. Bus. & Com. Code § 9.102(a)(73)(B)); and a consigner (Tex. Bus. & Com. Code § 9.102(a)(73)(C)). When a secured party acts as a representative for holders of secured obligations, the representative may include not just an indenture trustee "or the like" but also any trustee, agent, or collateral agent. Tex. Bus. & Com. Code § 9.102(a)(73)(E).

Debtor and Obligor: The debtor is the person who has a property interest, other than a security interest or other lien, in the collateral. Tex. Bus. & Com. Code § 9.102(a)(28)(A). The debtor also includes a seller of accounts, chattel paper, payment intangibles, or promissory notes (Tex. Bus. & Com. Code § 9.102(a)(28)(B)); a person who has a property interest in collateral subject to an agricultural lien (Tex. Bus. & Com. Code § 9.102(a)(28)(A)); and a consignee (Tex. Bus. & Com. Code § 9.102(a)(28)(C)). The obligor is the person who owes the secured obligation. Tex. Bus. & Com. Code § 9.102(a)(60).

Secondary Obligor: A secondary obligor is a person who is secondarily obligated on the secured obligation or who has a right of recourse against others with respect to the secured obligation. Tex. Bus. & Com. Code § 9.102(a)(72). For example, a guarantor is a secondary obligor.

§ 9.3:3 Collateral Categories

Chapter 9 classifies collateral into categories.

Goods: Goods are all things that are movable at the time the security interest attaches, including fixtures. Tex. Bus. & Com. Code

§ 9.102(a)(44). Money, documents, instruments, investment property, accounts, chattel paper, general intangibles, deposit accounts, letter-of-credit rights, and minerals before extraction are not goods. Software embedded in goods and customarily viewed as a part of the goods (for example, the computer chip in the airbag in an automobile) is considered goods. There are four subcategories of goods: consumer goods, inventory, farm products, and equipment. Tex. Bus. & Com. Code § 9.102(a)(23), (a)(33), (a)(34), (a)(48).

Consumer goods are goods used or bought for use primarily for personal, family, or household purposes. Tex. Bus. & Com. Code § 9.102(a)(23).

Inventory consists of goods, other than farm products, held by a person for sale or lease or consisting of raw materials, work in process, or materials consumed in business. Tex. Bus. & Com. Code § 9.102(a)(48).

Farm products are crops, livestock, or other supplies produced or used in farming operations, and they include products of crops or livestock in their unmanufactured state. For goods to be farm products, the debtor has to be engaged in farming operations with respect to the goods. Farming operations include aquatic farming operations. Farm products include aquatic goods produced in aquacultural operations. *See* Tex. Bus. & Com. Code § 9.102(a)(34), (a)(35).

Equipment is the residual subcategory of goods. It consists of goods that are not consumer goods, inventory, or farm products. Tex. Bus. & Com. Code § 9.102(a)(33).

Investment Property: Investment property comprises certificated and uncertificated securities, securities accounts, and security entitlements, all of which are defined in Texas UCC chapter 8. Tex. Bus. & Com. Code § 9.102(a)(49); *see* Tex. Bus. & Com. Code § 8.102(a)(15) (defining "security"), § 8.501 (defining "securities account"), § 8.102(a)(17) (defining "security entitlement"). Investment property also includes commodity contracts (*see* Tex. Bus. & Com. Code § 9.102(a)(15)) and commodity accounts (*see* Tex. Bus. & Com. Code § 9.102(a)(14)). Tex. Bus. & Com. Code § 9.102(a)(49).

Other Semi-Intangibles: Certain writings or records represent other rights of the debtor. These are defined in chapter 9 as documents, instruments, and chattel paper.

Documents: A document is a document of title, such as a bill of lading or warehouse receipt, including a deemed warehouse receipt under Business and Commerce Code section 7.201(b). Tex. Bus. & Com. Code § 9.102(a)(30); *see also* Tex. Bus. & Com. Code §§ 1.201(b)(16), 7.102(a)(5), 7.201(b).

A document may be electronic or tangible. *See* Tex. Bus. & Com. Code § 1.201(b)(16).

Instruments: An instrument is a negotiable instrument governed by Texas UCC chapter 3 or another writing evidencing a right to the payment of money that, in the ordinary course of business, is transferred by delivery with any necessary endorsement or assignment. A negotiable instrument or other writing is not an instrument, as defined, if it is a lease or investment property. Tex. Bus. & Com. Code § 9.102(a)(47). A credit card slip is not an instrument. Tex. Bus. & Com. Code § 9.102(a)(47)(iii). The Texas legislature has adopted nonuniform language providing that a nonnegotiable certificate of deposit is not an instrument. Tex. Bus. & Com. Code § 9.102(a)(47)(iv).

The term *promissory note* is a subcategory of the collateral category "instrument." Tex. Bus. & Com. Code § 9.102(a)(66). A promissory note is an instrument evidencing a promise to pay (rather than an order to pay, such as a check). An instrument, such as a certificate of deposit, by a bank acknowledging receipt of funds is not a promissory note. Tex. Bus. & Com. Code § 9.102(a)(66).

Chattel Paper: Chattel paper means writings or records that evidence both a monetary obligation and a security interest in or a lease of specific goods. A charter for the use or hire of a vessel is not chattel paper. Tex. Bus. & Com. Code § 9.102(a)(11). Chattel paper may be evidenced by writings or electronic records. Tex. Bus. & Com. Code § 9.102(a)(11), (a)(70) (defining "record"). Chattel paper also includes a monetary obligation secured by a security interest in specific goods and software used in those specific goods. Tex. Bus. & Com. Code § 9.102(a)(11).

Letter-of-Credit Rights: Chapter 9 uses the term *letter-of-credit right* to mean a right to payment or performance under a letter of credit, whether the letter of credit is written or electronic. The term does not include the debtor's drawing rights as beneficiary under the letter of credit. Tex. Bus. & Com. Code § 9.102(a)(51). A letter-of-credit right may be a supporting obligation (see the discussion in this section below) or original collateral.

Other Intangibles: Pure intangibles that are not investment property are accounts, deposit accounts, commercial tort claims, or general intangibles.

Accounts: "Account" is defined to include a right to payment, whether earned by performance or not, for property (real or personal, tangible and intangible, not just goods) sold; for services rendered; for intellectual property licensed; for a suretyship obligation incurred; for a policy of insurance issued; arising out of the use of a credit card; and as government sponsored or licensed lottery winnings. A charter for the lease or hire of a vessel is an account. In addition, a health-care-insurance receivable is a subcategory of the collateral category account. Tex. Bus. & Com. Code § 9.102(a)(2).

A health-care-insurance receivable is an interest in or claim under a policy of insurance that is a right to payment of a monetary obligation for health-care goods or services provided. Tex. Bus. & Com. Code § 9.102(a)(46).

Deposit Accounts: A deposit account is a demand, time, savings, passbook, or similar account maintained with a bank (*see* Tex. Bus. & Com. Code § 9.102(a)(8), defining "bank") but does not include investment property or an account evidenced by an instrument. Tex. Bus. & Com. Code § 9.102(a)(29). As defined, a deposit account includes an uncertificated certificate of deposit, for which there is no separate writing evidencing the bank's obligation to pay. The Texas legislature has adopted nonuniform changes to the definition of deposit account to include a nonnegotiable certificate of deposit and to the definition of instrument to exclude from the latter a nonnegotiable certificate of deposit. Tex. Bus. & Com. Code § 9.102(a)(29), (a)(47). The Texas UCC also has a definition for the term *nonnegotiable certificate of deposit*. *See* Tex. Bus. & Com. Code § 9.102(a)(59). Accordingly, the official comment 12 to Tex. Bus. & Com. Code § 9.102 is not accurate for a nonnegotiable certificate of deposit governed by the Texas UCC's version of revised chapter 9.

Commercial Tort Claims: A commercial tort claim is a claim of an organization (*see* Tex. Bus. & Com. Code § 1.201(b)(25), defining "organization") arising in tort. Tex. Bus. & Com. Code § 9.102(a)(13)(A). A commercial tort claim is also a claim of an individual arising in tort if the claim arose out of the individual's business and does not include damages for death or personal injury. Tex. Bus. & Com. Code § 9.102(a)(13)(B). After a commercial tort claim is contractually settled, it ceases to be a commercial tort claim. A right to payment of the contractually settled commercial tort claim may be evidenced by an instrument, chattel paper, or the settlement agreement itself. In the latter case, the right to payment is a payment intangible. *See* Tex. Bus. & Com. Code § 9.109 cmt. 15.

General Intangibles: General intangibles are any personal property other than goods, accounts, chattel paper, commercial tort claims, deposit accounts, documents, instruments, investment property, letter-of-credit rights, or money. Tex. Bus. & Com. Code § 9.102(a)(42). There are two special subcategories within the category of general intangibles: payment intangibles and software.

A payment intangible is a general intangible under which the principal obligation of the account debtor (*see* Tex. Bus. & Com. Code § 9.102(a)(3), defining "account debtor") is to pay money. Tex. Bus. & Com. Code § 9.102(a)(62).

Software is a computer program and includes related supporting information. However, software embedded in goods and customarily viewed as a part of the goods is treated as part of the goods and not as software under chapter 9. Tex. Bus. & Com. Code § 9.102(a)(76).

Not all intangible personal property included in the collateral category of a general intangible is a payment intangible or software. Intangible personal property exists that is neither a payment intangible nor software that nevertheless is a general intangible.

Proceeds: Proceeds are generally not considered a separate category of collateral. Rather, a secured party has a claim to proceeds that is derived from the secured party's security interest in other collateral. Proceeds include whatever is acquired on the sale, lease, license, exchange, or other disposition of collateral (Tex. Bus. & Com. Code § 9.102(a)(65)(A)) and also include collections of and distributions with respect to collateral (Tex. Bus. & Com. Code § 9.102(a)(65)(B)), rights arising out of collateral (Tex. Bus. & Com. Code § 9.102(a)(65)(C)), and claims, including insurance payable, for loss, defects, or damage to collateral (Tex. Bus. & Com. Code § 9.102(a)(65)(D), (a)(65)(E)). Cash proceeds are a subcategory of proceeds and consist of proceeds that are money, checks, deposit accounts, or the like. Tex. Bus. & Com. Code § 9.102(a)(9).

Supporting Obligations: A supporting obligation is a credit enhancement, such as a guaranty and letter-of-credit right, that supports underlying collateral consisting of an account, chattel paper, a document, a general intangible, an instrument, or investment property. Tex. Bus. & Com. Code § 9.102(a)(78). A supporting obligation is incident to the collateral it supports. Collections of and distributions with respect to a supporting obligation are proceeds of the underlying collateral and of the supporting obligation itself. This characterization as proceeds has significance under the priority rules for proceeds.

§ 9.4 Creation and Attachment of Security Interest

§ 9.4:1 Attachment of Security Interest Generally

A security agreement may provide for or create a security interest. Tex. Bus. & Com. Code § 9.102(a)(74). A security interest is not enforceable against a debtor until it attaches. Tex. Bus. & Com. Code § 9.203(a). Attachment occurs if—

1. value has been given (see section 9.4:2 below);
2. the debtor has rights in the collateral (see section 9.4:3 below); and
3. one of these conditions is met:
   a. the debtor has authenticated a security agreement that contains a description of the collateral (see section 9.4:4 below);

b. under a security agreement with the debtor, the secured party has possession of the collateral (other than a certificated security) (see section 9.4:5 below); or

c. the secured party has control of the collateral if the collateral is investment property, a deposit account, electronic chattel paper, a letter-of-credit right, or an electronic document (see section 9.4:6 below).

Tex. Bus. & Com. Code § 9.203(b).

§ 9.4:2 Value

Value includes any consideration sufficient to support a simple contract. Examples include lending money, making a binding commitment to lend money, issuing a guarantee, or acting as an accommodation party. Value also includes satisfaction, in whole or in part, of a preexisting claim. Tex. Bus. & Com. Code § 1.204.

§ 9.4:3 Rights in Collateral

A debtor may grant a security interest only in those rights in collateral that the debtor holds. Similarly, a secured party may not enjoy greater rights in the collateral than the debtor holds, unless the Texas UCC provides otherwise. Tex. Bus. & Com. Code § 9.203(b) cmt. 6. The power of a debtor to transfer collateral is sufficient to satisfy the rights-in-the-collateral requirement. Tex. Bus. & Com. Code § 9.203(b)(2). Attachment of a security interest is conditioned on the debtor's having rights in the collateral or the power to transfer rights in the collateral to a secured party. Limited rights in collateral, short of full ownership, are sufficient for a security interest to attach. A security interest attaches only to those rights a debtor has in collateral, however broad or limited those rights may be.

A security agreement may create or provide for a security interest in after-acquired collateral. Tex. Bus. & Com. Code § 9.204(a). A security interest in after-acquired collateral attaches when the debtor acquires rights in the after-acquired collateral.

§ 9.4:4 Security Agreement

Purpose and Effect: A debtor's authentication of a security agreement describing the collateral provides evidence, similar to the evidence required to satisfy the statute of frauds, that the parties intend to create a security interest in the described collateral. That action also renders the security interest enforceable against the debtor and results in the security interest attaching to the described collateral. Tex. Bus. & Com. Code § 9.203(a), (b)(3)(A).

Authenticated by Debtor: A security agreement must be authenticated by the debtor. Tex. Bus. & Com. Code § 9.203(b)(3)(A). The term *authenticated* includes a signature on a writing; a process of adopting or accepting a retrievable electronic transmission; and attaching to or logically associating with a retrievable electronic record an electronic sound, symbol, or process with the intent of adopting or accepting that record. Tex. Bus. & Com. Code § 9.102(a)(7), (a)(70).

Reasonable Identification of Collateral: Chapter 9 requires security agreements to reasonably identify the collateral. Tex. Bus. & Com. Code §§ 9.108(a), 9.203(b)(3)(A). Reasonable identification of collateral may be by specific listing, category, type, quantity, computational formula, or any method under which the identity of the collateral is objectively determinable. Tex. Bus. & Com. Code § 9.108(b). In a security agreement, an all-asset description is, however, insufficient. Tex. Bus. & Com. Code § 9.108(c). A description by type alone is insufficient if the collateral is a commercial tort claim or, in a consumer transaction, if the collateral is consumer goods, a security entitlement, a securities account, or a commodity account. Tex. Bus. & Com. Code § 9.108(e). If the collateral is timber to be cut, a real estate description is required in the security agreement. Tex. Bus. & Com. Code § 9.203(b)(3)(A).

After-Acquired Property: Security agreements may contain after-acquired property clauses. Tex. Bus. & Com. Code § 9.204(a). A secured party generally may not obtain a security interest in after-acquired consumer goods unless the debtor acquires rights in the consumer goods within ten days after the secured party gives value. Tex. Bus. & Com. Code § 9.204(b)(1). A security interest in a commercial tort claim attaches only to one existing at the time the security agreement is entered into. A security interest will not attach to an after-acquired commercial tort claim. Tex. Bus. & Com. Code § 9.204(b)(2).

Future Advances and Cross-Collateralization: A security interest under chapter 9 may secure future advances, and the security agreement may provide for cross-collateralization of obligations. Tex. Bus. & Com. Code § 9.204(c). Comment 5 to section 9.204 expressly rejects the holdings of cases that require future advances to be of the same type or otherwise related to the original advance. Tex. Bus. & Com. Code § 9.204 cmt. 5.

§ 9.4:5 Possession

Possession of collateral by a secured party pursuant to a security agreement with (but not necessarily authenticated by) a debtor also evidences that the parties intend to create a security interest in the possessed collateral. If a secured party so possesses the collateral, the security interest is enforceable against the debtor and attaches. Tex. Bus. & Com. Code § 9.203(a), (b)(3)(B), (b)(3)(C). A secured party may possess the collateral itself or through a third party who possesses the collateral. Generally, a secured party will not rely on possession of the collateral pursuant to an unauthenticated security agreement with the debtor to create an enforceable, attached security interest in collateral. Rather, secured parties will generally obtain an authenticated security agreement, as described in section 9.4:4 above. In addition to being a means of causing a security interest to attach to collateral, possession is also a means of perfecting a security interest. Perfection by possession is more likely to occur than attachment by possession. Therefore, a more detailed discussion of the requirements of possession is contained at section 9.5:4 below, which discusses perfection by possession.

§ 9.4:6 Control

Control under chapter 9, as a method of attachment and perfection of a security interest, applies to investment property, deposit accounts, electronic chattel paper, electronic documents, and letter-of-credit rights. Tex. Bus. & Com. Code § 9.203(b)(3)(D). Control under chapter 9 does not have its common, colloquial meaning. Rather, control as used in chapter 9 has specific meanings, and specified actions must be taken to obtain control. Moreover, different actions are required to obtain control of different types of collateral. The actions to obtain control of a deposit account are set forth in section 9.104, of electronic chattel paper in section 9.105 (see also Tex. Bus. & Com. Code § 9.102(a)(31), defining "electronic chattel paper"), of investment property in sections 9.106 and 8.106, of electronic documents in section 7.106, and of letter-of-credit rights in section 9.107. Additionally, the secured party must have control of the collateral pursuant to the debtor's security agreement. Tex. Bus. & Com. Code § 9.203(b)(3)(D). Another agreement with a third party—for example, a bank for a deposit account or a broker for a securities account—may be the agreement that establishes control of the collateral. Although attachment by control without a debtor-authenticated security agreement is possible, secured parties generally will obtain a debtor-authenticated security agreement as described in section 9.4:4 above and rely on control for perfection of the security interest, not attachment. Perfection by control is discussed in section 9.5:5 below.

§ 9.5 Perfection of Security Interest

§ 9.5:1 Perfected Security Interest Generally

An unperfected security interest is subordinate to the rights of a person who becomes a lien creditor before the security interest is perfected. Tex. Bus. & Com. Code § 9.317(a)(2). Stated another way, a perfected security interest prevails over a judgment creditor using the judicial process to obtain a judgment lien on the collateral, including a trustee in bankruptcy that has the status of a lien creditor on the commencement of a bankruptcy proceeding for the debtor. Only an attached security interest may be a perfected security interest. Tex. Bus. & Com. Code § 9.308(a).

§ 9.5:2 Methods of Perfection

There are four basic methods of perfecting an attached security interest. First, a properly completed financing statement (*see* Tex. Bus. & Com. Code § 9.102(a)(39)) may be filed in the appropriate UCC filing offices. Second, the collateral may be in the possession of the secured party. Third, the secured party may have control of the collateral. Fourth, in a few cases, attachment of a security interest automatically perfects the security interest. For a specific category of collateral, there may be only one method of perfection or several.

§ 9.5:3 Perfection by Filing

A security interest in many types of collateral may be perfected by filing a properly completed financing statement or statements in the appropriate UCC filing offices. For certain types of collateral, a properly completed financing statement must be filed in the appropriate UCC filing offices to perfect a security interest in that collateral. Tex. Bus. & Com. Code § 9.310(a). Filing a properly completed financing statement is the only method of perfecting a security interest in accounts, a commercial tort claim, and general intangibles except for a security interest arising out of certain sales of accounts or payment intangibles. Filing a properly completed financing statement is an alternative method of perfecting a security interest in goods (other than goods governed by a certificate of title or another form of registration), negotiable documents, instruments, chattel paper, and investment property. If filing a financing statement is an alternative method of perfecting a security interest in collateral, then, with certain exceptions for goods, generally a secured party that perfects its security interest by another method can obtain priority over the secured party who perfects by filing.

Contents of Financing Statement: A financing statement under chapter 9 must (1) set forth the debtor's name (rules for determining a debtor's name are contained in Tex. Bus. & Com. Code § 9.503(a); see also section 9.14:2 below); (2) set forth the debtor's mailing address; (3) indicate whether the debtor is an individual or an organization; (4) if the debtor is an individual, indicate the debtor's surname; (5) indicate the name of the secured party or the secured party's representative; (6) list the mailing address of the secured party or its representative; and (7) indicate the collateral covered by the financing statement. Tex. Bus. & Com. Code §§ 9.502(a), 9.516(b)(3), (b)(4), (b)(5). If the collateral is timber to be cut, as-extracted collateral (defined in Tex. Bus. & Com. Code

§ 9.102(a)(6)), or fixtures, additional information must be included on the financing statement. Tex. Bus. & Com. Code §§ 9.502(b), (c), 9.516(b)(3)(D). A secured party may file a financing statement without the debtor's signature if the debtor authorizes the filing. Tex. Bus. & Com. Code § 9.509(a)(1). By entering into a security agreement, a debtor automatically authorizes the filing of a financing statement covering collateral described in the security agreement. Tex. Bus. & Com. Code § 9.509(b). A secured party needs separate, express authorization from the debtor to file a financing statement before the debtor has entered into a security agreement. Even though an all-asset collateral description is insufficient in a security agreement, an indication in a financing statement that the collateral is all assets or all personal property is sufficient. Tex. Bus. & Com. Code § 9.504. A financing statement containing minor errors that are not seriously misleading may be effective. Tex. Bus. & Com. Code § 9.506(a).

Where to File in a State: Chapter 9 contains choice-of-law rules to determine the jurisdiction in which filings must be made. Those rules are discussed in section 9.6 below. Chapter 9, like the official text of Uniform Commercial Code article 9, generally requires that financing statements be filed in only one office in a jurisdiction. For Texas, that is the office of the secretary of state. Local filings are required only for as-extracted collateral (defined in section 9.102(a)(6)), timber to be cut, or fixtures. Tex. Bus. & Com. Code § 9.501(a)(1). The local filing office is the real estate recording office for a mortgage on the related real property.

What Constitutes Filing: Communication of the financing statement to the filing office and tender of the correct filing fee, the so-called tender rule, constitutes filing. Tex. Bus. & Com. Code § 9.516(a). The word *communication* (defined in Tex. Bus. & Com. Code § 9.102(a)(18)) is used to accommodate electronic filing. Chapter 9 sets forth the reasons a filing office may refuse to accept a financing statement for filing, rendering the filing ineffective. Tex. Bus. & Com. Code § 9.516(b). Under section 9.520(a) of the Texas Business and Commerce Code, a filing office may refuse to accept a financing statement or an amendment or other record related to a financing statement only for a reason set forth in section 9.516(b). If a filing office could reject the filing, but nevertheless accepts it, the filing is effective if the financing statement contains sufficient information under sections 9.502(a) and (b). Tex. Bus. & Com. Code § 9.520(c). If a filing office refuses to accept a financing statement or other record for filing for an impermissible reason, the financing statement or record is deemed as effective as if it were filed, except against a purchaser for value of the collateral that reasonably relies on the absence of the filing. Tex. Bus. & Com. Code § 9.516(d).

How Filings Are Indexed: Filings under chapter 9 are to be indexed according to the name of the debtor so they can be located by subsequent searchers. Tex. Bus. & Com. Code § 9.519(c)(1), (f)(1). Once an initial filing is made, the filing office is required to index any amendment, assignment, or continuation statement relating to the initial filing in a way that links it to the initial filing. Tex. Bus. & Com. Code § 9.519(c)(1), (f)(2). The filing office may not delete its records pertaining to any financing statement until at least one year after the financing statement has lapsed. Tex. Bus. & Com. Code § 9.522(a).

Continuation; Lapse; Termination: Filings generally expire after five years and must be continued within six months before the end of the five-year period by the filing of a continuation statement. Tex. Bus. & Com. Code § 9.515. A filing office may reject a continuation statement that is not filed during that period. Tex. Bus. & Com. Code §§ 9.516(b)(3)(B)(ii), 9.516(b)(7). If an initial financing statement is filed in connection with a public finance transaction (defined in Tex. Bus. & Com. Code § 9.102(a)(68)) or a manufactured-home transaction (defined in Tex. Bus. & Com. Code § 9.102(a)(54)) and the financing statement indicates that fact, the financing statement is effective for thirty years. Tex. Bus. & Com. Code § 9.515(b). If a financing statement lapses, a security interest perfected by the filing becomes unperfected (unless perfected by another method such as possession) and is deemed never to have been perfected against a purchaser for value. Tex. Bus. & Com. Code § 9.515(c). When the secured obligation has been satisfied and the secured party has no obligation to extend credit, the secured party is obligated to file, or in a commercial transaction provide to the debtor, a termination statement. Tex. Bus. & Com. Code § 9.513. A debtor may file a termination statement if the secured party is required to file or provide the termination statement and has failed to do so. Tex. Bus. & Com. Code § 9.509(d)(2). A termination statement filed by a debtor must indicate that the debtor authorized the filing of the termination statement. Tex. Bus. & Com. Code § 9.509(d)(2).

Bogus Filings: There used to be no nonjudicial means for a debtor to correct a financing statement filed against the debtor that the debtor believed was wrongful, a so-called bogus or fraudulent filing. Chapter 9 permits a debtor who believes that a filing concerning the debtor is inaccurate or was wrongfully filed to file an information statement containing the basis for the debtor's belief that the record is inaccurate or was wrongfully filed. The information statement becomes part of the filing record but does not affect the effectiveness of an initial financing statement or other filed record. Tex. Bus. & Com. Code § 9.518. Texas has adopted a nonuniform additional section in chapter 9 that permits an owner of property covered by a fraudulent filing to recover civil penalties against the filer and to sue to request release of the filing. Tex. Bus. & Com. Code § 9.5185. Certain financing statements by inmates and their representatives are presumptively fraudulent. For special restrictions on filings by such parties, see Tex. Civ. Prac. & Rem. Code §§ 12.001–.007 and Tex. Gov't Code §§ 51.901, 405.022. See also section 2.113 in this manual for a description of criminal and other civil actions that may be brought against a fraudulent filer.

Other Filing Provisions: Additional details concerning financing statements and the UCC filing system are contained in subchapter E of chapter 9.

§ 9.5:4 Perfection by Possession

A secured party may perfect a security interest by having possession, by itself or through a third party, of the collateral. Types of collateral that may or must be perfected by possession are summarized in the following paragraphs.

Money: The only way a secured party may perfect its security interest in money (defined in Texas Business and Commerce Code section 1.201(b)(24)) is by possession. Tex. Bus. & Com. Code § 9.312(b)(3).

Instruments: A secured party may perfect a security interest in an instrument by either filing or possession. Tex. Bus. & Com. Code §§ 9.312(a), 9.313(a). The priority of a security interest in an instrument differs depending on whether perfection is by filing or possession. There is a separate perfection rule for a sale of an instrument that is a promissory note. Such a sale is a security interest under section 1.201(b)(35) and section 9.109(a)(3). A security interest arising out of a sale of a promissory note is perfected automatically, without additional action, when it attaches. Tex. Bus. & Com. Code § 9.309(4).

Even though a secured party may perfect a security interest in an instrument by merely obtaining possession of the instrument without obtaining an endorsement of the instrument, a secured party will want to obtain an endorsement to be entitled to holder-in-due-course status under Texas UCC chapter 3. Tex. Bus. & Com. Code §§ 3.302(a), 3.201 (defining "negotiation").

Letter-of-Credit Rights: Under chapter 9, possession of a written letter of credit does not perfect a security interest in proceeds under the letter of credit. Instead, a security interest in a letter-of-credit right that is a supporting obligation (defined in Tex. Bus. & Com. Code § 9.102(a)(78)) is automatically perfected if the security interest in the related collateral is perfected. Tex. Bus. & Com. Code § 9.308(d). If a letter-of-credit right is original collateral, and not a supporting obligation to other collateral, a security interest therein may be perfected only by control. Tex. Bus. & Com. Code § 9.312(b)(2).

Certificated Securities: Under chapter 9, a secured party's taking delivery of a certificated security under section 8.301 and Tex. Bus. & Com. Code § 9.313(a) perfects its security interest. Like mere possession of an instrument, a secured party's taking delivery of a certificated security under section 8.301, without an endorsement, perfects the secured party's security interest in the certificated security. The secured party will want to obtain an endorsement to be entitled to "protected purchaser" status under Texas UCC chapter 8 (*see* Tex. Bus. & Com. Code §§ 8.303, 8.106(b)(1)) and the priority status afforded a secured party in control of a certificated security. Tex. Bus. & Com. Code § 9.328(1), (5).

If the collateral is a certificated security in registered form, attachment of a security interest occurs when the certificated security is delivered to the secured party under Texas Business and Commerce Code section 8.301. Tex. Bus. & Com. Code §§ 9.203(b)(3)(C), 9.313(e). Delivery of a certificated security to a secured party occurs when the secured party acquires possession of the certificated security, when a third party (who is not a securities intermediary) acquires possession of the certificated security on behalf of the secured party, or when a third party (who is not a securities intermediary) who already has possession of the certificated security acknowledges that it holds the certificated security for the secured party. Tex. Bus. & Com. Code § 8.301(a)(1), (a)(2).

Delivery of a certificated security to a secured party for purposes of attaching and perfecting a security interest in the security certificate by possession also occurs when a securities intermediary (for example, a securities broker), acting on behalf of the secured party, acquires possession of the security certificate. The certificate must be in registered form and registered in the name of the secured party, payable to the order of the secured party, or endorsed to the secured party, not to the securities intermediary or in blank. Tex. Bus. & Com. Code § 8.301(a)(3).

Certificated securities are seldom endorsed on the back in the space provided for an endorsement by the registered owner to a purchaser, including a secured party. Rather, the general practice is for the registered owner to sign a stock power with respect to the certificated security. Frequently stock powers are signed in blank, that is, without designating the transferee of the certificate. If a secured party intends to perfect a security interest in a certificated security by possession, which occurs by delivery of the certificated security to a securities intermediary or broker that acts on behalf of the secured party, the secured party should take care to ensure that the security is in registered form and is appropriately endorsed, either on the back of the certificate or by an appropriate stock or bond power.

If a secured party intends to perfect its security interest by delivery of a certificated security to a securities intermediary, as described above, the secured party should also take steps to ensure that the securities intermediary retains possession of the certificated security. After a securities intermediary acquires a certificated security for a customer, in this case for the secured party, the securities intermediary often credits the security to a securities account held by the securities intermediary for its customer. The securities intermediary usually will not retain possession of the certificated security but rather will transfer the certificated security to the securities intermediary's clearing corporation. The records of the securities intermediary will reflect the securities credited to its customer's account. The secured party in such a situation would have to rely on "control" (see section 9.5:5 below) as the method of maintaining the perfected status of its security interest, even if the security certificate was appropriately delivered to the securities intermediary to initially perfect the secured party's security interest by possession.

Chattel Paper: A security interest in tangible chattel paper may be perfected by possession. Tex. Bus. & Com. Code § 9.313(a). A security interest in electronic chattel paper may not be perfected by possession but may be perfected by control or filing. Tex. Bus. & Com. Code §§ 9.312(a), 9.314(a).

Other Collateral: Other collateral that may be perfected by the secured party's taking possession of the collateral includes goods and tangible negotiable documents. Tex. Bus. & Com. Code § 9.313(a).

Possession by Third Parties: A secured party desiring to perfect a security interest in collateral by possession when the collateral (other than a certificated security or goods covered by a document) is in the possession of a third party must obtain an authenticated record (for example, a signed writing) from the possessor of the collateral acknowledging that it is holding the collateral for the secured party. Tex. Bus. & Com. Code § 9.313(c)(1) (compare with Tex. Bus. & Com. Code §§ 8.106(a), (b), 8.301(a)(2) for certificated securities). The third party in possession of the collateral may not be the debtor or a lessee in the ordinary course from the debtor. Tex. Bus. & Com. Code § 9.313(c). If a secured party or a third party on behalf of the secured party has possession of collateral, possession is not relinquished if the collateral is delivered with appropriate instructions to a possible purchaser of the collateral (other than the debtor or an ordinary-course lessee of the collateral) for inspection or return. Tex. Bus. & Com. Code § 9.313(h).

§ 9.5:5 Perfection by Control

Perfection of a security interest by control applies to investment property, deposit accounts, electronic chattel paper, electronic documents, and letter-of-credit rights. Tex. Bus. & Com. Code §§ 7.106, 9.104–.107, 9.314(a).

Investment Property: A security interest in investment property may be perfected by control or filing. Tex. Bus. & Com. Code §§ 9.312(a), 9.314(a). A secured party that has control of investment property has priority over another secured party that perfects its security interest in the same property by filing a financing statement. Tex. Bus. & Com. Code § 9.328(1). Generally, chapter 9 defers to Texas UCC chapter 8 to set forth the requirements for control of investment property. Tex. Bus. & Com. Code § 9.106(a). Control of investment property includes delivery, with endorsement, of a certificated security to the secured party; an agreement by the issuer of an uncertificated security that the issuer will honor instructions from the secured party without further consent of the debtor; and an agreement by a bank, broker, or other securities intermediary holding a securities account or by a commodity intermediary that it will honor instructions from the secured party concerning the account without further consent of the debtor. Banks, brokers, and other securities intermediaries that regularly hold securities accounts for their customers typically require the use of their own form of a so-called control agreement. Control also includes registering a security, a securities account, or a commodity account in the name of the secured party. If a secured party is the debtor's securities intermediary or commodity intermediary, the secured party automatically has control. Tex. Bus. & Com. Code §§ 8.106, 9.106.

Deposit Accounts: A secured party may perfect a security interest in a deposit account as original collateral only by obtaining control of the deposit account. Tex. Bus. & Com. Code §§ 9.312(b)(1), 9.314(a). Filing a financing statement does not perfect a security interest in a deposit account as original collateral. Tex. Bus. & Com. Code § 9.312 cmt. 5. A secured party has control of a deposit account if it is the depositary bank or if the deposit account is in the secured party's name. A secured party also has control if the depositary bank agrees to comply with instructions from the secured party concerning the deposit account without further consent from the debtor. Tex. Bus. & Com. Code § 9.104(a). Form 9-19 is a form of deposit account control agreement that restricts the ability of the debtor to use the account. Form 9-20 is a form of deposit account control agreement that allows the debtor to use the account before an event of default. Banks typically require the use of their own form of deposit account control agreement.

Electronic Chattel Paper: A security interest in electronic chattel paper may be perfected by filing or by control. Tex. Bus. & Com. Code §§ 9.312(a), 9.314(a).

The requirements for control of electronic chattel paper are in Tex. Bus. & Com. Code § 9.105.

Letter-of-Credit Rights: A secured party may perfect its security interest in a letter-of-credit right that is not a supporting obligation for other collateral only by obtaining control of the letter-of-credit right. Tex. Bus. & Com. Code §§ 9.312(b)(2), 9.314(a). A secured party has control of a letter-of-credit right if the issuer or nominated person has consented to an assignment of proceeds of the letter of credit under Texas Business and Commerce Code section 5.114(c). Tex. Bus. & Com. Code § 9.107.

Electronic Documents: A security interest in an electronic document of title may be perfected by filing or by control. Tex. Bus. & Com. Code §§ 9.312(a), 9.314(a). A secured party has control of an electronic document of title if a system employed for evidencing the transfer of interests in the electronic document reliably establishes the secured party as the person to which the electronic document was issued or transferred. Tex. Bus. & Com. Code § 7.106(a).

§ 9.5:6 Automatic Perfection

In some cases, a security interest is automatically perfected if it has attached; no additional action other than attachment is necessary to perfect the security interest. Tex. Bus. & Com. Code § 9.309.

Automatic Perfection: The security interests that are automatically perfected on attachment under chapter 9 are—

1. a purchase-money security interest in consumer goods;
2. a sale of payment intangibles and promissory notes;
3. an assignment of accounts that does not, alone or in conjunction with other assignments to the same assignee, transfer a significant part of the outstanding accounts of the assignor;
4. an assignment of payment intangibles that does not, alone or in conjunction with other assignments to the same

assignee, transfer a significant part of the payment intangibles of the assignor;

5. a security interest arising under Texas UCC chapter 2, 2A, or 4;

6. a security interest in investment property created by a securities intermediary or commodity intermediary;

7. for a temporary period, a security interest in instruments, certificated securities, and negotiable documents;

8. an assignment of a health-care-insurance receivable to the health-care provider;

9. for a temporary period, a security interest in proceeds;

10. a sale by an individual of lottery winnings; and

11. a security interest in favor of an issuer or nominated person in documents presented to the issuer or nominated person for draw under a letter of credit.

Tex. Bus. & Com. Code §§ 9.309(1)–(8), (10), (11), (14), 9.312(e), 9.315(d). *See* Tex. Bus. & Com. Code § 5.118.

Supporting Obligation: If a security interest in an account, chattel paper, document, general intangible, instrument, or investment property is perfected, a security interest in a supporting obligation for that collateral is automatically perfected. Tex. Bus. & Com. Code §§ 9.203(f), 9.308(d). A supporting obligation is a letter-of-credit right or secondary obligation, such as a guaranty, that supports the payment or performance of an account, chattel paper, document, general intangible, instrument, or investment property. Tex. Bus. & Com. Code § 9.102(a)(78).

§ 9.5:7 Other Perfection Provisions under Chapter 9

The temporary automatic perfection periods for instruments, certificated securities, and negotiable documents is twenty days (Tex. Bus. & Com. Code § 9.312(e)), as is the temporary perfection period of a security interest in proceeds. Tex. Bus. & Com. Code § 9.315(d). A financing statement must be filed to perfect a security interest in a beneficiary's interest in a common-law trust. Tex. Bus. & Com. Code § 9.309(13). A security interest in titled-goods inventory held for sale or lease by a dealer in the business of selling goods of that kind is perfected by filing, not by notation of the security interest on the certificate of title. A security interest in titled-goods inventory held for sale or lease by a person in the business of leasing such goods is perfected by notation on the certificate of title and not by filing. Tex. Bus. & Com. Code § 9.311(d).

§ 9.5:8 Other Means of Perfection

Federal and state statutes may provide a means of perfecting a security interest in vessels, aircraft, intellectual property, and titled goods (such as motor vehicles that are not inventory of a dealer). Compliance with these forms of perfection constitutes perfection by filing under chapter 9. Tex. Bus. & Com. Code § 9.311(a), (b).

Former Tex. Bus. & Com. Code § 9.343 (repealed by Acts 2021, 87th Leg., R.S., ch. 284, § 5 (H.B. 3794), eff. Sept. 1, 2021), which provided for "a security interest in favor of interest owners, as secured parties, to secure the obligations of the first purchaser of oil and gas production, as debtor, to pay the purchase price," was replaced with Tex. Prop. Code § 67.002 because of the holding in *In re First River Energy, L.L.C.*, 986 F.3d 914 (5th Cir. 2021), in which the Texas priority lien of Tex. Bus. & Com. Code § 9.343 was not given effect under Delaware law (the jurisdiction of the bankrupt debtor), as Delaware did not have a similar nonuniform provision. The case did uphold an Oklahoma statutory lien outside of the Uniform Commercial Code that provided priority to an Oklahoma producer. The replacement of Tex. Prop. Code § 67.002 for the prior Tex. Bus. & Com. Code § 9.343 is intended to follow the Oklahoma statutory scheme.

§ 9.6 Choice of Law

§ 9.6:1 Choice of Law Generally

Chapter 9 contains choice-of-law provisions that determine which jurisdiction's law governs attachment of a security interest, perfection of a security interest, and priority over another interest. If a dispute occurs in a UCC jurisdiction, the choice-of-law rules in chapter 9 of the forum jurisdiction determine which jurisdiction's laws the forum jurisdiction is required to apply. The choice-of-law rules in the UCC do not address which law a non-UCC jurisdiction would apply.

§ 9.6:2 Contract Choice of Law

If a security agreement specifies a governing law, and if the transaction has a reasonable relationship with the chosen jurisdiction, the forum jurisdiction should apply the law of the jurisdiction specified in the security agreement to determine the contractual rights and obligations of the debtor and the secured party. Tex. Bus. & Com. Code § 1.301(a). Regardless of the jurisdiction chosen by the parties to govern their rights and obligations, the secured party and the debtor by their contract may not vary the mandatory choice-of-law rules in chapter 9 concerning perfection and priority of a security interest. Tex. Bus. & Com. Code § 1.301(b). *See also* Tex. Bus. & Com. Code ch. 271.

§ 9.6:3 Perfection

General Rule—Location of Debtor: Except as noted below, the law of the jurisdiction in which the debtor is located governs perfection of a security interest in collateral. Tex. Bus. & Com. Code § 9.301(1). For a debtor with multistate operations, if a security interest in collateral is perfected by filing, the jurisdiction in which the debtor is located is the filing jurisdiction. Because of the importance of the location of the debtor to the choice-of-law rule, chapter 9 provides rules to determine a debtor's location.

Registered organizations: A registered organization is one formed or organized in a state or the United States by the filing with, issuance of a public organic document by, or enactment of legislation by the state or the United States. Tex. Bus. & Com. Code § 9.102(a)(71) (defining "registered organization"); *see also* Tex. Bus. & Com. Code § 1.201(b)(25) (defining "organization"); Tex. Bus. & Com. Code § 9.102(a)(68–a) (defining "public organic record"); Tex. Bus. & Com. Code § 9.102(a)(77) (limiting the definition of "state" to jurisdictions in the United States and its territories and possessions). A registered organization that is organized under the law of a state is located in that state. Tex. Bus. & Com. Code § 9.307(e). For example, if a debtor is a corporation, limited liability company, or limited partnership organized under the laws of a particular state, the debtor is located in that state. *See* Tex. Bus. & Com. Code §§ 9.102 cmt. 11, 9.307 cmt. 4.

Other debtors: If the debtor is an individual, the debtor is located at his residence. If the debtor is an organization but is not a registered organization, the debtor is located at the debtor's place of business if the debtor has only one place of business or at the debtor's chief executive office if the debtor has more than one place of business. Tex. Bus. & Com. Code § 9.307(b).

Foreign debtors: If the debtor is located in a jurisdiction outside the United States and that jurisdiction does not provide for a public filing system for nonpossessory security interests for a secured party to prevail over a subsequent lien creditor, the debtor is deemed to be located in the District of Columbia. Tex. Bus. & Com. Code § 9.307(c).

Possessory Security Interests: If a security interest is perfected by possession, the law of the jurisdiction in which the collateral is located governs perfection (that is, the requirements of possession) and priority of that security interest. Tex. Bus. & Com. Code § 9.301(2).

Fixtures: If a security interest in fixtures is perfected by a fixture filing, the law of the jurisdiction in which the fixtures are located governs whether perfection has occurred and the priority of conflicting security interests. Tex. Bus. & Com. Code § 9.301(3)(A).

Titled Goods: If goods are covered by a certificate of title (defined in Tex. Bus. & Com. Code § 9.102(a)(10)) issued by a particular jurisdiction, the law of the certificate-issuing jurisdiction governs whether perfection occurs. Tex. Bus. & Com. Code § 9.303(c). An exception to this rule for certificate-of-title goods applies if the goods are inventory. If titled goods are inventory, the law of the jurisdiction of the debtor's location determines whether a security interest is perfected. Tex. Bus. & Com. Code § 9.301. Under section 9.311(d), titled goods that are inventory of a person in the business of selling such goods are treated as ordinary goods for determining whether a security interest in such goods is perfected; a notation on a certificate of title for titled goods that are inventory of such a person is not necessary or effective to perfect a security interest. *See* Tex. Bus. & Com. Code § 9.303 cmt. 5.

Agricultural Liens: The law of the jurisdiction in which the farm products are located governs whether an agricultural lien on the farm products is perfected. Tex. Bus. & Com. Code § 9.302.

Investment Property: If a security interest in investment property is perfected by filing, the law of the jurisdiction in which the debtor is located governs perfection. Tex. Bus. & Com. Code § 9.305(c)(1). If a security interest in investment property collateral is perfected by a means other than filing, (1) if the collateral is a security certificate, the law of the jurisdiction in which the security certificate is located determines whether a security interest in the certificated security is perfected (Tex. Bus. & Com. Code § 9.305(a)(1)); (2) if the collateral is an uncertificated security, the law of the jurisdiction under which the issuer of the uncertificated security is organized governs perfection of a security interest in the uncertificated security or, if permitted by the law of that jurisdiction, the law of another jurisdiction specified by the issuer (Tex. Bus. & Com. Code § 8.110(d)); (3) if the collateral is a security account or a security entitlement, the agreement of the parties to the account or entitlement determines the jurisdiction governing perfection for the security account or security entitlement; if, however, the parties do not provide for a jurisdiction, the jurisdiction is determined by sections 8.110(e) and 9.305(a)(3) of the Texas Business and Commerce Code; and (4) if the collateral is a commodity account, the agreement of the parties to the account determines the jurisdiction governing perfection for the commodity account; if, however, the parties do not provide for a jurisdiction, the jurisdiction is determined by Tex. Bus. & Com. Code § 9.305(b).

Deposit Accounts: The law of the jurisdiction of the depositary bank governs perfection of a security interest in a deposit account. Tex. Bus. & Com. Code § 9.304(a). Chapter 9 contains rules for determining where a depositary bank is located. Tex. Bus. & Com. Code § 9.304(b). Those rules are similar to the rules for determining the location of a securities intermediary.

Letter-of-Credit Rights: The law of the jurisdiction of the issuer or nominated person of a letter of credit generally governs perfection of a security interest in a letter-of-credit right, other than a letter-of-credit right that is a supporting obligation. The issuer's or nominated person's jurisdiction is determined under section 5.116 of the Texas Business and Commerce Code. Tex. Bus. & Com. Code § 9.306. If the issuer's or nominated person's jurisdiction is not a state (defined in Tex. Bus. & Com. Code § 9.102(a)(77)), the law of the debtor's location determines perfection of a security interest in a letter-of-credit right. *See* Tex. Bus. & Com. Code § 9.306 cmts. 2, 3.

§ 9.6:4 Effect of Perfection or Nonperfection and Priority

The jurisdiction whose law governs the effect of perfection or nonperfection and priority of a security interest is sometimes different from the jurisdiction whose law governs perfection.

Tangible Negotiable Documents, Goods, Instruments, Money, and Tangible Chattel Paper: The jurisdiction whose law governs the effect of perfection or nonperfection and priority of a nonpossessory security interest (for example, one perfected by filing) is the jurisdiction in which the collateral is located. Tex. Bus. & Com. Code § 9.301(3)(C).

Certificated Securities: The jurisdiction whose law governs the effect of perfection or nonperfection and priority of a security interest in a certificated security is the jurisdiction in which the security certificate is located. Tex. Bus. & Com. Code § 9.305(a)(1).

Uncertificated Securities: The jurisdiction whose law governs the effect of perfection or nonperfection and priority of a security interest in an uncertificated security is the jurisdiction of the issuer of the uncertificated security. Tex. Bus. & Com. Code § 9.305(a)(2).

Security Entitlements, Security Accounts, Commodity Contracts, and Commodity Accounts: The jurisdiction whose law governs the effect of perfection or nonperfection and priority of a security interest in a security entitlement, security account, commodity contract, or commodity account is the jurisdiction of the securities intermediary or commodity intermediary. Tex. Bus. & Com. Code § 9.305(a)(3), (a)(4).

Other Collateral: Otherwise, generally the jurisdiction whose law governs perfection of a security interest also governs the effect of perfection or nonperfection and priority of that security interest. See section 9.301(1) for accounts, commercial tort claims, and general intangibles; section 9.301(2) for possessory security interests; section 9.301(3)(A) for fixtures; section 9.301(3)(B) for timber to be cut; section 9.301(4) for as-extracted collateral; section 9.302 for farm products; section 9.303(c) for certificate-of-title goods that are not inventory; and section 9.304 for deposit accounts.

§ 9.7 Cautions

This chapter of the manual does not cover all the issues involved in complex secured transactions. Rather, this chapter provides forms and analysis to create, attach, and perfect a security interest in straightforward secured transactions.

Certain types of collateral are subject to statutes that require other steps for perfecting the security interest and are beyond the scope of this manual. *See* Tex. Bus. & Com. Code §§ 9.109(c), (d), 9.311(a). The following are examples.

Titled Vehicles: If the title to the collateral is created by a certificate of title, such as for a car, boat, or trailer, proper perfection is by registering the lien on the title.

Patents, Copyrights, and Trademarks: The federal patent office registers liens on patent, copyright, and trademark rights.

Ships and Aircraft: Federal statutes govern perfection requirements for large ships and aircraft.

Additionally, issues not applicable to other types of collateral arise if the collateral consists of fixtures or farm products.

§ 9.7:1 Fixtures

Goods are fixtures if they become so related to particular real estate that an interest in them arises under the real property law of the state in which the real property is situated. Tex. Bus. & Com. Code § 9.102(a)(41). Texas cases have generally held that personalty becomes a fixture if it is affixed to realty in such a manner that it cannot be removed without damage to the realty. The intent of the "annexing party" is a major factor in the determination. Building materials incorporated into realty are not fixtures. Tex. Bus. & Com. Code § 9.334(a).

If the secured party has a deed-of-trust lien on real property, the secured party does not need a separate security interest in the fixtures on that real property or a separate financing statement filed in the real property records. A recorded deed of trust creates and perfects a lien on the fixtures as an interest in real property if the deed of trust contains certain information. Tex. Bus. & Com. Code § 9.502(c). The deed of trust as a security agreement and financing statement is discussed at section 8.9 in this manual.

Fixtures have characteristics of both real and personal property. This dual nature accounts for the special treatment of fixtures in the security agreement and the financing statement. In the security agreement, forms 9-1 through 9-4 in this chapter, the debtor warrants that the collateral is not a fixture except as provided in the agreement. The debtor also covenants to give the secured party certain rights if the collateral becomes a fixture.

In priority conflicts involving fixtures, the parties competing with the secured party are those with real estate interests, such as a lien on the real property to which the goods are affixed. *See* Tex. Bus. & Com. Code § 9.334 cmt. 4. If fixtures were treated like other personalty and if the financing statements were filed with the secretary of state, parties with real estate interests would not learn of the security interest by a title search. Thus, a security agreement and financing statement covering fixtures must describe the real estate, and the financing statement must be filed in the real property records. Tex. Bus. & Com. Code § 9.502(b).

If there is any doubt about whether collateral is or may become a fixture, the secured party should file a Uniform Commercial Code fixture filing. Sections 9.5:3 above and 9.14:5 below discuss additional rules for filing.

§ 9.7:2 Farm Products and Agricultural Liens

Creating and perfecting a security interest in farm products collateral requires action under two separate and distinct systems. Creating and perfecting a security interest against competing creditors is governed by Texas Business and Commerce Code chapter 9. Perfection of that same security interest in farm products against buyers in the ordinary course of business requires compliance with the federal Food Security Act of 1985. 7 U.S.C. § 1631.

Perfection under chapter 9 is normally accomplished by the execution of a security agreement and the filing of an appropriate financing statement. In Texas, perfection against buyers in the ordinary course of business under 7 U.S.C. § 1631 (so-called "superperfection") requires the creditor to deliver notice of the security interest to the purchaser of the farm product at any time within one year before the sale occurs. To determine which potential buyers must receive this notice, the secured party may require the debtor to list likely purchasers of the farm products collateral (see form 9-7 in this chapter). Texas has no central filing system for farm products liens under the Food Security Act. To be effective, the superperfection prenotification notice must be delivered to the farm products buyer before the sale of the farm products. The notice remains effective for only one year after it is delivered. Secured creditors should exercise diligence to determine that their prenotification notices are timely delivered and remain effective. Farm products are not infrequently sold under forward contracts. The date of a sale under a forward contract may be ambiguous. Additionally, farm products are often warehoused after harvest for an extended period. A notice may expire during the period that farm products are warehoused. A new notice, with its new one-year effectiveness, may have to be delivered to the farm products buyer of warehoused farm products.

The required contents of a prenotification notice are unique to the Food Security Act and are much more extensive than the information contained in a financing statement. See the prenotification statement at form 9-6 for the contents of the notice.

In addition, the perfection and priority of agricultural liens may be subject to rules outside of chapter 9 of the Texas Uniform Commercial Code. For example, notwithstanding the provisions of chapter 9, an agricultural lien granted under subchapter E of Texas Property Code chapter 70 has priority over certain prior liens if certain conditions are met. *See* Tex. Prop. Code § 70.4045. Similarly, the statutory trust created upon acceptance of commodities to which the Perishable Agricultural Commodities Act applies may also have priority over certain previously filed UCC liens. *See* 7 U.S.C. §§ 499a–499s; *see, e.g., Bocchi Americas Associates, Inc. v. Commerce Fresh Marketing, Inc.*, 515 F.3d 383 (5th Cir. 2008).

§ 9.7:3 Federal Tax Liens

A federal tax lien notice covering all personal property of a debtor may be filed in an office that is different from the office in which a financing statement against the debtor is filed. All personal property of a taxpayer that is a corporation or partnership is deemed located where the principal place of the business is located; for other taxpayers, at the taxpayer's residence; and for a taxpayer located outside of the United States, in the District of Columbia. 26 U.S.C. § 6323(f)(2)(B). Under section 14.002 of the Texas Property Code, a notice of a federal tax lien should be filed in the office of the secretary of state for a corporation or partnership whose principal executive office is in Texas and, in all other cases, in the office of the county clerk in the county in which the person against whom the lien applies resides when the notice is filed. Tex. Prop. Code § 14.002.

As referenced in Texas Property Code section 14.002, "corporation" may refer to any entity taxed as a corporation for federal income tax purposes, and "partnership" may refer to any entity treated as a partnership for federal income tax purposes. A single-member limited liability company that does not elect to be taxed as a corporation for federal income tax purposes and is disregarded for federal income tax purposes may also be disregarded for purposes of federal tax lien notice filings. A notice of a federal tax lien filing may be made against such a limited liability company under the name of its single-member owner, and the federal tax lien may attach to the otherwise (for state law purposes) separate property of the limited liability company. Searches for outstanding liens against a debtor should also be made in the offices in which a federal tax lien notice may have been filed.

§ 9.8 Deed of Trust as Security Agreement and Financing Statement

In addition to creating a lien on the real property conveyed, the deed of trust can be modified to create a security interest in other collateral. See form 8-1 in this manual. See also section 8.11, which describes the use of a deed of trust as security agreement and financing statement.

§ 9.9 Instructions for Completing Security Agreement Forms

In the following instructions for completing the security agreement, forms 9-1 through 9-4 in this chapter, different classifications of collateral are considered separately if appropriate; otherwise, the remarks apply to all classifications of collateral. Form 9-1 is designed for use if the collateral is consumer goods or documents with respect to goods, equipment, or inventory. If addendum form 9-5 is attached, form 9-1 may also be used if the collateral is farm products. Form 9-2 is designed for use if the collateral is accounts, chattel paper, general intangibles, or a commercial tort claim. Form 9-3 is designed for use if the collateral is instruments, including a promissory note, or investment property. Form 9-4 is designed for use if the collateral is a debtor's interest as a partner in a general or limited partnership or as a member in a limited liability company.

Parties and Name of Debtor: For general information about designation of parties and the name of the debtor, see sections 9.5:3 and 9.14:2 and chapter 3 in this manual.

Classification of Collateral: The secured party should list all classifications of the collateral subject to the security agreement. If the debtor and the secured party agree that the collateral is or may become a fixture, that fact should be noted in the classification, with language such as "equipment to become a fixture," and the security agreement should include a legal description of the real property. See section 9.3:3 above for a list of the classifications.

Collateral: Any description of personal property or real estate is sufficient, whether it is specific or not, if it reasonably identifies what is described. Tex. Bus. & Com. Code § 9.108. In a consumer transaction, however, a description by collateral type alone is not sufficient if the collateral is consumer goods, a security entitlement, a security account, or a commodity account. Tex. Bus. & Com. Code § 9.108(e). A description by type alone is also not sufficient for a commercial tort claim. Tex. Bus. & Com. Code § 9.108(e). Several examples of alternate clauses are included in the security agreement forms, but the attorney may use any description that meets the requirements of section 9.108. *See* Tex. Bus. & Com. Code § 9.108 cmt. 2.

Debtor's Representations Concerning Debtor and Locations: The security agreement forms have the debtor representing the location of the collateral, the location of the debtor's records concerning the collateral, and the location of the debtor. If a secured party has to enforce its security interest, the secured party will need to know where the collateral and records pertaining to the collateral are located. The debtor's location is important because under chapter 9 the filing jurisdiction generally depends on the location of the debtor. *See* Tex. Bus. & Com. Code § 9.301(1) and section 9.6:3 above. The filing jurisdiction under chapter 9 may be different from the jurisdiction in which the collateral is located. The security agreement may show the location where the debtor intends to keep the collateral and records concerning the collateral; the location of the debtor's place of business or chief executive office if the debtor has more than one place of business; if the debtor is an individual, the location of the debtor's place of business or chief executive office if the debtor has more than one place of business and the location of the debtor's residence; and, if the debtor is a registered organization, the jurisdiction in which the debtor is organized. For most purposes, a street address or other unambiguous location should be sufficient.

The remaining representations concerning the debtor deal with information needed to complete the financing statement form.

If the collateral is or will become timber to be cut, this part of the agreement should describe the land where the collateral is or will be located. Tex. Bus. & Com. Code § 9.203(b)(3)(A). The secured party should file a financing statement in the real property records to perfect its security interest in timber to be cut, as-extracted collateral, or fixtures. Tex. Bus. & Com. Code § 9.501(a)(1). Financing statements for these types of collateral require a description of the real property. Tex. Bus. & Com. Code § 9.502(b)(3). For general information about property descriptions, see section 3.8 in this manual.

Security agreement form 9-1 is drafted for consumer goods, equipment, or inventory. With addendum form 9-5, form 9-1 can also provide coverage for farm products. By appropriately wording paragraph H.14., the parties may incorporate the addendum into the agreement. Use of the addendum for farm products to security agreement form 9-1 together with additional forms for listing of potential buyers, commission merchants, and selling agents (form 9-7) and the prenotification statement (form 9-6) allows compliance with the federal Food Security Act (7 U.S.C. § 1631).

There are two methods for documenting a security interest in a note secured by real property. One method, use of the security agreement, is discussed in the following paragraphs. The other method, use of the collateral transfer of note and lien, is discussed in section 9.18 below.

Use of security agreement form 9-3, with appropriate alternate clauses, will create a security interest in the note. Chapter 9 provides that it governs a security interest in a secured obligation (such as a note secured by real property) notwithstanding that the underlying collateral (for example, the real property) is not governed by chapter 9. Tex. Bus. & Com. Code § 9.109(b). Furthermore, if a security interest attaches under chapter 9 to a secured obligation, the security interest automatically attaches to the security interest, mortgage, or other lien that secures the secured obligation. Tex. Bus. & Com. Code § 9.203(g). Additionally, perfection of the security interest in the secured obligation automatically perfects a security interest in the security interest, mortgage, or other lien that secures the secured obligation. Tex. Bus. & Com. Code § 9.308(e). If the note is secured by real property, a properly completed transfer-of-lien form should be filed in the real property records of the county clerk in the county in which the real property is located. See form 9-1. The transfer of lien provides notice to anyone searching the real property records of the secured party's interest in the real property. If the note is secured by personal property, a properly completed UCC3 financing statement amendment (form 9-14) should be filed in the appropriate place for the type of collateral covered. The assignment provides notice to anyone searching the personal property records of the secured party's interest in the personal property. See section 9.12 below for further discussion.

A secured party may perfect its security interest in a note by either filing a financing statement or obtaining possession of the note. Tex. Bus. & Com. Code §§ 9.312(a), 9.313(a). A secured party that has possession of an instrument may have priority over a secured party that perfects its security interest in the instrument by filing. Tex. Bus. & Com. Code § 9.330(d). For the secured party to become a holder or a holder in due course of the note, with all the benefits that entails under chapter 3 of the Texas Business and Commerce Code, the payee or, if different, the current holder of the note must endorse the note to the secured party. Among the advantages of a secured party becoming a holder in due course of the note is that the secured party also becomes the person entitled to enforce the note. Tex. Bus. & Com. Code § 3.301. The note transferred may be endorsed as follows:

> [**Date of transfer**]
>
> Pay to the order of [**name of secured party**] as collateral in accordance with the security agreement dated [**date**].
>
> [**Name of payee/holder**]

Additionally, notice of the security interest may be given to the maker of the note to prevent a prepayment of the note to the payee.

§ 9.10 Additional Clauses

§ 9.10:1 After-Acquired Property

The Texas Business and Commerce Code authorizes and validates a security interest in after-acquired property if the security agreement so provides. *See* Tex. Bus. & Com. Code § 9.204(a). The secured party may include the parenthetical language *whether now owned and all after-acquired collateral of the same classification* on forms 9-1 through 9-4 in this chapter, under the heading "Collateral," to include after-acquired property. No security interest attaches to after-acquired consumer goods (other than accessions) if they are given as additional security, unless the debtor acquires rights in the goods within ten days after the secured party gives value. Tex. Bus. & Com. Code § 9.204(b). Additionally, a security interest in a commercial tort claim attaches only to such a claim that exists when the security agreement is entered into and not to an after-acquired claim. Tex. Bus. & Com. Code § 9.204(b).

§ 9.10:2 Other Debt/Future Advances

The Texas Business and Commerce Code provides that a security interest secures future advances to the debtor if the security agreement so provides. *See* Tex. Bus. & Com. Code § 9.204(c). To secure future advances, include the appropriate optional language under the heading "Obligation" in forms 9-1 through 9-4 in this chapter or use a modified form of the all-indebtedness or other-indebtedness clauses in form 8-6 in this manual.

§ 9.10:3 Purchase-Money Security Interest

If the secured obligation is advanced as purchase money for the collateral, the security agreement should contain the appropriate clause from form 8-3 in this manual acknowledging the purchase-money security interest. Sections 9.317 and 9.324 contain special priority rules for purchase-money security interests. *See* Tex. Bus. & Com. Code §§ 9.317, 9.324. Section 9.103 contains rules for determining when a security interest is a purchase-money security interest. Tex. Bus. & Com. Code § 9.103.

§ 9.10:4 Attorney's Fee Provision

The attorney's fee provision in forms 9-1, 9-2, 9-3, and 9-4 in this chapter is in paragraph D.2. If the loan transaction to which the security agreement relates is governed by Texas Finance Code chapter 342, then section 502 of that chapter limits attorney's fees that may be charged and assessed to those assessed by a court. Tex. Fin. Code § 342.502(b)(2). A loan is governed by chapter 342 if it is made by a lender engaged in the business of making, arranging, or negotiating loans governed by that chapter; the interest rate exceeds 10 percent per year; the loan proceeds will be used for personal, family, or household use; and either the loan is not secured by a lien on real property or the loan is a secondary mortgage loan. Tex. Fin. Code § 342.005. See also the commentary on promissory notes at section 6.2:7 in this manual. If the related loan is governed by chapter 342, the attorney's fee clause should be modified as indicated.

§ 9.11 Additional Documents

For almost all transactions involving a security agreement, at least two other documents are necessary. The promissory note is described in chapter 6 in this manual, and the UCC1 financing statement, form 9-11, is described in section 9.13 below.

If a security agreement, like form 9-4, covers a debtor's interest as a partner in a general or limited partnership or as a member in a limited liability company, the secured party may need the consent of other partners, managers, or members, as applicable, to be able to create, attach, perfect, enforce, and foreclose its security interest. For entities formed under Texas law, a limited partnership agreement may restrict assignability of a partner's partnership interest in the limited partnership (*see* Tex. Bus. Orgs. Code § 153.251); a general partnership does not have to give effect to a transfer or assignment of a partner's partnership interest that is prohibited by its partnership agreement (*see* Tex. Bus. Orgs. Code § 152.405); and the regulations of a limited liability company may restrict assignability of a member's membership interest in the limited liability company (*see* Tex. Bus. Orgs. Code § 101.108(a)).

Partnership agreements and regulations of limited liability companies frequently contain provisions prohibiting any assignment, including a grant of a security interest, of a partner's or member's interest in the applicable entity and stating that any such purported assignment or grant of a security interest is void. Sometimes assignment of an interest is permitted after obtaining consent. The requirements for consent may vary widely. The attorney for the secured party should review the applicable partnership agreement, limited liability company regulations, or comparable document for an entity formed under the laws of another jurisdiction to determine the assignability of the debtor's interest in the entity and what consents may be required. Restrictions on assignability of personal property as security for an obligation are disfavored under chapter 9.

Generally, the interest of a partner in a general or limited partnership or of a member in a limited liability company is a general intangible under chapter 9 and not a security, certificated or uncertificated, under chapter 8. *See* Tex. Bus. & Com. Code § 8.103(c). Under chapter 9, a term in an agreement relating to a general intangible that prohibits, restricts, or requires consent to the assignment or transfer of, or creation, attachment, or perfection of a security interest in, the general intangible is ineffective to impair the creation, attachment, or perfection of a security interest or to render such creation, attachment, or perfection a default or breach of the agreement. Tex. Bus. & Com. Code § 9.408(a). Section 9.408 does not, however, apply to an interest in a partnership or a limited liability company. Tex. Bus. & Com. Code § 9.408(e). Thus, restrictions on assignability in a partnership agreement, in regulations of a limited liability company, or in comparable documents for partnership or limited liability companies formed under laws of other states are effective to prevent the creation, attachment, or perfection of a security interest in a partner's or member's interest in the entity and to render such creation, attachment, or perfection a default under the partnership agreement, limited liability company agreement, or other comparable document if so provided in the entity's documents.

Moreover, even if a security interest is created, attached, and perfected in a person's interest in such an entity and there are anti-assignment provisions in the entity's organizational documents, neither the entity nor its partners or members owe any duty to the secured party and the secured party may not enforce its security interest. Tex. Bus. & Com. Code § 9.408(d). Depending on the bargaining position of the parties and more likely depending on the relative ownership interest of the debtor in the entity, the secured party may be able to obtain the consent by the entity or other owners of the entity to the creation, attachment, perfection, and enforcement of its security interest. The required consent should come from the persons whose consent is required under the organizational documents of the entity to an outright assignment of an owner's interest in the entity. In paragraph C.5. of security agreement form 9-4, the debtor represents that it has obtained the consent of all persons necessary to authorize the secured party to exercise its rights under the security agreement. This provision should be modified if such a consent is required under the organizational documents of the entity in which the debtor has an interest but is not obtained. A form of a consent is at form 9-10.

§ 9.12 Assignment of Security Interest

The secured party may assign the security interest created by the security agreement either before or after the interest is perfected, in accordance with section 9.514 of the Texas Business and Commerce Code.

If the financing statement is not filed before assignment of the security interest, the financing statement may show the assignment by giving the assignee's name and address. Tex. Bus. & Com. Code § 9.514. One way to show the assignment is to prepare a form UCC1Ad financing statement addendum (form 9-12 in this chapter) to the UCC1 financing statement (form 9-11) to reflect the assignee of the secured party. The financing statement addendum should be attached to and filed with the financing statement.

If the financing statement is filed before the assignment, the parties should prepare a form UCC3 financing statement amendment (form 9-14), including the financing statement's file number and date of filing, the assignor's name, and the assignee's name and address. The financing statement amendment should be filed in the same filing office or offices as the assigned original financing statement. Tex. Bus. & Com. Code § 9.514. See section 9.15:2 below for additional instructions concerning the UCC3 financing statement amendment.

The assigning secured party should endorse the note and deliver it, the original security agreement, and the filing officer's acknowledgment copy of the original financing statement to the assignee.

§ 9.13 Financing Statement and Other UCC Forms

§ 9.13:1 Financing Statement Generally

The UCC1 financing statement, form 9-11 in this chapter, perfects a security interest for most classifications of collateral if it is filed with either the secretary of state in Austin or the county clerk, depending on the classification. Tex. Bus. & Com. Code § 9.501(a). *See also* Tex. Bus. & Com. Code § 9.310(a). The security agreement establishes the secured party's rights against the debtor, but perfection of the security interest by filing a financing statement, obtaining possession of the collateral, or obtaining control of the collateral establishes the rights of the secured party against competing parties, such as other secured creditors. Tex. Bus. & Com. Code § 9.201(a). *See* Tex. Bus. & Com. Code § 9.308 cmt. 2.

Filing a financing statement will not perfect a security interest in certain classifications of collateral. See section 9.5 above for an explanation of the different methods of perfecting a security interest and the type of collateral that may be perfected under each method.

Another exception to the financing statement requirement is a purchase-money security interest in consumer goods, which is perfected automatically. Even though this automatic perfection protects the retailer's rights against the consumer, retailers selling expensive merchandise often file a financing statement to protect themselves in case a debtor sells to another consumer. Without a financing statement on file, the subsequent sale would destroy the retailer's interest in the collateral. Tex. Bus. & Com. Code §§ 9.309, 9.320(b).

See section 9.5:3 above for a discussion of the contents of a financing statement. The financing statement is not intended to describe the full agreement of the parties but rather to give public notice of the security interest. *See* Tex. Bus. & Com. Code § 9.502 cmt. 2.

§ 9.13:2 Cautions

A financing statement is constructive notice to all parties of a secured party's rights in collateral. To give constructive notice of a security interest, the financing statement must be filed in the proper office. If there is doubt about the proper filing place, the attorney should file the financing statement in every place that might be appropriate. *See* Tex. Bus. & Com. Code § 9.501(a).

Certain types of collateral, such as motor vehicles and manufactured housing, are covered by other statutes and may require additional documentation, such as certificates of title. Other examples of such collateral include patents, trademarks, rolling stock, ships, and aircraft. *See* Tex. Bus. & Com. Code § 9.311(b).

§ 9.14 Instructions for Completing Form UCC1

§ 9.14:1 General Considerations for Completing Form UCC1

Nonstandard forms of financing statements should not be used in Texas. Texas filing offices may reject tendered written filings that are not on a standard form adopted by rule by the Texas secretary of state. Tex. Bus. & Com. Code § 9.5211.

See section 9.19 below for how to obtain a UCC1 and other financing statement forms. The attorney should review section 9.310(b) for a listing of collateral for which a financing statement is either unnecessary or ineffective in perfecting a security interest. See also section 9.5 above for a discussion of perfection of a security interest.

§ 9.14:2 Blocks 1, 2, and 3: Names of Debtor and Secured Party

For general information about designation of parties, see chapter 3 in this manual.

The debtor's correct name is crucial to the validity of the financing statement because records are indexed on that basis. The names of the debtor and of the secured party should appear on this form exactly as they appear on the security agreement. If the debtor is a registered organization, the debtor's name is the name stated to be the registered organization's name on the public organic record most recently filed with, issued by, or enacted by the debtor's jurisdiction of organization that states, amends, or restates the debtor's name. Tex. Bus. & Com. Code § 9.503(a)(1). For a Texas filing entity (as defined in Tex. Bus. Orgs. Code § 1.002(22)), this means that the debtor's name is the name stated to be the name of the filing entity on its certificate of formation or a restated certificate of formation and all amendments to an original or restated certificate of formation. Special rules apply for an entity that is a trust or a decedent's estate. Tex. Bus. & Com. Code § 9.503(a)(1), (a)(2), (a)(3), (f), (h). If the debtor is an individual, the financing statement must use the name of the debtor as shown on the most recently issued unexpired Texas driver's license or most recently issued unexpired Texas Department of Public Safety–issued identification certificate and indicate the debtor's surname. Tex. Bus. & Com. Code §§ 9.503(a)(4), (g), 9.516(b)(3). If the debtor does not have a driver's license or identification certificate, the financing statement must provide the individual name of the debtor or the surname and first personal name of the debtor. Tex. Bus. & Com. Code § 9.503(a)(5). A trade name is not a sufficient name of a debtor. Tex. Bus. & Com. Code § 9.503(c). Any name used for a debtor other than the correct name renders the financing statement insufficient and seriously misleading unless the name used is so similar to the debtor's correct name that a search under the debtor's correct name, using the filing office's standard search logic, would disclose the filing with the incorrect name. Tex. Bus. & Com. Code § 9.506(c).

If the debtor's name changes and the change renders the original form seriously misleading, the secured party must file a UCC3 financing statement amendment (form 9-14 in this chapter) with the correct name within four months of the change to continue the security interest. Tex. Bus. & Com. Code § 9.507(c). A filing is seriously misleading if a search under the changed, now correct name, using the filing office's standard search logic, would not disclose the filing under the former, now incorrect, name. Tex. Bus. & Com. Code § 9.506(c).

§ 9.14:3 Block 4: Classification and Description of Collateral

For a general discussion of the significance of classification of collateral, see section 9.3:3 above.

The Texas Business and Commerce Code specifies that the description of collateral in the financing statement is sufficient if it "indicates the collateral covered by the financing statement." Tex. Bus. & Com. Code § 9.502(a)(3). A financing statement indicates the collateral covered if it contains a description of the collateral under section 9.108 or indicates that it covers all assets or all personal property. Tex. Bus. & Com. Code § 9.504.

A financing statement that correctly describes the original collateral continues perfection in after-acquired property, proceeds, and future advances without specific reference to these interests in the financing statement. If a financing statement is recorded and the general description in the financing statement shows that a security interest exists, any affected creditor should contact the secured party to determine if the security interest extends to such after-acquired property, proceeds, or future advances.

If the collateral is timber to be cut, fixtures, or as-extracted collateral, the description in the financing statement must include a description of both the collateral and the real property where it is located. Tex. Bus. & Com. Code § 9.502(b). The real property description must be "sufficient to give constructive notice of a mortgage under the law of this state if the description were contained in . . . a mortgage." Tex. Bus. & Com. Code § 9.502(b)(3). For a general discussion of property descriptions, see section 3.8 in this manual.

§ 9.14:4 Concluding the Form

Block 3 of the form designates the secured party or its assignee. If the financing statement has been filed before assignment of the interest, the assignor should prepare a written assignment and also complete a form UCC3 financing statement amendment (form 9-14 in this chapter) for each UCC1 on file. Tex. Bus. & Com. Code

§ 9.514(b). See section 9.12 above for further suggestions.

A financing statement may be filed without the debtor's signature on it if the debtor authorizes the filing. *See* Tex. Bus. & Com. Code § 9.509(a)(1). By entering into a security agreement a debtor automatically authorizes the filing of a financing statement covering the collateral described in the security agreement. Tex. Bus. & Com. Code § 9.509(b). If a secured party wants to file a financing statement before the debtor has entered into a security agreement, the secured party needs separate express authorization from the debtor. One way to evidence the debtor's authorization is to have the debtor sign the financing statement. However, the UCC1 financing statement standard form does not provide a space for the debtor's signature. Another way to evidence the debtor's authorization is to have the debtor sign a statement, to which a copy of the completed form UCC1 is attached, authorizing the filing of the form.

§ 9.14:5 Filing

If Texas is the correct state in which to file a financing statement and no other statutory perfection rules apply, the proper office in which to file is determined by the classification of the collateral. Generally, the secretary of state's office in Austin is the proper place to file a financing statement.

Exceptions to this general rule involve collateral significantly related to real property. For timber to be cut or as-extracted collateral, or if the financing statement is filed as a fixture filing, the proper place to file is in the real property records of the county clerk in the county in which the related real property is located. However, if the secured party has a deed-of-trust lien on the real property and a security interest in the timber to be cut, as-extracted collateral, or fixtures, the secured party does not need to file a separate financing statement in the real property records, assuming that the deed of trust otherwise meets the requirements of a financing statement. Tex. Bus. & Com. Code § 9.502(b), (c).

The secretary of state accepts electronic filing of UCC financing statements through its website, **www.sos.state.tx.us/ucc/uccforms.shtml**.

A party in doubt about the proper place to file should file the statement in every possible place.

These rules apply only to Texas transactions. Filings may be required in other jurisdictions. See the discussion of perfection at section 9.6:3 above.

§ 9.15 Additional Documents

A typical security interest transaction requires a note, discussed in chapter 6 in this manual; a security agreement, forms 9-1 through 9-4 in this chapter; and a financing statement. Other documents that may be necessary include a form UCC1Ad financing statement addendum (form 9-12), a form UCC3 financing statement amendment (form 9-14), a form UCC3Ad financing statement amendment addendum (form 9-15), and a form UCC11 information request (form 9-16).

§ 9.15:1 Financing Statement Addendum

The form UCC1Ad financing statement addendum, form 9-12 in this chapter, serves several purposes.

The financing statement addendum may be used to identify an additional debtor, if there are more than two (the first two may be identified on the form UCC1 financing statement) (see item 11 of the form UCC1Ad); identify an additional secured party (see item 12 of the form); and reflect an assignment by the initial secured party to an assignee (see item 12 of the form). The form may also be used to indicate if the financing statement covers timber to be cut, as-extracted collateral, or fixtures (see item 13 of the form); if so the form provides space to include a description of the real estate (see item 14 of the form) and the name of the record owner (if the debtor does not have a record interest) (see item 15 of the form). The form also provides space for an expanded description of the collateral (see item 16 of the form). The form may be used to indicate whether the debtor is a trust, a trustee for property held in trust, a decedent's estate (see item 17 of the form), or a transmitting utility (see item 18 of the form) or to indicate whether the filing is for a manufactured housing transaction or a public finance transaction (see item 18 of the form).

The name of the first debtor, identified in item 1 on the form UCC1 financing statement, should be inserted in item 9 of the related financing statement addendum to relate the financing statement addendum to the financing statement. The remaining items of the form should be completed only if appropriate.

The form UCC1Ad financing statement addendum should be attached to and filed with its related form UCC1 financing statement and not filed separately.

§ 9.15:2 Financing Statement Amendment

The form UCC3 financing statement amendment, form 9-14 in this chapter, serves several purposes, some of which are discussed in sections 9.9, 9.12, 9.14:2, and 9.14:4 above, in relation to the security agreement and financing statement.

The form provides for continuation of a security interest beyond the five-year duration of the original filing (Tex. Bus. & Com. Code § 9.515); assignment of a security interest if the assignment is made after the original financing statement is filed (Tex. Bus. & Com. Code § 9.514(b)); termination of a security interest, which is a required procedure for the secured party if "there is no obligation secured by the collateral covered by the financing statement and no commitment to make an advance, incur an obligation, or otherwise give value" (Tex. Bus. & Com. Code § 9.513(a)(1), (c)(1)); partial release of collateral; and amendment of the financing statement.

A separate form UCC3 should be used for each form UCC1 already filed, and each form UCC3 should relate to a particular financing statement by giving the financing statement's file number and, because the Texas secretary of state does not use a unique number system that distinguishes among filings made in different years, the date of filing. The form UCC3 does not provide a separate block for the filing date of the related initial financing statement. The date of filing should be inserted in block 1a after the initial financing statement file number. The form UCC3 financing statement amendment should be filed in the same filing office or offices as the original financing statement to which it relates.

If, after a financing statement is filed in the correct state, the jurisdiction of the location of the debtor changes (for example, for a registered organization, the debtor changes its jurisdiction of organization; or for an organization that is not a registered organization, the debtor changes the state in which its place of business is located or, if the debtor has more than one place of business, the state in which its chief executive office is located; or for an individual debtor, the debtor changes his state of residence), the original filing is effective for only four months after the move. Tex. Bus. & Com. Code § 9.316(a)(2). The financing statement becomes ineffective to continue a perfected security interest unless the secured party files a form UCC3 in the state in which the debtor has relocated within the four-month period. Tex. Bus. & Com. Code § 9.316(a), (b). A mere change of an address within a state of the location of the collateral, the location of a debtor's place of business or chief executive office, or the location of an individual's residence does not render an original filing ineffective.

If, after a financing statement is filed using the debtor's then-correct name, the debtor's name changes and the change renders the original filed financing statement seriously misleading, a UCC3 financing statement amendment with the changed, now correct name of the debtor must be filed within four months of the name change to continue the perfection by filing of the security interest. Tex. Bus. & Com. Code § 9.507(c). An original filing becomes seriously misleading if a search under the changed, now correct name, using the filing office's standard search logic, would not disclose the filing under the former, now incorrect name. Tex. Bus. & Com. Code § 9.506(c).

§ 9.15:3 Financing Statement Amendment Addendum

The form UCC3Ad financing statement amendment addendum, form 9-15 in this chapter, is used to indicate additional information that cannot be included in the spaces provided in the form UCC3 financing statement amendment, form 9-14. It should be attached to and filed with the related form UCC3 financing statement amendment and not filed separately.

§ 9.15:4 Financing Statement Search

The form UCC11 information request, form 9-18 in this chapter, is the device commonly used to search for records of other secured interests in the property that may have priority over the interest being created. *See* Tex. Bus. & Com. Code § 9.523(c). To expedite this process, the attorney may use a private service that can complete a search quickly or an online service that can immediately verify the existence of a financing statement.

Like form UCC1, form UCC11 provides adequate instructions on its reverse side for completing the form.

§ 9.16 Extension and Termination

Most financing statements are effective for five years, after which they automatically expire. Tex. Bus. & Com. Code § 9.515(a). A financing statement filed in connection with a manufactured-home transaction or a public-finance transaction that indicates that fact is effective for thirty years from the date it is filed. Tex. Bus. & Com. Code § 9.515(b). The secured party may file a form UCC3 financing statement amendment (form 9-14 in this chapter) as a continuation statement not earlier than six months before the termination date. See sections 9.15:2 and 9.15:3 above. Once a financing statement has expired, the previous priority position is gone and a refiling of the financing statement will be effective on the date of refiling. Tex. Bus. & Com. Code § 9.515(c). The secretary of state accepts electronic filing of continuation and termination financing statements through its website, **www.sos.state.tx.us/ucc/uccforms .shtml**.

If after a financing statement is filed there is no longer an obligation secured by the collateral covered by the financing statement and there is no commitment to make an advance, incur an obligation, or otherwise give value, a termination statement on form UCC3 should be filed. Tex. Bus. & Com. Code § 9.513(a), (c). When a termination statement is filed the related financing statement ceases to be effective. Tex. Bus. & Com. Code § 9.513(d).

§ 9.17 Prefiling Financing Statement

A financing statement may be filed at any time, even before the security agreement is made. Tex. Bus. & Com. Code § 9.502(d). To fully protect the secured party, a financing statement can be filed, and then, after the filing office confirms that the secured party has the desired priority position, the funds can be advanced. The debtor must authorize the secured party to file a financing statement before a security agreement is made. See sections 9.5:3 and 9.14:4 above.

§ 9.18 Collateral Transfer of Note and Lien

§ 9.18:1 Security for Collateral Generally

In most secured transactions, the collateral (for example, the equipment) is the source of the security. However, in a transaction involving the pledge of a note secured by real property, the note itself may not be the primary source of security; the underlying real property may be the actual collateral. Therefore, the secured party and the attorney must carefully review the underlying transaction to understand the value of the collateral. The title policy, deed of trust, survey, financial reports, engineering reports, appraisals, and environmental reports may contain critical information.

§ 9.18:2 Instructions for Completing Collateral Transfer of Note and Lien

Parties: For general information about designation of parties, see chapter 3 in this manual.

Collateral Note: The collateral transfer of note and lien, form 9-8 in this chapter, contains a sample description of the note being pledged to the secured party. The description must be drafted to cover the actual note.

Current Balance: The current balance is that of the underlying collateral note. It is part of the debtor's representations in the agreement.

Collateral Note Security: The form contains a sample description of the deed of trust on the underlying collateral note. The description must be drafted to cover the actual deed of trust and other collateral documents.

Property Description: For general information on property descriptions, see chapter 3.

Obligation: The agreement should identify the note that the collateral secures.

The subheading "Other obligation" is appropriate if the form secures an obligation other than a note, such as the performance of a guaranty or indemnity or performance under a lease agreement.

Collateral Note Payments: Two alternate example clauses are shown on the agreement.

§ 9.18:3 Perfection

The security interest may be perfected by possession or by filing a financing statement covering the collateral note. A secured party that perfects its security interest in a collateral note by possession has priority over a secured party that perfects its security interest in the collateral note by filing a financing statement.

§ 9.18:4 Recording

It is recommended that the secured party record the collateral transfer of note and lien as soon as possible in the real property records, to put all parties dealing with the real property on notice of the secured party's interest in the collateral note and the real property securing the collateral note. Merely recording the collateral transfer of note and lien in the real property records does not perfect the secured party's security interest if the secured party (or a third party on its behalf) does not obtain possession of the collateral note or file a financing statement covering the note.

§ 9.18:5 Endorsement

To obtain the rights of a holder and of a holder in due course under Texas Business and Commerce Code chapter 3, the secured party must secure the payee's (or, if different, the current holder's) endorsement on the collateral note. Among the advantages of a secured party becoming a holder in due course of the collateral note is that the secured party also becomes the person entitled to enforce the collateral note. Tex. Bus. & Com. Code § 3.301. The endorsement may read as follows:

> Pay to the order of [**name of secured party**] as collateral in accordance with collateral transfer of note and lien dated [**date**].

After the debt is repaid, the secured party should return the collateral note to the debtor. Additionally, either the secured party should endorse the collateral note to the debtor, or the debtor, on reacquiring the collateral note, may cancel its endorsement to the secured party. Tex. Bus. & Com. Code § 3.207. If the collateral transfer of note and lien has been recorded, the secured party should sign a release of collateral transfer of note and lien (see form 10-21 in this manual), and that document should be recorded.

§ 9.18:6 Collateral Note Maker's Estoppel Certificate

As additional security for the loan, the secured party should consider requiring the collateral note maker to sign the certificate set forth as form 9-9 in this chapter.

§ 9.19 Obtaining UCC Forms

The UCC forms in this manual are available in a fill-in-the-blank format over the Internet from the Texas secretary of state at **www.sos.state .tx.us/ucc/uccforms.shtml**.

§ 9.20 Additional Resources

Collins, Susan E., and Paul Hodnefield. "UCC Update: Article 9." In *Advanced Business Law Course, 2007*. Austin: State Bar of Texas, 2007.

Kaiser, Stephanie E. "Article 9—Perfection, Priorities, and Other Unique Issues to be Aware Of." In *Collections and Creditors' Rights Course, 2018*. Austin: State Bar of Texas, 2018.

Kearney, Amy. "Uniform Commercial Code Impact on Real Estate." In *Advanced Real Estate Law Course, 2019*. Austin: State Bar of Texas, 2019.

Tarry, Stephen C. "Traps for the Unwary in Perfecting UCC Security Interests." In *Essentials of Business Law: Protecting Your Business Course, 2018*. Austin: State Bar of Texas, 2018.

Form 9-1

Security Agreement

[Goods, Including Documents Covering Goods, Equipment, Inventory, Consumer Goods, and Farm Products]

Basic Information

Date:

Debtor:

Debtor's Mailing Address:

Secured Party:

Secured Party's Mailing Address:

Classification of Collateral: [**select one or more of the following:** Documents covering goods/ Equipment/Equipment to become a fixture/Inventory/Consumer goods/Farm products]

Collateral (including all accessions):

All of Debtor's interest in the following personal property and all proceeds [**include if a purchase-money security interest in inventory is involved:** , including chattel paper or instruments constituting proceeds of the inventory and in proceeds of such chattel paper and instruments,] of such property, including [**describe the specific collateral or select one or more of the following:** documents, including documents of title, warehouse receipts, and bills of lading, covering equipment and/or inventory; equipment; inventory; consumer goods consisting of [**describe goods**]; and farm products [, wherever located]] [**include if applicable:** , and [all after-acquired collateral of the same classification/all products, increase, and offspring of the collateral]].

Obligation

Note

Date:

Original principal amount:

Borrower (Obligor):

Include either or both of the following if applicable.

Other debt/Future advances: The security interest also secures all other present and future debts and liabilities of Debtor and/or Obligor to Secured Party, including future advances.

Other obligation[s]:

Continue with the following.

A. Debtor's Representations Concerning Debtor and Locations

A.1. The collateral is located solely at [**address, city, state**].

Include one or more of the following paragraphs as applicable and modify paragraph numbers as appropriate.

A.2. [Debtor's place of business/Debtor's chief executive office] is located at [**address, city, state**].

Include the following if the debtor is an individual.

A.3. Debtor's residence is located at [**address, city, state**].

Include the following if the debtor is a corporation, limited partnership, or limited liability company.

A.3. Debtor's state of organization is [Texas/[**state**]], and Debtor's name, as shown in its public organic record, as amended, is exactly as set forth above.

Continue with the following.

A.4. Debtor's records concerning the Collateral are located at [**address, city, state**].

B. Granting Clause

Debtor grants to Secured Party a security interest in the Collateral and all its proceeds to secure the Obligation and all renewals, modifications, and extensions of the Obligation. Debtor authorizes Secured Party to file a financing statement describing the Collateral.

C. Debtor Represents the Following:

C.1. No financing statement covering the Collateral is filed in any public office [**include if the secured party has prefiled a financing statement or otherwise has a financing statement on file:** except any financing statement in favor of Secured Party].

C.2. Debtor owns the Collateral and has the authority to grant this security interest, free from any setoff, claim, restriction, security interest, or encumbrance except liens for taxes not yet due.

C.3. None of the Collateral is an accession to any goods, is commingled with other goods, is or will become an accession or part of a product or mass with other goods, or is or will become covered by a document except as provided in this agreement.

C.4. All information about Debtor's financial condition is or will be accurate when provided to Secured Party.

C.5. None of the Collateral is affixed to real estate.

Include the following if applicable if the debtor is an individual.

C.6. The Obligation was not incurred primarily for personal, family, or household purposes.

And/Or

C.7. The collateral was not acquired and will not be held primarily for personal, family, or household purposes.

Continue with the following.

D. Debtor Agrees to—

D.1. Defend the Collateral against all claims adverse to Secured Party's interest; pay all taxes imposed on the Collateral or its use; keep the Collateral free from liens, except for liens in favor of Secured Party or for taxes not yet due; keep the Collateral in Debtor's possession and ownership except as otherwise provided in this agreement; maintain the Collateral in good condition; and protect the Collateral against waste, except for ordinary wear and tear.

D.2. Pay all Secured Party's expenses, including reasonable attorney's fees and legal expenses **[include for a loan transaction subject to Texas Finance Code section 342.502:** assessed by a court], incurred to (a) obtain, preserve, perfect, defend, or enforce this agreement; (b) retake, hold, prepare for disposition, dispose, collect, or enforce the Collateral; or (c) collect or enforce the Obligation. These expenses will bear interest from the date of advance at the rate stated in the Note for matured, unpaid amounts and are payable on demand at the place where the Obligation is payable. These expenses and interest are part of the Obligation and are secured by this agreement.

D.3. Sign and deliver to Secured Party any documents or instruments that Secured Party considers necessary to obtain, maintain, and perfect this security interest in the Collateral. This includes a certificate of title for any Collateral covered by a certificate of title so that Secured Party may have the certificate of title reissued with its lien noted thereon.

D.4. Notify Secured Party immediately of any event of default and of any material change (a) in the Collateral, (b) in Debtor's Mailing Address, (c) in the location of any Collateral, (d) in any other representation in this agreement, or (e) that may affect this security interest, or of any change (f) in Debtor's name or (g) of any location set forth above to another state.

D.5. Use the Collateral primarily according to the stated classification.

D.6. Maintain accurate records of the Collateral at the address set forth above, furnish Secured Party any requested information related to the Collateral, and permit Secured Party to inspect and copy all records relating to the Collateral.

D.7. Permit Secured Party to inspect the Collateral.

Include the following if the collateral includes inventory and the security interest is a purchase-money security interest.

D.8. Deliver to Secured Party on receipt all chattel paper or instruments constituting proceeds of the inventory and, at Secured Party's request, deposit all checks, items, and other cash proceeds of the inventory in a special bank account designated by Secured Party, who alone will have power of withdrawal.

Continue with the following.

E. Debtor Agrees Not to—

E.1. Sell, transfer, or encumber any of the Collateral, except in the ordinary course of Debtor's business.

E.2. Except as permitted in this agreement, permit the Collateral to be affixed to any real estate, to become an accession to any goods, to be commingled with other goods, to become a fixture, accession, or part of a product or mass with other goods, or to be covered by a document, except a document in the possession of Secured Party.

Select one of the following.

Include the following if the debtor is a corporation, limited partnership, or limited liability company.

E.3. Change its name or jurisdiction of organization, merge or consolidate with any person, or convert to a different entity without notifying Secured Party in advance and taking action to continue the perfected status of the security interest in the Collateral.

Or

Include the following if the debtor is an entity other than a corporation, limited partnership, or limited liability company.

E.3. Change the state in which Debtor's place of business (or chief executive office if Debtor has more than one place of business) is located, change its name, or convert to a different entity without notifying Secured Party in advance and taking action to continue the perfected status of the security interest in the Collateral.

Or

Include the following if the debtor is an individual.

E.3. Change Debtor's name or state of residence without notifying Secured Party in advance and taking action to continue the perfected status of the security interest in the Collateral.

Continue with the following.

Include the following if the collateral includes inventory and the security interest is a purchase-money security interest.

E.4. Deliver any item of inventory to a buyer before the buyer delivers to Debtor a check, another item, money, an instrument, or chattel paper in full payment therefor or commingle any check, item, money, or other cash proceeds from the sale or lease of an item of inventory with any of Debtor's other funds or property.

Continue with the following.

F. Insurance and Risk of Loss

F.1. Debtor will insure the Collateral in accordance with Secured Party's reasonable requirements regarding choice of carrier, risks insured against, and amount of coverage. Policies must be written in favor of Debtor, be endorsed to name Secured Party as an additional insured or as otherwise directed in writing by Secured Party, and provide that Secured Party will receive at least ten days' notice before cancellation. Debtor must provide copies of the policies or evidence of insurance to Secured Party.

F.2. **COLLATERAL PROTECTION INSURANCE NOTICE**

In accordance with the provisions of section 307.052(a) of the Texas Finance Code, the Secured Party hereby notifies the Debtor as follows:

(A) the Debtor is required to:

(i) keep the collateral insured against damage in the amount the Secured Party specifies;

(ii) purchase the insurance from an insurer that is authorized to do business in the state of Texas or an eligible surplus lines insurer; and

(iii) name the Secured Party as the person to be paid under the policy in the event of a loss;

(B) the Debtor must, if required by the Secured Party, deliver to the Secured Party a copy of the policy and proof of the payment of premiums; and

(C) if the Debtor fails to meet any requirement listed in Paragraph (A) or (B), the Secured Party may obtain collateral protection insurance on behalf of the Debtor at the Debtor's expense.

F.3. Debtor assumes all risk of loss to the Collateral.

F.4. Debtor appoints Secured Party as attorney-in-fact to collect any returned unearned premiums and proceeds of any insurance on the Collateral and to endorse and deliver to Secured Party any payment from such insurance made payable to Debtor. Debtor's appointment of Secured Party as Debtor's agent is coupled with an interest and if Debtor is an individual will survive any disability of Debtor.

G. Default and Remedies

G.1. A default exists if—

a. Debtor, Obligor, or any secondary obligor fails to timely pay or perform any obligation or covenant in any written agreement between Secured Party and any of Debtor, Obligor, or secondary obligor;

b. any representation in this agreement or in any other written agreement between Secured Party and any of Debtor, Obligor, or secondary obligor is materially false when made;

c. a receiver is appointed for Debtor, Obligor, any secondary obligor, or any Collateral;

d. any Collateral is assigned for the benefit of creditors;

e. a bankruptcy or insolvency proceeding is commenced by Debtor, a partnership in which Debtor is a general partner, Obligor, or any secondary obligor;

f. a bankruptcy or insolvency proceeding is commenced against Debtor, a partnership in which Debtor is a general partner, Obligor, or any secondary obligor, and the proceeding continues without dismissal for sixty days, the party against whom the proceeding is commenced admits the material allegations of the petition against it, or an order for relief is entered;

g. any of the following parties is terminated, begins to wind up its affairs, is authorized to terminate or wind up its affairs by its governing body or persons, or any event occurs or condition exists that permits the termination or winding up of the affairs of any of the following parties: Debtor; a partnership of which Debtor is a general partner; Obligor; or any secondary obligor; or

h. any Collateral is impaired by loss, theft, damage, levy and execution, issuance of an official writ or order of seizure, or destruction, unless it is promptly replaced with collateral of like kind and quality or restored to its former condition.

G.2. If a default exists, Secured Party may—

a. demand, collect, convert, redeem, settle, compromise, receipt for, realize on, sue for, and adjust the Collateral either in Secured Party's or Debtor's name, as Secured Party desires, or take control of any proceeds of the Collateral and apply the proceeds against the Obligation;

b. take possession of any Collateral not already in Secured Party's possession, without demand or legal process, and for that purpose Debtor grants Secured Party the right to enter any premises where the Collateral may be located;

c. without taking possession, sell, lease, or otherwise dispose of the Collateral at any public or private sale in accordance with law; or

d. exercise any rights and remedies granted by law or this agreement.

G.3. Foreclosure of this security interest by suit does not limit Secured Party's remedies, including the right to sell the Collateral under the terms of this agreement. Secured Party may exercise all remedies at the same or different times, and no remedy is a defense to any other. Secured Party's rights and remedies include all those granted by law and those specified in this agreement.

G.4. Secured Party's delay in exercising, partial exercise of, or failure to exercise any of its remedies or rights does not waive Secured Party's rights to subsequently exercise those remedies or rights. Secured Party's waiver of any default does not waive any other default by Debtor. Secured Party's waiver of any right in this agreement or of any default is binding only if it is in writing. Secured Party may remedy any default without waiving it.

G.5. Secured Party has no obligation to clean or otherwise prepare the Collateral for sale.

G.6. Secured Party has no obligation to satisfy the Obligation by attempting to collect the Obligation from any other person liable for it. Secured Party may release, modify, or waive any collateral provided by any other person to secure any of the Obligation. If Secured Party attempts to collect the Obligation from any other person liable for it or releases, modifies, or waives any collateral provided by any other person, that will not affect Secured Party's rights against Debtor. Debtor waives any right Debtor may have to require Secured Party to pursue any third person for any of the Obligation.

G.7. If Secured Party must comply with any applicable state or federal law requirements in connection with a disposition of the Collateral, such compliance will not be considered to adversely affect the commercial reasonableness of a sale of the Collateral.

G.8. Secured Party may sell the Collateral without giving any warranties as to the Collateral. Secured Party may specifically disclaim any warranties of title or the like. This procedure will not be considered to adversely affect the commercial reasonableness of a sale of the Collateral.

G.9. If Secured Party sells any of the Collateral on credit, Debtor will be credited only with payments actually made by the purchaser and received by Secured Party for application to the indebtedness of the purchaser. If the purchaser fails to pay for the Collateral, Secured Party may resell the Collateral and Debtor will be credited with the proceeds of the sale.

G.10. If Secured Party purchases any of the Collateral being sold, Secured Party may pay for the Collateral by crediting the purchase price against the Obligation.

G.11. Secured Party has no obligation to marshal any assets in favor of Debtor or against or in payment of the Note, any of the Other Obligation[s], or any other obligation owed to Secured Party by Debtor or any other person.

G.12. If the Collateral is sold after default, recitals in the bill of sale or transfer will be prima facie evidence of their truth and all prerequisites to the sale specified by this agreement and by law will be presumed satisfied.

H. General

H.1. Secured Party may at any time—

a. take control of proceeds of insurance on the Collateral and reduce any part of the Obligation accordingly or permit Debtor to use the funds to repair or replace the Collateral and

b. purchase single-interest insurance coverage that will protect only Secured Party if Debtor fails to maintain insurance, and premiums for the insurance will become part of the Obligation.

H.2. Notice is reasonable if it is mailed, postage prepaid, to Debtor at Debtor's Mailing Address at least ten days before any public sale or ten days before the time when the Collateral may be otherwise disposed of without further notice to Debtor.

H.3. This security interest will attach to after-acquired consumer goods only to the extent permitted by law.

H.4. This security interest will neither affect nor be affected by any other security for any of the Obligation. Neither extensions of any of the Obligation nor releases of any of the Collateral will affect the priority or validity of this security interest.

H.5. This agreement binds, benefits, and may be enforced by the successors in interest of Secured Party and will bind all persons who become bound as debtors to this agreement. Assignment of any part of the Obligation and Secured Party's delivery of any part of the Collateral will fully discharge Secured Party from responsibility for that part of the Collateral. If such an assignment is made, Debtor will render performance under this agreement to the assignee. Debtor waives and will not assert against any assignee any claims, defenses, or setoffs that Debtor could assert against Secured Party except defenses that cannot be waived. All representations and obligations are joint and several as to each Debtor.

H.6. This agreement may be amended only by an instrument in writing signed by Secured Party and Debtor.

H.7. The unenforceability of any provision of this agreement will not affect the enforceability or validity of any other provision.

H.8. This agreement will be construed according to Texas law, without regard to choice-of-law rules of any jurisdiction. This agreement is to be performed in [**include if applicable in a consumer transaction:** , and has been signed by Debtor in,] the county of Secured Party's Mailing Address.

H.9. Interest on the Obligation secured by this agreement will not exceed the maximum amount of nonusurious interest that may be contracted for, taken, reserved, charged, or received under law. Any interest in excess of that maximum amount will be credited on the principal of the Obligation or, if that has been paid, refunded. On any acceleration or required or permitted prepayment, any such excess will be canceled automatically as of the acceleration or prepayment or, if already paid, credited on the principal of the Obligation or, if the principal of the Obligation has been paid, refunded. This provision overrides any conflicting provisions in this and all other instruments concerning the Obligation.

H.10. In no event may this agreement secure payment of any debt that may not lawfully be secured by a lien on real estate or create a lien otherwise prohibited by law.

H.11. When the context requires, singular nouns and pronouns include the plural.

H.12. Any term defined in sections 1.101 to 9.709 of the Texas Business and Commerce Code and not defined in this agreement has the meaning given to the term in the Code.

H.13. Except for inventory collateral, if the Obligation includes purchase money for the Collateral, Debtor's repayment of the Obligation will be applied on a first-in-first-out basis with the effect that the portion of the Obligation used to purchase a particular item of Collateral will be paid in the chronological order in which Debtor purchased the Collateral.

Include the following if the collateral is farm products.

H.14. The farm products addendum is attached to this agreement and incorporated into it for all purposes. [**Attach form 9-5 in this chapter.**]

Include the following if the collateral is equipment or inventory on which ad valorem taxes are assessed.

H.15. **Debtor waives and surrenders to Secured Party (a) Debtor's power to authorize anyone (other than Secured Party or Debtor) to pay ad valorem taxes on the Collateral and (b) Debtor's power to authorize a taxing entity to transfer its tax lien on the Collateral to anyone other than Secured Party. Debtor agrees and declares that any authorization from Debtor to another (other than Secured Party) to pay the taxes and transfer a tax lien on the Collateral is void.**

Continue with the following.

____
[**Name of debtor**]

Form 9-2

Security Agreement

[Accounts, Chattel Paper, General Intangibles, Commercial Tort Claims]

Basic Information

Date:

Debtor:

Debtor's Mailing Address:

Secured Party:

Secured Party's Mailing Address:

Classification of Collateral: [**select one or more of the following:** [Accounts/Chattel paper/ General intangibles/Commercial tort claim]]

Collateral:

All of Debtor's interest in the following personal property and all supporting obligations and proceeds of such property [**describe the specific collateral or select one or more of the following:** accounts; chattel paper; general intangibles; commercial tort claims arising out of Debtor's claim against [**name**] and other persons; and all rights to payment arising out of a judgment or settlement of such commercial tort claim, including under any instrument, chattel paper, or settlement agreement] [**include if applicable:** and all after-acquired collateral of the same classification].

Obligation

Note

Date:

Original principal amount:

Borrower (Obligor):

Include either or both of the following if applicable.

Other debt/Future advances: The security interest also secures all other present and future debts and liabilities of Debtor and/or Obligor to Secured Party, including future advances.

Other obligation[s]:

Continue with the following.

A. Debtor's Representations Concerning Debtor and Locations

A.1. The chattel paper collateral is located solely at [**address, city, state**].

Include one or more of the following paragraphs as applicable and modify paragraph numbers as appropriate.

A.2. [Debtor's place of business/Debtor's chief executive office] is located at [**address, city, state**].

Include the following if the debtor is an individual.

A.3. Debtor's residence is located at [**address, city, state**].

Include the following if the debtor is a corporation, limited partnership, or limited liability company.

A.3. Debtor's state of organization is [Texas/[**state**]], and Debtor's name, as shown in its public organic record, as amended, is exactly as set forth above.

Continue with the following.

A.4. Debtor's records concerning the Collateral are located at [**address, city, state**].

B. Granting Clause

Debtor grants to Secured Party a security interest in the Collateral and all its proceeds to secure the Obligation and all renewals, modifications, and extensions of the Obligation. Debtor authorizes Secured Party to file a financing statement describing the Collateral.

C. Debtor Represents the Following:

C.1. No financing statement covering the Collateral is filed in any public office [**include if the secured party has prefiled a financing statement or otherwise has a financing statement on file:** except any financing statement in favor of Secured Party].

C.2. Debtor owns the Collateral and has the authority to grant this security interest, free from any setoff, claim, restriction, security interest, or encumbrance except liens for taxes not yet due.

C.3. All information about Debtor's financial condition is or will be accurate when provided to Secured Party.

C.4. Each account and chattel paper in the Collateral is and will be the valid, legally enforceable obligation of a third-party account debtor or obligor.

C.5. If any Collateral or proceeds include obligations of third parties to Debtor, the transactions creating those obligations conform and will conform in all respects to applicable state and federal consumer credit law.

C.6. The chattel paper Collateral is in tangible, not electronic, form and has only one original counterpart. No person, other than Debtor or Secured Party, has actual or constructive possession of any chattel paper Collateral.

D. Debtor Agrees to—

D.1. Defend the Collateral against all claims adverse to Secured Party's interest; pay all taxes imposed on the Collateral; keep the Collateral free from liens, except for liens in favor of Secured Party or for taxes not yet due; and keep the Collateral in Debtor's possession and ownership except as otherwise provided in this agreement.

D.2. Pay all Secured Party's expenses, including reasonable attorney's fees and legal expenses [**include for a loan transaction subject to Texas Finance Code section 342.502:** assessed by a court], incurred to (a) obtain, preserve, perfect, defend, or enforce this agreement; (b) retake, hold, prepare for disposition, dispose, collect, or enforce the Collateral; or (c) collect or enforce the Obligation. These expenses will bear interest from the date of advance at the rate stated in the Note for matured, unpaid amounts and are payable on demand at the place where the Obligation is payable. These expenses and interest are part of the Obligation and are secured by this agreement.

D.3. Sign and deliver to Secured Party any documents or instruments that Secured Party considers necessary to obtain, maintain, and perfect this security interest in the Collateral.

D.4. Notify Secured Party immediately of any event of default and of any material change (a) in the Collateral, (b) in Debtor's Mailing Address, (c) in the location of any Collateral, (d) in any other representation or warranty in this agreement, or (e) that may affect this security interest, or of any change (f) in Debtor's name or (g) of any location set forth above to another state.

D.5. Use the Collateral primarily according to the stated classification.

D.6. Maintain accurate records of the Collateral at the address set forth above; furnish Secured Party any requested information related to the Collateral; and permit Secured Party to inspect and copy all records relating to the Collateral.

D.7. Preserve the liability of all obligors on the Collateral and preserve the priority of all security for the Collateral.

D.8. On Secured Party's demand, hold payments, including instruments, items, and money received as proceeds of the Collateral, separate and in an express trust for Secured Party and deposit all such payments received as proceeds of the Collateral in a special bank account designated by Secured Party, who alone will have power of withdrawal.

D.9. Inform Secured Party immediately of the rejection of property, a delay in delivery or performance, or a claim made in regard to any Collateral.

D.10. As trustee for Secured Party, keep returned property segregated from Debtor's other property until Secured Party has been paid the amount loaned against the related account and deliver the property on demand to Secured Party.

D.11. Pay Secured Party the unpaid amount of an account in the Collateral under any of the following conditions: if the account is not paid when due; if a purchaser rejects the property or services covered by the account; or if Secured Party rejects the account as unsatisfactory. Secured Party may retain the account in the Collateral and may charge any deposit account of Debtor with the unpaid amount.

D.12. Cause each chattel paper in the Collateral to have only one original counterpart and, at the request of Secured Party, (a) immediately deliver to Secured Party all current and after-acquired chattel paper Collateral in Debtor's possession and either endorse it to Secured Party's order or give Secured Party appropriate executed powers, (b) obtain the acknowledgment of any other person in possession of chattel paper Collateral of Secured Party's security interest in the Collateral, or (c) mark each chattel paper in the Collateral with a legend indicating that it is subject to a security interest under this agreement.

E. Debtor Agrees Not to—

E.1. Sell, transfer, or encumber any of the Collateral, except in the ordinary course of Debtor's business.

Select one of the following.

Include the following if the debtor is a corporation, limited partnership, or limited liability company.

E.2. Change its name or jurisdiction of organization, merge or consolidate with any person, or convert to a different entity without notifying Secured Party in advance and taking action to continue the perfected status of the security interest in the Collateral.

Or

Include the following if the debtor is an entity other than a corporation, limited partnership, or limited liability company.

E.2. Change the state in which Debtor's place of business (or chief executive office if Debtor has more than one place of business) is located, change its name, or convert to a different entity without notifying Secured Party in advance and taking action to continue the perfected status of the security interest in the Collateral.

Or

Include the following if the debtor is an individual.

E.2. Change Debtor's name or state of residence without notifying Secured Party in advance and taking action to continue the perfected status of the security interest in the Collateral.

Continue with the following.

E.3. Modify any agreement related to the Collateral.

E.4. Commingle the Collateral or any proceeds with any of Debtor's other funds or property.

F. Insurance and Risk of Loss

F.1. Debtor will insure the Collateral in accordance with Secured Party's reasonable requirements regarding choice of carrier, risks insured against, and amount of coverage. Policies must be written in favor of Debtor, be endorsed to name Secured Party as an additional insured or as otherwise directed in writing by Secured Party, and provide that Secured Party will receive at least ten days' notice before cancellation. Debtor must provide copies of the policies or evidence of insurance to Secured Party.

F.2. **COLLATERAL PROTECTION INSURANCE NOTICE**

In accordance with the provisions of section 307.052(a) of the Texas Finance Code, the Secured Party hereby notifies the Debtor as follows:

(A) the Debtor is required to:

(i) keep the collateral insured against damage in the amount the Secured Party specifies;

(ii) purchase the insurance from an insurer that is authorized to do business in the state of Texas or an eligible surplus lines insurer; and

(iii) name the Secured Party as the person to be paid under the policy in the event of a loss;

(B) the Debtor must, if required by the Secured Party, deliver to the Secured Party a copy of the policy and proof of the payment of premiums; and

(C) if the Debtor fails to meet any requirement listed in Paragraph (A) or (B), the Secured Party may obtain collateral protection insurance on behalf of the Debtor at the Debtor's expense.

F.3. Debtor assumes all risk of loss to the Collateral.

F.4. Debtor appoints Secured Party as attorney-in-fact to collect any returned unearned premiums and proceeds of any insurance on the Collateral and to endorse and deliver to Secured Party any payment from such insurance made payable to Debtor. Debtor's appointment of Secured Party as Debtor's agent is coupled with an interest and if Debtor is an individual will survive any disability of Debtor.

G. Default and Remedies

G.1. A default exists if—

a. Debtor, Obligor, or any secondary obligor fails to timely pay or perform any obligation or covenant in any written agreement between Secured Party and any of Debtor, Obligor, or secondary obligor;

b. any representation in this agreement or in any other written agreement between Secured Party and any of Debtor, Obligor, or secondary obligor is materially false when made;

c. a receiver is appointed for Debtor, Obligor, any secondary obligor, or any Collateral;

d. any Collateral is assigned for the benefit of creditors;

e. a bankruptcy or insolvency proceeding is commenced by Debtor, a partnership in which Debtor is a general partner, Obligor, or any secondary obligor;

f. a bankruptcy or insolvency proceeding is commenced against Debtor, a partnership in which Debtor is a general partner, Obligor, or any secondary obligor, and the proceeding continues without dismissal for sixty days, the party against whom the proceeding is commenced admits the material allegations of the petition against it, or an order for relief is entered;

g. any of the following parties is terminated, begins to wind up its affairs, is authorized to terminate or wind up its affairs by its governing body or persons, or any event occurs or condition exists that permits the termination or winding up of the affairs of any of the following parties: Debtor; a partnership of which Debtor is a general partner; Obligor; or any secondary obligor; or

h. any Collateral is impaired by loss, theft, damage, levy and execution, issuance of an official writ or order of seizure, or destruction, unless it is promptly replaced with collateral of like kind and quality or restored to its former condition.

G.2. If a default exists, Secured Party may—

a. demand, collect, convert, redeem, settle, compromise, receipt for, realize on, sue for, and adjust the Collateral either in Secured Party's or Debtor's name, as Secured Party desires, or take control of any proceeds of the Collateral and apply the proceeds against the Obligation;

b. take possession of any Collateral not already in Secured Party's possession, without demand or legal process, and for that purpose Debtor grants Secured Party the right to enter any premises where the Collateral may be located;

c. without taking possession, sell, lease, or otherwise dispose of the Collateral at any public or private sale in accordance with law;

d. exercise any rights and remedies granted by law or this agreement;

e. notify obligors on the Collateral to pay Secured Party directly and enforce Debtor's rights against such obligors; or

f. as Debtor's agent, make any endorsements in Debtor's name and on Debtor's behalf.

G.3. Foreclosure of this security interest by suit does not limit Secured Party's remedies, including the right to sell the Collateral under the terms of this agreement. Secured Party may exercise all remedies at the same or different times, and no remedy is a defense to any other. Secured Party's rights and remedies include all those granted by law and those specified in this agreement.

G.4. Secured Party's delay in exercising, partial exercise of, or failure to exercise any of its remedies or rights does not waive Secured Party's rights to subsequently exercise those remedies or rights. Secured Party's waiver of any default does not waive any other default by Debtor. Secured Party's waiver of any right in this agreement or of any default is binding only if it is in writing. Secured Party may remedy any default without waiving it.

G.5. Secured Party has no obligation to clean or otherwise prepare the Collateral for sale.

G.6. At any time Secured Party may contact obligors on the Collateral directly to verify information furnished by Debtor.

G.7. Secured Party has no obligation to collect any of the Collateral and is not liable for failure to collect any of the Collateral, for failure to preserve any rights pertaining to the Collateral, or for any act or omission on the part of Secured Party or Secured Party's officers, agents, or employees, except willful misconduct.

G.8. Secured Party has no obligation to satisfy the Obligation by attempting to collect the Obligation from any other person liable for it. Secured Party may release, modify, or waive any collateral provided by any other person to secure any of the Obligation. If Secured Party attempts to collect the Obligation from any other person liable for it or releases, modifies, or waives any collateral provided by any other person, that will not affect Secured Party's rights against Debtor. Debtor waives any right Debtor may have to require Secured Party to pursue any third person for any of the Obligation.

G.9. If Secured Party must comply with any applicable state or federal law requirements in connection with a disposition of the Collateral, such compliance will not be considered to adversely affect the commercial reasonableness of a sale of the Collateral.

G.10. Secured Party may sell the Collateral without giving any warranties as to the Collateral. Secured Party may specifically disclaim any warranties of title or the like. This procedure will not be considered to adversely affect the commercial reasonableness of a sale of the Collateral.

G.11. If Secured Party sells any of the Collateral on credit, Debtor will be credited only with payments actually made by the purchaser and received by Secured Party for application to the indebtedness of the purchaser. If the purchaser fails to pay for the Collateral, Secured Party may resell the Collateral and Debtor will be credited with the proceeds of the sale.

G.12. If Secured Party purchases any of the Collateral being sold, Secured Party may pay for the Collateral by crediting the purchase price against the Obligation.

G.13. Secured Party has no obligation to marshal any assets in favor of Debtor or against or in payment of the Note, any of the Other Obligation[s], or any other obligation owed to Secured Party by Debtor or any other person.

G.14. If the Collateral is sold after default, recitals in the bill of sale or transfer will be prima facie evidence of their truth and all prerequisites to the sale specified by this agreement and by law will be presumed satisfied.

H. General

H.1. Secured Party may at any time—

a. take control of proceeds of insurance on the Collateral and reduce any part of the Obligation accordingly or permit Debtor to use the funds to repair or replace the Collateral and

b. purchase single-interest insurance coverage that will protect only Secured Party if Debtor fails to maintain insurance, and premiums for the insurance will become part of the Obligation.

H.2. Notice is reasonable if it is mailed, postage prepaid, to Debtor at Debtor's Mailing Address at least ten days before any public sale or ten days before the time when the Collateral may be otherwise disposed of without further notice to Debtor.

H.3. This security interest will attach to an after-acquired commercial tort claim only to the extent permitted by law.

H.4. This security interest will neither affect nor be affected by any other security for any of the Obligation. Neither extensions of any of the Obligation nor releases of any of the Collateral will affect the priority or validity of this security interest.

H.5. This agreement binds, benefits, and may be enforced by the successors in interest of Secured Party and will bind all persons who become bound as debtors to this agreement. Assignment of any part of the Obligation and Secured Party's delivery of any part of the Collateral will fully discharge Secured Party from responsibility for that part of the Collateral. If such an assignment is made, Debtor will render performance under this agreement to the assignee. Debtor waives and will not assert against any assignee any claims, defenses, or setoffs that Debtor could assert against Secured Party except defenses that cannot be waived. All representations and obligations are joint and several as to each Debtor.

H.6. This agreement may be amended only by an instrument in writing signed by Secured Party and Debtor.

H.7. The unenforceability of any provision of this agreement will not affect the enforceability or validity of any other provision.

H.8. This agreement will be construed according to Texas law, without regard to choice-of-law rules of any jurisdiction. This agreement is to be performed in [**include if applicable in a consumer transaction:** , and has been signed by Debtor in,] the county of Secured Party's Mailing Address.

H.9. Interest on the Obligation secured by this agreement will not exceed the maximum amount of nonusurious interest that may be contracted for, taken, reserved, charged, or received under law. Any interest in excess of that maximum amount will be credited on the principal of the Obligation or, if that has been paid, refunded. On any acceleration or required or permitted prepayment, any such excess will be canceled automatically as of the acceleration or prepayment or, if already paid, credited on the principal of the Obligation or, if the

principal of the Obligation has been paid, refunded. This provision overrides any conflicting provisions in this and all other instruments concerning the Obligation.

H.10. In no event may this agreement secure payment of any debt that may not lawfully be secured by a lien on real estate or create a lien otherwise prohibited by law.

H.11. When the context requires, singular nouns and pronouns include the plural.

H.12. Any term defined in sections 1.101 to 9.709 of the Texas Business and Commerce Code and not defined in this agreement has the meaning given to the term in the Code.

____

[Name of debtor]

Form 9-3

Security Agreement
[Instruments, Investment Property]

Basic Information

Date:

Debtor:

Debtor's Mailing Address:

Secured Party:

Secured Party's Mailing Address:

Classification of Collateral: [**select one or both of the following:** [Instruments [and]/Investment property]]

Collateral:

All of Debtor's interest in the following personal property and all supporting obligations and proceeds of such property: [**describe the specific collateral as follows:** that certain [[**title of instrument**]/note], dated [**date**], in the original face amount of $[**amount**], issued by [**name**] as maker and payable to [**name**] as payee/all instruments or notes acquired by or payable to Debtor arising out of Debtor's sale of lots in the [**name**] subdivision otherwise known as [**insert legal description**]/[**number**] shares of [**describe class or series of preferred or common**] stock of [**name of corporation**] represented by certificate number[s] [**number[s]**], brokerage account number [**number**], maintained in the name of Debtor with [**name of broker or securities intermediary**]/

instruments, including promissory notes/investment property, including securities] [**include if applicable:** and all after-acquired collateral of the same classification].

Obligation

Note

Date:

Original principal amount:

Borrower (Obligor):

Include either or both of the following if applicable.

Other debt/Future advances: The security interest also secures all other present and future debts and liabilities of Debtor and/or Obligor to Secured Party, including future advances.

Other obligation[s]:

Continue with the following.

A. Debtor's Representations Concerning Debtor and Locations

Include one or more of the following paragraphs as applicable and modify paragraph numbers as appropriate.

A.1. [Debtor's place of business/Debtor's chief executive office] is located at [**address, city, state**].

Include the following if the debtor is an individual.

A.2. Debtor's residence is located at [**address, city, state**].

Include the following if the debtor is a corporation, limited partnership, or limited liability company.

A.2. Debtor's state of organization is [Texas/[**state**]], and Debtor's name, as shown in its public organic record, as amended, is exactly as set forth above.

A.3. Debtor's records concerning the Collateral are located at [**address, city, state**].

B. Granting Clause

Debtor grants to Secured Party a security interest in the Collateral and all its proceeds to secure the Obligation and all renewals, modifications, and extensions of the Obligation. Debtor authorizes Secured Party to file a financing statement describing the Collateral.

C. Debtor Represents the Following:

C.1. No financing statement covering the Collateral is filed in any public office [**include if the secured party has prefiled a financing statement or otherwise has a financing statement on file:** except any financing statement in favor of Secured Party].

C.2. Debtor owns the Collateral and has the authority to grant this security interest, free from any setoff, claim, restriction, security interest, or encumbrance except liens for taxes not yet due.

C.3. All information about Debtor's financial condition is or will be accurate when provided to Secured Party.

C.4. Each instrument and security, certificated or uncertificated, in the Collateral is and will represent the valid, legally enforceable obligation of the issuer thereof.

C.5. The transaction under which each instrument and security, certificated or uncertificated, in the Collateral was issued and transferred to Debtor conforms and will conform in all respects to applicable state and federal law, including securities law and consumer credit law.

D. Debtor Agrees to—

D.1. Defend the Collateral against all claims adverse to Secured Party's interest; pay all taxes imposed on the Collateral; keep the Collateral free from liens, except for liens in favor of Secured Party or for taxes not yet due; keep the Collateral in Debtor's possession and ownership except as otherwise provided in this agreement; maintain the Collateral in good condition; and protect the Collateral against waste, except for ordinary wear and tear.

D.2. Pay all Secured Party's expenses, including reasonable attorney's fees and legal expenses [**include for a loan transaction subject to Texas Finance Code section 342.502:** assessed by a court], incurred to (a) obtain, preserve, perfect, defend, or enforce this agreement; (b) retake, hold, prepare for disposition, dispose, collect, or enforce the Collateral; and (c) collect or enforce the Obligation. These expenses will bear interest from the date of advance at the rate stated in the Note for matured, unpaid amounts and are payable on demand at the place where the Obligation is payable. These expenses and interest are part of the Obligation and are secured by this agreement.

D.3. Sign and deliver to Secured Party any documents or instruments that Secured Party considers necessary to obtain, maintain, and perfect this security interest in the Collateral and take any action requested by Secured Party for Secured Party to obtain control of investment property in the Collateral.

D.4. Notify Secured Party immediately of any event of default and of any material change (a) in the Collateral, (b) in Debtor's Mailing Address, (c) in the location of any Collateral, (d) in any other representation or warranty in this agreement, or (e) that may affect this security interest, or of any change (f) in Debtor's name or (g) of any location set forth above to another state.

D.5. Use the Collateral primarily according to the stated classification.

D.6. Maintain accurate records of the Collateral at the address set forth above; furnish Secured Party any requested information related to the Collateral; and permit Secured Party to inspect and copy all records relating to the Collateral.

D.7. If the Collateral is not in the possession or control of Secured Party, permit Secured Party to inspect the Collateral.

D.8. Immediately deliver to Secured Party, with an assignment or endorsement, current and after-acquired instruments and certificated securities in the Collateral.

D.9. Preserve the liability of all obligors on the Collateral and preserve the priority of all security for the Collateral.

D.10. On Secured Party's demand, deposit all payments received as proceeds of the Collateral in a special bank account designated by Secured Party, who alone will have power of withdrawal.

D.11. Cause all obligors on the Collateral to pay and perform all their obligations and inform Secured Party immediately of the default in the payment or performance of any Collateral.

E. Debtor Agrees Not to—

E.1. Sell, transfer, or encumber any of the Collateral [**include if applicable:** except in the ordinary course of Debtor's business].

Select one of the following.

Include the following if the debtor is a corporation, limited partnership, or limited liability company.

E.2. Change its name or jurisdiction of organization, merge or consolidate with any person, or convert to a different entity without notifying Secured Party in advance and taking action to continue the perfected status of the security interest in the Collateral.

Or

Include the following if the debtor is an entity other than a corporation, limited partnership, or limited liability company.

E.2. Change the state in which Debtor's place of business (or chief executive office if Debtor has more than one place of business) is located, change its name, or convert to a different entity without notifying Secured Party in advance and taking action to continue the perfected status of the security interest in the Collateral.

Or

Include the following if the debtor is an individual.

E.2. Change Debtor's name or state of residence without notifying Secured Party in advance and taking action to continue the perfected status of the security interest in the Collateral.

Continue with the following.

E.3. Modify any term of any instrument or security in the Collateral.

E.4. Commingle any payment on the Collateral with any of Debtor's other funds or property.

F. Default and Remedies

F.1. A default exists if—

a. Debtor, Obligor, or any secondary obligor fails to timely pay or perform any obligation or covenant in any written agreement between Secured Party and any of Debtor, Obligor, or secondary obligor;

b. any representation in this agreement or in any other written agreement between Secured Party and any of Debtor, Obligor, or secondary obligor is materially false when made;

c. a receiver is appointed for Debtor, Obligor, any secondary obligor, or any Collateral;

d. any Collateral is assigned for the benefit of creditors;

e. a bankruptcy or insolvency proceeding is commenced by Debtor, a partnership in which Debtor is a general partner, Obligor, or any secondary obligor;

f. a bankruptcy or insolvency proceeding is commenced against Debtor, a partnership in which Debtor is a general partner, Obligor, or any secondary obligor, and the proceeding continues without dismissal for sixty days, the party against whom the proceeding is commenced admits the material allegations of the petition against it, or an order for relief is entered;

g. any of the following parties is terminated, begins to wind up its affairs, is authorized to terminate or wind up its affairs by its governing body or persons, or any event occurs or condition exists that permits the termination or winding up of the affairs of any of the following parties: Debtor; a partnership of which Debtor is a general partner; Obligor; or any secondary obligor; or

h. any Collateral is impaired by loss, theft, damage, levy and execution, issuance of an official writ or order of seizure, or destruction, unless it is promptly replaced with collateral of like kind and quality or restored to its former condition.

F.2. If a default exists, Secured Party may—

a. demand, collect, convert, redeem, settle, compromise, receipt for, realize on, sue for, and adjust the Collateral either in Secured Party's or Debtor's name, as Secured Party desires, or take control of any proceeds of the Collateral and apply the proceeds against the Obligation;

b. take possession of any Collateral not already in Secured Party's possession, without demand or legal process, and for that purpose Debtor grants Secured Party the right to enter any premises where the Collateral may be located;

c. without taking possession, sell, lease, or otherwise dispose of the Collateral at any public or private sale in accordance with law;

d. exercise any rights and remedies granted by law or this agreement;

e. notify obligors on the Collateral to pay Secured Party directly;

f. as Debtor's agent, make any endorsements in Debtor's name and on Debtor's behalf of any instruments in the Collateral and to any proceeds of the Collateral;

g. exercise and enforce all rights, including voting rights, available to an owner of the Collateral; and

h. transfer record ownership of any Collateral to Secured Party.

F.3. Foreclosure of this security interest by suit does not limit Secured Party's remedies, including the right to sell the Collateral under the terms of this agreement. Secured Party may exercise all remedies at the same or different times, and no remedy is a defense to any other. Secured Party's rights and remedies include all those granted by law and those specified in this agreement.

F.4. Secured Party's delay in exercising, partial exercise of, or failure to exercise any of its remedies or rights does not waive Secured Party's rights to subsequently exercise those remedies or rights. Secured Party's waiver of any default does not waive any other default by Debtor. Secured Party's waiver of any right in this agreement or of any default is binding only if it is in writing. Secured Party may remedy any default without waiving it.

F.5. Secured Party has no obligation to clean or otherwise prepare the Collateral for sale.

F.6. Other than exercising reasonable care to assure safe custody of the Collateral in its possession, Secured Party has no responsibility for the Collateral. Secured Party has no obligation to collect any of the Collateral and is not liable for failure to collect any of the Collateral, for failure to preserve any right pertaining to the Collateral, or for any act or omission on the part of Secured Party or Secured Party's officers, agents, or employees, except willful misconduct.

F.7. Secured Party has no obligation to satisfy the Obligation by attempting to collect the Obligation from any other person liable for it. Secured Party may release, modify, or waive any collateral provided by any other person to secure any of the Obligation. If Secured Party attempts to collect the Obligation from any other person liable for it or releases, modifies, or waives any collateral provided by any other person, that will not affect Secured Party's rights against Debtor. Debtor waives any right Debtor may have to require Secured Party to pursue any third person for any of the Obligation.

F.8. If Secured Party must comply with any applicable state or federal law requirements in connection with a disposition of the Collateral, such compliance will not be considered to adversely affect the commercial reasonableness of a sale of the Collateral.

F.9. Secured Party may sell the Collateral without giving any warranties as to the Collateral. Secured Party may specifically disclaim any warranties of title or the like. This procedure will not be considered to adversely affect the commercial reasonableness of a sale of the Collateral.

F.10. If Secured Party sells any of the Collateral on credit, Debtor will be credited only with payments actually made by the purchaser and received by Secured Party for application to the indebtedness of the purchaser. If the purchaser fails to pay for the Collateral, Secured Party may resell the Collateral and Debtor will be credited with the proceeds of the sale.

F.11. If Secured Party purchases any of the Collateral being sold, Secured Party may pay for the Collateral by crediting the purchase price against the Obligation.

F.12. Secured Party has no obligation to marshal any assets in favor of Debtor or against or in payment of the Note, any of the Other Obligation[s], or any other obligation owed to Secured Party by Debtor or any other person.

F.13. If the Collateral is sold after default, recitals in the bill of sale or transfer will be prima facie evidence of their truth and all prerequisites to the sale specified by this agreement and by law will be presumed satisfied.

G. General

G.1. Notice is reasonable if it is mailed, postage prepaid, to Debtor at Debtor's Mailing Address at least ten days before any public sale or ten days before the time when the Collateral may be otherwise disposed of without further notice to Debtor.

G.2. This security interest will neither affect nor be affected by any other security for any of the Obligation. Neither extensions of any of the Obligation nor releases of any of the Collateral will affect the priority or validity of this security interest.

G.3. This agreement binds, benefits, and may be enforced by the successors in interest of Secured Party and will bind all persons who become bound as debtors to this agreement. Assignment of any part of the Obligation and Secured Party's delivery of any part of the Collateral will fully discharge Secured Party from responsibility for that part of the Collateral. If such an assignment is made, Debtor will render performance under this agreement to the assignee. Debtor waives and will not assert against any assignee any claims, defenses, or setoffs that Debtor could assert against Secured Party except defenses that cannot be waived. All representations and obligations are joint and several as to each Debtor.

G.4. This agreement may be amended only by an instrument in writing signed by Secured Party and Debtor.

G.5. The unenforceability of any provision of this agreement will not affect the enforceability or validity of any other provision.

G.6. This agreement will be construed according to Texas law, without regard to choice-of-law rules of any jurisdiction. This agreement is to be performed in [**include if applicable in a consumer transaction:** , and has been signed by Debtor in,] the county of Secured Party's Mailing Address.

G.7. Interest on the Obligation secured by this agreement will not exceed the maximum amount of nonusurious interest that may be contracted for, taken, reserved, charged, or received under law. Any interest in excess of that maximum amount will be credited on the principal of the Obligation or, if that has been paid, refunded. On any acceleration or required or permitted prepayment, any such excess will be canceled automatically as of the acceleration or prepayment or, if already paid, credited on the principal of the Obligation or, if the

principal of the Obligation has been paid, refunded. This provision overrides any conflicting provisions in this and all other instruments concerning the Obligation.

G.8. In no event may this agreement secure payment of any debt that may not lawfully be secured by a lien on real estate or create a lien otherwise prohibited by law.

G.9. When the context requires, singular nouns and pronouns include the plural.

G.10. Any term defined in sections 1.101 to 9.709 of the Texas Business and Commerce Code and not defined in this agreement has the meaning given to the term in the Code.

____

[Name of debtor]

Form 9-4

Security Agreement
[Interest in Noncorporate Entity]

Basic Information

Date:

Debtor:

Debtor's Mailing Address:

Secured Party:

Secured Party's Mailing Address:

Classification of Collateral: General intangibles

Collateral:

All of Debtor's interest in the following personal property and all proceeds of that property [**describe the specific collateral as in the following example**]:

a. Debtor's undivided interest as a [general partner/limited partner/member] in and to that certain [general partnership/limited partnership/limited liability company] named [**name of company**] (the "Company"), described in the [[limited/general] partnership agreement/limited liability company [agreement/regulations]] of the Company dated [**date**], by and between Debtor and other [partners/members] of the Company, as amended or modified and in effect (the "Company Agreement"), together with all of Debtor's other rights, title, and interest of every kind and character whatever in and to the Company and under the Company Agreement; and

b. all of Debtor's share of profits, distributions, income, and surplus from the Company and Debtor's interest in specific properties of the Company on dissolution or otherwise.

Obligation

Note

Date:

Original principal amount:

Borrower (Obligor):

Include either or both of the following if applicable.

Other debt/Future advances: The security interest also secures all other present and future debts and liabilities of Debtor and/or Obligor to Secured Party, including future advances.

Other obligation[s]:

Continue with the following.

A. Debtor's Representations Concerning Debtor and Locations

Include one or more of the following paragraphs as applicable and modify paragraph numbers as appropriate.

A.1. [Debtor's place of business/Debtor's chief executive office] is located at [**address, city, state**].

Include the following if the debtor is an individual.

A.2. Debtor's residence is located at [**address, city, state**].

Include the following if the debtor is a corporation, limited partnership, or limited liability company.

A.2. Debtor's state of organization is [Texas/[**state**]], and Debtor's name, as shown in its public organic record, as amended, is exactly as set forth above.

Continue with the following.

A.3. The Company's state of organization is [Texas/[**state**]], and the Company's name, as shown in its organizational documents, as amended, is exactly as set forth above.

A.4. Debtor's records concerning the Collateral are located at [**address, city, state**].

B. Granting Clause

Debtor grants to Secured Party a security interest in the Collateral and all its proceeds to secure the Obligation and all renewals, modifications, and extensions of the Obligation. Debtor authorizes Secured Party to file a financing statement describing the Collateral.

C. Debtor Represents the Following:

C.1. No financing statement covering the Collateral is filed in any public office [**include if the secured party has prefiled a financing statement or otherwise has a financing statement on file:** except any financing statement in favor of Secured Party].

C.2. Debtor owns the Collateral and has the authority to grant this security interest, free from any setoff, claim, restriction, security interest, or encumbrance except liens for taxes not yet due.

C.3. All information about Debtor's financial condition is or will be accurate when provided to Secured Party.

C.4. An accurate copy of the Company Agreement has been delivered to Secured Party. There are no changes to the Company Agreement not reflected in the copy delivered to Secured Party.

C.5. Debtor has obtained the written consent of all persons required under the Company Agreement or otherwise to authorize the security interest created by this agreement and Secured Party's exercise of its rights hereunder. On request of Secured Party, Debtor will deliver to Secured Party an executed original of that consent.

D. Debtor Agrees to—

D.1. Defend the Collateral against all claims adverse to Secured Party's interest; pay all taxes imposed on the Collateral; keep the Collateral free from liens, except for liens in favor of Secured Party or for taxes not yet due; keep the Collateral in Debtor's possession and ownership except as otherwise provided in this agreement; maintain the Collateral in good condition; and protect the Collateral against waste, except for ordinary wear and tear.

D.2. Pay all Secured Party's expenses, including reasonable attorney's fees and legal expenses [**include for a loan transaction subject to Texas Finance Code section 342.502:** assessed by a court], incurred to (a) obtain, preserve, perfect, defend, or enforce this agreement; (b) retake, hold, prepare for disposition, dispose, collect, or enforce the Collateral; or (c) collect or enforce the Obligation. These expenses will bear interest from the date of advance at the rate stated in the Note for matured, unpaid amounts and are payable on demand at the place where the Obligation is payable. These expenses and interest are part of the Obligation and are secured by this agreement.

D.3. Sign and deliver to Secured Party any documents or instruments that Secured Party considers necessary to obtain, maintain, and perfect this security interest in the Collateral.

D.4. Notify Secured Party immediately of any event of default and of any material change (a) in the Collateral, (b) in Debtor's Mailing Address, (c) in the location of any Collateral, (d) in any other representation or warranty in this agreement, or (e) that may affect this security interest, or of any change (f) in Debtor's name or (g) of any location set forth above to another state.

D.5. Use the Collateral primarily according to the stated classification.

D.6. Maintain accurate records of the Collateral at the address set forth above; furnish Secured Party any requested information related to the Collateral; and permit Secured Party to inspect and copy all records relating to the Collateral.

D.7. Perform all obligations to be performed by Debtor under the Company Agreement.

D.8. Notify Secured Party of any default known to Debtor of any other person under the Company Agreement and of any notice of default given under the Company Agreement.

D.9. Enforce the obligations of other persons under the Company Agreement and at Secured Party's request, at Debtor's expense, take action requested by Secured Party to enforce the obligations of other persons and exercise the rights of Debtor under the Company Agreement.

E. Debtor Agrees Not to—

E.1. Sell, transfer, or encumber any of the Collateral [**include if applicable:** , except in the ordinary course of Debtor's business].

Select one of the following.

Include the following if the debtor is a corporation, limited partnership, or limited liability company.

E.2. Change its name or jurisdiction of organization, merge or consolidate with any person, or convert to a different entity without notifying Secured Party in advance and taking action to continue the perfected status of the security interest in the Collateral.

Or

Include the following if the debtor is an entity other than a corporation, limited partnership, or limited liability company.

E.2. Change the state in which Debtor's place of business (or chief executive office if Debtor has more than one place of business) is located, change its name, or convert to a different entity without notifying Secured Party in advance and taking action to continue the perfected status of the security interest in the Collateral.

Or

Include the following if the debtor is an individual.

E.2. Change Debtor's name or state of residence without notifying Secured Party in advance and taking action to continue the perfected status of the security interest in the Collateral.

Continue with the following.

E.3. Consent to or approve any modification of the Company Agreement.

E.4. Compromise or reduce any payment or distribution to be made to Debtor on the Collateral.

F. Secured Party Not Liable

Debtor remains liable under the Company Agreement for all its obligations thereunder. Secured Party has no liability thereunder because of this agreement. Secured Party is not liable, because of this agreement, for any obligation of Debtor under the Company Agreement.

G. Default and Remedies

G.1. A default exists if—

a. Debtor, Obligor, or any secondary obligor fails to timely pay or perform any obligation or covenant in any written agreement between Secured Party and any of Debtor, Obligor, or secondary obligor;

b. any representation in this agreement or in any other written agreement between Secured Party and any of Debtor, Obligor, or secondary obligor is materially false when made;

c. a receiver is appointed for Debtor, Obligor, any secondary obligor, or any Collateral;

d. any Collateral is assigned for the benefit of creditors;

e. a bankruptcy or insolvency proceeding is commenced by Debtor, the Company, a partnership in which Debtor is a general partner, Obligor, or any secondary obligor;

f. a bankruptcy or insolvency proceeding is commenced against Debtor, the Company, a partnership in which Debtor is a general partner, Obligor, or any secondary obligor, and the proceeding continues without dismissal for sixty days, the party against whom the proceeding is commenced admits the material allegations of the petition against it, or an order for relief is entered;

g. any of the following parties is terminated, begins to wind up its affairs, is authorized to terminate or wind up its affairs by its governing body or persons, or any event occurs or condition exists that permits the termination or winding up of the affairs of any of the following parties: Debtor; the Company; a partnership of which Debtor is a general partner; Obligor; or any secondary obligor; or

h. any Collateral is impaired by loss, theft, damage, levy and execution, issuance of an official writ or order of seizure, or destruction, unless it is promptly replaced with collateral of like kind and quality or restored to its former condition.

G.2. If a default exists, Secured Party may—

a. demand, collect, convert, redeem, settle, compromise, receipt for, realize on, sue for, and adjust the Collateral either in Secured Party's or Debtor's name, as Secured Party desires, or take control of any proceeds of the Collateral and apply the proceeds against the Obligation;

b. take possession of any Collateral not already in Secured Party's possession, without demand or legal process, and for that purpose Debtor grants Secured Party the right to enter any premises where the Collateral may be located;

c. without taking possession, sell, lease, or otherwise dispose of the Collateral at any public or private sale in accordance with law;

d. exercise any rights and remedies granted by law or this agreement;

e. notify obligors on the Collateral to pay Secured Party directly;

f. as Debtor's agent, make any endorsements in Debtor's name and on Debtor's behalf of any proceeds of the Collateral; or

g. exercise and enforce all rights, including voting rights, available to an owner of the Collateral.

G.3. Foreclosure of this security interest by suit does not limit Secured Party's remedies, including the right to sell the Collateral under the terms of this agreement. Secured Party may exercise all remedies at the same or different times, and no remedy is a defense to any other. Secured Party's rights and remedies include all those granted by law and those specified in this agreement.

G.4. Secured Party's delay in exercising, partial exercise of, or failure to exercise any of its remedies or rights does not waive Secured Party's rights to subsequently exercise those remedies or rights. Secured Party's waiver of any default does not waive any other default by Debtor. Secured Party's waiver of any right in this agreement or of any default is binding only if it is in writing. Secured Party may remedy any default without waiving it.

G.5. Secured Party has no obligation to clean or otherwise prepare the Collateral for sale.

G.6. Secured Party has no obligation to collect any of the Collateral and is not liable for failure to collect any of the Collateral, for failure to preserve any right pertaining to the Collateral, or for any act or omission on the part of Secured Party or Secured Party's officers, agents, or employees, except willful misconduct.

G.7. Secured Party has no obligation to satisfy the Obligation by attempting to collect the Obligation from any other person liable for it. Secured Party may release, modify, or waive any collateral provided by any other person to secure any of the Obligation. If Secured Party attempts to collect the Obligation from any other person liable for it or releases, modifies, or waives any collateral provided by any other person, that will not affect Secured Party's rights against Debtor. Debtor waives any right Debtor may have to require Secured Party to pursue any third person for any of the Obligation.

G.8. If Secured Party must comply with any applicable state or federal law requirements in connection with a disposition of the Collateral, such compliance will not be considered to adversely affect the commercial reasonableness of a sale of the Collateral.

G.9. Secured Party may sell the Collateral without giving any warranties as to the Collateral. Secured Party may specifically disclaim any warranties of title or the like. This procedure will not be considered to adversely affect the commercial reasonableness of a sale of the Collateral.

G.10. If Secured Party sells any of the Collateral on credit, Debtor will be credited only with payments actually made by the purchaser and received by Secured Party for application to the indebtedness of the purchaser. If the purchaser fails to pay for the Collateral, Secured Party may resell the Collateral and Debtor will be credited with the proceeds of the sale.

G.11. If Secured Party purchases any of the Collateral being sold, Secured Party may pay for the Collateral by crediting the purchase price against the Obligation.

G.12. Secured Party has no obligation to marshal any assets in favor of Debtor or against or in payment of the Note, any of the Other Obligation[s], or any other obligation owed to Secured Party by Debtor or any other person.

G.13. If the Collateral is sold after default, recitals in the bill of sale or transfer will be prima facie evidence of their truth and all prerequisites to the sale specified by this agreement and by law will be presumed satisfied.

H. General

H.1. Notice is reasonable if it is mailed, postage prepaid, to Debtor at Debtor's Mailing Address at least ten days before any public sale or ten days before the time when the Collateral may be otherwise disposed of without further notice to Debtor.

H.2. This security interest will neither affect nor be affected by any other security for any of the Obligation. Neither extensions of any of the Obligation nor releases of any of the Collateral will affect the priority or validity of this security interest.

H.3. This agreement binds, benefits, and may be enforced by the successors in interest of Secured Party and will bind all persons who become bound as debtors to this agreement. Assignment of any part of the Obligation and Secured Party's delivery of any part of the Collateral will fully discharge Secured Party from responsibility for that part of the Collateral. If such an assignment is made, Debtor will render performance under this agreement to the assignee. Debtor waives and will not assert against any assignee any claims, defenses, or setoffs that Debtor could assert against Secured Party except defenses that cannot be waived. All representations and obligations are joint and several as to each Debtor.

H.4. This agreement may be amended only by an instrument in writing signed by Secured Party and Debtor.

H.5. The unenforceability of any provision of this agreement will not affect the enforceability or validity of any other provision.

H.6. This agreement will be construed according to Texas law, without regard to choice-of-law rules of any jurisdiction. This agreement is to be performed in [**include if applicable in a consumer transaction:** , and has been signed by Debtor in,] the county of Secured Party's Mailing Address.

H.7. Interest on the Obligation secured by this agreement will not exceed the maximum amount of nonusurious interest that may be contracted for, taken, reserved, charged, or received under law. Any interest in excess of that maximum amount will be credited on the principal of the Obligation or, if that has been paid, refunded. On any acceleration or required or permitted prepayment, any such excess will be canceled automatically as of the acceleration or prepayment or, if already paid, credited on the principal of the Obligation or, if the

principal of the Obligation has been paid, refunded. This provision overrides any conflicting provisions in this and all other instruments concerning the Obligation.

H.8. In no event may this agreement secure payment of any debt that may not lawfully be secured by a lien on real estate or create a lien otherwise prohibited by law.

H.9. When the context requires, singular nouns and pronouns include the plural.

H.10. Any term defined in sections 1.101 to 9.709 of the Texas Business and Commerce Code and not defined in this agreement has the meaning given to the term in the Code.

____

[Name of debtor]

Form 9-5

Addendum to Security Agreement
[Farm Products]

Basic Information

Date:

Debtor:

Secured Party:

Date of Security Agreement:

This addendum applies to and is incorporated in the security agreement.

A. Supplemental Description of Farm Products Collateral

A.1. Type and description of farm products collateral: [**describe collateral and specify farm products collateral type according to USDA classification system at 9 C.F.R. § 205.206(a)**].

A.2. Amount of farm products collateral:

A.3. Crop year of farm products collateral:

A.4. [County/Counties] where farm products collateral located:

A.5. Real property where farm products collateral located:

A.6. Additional collateral:

The Collateral includes, with respect to both the Collateral and all products, increase, or offspring of the Collateral, the following: all seed, seed plants, and propagative materials of crops or plants; all sale or other proceeds; all insurance proceeds for loss, damage, or theft; all claims or causes of action relating to use, sale, lease, damage, or loss; all contracts, warehouse receipts, bills of lading, assignments, receipts, claims, drafts, checks, or causes of action relating to or representing any sale of the Collateral; all fees, charges, or things of value earned by livestock for reproductive services or uses of any kind; all copyrights and patents in any way relating to or arising out of the Collateral; all future-acquired property of Debtor of the same type or kind as the Collateral; and all additions to or replacement of the Collateral.

B. Debtor Agrees:

B.1. Conditions for Sale of Collateral. This security interest may not be waived or released unless the sale or other disposition is approved in advance in writing by Secured Party for the full value of the Collateral and the consideration from the sale or other disposition is actually delivered to Secured Party and finally paid. Debtor may not transfer or encumber the Collateral or engage in any transaction involving the Collateral with any buyer, commission merchant, or selling agent without seven days' prior written notice to Secured Party and without securing the prior written consent of Secured Party. Debtor may make no sale or other disposition of any of the Collateral unless the proceeds are paid by an instrument jointly payable to Debtor and Secured Party and delivered to Secured Party. Debtor will immediately remit to Secured Party all proceeds of the sale or other disposition or as much of the proceeds as necessary to fully discharge the Obligation.

B.2. Conditions for Collateral Storage. The Collateral may not be placed in storage at any storage facility issuing warehouse receipts for the Collateral without seven days' prior written notice to Secured Party. Any warehouse receipts issued for the Collateral must be nonnegotiable warehouse receipts naming Secured Party as the person entitled to possession of the Collateral. Debtor must immediately deliver all such receipts to Secured Party. Before placing any of the Collateral in storage, Debtor must advise the storage facility of the security interest of Secured Party in the Collateral.

B.3. Compliance with Federal Food Security Act. Debtor agrees to furnish Secured Party a list of the names and addresses of every buyer, commission merchant, and selling agent to or through whom Debtor may make any sale or other disposition of the Collateral. "Commission merchant" and "selling agent" have those meanings set out in 7 U.S.C. section 1631. Debtor agrees to notify Secured Party in writing of the identity of any buyer, selling agent, or commission merchant for any of the Collateral at least seven days before the sale or other disposition of any part of the Collateral as may be authorized by the security agreement. If Debtor makes an unauthorized sale or transfer of the Collateral, Debtor must account to Secured Party for the proceeds of the sale or other disposition within ten days.

NOTICE: VIOLATION OF THE FOREGOING MAY CONSTITUTE A CRIMINAL ACT UNDER THE PROVISIONS OF 7 U.S.C. SECTION 1631.

B.4. Additional Defaults. In addition to the defaults listed in the security agreement, a default exists if—

a. the Collateral is not maintained, preserved, or protected according to the standards of the industry or good agricultural husbandry; or

b. Debtor makes any sale or other disposition of any of the Collateral without complying with the provisions of this addendum.

B.5. Additional Remedies on Default. If a default exists, Secured Party, in addition to the remedies provided in the security agreement, may—

a. complete any and all growing, grazing, fattening, or other farming or ranching operations in connection with the Collateral reasonable to its sale or other disposition; or

b. incur reasonable expenses on behalf of Debtor in connection with the retaking, holding, storing, growing, nurturing, fattening, or grazing of the Collateral and in preparation of the Collateral for sale or other disposition.

Form 9-6

Prenotification Statement

[Notice of Security Interest]

Basic Information

To: [**name of buyer, commission merchant, or selling agent**]

Date:

Debtor:

Debtor's Mailing Address:

Debtor's Social Security No. or Federal Tax ID No.:

Secured Party:

Secured Party's Mailing Address:

Collateral:

1. Type and description of farm products collateral: [**describe collateral and specify farm products collateral type according to USDA classification system at 9 C.F.R. § 205.206(a)**].

2. Amount of farm products collateral:

3. Crop year of farm products collateral:

4. [County/Counties] where farm products collateral located:

5. Real property where farm products collateral located:

6. Additional collateral:

The Collateral includes, with respect to both the Collateral and all products, increase, or offspring of the Collateral, the following: all seed, seed plants, and propagative materials of crops or plants; all sale or other proceeds; all insurance proceeds for loss, damage, or theft; all claims or causes of action relating to use, sale, lease, damage, or loss; all contracts, warehouse receipts, bills of lading, assignments, receipts, claims, drafts, checks, or causes of action relating to or representing any sale of the Collateral; all fees, charges, or things of value earned by livestock for reproductive services or uses of any kind; all copyrights and patents in any way relating to or arising out of the Collateral; all future-acquired property of Debtor of the same type or kind as the Collateral; and all additions to or replacement of the Collateral.

Conditions for Waiver or Release of Security Interest

The security interest may not be waived or released unless the sale or other disposition is approved in advance in writing by Secured Party for the full value of the Collateral to be sold (as that value may be determined by Secured Party) and the consideration from the sale or other disposition is actually delivered to Secured Party and finally paid. Debtor may not transfer or encumber the Collateral or engage in any transaction involving the Collateral with any buyer, commission merchant, or selling agent without seven days' prior written notice to Secured Party and without securing the prior written consent of Secured Party. Any contract or agreement for the sale or other disposition of any of the Collateral must provide that the sales proceeds will be paid by an instrument jointly payable to Debtor and Secured Party and delivered to Secured Party. Debtor will immediately remit to Secured Party all proceeds of the sale or other disposition or as much of the proceeds as necessary to fully discharge the obligation.

Notice of Security Interest

Debtor or Secured Party has identified you as a potential buyer, commission merchant, or selling agent of the Collateral. You are hereby given notice pursuant to the Food Security

Act of 1985 that Debtor has given a security interest in the Collateral to Secured Party. This security interest covers the Collateral wherever located.

You will be subject to the security interest in the Collateral unless the Conditions for Waiver or Release of Security Interest are satisfied.

Satisfaction of the Conditions for Waiver or Release of Security Interest will not affect the security interest of the Secured Party in any proceeds from the sale or other disposition of the Collateral.

____

[Name of secured party]

Form 9-7

Listing of Potential Buyers, Commission Merchants, and Selling Agents

Basic Information

Date:

Debtor:

Debtor's Mailing Address:

Debtor's Social Security No. or Federal Tax ID No.:

Secured Party:

Secured Party's Mailing Address:

Collateral:

1. Type and description of farm products collateral: [**describe collateral and specify farm products collateral type according to USDA classification system at 9 C.F.R. § 205.206(a)**].

2. Amount of farm products collateral:

3. Crop year of farm products collateral:

4. [County/Counties] where farm products collateral located:

5. Real property where farm products collateral located:

6. Additional collateral:

The Collateral includes, with respect to both the Collateral and all products, increase, or offspring of the Collateral, the following: all seed, seed plants, and propagative materials of crops or plants; all sale or other proceeds; all insurance proceeds for loss, damage, or theft; all claims or causes of action relating to use, sale, lease, damage, or loss; all contracts, warehouse receipts, bills of lading, assignments, receipts, claims, drafts, checks, or causes of action relating to or representing any sale of the Collateral; all fees, charges, or things of value earned by livestock for reproductive services or uses of any kind; all copyrights and patents in any way relating to or arising out of the Collateral; all future-acquired property of Debtor of the same type or kind as the Collateral; and all additions to or replacement of the Collateral.

Debtor Agrees

Debtor is giving to Secured Party this list of potential buyers, commission merchants, and selling agents to or through whom Debtor may make a sale or other disposition of the Collateral. "Selling agent" and "commission merchant" have those meanings set out in 7 U.S.C. section 1631. Debtor is aware that any sale or other disposition of the Collateral to or through anyone not on this list is illegal unless Debtor notifies Secured Party in writing of the identity of the buyer, commission merchant, or selling agent at least seven days before the sale or other disposition or Debtor accounts to Secured Party for the proceeds of the sale within ten days after the sale or other disposition. Debtor agrees to keep this list current and to promptly notify Secured Party of any changes to this list. Debtor and Secured Party intend that the terms of this listing of potential buyers, commission merchants, and selling agents become part of the security agreement between the parties.

Debtor agrees that the Collateral may not be sold or otherwise disposed of free of the security interest of Secured Party unless the conditions for waiver or release of the security interest are satisfied.

List

List of Potential Buyers, Commission Merchants, and Selling Agents: [**list, including names, addresses, and telephone numbers**].

____

[**Name of debtor**]

Form 9-8

Collateral Transfer of Note and Lien

Basic Information

Date:

Debtor:

Debtor's Mailing Address:

Secured Party:

Secured Party's Mailing Address:

Classification of Collateral: Instrument

Collateral (including all accessions): All of Debtor's interest in the Collateral Note and the Collateral Note Security.

Collateral Note: $[**amount**] Note executed by [**maker**] and payable to the order of [**payee**] dated [**date**].

Current balance:

Collateral Note Security: Deed of Trust dated [**date**], recorded in [**recording data**].

Property description:

Obligation

Note in the amount of $[**amount**] executed by [**maker**] and payable to the order of [**payee**] dated [**date**].

Include either or both of the following if applicable.

Other debt/Future advances: The security interest also secures all other present and future debts and liabilities of Debtor to Secured Party, including future advances.

Other obligation:

Continue with the following.

Collateral Note Payments: All payments on the Collateral Note are to be made directly [to Secured Party/to Debtor until after the occurrence of an event of default, at which time Secured Party may notify the Collateral Note maker to make all future payments to Secured Party].

A. Granting Clause

Debtor grants to Secured Party a security interest in the Collateral and all its proceeds to secure Debtor's Obligation and all renewals of any of the Obligation.

B. Deliveries

Simultaneously with Debtor's execution and delivery to Secured Party of this agreement, Debtor has endorsed and delivered to Secured Party the original Collateral Note, thereby making Secured Party the person entitled to enforce the Collateral Note.

C. Debtor Represents the Following:

C.1. Debtor [**include if applicable:** owns the Collateral and] has the authority to grant this security interest, free from any setoff, claim, restriction, security interest, or encumbrance except liens for taxes not yet due.

C.2. All information about Debtor's financial condition is or will be accurate when provided to Secured Party.

C.3. The current balance of the Collateral Note is correct.

C.4. The Collateral Note has not been modified and is not in default.

C.5. There are no defenses or offsets to the Collateral Note.

C.6. The lien of the Collateral Note Security is a first lien.

C.7. The Collateral represents the valid, legally enforceable obligation of the Collateral Note maker.

C.8. Debtor will keep the records of payments on the Collateral Note at Debtor's Mailing Address.

D. Debtor Agrees to—

D.1. Defend the Collateral against all claims adverse to Secured Party's interest and keep the Collateral free from liens.

D.2. Pay all of Secured Party's expenses incurred, including reasonable attorney's fees and legal expenses [**include the following for a loan subject to Texas Finance Code section 342.502:** assessed by a court], to (a) obtain, preserve, perfect, defend, or enforce this agreement; (b) dispose of, collect, or enforce the Collateral; or (c) collect or enforce the Obligation. These expenses will bear interest from the date of advance at the highest rate allowed by law and are payable on demand at the place where the Obligation is payable. These expenses and interest will become part of the Obligation and will be secured by this agreement.

D.3. Sign any documents that Secured Party considers necessary to obtain, maintain, and perfect this security interest.

D.4. Notify Secured Party immediately of any material change in the Collateral; change in Debtor's name, address, or location; change in any representation in this agreement; change that may affect this security interest; or any default.

D.5. Maintain accurate records of the Collateral; furnish Secured Party any requested information related to the Collateral; and allow Secured Party to inspect and copy all records relating to the Collateral.

D.6. Perform all obligations required under the Collateral Note Security.

D.7. Preserve the liability of all obligors on the Collateral and preserve the priority of all security for the Collateral.

D.8. On Secured Party's demand, deposit all payments received as proceeds of the Collateral in a special bank account designated by Secured Party, who alone will have power of withdrawal.

D.9. Cause the Collateral Note maker to pay and perform all obligations under the Collateral Note and the Collateral Note Security and inform Secured Party immediately of default in the payment or performance of the Collateral Note.

E. Debtor Agrees Not to—

E.1. Renew, extend, or modify the Collateral Note or grant releases of any part of the property securing the Collateral Note.

E.2. Modify any terms in the Collateral Note Security.

E.3. Commingle any payments on the Collateral with any of Debtor's other funds or property.

F. Default and Remedies

F.1. A default exists if—

a. Debtor fails to timely pay or perform any Obligation, covenant, or liability in any written agreement between Debtor and Secured Party;

b. any representation in this agreement is materially false when made;

c. a receiver is appointed for Debtor or any of the Collateral;

d. the Collateral is assigned for the benefit of creditors;

e. to the extent permitted by law, a bankruptcy or insolvency proceeding is commenced against or by any of the following parties: Debtor; the Collateral Note maker; any partnership of which Debtor is a general partner; or any maker, drawer, acceptor, endorser, guarantor, surety, accommodation party, or other person liable on or for any part of the Obligation;

f. any of the following parties is terminated: Debtor; the Collateral Note maker; any partnership of which Debtor is a general partner; or any maker, drawer, acceptor, endorser, guarantor, surety, accommodation party, or other person liable on or for any part of the Obligation; or

g. default exists under the Collateral Note or the Collateral Note Security.

F.2. Secured Party may at any time—

a. take control of any proceeds of the Collateral;

b. release any Collateral in Secured Party's possession to any debtor, temporarily or otherwise;

c. take control of proceeds of insurance on the Collateral Note Security and reduce any part of the Obligation accordingly or permit Debtor to use such funds to repair or replace damaged or destroyed Collateral covered by insurance;

d. demand, collect, convert, redeem, settle, compromise, receipt for, realize on, sue for, and adjust the Collateral either in Secured Party's or Debtor's name, as Secured Party desires; or

e. exercise all other rights available to an owner of such Collateral.

F.3. If a default exists, Secured Party may—

a. declare the unpaid principal and earned interest of the Obligation immediately due in whole or part;

b. enforce the Obligation; and

c. exercise any rights and remedies granted by law or this agreement.

F.4. Foreclosure of this security interest by suit does not limit Secured Party's remedies, including the right to sell the Collateral under the terms of this agreement. Secured Party may exercise all remedies at the same or different times, and no remedy is a defense to any other. Secured Party's rights and remedies include all those granted by law or otherwise, in addition to those specified in this agreement.

F.5. If the Collateral is sold after default, recitals in the bill of sale or transfer will be prima facie evidence of their truth and all prerequisites to the sale specified by this agreement and by law will be presumed satisfied.

G. Collateral Note/Enforcement of Power of Sale

G.1. Debtor has endorsed and delivered the Collateral Note to Secured Party. Secured Party is the holder of the Collateral Note, the person entitled to enforce the Collateral Note, and the sole party with power to appoint a substitute trustee or request the trustee to act. Any foreclosure action requested by Debtor is void.

G.2. Any foreclosure sale under the Collateral Note Security will be at such time and on such terms as Secured Party may, in its discretion, approve. If Secured Party approves a bid from Debtor without payment in full of the Collateral Note, Debtor must provide a mortgagee's title insurance policy with only such exceptions as Secured Party approves and execute such additional security documents as Secured Party may require.

G.3. Debtor assigns, transfers, and conveys to Secured Party all amounts due on the Collateral Note. Collateral Note maker is directed to make payments on the Collateral Note in accordance with the Collateral Note payments provision above.

G.4. Debtor indemnifies Secured Party from all claims made against or incurred by Secured Party from any action in connection with the Collateral Note or the Collateral Note Security documents.

H. General

H.1. Notice is reasonable if it is mailed, postage prepaid, to Debtor at Debtor's Mailing Address at least ten days before any public sale or ten days before the time when the Collateral may be otherwise disposed of without further notice to Debtor.

H.2. This security interest will neither affect nor be affected by any other security for any of the Obligation. Neither extensions of any of the Obligation nor releases of any of the Collateral will affect the priority or validity of this security interest as to any third person.

H.3. This agreement binds, benefits, and may be enforced by the successors in interest of the parties, except as otherwise provided. Assignment of any part of the Obligation and Secured Party's delivery of any part of the Collateral will fully discharge Secured Party from responsibility for that part of the Collateral. All representations and obligations are joint and several as to each Debtor.

H.4. Secured Party's delay in exercising, partial exercise of, or failure to exercise any of its remedies or rights does not waive Secured Party's rights to subsequently exercise those remedies or rights. Secured Party's waiver of any default does not waive any further default by Debtor. Secured Party's waiver of any right in this agreement or of any default is binding only if it is in writing. Secured Party may remedy any default without waiving it.

H.5. This agreement may be amended only by an instrument in writing signed by Secured Party and Debtor.

H.6. The unenforceability of any provision of this agreement will not affect the enforceability or validity of any other provision.

H.7. This agreement will be construed according to Texas law. This agreement is to be performed in the county of Secured Party's Mailing Address.

H.8. Interest on the Obligation secured by this agreement will not exceed the maximum amount of nonusurious interest that may be contracted for, taken, reserved, charged, or received under law. Any interest in excess of that maximum amount will be credited on the principal of the Obligation or, if that has been paid, refunded. On any acceleration or required or permitted prepayment, any such excess will be canceled automatically as of the acceleration or prepayment or, if already paid, credited on the principal of the Obligation or, if the principal of the Obligation has been paid, refunded. This provision overrides any conflicting provisions in this and all other instruments concerning the Obligation.

H.9. In no event may this agreement secure payment of any debt that may not lawfully be secured by a lien on real estate or create a lien otherwise prohibited by law.

H.10. When the context requires, singular nouns and pronouns include the plural.

____
[Name of debtor]

Form 9-9

Collateral Note Maker's Estoppel Certificate

Basic Information

Date:

Debtor:

Debtor's Mailing Address:

Secured Party:

Secured Party's Mailing Address:

Collateral Note: Note dated [**date**], in the original principal amount of $[**amount**], executed by Collateral Note Maker and payable to Debtor as therein provided.

Collateral Note Maker:

Collateral Note Maker's Mailing Address:

Deed of Trust: Deed of trust securing Collateral Note, recorded in [**recording data**] of the real property records of [**county**] County, Texas.

Real Property:

A. Reason for and Reliance on Certificate

Debtor has requested that Secured Party make a loan to be secured by the Collateral Note, and Secured Party has agreed to do so. As a condition for this loan, Secured Party requires Collateral Note Maker to verify the following information concerning the Collateral

Note. Collateral Note Maker understands that Secured Party is relying on this information in connection with the closing of the loan.

B. Representations

Collateral Note Maker represents to Secured Party that—

B.1. True and complete copies of the Collateral Note and Deed of Trust are attached as Exhibits [**exhibit numbers/letters**].

B.2. The Collateral Note and Deed of Trust have not been modified.

B.3. The present unpaid balance of the Collateral Note is $[**amount**].

B.4. The amount of accrued unpaid interest on the Collateral Note is $[**amount**].

B.5. Collateral Note Maker has no claims, setoffs, or defenses to payment of the Collateral Note or against Debtor.

B.6. No default presently exists under the terms of the Collateral Note or Deed of Trust or any other loan documents.

Select one of the following.

B.7. No amount is being held in escrow by Debtor.

Or

B.7. The amount of $[**amount**] is presently being held in escrow by Debtor for the payment of taxes, insurance, or both, under the terms of the Collateral Note and Deed of Trust.

Continue with the following.

C. Agreement

Collateral Note Maker agrees with Secured Party that—

C.1. The Collateral Note and Deed of Trust will not be modified without Secured Party's prior written consent.

C.2. Collateral Note Maker has been furnished with a copy of the collateral transfer of note and lien dated [**date**] executed by Debtor to Secured Party and agrees to abide by its terms.

C.3. Secured Party is the current holder of the Collateral Note and is the only party entitled to receive payments on the Collateral Note.

Select one of the following.

C.4. Collateral Note Maker will make regularly scheduled monthly payments on the Collateral Note only to Debtor. On written request of Secured Party, Collateral Note Maker will make all payments on the Collateral Note directly to Secured Party.

Or

C.4. Collateral Note Maker will make all payments on the Collateral Note directly to Secured Party.

Continue with the following.

D. Debtor's Consent

Debtor joins in this agreement to evidence its consent to Collateral Note Maker's obligations hereunder.

____

[**Name of collateral note maker**]

____
[Name of debtor]

Include acknowledgments and attach exhibits.

Form 9-10

Consent and Agreement

Basic Information

Date:

Secured Party:

Secured Party's Mailing Address:

Debtor:

Company:

Company's Mailing Address:

Company is a [[general/limited] partnership/limited liability company] organized under the laws of the state of [Texas/[**state**]].

A. Background

Debtor and Secured Party are entering into a security agreement covering Debtor's interest in the Company.

The [partnership agreement/regulations/limited liability company agreement] of the Company (the "Company Agreement") contains terms restricting assignment of interests in the Company by its [partners/members] and conditioning effectiveness of any such assignment on the consent of the [general partner/managing general partner/general partner and a majority in interest of the limited partners/partners/manager/managing member/majority in interest of the members/members] of the Company. The undersigned and the Company are the persons whose consent must be obtained under the terms of the Company Agreement.

B. Agreement

The Company and the undersigned severally agree for the benefit of Secured Party as follows:

B.1. The Company and each of the undersigned consent to the creation, attachment, and perfection of a security interest in Debtor's interest in the Company and other collateral under Debtor's security agreement with Secured Party.

B.2. The Company agrees that if Secured Party delivers to the Company a notice stating that a default exists under Debtor's security agreement with Secured Party and directing the Company to deliver to Secured Party any profits, income, distributions (whether in money, specific property of the Company, or other assets), withdrawal, liquidation, and redemption proceeds, and any other proceeds payable to Debtor from time to time in respect of Debtor's interest in the Company, the Company will comply with that directive. The Company is not required to inquire as to or determine the validity of the factual matters in any such notice or the genuineness of any such notice. The undersigned consent to the Company's compliance with any such notice.

B.3. The undersigned consent to Secured Party's exercise of any of its rights and remedies under Debtor's security agreement with Secured Party, including the right to exercise any voting, consensual, or other management rights of Debtor and the right to sell or otherwise dispose of any of the collateral granted by Debtor under Debtor's security agreement with Secured Party. The undersigned agree that on Secured Party's exercise of any of its rights and remedies under Debtor's security agreement with Secured Party, any acquirer (whether by foreclosure or otherwise) of the [partnership/membership] interest of Debtor will become, without further consent by any of the undersigned, a substitute [partner/member] of the Company under the Company Agreement and the Company's other organizational documents, entitled to exercise any of the rights and remedies of Debtor thereunder; provided that such acquirer will not be liable for obligations of Debtor to contribute capital to the Company that arose before the acquirer's acquisition of Debtor's [partnership/membership] interest.

COMPANY:

____

[Name of company]

By: ____________________________

____

[Name and capacity]

____

[Name and capacity]

Form 9-11

UCC1 Financing Statement

Instructions for UCC Financing Statement (Form UCC1)

Please type or print this form. Be sure it is completely legible. Forms with handwritten entries may be rejected. Read and follow all Instructions.

Fill in form very carefully; mistakes may have important legal consequences. If you have questions, consult your attorney. The filing office cannot give legal advice.

Unless specifically required by applicable state law, DO NOT include social security numbers, driver's license numbers, financial account numbers or other non-public personally identifiable information anywhere on the form.

Form instructions are intended for paper forms. Electronic UCC filing parameters and instructions may differ from the below instructions.

Send completed form and any attachments to the filing office, with the required fee.

ITEM INSTRUCTIONS

A and B. To assist filing offices that might wish to communicate with filer, filer may provide information in item A and item B. These items are optional.
C. Complete item C if filer desires an acknowledgment sent to them.

1. Debtor's name. Carefully review applicable statutory guidance about providing the debtor's name. Enter only one Debtor name in item 1 -- either an organization's name (1a) or an individual's name (1b). If any part of the Individual Debtor's name will not fit in line 1b, check the box in item 1, leave all of item 1 blank, check the box in item 9 of the Financing Statement Addendum (Form UCC1Ad) and enter the Individual Debtor name in item 10 of the Financing Statement Addendum (Form UCC1Ad). Enter Debtor's correct name. Do not abbreviate words that are not already abbreviated in the Debtor's name. If a portion of the Debtor's name consists of only an initial or an abbreviation rather than a full word, enter only the abbreviation or the initial. If the collateral is held in a trust and the Debtor name is the name of the trust, enter trust name in the Organization's Name box in item 1a.

1a. Organization Debtor Name. "Organization Name" means the name of an entity that is not a natural person. A sole proprietorship is not an organization, even if the individual proprietor does business under a trade name. If Debtor is a registered organization (e.g., corporation, limited partnership, limited liability company), it is advisable to examine Debtor's current filed public organic records to determine Debtor's correct name. Trade name is insufficient. If a corporate ending (e.g., corporation, limited partnership, limited liability company) is part of the Debtor's name, it must be included. Do not use words that are not part of the Debtor's name.

1b. Individual Debtor Name. "Individual Name" means the name of a natural person; this includes the name of an individual doing business as a sole proprietorship, whether or not operating under a trade name. The term includes the name of a decedent where collateral is being administered by a personal representative of the decedent. The term does not include the name of an entity, even if it contains, as part of the entity's name, the name of an individual. Prefixes (e.g., Mr., Mrs., Ms.) and titles (e.g., M.D.) are generally not part of an individual name. Indications of lineage (e.g., Jr., Sr., III) generally are not part of the individual's name, but may be entered in the Suffix box. Enter individual Debtor's surname (family name) in Individual's Surname box, first personal name in First Personal Name box, and all additional names in Additional Name(s)/Initial(s) box.
If a Debtor's name consists of only a single word, enter that word in Individual's Surname box and leave other boxes blank.

For both organization and individual Debtors. Do not use Debtor's trade name, DBA, AKA, FKA, division name, etc. in place of or combined with Debtor's correct name; filer may add such other names as additional Debtors if desired (but this is neither required nor recommended).

For both organization and individual Debtors. Name variations may be optionally provided as additional debtors. Do not combine multiple names in one section. Provide each name variation and address as described in the instructions for item 2 below.

1c. Enter a mailing address for the Debtor named in item 1a or 1b.

2. Additional Debtor's name. If an additional Debtor is included, complete item 2, determined and formatted per Instruction 1. For additional Debtors, attach either Addendum (Form UCC1Ad) or Additional Party (Form UCC1AP) and follow Instruction 1 for determining and formatting additional names.

3. Secured Party's name. Enter name and mailing address for Secured Party or full Assignee who will be the Secured Party of record. For additional Secured Parties, attach either Addendum (Form UCC1Ad) or Additional Party (Form UCC1AP). Optional: Attach Addendum (Form UCC1Ad) giving Assignor Secured Party's name and mailing address in item 11.

4. Collateral. Use item 4 to indicate the collateral covered by this financing statement. If space in item 4 is insufficient, continue the collateral description in item 12 of the Addendum (Form UCC1Ad) or attach additional page(s) and incorporate by reference in item 12 (e.g., See Exhibit A).

Note: If this financing statement covers timber to be cut, covers as-extracted collateral, and/or is filed as a fixture filing, attach Addendum (Form UCC1Ad) and complete the required information in items 13, 14, 15, and 16. Consult applicable state UCC law for filing location.

5. If collateral is held in a trust or being administered by a decedent's personal representative, check the appropriate box in item 5. If more than one Debtor has an interest in the described collateral and the check box does not apply to the interest of all Debtors, the filer should consider filing a separate Financing Statement (Form UCC1) for each Debtor.

6a. If this financing statement relates to a Public-Finance Transaction, Manufactured-Home Transaction, or a Debtor is a Transmitting Utility, check the appropriate box in item 6a. If a Debtor is a Transmitting Utility and the initial financing statement is filed in connection with a Public-Finance Transaction or Manufactured-Home Transaction, check only that a Debtor is a Transmitting Utility.

6b. If this is an Agricultural Lien (as defined in applicable state's enactment of the Uniform Commercial Code) or if this is not a UCC security interest filing (e.g., a tax lien, judgment lien, etc.), check the appropriate box in item 6b and attach any other items required under applicable law.

7. Alternative Designation. If filer desires (at filer's option) to use the designations lessee and lessor, consignee and consignor, seller and buyer (such as in the case of the sale of a payment intangible, promissory note, account or chattel paper), bailee and bailor, or licensee and licensor instead of Debtor and Secured Party, check the appropriate box in item 7.

8. Optional Filer Reference Data. This item is optional and is for filer's use only to provide reference information the filer may find useful.

UCC FINANCING STATEMENT

FOLLOW INSTRUCTIONS

A. NAME & PHONE OF CONTACT AT SUBMITTER (optional)

B. E-MAIL CONTACT AT SUBMITTER (optional)

C. SEND ACKNOWLEDGMENT TO: (Name and Address)

SEE BELOW FOR SECURED PARTY CONTACT INFORMATION

THE ABOVE SPACE IS FOR FILING OFFICE USE ONLY

1\. DEBTOR'S NAME: Provide only <u>one</u> Debtor name (1a or 1b) (use exact, full name; do not omit, modify, or abbreviate any part of the Debtor's name); if any part of the Individual Debtor's name will not fit in line 1b, leave all of item 1 blank, check here ☐ and provide the Individual Debtor information in item 10 of the Financing Statement Addendum (Form UCC1Ad)

1a. ORGANIZATION'S NAME				
OR 1b. INDIVIDUAL'S SURNAME	FIRST PERSONAL NAME	ADDITIONAL NAME(S)/INITIAL(S)		SUFFIX
1c. MAILING ADDRESS	CITY	STATE	POSTAL CODE	COUNTRY

2\. DEBTOR'S NAME: Provide only <u>one</u> Debtor name (2a or 2b) (use exact, full name; do not omit, modify, or abbreviate any part of the Debtor's name); if any part of the Individual Debtor's name will not fit in line 2b, leave all of item 2 blank, check here ☐ and provide the Individual Debtor information in item 10 of the Financing Statement Addendum (Form UCC1Ad)

2a. ORGANIZATION'S NAME				
OR 2b. INDIVIDUAL'S SURNAME	FIRST PERSONAL NAME	ADDITIONAL NAME(S)/INITIAL(S)		SUFFIX
2c. MAILING ADDRESS	CITY	STATE	POSTAL CODE	COUNTRY

3\. SECURED PARTY'S NAME (or NAME of ASSIGNEE of ASSIGNOR SECURED PARTY): Provide only <u>one</u> Secured Party name (3a or 3b)

3a. ORGANIZATION'S NAME				
OR 3b. INDIVIDUAL'S SURNAME	FIRST PERSONAL NAME	ADDITIONAL NAME(S)/INITIAL(S)		SUFFIX
3c. MAILING ADDRESS	CITY	STATE	POSTAL CODE	COUNTRY

4\. COLLATERAL: This financing statement covers the following collateral:

5\. Check <u>only</u> if applicable and check <u>only</u> one box: Collateral is ☐ held in a Trust (see UCC1Ad, item 17 and Instructions) ☐ being administered by a Decedent's Personal Representative

6a. Check <u>only</u> if applicable and check <u>only</u> one box: ☐ Public-Finance Transaction ☐ Manufactured-Home Transaction ☐ A Debtor is a Transmitting Utility

6b. Check <u>only</u> if applicable and check <u>only</u> one box: ☐ Agricultural Lien ☐ Non-UCC Filing

7\. ALTERNATIVE DESIGNATION (if applicable): ☐ Lessee/Lessor ☐ Consignee/Consignor ☐ Seller/Buyer ☐ Bailee/Bailor ☐ Licensee/Licensor

8\. OPTIONAL FILER REFERENCE DATA:

FILING OFFICE COPY — UCC FINANCING STATEMENT (Form UCC1) (Rev. 07/01/23)

Form 9-12

UCC1Ad
Financing Statement Addendum

Instructions for UCC Financing Statement Addendum (Form UCC1Ad)

Please type or laser-print this form. Be sure it is completely legible. Read and follow all Instructions; use of the correct name for the Debtor is crucial. Fill in form very carefully; mistakes may have important legal consequences. If you have questions, consult your attorney. The filing office cannot give legal advice.

ITEM INSTRUCTIONS

9. **Name of first Debtor.** Enter name of first Debtor exactly as shown in item 1 of Financing Statement (Form UCC1) to which this Addendum relates. The name will not be indexed as a separate debtor. The Debtor name in this section is intended to cross-reference this Addendum with the related Financing Statement (Form UCC1).

   If the box in item 1 of the Financing Statement (Form UCC1) was checked because Individual Debtor name did not fit, the box in item 9 of this Addendum should be checked.

10. **Additional Debtor's name.** If this Addendum adds an additional Debtor, complete item 10 in accordance with Instruction 1 of Financing Statement (Form UCC1). For additional Debtors, attach either an additional Addendum or Additional Party (Form UCC1AP) and follow Instruction 1 of Financing Statement (Form UCC1) for determining and formatting additional names.

11. **Additional Secured Party's name or Assignor Secured Party's name.** If this Addendum adds an additional Secured Party, complete item 11 in accordance with Instruction 3 of Financing Statement (Form UCC1). For additional Secured Parties, attach either an additional Addendum or Additional Party (Form UCC1AP) and complete applicable items in accordance with Instruction 3 of Financing Statement (Form UCC1). In the case of a full assignment of the Secured Party's interest before the filing of this financing statement, if filer has provided the name and mailing address of the Assignee in item 3 of Financing Statement (Form UCC1), filer may enter Assignor Secured Party's name and mailing address in item 11.

12. **Additional Collateral Description.** If space in item 4 of Financing Statement (Form UCC1) is insufficient or additional information must be provided, enter additional information in item 12 or attach additional page(s) and incorporate by reference in item 12 (e.g., See Exhibit A). Do not include social security numbers or other personally identifiable information.

13-16. **Real Estate Record Information.** If this Financing Statement is to be filed in the real estate records and covers timber to be cut, covers as-extracted collateral, and/or is filed as a fixture filing, complete items 1-4 of the Financing Statement (Form UCC1), check the box in item 13, check the appropriate box in item 14, and complete the required information in items 15 and 16. If the Debtor does not have an interest of record, enter the name and address of the record owner in item 15. Provide a sufficient description of real estate in accordance with the applicable law of the jurisdiction where the real estate is located in item 16. If space in items 15 or 16 is insufficient, attach additional page(s) and incorporate by reference in items 15 or 16 (e.g., See Exhibit A), and continue the real estate record information. Do not include social security numbers or other personally identifiable information.

17. **Miscellaneous.** Under certain circumstances, additional information not provided on the Financing Statement (Form UCC1) may be required. Also, some states have non-uniform requirements. Use this space or attach additional page(s) and incorporate by reference in item 17 (e.g., See Exhibit A) to provide such additional information or to comply with such requirements; otherwise, leave blank. Do not include social security numbers or other personally identifiable information.

UCC FINANCING STATEMENT ADDENDUM

FOLLOW INSTRUCTIONS

9. NAME OF FIRST DEBTOR: Same as line 1a or 1b on Financing Statement; if line 1b was left blank because Individual Debtor name did not fit, check here ☐

9a. ORGANIZATION'S NAME

OR

9b. INDIVIDUAL'S SURNAME

FIRST PERSONAL NAME

ADDITIONAL NAME(S)/INITIAL(S) | SUFFIX

Reset

THE ABOVE SPACE IS FOR FILING OFFICE USE ONLY

10. DEBTOR'S NAME: Provide (10a or 10b) only one additional Debtor name or Debtor name that did not fit in line 1b or 2b of the Financing Statement (Form UCC1) (use exact, full name; do not omit, modify, or abbreviate any part of the Debtor's name) and enter the mailing address in line 10c

10a. ORGANIZATION'S NAME

OR

10b. INDIVIDUAL'S SURNAME

INDIVIDUAL'S FIRST PERSONAL NAME

INDIVIDUAL'S ADDITIONAL NAME(S)/INITIAL(S) | SUFFIX

10c. MAILING ADDRESS	CITY	STATE	POSTAL CODE	COUNTRY

11. ☐ ADDITIONAL SECURED PARTY'S NAME or ☐ ASSIGNOR SECURED PARTY'S NAME: Provide only one name (11a or 11b)

11a. ORGANIZATION'S NAME

OR

11b. INDIVIDUAL'S SURNAME	FIRST PERSONAL NAME	ADDITIONAL NAME(S)/INITIAL(S)	SUFFIX

11c. MAILING ADDRESS	CITY	STATE	POSTAL CODE	COUNTRY

12. ADDITIONAL SPACE FOR ITEM 4 (Collateral):

13. ☐ This FINANCING STATEMENT is to be filed [for record] (or recorded) in the REAL ESTATE RECORDS (if applicable)

14. This FINANCING STATEMENT: ☐ covers timber to be cut ☐ covers as-extracted collateral ☐ is filed as a fixture filing

15. Name and address of a RECORD OWNER of real estate described in item 16 (if Debtor does not have a record interest):

16. Description of real estate:

17. MISCELLANEOUS:

SECURED PARTY COPY — UCC FINANCING STATEMENT ADDENDUM (Form UCC1Ad) (Rev. 07/01/23)

Form 9-13

UCC1AP
Financing Statement Additional Party

Instructions for UCC Financing Statement Additional Party (Form UCC1AP)

Please type or laser-print this form. Be sure it is completely legible. Read and follow all Instructions; use of the correct name for the Debtor is crucial.

Fill in form very carefully; mistakes may have important legal consequences. If you have questions, consult your attorney. The filing office cannot give legal advice.

Use this form (multiple copies if needed) to continue adding additional Debtor or Secured Party names as needed when filing a UCC Financing Statement (Form UCC1).

ITEM INSTRUCTIONS

18. **Name of first Debtor.** Enter name of first Debtor exactly as shown in item 1 of Financing Statement (Form UCC1) to which this Additional Party relates. The name will not be indexed as a separate Debtor. If line 1b of the Financing Statement (Form UCC1) was left blank because the Individual Debtor name did not fit, check the box in item 18 and enter as much of the Individual Debtor name from item 10 that will fit. The Debtor name in this section is intended to cross-reference this Additional Party with the related Financing Statement (Form UCC1).

19-21. **Additional Debtor's name.** If this Additional Party adds additional Debtors, complete items 19, 20, and 21 in accordance with Instruction 1 of Financing Statement (Form UCC1).

22-23. **Additional Secured Party's name or Assignor Secured Party's name.** If this Additional Party form adds additional Secured Parties, complete items 22 and 23 in accordance with Instruction 3 of Financing Statement (Form UCC1). In the case of a full assignment of the Secured Party's interest before the filing of this financing statement, if filer has provided the name and mailing address of the Assignee in item 3 of Financing Statement (Form UCC1), filer may enter Assignor Secured Party's name and mailing address in items 22 and 23.

24. **Miscellaneous.** Under certain circumstances, additional information not provided on the Financing Statement (Form UCC1) may be required. Also, some states have non-uniform requirements. Use this space or attach additional page(s) and incorporate by reference in item 24 (e.g., See Exhibit A) to provide such additional information or to comply with such requirements; otherwise, leave blank. Do not include social security numbers or other personally identifiable information.

UCC FINANCING STATEMENT ADDITIONAL PARTY

FOLLOW INSTRUCTIONS

18. NAME OF FIRST DEBTOR: Same as line 1a or 1b on Financing Statement; if line 1b was left blank because Individual Debtor name did not fit, check here ☐

18a. ORGANIZATION'S NAME

OR 18b. INDIVIDUAL'S SURNAME

FIRST PERSONAL NAME

ADDITIONAL NAME(S)/INITIAL(S) | SUFFIX

Reset

THE ABOVE SPACE IS FOR FILING OFFICE USE ONLY

19. ADDITIONAL DEBTOR'S NAME: Provide only one Debtor name (19a or 19b) (use exact, full name; do not omit, modify, or abbreviate any part of the Debtor's name)

19a. ORGANIZATION'S NAME

OR 19b. INDIVIDUAL'S SURNAME | FIRST PERSONAL NAME | ADDITIONAL NAME(S)/INITIAL(S) | SUFFIX

19c. MAILING ADDRESS | CITY | STATE | POSTAL CODE | COUNTRY

20. ADDITIONAL DEBTOR'S NAME: Provide only one Debtor name (20a or 20b) (use exact, full name; do not omit, modify, or abbreviate any part of the Debtor's name)

20a. ORGANIZATION'S NAME

OR 20b. INDIVIDUAL'S SURNAME | FIRST PERSONAL NAME | ADDITIONAL NAME(S)/INITIAL(S) | SUFFIX

20c. MAILING ADDRESS | CITY | STATE | POSTAL CODE | COUNTRY

21. ADDITIONAL DEBTOR'S NAME: Provide only one Debtor name (21a or 21b) (use exact, full name; do not omit, modify, or abbreviate any part of the Debtor's name)

21a. ORGANIZATION'S NAME

OR 21b. INDIVIDUAL'S SURNAME | FIRST PERSONAL NAME | ADDITIONAL NAME(S)/INITIAL(S) | SUFFIX

21c. MAILING ADDRESS | CITY | STATE | POSTAL CODE | COUNTRY

22. ☐ ADDITIONAL SECURED PARTY'S NAME or ☐ ASSIGNOR SECURED PARTY'S NAME: Provide only one name (22a or 22b)

22a. ORGANIZATION'S NAME

OR 22b. INDIVIDUAL'S SURNAME | FIRST PERSONAL NAME | ADDITIONAL NAME(S)/INITIAL(S) | SUFFIX

22c. MAILING ADDRESS | CITY | STATE | POSTAL CODE | COUNTRY

23. ☐ ADDITIONAL SECURED PARTY'S NAME or ☐ ASSIGNOR SECURED PARTY'S NAME: Provide only one name (23a or 23b)

23a. ORGANIZATION'S NAME

OR 23b. INDIVIDUAL'S SURNAME | FIRST PERSONAL NAME | ADDITIONAL NAME(S)/INITIAL(S) | SUFFIX

23c. MAILING ADDRESS | CITY | STATE | POSTAL CODE | COUNTRY

24. MISCELLANEOUS:

FILING OFFICE COPY — UCC FINANCING STATEMENT ADDITIONAL PARTY (Form UCC1AP) (Rev. 07/01/23)

Form 9-14

UCC3
Financing Statement Amendment

Instructions for UCC Financing Statement Amendment (Form UCC3)

Please type or print this form. Be sure it is completely legible. Forms with handwritten entries may be rejected. Read and follow all Instructions.

Fill in form very carefully; mistakes may have important legal consequences. If you have questions, consult your attorney. The filing office cannot give legal advice.

Unless specifically required by applicable state law, DO NOT include social security numbers, driver's license numbers, financial account numbers or other non-public personally identifiable information anywhere on the form.

Form instructions are intended for paper forms. Electronic UCC filing parameters and instructions may differ from the below instructions.

Send completed form and any attachments to the filing office, with the required fee.

ITEM INSTRUCTIONS

A and B. To assist filing offices that might wish to communicate with filer, filer may provide information in item A and item B. These items are optional.

C. Complete item C if filer desires an acknowledgment sent to them. If filing in a filing office that returns an acknowledgment copy furnished by filer, present simultaneously with this form the Acknowledgment Copy or a carbon or other copy of this form for use as an acknowledgment copy.

Always complete items 1a and 9.

1a. File Number. Enter file number of initial financing statement to which this Amendment relates. Enter only one file number. If required by a local filing office or optionally when filing at the state level, the date of filing may be added after the initial financing statement file number.

1b. If this Amendment is to be filed in the real estate records or in any other filing office where the name of current Debtor is required for indexing purposes, check the box in item 1b and enter Debtor name in item 13 of Amendment Addendum (Form UCC3Ad). Complete item 13 in accordance with instructions on Amendment Addendum (Form UCC3Ad). If Debtor does not have an interest of record, enter the name and address of the record owner in item 16 of Amendment Addendum (Form UCC3Ad).

Note: Show purpose of this Amendment by checking box 2, 3, 4, 5, or 8 (in items 5 and 8 you must check additional boxes); also complete items 6, 7, and/or 8 as appropriate. Some filing offices may accept certain combinations of multiple actions on an Amendment. Filing offices that accept multiple actions may charge an additional fee. Consult the administrative rules of the designated filing office to determine the extent to which multiple actions will be accepted, indexed, and the applicable filing fees for multiple actions.

2. Termination. To terminate the effectiveness of the identified financing statement with respect to the security interest(s) of authorizing Secured Party, check box in item 2. See Instruction 9 below.

3. Assignment. To assign (1) some or all of Assignor's right to amend the identified financing statement, or (2) the Assignor's right to amend the identified financing statement with respect to some (but not all) of the collateral covered by the identified financing statement: Check box in item 3 and enter name of Assignee in item 7a or 7b; always enter the Assignee's mailing address in item 7c. Also enter name of Assignor in item 9. If assignment affects the right to amend the financing statement with respect to some (but not all) of the collateral covered by the identified financing statement, check the ASSIGN collateral box and indicate the particular collateral covered in item 8.

4. Continuation. To continue the effectiveness of the identified financing statement with respect to the security interest(s) of authorizing Secured Party, check box in item 4. Note: a continuation statement must be filed within six months before the lapse date. Consult filing office rules to determine the first and last days permitted for filing continuation statements.

5-7. Party Information Change. To indicate a party information change, check this box; also check additional boxes (as applicable) and complete items 5, 6, and/or 7 as appropriate.

To change the name and/or address of a party (items 5, 6, and 7): Check box in item 5 to indicate whether this Amendment relates to a Debtor or Secured Party of record; and check the CHANGE name and/or mailing address box in item 5 and enter name of affected party (current record name) in item 6a or 6b; and repeat or enter the new name in item 7a or 7b; always enter the party's mailing address in item 7c.

To add a party (items 5 and 7): Check box in item 5 to indicate whether this Amendment relates to a Debtor or Secured Party of record; and check the ADD name box in item 5 and enter the added party's name in item 7a or 7b; always enter the party's mailing address in item 7c. For additional Debtors or Secured Parties, attach Amendment Additional Party (Form UCC3AP), using correct name format.

To delete a party (items 5 and 6): Check box in item 5 to indicate whether this Amendment relates to a Debtor or Secured Party of record; and check the DELETE name box in item 5 and enter the deleted party's name in item 6a or 6b.

8. Collateral Change. To indicate a collateral change, check the applicable box and describe the change in item 8. If space in item 8 is insufficient, continue collateral description in item 14 of Amendment Addendum (Form UCC3Ad).

To add collateral: Check the ADD collateral box in item 8 and indicate the additional collateral.

To delete collateral: Check the DELETE collateral box in item 8 and indicate the deleted collateral. A partial release is a DELETE collateral change.

To restate covered collateral description: Check the RESTATE covered collateral box in item 8 and indicate the restated collateral.

To assign the right to amend the financing statement with respect to part (but not all) of the collateral covered by the identified financing statement: Comply with Instruction 3 above, check the ASSIGN collateral box in item 8 and describe the collateral subject to the partial assignment.

9. Name of Authorizing Party. Enter name of the party of record authorizing this Amendment. In most cases, the authorizing party is the Secured Party of record. If this is an Amendment (Assignment), enter the Assignor' secured party's name in item 9a or 9b. If this is an Amendment (Termination) authorized by a Debtor, check the box in item 9 and enter the name of the Debtor authorizing this Amendment in item 9a or 9b. If this Amendment (Termination) is to be filed or recorded in the real estate records, also enter, in item 12 of Amendment Addendum (Form UCC3Ad), the name of Secured Party of record. Optional: if there is more than one authorizing Secured Party or Debtor, enter additional name(s) in item 18 of the Amendment Addendum (Form UCC3Ad) or attach an exhibit listing the additional parties that authorized the amendment.

10. Optional Filer Reference Data. This item is optional and is for filer's use only. For filer's convenience of reference, filer may enter in item 10 any identifying information that filer may find useful.

UCC FINANCING STATEMENT AMENDMENT

FOLLOW INSTRUCTIONS

A. NAME & PHONE OF CONTACT AT SUBMITTER (optional)

B. E-MAIL CONTACT AT SUBMITTER (optional)

C. SEND ACKNOWLEDGMENT TO: (Name and Address)

SEE BELOW FOR SECURED PARTY CONTACT INFORMATION

THE ABOVE SPACE IS FOR FILING OFFICE USE ONLY

1a. INITIAL FINANCING STATEMENT FILE NUMBER

1b. ☐ This FINANCING STATEMENT AMENDMENT is to be filed [for record] (or recorded) in the REAL ESTATE RECORDS. Filer: attach Amendment Addendum (Form UCC3Ad) and provide Debtor's name in item 13.

2. ☐ TERMINATION: Effectiveness of the Financing Statement identified above is terminated with respect to the security interest(s) of Secured Part(y)(ies) authorizing this Termination Statement

3. ☐ ASSIGNMENT: Provide name of Assignee in item 7a or 7b, and address of Assignee in item 7c and name of Assignor in item 9
For partial assignment, complete items 7 and 9; check ASSIGN Collateral box in Item 8 and describe the affected collateral in item 8

4. ☐ CONTINUATION: Effectiveness of the Financing Statement identified above with respect to the security interest(s) of Secured Party authorizing this Continuation Statement is continued for the additional period provided by applicable law

5. PARTY INFORMATION CHANGE:

Check one of these two boxes:
This Change affects ☐ Debtor or ☐ Secured Party of record

AND Check one of these three boxes to:
☐ CHANGE name and/or address: Complete item 6a or 6b; and item 7a or 7b and item 7c
☐ ADD name: Complete item 7a or 7b, and item 7c
☐ DELETE name: Give record name to be deleted in item 6a or 6b

6. CURRENT RECORD INFORMATION: Complete for Party Information Change - provide only one name (6a or 6b)

	6a. ORGANIZATION'S NAME			
OR	6b. INDIVIDUAL'S SURNAME	FIRST PERSONAL NAME	ADDITIONAL NAME(S)/INITIAL(S)	SUFFIX

7. CHANGED OR ADDED INFORMATION: Complete for Assignment or Party Information Change - provide only one name (7a or 7b) (use exact, full name; do not omit, modify, or abbreviate any part of the Debtor's name)

	7a. ORGANIZATION'S NAME				
OR	7b. INDIVIDUAL'S SURNAME				
	INDIVIDUAL'S FIRST PERSONAL NAME				
	INDIVIDUAL'S ADDITIONAL NAME(S)/INITIAL(S)				SUFFIX
7c.	MAILING ADDRESS	CITY	STATE	POSTAL CODE	COUNTRY

8. COLLATERAL CHANGE: Check only one box: ☐ ADD collateral ☐ DELETE collateral ☐ RESTATE covered collateral ☐ ASSIGN* collateral

Indicate collateral:

*Check ASSIGN COLLATERAL only if the assignee's power to amend the record is limited to certain collateral and describe the collateral in Section 8

9. NAME OF SECURED PARTY OF RECORD AUTHORIZING THIS AMENDMENT: Provide only one name (9a or 9b) (name of Assignor, if this is an Assignment)
If this is an Amendment authorized by a DEBTOR, check here ☐ and provide name of authorizing Debtor

	9a. ORGANIZATION'S NAME			
OR	9b. INDIVIDUAL'S SURNAME	FIRST PERSONAL NAME	ADDITIONAL NAME(S)/INITIAL(S)	SUFFIX

10. OPTIONAL FILER REFERENCE DATA:

FILING OFFICE COPY — UCC FINANCING STATEMENT AMENDMENT (Form UCC3) (Rev. 07/01/23)

Form 9-15

UCC3Ad
Financing Statement Amendment Addendum

Instructions for UCC Financing Statement Amendment Addendum (Form UCC3Ad)

Please type or print this form. Be sure it is completely legible. Forms with handwritten entries may be rejected. Read and follow all Instructions.

Fill in form very carefully; mistakes may have important legal consequences. If you have questions, consult your attorney. The filing office cannot give legal advice.

Unless specifically required by applicable state law, DO NOT include social security numbers, driver's license numbers, financial account numbers or other non-public personally identifiable information anywhere on the form.

Form instructions are intended for paper forms. Electronic UCC filing parameters and instructions may differ from the below instructions.

Send completed form and any attachments to the filing office, with the related UCC3 Amendment Form and the correct fee.

ITEM INSTRUCTIONS

11. File Number. Enter file number of initial financing statement as shown in item 1a of Amendment (Form UCC3) to which this Amendment Addendum relates.

12. Name of Authorizing Party. Enter information exactly as shown in item 9 on Amendment (Form UCC3).

13. Name of Debtor on related Financing Statement. If this Amendment (Form UCC3) is to be filed in the real estate records or in any other filing office where the name of a current Debtor of record is required for indexing purposes, enter Debtor name in item 13a or 13b. Item 13 is intended to cross-reference the Amendment (Form UCC3) and Amendment Addendum with the related Financing Statement (Form UCC1). If more than one current Debtor, enter additional name(s) in item 14 or on additional Amendment Addendum (Form UCC3Ad). Do not use item 13 to change, add, or delete a Debtor name.

14. Additional Space for Item 8 (Collateral) or Other Information. If space in item 8 of Amendment (Form UCC3) is insufficient or other information must be provided, check the box to indicate the type of information in item 8 and then enter the additional collateral or other information in item 14 or attach additional page(s) and incorporate by reference in item 14 (e.g., See Exhibit A).

15-17. Real Estate Record Information. If this Amendment (Form UCC3) is to be filed in the real estate records, complete the required information (items 15, 16, and 17). If this Amendment (Form UCC3) covers timber to be cut, covers as-extracted collateral, and/or is filed as a fixture filing, check appropriate box in item 15. If the Debtor does not have an interest of record, enter the name and address of the record owner in item 16. Provide a sufficient description of real estate in accordance with the applicable law of the jurisdiction where the real estate is located in item 17. If space in items 16 or 17 is insufficient, attach additional page(s) and incorporate by reference in items 16 or 17 (e.g., See Exhibit A), and continue the real estate information. Do not include social security numbers or other personally identifiable information.

18. Miscellaneous. Under certain circumstances, additional information not provided on the Financing Statement Amendment (Form UCC3) may be required. Also, some states have non-uniform requirements. Use this space or attach additional page(s) and incorporate by reference in item 18 (e.g., See Exhibit A) to provide such additional information or to comply with such requirements; otherwise, leave blank. Do not include social security numbers or other personally identifiable information.

UCC FINANCING STATEMENT AMENDMENT ADDENDUM

FOLLOW INSTRUCTIONS

11. INITIAL FINANCING STATEMENT FILE NUMBER: Same as item 1a on Amendment form

12. NAME OF PARTY AUTHORIZING THIS AMENDMENT: Same as item 9 on Amendment form

12a. ORGANIZATION'S NAME

OR

12b. INDIVIDUAL'S SURNAME

FIRST PERSONAL NAME

ADDITIONAL NAME(S)/INITIAL(S)	SUFFIX

THE ABOVE SPACE IS FOR FILING OFFICE USE ONLY

13. Name of DEBTOR on related financing statement (Name of a current Debtor of record required for indexing purposes only in some filing offices - see Instruction item 13): Provide only one Debtor name (13a or 13b) (use exact, full name; do not omit, modify, or abbreviate any part of the Debtor's name); see Instructions if name does not fit

13a. ORGANIZATION'S NAME

OR

13b. INDIVIDUAL'S SURNAME	FIRST PERSONAL NAME	ADDITIONAL NAME(S)/INITIAL(S)	SUFFIX

14. ADDITIONAL SPACE FOR (CHECK ONE BOX): ☐ ITEM 8 (Collateral) OR ☐ OTHER INFORMATION (Please Describe)

15. This FINANCING STATEMENT AMENDMENT:

☐ covers timber to be cut ☐ covers as-extracted collateral ☐ is filed as a fixture filing

16. Name and address of a RECORD OWNER of real estate described in item 17 (if Debtor does not have a record interest):

17. Description of real estate:

18. MISCELLANEOUS:

FILING OFFICE COPY — UCC FINANCING STATEMENT AMENDMENT ADDENDUM (Form UCC3Ad) (Rev. 07/01/23)

Form 9-16

UCC3AP
Financing Statement Amendment Additional Party

Instructions for UCC Financing Statement Amendment Additional Party (Form UCC3AP)

Please type or laser-print this form. Be sure it is completely legible. Read and follow all Instructions; use of the correct name for the Debtor is crucial.
Fill in form very carefully; mistakes may have important legal consequences. If you have questions, consult your attorney. The filing office cannot give legal advice.
Use this form (multiple copies if needed) to continue adding additional Debtor or Secured Party names as needed when filing a UCC Financing Statement Amendment (Form UCC3).

ITEM INSTRUCTIONS

19. **File Number.** Enter file number of initial financing statement as shown in item 1a of Amendment (Form UCC3) to which this Amendment Addendum relates.

20. **Name of Authorizing Party.** Enter information exactly as shown in item 9 on Amendment (Form UCC3).

21-23. **Additional Debtor's name.** If this Amendment Additional Party adds additional Debtors, complete items 21, 22, and 23 in accordance with Instruction 1 of Financing Statement (Form UCC1).

24-25. **Additional Secured Party's name or Assignor Secured Party's name.** If this Amendment Additional Party adds additional Secured Parties, complete items 24 and 25 in accordance with Instruction 3 of Financing Statement (Form UCC1). In the case of an assignment of the Secured Party's interest, filer may enter Secured Party and/or Assignor Secured Party's name and mailing address information in items 24 and 25.

26. **Miscellaneous.** Under certain circumstances, additional information not provided on the Financing Statement Amendment (Form UCC3) may be required. Also, some states have non-uniform requirements. Use this space or attach additional page(s) and incorporate by reference in item 26 (e.g., See Exhibit A) to provide such additional information or to comply with such requirements; otherwise, leave blank. Do not include social security numbers or other personally identifiable information.

UCC FINANCING STATEMENT AMENDMENT ADDITIONAL PARTY

FOLLOW INSTRUCTIONS

19. INITIAL FINANCING STATEMENT FILE NUMBER: Same as item 1a on Amendment form

20. NAME OF PARTY AUTHORIZING THIS AMENDMENT: Same as item 9 on Amendment form

20a. ORGANIZATION'S NAME

OR

20b. INDIVIDUAL'S SURNAME

FIRST PERSONAL NAME

ADDITIONAL NAME(S)/INITIAL(S) | SUFFIX

THE ABOVE SPACE

21. ADDITIONAL DEBTOR'S NAME: Provide only one Debtor name (21a or 21b) (use exact, full name; do not omit, modify, or abbreviate any pa

21a. ORGANIZATION'S NAME

OR

21b. INDIVIDUAL'S SURNAME	FIRST PERSONAL NAME	ADDITIC
21c. MAILING ADDRESS	CITY	STATE

22. ADDITIONAL DEBTOR'S NAME: Provide only one Debtor name (22a or 22b) (use exact, full name; do not omit, modify, or abbreviate any pa

22a. ORGANIZATION'S NAME

OR

22b. INDIVIDUAL'S SURNAME	FIRST PERSONAL NAME	ADDITIC
22c. MAILING ADDRESS	CITY	STATE

23. ADDITIONAL DEBTOR'S NAME: Provide only one Debtor name (23a or 23b) (use exact, full name; do not omit, modify, or abbreviate any pa

23a. ORGANIZATION'S NAME

OR

23b. INDIVIDUAL'S SURNAME	FIRST PERSONAL NAME	ADDITIC
23c. MAILING ADDRESS	CITY	STATE

24. ☐ ADDITIONAL SECURED PARTY'S NAME or ☐ ASSIGNOR SECURED PARTY'S NAME: Provide only one nai

24a. ORGANIZATION'S NAME

OR

24b. INDIVIDUAL'S SURNAME	FIRST PERSONAL NAME	ADDITIC
24c. MAILING ADDRESS	CITY	STATE

25. ☐ ADDITIONAL SECURED PARTY'S NAME or ☐ ASSIGNOR SECURED PARTY'S NAME: Provide only one nai

Form 9-17

UCC5
Information Statement

Instructions for Information Statement (Form UCC5)

Please type or laser-print this form. Be sure it is completely legible. Read and follow all Instructions, especially Instructions 1a and 1b; correct identification of the initial record to which this Information Statement relates is crucial.
Fill in form very carefully; mistakes may have important legal consequences. If you have questions, consult your attorney. The filing office cannot give legal advice.
Send completed form and any attachments to the filing office, with the required fee.

Note: A person may file an Information Statement with respect to a record indexed under that person's name if the person believes the record was inaccurate or wrongfully filed, or a person may file an Information Statement with respect to a record if the person is a Secured Party of Record with respect to the financing statement to which the record relates and believes that the person that filed the record was not entitled to do so.

ITEM INSTRUCTIONS

A and B. To assist filing offices that might wish to communicate with filer, filer may provide information in item A and item B. These items are optional.
C. Complete item C if filer desires an acknowledgment sent to them. If filing in a filing office that returns an acknowledgment copy furnished by filer, present simultaneously with this form the Acknowledgment Copy or a carbon or other copy of this form for use as an acknowledgment copy.

Always complete items 1 and 5 and either 2a or 2b or 2c. Always complete item 3 with the basis for the box marked in item 2. You may also be required to complete item 4.

1a. **File number:** Enter file number of initial financing statement to which the record that is the object of this Information Statement relates. Enter only one file number.

1b. Enter record information to which this Information Statement relates. Indicate the type of record to which this Information Statement relates (e.g., Financing Statement or Amendment) or you may also insert additional information that you believe will assist in identifying the record (e.g., the record file number or the filing date of the record).

2a. **Record is inaccurate.** If this Information Statement is filed based upon the belief of the Debtor of Record that the record identified in item 1 is inaccurate, check box in item 2a, provide the basis for that belief in item 3, and indicate the manner in which the record should be amended to cure the inaccuracy.

2b. **Record was wrongfully filed.** If this Information Statement is filed based upon the belief of the Debtor of Record that the record identified in item 1 was wrongfully filed, check box in item 2b and provide the basis for that belief in item 3.

2c. **Record filed by person not entitled to do so.** If this Information Statement is filed based upon the belief of the Secured Party of Record that the person that filed the record identified in item 1b was not entitled to do so under Section 9-509, check box in item 2c and provide the basis for that belief in item 3.

3. **Basis.** Use this item to provide the basis for the box checked in item 2.

4. **Filing office date and time.** If this Information Statement relates to a record filed [or recorded] in a filing office described in Section 9-501(a)(1) and this Information Statement is filed in such a filing office, provide the date [and time] on which the initial financing statement identified in item 1a above was filed [or recorded].

5. **Name of Authorizing Party.** Enter name of the person filing this Information Statement. This name must be the same name as a Secured Party of Record or the name under which the record is indexed.

CAUTION:
This is not an amendment.

INFORMATION STATEMENT
FOLLOW INSTRUCTIONS

A. NAME & PHONE OF SUBMITTER (optional)

B. E-MAIL CONTACT OF SUBMITTER (optional)

C. SEND ACKNOWLEDGMENT TO: (Name and Address)

THE ABOVE SPACE IS FOR FILING OFFICE USE ONLY

1. Identification of the RECORD to which this INFORMATION STATEMENT relates

1a. INITIAL FINANCING STATEMENT FILE NUMBER	1b. RECORD INFORMATION TO WHICH THIS INFORMATION STATEMENT RELATES

2. Check one of these three boxes to indicate the claim made by this INFORMATION STATEMENT

2a. ☐ RECORD IS INACCURATE. Enter in item 3 the basis for the belief by the Debtor of Record identified in item 5 that the RECORD identified in item 1 is inaccurate and indicate the manner in which the person believes the RECORD should be amended to cure the inaccuracy

2b. ☐ RECORD WAS WRONGFULLY FILED. Enter in item 3 the basis for the belief by the Debtor of Record identified in item 5 that the RECORD identified in item 1 was wrongfully filed

2c. ☐ RECORD FILED BY PERSON NOT ENTITLED TO DO SO. Enter in item 3 the basis for the belief by the Secured Party of Record that the person that filed the RECORD identified in item 1 was not entitled to do so under UCC Section 9-509

3. Basis for claim of box checked in item 2

4. If this INFORMATION STATEMENT relates to a RECORD filed [or recorded] in a filing office described in Section 9-501(a)(1) and this INFORMATION STATEMENT is filed in such a filing office, provide the date [and time] on which the INITIAL FINANCING STATEMENT identified in item 1a above was filed [or recorded]

4a. DATE	4b. TIME

5. NAME of PERSON filing this INFORMATION STATEMENT

5a. ORGANIZATION'S NAME			
OR 5b. INDIVIDUAL'S SURNAME	FIRST PERSONAL NAME	ADDITIONAL NAME(S)/INITIAL(S)	SUFFIX

FILING OFFICE COPY — INFORMATION STATEMENT (Form UCC5) (Rev. 07/01/23)

Form 9-18

UCC11
Information Request

[redacted]

INFORMATION REQUEST

FOLLOW INSTRUCTIONS

A. NAME & PHONE OF CONTACT AT FILER (optional)	FILING OFFICE ACCT #
B. E-MAIL CONTACT AT FILER (optional)	
C. RETURN TO: (Name and Address)	

THE ABOVE SPACE IS FOR FILING OFFICE USE ONLY

1. DEBTOR'S NAME to be searched: Provide only one Debtor name (1a or 1b) (use exact full name; do not omit, modify or abbreviate any part of the Debtor's name)

1a. ORGANIZATION'S NAME

OR

1b. INDIVIDUAL'S SURNAME	FIRST PERSONAL NAME	ADDITIONAL NAME(S)/INITIAL(S)	SUFFIX

2. INFORMATION OPTIONS relating to UCC filings and other notices on file in the filing office that include the Debtor name identified in item 1:

2a. ☐ LISTING RELATING TO DEBTOR AT SPECIFIED CITY AND STATE ONLY — Filing office requested to furnish a search report listing all financing statements, related records, and other notices on file in filing office that include the Debtor's name identified in item 1 and show that Debtor's address in the city, state, and country indicated here:

CITY	STATE	COUNTRY

2b. ☐ INFORMATION REQUEST RESPONSE WITH FULL COPIES (CERTIFIED) — Filing office requested to furnish a search report listing all financing statements, related records, and other notices, showing date and time of filing and name and address of each Secured Party named therein, and also furnish an exact CERTIFIED COPY of ALL reported records (including all attachments)

2c. ☐ INFORMATION REQUEST RESPONSE WITHOUT COPIES — Filing office requested to furnish a search report (as described in 2b) listing all reported records, but to furnish NO COPIES of reported records

2d. ☐ INFORMATION REQUEST RESPONSE WITH PARTIAL COPIES (CERTIFIED) — Filing office requested to furnish a search report (as described in 2b) and also to furnish an exact CERTIFIED COPY of the FIRST PAGE ONLY of all reported records

3. ☐ SPECIFIED COPIES ONLY — Filing office requested to furnish an exact copy of each page of the financing statements, related records, and other notices (including all attachments) that are identified below by record number. Certain filing offices require additional identifying information — please complete if required

☐ CERTIFIED COPY REQUEST — Filing office requested to furnish CERTIFIED copies per request indicated in this item 3

Record Number	Date Record Filed (if required)	Type of Record and Additional Identifying Information (if required)

4. ☐ LISTING RELATING TO SECURED PARTY — Filing office requested to furnish a search report listing all financing statements, related records, and other notices (regardless of Debtor name) on file in filing office that include the Secured Party's name identified in item 4a or 4b. If a specified city, state, and country are being requested (optional), show that Secured Party's address in item 4c

4a. ORGANIZATION'S NAME

OR

4b. INDIVIDUAL'S SURNAME	FIRST PERSONAL NAME	ADDITIONAL NAME(S)/INITIAL(S)	SUFFIX

4c. CITY	STATE	COUNTRY

5. DELIVERY INSTRUCTIONS (request will be filled by mail sent to address shown in item C unless otherwise instructed here):

5a. ☐ FAX Delivery — Filing office requested to fax results of this Information Request to fax number indicated here: ( )

5b. ☐ Pick Up

5c. ☐ Other

Specify desired method here (if available from this office); provide delivery information (e.g., delivery service's name, addressee's account # with delivery service, addressee's phone #, etc.)

FILING OFFICE COPY (1) — INFORMATION REQUEST (Form UCC11) (Texas) (Rev. 07/19/12)

Office of the Secretary of State of Texas

Instructions for Information Request (Form UCC11) (Texas)

Please type or laser-print this form. Be sure it is completely legible. Read and follow all Instructions, especially Instruction 1; use of the correct name for the Debtor is crucial.

Fill in form very carefully; mistakes may have important legal consequences. If you have questions, consult your attorney. The filing office cannot give legal advice.

Send completed form parts 1 and 2 (labeled Filing Office Copy (1) and (2)) to the filing office, with the required fee.

ITEM INSTRUCTIONS

A and B. To assist filing offices that might wish to communicate with filer, filer may provide information in item A and item B. These items are optional.

C. Provide name and address of requestor in item C. This item is NOT optional.

1. **Debtor's name.** Enter only one Debtor name in item 1 -- either an organization's name (1a) or an individual's name (1b). Enter Debtor's correct name. Do not abbreviate words that are not already abbreviated in the Debtor's name.

1a. Organization Debtor Name. "Organization Name" means the name of an entity that is not a natural person. A sole proprietorship is not an organization, even if the individual proprietor does business under a trade name. If Debtor is a registered organization (e.g., corporation, limited partnership, limited liability company), it is advisable to examine Debtor's current filed public organic records to determine Debtor's correct name. Trade name is insufficient. If a corporate ending (e.g., corporation, limited partnership, limited liability company) is part of the Debtor's name, it must be included. Do not use words that are not part of the Debtor's name.

1b. Individual Debtor Name. "Individual Name" means the name of a natural person; this includes the name of an individual doing business as a sole proprietorship, whether or not operating under a trade name. The term includes the name of a decedent where collateral is being administered by a personal representative of the decedent. The term does not include the name of an entity, even if it contains, as part of the entity's name, the name of an individual. Prefixes (e.g., Mr., Mrs., Ms.) and titles (e.g., M.D.) are generally not part of an individual name. Indications of lineage (e.g., Jr., Sr., III) generally are not part of the individual's name, but may be entered in the Suffix box. Enter individual Debtor's surname (family name) in Individual's Surname box, first personal name in First Personal Name box, and all additional names in Additional Name(s)/Initial(s) box.

If a Debtor's name consists of only a single word, enter that word in Individual's Surname box and leave other boxes blank.

For both organization and individual Debtors. Do not use Debtor's trade name, DBA, AKA, FKA, division name, etc. in place of or combined with Debtor's correct name; filer may add such other names as additional Debtors if desired (but this is neither required nor recommended).

2. **Information Options.**

2a. To request a "Listing Relating to Debtor at Specified City and State Only" check box 2a and enter the city, state, and country in item 2a. This type of request will introduce a search criterion that narrows the scope of the search, which may result in an incomplete search (that fails to list all filings against a named Debtor) and requestor may fail to learn information that might be of value.

2b-2d. Check appropriate box (2b, 2c, or 2d) to specify whether search response should include all copies, no copies or partial copies.

3. **Specified Copies Only.** To request specified copies only, check the "Specified Copies Only" box and provide the record number(s) as requested. To request certified copies for record number(s) identified in item 3, also check the "Certified Copy Request" box.

4. **Listing relating to Secured Party.** To request a listing for a named Secured Party, check this box. Enter only one Secured Party name in item 4 -- either an organization's name (4a) or an individual's name (4b). If a specified city, state, and country is being requested (optional), enter that Secured Party's address in item 4c.

5. **Delivery Instructions.** Unless otherwise instructed, filing office will mail information to the name and address in item C. Check appropriate box (5a, 5b, or 5c) if optional delivery method is being requested.

5a. To request information to be faxed to the requestor, check the "FAX Delivery" box and provide fax number in specified area.

5b. To request information to be picked up from the filing office, check the "Pick Up" box.

5c. For other than mail, pick up or FAX, check the "Other" box and specify the other delivery method that is being requested. If requesting delivery service, provide delivery service's name and requestor's account number to bill for delivery charge. Filing office will not deliver by delivery service unless prepaid waybill or account number for billing is provided.

If requesting information from a county clerk filing office, contact county clerk to determine what services are offered by that office.

Form 9-19

Deposit Account Control Agreement

[Blocked Account]

Basic Information

Date:

Customer:

Customer's Mailing Address:

Secured Party:

Secured Party's Mailing Address:

Depository Bank:

Depository Bank's Mailing Address:

Security Agreement:

A. Notice and Acknowledgment of Security Interest

Depository Bank confirms that Depository Bank has established account number [**number**] (the "Specified Deposit Account") in the name of Customer. Customer and Secured Party notify Depository Bank of, and Depository Bank acknowledges, the security interest granted by Customer to Secured Party pursuant to the Security Agreement in all of Customer's right, title, and interest in the Specified Deposit Account and the funds on deposit therein. Depository Bank, Customer, and Secured Party agree that Secured Party has control over the Specified Deposit Account.

B. Control of Specified Deposit Account

B.1. Depository Bank agrees, without further consent of Customer, to (a) comply with all instructions originated by Secured Party for the disposition of funds in the Specified Deposit Account (the "Instructions") and disregard any instructions from Customer for the Specified Deposit Account and dispositions of its funds and (b) otherwise deal with the Specified Deposit Account as directed by Secured Party.

B.2. Customer is not permitted to operate and transact business through the Specified Deposit Account, including the directing of the disposition of funds from the Specified Deposit Account. Additionally, Customer may not, without Secured Party's prior written consent, close the Specified Deposit Account.

B.3. Secured Party's power under this Agreement to give Depository Bank Instructions includes, without limitation, the power to give stop payment orders for any items being presented to the Specified Deposit Account for payment. Customer confirms that Depository Bank should follow the Instructions even if the result of following the Instructions is that Depository Bank dishonors items presented for payment from the Specified Deposit Account. Customer confirms that Depository Bank will have no liability to Customer for the wrongful dishonor of such items in following the Instructions.

C. Certain Other Agreements

C.1. Depository Bank will not be liable to Customer for complying with the Instructions even if Customer notifies Depository Bank that Secured Party is not legally entitled to issue the Instructions, unless Depository Bank takes the action after it is served with an injunction, restraining order, or other legal process enjoining it from doing so, issued by a court of competent jurisdiction, and had a reasonable opportunity to act on the injunction, restraining order, or other legal process. Depository Bank need not investigate whether

Secured Party is entitled, under the Security Agreement or any other agreement between Secured Party and Customer, to give the Instructions.

C.2. Depository Bank will have no responsibility or liability to Secured Party for complying with any order or instruction, whether oral or written, concerning the Specified Deposit Account, except to the extent such compliance would violate (a) section B. above or (b) written instructions or orders previously received from Secured Party, but only to the extent Depository Bank received such instruction before the third Business Day after Depository Bank receives a contrary Instruction from Secured Party. "Business Day" means any day on which Depository Bank is not authorized or required to close. Depository Bank will not have any liability to Customer or Secured Party for losses or liabilities resulting from any failure to comply with instructions relating to the Specified Deposit Account or delay in complying with such instructions if (a) compliance with such instructions would require Depository Bank to violate any then-existing injunction or order of any court of competent jurisdiction, including, without limitation, in any bankruptcy case under title 11 of the United States Code, or (b) the failure or delay is due to circumstances beyond Depository Bank's reasonable control.

C.3. If any conflict between this Agreement and any other agreement between Depository Bank and Customer arises, the terms of this Agreement will prevail.

D. Account Information

Customer instructs Depository Bank, and Depository Bank agrees, to furnish to Secured Party, upon request of Secured Party, bank statements for the Specified Deposit Account that are customarily provided to customers of Depository Bank at the times such statements are normally provided to customers of Depository Bank, through the normal method of transmission, including United States mail, with a copy to Customer, at Customer's expense. Customer instructs Depository Bank, and Depository Bank agrees, to make available to Secured Party and Customer, upon request of Secured Party, copies of all daily debit and credit advices of the Specified Deposit Account and any other item reasonably requested by Secured Party. If Depository Bank receives any notice of a claim of a third party for the Specified Deposit Account or legal process of any kind relating to Customer, Depository Bank will make a reasonable effort to give notice to Secured Party and Customer of such legal process.

E. Governing Law

This Agreement will be construed according to Texas law, without regard to choice-of-law rules of any jurisdiction. Depository Bank agrees that Texas is Depository Bank's jurisdiction for all purposes.

F. Definitions; Rules of Construction

Any term defined in sections 1.101 to 9.709 of the Texas Business and Commerce Code and not defined in this Agreement has the meaning given to the term in the Code.

G. Returned Items; Fees and Expenses of Depository Bank

Depository Bank will not charge or debit, or exercise any right of offset or banker's lien against, the Specified Deposit Account except as provided in this section G. Depository Bank may charge the Specified Deposit Account for all customary and reasonable charges of Depository Bank resulting from the Specified Deposit Account, and Depository Bank may set off against the Specified Deposit Account for any items deposited in the Specified Deposit Account that are returned for any reason or otherwise not collected; for overdrafts on the Specified Deposit Account; and for all service charges, commissions, expenses, fees, and other items ordinarily chargeable to the Specified Deposit Account. Customer agrees to pay the amount of any customary fees and any returned item immediately upon demand to the extent that there are not sufficient funds in the Specified Deposit Account to cover such amount on the day of the debit. Secured Party agrees to reimburse Depository Bank for all charges and fees for which there were insufficient funds in the Specified Deposit Account to satisfy the amount thereof as a result and to the extent of the funds that Depository Bank forwarded to Secured Party pursuant to the terms of this Agreement. The provisions of this section G. shall survive termination of this Agreement.

Signed on [**date**].

[**Name of customer**]

By: ______________________________
[**Name and title of representative for customer**]

[**Name of depository bank**]

By: ______________________________
[**Name and title of representative for depository bank**]

[**Name of secured party**]

By: ______________________________
[**Name and title of representative for secured party**]

Form 9-20

Deposit Account Control Agreement

[Operating Account]

Basic Information

Date:

Customer:

Customer's Mailing Address:

Secured Party:

Secured Party's Mailing Address:

Depository Bank:

Depository Bank's Mailing Address:

Security Agreement:

A. Notice and Acknowledgment of Security Interest

Depository Bank confirms that Depository Bank has established account number [**number**] (the "Specified Deposit Account") in the name of Customer. Customer and Secured Party notify Depository Bank of, and Depository Bank acknowledges, the security interest granted by Customer to Secured Party pursuant to the Security Agreement in all of Customer's right, title, and interest in the Specified Deposit Account and the funds on deposit therein. Depository Bank, Customer, and Secured Party agree that Secured Party has control over the Specified Deposit Account.

B. Control of Specified Deposit Account

B.1. Depository Bank agrees, without further consent of Customer, to (a) comply with all instructions originated by Secured Party for the disposition of funds in the Specified Deposit Account (the "Instructions") and disregard any instructions from Customer for the Specified Deposit Account and dispositions of its funds except as set forth in paragraph B.2. below and (b) otherwise deal with the Specified Deposit Account as directed by Secured Party.

B.2. Before the receipt of written notice (a "Default Notice") from Secured Party referencing the Security Agreement and stating that an "Event of Default" has occurred pursuant to the Security Agreement, Depository Bank may permit Customer to operate and transact business through the Specified Deposit Account, including making withdrawals from and writing checks on the Specified Deposit Account, provided that without Secured Party's written consent, Customer may not close the Specified Deposit Account.

B.3. Subject to paragraph B.4. below, after receipt by Depository Bank of a Default Notice (and until Depository Bank receives a written withdrawal of such notice), (a) Secured Party shall have exclusive dominion and control over the Specified Deposit Account, (b) neither Customer nor any person acting through or on behalf of Customer shall have any right to access or to withdrawal from the Specified Deposit Account, and (c) Depository Bank shall not comply with any instructions originated by Customer or any such person directing disposition of funds in the Specified Deposit Account.

B.4. Any Default Notice shall be in writing, shall refer to this Agreement, and shall include clear and specific instructions for the disposition of funds in the Specified Deposit Account. Depository Bank shall have a period not exceeding three Business Days following the date on which Depository Bank receives a Default Notice to act on such Default Notice. Depository Bank may rely on a Default Notice notwithstanding any other or conflicting information it may receive from Customer. As used in this Agreement, the term "Business Day" means any day on which Depository Bank is not authorized or required to close.

B.5. Secured Party's power under this Agreement to give Depository Bank Instructions includes, without limitation, the power to give stop payment orders for any items being presented to the Specified Deposit Account for payment. Customer confirms that Depository Bank should follow the Instructions even if the result of following the Instructions is that Depository Bank dishonors items presented for payment from the Specified Deposit Account. Customer confirms that Depository Bank will have no liability to Customer for the wrongful dishonor of such items in following the Instructions.

C. Certain Other Agreements

C.1. Depository Bank will not be liable to Customer for complying with the Instructions even if Customer notifies Depository Bank that Secured Party is not legally entitled to issue the Instructions, unless Depository Bank takes the action after it is served with an injunction, restraining order, or other legal process enjoining it from doing so, issued by a court of competent jurisdiction, and had a reasonable opportunity to act on the injunction, restraining order, or other legal process. Depository Bank need not investigate whether Secured Party is entitled, under the Security Agreement or any other agreement between Secured Party and Customer, to give the Instructions.

C.2. Depository Bank will have no responsibility or liability to Secured Party for complying with any order or instruction, whether oral or written, concerning the Specified Deposit Account, except to the extent such compliance would violate (a) section B. above or (b) written instructions or orders previously received from Secured Party, but only to the extent Depository Bank received such instruction before the third Business Day after Depository Bank receives a contrary Instruction from Secured Party. Depository Bank will not have any liability to Customer or Secured Party for losses or liabilities resulting from any failure to comply with instructions relating to the Specified Deposit Account or delay in complying with such instructions if (a) compliance with such instructions would require Depository Bank to violate any then-existing injunction or order of any court of competent jurisdiction, including, without limitation, in any bankruptcy case under title 11 of the United States Code, or (b) the failure or delay is due to circumstances beyond Depository Bank's reasonable control.

C.3. If any conflict between this Agreement and any other agreement between Depository Bank and Customer arises, the terms of this Agreement will prevail.

D. Account Information

Customer instructs Depository Bank, and Depository Bank agrees, to furnish to Secured Party, upon request of Secured Party, bank statements for the Specified Deposit Account that are customarily provided to customers of Depository Bank at the times such statements are normally provided to customers of Depository Bank, through the normal method of transmission, including United States mail, with a copy to Customer, at Customer's expense. Customer instructs Depository Bank, and Depository Bank agrees, to make available to Secured Party and Customer, upon request of Secured Party, copies of all daily debit and credit advices of the Specified Deposit Account and any other item reasonably requested by Secured Party. If Depository Bank receives any notice of a claim of a third party for the Specified Deposit Account or legal process of any kind relating to Customer, Depository Bank will make a reasonable effort to give notice to Secured Party and Customer of such legal process.

E. Governing Law

This Agreement will be construed according to Texas law, without regard to choice-of-law rules of any jurisdiction. Depository Bank agrees that Texas is Depository Bank's jurisdiction for all purposes.

F. Definitions; Rules of Construction

Any term defined in sections 1.101 to 9.709 of the Texas Business and Commerce Code and not defined in this Agreement has the meaning given to the term in the Code.

G. Returned Items; Fees and Expenses of Depository Bank

Depository Bank will not charge or debit, or exercise any right of offset or banker's lien against, the Specified Deposit Account except as provided in this section G. Depository Bank may charge the Specified Deposit Account for all customary and reasonable charges of Depository Bank resulting from the Specified Deposit Account, and Depository Bank may set off against the Specified Deposit Account for any items deposited in the Specified Deposit Account that are returned for any reason or otherwise not collected; for overdrafts on the Specified Deposit Account; and for all service charges, commissions, expenses, fees, and other items ordinarily chargeable to the Specified Deposit Account. Customer agrees to pay the amount of any customary fees and any returned item immediately upon demand to the extent that there are not sufficient funds in the Specified Deposit Account to cover such amount on the day of the debit. Secured Party agrees to reimburse Depository Bank for all charges and fees for which there were insufficient funds in the Specified Deposit Account to satisfy the amount thereof as a result and to the extent of the funds that Depository Bank forwarded to Secured Party pursuant to the terms of this Agreement. The provisions of this section G. shall survive termination of this Agreement.

Signed on **[date]**.

[Name of customer]

By: ______________________________
[Name and title of representative for customer]

[Name of depository bank]

By: ________________________________

[Name and title of representative for depository bank]

[Name of secured party]

By: ________________________________

[Name and title of representative for secured party]

Chapter 10

Ancillary Loan Documents

Forms

Chapter 10

Ancillary Loan Documents

§ 10.1 General Considerations for Transfer of Note and Lien

The transfer of note and lien, form 10-1 in this chapter, is used to transfer ownership of a note or other obligation and the lien securing it to another party. This type of transfer is a real property transaction not subject to the Uniform Commercial Code provisions governing secured transactions. The transfer instrument must be acknowledged and filed in the real property records of the county in which the land is located, or, like other documents concerning the conveyance of real property, it is void as to a creditor or subsequent purchaser for valuable consideration without notice. Tex. Prop. Code § 13.001(a).

The holder of the note must endorse it in favor of the transferee and deliver both the transfer instrument and the note to the transferee. Any special terms included in the transfer instrument, such as a negation of recourse or of representations or warranties, should also be noted in the endorsement on the note. An allonge may be used to reflect the endorsement. See form 10-25.

If the note and lien are being pledged as collateral, the transaction is subject to the Texas Uniform Commercial Code. The proper procedure for effecting a security interest is outlined in chapter 9 in this manual.

§ 10.1:1 Cautions for Transfer of Lien

The borrower must receive actual notice of the transfer of the note and lien. If the borrower continues to make payments to the prior holder and has not received actual notice, the transferee has no recourse against the borrower. Accordingly, the transferee should either notify the borrower of the transfer or make certain that the prior holder informs the borrower of the transfer.

§ 10.1:2 Instructions for Completing Transfer of Lien

Form 10-1 in this chapter is drafted with the assumption that the parties will not wish to show the actual consideration for the transfer. However, a description of the consideration could be added at any suitable place.

The note is frequently secured by two liens, such as a vendor's lien and a deed-of-trust lien. All liens should be listed, even if the attorney for the note holder making the transfer has access only to the recording information for the deed of trust. If recording information for all documents is available, it should be included, but a simple notation of a lien other than the one described by recording information is adequate.

For information about the property description, see section 3.8 in this manual.

§ 10.1:3 Additional Clauses: Negation of Recourse and Representations and Warranties

If the holder is being paid in full, the holder has the option to sign a release. The transferee, however, will most likely want a transfer instrument. In that case, the holder will not want to incur any liability beyond that which the holder would incur by signing a release. To do so, the holder will make the transfer without recourse. Merely making the transfer without recourse does not negate the transfer warranties of Texas Business and Commerce Code section 3.416. *See* Tex. Bus. & Com. Code § 3.416 cmt. 3. To negate the transfer warranties, the words *without warranties* or other specific reference must be included in the transfer instrument. *See* Tex. Bus. & Com. Code § 3.416 cmt. 5. The words *without recourse against or without representation or warranty by* should be added to the endorsement of the note and a statement added to the transfer of note and lien to accomplish this purpose. There are some representations that the holder can make that will not result in liability beyond that of signing a release. First, the holder is the correct person to make the transfer, that is, the holder is the person entitled to enforce the note. Second, the payoff amount, the outstanding principal and interest, is correctly stated. Third, if true, the note is not overdue. This last representation helps the transferee obtain holder-in-due-course status. *See* Tex. Bus. & Com. Code § 3.302(a)(2)(C).

§ 10.1:4 Endorsement of Note

The note transferred should be endorsed and dated, and if the transfer is without recourse against or representation or warranty by the holder, except as stated, that fact should be noted:

> [**Date of transfer**]
>
> Pay to the order of [**name**] [without recourse against [and/or] without representation or warranty by, except as stated in a separate transfer of note and lien, [**name of holder**]].
>
> [**Signature of holder**]

Alternatively, the holder of the note may endorse the note in favor of the transferee by use of an allonge, form 10-25 in this chapter. As described in section 10.1 above, any special terms included in the transfer instrument, such as a negation of recourse or of representations or warranties, should also be noted in the allonge used to endorse the note. The holder of the note should affix the allonge to the note and deliver the transfer instrument together with the note and allonge to the transferee.

§ 10.1:5 Confidentiality Notice

Instruments transferring an interest in real property to or from an individual must contain the confidentiality notice required by Tex. Prop. Code § 11.008. An instrument is defined as "a deed, deed of trust, or any other record recorded by a county clerk related to real property, including a mineral lease, a mechanic's lien, and the release of a mechanic's lien." Tex. Prop. Code § 11.008(a). See section 3.17 in this manual.

§ 10.2 General Considerations for Release of Lien and Partial Release of Lien

Although payment of a debt extinguishes the liens that secure it even without a formal release, the lienholder has a duty to provide a written release. After paying the debt, the borrower may bring suit against a lienholder who refuses to provide a release and may recover actual damages incurred because of the refusal. *Bayless v. Strahan*, 182 S.W.2d 262 (Tex. App.—Amarillo 1944, writ ref'd w.o.m.).

The release should be filed in the real property records of the county in which the lien is recorded.

§ 10.2:1 Cautions for Partial Release

Only the portion of the property to be released from the lien should be described in the partial release, form 10-3 in this chapter.

If the lien instrument does not authorize partial releases, the lienholder is not required to grant a partial release. If the lienholder nevertheless agrees to a partial release, obtaining the written consent of any junior lienholder may be considered, although obtaining a junior lienholder's consent is not general practice.

If the note secured by the lien has makers or guarantors who are not grantors in the lien instrument, their written consent to the partial release is probably necessary unless the note or guaranty provides for their continuing liability after a partial release.

If the lien is insured by a mortgagee's title policy, an endorsement of the policy should be obtained. Title companies may require a premium for endorsement. Procedural Rule P-9.b(3), *Basic Manual of Rules, Rates and Forms for the Writing of Title Insurance in the State of Texas*.

§ 10.2:2 Instructions for Completing Release

Notes are frequently secured by more than one lien, such as a vendor's lien and deed-of-trust lien, and all of them should be included in the release. If recording information for all documents is available, it should be included under the heading "Note and Lien Are Described in the Following Documents." Even if some recording information is not available, all lien documents should be described as fully as possible.

For information about the property description, see section 3.8 in this manual.

§ 10.2:3 Instructions for Completing Partial Release

A partial release should include a description of all liens securing the note. If recording information for all documents is available, it should be included under the heading "Note and Lien Are Described in the Following Documents." Even if some recording information is not available, all lien documents should be described as fully as possible.

§ 10.2:4 Additional Clauses for Use with Partial Release

A partial release clause in a lien instrument or a prepayment clause in a note should state how any allowable prepayment will be applied. If those clauses do not adequately explain the application of a prepayment, a clause serving that purpose should be added to form 10-3 in this chapter after the sentence releasing the lien. The prepayment clauses suggested in form 6-3 in this manual may serve as appropriate models for drafting this type of clause.

§ 10.3 General Considerations for Modification and Extension Agreement

Form 10-4 in this chapter is appropriate for extending the time or manner of payment of a note secured by a deed-of-trust lien on property or for modifying the terms of the note. If instead the parties want to reinstate a note and pay it as originally written, they should use a different form. See the suggested reinstatement agreement at form 14-6 in this manual.

The legality of extensions and their effect on the statute of limitations are governed by Tex. Civ. Prac. & Rem. Code §§ 16.035–.037. The form expressly requires the obligor to assume payment of the note, even if the obligor was not the original borrower. This requirement accords with section 16.036, which provides that the extension of a note likewise extends the statute of limitations for foreclosure of a lien only if the extension is executed by the "party or parties primarily liable for a debt." Therefore a party who buys the property subject to the lien without assuming the note should not execute this extension form, for the party would become liable for payment of the note.

Many attorneys advise their clients to obtain written consent from all junior or inferior lien claimants and holders before agreeing to an extension. Numerous cases, however, have held that junior lienholders who acquire their liens while the first lien and first-lien note are intact are bound by the terms of a valid extension agreement. *See Yates v. Darby*, 131 S.W.2d 95, 101 (Tex. 1939).

§ 10.3:1 Cautions for Modification and Extension Agreement

If a loan policy covers the interest of the note holder, it should be examined carefully. Policies written before March 1, 1983, limit the policy protection to the final maturity date of the note as originally written plus the applicable limitations period. There is also no loan policy endorsement available for increased value.

§ 10.3:2 Instructions for Completing Modification and Extension Agreement

The property description should match that on the note, if any, and the deed of trust.

The period of extension must be definite, or the extension will not be enforceable.

After being acknowledged, the form must be recorded in the county in which the land is located to provide notice to third parties.

If a party to a modification or extension agreement is an individual, the practitioner must include the confidentiality notice required by Tex. Prop. Code § 11.008. See section 3.17 in this manual.

§ 10.4 Assignment of Rent

Texas has adopted an assignment of rents act. *See* Tex. Prop. Code ch. 64. Under the act, an enforceable security instrument (meaning a deed of trust, mortgage, or other contract lien on an interest in real property) creates an assignment of rents arising from the real property, unless the security instrument provides otherwise or an assignment of rents is governed by article XVI, § 50(a)(6), (a)(7), or (a)(8), of the Texas Constitution (Texas home equity, reverse mortgage, or conversion of manufactured home liens). The assignment of rents is a security interest in all accrued and unaccrued rents, regardless of the form of the document creating the assignment of rents. Tex. Prop. Code § 64.051. The security interest is perfected upon recording the security instrument in the real property records of the county where any part of the real property is located. Tex. Prop. Code § 64.052.

The assignee may enforce an assignment of rents by giving notice to the assignor demanding that all rents accrued but not paid and unaccrued rents be sent to the assignee when collected by the assignor. An assignee may not enforce an assignment of rents by notice to the assignor if the property is a one-to-four-family residence that is the assignor's homestead on the date the security instrument was signed and the date of prospective enforcement. Tex. Prop. Code § 64.054. The assignee may also enforce an assignment of rents by giving notice, a form of which is included in the statute, to the tenant that all rents accrued but not paid and unaccrued rents be paid to the assignee when rent payments are due. After a tenant receives notice from an assignee to pay rents to the assignee, the tenant's obligation to pay rents is discharged by paying rents to the assignee. If a tenant is occupying the premises as his primary residence, the tenant's obligation to pay rents is also discharged by continuing to pay rents to the assignor/landlord. For other tenants, the obligation to pay rents is not discharged by continuing to pay rents to the assignor/landlord after receipt of the notice from the assignee. Tex. Prop. Code §§ 64.055, 64.056.

Unless otherwise agreed, an assignee that collects rents must apply the collected rents in a stipulated order. Tex. Prop. Code § 64.058. The order of application for collected rents is different than the order of application of foreclosure proceeds under the Texas Property Code. Unless otherwise agreed, a subordinate creditor that enforces its assignment of rents and collects rents before receipt of a turnover notice from an assignee with priority is not obligated to turn over to the assignee with priority rents collected before receipt of the turnover demand. Tex. Prop. Code § 64.060. If an assignee's security interest in rents is perfected, the assignee's security interest attaches to identifiable proceeds and is perfected as to identifiable cash proceeds. Tex. Prop. Code § 64.061.

§ 10.5 Borrowing Resolutions

Form 10-6 in this chapter provides examples of resolutions authorizing an entity to guarantee a loan or borrow funds and mortgage real property as security for the loan. These resolutions may be incorporated into one of the certificates of resolutions included in chapter 26, forms 26-9 through 26-14, in this manual. The requirements for meeting and voting for for-profit corporations are found in chapter 21 of the Texas Business Organizations Code. *See* Tex. Bus. Orgs. Code §§ 21.411–.416. The requirements for meeting and voting for limited liability companies are found in chapter 101 of the Code. *See* Tex. Bus. Orgs. Code §§ 101.353–.358.

§ 10.6 Collection and Payment Agreement

Form 10-7 in this chapter may be used in wraparound loan transactions. See section 8.3 in this manual for commentary on wraparound loan transactions.

§ 10.7 Homestead Affidavits

Forms 10-8 and 10-9 in this chapter designate property as a rural homestead or urban homestead. Constitutional and statutory prohibitions against mortgaging or encumbering the homestead (except for purchase money, taxes, owelty of partition, refinance, improvements, home equity loans, reverse mortgages, or conversion of a manufactured home) and against one spouse's selling or abandoning the homestead without the consent of the other may limit the ability to borrow against or transfer the property. The voluntary designation of homestead in the real property records may free property that is not claimed as homestead from these limitations. A purchaser or lender for value without actual knowledge is entitled to conclusively rely on an affidavit that disclaims property as homestead or designates other property as the homestead of the affiant. Tex. Const. art. XVI, § 50(d). Both spouses should join in the designation of a homestead. Form 10-8 may be used by a lender making a loan to be secured by the borrower's nonhomestead property. See clauses 8-9-2 and 8-9-3 in this manual for homestead disclaimer and designation clauses suggested for use in a deed of trust. Form 10-9 is an example of an affidavit appropriate for loans to be secured by the borrower's homestead.

§ 10.8 Lender's Estoppel Certificate

A lender considering a loan to be secured by a subordinate lien on real property already encumbered by a prior lien often will require, as a condition to making the loan, that the borrower obtain an estoppel certificate from the prior lienholder. Form 10-10 in this chapter requires the prior lienholder to confirm important information regarding the prior lienholder's note and deed of trust. Some of the provisions of this form may have to be modified or deleted to obtain the prior lienholder's agreement to execute this form.

§ 10.9 Lienholder's Subordination to Oil, Gas, and Mineral Lease

Form 10-11 in this chapter is used if an oil, gas, and mineral lease is given on real property already encumbered by a deed-of-trust lien or other lien. This form provides that the lease will not be affected by foreclosure of the lien if the lease is maintained according to its terms.

§ 10.10 Notice from Lender's Attorney to Borrower

Form 10-12 in this chapter is an example of a written disclosure confirming that the lender's attorney does not represent the borrower. As with all forms, this letter should be modified to reflect the specific details of the loan transaction. See section 1.6:4 in this manual for commentary regarding an attorney's communications with unrepresented parties.

§ 10.11 Subordination of Lien

Form 10-13 in this chapter is used if a new deed-of-trust lien is made superior to an existing deed-of-trust lien. The new lender typically requires the subordination of existing liens to the newly created lien.

§ 10.12 Notice of Final Agreement

Loans made by banks, savings and loan associations, and credit unions in excess of $50,000 must be in writing and be signed by the party to be bound or by that party's authorized representative. Tex. Bus. & Com. Code § 26.02(b). Written loan documents evidencing loans in excess of $50,000 may not be varied by oral agreements if the financial institution gives the obligor, on or before execution of the loan documents, a written notice stating substantially the following:

> This written loan agreement represents the final agreement between the parties and may not be contradicted by evidence of prior, contemporaneous, or subsequent oral agreements of the parties. There are no unwritten oral agreements between the parties.

The notice may be in a separate document signed by the obligor or incorporated into one or more of the loan documents and must be conspicuous. Form 10-14 in this chapter may be used by financial institutions to satisfy the requirements of section 26.02 of the Texas Business and Commerce Code.

§ 10.13 General Considerations for Guaranty

Form 10-15 in this chapter is an unconditional guaranty of payment. It allows the lender to pursue the guarantor without first pursuing the principal obligor on the default of the principal obligor. This form should be distinguished from a guaranty of collection, which requires the lender to use reasonable diligence to compel payment by the principal obligor before pursuing the guarantor. This form may be modified to become a limited guaranty by describing the guaranteed indebtedness as limited to a specific dollar amount or a specific percentage of the borrower's debt to the lender. Although this form contains several waivers by the guarantor of various defenses to the enforcement of a guaranty, many attorneys recommend that the guarantor's written consent be obtained at the time of any modification of the guaranteed indebtedness. If the guarantor is a corporation, the lender should require a specific resolution of the corporation's board of directors authorizing the execution of the guaranty and declaring that the guaranty may reasonably be expected to benefit the corporation. *See* Tex. Bus. Orgs. Code § 2.104(c).

In *Moayedi v. Interstate 35/Chisam Road, L.P.*, 438 S.W.3d 1, 6 (Tex. 2014), the Texas Supreme Court held that a guarantor may waive his right to offset under section 51.003 of the Texas Property Code.

§ 10.14 Home Loans

"Home loan" is defined as a loan that is made to one or more individuals for personal, family, or household purposes and secured in whole or part by either a manufactured home (as defined by Texas Finance Code section 347.002), used or to be used as a borrower's principal residence, or real property improved by a dwelling designed for occupancy by four or fewer families and used or to be used as a borrower's principal residence. Tex. Fin. Code § 343.001(2). A lender, mortgage banker, or licensed mortgage broker must provide each applicant for a home loan with a notice of penalties for making false or misleading written statements. Tex. Fin. Code § 343.105. Form 10-19 in this chapter may be used to provide the statutorily required notice. As used in chapter 343 of the Finance Code, a home loan excludes a reverse mortgage or an "open-end account" as defined by Finance Code section 301.002. Tex. Fin. Code § 343.002(b). Two types of home loans are addressed in the statute: low-rate home loans and high-cost home loans.

§ 10.14:1 Low-Rate Home Loans

A low-rate home loan is a home loan that at its inception carries an interest rate two percentage points or more below the yield on treasury securities having comparable periods of maturity to the loan maturity, except that if the loan's interest rate is a discounted introductory rate or a rate that automatically steps up over time, the fully indexed rate or the fully stepped-up rate, as appropriate, is used instead of the rate at the loan's inception to determine if the loan is a low-rate home loan. Tex. Fin. Code § 343.101(a). A lender may not replace or consolidate a low-rate home loan directly made by a governmental or nonprofit lender before the seventh anniversary of the date of the loan unless the new or consolidated loan has a lower interest rate and requires payment of a lesser amount of points and fees than the original loan or is a restructure to avoid foreclosure. Tex. Fin. Code § 343.101(b). A restructure is defined as a change in the payment schedule or other terms of a home loan as a result of the borrower's default. Tex. Fin. Code § 343.001(3).

§ 10.14:2 High-Cost Home Loans

A high-cost home loan is a home loan that (1) is made to one or more individuals for personal, family, or household purposes; (2) is secured in whole or part by (a) a manufactured home (as defined by Tex. Fin. Code § 347.002) used or to be used as the borrower's principal residence or (b) real property improved by a dwelling designed for occupancy by four or fewer families and used or to be used as the borrower's principal residence; (3) has a principal amount equal to or less than one-half of the maximum conventional loan amount for first mortgages as established and adjusted by the Federal National Mortgage Association; (4) is not a reverse mortgage or an "open-end account" as defined by Tex. Fin. Code § 301.002; and (5) is a credit transaction described by 12 C.F.R. § 1026.32, except that the term includes a residential mortgage transaction, as defined by 12 C.F.R. § 1026.2, if the total loan amount is $20,000 or more and (a) the annual percentage rate exceeds the rate indicated in 12 C.F.R. § 1026.32(a)(1)(i) or (b) the total points and fees payable by the consumer at or before the loan closing will exceed the amount indicated in 12 C.F.R. § 1026.32(a)(1)(ii). Tex. Fin. Code § 343.201(1). Points and fees have the meaning assigned by 12 C.F.R. § 1026.32(b). Tex. Fin. Code § 343.201(2).

A high-cost home loan may not contain a provision for a scheduled payment that is more than twice as large as the average of earlier scheduled monthly payments unless the balloon payment becomes due not less than sixty months after the date of the loan. This prohibition does not apply if the payment schedule is adjusted to account for the seasonal or otherwise irregular income of the borrower or if the loan is a bridge loan in connection with the acquisition or construction of a dwelling intended to become the borrower's principal dwelling. Tex. Fin. Code § 343.202.

A high-cost home loan may not provide for a payment schedule with regular periodic payments that cause the principal balance to increase except for any negative amortization as a consequence of a temporary forbearance, bridge loan, or restructure sought by the borrower. Tex. Fin. Code § 343.203. A high-cost home loan also may not contain a provision for a prepayment penalty. Tex. Fin. Code § 343.205.

A bridge loan under Finance Code chapter 343 refers to temporary or short-term financing that requires payment of only interest until the entire unpaid balance is due. Tex. Fin. Code § 343.001(1).

A high-cost home loan lender may also not engage in a pattern or practice of extending consumer credit based on the consumer's collateral without regard to an obligor's repayment ability, including an obligor's current and expected income, current obligations, employment status, and other financial resources, other than an obligor's equity in the dwelling that secures repayment of the loan. Tex. Fin. Code § 343.204(b). The term *obligor* as used in section 343.204(b) refers to all persons obligated to pay a high-cost home loan, including borrowers, cosigners, and guarantors. Tex. Fin. Code § 343.204(a).

§ 10.14:3 Credit Life, Disability, or Unemployment Insurance

Lenders must provide a statutory insurance disclosure to each home loan applicant, which must be made by hand delivery or mail not later than the third business day after the date the lender receives a home loan application. Tex. Fin. Code § 343.104. Form 10-16 in this chapter may be used to provide the statutorily required insurance disclosure.

§ 10.15 Certification of Trust

A person other than a beneficiary is not required to inquire into the extent of the trustee's powers or the propriety of the exercise of those powers if the person deals with the trustee in good faith and obtains a certification of trust. *See* Tex. Prop. Code § 114.081(b). Instead of providing a copy of a trust instrument to a third party, the trustee may provide a certification of trust that contains, among other things, representations about the power of the trustee to take actions on behalf of the trust. Any party without actual knowledge to the contrary may rely on the representations in the certification of trust in dealing with the trustee. A person who in good faith enters into a transaction relying on a certification of trust may enforce the transaction against the trust property as if the representations contained in the certification of trust are correct. A mortgage loan made to a revocable living trust that holds title to a person's residence may be subject to Fannie Mae requirements for approval. Any certification of trust provided to Fannie Mae for review must (1) identify the settlor, trustee, and primary beneficiaries of the trust; (2) confirm whether the trust is revocable during the settlor's lifetime; and (3) verify whether the trustee's powers include the ability to mortgage trust property. If a certification of trust does not contain that information, a mortgage lender will request a copy of the trust instrument to review for compliance with Fannie Mae requirements. Form 10-29 of this manual includes a checklist for reviewing revocable trusts.

Form 10-20 in this chapter provides an example of a certification of trust. The statute allows a recipient of a certification of trust to require the trustee to furnish copies of the excerpts from the original trust instrument and later amendments to the trust instrument that designate the trustee and confer on the trustee the power to act in the pending transaction. *See* Tex. Prop. Code § 114.086(e). The statute does not provide protection to parties with knowledge contrary to the contents of the certification.

A person making a demand for the trust instrument in addition to a certification of trust or excerpts as provided by the statute is liable for damages if the court determines that the person did not act in good faith in making the demand. Tex. Prop. Code § 114.086(i).

§ 10.16 Subordination, Nondisturbance, and Attornment Agreement

A subordination, nondisturbance, and attornment agreement (SNDA) deals with the issues of existing commercial tenants' and lienholders' rights as they relate to present and future financing. This agreement is an acknowledgment by a landlord, tenant, and lienholder of their respective rights and obligations, and it provides assurance to the parties that present rights and obligations will be preserved should the landlord default on its loan and the lender foreclose. The tenant agrees to continue to be a tenant of the landlord or purchaser on foreclosure, and the lienholder agrees not to foreclose the rights of the tenant on foreclosure of the lien. Form 25-16 in this manual provides an example of a simple SNDA. Language also may be incorporated in the lease agreement if the situation warrants its incorporation. When drafting an SNDA, the attorney may also need to address various other issues applicable to the different types of commercial properties.

§ 10.17 Assumption Agreement

Form 10-22 in this chapter is an example of an assumption agreement used to document a third party's assumption of an obligation to pay an indebtedness secured by a vendor's lien or deed-of-trust lien on real property. Alternative paragraphs are included to distinguish between an assumption of debt where the original borrower is released or not released from liability to pay the assumed indebtedness. If the original borrower is not released from liability to pay the assumed indebtedness, a practitioner should review sections 8.6 and 8.7 in this manual concerning the use and effect of a deed of trust to secure assumption.

§ 10.18 Lender's Rescission and Waiver of Acceleration of Indebtedness Secured by Lien on Real Property

A lender may use forms 10-23 and 10-24 in this chapter to rescind and waive the acceleration of an indebtedness secured by a lien on real property before the limitations period expires, following the requirements of section 16.038 of the Texas Civil Practice and Remedies Code, and to document the lender's compliance with the written notice requirement to the borrower.

§ 10.19 Assignment of Architect's Contract and Consent; Assignment of Construction Contract and Consent

Commercial construction lenders typically require an assignment of the borrower's rights in contracts for the completion of the project, such as contracts with architects, engineers, and contractors. These assignments and the related consents are intended to give lenders the ability to complete the project upon a borrower's default by using the services of these professionals. Some lenders include an assignment of these contracts in the deed of trust, while others use a stand-alone collateral assignment. Form 10-26 in this chapter is a short-form collateral assignment of an architect's contract, and form 10-27 is a short-form collateral assignment of a construction contract. Each could be modified for use with other building professionals. Such assignments are technically security agreements under the Uniform Commercial Code that would be perfected in the same manner as any other security interest in a general intangible. See chapter 9 in this manual.

In the "Basic Information" section of form 10-26, the "Architect's Agreement" would identify the contract between the architect and the borrower (such as by date, project number, or other details assigned by the architect and the borrower). "Plans" would identify the plans drawn by the architect, such as by date, number of pages, or other identifying information. "Project" would identify the construction project as the architect and the borrower have designated it, such as "Mixed-Use Development on Washington Avenue, Houston" or "West End Shopping Center, Dallas, Texas." The form assumes that the borrower and lender will execute a construction loan agreement. Form 10-18 includes representative terms that may be included in a construction loan agreement. The alternative sections E.1. and E.2. in form 10-26 address the obligation of the lender to reimburse the architect for certain amounts due to the architect and are typically a subject of negotiation between the lender and the architect. Similarly, in the "Basic Information" section of form 10-27, the "Construction Contract" would identify the construction contract between the contractor and the borrower (such as by date, project number, or other details assigned by the contractor and the borrower). As in the case of alternative sections E.1. and E.2. in form 10-26, the obligation of the lender to reimburse the contractor for certain amounts due the contractor is typically a subject of negotiation between the lender and the contractor. Sections E.1. and E.2. in form 10-27 are examples of the types of clauses that the lender and contractor might use.

§ 10.20 Other Loan Documents

For other forms in this manual related to loan transactions, see the following:

- mechanic's lien contract and related forms—chapter 20;
- reinstatement agreement—form 14-6; and
- closing instructions letters—forms 26-15 through 26-18.

§ 10.21 Additional Resources

Barton, J. Cary. "Negotiating Guaranty Agreements from the Guarantor's Perspective." In *Advanced Real Estate Drafting Course, 2016*. Austin: State Bar of Texas, 2016.

Conoly, David Z. "Collateral Transfer of a Promissory Note." In *Advanced Real Estate Drafting Course, 2020*. Austin: State Bar of Texas, 2020.

———. "Foreclosure on a Collateral Transfer of Note & Lien." In *Advanced Real Estate Law Course, 2020*. Austin: State Bar of Texas, 2020.

Crow, Richard A. "Collateral Transfer of a Promissory Note." In *Advanced Real Estate Drafting Course, 2021*. Austin: State Bar of Texas, 2021.

Erwin, K. Gregory. "Texas Annotated Guaranty." In *Advanced Real Estate Strategies Course, 2015*. Austin: State Bar of Texas, 2015.

Form 10-1

Transfer of Note and Lien

Notice of confidentiality rights: If you are a natural person, you may remove or strike any or all of the following information from any instrument that transfers an interest in real property before it is filed for record in the public records: your Social Security number or your driver's license number.

Basic Information

Date:

Holder of Note and Lien ("Holder"):

Holder's Mailing Address:

Transferee:

Transferee's Mailing Address:

Note

Date:

Original principal amount:

Borrower:

Lender:

Unpaid principal and interest:

[Maturity date:]

Note and Lien Are Described in the Following Documents ("Lien Documents"): [**include recording information**]

Property (including any improvements):

Prior Lien(s): [**include recording information**]

Transfer of Note and Lien

Holder transfers the Note and the liens and security interests ("Lien") on the Property granted in the Lien Documents to Transferee.

[**Include if applicable:** This transfer is without recourse against [and/or] without representation or warranty by Holder, except that] Holder represents that Holder is the person entitled to enforce the Note [**include if applicable:** , the Note is not overdue,] and the unpaid principal and interest on the Note are correctly stated.

Holder expressly waives and releases all present and future rights to establish or enforce the liens described in this instrument as security for payment of any future or other indebtedness.

When the context requires, singular nouns and pronouns include the plural.

____

[**Name of holder**]

Include acknowledgment.

Form 10-2

Release of Lien

Notice of confidentiality rights: If you are a natural person, you may remove or strike any or all of the following information from any instrument that transfers an interest in real property before it is filed for record in the public records: your Social Security number or your driver's license number.

Basic Information

Date:

Holder of Note and Lien:

Holder's Mailing Address:

Note

Date:

Original principal amount:

Borrower:

Lender:

[Maturity date:]

Note and Lien Are Described in the Following Documents ("Lien Documents"): [**include recording information**]

Property (including any improvements): [**include legal description of real property and personal property to be released**]

Release of Lien and Security Interests

Holder is the owner and holder of the Note and Lien.

Select one of the following.

Holder releases the Property from all liens and security interests held by Holder granted in the Lien Documents and any other instruments, including other instruments recorded in the official public records of the county where the Property is located.

Or

Holder releases the Property from all liens and security interests held by Holder granted in the Lien Documents.

Continue with the following.

When the context requires, singular nouns and pronouns include the plural.

____

[**Name of holder**]

Include acknowledgment.

Form 10-3

Partial Release of Lien

Notice of confidentiality rights: If you are a natural person, you may remove or strike any or all of the following information from any instrument that transfers an interest in real property before it is filed for record in the public records: your Social Security number or your driver's license number.

Basic Information

Date:

Holder of Note and Lien:

Holder's Mailing Address:

Note

Date:

Original principal amount:

Borrower:

Lender:

[Maturity date:]

Note and Lien Are Described in the Following Documents: [**include recording information**]

Property (including any improvements) to Be Released from Lien ("Property"):

Partial Release of Lien

For value received, Holder of Note and Lien releases only the Property from the Lien and from all liens held by Holder of Note and Lien, without regard to how they were created or evidenced.

When the context requires, singular nouns and pronouns include the plural.

____

[**Name of holder**]

Include acknowledgment.

Form 10-4

Modification and Extension Agreement

Notice of confidentiality rights: If you are a natural person, you may remove or strike any or all of the following information from any instrument that transfers an interest in real property before it is filed for record in the public records: your Social Security number or your driver's license number.

Basic Information

Date:

Holder of Note and Lien:

Holder's Mailing Address:

Obligor:

Obligor's Mailing Address:

Note

Date:

Original principal amount:

Borrower:

Lender:

[Maturity date:]

Unpaid Principal and Interest on Note:

Lien Documents: [**include recording information**]

Property (including any improvements):

Extended Maturity Date of Note:

Modified Terms:

Obligor's Covenants and Warranties

The Note is secured by liens against the Property. Whether Obligor is primarily liable on the Note or not, Obligor nevertheless agrees to pay the Note and comply with the obligations expressed in the Lien Documents.

For value received, Obligor renews the Note and promises to pay to the order of Holder of Note and Lien, according to the Modified Terms, the Unpaid Principal and Interest on Note. All unpaid amounts are due by the Extended Maturity Date of Note. Obligor also extends the liens described in the Lien Documents.

The Note and the Lien Documents continue as written, except as provided in this agreement.

Obligor warrants to Holder of Note and Lien that the Note and the Lien Documents, as modified, are valid and enforceable and represents that they are not subject to rights of offset, rescission, or other claims.

When the context requires, singular nouns and pronouns include the plural.

____

[Name of obligor]

____

[Name of holder]

Include acknowledgments.

Form 10-5

Assignment of Rent

Notice of confidentiality rights: If you are a natural person, you may remove or strike any or all of the following information from any instrument that transfers an interest in real property before it is filed for record in the public records: your Social Security number or your driver's license number.

Basic Information

Date:

Assignor:

Assignor's Mailing Address:

Assignee:

Assignee's Mailing Address:

Note

Date:

Original principal amount:

Borrower:

Lender:

Deed of Trust

Date:

Borrower:

Lender:

Trustee:

Property:

Current Leases: **[include recording information if available]**

Clauses and Covenants

For value received, as a supplement to the Deed of Trust, Assignor collaterally assigns to Assignee all current and future rent from the Property. Leases are not assigned.

A. Assignor's Representations

Assignor represents the following:

A.1. This assignment is valid and enforceable.

A.2. The Current Leases are valid, have not been modified or amended except as stated, have not been previously assigned, and are subject to no security interests.

A.3. Without the prior written consent of Assignee, Assignor will not modify any material term in any lease covering the Property, exercise or forfeit any option in a lease, or accept payment of rent more than one month before its regular monthly payment date.

A.4. Assignor will perform all the obligations of the lessor in all leases covering the Property.

A.5. Assignor will promptly inform Assignee of all material events concerning the leases covering the Property.

A.6. Assignor will keep accurate records of all aspects of leases covering the Property and on request will make them available for Assignee's examination.

A.7. Assignor will apply all rent from the Property to payment of the Note and performance of the obligations in the Deed of Trust, but if the rent exceeds the amount due under the Note and the Deed of Trust, Assignor may retain the excess.

B. Default and Remedies

B.1. If a default exists in payment of the Note or performance of any obligation in the Deed of Trust or this assignment and the default continues after any required notice of the default and the time allowed to cure, Assignee may—

a. exercise Assignee's rights with respect to rent under the Texas Property Code as then in effect;

b. increase or reduce rent or change the terms of any lease, if permitted;

c. enter into new leases in the name of Assignor or otherwise on terms that Assignee chooses; and

d. sue for the collection of unpaid rent, to cancel any lease in default, and for possession of any portion of the Property covered by a lease in default.

B.2. Assignee will apply all rent collected under this assignment as required by the Texas Property Code as then in effect.

B.3. Assignee may elect not to collect rent under this assignment, but that election will not prejudice Assignee's right to collect rent subsequently. Assignee will never be liable for failure to collect rent but will be accountable for rent received before foreclosure of the Deed of Trust.

B.4. By exercising rights and remedies under this assignment, Assignee does not waive the right to enforce the Note or the Deed of Trust.

C. General Provisions

C.1. Assignee's collection of rent from the Property does not relieve Assignor of any obligations in the Note and the Deed of Trust.

C.2. Neither acceptance of this assignment nor any other act of Assignee under this assignment will be construed as a waiver of the priority of the Deed of Trust lien as to any lease or contract.

C.3. This assignment binds, benefits, and may be enforced by the successors in interest of the parties.

C.4. This assignment terminates on release of the Deed of Trust. At Assignor's expense, Assignee will sign a release of this assignment in recordable form.

C.5. Assignee does not have or assume any obligations as lessor to any occupant of the Property.

C.6. Assignee may exercise Assignee's rights and remedies in this assignment without taking possession of the Property.

C.7. When the context requires, singular nouns and pronouns include the plural.

____
[Name of assignor]

Include acknowledgment.

Form 10-6

Consent Resolutions

Corporation, Written Consent of Sole Director

Clause 10-6-1

[Name of corporation]

Written Consent of Sole Director

The undersigned, being the sole member of the board of directors of [**name of company**], a Texas corporation (the "Company"), acting pursuant to the provisions of [section 6.201 of the Texas Business Organizations Code], adopts by consent the following resolutions: [**insert resolution recitals (see clauses 10-6-5 and 10-6-6)**].

____
[**Name of sole director**]
Date:

Corporation, Unanimous Written Consent

Clause 10-6-2

[Name of corporation]

Unanimous Written Consent of Board of Directors

The undersigned, being all the members of the board of directors of [**name of company**], a Texas corporation (the "Company"), acting pursuant to the provisions of [section 6.201 of the Texas Business Organizations Code], adopt by consent the following resolutions: [**insert resolution recitals (see clauses 10-6-5 and 10-6-6)**].

____
[Name of director]
Date:

> Repeat for each director.

Limited Liability Company, Written Consent of Sole Member

Clause 10-6-3

[Name of limited liability company]

Written Consent of the [Sole Member/Manager]

The undersigned, being the [sole member/manager] of [**name of company**], a Texas limited liability company (the "Company"), acting pursuant to the provisions of [article 2.23(B)(1) of the Texas Limited Liability Company Act, Tex. Rev. Civ. Stat. Ann. art. 1528n/section 6.201 of the Texas Business Organizations Code], adopts by consent the following resolutions: [**insert resolution recitals (see clauses 10-6-5 and 10-6-6)**].

____
[Name of [sole member/manager]]
Date:

Limited Liability Company, Unanimous Written Consent

Clause 10-6-4

[Name of limited liability company]

Unanimous Written Consent of [Members/Managers]

The undersigned, being all the [members/managers of the board of managers] of [**name of company**], a Texas limited liability company (the "Company"), acting pursuant to the provisions of [article 2.23(B)(1) of the Texas

Limited Liability Company Act, Tex. Rev. Civ. Stat. Ann. art. 1528n/section 6.201 of the Texas Business Organizations Code], adopt by consent the following resolutions: [**insert resolution recitals (see clauses 10-6-5 and 10-6-6)**].

____
[**Name of [member/manager]**]
Date:

Repeat for each member or manager.

Borrowing Resolution Recitals

Clause 10-6-5

[The Company is the general partner of [**name**], a [Texas/[**state**]] limited partnership ("Borrower")]. RESOLVED, that [the Company/Borrower] is authorized to borrow the amount of $[**amount**] from [**name of lender**] ("Lender") to [purchase certain land and improvements located in [**county**] County, Texas, (the "Property")/[**state other purpose of use of loan proceeds**]] and to enter into a promissory note (the "Note") in the principal amount of $[**amount**], payable to the order of Lender.

RESOLVED FURTHER, that to secure the payment of the Note, [the Company/Borrower] is authorized to enter into a deed of trust (the "Deed of Trust") covering the Property and any necessary modifications, extensions, increases, and renewals of the Deed of Trust.

RESOLVED FURTHER, that [the Company/Borrower] is authorized to enter into any assignments, pledges, mortgages, deeds of trust, security agreements, and other documents and instruments concerning the Property, or any real or personal property, or any interest therein, owned by [the Company/

Borrower] that may be necessary or appropriate, or required by Lender, to evidence and secure the payment of the Note.

Include if applicable.

RESOLVED FURTHER, that [the Company/Borrower] is authorized to contract for the issuance by Lender of letters of credit, to discount with Lender notes, acceptances, and evidences of indebtedness payable to or due [the Company/Borrower], to endorse the same and execute any contracts and instruments for repayment thereof to Lender as Lender may require, to enter into foreign exchange transactions with or through Lender, and to enter into interest-rate hedging transactions with Lender in connection with the Note.

Continue with the following, selecting the appropriate alternative.

RESOLVED FURTHER, that [**name of individual**] (the "Authorized Representative") is authorized to execute and deliver, on behalf of and in the name of [the Company/Borrower], the Note, the Deed of Trust, and any other agreements, documents, or instruments, and to take or cause to be taken any action necessary or appropriate in connection with the Note and the Deed of Trust or to accomplish the purposes of these resolutions, in the form and with the provisions the Authorized Representative may deem proper.

Or

RESOLVED FURTHER, that the president or any vice president of [the Company/Borrower] is authorized to execute and deliver, on behalf of and in the name of [the Company/Borrower], the Note, the Deed of Trust, and any other agreements, documents, or instruments, and to take or cause to be taken any action necessary or appropriate in connection with the Note and the Deed of Trust or to accomplish the purposes of these resolutions, in the form and with the provisions that the officers may deem proper.

Continue with the following.

RESOLVED FURTHER, that [the Company/Borrower] confirms and ratifies all actions previously taken by any officer or other representative of [the Company/Borrower] with respect to the loan evidenced by the Note and all documents executed in connection with the loan.

Corporate Guaranty Resolution Recitals

Clause 10-6-6

[**Name of lender**] ("Lender") has agreed to make a loan in the amount of $[**amount**] to [**name of borrower**] ("Borrower") to be evidenced by a note, in the original principal amount of $[**amount**], payable to the order of Lender (the "Note"), which is secured by a deed of trust (the "Deed of Trust") covering the property described in the Deed of Trust.

As a condition to making the loan, Lender has requested that the Company guarantee [a portion of] the indebtedness evidenced by the Note and the obligations of Borrower under the Deed of Trust and any other document executed by Borrower evidencing or securing the Note (the "Guaranteed Obligations").

RESOLVED, that the Company reasonably may be expected to benefit, either directly or indirectly, from guaranteeing the Guaranteed Obligations.

RESOLVED FURTHER, that the Company is authorized to enter into a guaranty (the "Guaranty") guaranteeing the Guaranteed Obligations.

RESOLVED FURTHER, that **[name of individual]** (the "Authorized Representative") is authorized to execute and deliver, on behalf of and in the name of the Company, the Guaranty and any other agreements, documents, or instruments, and to take or cause to be taken any action necessary or appropriate in connection with the Guaranty or to accomplish the purposes of these resolutions, in the form and with the provisions the Authorized Representative may deem proper.

Or

RESOLVED FURTHER, that the president or any vice president of the Company is authorized to execute and deliver, on behalf of and in the name of the Company, the Guaranty and any other agreements, documents, or instruments, and to take or cause to be taken any action necessary or appropriate in connection with the Guaranty or to accomplish the purposes of these resolutions, in the form and with the provisions that the officers may deem proper.

Continue with the following.

RESOLVED FURTHER, that the Company confirms and ratifies all actions previously taken by any officer or other representative of the Company on behalf of the Company with respect to the Guaranty and all documents executed in connection with the Guaranty.

Form 10-7

Collection and Payment Agreement

Basic Information

Date:

Borrower:

Borrower's Mailing Address:

Lender:

Lender's Mailing Address:

Collection Agent:

Collection Agent's Mailing Address:

Prior Note

Date:

Original principal amount:

Maker:

Payee:

Holder:

Holder's mailing address:

Maturity date:

[Terms:]

Secured by deed of trust

Date:

Recorded in:

Wraparound Note

Date:

Original principal amount:

Maker: Borrower

Payee: Lender

Maturity date:

[Terms:]

Secured by Wraparound Deed of Trust

Date:

Recorded in:

Property (including any improvements):

Particulars of the Agreement

Day of month by which Borrower's deposit must be made:

Date of first deposit:

Amount of deposit for escrow account under Wraparound Note:

Monthly principal and interest due on Wraparound Note:

Collection Agent's fee:

Monthly principal and interest due on Prior Note:

Amount of deposit for escrow account under Prior Note:

Clauses and Covenants

Lender has sold the Property to Borrower, and as partial consideration Borrower has executed and delivered to Lender the Wraparound Note, a copy of which is attached to this agreement. Lender is required to make payments to Holder of the Prior Note, a copy of which is attached to this agreement, according to its terms. Borrower, Lender, and Collection Agent enter into this agreement to facilitate payment of both notes.

A. Borrower's Duties

A.1. Borrower will deposit in Lender's account with Collection Agent on or before each monthly due date an amount equal to the required monthly installment of principal and interest due under the Wraparound Note plus any required monthly payment to the tax and insurance escrow account.

A.2. Borrower will promptly submit to Collection Agent and Lender copies of bills for ad valorem taxes on the Property and for insurance policy premiums on the Property if Borrower receives such bills.

A.3. Borrower will pay Collection Agent one-half of the annual fee for its services as specified below. Borrower also agrees to reimburse Collection Agent for any extraordinary expenses incurred as a result of Borrower's delinquency or default in making deposits.

B. Lender's Duties

B.1. Before the time specified for Borrower to make the first deposit, Lender will open a special account with Collection Agent and will notify Borrower of any information relevant to making deposits to the account.

B.2. Lender will pay Collection Agent one-half of the annual fee for its services as specified below.

B.3. Lender will notify Borrower and Collection Agent of any adjustment in the amount of the monthly escrow account payment that may become necessary.

C. Collection Agent's Duties

C.1. Within [**number**] business days after each of Borrower's monthly deposits to Lender's special account, Collection Agent will pay on behalf of Lender the required payments due on the Prior Note.

C.2. After paying all amounts then due under the Prior Note, Collection Agent will pay or credit the remaining balance to Lender each month.

C.3. Collection Agent will promptly forward to Lender and Borrower copies of its documents transmitting all payments.

C.4. Unless specified otherwise in this agreement, on termination of this agreement Collection Agent will pay any amounts in Lender's special account to Lender.

D. General Provisions

D.1. No interest will be paid on funds in Lender's account.

D.2. This agreement will terminate on the occurrence of any of the following events or conditions:

a. The full and final payment of either the Wraparound Note or the Prior Note.

b. Written notice from Lender and Borrower to Collection Agent. Collection Agent will then transfer all amounts in Lender's account to any successor Collection Agent and be released from further liability. If Lender and Borrower fail to appoint a successor collection agent within thirty days, Collection Agent is unconditionally authorized to deposit the balance of the account with a court of proper jurisdiction.

c. Acceleration of maturity of the Wraparound Note by Lender. In this event, Lender may terminate this agreement by giving notice to Collection Agent and Borrower.

d. Collection Agent's resignation. Collection Agent may resign by giving Borrower and Lender written notice at least thirty days before the effective date of the resignation. On such resignation, the balance of the account will be transferred according to written instructions from Borrower and Lender. If Collection Agent does not receive written instructions within thirty days after mailing the notice, Collection Agent is unconditionally authorized to deposit the balance of the account with a court of proper jurisdiction.

D.3. Any notice required or permitted under this agreement must be in writing. Any notice required by this agreement will be deemed to be given (whether received or not) the earlier of receipt or three business days after being deposited with the United States Postal Service, postage prepaid, certified mail, return receipt requested, and addressed to the intended recipient at the address shown in this agreement. Notice may also be given by regular mail, personal delivery, courier delivery, or email and will be effective when received. Any address for notice may be changed by written notice given as provided herein.

D.4. Collection Agent may rely on any document that it reasonably believes to be authentic in making any delivery of money under this agreement. Collection Agent is not liable for harm resulting from any of its acts or omissions unless the acts or omissions constitute willful misconduct or gross negligence. Borrower and Lender agree that Collection Agent's liabilities and obligations are strictly limited to those enumerated in this agreement. Borrower and Lender also indemnify Collection Agent against all liability, loss, and expense that Collection Agent may incur in exercising any authority granted to it by this agreement.

D.5. This agreement binds, benefits, and may be enforced by the successors in interest of the parties.

D.6. When the context requires, singular nouns and pronouns include the plural.

____
[Name of borrower]

____
[Name of lender]

____
[Name of collection agent]

Form 10-8

Designation of Homestead and Affidavit of Nonhomestead

Date:

Affiant:

Affiant's Homestead Property:

> For a rural homestead, indicate the number of acres designated, not to exceed 200 acres if the homestead of a family or 100 acres if the homestead of a single adult. If there is more than one survey, include the number of acres in each. For an urban homestead, indicate the number of acres designated, not to exceed 10 acres.

Current Record Title Holder of Affiant's Homestead Property:

Affiant's Nonhomestead Property:

[Lender:]

Affiant on oath swears that the following statements are true and are within the personal knowledge of Affiant:

1. My full legal name is [**full legal name of affiant**], and I am over the age of eighteen years.

2. I currently reside at [**current residence address**].

3. I do not now intend or ever intend to reside on, use in any manner, or claim Affiant's Nonhomestead Property as a business or residence homestead.

4. I disclaim all homestead right, interest, and exemption in Affiant's Nonhomestead Property.

5. I now own and reside on, use, claim, and designate Affiant's Homestead Property as my only legal homestead, exempt from forced sale under the constitution and laws of Texas.

6. This affidavit and this designation are made to [induce Lender to make a loan secured by a deed of trust on Affiant's Nonhomestead Property/[**state other purpose of affidavit**]].

____
[**Name of affiant**]

SUBSCRIBED AND SWORN TO before me on __________________ by [**name of affiant**].

____
Notary Public, State of Texas

Form 10-9

Affidavit of Homestead

Date:

Affiant:

Affiant's Homestead Property ("Property"):

> For a rural homestead, indicate the number of acres designated, not to exceed 200 acres if the homestead of a family or 100 acres if the homestead of a single adult. If there is more than one survey, include the number of acres in each. For an urban homestead, indicate the number of acres designated, not to exceed 10 acres.

Current Record Title Holder of Affiant's Homestead Property:

Lender:

Lender's Address:

Affiant on oath swears that the following statements are true and are within the personal knowledge of Affiant:

1. My full legal name is [**full legal name of affiant**], and I am over the age of eighteen years.

2. I currently reside at [**current residence address**].

3. I acknowledge that Lender is taking a security interest in the Property and I will use and claim the Property as my homestead.

4. I acknowledge that I am obtaining a loan ("Loan") from Lender for a part of the purchase price of the Property.

5. I confirm that Lender has informed me that, as a condition of obtaining the Loan from Lender, I must occupy the Property as my primary residence after the closing so that the Property will constitute my homestead.

6. I also confirm that Lender has informed me that my failure to occupy the Property as my primary residence will impair Lender's security for the Loan and that Lender would not have made the Loan but for my representation and stated intention that the Property will be used as my homestead and residence.

7. I further confirm that I have been informed that, if I cease to occupy the Property as my residence, Lender may accelerate all amounts then due and owing to Lender with respect to the Loan and exercise all rights granted to Lender in the instruments evidencing and securing the Loan.

8. I understand that, if Lender accelerates the Loan in such circumstances, the entire loan balance will be immediately due and payable, and if I fail to pay the amounts due, Lender may institute collection proceedings against me, including, without limitation, nonjudicial foreclosure sale in accordance with the terms and conditions of the deed of trust encumbering the Property that I have executed to secure payment of the Loan.

____
[Name of affiant]

SUBSCRIBED AND SWORN TO before me on ________________ by **[name of affiant]**.

____
Notary Public, State of Texas

Form 10-10

Lender's Estoppel Certificate

Basic Information

Date:

Borrower:

Borrower's Mailing Address:

Prior Lender:

Prior Lender's Mailing Address:

Prior Lender's Note: Note dated [**date**], in the original principal amount of $[**amount**], executed by Borrower and payable to Prior Lender.

Prior Lender's Deed of Trust: [**include recording information**]

Subordinate Lender:

Subordinate Lender's Mailing Address:

Subordinate Lender's Loan:

Property:

Clauses and Covenants

Borrower has requested Subordinate Lender to make a loan to be secured by the Property, and Subordinate Lender has agreed that the liens securing the note evidencing Subordinate Lender's Loan will be subordinate to the liens securing Prior Lender's Note. As a condition to making Subordinate Lender's Loan, however, Subordinate Lender requires Prior Lender to verify the following information concerning Prior Lender's Note. Prior Lender understands that Subordinate Lender will rely on this information in connection with the closing of Subordinate Lender's Loan.

1. Prior Lender certifies to Subordinate Lender the following:

   a. True copies of Prior Lender's Note and Prior Lender's Deed of Trust are attached as Exhibits [**exhibit numbers/letters**].

   b. Prior Lender's Note and Prior Lender's Deed of Trust have not been renewed, extended, modified, or amended [**include if applicable:** , except as evidenced by the documents attached as Exhibits [**exhibit numbers/letters**]].

   c. Prior Lender is the present owner and holder of Prior Lender's Note.

   d. The unpaid principal balance of Prior Lender's Note as of Date is $[**amount**].

   e. The amount of accrued unpaid interest on Prior Lender's Note as of Date is $[**amount**].

   f. All amounts required to be paid as of Date under the terms of Prior Lender's Note and Prior Lender's Deed of Trust and any other loan documents have been paid in full.

   g. No default exists under the terms of Prior Lender's Note or Prior Lender's Deed of Trust or any other loan documents.

   h. The amount of $[**amount**] is held in escrow by Prior Lender for the payment of taxes and other amounts required to be escrowed under the terms of Prior Lender's Note and Prior Lender's Deed of Trust.

2. Prior Lender agrees that Prior Lender's Deed of Trust will not secure any indebtedness other than the indebtedness evidenced by Prior Lender's Note, and Prior Lender waives the provisions of any future advance or dragnet clause that would cause Prior Lender's Deed of Trust to secure other indebtedness of Borrower.

3. Prior Lender agrees that Subordinate Lender's Loan will not cause Prior Lender's Note to be in default, and Prior Lender waives the provisions of any due-on-sale clause or due-on-encumbrance clause that would make Subordinate Lender's Loan a default under Prior Lender's Note or Prior Lender's Deed of Trust.

4. Prior Lender agrees to give Subordinate Lender written notice of default not less than [**number**] days before any acceleration of the unpaid balance of Prior Lender's Note. Any notice required or permitted under this agreement must be in writing. Any notice required by this agreement will be deemed to be given (whether received or not) the earlier of receipt or three business days after being deposited with the United States Postal Service, postage prepaid, certified mail, return receipt requested, and addressed to the intended recipient at the address shown in this agreement. Notice may also be given by regular mail, personal delivery, courier delivery, or email and will be effective when received. Any address for notice may be changed by written notice given as provided herein.

5. Prior Lender agrees to accept payments on Prior Lender's Note from Subordinate Lender with the understanding that Subordinate Lender in no way obligates itself to make any payments.

6. If Prior Lender transfers Prior Lender's Note to any other party, Prior Lender agrees to notify the transferee of the terms of this estoppel certificate and obtain the transferee's consent to its terms and conditions.

____

[**Name of prior lender**]

Form 10-11

Lienholder's Subordination to Oil, Gas, and Mineral Lease

Basic Information

Date:

Lienholder:

Deed of Trust

Date:

Grantor:

Beneficiary:

Property:

Recording information:

Lease

Date:

Lessor:

Lessee:

Recording information:

Clauses and Covenants

The property described in the Lease includes [all/part] of the Property encumbered by the Deed of Trust. For value received, Lienholder, owner of the Deed of Trust lien, subordinates the lien to the Lease and ratifies the Lease.

If the Deed of Trust lien is foreclosed, the sale of the Property will not affect the Lease if the Lease is maintained according to its terms.

____

[Name of lienholder]

Include acknowledgment.

Form 10-12

Notice from Lender's Attorney to Borrower

Basic Information

Date:

Borrower:

Lender:

Loan: Loan evidenced by a note dated [**date**] in the original principal amount of $[**amount**], executed by Borrower, payable to Lender, and secured by a deed of trust on the property described therein.

Attorney:

Disclosure of Relationship

This notice discloses the relationship between Attorney, Borrower, and Lender.

1. Lender has engaged Attorney to prepare the note, deed of trust, and other documents relating to the Loan.

2. Attorney has not researched or examined title to the property and makes no representation or warranty about the condition of title, access to the property, or any other matter that might be revealed by an examination of a survey, title commitment, or the property itself. In preparing the documents, Attorney has relied on information provided by other parties, including the title company. If Borrower is purchasing the property, Borrower is cautioned to assure itself that the deed to Borrower conveys what Borrower has contracted to purchase and otherwise conforms with the earnest money contract.

3. Attorney represents only Lender and no other party involved in this transaction, although Attorney's legal fees may be paid by Borrower.

4. Attorney's legal fees are based on a per document or per transaction charge rather than an hourly fee. The legal fees are intended to provide fair compensation for time and labor involved in information gathering, document preparation, processing, and review. No charge has been made for preparation of Truth in Lending disclosures or for any disclosures required by the Real Estate Settlement and Procedures Act, if Attorney has prepared any of those documents.

5. Borrower has the right to be represented by its own attorney and to have its attorney review the Loan documents (including the deed, if there is one) and closing documents and be present at the closing of the Loan.

6. If any documents to be used are prepared by someone other than Attorney, Lender reserves the right to have Attorney review and approve those documents to ensure they properly protect Lender's interests.

By signing below, Borrower indicates that it has been notified of and understands its right to independent legal counsel and that Attorney represents only the interests of Lender and not those of Borrower or any other party.

____

[**Name of borrower**]

NOTE TO TITLE COMPANY OR CLOSER: Please return the executed original of this notice to [**name and address**].

Form 10-13

Subordination of Lien

Basic Information

Date:

Subordinating Party:

Subordinated Lien

Date:

Grantor:

Beneficiary:

Note Secured by Subordinated Lien: Note dated [**date**], in the original principal amount of $[**amount**].

Recording information:

Superior Lien

Date:

Borrower:

Lender:

Note Secured by Superior Lien: Note dated [**date**], in the original principal amount of $[**amount**].

Recording information:

Property:

Terms of Subordination

Subordinating Party is the owner and holder of the Subordinated Lien, which is a lien against the Property.

For value received, Subordinating Party subordinates the Subordinated Lien against the Property to the Superior Lien and agrees that the Subordinated Lien will remain subordinate to the Superior Lien regardless of the frequency or manner of renewal, extension, change, or alteration of the Superior Lien or the Note Secured by Superior Lien.

When the context requires, singular nouns and pronouns include the plural.

____

[Name of subordinating party]

Include acknowledgment.

Form 10-14

Notice of Final Agreement

Date:

Borrower:

Lender:

To: Borrower and all other debtors and obligors with respect to the Loan identified below.

1. THE WRITTEN LOAN AGREEMENT REPRESENTS THE FINAL AGREEMENT BETWEEN THE PARTIES AND MAY NOT BE CONTRADICTED BY EVIDENCE OF PRIOR, CONTEMPORANEOUS, OR SUBSEQUENT ORAL AGREEMENTS OF THE PARTIES.

THERE ARE NO UNWRITTEN ORAL AGREEMENTS BETWEEN THE PARTIES.

2. As used in this notice:

"Obligor" means any entity or individual who (a) is obligated to pay the Loan or (b) otherwise is or becomes obligated to pay the Loan (for example, as cosigner or guarantor) or (c) has pledged any property as security for the Loan.

"Loan" means the loan by Lender that is to be evidenced by the note dated [**date**] executed by Borrower, payable to the order of Lender, in the original principal amount of $[**amount**] as modified and extended by Borrower.

"Written Loan Agreement" means one or more promises, notes, agreements, undertakings, security agreements, deeds of trust, or other documents, or commitments, or any combination of actions or documents relating to the Loan.

3. Each Borrower and Obligor who signs below acknowledges, represents, and warrants to Lender that Lender has given and each respective Borrower and Obligor has received a copy of this notice on or before the execution of any Loan Agreement.

____

[Name of lender]

____

[Name of borrower]

____

[Name of obligor]

Form 10-15

Guaranty

Basic Information

Date:

Guarantor:

Guarantor's Mailing Address:

Borrower:

Borrower's Mailing Address:

Lender:

Lender's Mailing Address:

Guaranteed Indebtedness: The debt evidenced by the note dated **[date]**, in the original principal amount of $**[amount]**, executed by Borrower and payable to the order of Lender, the obligations under the deed of trust executed in connection with the note and any other document executed by Borrower evidencing or securing the note (collectively, the "Loan Documents"), plus all interest, penalties, expenses, attorney's fees, and other collection costs as provided in the Loan Documents.

Clauses and Covenants

1. Guarantor agrees to pay, when due or declared due, the Guaranteed Indebtedness to Lender at Lender's Mailing Address.

2. Guarantor waives (a) diligence in preserving liability of any person on the Guaranteed Indebtedness and in collecting or bringing suit to collect the Guaranteed Indebtedness; (b) all rights of Guarantor under chapter 43 of the Texas Civil Practice and Remedies Code, section 17.001 of the Texas Civil Practice and Remedies Code, [and] rule 31 of the Texas Rules of Civil Procedure [**include if applicable:** , and sections 51.003, 51.004, and 51.005 of the Texas Property Code]; (c) protest; (d) notice of extensions, increases, renewals, or rearrangements of the Guaranteed Indebtedness; and (e) notice of acceptance of this guaranty, of creation of the Guaranteed Indebtedness, of failure to pay the Guaranteed Indebtedness as it matures, of any other default, of adverse change in Borrower's financial condition, of release or substitution of collateral, of intent to accelerate, of acceleration, and of subordination of Lender's rights in any collateral, and every other notice of every kind. Guarantor's obligations under this guaranty will not be altered nor will Lender be liable to Guarantor because of any action or inaction of Lender in regard to a matter waived or of which notice is waived by Guarantor in the preceding sentence.

3. Guarantor agrees to pay reasonable attorney's fees and other collection costs if an attorney is retained to enforce this guaranty for collection.

4. This guaranty is an absolute, irrevocable, unconditional, and continuing guaranty of payment and performance and not of collection.

5. Lender need not resort to Borrower or any other person or proceed against collateral before pursuing its rights against Guarantor or any other guarantor. Lender's action or inaction with respect to any right of Lender under the law or any agreement will not alter the obligation of Guarantor hereunder. Lender may pursue any remedy against Borrower or any collateral or under any other guaranty without altering the obligations of Guarantor hereunder and without liability to Guarantor, even though Lender's pursuit of such remedy may result in Guarantor's loss of rights of subrogation or to proceed against others for reimbursement of contribution or any other right.

6. Guarantor will remain liable for the Guaranteed Indebtedness even though the Guaranteed Indebtedness may be unenforceable against or uncollectible from Borrower or any other person because of incapacity, lack of power or authority, discharge, or any other reason.

7. Guarantor consents and acknowledges that Guarantor's obligations will not be released by (a) the renewal, extension, or modification of the Guaranteed Indebtedness or any of the Loan Documents; (b) the insolvency, bankruptcy, liquidation, or dissolution of Borrower or any other obligor; (c) the failure of Lender to properly obtain, perfect, or preserve any security interest or lien in any collateral for the Guaranteed Indebtedness; (d) the release, substitution, or addition of any collateral for the Guaranteed Indebtedness; or (e) the failure of Lender to exercise diligence, commercial reasonableness, or reasonable care in the preservation, enforcement, or sale of any of the collateral.

8. Lender need not notify Guarantor that Lender has sued Borrower, but if Lender gives written notice to Guarantor that it has sued Borrower, Guarantor will be bound by any judgment or decree, to the extent permitted by law.

9. Lender may sue any guarantor without impairing Lender's rights against any other guarantor, with or without making Borrower a party. Lender may settle with Borrower or any other guarantor for such amounts as it may elect or may release Borrower or any guarantor or any collateral securing the Guaranteed Indebtedness without impairing Lender's right to collect the Guaranteed Indebtedness from Guarantor.

10. This guaranty binds Guarantor and Guarantor's heirs, successors, and assigns, and it benefits and may be enforced by Lender and Lender's successors in interest. When the context requires, singular nouns and pronouns include the plural. This guaranty will be construed under the laws of the state of Texas, without regard to choice-of-law rules of any jurisdiction. The provisions of this guaranty are severable. If a court of competent jurisdiction finds that

any provision of this guaranty is unenforceable, then the remaining provisions will remain in effect without the unenforceable parts.

11. FINAL AGREEMENT: THIS WRITTEN AGREEMENT REPRESENTS THE FINAL AGREEMENT BETWEEN THE PARTIES AND MAY NOT BE CONTRADICTED BY EVIDENCE OF PRIOR, CONTEMPORANEOUS, OR SUBSEQUENT ORAL AGREEMENTS OF THE PARTIES. THERE ARE NO UNWRITTEN ORAL AGREEMENTS BETWEEN THE PARTIES.

____
[Name of guarantor]

Form 10-16

This disclosure, set forth in Tex. Fin. Code § 343.104, must be made by hand delivery or mail not later than the third business day after the date the lender receives a home loan application. Tex. Fin. Code § 343.001 defines "home loan" for purposes of the required disclosure.

Insurance Notice to Applicant

You may elect to purchase credit life, disability, or involuntary unemployment insurance in conjunction with this mortgage loan. If you elect to purchase this insurance coverage, you may pay for it either on a monthly premium basis or with a single premium payment at the time the lender closes this loan. If you choose the single premium payment, the cost of the premium will be financed at the interest rate provided for in the mortgage loan.

This insurance is NOT required as a condition of closing the mortgage loan and will be included with the loan only at your request.

You have the right to cancel this credit insurance once purchased. If you cancel it within 30 days of the date of your loan, you will receive either a full refund or a credit against your loan account. If you cancel this insurance at any other time, you will receive either a refund or credit against your loan account of any unearned premium. YOU MUST CANCEL WITHIN 30 DAYS OF THE DATE OF THE LOAN TO RECEIVE A FULL REFUND OR CREDIT.

To assist you in making an informed choice, the following estimates of premiums are being provided along with an example of the cost of financing. The examples assume that the term of the insurance product is [**number**] years and that the interest rate is [**percent**] percent (a rate that has recently been available for the type of loan you are seeking). PLEASE NOTE THAT THE ACTUAL LOAN TERMS YOU QUALIFY FOR MAY VARY FROM THIS EXAMPLE. "Total amount paid" is the amount that would be paid if you financed only the total insurance premium for a [**number**] year period and is equal to the amount you would have paid if you made all scheduled payments. This is NOT the total of payments on your loan.

CREDIT LIFE INSURANCE: Estimated premium of $[**amount**]

DISABILITY INSURANCE: Estimated premium of $[**amount**]

INVOLUNTARY UNEMPLOYMENT INSURANCE: Estimated premium of $[**amount**]

TOTAL INSURANCE PREMIUMS: $[**amount**]

TOTAL AMOUNT PAID: $[**amount**]

Include the following language if an acknowledgment of receipt is desired.

The undersigned acknowledge[s] receipt of the foregoing notice on [**date**].

Continue with the following.

____

[**Name of applicant**]
Date:

Include additional signature lines for each applicant.

Form 10-17

Loan Agreement

[Borrower's Required Insurance Coverages]

Basic Information

Date:

Borrower:

Mailing address:

Phone:

Email:

Type of entity:

State of organization:

Federal tax identification number:

Lender:

Mailing address:

Phone:

Email:

Loan officer:

Guarantor:

Mailing address:

Phone:

Email:

Title Company:

Mailing address:

Phone:

Email:

Note

Date:

Original Principal Amount:

Maturity date:

Loan Commitment Fee:

Use of Loan Proceeds:

Collateral

Real Property:

Prior liens: [**include recording information**]

Personal property:

Prior security interests: [**include recording information**]

Loan Documents

Loan agreement/note: [**list other loan documents, i.e., deed of trust, security agreement, guaranty, etc.**]

Financial Covenants:

Additional Loan Requirements:

The Loan

Subject to the terms and conditions of this agreement, Lender will lend Borrower the Original Principal Amount as represented by the Note (the "Loan"), and Borrower agrees to pay the Note.

Clauses and Covenants

A. Conditions Precedent to Loan

The obligation of Lender to make the Loan is conditioned on—

A.1. the execution and delivery of the Loan Documents;

A.2. the accuracy, in all material respects, of all representations and warranties in the Loan Documents;

A.3. no default existing under the Loan Documents;

A.4. payment of the Loan Commitment Fee and all expenses incurred by Lender in connection with the Loan Documents; and

A.5. Lender's receipt, in a form acceptable to Lender, of—

a. opinion of Borrower's counsel as to Borrower's authority to execute and deliver the Loan Documents; the enforceability of the Loan Documents;

the nonusurious nature of the Loan [**include if applicable:** ; and the validity of Borrower's organization];

b. certification from Borrower's authorized representative for any Borrower that is an entity attaching (i) a copy of Borrower's organizational documents, (ii) the approval of Borrower's governing authority for the execution and delivery of the Loan Documents, and (iii) specimen signatures from all Borrower representatives authorized to execute the Loan Documents;

c. certification from governmental authorities for any Borrower that is an entity confirming Borrower's existence [**include if applicable:** and Borrower's account status with the Texas comptroller of public accounts];

d. appraisal of the Real Property;

e. survey plat of the Real Property;

f. environmental assessment of the Real Property;

g. commitment for issuance of a loan policy of title insurance in the Original Principal Amount insuring the validity of Lender's lien on the Real Property and confirming that no liens exist on the Real Property other than those liens permitted by the Loan Documents;

h. financing statement reports on the Personal Property issued by all applicable filing officers confirming no financing statements are filed on the Personal Property other than those financing statements permitted by the Loan Documents;

i. financial statement on Borrower [**include if applicable:** and financial statement on Guarantor]; and

j. proof of insurance required by the Loan Documents

together with all other documents, instruments, and certificates reasonably requested by Lender.

B. Borrower's Representations

To induce Lender to enter into this agreement and to make the Loan, Borrower represents to Lender that—

B.1. Borrower—

a. has the power and authority needed to execute and deliver the Loan Documents and to perform Borrower's obligations under the Loan Documents; and

b. possesses all permits, registrations, approvals, consents, licenses, trademarks, trademark rights, trade names, trade name rights, and copyrights needed to conduct Borrower's business[./ and;]

c. [**include if applicable:** was validly formed and exists under the laws of the State of Organization[./ and;]]

d. [**include if applicable:** is in good standing under the laws of the State of Organization and all other jurisdictions where the nature of Borrower's business makes qualification necessary[./ and;]]

e. [**include if applicable:** is qualified to do business under the laws of the State of Organization and all other jurisdictions where the nature of Borrower's business makes qualification necessary.]

B.2. the execution, delivery, and performance of the Loan Documents executed by Borrower have been duly authorized and do not and will not (a) contravene or violate any legal requirement; (b) result in the breach of, or constitute a default under, any instrument to which Borrower is a party or by which any of Borrower's property may be bound or affected; or (c) result in a requirement to create any lien on any of Borrower's property other than liens granted to Lender on the Collateral;

B.3. the Loan Documents are legal, valid, and binding obligations of the parties executing the documents;

B.4. Borrower has good and indefeasible title to the Real Property and has good title to the Personal Property, free and clear of all liens except (a) as disclosed in the Loan Documents; (b) liens for ad valorem taxes, general and special assessments, and other governmental charges not yet due or payable; and (c) liens granted to Lender;

B.5. Borrower's financial statements delivered to Lender fairly present the financial condition and the results of Borrower's operations as of the dates and for the periods indicated, and no material adverse change has occurred in the assets, liabilities, financial condition, or business of Borrower since the dates of the financial statements;

B.6. Borrower has no knowledge of any litigation or administrative claim, action, or proceeding, pending or threatened, against Borrower or directly involving the Collateral before or by any governmental authority that, if adversely determined, could have a material adverse effect on Borrower;

B.7. there is no outstanding adverse judgment, writ, order, injunction, award, or decree affecting Borrower or the Collateral;

B.8. Borrower is not in default under any agreement to which Borrower is bound or to which any of the collateral is subject that could have a material adverse effect on Borrower or the Collateral;

B.9. all information and documentation supplied to Lender and all statements made to Lender by or on behalf of Borrower are correct and complete in all material respects as of the date made;

B.10. Borrower has no knowledge of the Real Property's being used for the production, release, or disposal of hazardous wastes or materials;

B.11. the Real Property is taxed and billed separately from any other property for ad valorem tax purposes;

B.12. no part of the Real Property is located within a flood zone;

B.13. Borrower's financial records have been prepared and maintained in accordance with good accounting practices consistently applied and reflect all moneys due or to become due from or to Borrower; and

B.14. Borrower has filed all required tax returns and paid all taxes shown thereon to be due, except those for which extensions have been obtained and those that are being contested in good faith and for which appropriate reserves have been established and disclosed in writing to Lender.

C. Affirmative Covenants

Borrower will—

C.1. apply all proceeds from the sale, collection, or other disposition of the Collateral to amounts owing on the Note unless the Loan Documents authorize an alternate use of the proceeds;

C.2. comply with the Additional Loan Requirements;

C.3. comply with the Financial Covenants;

C.4. operate Borrower's business in accordance with all applicable legal requirements;

C.5. keep at Borrower's address, or such other place as Lender may approve, accounts and records reflecting the operation of Borrower's business and copies of all written contracts, leases, and other instruments that affect the Collateral;

C.6. prepare Borrower's financial records in compliance with good accounting practices consistently applied;

C.7. permit Lender to examine and make copies of Borrower's books, records, contracts, leases, and other instruments at any reasonable time;

C.8. deliver to Lender, at Lender's request from time to time, Borrower's tax returns and [audited/reviewed/compiled/internally prepared] financial statements of Borrower prepared in accordance with good accounting practices consistently applied, in detail reasonably satisfactory to Lender and certified to be true and correct by [**include if applicable:** the chief financial officer of] Borrower [**include if applicable:** and accompanied by an opinion of an independent certified public accountant];

Include if applicable.

C.9. deliver to Lender, at Lender's request from time to time, tax returns of Guarantor, and [audited/reviewed/compiled/internally prepared] financial statements of Guarantor prepared in accordance with good accounting practices consistently applied, in detail reasonably satisfactory to Lender and certified to be true and correct by [**include if applicable:** the chief financial officer of] Guarantor [**include if applicable:** and accompanied by an opinion of an independent certified public accountant];

Continue with the following.

C.10. execute, acknowledge as required, and deliver to Lender, at Lender's request from time to time, at Borrower's expense, any document needed by Lender to (a) correct any defect, error, omission, or ambiguity in the Loan Documents; (b) comply with Borrower's obligations under the Loan Documents; (c) make subject to and perfect the liens and security interests of the Loan Documents any property intended to be covered thereby; and (d) protect, perfect, or preserve the liens and the security interests of the Loan Documents against third persons or make any recordings, file any notices, or obtain any consents requested by Lender in connection therewith;

C.11. notify Lender promptly (a) on acquiring knowledge of the occurrence of any event of default under the Loan Documents; (b) if any of Borrower's property is surrendered in satisfaction of a debt or obligation [**include if applicable:** or on acquiring knowledge that any of Guarantor's property was surrendered in satisfaction of a debt or obligation]; and (c) of any litigation, arbitration, mediation, or proceedings before any governmental agency that could have a material adverse effect on Borrower or the Collateral [**include if applicable:** or on acquiring knowledge of any litigation, arbitration, mediation, or proceedings before any governmental agency that could have a material adverse effect on Guarantor];

C.12. pay promptly on demand all expenses in connection with (a) the negotiation, preparation, execution, filing, recording, rerecording, modification, and supplementation of the Loan Documents; (b) the collection of the Note; (c) the protection of the Collateral; (d) the collection, enforcement, sale, or other disposition of the Collateral; and (e) the performance by Lender of any of Borrower's obligations under the Loan Documents;

C.13. use the Note proceeds for the purposes permitted in this agreement[./; and]

Include if applicable.

C.14. do all things necessary to preserve Borrower's existence, qualifications, rights, and franchises in all jurisdictions where Borrower does business.

D. Negative Covenants

Borrower will not—

D.1. use or allow the use of the Collateral in any manner that (a) constitutes a public or private nuisance; (b) makes void, voidable, or cancelable, or increases the premium of, any insurance required by the Loan Documents; or (c) lessens the value of the Collateral, other than as a result of ordinary wear and tear from the Collateral's intended use;

D.2. purchase, acquire, or lease any property from, or sell, transfer, or lease any property to, any equity owner, manager, director, officer, agent, or employee of Borrower, or any person or entity controlled by, controlling, or under common control with Borrower, except on terms then customarily available between unrelated parties in substantially similar transactions;

D.3. lend money to, or guarantee the payment or performance of any liability or obligation of, any person, except short-term loans to Borrower's employees that, in the aggregate, do not exceed $[**amount**];

D.4. materially change the nature of Borrower's business or enter into any business that is substantially different from Borrower's existing business;

D.5. incur any indebtedness other than the Note, except short-term indebtedness to trade creditors incurred in the ordinary course of Borrower's business that, in the aggregate, does not exceed $[**amount**];

D.6. create or permit any mortgage, security interest, or lien on any Collateral other than mortgages, security interests, or liens existing at the date of this agreement and disclosed to Lender or created pursuant to the Loan Documents;

D.7. purchase or redeem any of Borrower's ownership interests, declare or pay any dividends, or make any distribution to the holders of any of Borrower's ownership interests (to the extent Borrower is an entity);

D.8. sell, transfer, convey, or lease any Collateral except for sales in the ordinary course of business and on the conditions provided in the Loan Documents; [or]

D.9. acquire all or substantially all of the assets or ownership interests of any third party[./; or]

Include if applicable.

D.10. liquidate or dissolve, or become a party to any merger or consolidation.

E. Default and Remedies

E.1. A default exists if—

a. Borrower fails to timely pay the Note;

b. a party fails to perform any obligation or covenant in any of the Loan Documents;

c. any representation made by a party in any of the Loan Documents is false in any material respect when made;

d. a receiver is appointed for any party executing any of the Loan Documents, or for any of the Collateral;

e. any Collateral is assigned for the benefit of creditors;

f. a bankruptcy or insolvency proceeding is commenced by a party executing any of the Loan Documents;

g. a bankruptcy or insolvency proceeding is commenced against a party executing any of the Loan Documents, and the proceeding continues without dismissal for sixty days, the party against whom the proceeding is commenced admits the material allegations of the petition against it, or an order for relief is entered;

h. any of the following parties is terminated, begins to wind up its affairs, is authorized by its governing body or persons to terminate or wind up its affairs, or any event occurs or condition exists that permits the termination or winding up of the affairs of any of the following parties: Borrower, a partnership of which Borrower is a general partner, or any other obligated party executing any of the Loan Documents; or

i. any Collateral is impaired by uninsured loss, theft, damage, or destruction, or by levy and execution, or by issuance of an official writ or order of seizure, unless it is promptly replaced with collateral of like kind and quality or restored to its former condition.

E.2. If a default exists, Lender may—

a. declare the unpaid principal balance, earned interest, and any other amounts owed on the Note immediately due; and

b. exercise against Borrower, the Collateral, and any other party executing the Loan Documents any rights and remedies available to Lender under the Loan Documents.

Include if applicable.

E.3. Notwithstanding any other provision in the Loan Documents, in the event of a default, before exercising any of Lender's remedies under the Loan Documents, Lender will first give Borrower notice of default and Borrower will have ten days after delivery of notice in which to cure the default. If the default is not cured within ten days after notice is delivered, Borrower and each surety, endorser, and guarantor waive all demand for payment, presentation for payment, notice of intention to accelerate maturity, notice of acceleration of maturity, protest, and notice of protest, to the extent permitted by law.

Continue with the following.

F. General Provisions

F.1. Any notice required or permitted under this agreement must be in writing. Any notice required by this agreement will be deemed to be given (whether received or not) the earlier of receipt or three business days after being deposited with the United States Postal Service, postage prepaid, certified mail, return receipt requested, and addressed to the intended recipient at the address provided in this agreement. Notice may also be given by regular mail, personal delivery, courier delivery, or email and will be effective when received. Any address for notice may be changed by notice given as provided herein.

F.2. The Loan Documents, including any of their exhibits and attachments, constitute the entire agreement of the parties. There are no representations, agreements, or promises by Lender pertaining to the Loan that are not in those documents.

F.3. This agreement may be amended only by an instrument in writing signed by the parties.

F.4. Borrower may not assign this agreement or any of Borrower's rights under it without Lender's prior written consent, and any attempted assignment is void. This agreement binds, benefits, and may be enforced by the parties and their successors in interest.

F.5. Borrower authorizes Lender to charge any amount due Lender under the Loan Documents against any of Borrower's deposit accounts with Lender.

F.6. Except as otherwise provided in the Loan Documents, Borrower waives all demand for payment, presentation for payment, notice of intention to accelerate maturity, notice of acceleration of maturity, protest, and notice of protest, to the extent permitted by law.

F.7. No remedy, right, or power conferred on Lender in this agreement is intended to be exclusive of any other remedy, right, or power now or hereafter existing at law, in equity, or otherwise, and all remedies, rights, and powers are cumulative.

F.8. This agreement will be construed under the laws of the state of Texas, without regard to choice-of-law rules of any jurisdiction. This agreement is to be performed where the Note is payable.

F.9. Interest on the Note will not exceed the maximum amount of nonusurious interest that may be contracted for, taken, reserved, charged, or received under law. Any interest in excess of that maximum amount will be credited on the principal of the Note or, if that has been paid, refunded. On any acceleration or required or permitted prepayment, any excess will be canceled automatically as of the acceleration or prepayment or, if already paid, credited on the principal of the Note or, if the principal of the Note has been paid, refunded. This provision overrides any conflicting provisions in this and all other Loan Documents.

F.10. It is not a waiver of default if the nondefaulting party fails to declare immediately a default or delays taking any action. Pursuit of any remedies set forth in this agreement does not preclude pursuit of other remedies in the other Loan Documents or provided by law.

F.11. There are no third-party beneficiaries of this agreement.

F.12. If any provision of this agreement is determined to be invalid or unenforceable, the validity or enforceability of any other provision will not be affected.

F.13. The rule of construction that ambiguities in a document will be construed against the party who drafted it will not be applied in interpreting this agreement.

F.14. The parties' relationship is an ordinary commercial relationship, and the parties do not intend to create the relationship of principal and agent, partnership, joint venture, or any other special relationship. Lender in exercising Lender's rights and performing Lender's obligations under the Loan Documents owes no fiduciary duty to Borrower.

F.15. If this agreement is executed in multiple counterparts, all counterparts taken together will constitute this agreement.

F.16. If Lender agrees to waive or defer any of the requirements of this agreement as a condition precedent to the advance of the proceeds of the Note, Borrower will provide any deferred information or documentation within thirty days after the advance.

F.17. In the event of any conflict among the provisions of this Loan Agreement and any of the Loan Documents, the more restrictive provision will control.

F.18. When the context requires, singular nouns and pronouns include the plural.

F.19. The term *Note* includes all extensions and renewals of the Note.

THE WRITTEN LOAN AGREEMENT REPRESENTS THE FINAL AGREEMENT BETWEEN THE PARTIES AND MAY NOT BE CONTRADICTED BY EVIDENCE OF PRIOR, CONTEMPORANEOUS, OR SUBSEQUENT ORAL AGREEMENTS OF THE PARTIES.

THERE ARE NO UNWRITTEN ORAL AGREEMENTS BETWEEN THE PARTIES.

Signed on [**date**].

____

[**Name of borrower**]

____

[**Name of lender**]

Attach insurance rider if applicable.

Insurance Rider to Loan Agreement

> Texas law prohibits additional insured coverage in a construction contract; in an agreement collateral to or affecting a construction contract, except that pertaining to a single family house, townhouse, duplex, or directly related land development; to a public works project of a municipality; or in other exceptions or exclusions set out in Texas Insurance Code chapter 151. *See* Tex. Ins. Code ch. 151. See section 17.2:4 in this manual.

Loan Agreement

Date:

Borrower:

Lender:

This insurance rider is part of the Loan Agreement.

Borrower's Required Insurance Coverages

Type of Insurance or Endorsement	Minimum Policy or Endorsement Limit	
General Liability Insurance Policy Required of Borrower		
☐ Commercial general liability (occurrence basis)	Per occurrence:	$____________
	General aggregate:	$____________
	Products-completed operations aggregate:	$____________
	Personal and advertising injury:	$____________
	Damage to premises rented to you:	$____________
	Medical expense:	$____________

Required Endorsements to Borrower's General Liability Policy

☐	Designated location(s) general aggregate limit	$__________
☐	Liquor liability	$__________
☐	______________________________	$__________

Include any other desired endorsements. See chapter 17.

Additional Liability Insurance Policies Required of Borrower

☐	Workers' compensation	$500,000
☐	Employer's liability	$__________
☐	Business automobile liability	$__________
☐	Garage	$__________
☐	Crime (or fidelity)	$__________
☐	Innkeepers	$__________
☐	Excess liability	$__________
	Or	
☐	Umbrella liability (occurrence basis)	$__________

Commercial Property Insurance Policies Required of Borrower If No Construction Is Contemplated or, If Construction Is Contemplated, for the Period After Construction Is Completed

☐	Causes of loss—special form	100 percent of replacement cost of the Property on an agreed-value basis

Required Endorsements to Borrower's Commercial Property Policy

☐	Business income and additional expense	Sufficient limits to address reasonably anticipated business interruption losses for a period of ____ months
☐	Boiler and machinery	$__________

☐	Flood (if Property is located within a 100-year floodplain (FEMA Flood Zone "A" or any subdesignation of Zone "A"))	$__________
☐	Earth movement	$__________
☐	Ordinance or law coverage	$__________
☐	Terrorism coverage	$__________
☐	Glass	Sufficient limits to cover plate glass
☐	Signs	Sufficient limits to cover exterior signage

Include any other desired endorsements. See chapter 17.

General Insurance Requirements

1. The commercial general liability policy must be endorsed to name Lender as an "additional insured" and must not be endorsed to exclude the partial, contributory, or comparative negligence of Lender from the definition of "insured contract."

2. Additional insured endorsements must not exclude coverage for the sole or contributory ordinary negligence of Lender.

3. Property insurance policies must contain waivers of subrogation of claims against Lender.

4. Certificates of insurance and copies of any additional insured and waiver of subrogation endorsements with respect to Borrower's insurance must be delivered by Borrower to Lender on the date of this agreement and at least [**number**] days before the expiration of the current policies.

5. Borrower may carry a business owner's insurance policy, commercial package insurance policy, or other package insurance policy rather than separate commercial property and general liability insurance policies described above, provided that such package policy contains the minimum insurance coverages, endorsements, and limits set forth in this agreement.

Include paragraph 6, 7, or 8 as applicable.

6. If Borrower will employ a third-party manager for the Real Property, Borrower will require that the third-party manager carry the property and liability insurance policies described in Exhibit [**exhibit number/letter**] to this agreement.

And/Or

7. If all or a portion of the Property is to be constructed during the construction period, Borrower will maintain, in lieu of the commercial property insurance described above, the builder's risk insurance described in Exhibit [**exhibit number/letter**] and require that the general contractor and architect carry the liability insurance policies described in Exhibit [**exhibit number/letter**].

And/Or

8. Certificates of insurance and copies of any additional insured endorsements with respect to a third-party manager's, contractor's, subcontractor's, or architect's insurance must be delivered by Borrower to Lender before such party enters the Property and thereafter at least [**number**] days before the expiration of the policies.

Exhibit [exhibit number/letter] to

Insurance Rider to Loan Agreement

Mark applicable boxes.

Additional Insurance Policies Required during Construction Period

FROM GENERAL CONTRACTOR

Type of Insurance or Endorsement	**Minimum Policy or Endorsement Limit**	

General Liability Insurance Policy Required of General Contractor

☐ Commercial general liability (occurrence basis)	Per occurrence:	$__________
	General aggregate:	$__________
	Products-completed operations aggregate:	$__________
	Personal and advertising injury:	$__________
	Damage to premises rented to you:	$__________
	Medical expense:	$__________

Required Endorsements to General Contractor's General Liability Policy

☐ Designated construction project(s) general aggregate limit $__________

☐ ______________________________________ $__________

Include any other desired endorsements. See chapter 17 in this manual.

Additional Liability Insurance Policies Required of General Contractor

☐ Workers' compensation	$500,000
☐ Employer's liability	$__________
☐ Business automobile liability	$__________

☐ Professional liability $__________
☐ Excess liability $__________

Or

☐ Umbrella liability (occurrence basis) $__________

Commercial Property Insurance Policies Required of General Contractor for General Contractor's Personal Property and Equipment

☐ Causes of loss—special form 100 percent of replacement cost of the general contractor's personal property and equipment

FROM ARCHITECT

Type of Insurance or Endorsement	**Minimum Policy or Endorsement Limit**

Professional Liability Insurance Policy Required of Architect

☐ Professional liability $__________

FROM BORROWER OR GENERAL CONTRACTOR

Type of Insurance or Endorsement	**Minimum Policy or Endorsement Limit**

Builder's Risk Insurance Policy Required of Borrower or General Contractor

☐ Builder's risk on a "completed value" basis 100 percent of replacement cost of the improvements to be constructed on the Property

Required Endorsements to Borrower's or General Contractor's Builder's Risk Insurance Policy

☐ Contract penalties $__________
☐ Collapse $__________
☐ Debris removal additional limit $__________

- ☐ Earthquake $___________
- ☐ Expediting expenses $___________
- ☐ Ordinance or law $___________
- ☐ Pollutant cleanup and removal $___________
- ☐ Preservation of property $___________
- ☐ Testing $___________
- ☐ Flood (if Property is located within a 100-year floodplain (FEMA Flood Zone "A" or any subdesignation of Zone "A")) $___________
- ☐ Occupancy of up to ____% of covered property to be permitted $___________

Form 10-18

Additional Clauses for Loan Agreements

Capital Expenditures

Clause 10-18-1

Borrower will not make any expenditures for fixed assets in excess of [**amount**] dollars ($[**amount**]) in any [fiscal/calendar] year. "Fixed assets" means tangible property that has a useful life in excess of [**number**] years.

Working Capital

Clause 10-18-2

Borrower will maintain at all times an excess of current assets over current liabilities of not less than [**amount**] dollars ($[**amount**]). "Current assets" means the sum of Borrower's cash, marketable securities, and other similar assets that are reasonably expected to be converted into cash or applied within twelve months of the date of determination. "Current liabilities" means the sum of all money owed by Borrower that is payable on demand or within twelve months of the date of determination.

Liquidity Ratio

Clause 10-18-3

Borrower will at all times maintain a ratio of the sum of cash and marketable securities to current liabilities of not less than [**number**] to 1. "Current liabilities" means the sum of all money owed by Borrower that is payable on demand or within twelve months of the date of determination.

Current Ratio

Clause 10-18-4

Borrower will maintain at all times a ratio of current assets to current liabilities of not less than [**number**] to 1. "Current assets" means the sum of Borrower's cash, marketable securities, and other assets that are reasonably expected to be converted into cash or applied within twelve months of the date of determination. "Current liabilities" means the sum of all money owed by Borrower that is payable on demand or within twelve months of the date of determination.

Debt Service Coverage

Clause 10-18-5

Borrower will maintain a ratio of net operating income to debt service for the [calendar/fiscal] year of not less than [**number**] to 1. "Net operating income" means gross income less operating expenses. "Debt service" means principal and interest payments on all debts with a maturity in excess of one year.

Loan-to-Value Ratio

Clause 10-18-6

Borrower will maintain a loan-to-value ratio on the [Collateral/Real Property/Personal Property] of [**ratio**] or less. The value of the [Collateral/Real Property/Personal Property] shall be the fair market value of the [Collateral/Real Property/Personal Property] as determined by [Lender/an appraisal acceptable to Lender]. "Loan" means the principal of any indebtedness secured by a [lien/security interest] on the [Collateral/Real Property/Personal Property].

Conditions to Lender's Obligations to Make Loan Advances

Clause 10-18-7

G. Conditions to Lender's Obligations to Make Loan Advances

Lender is not obligated to make any advance, including any after the first advance, of loan proceeds hereunder unless the following conditions have been satisfied, with proof provided in a form and sufficiency as Lender may reasonably request:

G.1. Lender must have received and approved (a) copies of the Plans and Specifications for the construction of the improvements on the Real Property (the "Improvements") (the "Plans"), any leases of personal property to be used in the construction of the Improvements (the "Equipment Leases"), any contracts between Borrower and contractors and subcontractors for the construction of the Improvements (the "Construction Contracts"), and any contracts between Borrower and any architects and engineers responsible for drafting the Plans (the "Architect's Agreement") that may be requested by Lender; (b) all presently procurable authorizations and permits required by any federal, state, or local governmental authority (a "Governmental Authority") for the construction of the Improvements, including those required for the use and operation of the Real Property and the Improvements (the "Property") for the purposes contemplated by the Plans; (c) a current title report from the Title Company describing the Real Property with attached copies of all instruments that appear as exceptions in the report; (d) an original current survey of each lot certified to Lender and the Title Company showing the locations of the perimeter of each lot within the Real Property by courses and distances, all easements and rights-of-way (identified as recorded in public records), the proposed building lines, the lines of the streets abutting the Real Property and the width thereof, encroachments, and the extent thereof in feet and inches upon the Real Property, the relation of the proposed Improvements by distances to the perimeter of the Real Property, the proposed building lines and the street lines, and if the Real Property is described as being on a filed map or plat, a legend relating the survey to the map or plat; (e) financial statements of Borrower; (f) advice from an architect or civil engineer and, if Lender elects, an independent architect or civil engineer approving the Plans and indicating that the construction contracts are acceptable and satisfactorily provide for the construction of the Improvements; (g) the policies of insurance required by the Deed of Trust and this Agreement accompanied by evidence of the payment of the policies' premiums; (h) a satisfactory "As Built" appraisal of the Improvements proposed for each lot in the Property; (i) Assignment of Architect's Agreement and consent of the architect; and (j) assignment of the Construction Contract and consent of the architect.

G.2. The Deed of Trust must have been executed by the parties to this Agreement and recorded in the office of the county clerk of each county in which any part of the Real Property is located, with all filing fees paid, all before commencement of any construction on any part of the Property and the placing of any material or equipment on the Property.

G.3. Lender must have received financing statements with proof of filing in the appropriate offices in the State of Texas and, if applicable, in other jurisdictions, and other things and instruments necessary or appropriate in the opinion of Lender to perfect a security interest in the property covered by the

Deed of Trust in accordance with the Texas Uniform Commercial Code, and Lender must have received proof that no prior financing statements from Borrower as debtor or from any other party affecting any of the Property have been filed in any such office in favor of any other party.

G.4. Lender must have received the Title Insurance showing the lien on the owner's interest in favor of Lender as holder of the Note, to be valid, first, and prior lien on the Real Property free and clear of all defects and encumbrances except as Lender approves. The Title Insurance must not contain any survey exceptions not already approved by Lender, and the status of title to the owner's interest shown therein shall otherwise be satisfactory to Lender.

G.5. The representations and warranties made in section B of this Agreement shall be true and correct on the date of the advance with the same effect as if made on that date.

G.6. There must be no default under this Agreement, the Note, or any of the Loan Documents.

G.7. Lender must have received the Note, Deed of Trust, and Loan Documents, all properly executed by the respective parties thereto.

G.8. An endorsement to the title policy or affidavit acceptable to Lender must state that there has been, as of the date of the requested advance, no change in the state of title and no survey exceptions not previously approved by Lender.

G.9. The Improvements, to the extent any have been made before the date of the advance, must not have been materially injured or damaged by fire or other casualty unless Lender has received insurance proceeds sufficient in the judgment of Lender and, if Lender elects, an independent supervising architect, to effect the satisfactory restoration of the Improvements and to permit their completion before the completion date.

G.10. Lender must have received (a) a proper request for advance from Borrower; (b) if construction has been performed before the advance, advice from an architect or inspector providing the opinion that the construction of the Improvements was performed in accordance with the Plans; (c) for advances after the first advance, a copy of a valid building permit issued for the Improvements; and (d) for advances after the first advance, Lender must have received (i) a notice of title continuation or an endorsement of the Title Insurance already delivered indicating that since the last preceding advance, there has been no change in the state of title and no survey exceptions not already approved by Lender, which endorsement shall have the effect of increasing the coverage of the Title Insurance by an amount equal to the advance then being made if the Title Insurance does not by its terms provide for such additional coverage without such an endorsement, and (ii) a forms or foundation survey satisfactory to Lender in its sole and absolute discretion.

G.11. All legal matters incident to this Agreement and the transactions contemplated by it must be satisfactory to counsel to Lender.

G.12. Lender must have received executed affidavits of contractor and Borrower duly and truthfully subscribed and sworn to evidencing any matter that Lender has requested.

[*G.13.* Lender, if it so requests, must have received one or more photographs of the Property taken on or after the date of the filing of the Deeds of

Trust and, if on the date of the filing, on or after the time of the filing. The photograph(s) must clearly show that there has not been actual commencement on the Property or any delivery of material to the Property. The photograph(s) must be signed on the back by the photographer for identification to an accompanying affidavit, and each photograph must include on its back the photographer's written description of the general area of the Property shown in the photograph and of the location from which the photograph was taken. The accompanying affidavit must be sworn and subscribed to by the photographer and certify that the photograph(s) were taken of the Property by the photographer at the date and time or times stated in the affidavit. Borrower shall pay the expenses of satisfying this condition.]

Form 10-19

This notice must be provided on a separate document, be in at least fourteen-point type, and use the below or substantially similar language. Tex. Fin. Code § 343.105.

Notice of Penalties for Making False or Misleading Written Statement (Pursuant to Section 343.105, Texas Finance Code)

Warning: Intentionally or knowingly making a materially false or misleading written statement to obtain property or credit, including a mortgage loan, is a violation of Section 32.32, Texas Penal Code, and, depending on the amount of the loan or value of the property, is punishable by imprisonment for a term of 2 years to 99 years and a fine not to exceed $10,000.

[I/We], the undersigned home loan applicant(s), represent that [I/we] have received, read, and understand this notice of penalties for making a materially false or misleading written statement to obtain a home loan.

[I/We] represent that all statements and representations contained in [my/our] written home loan application, including statements or representations regarding [my/our] identity, employment, annual income, and intent to occupy the residential real property secured by the home loan, are true and correct as of the date of loan closing.

____
[Name of borrower/loan applicant]

Repeat signature lines as necessary.

Form 10-20

Certification of Trust

Basic Information

Date:

Trust:

Trustee:

Trustee's Mailing Address:

Repeat as necessary.

Settlor:

Repeat as necessary.

Include the following terms as applicable.

Note

Date:

Original principal amount:

Borrower:

Lender:

Deed of Trust

Date:

Grantor:

Beneficiary:

Recording information:

Property:

Buyer:

Continue with the following.

Terms of Certification

1. Trustee is a currently acting trustee of the Trust under an instrument executed on [**date**], and the Trust exists.

Select one of the following.

2. The Trust powers include at least all those trust powers granted a trustee by subchapter A, chapter 113, of the Texas Property Code.

Or

2. The Trust powers include the power to, and the Trustee is authorized to

Select as applicable.

borrow money in the amount of $[**amount**] from Lender to [purchase the Property/[**state other purpose or use of loan proceeds**]] and to enter into the Note, payable to the order of Lender [;/.]

And/Or

grant security interests in or liens on all or certain assets of the Trust, including entering into the Deed of Trust covering the Property and any necessary modifications, extensions, increases, and renewals of the Deed of Trust [;/.]

And/Or

enter into any assignments, pledges, mortgages, deeds of trust, security agreements, and other documents and instruments concerning the Property, or any real or personal property, or any interest therein, owned by the Trust that may be necessary or appropriate or required by Lender to evidence and secure the payment of the Note [;/.]

And/Or

contract for the issuance by Lender of letters of credit, to discount with Lender notes, acceptances, and evidences of indebtedness payable to or due the Trust, to endorse the same and execute any contracts and instruments for repayment thereof to Lender as Lender may require, to enter into foreign exchange transactions with or through Lender, and to enter into interest-rate hedging transactions with Lender in connection with the Note [;/.]

And/Or

execute deeds or other instruments of conveyance [;/.]

And/Or

enter into a guaranty guaranteeing [a portion of] the obligations of Borrower to Lender [;/.]

And/Or

[**state other purpose of certification**].

Select one of the following.

3. The Trust is irrevocable.

Or

3. The Trust is revocable, and the power to revoke the Trust is held by [**name**].

Continue with the following.

4. Under the terms of the Trust, [all/[**number**]] of the currently acting trustees are required to sign documents in order to exercise the powers of the trustees.

5. Title to the Trust property should be taken in the following manner: [**describe**].

6. The Trust has not been revoked, modified, or amended in any manner that would cause the representations contained in this Certification to be incorrect.

Include one of the following if applicable.

7. The Settlor is the primary beneficiary of the Trust.

Or

7. The Settlor is not the primary beneficiary of the Trust.

Trustee:

____

[**Name of trustee**]

Repeat signature lines as necessary.

Form 10-21

Release of Collateral Transfer of Note and Lien

Notice of confidentiality rights: If you are a natural person, you may remove or strike any or all of the following information from any instrument that transfers an interest in real property before it is filed for record in the public records: your Social Security number or your driver's license number.

Basic Information

Date:

Secured Party:

Secured Party's Mailing Address:

Debtor:

Debtor's Mailing Address:

Collateral Note: $[**amount**] Note executed by [**maker**] and payable to the order of [**payee**] dated [**date**].

Collateral Note Security: Deed of Trust dated [**date**], recorded in [**recording data**].

Collateral Transfer of Note and Lien

Date:

Recorded: [**recording data**]

Purpose of Collateral Transfer of Note and Lien

In the Collateral Transfer of Note and Lien, Debtor granted to Secured Party a security interest in the Collateral Note and the Collateral Note Security, each as described in the Collateral Transfer of Note and Lien.

Release

Secured Party releases Secured Party's security interest in the Collateral Note and Collateral Note Security.

No Release of Underlying Collateral Note Debt and Collateral Note Security

Secured Party's release of its security interest in the Collateral Note and the Collateral Note Security does not affect or release (1) the indebtedness owing to Debtor on the Collateral Note and (2) the liens held by Debtor under the Collateral Note Security documents on the property described in those documents.

When the context requires, singular nouns and pronouns include the plural.

____
[Name of secured party]

Include acknowledgment.

Form 10-22

Assumption Agreement

Notice of confidentiality rights: If you are a natural person, you may remove or strike any or all of the following information from any instrument that transfers an interest in real property before it is filed for record in the public records: your Social Security number or your driver's license number.

Basic Information

Date:

Transferor:

Transferor's Original Mailing Address:

Assuming Party:

Assuming Party's Mailing Address:

Holder of Note and Lien ("Holder"):

Holder's Mailing Address:

Note

Date:

Original Principal Amount:

Borrower:

Lender:

Unpaid Principal Amount:

Accrued but Unpaid Interest:

Maturity Date:

[Extended Maturity Date of Note:]

Property (including any improvements):

Note and Lien(s) Are Described in the Following Documents ("Lien Documents"): [**include recording information**]

Modified Terms:

Agreement of the Parties

For good and valuable consideration, Transferor, Assuming Party, and Holder are entering into this agreement.

1. Assuming Party and Transferor warrant to Holder that the Note and the Lien Documents, as modified by this agreement, are valid and enforceable, and represent to Holder that the Note and Lien Documents are not subject to rights of offset, rescission, or other claims.

Select one of the following.

2. Assuming Party—

a. promises to perform all of Borrower's obligations under the Note and promises to pay to the order of Holder (i) the Unpaid Principal Amount, (ii) the Accrued but Unpaid Interest, and (iii) all other amounts now or hereafter due and owing on the Note; and

b. agrees to perform all obligations of grantor [**include if applicable:** and debtor/obligor] under the Lien Documents.

Or

2. Assuming Party and Transferor—

   a. promise to perform all of Borrower's obligations under the Note and promise to pay to the order of Holder (i) the Unpaid Principal Amount, (ii) the Accrued but Unpaid Interest, and (iii) all other amounts now or hereafter due and owing on the Note; and

   b. agree to perform all obligations of grantor [**include if applicable:** and debtor/ obligor] under the Lien Documents.

Select one of the following.

3. Holder consents to Transferor's conveyance of the Property to Assuming Party and Assuming Party's assumption of Transferor's obligations under the Note and the Lien Documents, and Holder releases Transferor from Transferor's obligations to Holder under the Note and the Lien Documents.

[**Include if applicable:** All unpaid amounts owing on the Note are due by the Extended Maturity Date of Note. Assuming Party also extends the liens described in the Lien Documents.]

Or

3. Holder consents to Transferor's conveyance of the Property to Assuming Party and Assuming Party's assumption of Transferor's obligations under the Note and the Lien Documents, but Holder's consent does not release Transferor from Transferor's obligations to Holder under the Note and the Lien Documents.

[**Include if applicable:** All unpaid amounts owing on the Note are due by the Extended Maturity Date of Note. Transferor and Assuming Party also extend the liens described in the Lien Documents.]

Continue with the following.

4. The Note and the Lien Documents continue as written, except as provided in this agreement.

5. When the context requires, singular nouns and pronouns include the plural.

____
[Name of transferor]

____
[Name of assuming party]

____
[Name of holder]

Include acknowledgments.

Form 10-23

Lender's Rescission and Waiver of Acceleration of Note

Date:

Note

Date:

Original Principal Amount:

Borrower:

Lender:

Original Stated Maturity Date:

Accelerated Maturity Date:

Rescission Date:

Deed of Trust

Date:

Grantor:

Lender:

Recording information:

Property:

[Guarantor:]

Lender, as of the Accelerated Maturity Date, accelerated the maturity of the Note.

Lender hereby rescinds and waives, as of the Rescission Date, its acceleration of the maturity of the Note. Lender hereby reinstates the payment terms of the Note, and the obligation evidenced by the Note will be governed by Texas Civil Practice and Remedies Code section 16.035 as if no acceleration had occurred.

A copy of this rescission and waiver, in accordance with Texas Civil Practice and Remedies Code section 16.038 has been served on each debtor who, according to Lender's records, is obligated to pay the Note.

____

[Name of lender]

Form 10-24

Affidavit of Mailing of Lender's Rescission and Waiver of Acceleration of Note

Date:

Affiant:

Note

Date:

Original principal amount:

Borrower:

Mortgagee:

Original stated maturity date:

Accelerated maturity date:

Rescission Date:

Deed of Trust

Date:

Grantor:

Mortgagee:

[Servicer: [**include name of servicer if servicer is not mortgagee**]]

Recording information:

Property: [**Insert property description and include the following if applicable:** including all personal property secured by the security agreement included in the Deed of Trust.]

Affiant on oath swears that the following statements are true and are within the personal knowledge of Affiant:

1. This affidavit is made with respect to Mortgagee's rescission and waiver, as of the Rescission Date, of Mortgagee's prior acceleration of the maturity of the Note.

2. Attached to this affidavit is a copy of the letter and accompanying Lender's Rescission and Waiver of Acceleration of Note (collectively, the "Written Notice") served by [first-class mail/certified mail] on each debtor obligated to pay the Note, in compliance with Texas Civil Practice and Remedies Code section 16.038, by [Mortgagee/Servicer/an attorney representing Mortgagee], either personally or by an agent, depositing a copy of the Written Notice in the United States mail, postage prepaid, addressed to each debtor obligated to pay the Note at each debtor's last known address.

____
[**Name of affiant**]

SUBSCRIBED AND SWORN TO before me on __________________ by [**name of affiant**].

____
Notary Public, State of Texas

After recording return to:
[**name and address**]

Include attachments.

Form 10-25

Allonge

Basic Information

Date:

Holder of Note ("Holder"):

Holder's Mailing Address:

Transferee:

Transferee's Mailing Address:

Note

Date:

Original principal amount:

Borrower:

Lender:

Unpaid principal and interest:

[Maturity date:]

Transfer of Note

Reference is made to the Note. This Allonge is to be attached to and made a permanent part of the Note.

Pay the Note to the order of Transferee.

[**Include if applicable:** This transfer is without recourse against [and/or] without representation or warranty by Holder, except that] Holder represents that Holder is the person entitled to enforce the Note [**include if applicable:** , the Note is not overdue,] and the unpaid principal and interest on the Note are correctly stated.

When the context requires, singular nouns and pronouns include the plural.

____

[**Name of holder**]

Form 10-26

Assignment of Architect's Agreement and Consent

Basic Information

Date:

Borrower:

Borrower's Mailing Address:

Lender:

Lender's Mailing Address:

Architect:

Architect's Mailing Address:

Architect's Agreement:

Plans:

Project:

Construction Loan Agreement

Date:

Loan (amount):

Deed of Trust:

Date:

Trustee:

Property:

A. Background

A.1. Borrower is entering into the Construction Loan Agreement with Lender under which Lender will provide the Loan for construction of the Project.

A.2. As security for the Loan, Borrower has executed and delivered the Deed of Trust.

A.3. It is a requirement for the advance of the Loan that Lender, Borrower, and Architect enter into this Assignment of Architect's Agreement and Consent.

B. Assignment

B.1. Borrower hereby assigns to Lender the Architect's Agreement and its rights to all Plans as security for the Loan.

B.2. Borrower and Architect, by executing this Assignment, agree that Lender does not assume any of Borrower's obligations or duties concerning the Plans or the Architect's Agreement, including but not limited to the obligation to pay for the preparation of the Plans or to compensate Architect for performance of the Architect's Agreement. Borrower agrees to indemnify and hold Lender harmless against and from any loss, cost, liability, or expense (including but not limited to reasonable attorney's fees) resulting from any failure of Borrower to perform its obligations or duties under the Architect's Agreement or with regard to the Plans.

B.3. Borrower hereby irrevocably constitutes and appoints Lender as its attorney-in-fact to demand, receive, and enforce Borrower's rights with respect to the Plans or the Architect's Agreement; to give appropriate receipts, releases, and satisfactions for and on behalf of

Borrower; and to do all acts in the name of Borrower or in the name of Lender with the same force and effect as Borrower could do if this Assignment had not been made.

C. Borrower's Representations and Warranties

Borrower hereby represents and warrants to and agrees with Lender as follows:

C.1. Exhibit A attached hereto is a complete and accurate description of all of the Plans.

C.2. The Plans have no modifications except as described in Exhibit A.

C.3. Borrower agrees that it will deliver a true and correct copy of the Architect's Agreement to Lender.

C.4. Lender may use the Plans or the Architect's Agreement for any purpose relating to the Project including but not limited to inspections of construction and the completion of the Project.

C.5. Lender's acceptance of this Assignment shall not constitute approval of the Plans by Lender. Lender has no liability or obligation whatsoever in connection with the Plans and no responsibility for their adequacy or for the construction of the Project contemplated by the Plans. Lender has no duty to inspect the Project, and if Lender should inspect the Project, Lender shall have no liability or obligation to Borrower arising out of such inspection. No such inspection nor any failure by Lender to make objections after any such inspection shall constitute a waiver of Lender's right thereafter to insist that the Project be constructed in accordance with the Plans.

C.6. Borrower has made no previous assignment of its interest in the Plans or the Architect's Agreement and agrees not to assign, sell, pledge, transfer, mortgage, or otherwise encumber its interest in the Plans or the Architect's Agreement as long as this Assignment is in effect.

D. Architect's Representations

Architect represents and warrants to Lender that as of the date hereof:

D.1. Architect has not reached any agreement or entered into any contract, written or oral, with respect to the construction of the Project, other than the Architect's Agreement, which has been duly executed and is in full force and effect.

D.2. The attached copy of the Architect's Agreement is true, correct, and complete, and it has no amendments or modifications (other than those attached, if any).

D.3. Architect has no counterclaims, rights of setoff, or defenses to Borrower's enforcement of Borrower's rights under the Architect's Agreement.

D.4. To the best of Architect's knowledge, (a) the Plans have been or will be approved by all appropriate applicable Governmental Authorities (as defined in the Construction Loan Agreement); (b) such Plans are the plans to be used in actual construction of the Project; (c) the Plans are sufficient to the extent indicated in the Architect's Agreement for the construction of the Project; (d) if the Project is constructed in accordance with the Plans, it will not violate any applicable and enforced codes and requirements as interpreted by the appropriate agency; (e) all Required Permits (as defined in the Construction Loan Agreement) have been or will be obtained; (f) the attached list is a comprehensive list of the plans and drawings by name, page number, and date; and (g) there have been no modifications thereof except as described in Exhibit A.

E. Default and Remedies

Architect consents and agrees in all respects to the creation in favor of Lender by Borrower of a security interest in Borrower's rights in the Architect's Agreement as security for the full and complete payment and performance of Borrower's indebtedness and obligations to Lender, and Architect further agrees with Lender as follows:

Select one of the following.

E.1. If a default occurs in connection with the Loan, Architect will, upon notice from Lender, and at Lender's election, (a) complete the performance of the work in accordance with the Architect's Agreement for the benefit of Lender notwithstanding any previous default thereunder by Borrower, and Architect agrees that Lender's rights in this agreement are solely to protect its rights as a lender, and Lender shall have no liability to Architect whatsoever by reason of any such default by Borrower unless Architect receives notice from Lender as provided herein to complete the performance of the work in accordance with the Architect's Agreement, and that Architect shall not seek payment from Lender for any performance of the work performed before Lender's notice, provided that Architect is paid, in accordance with the Architect's Agreement, for all work thereafter rendered by Architect for the benefit of Lender; or (b) immediately cease performance of the work in accordance with the Architect's Agreement and vacate the Project.

Or

E.1. If a default occurs in connection with the Loan, Architect will, upon notice from Lender, and at Lender's election, (a) complete the performance of the work in accordance with the Architect's Agreement for the benefit of Lender notwithstanding any previous default thereunder by Borrower, and Architect agrees that Lender's rights in this agreement are solely to protect its rights as a lender, and Lender shall have no liability to Architect whatsoever by reason of any such default by Borrower unless Architect receives notice from

Lender as provided herein to complete the performance of the work in accordance with the Architect's Agreement, in which case Lender shall be responsible for payment of amounts due to Architect, whether performed before or after receipt of notice from Lender; or (b) immediately cease performance of the work in accordance with the Architect's Agreement and vacate the Project.

Select one of the following.

E.2. Upon the occurrence of a default by Borrower under the Loan, Architect will not exercise any remedies thereunder (other than the cessation of the work for monetary defaults pending either the cure thereof or the request by Lender that, in accordance with paragraph E.1., Architect complete the work for the benefit of Lender) until it has notified Lender in writing and granted Lender thirty days (or a reasonable time if the default cannot be cured in thirty days) after receipt by Lender of that notice, during which Lender shall be entitled, but not obligated, to cure the default.

Or

E.2. Upon the occurrence of a default by Borrower under the Loan, Architect will not exercise any remedies thereunder (other than the cessation of the work for monetary defaults pending the cure thereof) until it has notified Lender in writing and granted Lender thirty days (or a reasonable time if the default cannot be cured in thirty days) after receipt by Lender of that notice, during which Lender shall be entitled, but not obligated, to cure the default.

Continue with the following.

E.3. In the event any of the proceeds of the Loan are disbursed by Lender directly to Architect, Architect will receive all such disbursements, will hold them as a trust fund for paying the costs of the work under the Architect's Agreement, and will apply them only to the payment of such costs and for no other purposes.

E.4. Upon request by Lender, Architect shall furnish to Lender a current list of all persons or firms with whom Architect has entered into subcontracts or other agreements relating to the work in connection with the Project, together with a statement of the status of each such subcontract or agreement and the respective amounts, if any, owed by Architect thereunder.

E.5. After execution and delivery of the Architect's Agreement, Architect will not amend the Architect's Agreement without the prior written consent of Lender, except upon terms similar to those negotiated by and between Lender and Borrower in the Construction Loan Agreement.

E.6. Lender and Lender's successors may use the Plans for any purpose relating to the Project including but not limited to inspections of construction and the completion of the Project without any further cost to Lender or its successors, regardless of whether Architect is retained to complete the Project.

F. General Provisions

F.1. Architect hereby subordinates all liens in its favor to the Deed of Trust and all other liens in favor of Lender with the same force and effect as though the Deed of Trust and any other instrument creating or evidencing liens in favor of the Lender had been executed, delivered, and recorded before the creation or inception of the liens in favor of Architect.

F.2. Nothing herein shall be construed to impose upon Lender any duty to see to the application of the proceeds of the Loan. Architect acknowledges that Lender is obligated with respect thereto only to Borrower and to no other person or entity.

F.3. This instrument shall be binding upon Architect and its heirs, personal representatives, successors, and assigns and shall inure to the benefit of Lender and its successors and assigns.

____
[Name of architect]

____
[Name of borrower]

____
[Name of lender]

Exhibit A

Plans

Attach plans.

Form 10-27

Assignment of Construction Contract and Consent

Basic Information

Date:

Borrower:

Borrower's Mailing Address:

Lender:

Lender's Mailing Address:

Contractor:

Contractor's Mailing Address:

Construction Contract:

Plans:

Project:

Construction Loan Agreement

Date:

Loan (amount):

Deed of Trust:

Date:

Trustee:

Property:

A. Background

A.1. Borrower is entering into the Construction Loan Agreement with Lender under which Lender will provide the Loan for construction of the Project.

A.2. As security for the Loan, Borrower has executed and delivered the Deed of Trust.

A.3. It is a requirement for the advance of the Loan that Lender, Borrower, and Contractor enter into this Assignment of Construction Contract and Consent.

B. Assignment

B.1. Borrower hereby assigns to Lender the Construction Contract as security for the Loan.

B.2. Borrower and Contractor, by executing this Assignment, agree that Lender does not assume any of Borrower's obligations or duties concerning the Construction Contract, including but not limited to the obligation to compensate Contractor for performance of the Construction Contract. Borrower agrees to indemnify and hold Lender harmless against and from any loss, cost, liability, or expense (including but not limited to reasonable attorney's fees) resulting from any failure of Borrower to perform its obligations or duties under the Construction Contract.

B.3. Borrower hereby irrevocably constitutes and appoints Lender as its attorney-in-fact to demand, receive, and enforce Borrower's rights with respect to the Construction Contract; to give appropriate receipts, releases, and satisfactions for and on behalf of Borrower;

and to do all acts in the name of Borrower or in the name of Lender with the same force and effect as Borrower could do if this Assignment had not been made.

C. Borrower's Representations and Warranties

Borrower hereby represents and warrants to and agrees with Lender as follows:

C.1. Exhibit A attached hereto is a true and complete copy of the Construction Contract.

C.2. The Construction Contract has no modifications except as described in Exhibit A.

C.3. Lender may use the Construction Contract for any purpose relating to the Project including but not limited to inspections of construction and the completion of the Project.

C.4. Lender's acceptance of this Assignment shall not constitute approval by Lender of the Contractor, the Construction Contract, or any other contractors, subcontractors, or suppliers. Lender has no liability or obligation whatsoever in connection with the construction of the Project. Lender has no duty to inspect the Project, and if Lender should inspect the Project, Lender shall have no liability or obligation to Borrower arising out of such inspection. No such inspection nor any failure by Lender to make objections after any such inspection shall constitute a waiver of Lender's right thereafter to insist that the Project be constructed in accordance with the Construction Contract.

C.5. Borrower has made no previous assignment of its interest in the Construction Contract and agrees not to assign, sell, pledge, transfer, mortgage, or otherwise encumber its interest in the Construction Contract as long as this Assignment is in effect.

D. Contractor's Representations

Contractor represents and warrants to Lender that as of the date hereof:

D.1. Contractor has not reached any agreement or entered into any contract, written or oral, with respect to the construction of the Project, other than the Construction Contract, which has been duly executed and is in full force and effect.

D.2. The attached copy of the Construction Contract is true, correct, and complete, and it has no amendments or modifications (other than those attached, if any).

D.3. Contractor has no counterclaims, rights of setoff, or defenses to Borrower's enforcement of Borrower's rights under the Construction Contract.

D.4. To the best of Contractor's knowledge, (a) all Required Permits (as defined in the Construction Loan Agreement) have been or will be obtained; (b) the attached list is a comprehensive list of all subcontractors, materialmen, and suppliers that will work on the Project; and (c) there have been no modifications to the Construction Contract except as described in Exhibit A.

E. Default and Remedies

Contractor consents and agrees in all respects to the creation in favor of Lender by Borrower of a security interest in Borrower's rights in the Construction Contract as security for the full and complete payment and performance of Borrower's indebtedness and obligations to Lender, and Contractor further agrees with Lender as follows:

Select one of the following.

E.1. If a default occurs in connection with the Loan, Contractor will, upon notice from Lender, and at Lender's election, (a) complete the performance of the work in accordance with the Construction Contract for the benefit of Lender notwithstanding any previous default thereunder by Borrower, and Contractor agrees that Lender's rights in this agreement are solely to protect its rights as a lender, and Lender shall have no liability to Contractor whatsoever by reason of any such default by Borrower unless Contractor receives notice from

Lender as provided herein to complete the performance of the work in accordance with the Construction Contract, and that Contractor shall not seek payment from Lender for any performance of the work performed before Lender's notice, provided that Contractor is paid, in accordance with the Construction Contract, for all work thereafter rendered by Contractor for the benefit of Lender; or (b) immediately cease performance of the work in accordance with the Construction Contract and vacate the Project.

Or

E.1. If a default occurs in connection with the Loan, Contractor will, upon notice from Lender, and at Lender's election, (a) complete the performance of the work in accordance with the Construction Contract for the benefit of Lender notwithstanding any previous default thereunder by Borrower, and Contractor agrees that Lender's rights in this agreement are solely to protect its rights as a lender, and Lender shall have no liability to Contractor whatsoever by reason of any such default by Borrower unless Contractor receives notice from Lender as provided herein to complete the performance of the work in accordance with the Construction Contract, in which case Lender shall be responsible for payment of amounts due to Contractor, whether performed before or after receipt of notice from Lender; or (b) immediately cease performance of the work in accordance with the Construction Contract and vacate the Project.

Select one of the following.

E.2. Upon the occurrence of a default by Borrower under the Loan, Contractor will not exercise any remedies thereunder (other than the cessation of the work for monetary defaults pending either the cure thereof or the request by Lender that, in accordance with paragraph E.1., Contractor complete the work for the benefit of Lender) until it has notified Lender in writing and granted Lender thirty days (or a reasonable time if the default cannot be cured in thirty days) after receipt by Lender of that notice, during which Lender shall be entitled, but not obligated, to cure the default.

Or

E.2. Upon the occurrence of a default by Borrower under the Loan, Contractor will not exercise any remedies thereunder (other than the cessation of the work for monetary defaults pending the cure thereof) until it has notified Lender in writing and granted Lender thirty days (or a reasonable time if the default cannot be cured in thirty days) after receipt by Lender of that notice, during which Lender shall be entitled, but not obligated, to cure the default.

Continue with the following.

E.3. In the event any of the proceeds of the Loan are disbursed by Lender directly to Contractor, Contractor will receive all such disbursements, will hold them as a trust fund for paying the costs of the work under the Construction Contract, including labor, materials, and supplies, and will apply them only to the payment of such costs and for no other purposes.

E.4. Upon request by Lender, Contractor shall furnish to Lender a current list of all persons or firms with whom Contractor has entered into subcontracts or other agreements relating to the work in connection with the Project, together with a statement of the status of each such subcontract or agreement and the respective amounts, if any, owed by Contractor thereunder.

E.5. After execution and delivery of the Construction Contract, Contractor will not amend the Construction Contract without the prior written consent of Lender, except upon terms similar to those negotiated by and between Lender and Borrower in the Construction Loan Agreement.

F. General Provisions

F.1. Contractor hereby subordinates all liens in its favor to the Deed of Trust and all other liens in favor of Lender with the same force and effect as though the Deed of Trust and any other instrument creating or evidencing liens in favor of the Lender had been executed, delivered, and recorded before the creation or inception of the liens in favor of Contractor.

F.2. Nothing herein shall be construed to impose upon Lender any duty to see to the application of the proceeds of the Loan. Contractor acknowledges that Lender is obligated with respect thereto only to Borrower and to no other person or entity.

F.3. This instrument shall be binding upon Contractor and its heirs, personal representatives, successors, and assigns and shall inure to the benefit of Lender and its successors and assigns.

____
[Name of contractor]

____
[Name of borrower]

____
[Name of lender]

Exhibit A

Construction Contract

Attach construction contract.

Form 10-28

Loan Agreement
[Construction]

Date:

Borrower:

Mailing address:

Lender:

Mailing address:

Phone:

Loan no.:

Loan officer:

Guarantor:

Mailing address:

Title Company:

GF #:

Note

Date:

Original Principal Amount:

Maturity Date:

Loan Origination Fee:

Use of Loan Proceeds:

Collateral

Real Property: As described in Exhibit A attached to this Loan Agreement

Prior liens: [None/[**include recording information**]]

Personal Property: As described in the Deed of Trust, Security Agreement, Assignment of Rents, Collateral Assignment of Leases, and Financing Statement

Loan Documents (all dated to be effective as of the date of the Note)

Loan Agreement (Construction)

Promissory Note

Deed of Trust, Security Agreement, Assignment of Rents, Collateral Assignment of Leases, and Financing Statement

Errors and Omissions Agreement

Notice of Final Agreement

Business Purpose Affidavit

Notice to Borrower from Lender's Attorney

Guaranty Agreement:

Certificate of Resolutions

Affidavit of No Prior Activity

Affidavits of Completion

Contractor's Agreement and Consent

Agreement to Provide Ongoing Information

Financial Covenants

"Financial Statements" means statements of Borrower and Guarantor prepared in accordance with the requirements of paragraphs C.8. and C.9. of this Loan Agreement.

The Financial Statements delivered to Lender are true and correct in all respects, have been prepared in accordance with sound principles consistently followed, and fully and accurately present the financial condition of those statements' subjects as of those statements' dates, and no materially adverse change has occurred in that financial condition since.

Borrower and Guarantor will deliver to Lender true and correct copies of the federal income tax returns of Borrower and Guarantor for the prior year and each tax year there is an outstanding balance on the Note, each return within thirty days of its filing, but in no event later than May 15th in any tax year, unless the filing is extended based on any permitted extension, but not later than the final due date for any return.

Borrower will furnish to Lender at Closing and annually thereafter a current rent roll for all properties owned by Borrower under lease listing each tenant, a description of the tenant's space, the rent amount, the status of the rent due under the lease, and the remaining term of the lease.

All financial information provided will substantiate to Lender's satisfaction that Borrower thereafter continuously maintains from Borrower's collective income sources a ratio of Net Operating Income to Debt Service for each calendar year beginning sixty days after 2023 year-end of not less than 1.20 (the "Debt Service Coverage Ratio"). "Net Operating Income" means gross income less operating expenses before income taxes, distributions to equity owners, dividends, depreciation, and amortization (also known as "EBITDA"). "Debt service" means principal and interest payments on all debts with a maturity in excess of one year. Failure to continuously maintain the Debt Service Coverage Ratio shall be a default under this Loan Agreement and the Promissory Note.

Buyer will fund at closing and thereafter maintain an Interest Reserve Account in the initial amount of no less than $**[amount]** and will continuously maintain this account until the Maturity Date. Funds in the Interest Reserve Account may be released at Lender's sole discretion for budgeted and Lender-approved expenses including interest due on the Note. The Reserve Account is subject to the security interest granted to Lender in the Deed of Trust, and all Obligors hereby grant Lender that Security Interest pursuant to the terms set out in the Deed of Trust.

The Loan

Subject to the terms and conditions of this Loan Agreement, Lender will lend Borrower the Original Principal Amount as represented by the Note (the "Loan"), and Borrower agrees to pay the Note.

Clauses and Covenants

A. Conditions Precedent to Loan

The obligation of Lender to make the Loan is conditioned on—

A.1. the execution and delivery of the Loan Documents;

A.2. the accuracy, in all material respects, of all representations and warranties in the Loan Documents;

A.3. no default existing under the Loan Documents;

A.4. payment of the Loan Origination Fee, set out above, and all expenses incurred by Lender in connection with the Loan Documents; and

A.5. Lender's receipt, in a form acceptable to Lender, of—

A.5.a. certification from Borrower's authorized representative for any Borrower that is an entity attaching (i) a copy of Borrower's organizational documents, (ii) the approval of Borrower's governing authority for the execution and delivery of the Loan Documents, and (iii) specimen signatures from all Borrower representatives authorized to execute the Loan Documents;

A.5.b. certification from governmental authorities for any Borrower that is an entity confirming Borrower's existence and Borrower's account status with the Texas Comptroller of Public Accounts;

A.5.c. appraisal of the Real Property;

A.5.d. survey plat of the Real Property;

A.5.e. commitment for issuance of a loan policy of title insurance in the Original Principal Amount insuring the validity of Lender's lien on the Real Property and confirming that no liens exist on the Real Property other than those liens permitted by the Loan Documents;

A.5.f. financing statement reports on the Personal Property issued by all applicable filing officers confirming no financing statements are filed on the Personal Property other than those financing statements permitted by the Loan Documents;

A.5.g. financial statement on Borrower and financial statement on Guarantor;

A.5.h. proof of insurance required by the Loan Documents; and

A.5.i. all other documents, instruments, and certificates reasonably requested by Lender.

B. Borrower's Representations

To induce Lender to enter into this Loan Agreement and to make the Loan, Borrower represents to Lender that—

B.1. Borrower—

B.1.a. has the power and authority needed to execute and deliver the Loan Documents and to perform Borrower's obligations under the Loan Documents;

B.1.b. possesses all permits, registrations, approvals, consents, licenses, trademarks, trademark rights, trade names, trade name rights, and copyrights needed to conduct Borrower's business;

B.1.c. was validly formed and exists under the laws of the state of organization;

B.1.d. is in good standing under the laws of the state of organization and all other jurisdictions where the nature of Borrower's business makes qualification necessary; and

B.1.e. is qualified to do business under the laws of the state of organization and all other jurisdictions where the nature of Borrower's business makes qualification necessary.

B.2. the execution, delivery, and performance of the Loan Documents executed by Borrower have been duly authorized and do not and will not (a) contravene or violate any legal requirement; (b) result in the breach of, or constitute a default under, any instrument to which Borrower is a party or by which any of Borrower's property may be bound or affected;

or (c) result in a requirement to create any lien upon any of Borrower's property other than liens granted to Lender on the Collateral;

B.3. the Loan Documents are legal, valid, and binding obligations of the parties executing the documents;

B.4. Borrower has good and indefeasible title to the Real Property and has good title to the Personal Property, free and clear of all liens except (a) as disclosed in the Loan Documents; (b) liens for ad valorem taxes, general and special assessments, and other governmental charges not yet due or payable; and (c) liens granted to Lender;

B.5. Borrower's financial statements delivered to Lender fairly present the financial condition and the results of Borrower's operations as of the dates and for the periods indicated, and no material adverse change has occurred in the assets, liabilities, financial condition, or business of Borrower since the dates of the financial statements;

B.6. Borrower has no knowledge of any litigation or administrative claim, action, or proceeding, pending or threatened, against Borrower or directly involving the Collateral before or by any governmental authority that, if adversely determined, could have a material adverse effect on Borrower;

B.7. there is no outstanding adverse judgment, writ, order, injunction, award, or decree affecting Borrower or the Collateral;

B.8. Borrower is not in default under any agreement to which Borrower is bound or to which any of the collateral is subject that could have a material adverse effect on Borrower or the Collateral;

B.9. all information and documentation supplied to Lender and all statements made to Lender by or on behalf of Borrower are correct and complete in all material respects as of the date made;

B.10. except as disclosed in an environmental report previously provided to Lender, Borrower has no knowledge of the Real Property's being used for the production, release, or disposal of hazardous wastes or materials in violation of applicable environmental laws;

B.11. the Real Property is taxed and billed separately from any other property for ad valorem tax purposes;

B.12. except as disclosed on the survey previously provided to Lender, no part of the Real Property is located within a flood zone;

B.13. Borrower's financial records have been prepared and maintained in accordance with good accounting practices consistently applied and reflect all moneys due or to become due from or to Borrower; and

B.14. Borrower has filed all required tax returns and paid all taxes shown due on them, except those for which extensions have been obtained and those that are being contested in good faith and for which appropriate reserves have been established and disclosed in writing to Lender.

C. Affirmative Covenants

Borrower will—

C.1. apply all proceeds from the sale, collection, or other disposition of the Collateral to amounts owing on the Note unless the Loan Documents authorize an alternate use of the proceeds;

C.2. comply with the Additional Loan Requirements;

C.3. comply with the Financial Covenants;

C.4. operate Borrower's business in accordance with all applicable legal requirements;

C.5. keep at Borrower's address, or such other place as Lender may approve, accounts and records reflecting the operation of Borrower's business and copies of all written contracts, leases, and other instruments that affect the Collateral;

C.6. prepare Borrower's financial records in compliance with good accounting practices consistently applied;

C.7. permit Lender to examine and make copies of Borrower's books, records, contracts, leases, and other instruments at any reasonable time;

C.8. deliver to Lender, annually and at Lender's request from time to time, Borrower's tax returns and internally prepared financial statements of Borrower prepared in accordance with good accounting practices consistently applied, in detail reasonably satisfactory to Lender and certified to be true and correct by Borrower;

C.9. deliver to Lender, annually and at Lender's request from time to time, Guarantor's tax returns and internally prepared financial statements prepared in accordance with good accounting practices consistently applied, in detail reasonably satisfactory to Lender and certified to be true and correct by Guarantor;

C.10. execute, acknowledge as required, and deliver to Lender, at Lender's request from time to time, at Borrower's expense, any document needed by Lender to (a) correct any defect, error, omission, or ambiguity in the Loan Documents; (b) comply with Borrower's obligations under the Loan Documents; (c) make subject to the Loan Documents, and perfect those documents' liens on and security interests in, any property intended to be covered thereby; and (d) protect, perfect, or preserve the liens and security interests of the Loan Documents against third parties or make any recordings, file any notices, or obtain any consents requested by Lender in connection therewith;

C.11. notify Lender promptly (a) on acquiring knowledge of the occurrence of any event of default under the Loan Documents; (b) if any of Borrower's property is surrendered in satisfaction of a debt or obligation or on acquiring knowledge that any of Guarantor's property was surrendered in satisfaction of a debt or obligation; and (c) of any litigation, arbitration, mediation, or proceedings before any governmental agency that could have a material adverse effect on Borrower or the Collateral or on acquiring knowledge of any litigation, arbitration, mediation, or proceedings before any governmental agency that could have a material adverse effect on Guarantor;

C.12. pay promptly on demand all expenses in connection with (a) the negotiation, preparation, execution, filing, recording, rerecording, modification, and supplementation of the Loan Documents; (b) the collection of the Note; (c) the protection of the Collateral; (d) the collection, enforcement, sale, or other disposition of the Collateral; and (e) the performance by Lender of any of Borrower's obligations under the Loan Documents;

C.13. use the Note proceeds for the purposes permitted in this Loan Agreement; and

C.14. do all things necessary to preserve Borrower's existence, qualifications, rights, and franchises in all jurisdictions where Borrower does business.

D. Negative Covenants

Borrower will not—

D.1. use or allow the use of the Collateral in any manner that (a) constitutes a public or private nuisance; (b) makes void, voidable, or cancelable, or increases the premium of, any insurance required by the Loan Documents; or (c) lessens the value of the Collateral, other than as a result of ordinary wear and tear from the Collateral's intended use;

D.2. purchase, acquire, or lease any property from, or sell, transfer, or lease any property to, any equity owner, manager, director, officer, agent, or employee of Borrower, or any person or entity controlled by, controlling, or under common control with Borrower, except on terms then customarily available between unrelated parties in substantially similar transactions;

D.3. lend money to, or guarantee the payment or performance of any liability or obligation of, any person, except short-term loans to Borrower's employees that, in the aggregate, do not exceed $[**amount**];

D.4. materially change the nature of Borrower's business or enter into any business that is substantially different from Borrower's existing business;

D.5. incur any indebtedness other than the Note, except short-term indebtedness to trade creditors incurred in the ordinary course of Borrower's business that, in the aggregate, does not exceed $[**amount**];

D.6. create or permit any mortgage, security interest, or lien on any Collateral other than mortgages, security interests, or liens existing at the date of this Loan Agreement and disclosed to Lender or created pursuant to the Loan Documents;

D.7. purchase or redeem any of Borrower's ownership interests, declare or pay any dividends, or make any distribution to the holders of any of Borrower's ownership interests (to the extent Borrower is an entity);

D.8. sell, transfer, convey, or lease any Collateral except for sales or leases in the ordinary course of business and on the conditions provided in the Loan Documents;

D.9. acquire all or substantially all of the assets or ownership interests of any third party; or

D.10. liquidate or dissolve, or become a party to any merger or consolidation.

E. Default and Remedies

E.1. A default exists, subject to any notice and opportunity to cure rights set forth in the Loan Documents, if—

E.1.a. Borrower fails to timely pay the Note;

E.1.b. a party fails to perform any obligation or covenant in any of the Loan Documents;

E.1.c. any representation made by a party in any of the Loan Documents is false in any material respect when made;

E.1.d. a receiver is appointed for any party executing any of the Loan Documents, or for any of the Collateral;

E.1.e. any Collateral is assigned for the benefit of creditors;

E.1.f. a bankruptcy or insolvency proceeding is commenced by a party executing any of the Loan Documents;

E.1.g. a bankruptcy or insolvency proceeding is commenced against a party executing any of the Loan Documents, and the proceeding continues without dismissal for sixty days, the party against whom the proceeding is commenced admits the material allegations of the petition against it, or an order for relief is entered;

E.1.h. any of the following parties is terminated, begins to wind up its affairs, is authorized by its governing body or persons to terminate or wind up its affairs, or any event occurs or condition exists that permits the termination or winding up of the affairs of any of the following parties: Borrower, a partnership of which Borrower is a general partner, or any other obligated party executing any of the Loan Documents; or

E.1.i. any Collateral is impaired by uninsured loss, theft, damage, or destruction, or by levy and execution, or by issuance of an official writ or order of seizure, unless it is promptly replaced with collateral of like kind and quality or restored to its former condition.

E.2. If a default exists, Lender may—

E.2.a. declare the unpaid principal balance, earned interest, and any other amounts owed on the Note immediately due; and

E.2.b. exercise against Borrower, the Collateral, and any other party executing the Loan Documents, any rights and remedies available to Lender under the Loan Documents.

E.3. Notwithstanding any other provision in the Loan Documents, in the event of a default, before exercising any of Lender's remedies under the Loan Documents, Lender will first give Borrower notice of default and Borrower will have ten days after delivery of notice of any monetary payment default and thirty days after notice of any other event of default (the "Cure Period") in which to cure the default. If the default is not cured before the expiration of the applicable Cure Period, Borrower and each surety, endorser, and guarantor waive all demand for payment, presentation for payment, notice of intention to accelerate maturity, notice of acceleration of maturity, protest, and notice of protest, to the extent permitted by law.

F. General Provisions

F.1. Any notice required or permitted under this Loan Agreement must be in writing. Any notice required by this Loan Agreement will be deemed to be delivered (whether actually received or not) when deposited with the United States Postal Service, postage prepaid, certified mail, return receipt requested, and addressed to the intended recipient at the address provided in this Loan Agreement. Notice may also be given by regular mail, personal delivery, courier delivery, facsimile transmission, or other commercially reasonable means and will be effective when actually received. Any address for notice may be changed by notice delivered as provided herein.

F.2. The Loan Documents, including any of their exhibits and attachments, constitute the entire agreement of the parties. There are no representations, agreements, or promises by Lender pertaining to the Loan that are not in those documents.

F.3. This Loan Agreement may be amended only by an instrument in writing signed by the parties.

F.4. Borrower may not assign this Loan Agreement or any of Borrower's rights under it without Lender's prior written consent, and any attempted assignment is void. This Loan Agreement binds, benefits, and may be enforced by the parties and their successors in interest.

F.5. Borrower authorizes Lender to charge any amount due Lender under the Loan Documents against any of Borrower's deposit accounts with Lender.

F.6. Except as otherwise provided in the Loan Documents, Borrower waives all demand for payment, presentation for payment, notice of intention to accelerate maturity, notice of acceleration of maturity, protest, and notice of protest, to the extent permitted by law.

F.7. No remedy, right, or power conferred on Lender in this Loan Agreement is intended to be exclusive of any other remedy, right, or power now or hereafter existing at law, in equity, or otherwise, and all remedies, rights, and powers are cumulative.

F.8. This Loan Agreement will be construed under the laws of the state of Texas, without regard to choice-of-law rules of any jurisdiction. This Loan Agreement is to be performed where the Note is payable.

F.9. Interest on the Note will not exceed the maximum amount of nonusurious interest that may be contracted for, taken, reserved, charged, or received under law. Any interest in excess of that maximum amount will be credited on the principal of the Note or, if that has been paid, refunded. On any acceleration or required or permitted prepayment, any excess will be canceled automatically as of the acceleration or prepayment or, if already paid, credited on the principal of the Note or, if the principal of the Note has been paid, refunded. This provision overrides other provisions in this and all other Loan Documents.

F.10. It is not a waiver of default if the nondefaulting party fails to declare immediately a default or delays taking any action. Pursuit of any remedies set forth in this Loan Agreement does not preclude pursuit of other remedies in the other Loan Documents or provided by law.

F.11. There are no third-party beneficiaries of this Loan Agreement.

F.12. If any provision of this Loan Agreement is determined to be invalid or unenforceable, the validity or enforceability of any other provision will not be affected.

F.13. The rule of construction that ambiguities in a document will be construed against the party who drafted it will not be applied in interpreting this Loan Agreement.

F.14. The parties' relationship is an ordinary commercial relationship, and the parties do not intend to create the relationship of principal and agent, a partnership, a joint venture, or any other special relationship. Lender in exercising Lender's rights and performing Lender's obligations under the Loan Documents owes no fiduciary duty to Borrower.

F.15. If this Loan Agreement is executed in multiple counterparts, all counterparts taken together will constitute this Loan Agreement.

F.16. If Lender agrees to waive or defer any of the requirements of this Loan Agreement as a condition precedent to the advance of the proceeds of the Note, Borrower will provide any deferred information or documentation within thirty days after the advance.

F.17. In the event of any conflict among the provisions of this Loan Agreement and any of the Loan Documents, the more restrictive provision will control.

F.18. When the context requires, singular nouns and pronouns include the plural.

F.19. The term Note includes all extensions and renewals of the Note.

G. Conditions to Lender's Obligations to Make Loan Advances

Lender is not obligated to make any advance, including any after the first advance, of loan proceeds hereunder unless the following conditions have been satisfied, with proof provided in a form and sufficiency as Lender may reasonably request:

G.1. Lender must have received and approved (a) copies of the plans, equipment leases, and any construction contracts that may be requested by Lender; (b) all presently procurable authorizations and permits required by any Governmental Authority for the construction of the Improvements (as defined in the Deed of Trust), including those required for the use and operation of the Property for the purposes contemplated by the plans; (c) a current title report from the Title Insurer describing the Property with attached copies of all instruments that appear as exceptions in the report; (d) an original current survey of each lot certified to Lender and the Title Insurer showing the locations of the perimeter of each lot within the Property by courses and distances, all easements and rights-of-way (identified as recorded in public records), the proposed building lines, the lines of the streets abutting the Property and the width thereof, encroachments, and the extent thereof in feet and inches upon the Property, the relation of the proposed Improvements by distances to the perimeter of the Property, the proposed building lines and the street lines, and if the Property is described as being on a filed map or plat, a legend relating the survey to the map or plat; (e) the Financial Statements; (f) advice from an architect or civil engineer and, if Lender elects, an independent architect or civil engineer approving the plans and indicating that the construction contracts are acceptable and satisfactorily provide for the construction of the Improvements; (g) the policies of insurance required by the Deeds of Trust and this Loan Agreement accompanied by evidence of the payment of the policies' premiums; and (h) a satisfactory "As Built" appraisal of the Improvements proposed for each lot in the Property.

G.2. The Deed of Trust must have been executed by the parties to this Loan Agreement and recorded in the office of the county clerk of each county in which any part of the Real Property is located, with all filing fees paid, all before commencement of any construction on any part of the Property and the placing of any material or equipment on the Property.

G.3. Lender must have received financing statements with proof of filing in the appropriate offices in the State of Texas and other things and instruments necessary or appropriate in the opinion of Lender to perfect a security interest in the property covered by the Deed of Trust in accordance with the Texas Uniform Commercial Code, and Lender must have received proof that no prior financing statements from Borrower as debtor or from any other party affecting any of the Property have been filed in any such office in favor of any other party.

G.4. Lender must have received the Title Insurance showing the lien on the owner's interest in favor of Lender as holder of the Note, to be valid, first, and prior lien on the Property free and clear of all defects and encumbrances except as Lender approves. The Title Insurance must not contain any survey exceptions not already approved by Lender, and the status of title to the owner's interest shown therein shall otherwise be satisfactory to Lender.

G.5. The representations and warranties made in section B of this Loan Agreement shall be true and correct on the date of the advance with the same effect as if made on that date.

G.6. There must be no default under this Loan Agreement, the Note, or any of the security instruments.

G.7. Lender must have received the Note, Deed of Trust, and Loan Documents, all properly executed by the respective parties thereto.

G.8. An endorsement to the title policy or affidavit acceptable to Lender must state that there has been, as of the date of the requested advance, no change in the state of title and no survey exceptions not previously approved by Lender.

G.9. The Improvements, to the extent any have been made before the date of the advance, must not have been materially injured or damaged by fire or other casualty unless Lender has received insurance proceeds sufficient in the judgment of Lender and, if Lender elects, an independent supervising architect, to effect the satisfactory restoration of the Improvements and to permit their completion before the completion date.

G.10. Lender must have received (a) a proper request for advance from Borrower; (b) if construction has been performed before the advance, advice from an architect or inspector providing the opinion that the construction of the Improvements was performed in accordance with the plans; (c) for advances after the first advance, a copy of a valid building permit issued for the Improvements; and (d) for advances after the first advance, Lender must have received (i) a notice of title continuation or an endorsement of the Title Insurance already delivered indicating that since the last preceding advance, there has been no change in the state of title and no survey exceptions not already approved by Lender, which endorsement shall have the effect of increasing the coverage of the Title Insurance by an amount equal to the advance then being made if the Title Insurance does not by its terms provide for such additional coverage without such an endorsement, and (ii) a forms or foundation survey satisfactory to Lender in its sole and absolute discretion.

G.11. All legal matters incident to this Loan Agreement and the transactions contemplated by it must be satisfactory to counsel to Lender.

G.12. Lender must have received executed affidavits of contractor and Borrower duly and truthfully subscribed and sworn to evidencing any matter that Lender has requested.

G.13. Lender, if it so requests, must have received one or more photographs of the Property taken on or after the date of the filing of the Deeds of Trust and, if on the date of the filing, on or after the time of the filing. The photograph(s) must clearly show that there has not been actual commencement on the Property or any delivery of material to the Property. The photograph(s) must be signed on the back by the photographer for identification to an accompanying affidavit, and each photograph must include on its back the photographer's written description of the general area of the Property shown in the photograph and of the location from which the photograph was taken. The accompanying affidavit must be sworn and subscribed to by the photographer and certify that the photograph(s) were taken of the Property by the photographer at the date and time or times stated in the affidavit. Borrower shall pay the expenses of satisfying this condition.

THE WRITTEN LOAN AGREEMENT REPRESENTS THE FINAL AGREEMENT BETWEEN THE PARTIES AND MAY NOT BE CONTRADICTED BY EVIDENCE OF PRIOR, CONTEMPORANEOUS, OR SUBSEQUENT ORAL AGREEMENTS OF THE PARTIES. THERE ARE NO UNWRITTEN ORAL AGREEMENTS BETWEEN THE PARTIES.

Signed on [**date**].

Remainder of page intentionally left blank. Separate signature page follows.

Lender:
[Name of entity]

By:

____
[Name of representative]
[Title]

Borrower:
[Name of entity], [a/an] **[type of entity]**

By:

____
[Name of representative]
[Title]

Guarantor:

By:

____
[Name of representative]
[Title]

Exhibit A

Description of Real Property Used as Collateral

Include legal description of the land.

Form 10-29

This checklist is for reviewing Fannie Mae inter vivos revocable trusts. See Fannie Mae's *Selling Guide* for the most updated version of these requirements, as they are subject to revision. An online version of Fannie Mae's *Selling Guide*, part B2-2-05, "Inter Vivos Revocable Trusts" (10/31/2017), is currently accessible at: **https://selling-guide.fanniemae.com/Selling-Guide/Origination-thru-Closing/Subpart-B2-Eligibility/Chapter-B2-2-Borrower-Eligibility/1032996281/B2-2-05-Inter-Vivos-Revocable-Trusts-10-31-2017.htm**.

Inter Vivos Revocable Trust Review Checklist

Date:

Loan Number:

Property:

Trust Name:

Settlor Name(s):

Trustee Name(s):

Fannie Mae Inter Vivos Revocable Trust Requirements

A certification of trust that meets all of the following requirements and the requirements of Texas Property Code section 114.086 is acceptable.

Requirement	Yes	No
1. The trust is established by one or more natural persons, solely or jointly.		
2. The trust was created during Settlor's lifetime.		
3. The trust becomes effective during Settlor's lifetime.		

Requirement	Yes	No
4. The trust can be amended or revoked by Settlor at any time, for any reason, during Settlor's lifetime.		
5. The primary beneficiary of the trust must be the individual(s) establishing the trust. If the trust is established jointly, there may be more than one primary beneficiary as long as the income or assets of at least one of the individuals establishing the trust will be used to qualify for the mortgage.		
6. The trustee(s) must be either (a) the individual establishing the trust (or at least one of the individuals, if there are two or more) or (b) an institutional trustee that customarily performs trust functions in and is authorized to act as trustee under the laws of the applicable state.		
7. The trustee(s) must have the power to mortgage the security property for the purpose of securing a loan to the individual(s) who are the borrower(s) under the mortgage or deed-of-trust note.		

Chapter 11

Home Equity Loan Documents

I. Home Equity Loans Generally

II. Reverse Mortgage Loans

III. General Instructions for Completing Forms

IV. Additional Resources

Forms

Chapter 11

Home Equity Loan Documents

I. Home Equity Loans Generally

§ 11.1 Home Equity Loan General Considerations

Article XVI, section 50, of the Texas Constitution allows a lien on homestead property to secure a home equity loan. In a departure from prior Texas practice, the validity of such a lien is generally not dependent on the use to which the loan proceeds are applied. Constitutional provisions authorizing home equity lending continue, however, to reflect a strong public policy solicitous of the homestead as the last shield against destitution. Home equity loans are authorized only on satisfaction of a number of significant constitutional safeguards and restrictions aimed at protecting homestead owners.

These restrictions are nonseverable and nonwaivable. Each must be satisfied to create a valid lien. Strict compliance with the requirements of the Texas Constitution is required. *See Toler v. Fertitta*, 67 S.W.2d 229, 230 (Tex. Comm'n App. 1934, holding approved).

Regulatory Commentary: Regulations and official commentary pertaining to home equity lending are available from the following different sources.

1. *Interpretive rules of Finance Commission and Credit Union Commission:* The constitution authorizes the legislature to delegate the authority to issue interpretations of the home equity lending provisions of the constitution. *See* Tex. Const. art. XVI, § 50(u). The legislature, acting pursuant to this amendment, delegated interpretive authority over the home equity provisions to the Finance Commission of Texas and the Texas Credit Union Commission, which in turn have jointly issued interpretations of home equity lending law. *See* Tex. Fin. Code §§ 11.308, 15.413. The interpretive rules are codified in 7 Tex. Admin. Code ch. 153, which may be accessed at **https://texreg.sos.state.tx.us/public/readtac$ext.ViewTAC?tac_view=4&ti=7&pt=8&ch=153&rl=Y**. *See* 7 Tex. Admin. Code §§ 153.1–.96.

   Lenders authorized by the constitution to make home equity extensions of credit are afforded substantial protections when relying on these interpretations. No act or omission is deemed to violate a home equity constitutional provision if the act or omission conforms to an interpretation of the provision that is in effect at the time of the act or omission and made by a state agency to which the power of interpretation is delegated or by an appellate court of this state or the United States. Tex. Const. art. XVI, § 50(u). However, the validity of certain of the interpretations has been successfully attacked in *Texas Bankers Ass'n v. Ass'n of Community Organizations for Reform Now (ACORN)*, 303 S.W.3d 404 (Tex. App.—Austin 2010, pet. granted). As a result, 7 Tex. Admin.

Code §§ 153.1(11), 153.5(3) (defining interest) and § 153.5(4), (6), (8), (9), (12) (incorporating that definition) have been held constitutionally invalid, and 7 Tex. Admin. Code §§ 153.13, 153.18, 153.20, 153.22, 153.84 have been revised by the commissions to rectify invalid provisions found by the lower court. The Supreme Court of Texas granted a petition for review of the decision to determine (1) whether deference to agency interpretations should be the standard for appellate review when state agencies, in this case the Finance Commission of Texas and the Credit Union Commission, have been delegated the authority to interpret constitutional home equity provisions by the constitution and statutes of this state; (2) whether the Finance Code's definition of "interest" was properly applied in agency interpretations for purposes of determining the constitutional 3 percent fee cap; and (3) whether agency interpretations should be upheld that allow the signing of an equity loan by power of attorney instead of a required signing by homeowners at locations specified by the constitution. On unopposed motion, the court also ordered ACORN dismissed as a party because of its intervening dissolution and ordered the style of the cause corrected to read *Finance Commission of Texas et al. v. Valerie Norwood et al.*, No. 10-0121, 54 Tex. Sup. Ct. J. 1077 (Tex. Feb. 25, 2011). In an opinion issued on June 21, 2013, the Texas Supreme Court decided (1) that agency interpretations are subject to the same standard of review as courts of appeals, which are reviewed, as a matter of law, *de novo*; (2) that the agency interpretation of the 3 percent fee cap, tying it to the meaning of the Finance Code definition of "interest," was invalid ("interest" as used in that provision means the amount determined by multiplying the loan principal by the interest rate); and (3) that execution of a power of attorney used in an equity loan transaction must occur only at the office of a lender, an attorney at law, or a title company. *Finance Commission of Texas v. Norwood*, 418 S.W.3d 566 (Tex. 2013). On January 24, 2014, on a motion for rehearing filed by the Texas Bankers Association, a supplemental opinion was issued to clarify that per diem interest and discount points were not subject to the 3 percent fee cap and to reaffirm the court's decision relating to the execution of a power of attorney used in an equity loan transaction. *Finance Commission of Texas*, 418 S.W.3d at 595–97.

2. *1998 OCCC Commentary:* On October 7, 1998, the Office of the Consumer Credit Commissioner (OCCC), the Texas Department of Banking, the Savings and Loan Department, and the Credit Union Department issued their joint Regulatory Commentary on Equity Lending Procedures to provide initial guidance to lenders and consumers concerning the regulatory views of the participating agencies. This regulatory commentary is referred to in this chapter as the "1998 OCCC Commentary." Though the 1998 OCCC Commentary has been supplanted by title 7, chapter 153, of the Texas Administrative Code (Home Equity Lending) (*see* 29 Tex. Reg. 84 (2004)), it retains vitality by helping practitioners understand home equity lending restrictions. The 1998 OCCC Commentary is accessible on the OCCC website at **https://occc.texas.gov**.

3. *Department of Insurance procedural rules:* The Texas Department of Insurance adopted title insurance coverages specifically for home equity loans along with accompanying procedural rules: (1) Equity Loan Mortgage Endorsement (T-42) and accompanying Procedural Rule P-44 and (2) Supplemental Coverage Equity Loan Mortgage Endorsement (T-42.1) and accompanying Procedural Rule P-47. These endorsements and procedural rules provide underwriting guidelines that interpret the constitutional requirements for a home equity lien.

Limitation of Chapter: The commentary and forms in this chapter are applicable to a first-lien home equity loan. Texas Finance Code chapter 342 imposes additional duties, prohibitions, and disclosure requirements in connection with secondary mortgage loans. Attorneys are cautioned that some forms in this chapter may require modification for use with a secondary mortgage loan transaction.

The checklist in this chapter (form 11-10) is included for practical guidance and to identify issues for attorneys reviewing Texas home equity transactions. Lenders and investors may impose their own requirements for Texas home equity reviews. Attorneys are cautioned to follow the lender and investor guidelines applicable to their specific Texas home equity transaction.

Model Forms and Regulations: Home equity loans regulated by the OCCC must be written in plain language designed to be easily understood by the average consumer and must be printed in an easily readable font and type size. Tex. Fin. Code § 341.502(a). The Finance Commission has adopted rules governing loan contracts subject to Texas Finance Code section 341.502, including model loan contracts that in certain cases may be required for use. *See* 7 Tex. Admin. Code ch. 90. Home equity loans that are regulated by the OCCC and therefore subject to these plain language and model form requirements include only loans that (1) provide for an interest rate exceeding 10 percent a year, (2) are extended primarily for personal, family, or household use, (3) are a secondary mortgage loan, and (4) are made by a person engaged in the business of making such loans licensed by the OCCC (other than a bank, savings and loan, or credit union). Tex. Fin. Code §§ 341.101–.103, 342.005; Tex. Att'y Gen. Op. No. JC-0513 (2002). These requirements do not apply to first-lien home equity loans or home equity loans made by traditional lenders.

§ 11.2 Home Equity Loans Closed before January 1, 2018

The rules governing home equity loans changed significantly on January 1, 2018. Where applicable, this chapter will identify provisions affected by the changes. The laws in effect at the time the home equity loan was closed govern the validity of the home equity loan. If an existing home equity loan is being analyzed for compliance, the closing date should be noted and the corresponding rules applied to the analysis. The January 1, 2018, changes are summarized below:

1. For home equity loans closed prior to January 1, 2018, closing costs should not exceed 3 percent of the loan amount. The January 1, 2018, amendments reduced the fee limitation to 2 percent but excluded some of the most expensive fees of a typical closing from the fees included in the limitation: appraisal fees, title fees, and survey fees. For a detailed analysis of which fees are included in the constitutional fee limitation, see section 11.6 below.
2. Before January 1, 2018, a home equity loan could not be secured by a homestead with an agricultural use tax exemption, unless the tract was used

primarily for the production of milk. The 2018 amendments removed this restriction, and home equity loans closed on or after January 1, 2018, may be secured by homesteads with an agricultural use tax exemption.

3. Before January 1, 2018, if a new mortgage loan was made and any portion of the loan proceeds were used to extinguish an existing home equity loan, the new loan had to be a home equity loan or a reverse mortgage. The 2018 amendments created a new procedure by which lenders may refinance an existing home equity loan with a conventional mortgage. Beginning January 1, 2018, a home equity loan may now be refinanced into a conventional loan if (a) at least one year has elapsed since the home equity loan was closed; (b) there is no advance of new money (except closing costs); (c) the new principal loan balance does not exceed 80 percent of the property's fair market value on the day of refinance; and (d) the owner is provided with a new disclosure twelve days before closing, advising owner of the risks of refinancing into a non–home equity loan.

4. For a home equity line of credit (HELOC) originated prior to January 1, 2018, there is a loan-to-value restriction on additional advances: no advances after the initial advance at closing may be made if the sum of all indebtedness secured by the homestead exceeds 50 percent of the fair market value of the property at the time the HELOC was closed. For HELOCs originated on or after January 1, 2018, the loan-to-value limit on additional advances is 80 percent.

§ 11.3 Authorized Lenders

The seven categories of lenders that may make home equity loans are—

1. a bank, savings and loan association, savings bank, or credit union doing business under Texas or federal law, including a subsidiary of a bank, savings and loan association, savings bank, or credit union;
2. a federally chartered lending instrumentality;
3. a person approved as a mortgagee by the United States government to make federally insured loans;
4. a person licensed to make regulated loans under Texas law;
5. a seller financing all or part of the homestead purchase;
6. a person related to the borrower within the second degree of affinity or consanguinity;
7. a person regulated under Texas law as a mortgage banker or mortgage company; or
8. a bank chartered under the laws of another state that does business in Texas in accordance with state law, including being registered with the Texas Secretary of State.

Tex. Const. art. XVI, § 50(a)(6)(P), 7 Tex. Admin. Code § 153.17(2). To qualify as a mortgage company under category 7 above, a lender must obtain a license under Texas Finance Code chapter 156, the Residential Mortgage Loan Company Licensing and Registration Act. To qualify as a mortgage banker under category 7 above, a lender must obtain a license under Texas Finance Code chapter 157, the Mortgage Banker Registration and Residential Mortgage Loan Originator License Act. 7 Tex. Admin. Code § 153.17(3).

§ 11.3:1 Financial Institutions

Some questions remain regarding the eligibility of a financial institution chartered in a foreign state to make a home equity loan. Such institutions are generally considered to be exempt from Texas usury law under 12 U.S.C. § 1831d. Such institutions may make loans to Texas residents under the usury laws of their home states. The 1998 OCCC Commentary recognizes that a financial institution chartered and doing business in a foreign state is not subject to licensure as a Texas-regulated lender but offers no direct opinion on whether such an institution would be recognized under the Texas Constitution as an authorized home equity lender. 1998 OCCC Commentary, at 9.

§ 11.3:2 HUD-Approved Mortgagees

A person approved by the United States government as a mortgagee to make federally insured loans is an authorized home equity lender. The Department of Housing and Urban Development (HUD) approves lenders to make federally insured loans. Federal Housing Administration (FHA) and HUD direct endorsement or nonsupervised mortgagees are eligible to make home equity loans. Correspondents to a HUD-approved mortgagee are not authorized to make home equity loans unless they qualify under another category of authorized lender. 7 Tex. Admin. Code § 153.17(2). Unless a HUD-approved mortgagee is also a bank, savings and loan association, or credit union, the mortgagee must obtain a license from the Office of Consumer Credit Commissioner to make junior-lien home equity loans. Tex. Fin. Code §§ 124.005, 339.005, 341.103–.104, 342.051.

§ 11.3:3 State-Regulated Lenders

A lender authorized under Texas Finance Code chapter 341 must still meet both constitutional and statutory qualifications to make a home equity loan. Generally, a nondepository lender that makes, negotiates, arranges, or transacts a secondary mortgage loan governed by Finance Code chapter 342 must comply with the licensing provisions of that chapter. *See* 7 Tex. Admin. Code § 153.17(1), (3). Residential mortgage loan originators licensed under chapter 156 of the Finance Code, federal and state banks, savings banks, and savings and loan associations are expressly exempt from the licensing requirements of chapter 342. *See* Tex. Fin. Code § 342.051(c)(1), (f). Exempt lenders are nevertheless thought to be subject to the substantive provisions of that chapter applicable to secondary mortgage loans. However, chapter 342 and other chapters of subtitle B, title 4, of the Finance Code do not apply to a credit union's extension of credit unless the agreement that evidences the transaction specifically provides otherwise. *See* Tex. Fin. Code § 124.005.

§ 11.3:4 Mortgage Banker or Mortgage Company

A person regulated by the state of Texas as a mortgage banker or mortgage company is authorized by the constitution to make a home equity loan. Tex. Const. art. XVI, § 50(a)(6)(P)(vi).

§ 11.3:5 Loans by Relatives

A person related to the borrower within the second degree of affinity or consanguinity may make a home equity loan. Tex. Const. art. XVI, § 50(a)(6)(P)(v). The Texas Government Code gives instructions for computing degrees of affinity and consanguinity. *See* Tex. Gov't Code §§ 573.021–.025. Individuals also are exempt under licensing and registration requirements of Texas Finance Code chapter 180 when offering or negotiating a residential mortgage loan with, or on behalf of, an immediate family member of the individual. *See* Tex. Fin. Code § 180.003(a)(2). An "immediate family member" for this purpose means the spouse, child, sibling, parent, grandparent, or grandchild of an individual. The term also includes a stepparent, stepchild, and step-sibling and a relationship established by adoption. *See* Tex. Fin. Code § 180.002(8).

§ 11.3:6 Redlining Restrictions

A lender otherwise authorized to make a home equity loan is ineligible to make such a loan if found by a federal regulatory agency to have engaged in the practice of refusing to make loans because the debtor resides or the property is located in a certain area. Tex. Const. art. XVI, § 50(a)(6)(P). No provision is made in the constitution to rehabilitate or requalify lenders who were once found to have done this.

§ 11.4 Restriction on Loan-to-Value Ratio

The principal amount of a home equity loan when added to the aggregate total of all other indebtedness secured by a lien against the homestead may not exceed 80 percent of the fair market value of the homestead on the date that the extension of credit is made. Tex. Const. art. XVI, § 50(a)(6)(B). For the purpose of this calculation, the principal amount of a home equity loan is the sum of cash advances and charges made at the inception of the loan to the extent that the charges are financed in the principal amount of the note. 7 Tex. Admin. Code § 153.3(1). The 80 percent limit applies to the principal balance of all outstanding debt secured by the homestead on the date that the extension of credit is made. 7 Tex. Admin. Code § 153.3(2). The principal amount of a home equity loan does not include interest accrued after the date that the extension of credit is made (other than any interest capitalized and added to the principal balance on the date that the extension of credit is made) or amounts advanced by the lender after closing as the result of default, including, for example, ad valorem taxes, hazard insurance premiums, and authorized collection costs, including attorney's fees. 7 Tex. Admin. Code § 153.3(3). With a closed-end multiple advance loan, the principal balance includes contractually obligated future advances not yet disbursed. 7 Tex. Admin. Code § 153.3(4).

Valuation: The lender and owner must sign a written acknowledgment of the fair market value of the homestead property on the date that the extension of credit is made. Tex. Const. art. XVI, § 50(a)(6)(Q)(ix). A lender may sign the written acknowledgment before or at closing. 7 Tex. Admin. Code § 153.26(2). An authorized agent may sign the written acknowledgment on behalf of the lender. 7 Tex. Admin. Code § 153.26(3). The owner and lender may sign the written acknowledgment electronically in accordance with state and federal law governing electronic signatures and delivery of electronic documents. The Texas Uniform Electronic Transactions Act (UETA) and the Electronic Signatures in Global and National Commerce Act (E-Sign Act) include requirements for electronic signatures and delivery. 7 Tex. Admin. Code § 153.26(4). A lender or assignee for value may conclusively rely on the fair market value established by this written acknowledgment if that value is established by appraisal or evaluation prepared in accordance with any applicable state or federal requirement and the lender or assignee has no actual knowledge at the time that the loan is made that the fair market value established by the written acknowledgment is incorrect. Tex. Const. art. XVI, § 50(h). The appraisal or evaluation should be attached to the written acknowledgement of value executed by the borrower at closing. *See* Procedural Rule P-47, *Basic Manual of Rules, Rates and Forms for the Writing of Title Insurance in the State of Texas*.

Federal banking regulators have issued regulations establishing the minimum criteria for valuations of real estate. An "appraisal" by a state certified or licensed appraiser is generally required for transactions valued at more than $400,000. An "evaluation" is required for transactions of $400,000 and less. *See* 12 C.F.R.

§§ 34.43(a), (b), 225.63(a), (b), 323.3(a), (b), 564.3(a), (b).

Federal Financial Institutions Examination Council Interagency Appraisal Evaluation Guidelines issued by federal banking regulators provide further specifications for an evaluation. The evaluation must (1) be written; (2) include the preparer's name, address, signature, and date of the evaluation; (3) describe the collateral, its condition, and its current and projected use; (4) describe the source of information used in the analysis; (5) describe the analysis and supporting information; and (6) provide an estimate of the real estate's market value, with any limiting conditions. Interagency Appraisal and Evaluation Guidelines in Commercial Real Estate and Construction Lending, Comptroller's Handbook, Appendix E (Comptroller of the Currency, November 1995), available at **www.occ.gov/publications-and-resources/publications/comptrollers-handbook/index-comptrollers-handbook.html**. Qualifying evaluations and appraisals may be performed by lender employees or agents as long as the appraiser or evaluator is independent from the loan decision. Home equity loans made by FDIC-insured institutions must be supported by an appraisal or evaluation complying with these federal requirements.

In some cases, constitutional restrictions against additional collateral for home equity loans may require the partition, subdivision, and replatting of a tract into separate homestead and nonhomestead parcels. The proper apportioning of value between the homestead tract and the nonhomestead tract is essential to compliance with loan-to-value limits. This apportionment of value should take into account that the partitioned unsecured tract may have critical value to the homestead because it provides access to a public street or, conversely, it may have no value save in conjunction with the disposition of the entire property. *See In re Tinsley*, 217 B.R. 188 (Bankr. N.D. Tex. 1997).

§ 11.5 Restrictions on Open-End Credit

A home equity loan must be for a definite original principal amount. The credit may not be in the form of an open-end account that may be debited from time to time or from which credit may be extended from time to time *unless* the open-end account qualifies as a home equity line of credit. Tex. Const. art. XVI, § 50(a)(6)(F).

The 1998 OCCC Commentary provides that open-end credit is defined by Tex. Rev. Civ. Stat. art. 5069–1B.002(14) (since codified as Tex. Fin. Code § 301.002(a)(14)) as an account under a written contract between a creditor and an obligor in connection with which—

1. the creditor reasonably contemplates repeated transactions and the obligor is authorized to make purchases or borrow money;
2. interest may be charged from time to time on an outstanding unpaid balance; and
3. the amount of the credit that may be extended during the term of the account is generally made available to the extent that any outstanding balance is repaid.

1998 OCCC Commentary, at 5.

The 1998 OCCC Commentary provides that amounts advanced by the lender after closing as a result of default for ad valorem taxes, hazard insurance premiums, and authorized collection costs, including reasonable attorney's fees, are not contemplated repeated transactions that render the loan an open-end account. 1998 OCCC Commentary, at 5.

Home Equity Line of Credit (HELOC): A home equity loan may be of the open-end account type if it qualifies as a home equity line of credit or HELOC. Tex. Const. art. XVI,

§ 50(a)(6)(F). A HELOC is a form of open-end account that may be debited from time to time, under which credit may be extended from time to time, and under which the borrower requests advances, repays money, and reborrows money. 7 Tex. Admin. Code § 153.82. To qualify as a HELOC, a home equity loan must meet eight additional constitutional requirements:

1. Borrower-Requested Advances. With a HELOC, credit may be extended to the borrower from time to time. However, any advances must be borrower-requested. Tex. Const. art. XVI, § 50(t)(1). Only a borrower named in the HELOC may request an advance. An owner may request an advance only if also named as a borrower. A HELOC may contain provisions that restrict which borrowers may request an advance or may require that all borrowers consent to the advance. 7 Tex. Admin. Code § 153.82.

2. Minimum Advances. No single debit or advance on a HELOC may be for less than $4,000. Tex. Const. art. XVI, § 50(t)(2).

3. Restriction against Credit/Debit Cards or Preprinted Checks Not Solicited by Borrower. Advances on a HELOC may not be made by credit card, debit card, or similar device or by preprinted check unsolicited by a borrower. Tex. Const. art. XVI, § 50(t)(3). A borrower may from time to time specifically request preprinted checks for use in obtaining a HELOC advance but may not request the lender to periodically send preprinted checks to the borrower. A borrower may use a check reorder form, which may be included with preprinted checks, as a means of requesting a specific number of preprinted checks. 7 Tex. Admin. Code § 153.84(2).

   A lender may offer one or more nonprohibited devices or methods for a borrower to request a HELOC loan advance. 7 Tex. Admin. Code § 153.84(1). The request may be made in person, but this is not required. 7 Tex. Admin. Code § 153.84(3). Permissible advance requests may be made by contacting the lender directly, by telephonic fund transfers, and by electronic fund transfers. Examples of devices to obtain a HELOC advance that are not "prohibited similar devices" to those specifically prohibited by the constitution include prearranged drafts, preprinted checks requested by the borrower, or written transfer instructions. 7 Tex. Admin. Code § 153.84(1).

4. Restriction on Fees. The restriction on closing expenses generally applicable to home equity loans is equally applicable to HELOCs. All such fees must be charged or collected only at the time of the initial extension of credit. No fee may be charged or collected in connection with any subsequent debit or advance. Tex. Const. art. XVI, § 50(t)(4). For the purpose of this restriction, the date of the initial extension of credit is the closing date of the HELOC. 7 Tex. Admin. Code § 153.85(b).

5. Restriction on Loan-to-Value Ratio. The 80 percent restriction on loan-to-value generally applicable to home equity loans also applies to HELOCs. The maximum principal amount that may be extended under the line of credit, when added to the aggregate total of the outstanding principal balances of all indebtedness secured by the homestead on the date of the extension of credit, may not exceed the 80 percent loan-to-value limit.

Tex. Const. art. XVI, § 50(t)(5). The maximum principal amount that may be outstanding on a HELOC at any time is determined as of the date of loan closing and does not change during the term of the HELOC. 7 Tex. Admin. Code § 153.86(3). The following amounts, when added together, must be equal to or less than 80 percent of the fair market value of the property: (1) the amount of the advance; (2) the principal amount of the HELOC at the time of the advance; and (3) the principal balance outstanding on all other debts secured by the homestead calculated as of the date of closing of the HELOC. 7 Tex. Admin. Code § 153.86(1), (4).

6. Loan-to-Value Limit on Additional Advances. For HELOCs closed before January 1, 2018, no additional advances may be made if the total principal amount outstanding exceeds an amount equal to 50 percent of the fair market value of the homestead as determined on the date of the original extension of credit. Tex. Const. art. XVI, § 50(t)(6) (repealed Jan. 1, 2018); 7 Tex. Admin. Code § 153.87, *repealed by* 43 Tex. Reg. 1839, 1839 (2018). To calculate the total principal amount outstanding for the purposes of determining the 50 percent threshold, the following amounts are added: (1) the principal amount of the HELOC at the time of the proposed advance and (2) the principal balance outstanding on all other debts secured by the homestead calculated as of the date of closing of the HELOC. 7 Tex. Admin. Code § 153.86(1), (4). If the total principal amount of the HELOC exceeds the 50 percent limitation but then is paid down to an amount equal to or less than 50 percent of the fair market value, subsequent advances are permitted subject to all other HELOC restrictions (for example, minimum advance limit and loan-to-value limit). For HELOCs closed on or after January 1, 2018, an 80 percent loan-to-value restriction applies to additional advances. Tex. Const. art. XVI, § 50(t)(5); 7 Tex. Admin. Code § 153.86.

7. Restriction against Unilateral Lender Amendments. A lender or holder of a HELOC may not unilaterally amend the extension of credit. Tex. Const. art. XVI, § 50(t)(7).

8. Restriction on Amortization. A HELOC must be repayable in regular periodic installments. The installments must be repayable not more often than every fourteen days and not less often than monthly. The installments must commence not later than two months from the date of the extension of credit. During the period in the loan term during which the borrower may request advances, the amount of each installment must be at least equal to the accrued interest on the loan. During the period in the loan term after which the borrower may not request additional advances, the amount of the installments must be substantially equal and sufficient to retire the indebtedness over the remaining term of the loan. Tex. Const. art. XVI, § 50(t)(8).

While installments on a HELOC are required to begin not later than two months from the date of the extension of credit, this does not apply when no advance is made at the time of closing. If no advance is made at closing, the repayment period is not required to begin until after the first advance. 7 Tex. Admin. Code § 153.88(b). While HELOC borrowers cannot be *required* to make loan installments more frequently than every fourteen days, this does not prohibit a borrower from voluntarily making payments on a schedule that is more frequent than that required by the lender. 7 Tex. Admin. Code § 153.88(c).

§ 11.6 Restriction on Fees

For home equity loans closed on or after January 1, 2018, closing expenses, other than interest or bona fide discount points used to buy down the interest rate, may not exceed 2 percent of the original principal amount of the loan. Loan closing expenses subject to this restriction include any fees paid to anyone to originate, evaluate, maintain, record, insure, or service the extension of credit, excluding fees for:

(i) an appraisal performed by a third party appraiser;

(ii) a property survey performed by a state registered or licensed surveyor;

(iii) a state base premium for a mortgagee policy of title insurance with endorsements established in accordance with state law; or

(iv) a title examination report if its cost is less than the state base premium for a mortgagee policy of title insurance without endorsements established in accordance with state law.

Tex. Const. art. XVI, § 50(a)(6)(E).

For home equity loans closed before January 1, 2018, closing expenses, other than interest, may not exceed 3 percent of the original principal amount of the loan. Appraisal fees, survey fees, title insurance premiums, and title search fees are included in the 3 percent loan fee calculation.

The 2 percent (3 percent for pre-2018 loans) fee limit applies only to charges, other than interest, that are required by the lender to be paid by the borrower or the borrower's spouse at the inception of the loan. Charges after loan closing for such matters as contractually permitted force-placed insurance premiums, returned check fees, late fees, and debt collection and foreclosure costs are subsequent events that are not subject to the fee limitation. *See* 7 Tex. Admin. Code § 153.5(19).

§ 11.6:1 Interest

Interest is specifically excluded from the fee limitation. Tex. Const. art. XVI, § 50(a)(6)(E). "Interest" had been interpreted by the Texas Finance Commission and Credit Union Commission in 2004 for purposes of the fee limitation to mean interest as defined by Tex. Fin. Code § 301.002(a)(4) and as interpreted by Texas courts. *See* 7 Tex. Admin. Code §§ 153.1(11), 153.5(3). Finance Code section 301.002, which is located in the subtitle of the Code governing usury, defines interest in pertinent part as "compensation for the use, forbearance, or detention of money." *See* Tex. Fin. Code § 301.002(a)(4). However, the supreme court invalidated this broad interpretation of interest as contrary to the intent and meaning of the constitution in *Finance Commission of Texas v. Norwood*, 418 S.W.3d 566 (Tex. 2013). The case reached the supreme court on petition for review of *Texas Bankers Ass'n v. Ass'n of Community Organizations for Reform Now (ACORN)*, 303 S.W.3d 404 (Tex. App.—Austin 2010, pet. granted), which was so styled and popularly referred to as the "ACORN" case before the supreme court ordered ACORN to be dismissed as a party because of its intervening dissolution and the style of the cause corrected to read *Finance Commission of Texas et al. v. Valerie Norwood et al.*, No. 10-0121, 54 Tex. Sup. Ct. J. 1077 (Tex. Feb. 25, 2011).

By adopting a definition of interest that is tied to a statute that can be amended by the legislature from time to time, the supreme court found that the commission's interpretation "utterly defeats the clear purpose of constitutionalizing it, which was to place the [fee] limitation beyond the Legislature's power to change without ratification by the voters." *Finance Commission of Texas*, 418 S.W.3d at 587. Moreover, the supreme court found implausible that the legislature intended that the same definition of interest that applies to and strengthens the consumer protections of usury would be applied to determining the constitutional fee limitation, which it weakens, although both are intended as consumer protections. Instead, the court adopted what it characterized as a narrower and "well-understood meaning of 'interest': the amount equal to the loan principal multiplied by the interest rate." *Finance Commission of Texas*, 418 S.W.3d at 587. The court concluded that "consistent with the [legislative] history, purpose, and text of Section 50(a)(6)(E), 'interest' as used in that provision means the amount determined by multiplying the loan principal by the interest rate." *Finance Commission of Texas*, 418 S.W.3d at 588. The court noted, however, that "this narrower definition of interest does not limit the amount a lender can charge for a loan, [but instead] limits only what part of the total charge can be paid in front-end fees rather than interest paid over time." *Finance Commission of Texas*, 418 S.W.3d at 588 n.104.

Per diem interest and discount points are considered "interest" and not subject to the constitutional fee limitation. *Finance Commission of Texas*, 418 S.W.3d at 596; 7 Tex. Admin. Code § 153.1(11). Discount points, to be excluded from the fee limitation, must truly correspond to a reduced interest rate. 7 Tex. Admin. Code § 153.5(3)(B).

§ 11.6:2 Voluntary Optional Fees

Optional charges not required by the lender but paid at the sole discretion of the borrower are not fees subject to the fee limitation. 7 Tex. Admin. Code § 153.5(1). If the borrower chooses to pay premiums for certain insurance coverage (for example, credit life, credit accident, or health insurance coverage), the premiums are excluded from the fee limitation. 7 Tex. Admin. Code § 153.5(2) If the lender required these same coverages, the premiums would be included in the fee limitation.

§ 11.6:3 Fees to Originate

Fees to originate a home equity loan are subject to the fee limitation. 7 Tex. Admin. Code § 153.5(6). Fees required to be paid by the borrower to third parties for separate and additional consideration for activities relating to originating the loan are fees subject to the limit. Attorney's fees for document preparation and broker's fees are considered fees to originate a loan. However, charges for loan origination that third parties absorb and do not require the borrower or borrower's spouse to pay are not fees subject to the limit. 7 Tex. Admin. Code § 153.5(7).

§ 11.6:4 Fees Absorbed by Lender

Charges that the lender absorbs that might otherwise be paid by the borrower or borrower's spouse are not fees subject to the limitation. 7 Tex. Admin. Code § 153.5(5).

§ 11.6:5 Fees to Evaluate

Fees to evaluate the credit decision for a home equity loan are subject to the fee limitation. This includes fees collected to cover the expenses of a credit report, flood zone determination, tax certificate, or inspection. 7 Tex. Admin. Code § 153.5(8).

For home equity loans closed on or after January 1, 2018, appraisal fees, survey fees, and title report fees are excluded from the 2 percent fee limit. Tex. Const. art. XVI, § 50(a)(6)(E)(i)–(a)(6)(E)(iv). For home equity loans closed before January 1, 2018, appraisal fees, survey fees, and title report fees are included in the 3 percent fee limit.

§ 11.6:6 Fees to Maintain

Fees to maintain a home equity loan are subject to the fee limitation. Fees paid at the inception of the loan as compensation for performing a service for the life of the loan (for example, flood zone determination fee or tax service fee) are subject to the limit. Also included in the limit are fees to maintain the loan customarily paid at the inception of the home equity loan but deferred for later payment. 7 Tex. Admin. Code § 153.5(9).

§ 11.6:7 Fees to Record

Fees paid to public officials and others for the purposes of recording public documents evidencing the lien are fees subject to the fee limit. 7 Tex. Admin. Code § 153.5(10).

§ 11.6:8 Fees to Insure

For home equity loans closed on or after January 1, 2018, a mortgagee's title insurance premium with endorsements is excluded from the 2 percent fee limit. Tex. Const. art. XVI, § 50(a)(6)(E)(iii).

For home equity loans closed before January 1, 2018, premiums to insure a home equity loan (for example, title insurance) are fees subject to the 3 percent limit.

Premiums that the borrower or borrower's spouse are required to pay to purchase homeowner's insurance are not fees subject to the fee limitation. This includes fire and extended coverage insurance and flood insurance. Though the failure to maintain insurance is generally an event of default on the home equity loan, it is not a condition to the extension of the credit. A lender may collect and escrow premiums for this insurance and include the premium in the periodic payment amount or principal amount. If the lender sells insurance to the borrower, the lender must also comply with all applicable law concerning the sale of insurance in connection with a mortgage loan. 7 Tex. Admin. Code § 153.5(20).

§ 11.6:9 Fees to Service

Any fee charged to or paid by an owner at the inception of the loan transaction to service a home equity loan is a fee subject to the fee limitation. Also, subject to the limit are fees to service a loan customarily paid at the inception of the home equity loan but deferred for later payment. 7 Tex. Admin. Code § 153.5(12).

§ 11.6:10 Escrow Funds

A lender may provide escrow services in a home equity loan transaction. Funds deposited by the borrower into the escrow account for the payment of taxes, insurance premiums, maintenance or homeowners' association assessments, or similar purposes remain the property of the borrower and are not considered fees subject to the fee limitation. However, a lender must not contract for a right of offset against escrow funds. This would result in a violation of prohibitions against additional collateral. 7 Tex. Admin. Code § 153.5(18).

§ 11.6:11 Fees to Subdivide or Replat

In some situations constitutional restrictions against additional collateral for a home equity loan may require the subdivision or replatting of a tract into separate homestead and nonhomestead parcels. Fannie Mae policy for the purchase of home equity loans suggests that all lender-required costs incurred by the borrower to resurvey, subdivide, or replat the property are fees subject to the fee limitation. Fannie Mae Lender Letter LL02-98 (May 28, 1998).

§ 11.6:12 Subsequent Events

The fee limitation applies only to fees contracted for or paid by an owner or owner's spouse at the inception of the loan. If the owner fails to perform covenants in the credit documents resulting in the lender's later assessment of costs to the owner, such postclosing costs are not subject to the limit. Examples of these costs include lender-acquired homeowner's insurance, late charges, returned check fees, collection costs, and foreclosure costs. 7 Tex. Admin. Code § 153.5(19). However, if the loan is subsequently modified, the original loan and its subsequent modification are regarded as a single transaction for purposes of calculating the fee limitation (that is, any fees paid in connection with the loan modification when added to fees charged at loan closing cannot exceed the applicable fee limitation). A modification for this purpose occurs when one or more terms of the loan are amended by written agreement between the lender and owner in which the original promissory note is not satisfied and replaced with a new debt instrument. *See* 7 Tex. Admin. Code § 153.14(2)(D).

§ 11.6:13 Secondary Mortgage Loans

A secondary mortgage loan as defined by Tex. Fin. Code § 342.001(4) is subject to certain statutory fee limitations. *See* Tex. Fin. Code §§ 342.307, 342.308, 342.502. A home equity loan also constituting a secondary mortgage loan must comply with both the constitutional and statutory fee limitations. 7 Tex. Admin. Code § 153.5(13).

§ 11.7 Restriction against Recourse Debt

A home equity loan must be a nonrecourse loan with no personal liability against the owner or the owner's spouse. Tex. Const. art. XVI, § 50(a)(6)(C). The lender may look to recover only against the homestead property and not pursue a deficiency judgment against any owner or any owner's spouse. 7 Tex. Admin. Code § 153.4(2). If the owner or the spouse of the owner cosigns the home equity loan or consents to the home equity lien, the loan must not give the lender personal recourse against either the owner or the spouse. 7 Tex. Admin. Code § 153.4(1). Lenders may report delinquent loan payments to credit reporting agencies without violating the prohibition against personal liability. *Melton v. CU Members Mortgage*, 586 S.W.3d 26 (Tex. App.—Austin 2019, pet. denied).

Fraud: The lender may have recourse against the owner or owner's spouse if the owner or spouse obtains the extension of credit by actual fraud. Tex. Const. art. XVI, § 50(a)(6)(C). Actual fraud requires a showing of dishonesty of purpose or intentional breach of duty that is designed to injure another or to gain an undue or unconscientious advantage. 7 Tex. Admin. Code § 153.4(3).

§ 11.8 Restriction against Prepayment Penalties

Home equity loans must be capable of being paid in advance without penalty or other charge. Tex. Const. art. XVI, § 50(a)(6)(G). A lockout provision in a loan contract prohibiting a buyer from paying early is considered a prepayment penalty. 7 Tex. Admin. Code § 153.7(2).

There is no express constitutional prohibition against note provisions applying principal prepayment to the last of the principal payments becoming due or providing that any partial prepayment would not alter the amount or timing of scheduled monthly payments. 1998 OCCC Commentary, at 5.

§ 11.9 Restriction against Additional Collateral

The homestead is the only collateral that may secure a home equity loan. The constitution expressly prohibits the credit from being secured by any other real or personal property. *See* Tex. Const. art. XVI, § 50(a)(6)(H).

§ 11.9:1 Incidental Collateral

A lender and an owner may enter into an agreement whereby a lender may acquire a security interest in items "incidental" to the homestead collateral. Items not considered additional real or personal property collateral are—

1. escrow funds for the payment of taxes and insurances;
2. an undivided interest in a condominium unit, a planned unit development, or the right to use and enjoy certain property owned by an association;
3. insurance proceeds related to the homestead;
4. condemnation proceeds;
5. fixtures; or
6. easements necessary or beneficial to the use of the homestead including access easements for ingress and egress.

7 Tex. Admin. Code § 153.8(1).

§ 11.9:2 Guaranty

A guaranty or obligation of a cosigner or surety is considered additional collateral not permissible in connection with a home equity loan. A guaranty of a home equity loan is also deemed inconsistent with Tex. Const. art. XVI, § 50(a)(6)(C) (prohibition against personal recourse). 7 Tex. Admin. Code § 153.8(2). This prohibition against guaranties prevents borrowers from obtaining a home equity loan through the U.S. Department of Veterans Affairs cash-out refinance program, which provides a guaranty by the federal government. Tex. Att'y Gen. Op. No. KP-0183 (2018).

§ 11.9:3 Cross-Collateral Provisions

If the borrower has other loans with the home equity lender secured by nonhomestead property (for example, a loan to purchase a car or boat), the security documents on these other loans may sometimes provide that this other collateral secures all debt of the borrower with that lender. Such a cross-collateral provision violates the constitutional prohibition against other collateral for a home equity loan. 7 Tex. Admin. Code § 153.8(4).

§ 11.9:4 Right of Offset

A contractual right of offset is prohibited additional collateral to a home equity loan. 7 Tex. Admin. Code § 153.8(3).

§ 11.9:5 Undivided Interest in Tenancy in Common

A debtor's undivided interest in a tenancy in common will sustain a homestead claim. *See Laster v. First Huntsville Properties Co.*, 826 S.W.2d 125, 131 (Tex. 1991).

§ 11.9:6 Homestead Exceeding Maximum

An urban homestead consists of not more than ten contiguous acres of land located in a city, town, or village, together with improvements thereon. Rural homesteads may be up to one hundred acres for single adults and two hundred acres for a family. Tex. Const. art. XVI, §§ 50, 51; Tex. Prop. Code § 41.002. For a homestead established on a tract that exceeds the maximum allowable land area, the excess is considered additional real property, which may not secure a home equity loan. 7 Tex. Admin. Code § 153.8(5).

The inclusion of nonhomestead acreage may invalidate a home equity lien. Tex. Const. art. XVI, § 50(a)(6)(H). Procedural Rule P-47 requires as a condition to insuring a home equity lien against invalidity for inclusion of additional collateral that each owner execute an affidavit stating that (1) all the property is the homestead of the owner and owner's spouse; (2) no portion of the property is nonhomestead; and (3) the owner and spouse claim no other property as homestead except as described in the affidavit. Procedural Rule P-47, *Basic Manual of Rules, Rates and Forms for the Writing of Title Insurance in the State of Texas*.

There is no provision in Tex. Const. art. XVI, § 50, upholding the validity of a home equity lien if the collateral includes only de minimus acreage in excess of the maximum acreage. Procedural Rule P-47 requires, as a condition to insuring against invalidity for inclusion of excess acreage, that the insured obtain a surveyor's certificate or letter stating the exact acreage or square footage of the collateral or that a computation of the acreage be made by a software program designed to compute acreage and generate drawings of land from the entry of boundary description calls.

§ 11.9:7 Options to Purchase

If the home equity lien extends to the maximum permitted acreage, lenders may risk invalidating the lien by taking an option to purchase an adjacent property deemed necessary to realize full value for the collateral. Fannie Mae policy for the purchase of home equity loans prohibits the lender taking such an option on adjacent acreage under circumstances in which such an interest could be construed as additional collateral. Fannie Mae Lender Letter LL02-98 (May 28, 1998).

§ 11.9:8 Distinguishing Rural and Urban Homestead

A home equity loan secured by property exceeding ten acres must be secured by a rural homestead. The proper classification of the homestead as rural or urban in certain cases is critical to the validity of the home equity lien.

Whether a homestead is urban or rural is a question of fact. The Texas legislature in 1999 enacted a detailed test for classifying homesteads as urban or rural. Tex. Prop. Code § 41.002(c). If a homestead does not meet the statutory definition of urban, it is classified as rural. The statute is the exclusive vehicle for distinguishing between rural and urban homesteads. *In re Bouchie*, 324 F.3d 780 (5th Cir. 2003).

A homestead is considered to be urban if, at the time the designation is made, the property is—

(1) located within the limits of a municipality or its extraterritorial jurisdiction or a platted subdivision; and

(2) served by police protection, paid or volunteer fire protection, and at least three of the following services provided by a municipality or under contract to a municipality:

- (A) electric;
- (B) natural gas;
- (C) sewer;
- (D) storm sewer; and
- (E) water.

Tex. Prop. Code § 41.002(c).

§ 11.9:9 Distinguishing Family and Single Adult Homestead

A rural single adult homestead is limited to one hundred acres. A rural family homestead may include up to two hundred acres. Tex. Const. art. XVI, §§ 50, 51; Tex. Prop. Code § 41.002. Thus, a home equity loan secured by property exceeding one hundred acres may be secured by a family rural homestead only. The proper classification of the property in such cases as a family or single adult homestead is critical to the validity of the home equity lien.

No definition of the word *family* is supplied by the constitution. Case authorities provide that a family consists of (1) a group of people having the social status of a family living subject to one domestic government; (2) with the head of the family legally or morally obligated to support at least one other family member; and (3) a corresponding dependence by the other family members for this support. *NCNB Texas National Bank v. Carpenter*, 849 S.W.2d 875, 879–80 (Tex. App.—Fort Worth 1993, no writ).

A married person with a living spouse can have only a family homestead interest. The spouses in a marriage together enjoy the benefits of the family homestead exemption. The constitution gives each spouse a separate and undivided possessory interest in the homestead, which may be lost only by death or abandonment and may not be compromised by either his heirs or the other spouse. Abandonment by one spouse of his homestead interest does not affect the character of the property as family homestead or the protection of the family homestead from judgment creditors as long as the other spouse occupies the property as a home. *Salomon v. Lesay*, 369 S.W.3d 540 (Tex. App.—Houston [1st Dist.] 2012, no pet.).

§ 11.10 Restriction on Number of Home Equity Loans

There may be only one home equity loan or reverse mortgage on the owner's homestead at any given time regardless of the aggregate total outstanding debt against the homestead. There is no corresponding restriction on the number of purchase-money, improvement, tax, or owelty liens on the same homestead. Tex. Const. art. XVI, § 50(a)(6)(K); 7 Tex. Admin. Code § 153.10(1). If the property ceases to be the homestead of the owner, the lender may treat a previous home equity lien as a nonhomestead lien for the purposes of this restriction. 7 Tex. Admin. Code § 153.10(2).

§ 11.11 Restriction on Frequency of Home Equity Loans

Home equity loans cannot be closed more frequently than one year after the closing date of the last such loan made on the same property. Tex. Const. art. XVI, § 50(a)(6)(M)(iii). A home equity loan cannot be refinanced until the expiration of one year after its original closing date. 7 Tex. Admin. Code § 153.14(1)(A). A new home equity loan cannot be made before the expiration of one year even if the previous home equity loan has been paid in full. 7 Tex. Admin. Code § 153.14(1)(B).

Effect of State of Emergency: A home equity loan may be closed before the first anniversary date of a prior home equity loan on the same property if the owner on oath requests an earlier closing due to a state of emergency that (1) has been declared by the President of the United States or governor as provided by law and (2) applies to the area where the homestead is located. Tex. Const. art. XVI, § 50(a)(6)(M)(iii). A state of emergency includes a national emergency declared by the president of the United States under the National Emergencies Act, 50 U.S.C. §§ 1601–1651. 7 Tex. Admin. Code § 153.14(3)(A). A state of emergency also includes a state of disaster declared by the governor of Texas under Texas Government Code chapter 418. 7 Tex. Admin. Code § 153.14(3)(B).

Modification of Home Equity Loans: A home equity loan may be modified before the expiration of one year from the date of the original closing. A modification is a transaction in which one or more terms of the home equity loan are modified but the note is not satisfied and replaced. 7 Tex. Admin. Code § 153.14(2). Any modification of a home equity loan must be agreed to in writing by both the borrower and lender unless the law otherwise requires. An example of a modification that is not required to be in writing is the modification required under the Servicemembers Civil Relief Act. 7 Tex. Admin. Code § 153.14(2)(A). Any modification of a home equity loan may not include the advance of additional funds nor include new terms that would not have been permitted by applicable law on the date of the original loan closing. 7 Tex. Admin. Code § 153.14(2)(B), (2)(C). Any fees paid by the borrower for the modification are fees subject to the fee limitation. 7 Tex. Admin. Code § 153.14(2)(D).

§ 11.12 Restriction on Amortization of Home Equity Loans

No balloon payments are allowed with closed-end home equity loans. The loan must be scheduled at closing to be repaid in substantially equal periodic installments. The installments must be payable not more often than every fourteen days or any less often than monthly. The installments must begin no later than two months from the date the extension of credit is made. The date the extension of credit is made refers to the closing date, or the date the borrower signs the loan documents, not the date the loan is funded. 7 Tex. Admin. Code § 153.11(2)–(3). Each installment payment must equal or exceed the amount of accrued interest on the note as of the date of that installment and contribute to the repayment of some amount of principal. A home equity loan may not contain a "negative amortization" feature, in which scheduled payments in the early years of the loan are in an amount less than the accruing interest and the resulting interest deficits are capitalized into the loan principal. Tex. Const. art. XVI, § 50(a)(6)(L); 7 Tex. Admin. Code §§ 153.11, 153.16(2).

There are special amortization rules for home equity loans qualifying as a home equity line of credit. *See* Tex. Const. art. XVI, § 50(a)(6)(L)(ii). See section 11.5 above.

§ 11.12:1 Subsequent Events

The constitutional restriction does not prohibit a lender from agreeing with the borrower to modify an equity loan if the modification does not satisfy and replace the original equity loan and does not create a new extension of credit. The modification may include a deferment of the borrower's original obligation, and may include amounts that are past due under the equity loan (e.g., accrued but unpaid interest, taxes, and insurance). 7 Tex. Admin. Code § 153.11(1). However, the first payment must begin within two months of closing, notwithstanding any allowable payment deferral. 7 Tex. Admin. Code § 153.11(2). The constitutional restriction on amortization does not preclude a lender's recovery of amounts made necessary by the borrower's failure to perform loan covenants such as taxes, adverse liens, insurance premiums, collections costs, and similar items. 7 Tex. Admin. Code § 153.11(5).

§ 11.12:2 Prepaid Interest

Scheduled periodic payments must begin no later than two months from the date that the extension of credit is made. This effectively limits prepaid interest to a maximum of one period's interest (first scheduled periodic payment would include interest in arrears for the preceding period). Tex. Const. art. XVI,

§ 50(a)(6)(L). Nothing in this provision limits or otherwise affects a lender's ability to charge or collect mortgage discount points with a corresponding interest rate reduction.

§ 11.13 Restriction on Interest

Interest on a home equity loan may be for any fixed or variable rate authorized by statute. Tex. Const. art. XVI, § 50(a)(6)(O).

§ 11.13:1 Variable Rate Notes

A home equity loan may be made on a variable interest rate tied to an external index. 7 Tex. Admin. Code § 153.16(3). If a variable interest rate is used, payment adjustments must be regularly made in amounts sufficient to fully amortize the outstanding loan balance in substantially equal successive payments between interest rate adjustments. 7 Tex. Admin. Code § 153.16(4)(A). The scheduled payment amount between each payment change date should be substantially equal and the amount of the payment should equal or exceed the amount of interest scheduled to accrue between each payment date and retire a portion of the principal. 7 Tex. Admin. Code § 153.16(4)(B). A home equity loan may contain an adjustable rate of interest that provides a maximum fixed interest rate pursuant to a schedule of stepped or tiered rates or provides a lower initial interest rate through the use of a discounted rate at the beginning of the loan. 7 Tex. Admin. Code § 153.16(5).

§ 11.13:2 Interest Rate

Interest rates on home equity loans must comply with all applicable constitutional and statutory provisions. 7 Tex. Admin. Code § 153.16(1). Tex. Const. art. XVI, § 11, permits interest rates of 10 percent or less on credit transactions unless alternative interest rates are specified by the legislature by statute. Interest rates of first-lien mortgages are nominally controlled by Tex. Fin. Code tit. 4, subtit. A. However, Congress by the enactment of the Depository Institutions Deregulation and Monetary Control Act of 1980 (12 U.S.C. § 1735f–7a) and the Alternative Mortgage Transaction Parity Act (12 U.S.C. §§ 3801–3806) preempted state interest rate limitations on first-lien residential mortgage loans. Secondary mortgage loans that exceed the constitutional rate of 10 percent are controlled by Texas Finance Code chapter 342, subchapter G. Chapter 124 of the Code and federal law provide for maximum rates on certain loans by credit unions. *See* 7 Tex. Admin. Code § 153.16(1).

§ 11.14 Restriction on Basis for Acceleration

The maturity of a home equity loan may not be accelerated because of a decrease in the market value of the homestead or the owner's default under some other indebtedness not secured by a prior valid encumbrance against the homestead. Tex. Const. art. XVI, § 50(a)(6)(J).

§ 11.14:1 Decrease in Value

The constitution does not prohibit the acceleration of a home equity loan because of a default by the owner of covenants contained in the loan, including covenants not to commit waste or remove property that indirectly bears on the market value of the homestead. 7 Tex. Admin. Code § 153.9(1).

§ 11.14:2 Cross-Default

A home equity loan can contain a cross-default provision only if the lien associated with the home equity loan is subordinate to the lien that is referenced by the cross-default clause. 7 Tex. Admin. Code § 153.9(2).

§ 11.15 Restriction against Confession of Judgment or Waiver of Citation

A home equity borrower may not be required to sign any confession of judgment or power of attorney allowing a confession of judgment or appearance for the debtor by a third party in a judicial proceeding. Tex. Const. art. XVI, § 50(a)(6)(Q)(iv); Tex. Civ. Prac. & Rem. Code § 30.001.

§ 11.16 Restriction against Assignment of Wages

A borrower may not be required to make an assignment of wages as security for a home equity loan. Tex. Const. art. XVI, § 50(a)(6)(Q)(ii).

§ 11.17 Restriction against Same Creditor Payoffs

A lender may not require a borrower to apply the loan proceeds of a home equity loan to pay off any other extension of credit by that same lender except one already validly secured by the homestead. Tex. Const. art. XVI, § 50(a)(6)(Q)(i). This provision precludes a creditor from demanding a security interest in the debtor's homestead as a condition for granting a forbearance, rearrangement, or recasting of an indebtedness not already secured by the homestead.

§ 11.17:1 Required Payment of Debt Secured by Homestead

A lender may require a debt secured by the homestead to be paid by the proceeds of a home equity loan. 7 Tex. Admin. Code § 153.18(2).

§ 11.17:2 Payoffs of Other Creditors

An owner is generally entitled to use the loan proceeds of a home equity loan for any lawful purpose at the owner's discretion. The lender may require that the loan proceeds be used to pay off, prepay, or reduce existing debt to another lender (for example, if underwriting guidelines based on earnings require that the debtor's monthly obligations be reduced to qualify for a loan). *See* 7 Tex. Admin. Code § 153.18(2).

§ 11.17:3 Other Restrictions Prohibited

Other than requiring loan proceeds to be paid on debt secured by the homestead or requiring payment of debt to another lender, the home equity lender may not otherwise specify or restrict the use of the loan proceeds. 7 Tex. Admin. Code § 153.18(1).

§ 11.17:4 Voluntary Payoffs to Same Creditor

The constitution prohibits the home equity lender only from *requiring* the debtor to pay off existing nonhomestead debt to that same lender. An owner is not precluded from voluntarily paying off existing nonhomestead debt to the home equity lender. 7 Tex. Admin. Code § 153.18.

§ 11.18 Required Preloan Disclosures

§ 11.18:1 Twelve-Day Disclosure for Home Equity Loans

The Texas Constitution requires a preloan disclosure specifying certain restrictions on home equity lending. Tex. Const. art. XVI, § 50(g). The required disclosure is reproduced as form 11-1 in this chapter. The text of the preloan disclosure is intended as a summary of the borrower's rights under the constitution. In case of any conflict between the substantive provisions of Tex. Const. art. XVI, § 50, and the text of the preloan disclosure, the substantive provisions are controlling. A lender may supplement the consumer disclosure to clarify any discrepancies or inconsistencies. Tex. Const. art. XVI, § 50(g); 7 Tex. Admin. Code § 153.51(3).

A home equity loan may not be closed before the twelfth calendar day after the later of the date that the borrower submits a loan application to the lender or the date that the lender provides all owners with a preloan disclosure in a separate instrument. Tex. Const. art. XVI, § 50(g); 7 Tex. Admin. Code §§ 153.12, 153.51. One copy of the required consumer disclosure may be provided to married owners. 7 Tex. Admin. Code § 153.12. A lender may provide the consumer disclosure electronically in accordance with state and federal law governing electronic signatures and delivery of electronic documents. The Texas Uniform Electronic Transactions Act (UETA) and the Electronic Signatures in Global and National Commerce Act (E-Sign Act) include requirements for electronic signatures and delivery. 7 Tex. Admin. Code § 153.51(2).

If the discussions with the borrower are conducted primarily in a language other than English, the lender must provide the borrower with an additional copy of the notice, before the loan closing, that is translated in the written language in which the discussions were conducted. Tex. Const. art. XVI, § 50(g). The Office of the Consumer Credit Commissioner has provided a Spanish language translation of the notice on its website at **https://occc.texas.gov**.

If the owner has executed a power of attorney in the manner described by title 7, section 153.15(2), of the Texas Administrative Code, then the lender may provide the consumer disclosure to the attorney-in-fact instead of providing it to the owner. 7 Tex. Admin. Code § 153.51(5).

Computation of Time: In computing the expiration of the twelve-day cooling-off period, the date that the disclosure is made is not counted. The twelve-day cooling-off period commences on the day after the lender provides the required preloan disclosure. The loan may be closed at any time on the twelfth day of the notice period. 7 Tex. Admin. Code § 153.12. The lender may establish verifiable procedures to ensure that the owner receives the required notice within the required time frame. 7 Tex. Admin. Code § 153.51(3).

The constitution does not prohibit the required notice being delivered by mail. Government regulations adopted a "mailbox rule." If a lender mails the notice to the borrower, a reasonable period of time should be allowed for delivery. A three-calendar-day period not including Sundays and federal legal public holidays constitutes a rebuttable presumption for sufficient mailing and delivery. 7 Tex. Admin. Code § 153.51(1).

Loan Application: An application is sufficient if submitted to an agent acting on behalf of a lender. 7 Tex. Admin. Code § 153.12(1). An application may be taken orally or electronically. It does not have to be in writing. 7 Tex. Admin. Code § 153.12(2).

§ 11.18:2 One-Day Disclosure

A home equity loan must not be closed until one business day after the owner of the homestead receives a copy of the final loan application, if not previously provided, and a final itemized disclosure of the actual fees, points, interest, costs, and charges that will be charged at closing. Tex. Const. art. XVI, § 50(a)(6)(M)(ii). The home equity loan may be closed at any time during normal business hours on the next business day following the calendar day on which the borrower receives the one-day preloan disclosure or any date thereafter. 7 Tex. Admin. Code § 153.13(6). A lender may satisfy this disclosure requirement by delivery to the borrower of a properly completed closing disclosure for a closed-end home equity loan. 7 Tex. Admin. Code § 153.13(3)(A). A lender may provide the preclosing disclosure electronically in accordance with state and federal law governing electronic signatures and delivery of electronic documents. The Texas Uniform Electronic Transactions Act (UETA) and the Electronic Signatures in Global and National Commerce Act (E-Sign Act) include requirements for electronic signatures and delivery. 7 Tex. Admin. Code § 153.13(4). For an HELOC, a lender may satisfy this disclosure requirement by delivery to the borrower of a properly completed account-opening disclosure under Regulation Z. 12 C.F.R. § 1026.6(a). 7 Tex. Admin. Code § 153.13(3)(B).

§ 11.18:3 Bona Fide Emergency

If a bona fide emergency or other good cause exists and the lender obtains the written consent of the owner, the lender may provide the documentation to the owner or the lender may modify previously provided documentation on the day of closing. Tex. Const. art. XVI, § 50(a)(6)(M)(ii). The bona fide emergency must occur before the closing date. A home equity loan secured by a homestead in an area designated by the Federal Emergency Management Agency (FEMA) as a disaster area is an example of a bona fide emergency if the homestead is damaged during FEMA's declared incident period. 7 Tex. Admin. Code § 153.13(4).

§ 11.18:4 Other Good Cause

A condition that would cause the owner "financial impact or an adverse consequence" is an example of other good cause that would allow the required one-day preloan disclosure to be given or modified on the day of closing. 7 Tex. Admin. Code § 153.13(5)(A)(i). Another example of good cause occurs when the modified disclosure contains only a de minimus variance from the prior disclosure. To qualify as a de minimus variance, one or more of the actual disclosed fees, costs, points, and charges must be less than the initial preloan disclosure or, if greater than the amounts given in the initial preloan disclosure, not vary by the greater of $100 or 0.125 percent of the principal amount of the home equity loan at closing. 7 Tex. Admin. Code § 153.13(5)(B)(i).

§ 11.19 Borrower's Right of Rescission

The homestead owner or the owner's spouse may rescind a home equity loan transaction without penalty or charge within three days after the date that the extension of credit is made. Tex. Const. art. XVI, § 50(a)(6)(Q)(viii). The borrower's spouse has this right of rescission even if the spouse has no record title to or community property interest in the homestead. 7 Tex. Admin. Code § 153.25(1). Funding of a home equity loan should be delayed until after the expiration of the rescission period.

§ 11.19:1 Calculation of Rescission Period

The rescission period begins at closing (the signing of the loan documents) and continues for three calendar days. If the third calendar day falls on a Sunday or federal legal public holiday, the right of rescission is extended to the next calendar day that is not a Sunday or a federal legal public holiday. 7 Tex. Admin. Code § 153.25(2). Loan proceeds may be disbursed on the day following the expiration of the rescission period.

§ 11.19:2 Truth in Lending Act

A home equity loan transaction may be subject to the provisions of the Truth in Lending Act and Regulation Z, which permit the borrower three business days to rescind a mortgage loan in applicable transactions. For a complete discussion of right of rescission procedures under the Truth in Lending Act and Regulation Z, see chapter 12 in this manual. A lender's compliance with the right of rescission procedures of the Truth in Lending Act and Regulation Z will satisfy the requirements of the constitution for a home equity loan if the notices are given to all owners of the homestead and to each spouse of an owner. 7 Tex. Admin. Code § 153.25(3).

§ 11.20 Requirements for Loan Documents

§ 11.20:1 Written Contract Required

A home equity lien must be a voluntary lien created under a written agreement. Tex. Const. art. XVI, § 50(a)(6)(A).

Plain Language and Font Requirements: A home equity loan contract for a home equity loan regulated by the Office of the Consumer Credit Commissioner (OCCC) must be written in plain language designed to be easily understood by the average consumer and must be printed in an easily readable font and type size. See the discussion in section 11.1 above.

Model Forms: In addition to requiring plain-language contracts, the Finance Code empowers the Finance Commission to adopt rules governing loan contracts subject to that section and to adopt model loan contracts. Tex. Fin. Code § 341.502(b). A lender may use either a model contract or its own nonstandard contract if the nonstandard contract has been submitted to, but not disapproved by, the OCCC. See the discussion in section 11.1 above.

§ 11.20:2 Required Loan Conditions

The constitution states that a home equity loan is an extension of credit made on specified conditions. Some of the conditions are self-actuating. *See* Tex. Const. art. XVI, § 50(a)(6)(Q). Tex. Const. art. XVI, § 50(a)(6)(Q)(vi), requires that "the security instruments securing the extension of credit contain a disclosure that the extension of credit is the type of credit defined by Section 50(a)(6), Article XVI, Texas Constitution." Practitioners differ as to whether the remaining conditions listed at Tex. Const. art. XVI, § 50(a)(6)(Q), must be included in the home equity loan documents. The home equity extension of credit, form 11-2 in this chapter, includes the conditions. In the absence of definitive authority on this question, the attorney is cautioned to exercise professional judgment regarding the inclusion of these conditions. If the conditions are included in the home equity extension of credit, the conditions may affect the negotiability of the instrument under chapter 3 of the Texas Business and Commerce Code. However, there is some dated authority that a nonrecourse note is by its very nature nonnegotiable. *Hinckley v. Eggers*, 587 S.W.2d 448, 450 (Tex. App.—Dallas 1979, writ ref'd n.r.e.).

§ 11.20:3 Required Disclosure

The security documents for a home equity loan must disclose that the credit is an equity loan subject to Tex. Const. art. XVI, § 50(a)(6). This disclosure should appear in the mortgage instrument bold-faced, capitalized, underlined, or otherwise conspicuously set out from the surrounding material. 1998 OCCC Commentary, at 10.

§ 11.20:4 Restriction against Blanks Left in Instruments

The borrower in a home equity loan transaction may not sign any instrument in which blanks for substantive terms of agreement are left to be filled in. Tex. Const. art. XVI, § 50(a)(6)(Q)(iii). The prohibited blanks refer to loan contract terms and not signature blocks that must be signed to execute the document. 7 Tex. Admin. Code § 153.20. No guidance is provided regarding blanks for recording information unknown at the time of closing.

The constitution does not specify the instruments to which this restriction applies. Procedural Rule P-47 requires, as a condition to insuring a home equity lien against invalidity for impermissible blanks, that no such blanks appear in (1) the written acknowledgement of the fair market value, (2) the insured mortgage, (3) the promissory note, or (4) any affidavits of compliance with Tex. Const. art. XVI, § 50(a)(6). *See* Procedural Rule P-47, *Basic Manual of Rules, Rates and Forms for the Writing of Title Insurance in the State of Texas.*

§ 11.20:5 Required Copies

The borrower at closing must receive a copy of the final loan application and all executed documents signed by the borrower at closing and related to the extension of credit. Tex. Const. art. XVI, § 50(a)(6)(Q)(v). It is not required that signed copies be provided as long as the copies accurately reflect the documents that the borrower actually signed at closing. *Pelt v. U.S. Trust N.A.*, 359 F.3d 764, 768 (5th Cir. 2004).

Except for the requirement that the borrower receive a copy of the final loan application, the constitution does not require the lender to provide copies of documents signed by the borrower before closing but related to the extension of credit. *See* 7 Tex. Admin. Code § 153.22. A lender may provide documents electronically in accordance with state and federal law governing electronic signatures and delivery of electronic documents. The Texas Uniform Electronic Transactions Act (UETA) and the Electronic Signatures in Global and National Commerce Act (E-Sign Act) include requirements for electronic signatures and delivery. 7 Tex. Admin. Code § 153.22(3).

§ 11.20:6 Required Signatories

A written instrument creating a home equity lien must be signed by each owner and each owner's spouse (regardless of whether the spouse claims ownership or other interest in the property or is liable on the debt). Tex. Const. art. XVI, § 50(a)(6)(A). A spouse or owner who is not a maker of the note may consent to the lien by signing a written consent to the mortgage instrument. The consent may be included in the mortgage instrument or a separate document. 7 Tex. Admin. Code § 153.2(2).

A lender, at the lender's option, may require each owner and each owner's spouse to consent to the home equity loan. This is in addition to the consent required for the lien. 7 Tex. Admin. Code § 153.2(3).

A trustee may sell or encumber a homestead property for which the trustee holds title in a "qualifying trust" without the joinder of either spouse with a beneficial interest in the trust unless expressly prohibited by the instrument or court order creating the trust. A married person who transfers homestead property to the trustee of a qualifying trust, however, must comply with the requirements relating to the joinder of the person's spouse as provided by chapter 5 of the Texas Family Code. Tex. Prop. Code § 41.0021.

§ 11.20:7 Junior-Lien Requirements

If a home equity loan is subordinate to another lien on the property, the loan may also be governed by Texas Finance Code chapter 342 unless the interest rate is 10 percent per year or less. *See* Tex. Fin. Code §§ 342.001(4), 342.005. The loan documents must comply with the requirements applicable to secondary mortgage loans. 1998 OCCC Commentary, at 4–5. If the mortgagee has a license from the Office of Consumer Credit Commissioner, both the home equity extension of credit (promissory note) (form 11-2 in this chapter) and deed of trust (home equity loan) (form 11-3) must contain the name, mailing address, and telephone number of the OCCC. Tex. Fin. Code § 14.104. See clause 8-9-24 in this manual for an example of such a disclosure. Additionally, the printed language in the home equity extension of credit and the deed of trust must be modified slightly. In the deed of trust, in paragraph B.4., the phrase "in a form acceptable to Lender" must be struck so that the obligation reads "maintain an insurance policy that . . . ." This change is necessary because

Finance Code sections 342.404, 342.405, and 342.413 prohibit a lender from approving the selection of insurance. *See* Tex. Fin. Code §§ 342.404, 342.405, 342.413. Also, Finance Code section 342.404 provides that if insurance is required in connection with a loan made under that chapter, the lender must furnish the borrower a statement like clause 11-4-8, which may be added to the home equity deed of trust as a numbered paragraph under "General Provisions." *See* Tex. Fin. Code § 342.404.

The same chapter imposes other requirements if the mortgagee sells or procures insurance related to the loan at a rate not fixed or approved by the State Board of Insurance. *See* Tex. Fin. Code § 342.405.

Finance Code section 342.307 limits the enforcement fees that may be included in secondary mortgage loan documents. To comply with this section for a home equity loan that is also a secondary mortgage loan, in the home equity extension of credit (promissory note) (form 11-2), the alternative indicated attorney's fee provision should be used. In the deed of trust (form 11-3), in paragraph E.10., after the words "an attorney" add "who is not an employee of Lender."

If the prior lien instrument contains a due-on-sale clause, the home equity deed of trust may violate the due-on-sale clause.

§ 11.20:8 Home Loans

A home equity loan may also be subject to the requirements of Texas Finance Code chapter 343, regulating certain types of "home loans." See section 10.14 in this manual.

§ 11.21 Restriction on Place of Closing

A home equity loan may be closed only at the offices of the lender, an attorney at law, or a title company. Tex. Const. art. XVI, § 50(a)(6)(N). The place of closing must be the permanent physical address of the office or branch office of the lender, attorney, or title company so that the closing occurs in an authorized physical location other than the homestead. 7 Tex. Admin. Code § 153.15(1). The closing may occur in any area located at the permanent physical address of the lender, attorney, or title company (e.g., indoor office, parking lot). 7 Tex. Admin. Code § 153.15(1). This provision is intended to protect homeowners from coercive conduct in an equity loan closing conducted at the "kitchen table" of one's home.

"Closing" as construed by the Texas Supreme Court in *Finance Commission of Texas v. Norwood*, 418 S.W.3d 566 (Tex. 2013), is a process that includes not just the final action of executing documents and funding the loan but also the initial action of obtaining required consents. Accordingly, the supreme court concluded that a homeowner's executing a required consent or a power of attorney is part of the closing process and also must occur only at one of the locations authorized by Tex. Const. art. XVI, § 50(a)(6)(N). *Finance Commission of Texas*, 418 S.W.3d at 588; *see also* 7 Tex. Admin. Code § 153.15(3). The court further concluded that the commission's interpretations of section 50(a)(6)(N) (which in part authorized a lender to accept a properly executed power of attorney allowing the attorney-in-fact to execute loan documents on behalf of the homeowner or to receive consents of the homeowner required under section 50(a)(6)(A) by mail or other delivery of the homeowner's signature) contradict the intent and purpose of the text of the provision and are therefore invalid. *Finance Commission of Texas*, 418 S.W.3d at 588–89. Although Fannie Mae generally allows a duly appointed attorney-in-fact to sign the security instrument or note on the borrower's behalf when certain conditions are met, its Selling Guide has been updated with respect to loans purchased on or after February 1, 2014, to prohibit the use of a power of attorney in cash-out refinance transactions and other transactions in connection with Texas section 50(a)(6) mortgage loans. See Fannie Mae, Selling Guide Announcement SEL-2013-08 (Oct. 22, 2013).

§ 11.21:1 Offices of Lender

A home equity loan may not be closed in the offices of a mere loan broker. To qualify as a lender, the party must advance funds directly to the borrower or be identified as the payee of the note. 7 Tex. Admin. Code § 153.15.

§ 11.21:2 Offices of Title Company

The offices of a title company include the leased or owned Texas office location of a title insurance company or (1) a direct operation, (2) a title insurance agent, or (3) an attorney conducting the attorney's business in the name of the title insurance company, direct operation, or title insurance agent (if the attorney or the attorney's bona fide employees are escrow officers under Tex. Ins. Code § 2501.003(4)). Procedural Rule P-44, *Basic Manual of Rules, Rates and Forms for the Writing of Title Insurance in the State of Texas*. The phrase *title company* refers to an agent of a title insurance company. A company merely performing title abstractions is not within the definition of a title company. *Rooms With A View, Inc. v. Private National Mortgage Ass'n*, 7 S.W.3d 840, 846–47 (Tex. App.—Austin 1999, pet. denied).

§ 11.22 Restriction on Release or Transfer of Note

Within a reasonable time after repayment of a home equity loan, the lender must cancel and return the promissory note to the borrower and deliver in a recordable form a release of lien. If the loan is being refinanced, a lender may deliver an endorsement and assignment of the lien. Tex. Const. art. XVI, § 50(a)(6)(Q)(vii). The lender is required to provide these copies without charge. 7 Tex. Admin. Code § 153.24(1). The lender is not required, however, to record or pay for the recording of the release of lien. 7 Tex. Admin. Code § 153.24(2). Thirty days is a reasonable time for the lender to perform the duties required by this section. 7 Tex. Admin. Code § 153.24(3). An affidavit of lost note or imaged note, or equivalent, may be returned to the owner in lieu of the original note if the original note has been lost or imaged. 7 Tex. Admin. Code § 153.24(4).

§ 11.23 Restriction on Refinancing

The refinancing of a debt, any portion of which is secured by a home equity lien, may be made only by an extension of credit meeting all of the constitutional requirements of a home equity loan or reverse mortgage, unless the refinancing meets all of the following conditions of Tex. Const. art. XVI, § 50(f)(2):

1. One-Year Prohibition. The refinance is not closed before the first anniversary of the date the extension of credit was closed. Tex. Const. art. XVI, § 50(f)(2)(A).

2. Prohibition on Additional Funds. The refinanced extension of credit does not include the advance of any additional funds other than (a) funds advanced to refinance a debt described by Tex. Const. art. XVI, § 50(a)(1)–(a)(7); or (b) actual costs and reserves required by the lender to refinance the debt.

3. Eighty Percent Loan-to-Value Limitation. The refinance is of a principal amount that, when added to the aggregate total of all indebtedness secured by the homestead, does not exceed 80 percent of the fair market value of the homestead on the date of the refinance.

4. Twelve-Day Notice. The lender provides the owner the notice contained

in form 11-8 of this chapter within three business days of loan application and at least twelve days before the refinance is closed. Tex. Const. art. XVI, § 50(f)(2)(D).

5. Affidavit of Compliance. An affidavit executed by the owner or the owner's spouse acknowledging that the requirements of Tex. Const. art. XVI, § 50(f)(2) have been met conclusively establishes that the requirements of Tex. Const. art. XVI, § 50(a)(4) have been met. See form 11-9 for a sample affidavit.

Additionally, any refinance of a debt against homestead to secure a debt for purchase money, taxes, owelty of partition, federal tax lien, or improvements that includes the advance of additional funds may not be secured by a valid lien against the homestead unless (1) the additional funds advanced are to pay taxes, an owelty of partition, or improvements; (2) the new loan is made as a home equity loan or reverse mortgage; or (3) the additional funds are for reasonable costs necessary to refinance such debt. Tex. Const. art. XVI, § 50(e); *see* 7 Tex. Admin. Code § 153.41.

§ 11.24 Forfeiture Provision

Constitutional provisions for home equity lending contain a forfeiture provision for loans failing to meet constitutional requirements. If a lender or holder fails to comply with the lender's or holder's constitutionally mandated obligations within sixty days after notice of the violation by the borrower, the lender or holder forfeits all principal and interest on the note. Tex. Const. art. XVI, § 50(a)(6)(Q)(x). Only a violation of a constitutionally mandated provision in the extension of credit will trigger a forfeiture. *Vincent v. Bank of America*, 109 S.W.3d 856 (Tex. App.—Dallas 2003, no pet.) (citing an earlier version of Tex. Const. art. XVI, § 50(a)(6)(Q)(x)).

§ 11.25 Cure Provisions

If a lender fails to comply with constitutional restrictions on home equity lending, the lender may avoid a forfeiture of all principal and interest and enforce an otherwise invalid lien by timely curing the failure in the manner specified by the Texas Constitution. Constitutional curative measures are equally available to cure lender noncompliance in an original home equity loan or in the refinance of a home equity loan. Tex. Const. art. XVI, § 50(a)(6)(Q)(x); 7 Tex. Admin. Code § 153.95(a); *In re Adams*, 307 B.R. 549, 553–54 (Bankr. N.D. Tex. 2004). Cure procedures are specific to certain identified home equity lending violations.

§ 11.25:1 Violation of Restriction on Fees, Restriction on Prepayment Penalties, or Restriction on Interest

In the event of a violation of the constitutional restrictions found at Tex. Const. art. XVI, § 50(a)(6)(E) (restriction on fees), Tex. Const. art. XVI, § 50(a)(6)(G) (restriction on prepayment penalties), or Tex. Const. art. XVI, § 50(a)(6)(O) (restriction on interest), the lender may cure the violation by refunding the borrower the amount of any overcharge. *See* Tex. Const. art. XVI, § 50(a)(6)(Q)(x)(a). The cure is effective when the lender credits the borrower's account with a refund, places the refund in the mail or other delivery carrier, or delivers the refund in person. A cure may also be made using any other delivery method agreed to by the borrower in writing after the lender receives notice of the lender's failure to comply. 7 Tex. Admin. Code § 153.94(a).

§ 11.25:2 Violation of Restriction on Loan-to-Value Ratio

In the event of a violation of the constitutional restriction found at Tex. Const. art. XVI, § 50(a)(6)(B) (restriction on loan-to-value ratio), the lender may cure the violation by sending the borrower written acknowledgment that the lien is valid only to the extent that the loan amount does not exceed the loan-to-value restriction. *See* Tex. Const. art. XVI, § 50(a)(6)(Q)(x)(b). The cure is effective when the lender places the acknowledgment in the mail or other delivery carrier or delivers the acknowledgment in person. A cure may also be made using any other delivery method that the borrower agrees to in writing after the lender receives notice of the lender's failure to comply. 7 Tex. Admin. Code § 153.94(a).

§ 11.25:3 Violation of Restriction against Additional Collateral or Restriction on Qualifying Agricultural Homestead (for Pre-2018 Loans)

In the event of a violation of the constitutional restrictions found at Tex. Const. art. XVI, § 50(a)(6)(H) (restriction against additional collateral), or Tex. Const. art. XVI, § 50(a)(6)(I) (restriction on qualifying agricultural homestead), the lender may cure the violation by sending the borrower an acknowledgment that the home equity loan is not secured by the prohibited additional collateral or nonqualifying agricultural property (for pre-2018 loans). *See* Tex. Const. art. XVI, § 50(a)(6)(Q)(x)(b). The cure is effective when the lender places the acknowledgment in the mail or other delivery carrier or delivers the acknowledgment in person. A cure may also be made using any other delivery method that the borrower agrees to in writing after the lender receives notice of the lender's failure to comply. 7 Tex. Admin. Code § 153.94(a).

§ 11.25:4 Violation of Restriction against Prohibited Amount, Percentage, Term, or Other Provision

In the event of a violation involving some other prohibited amount, percentage, term, or other provision, the lender may cure the violation by sending written notice to the borrower amending the prohibited provision and adjusting the account of the borrower to ensure that the borrower is not required to pay more than an amount permitted by the constitution or that the borrower is not subject to any other term or provision prohibited by the constitution. *See* Tex. Const. art. XVI, § 50(a)(6)(Q)(x)(c). The cure is effective when the lender makes the necessary adjustment to the borrower's account and places the required notice in the mail or other delivery carrier or personally delivers the notice to the borrower. A cure may also be made using any other delivery method agreed to by the borrower in writing after the lender receives notice of the lender's failure to comply. 7 Tex. Admin. Code § 153.94(a).

§ 11.25:5 Violation of Requirement for Delivery of Documents

In the event of a violation of the constitutional restriction found at Tex. Const. art. XVI, § 50(a)(6)(Q)(v) (requirement for delivery to the borrower of copies of all documents signed by the borrower), the lender may cure the violation by delivering the required documents to the borrower. *See* Tex. Const. art. XVI, § 50(a)(6)(Q)(x)(d). The cure is effective when the lender delivers the required documents by placing them in the mail or other delivery carrier or by personally delivering the documents to the borrower. A cure may also be made using any other delivery method agreed to by the borrower in writing after the lender receives notice of the lender's failure to comply. 7 Tex. Admin. Code § 153.94(a).

§ 11.25:6 Violation of Requirement for Acknowledgment of Fair Market Value of Homestead

In the event of a violation of the constitutional restriction found at Tex. Const. art. XVI, § 50(a)(6)(Q)(ix) (requirement that lender and borrower sign a written acknowledgment of the fair market value of the homestead), the lender may cure the violation by obtaining the appropriate signatures on the required acknowledgment of fair market value. *See* Tex. Const. art. XVI, § 50(a)(6)(Q)(x)(d).

§ 11.25:7 Violation of Restriction on Number of Home Equity Loans

In the event of a violation of the restriction found at Tex. Const. art. XVI, § 50(a)(6)(K) (antistacking provision allowing only one home equity loan on a homestead at a time), the lender may cure the violation by sending the borrower a written acknowledgment that the accrual of interest and all of the borrower's obligations under the extension of credit are abated while any prior lien remains secured by the homestead. *See* Tex. Const. art. XVI, § 50(a)(6)(Q)(x)(e). The cure is effective when the lender places the acknowledgment in the mail or other delivery carrier or personally delivers the acknowledgment to the debtor. A cure may also be made using any other delivery method agreed to by the borrower in writing after the lender receives notice of the lender's failure to comply. 7 Tex. Admin. Code § 153.94(a).

§ 11.25:8 "Catch-All" Cure Provision

In the event of a violation of constitutional restrictions on home equity lending that cannot be cured by any of the above cure provisions, the lender may cure the violation by refunding or crediting the borrower $1,000 and offering to refinance the extension of credit for the borrower for the remaining term at no cost to the borrower, on the same terms, including interest, as the original extension of credit together with any modifications necessary to comply with the constitution. *See* Tex. Const. art. XVI, § 50(a)(6)(Q)(x)(f). The lender must make a $1,000 refund or give a $1,000 credit. 7 Tex. Admin. Code § 153.96(b)(1). Additionally, the lender must either modify or refinance. If modification is elected, the modification may be made without completing the requirements of a refinance. If a refinance is elected, the refinance must meet all constitutional requirements for a home equity loan. 7 Tex. Admin. Code § 153.96(b).

The catch-all cure provision presupposes the debtor's compliance and cooperation with the lender's attempted cure. The debtor may not block the lender's cure by the debtor's refusal to cooperate. The cure protection afforded the lender is complete on the refund or credit of the $1,000 and the timely delivery of an offer to modify or refinance. 7 Tex. Admin. Code § 153.96; *In re Adams*, 307 B.R. 549, 560 (Bankr. N.D. Tex. 2004). The offer to modify or refinance is delivered by placing the offer in the mail or with other delivery carriers or by personal delivery to the borrower. 7 Tex. Admin. Code § 153.96(a)(2). After the borrower accepts an offer to modify or refinance, the lender or holder must complete, or make a good-faith effort to complete, the modification or refinance with a reasonable time not to exceed ninety days. 7 Tex. Admin. Code § 153.96(d).

§ 11.25:9 Noncurable Violations

Any violation of Tex. Const. art. XVI, § 50(a)(6)(P) (prohibition against home equity loans made by an unauthorized lender), or Tex. Const. art. XVI, § 50(a)(6)(A) (requirement that home equity liens be created by written agreement with the consent of each owner and each owner's spouse), are noncurable and result in the forfeiture of all principal and interest on the home equity loan. An exception to this rule applies in the case in which one spouse fails to consent by signature to the home equity loan but subsequently does consent. *See* Tex. Const. art. XVI, § 50(a)(6)(Q)(xi).

§ 11.25:10 Burden of Proof to Show Cure

The lender bears the burden of showing the lender's compliance with any cure provision relied on by the lender to cure a violation. 7 Tex. Admin. Code §§ 153.94(b), 153.96(c).

§ 11.25:11 Timeliness of Cure

To timely cure a violation of a home equity lending restriction, the lender must comply with the cure provisions within sixty days after the lender is notified of the violation by the borrower. Tex. Const. art. XVI, § 50(a)(6)(Q)(x). The sixty-day cure period begins the day after the lender or holder receives the borrower's notification to the lender or holder. If the borrower mails the notification to the lender or holder, a rebuttable presumption arises that the delivery date is the date indicated on the certified mail receipt or other carrier-delivery receipt signed by the lender or holder. This does not preclude other methods of delivering the notification. However, with other methods of delivery, the borrower has the burden of proving delivery. *See* 7 Tex. Admin. Code §§ 153.92, 153.93. After the commencement of the sixty-day cure period, all calendar days are counted up to day sixty. If day sixty falls on a Sunday or a federal legal public holiday, the cure period is extended to include the next day that is not a Sunday or a federal legal public holiday. 7 Tex. Admin. Code § 153.92(a). If a borrower provides inadequate notice of the alleged violation, the sixty-day cure period does not begin to run. 7 Tex. Admin. Code § 153.92(b).

If a lender or holder appropriately cures the violation before receiving notice of the violation from the borrower, the cure is as effective as if the lender or holder had timely cured the violation after receiving notice from the borrower. 7 Tex. Admin. Code § 153.95(b).

§ 11.25:12 Requirements for Borrower's Notification of Lender's Failure to Comply

The borrower notifies the lender or holder of an alleged failure to comply with an obligation by taking reasonable steps to give notice of the failure. The notification must include an identification of the borrower, an identification of the loan, and a description of the alleged failure to comply. The notice need not cite the section of the constitution allegedly violated. 7 Tex. Admin. Code § 153.91.

To designate a point of contact for receipt of notice of failure to comply, the lender or holder may make at closing a reasonably conspicuous designation in writing of a location where the borrower may deliver written or oral notice of violation of home equity restrictions. The designation may include a mailing address, a physical address, telephone number, email, or other point of contact. The lender or holder may change this point of contact by conspicuous written notice to the borrower. The change is effective when sent by the lender or holder. 7 Tex. Admin. Code § 153.93.

§ 11.25:13 Statute of Limitations

The Texas Supreme Court ruled in 2016 that the four-year residual limitations period of Tex. Civ. Prac. & Rem. Code § 16.051 does not apply to constitutional infirmities under Tex. Const. art. XVI, § 50(a)(6). *Wood v. HSBC Bank USA, N.A.*, 505 S.W.3d 542 (Tex. 2016). Consequently, a borrower may bring an action against his home equity lender for constitutional violations at any time during the life of the loan if the lender fails to correct the alleged defects after notification of the defect. This Texas Supreme

Court decision reversed the precedent set in *Priester v. JP Morgan Chase Bank*, 708 F.3d 667 (5th Cir. 2013), which applied the four-year residual limitations period to home equity loan violations.

§ 11.25:14 Equitable Subrogation

Even if a lender fails to timely cure a constitutional defect, rendering its lien invalid, a lender may still rely on the doctrine of equitable subrogation to reduce their loss to the extent home equity loan proceeds were used to extinguish a valid lien. A lender who discharges a prior, valid lien on the borrower's homestead property is entitled to subrogation, even if the lender failed to correct a curable defect in the loan documents. *Federal Home Loan Mortgage Corp. v. Zepeda*, 601 S.W.3d 763, 769 (Tex. 2020).

§ 11.26 Nonseverability Provision

Home equity lending is authorized only on condition that none of the constitutional restrictions ever be preempted by federal law. To this end, Tex. Const. art. XVI, § 50(j), contains a "poison pill" provision that all home equity provisions are nonseverable and that none would have been enacted without the other. If any home equity provision is held to be preempted by federal law, all home equity lending provisions are rendered invalid. In such a case, a savings provision upholds the validity of home equity loans made before the decision holding any aspect of home equity lending preempted by federal law. Tex. Const. art. XVI, § 50(j).

§ 11.27 Truth in Lending

A home equity loan may be subject to the Truth in Lending Act and its accompanying Regulation Z. See the discussion of this subject in section 11.19:2 above and chapter 12 in this manual.

[Sections 11.28 through 11.30 are reserved for expansion.]

II. Reverse Mortgage Loans

§ 11.31 Overview of Reverse Mortgage Loans

Reverse mortgage loans secured on Texas homestead properties were first authorized by constitutional amendment effective January 1, 1998. Tex. Const. art. XVI, § 50(a)(7), authorizes reverse mortgages, and Tex. Const. art. XVI, § 50(k)–(r), (v), defines and governs them. There are currently no enabling statutes that implement these constitutional provisions or interpretive rule making, although the power to interpret constitutional reverse mortgage provisions has been expressly delegated to the Texas Finance Commission and the Texas Credit Union Commission. *See* Tex. Fin. Code §§ 11.308, 15.413.

Reverse mortgages are a type of home equity loan for which only senior homeowners, age sixty-two or older, are eligible. Tex. Const. art. XVI, § 50(k)(2). The loans are meant to provide senior homeowners the resources needed to remain in their homes for their remaining lives, if they so desire, by converting their home equity into annuity-like periodic payments, or advances, to the homeowners for life (referred to as a "tenure" option) or, if preferred, a term of years (referred to as a "term" option) that may be used to pay for housing costs, medical care, and other costs of living. A homeowner under a reverse mortgage may also elect to receive a single advance at loan settlement (referred to as a "lump sum" option) or multiple unscheduled advances under a line of credit. Tex. Const. art. XVI, § 50(p).

A reverse mortgage is a nonrecourse obligation generally based on an owner's equity in the owner's homestead property, and the owner is not required to demonstrate general creditworthiness or a source of income or other assets with which to repay the loan. Any Texas resident age sixty-two or older who owns and occupies as a principal dwelling a single-family home, a qualified condominium unit or townhouse, or a permanently attached and qualified manufactured home in which there is sufficient appraised home equity should qualify for a reverse mortgage. *See* Tex. Const. art. XVI, § 50(k)(2), (k)(4). Home equity means the appraised market value of the homestead property minus the outstanding balance of all mortgages and liens secured on the homestead property. *See* Tex. Const. art. XVI, § 50(a)(6)(B).

An owner generally is not obligated to make any repayments of principal or interest during the term of a reverse mortgage as long as the owner continues to occupy the home as a principal residence and keeps property tax and insurance payments current. Tex. Const. art. XVI, § 50(k)(6). Advances made to a homestead owner under a reverse mortgage accrue interest, including interest on interest, until the occurrence of a maturity event, when the full loan balance of principal and interest is repaid to the lender in one final lump-sum payment, typically from sales proceeds when the homestead property is sold by the owner or by the owner's estate after the owner dies. Maturity events are strictly limited by the constitution. A reverse mortgage generally cannot be called due and payable until (1) the homeowner sells or transfers the homestead property; (2) the homeowner permanently abandons the property for twelve consecutive months without obtaining the lender's prior approval or, if the loan is used for the purchase of a homestead property, the borrower fails to timely occupy the homestead property as the borrower's principal residence within a specified period after loan closing stipulated in the written loan agreement; or (3) the homeowner (or, if married, the last of the homeowners) dies. Tex. Const. art. XVI, § 50(k)(6)(A)–(k)(6)(C). The lender in some cases may, however, call the loan due if discovering the owner has committed actual fraud in obtaining the loan; has defaulted on contractual obligations in the deed of trust to repair and maintain, pay taxes and assessments on, or insure the homestead property; or has failed to maintain the lender's first-lien priority on the homestead property. Tex. Const. art. XVI, § 50(k)(6)(D).

Texas procedural rules provide the authority for title insurance companies to insure the validity of reverse mortgage liens and for lenders to foreclose reverse mortgage liens under conditions permitted by the Texas Constitution. Specifically, the Texas Commissioner of Insurance has adopted a reverse mortgage endorsement (T-43) to the standard mortgagee's form of title insurance policy in Procedural Rule P-45, and the Supreme Court of Texas has adopted revisions to rules 735 and 736 of the Texas Rules of Civil Procedure to provide for an expedited procedure for foreclosing reverse mortgage loans requiring a court order as a condition to foreclosure. *See* Tex. R. Civ. P. 735–736; Procedural Rule P-45, *Basic Manual of Rules, Rates and Forms for the Writing of Title Insurance in the State of Texas*.

Although the Texas reverse mortgage is a particular type of home equity loan, it is important to note that the numerous conditions imposed on home equity loans under section 50(a)(6) described in part I. of this chapter are inapplicable to reverse mortgages authorized by section 50(a)(7). The limitations under section 50(a)(6), for example, restricting the permitted loan-to-value ratio (80 percent) and fees and charges (3 percent) and imposing cooling off and rescission rights and numerous other conditions, are not carried over to the reverse mortgage provisions. Reverse mortgages nevertheless have their own subset of consumer protections spelled out in subsections 50(k)–(p) and 50(v), all of which must be strictly observed to create a valid and enforceable lien on a homestead property.

§ 11.32 Consensual Homestead Lien by Senior Homeowner and Spouse

A reverse mortgage loan may be made only to, and only with the consent of, a person who is, or whose spouse is, sixty-two years of age or older. It may be secured by only a voluntary lien on the owner's homestead property created by a written agreement between the lender, each owner of the homestead property, and the spouse of each owner. Each owner's spouse must consent to the lien securing a reverse mortgage regardless of whether the spouse claims an ownership interest in the property or is an applicant for, or obligor on, the debt. Any homestead property, urban or rural, is eligible as security for a reverse mortgage (with no disqualifying exception for homestead property designated for agricultural use for property tax purposes, unlike Tex. Const. art. XVI, § 50(a)(6), home equity loans). Tex. Const. art. XVI, § 50(k)(1), (k)(2).

§ 11.33 Nonrecourse Debt

A reverse mortgage must be made without recourse for personal liability against any owner or the spouse of any owner. Tex. Const. art. XVI, § 50(k)(3). A reverse mortgage is typically repaid from sales proceeds on the sale of the homestead property by the borrower or the sale by the borrower's estate after the borrower, or the last of the borrowers, dies. If a reverse mortgage is not paid when due, the lender or note holder must look to recovery against the homestead property under its security interest as its exclusive remedy. The homeowner, therefore, will never owe more than the loan balance or the value of the homestead property, whichever is less, and no assets other than the homestead property may be used to repay the debt. Neither the borrower's estate nor the heirs of the estate have any liability for any deficiency that may result from the sale of the homestead property. Tex. Const. art. XVI, § 50(k)(3).

§ 11.34 Advances Based on Equity in Homestead

Advances under a reverse mortgage must be based on the equity in the owner's homestead property or the equity the owner will invest when purchasing a homestead property that the borrower will occupy as a principal residence. Tex. Const. art. XVI, § 50(k), was amended effective January 1, 2014, to authorize a reverse mortgage to be used to finance the purchase of a Texas homestead, and thereby to qualify Texas homeowners for the first time to participate in the Federal Housing Administration's "HECM for Purchase" loan program. *See* Tex. S.J. Res. 18, 83d Leg., R.S., 2013 Tex. Gen. Laws Pamph. 3, at A-7. Owners are not disqualified for a reverse mortgage because they lack income or other assets for repaying the loan. Tex. Const. art. XVI, § 50(k)(4). For purposes of determining eligibility under any state statute relating to payments, allowances, benefits, or services on a "means-tested" basis (including expressly supplemental security income, low-income energy assistance, property tax relief, medical assistance, and general assistance), reverse mortgage advances made to the borrower are considered loan proceeds and not income, and undisbursed funds under a reverse mortgage loan are considered equity in the home and not loan proceeds. Tex. Const. art. XVI, § 50(o).

§ 11.35 No Repayment Until Maturity Event Occurs; Grounds for Foreclosure

The borrower must have no legal obligation to repay a reverse mortgage, or any portion of its principal or interest, until the loan balance is due on the occurrence of one of the following maturity events: (1) the last surviving borrower dies, (2) the homestead property is sold or transferred, or (3) all borrowers cease occupying the homestead property as their principal residence for twelve consecutive months (without the lender's prior written approval) or, if the loan is used for the purchase of a homestead property, the borrower fails to timely occupy the homestead property as the borrower's principal residence within a specified period after loan closing stipulated in the written agreement creating the lien on the property. The lender may also require payment of all principal and interest if the borrower commits actual fraud in connection with the loan; defaults on an obligation provided for in the loan documents to repair and maintain, pay taxes and assessments on, or insure the homestead property; or fails to maintain the priority of the lender's lien on the homestead property. Tex. Const. art. XVI, § 50(k)(6)(A)–(k)(6)(D).

A reverse mortgage debt may be accelerated and declared due and payable only after the occurrence of one of the foregoing constitutional grounds for foreclosure, notice by the lender to the borrower of a claimed ground for foreclosure, and an opportunity for the borrower to remedy the claimed ground for foreclosure in the manner and within a period stipulated by the Texas Constitution. The lender must first give written notice to the borrower that one of these grounds for foreclosure exists and give the borrower an opportunity to cure the ground for foreclosure. Notice must be given in the same manner provided for a notice by mail related to the foreclosure of liens for home equity loans under section 50(a)(6). The owner must be given at least thirty days to either (1) remedy the condition creating the ground for foreclosure, (2) pay the reverse mortgage debt secured by the homestead property from proceeds of the sale of the homestead property or from any other sources, or (3) convey the homestead property to the lender by deed in lieu of foreclosure. A cure period of only twenty days must be given the owner if the claimed ground for foreclosure is a failure of the borrower to maintain the priority of the reverse mortgage lien under section 50(k)(6)(D)(iii). Tex. Const. art. XVI, § 50(k)(10).

§ 11.36 Permitted Uses of Loan Funds

Proceeds from a reverse mortgage may be used by senior homeowners for any purpose, although most often loan proceeds are regarded as a supplement to Social Security benefits and pension payments and used by homeowners to maintain their homes in a good state of repair, pay property taxes and insurance when due, and defray medical and other ordinary costs of living. Significantly, advances under a reverse mortgage are not taxable as income and generally do not affect senior homeowners' eligibility for Social Security or Medicare benefits. *See* Tex. Const. art. XVI, § 50(o). (However, senior homeowners electing a lump-sum advance of proceeds should seek counseling regarding their continued eligibility for Medicaid benefits if retaining the advance as a liquid asset.)

§ 11.37 Foreclosure under Power of Sale and by Court Order

Foreclosure based on either of the grounds set out in Tex. Const. art. XVI, § 50(k)(6)(A), (k)(6)(B), that all borrowers have died or that the homestead property securing the loan has been sold or otherwise transferred, may be carried out under the power of sale contained in the deed of trust securing the loan and the requirements of section 51.002 of the Texas Property Code, pertaining to contractual liens. Tex. Const. art. XVI, § 50(k)(11).

If the foreclosure is for any other ground, however, a reverse mortgage lien may be foreclosed on only by court order pursuant to rules 735 and 736 of the Texas Rules of Civil Procedure. Tex. Const. art. XVI, § 50(k)(11). Rule 735 provides several judicial foreclosure options for a lender foreclosing a reverse mortgage on grounds other than under section 50(k)(6)(A) or (k)(6)(B). Under rule 735, the lender may file (1) a suit seeking judicial foreclosure, (2) a suit or counterclaim seeking a final judgment that includes an order allowing foreclosure under the security instrument, or (3) an application for an order allowing foreclosure under rule 736 pertaining to expedited foreclosure proceedings. Tex. R. Civ. P. 735. Under the expedited procedures of rule 736, a lender may file a verified application in the district court of the county in which the homestead property is located seeking a court order allowing a foreclosure in accordance with the power of sale under the security instrument and section 51.002 of the Property Code. Under the rule, if no response is timely made, the court must grant the application without further notice or hearing if the application complies in form and content with the requirements of the rule and a copy of the notice and certificate of service has then been on file with the clerk of the court for at least ten days. If a response is made, however, a hearing on the application must be set promptly after reasonable notice to the parties and, in any case, not later than ten business days after a request for hearing by either party. The rule calls for a streamlined hearing in which no discovery is allowed and the court's action in granting or denying the order may not be appealed. On hearing, if the court determines that the applicant has proved that a valid debt exists that is secured by a valid lien on the homestead property created under Texas Constitution, article XVI, section 50(a)(7), the court must grant the application and issue an order to proceed with foreclosure pursuant to the power of sale. Tex. R. Civ. P. 736.

A four-year limitations period applies to actions to foreclose a reverse mortgage lien on a homestead property once a ground for foreclosure has occurred. On the expiration of the four-year limitations period, the real property lien and a power of sale to enforce it become void. *See* Tex. Civ. Prac. & Rem. Code § 16.035(a), (d). Practitioners are cautioned that the accrual date for such an action is not the date that the reverse mortgage debt is accelerated and declared due and payable, but instead the lender's cause of action to enforce a reverse mortgage lien accrues when one or more of the constitutional conditions to foreclosure has occurred. If the ground for foreclosure is the death of the last surviving borrower, the cause of action accrues on the date of that death—a fact that could be undiscovered by the lender for some extended period of time. *See Financial Freedom Senior Funding Corp. v. Horrocks*, 294 S.W.3d 749 (Tex. App.—Houston [14th Dist.] 2009, no pet.).

§ 11.38 No Closing until Delivery of Twelve-Day Consumer Notice and Certification of Required Counseling

A reverse mortgage may not be closed before the twelfth calendar day after the date the lender provides to the prospective borrower a statutory notice on a separate instrument, which the lender or originator and the borrower must sign for the notice to take effect. See form 11-7 in this chapter for the text of the notice.

Furthermore, a reverse mortgage may not be closed until the prospective borrower and the spouse of the prospective borrower attest in writing that the prospective borrower and the spouse of the prospective borrower received counseling regarding the advisability and availability of reverse mortgages and other financial alternatives that was completed not earlier than the 180th day nor later than the fifth day before the date the extension of credit is closed. *See* Tex. Const. art. XVI, § 50(k)(8), (k)(9).

§ 11.39 Advances According to Authorized Payment Plan (Including Line-of-Credit Method)

The proceeds of a reverse mortgage must be disbursed to the borrower in one or more payments of principal, generally referred to as advances, according to an agreed payment plan. The total loan obligation, generally referred to as the balance, is the sum of all advances due at loan maturity (including any amounts advanced to cover closing and other costs) plus accrued interest, including interest on interest, and other finance charges, such as mortgage insurance premiums and servicing fees. Line-of-credit advances under a Texas reverse mortgage were first authorized effective November 8, 2005. Tex. S.J. Res. 7, 79th Leg., R.S., 2005 Tex. Gen. Laws Pamph. 1, at A-1. As amended, Tex. Const. art. XVI, § 50(p), expressly permits a line-of-credit method of advances in which an initial advance may be made at any time and future advances may be made at times and in amounts requested by the borrower until the credit limit established by the loan documents is reached (and, thereafter, subsequent advances may be made at times and in amounts requested by the borrower to the extent that the outstanding balance is repaid). Tex. Const. art. XVI, § 50(p)(2)–(p)(4).

In addition, if the borrower fails to timely pay any of the following for which the borrower is obligated under the loan documents, the lender may at any time, to the extent necessary to protect the lender's interest in or the value of the homestead property, advance amounts on behalf of the borrower to pay (1) property taxes, (2) assessments, (3) insurance, (4) costs of repairs and maintenance (when performed by persons who are not employed by or affiliated with the lender), or (5) any lien that has or may obtain priority over the reverse mortgage lien. Tex. Const. art. XVI, § 50(p)(6).

§ 11.40 Prohibitions against Use of Credit Cards and Similar Devices, Transaction Fees, and Unilateral Amendments of Terms

A reverse mortgage must provide that (1) an owner may not use a credit card, debit card, preprinted solicitation check, or similar device to obtain an advance; (2) a lender may not charge a transaction fee after closing solely in connection with any debit or advance; and (3) a lender or holder of the reverse mortgage may not unilaterally amend the terms of the extension of credit. Tex. Const. art. XVI, § 50(v).

§ 11.41 Future Advances; Priority of Lien

Advances made and to be made in the future under a recorded reverse mortgage, and interest on those advances, have lien priority over any subsequently filed lien. Therefore, future advances under a reverse mortgage recorded in the real property records of the county in which the homestead property is located will have lien priority over any other lien filed for record after the reverse mortgage instrument has been recorded. Tex. Const. art. XVI, § 50(*l*).

§ 11.42 Interest; Shared Appreciation

Interest may be charged on a reverse mortgage loan at any fixed or adjustable rate that the parties may agree on (and which, if secured by other than a first lien, does not exceed the maximum lawful rate under the Texas Finance Code), and interest may accrue and be compounded during the term of the loan according to the terms of the loan agreement. Furthermore, interest expressly may be contingent on appreciation in the fair market value of the homestead property, apparently allowing for lenders to charge "equity share" fees based on the appreciation of appraised value of the homestead when the loan matures. Tex. Const. art. XVI, § 50(m).

§ 11.43 Reducing or Failing to Make Advances; Forfeiture

If an adjustable rate of interest is charged, the lender under a reverse mortgage is expressly prohibited from reducing the amount or number of advances made to the borrower because of an adjustment in the interest rate. Tex. Const. art. XVI, § 50(k)(5). The lender is obligated to make loan advances as required by the loan documents under the penalty of forfeiture. If the lender fails for any reason to make loan advances according to the terms of the loan documents and, after notice from the borrower, fails to cure the default as required in the loan documents, the constitution provides that the lender forfeits all principal and interest on the reverse mortgage. This forfeiture provision does not apply, however, when a governmental agency, such as the Federal Housing Administration under its Home Equity Conversion Mortgage reverse mortgage insurance, takes an assignment of the loan to cure the default. Tex. Const. art. XVI, § 50(k)(7).

§ 11.44 Preemptive Authority

Texas reverse mortgage law as authorized and effected by the constitution expressly supersedes any statutes, including the Texas Property Code, that purport to limit encumbrances that may be fixed on homestead property. Furthermore, a reverse mortgage may be made without regard to any other conflicting state law, including any purported limitations on future advances; any requirement that a maximum loan amount be stated in the reverse mortgage loan documents or that a percentage of reverse mortgage proceeds be advanced before the assignment of the reverse mortgage; or any prohibition on balloon payments, compound interest or interest on interest, or contracting for, charging, or receiving any rate of interest authorized by Texas law. Tex. Const. art. XVI, § 50(q).

§ 11.45 Title Insurance Considerations

The Texas Reverse Mortgage Endorsement (T-43) and Procedural Rule P-45, *Basic Manual of Rules, Rates and Forms for the Writing of Title Insurance in the State of Texas*, insure against claims of lien invalidity of a covered reverse mortgage arising out of a lender's failure to satisfy certain of the constitutional conditions. *See* Procedural Rule P-45, *Basic Manual of Rules, Rates and Forms for the Writing of Title Insurance in the State of Texas*.

The Texas Reverse Mortgage Endorsement (T-43) to the Mortgagee Policy of Title Insurance (T-2) excludes from coverage any loss or damage based on usury or on any consumer credit protection or truth-in-lending law or violation of any subsections of Tex. Const. art. XVI, § 50(k)(3)–(k)(11), (m), (p), (v), and any regulatory or statutory requirements for a mortgage made pursuant to Tex. Const. art. XVI, § 50(a)(7), *except as expressly provided in paragraph 3 of the endorsement*. Form T-43, in paragraphs 1 and 2, insures the validity of future advances made under a reverse mortgage, with certain exceptions, up to the outstanding aggregate amount of loan proceeds actually disbursed and the amount of its unpaid, accrued interest as of the time a loss occurs under the policy. In paragraph 3, form T-43 expressly insures against loss sustained by the lender under the mortgagee policy because of invalidity or unenforceability of the reverse mortgage lien by reason of any of the following: (1) the failure of the insured mortgage to be created under a written agreement with the consent of each owner of the insured homestead property and each owner's spouse; (2) the failure of the insured mortgage to be made to a person who is, or whose spouse is, sixty-two years of age or older; (3) the failure of the written document purporting to be made pursuant to Tex. Const. art. XVI, § 50(k)(8), to be executed by the homeowner on the date that the insured mortgage and promissory note it secures are executed by the owner (provided that the policy does not insure that the document itself complies with section 50(k)(8)); and (4) the failure of the title company or its agents to furnish the homeowner a copy of written notice purporting to be made pursuant to Tex. Const. art. XVI, § 50(k)(9), on the date that the owner executed the insured mortgage and promissory note it secures (provided that the policy does not insure that the written document itself complies with section 50(k)(9)).

While attachment of the T-43 endorsement to any mortgagee policy of title insurance issued in connection with a reverse mortgage loan is mandatory, under Procedural Rule P-45 the issuing agency may delete any of these four subdivisions of paragraph 3 if it does not consider the additional risk insurable and must delete all four subdivisions if the promissory note and the insured mortgage instrument for the loan are not executed by the borrower at the office of the title company. Furthermore, the insuring agency must delete the second subdivision of paragraph 3 if the age of the owner or spouse is not verifiable "with government issued photographic identification" furnished the title agency and must delete the second and fourth subdivisions if the related documents furnished by the insured are not executed by the homeowner at the office of the title company on the date that the insured mortgage and promissory note it secures are executed. Procedural Rule P-45, *Basic Manual of Rules, Rates and Forms for the Writing of Title Insurance in the State of Texas*.

§ 11.46 Truth-in-Lending Disclosure Considerations

Reverse mortgage loans are subject to the federal Truth in Lending Act, 15 U.S.C. §§ 1601–1667f, and its Regulation Z, 12 C.F.R. pt. 1026. In addition to other consumer disclosures required under the Truth in Lending Act, the lender in a reverse mortgage is required to provide the borrower written disclosures under 12 C.F.R. § 1026.33 of the total annual loan cost of credit in the form of appendix K, paragraph (d), of Regulation Z. Generally referred to as the "Total Annual Loan Cost Rate Disclosure," or "TALC," this disclosure contains (1) a statement that the borrower is not obligated to complete the transaction merely because the borrower has received the disclosures or has signed an application for a reverse mortgage loan; (2) a good-faith projection of the total cost of the credit expressed as a table of "Total Annual Loan Cost Rates," using that term, that reflects (a) costs and charges to the borrower, (b) payments (advances) to, or for the benefit of, the borrower, (c) additional compensation to the lender (such as shared appreciation the lender is entitled to), (d) any limitations on the borrower's liability (such as nonrecourse limits), (e) assumed appreciation rates for the dwelling securing the loan at rates of 0 percent, 4 percent, and 8 percent, and (f) assumed loan periods, alternatively, of two years, the actuarial life expectancy of the borrower (or youngest of the borrowers), and that same life expectancy multiplied by a factor of 1.4 and rounded to the nearest full year (and, at the option of the borrower, that same actuarial life expectancy multiplied by a factor of 0.5 and rounded to the nearest full year); (3) an itemization of loan terms, charges, the age of the youngest borrower, and the appraised property value; and (4) an explanation of the total annual loan cost rates as provided in the model form. 12 C.F.R. § 1026.33, pt. 1026 app. K(d).

§ 11.47 Federal Home Equity Conversion Mortgage (HECM) Loan Program

More than 90 percent of all reverse mortgage loan originations nationwide are made under the Home Equity Conversion Mortgage (HECM) program insured by the Federal Housing Administration (FHA) under the Department of Housing and Urban Development (HUD). The HECM program in Texas is regulated by HUD Handbook 4235.1 Rev-1, as supplemented and amended from time to time, and mortgagee letters ML 00-09 and ML 00-10, each dated March 8, 2000; ML 00-34, dated August 30, 2000 (supplementing ML 00-09); ML 00-39, dated November 7, 2000 (supplementing ML 00-09, ML 00-10, and ML 00-34); and ML 06-06, dated March 17, 2006 (in part replacing the guidance set out in ML 00-09, ML 00-34, and ML 00-39). Regulations for the HECM program are codified in 24 C.F.R. pt. 206. Effective January 1, 2014, Tex. Const. art. XVI, § 50(k), was amended to authorize a reverse mortgage also to be used to finance the purchase of a Texas homestead. Texas homeowners are now able to participate in the FHA's "HECM for Purchase" loan program for the first time. *See* Tex. S.J. Res. 18, 83d Leg., R.S., 2013 Tex. Gen. Laws Pamph. 3, at A-7.

Model forms set out in full and attached to ML 00-39 replaced earlier versions of Texas model forms published in ML 00-09 and ML 00-34, which at that time constituted the only forms approved by HUD for use to document an HECM loan in Texas. These model forms included Texas forms of a home equity conversion loan agreement, an adjustable rate deed of trust, an adjustable rate note, an adjustable rate second deed of trust, an adjustable rate second note, and a repair rider. With the adoption of the 2005 constitutional amendment authorizing line-of-credit advances under a Texas reverse mortgage loan, however, HUD chose not to publish revised model forms and instead imposed on approved mortgagees the obligation, in consultation with their attorneys, to adapt all forms to ensure compliance with FHA requirements and the Texas Constitution and statutes. These requirements are set forth in ML 06-06, issued March 17, 2006, which authorizes Texas borrowers to choose a line-of-credit payment option, a modified tenure option (a combination of tenure and line-of-credit payment options), or a modified term option (a combination of term and line-of-credit payment options) and provides guidance regarding such matters as the adaptation and preparation of the form of loan documents, including the repair rider, the timing of loan closings and disbursements by the lender, the conditions under which the loan may be accelerated under applicable Texas law, and procedures to be followed under Texas law to conduct foreclosures. ML 06-06 expressly replaces guidance previously issued in ML 00-09, ML 00-34, and ML 00-39 on the same topics.

Model Texas forms were set out as attachments to HUD ML 00-39, dated November 7, 2000, with such adaptations by counsel as may be necessary to conform the instruments to state or local requirements. When adapting these model forms to Texas law and practices, counsel must consult the footnotes to each model form regarding state-specific modifications; instructions in chapter 6 to Handbook 4235.1 Rev-3; Handbook 4165.1 Rev-1 Chg-3, issued November 30, 1995, regarding model mortgage and note forms; ML 97-15; ML 00-09 regarding Texas modifications of the loan agreement form and repair rider; and ML 06-06 regarding line-of-credit terms and other provisions of the 2005 constitutional amendment.

[Sections 11.48 through 11.50 are reserved for expansion.]

III. General Instructions for Completing Forms

§ 11.51 Introduction to Form General Instructions

For information about completing forms generally, see chapter 3 in this manual. In most forms the information that the attorney must provide is listed at the beginning of the form. Of course, the attorney may add other specific provisions, references, exhibits, and riders as necessary for each specific transaction.

The forms in this chapter are applicable to a first-lien home equity loan. Tex. Fin. Code ch. 342 imposes additional duties, prohibitions, and disclosure requirements in connection with secondary mortgage loans. Attorneys are cautioned that some forms in this chapter may require modification for use with a secondary mortgage loan transaction.

A home equity loan transaction may require documentation in addition to that provided by this chapter. For example, a "loan agreement" as defined in Texas Business and Commerce Code section 26.02 requires the notice prescribed therein. Form 10-14 in this manual, notice of final agreement, may be modified for use in a home equity transaction. Each transaction is unique, and the practitioner must use individual judgment in ensuring that all required documentation has been adequately prepared.

A home equity loan transaction must be closed at the offices of the lender, an attorney at law, or a title company. Tex. Const. art. XVI, § 50(a)(6)(N). The owner may not be required to sign any instrument in which blanks are left to be filled in. Tex. Const. art. XVI, § 50(a)(6)(Q)(iii). The lender must provide copies of all instruments related to the loan to the homestead owner at the time of closing. Tex. Const. art. XVI, § 50(a)(6)(Q)(v).

§ 11.52 Instructions for Completing Notice Concerning Extensions of Credit

The notice concerning extensions of credit (form 11-1 in this chapter) defined by section 50(a)(6), article XVI, of the Texas Constitution is the preloan disclosure required to be given to the homestead owner under Tex. Const. art. XVI, § 50(g). The home equity loan cannot be closed until the twelfth day after the notice is given. If discussions with the borrower are conducted primarily in a language other than English, the lender must provide the owner with an additional copy of the notice translated into the written language in which discussions were conducted. The Office of the Consumer Credit Commissioner has provided a Spanish language translation of the notice on its website at **https://occc.texas.gov**. No foreign-language translations of forms are included in this manual.

§ 11.53 Instructions for Completing Home Equity Extension of Credit (Promissory Note)

The form for the home equity extension of credit (form 11-2 in this chapter) is principally adapted from form 6-1 (promissory note) in this manual and is redesignated to conform with the terminology used in Tex. Const. art. XVI, § 50(a)(6). The attorney is referred to chapter 6 in this manual for general commentary and instructions for completing promissory notes.

Note that the extension of credit makes no provision for late charges. The attorney is referred to section 6.4:3 and the clauses referenced therein for commentary and instructions on late charges.

As reflected in the "Terms of Payment" paragraph, the home equity extension of credit must be repaid in substantially equal successive periodic installments. Tex. Const. art. XVI, § 50(a)(6)(L). The installments must begin not later than two months from the date of the instrument. Each installment must equal or exceed the amount of accrued interest as of the date of the scheduled installment.

The home equity extension of credit can be converted for a variable rate of interest by deleting the heading for "Annual Interest Rate" and modifying the heading "Terms of Payment" to read "Terms of Payment, Including Variable Interest Rate on Unpaid Principal." A variable rate interest clause appears at clause 6-2-18.

The security for payment for a home equity extension of credit is fixed by Tex. Const. art. XVI, § 50(a)(6)(A), (a)(6)(H). The home equity extension of credit may be secured only by a lien on the borrower's homestead. Additional collateral is prohibited. The home equity extension of credit has no provision referring to a guaranty or guarantor. A guaranty is construed as prohibited additional collateral.

As required by Tex. Const. art. XVI, § 50(a)(6)(C), the home equity extension of credit is a nonrecourse obligation. In addition, the home equity extension of credit contains many other limitations and restrictions unique to home equity lending and required by Tex. Const. art. XVI, § 50(a)(6). These restrictions are discussed in detail in the commentary in this chapter. A lender forfeits all principal and interest if the lender fails to cure a failure to comply with constitutional restrictions on home equity lending after sixty days' notice of the violation given by the borrower. Tex. Const. art. XVI, § 50(a)(6)(Q)(x). These cure provisions are discussed in detail in section 11.25 above.

If the lender of a home equity extension of credit has a license from the Office of Consumer Credit Commissioner, the home equity extension of credit must contain the name, mailing address, and telephone number of the OCCC. Tex. Fin. Code § 14.104. Additionally, if the home equity loan is a secondary mortgage loan, the alternative attorney's fee provision should be used. See section 8.4 for a discussion of secondary mortgage loans and see the discussion in section 11.20:7 above concerning alternative provisions.

§ 11.54 Instructions for Completing Deed of Trust (Home Equity Loan)

The form for the deed of trust (form 11-3 in this chapter) is adapted from form 8-1 in this manual. The attorney is referred to chapter 8 for general commentary and instructions for completing deeds of trust.

A lien securing a home equity loan may be foreclosed only after court order. Tex. Const. art. XVI, § 50(a)(6)(D). The power of sale of the deed of trust (home equity loan) is conditioned on the lender obtaining a court order allowing foreclosure under any proceeding authorized by the Texas Rules of Civil Procedure and other applicable law.

A question remains whether the assignment of rents in a deed of trust securing a home equity loan constitutes prohibited additional collateral under Tex. Const. art. XVI, § 50(a)(6)(H). The deed of trust (home equity loan) does not contain an assignment of rents clause. In the absence of definitive authority on this question, the attorney is cautioned to exercise professional judgment regarding this provision.

If the home equity extension of credit is a junior lien and if the lender is a bank, savings and loan association, credit union, or lender with a license from the Office of Consumer Credit Commissioner, the deed of trust (home equity) should be modified as discussed in section 11.20:7 above to comply with requirements applicable to secondary mortgage loans governed by Texas Finance Code chapter 342.

The deed of trust (home equity loan) also contains a notice of confidentiality rights as required by Tex. Prop. Code § 11.008(b). See section 3.17 in this manual.

§ 11.55 Instructions for Completing Home Equity Certificate and Agreement

The home equity certificate and agreement contains a written acknowledgment of the fair market value of the homestead as required by Tex. Const. art. XVI, § 50(a)(6)(Q)(ix). The acknowledgment of value is necessary to assure compliance with the 80 percent loan-to-value restriction of Tex. Const. art. XVI, § 50(a)(6)(B). The acknowledgment is conclusive evidence of the fair market value of the homestead if the acknowledgment is made under the conditions set out at Tex. Const. art. XVI, § 50(h). To comply with restrictions against additional collateral, the home equity compliance certificate and agreement (form 11-5 in this chapter) contains a waiver by the lender of cross-collateral provisions contained in other debt instruments. In addition, the form contains other representations and warranties to be made by the borrower at closing, evidencing compliance with certain constitutional requirements for creating a valid home equity lien.

The home equity certificate and agreement must be signed on the date that the extension of credit is made. Tex. Const. art. XVI, § 50(a)(6)(Q)(ix).

§ 11.56 Instructions for Completing Election Regarding Right of Rescission

The election regarding right of rescission (form 11-6 in this chapter) confirms the borrower's election to rescind or decline to rescind the home equity extension of credit under Tex. Const. art. XVI, § 50(a)(6)(Q)(viii). For married couples, a separate notice of right of rescission should be given by each spouse. Funding of the home equity loan should be delayed until the rescission period has expired.

§ 11.57 Instructions for Completing Notice Concerning Refinance of Existing Home Equity Loan

The notice concerning refinance of an existing home equity loan (form 11-8 in this chapter) is the preloan disclosure required to be given to the homestead owner under Tex. Const. art. XVI, § 50(f)(2), when an existing home equity loan will be refinanced into a conventional mortgage. The refinance disclosure must be given not later than the third business day after the date the owner submits the loan application and at least twelve days before the refinance is closed. The refinance disclosure must be given to all owners within the prescribed time limits. One copy of the refinance disclosure may be provided to married owners. 7 Tex. Admin. Code § 153.45(4). A lender may provide the refinance disclosure electronically in accordance with state and federal law governing electronic signatures and delivery of electronic documents. The Texas Uniform Electronic Transactions Act (UETA) and the Electronic Signatures in Global and National Commerce Act (E-Sign Act) include requirements for electronic signatures and delivery. 7 Tex. Admin. Code § 153.45(4)(E).

§ 11.58 Instructions for Completing Affidavit of Compliance

The affidavit of compliance (form 11-9 in this chapter), if signed by the owner or owner's spouse, provides conclusive proof that all requirements of Tex. Const. art. XVI, § 50(f)(2), have been met. The affidavit of compliance should be signed by the owner or owner's spouse at closing.

[Sections 11.59 and 11.60 are reserved for expansion.]

IV. Additional Resources

§ 11.61 Additional Resources

Alsup, J. Alton. "Documenting Compliance with the New Texas Home Equity Reform Amendment." In *Advanced Real Estate Drafting Course, 2005*. Austin: State Bar of Texas, 2005.

———. "Lines of Credit under Texas Home Equity and Reverse Mortgage Law." In *Advanced Real Estate Law Course, 2006*. Austin: State Bar of Texas, 2006.

Baggett, W. Mike. "Foreclosure Update Including Foreclosing Home Equity Loans." In *Advanced Real Estate Strategies Course, 2008*. Austin: State Bar of Texas, 2008.

Baird, Michael Fritz. "Residential Real Estate Lending Update." In *Advanced Real Estate Drafting Course, 2020*. Austin: State Bar of Texas, 2020.

Baird, Morton W. II, and Michael F. Baird. "Issues in Home Equity Financing." In *Advanced Real Estate Law Course, 2015*. Austin: State Bar of Texas, 2015.

Bastian, G. Tommy. "Home Equity Lending—Updates and Issues." In *Advanced Real Estate Law Course, 2018*. Austin: State Bar of Texas, 2018.

Beyer, Gerry W. *Real Property*. 2nd ed. West's Texas Forms 13–15. St. Paul, MN: West, 2001. Supplement 2014.

Cockerell, Perry. "Developments in Texas Home Equity Litigation in Bankruptcy Court." In *Advanced Real Estate Law Course, 2016*. Austin: State Bar of Texas, 2016.

Jenkins, Christina. "Ancillary Document Reviews in Residential Mortgage Transactions." In *Advanced Real Estate Law Course, 2021*. Austin: State Bar of Texas, 2021.

Jenkins, Christina, and David Pederson. "Texas Home Equity: A Big Win for Lenders." 58 *Real Estate, Probate & Trust Law Reporter* 3 (2020).

McConnell, Paul. "Equitable Subrogation—Home Equity, Intervening Liens, and Zepeda." In *Texas Land Title Institute, 2021*. Austin: Texas Land Title Institute, 2021.

St. Claire, Frank A., and William V. Dorsaneo III. *Texas Real Estate Guide*. New York: Matthew Bender & Co., 2001.

Vandergriff, Connie J. "How to Cure Home Equity Loans." In *Advanced Real Estate Drafting Course, 2018*. Austin: State Bar of Texas, 2018.

Form 11-1

Notice Concerning Extensions of Credit

NOTICE CONCERNING EXTENSIONS OF CREDIT DEFINED BY

SECTION 50(a)(6), ARTICLE XVI, TEXAS CONSTITUTION:

SECTION 50(a)(6), ARTICLE XVI, OF THE TEXAS CONSTITUTION ALLOWS CERTAIN LOANS TO BE SECURED AGAINST THE EQUITY IN YOUR HOME. SUCH LOANS ARE COMMONLY KNOWN AS EQUITY LOANS. IF YOU DO NOT REPAY THE LOAN OR IF YOU FAIL TO MEET THE TERMS OF THE LOAN, THE LENDER MAY FORECLOSE AND SELL YOUR HOME. THE CONSTITUTION PROVIDES THAT:

(A) THE LOAN MUST BE VOLUNTARILY CREATED WITH THE CONSENT OF EACH OWNER OF YOUR HOME AND EACH OWNER'S SPOUSE;

(B) THE PRINCIPAL LOAN AMOUNT AT THE TIME THE LOAN IS MADE MUST NOT EXCEED AN AMOUNT THAT, WHEN ADDED TO THE PRINCIPAL BALANCES OF ALL OTHER LIENS AGAINST YOUR HOME, IS MORE THAN 80 PERCENT OF THE FAIR MARKET VALUE OF YOUR HOME;

(C) THE LOAN MUST BE WITHOUT RECOURSE FOR PERSONAL LIABILITY AGAINST YOU AND YOUR SPOUSE UNLESS YOU OR YOUR SPOUSE OBTAINED THIS EXTENSION OF CREDIT BY ACTUAL FRAUD;

(D) THE LIEN SECURING THE LOAN MAY BE FORECLOSED UPON ONLY WITH A COURT ORDER;

(E) FEES AND CHARGES TO MAKE THE LOAN MAY NOT EXCEED 2 PERCENT OF THE LOAN AMOUNT, EXCEPT FOR A FEE OR CHARGE FOR AN APPRAISAL PERFORMED BY A THIRD-PARTY APPRAISER, A PROPERTY SURVEY PERFORMED BY A STATE-REGISTERED OR LICENSED

SURVEYOR, A STATE BASE PREMIUM FOR A MORTGAGEE POLICY OF TITLE INSURANCE WITH ENDORSEMENTS, OR A TITLE EXAMINATION REPORT;

(F) THE LOAN MAY NOT BE AN OPEN-END ACCOUNT THAT MAY BE DEBITED FROM TIME TO TIME OR UNDER WHICH CREDIT MAY BE EXTENDED FROM TIME TO TIME UNLESS IT IS A HOME EQUITY LINE OF CREDIT;

(G) YOU MAY PREPAY THE LOAN WITHOUT PENALTY OR CHARGE;

(H) NO ADDITIONAL COLLATERAL MAY BE SECURITY FOR THE LOAN;

(I) (REPEALED);

(J) YOU ARE NOT REQUIRED TO REPAY THE LOAN EARLIER THAN AGREED SOLELY BECAUSE THE FAIR MARKET VALUE OF YOUR HOME DECREASES OR BECAUSE YOU DEFAULT ON ANOTHER LOAN THAT IS NOT SECURED BY YOUR HOME;

(K) ONLY ONE LOAN DESCRIBED BY SECTION 50(a)(6), ARTICLE XVI, OF THE TEXAS CONSTITUTION MAY BE SECURED WITH YOUR HOME AT ANY GIVEN TIME;

(L) THE LOAN MUST BE SCHEDULED TO BE REPAID IN PAYMENTS THAT EQUAL OR EXCEED THE AMOUNT OF ACCRUED INTEREST FOR EACH PAYMENT PERIOD;

(M) THE LOAN MAY NOT CLOSE BEFORE 12 DAYS AFTER YOU SUBMIT A LOAN APPLICATION TO THE LENDER OR BEFORE 12 DAYS AFTER YOU RECEIVE THIS NOTICE, WHICHEVER DATE IS LATER AND MAY NOT WITHOUT YOUR CONSENT CLOSE BEFORE ONE BUSINESS DAY AFTER THE DATE ON WHICH YOU RECEIVE A COPY OF YOUR LOAN APPLICATION IF NOT PREVIOUSLY PROVIDED AND A FINAL ITEMIZED DISCLOSURE OF THE ACTUAL FEES, POINTS, INTERESTS, COSTS, AND CHARGES THAT WILL BE CHARGED AT CLOSING; AND IF YOUR HOME WAS SECURITY FOR THE SAME TYPE OF LOAN WITHIN THE PAST YEAR, A NEW LOAN SECURED BY THE SAME PROPERTY MAY NOT CLOSE BEFORE ONE YEAR HAS PASSED FROM THE CLOSING

DATE OF THE OTHER LOAN, UNLESS ON OATH YOU REQUEST AN EARLIER CLOSING DATE DUE TO A DECLARED STATE OF EMERGENCY;

(N) THE LOAN MAY CLOSE ONLY AT THE OFFICE OF THE LENDER, TITLE COMPANY, OR AN ATTORNEY AT LAW;

(O) THE LENDER MAY CHARGE ANY FIXED OR VARIABLE RATE OF INTEREST AUTHORIZED BY STATUTE;

(P) ONLY A LAWFULLY AUTHORIZED LENDER MAY MAKE LOANS DESCRIBED BY SECTION 50(a)(6), ARTICLE XVI, OF THE TEXAS CONSTITUTION;

(Q) LOANS DESCRIBED BY SECTION 50(a)(6), ARTICLE XVI, OF THE TEXAS CONSTITUTION MUST:

(1) NOT REQUIRE YOU TO APPLY THE PROCEEDS TO ANOTHER DEBT EXCEPT A DEBT THAT IS SECURED BY YOUR HOME OR OWED TO ANOTHER LENDER;

(2) NOT REQUIRE THAT YOU ASSIGN WAGES AS SECURITY;

(3) NOT REQUIRE THAT YOU EXECUTE INSTRUMENTS WHICH HAVE BLANKS FOR SUBSTANTIVE TERMS OF AGREEMENT LEFT TO BE FILLED IN;

(4) NOT REQUIRE THAT YOU SIGN A CONFESSION OF JUDGMENT OR POWER OF ATTORNEY TO ANOTHER PERSON TO CONFESS JUDGMENT OR APPEAR IN A LEGAL PROCEEDING ON YOUR BEHALF;

(5) PROVIDE THAT YOU RECEIVE A COPY OF YOUR FINAL LOAN APPLICATION AND ALL EXECUTED DOCUMENTS YOU SIGN AT CLOSING;

(6) PROVIDE THAT THE SECURITY INSTRUMENTS CONTAIN A DISCLOSURE THAT THIS LOAN IS A LOAN DEFINED BY SECTION 50(a)(6), ARTICLE XVI, OF THE TEXAS CONSTITUTION;

(7) PROVIDE THAT WHEN THE LOAN IS PAID IN FULL, THE LENDER WILL SIGN AND GIVE YOU A RELEASE OF LIEN OR AN ASSIGNMENT OF THE LIEN, WHICHEVER IS APPROPRIATE;

(8) PROVIDE THAT YOU MAY, WITHIN 3 DAYS AFTER CLOSING, RESCIND THE LOAN WITHOUT PENALTY OR CHARGE;

(9) PROVIDE THAT YOU AND THE LENDER ACKNOWLEDGE THE FAIR MARKET VALUE OF YOUR HOME ON THE DATE THE LOAN CLOSES; AND

(10) PROVIDE THAT THE LENDER WILL FORFEIT ALL PRINCIPAL AND INTEREST IF THE LENDER FAILS TO COMPLY WITH THE LENDER'S OBLIGATIONS UNLESS THE LENDER CURES THE FAILURE TO COMPLY AS PROVIDED BY SECTION 50(a)(6)(Q)(x), ARTICLE XVI, OF THE TEXAS CONSTITUTION; AND

(R) IF THE LOAN IS A HOME EQUITY LINE OF CREDIT:

(1) YOU MAY REQUEST ADVANCES, REPAY MONEY, AND REBORROW MONEY UNDER THE LINE OF CREDIT;

(2) EACH ADVANCE UNDER THE LINE OF CREDIT MUST BE IN AN AMOUNT OF AT LEAST $4,000;

(3) YOU MAY NOT USE A CREDIT CARD, DEBIT CARD, OR SIMILAR DEVICE, OR PREPRINTED CHECK THAT YOU DID NOT SOLICIT, TO OBTAIN ADVANCES UNDER THE LINE OF CREDIT;

(4) ANY FEES THE LENDER CHARGES MAY BE CHARGED AND COLLECTED ONLY AT THE TIME THE LINE OF CREDIT IS ESTABLISHED AND THE LENDER MAY NOT CHARGE A FEE IN CONNECTION WITH ANY ADVANCE;

(5) THE MAXIMUM PRINCIPAL AMOUNT THAT MAY BE EXTENDED, WHEN ADDED TO ALL OTHER DEBTS SECURED BY YOUR HOME, MAY NOT EXCEED 80 PERCENT OF THE FAIR MARKET VALUE OF YOUR HOME ON THE DATE THE LINE OF CREDIT IS ESTABLISHED;

(6) IF THE PRINCIPAL BALANCE UNDER THE LINE OF CREDIT AT ANY TIME EXCEEDS 80 PERCENT OF THE FAIR MARKET VALUE OF YOUR HOME, AS DETERMINED ON THE DATE THE LINE OF CREDIT IS ESTABLISHED, YOU MAY NOT CONTINUE TO REQUEST ADVANCES UNDER THE LINE OF CREDIT UNTIL THE BALANCE IS LESS THAN 80 PERCENT OF THE FAIR MARKET VALUE; AND

(7) THE LENDER MAY NOT UNILATERALLY AMEND THE TERMS OF THE LINE OF CREDIT.

THIS NOTICE IS ONLY A SUMMARY OF YOUR RIGHTS UNDER THE TEXAS CONSTITUTION. YOUR RIGHTS ARE GOVERNED BY SECTION 50, ARTICLE XVI, OF THE TEXAS CONSTITUTION, AND NOT BY THIS NOTICE.

I have received a copy of this notice concerning extensions of credit defined by section 50(a)(6), article XVI, of the Texas Constitution.

____
[Name of borrower]
Date:

Form 11-2

Home Equity Extension of Credit
[Promissory Note]

Basic Information

THE LOAN EVIDENCED BY THIS INSTRUMENT IS AN EXTENSION OF CREDIT AS DEFINED BY SECTION 50(a)(6), ARTICLE XVI, OF THE TEXAS CONSTITUTION ("HOME EQUITY EXTENSION OF CREDIT").

Date:

Borrower:

Borrower's Mailing Address:

Lender:

Place for Payment:

Principal Amount:

Annual Interest Rate:

Maturity Date:

Annual Interest Rate on Matured, Unpaid Amounts:

Terms of Payment (principal and interest): The Principal Amount and interest are due and payable in equal periodic installments of [**amount**] DOLLARS ($[**amount**]), on the [**specify**] day[s] of each month, beginning [**date**] and continuing until the unpaid principal and accrued, unpaid interest have been paid in full. Payments will be applied first to accrued interest and the remainder to the Principal Amount.

Security for Payment: This Home Equity Extension of Credit is secured by a deed of trust dated [**date**] from [Borrower/[**name of grantor in deed of trust**]] to [**name of trustee**], trustee, which covers the following real property: [**property description**] (the "Property").

A. Promise to Pay

Borrower promises to pay to the order of Lender the Principal Amount plus interest at the Annual Interest Rate. This Home Equity Extension of Credit is payable at the Place for Payment and according to the Terms of Payment. All unpaid amounts are due by the Maturity Date. If any amount is not paid either when due under the Terms of Payment or on acceleration of maturity, Borrower promises to pay any unpaid amount plus interest from the date the payment was due to the date of payment at the Annual Interest Rate on Matured, Unpaid Amounts.

B. Default and Remedies

If Borrower defaults in the payment of this Home Equity Extension of Credit or in the performance of any obligation in any instrument securing this Home Equity Extension of Credit, Lender may declare the unpaid principal balance and earned interest on the Home Equity Extension of Credit due. Borrower waives all demand for payment, presentation for payment, notice of intention to accelerate maturity, notice of acceleration of maturity, protest, and notice of protest, to the extent permitted by law.

C. Attorney's Fees

> Include the following paragraph only if the loan is not a secondary mortgage loan.

Borrower also promises to pay reasonable attorney's fees and court and other costs if an attorney is retained to collect or enforce the Home Equity Extension of Credit. These expenses will bear interest from the date of advance at the Annual Interest Rate on Matured, Unpaid

Amounts. Borrower will pay Lender these expenses and interest on demand at the Place for Payment. These expenses and interest will become part of the Home Equity Extension of Credit and will be secured by the Security for Payment.

Include the following paragraph for a secondary mortgage loan.

Borrower also promises to pay reasonable attorney's fees and court costs and other fees incurred if this Home Equity Extension of Credit is placed in the hands of an attorney who is not an employee of Lender to collect or enforce the Home Equity Extension of Credit. Borrower will pay Lender these expenses on demand at the Place for Payment. These expenses will become part of the Home Equity Extension of Credit and will be secured by the Security for Payment.

Continue with the following.

D. Loan Conditions

The Home Equity Extension of Credit is made on condition that—

D.1. Borrower not be required to apply the proceeds of the Home Equity Extension of Credit to repay another debt except debt secured by the Property or debt to another lender;

D.2. Borrower not assign wages as security for the Home Equity Extension of Credit;

D.3. Borrower not sign any instrument in which blanks are left to be filled in;

D.4. Borrower not sign a confession of judgment or power of attorney to Lender or to a third person to confess judgment or to appear for Borrower in a judicial proceeding;

D.5. Lender, at the time the Home Equity Extension of Credit is made, provide Borrower a copy of all documents signed by Borrower related to the Home Equity Extension of Credit;

D.6. within a reasonable time after termination and full payment of the Home Equity Extension of Credit, Lender cancel and return the Home Equity Extension of Credit to Borrower and deliver, in recordable form, a release of the lien securing the Home Equity Extension of Credit or a copy of an endorsement or assignment of the lien to a lender that is refinancing the Home Equity Extension of Credit;

D.7. Borrower and Borrower's spouse may, within three days after the Home Equity Extension of Credit is made, rescind the Home Equity Extension of Credit without penalty or charge;

D.8. Borrower and Lender sign a written acknowledgment of the fair market value of the Property on the date the Home Equity Extension of Credit is made;

D.9. except as otherwise provided in this paragraph, Lender or any holder of the Home Equity Extension of Credit will forfeit all principal and interest of the Home Equity Extension of Credit if Lender or the holder fails to comply with Lender's or the holder's obligations under Tex. Const. art. XVI, § 50(a)(6), and fails to correct the failure not later than the sixtieth day after the date that the Lender or the holder is notified by Borrower of failure to comply; except as otherwise provided in this paragraph, Lender or holder may correct a failure to comply with Tex. Const. art. XVI, § 50(a)(6), by—

a. paying to Borrower an amount equal to any overcharge paid by Borrower under or related to the Home Equity Extension of Credit if Borrower has paid an amount that exceeds an amount stated in Tex. Const. art. XVI, § 50(a)(6)(E), (a)(6)(G), or (a)(6)(O);

b. sending Borrower a written acknowledgment that the lien securing the Home Equity Extension of Credit is valid only in the amount that the Home Equity Extension of Credit does not exceed the percentage described by Tex. Const. art. XVI, § 50(a)(6)(B), if applicable, or is not secured by property described in Tex. Const. art. XVI, § 50(a)(6)(H) or (a)(6)(I), if applicable;

c. sending Borrower a written notice modifying any other amount, percentage, term, or other provision prohibited by Tex. Const. art. XVI, § 50(a)(6), to a permitted amount, percentage, term, or other provision and adjusting the account of Borrower to ensure that Borrower is not required to pay more than an amount permitted by Tex. Const. art. XVI, § 50, and is not subject to any other term or provision prohibited by Tex. Const. art. XVI, § 50;

d. delivering the required documents to Borrower if Lender or holder fails to comply with Tex. Const. art. XVI, § 50(a)(6)(Q)(v), or obtaining the appropriate signatures if Lender or holder fails to comply with Tex. Const. art. XVI, § 50(a)(6)(Q)(ix);

e. sending Borrower a written acknowledgment, if the failure to comply is prohibited by Tex. Const. art. XVI, § 50(a)(6)(K), that the accrual of interest and all of Borrower's obligations under the Home Equity Extension of Credit are abated while any prior lien prohibited under Tex. Const. art. XVI, § 50(a)(6)(K), remains secured by the homestead; or

f. if the failure to comply cannot be cured by (a)–(e) above, curing the failure to comply by refund or credit to Borrower of $1,000 and offering Borrower the right to refinance the Home Equity Extension of Credit with Lender or holder for the remaining term of this Home Equity Extension of Credit at no cost to Borrower on the same terms, including interest, as the original Home Equity Extension of Credit with any modifications necessary to comply with Tex. Const. art. XVI, § 50, or terms on which Borrower and

Lender or holder otherwise agree that comply with Tex. Const. art. XVI, § 50;

D.10. Lender or any holder of this Home Equity Extension of Credit shall forfeit all principal and interest of this Home Equity Extension of Credit if this Home Equity Extension of Credit is made by a person other than a person described in Tex. Const. art. XVI, § 50(a)(6)(P), or if the lien is not created under a written agreement with consent of Borrower and Borrower's spouse, unless Borrower and Borrower's spouse who did not initially consent subsequently consent to this Home Equity Extension of Credit;

D.11. the Home Equity Extension of Credit is without recourse for personal liability against Borrower or Borrower's spouse unless the Home Equity Extension of Credit was obtained by actual fraud;

D.12. the Home Equity Extension of Credit is not a form of open-end account that may be debited from time to time or under which credit may be extended from time to time unless this Home Equity Extension of Credit is a home equity line of credit as defined by Tex. Const. art. XVI, § 50(t);

D.13. the Home Equity Extension of Credit is payable in advance without penalty or charge; unless Lender agrees otherwise in writing, prepayments will be applied to the last maturing principal; installments will continue as scheduled until the Principal Amount and all accrued interest are paid;

D.14. the Home Equity Extension of Credit may not be accelerated because of a decrease in the market value of the Property or Borrower's default under other indebtedness not secured by a prior valid encumbrance against the Property; and

D.15. the Home Equity Extension of Credit is closed only at the office of Lender, an attorney at law, or a title company.

E. Prepayments

Borrower may at any time make full or partial prepayments on the principal without paying any penalty, in addition to making regularly scheduled payments. Unless Lender agrees otherwise in writing, the making of partial prepayments will not alter the dates or amounts of regularly scheduled payments.

F. Usury Savings

Interest on the debt evidenced by this Home Equity Extension of Credit will not exceed the maximum rate or amount of nonusurious interest that may be contracted for, taken, reserved, charged, or received under law. Any interest in excess of that maximum amount will be credited on the Principal Amount or, if the Principal Amount has been paid, refunded. On any acceleration or required or permitted prepayment, any excess interest will be canceled automatically as of the acceleration or prepayment or, if the excess interest has already been paid, credited on the Principal Amount or, if the Principal Amount has been paid, refunded. Loan charges, fees, or similar amounts other than interest will not exceed the maximum amount or rate that may be contracted for, taken, reserved, charged, or received under law. Any loan charges, fees, or similar amounts other than interest in excess of that maximum rate or amount will be credited on the Principal Amount or, if the Principal Amount has been paid, refunded. This provision overrides any conflicting provisions in this Home Equity Extension of Credit and all other instruments concerning the debt.

G. Other Clauses

Borrower will provide written notice to Lender or a holder of Lender's on the holder's failure to comply with any obligations of Tex. Const. art. XVI, § 50, the deed of trust, or applicable law delivered by certified or registered mail, licensed courier, or express mail service providing proof of delivery.

When the context requires, singular nouns and pronouns include the plural.

____
[Name of borrower]

Form 11-3

Deed of Trust

[Home Equity Loan]

Notice of confidentiality rights: If you are a natural person, you may remove or strike any or all of the following information from any instrument that transfers an interest in real property before it is filed for record in the public records: your Social Security number or your driver's license number.

THE LOAN SECURED BY THIS DEED OF TRUST IS AN EXTENSION OF CREDIT AS DEFINED BY SECTION 50(a)(6), ARTICLE XVI, OF THE TEXAS CONSTITUTION.

Basic Information

Date:

Grantor:

Grantor's Mailing Address:

Trustee:

Trustee's Mailing Address:

Lender:

Lender's Mailing Address:

Home Equity Extension of Credit (Promissory Note)

Date:

Original principal amount:

Borrower:

Lender:

Maturity date:

Property (including any improvements):

Prior Lien: **[include recording information]**

Other Exceptions to Conveyance and Warranty:

A. Granting Clause

For value received and to secure payment of the Home Equity Extension of Credit, Grantor conveys the Property to Trustee in trust. Grantor warrants and agrees to defend the title to the Property, subject to the Other Exceptions to Conveyance and Warranty. On payment of the Home Equity Extension of Credit and all other amounts secured by this deed of trust, this deed of trust will have no further effect.

B. Grantor's Obligations

Grantor agrees to—

B.1. keep the Property in good repair and condition;

B.2. pay all taxes and assessments on the Property before delinquency, not authorize a taxing entity to transfer its tax lien on the Property to anyone other than Lender, and not request a deferral of the collection of taxes pursuant to section 33.06 of the Texas Tax Code;

B.3. defend title to the Property subject to the Other Exceptions to Conveyance and Warranty and preserve the lien's priority as it is established in this deed of trust;

B.4. maintain, in a form acceptable to Lender, an insurance policy that—

a. covers all improvements for their full insurable value as determined when the policy is issued and renewed, unless Lender approves a smaller amount in writing;

b. contains an 80 percent coinsurance clause;

c. provides fire and extended coverage, including windstorm coverage;

d. protects Lender with a standard mortgage clause;

e. provides flood insurance at any time the Property is in a flood hazard area; and

f. contains such other coverage as Lender may reasonably require;

B.5. comply at all times with the requirements of the 80 percent coinsurance clause;

B.6. deliver the insurance policy to Lender within ten days of the date of this deed of trust and deliver renewals to Lender at least fifteen days before expiration;

B.7. obey all laws, ordinances, and restrictive covenants applicable to the Property;

B.8. keep any buildings occupied as required by the insurance policy; and

B.9. if the lien of this deed of trust is not a first lien, pay or cause to be paid all prior lien notes and abide by or cause to be abided by all prior lien instruments.

C. Lender's Rights

C.1. Lender may appoint in writing a substitute trustee, succeeding to all rights and responsibilities of Trustee.

C.2. If the proceeds of the Home Equity Extension of Credit are used to pay any debt secured by prior liens, Lender is subrogated to all the rights and liens of the holders of any debt so paid.

C.3. Lender may apply any proceeds received under the insurance policy either to reduce the Home Equity Extension of Credit or to repair or replace damaged or destroyed improvements covered by the policy. If Lender reasonably determines that repairs to the improvements are economically feasible, Lender will make the insurance proceeds available to Grantor for repairs.

C.4. Notwithstanding the terms of the Home Equity Extension of Credit to the contrary, and unless applicable law prohibits, all payments received by Lender from Grantor under the Home Equity Extension of Credit or this deed of trust may, at Lender's discretion, be applied first to amounts payable under this deed of trust and then to amounts due and payable to Lender under the Home Equity Extension of Credit, to be applied to principal or interest in the order Lender in Lender's discretion determines.

C.5. If Grantor fails to perform any of Grantor's obligations, including obligations contained in the Home Equity Extension of Credit or any instrument securing the Home Equity Extension of Credit, Lender may perform those obligations and be reimbursed by Grantor on demand for any amounts so paid, including attorney's fees, plus interest on those amounts from the dates of payment at the rate stated in the Home Equity Extension of Credit for matured, unpaid amounts. The amount to be reimbursed will be secured by this deed of trust.

C.6. If there is a default in the payment of the Home Equity Extension of Credit or if Grantor fails to perform any of Grantor's obligations in any instrument securing the Home Equity Extension of Credit, and the default continues after any required notice of default and time allowed to cure, Lender may—

a. declare the unpaid principal balance and earned interest on the Home Equity Extension of Credit immediately due; and

b. foreclose this lien under any proceeding authorized by the Texas Rules of Civil Procedure and other applicable law.

C.7. The lien of this deed of trust may be foreclosed only by court order. On obtaining a court order allowing a foreclosure of this lien under this deed of trust and the Texas Property Code as then in effect, Lender may—

a. direct Trustee to foreclose this lien, in which case Lender or Lender's agent will cause notice of the foreclosure sale to be given as provided by the Texas Property Code as then in effect; and

b. purchase the Property at any foreclosure sale by offering the highest bid and then have the bid credited on the Home Equity Extension of Credit.

C.8. Lender may remedy any default without waiving it and may waive any default without waiving any prior or subsequent default.

D. Trustee's Rights and Duties

If directed by Lender to foreclose this lien, Trustee will—

D.1. either personally or by agent give notice of the foreclosure sale as required by the Texas Property Code as then in effect;

D.2. sell and convey all or part of the Property "AS IS" to the highest bidder for cash with a general warranty binding Grantor, subject to the Prior Lien and to the Other Exceptions to Conveyance and Warranty and without representation or warranty, express or implied, by Trustee;

D.3. from the proceeds of the sale, pay, in this order—

a. expenses of foreclosure, including a reasonable commission to Trustee;

b. to Lender, the full amount of principal, interest, attorney's fees, and other charges due and unpaid;

c. any amounts required by law to be paid before payment to Grantor; and

d. to Grantor, any balance; and

D.4. be indemnified by Lender against all costs, expenses, and liabilities incurred by Trustee for acting in the execution or enforcement of the trust created by this deed of trust, which includes all court and other costs, including attorney's fees, incurred by Trustee in defense of any action or proceeding taken against Trustee in that capacity.

E. General Provisions

E.1. If any of the Property is sold under this deed of trust, Grantor must immediately surrender possession to the purchaser. If Grantor does not, Grantor will be a tenant at sufferance of the purchaser, subject to an action for forcible detainer.

E.2. Recitals in any trustee's deed conveying the Property will be presumed to be true.

E.3. Proceeding under this deed of trust, filing suit for foreclosure, filing application for expedited foreclosure proceeding, or pursuing any other remedy will not constitute an election of remedies.

E.4. This lien will remain superior to liens later created even if the time of payment of all or part of the Home Equity Extension of Credit is extended or part of the Property is released.

E.5. If any portion of the Home Equity Extension of Credit cannot be lawfully secured by this deed of trust, payments will be applied first to discharge that portion to the extent permitted by law.

E.6. Grantor assigns to Lender all amounts payable to or received by Grantor from condemnation of all or part of the Property, from private sale in lieu of condemnation, and from damages caused by public works or construction on or near the Property. After deducting any expenses incurred, including attorney's fees and court and other costs, Lender will either release any remaining amounts to Grantor or apply such amounts to reduce the Home Equity Extension of Credit. Lender will not be liable for failure to collect or to exercise diligence in collecting any such amounts. Grantor will immediately give Lender notice of any actual or threatened proceedings for condemnation of all or part of the Property.

E.7. Interest on the debt secured by this deed of trust will not exceed the maximum amount of nonusurious interest that may be contracted for, taken, reserved, charged, or received under law. Any interest in excess of that maximum amount will be credited on the principal of the debt or, if that has been paid, refunded. On any acceleration or required or permitted prepayment, any such excess will be canceled automatically as of the acceleration or prepayment or, if already paid, credited on the principal of the debt or, if the principal of the debt has been paid, refunded. Loan charges, fees, or similar amounts other than interest will not exceed the maximum amount or rate that may be contracted for, taken, reserved, charged, or received under law. Any loan charges, fees, or similar amounts other than interest in excess of that maximum rate or amount will be credited on the principal of the debt or, if the principal of the debt has been paid, refunded. This provision overrides any conflicting provisions in this and all other instruments concerning the Home Equity Extension of Credit.

E.8. In no event may this deed of trust secure payment of any debt that may not lawfully be secured by a lien on real estate or create a lien otherwise prohibited by law.

E.9. Grantor waives all demand for payment, presentation for payment, notice of intention to accelerate maturity, notice of acceleration of maturity, protest, and notice of protest to the extent permitted by applicable law.

E.10. Grantor agrees to pay reasonable attorney's fees, trustee's fees, and court and other costs of enforcing Lender's rights under this deed of trust if an attorney [**include if the transaction is a secondary mortgage loan:** who is not an employee of Lender] is retained for its enforcement.

E.11. If any provision of this deed of trust is determined to be invalid or unenforceable, the validity or enforceability of any other provision will not be affected.

E.12. The term *Home Equity Extension of Credit* includes all extensions and renewals of the Home Equity Extension of Credit and all amounts secured by this deed of trust.

E.13. This deed of trust binds, benefits, and may be enforced by the successors in interest of all parties.

E.14. If Grantor and Borrower are not the same person, the term *Grantor* includes Borrower.

E.15. Grantor represents to Lender that all of the Property is Grantor's homestead.

E.16. The Home Equity Extension of Credit will conform strictly to the provisions of the Texas Constitution applicable to extensions of credit as defined by Tex. Const. art. XVI, § 50(a)(6). In no event will Grantor or Lender be obligated to perform any act or be bound by any requirement that would conflict therewith. If any term, obligation, privilege, or right of the Home Equity Extension of Credit, this deed of trust, any instrument to which Lender is subrogated hereunder, any instrument renewed or extended hereby, or any other document executed in connection with the Home Equity Extension of Credit fails to conform to Tex. Const. art. XVI, § 50(a)(6), or in the event Lender or any holder of the Home Equity Extension of Credit fails to comply with Tex. Const. art. XVI, § 50(a), then, to the extent provided by applicable law, such violation may be cured as set out in Tex. Const. art. XVI, § 50(a)(6).

____

[Name of grantor]

Include acknowledgment.

Form 11-4

Additional Clauses for Deeds of Trust (Home Equity Loan)

Refinance and Extension of Existing Texas Home Equity Deed of Trust

Clause 11-4-1

The Note secured by this Security Instrument is given to refinance and extend the amount left owing and unpaid by Grantor upon that one certain Promissory Note in the original principal amount of [**amount**] DOLLARS ($[**amount**]), which is dated [**date**], executed by [**name**], and payable to the order of [**name**], secured by a Texas Home Equity Security Instrument from [**name**] to [**name**], dated [**date**] and recorded in [**recording data**] of the real property records of [**county**] County, Texas against the Property. Lender is subrogated to all rights and remedies of the holder of the obligations. The lien is hereby refinanced, extended and continued in full force and effect to secure the payment of the Note secured by this Security Instrument. The lien is a lien described in section 50(a)(4), article 16, of the Texas Constitution.

Extension of Mechanic's Lien Contract and Security for Cash Advanced

Clause 11-4-2

The Home Equity Extension of Credit renews and extends the balance of [**amount**] DOLLARS ($[**amount**]) that Grantor owes on a prior note in the original principal amount of [**amount**] DOLLARS ($[**amount**]), which is dated [**date**], executed by [**name**], and payable to the order of [**name**]. The prior note is secured by a mechanic's lien contract creating a lien on the Property, dated [**date**] and recorded in [**recording data**] of the real property records of [**county**] County, Texas. [**Include if applicable:** The prior note and the lien securing it have been transferred to Lender.] The Home Equity Extension of Credit also represents **[amount]** DOLLARS ($**[amount]**) in cash that Lender advanced to Grantor on **[date]** at Grantor's request. Grantor acknowledges that the lien securing the prior note is valid, that it subsists against the Property, and that by this deed of trust it is renewed and extended in full force until the Home Equity Extension of Credit is paid.

To Pay Ad Valorem Taxes and Security for Cash Advanced

Clause 11-4-3

The Home Equity Extension of Credit represents **[amount]** DOLLARS ($**[amount]**) in cash that, at Grantor's request, Lender advanced to pay the following taxes [**include if applicable:** , including penalties, interest, and collection expenses,] assessed and owed on the Property, which Grantor now owns: **[amount]** DOLLARS ($**[amount]**) to **[county]** County in payment of taxes for the years **[specify]**; and **[amount]** DOLLARS ($**[amount]**) to the city of **[city]** in payment of taxes for the years **[specify]**. The Home Equity Extension of Credit also represents **[amount]** DOLLARS ($**[amount]**) in cash that Lender advanced to Grantor on **[date]** at Grantor's request.

To Pay Income Taxes and Security for Cash Advanced

Clause 11-4-4

The Home Equity Extension of Credit includes **[amount]** DOLLARS ($**[amount]**) that, at Grantor's request, Lender advanced to the United States Internal Revenue Service to discharge federal tax lien number **[number]**, which is recorded in **[recording data]** of the federal tax lien records of **[county]** County, Texas. Grantor acknowledges this federal tax lien to be valid and subsisting, and the same is renewed and extended by this deed of trust until the Home Equity Extension of Credit is fully paid. This Home Equity Extension of Credit also represents [**amount**] DOLLARS ($[**amount**]) in cash that Lender advanced to Grantor on [**date**] at Grantor's request.

Tax and Insurance Reserve or Escrow Account

Clause 11-4-5

Grantor agrees to make an initial deposit in a reasonable amount to be determined by Lender and then make periodic payments to a fund for taxes and insurance premiums on the Property. Periodic payments will be made on the payment dates specified in the Home Equity Extension of Credit, and each payment will be in an amount that Lender estimates will be sufficient to pay taxes and insurance premiums. The fund will accrue no interest, and Lender will hold it without bond in escrow and use it to pay the taxes and insurance premiums. If Grantor has complied with the requirements of this paragraph, Lender must pay taxes before [the end of the calendar year/delinquency]. Grantor agrees to make additional deposits on demand if the fund is ever insufficient for its purpose. If an excess accumulates in the fund, Lender may either credit it to future periodic deposits until the excess is exhausted or refund it to Grantor. When Grantor makes the final payment on the Home Equity Extension of Credit, Lender will credit to that payment the whole amount then in the fund [**include if applicable:** or, at Lender's option, refund it after the Home Equity Extension of Credit is paid]. If this deed of trust is foreclosed, any balance in the fund over that needed to pay taxes, including taxes accruing but not yet payable, and to pay insurance premiums will be paid under section D., "Trustee's Rights and Duties." [**Include if applicable:** If the Property is transferred, any balance then in the fund will still be subject to the provisions of this paragraph and will inure to the benefit of the transferee.] Deposits to the fund described in this paragraph are in addition to the periodic payments provided for in the Home Equity Extension of Credit.

Assignment of Insurance Policies

Clause 11-4-6

If the Property is transferred by foreclosure, the transferee will acquire title to all insurance policies on the Property.

Evidence of Payment of Taxes

Clause 11-4-7

Clause 11-4-7 should not be used if the escrow clause at 11-4-5 is used.

Grantor agrees to furnish on Lender's request evidence satisfactory to Lender that all taxes and assessments on the Property have been paid when due.

Consumer Credit Insurance Notice

Clause 11-4-8

GRANTOR MAY FURNISH ANY INSURANCE REQUIRED BY THIS DEED OF TRUST EITHER THROUGH EXISTING POLICIES OWNED OR CONTROLLED BY GRANTOR OR THROUGH EQUIVALENT COVERAGE FROM ANY INSURANCE COMPANY AUTHORIZED TO TRANSACT BUSINESS IN TEXAS.

Due-on-Sale Clause

Clause 11-4-9

If Grantor transfers any part of the Property without Lender's prior written consent, Lender may declare the debt secured by this deed of trust immediately payable and invoke any remedies provided in this deed of trust for default. If the Property is residential real property containing less than five dwelling units or a residential manufactured home occupied by Grantor, exceptions to this provision are limited to (a) a subordinate lien or encumbrance that does not transfer rights of occupancy of the Property; (b) creation of a purchase-money security interest for household appliances; (c) transfer by devise, descent, or operation of law on the death of a co-Grantor; (d) grant of a leasehold interest of three years or less without an option to purchase; (e) transfer to a spouse or children of Grantor or between co-Grantors; (f) transfer to a relative of Grantor on Grantor's death; and (g) transfer to an inter vivos trust in which Grantor is or remains a beneficiary and occupant of the Property.

Subordinate Lien Clauses

Clause 11-4-10

The lien created by this deed of trust is subordinate to the lien securing payment of a note, and any renewals, extensions, and modifications thereof, in the original principal amount of [**amount**] DOLLARS ($[**amount**]), which is dated [**date**], executed by [**name**], payable to the order of [**name**], and more fully described in a deed of trust recorded in [**recording data**] of the real property records of [**county**] County, Texas. If default occurs in payment of any part of principal or interest of that $[**amount**] note or in observance of any covenants of the deed of trust securing it, the entire debt secured by this deed of trust will immediately become payable at the option of Lender.

Or

Clause 11-4-11

If Grantor fails to pay any part of principal or interest secured by a prior lien or liens on the Property when it becomes payable or defaults on any prior lien instrument, the entire debt secured by this deed of trust will immediately become payable at the option of Lender.

Form 11-5

Home Equity Compliance Certificate and Agreement

Basic Information

Date:

Borrower:

[Borrower's Spouse:]

Borrower's Mailing Address:

[Borrower's Spouse's Mailing Address:]

Lender:

Lender's Mailing Address:

Home Equity Extension of Credit (Promissory Note)

Date:

Original principal amount:

Maturity date:

Property (including any improvements):

Fair Market Value of the Property:

A. Agreement of Parties

A.1. Borrower and Lender acknowledge and agree on the Fair Market Value of the Property and have signed a written acknowledgment of the Fair Market Value of Property on the date the Home Equity Extension of Credit is made.

A.2. The Home Equity Extension of Credit is not secured by any additional real or personal property other than the Property. Any provision contained in any other agreement between the Parties or any third party that gives Lender a security interest in any personal or real property other than the Property will not apply to the Home Equity Extension of Credit.

B. Representation and Warranties of Borrower

Borrower represents and warrants the following:

B.1. The Fair Market Value of the Property is an accurate value estimate based on an appraisal or evaluation not disputed by Borrower.

B.2. The original principal amount of the Home Equity Extension of Credit, when added to the aggregate total of the outstanding principal balances of any other indebtedness secured by valid encumbrances of record against the Property, does not exceed 80 percent of the Fair Market Value of the Property.

B.3. Borrower has not been required to pay, in addition to any interest, fees to any person that are necessary to originate, evaluate, maintain, record, insure, or service the Home Equity Extension of Credit that exceed, in the aggregate, 3 percent of the original principal amount of the Home Equity Extension of Credit.

B.4. The lien securing the Home Equity Extension of Credit is a voluntary lien on the Property created with the consent of all owners and their spouses.

B.5. The Home Equity Extension of Credit is not secured by any additional property other than the collateral.

Select one of the following.

B.6. The Home Equity Extension of Credit is the only debt secured by the Property.

Or

B.6. The Home Equity Extension of Credit is the only loan made pursuant to section 50(a)(6) of article 16 of the Texas Constitution and the only debt secured by the Property except the debts and liens described in the following documents: [**specify**].

Continue with the following.

B.7. The closing of the Home Equity Extension of Credit did not occur before the twelfth day after the later of the date that Borrower submitted a loan application to Lender for the Home Equity Extension of Credit or the date that Lender provided Borrower a copy of a notice concerning the Home Equity Extension of Credit making all disclosures required by section 50(g), article XVI, of the Texas Constitution.

Select one of the following.

B.8. The closing of the Home Equity Extension of Credit did not occur before one business day after the date that Borrower received a copy of the loan application if not previously provided and a final itemized disclosure of the actual fees, points, interest, costs, and charges that were charged at closing.

Or

B.8. Borrower understands that under the Texas Constitution this home equity loan may not be closed before one business day after the date that Borrower receives a copy of the loan application if not previously provided and a final itemized disclosure of actual fees, points, interest, costs, and charges to be charged at the closing of the loan unless Borrower consents in writing for this information to be originally given or modified on the date of closing because of the existence of a bona fide emergency or other good cause. Borrower acknowledges the existence of a bona fide emergency or other good cause being [**specify nature of bona fide emergency or other good cause; *see* 7 Tex. Admin. Code § 153.13**] and consents to Lender providing a final itemized disclosure of actual fees, points, interest, costs, and charges to be charged on the loan on the loan closing date.

Select one of the following.

B.9. The closing of the Home Equity Extension of Credit did not occur before the first anniversary of the closing date of any other home equity extension of credit made under section 50(a)(6), article XVI, of the Texas Constitution and secured by part or all of the Property.

Or

B.9. Borrower requests a closing of the Home Equity Extension of Credit before the first anniversary of the closing date of any other extension of credit made under section 50(a)(6), article XVI, of the Texas Constitution and secured by part or all of the property due to an emergency that has been declared by the President of the United States or the governor as provided by law and that applies to the area where the property is located.

Continue with the following.

B.10. The closing of the Home Equity Extension of Credit has taken place at the office of Lender, an attorney at law, or a title company.

Select one of the following.

B.11. Borrower has not been required to apply the proceeds of the Home Equity Extension of Credit to repay another debt.

Or

B.11. Borrower has not been required to apply the proceeds of the Home Equity Extension of Credit to repay another debt except debt to another lender.

Or

B.11. Borrower has not been required to apply the proceeds of the Home Equity Extension of Credit to repay another debt except debt secured by the Property.

Or

B.11. Borrower has not been required to apply the proceeds of the Home Equity Extension of Credit to repay another debt except debt to another lender and debt secured by the Property.

Continue with the following.

B.12. Borrower has not assigned wages as security for the Home Equity Extension of Credit or signed a confession of judgment or power of attorney to Lender or anyone to confess judgment or appear for Borrower in a judicial proceeding.

B.13. Borrower has not signed any instrument relating to the Home Equity Extension of Credit in which blanks relating to substantive terms of the agreement were left to be filled in.

B.14. Borrower has received, as of the time the Home Equity Extension of Credit was made, a copy of the loan application and all executed documents signed by Borrower at closing related to the Home Equity Extension of Credit.

B.15. All of the Property is the homestead of Borrower. No portion of the Property is nonhomestead.

Select one of the following.

B.16. The Home Equity Extension of Credit is not a form of open-end account that may be debited from time to time or under which credit may be extended from time to time.

Or

B.16. The Home Equity Extension of Credit is a home equity line of credit constituting an open-end account that may be debited from time to time and under which credit may be extended from time to time subject to the restrictions found at Tex. Const. art. XVI, § 50(t).

Continue with the following.

B.17. Borrower has been advised that Borrower may, within three days after the Home Equity Extension of Credit is made, rescind the Home Equity Extension of Credit without penalty or charge. [**Include if applicable:** Borrower's Spouse has been advised that Borrower's Spouse may, within three days after the Home Equity Extension of Credit is made, rescind the Home Equity Extension of Credit without penalty or charge.]

B.18. Borrower understands and agrees that Lender is relying on the truth and accuracy of each of the representations and warranties in this Certificate and Agreement. Borrower acknowledges that Lender would not make the Home Equity Extension of Credit if any of the representations and warranties were not true and accurate.

____

[Name of borrower]

SUBSCRIBED AND SWORN TO before me on ________________ by **[name of affiant]**.

____

Notary Public, State of Texas

Include the following if applicable.

____

[Name of borrower's spouse]

SUBSCRIBED AND SWORN TO before me on __________________ by [**name of affiant**].

____
Notary Public, State of Texas

Continue with the following.

____
[**Name of lender**]

SUBSCRIBED AND SWORN TO before me on __________________ by [**name of affiant**].

____
Notary Public, State of Texas

Form 11-6

Note: For married couples, a separate election regarding right of rescission should be given by each spouse.

Election Regarding Right of Rescission

Date:

Borrower:

[Borrower's Spouse:]

Borrower's Mailing Address:

[Borrower's Spouse's Mailing Address:]

Lender:

Lender's Mailing Address:

Home Equity Extension of Credit

Date:

Original principal amount:

In accordance with Tex. Const. art. XVI, § 50(a)(6)(Q)(viii), [Borrower/Borrower's Spouse] provides Lender with the following notice regarding the Home Equity Extension of Credit:

☐ I have elected not to rescind the Home Equity Extension of Credit. I acknowledge that more than three days have expired from the date that the Home Equity Extension of Credit was made.

☐ I have elected to rescind the Home Equity Extension of Credit. This notice is given within three days from the date that the Home Equity Extension of Credit was made.

____

[**Name of [borrower/borrower's spouse]**]

Form 11-7

This form provides the notice required by Tex. Const. art. XVI, § 50(k)(9), as amended November 5, 2013.

IMPORTANT NOTICE TO BORROWERS RELATED TO YOUR REVERSE MORTGAGE

UNDER THE TEXAS TAX CODE, CERTAIN ELDERLY PERSONS MAY DEFER THE COLLECTION OF PROPERTY TAXES ON THEIR RESIDENCE HOMESTEAD. BY RECEIVING THIS REVERSE MORTGAGE YOU MAY BE REQUIRED TO FORGO ANY PREVIOUSLY APPROVED DEFERRAL OF PROPERTY TAX COLLECTION AND YOU MAY BE REQUIRED TO PAY PROPERTY TAXES ON AN ANNUAL BASIS ON THIS PROPERTY.

THE LENDER MAY FORECLOSE THE REVERSE MORTGAGE AND YOU MAY LOSE YOUR HOME IF:

(A) YOU DO NOT PAY THE TAXES OR OTHER ASSESSMENTS ON THE HOME EVEN IF YOU ARE ELIGIBLE TO DEFER PAYMENT OF PROPERTY TAXES;

(B) YOU DO NOT MAINTAIN AND PAY FOR PROPERTY INSURANCE ON THE HOME AS REQUIRED BY THE LOAN DOCUMENTS;

(C) YOU FAIL TO MAINTAIN THE HOME IN A STATE OF GOOD CONDITION AND REPAIR;

(D) YOU CEASE OCCUPYING THE HOME FOR A PERIOD LONGER THAN 12 CONSECUTIVE MONTHS WITHOUT THE PRIOR WRITTEN APPROVAL FROM THE LENDER OR, IF THE EXTENSION OF CREDIT IS USED FOR THE PURCHASE OF THE HOME, YOU FAIL TO TIMELY OCCUPY THE HOME AS YOUR PRINCIPAL RESIDENCE WITHIN A PERIOD OF TIME AFTER THE EXTENSION OF CREDIT IS MADE THAT IS STIPULATED IN THE WRITTEN AGREEMENT CREATING THE LIEN ON THE HOME;

(E) YOU SELL THE HOME OR OTHERWISE TRANSFER THE HOME WITHOUT PAYING OFF THE LOAN;

(F) ALL BORROWERS HAVE DIED AND THE LOAN IS NOT REPAID;

(G) YOU COMMIT ACTUAL FRAUD IN CONNECTION WITH THE LOAN; OR

(H) YOU FAIL TO MAINTAIN THE PRIORITY OF THE LENDER'S LIEN ON THE HOME, AFTER THE LENDER GIVES NOTICE TO YOU, BY PROMPTLY DISCHARGING ANY LIEN THAT HAS PRIORITY OR MAY OBTAIN PRIORITY OVER THE LENDER'S LIEN WITHIN 10 DAYS AFTER THE DATE YOU RECEIVE THE NOTICE, UNLESS YOU:

(1) AGREE IN WRITING TO THE PAYMENT OF THE OBLIGATION SECURED BY THE LIEN IN A MANNER ACCEPTABLE TO THE LENDER;

(2) CONTEST IN GOOD FAITH THE LIEN BY, OR DEFEND AGAINST ENFORCEMENT OF THE LIEN IN, LEGAL PROCEEDINGS SO AS TO PREVENT THE ENFORCEMENT OF THE LIEN OR FORFEITURE OF ANY PART OF THE HOME; OR

(3) SECURE FROM THE HOLDER OF THE LIEN AN AGREEMENT SATISFACTORY TO THE LENDER SUBORDINATING THE LIEN TO ALL AMOUNTS SECURED BY THE LENDER'S LIEN ON THE HOME.

IF A GROUND FOR FORECLOSURE EXISTS, THE LENDER MAY NOT COMMENCE FORECLOSURE UNTIL THE LENDER GIVES YOU WRITTEN NOTICE BY MAIL THAT A GROUND FOR FORECLOSURE EXISTS AND GIVES YOU AN OPPORTUNITY TO REMEDY THE CONDITION CREATING THE GROUND FOR FORECLOSURE OR TO PAY THE REVERSE MORTGAGE DEBT WITHIN THE TIME PERMITTED BY SECTION 50(k)(10), ARTICLE XVI, OF THE TEXAS CONSTITUTION. THE LENDER MUST OBTAIN A COURT ORDER FOR FORECLOSURE EXCEPT THAT A COURT ORDER IS NOT REQUIRED IF THE FORECLOSURE OCCURS BECAUSE:

(1) ALL BORROWERS HAVE DIED; OR

(2) THE HOMESTEAD PROPERTY SECURING THE LOAN IS SOLD OR OTHERWISE TRANSFERRED.

YOU SHOULD CONSULT WITH YOUR HOME COUNSELOR OR AN ATTORNEY IF YOU HAVE ANY CONCERNS ABOUT THESE OBLIGATIONS BEFORE YOU CLOSE YOUR REVERSE MORTGAGE LOAN. TO LOCATE AN ATTORNEY IN YOUR AREA, YOU MAY WISH TO CONTACT THE STATE BAR OF TEXAS.

THIS NOTICE IS ONLY A SUMMARY OF YOUR RIGHTS UNDER THE TEXAS CONSTITUTION. YOUR RIGHTS ARE GOVERNED IN PART BY SECTION 50, ARTICLE XVI, OF THE TEXAS CONSTITUTION, AND NOT BY THIS NOTICE.

____
[Name of borrower]

____
[Name of lender/originator]

Form 11-8

Notice Concerning Refinance of Existing Home Equity Loan to Non–Home Equity Loan under Section 50(f)(2), Article XVI, Texas Constitution

YOUR EXISTING LOAN THAT YOU DESIRE TO REFINANCE IS A HOME EQUITY LOAN. YOU MAY HAVE THE OPTION TO REFINANCE YOUR HOME EQUITY LOAN AS EITHER A HOME EQUITY LOAN OR AS A NON–HOME EQUITY LOAN, IF OFFERED BY YOUR LENDER.

HOME EQUITY LOANS HAVE IMPORTANT CONSUMER PROTECTIONS. A LENDER MAY ONLY FORECLOSE A HOME EQUITY LOAN BASED ON A COURT ORDER. A HOME EQUITY LOAN MUST BE WITHOUT RECOURSE FOR PERSONAL LIABILITY AGAINST YOU AND YOUR SPOUSE.

IF YOU HAVE APPLIED TO REFINANCE YOUR EXISTING HOME EQUITY LOAN AS A NON–HOME EQUITY LOAN, YOU WILL LOSE CERTAIN CONSUMER PROTECTIONS. A NON–HOME EQUITY REFINANCED LOAN:

(1) WILL PERMIT THE LENDER TO FORECLOSE WITHOUT A COURT ORDER;

(2) WILL BE WITH RECOURSE FOR PERSONAL LIABILITY AGAINST YOU AND YOUR SPOUSE; AND

(3) MAY ALSO CONTAIN OTHER TERMS OR CONDITIONS THAT MAY NOT BE PERMITTED IN A TRADITIONAL HOME EQUITY LOAN.

BEFORE YOU REFINANCE YOUR EXISTING HOME EQUITY LOAN TO MAKE IT A NON–HOME EQUITY LOAN, YOU SHOULD MAKE SURE YOU UNDERSTAND THAT YOU ARE WAIVING IMPORTANT PROTECTIONS THAT HOME EQUITY LOANS PROVIDE UNDER THE LAW AND SHOULD CONSIDER CONSULTING WITH AN ATTORNEY OF YOUR CHOOSING REGARDING THESE PROTECTIONS.

YOU MAY WISH TO ASK YOUR LENDER TO REFINANCE YOUR LOAN AS A HOME EQUITY LOAN. HOWEVER, A HOME EQUITY LOAN MAY HAVE A HIGHER INTEREST RATE AND CLOSING COSTS THAN A NON–HOME EQUITY LOAN.

Form 11-9

Affidavit of Compliance (Pursuant to Section 50(f)(2), Article XVI, Texas Constitution)

Date:

Affiant[s]: [**name of owner**] [**include if applicable:**, [**name of owner's spouse**]]

Lender:

Home Equity Loan: [**include recording information**]

Property:

Affiant[s] on oath swear[s] that the following statements are true and within the personal knowledge of Affiant[s]:

1. I am a borrower named in the Note or the owner or spouse of any owner of the Property described in the Deed of Trust (which term includes any riders thereto), both dated [**date**], evidencing and securing a debt payable to the Lender and providing for a lien pursuant to section 50(a)(4), article XVI, of the Texas Constitution upon and against the Property (the "Loan").

2. The Loan is secured by homestead property as defined under applicable Texas law.

3. All of the following conditions are met in connection with the Loan:

   a. The Property is not the subject of a Home Equity Loan that was closed within one year before the date of this Affidavit.

   b. The Loan does not include the advance of any additional funds, other than:

i. funds advanced to refinance a valid debt described by sections 50(a)(1) through (a)(7), article XVI, of the Texas Constitution; or

ii. actual costs and reserves required Lender to refinance the debt.

4. The principal amount of the Loan when added to the aggregate total of the outstanding principal balances of all other indebtedness secured by valid encumbrances of record against the Property does not exceed 80 percent of the fair market value of the Property on the date the Loan is made.

5. Lender provided me with the written notice required by section 50(f)(2)(D), article XVI, of the Texas Constitution not later than the third business day after the date I submitted my loan application to Lender and at least twelve days before the date the Loan is closed.

____
[Name of owner]

SUBSCRIBED AND SWORN TO before me on __________________ by **[name of affiant]**.

____
Notary Public, State of Texas

Include the following if applicable.

____
[Name of owner's spouse]

SUBSCRIBED AND SWORN TO before me on __________________ by **[name of affiant]**.

____
Notary Public, State of Texas

Include the following if applicable.

____
[Name of nonborrowing owner]

SUBSCRIBED AND SWORN TO before me on ________________ by [name of affiant].

____
Notary Public, State of Texas

Include the following if applicable.

____
[Name of nonborrowing owner's spouse]

SUBSCRIBED AND SWORN TO before me on ________________ by [name of affiant].

____
Notary Public, State of Texas

Form 11-10

This Texas home equity review form is provided as a sample and should not be relied on as a substitute for independent legal counsel and review of a specific loan transaction.

"Investor" means the end purchaser of the loan.

[Name of investor]

Texas Home Equity Attorney Opinion, Checklist, and Lender Certification

Loan Number:

Borrower:

Property Address:

Lender:

Investor:

Investor purchasing guidelines require Lender to engage a licensed Texas attorney to provide this opinion and certification of a Texas home equity loan pursuant to article XVI, section 50(a)(6), of the Texas Constitution. Lender has submitted the following documents for attorney review (collectively, the "Loan Documents"):

1. Fully executed Texas home equity loan package
2. Appraisal
3. Initial loan application and twelve-day notice
4. Loan estimate
5. Title commitment

Sections A, B, and C of this form must be completed before the file is delivered for purchase.

A. Attorney Opinion Statement

After reviewing the loan file, Lender's certification, and the requirements for Texas home equity loans set forth in article XVI, section 50(a)(6), of the Texas Constitution, I am issuing the following opinion:

______ Yes, the loan satisfies the requirements for Texas home equity loans.

______ No, the loan does not satisfy the requirements for Texas home equity loans.

B. Attorney Compliance Review

§ 50(a)(6) Subsection	Attorney Findings and Conclusions
A	The loan is secured by a voluntary lien on the homestead created under a written agreement with the consent of each owner and each owner's spouse.
B	The loan is of a principal amount that when added to the aggregate total of the outstanding principal balances of all other indebtedness secured by valid encumbrances of record against the homestead does not exceed 80 percent of the fair market value of the homestead on the date the extension of credit is made.
C	The loan is without recourse for personal liability against each owner and the spouse of each owner, unless the owner or spouse obtained the extension of credit by actual fraud.
D	The loan is secured by a lien that may be foreclosed upon only by a court order.
E	The loan does not require the owner or the owner's spouse to pay, in addition to any interest or any bona fide discount points used to buy down the interest rate, any fees to any person that are necessary to originate, evaluate, maintain, record, insure, or service the extension of credit that exceed, in the aggregate, two percent of the original principal amount of the extension of credit, excluding fees for: (i) an appraisal performed by a third party appraiser; (ii) a property survey performed by a state registered or licensed surveyor; (iii) a state base premium for a mortgagee policy of title insurance with endorsements established in accordance with state law; or (iv) a title examination report if its cost is less than the state base premium for a mortgagee policy of title insurance without endorsements established in accordance with state law.

§ 50(a)(6) Subsection	Attorney Findings and Conclusions
F	The loan is not a form of open-end account that may be debited from time to time.
G	The loan is payable in advance without penalty or other charge.
H	The loan is not secured by any additional real or personal property other than the homestead.
I	(Repealed)
J	The loan may not be accelerated because of a decrease in the market value of the homestead or because of the owner's default under other indebtedness not secured by a prior valid encumbrance against the homestead.
K	The debt evidenced by the Loan Documents is the only debt secured by the homestead at the time the extension of credit is made unless the other debt was made for a purpose described by section 50(a)(1)–(a)(5) or section 50(a)(8), article XVI, of the Texas Constitution.
L	The loan is scheduled to be repaid in substantially equal successive periodic installments, not more often than every fourteen days and not less often than monthly, beginning no later than two months from the date the extension of credit is made, each of which equals or exceeds the amount of accrued interest as of the date of the scheduled installment.
M(i)	The loan was not closed before the twelfth day after the later of the date that the owner of the homestead submits a loan application to the lender for the extension of credit or the date that the lender provides the owner a copy of the notice prescribed by section 50(g), article XVI, of the Texas Constitution.
M(ii)	The loan was not closed before one business day after the date that the owner of the homestead receives a copy of the loan application if not previously provided and a final itemized disclosure of the actual fees, points, interest, costs, and charges that will be charged at closing.
M(iii)	The loan was not closed before the first anniversary of the closing date of any other extension of credit described by section 50(a)(6), article XVI, of the Texas Constitution secured by the same homestead property.
N	The loan was closed only at the office of the lender, an attorney at law, or a title company.
O	The loan permits a lender to contract for and receive any fixed or variable rate of interest authorized under statute.

§ 50(a)(6) Subsection	Attorney Findings and Conclusions
P	The loan is made by one of the following that has not been found by a federal regulatory agency to have engaged in the practice of refusing to make loans because the applicants for the loans reside or the property proposed to secure the loans is located in a certain area: (i) a bank, savings and loan association, savings bank, or credit union doing business under the laws of this state or the United States, including a subsidiary of a bank, savings and loan association, savings bank, or credit union described by this subparagraph; (ii) a federally chartered lending instrumentality or a person approved as a mortgagee by the United States government to make federally insured loans; (iii) a person licensed to make regulated loans, as provided by statute of this state; (iv) a person who sold the homestead property to the current owner and who provided all or part of the financing for the purchase; (v) a person who is related to the homestead property owner within the second degree of affinity or consanguinity; or (vi) a person regulated by this state as a mortgage banker or mortgage company.
Q(i)	The loan was made on the condition that the owner of the homestead is not required to apply the proceeds of the extension of credit to repay another debt except debt secured by the homestead or debt to another lender.
Q(ii)	The loan was made on the condition that the owner of the homestead not assign wages as security for the extension of credit.
Q(iii)	The loan was made on the condition that the owner of the homestead not sign any instrument in which blanks relating to substantive terms of agreement are left to be filled in.
Q(iv)	The loan was made on the condition that the owner of the homestead not sign a confession of judgment or power of attorney to the lender or to a third person to confess judgment or to appear for the owner in a judicial proceeding.
Q(v)	The loan was made on the condition that at the time the extension of credit was made, the owner of the homestead shall receive a copy of the final loan application and all executed documents signed by the owner at closing related to the extension of credit.
Q(vi)	The loan was made on the condition that the security instruments securing the extension of credit contain a disclosure that the extension of credit is the type of credit defined by section 50(a)(6), article XVI, of the Texas Constitution.
Q(vii)	The loan was made on the condition that within a reasonable time after termination and full payment of the extension of credit, the lender cancel and return the promissory note to the owner of the homestead and give the owner, in recordable form, a release of the lien securing the extension of credit or a copy of an endorsement and assignment of the lien to a lender that is refinancing the extension of credit.

§ 50(a)(6) Subsection	Attorney Findings and Conclusions
Q(viii)	The loan was made on the condition that the owner of the homestead and any spouse of the owner may, within three days after the extension of credit is made, rescind the extension of credit without penalty or charge.
Q(ix)	The loan was made on the condition that the owner of the homestead and the lender sign a written acknowledgment as to the fair market value of the homestead property on the date the extension of credit is made.

Attorney Certification and Signature

I certify that I am a licensed Texas attorney and have personally completed or overseen the review set forth above. I understand that this document constitutes an opinion of counsel on the matters set forth herein, and that my client, Investor, and Lender are entitled to rely on it as such.

My review has been based solely on the documentation provided by Lender, and Lender understands that in preparing this opinion, I have not made any independent inquiry or investigation beyond those documents.

By:______________________________
Printed Name:
Title:
[Firm Name:]
Date:

C. Texas 50(a)(6) Certification of Lender

This certification must be signed by an authorized representative of the original lender. This certification must be completed and may not be altered in any way.

Lender:

Borrower:

Loan/File Number:

By executing this document, I certify the following on behalf of Lender:

1. Each person consenting to the lien in this transaction did so voluntarily.

2. There is no additional collateral securing this transaction.

3. The loan was not closed before the twelfth day after the later of (a) the date the owner submitted an application to Lender for the loan or (b) the date that Lender provided the owner with a copy of the notice required by article XVI, section 50(g), of the Texas Constitution (the "Notice").

4. The loan was not closed before the first business day after the owner received a copy of the application, as well as a final, itemized disclosure of the actual fees, points, interest, costs, and charges that would be charged at closing (unless a bona fide emergency existed and Lender obtained the written consent of the owner to (a) provide the document to the owner on the date of closing or (b) modify the previously disclosed information on the date of closing).

5. Lender has not been found by a federal regulatory agency to have engaged in the practice of refusing to make loans because the applicant(s) reside, or the property proposed to secure the loan is located, in a certain area.

6. Lender did not require the owner to apply the loan proceeds to repay another debt (except debt secured by the homestead or debt owed to another lender).

7. Lender did not require the owner to assign wages as security for the loan.

8. Lender did not permit the owner to sign any instrument in which blanks relating to substantive loan terms are left to be filled in.

9. Lender did not require the owner to sign a confession of judgment, or power of attorney to Lender or to a third person to confess judgment, or to appear for the owner in a judicial proceeding.

10. At the time of the loan closing, Lender provided the owner with copies of all documents signed by the owner related to the extension of credit, including a copy of the final application.

11. At the time of the payment of value or advance of funds, Lender had no knowledge that the fair market value stated in the Acknowledgment of Fair Market Value was incorrect.

12. Lender is a bank, savings and loan association, savings bank, or credit union doing business under the laws of the United States, and as such may make Texas home equity loans.

13. If the discussions with Borrower were conducted primarily in a language other than English, Lender provided, before closing, an additional copy of the Notice translated into the written language in which the discussions were conducted.

By:______________________________
Printed Name:
Title:
Date:

Chapter 12

Federal Consumer Disclosure Documents

I. Truth-in-Lending Disclosure Documents

II. RESPA Consumer Disclosure Documents

Forms

Chapter 12

Federal Consumer Disclosure Documents

I. Truth-in-Lending Disclosure Documents

§ 12.1 Overview of the Truth in Lending Act and Regulation Z

§ 12.1:1 Source of Authority

The federal Truth in Lending Act, 15 U.S.C. §§ 1601–1667f, requires a creditor extending consumer credit, including mortgage credit secured by a dwelling, to make meaningful disclosures of actual credit terms that enable the consumer to more readily compare those terms with the terms of competitors and make an informed decision regarding the use and costs of credit. The Act is implemented by Regulation Z (12 C.F.R. pt. 1026), which is an official interpretive rule adopted and published by the BCFP, and the official staff interpretations of Regulation Z (12 C.F.R. pt. 1026, supp. I), which the BCFP staff updates and publishes annually. Reliance on and good-faith compliance with Regulation Z and the official staff interpretations afford creditors protection from civil liability and administrative penalties for failure to comply with disclosure and other requirements imposed on creditors under the Act. *See* 15 U.S.C. § 1640(f). Closed-end credit, including traditional mortgage loans, is regulated under subpart C of Regulation Z, 12 C.F.R. §§ 1026.17–.24.

§ 12.1:2 Coverage

Generally, the Act covers any credit transaction in which a creditor offers or extends a consumer credit at or below a threshold amount adjusted on January 1 each year that is primarily for personal, family, or household purposes and for which a finance charge is made in connection with the credit or, by written agreement, the credit is to be repaid in more than four installments. 12 C.F.R. § 1026.3(b). The threshold amount in 2015 was $54,600 and will adjust in tandem with the annual percentage increase in the Consumer Price Index in effect on June 1 of the preceding year. *See* Official Interpretation to 12 C.F.R. § 1026.3(b), Comment 3(b)-1. As discussed below, the Act also covers most consumer credit transactions secured by real property (or by personal property, such as a mobile home, used or intended to be used as the borrower's principal dwelling) regardless of the loan amount. For the Act to apply in any case, the creditor must be a person (including a natural person or a corporate or other business organization) who regularly extends credit of this type, which generally means that the person has extended credit more than twenty-five times in the preceding calendar year or more than five times for transactions secured by a dwelling during the preceding or current calendar year, and the consumer must be a natural person. *See* 15 U.S.C. § 1603.

For the purposes of providing disclosures under the TILA-RESPA Integrated Disclosures Rule (TRID), the rule applies to most closed-end consumer credit transactions secured by real property but does not apply to home equity lines of credit, reverse mortgages, or chattel-dwelling loans such as mobile homes or other dwellings that are not attached to real property. 12 C.F.R. § 1026.19. Loans made by a person or entity not considered to be a creditor are not covered by the rule. 12 C.F.R. § 1026.2(a)(17). Certain transactions, such as down payment assistance loans, have a partial exemption. 12 C.F.R. § 1026.3(h). Construction-only loans and loans secured by vacant land or by twenty-five or more acres are not subject to RESPA but are still subject to the disclosure requirements of TRID. *See* 12 C.F.R. §§ 1024.5, 1026.19. Credit extended to land trusts or trusts for tax or estate planning purposes is also covered. Official Interpretation to 12 C.F.R. § 1026.3(a), Comment 3(a)-10.

§ 12.1:3 Required Consumer Disclosures

Written disclosures must be made for each credit transaction subject to the Act before consummation; must reflect the terms of the actual legal obligation between the parties; and must show the calculated annual percentage rate (APR), finance charge, amount financed, payment schedule, and total of payments and other material disclosures of the cost of credit within permitted tolerances for accuracy. Creditors must disclose information germane to a loan transaction, including the loan details, payment schedule, loan fees, cash to close, service providers, escrows, and relevant state law provisions. All of this information must be provided in a dynamic format, such that the form changes with changes in the loan data and contains only provisions that reflect the terms of the loan transaction. Creditors are further required to ensure that the disclosures are clearly and conspicuously in writing in a form that the consumer can keep. 12 C.F.R. §§ 1026.17, 1026.18.

The initial disclosure is referred to as the loan estimate (LE); the final disclosure is referred to as the closing disclosure (CD). For loan transactions not subject to the new disclosure requirements (home equity lines of credit, reverse mortgages, mortgages secured by mobile homes, mortgages secured by dwellings (other than cooperative units) not attached to real property), the initial and final TIL disclosure statements, good-faith estimate, and HUD-1, as applicable, are still used. 12 C.F.R. § 1026.19(e), (f). The following consumer disclosures, as applicable, are required under the Act and Regulation Z.

Early Disclosures: Creditors must make early disclosures to the consumer within three business days after loan application and at least seven business days before loan closing. *See* 12 C.F.R. § 1026.19(e)(1)(iii). The disclosures must be made before the consumer pays any fee other than a bona fide and reasonable fee for obtaining credit history. *See* 12 C.F.R. § 1026.19(e)(2)(i)(B).

Correction Disclosures: Creditors are permitted to provide a revised LE only if there is a "changed circumstance" defined as (1) an extraordinary event beyond the control of any interested party or other unexpected event specific to the consumer or transaction; (2) information specific to the consumer or transaction that the creditor relied on when providing the disclosures that was inaccurate or changed after the disclosures were provided; or (3) new information specific to the consumer or transaction that the creditor did not rely on when providing the original disclosures. 12 C.F.R. § 1026.19(e)(3)(iv)(A). Revised CDs must be received no later than three days before loan consummation if the disclosed APR becomes inaccurate, the loan product changes, or a prepayment penalty is added; for any other changes, the creditor must ensure receipt of the revised CD at or before loan consummation. 12 C.F.R. § 1026.19(f)(2)(i). If a subsequent event causes the disclosure of the APR to be inaccurate outside of permitted tolerances, the creditor must make a correction disclosure of the APR and all other changed terms at least three business days before loan consummation. *See* 12 C.F.R. § 1026.19(a)(2)(ii).

Final Disclosures: Creditors must ensure that the borrower receives a final CD no later than three business days before loan consummation. *See* 12 C.F.R. § 1026.19(f).

Notice of Right of Rescission: If a security interest is or will be retained or acquired in the consumer's principal dwelling in connection with a mortgage loan, the Act provides the consumer a right to rescind the loan transaction within three business days. The consumer may exercise the right to rescind until midnight of the third business day after loan consummation, delivery of notice of right of rescission, or delivery of the material disclosures, whichever occurs last. Certain loan transactions, including a loan to finance the purchase or initial construction of the consumer's principal dwelling, are exempt from the right of rescission. *See* 12 C.F.R. § 1026.23(f). Certain required disclosures, such as the amount of the finance charge, the amount financed, and the APR, are regarded as *material* disclosures and must be provided to the consumer before the prescribed three-business-day rescission period begins to run. The failure to timely provide these material disclosures within prescribed tolerances for accuracy not only subjects the creditor to substantial liability under the Act for administrative penalties and costs, restitution, and civil damages but may also have the legal effect of extending the rescission period for up to three years after loan closing. *See* 12 C.F.R. § 1026.23(a)(3). The content and model form of the required rescission notice is set out in 12 C.F.R. § 1026.23(b)(1), (b)(2) and appendix H to Regulation Z.

Variable-Rate Loan Disclosures: Special disclosure requirements apply to variable-rate transactions secured by a principal dwelling under 12 C.F.R. § 1026.19(b), requiring (1) delivery to the consumer at the time of loan application of detailed written adjustable-rate mortgage loan program disclosures and a preprinted disclosure booklet titled Consumer Handbook on Adjustable Rate Mortgages, published by the BCFP, and (2) a loan program disclosure for each variable-rate program for which the consumer expresses an interest, with periodic written disclosures of adjustments made to the interest rate in a variable-rate transaction subject to section 1026.19(b). *See* 12 C.F.R. § 1026.20(c). Home equity lines of credit and other open-end credit secured by residential dwellings require written disclosures and are subject to substantive rules under subpart B, 12 C.F.R. §§ 1026.5–.13.

Loan Assumption Disclosures: A creditor must provide a consumer new written disclosures when the consumer assumes an existing residential mortgage obligation with the written consent of the creditor and the creditor agrees to accept that consumer as the principal obligor. *See* 12 C.F.R. § 1026.20(b).

Mortgage Loan Sale Disclosure: Creditors that purchase or accept the sale and assignment of a whole loan secured by a consumer's principal dwelling on or after May 29, 2009, must provide the borrower obligated under the loan a written notice within thirty days after the sale or assignment containing information identifying the new creditor, the date of transfer of the loan, the location where the transfer of the loan is recorded, and other relevant information about the creditor. 12 C.F.R. § 1026.39.

HOEPA and Higher-Priced Loan Disclosures: Special rules regarding high-rate, high-cost loans (generally referred to as "Section 32," or Home Ownership and Equity Protection Act (HOEPA) loans) are set out under subpart E, 12 C.F.R. §§ 1026.31, 1026.32, 1026.34. Creditors making HOEPA loans must furnish consumers a written disclosure meeting the requirements of section 1026.32(c) at least three business days before loan consummation and abide by certain substantive terms of that section. Special rules effective October 1, 2009, regarding a new category of higher-priced mortgage loans (HPMLs) are also set out in 12

C.F.R. § 1026.35. The Home Ownership and Equity Protection Act is codified at 15 U.S.C. § 1639.

Reverse Mortgage Loan Disclosures: Creditors making reverse mortgage loans subject to 12 C.F.R. § 1026.33(a) must provide consumers an additional written disclosure of the "total annual loan cost of credit" (generally referred to as the "TALC" disclosure) in content set out in 12 C.F.R. § 1026.33(b) and substantially in the model form found in 12 C.F.R. pt. 1026 app. K(d).

§ 12.1:4 Certain Consumer Protection Provisions

Regulation Z contains various substantive provisions intended to protect consumers from certain unfair, deceptive, and abusive practices of originators and servicers of home mortgage loans. *See* 73 Fed. Reg. 44,522 (July 30, 2008).

Prohibited Deceptive Advertising: Advertising rules targeting deceptive and misleading practices apply to all consumer credit transactions secured by dwellings. Advertisements occurring on or after October 1, 2009, that promote mortgage credit secured by a dwelling are regulated by extensive new advertising rules set out in amendments to 12 C.F.R. §§ 1026.16, 1026.24 (open- and closed-end credits, respectively). The rules are intended to ensure that advertisements for credit clearly and conspicuously provide accurate and balanced information about rates, monthly payments, and other loan features and that several deceptive and misleading advertising practices are banned. The advertising regulations apply to any advertisement (including promotional materials accompanying applications) in any medium promoting a credit transaction secured by a dwelling (except radio and television advertisements, to which new alternative regulations apply).

Unfair or deceptive acts and practices in home mortgage advertising are also regulated by a final rule of the Federal Trade Commission (FTC) for business entities under its regulatory jurisdiction, including "nondepository covered persons" such as independent mortgage bankers and brokers. *See* 76 Fed. Reg. 43,826 (July 22, 2011); 16 C.F.R. pt. 321. The regulations prohibit any misrepresentation in any commercial communication regarding any term or feature of any mortgage credit product and impose certain recordkeeping requirements. Rulemaking authority of the FTC was transferred to the BCFP on July 21, 2011, pursuant to Title X of the Dodd-Frank Act, but the FTC, the BCFP, and any state's attorney general or other authorized state officer have statutory authority to bring enforcement actions and seek civil penalties under these deceptive advertising regulations.

Prohibited Coercion of Appraisers: Creditors, mortgage brokers, and their affiliates are prohibited from coercing, influencing, or otherwise encouraging an appraiser to misstate or misrepresent the value of a consumer's principal dwelling securing a covered loan. Any creditor who knows at or before a loan closing of a violation of these anticoercion regulations is prohibited from extending credit based on such an appraisal unless the creditor documents that it has acted with reasonable diligence to determine that the appraisal does not materially misstate or misrepresent the value of the appraised property. *See* 12 C.F.R. § 1026.42.

Prohibited Servicing Practices: Mortgage servicers of loans secured by principal dwellings are prohibited from (1) failing to timely credit payments as of the date of receipt, with certain exceptions, (2) imposing a late charge on a consumer in connection with the receipt of a payment when the only delinquency is attributable to a late fee or delinquency charge assessed on an earlier payment (and the current payment is otherwise a full payment made on or before its due date or within an applicable grace period), and (3) failing to provide an accurate payoff statement within a reasonable time after receiving a request for it by a consumer (or a person acting on behalf of a consumer). *See* 12 C.F.R. § 1026.36(c).

Prohibited Steering and Certain Loan Originator Compensation Practices: Effective for closed-end loans secured by a dwelling for which creditors receive the application on or after April 1, 2011, amendments to 12 C.F.R. § 1026.36 prohibit three certain loan originator compensation practices:

1. *Compensation based on loan terms:* Mortgage brokers and other loan originators are prohibited from charging or receiving compensation based on any terms and conditions of the loan transaction other than the loan amount. This has the effect of prohibiting creditors from paying so-called yield-spread premiums to mortgage brokers (that is, compensation based on spreads in the interest rate) although paying a fee based on a fixed percentage of the loan amount is authorized. "Compensation," for purposes of the rule, means all amounts paid to and retained by the mortgage broker or other loan originator from salaries, commissions, annual or periodic bonuses, incentive compensation, or awards of merchandise, services, trips, or similar prizes but does not include fees charged to the consumer that are passed through by the loan originator to third-party providers to pay for services such as a property appraisal and a consumer credit report.

2. *Receiving compensation from both creditor and consumer:* Mortgage brokers and other loan originators are prohibited from directly receiving compensation from both the creditor, or any other person, and the consumer in the same loan transaction. That is to say, if any loan originator receives compensation directly from a consumer in a loan transaction, neither the creditor nor any other person may provide any compensation to the loan originator, directly or indirectly, in connection with that same loan transaction.

3. *Steering consumer to loan not in consumer's interest for greater compensation:* Mortgage brokers and other loan originators are prohibited from steering consumers to consummate a loan not in the consumer's interest in order to receive greater compensation from the creditor for the loan than for other loan transactions that the loan originator offered or could have offered the consumer and for which the consumer likely could have qualified. "Steering" for this purpose means advising, counseling, or otherwise influencing a consumer to accept and actually consummate a particular loan transaction. "Safe harbor" procedures are set out in the C.F.R. that may be relied on to assure compliance under which the consumer must be presented with various loan options from a significant number of creditors to choose from.

The new rule applies to all loan originators, including mortgage brokers and loan officers employed by mortgage brokers, mortgage bankers, and financial institutions that, for compensation, arrange, negotiate, or otherwise obtain a consumer loan for another person. Managers, administrative staff, and other employees of such loan originators who do not engage in these activities (and whose compensation is not based on where any particular loan is originated) are not considered loan originators. The rule also applies to creditors who close transactions that are table funded (that is, closings in which the creditor named as payee on the promissory note does not actually fund the loan from its own resources or a bona fide warehouse line of credit for which it is obligated, but instead obtains funding by another party who is immediately assigned the loan). 12 C.F.R. § 1026.36(d), (e).

Prohibited Practices Applicable to HOEPA and HPML Loans: Certain consumer protections apply only to so-called high-rate, high-cost loans ("Section 32" or HOEPA loans), which bear interest rates or fees above a certain percentage or amount described in 12 C.F.R. § 1026.32 and a new category of HPMLs, which bear interest rates above standards described in 12 C.F.R. § 1026.35.

1. *Prohibited lending without regard to repayment ability:* Creditors are prohibited from extending credit for HOEPA loans or HPMLs to any consumer based on the value of the consumer's collateral without regard to the consumer's ability as of the date of consummation to repay the loan from sources other than the collateral itself. Creditors are required to verify each borrower's income and assets relied on in underwriting the loan and are prohibited from relying on stated amounts of income, including expected income, or assets unless the creditor verifies such amounts according to standards set out in the rules. *See* 12 C.F.R. §§ 1026.34(a)(4), 1026.35.
2. *Restrictions on prepayment penalties:* HOEPA loans and HPMLs may provide for a prepayment penalty only if (1) the penalty is otherwise permitted by state or other applicable law; (2) the source of prepayment funds is not a refinancing by the same creditor or its affiliate; (3) the prepayment penalty will not apply after the two-year period following loan consummation; and (4) the amount of the periodic payment of principal, interest, or both does not change during the four-year period following loan consummation. HOEPA loans have one additional condition not applicable to HPMLs: the consumer's total monthly debt payments (including amounts owed under the mortgage loan) may not exceed 50 percent of the consumer's gross monthly income as of the date of loan consummation and as verified under the standards set out in the regulations. *See* 12 C.F.R. §§ 1026.32(d)(6), 1026.35.
3. *Mandatory escrow accounts:* Before consummating a first-lien HPML, the creditor must establish, and thereafter maintain, an escrow account to collect reserves from the consumer for the payment of property taxes and premiums for mortgage-related insurance required by the creditor. The creditor or loan servicer may permit a consumer to cancel the mandatory escrow account if the consumer requests cancellation in a dated written request received by the creditor no earlier than 365 days after loan consummation. Mandatory escrow account regulations apply to covered loans for which applications are received on or after April 1, 2010, or, if such loans are secured by manufactured housing, October 1, 2010. *See* 12 C.F.R. § 1026.35(b).

§ 12.2 General Considerations for Disclosures

This chapter discusses four of the forms designed to comply with the consumer disclosure requirements applicable to closed-end credit under the Truth in Lending Act and Regulation Z. The following forms are the model forms in appendix H of Regulation Z:

- loan estimate (fixed-rate loan) (from app. H-24(B)) (available at **https://s3.amazonaws.com/files.consumerfinance.gov/f/documents/cfpb_kbyo_guide-loan-estimate-and-closing-disclosure-forms_v2.0.pdf**);
- closing disclosure (fixed-rate loan) (from app. H-25(B)) (available at **https://s3.amazonaws.com/files.consumerfinance.gov/f/documents/cfpb_kbyo_guide-loan-estimate-and-closing-disclosure-forms_v2.0.pdf**);
- truth-in-lending (sale) disclosure statement (from app. H-1);
- truth-in-lending (loan) disclosure statement (from app. H-2);
- notice of right of rescission (general) (from app. H, clause H-8) (form 12-1 in this chapter); and
- notice of right of rescission (refinancing) (from app. H, clause H-9) (form 12-2).

The forms may require modification to comply with federal and state consumer laws.

Regulation Z, a complex set of rules, mandates making certain disclosures at specified times to any person who obtains consumer credit from a creditor. "Consumer credit" means credit offered or extended to a consumer primarily for personal, family, or household purposes. A "creditor" is the person to whom a consumer credit obligation is initially payable. A creditor must give the consumer (the borrower) truth-in-lending disclosures in a consumer credit transaction if the creditor regularly extends consumer credit that is subject to a finance charge or that is payable by written agreement in more than four installments, not including a down payment, and to whom the obligation is initially payable. A person "regularly extends consumer credit" only if credit is extended in the current or preceding calendar year more than twenty-five times for general transactions or more than five times for transactions secured by dwellings. 12 C.F.R. § 1026.2. A credit transaction, other than one secured by real property or personal property used as the principal dwelling of the consumer, is exempt from Regulation Z if the total amount financed in the transaction exceeds the threshold amount. 12 C.F.R. § 1026.3(b).

By these definitions, most entities providing credit for home equity financing transactions or for building or improving homes are subject to the requirements of Regulation Z. Chapter 20 in this manual describes transactions involving mechanic's liens and suggests which of those transactions require use of these forms.

For a description of home equity financing transactions, see chapter 11.

§ 12.2:1 Disclosure Statements

General requirements for the disclosure statements applicable to closed-end credit are set forth in 12 C.F.R. §§ 1026.17, 1026.18. Among other requirements, the disclosures must be made "clearly and conspicuously in writing, in a form that the consumer may keep." They must be segregated from other information, and they "shall not contain any information not directly related to the disclosures required under § 1026.18 or § 1026.47." 12 C.F.R. § 1026.17(a). These disclosures may be provided to the consumer in electronic form, subject to compliance with the consumer consent and other applicable provisions of the Electronic Signatures in Global and National Commerce Act (E-Sign Act). 15 U.S.C. §§ 7001–7031.

If the creditor is the seller, the (sale) disclosure is used.

Generally, disclosures must be made before the transaction is consummated, but certain transactions involving residential mortgages, mail or telephone orders, or a series of sales have different timing requirements. 12 C.F.R. § 1026.17(b). Disclosures for most residential mortgage transactions, for example, must be given at the time of loan application or delivered or placed in the mail not later than three business days after the creditor receives the consumer's written loan application. Redisclosure may be required before loan consummation if there is a changed circumstance, if the disclosed annual percentage rate terms change before loan settlement, or if a subsequent event makes disclosed terms inaccurate. 12 C.F.R. §§ 1026.17(f), 1026.19(a).

§ 12.2:2 Notices of Right of Rescission

The two notices of right of rescission, forms 12-1 and 12-2 in this chapter, differ only to the extent that one applies to original financing and the other to refinancing. A refinancing involves the satisfaction of one financing transaction with a new financing transaction by the same lender and borrower. 12 C.F.R. § 1026.20(a). In either case the notice provides a cooling-off period of three business days after a person obtains credit involving a lien against the person's principal dwelling. During this period the homeowner may rescind the transaction.

Regulations governing the right to rescind appear at 12 C.F.R. § 1026.23, and forms 12-1 and 12-2 are drafted in accordance with that section.

Creditors subject to truth-in-lending requirements should provide the appropriate notice of right of rescission, form 12-1 or 12-2, if a transaction creates a lien or other security interest in a consumer's principal dwelling, except when the transaction finances the acquisition or initial construction of the dwelling. 12 C.F.R. § 1026.23. Typical transactions requiring this form are a refinancing of a residential mortgage transaction by a new creditor, a home equity extension of credit, and a home improvement loan secured by a mechanic's lien. A consumer's principal dwelling may be an ordinary residence, a condominium, a cooperative unit, a mobile home, or a trailer. A person may have only one principal dwelling, and it may or may not be attached to real property. *See* 12 C.F.R. § 1026.2(a)(19).

All persons who have ownership interests in the dwelling used as security and who use it as their principal dwelling may be entitled to rescind the transaction. 12 C.F.R. § 1026.23(a).

Transactions exempt from the right of rescission and this notice requirement are described in 12 C.F.R. § 1026.23(f). A refinancing by the same creditor of an extension of credit already secured by the consumer's principal dwelling is subject to the right of rescission only to the extent that the new loan amount exceeds the sum of the unpaid principal balance and accrued finance charges of the existing extension of credit and closing costs related to the refinancing transaction. Certain other transactions are also exempt from the right of rescission, including a residential mortgage transaction to finance the acquisition or initial construction of a principal residence. 12 C.F.R. § 1026.23(f).

§ 12.2:3 References

Regulation Z requires strict compliance, and even minor errors or omissions in drafting truth-in-lending documents may lead to administrative enforcement actions, statutory penalties, and individual and class actions for civil liability against creditors. *See* 15 U.S.C. § 1640. Accordingly, attorneys should consult Regulation Z itself, especially the sections addressing these forms (12 C.F.R. §§ 1026.17–.24), for aid in drafting the documents. Section 1026.18 establishes contents for the disclosure statements, and section 1026.23 governs the right of rescission. Regulation Z is published in title 12 of the Code of Federal Regulations, part 1026.

The official commentary to Regulation Z offers additional useful information; commentaries are issued periodically by officials in the BCFP, and are available online at **www.consumerfinance.gov/rules-policy/regulations/1026**.

§ 12.3 Cautions

The disclosure statements must be completed in compliance with 12 C.F.R. § 1026.18. That section provides, among many other requirements, that if the consumer wishes to have an itemization of the amount financed, the itemization must be given in a separate writing.

For the notices of right of rescission, the creditor should observe certain cautions during the three-business-day cooling-off period: other than money in escrow, no funds should be disbursed; no improvements to the property should be made; no service related to the transaction should be provided to the consumer; and no goods or materials for construction should be delivered to the property. If the consumer rescinds the transaction, within twenty calendar days the creditor must return any money or property received from the consumer. 12 C.F.R. § 1026.23(d).

Any disclosure statements required at consummation, including notices of the right of rescission, and other documents related to the transaction should be signed or delivered to the consumer at loan settlement. The creditor must provide each consumer entitled to rescind two copies of the notice of the right to rescind. A consumer may exercise the right to rescind until midnight of the third business day following the last to occur of loan consummation, delivery of the material disclosures, or delivery of the notices of the right of rescission. A consumer may rescind by written notice to the creditor, which is effective when mailed, sent by other means, or delivered to the creditor. The creditor must delay disbursing funds and otherwise performing under the extension of credit until the rescission period has expired and the creditor is reasonably satisfied that the consumer has not rescinded. Failure of the creditor to deliver required notices or statements can subject the creditor to statutory penalties and civil liability for damages and have the further legal effect of extending the period during which the consumer may rescind the transaction for up to three years after the date of consummation. 12 C.F.R. § 1026.23(a).

§ 12.4 Instructions for Completing Disclosure Statements

Attorneys completing the disclosure statements should follow closely the instructions in 12 C.F.R. § 1026.18 and should also consult the more detailed instructions promulgated by the BCFP (see section 12.2:3 above).

Disclosures not relevant to the transaction may be omitted; for example, the total sale price may be omitted in a loan transaction.

The creditor must be identified at least by name, but this disclosure may appear apart from the other disclosures. When a transaction involves multiple creditors, any one of them may make the disclosures, but the disclosing creditor must be identified. 12 C.F.R. §§ 1026.17(d), 1026.18(a).

The annual percentage rate is determined by methods set forth in 12 C.F.R. § 1026.22. The BCFP provides other useful aids for this calculation, including appendix J of Regulation Z and annual percentage rate tables available from the Board.

"Finance charge" is defined in 12 C.F.R. § 1026.4, which offers several examples and lists certain charges excluded from the finance charge. Calculating this charge is central to the disclosure statements, so it should be done with great care. Generally, any charge payable directly or indirectly by the consumer that is imposed directly or indirectly by the creditor as an incident to or condition of the extension of credit constitutes a finance charge unless the charge is expressly excluded under 12 C.F.R. § 1026.4. Most notable among the exclusions are charges of a type that would be payable in a comparable cash transaction and the "real estate related fees" enumerated in 12 C.F.R. § 1026.4(c)(7).

Section 1026.4 also excludes some insurance premiums under certain conditions. Many creditors find this exclusion highly desirable. Premiums for credit life, accident, health, or loss-of-income insurance may be excluded under the following conditions: the creditor does not require such coverage and discloses that fact; the creditor discloses the premium for the initial term of insurance coverage; and the consumer signs or initials an affirmative written request for the insurance after receiving the required disclosures. Premiums for insurance against loss of or damage to property or against liability arising from the ownership or use of property may be excluded under the following conditions: the coverage may be obtained from a person of the consumer's choice, and that fact is disclosed; and if it is obtained from or through the creditor, the creditor discloses the premium for the initial term of coverage.

Determination of the amount financed under 12 C.F.R. § 1026.18(b) requires determining the principal loan amount or cash price less any down payment, adding other amounts financed except the finance charge, and subtracting any prepaid finance charge. The creditor may include other items in this amount, such as rebates or loan premiums.

If the consumer wants an itemization of the amount financed or if the creditor prefers to supply one as a matter of course, it must be provided in a separate document at the same time as other disclosures required by section 1026.18. A model for this disclosure appears in appendix H-3 of Regulation Z.

In the late-payment disclosure, the creditor must reveal any charge that may be imposed before maturity due to a late payment, other than a deferral or extension charge. 12 C.F.R. § 1026.18(*l*). If the creditor merely continues to assess interest at the rate charged before default, that fact need not be disclosed.

For a home equity extension of credit (see chapter 11 in this manual), the description of the security should be inserted as "your home."

Regulation Z requires that the disclosure statement include an appropriate version of the assumption policy model clause when the transaction involves a residential mortgage. 12 C.F.R. § 1026.18(q). A "residential mortgage transaction" is defined as a transaction in which a "consensual security interest is created or retained in the consumer's principal dwelling to finance the acquisition or initial construction of that dwelling." 12 C.F.R. § 1026.2(a)(24). For this type of transaction, the appropriate form of this model clause (H-6), which can be found at appendix H of Regulation Z, should be added to the disclosure statement.

Appendix H of Regulation Z offers other model clauses that may be suitable for the disclosure statements: variable rate (H-4), demand feature (H-5), and required deposit (H-7).

The truth-in-lending disclosure statements are designed for simple, fixed-interest-rate transactions. If a variable-interest-rate transaction is involved, the disclosure statement forms in this manual must be revised to include variable-interest-rate disclosures. Additionally, if the interest rate on a loan secured by a consumer's principal dwelling, such as a home equity extension of credit or credit for building or improving a consumer's home, may increase after funding and the term of the credit exceeds one year, variable-interest-rate disclosures in addition to those contained in the truth-in-lending disclosure statement must be given by the creditor to the borrower at the earlier of the time the borrower either receives the loan application form or pays a nonrefundable fee. *See* 12 C.F.R. § 1026.19(b). These variable-rate mortgage loan disclosures are extensive and include twelve features of the variable-rate loan program that must be disclosed. The disclosures would thus be unique to any specific loan program offered by a creditor, and it would be impractical for this manual to provide a model variable-rate mortgage loan disclosure form. If a variable-rate credit secured by the consumer's principal dwelling is desired, the attorney should be sure that the creditor has given appropriate variable-rate disclosures to the borrower.

The other information required in the disclosure statements should be provided in careful accordance with the guidelines of 12 C.F.R. § 1026.18 and the BCFP's commentary on that section.

§ 12.5 Instructions for Completing Notices of Right of Rescission

The attorney should be careful to use the appropriate model form for the notice of right of rescission. The refinancing notice of right of rescission (form 12-2 in this chapter) should be used only for refinancings by the same creditor. See section 12.2:2 above. The general form (form 12-1) should be used in other consumer credit transactions requiring the notice.

The date of the transaction is the date the consumer initially becomes obligated, either by signing a note or retail installment contract (home improvement) or by assuming a contractual obligation, whichever is first.

The creditor's name and mailing address must be provided.

The date of the end of the rescission period must be stated accurately; it is the third business day following the date of the transaction specified on the form. A definition of "business day" is given in 12 C.F.R. § 1026.2(a)(6).

Finally, the consumer should sign the form to acknowledge its receipt.

§ 12.6 Additional Documents

For other documents related to mechanic's lien transactions that may require a disclosure statement and notice of right of rescission, see chapter 20 in this manual.

§ 12.7 Other Comments

Regulation Z requires that creditors give consumers the disclosure statements "in a form that the consumer may keep." 12 C.F.R. § 1026.17(a). Also, the creditor must retain evidence of compliance, such as by keeping a copy of the executed form showing the consumer's acknowledgment of receiving it, for two years after the date disclosures are required to be made or action is required to be taken. 12 C.F.R. § 1026.25. The form need not be filed or recorded.

Each consumer entitled to rescission must be provided two copies of the notice of right of rescission, one for potential use in canceling the transaction and one for recordkeeping. Each person whose ownership interest in the dwelling is subject to the security interest and who also uses it as his or her principal dwelling should receive two copies of the notice (one copy to each if the notice is provided in electronic form in accordance with the consumer consent and other applicable provisions of the E-Sign Act). As with the disclosure statement, the creditor should also keep a copy of the executed form for two years.

During the three-business-day rescission period provided by the notice, the creditor may accrue finance charges on the amount loaned.

Consumers may waive the right to rescind by providing a signed, dated statement that the loan is necessary to cope with a bona fide personal financial emergency. The waiver form must describe the emergency and specifically waive the right to rescind. Printed or otherwise standard waiver forms generally may not be used for this purpose, and everyone entitled to rescind must sign the waiver. 12 C.F.R. § 1026.23(e).

The borrower may not be charged for the preparation of truth-in-lending documents. If an attorney for the lender prepares truth-in-lending documents, the lender should pay any fee for that service separately and may not charge or pass through to the borrower (as part of loan settlement or closing costs or otherwise) that fee. 12 U.S.C. § 2610.

[Sections 12.8 through 12.10 are reserved for expansion.]

II. RESPA Consumer Disclosure Documents

§ 12.11 Overview of the Real Estate Settlement Procedures Act

§ 12.11:1 Source of Authority

The Real Estate Settlement Procedures Act of 1974 (RESPA), 12 U.S.C. §§ 2601–2617, is a federal consumer disclosure and protection statute intended to ensure consumers are provided greater and more timely information on the nature and costs of the settlement process and are protected from unnecessarily high settlement charges caused by abusive settlement practices, such as kickbacks or referral fees that tend to increase the costs of settlement services.

RESPA was implemented by Regulation X, 12 C.F.R. pt. 1024, which was an official interpretive rule adopted and published by the Department of Housing and Urban Development (HUD) under its previously congressionally delegated authority to interpret and implement the statute. The Bureau of Consumer Financial Protection (BCFP) has enforcement authority. The BCFP reissued its regulation of these statutes under 12 C.F.R. pt. 1024. Regulation X provides "reliance on rule" protections to lenders and other settlement service providers. No provision of Regulation X imposing liability will apply to any act done or omitted in good-faith compliance with Regulation X or any other official HUD rule, regulation, or interpretation, even if after the act or omission has occurred the rule, regulation, or interpretation is amended, rescinded, or determined by judicial or other means to be invalid for any reason. *See* 12 U.S.C. § 2617(b).

§ 12.11:2 Coverage

RESPA applies to all *federally related mortgage loans*, a term broadly defined by regulation in 12 C.F.R. § 1024.5(a) to include virtually any mortgage loan made by a creditor in the United States that is secured by a lien on a one- to four-family residential dwelling. Certain loans, such as business purpose loans, loans secured by vacant land, and temporary financing, such as a construction loan, with a term of less than two years that is not convertible to permanent financing, are exempt from coverage. See the exemptions at 12 C.F.R. § 1024.5(b).

§ 12.11:3 Consumer Disclosures

Generally, RESPA requires that loan originators provide written disclosures to loan applicants and borrowers at various stages of loan origination, settlement, and servicing of a federally related mortgage loan. The rules regulating the form, content, and timing of these required consumer disclosures and certain other key provisions are summarized below.

Loan Estimate: A loan originator, either the lender or the mortgage broker, of a federally related mortgage loan must provide a loan applicant a loan estimate (LE) within three business days after receiving an application (or information sufficient to complete an application). The lender or mortgage broker must provide the LE by hand delivery or by placing the LE in the mail within the three-business-day period. The LE is an estimate of all fees and charges a borrower is likely to incur at loan closing that must be accurate within narrow permitted tolerances; the applicant can comparison shop estimated costs among competing lenders and brokers. "Application," for this purpose, is defined in 12 C.F.R. § 1024.2(b). The form, content, and timing of a standardized LE disclosure must comply with the requirements of 12 C.F.R. § 1025.7 and appendix C, as amended.

Special Information Booklets: A mortgage lender or mortgage broker must provide loan applicants a preprinted special information booklet within three business days after receiving a loan application (unless the application is declined or withdrawn within that three-day period) consisting as applicable of either *Your Home Loan Toolkit—A Step-by-Step Guide* (accessible at **https://files.consumerfinance.gov/f/201503_cfpb_your-home-loan-toolkit-web.pdf**), in the case of closed-end credits to purchase a home, or *When Your Home is On the Line: What You Should Know about Home Equity Lines of Credit* (Consumer Financial Protection Bureau), in the case of open-end credit plans. *See* 12 C.F.R. §§ 1024.6, 1026.19(g).

Escrow Account Notices: When escrow accounts are established and maintained by the lender to reserve for property tax and insurance premium payments, the lender or loan servicer must provide the borrower an initial escrow account statement at loan settlement (or within forty-five days after settlement), and thereafter the servicer must provide the borrower an annual escrow account statement within thirty days after the end of each account computation year (which need not be a calendar year). The initial notice must itemize the amounts of the required initial deposit to the account to be collected from the borrower at loan settlement, the monthly deposits to be collected from the borrower during the twelve months thereafter, and the amounts and timing of payments from the account for that twelve-month computation year. RESPA, section 10, substantively regulates the maximum amount, including any cushion, that a mortgage lender may require the borrower to reserve in an escrow account and the method of analyzing and accounting for escrow balances, including any surpluses, shortages, and deficiencies that may occur. *See* 12 C.F.R. § 1024.17. The form and content of the initial and annual escrow account statements must comply with the requirements of sections 1024.17(h) and 1024.17(i), respectively, and the Public Guidance Documents referenced therein.

Loan Servicing Transfer Notices: Mortgage lenders, mortgage brokers who anticipate using table funding (that is, closings in which the note is made payable to the mortgage broker and the loan proceeds are advanced by an investor on contemporaneous assignment of the note and security instrument), and dealers of manufactured homes who anticipate a first-lien dealer loan must provide loan applicants a servicing disclosure statement at the time of application or within three business days after submission of an application that indicates whether the servicing of the loan may be assigned, sold, or transferred at any time while the loan is outstanding. The form, content, and timing of the servicing disclosure statement must generally conform to the model format set out in appendix MS-1 to Regulation X, 12 C.F.R. pt. 1024. *See* 12 C.F.R. § 1024.33(b). The term *servicing* generally refers to such contract administration services as collecting scheduled monthly or other periodic payments from the borrower, remitting principal and interest payments to the holder of the loan, disbursing property tax and insurance premium payments from escrow accounts when due, maintaining accounting and business records of account activity, and providing notices and reports required by law or the terms of the mortgage contract. The term *servicer* generally refers to the entity or other person responsible for performing servicing. These terms are defined in 12 C.F.R. § 1024.2.

A written notice of transfer also must be provided to the borrower on the actual assignment, sale, or transfer of servicing by the transferor servicer at least fifteen days before the effective date of the transfer and by the transferee servicer not later than fifteen days after the effective date. A combined written notice of transfer by the transferor and transferee given at loan settlement also satisfies these timing requirements. The notice of transfer must include such information as the effective date of the transfer of servicing; the date on which the transferor servicer will cease accepting payments on the loan and the date the transferee servicer will begin to accept the payments; the names, addresses, and toll-free numbers of the transferor and transferee servicers where inquiries regarding the servicing transfer may be directed; a statement of the borrower's rights regarding complaint resolution; and other content as set out in appendix MS-2 to Regulation X, 12 C.F.R. pt. 1024. A late fee may not be charged for any misdirected payments by a borrower during the sixty-day period beginning on the effective date of the transfer, and misdirected payments may not be treated as late for credit reporting or other purposes. *See* 12 C.F.R. § 1024.33(c).

Affiliated Business Arrangement Disclosure Statement: Any mortgage lender, mortgage broker, real estate broker, or other person or entity in a position to refer settlement service business that refers a borrower or other person to an affiliated business to perform a settlement service must provide the borrower or other person to whom the referral is made a written affiliated business arrangement disclosure statement. The disclosure statement must generally be in the format of appendix D to Regulation X, 12 C.F.R. pt. 1024. The statement must describe the nature of the relationship between the person making the referral and the referred settlement service provider, set out the estimated charge or range of charges by the provider for the settlement services, and disclose that the borrower or other person is not required to use the referred service provider and is free to "shop around" for the best services and rates that may be available from other service providers. An affiliated business arrangement exists when a person or entity in a position to refer settlement service business, or an associate of such a person, has an affiliate relationship with, or a direct or beneficial interest of more than 1 percent in, a provider of settlement services and directly or indirectly refers such settlement service business to that provider (or affirmatively influences the selection of that affiliated provider). The disclosure statement must be on a sheet of paper separate from other disclosures and be provided at the time the referral is made. If a lender makes the referral to a borrower, the disclosure may be provided at the time the good-faith estimate disclosure is provided to the borrower. *See* 12 C.F.R. § 1024.15.

§ 12.11:4 Prohibition against Kickbacks and Unearned Fees

RESPA, section 8, prohibits kickbacks, referral fees, and unearned fees in connection with federally related mortgage loans. 12 U.S.C. § 2607. Specifically, section 8, as interpreted by Regulation X, provides that "[n]o person shall give and no person shall accept any fee, kickback or other *thing of value* pursuant to any agreement or *understanding*, oral or otherwise, that business incident to or part of a *settlement service* involving a federally related mortgage loan shall be *referred* to any person." 12 C.F.R. § 1024.14(b) (emphasis added). Payment of a fee or other thing of value in consideration of a referral of a settlement service or an agreement to split or pay a portion of a fee charged for the performance of a settlement service with a person referring the business, other than for the reasonable value of services actually performed by the person accepting the payment, is a violation of section 8. A violation implicates both the party giving and the party receiving the unlawful kickback, referral fee, or other thing of value. Moreover, against the weight of judicial authority, the BCFP construes section 8 to prohibit unearned fees even when the fee is not split between two parties, including a charge by any person for which no or nominal services are performed or for which duplicative fees are charged. Section 8 violations are rife with enforcement actions by the BCFP and civil litigation under private rights of action, including class action.

Practitioners are cautioned that section 8 violations are most often inferred from specific facts, and careful analysis of all relevant facts is often required to determine if a violation has occurred. Key elements of the offense are broadly construed. A "referral," for example, includes any oral or written action directed to the borrower or other person that has the effect of affirmatively influencing the person's selection of a particular provider of a settlement service for which the person will be charged. 12 C.F.R. § 1024.14(f). An "understanding" need not be written or oral, but may be inferred from a practice, pattern, or course of conduct. 12 C.F.R. § 1024.14(e). Moreover, a "thing of value" does not require a transfer of money and may be any of a number of seemingly unrelated benefits to the party making a referral: discounts, credits, equity adjustments, deferred rents, debt reduction or forgiveness, free promotions and advertising, assumption of business expenses, expense-paid travel and vacations, and any other imaginable benefit. 12 C.F.R. § 1024.14(d).

Section 8, however, expressly permits payment to attorneys, title agents, or other settlement service providers for goods or facilities actually furnished or services actually performed; fee splits between real estate agents and real estate brokers pursuant to cooperative brokerage agreements; and compensation by an employer to its own employees for referrals either to the employer or to an affiliated business. *See* 12 C.F.R. § 1024.14(g)(1).

Referrals of borrowers or other persons to affiliates to perform settlement services are permitted under strict guidelines for affiliated business arrangements set out in 12 C.F.R. § 1024.15, which requires that written disclosure of the business arrangement is timely made in the form of an affiliated business arrangement disclosure statement described above, that the borrower or other person is not required to use any particular provider of the service, and that the only thing of value that is received from the arrangement is a bona fide return on the ownership interest the referring party may have in the affiliate or a franchise relationship. A prohibited "required use" for this purpose is defined in 12 C.F.R. § 1024.2.

Caution: HUD published an "Advanced Notice of Proposed Rulemaking" in the Federal Register on June 3, 2010, at 75 Fed. Reg. 31,334 to strengthen and clarify the RESPA, section 8, prohibition against the "required use" of affiliated settlement service providers, examining in particular the practice of homebuilders' conditioning construction discounts or discounted upgrades on the use of the homebuilder's affiliated mortgage lender.

HUD's Statement of Policy 1996-2 Regarding Sham Controlled Business Arrangements, 61 Fed. Reg. 29,258 (June 7, 1996), provides guidance on the affiliated business arrangement exemption to section 8 prohibitions against referral fees. According to the policy statement, Congress did not intend this exemption to promote disguised referral fee payments through sham arrangements or shell entities for which there is no bona fide business purpose. By definition, for this exemption to apply, the person or entity receiving the referral must be a bona fide provider of settlement services. If the person or entity is not, considering particular factors enumerated in the policy statement, the arrangement would not qualify for the exemption even if the three safe harbor conditions of 12 C.F.R. § 1024.15 are otherwise met.

HUD's Statement of Policy 1996-3, Rental of Office Space, Lock-outs, and Retaliation, 61 Fed. Reg. 29,264 (June 7, 1996), also addresses the application of section 8 to the practice of settlement service providers (such as mortgage lenders) leasing desks or office space at real estate brokerage offices in anticipation of loan referrals. This practice is permitted only if the general market value of the desk rental or other arrangement is paid by the settlement service provider. The "general market value" for this purpose, which also may include an appropriate portion of the cost for related office services actually provided under the arrangement (such as secretarial service, utilities, telephone, and other office equipment), means the rental amount that a *non–settlement service provider* (that is, one who would not be renting in anticipation of referrals) would pay for the same amount of space and services in the same or a comparable building.

HUD's interpretive rule published June 25, 2010, in the Federal Register at 75 Fed. Reg. 36,271 addressed the application of section 8 to payments by home warranty companies to real estate brokers and agents for services performed in connection with home sales transactions in which a home warranty is sold to the purchaser. HUD concluded that a broker or agent may not be compensated by a home warranty company for marketing services directed to particular homebuyers or sellers and deemed any payments by a home warranty company to a broker or agent to be lawful only if services are actually performed by the broker or agent, are not nominal and are necessary and distinct from the primary services performed by the real estate broker or agent in the same transaction, and are services for which there is no duplicative charge. For example, conducting actual inspections of items to be covered by the home warranty to identify preexisting conditions, recording serial numbers of the items, documenting the condition of the items by taking photographs, and preparing a report to the home warranty company of findings may be compensable services. Any payment for compensable services nevertheless must reasonably relate in amount to the value of services actually performed.

Persons violating section 8, on conviction, may be fined not more than $10,000, imprisoned for not more than one year, or both. Any person violating section 8 provisions also is jointly and severally liable to the person or persons charged for the settlement service involved in the violation in an amount equal to three times the amount of any charge paid for the service. In any private action brought under section 8, the court may award court costs and reasonable attorney's fees to the prevailing party. *See* 12 U.S.C. § 2607(d); 12 C.F.R. § 1024.14(a). Violations may also be grounds for disbarment, suspension, or ineligibility of lenders participating in federally insured or guaranteed loan programs or for enforcement actions by federal or state agencies having supervisory authority over lenders. 12 C.F.R. § 1024.14.

§ 12.11:5 Prohibition against Required Use of Particular Title Company

RESPA, section 9, provides that no seller of property that will be purchased with the assistance of a federally related mortgage loan may require that, as a condition of selling the property, title insurance covering the property must be purchased by the buyer from any particular title company. 12 U.S.C. § 2608. This provision is thought by some practitioners to be inapplicable to Texas practice, in which the seller customarily purchases and pays the premium for the owner's title insurance policy. An offer of a discounted package or of discounts or rebates for the purchase of multiple settlement services as an inducement to the buyer to use a particular title company may be permitted without violating this prohibition against a required use. See the definition of "required use" at 12 C.F.R. § 1024.2. Any seller who violates section 9 is liable to the buyer in an amount equal to three times all charges paid for the title insurance. *See* 12 U.S.C. § 2608; 12 C.F.R. § 1024.14.

§ 12.11:6 Prohibition against Charging for Preparation of Regulatory Disclosures

RESPA, section 12, provides that no fee or charge may be imposed or charged by a lender of a federally related mortgage loan, or by the servicer of the loan, for the preparation and distribution to the borrower or other person of a HUD-1 or HUD-1A settlement statement; escrow account notices and statements required by RESPA, section 10; or statements required by the Truth in Lending Act. *See* 12 U.S.C. § 2610; 12 C.F.R. § 1024.12.

§ 12.11:7 Prohibition against Collecting Excessive Escrow Deposits

RESPA, section 10, substantively limits the amounts that a lender of a federally related mortgage loan may require the borrower to deposit in any escrow account established by the lender to ensure timely payment of property taxes, insurance premiums, or other property charges. 12 U.S.C. § 2609. When establishing the account, typically at loan closing, the lender may require an initial deposit equal to the proportion of total annual costs reasonably anticipated to be paid from the account for the period beginning with the date on which the costs were last paid (or the date on which each of the costs would have been paid under the normal lending practices of the lender and local custom) and ending on the due date of the first installment payment under the mortgage loan plus an additional reserve (for unanticipated disbursements) of no more than one-sixth of the total of all such costs to be paid from the escrow account over the ensuing twelve-month period (that is, a two-month cushion). Thereafter, a lender may not require the borrower to deposit in any such escrow account in any month a sum greater than one-twelfth of the total of the estimated taxes, insurance premiums, and other charges that are reasonably anticipated to be paid from the account during the ensuing twelve months plus a cushion of no more than one-sixth of the monthly amount. If a lender conducts an account analysis, however, and determines there is or will be a deficiency in the escrow account, the lender may require the borrower to make additional monthly deposits to the account to avoid or eliminate the deficiency, subject to substantive and procedural rules set out in Regulation X, 12 C.F.R. § 1024.17(f). Violations of section 10 of RESPA are subject to civil penalties set out in 12 U.S.C. § 2609(d).

§ 12.12 Upcharges Prohibited

The amount stated on the HUD-1 or HUD-1A settlement statement for any itemized settlement service must not exceed the amount actually received by the settlement service provider for that service (unless the charge is an average charge in accordance with 12 C.F.R. § 1024.8(b)(2)). Third-party fees disclosed on the good-faith estimate (GFE) may not exceed the estimated amounts to be paid the third-party settlement service providers, and such fees reported on the HUD-1 may not exceed the amounts actually paid to such third parties. Thus, even earned markups that were permitted based on the value of actual services performed by the lender or mortgage broker in connection with services principally performed by third parties now appear to be prohibited.

§ 12.13 Additional Resources

Bureau of Consumer Financial Protection, *TILA-RESPA Integrated Disclosure—Guide to the Loan Estimate and Closing Disclosure Forms*, **https://s3.amazonaws.com/files.consumerfinance.gov/f/documents/cfpb_kbyo_guide-loan-estimate-and-closing-disclosure-forms_v2.0.pdf**.

Hall, Kenneth F. *Mortgage and Consumer Loan and Lease Disclosure Handbook*. 2015–2016 ed. Thomson Reuters, 2015.

Form 12-1

This form is based on the model form at 12 C.F.R. pt. 226 app. H, clause H-8.

Truth-in-Lending Notice of Right of Rescission

[Notice of Right to Cancel—General]

[**Identification of transaction**]

Your Right to Cancel

You are entering into a transaction that will result in a [mortgage on/lien on/security interest in] your home. You have a legal right under federal law to cancel this transaction, without cost, within three business days from whichever of the following events occurs last:

1. the date of the transaction, which is [**date**]; or

2. the date you received your Truth-in-Lending disclosures; or

3. the date you received this notice of your right to cancel.

If you cancel the transaction, the [mortgage/lien/security interest] is also canceled. Within twenty calendar days after we receive your notice, we must take the steps necessary to reflect the fact that the [mortgage on/lien on/security interest in] your home has been canceled, and we must return to you any money or property you have given to us or to anyone else in connection with this transaction.

You may keep any money or property we have given you until we have done the things mentioned above, but you must then offer to return the money or property. If it is impractical or unfair for you to return the property, you must offer its reasonable value. You may offer to return the property at your home or at the location of the property. Money must be returned to the address below.

If we do not take possession of the money or property within twenty calendar days of your offer, you may keep it without further obligation.

How to Cancel

If you decide to cancel this transaction, you may do so by notifying us in writing, at [**creditor's name and business address**].

You may use any written statement that is signed and dated by you and states your intention to cancel, or you may use this notice by signing and dating the notice of cancellation below. Keep one copy of this notice because it contains important information about your rights.

If you cancel by mail or telegram, you must send the notice not later than midnight of [**date**] (or midnight of the third business day following the latest of the three events listed above). If you send or deliver your written notice to cancel in some other way, it must be delivered to the above address no later than that time.

In this agreement "you" and "your" refer to the consumer, and "we" and "us" refer to the creditor.

Consumer acknowledges receipt of the completed Truth-in-Lending Notice of Right of Rescission.

____

Consumer's signature

Date:

Notice of Cancellation

I WISH TO CANCEL.

____
Consumer's signature
Date:

Form 12-2

This form is based on the model form at 12 C.F.R. pt. 226 app. H, clause H-9.

Truth-in-Lending Notice of Right of Rescission

[Notice of Right to Cancel—Refinancing]

[**Identification of transaction**]

Your Right to Cancel

You are entering into a new transaction to increase the amount of credit previously provided to you. Your home is the security for this new transaction. You have a legal right under federal law to cancel this new transaction, without cost, within three business days from whichever of the following events occurs last:

1. the date of this new transaction, which is [**date**]; or
2. the date you received your new Truth-in-Lending disclosures; or
3. the date you received this notice of your right to cancel.

If you cancel this new transaction, it will not affect any amount that you presently owe. Your home is the security for that amount. Within twenty calendar days after we receive your notice of cancellation of this new transaction, we must take the steps necessary to reflect the fact that your home does not secure the increase of credit. We must also return any money you have given to us or anyone else in connection with this new transaction.

You may keep any money we have given you in this new transaction until we have done the things mentioned above, but you must then offer to return the money at the address below.

If we do not take possession of the money within twenty calendar days of your offer, you may keep it without further obligation.

How to Cancel

If you decide to cancel this new transaction, you may do so by notifying us in writing, at [**creditor's name and business address**].

You may use any written statement that is signed and dated by you and states your intention to cancel, or you may use this notice by signing and dating the notice of cancellation below. Keep one copy of this notice because it contains important information about your rights.

If you cancel by mail or telegram, you must send the notice no later than midnight of [**date**] (or midnight of the third business day following the latest of the three events listed above).

If you send or deliver your written notice to cancel in some other way, it must be delivered to the above address no later than that time.

In this agreement "you" and "your" refer to the consumer, and "we" and "us" refer to the creditor.

Consumer acknowledges receipt of the completed Truth-in-Lending Notice of Right of Rescission.

____
Consumer's signature
Date:

Notice of Cancellation

I WISH TO CANCEL.

____
Consumer's signature
Date:

Chapter 13

Residential Contracts for Deed

Chapter 13

Residential Contracts for Deed

§ 13.1 Removal from Manual; Use of Contracts for Deed in Texas

The Real Estate Forms Committee has removed the chapter on residential contracts for deed. For decades, these transactions have been subject to legislative scrutiny as reflected by the many amendments to Texas Property Code title 2, chapter 5, subchapter D. The legislative intent behind the amendments was to remedy what were perceived as seller abuses of contracts for deed. For example, a seller might collect a large down payment and then, if the buyer fell behind, use the eviction process to repossess the property as if the buyer were merely a tenant.

Contracts for deed, sometimes referred to as "installment land contracts" or "rent-to-own" financing arrangements, are legal and have been used and litigated in Texas for seller-financed property sales for more than a hundred years. *See Taber v. Dallas Co.*, 106 S.W. 332, 335 (Tex. 1908). As set out below, the risks associated with the use of contracts for deed outweigh their usefulness. This is especially true since a deed, note, and deed of trust can be used to document the transaction and protect the interests of seller and buyer. *See, e.g., Smith v. Davis*, 462 S.W.3d 604 (Tex. App.—Tyler 2015, pet. denied); *Morton v. Nguyen*, 369 S.W.3d 659 (Tex. App.—Houston [14th Dist.] 2012), *rev'd on other grounds, Morton v. Nguyen*, 412 S.W.3d 506 (Tex. 2013).

Texas Property Code title 2, chapter 5, subchapter D, "Executory Contract for Conveyance," sections 5.061 through 5.087, refers to contracts for deed as "executory contracts," which evidence transactions that are incomplete or unfinished in a material respect, namely, the delivery of the deed. This statute applies to "the conveyance of real property used or to be used as the purchaser's residence or as the residence of a person related to the purchaser within the second degree by consanguinity or affinity, as determined under Chapter 573, Government Code." Tex. Prop. Code § 5.062(a). "[A] lot measuring one acre or less is presumed to be residential property." Tex. Prop. Code § 5.062(a)(1). An option to purchase real property that includes a residential lease agreement is considered to be an executory contract for conveyance of real property. *See* Tex. Prop. Code § 5.062(a)(2). In 2005, section 5.0621 was enacted to clarify that this statute and Texas Property Code chapter 92, "Residential Tenancies," apply to the residential lease agreement referenced in Tex. Prop. Code § 5.062(a)(2). *See* Tex. Prop. Code § 5.0621.

The statute sets out specific transactions that are excluded, including transactions where the seller delivers a deed within 180 days or where the purchaser is related to the seller within the second degree by consanguinity or affinity, as determined under chapter 573 of the Government Code. *See* Tex. Prop. Code § 5.062(c), (d).

§ 13.2 Seller's Risks Associated with Contracts for Deed

Texas Property Code title 2, chapter 5, subchapter D, sets out many rules creating burdens and risks for the seller, including the following provisions. A contract for deed must be recorded. *See* Tex. Prop. Code § 5.076. Before a contract for deed is signed by a buyer, a seller must provide the buyer with a survey or plat of a current survey, copies of documents encumbering the title to the property, a statement of the condition of the property as outlined in the statute, a tax certificate and legible copies of any insurance policies, and a written statement setting out the financial terms. *See* Tex. Prop. Code §§ 5.069–.071. A violation of these disclosure requirements is a "false, misleading, or deceptive act or practice within the meaning of Section 17.46, Business & Commerce Code." Tex. Prop. Code § 5.070(b)(1). A contract for deed must contain certain statutory language, or the buyer can rescind the contract at any time and be entitled to a full refund of all sums paid to seller. *See* Tex. Prop. Code § 5.074. A buyer also has a right to convert a contract for deed to a deed, note, and deed of trust. *See* Tex. Prop. Code § 5.081.

A seller must provide a buyer with an annual accounting statement by January 31 including the amount paid and the remaining amount owed under the contract. *See* Tex. Prop. Code § 5.077(a), (b). A seller who conducts only one transaction in a twelve-month period and fails to comply with the annual accounting requirements can be assessed penalties of $100 for each annual accounting statement that is not delivered, plus attorney's fees. *See* Tex. Prop. Code § 5.077(c). A seller who conducts two or more transactions in a twelve-month period and fails to comply with the annual accounting requirements can be assessed penalties of $250 per day for each day after January 31 that the annual accounting statement is not delivered, not to exceed the fair market value of the property, plus reasonable attorney's fees. *See* Tex. Prop. Code § 5.077(d).

There are additional restrictions and prohibitions against selling under an executory contract if there is a mortgage on the property. *See* Tex. Prop. Code § 5.085. A violation of Tex. Prop. Code § 5.085 is a "false, misleading, or deceptive act or practice within the meaning of Section 17.46, Business & Commerce Code." Tex. Prop. Code § 5.085(c)(1).

When a client presents the opportunity to sell or buy real property under an executory contract, all circumstances and alternatives should be considered and evaluated. A client should be provided with not only the statutory requirements applicable to contracts for deed, but also the benefits of structuring the transaction with a deed, note, and deed of trust.

§ 13.3 Additional Resources

McGarvey, Cassie. "Contracts for Deed and Wraparound Mortgages: Navigating High-Risk Financing." In *Real Estate Law 101 Course, 2022*. Austin: State Bar of Texas, 2022.

Orozco, Francisco J., Jr. "Contracts for Deed Strategies and Pitfalls." In *Soaking Up Some CLE Course, 2022*. Austin: State Bar of Texas, 2022.

Chapter 14

Foreclosure Documents

Chapter 14

Foreclosure Documents

§ 14.1 General Considerations for Foreclosure Documents

This chapter summarizes the nonjudicial foreclosure process for real and personal property. The forms in this chapter are drafted specifically for the loan documents in this manual. Foreclosure by a mortgage servicer on behalf of a mortgagee requires a special notice of sale. See form 14-13 in this chapter. The attorney is cautioned that these letters and documents are provided as examples only and should not be used as standard forms. As each foreclosure is unique and requires careful consideration, the attorney must tailor the forms to fit the facts of the case. A complete analysis of Texas foreclosure law is beyond the scope of this manual.

For a thorough discussion of Texas foreclosure law, with additional forms and examples, see William H. Locke, Jr., Ralph Martin Novak, Jr. G. Tommy Bastian & Sara E. Dysart, eds., *Texas Foreclosure Manual*, State Bar of Texas (2023 ed.). See also section 14.12 for related bibliographical material.

§ 14.2 Real Estate Foreclosures

§ 14.2:1 Real Estate Foreclosures Generally

A real property foreclosure must be conducted by a trustee or substitute trustee in strict compliance with Tex. Prop. Code §§ 51.0001, 51.002, 51.0021, 51.0025, 51.0074, 51.0075, 51.009, 51.015 and with any requirements set out in the deed of trust. A trustee or substitute trustee foreclosing on residential real estate should also satisfy any applicable requirements of chapter 22 of the Texas Business and Commerce Code.

The attorney must carefully review all loan documents to determine if additional notices, postings, or procedures apply to the foreclosure. For example, the prior version of the foreclosure statute required posting the foreclosure notice in three public places. That language was incorporated into many old deed-of-trust forms. Even though the law no longer requires these postings, if the deed of trust includes the language, the postings must be made. *Harwath v. Hudson*, 654 S.W.2d 851, 854 (Tex. App.—Dallas 1983, writ ref'd n.r.e.).

Many deed-of-trust forms have a foreclosure section that essentially tracks the language of section 51.002 of the Property Code. Sections 51.0001, 51.0021, 51.0025, 51.0075, and 51.009 regulate foreclosures by mortgage servicers. The deed of trust and security agreement forms in this manual do not repeat the statutory language but instead require the mortgagee or mortgage servicer to foreclose in accordance with the law then in effect.

§ 14.2:2 Statutory Requirements

In Texas, a nonjudicial foreclosure sale must be conducted by a trustee or substitute trustee on the first Tuesday of a month or, if the first Tuesday of the month occurs on January 1 or July 4, on the first Wednesday of the month, in the county in which part or all of the real estate is located. Tex. Prop. Code § 51.002. The sale must take place at the county courthouse in the county in which the property is located unless the commissioner's court designates another public place within a reasonable proximity to the county courthouse. Tex. Prop. Code § 51.002(h). The commissioner's court designation of sales location must be recorded in the real property records of that county, but will not be effective before the ninetieth day after the designation is recorded. Tex. Prop. Code § 51.002(h). A designation by a commissioner's court is not a ground for challenging or invalidating any sale. Tex. Prop. Code § 51.002(h). If the first Tuesday falls on a courthouse holiday in any month other than January or July, the sale may still be conducted. *Koehler v. Pioneer American Insurance Co.*, 425 S.W.2d 889, 891 (Tex. App.—Fort Worth 1968, no writ). The holding in *Koehler* is not applicable to the months of January and July. Tex. Prop. Code § 51.002(a–1). Because deed of trust terms are strictly construed, the holding in *Harwath v. Hudson*, 654 S.W.2d 851 (Tex. App.—Dallas 1983, writ ref'd n.r.e.), should be considered when a deed of trust includes language restricting a foreclosure sale to the first Tuesday of the month if a trustee or substitute trustee intends to conduct a first Wednesday foreclosure sale. If the deed of trust covers property that lies in two or more counties, the notice should provide where the sale is to take place. The notice must be posted in all counties in which the real property is located. Tex. Prop. Code § 51.002(b). If the deed of trust covers multiple properties located in different counties, all properties can be foreclosed in one sale, even if the tracts are not contiguous. *Bateman v. Carter-Jones Drilling Co.*, 290 S.W.2d 366, 370 (Tex. App.—Texarkana 1956, writ ref'd n.r.e.); *Dall v. Lindsey*, 237 S.W.2d 1006, 1009–10 (Tex. App.—Amarillo 1951, writ ref'd n.r.e.); *see also Lewis v. Dainwood*, 130 S.W.2d 456, 457 (Tex. App.—San Antonio 1939, writ ref'd).

Section 51.0001 of the Texas Property Code recognizes the effects of the national Mortgage Electronic Registration System and the securitization of mortgages. This section added definitions of "book entry system," "debtor's last known address," "mortgage servicer," "mortgagee," "mortgagor," "security instrument," "substitute trustee," and "trustee."

Section 51.002(b) of the Property Code has three requirements for a foreclosure sale: (1) the mortgage servicer must give written notice of the sale to all debtors obligated to pay the debt, (2) the notice of the sale must be posted at the county courthouse of each county in which the property is located designating the county in which the property will be sold, and (3) a notice of the sale must be filed with the county clerk of each county in which the property is located. These steps must be completed at least twenty-one days before the sale date. Tex. Prop. Code § 51.002(b). However, if the courthouse or county clerk's office is closed because of inclement weather, natural disaster, or other act of God, the notices required by section 51.002(b) may be posted or filed up to forty-eight hours after the courthouse or county clerk's office reopens for business. Tex. Prop. Code § 51.002(b–1).

Additionally, the Property Code requires the mortgage servicer to give at least twenty days' notice of default before posting the property for foreclosure if the property is the debtor's residence. Tex. Prop. Code § 51.002(d).

Property Code section 51.002 requires the mortgage servicer to serve written notice of the sale on "each debtor who, according to the records of the mortgage servicer of the debt, is obligated to pay the debt." *See* Tex. Prop. Code § 51.002(b)(3). Although a guarantor has been held not to be such a debtor, many attorneys elect to send a notice of the foreclosure sale to a guarantor in the same manner as sent to the debtor. *See Long v. NCNB—Texas National Bank*, 882 S.W.2d 861, 866 (Tex. App.—Corpus Christi–Edinburg 1994, no writ; *Bishop v. National Loan Investors, L.P.*, 915 S.W.2d 241, 245 (Tex. App.—Fort Worth 1995, writ denied).

The notice must designate the county in which the property will be sold. Tex. Prop. Code § 51.002(b)(1). If no area has been designated for foreclosure sales by the county commissioner's court, the notice of sale must designate the area where the sale is to take place. Tex. Prop. Code § 51.002(a). The notice of sale also must state the earliest time at which the sale will begin and the names and street addresses for the trustees or substitute trustees. Tex. Prop. Code §§ 51.002(b), 51.0075(e). The notice must also include conspicuous language regarding the rights of members of the armed forces. Tex. Prop. Code § 51.002(i). Beyond these requirements (and the disclosure required if a mortgage servicer is administering the foreclosure sale on behalf of the mortgagee that is discussed below in this section) there is little statutory or judicial guidance concerning the content of the notice.

The sale must take place between the hours of 10:00 A.M. and 4:00 P.M. on the first Tuesday of a month or, if the first Tuesday of the month occurs on January 1 or July 4, on the first Wednesday of the month. The sale must begin at the time stated in the notice of sale or not later than three hours after the time listed in the notice of sale. Tex. Prop. Code § 51.002(a), (c); Tex. Civ. Prac. & Rem. Code § 34.041.

The sale must be a public auction with the trustee announcing the property to those gathered at the courthouse and offering the property for sale to the highest bidder for cash. Often the mortgagee is the only bidder. Section 51.0075(f) of the Property Code allows the foreclosure purchaser and the trustee or substitute trustee to agree on a reasonable time after acceptance of the bid within which to deliver the purchase price; otherwise, the purchase price is payable without delay after acceptance of the bid. Most trustees will accept, and some may prefer, the cash bid in the form of a cashier's check or a certified check.

A mortgage servicer may administer a foreclosure for a mortgagee if two requirements are met. First, there must be an agreement between the mortgagee and mortgage servicer granting the mortgage servicer the right to service the mortgage. Second, the notice of sale must disclose that the mortgage servicer is representing the mortgagee servicing agreement, the name of the mortgagee, and the address of the mortgagee or the mortgage servicer authorized to service the mortgage. Tex. Prop. Code § 51.0025. Trustees or substitute trustees can set reasonable conditions for conducting the public sale if the conditions are announced before the bidding is opened for the first sale of the day held by the trustee or substitute trustee. Tex. Prop. Code § 51.0075(a). A purchaser at the foreclosure sale acquires the property "AS IS" without any express or implied warranties except warranties of title from the mortgagor. *Sandel v. Burney*, 714 S.W.2d 40 (Tex. App.—San Antonio 1986, no writ). The purchase is made at the purchaser's own risk. Tex. Prop. Code § 51.009(1). A purchaser at foreclosure is not a consumer. Tex. Prop. Code § 51.009(2).

§ 14.2:3 Suit for Deficiency—Real Property

A person liable on the debt, including a guarantor, may introduce evidence of the fair market value of the property as of the date of the foreclosure sale. Tex. Prop. Code §§ 51.003, 51.005. The attorney should discuss these rights with the mortgagee-client before foreclosure to decide if a deficiency is likely and if so whether it would be prudent to obtain an appraisal to document fair market value and if a judicial foreclosure is a better alternative.

The rights granted to an obligor, including a guarantor, in sections 51.003 and 51.005 may be waived. *See LaSalle Bank N.A. v. Sleutel*, 289 F.3d 837, 841–42 (5th Cir. 2002); *Segal v. Emmes Capital, L.L.C.*, 155 S.W.3d 267, 279–

80 (Tex. App.—Houston [1st Dist.] 2004, pet. dismissed).

§ 14.2:4 Residential Property

If the property is used as the borrower's residence, the mortgagee or mortgage servicer must allow the borrower at least twenty days to cure the default before accelerating the maturity of the debt and giving the twenty-one-day foreclosure notice. Tex. Prop. Code § 51.002(d). The delinquent payment of ad valorem taxes may not be considered a default under a deed of trust or other contract lien if the owner of the residence has entered into an installment agreement for the payment of such taxes under section 33.02 of the Texas Tax Code. Tex. Prop. Code § 51.0011.

A trustee or substitute trustee conducting a residential real property foreclosure may contract with an attorney to advise the trustee or substitute trustee and to administer or perform any of the trustee's or substitute trustee's functions or responsibilities under the deed of trust and chapter 51 of the Texas Property Code. Tex. Bus. & Com. Code § 22.003. The trustee or substitute trustee may also contract with an auction company to arrange, manage, sponsor, or advertise a residential real property foreclosure sale. Tex. Bus. & Com. Code § 22.003.

For residential real property foreclosures, a trustee or substitute trustee must also satisfy any applicable requirements of sections 22.004, 22.005, and 22.006 of the Texas Business and Commerce Code. If the successful bidder is not the mortgagee or the mortgage servicer, the trustee or substitute trustee must obtain the name, address, and other required information on certain parties submitting the highest and best bid. Tex. Bus. & Com. Code § 22.004. The trustee or substitute trustee must also provide the winning bidder a receipt for the sale proceeds tendered, deliver or record the deed, and account for and distribute the sale proceeds, including maintaining the sale proceeds in a separate account, and maintaining a written record of all deposits and disbursements from the account. Tex. Bus. & Com. Code §§ 22.005, 22.006.

A trustee or substitute trustee conducting a residential real property foreclosure may recover (1) the trustee's or substitute trustee's reasonable actual costs, (2) reasonable attorney's fees incurred by the trustee or substitute trustee, (3) reasonable trustee's or substitute trustee's fees, and (4) the trustee's or substitute trustee's reasonable attorney's fees in a suit based on a claim related to the sale if the suit is found to be groundless, in each instance payable from the sale proceeds in excess of the amount owed on the indebtedness secured by the residential real property. Tex. Bus. & Com. Code § 22.006. Certain trustee's or substitute trustee's fees and expenses in a residential real property foreclosure are presumed to be reasonable if they do not exceed the amounts provided by law. Tex. Bus. & Com. Code § 22.006.

§ 14.2:5 Federal Interests

If the federal government has a property interest that would be extinguished through foreclosure, including a security interest, lien, or mortgage, the government's consent may be required to eliminate that interest; the government has a one-year right of redemption for certain liens eliminated by foreclosure of a superior lien without its consent. 12 U.S.C. § 1825(b)(2); 28 U.S.C. § 2410(c).

Before foreclosure, the federal tax lien records of the county in which the real property is located should be examined. If personal property secures the loan, the federal tax lien records of the secretary of state's office or other appropriate office should also be examined. *See* 26 U.S.C. § 6323(f)(1)(A). If the property is encumbered by an inferior federal tax lien filed more than thirty days before the scheduled foreclosure sale, the mortgagee or mortgage servicer must give a special notice to the Internal Revenue Service at least twenty-five days in advance of the sale. *See* 26 U.S.C. § 7425(b), (c). The Internal Revenue Code provides that unless a proper notice is given, a foreclosure sale will not affect the subordinate tax lien. In the case of real property, the IRS has a 120-day right of redemption following the sale, provided a proper notice was given. 26 U.S.C. § 7425(d).

§ 14.2:6 Beachfront Property

If the property is located seaward of the Gulf Intracoastal Waterway, as defined in Tex. Nat. Res. Code § 61.025, the purchaser should receive the statutory notice specified by that section. *See* Tex. Att'y Gen. Op. No. JM-834 (1987). See also section 2.43 in this manual.

§ 14.2:7 Personal Property Included in Deed of Trust

If the deed of trust includes a security agreement for personal property, the real property foreclosure sale can include the personal property in which a security interest is granted in the deed of trust as part of the foreclosure. *See* Tex. Bus. & Com. Code § 9.604(a). If personal property is sold in connection with the foreclosure sale of real property, the commercially reasonable standard of the Texas Business and Commerce Code does not govern the sale. *Huddleston v. TCB-Dallas*, 756 S.W.2d 343 (Tex. App.—Dallas 1988, writ denied).

§ 14.2:8 Deed in Lieu of Foreclosure

The Supreme Court of Texas has ruled that there is no such thing as a "deed in lieu of foreclosure." *Flag-Redfern Oil Co. v. Humble Exploration Co.*, 744 S.W.2d 6, 8 (Tex. 1987). The supreme court held that a deed in lieu of foreclosure is merely a conveyance by the borrower as a payment for the debt and that, because the deed does not have the effect of a lien foreclosure, the deed does not extinguish any subordinate liens. Deeds in lieu of foreclosure are, however, recognized by statute in Texas. Tex. Prop. Code § 51.006. A creditor who accepts a deed in lieu of foreclosure may void that deed within four years of accepting it if the debtor fails to disclose a lien before executing the deed and the creditor has no personal knowledge of the undisclosed lien. Tex. Prop. Code § 51.006(b). Some borrowers prefer to execute a deed in lieu of foreclosure to avoid the publicity associated with a public foreclosure. Before advising a client about a deed-in-lieu transaction, the attorney should review the law on this subject. See the articles listed in section 14.12 below. For an example of a deed in lieu of foreclosure, see form 5-13 in this manual.

§ 14.2:9 Home Equity Loan Lien Foreclosure

Tex. Const. art. XVI, § 50(a)(6), authorizes a voluntary lien on a Texas homestead for a home equity loan. (See chapter 11 in this manual for a discussion of home equity loans.) A lien on a Texas homestead securing the payment of a home equity loan may be foreclosed only by court order. Tex. Const. art. XVI, § 50(a)(6)(D). Article XVI, section 50(r), directs the Texas Supreme Court to promulgate rules of civil procedure for an expedited court order, and, acting pursuant to that authority, the Texas Supreme Court adopted rules 735 and 736 of the Texas Rules of Civil Procedure. The court approved forms for expedited foreclosure proceedings on February 10, 2014 (Misc. Docket No. 14-9047, Feb. 10, 2014). The forms may be found at **www.txcourts.gov/media/847145/expedited-foreclosure-forms-for-website.pdf**. Although rules 735 and 736 do require a judicial order before proceeding with the foreclosure of a home equity loan lien, those rules do not otherwise change existing Texas real property foreclosure law. *See* Tex. R. Civ. P. 735.2. The right of a lender to foreclose a home equity loan lien therefore remains conditioned on an underlying default on the home equity loan. (See forms

14-31 and 14-32 in this chapter for a notice of default and notice of acceleration letters on a home equity loan.)

Rules 735 and 736 were substantially amended effective January 1, 2012.

Rule 736 provides the procedure for obtaining a court order to allow foreclosure of a lien containing a power of sale in a security instrument securing a home equity loan. Tex. R. Civ. P. 735.1. Forms 14-33 through 14-38 are some of the forms promulgated by the supreme court. In addition, the practitioner should review section 14.4:5 below for additional information on consumer debt collection activities.

Rule 736 establishes an expedited judicial procedure for obtaining a court order that allows a lender to proceed with the foreclosure of a home equity loan lien. Under the rule, a lender files an application (see form 14-33) in any court with appropriate jurisdiction in any county where all or any part of the real property is located, including probate courts. Tex. R. Civ. P. 736.1(a). The required contents of the application were changed when the rule was amended and are set out in detail in Tex. R. Civ. P. 736.1(d).

The process for service of a rule 736 application changed effective January 1, 2012. Under the previous rule, the applicant or applicant's attorney mailed the application to the obligor and obligor's attorney. The new rule requires the clerk of the court to prepare and serve a citation by both certified and regular mail for each respondent named in the application. A citation addressed to "the occupant of the property" must also be issued. Tex. R. Civ. P. 736.3(a), (b). Other requirements for service by the clerk of the court may be found in Tex. R. Civ. P. 736.3.

A response to an application for a court order permitting the lender to proceed with the foreclosure of a home equity loan lien is due on the first Monday following the expiration of thirty-eight days from the date the citation was placed in the custody of the United States Postal Service. Tex. R. Civ. P. 736.5(b).

The response must be signed in accordance with rule 57 and may be in the form of a general denial under rule 92, except that the respondent must affirmatively plead the defenses relied on as set out in rule 736.5(c)(1)–(5). Tex. R. Civ. P. 736.5(c). The response may not state an independent claim for relief, and the court is required to strike any such claim without a hearing. Tex. R. Civ. P. 736.5(d).

The court must not conduct a hearing unless a response is filed. Tex. R. Civ. P. 736.6.

No discovery is permitted in a proceeding governed by rule 736, and the only issue to be determined is whether a party may obtain an order to proceed with foreclosure under applicable law and the terms of the loan agreement, contract, or lien sought to be foreclosed. Tex. R. Civ. P. 735.2, 736.4.

An order under rule 736 is without prejudice and has no res judicata, collateral estoppel, estoppel by judgment, or other effect in any other judicial proceeding. Tex. R. Civ. P. 736.9.

If no response to the application is filed by the due date, the petitioner may file a motion and proposed order to obtain a default order. A default order must be granted by the court no later than thirty days after a motion is filed and served in accordance with the rules. The return of service must be on file with the clerk of the court for at least ten days before the court may grant the application. Tex. R. Civ. P. 736.7. The granting or denial of the application is not an appealable order. Tex. R. Civ. P. 736.8(c).

An order (see form 14-38) granting an application that allows a lender to proceed with foreclosure of a home equity loan lien must describe—

1. the material facts establishing the basis for foreclosure,
2. the property to be foreclosed by commonly known mailing address and legal description,
3. the name and last known address of each respondent subject to the order, and
4. the recording or indexing information of each lien to be foreclosed.

Tex. R. Civ. P. 736.8(b).

A proceeding under rule 736 is automatically stayed if a respondent files a separate, original proceeding in a court of competent jurisdiction that puts in issue any matter relating to the foreclosure before 5:00 P.M. on the Monday before the scheduled foreclosure sale. Tex. R. Civ. P. 736.11(a). A stayed proceeding is to be dismissed if no order has been granted. If an order has been signed, the court must vacate the rule 736 order. Tex. R. Civ. P. 736.11(c).

§ 14.2:10 Property Owned by Military Servicemember

Property Code section 51.015 (1) prohibits any nonjudicial foreclosure of a dwelling owned by military personnel on active duty or within nine months after their active duty concludes; (2) provides that a court may, during the same active duty period and the nine months subsequent, either (a) stay a proceeding to judicially foreclose or enforce a mortgage lien or (b) modify the terms of any such mortgage, as necessary to preserve the interests of the parties; (3) authorizes the court to also issue similar orders of stay or take other actions to protect dependents of active duty personnel and third-party guarantors of the loan obligation; and (4) imposes a criminal penalty (class A misdemeanor) on any person who knowingly causes a foreclosure or seizure of property protected as set forth above. A borrower or guarantor may voluntarily waive these protections by written agreement contained in an instrument separate from the loan obligation. Tex. Prop. Code § 51.015. Property Code section 51.015 includes many of the same protections for military servicemembers as does the federal Servicemember's Civil Relief Act.

§ 14.3 Personal Property Foreclosures

The foreclosure rules for personal property secured transactions are found at Tex. Bus. & Com. Code §§ 9.601–.628. There are four ways to foreclose a security interest in personal property collateral: as part of a real property foreclosure; by public disposition; by private disposition; and through strict foreclosure, accepting the property with or without a claim for a deficiency. Without foreclosing, a secured party may also collect amounts owed on collateral and enforce obligations of persons obligated on collateral.

A detailed discussion of the rules of personal property foreclosure is beyond the scope of this manual. Attorneys are encouraged to review the relevant provisions of chapter 9 of the Texas Business and Commerce Code and applicable case law before foreclosing a security interest in personal property.

A disposition of personal property collateral must be commercially reasonable, whether the disposition is public or private. Tex. Bus. & Com. Code § 9.610(b). This requirement cannot be waived or varied. Tex. Bus. & Com. Code § 9.602(7). The term *commercially reasonable* is a term of art, the meaning of which has been heavily litigated. The attorney should review the relevant case law on the particular type of personal property being disposed of to properly advise the client. Section 9.627 of the Code also gives guidelines for determining if conduct was commercially reasonable. Tex. Bus. & Com. Code § 9.627.

§ 14.3:1 Real Estate Foreclosure

If the security agreement covers both real and personal property, the secured party may elect to foreclose both under the real property laws. In that event, chapter 9 rules do not apply. Tex. Bus. & Com. Code § 9.604(a). For a discussion of the real property foreclosure rules, see section 14.2 above.

§ 14.3:2 Public Disposition vs. Private Disposition

The law of public and private foreclosure disposition of personal property collateral is found at Tex. Bus. & Com. Code §§ 9.610–.619, 9.623–.628. A disposition includes a sale, lease, or license of personal property collateral. A public disposition is not defined in the Texas Uniform Commercial Code. The official comment to section 9.610 states that although "public disposition" is not defined, it is one at which the price is determined after the public has had a meaningful opportunity for competitive bidding. In other words, a "public disposition" is a disposition at an auction open to the public. "Meaningful opportunity" is meant to imply that some form of advertisement or public notice must precede the sale (or other disposition) and that the public must have access to the sale or disposition. Tex. Bus. & Com. Code § 9.610 cmt. 7.

Conversely, although a private disposition also is not defined in the Texas UCC, some commentators believe that a "private disposition" is any disposition that is not a "public disposition."

A public-sale foreclosure or other public disposition of personal property collateral is more difficult for the secured party because every aspect of the disposition must be commercially reasonable. Tex. Bus. & Com. Code § 9.610(b). Unlike a real estate foreclosure, for which a courthouse public auction is authorized, a public auction disposition of personal property collateral is appropriate only if that method of disposition is commercially reasonable for the collateral involved. With the existence of Internet auction sites, many types of personal property are sold at an Internet public auction. However, there may be some types of personal property for which a public auction disposition is not commercially reasonable. The manner of disposition must be commercially reasonable. A public auction disposition must be conducted fairly. Adequate advertising should precede the disposition to solicit potential bidders. Merely advertising in a local newspaper may not be "commercially reasonable," particularly if a potential buyer for the property would ordinarily look elsewhere for advertisements offering that type of property for sale. The time and place of the public auction must be commercially reasonable. If there is a usual place or market for a public auction disposition of property of the type involved that is reasonably available, the collateral should be disposed of there. Tex. Bus. & Com. Code § 2.706(d)(2). "[I]f such 'usual' place or market is not reasonably available, a duly advertised public [disposition] may be held at another place if it is one which prospective bidders may reasonably be expected to attend, as distinguished from a place where there is no demand whatsoever for [property] of the kind." Tex. Bus. & Com. Code § 2.706 cmt. 9. The collateral should be available for reasonable inspection by prospective bidders, either at the public auction disposition or at another place made known to the bidders. Tex. Bus. & Com. Code § 2.706(d)(3). In a transaction, other than a consumer transaction, if a secured party's compliance with the provisions of chapter 9 is placed in issue, the secured party has the burden of establishing that its collection, enforcement, or disposition of the collateral complied with the statutory requirements. Tex. Bus. & Com. Code § 9.626(a)(2). A secured party should consider how it will establish that all aspects of its public auction disposition of collateral meet the commercially reasonable requirement before deciding to proceed in that manner. A secured party may elect to conduct a private disposition. A private disposition may offer lower transaction costs to the secured party. A private disposition must be an arm's-length transaction.

There are two primary distinctions between a public disposition and a private disposition of personal property collateral. First, the secured party may purchase the collateral at a public disposition but generally may not do so at a private disposition. Tex. Bus. & Com. Code § 9.610(c). Second, the debtor is entitled to notification of "the time and place" of a public disposition but is merely entitled to notification of "the time after which" a private disposition is to be made. Tex. Bus. & Com. Code § 9.613(1)(E).

§ 14.3:3 Rules for Foreclosure

The property may be sold or otherwise disposed of as a unit or in parcels and at any time and place and on any terms. Tex. Bus. & Com. Code § 9.610(b). However, every aspect of the disposition must be commercially reasonable. Tex. Bus. & Com. Code § 9.610(b). The obligation of the secured party to proceed in a commercially reasonable manner may not be waived by the debtor. Tex. Bus. & Com. Code § 9.602(7).

Except as described below, the secured party must send a proper notification of disposition of collateral to the debtor and to any secondary obligor. Additionally, if the collateral is other than consumer goods, notice must be sent to any other person from whom the secured party has received, before the notification date, notification of a claim of an interest in the collateral and to any other secured party that has filed a financing statement that meets the requirements set out in section 9.611(c)(3)(B) or that has complied with certificate of title or other title registration laws. Tex. Bus. & Com. Code § 9.611(c). Thus, for a disposition of collateral other than consumer goods, the foreclosing secured party has the duty of conducting a Uniform Commercial Code financing statement search to discover other potential secured parties and to notify any that are discovered. The attorney advising the secured party should carefully review section 9.611 and its comments to determine the filing offices to search and the period within which the search should be conducted. In a transaction other than a consumer transaction, a proper notification sent after default and ten or more days before the earliest time of disposition is deemed to be reasonable. Tex. Bus. & Com. Code § 9.612(b). The secured party need not give notice of disposition of the collateral if the property is perishable, threatens to decline speedily in value, or sells on a recognized market (such as a publicly listed stock). Tex. Bus. & Com. Code § 9.611(d). The debtor or a secondary obligor may waive its rights, but not the rights of other parties, to receive a notice of disposition of collateral by written waiver signed after default. Tex. Bus. & Com. Code § 9.624.

The contents of a proper notice of disposition of collateral are set forth in section 9.613 for collateral other than consumer goods and in section 9.614 for consumer goods collateral. Those sections also include model forms, which when completed are deemed to provide sufficient information concerning the disposition. The debtor may not waive, or agree that the secured party may vary from, the notification requirements of those sections. *See* Tex. Bus. & Com. Code § 9.602(7). Notices to consumers must also comply with the federal Fair Debt Collection Practices Act (15 U.S.C. §§ 1692–1692p) and the Texas Debt Collection Act (Tex. Fin. Code §§ 392.001–.404).

The secured party may buy personal property collateral at a public disposition. Tex. Bus. & Com. Code § 9.610(c)(1). The secured party may buy personal property collateral at a private disposition only if the property is of a kind that is customarily sold on a recognized market or is the subject of widely distributed standard price quotations. Tex. Bus. & Com. Code § 9.610(c)(2).

If a foreclosing secured party does not comply with section 9.601 *et seq.*, a court may order or restrain collection, enforcement, or disposition of collateral on appropriate terms and conditions. Tex. Bus. & Com. Code § 9.625(a). This section also sets out the damages for which a secured party may be liable, including minimum penalties in consumer transactions and nonconsumer transactions. *See* Tex. Bus. & Com. Code § 9.625(b)–(g).

A contract for sale, lease, license, or other disposition of personal property as a result of a foreclosure includes the warranties relating to title, possession, quiet enjoyment, and the like that by operation of law accompany a voluntary disposition of like-kind property. Tex. Bus. & Com. Code § 9.610(d). These warranties may be disclaimed or modified. The manner and the approved language for disclaiming or modifying warranties are set out in Tex. Bus. & Com. Code § 9.610(e), (f).

§ 14.3:4 Strict Foreclosure

The law of strict foreclosure is found at Tex. Bus. & Com. Code §§ 9.620–.622. The secured party may accept personal property collateral in full or partial satisfaction of the secured obligation only under the circumstances set forth in section 9.620. A secured party may not accept collateral in partial satisfaction of a secured obligation in a consumer transaction. Tex. Bus. & Com. Code § 9.620(g).

A secured party that wants to accept personal property collateral in full or partial satisfaction of a secured obligation in a nonconsumer transaction must obtain the debtor's consent. The secured party must send its proposal to do so to any person from whom the secured party has received, before the debtor consented to the acceptance, a notice of a claim of interest in the collateral and to any other secured party or lienholder that has a perfected security interest in the collateral either because of a filed financing statement that meets the requirements of section 9.621(a)(2) or because of compliance with certificate of title or other title registration laws. Tex. Bus. & Com. Code § 9.621(a). If the secured party proposes to accept the collateral in partial satisfaction of the secured obligation, the secured party must also notify any secondary obligor. Tex. Bus. & Com. Code § 9.621(b). A secured party that proposes to accept personal property collateral in full or partial satisfaction of a secured obligation thus has a duty to conduct a UCC financing statement search to discover other potential secured parties and to notify those that have filed a proper financing statement of the secured party's proposal. Moreover, a secured party that accepts personal property collateral is liable to another secured party that should have been notified, but was not, for any loss resulting from the failure of the enforcing secured party to notify the other secured party. Tex. Bus. & Com. Code § 9.625(b). The debtor may consent to the acceptance of collateral in partial satisfaction of the secured obligation only by a record authenticated after default. The debtor may consent to acceptance of collateral in full satisfaction of the secured obligation by authenticating a record (for example, signing a writing) after default or by failing to object to a properly sent proposal within twenty days after the proposal is sent. Tex. Bus. & Com. Code § 9.620(c)(2).

The secured party may not use strict foreclosure if—

1. the debtor does not consent (Tex. Bus. & Com. Code § 9.620(a)(1));
2. the secured party timely receives objection in writing from a party entitled to notice of the proposed strict foreclosure (Tex. Bus. & Com. Code § 9.620(a)(2));
3. the secured party is foreclosing a security interest in consumer goods and the debtor is in possession of the goods

(Tex. Bus. & Com. Code § 9.620(a)(3));

4. the secured party is foreclosing a security interest in consumer goods and the debtor has paid more than 60 percent of the principal amount of the obligation (Tex. Bus. & Com. Code § 9.620(e)); or

5. in a consumer transaction, the secured party does not propose to satisfy the secured obligation in full (Tex. Bus. & Com. Code § 9.620(g)).

After default, the debtor may waive or modify limitations 1., 3., and 4. by an authenticated agreement. Tex. Bus. & Com. Code §§ 9.620(a)(4), 9.624(b).

§ 14.3:5 Suit for Deficiency—Personal Property

The procedure for determining a deficiency or surplus is found in Tex. Bus. & Com. Code §§ 9.615, 9.626.

In a consumer goods transaction in which either the debtor is entitled to a surplus or a consumer obligor is liable for a deficiency, the secured party must send a written explanation of the surplus or deficiency. If a surplus exists, the secured party must send an explanation of the surplus before or when the secured party accounts to the debtor and pays any surplus or within fourteen days of the debtor's request for an explanation, whichever comes first. If a deficiency exists, the secured party must send an explanation of the deficiency when the secured party first makes written demand for the deficiency or within fourteen days of the debtor's request for an explanation, whichever comes first. Tex. Bus. & Com. Code § 9.616(b). A debtor or consumer obligor is entitled without charge to one response to a request for an explanation of the surplus or deficiency during any six-month period in which the secured party does not send one. The secured party may require payment of a charge not exceeding $25 for each additional response. Tex. Bus. & Com. Code § 9.616(e).

The rules for an action to collect a deficiency other than in a consumer transaction are set forth in section 9.626. This section provides for the determination of the deficiency when the secured party fails to comply with the procedures set forth in section 9.601 *et seq.* Under this section, the liability of a debtor or a secondary obligor for a deficiency is limited to an amount by which the sum of the secured obligation, expenses, and attorney's fees exceeds the greater of the proceeds the secured party realized or the amount the proceeds would have been if the secured party had proceeded in compliance with those provisions. Tex. Bus. & Com. Code § 9.626(a). A court may not infer from section 9.626 the nature of the proper rule in consumer transactions and may continue to apply existing principles. Tex. Bus. & Com. Code § 9.626(b). *See Greathouse v. Charter National Bank—Southwest*, 851 S.W.2d 173 (Tex. 1992); *Tanenbaum v. Economics Laboratory, Inc.*, 628 S.W.2d 769 (Tex. 1982).

§ 14.3:6 Cautions

The lender's rights are governed by subchapter F of article 9 of the Uniform Commercial Code (Tex. Bus. & Com. Code §§ 9.601–.628) and the security agreement. Certain provisions, noted in Tex. Bus. & Com. Code § 9.602, cannot be altered by the parties. Before exercising any contractual right under the security agreement, the attorney should review these subchapters.

§ 14.3:7 Secured Party's Collection Rights—Accounts, Intangibles, and Instruments

After default, or earlier if agreed, the secured party may notify an account debtor or other person obligated on collateral, such as the maker of a Business and Commerce Code chapter 3 negotiable instrument, to make payment or otherwise render performance directly to the secured party. Tex. Bus. & Com. Code § 9.607(a). This remedy may enhance the secured party's recovery because payments on the collateral would otherwise be paid to the debtor. This procedure requires no prior notice to the debtor. *Cullen Frost Bank v. Dallas Sportswear Co.*, 730 S.W.2d 668, 669–70 (Tex. 1987). If a debtor or secondary obligor will be liable for a deficiency, a secured party must proceed in a commercially reasonable manner in collecting or enforcing the obligation of an account debtor or other person obligated on collateral. Tex. Bus. & Com. Code § 9.607(c).

§ 14.3:8 Right of Possession

After default, unless otherwise agreed, the secured party may take possession of tangible personal property collateral. Tex. Bus. & Com. Code § 9.609. The repossession must not breach the peace. This nonjudicial self-help remedy is useful in allowing the secured party to obtain possession without delay.

§ 14.3:9 Right of Redemption

A debtor, any secondary obligor, or any junior secured party or lienholder may redeem the collateral from the secured party at any time before (1) the secured party has collected the collateral under section 9.607, (2) the secured party has disposed of the collateral or entered into a contract to dispose of the collateral under section 9.610; or (3) the secured party has accepted the collateral in full or partial satisfaction of the obligation under section 9.622. *See* Tex. Bus. & Com. Code §§ 9.607, 9.610, 9.622. To redeem the collateral, a person must fulfill all obligations secured by the collateral and pay certain expenses and attorney's fees. Tex. Bus. & Com. Code § 9.623(b).

§ 14.3:10 Secured Party's Liability

If a secured party has not complied with section 9.601 *et seq.*, a court may order or restrain collection, enforcement, or disposition of collateral. Tex. Bus. & Com. Code § 9.625(a). Further, a secured party is liable for damages in the amount of any loss caused by a failure to comply with Texas Business and Commerce Code chapter 9. Tex. Bus. & Com. Code § 9.625(b). In addition, certain violations of chapter 9 render a noncomplying secured party liable for statutory minimum penalties. Tex. Bus. & Com. Code § 9.625(e), (f).

Chapter 9 requires the secured party's collection and enforcement rights to be exercised in a commercially reasonable manner. Evidence that a better price could have been obtained under a different foreclosure proceeding does not of itself establish that the sale was commercially unreasonable. A sale under judicial approval is deemed to be commercially reasonable, but the UCC does not require a secured party to seek such approval. *See* Tex. Bus. & Com. Code § 9.627.

§ 14.4 Foreclosure Documents

§ 14.4:1 Foreclosure Documents Applicable to Real Property and Personal Property

The appropriate forms to use in any foreclosure depend on the facts of the specific situation. The forms in this chapter are examples of foreclosure documents to be used with the forms in this manual, without modification of their principal terms. Use of modified State Bar forms or other forms could significantly change the foreclosure document requirements.

Sections 14.4:2 through 14.10 below provide a chronological analysis of the foreclosure process and references to forms for compliance.

§ 14.4:2 Document Review

The attorney should review with the client all the loan documents for the transaction. In transactions that cover long time periods, there may be modification agreements that would affect the foreclosure process. For example, a subordinate creditor may have obtained an agreement from the first secured creditor to receive a special notice of default or foreclosure. The attorney should verify with the client that no such agreements exist.

§ 14.4:3 Statute of Limitations

The attorney should confirm that the statute of limitations has not barred any right to relief. A sale of real property under a power of sale contained in a deed of trust must be made not later than four years after the day the cause of action accrues. Tex. Civ. Prac. & Rem. Code § 16.035(b). However, a mortgage servicer may foreclose a security interest in personal property collateral notwithstanding that there is a limitations defense to the debt. *Miller, Hiersche, Martens & Hayward, P.C. v. Bent Tree National Bank*, 894 S.W.2d 828, 830 (Tex. App.—Dallas 1995, no writ).

§ 14.4:4 Current Title, Abstract, and Tax Searches

The attorney should verify current information about the collateral and its ownership. Because tax liens are accorded priority over most other claims, the client must know the amounts of any delinquent taxes to be able to decide if the foreclosure is economically feasible. *See* Tex. Tax Code § 32.05.

The attorney should advise the client that title insurance coverage may be available. The limited preforeclosure policy (form T-98) is issued in connection with a mortgage in default to the named mortgagee or its assignee, a loan servicer, a trustee, or an attorney and insures as to matters recorded since the mortgage, including involuntary liens such as federal tax liens. See Procedural Rule P-43, *Basic Manual of Rules, Rates and Forms for the Writing of Title Insurance in the State of Texas*, available at **www.tdi.texas.gov/title/titlem4g.html#P-43**.

§ 14.4:5 Consumer Transactions

Fair Debt Collection Practices Act Notice: The forms in this chapter are drafted for use in nonconsumer transactions, to which federal and state fair debt collection acts do not apply. The Texas Property Code provides that a trustee or a substitute trustee is not a debt collector under Texas law. Tex. Prop. Code § 51.0075(b). If, however, the attorney wishes to try to adapt these forms for a consumer transaction, the notice contained in clause 14-7-1 in this chapter should be incorporated in the first correspondence the attorney has with the consumer. Additional modifications to the forms also may be required. Case law is unclear, and there is no Fifth Circuit authority on what additional collection efforts, if any, may be made during the thirty-day period during which the consumer may request debt verification. Nothing may be included with the notice that negates the notice or would lead an unsophisticated person to misunderstand the right to contest the debt. *Chauncey v. JDR Recovery Corp.*, 118 F.3d 516, 519 (7th Cir. 1997) (demand that payment be received within thirty days or "a decision to pursue other avenues to collect the amount due will be made" found to contradict notice); *Terran v. Kaplan*, 109 F.3d 1428, 1434 (9th Cir. 1997) (statement that "[u]nless an immediate telephone call is made . . . we may find it necessary to recommend to our client that they proceed with legal action" held not a demand for payment and thus not contradictory or overshadowing). The safest course of action would be to send only the notice found in clause 14-7-1 and wait thirty days before making any other collection efforts. The attorney, as a debt collector under the federal and state acts, can be personally liable to the consumer for failure to comply with the acts and should review this area of the law with care. See section 2.96 in this manual and the materials in section 14.12 below.

Fair Credit Reporting Act: Any financial institution that extends credit to an individual and regularly and in the ordinary course of business reports negative information to a credit bureau must give its individual customers a clear and conspicuous written notice about reporting negative information. A financial institution complies with the notice requirement if the institution uses a model notice promulgated by the Board of Governors of the Federal Reserve System. There are two model notices, one that may be used before reporting negative information to a credit bureau and one that may be used after reporting negative information to a credit bureau. If the financial institution did not include the notice in its initial loan documentation or related communication, the notice should be given with the first correspondence concerning the foreclosure. 15 U.S.C. § 1681s–2(a)(7); 12 C.F.R. pt. 222. The model forms of notice are found in clauses 14-7-2 and 14-7-3 in this chapter. See section 2.95 in this manual.

§ 14.5 Notices

All foreclosure notices must be sent by certified mail and should be sent return receipt requested. For real estate foreclosures, the notice must be addressed to the debtor at the debtor's last known address. Tex. Prop. Code § 51.002(e). For personal property foreclosures, the notice should be sent to the address specified in the security agreement or other agreement or, if none, to any address reasonable under the circumstances. Tex. Bus. & Com. Code § 1.201(b)(36). For foreclosure of a debt secured by a debtor's residence there is a presumption that the residential address is to be used for notice unless the debtor notifies the mortgage servicer otherwise. Tex. Prop. Code § 51.0001(2)(A). For all other debts the notices are sent to the last known address of the debtor as shown by the records of the mortgage servicer. Tex. Prop. Code § 51.0001(2)(B). If there is doubt about the proper address, it is good practice to send the notice to each address in the file. If two borrowers reside at the same address, the attorney may wish to send the letter separately to each person at the address. Some attorneys also send a copy of the letter to each party by first-class mail to attempt actual delivery if the certified mail is not accepted by the borrower. That attempt should be noted on the letter.

The mortgage servicer must give at least twenty days' notice of default before posting the property for foreclosure if the property is the debtor's residence. Tex. Prop. Code § 51.002(d). See the notice of default and intent to accelerate, form 14-4 in this chapter.

A debtor is required to inform the mortgage servicer of any change of address of the debtor. Tex. Prop. Code § 51.0021. Form 14-2 is a "Notice of Change of Debtor's Address" to comply with this requirement.

§ 14.5:1 Letter to Reinstate Default Provisions

If the mortgagee has not insisted on strict performance of the loan documents in the past, the mortgagee should advise the borrower of its decision to strictly enforce the agreements in the future. *Dhanani Investments, Inc. v. Second Master Bilt Homes, Inc.*, 650 S.W.2d 220, 222 (Tex. App.—Fort Worth 1983, no writ). See form 14-1 in this chapter.

§ 14.5:2 Notice of Maturity and Demand for Payment

If the note has matured by its own terms, the mortgagee or mortgage servicer should demand payment. See form 14-3 in this chapter.

§ 14.5:3 Notice of Default and Intent to Accelerate

The notices of default and of intent to accelerate are waived in the promissory note form (see form 6-1 in this manual). However, Texas courts deem acceleration a harsh remedy. *Shumway v. Horizon Credit Corp.*, 801 S.W.2d 890, 892–93 (Tex. 1991). Even if notices of default and of intent to accelerate have been expressly waived, many attorneys elect to send this notice, viewing the waiver more as a safeguard to protect the mortgagee from the complications of minor technicalities than as a license to foreclose on borrowers without notice or demand. See form 14-4 in this chapter.

§ 14.5:4 Notice of Acceleration

The notice of acceleration is used if the mortgagee or mortgage servicer gives notice of intent to accelerate and the borrower fails to cure the default. See form 14-5 in this chapter.

§ 14.5:5 Reinstatement Agreement

Sometimes the mortgagee and the borrower will agree to continue the payment terms of the note after acceleration. However, once the maturity of a note is accelerated, limitations on the entire debt will begin to run. A reinstatement agreement should rescind the acceleration and reinstate the payment provisions in the note. See form 14-6 in this chapter.

§ 14.5:6 Affidavit of Posting and Filing

The affidavit of posting and filing is not required by law, but it serves to document where and when the notice was distributed and will normally be required by title companies. See form 14-8 in this chapter. If a newspaper or other public advertisement is used, the company publishing the notice should provide an affidavit of the publication, and the attorney should provide a copy of the page for the client's file. Some attorneys prefer to use a certificate form instead of an affidavit.

§ 14.5:7 Affidavit of Mailing

The affidavit of mailing is not required by law, but it serves to document legal notice mailing compliance and will normally be required by title companies. See form 14-9 in this chapter. Such an affidavit, completed and signed by a person knowledgeable of the facts, is prima facie evidence of service. Tex. Prop. Code § 51.002(e). Some attorneys prefer to use a certificate form instead of an affidavit.

§ 14.6 Foreclosure Documents Unique to Real Property

§ 14.6:1 Appointment of Substitute Trustee

Forms 14-10 and 14-11 in this chapter may be used if the mortgagee or mortgage servicer wishes for someone other than the trustee named in the deed of trust to act. The appointment may also be made in the notice of trustee's sale. See section 14.6:2 below. If required by the deed of trust, the appointment of substitute trustee must be recorded in the real property records before posting the notice of foreclosure.

§ 14.6:2 Notice of Trustee's Sale

Form 14-12 in this chapter has been adapted to include personal property that may be covered by the deed of trust and that the mortgagee may wish to foreclose on with the foreclosure of the real property. See section 14.2:7 above. Note that, once appointed, the substitute trustee is the trustee under the deed of trust and is referred to as such rather than as the substitute trustee.

The appointment or authorization of a trustee or substitute trustee made in a notice of sale is effective as of the date of the notice if the notice—

1. complies with sections 51.002 and 51.0075(e) of the Texas Property Code;
2. is signed by an attorney or agent of the mortgagee or mortgage servicer; and
3. contains a statement in all capital letters, bold-faced type, to read as follows:

   THIS INSTRUMENT APPOINTS THE SUBSTITUTE TRUSTEE(S) IDENTIFIED TO SELL THE PROPERTY DESCRIBED IN THE SECURITY INSTRUMENT IDENTIFIED IN THIS NOTICE OF SALE. THE PERSON SIGNING THIS NOTICE IS THE ATTORNEY OR AUTHORIZED AGENT OF THE MORTGAGEE OR MORTGAGE SERVICER.

See Tex. Prop. Code § 51.0076. Form 14-13 allows a mortgage servicer to administer a foreclosure under Tex. Prop. Code § 51.0025.

§ 14.6:3 Agenda of Public Sale

Forms 14-14 and 14-15 in this chapter, although not required by law, serve to document the sale.

§ 14.6:4 Trustee's Deed

Form 14-16 in this chapter has been adapted to include personal property that may be covered by the deed of trust and that the mortgagee may wish to foreclose on with the foreclosure of the real property. See section 14.2:7 above. Note that, once appointed, the substitute trustee is the trustee under the deed of trust and is referred to as such rather than as the substitute trustee.

Deeds transferring an interest to or from an individual, including a trustee, must contain the confidentiality notice required by Tex. Prop. Code § 11.008. See section 3.17 in this manual.

§ 14.6:5 Foreclosure Affidavit

Form 14-17 in this chapter, although not required by law, serves to document the legal requirements of the sale. Title companies will normally require an affidavit from the trustee attesting to these matters. This form may be used as a stand-alone document or may be attached to the trustee's deed. It may also be used in conjunction with the affidavit of posting and filing (form 14-8) and the affidavit of mailing (form 14-9) with the appropriate modifications.

§ 14.6:6 Notice and Affidavit of Advancement

If the mortgagee advances funds to cure a default under the deed of trust to secure assumption or a similar form used to secure performance, the mortgagee should use the notice of advancement (form 14-18 in this chapter) and the affidavit of advancement (form 14-19) to protect its rights and put parties on notice of the payment.

§ 14.6:7 IRS Notice Letter

If the property is subject to an Internal Revenue Service lien, the notification letter at form 14-20 in this chapter may be used. See section 14.2:5 above for information about the IRS lien.

§ 14.6:8 Rescission of Nonjudicial Foreclosure Sale

Texas Property Code section 51.016 provides a nonexclusive method for rescission of a nonjudicial foreclosure sale of residential real property, as defined in section 51.016(a). *See* Tex. Prop. Code § 51.016. Not later than the fifteenth day after the date of a foreclosure sale, a mortgagee, trustee, or substitute trustee may rescind the sale if one or more of these statutory reasons listed in section 51.016(b) exists:

1. the statutory requirements for the sale were not satisfied;
2. the default leading to the sale was cured before the sale;
3. a receivership or dependent probate administration involving the property was pending at the time of sale;
4. a condition specified in the conditions of sale prescribed by the trustee or substitute trustee before the sale and made available in writing to prospective bidders at the sale was not met;
5. the mortgagee or mortgage servicer and the debtor agreed before the sale to cancel the sale based on an enforceable written agreement by the debtor to cure the default; or
6. at the time of the sale, a court-ordered or automatic stay of the sale imposed in a bankruptcy case filed by a person with an interest in the property was in effect.

Tex. Prop. Code § 51.016(b).

The party rescinding the sale must serve written notice of rescission on the purchaser and each debtor obligated to pay the debt that describes the reason for the rescission and includes recording information for any affected trustee's deed. Tex. Prop. Code § 51.016(c)(1). See form 14-40 in this chapter. This notice must be served by certified mail in the county where all or a part of the property is located. Tex. Prop. Code § 51.016(c)(2), (d). The rescinding mortgagee, trustee, or substitute trustee shall record in the real property records of the county in which the written notice of rescission is filed an affidavit stating the date the bid amount was returned together with the certified mail, electronic or wire transfer, or courier service delivery tracking information. Tex. Prop. Code § 51.016(f). See form 14-41. This affidavit is prima facie evidence of the return of the bid amount. Tex. Prop. Code § 51.016(g). A completed rescission restores the mortgagee and debtor to their respective title, rights, and obligations under the instrument relating to the foreclosed property that existed immediately before the sale. Tex. Prop. Code § 51.016(h). No action challenging the effectiveness of a rescission under this section may be commenced, unless filed on or before the thirtieth calendar day after the notices of rescission are filed for recording. Tex. Prop. Code § 51.016(j). A rescission under this section is not effective as to a creditor or subsequent good-faith purchaser for value. Tex. Prop. Code § 51.016(i). Damages in a suit challenging the effectiveness of the rescission or resulting from the rescission are substantially limited to the amount of the bid price. *See* Tex. Prop. Code § 51.016(k), (*l*). Specific performance is not available. Tex. Prop. Code § 51.016(k).

§ 14.7 Foreclosure Documents for Public Disposition of Personal Property

§ 14.7:1 Waiver of Right to Notice after Default

A debtor or secondary obligor may waive its rights (but not the rights of other parties) to notice of a public disposition of personal property collateral, but the waiver must be signed after the default has occurred. Tex. Bus. & Com. Code § 9.624(a). See form 14-21 in this chapter for a waiver.

§ 14.7:2 Notice of Public Disposition

The posted notice of public sale can be used for public posting and advertisement of the sale. The attorney should consider advising the client about the requirements of a commercially reasonable sale and the risks associated with it. See form 14-23 in this chapter for a notice of public sale.

Texas Business and Commerce Code section 9.613 sets forth an approved form for notice of public or private disposition of personal property collateral other than consumer goods. *See* Tex. Bus. & Com. Code § 9.613. The approved form for notification of public or private disposition of personal property collateral that consists of consumer goods is set out in section 9.614. *See* Tex. Bus. & Com. Code § 9.614. Notice must be sent to the debtor, any secondary obligor, and, if the collateral is other than consumer goods, any other person from whom the secured party has received, before the notification date, an authenticated claim of interest in the collateral, and any other secured party or lienholder described in section 9.611(c)(3)(B), (c)(3)(C). *See* Tex. Bus. & Com. Code § 9.611(c). See form 14-28 for a notice if the collateral is consumer goods and form 14-29 for a notice if the collateral is not consumer goods.

§ 14.7:3 Agenda of Public Sale

The agenda of public sale is not required by the Uniform Commercial Code, but it serves to document that the sale was completed. See form 14-24 in this chapter.

§ 14.7:4 Bill of Sale

The bill of sale evidences the transfer of ownership of the personal property to the successful bidder. See form 14-25 in this chapter. If applicable, a disclaimer of warranties should be included. To disclaim warranties, the attorney must use language similar to that provided in Tex. Bus. & Com. Code § 9.610(f).

§ 14.8 Strict Foreclosure of Personal Property

§ 14.8:1 Notice of Strict Foreclosure

The notice of strict foreclosure notifies the debtor and others required to be notified of the secured party's proposal to accept personal property collateral in satisfaction of the debt. *See* Tex. Bus. & Com. Code §§ 9.620–.622. See form 14-26 in this chapter for a notice of strict foreclosure.

§ 14.8:2 Consent to Strict Foreclosure

The debtor must consent to the secured party's proposal to accept the collateral in satisfaction of the debt. Tex. Bus. & Com. Code § 9.620(a)(1), (c). The consent may be an express consent made by the debtor agreeing to the secured party's proposal in a writing signed after default. Tex. Bus. & Com. Code § 9.620(c)(1), (c)(2). See form 14-22 in this chapter for a consent form.

§ 14.8:3 Objection to Strict Foreclosure

A letter of objection notifies the secured party of a person's objection to the secured party's proposal to accept the collateral in satisfaction of the debt. See form 14-27 in this chapter. The letter may be sent by any person to whom the secured party sent its proposal to accept the collateral. To be effective, the objection letter must be received by the secured party within twenty days after the date the secured party sends its proposal. Tex. Bus. & Com. Code § 9.620(c)(2)(C), (d)(1), (d)(2)(A).

§ 14.9 Private Disposition of Personal Property

§ 14.9:1 Waiver of Notice after Default

A debtor or secondary obligor may waive its rights (but not the rights of other parties) to notice of a private disposition of personal property collateral, but the waiver must be signed after the default has occurred. Tex. Bus. & Com. Code § 9.624(a). See form 14-21 in this chapter for a waiver.

§ 14.9:2 Notice of Private Disposition

Texas Business and Commerce Code section 9.613 sets forth an approved form for notice of public or private disposition of personal property collateral other than consumer goods. *See* Tex. Bus. & Com. Code § 9.613. The approved form for notification of public or private disposition of personal property collateral that consists of consumer goods is set out in Tex. Bus. & Com. Code § 9.614. Notice must be sent to the debtor, any secondary obligor, and, if the collateral is other than consumer goods, any other person from whom the secured party has received, before the notification date, an authenticated claim of interest in the collateral, and any other secured party or lienholder described in section 9.611(c)(3)(B), (c)(3)(C). Tex. Bus. & Com. Code § 9.611(c). See form 14-28 in this chapter for a notice if the collateral is consumer goods and form 14-29 for a notice if the collateral is not consumer goods.

§ 14.9:3 Memorandum of Private Sale

The agenda of private sale is not required by the Uniform Commercial Code, but it serves to document that the sale was completed. See form 14-30 in this chapter.

§ 14.9:4 Bill of Sale

The bill of sale evidences the transfer of ownership of the personal property to the buyer at the private foreclosure sale. See form 14-25 in this chapter. If applicable, a disclaimer of warranties should be included. To disclaim warranties, the attorney must use language similar to that provided in Tex. Bus. & Com. Code § 9.610(f).

§ 14.10 Security Interest Included in Deed of Trust

If the deed of trust contains the security interest covering personal property, the lienholder may foreclose the personal property lien with the real property foreclosure. Tex. Bus. & Com. Code § 9.604(a).

§ 14.11 Collateral Transfer of Note and Lien Foreclosure

The collateral transfer of note and lien form creates a security interest in an instrument, the collateral promissory note. The foreclosure of the collateral note under a collateral transfer is governed by the Texas Business and Commerce Code rather than by the Texas Property Code. *See* Tex. Bus. & Com. Code §§ 9.601–.628. The secured party may select any procedure applicable to the situation: strict foreclosure, public disposition, or private disposition. Without foreclosing on the collateral note, the secured party may collect and enforce the collateral note, including, if the collateral note is in default, accelerating the collateral note and exercising any foreclosure remedy contained in the underlying deed of trust. See the collateral transfer of note and lien, form 9-8 in this manual.

§ 14.12 Additional Resources

Austin, Judd A., Jr. "HOA Collections and Foreclosures: New Statutes & New Rules." In *Advanced Real Estate Drafting Course, 2012*. Austin: State Bar of Texas, 2012.

Ayers, R. Glen. "Mortgage Foreclosure in an Age of Securization: Missing Original Notes and Other Problems for Creditors." In *Advanced Real Estate Law Course, 2009*. Austin: State Bar of Texas, 2009.

Bastian, G. Tommy. "Expedited Foreclosure Home Equity, Home Equity Line of Credit, Reverse Mortgage, and Tax Lien Transfer and Property Tax Loan Forms for the New Supreme Court Rules." In *Advanced Real Estate Drafting Course, 2012*. Austin: State Bar of Texas, 2012.

———. "Foreclosure of Farm and Ranch Real Property." In *Advanced Real Estate Strategies Course, 2008*. Austin: State Bar of Texas, 2008.

———. "How Securitization Changed Residential Foreclosures." In *Advanced Real Estate Law Course, 2010*. Austin: State Bar of Texas, 2010.

———. "Rule 735 and 736 Foreclosures: Tax Lien Transfers." In *Advanced Real Estate Law Course, 2009*. Austin: State Bar of Texas, 2009.

———. "Rule 736 Promulgated Forms." In *Advanced Real Estate Drafting Course, 2014*. Austin: State Bar of Texas, 2014.

———. "Texas Foreclosures: Myths and Reality." In *Advanced Real Estate Law Course, 2011*. Austin: State Bar of Texas, 2011.

Baucum, Michael. "Alternatives to Foreclosure—Ideas and Forms." In *Advanced Real Estate Drafting Course, 2015*. Austin: State Bar of Texas, 2015.

Biel, Frederick J. "Commercial Foreclosures: Selected Documentation and Procedural Issues." In *Advanced Real Estate Strategies Course, 2010*. Austin: State Bar of Texas, 2010.

———. "Servicing, Foreclosing, and Re-Selling Non-Securitized Single Family Residential Real Estate Secured Notes." In *Advanced Real Estate Law Course, 2011*. Austin: State Bar of Texas, 2011.

———. "UCC Related Foreclosure Matters—Commercial Reasonableness and Its Impact on Deficiency and Surplus Claims under Chapter 9." In *Advanced Real Estate Law Course, 2013*. Austin: State Bar of Texas, 2013.

Burns, Randolph L. "Looking at a Receivership Issue? Here's What You Need to Know." In *Advanced Real Estate Law Course, 2012*. Austin: State Bar of Texas, 2012.

Derber, David P. "Personal Property Foreclosures." In *Advanced Real Estate Strategies Course, 2010*. Austin: State Bar of Texas, 2010.

Doggett, Mary Belan, and Yanira M. Reyes. "Foreclosure of Transferred Ad Valorem Tax Liens." In *Advanced Real Estate Law Course, 2012*. Austin: State Bar of Texas, 2012.

Dysart, Sara E. "Attorney Acting as Substitute Trustee in a Non-Judicial Foreclosure Sale." In *Advanced Real Estate Strategies Course, 2008*. Austin: State Bar of Texas, 2008.

———. "Planning for Defaults, Workouts, and Foreclosures." In *Advanced Real Estate Strategies Course, 2010*. Austin: State Bar of Texas, 2010.

———. "Workouts, Deeds in Lieu and Foreclosure." In *State Bar College "Summer School" Course, 2010*. Austin: State Bar of Texas, 2010.

Grantham, Terry L. "The Trustee's Role in Foreclosures: 'Ten Things Every Foreclosure Trustee Needs to Know.'" In *Advanced*

Real Estate Law Course, 2009. Austin: State Bar of Texas, 2009.

Guzman, Leann D. "Sales, Purchases, and Redemption of Tax-Foreclosed Property." In *Advanced Real Estate Law Course, 2012*. Austin: State Bar of Texas, 2012.

Howard, C. Elaine. "Problems with Foreclosures: A Legal Analysis of Current Events." In *7th Annual John Huffaker Agricultural Law Course, 2013*. Austin: State Bar of Texas, 2013.

Johnson, Leslie S. "Unwrapping the Wrap Mortgage." In *Advanced Real Estate Law Course, 2022*. Austin: State Bar of Texas, 2022.

Locke, William H., Jr., and Ralph Martin Novak, Jr. "Texas Foreclosure Experiences (So Many Ways to Leave Your Lover)." In *Advanced Real Estate Strategies Course, 2022*. Austin: State Bar of Texas, 2022.

Locke, William H., Jr., Ralph Martin Novak, Jr., G. Tommy Bastian, and Sara E. Dysart, eds. *Texas Foreclosure Manual*. 2023 ed. Austin: State Bar of Texas, 2023.

Melamed, Richard. "Excess Proceeds and How to Get Them." In *Advanced Real Estate Drafting Course, 2021*. Austin: State Bar of Texas, 2021.

Morris, Brian T. "Post Foreclosure Attacks on Sale, Collection of Deficiency, Limitations and Related Matters." In *Advanced Real Estate Strategies Course, 2022*. Austin: State Bar of Texas, 2022.

Pattillo, Andy. "Texas Foreclosures and Evictions 101." In *Real Estate Law 101 Course, 2020*. Austin: State Bar of Texas, 2020.

Tapley, Katherine A. "Deeds in Lieu of Foreclosure." In *Advanced Real Estate Drafting Course, 2021*. Austin: State Bar of Texas, 2021.

———. "Practice Tips Related to Loan Defaults and Workouts." In *Advanced Real Estate Strategies Course, 2022*. Austin: State Bar of Texas, 2022.

Tomek, David W. "Real Property Foreclosures: Legal Considerations, Documentation, and Notable Recent Developments." In *5th Annual John Huffaker Agricultural Law Course, 2011*. Austin: State Bar of Texas, 2011.

Wilbanks, Erwin. "Common Errors in Foreclosure." In *Advanced Real Estate Law Course, 2010*. Austin: State Bar of Texas, 2010.

Form 14-1

Letter to Reinstate Default Provisions

[**Date**]

[**Name and address of borrower**]

See section 14.5 in this chapter.

Re: [**describe note and loan documents**]

[**Salutation**]

In the past, you have been delinquent in your monthly payments, and the mortgagee has accepted the late payments without assessing a penalty. Please be advised, however, that all future payments must be received by the due date, or the mortgagee will exercise its rights under the loan documents.

Include clause 14-7-1 if this is the first correspondence from the attorney to a debtor who is a consumer. See section 14.4:5.

If you have any questions, please consult your legal counsel.

Sincerely yours,

____
[**Name of attorney**]

Certified Mail No. [**number**]
Return Receipt Requested
c: [**name of borrower**], by first-class mail

Form 14-2

Notice of Change of Debtor's Address

Date:

Debtor:

Debtor's Old Mailing Address:

Debtor's New Mailing Address:

Trustee:

Trustee's Mailing Address:

Mortgagee:

Mortgagee's Mailing Address:

Obligation

Note

Date:

Original principal amount:

Debtor:

Grantor: (if different)

Lender:

Maturity date:

Property (including any improvements):

This is notice to Lender and its mortgage servicers of the change in Debtor's mailing address.

____

[Name of [grantor/debtor]]

Form 14-3

Notice of Maturity and Demand for Payment

[**Date**]

[**Name and address of borrower**]

See section 14.5 in this chapter.

Re: [**describe note and loan documents**]

[**Salutation**]

The referenced note matured on [**date**] and remains unpaid.

Select one of the following.

Demand is made for the immediate payment of all unpaid principal and all accrued but unpaid interest. Please contact [**name**] for the current payoff information.

Or

Demand is made for the immediate payment of $[**amount**] principal and $[**amount**] accrued but unpaid interest through [**date**], together with additional interest at the rate of $[**amount**] per day until paid.

Continue with the following.

Please be advised that if the payment is not received by [**date**], the mortgagee will exercise its rights under the loan documents.

Include clause 14-7-1 if this is the first correspondence from the attorney to a debtor who is a consumer. See section 14.4:5.

If you have any questions, please consult your legal counsel.

Sincerely yours,

____
[**Name of attorney**]

Certified Mail No. [**number**]
Return Receipt Requested
c: [**name of borrower**], by first-class mail

Form 14-4

Notice of Default and Intent to Accelerate

[**Date**]

[**Name and address of borrower**]

See section 14.5 in this chapter.

Re: [**describe note and loan documents**]

[**Salutation**]

This letter is to give you notice of default under the referenced loan documents. This default consists of [**describe default**].

Select one of the following. Use the first paragraph if the property is not the debtor's principal residence. Use the second paragraph if the property is the debtor's principal residence; see section 14.2:4.

Unless the default is cured by [**date**], the mortgagee intends to enforce its rights and remedies under the loan documents. Specifically, the mortgagee intends to accelerate the maturity of the note and demand payment for the full unpaid principal balance, together with accrued but unpaid interest and all fees and expenses, as allowed by law. If the amount due is not timely paid, the mortgagee intends to foreclose the lien under the loan documents. [**Include if applicable:** In addition, the mortgagee demands that you pay to the mortgagee the proceeds of all accrued but unpaid rent as of the date you receive this letter and all rent that accrues after you receive this letter. Payment of the proceeds should be made to [**name of mortgagee and address for payments**]. The tenant[s] will be instructed to pay all rents to the mortgagee until further notice, in accordance with [the deed of trust/[**specify instrument**]] and the Texas Property Code.]

Or

You are notified that if the default is not cured within twenty days from the date of posting of this letter, the mortgagee intends to enforce its rights under the loan documents. Specifically, the mortgagee intends to accelerate the maturity of the note and demand payment for the full unpaid principal balance, together with accrued but unpaid interest and all fees and expenses, as allowed by law. If the amount due is not timely paid, the mortgagee intends to foreclose the lien under the loan documents.

Continue with the following.

Include clause 14-7-1 if this is the first correspondence from the attorney to a debtor who is a consumer. See section 14.4:5.

If you have any questions, please consult your legal counsel.

Sincerely yours,

____

[Name of attorney]

Certified Mail No. **[number]**
Return Receipt Requested
c: **[name of borrower]**, by first-class mail

Form 14-5

Notice of Acceleration

[**Date**]

[**Name and address of borrower**]

See section 14.5 in this chapter.

Re: [**describe note and loan documents**]

[**Salutation**]

Because of the failure to cure the default under the referenced loan documents, the mortgagee has accelerated the maturity of the note.

Select one of the following.

Demand is made for the payment of all unpaid principal and all accrued but unpaid interest. Please contact [**name**] for the current payoff information.

Or

Demand is made for the payment of $[**amount**] principal and $[**amount**] accrued but unpaid interest through [**date**], together with additional interest at the rate of $[**amount**] per day until paid.

Continue with the following.

If the amount due is not paid, the mortgagee intends to foreclose the lien under the loan documents in accordance with the enclosed notice of sale.

[**Include if applicable:** The mortgagee demands that you pay to the mortgagee the proceeds of all accrued but unpaid rent as of the date you receive this letter and all rent that accrues after you receive this letter in accordance with the loan documents and the Texas

Property Code. Payment of the proceeds should be made to [**name of mortgagee and address for payments**]. The tenant[s] will be instructed to pay all rents to the mortgagee until further notice, in accordance with [the deed of trust/[**specify instrument**]] and the Texas Property Code.]

> Include clause 14-7-1 if this is the first correspondence from the attorney to a debtor who is a consumer. See section 14.4:5.

If you have any questions, please consult your legal counsel.

Sincerely yours,

____

[**Name of attorney**]

Certified Mail No. [**number**]
Return Receipt Requested
c: [**name of borrower**], by first-class mail

Form 14-6

Reinstatement Agreement

Date:

Deed of Trust

Date:

Grantor:

Mortgagee:

Recording information:

Property:

Note

Date:

Principal amount:

Mortgagee:

Borrower:

[**Include if the owner is different from the borrower:** Owner of Property:]

[Guarantor:]

Borrower has defaulted in payment of the Note, and Mortgagee has accelerated the maturity of the Note. At Borrower's request and for valuable consideration, Mortgagee rescinds the acceleration, and Mortgagee and Borrower reinstate the payment terms of the Note.

Borrower agrees to pay the Note according to its terms and to comply with all provisions of the Deed of Trust. This agreement does not replace the Note or the Deed of Trust. It only reinstates those documents as written.

Borrower and Mortgagee agree that the unpaid principal balance of the Note is $[**amount**] and the interest is paid through [**date**].

Include the following if applicable.

Guarantor consents to the reinstatement of the Note under the terms of this agreement.

And/Or

Owner of Property consents to the reinstatement of the Note under the terms of this agreement.

Continue with the following.

Mortgagee's acceptance of this agreement and rescission of the acceleration will not prejudice Mortgagee's rights regarding future defaults under the Note or the Deed of Trust.

As a material inducement to Mortgagee to execute this agreement, Borrower [**include either or both if applicable:** and Guarantor/and Owner of Property] acknowledge[s] that:

1. The current principal balance of the Note is $[**amount**], and the interest is paid through [**date**].

2. The liens and security interests of the Deed of Trust are valid and subsisting liens against the Property and are renewed to secure the payment of the Note and the obligations of the Deed of Trust.

3. There are no claims or offsets against or defenses or counterclaims to the Note and the obligations secured by the Deed of Trust.

____
[Name of borrower]

____
[Name of mortgagee]

Include signature lines for the guarantor and the owner if applicable. Include acknowledgments.

Form 14-7

Additional Clauses for Foreclosure Documents

Fair Debt Collection Act Notice

> If this notice is sent in a letter as suggested in section 14.4:5 in this chapter, a sentence describing the debt should be included following the internal address.

Clause 14-7-1

In accordance with federal and Texas laws regarding fair debt collections, unless you, within thirty days after receipt of this notice, dispute the validity of the debt set forth above, or any portion thereof, the indebtedness will be assumed to be valid. If you notify the undersigned in writing within the thirty-day period that the indebtedness, or any portion thereof, is disputed, I will obtain a verification of the indebtedness and will mail that verification to you. On my receipt of your written request within the thirty-day period, I will forward to you the name and address of the original creditor, if different from the current creditor.

I am attempting to collect this indebtedness, and any information obtained will be used for that purpose. This letter is being sent to your attention in accordance with federal law.

Fair Credit Reporting Act Notices

Clause 14-7-2

We may report information about your account to credit bureaus. Late payments, missed payments, or other defaults on your account may be reflected in your credit report.

Clause 14-7-3

We have told a credit bureau about a late payment, missed payment, or other default on your account. This information may be reflected in your credit report.

Form 14-8

Affidavit of Posting and Filing

Date:

Affiant:

If the affidavit is to be attached to the trustee's deed and has been incorporated by reference, the following may be omitted.

Deed of Trust

Date:

Grantor:

Mortgagee:

Recording information:

Property: [**Insert property description and include the following if applicable:** , including all personal property secured by the security agreement included in the Deed of Trust.]

Continue with the following.

Affiant on oath swears that the following statements are true and are within the personal knowledge of Affiant:

1. This affidavit is made with respect to the foreclosure of the Deed of Trust that occurred on [**date**].

2. Attached to this affidavit is a copy of the Notice of Trustee's Sale, file-stamped by the county clerk's office.

3. Affiant posted a copy of the Notice of Trustee's Sale on [**date**] at the place at [the/each] courthouse designated in the notice [**include if applicable:** , being the area designated by the county commissioner's court for foreclosure sales,] and filed the Notice of Trustee's Sale in the office of the county clerk for [the/each] county in which the property is located.

____
[**Name of affiant**]

SUBSCRIBED AND SWORN TO before me on ______________ by [**name of affiant**].

____
Notary Public, State of Texas

Form 14-9

Affidavit of Mailing

Date:

Affiant:

> If the affidavit is to be attached to the trustee's deed and has been incorporated by reference, the following may be omitted.

Deed of Trust

Date:

Grantor:

Mortgagee:

Recording information:

Property: [**Insert property description and include the following if applicable:** , including all personal property secured by the security agreement included in the Deed of Trust.]

> Continue with the following.

Affiant on oath swears that the following statements are true and are within the personal knowledge of Affiant:

1. This affidavit is made with respect to the foreclosure of the Deed of Trust that occurred on [**date**].

> Select one of the following.

2. Attached to this affidavit is a copy of the letter sent to each debtor obligated to pay the debt at the address required by the Deed of Trust and the Texas Property Code.

Or

2. At least twenty-one days before the trustee's sale, Affiant, either personally or by agent, served notice of the sale on [**date**] on each debtor, at the address for that debtor as shown by Mortgagee's records, who [is/are]: [**list name[s] and address[es]**].

Continue with the following.

Each notice was served by certified mail, postage prepaid, properly addressed to each debtor listed above at the address[es] stated.

____

[**Name of affiant**]

SUBSCRIBED AND SWORN TO before me on ____________________ by [**name of affiant**].

____

Notary Public, State of Texas

Form 14-10

Appointment of Substitute Trustee[s]
[Mortgagee]

Date:

Borrower:

Borrower's Address:

Mortgagee:

Mortgagee's Address:

Mortgage Servicer:

Mortgage Servicer's Address:

Substitute Trustee:

Substitute Trustee's Address:

Repeat as necessary for multiple trustees.

Deed of Trust

Date:

Grantor:

Mortgagee:

Recording information:

Property: [**Insert property description and include the following if applicable:** , including all personal property secured by the security agreement included in the Deed of Trust.]

The Deed of Trust and section 51.0075 of the Texas Property Code allow Mortgagee to remove the trustee[s] and appoint [a] substitute trustee[s]. Mortgagee removes the present trustee[s] and appoints Substitute Trustee[s] as the trustee[s] under the Deed of Trust. Mortgagee directs Substitute Trustee[s] to foreclose the lien of the Deed of Trust in accordance with its terms and the laws of the state of Texas.

____
[**Name of mortgagee**]

Include acknowledgment.

Form 14-11

Appointment of Substitute Trustee[s]

[Mortgage Servicer]

Date:

Borrower:

Borrower's Address:

Mortgagee:

Mortgagee's Address:

Mortgage Servicer:

Mortgage Servicer's Address:

Substitute Trustee:

Substitute Trustee's Address:

Repeat as necessary for multiple trustees.

Deed of Trust

Date:

Grantor:

Mortgagee:

Recording information:

Property: [**Insert property description and include the following if applicable:**, including all personal property secured by the security agreement included in the Deed of Trust.]

Sections 51.0001(7) and 51.0075 of the Texas Property Code allow a mortgage servicer to remove the trustee[s] and appoint [a] substitute trustee[s]. Mortgage Servicer removes the present trustee[s] and appoints Substitute Trustee[s] as the trustee[s] under the Deed of Trust. Mortgage Servicer directs Substitute Trustee[s] to foreclose the lien of the Deed of Trust in accordance with its terms and the laws of the state of Texas.

____
[**Name of mortgage servicer**]

Include acknowledgment.

Form 14-12

Notice of Trustee's Sale
[Mortgagee]

Date:

[Trustee/Substitute Trustee]:

[Trustee/Substitute Trustee]'s Address:

Repeat as necessary for multiple trustees.

Mortgagee:

Note:

Deed of Trust

Date:

Grantor:

Mortgagee:

Recording information:

Property: [**Insert property description and include the following if applicable:** including all personal property secured by the security agreement included in the Deed of Trust.]

County:

Date of Sale (first Tuesday of month):

Time of Sale:

Place of Sale: [**Designate county location where sale will take place (may be other than courthouse)**]

ASSERT AND PROTECT YOUR RIGHTS AS A MEMBER OF THE ARMED FORCES OF THE UNITED STATES. IF YOU ARE OR YOUR SPOUSE IS SERVING ON ACTIVE MILITARY DUTY, INCLUDING ACTIVE MILITARY DUTY AS A MEMBER OF THE TEXAS NATIONAL GUARD OR THE NATIONAL GUARD OF ANOTHER STATE OR AS A MEMBER OF A RESERVE COMPONENT OF THE ARMED FORCES OF THE UNITED STATES, PLEASE SEND WRITTEN NOTICE OF THE ACTIVE DUTY MILITARY SERVICE TO THE SENDER OF THIS NOTICE IMMEDIATELY.

[[**Name[s] of trustee[s]**] [is/are] Trustee[s] under the Deed of Trust/Mortgagee has appointed [**name[s] of trustee[s]**] as Trustee[s] under the Deed of Trust]. Mortgagee has instructed Trustee[s] to offer the Property for sale toward the satisfaction of the Note.

Include the following if appointing a substitute trustee in this notice.

THIS INSTRUMENT APPOINTS THE SUBSTITUTE TRUSTEE(S) IDENTIFIED TO SELL THE PROPERTY DESCRIBED IN THE SECURITY INSTRUMENT IDENTIFIED IN THIS NOTICE OF SALE. THE PERSON SIGNING THIS NOTICE IS THE ATTORNEY OR AUTHORIZED AGENT OF THE MORTGAGEE OR MORTGAGE SERVICER.

Continue with the following.

Notice is given that on the Date of Sale, Trustee[s] will offer the Property for sale at public auction at the Place of Sale, to the highest bidder for cash, "AS IS." [**Include if applicable:** THERE WILL BE NO WARRANTY RELATING TO TITLE, POSSESSION, QUIET ENJOYMENT, OR THE LIKE FOR THE PERSONAL PROPERTY IN THIS DISPOSITION.] The sale will begin at the Time of Sale or not later than three hours thereafter. This sale will be conducted subject to the right of rescission contained in section 51.016 of the Texas Property Code.

____
[Name of trustee]

Repeat signature line as necessary.

Include the following if appointing a substitute trustee in this notice.

____
[Name of attorney or authorized agent of the mortgagee]

Form 14-13

Notice of Trustee's Sale
[Mortgage Servicer]

Date:

[Trustee/Substitute Trustee]:

[Trustee/Substitute Trustee]'s Address:

Repeat as necessary for multiple trustees.

Mortgagee:

Mortgagee's Address:

Mortgage Servicer:

Mortgage Servicer's Address:

Note:

Deed of Trust

Date:

Grantor:

Mortgagee:

Recording information:

Property: [**Insert property description and include the following if applicable:** including all personal property secured by the security agreement included in the Deed of Trust.]

County:

Date of Sale (first Tuesday of month):

Time of Sale:

Place of Sale: [**Designate county location where sale will take place (may be other than courthouse)**]

ASSERT AND PROTECT YOUR RIGHTS AS A MEMBER OF THE ARMED FORCES OF THE UNITED STATES. IF YOU ARE OR YOUR SPOUSE IS SERVING ON ACTIVE MILITARY DUTY, INCLUDING ACTIVE MILITARY DUTY AS A MEMBER OF THE TEXAS NATIONAL GUARD OR THE NATIONAL GUARD OF ANOTHER STATE OR AS A MEMBER OF A RESERVE COMPONENT OF THE ARMED FORCES OF THE UNITED STATES, PLEASE SEND WRITTEN NOTICE OF THE ACTIVE DUTY MILITARY SERVICE TO THE SENDER OF THIS NOTICE IMMEDIATELY.

[[**Name[s] of trustee[s]**] [is/are] Trustee[s] under the Deed of Trust/[Mortgagee/Mortgage Servicer] has appointed [**name[s] of trustee[s]**] as Trustee[s] under the Deed of Trust]. [Mortgagee/Mortgage Servicer] has instructed Trustee[s] to offer the Property for sale toward the satisfaction of the Note. This foreclosure is being administered by Mortgage Servicer. Mortgage Servicer is representing Mortgagee under a servicing agreement.

Include the following if appointing a substitute trustee in this notice.

THIS INSTRUMENT APPOINTS THE SUBSTITUTE TRUSTEE(S) IDENTIFIED TO SELL THE PROPERTY DESCRIBED IN THE SECURITY INSTRUMENT IDENTIFIED IN THIS NOTICE OF SALE. THE PERSON SIGNING THIS NOTICE IS THE ATTORNEY OR AUTHORIZED AGENT OF THE MORTGAGEE OR MORTGAGE SERVICER.

Continue with the following.

Notice is given that on the Date of Sale, Trustee[s] will offer the Property for sale at public auction at the Place of Sale, to the highest bidder for cash, "AS IS." [**Include if applicable:** THERE WILL BE NO WARRANTY RELATING TO TITLE, POSSESSION, QUIET ENJOYMENT, OR THE LIKE FOR THE PERSONAL PROPERTY IN THIS DISPOSITION.] The sale will begin at the Time of Sale or not later than three hours thereafter. This sale will be conducted subject to the right of rescission contained in section 51.016 of the Texas Property Code.

____

[**Name of trustee**]

Repeat signature line as necessary.

Include the following if appointing a substitute trustee in this notice.

____

[**Name of attorney or authorized agent of the mortgagee**]

Form 14-14

Note: On the first sale of the day by a trustee or a substitute trustee an announcement of the reasonable conditions for conducting the public sale may be made pursuant to Tex. Prop. Code § 51.0075(a). Tex. Prop. Code § 51.0075(f) was amended in 2009 to allow the foreclosure purchaser and the trustee or substitute trustee to agree on a reasonable time after acceptance of the bid within which to deliver the purchase price; otherwise, the purchase price is payable without delay after acceptance of the bid.

Agenda of Public Foreclosure Sale

[**county**] County, Texas, [**date**]

I am [**name of trustee**], Trustee under the Deed of Trust recorded in [**recording data**] of the real property records of [**county**] County, Texas. [**Name of mortgagee or mortgage servicer**] has instructed me to sell, at public auction, the property described in the Deed of Trust,

Include one or both of the following.

together with the personal property that is subject to the security interest granted in the Deed of Trust[.]

And/Or

but not including any property previously released from the Deed of Trust, including but not limited to the property described in Exhibit [**exhibit letter/number**] attached hereto.

Continue with the following.

This is to be an "AS IS" sale. This sale will be conducted subject to the right of rescission contained in section 51.016 of the Texas Property Code.

The property is [**read legal description or offer a copy for review. If appropriate, provide beachfront notice. See TREC form no. 33-2 at www.trec.texas.gov/forms/addendum-coastal-area-property**].

[**Include if applicable:** THERE WILL BE NO WARRANTY RELATING TO TITLE, POSSESSION, QUIET ENJOYMENT, OR THE LIKE FOR THE PERSONAL PROPERTY IN THIS DISPOSITION.]

I now call for cash bids on the property. Each bidder will please state his or her name, for whom the bid is being made, and the amount of each bid made. [**Include if applicable:** All bidders must execute an acknowledgment of receipt of the beachfront notice in order to bid.]

Bids in the order made:

1. Name:

   Representing:

   Amount bid:

Repeat above information as needed.

Are there any further bids?

When there are no further bids, select one of the following.

If the bidder has requested, and the trustee agrees to grant the bidder, a reasonable time to obtain the amount of the bid, select the following.

Hearing no further bids, this sale is adjourned until ____________, at which time this sale will reconvene at this location if the bidder has not delivered cash to me, as Trustee, in the amount of the bidder's bid; provided, however, that if the bidder delivers the cash bid, the property will be sold to the bidder without further notice, and this sale will be concluded.

The time for reconvening the sale must allow time to complete the sale by 4:00 P.M. and bidding on behalf of the beneficiary should commence at its minimum bid. If the sale is reconvened, this agenda should be reread in full.

If the bidder has not requested time to obtain the amount of the bid, select the following.

Hearing no further bids, the property is sold to ________________________, who made the highest and best bid.

This concludes the sale.

Continue with the following.

____
[Name of trustee]

Form 14-15

Note: On the first sale of the day by a trustee or a substitute trustee an announcement of the reasonable conditions for conducting the public sale may be made pursuant to Tex. Prop. Code § 51.0075(a). Tex. Prop. Code § 51.0075(f) was amended in 2009 to allow the foreclosure purchaser and the trustee or substitute trustee to agree on a reasonable time after acceptance of the bid within which to deliver the purchase price; otherwise, the purchase price is payable without delay after acceptance of the bid.

Agenda of Public Foreclosure Sale of Residential Real Property

[**county**] County, Texas, [**date**]

I am [**name of trustee**], Trustee under the Deed of Trust recorded in [**recording data**] of the real property records of [**county**] County, Texas. [**Name of mortgagee or mortgage servicer**] has instructed me to sell, at public auction, the property described in the Deed of Trust,

Include one or both of the following.

together with the personal property that is subject to the security interest granted in the Deed of Trust[.]

And/Or

but not including any property previously released from the Deed of Trust, including but not limited to the property described in Exhibit [**exhibit letter/number**] attached hereto.

Continue with the following.

This is to be an "AS IS" sale. This sale will be conducted subject to the right of rescission contained in section 51.016 of the Texas Property Code.

The property is [**read legal description or offer a copy for review. If appropriate, provide beachfront notice. See TREC form no. 33-2 at www.trec.texas.gov/forms/addendum-coastal-area-property**].

[**Include if applicable:** THERE WILL BE NO WARRANTY RELATING TO TITLE, POSSESSION, QUIET ENJOYMENT, OR THE LIKE FOR THE PERSONAL PROPERTY IN THIS DISPOSITION.]

I now call for cash bids on the property. Each bidder will please state his or her name, for whom the bid is being made, and the amount of each bid made. [**Include if applicable:** All bidders must execute an acknowledgment of receipt of the beachfront notice in order to bid.]

Bids in the order made:

1. Name:

   Representing:

   Amount bid:

Repeat above information as needed.

Are there any further bids?

Include the following information, as required by Tex. Bus. & Com. Code § 22.004, for the winning bidder other than the mortgagee or mortgage servicer.

Bidder submitting the highest and best bid:

Name:

Address:

Telephone number:

Email address:

Taxpayer identification number:

Bidder's principal (if bidder is acting as an agent):

Name of individual or organization:

Name of organization's contact person:

Address:

Telephone number:

Email address:

Grantee in deed:

Name:

Address:

Party tendering payment of highest and best bid:

Name:

Address:

Telephone number:

Email address:

Government-issued photo identification: [attach copy]

Select one of the following.

If the bidder has requested, and the trustee agrees to grant the bidder, a reasonable time to obtain the amount of the bid, select the following.

Hearing no further bids, this sale is adjourned until ____________, at which time this sale will reconvene at this location if the bidder has not delivered cash to me, as Trustee, in the amount of the bidder's bid; provided, however, that if the bidder delivers the cash bid, the property will be sold to the bidder without further notice, and this sale will be concluded.

> The time for reconvening the sale must allow time to complete the sale by 4:00 P.M. and bidding on behalf of the beneficiary should commence at its minimum bid. If the sale is reconvened, this agenda should be reread in full.

> If the bidder has not requested time to obtain the amount of the bid, select the following.

Hearing no further bids, the property is sold to ______________________, who made the highest and best bid.

This concludes the sale.

> Continue with the following.

____
[Name of trustee]

Form 14-16

Trustee's Deed [with Bill of Sale]

Notice of confidentiality rights: If you are a natural person, you may remove or strike any or all of the following information from any instrument that transfers an interest in real property before it is filed for record in the public records: your Social Security number or your driver's license number.

Date:

Trustee:

Deed of Trust

Date:

Grantor:

Mortgagee:

Recording information:

Property: [**Insert property description and include the following if applicable:** , including all personal property secured by the security agreement included in the Deed of Trust.]

Note

Date:

Principal amount:

Borrower:

Mortgagee:

Date of Sale (first Tuesday of month):

Time of Sale:

Place of Sale:

Buyer:

Buyer's Mailing Address:

[Amount of Sale:]

A default existed under the Deed of Trust and Mortgagee or its agent directed Trustee to enforce the trust.

Notices stating the time, place, and terms of sale of the Property were posted and filed and [**include if applicable:** as shown by the affidavit attached to this deed and incorporated in it by this reference] Mortgagee either personally or by agent served notice of the sale to each debtor, as required by section 51.002 of the Texas Property Code. In accordance with that statute and the Deed of Trust, Trustee sold the Property to Buyer, who was the highest bidder at the public auction [**include if the amount of sale is completed:** , for the Amount of Sale]. The sale was made on the Date of Sale, began at the Time of Sale or not later than three hours thereafter, and was concluded by 4:00 P.M.

Trustee, subject to any prior liens, the right of rescission contained in section 51.016 of the Texas Property Code, and other exceptions to conveyance and warranty in the Deed of Trust and for the [bid price/Amount of Sale] paid by Buyer as consideration, grants, sells, and conveys the Property to Buyer, "AS IS," together with all and singular the rights and appurtenances thereto in any way belonging, to have and to hold it to Buyer and Buyer's heirs, successors, and assigns forever. Trustee binds Grantor and Grantor's heirs and successors to warrant and forever defend all and singular the Property to Buyer and Buyer's heirs, successors, and assigns against every person whomsoever lawfully claiming or to claim the same or any part thereof, except as to the prior liens and other exceptions to conveyance and warranty in the Deed of Trust.

Include the following if applicable.

TRUSTEE HAS NOT MADE, AND DOES NOT MAKE, ANY REPRESENTATION, EXPRESS OR IMPLIED, WITH RESPECT TO THE PERSONAL PROPERTY, AND THE PERSONAL PROPERTY IS SOLD TO BUYER "AS IS, WHERE IS, AND WITH ALL FAULTS." THERE IS NO WARRANTY RELATING TO TITLE, POSSESSION, QUIET ENJOYMENT, OR THE LIKE IN THIS DISPOSITION OF PERSONAL PROPERTY.

Continue with the following.

____
[Name of trustee]

Include acknowledgment.

Form 14-17

Foreclosure Affidavit

Date:

Affiant:

> If the affidavit is to be attached to the trustee's deed and has been incorporated by reference, the following may be omitted.

Deed of Trust

Date:

Grantor:

Mortgagee:

Recording information:

Property: [**Insert property description and include the following if applicable:**, including all personal property secured by the security agreement included in the Deed of Trust.]

> Continue with the following.

Affiant on oath swears that the following statements are true and are within the personal knowledge of Affiant:

1. This affidavit is made with respect to the foreclosure of the Deed of Trust that occurred on [**date**].

2. Attached to this affidavit is a copy of the Notice of Trustee's Sale, file-stamped by the county clerk's office.

3. The trustee's sale took place on [**date**] at approximately [**time**] at the place at the courthouse designated in the notice [**include if applicable:** , being the area designated by the county commissioner's court for foreclosure sales].

Select one of the following.

4. Attached to this affidavit is a copy of the letter sent to each debtor obligated to pay the debt at the address required under the Texas Property Code.

Or

4. At least twenty-one days before the trustee's sale, Affiant, either personally or by agent, served notice of the sale on each debtor, at the address for that debtor as shown by Mortgagee's records, who [is/are]: [**list name[s] and address[es]**].

Continue with the following.

The [notice[s]/letter[s]] [was/were] served on [**date**] by certified mail, postage prepaid, properly addressed to each debtor listed above at the address[es] stated.

5. To the best of Affiant's knowledge, the debtor[s] [was/were] alive on the date of the trustee's sale.

Select one of the following.

6. [**Name of grantor**] is a servicemember in military service, as those terms are defined in 50 U.S.C. § 3911; however, the obligation described in the mortgage originated after [**name**] began military service on [**date**].

Or

6. [**Name of grantor**] is a servicemember in military service, as those terms are defined in 50 U.S.C. § 3911, and the obligation described in the mortgage originated before [**name**] began military service on [**date**]. However, [**name**], during [his/her] military service,

executed and delivered a written waiver of rights and protections provided by 50 U.S.C. §§ 3901–4043, and a copy of the waiver is attached to this affidavit.

Or

6. [**Name of grantor**] was not a servicemember in military service, as those terms are defined in 50 U.S.C. § 3911, or at any time within ninety days preceding the date of the trustee's sale.

Include the following if applicable.

7. Attached to this affidavit is a copy of the notice sent to the Internal Revenue Service regarding the tax liens described therein.

Continue with the following.

____
[**Name of affiant**]

SUBSCRIBED AND SWORN TO before me on ________________ by [**name of affiant**].

____
Notary Public, State of Texas

Form 14-18

Notice of Advancement and Demand for Payment

[**Date**]

[**Name and address of borrower**]

See section 14.5 in this chapter.

Re: [**describe note and loan documents**]

[**Salutation**]

This letter is to give you notice of default under the referenced loan documents. This default consists of your failure to pay the loan that you assumed and agreed to pay. The mortgagee has paid $[**amount**] to [**name of mortgage company**].

Demand is made for the immediate payment of $[**amount**], with interest as allowed by the deed of trust. Unless the default is cured by [**date**], the mortgagee intends to foreclose its lien under the loan documents.

Include clause 14-7-1 if this is the first correspondence from the attorney to a debtor who is a consumer. See section 14.4:5.

If you have any questions, please consult your legal counsel.

Sincerely yours,

____

[**Name of attorney**]

Certified Mail No. [**number**]
Return Receipt Requested
c: [**name of borrower**], by first-class mail

Form 14-19

Affidavit of Advancement

Date:

Affiant:

Deed of Trust to Secure Assumption

Date:

Grantor:

Grantor's address:

Mortgagee:

Mortgagee's address:

Trustee:

Trustee's address:

Recording information:

Property:

Amount Advanced:

Affiant on oath swears that the following statements are true and are within the personal knowledge of Affiant:

Affiant is Mortgagee in the Deed of Trust to Secure Assumption. Grantor has defaulted in the performance of the loan assumed, and Affiant has advanced the Amount Advanced to cure the default. Affiant has given notice of the advancement to Grantor and has demanded to be reimbursed.

____
[Name of affiant]

SUBSCRIBED AND SWORN TO before me on __________________ by **[name of affiant]**.

____
Notary Public, State of Texas

Form 14-20

IRS Notice Letter

[**Date**]

District Director
Internal Revenue Service
[**Address**]
Attention: Technical Support Group Manager

Re: Notice of nonjudicial foreclosure sale on property
Taxpayer:

[**Salutation**]

This letter is notice as required under section 7425 of the Internal Revenue Code and Treasury Regulations section 301.7425–3(a) that property encumbered by a deed-of-trust lien granted by [**name of borrower**] is being nonjudicially foreclosed pursuant to the authority granted in the deed of trust. [**Name of mortgagee**], holder of the deed-of-trust lien, gives notice of the proposed nonjudicial sale of the property.

1. *Name and Address of Creditor*. The name and address of the person for whom this notice is submitted is [**name of mortgagee**]. This creditor is the current owner and holder of the deed of trust and the promissory note[s] secured by it, which are described as follows: [**describe deed of trust and promissory note[s]**].

2. *Tax Lien Descriptions*. A copy of each of the following notices of federal tax lien potentially affecting the property to be sold is enclosed:

Place filed: [**county**] County, Texas

Date filed:

Recording data:

Tax amount:

Taxpayer:

Repeat above information as needed.

3. *Description and Location of Property*. A detailed description, including location of the property affected by this notice, is [**include property description and any other relevant data**].

The street address of the property is [**address**].

4. *Date, Time, and Place of Foreclosure Sale*. The date, time, place, and terms of the proposed sale are as follows:

Date:

Time: Between the hours of 10:00 A.M. and 4:00 P.M. and to begin no earlier than [**time**] and no later than three hours thereafter.

Place:

Terms: To the highest bidder for cash.

5. *Debt*. The approximate amount of the principal obligation, including interest, secured by the lien sought to be enforced and a description of the other expenses (such as legal expenses and selling costs) that may be charged against the sale proceeds are as follows:

Principal balance:

Interest through [**date**]:

Daily accrual:

Legal and sale expenses: Estimated range of expenses is from $[**amount**] to $[**amount**].

Include the following if applicable.

6. *Property within District.* The property within your district is referred to in the mortgagee title policy held by [**name of mortgagee**], which covers the tract and related improvements and which has been included if available.

Continue with the following.

7. *Acknowledgment of Notice Requested.* Please acknowledge receipt of this notice by returning a file-stamped copy of this letter in the enclosed envelope. If you have any questions, please do not hesitate to call.

Sincerely yours,

____

[**Name of attorney**]

c: [**name of client**]

Form 14-21

Waiver of Rights after Default

Date:

Security Agreement

Date:

Lender (Secured Party):

Debtor:

Collateral:

Note

Date:

Amount:

Borrower (Obligor):

[Secondary Obligor:]

[Debtor/Secondary Obligor] acknowledges that a default exists under the Note and the Security Agreement. [Debtor/Secondary Obligor] waives all further notices of disposition of the collateral, pursuant to section 9.624(a) of the Texas Business and Commerce Code.

Include the following if a waiver of disposition of consumer goods collateral is desired. See section 14.3:4 in this chapter for requirements for using a waiver.

Further, [Debtor/Secondary Obligor] waives the right to require Secured Party to dispose of the collateral within ninety days pursuant to section 9.620(e) of the Texas Business and Commerce Code.

> Include the following if a waiver of the right to redeem the collateral is desired. Note: This waiver may not be used in a consumer goods transaction.

[Debtor/Secondary Obligor] acknowledges that the collateral is not consumer goods and waives its right to redeem the collateral.

> Continue with the following.

____
[Name of debtor or secondary obligor]

Form 14-22

Debtor's Consent to Acceptance of Collateral

Date:

Security Agreement

Date:

Lender (Secured Party):

Debtor:

Collateral:

Note

Date:

Amount:

Borrower (Obligor):

[Secondary Obligor:]

[Debtor/Secondary Obligor] acknowledges receipt of a proposal from Lender to accept the collateral in [full/partial] satisfaction of the obligation. [Debtor/Secondary Obligor] consents to the acceptance of the collateral as proposed by Lender.

[Debtor/Secondary Obligor] acknowledges that a default has occurred under the Note and the Security Agreement [./and/,] [**include if the collateral is consumer goods:** that Debtor is not in possession of the collateral at this time[./, and]] [**include if applicable:** that 60 percent of the cash price has not been paid in a consumer purchase-money transaction or 60 percent of the principal amount of the obligation has not been paid in a consumer non-purchase-money transaction]. **[If 60 percent of the cash price has been paid in a consumer purchase-money transaction or 60 percent of the principal amount of the obligation has been paid in a consumer non-purchase-money transaction, include:** Further, [Debtor/Secondary Obligor] waives its right to require disposition of the collateral within ninety days pursuant to section 9.620(e) of the Texas Business and Commerce Code.]

____

[Name of debtor or secondary obligor]

Form 14-23

[Posted] Notice of Public Sale

Date:

Security Agreement

Date:

Debtor:

Lender (Secured Party):

Collateral:

Note

Date:

Amount:

Borrower (Obligor):

Lender (Secured Party):

[Secondary Obligor:]

Date of Sale:

Place of Sale:

Time of Sale:

A default exists under the Security Agreement. Secured Party will sell the Collateral at public auction to the highest bidder for cash at the Place of Sale on the Date of Sale to satisfy the debt secured by the Security Agreement. The sale will begin at the Time of Sale.

[**Include if applicable:** THERE WILL BE NO WARRANTY RELATING TO TITLE, POSSESSION, QUIET ENJOYMENT, OR THE LIKE FOR THE PERSONAL PROPERTY IN THIS DISPOSITION.]

____

[**Name of lender**]

Form 14-24

Agenda of Public Foreclosure Sale
Held on [date]
[Personal Property]

I am **[name]**, **[title]**. **[Name of debtor]** signed a security agreement in favor of **[name of lender]**, the lender, granting a security interest in **[describe collateral]**, the property in this sale. The lender has authorized me to sell the property at public auction. The property is **[read itemized list of property or offer a copy for review]**. **[Include if applicable:** THERE WILL BE NO WARRANTY RELATING TO TITLE, POSSESSION, QUIET ENJOYMENT, OR THE LIKE FOR THE PERSONAL PROPERTY IN THIS DISPOSITION.]

I now call for cash bids on the property. Each bidder will please state his or her name, for whom the bid is being made, and the amount of each bid made.

Bids in the order made:

1. Name:

   Representing:

   Amount bid:

> Repeat above information as needed.

Are there any further bids?

> If the successful bidder is not the lender, continue with the following.

Does the bidder require time to obtain cash in the amount of its bid?

> If the answer is "yes," continue with the following.

Hearing no further bids, this sale is adjourned until ____________, at which time this sale will reconvene at this location if the bidder has not delivered cash to me in the amount of the bidder's bid; provided, however, that if the bidder delivers the cash bid, the property will be sold to the bidder without further notice, and this sale will be concluded.

If the sale is reconvened, this agenda should be reread in full.

If the answer is "no" or if the successful bidder is the lender, continue with the following.

Hearing no further bids, the property is sold to ____________________, who made the highest and best bid.

This concludes the sale.

Continue with the following.

____

[Name of trustee]

Form 14-25

Bill of Sale

Date:

Security Agreement

Date:

Debtor:

Lender (Secured Party):

Property:

Note

Date:

Amount:

Borrower (Obligor):

Lender (Secured Party):

Date of Sale:

Place of Sale:

Time of Sale:

Buyer:

A default occurred under the Security Agreement. Notices stating the time, place, and terms of sale of the property were sent to Debtor, any secondary obligor, and other persons to whom Lender is required to send such notice by the laws of the state of Texas. At the foreclosure sale for the Property, Lender accepted Buyer's bid, which was the highest bid.

Lender, subject to the prior liens and other exceptions to conveyance and warranty in the Security Agreement and for the amount of sale paid by Buyer as consideration, sells and conveys the Property to Buyer.

Include the following if applicable.

LENDER HAS NOT MADE, AND DOES NOT MAKE, ANY REPRESENTATION, EXPRESS OR IMPLIED, WITH RESPECT TO THE PROPERTY, AND THE PROPERTY IS SOLD TO BUYER "AS IS, WHERE IS, AND WITH ALL FAULTS." [**Include if applicable:** THERE IS NO WARRANTY RELATING TO TITLE, POSSESSION, QUIET ENJOYMENT, OR THE LIKE IN THIS DISPOSITION OF PERSONAL PROPERTY.]

Continue with the following.

____

[Name of lender]

Form 14-26

Notice of Strict Foreclosure

[**Date**]

[**Name and address of borrower**]

Re: [**describe property, note, and loan documents**]

[**Salutation**]

This letter is to give you notice that [**name of lender**], the lender, proposes to accept the Property described above in [full/partial] satisfaction of the obligations under the note and security agreement, as provided in sections 9.620 through 9.622 of the Texas Business and Commerce Code. This proposal is [unconditional/subject only to the condition that any property not in the possession of the lender be preserved and maintained].

If the lender receives within twenty-one days from the date of this letter your written objection to this proposal, the lender will dispose of the Property at either a public or a private disposition or will undertake to collect from or enforce an obligation of any person obligated on the Property, as allowed by law.

Include the following if applicable.

A copy of this letter has been sent to the secured party[ies], lienholder[s], or other persons below, as required by law.

Continue with the following.

If you have any questions, please consult your legal counsel.

Sincerely yours,

____

[Name of attorney]

Certified Mail No. **[number]**
Return Receipt Requested
c: **[name of borrower]**, by first-class mail
[c: **[name[s] of secured party[ies] and other persons required by Tex. Bus. & Com. Code §§ 9.620–.621]**]

Form 14-27

Objection to Proposal to Accept Collateral in [Full/Partial] Satisfaction of Obligation

[Date]

[Name and address of lender]

Security Agreement

Date:

Debtor:

Lender (Secured Party):

Collateral:

Note

Date:

Amount:

Borrower (Obligor):

[Secondary Obligor:]

Lender (Secured Party):

[Salutation]

This letter is to notify you of an objection to your proposal to accept the collateral dated **[date of lender's proposal]**.

____
[Name of debtor or person objecting]

Form 14-28

This form is for use in consumer goods transactions.

Notice of Our Plan to Sell Property

[Date]

[Name and address of borrower]
[Name and address of any obligor who is also a debtor]

Re: **[describe property, note, and loan documents]**

[Salutation]

We have your **[describe collateral]** because you broke promises in our agreement.

> Select one of the following. Include the first paragraph for a public disposition. Include the second paragraph for a private disposition.

We will sell **[describe collateral]** at public sale. A sale could include a lease or license. The sale will be held on **[date]** at **[time]** at **[place]**. You may attend the sale and bring bidders if you want.

> Or

We will sell **[describe collateral]** at private sale sometime after **[date]**. A sale could include a lease or license.

> Continue with the following.

The money that we get from the sale (after paying our costs) will reduce the amount you owe. If we get less money than you owe, you [will/will not] still owe us the difference. If we get more money than you owe, you will get the extra money, unless we must pay it to someone else.

You can get the property back at any time before we sell it by paying us the full amount you owe (not just the past-due payments), including our expenses. To learn the exact amount you must pay, call us at [**telephone number**]. If you want us to explain to you in writing how we have figured the amount that you owe us, you may call us at [**telephone number**] [**include if applicable:** or write us at [**address of secured party**]] and request a written explanation. [**Include if applicable:** We will charge you $[**amount**] for the explanation if we sent you another written explanation of the amount you owe us within the last six months.]

If you need more information about the sale, call us at [**telephone number**] or write us at [**address of secured party**].

[**Include if applicable:** We are sending this notice to the following people who have an interest in [**describe collateral**] or who owe money under your agreement: [**list names of all other debtors and obligors, if any**].]

____

[**Name of lender**]

Form 14-29

This form is for use in transactions other than those for consumer goods.

Notification of Disposition of Collateral

[**Date**]

[**Name and address of debtor, obligor, or other person to whom the notice is sent**]
[**Name, address, and telephone number of secured party**]
[**Include only if debtor is not an addressee:** Name[s] of Debtor[s]: [**name[s]**]]

> Select one of the following. Include the first paragraph for a public disposition. Include the second paragraph for a private disposition.

We will [sell/lease/license] the [**describe collateral**] [**include if applicable:** to the highest qualified bidder] in public on [**date**] at [**time**] at [**place**].

> Or

We will [sell/lease/license] the [**describe collateral**] privately sometime after [**date**].

> Continue with the following.

You are entitled to an accounting of the unpaid indebtedness secured by the property that we intend to [sell/lease/license] [**include if applicable:** for a charge of $[**amount**]]. You may request an account by calling us at [**telephone number**].

____
[**Name of lender**]

Certified Mail No. [**number**]
Return Receipt Requested
c: [**name of debtor**], by first-class mail

Form 14-30

Memorandum of Private Foreclosure Sale
Held on [date]

I am [**name**], [**title**]. [**Name of debtor**] signed a security agreement in favor of [**name of lender**], the lender, granting a security interest in [**describe collateral**], the property in this sale. The lender has given notice to Debtor and any secondary obligor that after [**date**] the property would be sold at a private sale. The property is [**read itemized list of property or offer a copy for review**]. [**Include if applicable:** THERE WILL BE NO WARRANTY RELATING TO TITLE, POSSESSION, QUIET ENJOYMENT, OR THE LIKE FOR THE PERSONAL PROPERTY IN THIS DISPOSITION.]

I now call for cash bids on the property. Each bidder will please state his or her name, for whom the bid is being made, and the amount of each bid made.

1. Name:

   Representing:

   Amount bid:

Repeat above information as needed.

Are there any further bids?

If the successful bidder is not the lender, continue with the following.

Does the bidder require time to obtain cash in the amount of its bid?

If the answer is "yes," continue with the following.

Hearing no further bids, this sale is adjourned until ____________, at which time this sale will reconvene at this location if the bidder has not delivered cash to me in the amount of the bidder's bid; provided, however, that if the bidder delivers the cash bid, the property will be sold to the bidder without further notice, and this sale will be concluded.

If the sale is reconvened, this agenda should be reread in full.

If the answer is "no" or if the successful bidder is the lender, continue with the following.

Hearing no further bids, the property is sold to ______________________, who made the highest and best bid.

This concludes the sale.

Continue with the following.

____

[Name of person conducting sale]

Form 14-31

Notice of Default

[Home Equity Loan]

[Date]

[Name and address of borrower]

Re: **[describe note and loan documents]**

[Salutation]

This letter is to give you notice of default under the referenced loan documents on your Texas Constitution article XVI, section 50(a)(6), home equity loan. This default consists of **[describe default; if the default is monetary, include the amount in default and the name of the mortgagee.]**. I am attempting to collect this indebtedness, and any information obtained will be used for that purpose. This letter is being sent to your attention in accordance with state and federal law.

You are notified that if the default is not cured within twenty days from the date of posting of this letter, the mortgagee will enforce its rights under the loan documents. Specifically, the mortgagee will accelerate the maturity of your home equity note and declare due and payable the unpaid principal balance, together with accrued but unpaid interest and fees and expenses allowed by law. If the amount due is not timely paid, the mortgagee will seek a court order allowing the mortgagee to foreclose the lien you granted on your homestead under the loan documents in accordance with Texas Constitution article XVI, section 50(a)(6), and rules 735 and 736 of the Texas Rules of Civil Procedure.

In accordance with federal laws regarding fair debt collections, unless you, within thirty days after receipt of this notice, dispute the validity of the debt set forth above, or any portion thereof, the indebtedness will be assumed to be valid. If you notify the undersigned in writing within the thirty-day period that the indebtedness, or any portion thereof, is disputed, I will obtain a verification of the indebtedness, and I will mail you that verification. If within the same thirty-day period you request in writing the name and address of the original mortgagee, and if the original mortgagee is different from the current lender, I will furnish you with that information. Federal laws do not require that I wait until the end of the thirty-day period before taking action to collect the debt. If, however, you have requested verification of the debt or the name and address of the original mortgagee within the thirty-day period, I will cease collection activities until the requested information has been mailed to you.

If you have any questions, please consult your legal counsel.

Sincerely yours,

____

[**Name of attorney**]

Certified Mail No. [**number**]
Return Receipt Requested
c: [**name of borrower**], by first-class mail

Form 14-32

Notice of Acceleration
[Home Equity Loan]

[**Date**]

[**Name and address of borrower**]

Re: [**describe note and loan documents**]

[**Salutation**]

By letter dated [**date of letter**], I notified you of a default under the referenced loan documents on your Texas Constitution article XVI, section 50(a)(6), home equity loan. I am attempting to collect this indebtedness, and any information obtained will be used for that purpose.

Because the default on your home equity note has not been cured, the mortgagee has accelerated the maturity of your note, declaring all unpaid principal, together with accrued but unpaid interest and fees and expenses allowed by law, immediately due and payable. The mortgagee will now seek a court order allowing the mortgagee to foreclose the lien you granted on your homestead under the loan documents in accordance with Texas Constitution article XVI, section 50(a)(6), and rules 735 and 736 of the Texas Rules of Civil Procedure.

If you have any questions, please consult your legal counsel.

Sincerely yours,

____

[**Name of attorney**]

Certified Mail No. [**number**]
Return Receipt Requested
c: [**name of borrower**], by first-class mail

Form 14-33

The Texas Supreme Court approved forms for expedited foreclosure proceedings on February 10, 2014. The forms may be found on the court's website, **www.txcourts.gov/media/847145/expedited-foreclosure-forms-for-website.pdf**. The form below is a reproduction of the form in the order.

Cause No.: ___________

In Re: Order for Foreclosure Concerning ____________________ **[*property address*] Under Tex. R. Civ. P. 736**	§ § § §	**In the** ________ **[*type of court, e.g., district, county, or probate*] Court**
Petitioner:	§ § §	
____________	§ § § §	_________ **County, Texas**
Respondent(s):	§ § §	
____________	§ §	________ **[*court designation*]**

Application for an Expedited Order Under Rule 736 on a Home Equity, Reverse Mortgage, or Home Equity Line of Credit Loan

1. Petitioner is _________, whose last known address is ____________________.

2. Respondent is________, whose last known address is ____________________.

3. The property encumbered by the _________ [*loan agreement, contract, or lien*] sought to be foreclosed is commonly known as ______________ [*street address of the property*] with the following legal description:

____

[*legal description of the property*]

4. Petitioner alleges:

A. The type of lien sought to be foreclosed is a ___________ [*see liens described in Texas Rule of Civil Procedure 735.1(a)*] under _________ [*state the statutory or constitutional authority for the lien*]. The lien is indexed at _______________ [*volume/page, instrument number, or clerk's file number*] and recorded in the real property records of ________ County, Texas.

B. Petitioner has authority to seek foreclosure of the lien because _______________.

C. The name of each Respondent obligated to pay the underlying debt or obligation evidenced by the _________ [*loan agreement, contract, or lien*] encumbering the property sought to be foreclosed is ____________________.

D. The name of each Respondent who is a mortgagor of the lien instrument sought to be foreclosed, but who is not a maker or assumer of the underlying debt, is ____.

E. As of _________ [*a date that is no more than sixty days prior to the date that the application is filed*]:

(i) [*If the default is monetary.*] ______ [*number and frequency of payments (e.g., monthly)*] have not been paid. The amount required to cure the default is _______. According to Petitioner's records, all lawful offsets, payments, and credits have been applied to the account in default.

(ii) [*If the lien secures a reverse mortgage or the default is nonmonetary.*] The facts creating the default and Petitioner's authority to enforce the lien are __________.

(iii) The total amount to pay off the __________ [*loan agreement, contract, or lien*] is __________.

F. Notice to cure the default has been sent by certified mail to each Respondent who is obligated to pay the underlying debt or obligation. The opportunity to cure has expired.

G. Before this application was filed, any other action required to initiate a foreclosure proceeding by Texas law or the _______ [*loan agreement, contract, or lien*] sought to be foreclosed was performed.

5. **Legal action is not being sought against the occupant of the property unless the occupant is named as a Respondent in this application.**

6. **If Petitioner obtains a court order, Petitioner will proceed with foreclosure of the property in accordance with applicable law and the terms of the _________ [*loan agreement, contract, or lien*] sought to be foreclosed.**

7. The following documents are attached to this application:

A. An affidavit or declaration of material facts describing the basis for foreclosure.

B. The ______ [*note, original recorded lien, or other documentation*] establishing the lien.

C. [*If the lien has been assigned.*] The current assignment of the lien recorded in the real property records of the county where the property is located.

D. A copy of each default notice required to be mailed to any Respondent under Texas law and the __________ [*loan agreement, contract, or lien*] sought to be foreclosed, and the __________ [*USPS Tracking report, return receipt, or other proof*] demonstrating that a notice was sent by certified mail before this application was filed.

8. **Assert and protect your rights as a member of the armed forces of the United States. If you or your spouse is serving on active military duty, including active military duty as a member of the Texas National Guard or the National Guard of another state or as a member of a reserve component of the armed forces of the United States, please send written notice of the active duty military service to Petitioner or Petitioner's attorney immediately.**

9. *Prayer for Relief:* Petitioner seeks an expedited order under Rule 736 so that it may proceed with foreclosure in accordance with applicable law and terms of the __________ [*loan agreement, contract, or lien*] sought to be foreclosed.

____
[*Petitioner's signature block*]

Form 14-34

The Texas Supreme Court approved forms for expedited foreclosure proceedings on February 10, 2014. The forms may be found on the court's website, **www.txcourts.gov/media/847145/expedited-foreclosure-forms-for-website.pdf**. The form below is a reproduction of the form in the order.

Cause No. ____________

In Re: Order for Foreclosure Concerning ________________ [*property address*] Under Tex. R. Civ. P. 736	§	**In the ______ [*type of court, e.g., district, county, or probate*] Court**
Petitioner:	§	
____________	§	**________ County, Texas**
Respondent(s):	§	
____________	§	**______ [*court designation*]**

Affidavit in Support of Petitioner's Application for an Expedited Order Under Rule 736

State of Texas

County of __________

Before me, the undersigned notary, on this day personally appeared __________ [*name of affiant*], and stated under oath:

1. My name is ____________________ [*first, middle, and last name*]. I am an adult and of sound mind.

2. I am ________________ [*job title or position*] of ______________ [*name of affiant's employer*], whose address is __________________ [*street address, city, state, and zip code*]. My affidavit concerns the account of ____________ [*name of each person who is obligated for the underlying debt or lien sought to be foreclosed*] ("Obligor"). ____________________. [*Explain the relationship between the affiant or the affiant's employer and Petitioner (e.g., affiant's employer is the agent for loan service*

administration for Petitioner) and the connection or role of the affiant or the affiant's employer with respect to the servicing or foreclosure of Obligor's account (e.g., mortgagee or mortgage servicer).]

3. I have read and understand the purpose of the application to which my affidavit is attached and adopt by reference the statements made in it. I am the authorized agent or representative of Petitioner with respect to Obligor's account, and in that capacity, I am authorized to make this affidavit on Petitioner's behalf. My testimony is based on my experience, my knowledge of the usual business practices of __________ [*affiant's employer*] and the servicing industry in general, my job responsibilities, and the servicing records for Obligor's account.
4. Through my job responsibilities, I have access to and have reviewed the servicing records and data for Obligor's account, including electronic and computer generated records and data compilations. The records attached to the application are the original records or exact duplicates of the original records kept in the servicing file for Obligor's account.
5. Based on the regular practices of _______ [*affiant's employer*] and the servicing industry in general, these records:
   a. were made at or near the time of each act, event, or condition set forth in the records;
   b. were made by, or from information transmitted by, a person engaged in the servicing of Obligor's account who had actual knowledge of the acts, events, or conditions recorded; and
   c. are the kind of records that are kept in the regular course of servicing loan agreements.
6. It is the regular practice of businesses engaged in the servicing of loan agreements or other contracts requiring the collection of money to keep accurate records on debits and credits to an account, an account's balance, the collateral securing the right to the

lienholder's right to repayment, and efforts to enforce the underlying debt if the Obligor has defaulted. These records are relied upon for accuracy by all persons engaged in the servicing and enforcement of a loan agreement. There is no indication that the servicing records for Obligor's account are untrustworthy.

7. Based on the servicing records for Obligor's account, ________________. [*State all facts demonstrating the basis for foreclosure, including, if applicable, the number of unpaid scheduled payments, the amounts required to cure the default and payoff the loan, and the credits and offsets that have been applied to Obligor's account. Describe proof (e.g., USPS Tracking report, return receipt, or other proof) that Obligor was given notice of the default by certified mail.*]
8. I sign this affidavit based on the personal knowledge that I have obtained by reviewing the servicing records for Obligor's account. The statements made in the application and my affidavit are true and correct as of the date stated.

Signed this _____ day of _____________, 20__

____
[*printed name and title of affiant*]

____
[*signature of affiant*]

Signed under oath before me on _______________, 20___.

[*notary's seal*]

____
Notary Public in and for the State of Texas

My commission expires: ________.

Form 14-35

The Texas Supreme Court approved forms for expedited foreclosure proceedings on February 10, 2014. The forms may be found on the court's website, **www.txcourts.gov/media/847145/expedited-foreclosure-forms-for-website.pdf**. The form below is a reproduction of the form in the order.

Cause No. ____________

In Re: Order for Foreclosure Concerning ____________________ [*property address*] Under Tex. R. Civ. P. 736	§	**In the ______ [*type of court, e.g., district, county, or probate*] Court**
Petitioner:	§	
____________	§	**______ County, Texas**
Respondent(s):	§	
____________	§	**____ [*court designation*]**

Declaration in Support of Petitioner's Application for an Expedited Order Under Rule 736

I, ______________ [*name*], declare:

1. My name is ______________________ [*first, middle, and last name*]. I am an adult and of sound mind.
2. I am __________________ [*job title or position*] of _______________ [*name of declarant's employer*], whose address is __________________ [*street address, city, state, and zip code*]. My declaration concerns the account of _____________ [*name of each person who is obligated for the underlying debt or lien sought to be foreclosed*] ("Obligor"). ___________________. [*Explain the relationship between the declarant or the declarant's employer and Petitioner (e.g., declarant's employer is the agent for loan service administration for Petitioner) and the connection or role of the declarant or the declarant's employer with respect to the servicing or foreclosure of Obligor's account (e.g., mortgagee or mortgage servicer).*]

3. I have read and understand the purpose of the application to which my declaration is attached and adopt by reference the statements made in it. I am the authorized agent or representative of Petitioner with respect to Obligor's account, and in that capacity, I am authorized to make this declaration on Petitioner's behalf. My testimony is based on my experience, my knowledge of the usual business practices of ________ [*declarant's employer*] and the servicing industry in general, my job responsibilities, and the servicing records for Obligor's account.
4. Through my job responsibilities, I have access to and have reviewed the servicing records and data for Obligor's account, including electronic and computer generated records and data compilations. The records attached to the application are the original records or exact duplicates of the original records kept in the servicing file for Obligor's account.
5. Based on the regular practices of _______ [*declarant's employer*] and the servicing industry in general, these records:
   a. were made at or near the time of each act, event, or condition set forth in the records;
   b. were made by, or from information transmitted by, a person engaged in the servicing of Obligor's account who had actual knowledge of the acts, events, or conditions recorded; and
   c. are the kind of records that are kept in the regular course of servicing loan agreements.
6. It is the regular practice of businesses engaged in the servicing of loan agreements or other contracts requiring the collection of money to keep accurate records on debits and credits to an account, an account's balance, the collateral securing the right to the lienholder's right to repayment, and efforts to enforce the underlying debt if the Obligor has defaulted. These records are relied upon for accuracy by all persons engaged in the servicing and enforcement of a loan agreement. There is no indication that the servicing records for Obligor's account are untrustworthy.

7. Based on the servicing records for Obligor's account, ________________. [*State all facts demonstrating the basis for foreclosure, including, if applicable, the number of unpaid scheduled payments, the amounts required to cure the default and payoff the loan, and the credits and offsets that have been applied to Obligor's account. Describe proof (e.g., USPS Tracking report, return receipt, or other proof) that Obligor was given notice of the default by certified mail.*]
8. I sign this declaration based on the personal knowledge that I have obtained by reviewing the servicing records for Obligor's account. The statements made in the application and my declaration are true and correct as of the date stated.

JURAT

My name is ________________ [*first, middle, and last*], my date of birth is ________________, and my address is ________________ [*street, city, state, zip code, and country*]. I declare under penalty of perjury that the foregoing is true and correct.

Executed on the ____ day of ______ [*month*], ______ [*year*].

____
[*signature of declarant*]

Form 14-36

The Texas Supreme Court approved forms for expedited foreclosure proceedings on February 10, 2014. The forms may be found on the court's website, **www.txcourts.gov/media/847145/expedited-foreclosure-forms-for-website.pdf**. The form below is a reproduction of the form in the order.

Cause No. ____________

In Re: Order for Foreclosure Concerning ____________________ [*property address*] Under Tex. R. Civ. P. 736	§	**In the ______ [*type of court, e.g., district, county, or probate*] Court**
Petitioner:	§	
____________	§	**______ County, Texas**
Respondent(s):	§	
____________	§	**______ [*court designation*]**

Military Status Affidavit

State of Texas

County of ________

Before me, the undersigned notary, on this day personally appeared __________ [*name of affiant*], and stated under oath:

1. My name is ____________________ [*first, middle, and last name*]. I am an adult and of sound mind.

2. Respondent's name is ______________________________.

3. I am _________ [*job title or position*] of ___________ [*name of the affiant's employer*]. ____________________. [*Explain relationship between affiant's employer and Petitioner.*] I have personal knowledge of the facts set forth in this affidavit. These facts are true and correct.

4. [*Choose one*]

   a. I know that Respondent is **not** currently in the military because I asked the U.S. Department of Defense to check its Defense Manpower Data Center (DMDC) database. DMDC notified me that Respondent is not on active duty in any of the armed forces. I attach a true copy of the DMDC verification. [*You can print a copy of the DMDC verification from this web address: https://www.dmdc.osd.mil/appj/scra/scraHome.do.*]

   b. I know that Respondent is **not** currently in the military because ________________. [*State facts that would render a person ineligible for military service, such as being in prison or having a serious disability.*]

   c. I am unable to determine if Respondent is in military service.

   d. Respondent is in the military now.

5. [*If Respondent was previously in the military.*] Respondent's period of military service ended more than ____ months before this proceeding was filed.

____
[*signature of affiant*]

Signed under oath before me on ______________, 20___.

[*notary's seal*]

____
Notary Public in and for the State of Texas

My commission expires:________.

Form 14-37

The Texas Supreme Court approved forms for expedited foreclosure proceedings on February 10, 2014. The forms may be found on the court's website, **www.txcourts.gov/media/847145/expedited-foreclosure-forms-for-website.pdf**. The form below is a reproduction of the form in the order.

Cause No. ______________

In Re: Order for Foreclosure Concerning ____________________ [*property address*] Under Tex. R. Civ. P. 736	§	**In the ______ [*type of court, e.g., district, county, or probate*] Court**
Petitioner:	§	
______________	§	**________ County, Texas**
Respondent(s):	§	
______________	§	**______ [*court designation*]**

Military Status Declaration

I, ______________ [*name*], declare:

1. My name is ______________________ [*first, middle, and last name*]. I am an adult and of sound mind.

2. Respondent's name is ________________________________.

3. I am __________ [*job title or position*] of _____________ [*name of the declarant's employer*]. ________________________. [*Explain relationship between declarant's employer and Petitioner.*] I have personal knowledge of the facts set forth in this affidavit. These facts are true and correct.

4. [*Choose one*]

   e. I know that Respondent is **not** currently in the military because I asked the U.S. Department of Defense to check its Defense Manpower Data Center (DMDC) database. DMDC notified me that Respondent is not on active duty in any of the armed forces. I attach a true copy of the DMDC verification. [*You can print a copy of the DMDC verification from this web address: https://www.dmdc.osd.mil/appj/scra/scraHome.do.*]

f. I know that Respondent is **not** currently in the military because ________________. [*State facts that would render a person ineligible for military service, such as being in prison or having a serious disability.*]

g. I am unable to determine if Respondent is in military service.

h. Respondent is in the military now.

5. [*If Respondent was previously in the military.*] Respondent's period of military service ended more than ____ months before this proceeding was filed.

JURAT

My name is _______________ [*first, middle, and last*], my date of birth is _________________, and my address is ___________________ [*street, city, state, zip code, and country*]. I declare under penalty of perjury that the foregoing is true and correct.

Executed on the ____ day of ______ [*month*], ______ [*year*].

____
[*signature of declarant*]

Form 14-38

The Texas Supreme Court approved forms for expedited foreclosure proceedings on February 10, 2014. The forms may be found on the court's website, **www.txcourts.gov/media/847145/expedited-foreclosure-forms-for-website.pdf**. The form below is a reproduction of the form in the order.

Cause No.: ______________

In Re: Order for Foreclosure Concerning ________________ [*property address*] Under Tex. R. Civ. P. 736	§	**In the _______ [*type of court, e.g., district, county, or probate*] Court**
Petitioner:	§	
______________	§	**_________ County, Texas**
Respondent(s):	§	
______________	§	**_______ [*court designation*]**

Default Order

1. On this day, the Court considered Petitioner's motion for a default order granting its application for an expedited order under Rule 736. Petitioner's application complies with the requirements of Texas Rule of Civil Procedure 736.1.
2. The name and last known address of each Respondent subject to this order is __________________. Each Respondent was properly served with the citation, but none filed a response within the time required by law. The return of service for each Respondent has been on file with the court for at least ten days.
3. The property that is the subject of this foreclosure proceeding is commonly known as _________________ [*street address of the property*] with the following legal description:

____

[*legal description of the property*]

4. The lien to be foreclosed is indexed or recorded at ________________ [*volume/page, instrument number, or clerk's file number*] and recorded in the real property records of __________ County, Texas.

5. The material facts establishing Respondent's default are alleged in Petitioner's application and the supporting __________ [*affidavit or declaration*]. Those facts are adopted by the court and incorporated by reference in this order.

6. Based on the ______ [*affidavit or declaration*] of Petitioner, no Respondent subject to this order is protected from foreclosure by the Servicemembers Civil Relief Act, 50 U.S.C. App. § 501 *et seq.*

7. Therefore, the Court grants Petitioner's motion for a default order under Texas Rules of Civil Procedure 736.7 and 736.8. Petitioner may proceed with foreclosure of the property described above in accordance with applicable law and the __________ [*loan agreement, contract, or lien*] sought to be foreclosed.

8. This order is not subject to a motion for rehearing, a new trial, a bill of review, or an appeal. Any challenge to this order must be made in a separate, original proceeding filed in accordance with Texas Rule of Civil Procedure 736.11.

SIGNED this _____ day of _________, 20__.

____
JUDGE PRESIDING

Form 14-39

Demand to Pay Proceeds of Rent

[**Date**]

[**Name and address of borrower**]

Re: [**describe note and loan documents**]

[**Salutation**]

A default exists under the referenced loan documents.

Demand is made for the payment of the proceeds of all accrued but unpaid rent as of the date you receive this letter and all rent that accrues after you receive this letter in accordance with the Texas Property Code. Payment of the proceeds should be made to [**name of mortgagee and address for payments**]. The tenant[s] will be instructed to pay all rents to the mortgagee until further notice, in accordance with [the deed of trust/[**specify instrument**]] and the Texas Property Code.

> Include clause 14-7-1 in this chapter if this is the first correspondence from the attorney to a debtor who is a consumer. See section 14.4:5.

If you have any questions, please consult your legal counsel.

Sincerely yours,

____

[**Name of attorney**]

Certified Mail No. [**number**]
Return Receipt Requested
c: [**name of borrower**], by first-class mail

Form 14-40

Notice of Rescission of Trustee's Sale

Notice of confidentiality rights: If you are a natural person, you may remove or strike any or all of the following information from any instrument that transfers an interest in real property before it is filed for record in the public records: your Social Security number or your driver's license number.

Date:

[Trustee/Substitute Trustee]:

[Trustee/Substitute Trustee]'s Address:

Repeat as necessary for multiple trustees.

Debtor[s]:

[Debtor's/Debtors'] Address[es]:

Buyer[s]:

[Buyer's/Buyers'] Address[es]:

Note

Date:

Principal amount:

Borrower:

Mortgagee:

Trustee's Deed

Date:

Trustee:

Buyer:

Recording information:

Property: [**Insert property description and include the following if applicable:** , including all personal property secured by the security agreement included in the Deed of Trust.]

County:

Date of Sale (first Tuesday of month):

Time of Sale:

Place of Sale: [**Designate county location where sale will take place (may be other than courthouse)**]

Notice is given that on the Date of Sale, Trustee[s] offered the Property for sale at public auction at the Place of Sale, to the highest bidder for cash, "AS IS." The sale was struck off at the Time of Sale to Buyer[s].

The foreclosure sale is rescinded by the Trustee[s] because one or more of the statutory reasons listed below exist:

1. the statutory requirements for the sale were not satisfied;

2. the default leading to the sale was cured before the sale;

3. a receivership or dependent probate administration involving the Property was pending at the Time of Sale;

4. a condition specified in the conditions of sale prescribed by the Trustee[s] or Substitute Trustee[s] before the sale and made available in writing to prospective bidders at the sale was not met;

5. the Mortgagee or mortgage servicer and the Debtor[s] agreed before the sale to cancel the sale based on an enforceable written agreement by the Debtor[s] to cure the default; or

6. at the Time of Sale, a court-ordered or automatic stay of the sale imposed in a bankruptcy case filed by a person with an interest in the Property was in effect.

____

[Name of trustee]

Repeat signature line as necessary.

Form 14-41

Affidavit of Return of Bid Amount

Date:

Affiant:

Trustee's Deed

Date:

Trustee:

Buyer:

Recording information:

Property: [**Insert property description and include the following if applicable:** , including all personal property secured by the security agreement included in the Deed of Trust.]

Tracking Information: [**certified mail, electronic or wire transfer, or delivery service tracking information**]

Affiant on oath swears that the following statements are true and are within the personal knowledge of Affiant:

1. This affidavit is made with respect to the rescission of a foreclosure sale evidenced by the Trustee's Deed.

2. On the date shown above, the bid amount for the Trustee's Deed was returned to the Buyer by the method shown in the Tracking Information.

____
[Name of affiant]

SUBSCRIBED AND SWORN TO before me on ____________________ by **[name of affiant]**.

____
Notary Public, State of Texas

[Chapter 15 is reserved for expansion.]